# THE LETTERS OF
# T. S. ELIOT
# VOLUME 3

By T. S. Eliot

THE COMPLETE POEMS AND PLAYS

*verse*

COLLECTED POEMS 1909–1962

FOUR QUARTETS

THE WASTE LAND AND OTHER POEMS

THE WASTE LAND:
A Facsimile and Transcript of the Original Drafts
edited by Valerie Eliot

INVENTIONS OF THE MARCH HARE:
POEMS 1909–1917
edited by Christopher Ricks

SELECTED POEMS

*plays*

MURDER IN THE CATHEDRAL

THE FAMILY REUNION

THE COCKTAIL PARTY

THE CONFIDENTIAL CLERK

THE ELDER STATESMAN

*literary criticism*

THE SACRED WOOD

SELECTED ESSAYS

THE USE OF POETRY AND THE USE OF CRITICISM

VARIETIES OF METAPHYSICAL POETRY
edited by Ronald Schuchard

TO CRITICIZE THE CRITIC

ON POETRY AND POETS

FOR LANCELOT ANDREWES

SELECTED PROSE OF T. S. ELIOT
edited by Frank Kermode

*social criticism*

THE IDEA OF A CHRISTIAN SOCIETY
edited by David Edwards

NOTES TOWARDS THE DEFINITION OF CULTURE

*letters*

THE LETTERS OF T. S. ELIOT
Volume 1: 1898–1922
Revised Edition
edited by Valerie Eliot and Hugh Haughton

THE LETTERS OF T. S. ELIOT
Volume 2: 1923–1925
edited by Valerie Eliot and Hugh Haughton

THE LETTERS OF T. S. ELIOT
Volume 3: 1926–1927
edited by Valerie Eliot and John Haffenden

THE LETTERS OF

# T. S. Eliot

EDITED BY

VALERIE ELIOT

AND

JOHN HAFFENDEN

VOLUME 3

1926–1927




*faber and faber*

LONDON

First published in 2012
by Faber and Faber Limited
74–77 Great Russell Street, London WC1B 3DA

Typeset by Donald Sommerville
Printed in England by T. J. International,
Padstow, Cornwall



A CIP record for this book is available from the British Library

ISBN 978-0-571-14085-5

2 4 6 8 10 9 7 5 3 1

# CONTENTS

# ILLUSTRATIONS

# ACKNOWLEDGEMENTS

For help and advice in many capacities, the publishers and editors would like to thank the following individuals and institutions. (Sadly, some of those named below are now deceased, but we wish still to put on record our gratitude to them.) Dr Donald Adamson; The American Jewish Archives, Cincinnati, Ohio; Dr Norma Aubertin-Potter, Librarian in Charge, Codrington Library, All Souls College, Oxford; Joan Bailey; Owen Barfield; Tansy Barton, Special Collections Administrator, Senate House Library, London; H. Baugh; T. O. Beachcroft; Anne Olivier Bell; Bibliothèque Nationale, Paris; Kenneth Blackwell, McMaster University; Michael Harry Blechner, McFarlin Library, University of Tulsa; Mary Boccaccio, McKeldin Library, University of Maryland; John Bodley; William H. Bond; University of Bonn Library; Ann Bowden, Harry Ransom Humanities Research Center, University of Texas at Austin; British Library; Valerie Brokenshire; Jewel Spears Brooker; Robert Brown, Archivist, Faber & Faber Ltd; Penelope Bulloch, Balliol College Library; Professor P. H. Butter; William R. Cagle and Saundra Taylor, Lilly Library; University of California, Los Angeles; Douglas Campbell; Humphrey Carpenter; François Chapon; Mrs Charlton; Dr Joseph Chiari; Alexander P. Clark, Firestone Library, Princeton University; Alan Clodd; Marguerite Cohn; John Constable; Joyce Crick; Arthur Crook; Tony Cuda; Roy Davids; Dr A. Deiss, General Secretariat, Swiss Medical Institutions; Giles de la Mare; the Literary Trustees of Walter de la Mare; Rodney G. Dennis; Valentine Dobrée; Bibliothèque Littéraire Jacques Doucet; Kenneth W. Duckett, Southern Illinois University at Carbondale; Ellen S Dunlap, Harry Ransom Humanities Research Center; Peter du Sautoy; Donald D. Eddy, Cornell University Library; Sarah Ethier, University of Wisconsin-Milwaukee Libraries; Matthew Evans; Sir Richard Faber KCVO; Elizabeth A. Falsey; Christopher Farley; David Farmer, Harry Ransom Humanities Research Center (and Warren Roberts, Mary Hirth, Mrs Sally Leach, and other members of staff); Anton Felton, Continuum Ltd; Mrs Harry Fine; Mrs Burnham Finney; Henri Fluchere; Fondren Library; Jennifer Formichelli; Donald Gallup; Special Collections, Isabella Stewart Gardner Museum, Boston, Mass.; K. C. Gay, Lockwood Memorial Library, Buffalo; Herbert Gerwing, University of Victoria; Mrs Ghika; R. C. Giles; Robert Giroux;

Estate of Enid Goldsmith; Professor Warwick Gould; Herbert T. Greene; J. C. Hall; K. J. Hall, Assistant Manager, Lloyds Bank Ltd, Worcester Trust Branch; Dr Michael Halls; Saskia Hamilton; Sir Rupert Hart-Davis; Harvard University Archives; Professor E. N. Hartley, Institute Archives, MIT; Michael Hastings; The Library, Haverford College; Cathy Henderson, Harry Ransom Humanities Research Center; Robert Henderson; David Higham Associates Ltd; Robert W. Hill, New York Public Library; Michael Hofmann; Michael Holroyd; Hornbake Library, University of Maryland; Lélia Howard; Penelope Hughes-Hallett; J. W. Hunt, Royal Military Academy, Sandhurst; Jeremy Hutchinson; Lord Hutchinson; Carolyn Jakeman; Iman Javadi; Robin Jackson, The British Academy; P. D. James; Dorothy O. Johansen, Reed College, Portland, Oregon; Gregory A. Johnson, Alderman Library, University of Virginia; William Jovanovich; William L. Joyce, Princeton University Library; Paul Keegan; Professor John Kelly, St John's College, Oxford; Dr P. Kelly, National Library of Scotland; Mary Kiffer, Assistant Secretary, John Simon Guggenheim Memorial Foundation, New York; Modern Archives Centre, King's College, Cambridge; Monique Kuntz, Bibliothèque Municipale, Vichy; Major N. Aylward Leete; Mrs Dorothy Milburn Léger; Lockwood Memorial Library; Kenneth A. Lohf; London Library; Mrs Pat Lowe; Richard M. Ludwig, Princeton University Library; Jim McCue; Mary C. McGreenery, Harvard Alumni Records; Ed Maggs; Professor B. K. Matilal; Francis Mattson, Berg Collection, New York Public Library; R. Russell Maylone, Northwestern University Library; Bernard Meehan, Keeper of Manuscripts, Trinity College, Dublin; Mrs Edward S. Mills; University Library, Missouri History Museum; Joe Mithenson; Kate Mole, Librarian/Archivist, The British Academy; Frank Vigor Morley; Leslie Morris, Houghton Library, Harvard University; Lewis Morris; Tim Munby; Mary Middleton Murry; New College, Oxford; Richard Ollard; Anne Owen; Martin Page; Stephen Page; Alasdair Paterson, University of Exeter Library; Fondation Saint-John Perse; Lord Quinton; Craig Raine; Angela Raspin, London School of Economics; Benedict Read; Real Academia de la Historia, Madrid; Dr R. T. H. Redpath; Joseph Regenstein Library, University of Chicago; Canon Pierre Riches; Helene Ritzerfeld; Adam Roberts; Galleria Nazionale d'Arte Moderna, Rome; Rosenbach Museum & Library; Anthony Rota; Mme Agathe Rouart-Valéry; Carol Z. Rothkopf; A. L. Rowse; Lord Russell; Mrs N. Ryan; Professor Alfred W. Satterthwaite; Marcia Satterthwaite; Schiller-Nationalmuseum, Marbach am Neckar; Gerd Schmidt; Susan Schreibman; Rev. Karl Schroeder, SJ; Professor Ronald Schuchard; Grace Schulman; Timothy and Marian

Seldes; Christopher Sheppard, Brotherton Collection, Leeds University Library; Ethel C. Simpson, Trustee, John Gould Fletcher Literary Estate; Samuel A. Sizer, Special Collections, University Libraries, University of Arkansas; Janet Adam Smith; Theodora Eliot Smith; Natasha Spender; Sir Stephen Spender; Tom Staley, Harry Ransom Humanities Research Center, University of Texas at Austin; Dom Julian Stead; Alix Strachey; James Strachey; Kendon L. Stubbs, University of Virginia Library; Barbara Sturtevant; University of Sussex Library; Lola L. Szladits, Berg Collection; Elizabeth Stege Teleky; David S. Thatcher, University of Victoria, British Columbia; Alan G Thomas; Dr Michael J Tilby; Professor Kathleen Tillotson; Trinity College, Cambridge; Francois Valéry; Judith Robinson-Valéry; The Paul Valéry Collection, Bibliothèque Nationale, Paris; University of Virginia Library; Michael J Walsh; Jemma Walton; J. Waterlow; Dave Watkins; Dr George Watson; John Weightman; John Wells, Cambridge University Library; James White, National Gallery of Ireland; Brooke Whiting, Department of Special Collections, University Research Library, University of California, Los Angeles; Widener Library, Harvard University; Helen Willard; Professor David G. Williams; Dr Charlotte Williamson; Professor George Williamson; Patricia Willis, Beinecke Rare Book and Manuscript Library, Yale University; Harriet Harvey Wood; Woodson Research Center, Rice University; Dr Daniel H. Woodward, Huntington Library; Yale University Archives; Michael Yeats.

We are immensely grateful to the following individuals and institutions for making available all of the T. S. Eliot letters in their care: Donald Adamson Collection; the late Owen Barfield; Jacob Rader Center of the American Jewish Archives, Cincinnati, Ohio; Archives Nationales, Paris; Special Collections, University Libraries, University of Arkansas;; The Beinecke Rare Book and Manuscript Library, Yale University; Henry W. and Albert A. Berg Collection of English and American Literature, the New York Public Library; The Bodleian Library, Oxford University; Universitäts und Landesbibliothek, Bonn University British Library, London; The Brotherton Collection, Leeds University Library; Rare Books and Manuscripts Division, Butler Library, Columbia University, New York; Fondazione Camillo Caetani; Cambridge University Library; Dorothy Collins; Department of Rare Books, Olin Library, Cornell University; Robert Craft; Walter De la Mare Estate; Special Collections, University Library, Durham University; Exeter University Library; Faber & Faber Archive, London; Dominique Fernandez; Angel Flores; Galleria Nazionale d'Arte Moderna, Rome; Guggenheim Foundation, New York; University Archives, Harvard University; Herrick Memorial

Library, Alfred University, New York; Hidehiko Shindo; The Houghton Library, Harvard University; House of Books, New York; Lelia Howard; Huntington Library, California; Modern Archive Centre, King's College, Cambridge; Lilly Library, Indiana University, Bloomington; Special Collections and University Archives, McFarlin Library, University of Tulsa; Mills Memorial Library, McMaster University. Hamilton, Ontario; Old Library, Magdalene College, Cambridge; Morris Library, Southern Illinois University at Carbondale; Lewis Morris; National Library of Scotland, Edinburgh; Special Collections, Northwestern University Library, Evanston, Illinois; Oxford University Press Archive; Fondation Saint-John Perse, Aix-en-Provence; Pierpont Morgan Library, New York; Department of Rare Books and Special Collections, Princeton University Library; Reading University Library; Rosenbach Museum and Library, Philadelphia; Grace Schulman; Timothy and Marian Seldes; Manuscript Collections, University of Sussex Library; Syracuse University Library; The Library, Trinity College, Dublin; The Harry Ransom Humanities Research Center, University of Texas at Austin; Department of Special Collections, McFarlin Library, University of Tulsa, Oklahoma; University of California at Los Angeles; Special Collections, McPherson Library, University of Victoria, British Columbia; Alderman Library, University of Virginia Library; Dr Charlotte Williamson.

For permission to quote from copyright material, we thank Alastair Kershaw (Richard Aldington); The Ezra Pound Literary Property Trust, and James Laughlin (Ezra Pound); The Bertrand Russell Estate and McMaster University (Bertrand Russell).

Special thanks go to Tom Chandler for copy-editing, to Donald Sommerville for typesetting, and to Debbie Whitfield for her steadfast commitment and hard work.

*The editors and publishers apologise if any person or estate has been overlooked. They would be grateful to be informed if any copyright notice has been omitted, or if there have been any changes of ownership or location.*

# PREFACE

Volume 3 of the *Letters of T. S. Eliot* brings the poet to the age of thirty-nine. In the period covered by this collection, Eliot determines upon a new course for his life and work. Forsaking the Unitarianism of his immediate family, he is received into the Church of England; and he is naturalised as a British citizen. 'I don't like being a squatter,' he later says. 'I might as well take the full responsibility.' He was to remark too, 'I should think it unseemly for a naturalized British subject to support any but the church as by law established.' (*Time* magazine observed: 'Last week a sleek, brilliant citizen of the U. S. became a subject of His Britannic Majesty King George V.') This radical alteration of the intellectual and spiritual direction of his career is to be made public, dramatically and controversially, when he declares his 'point of view', in *For Lancelot Andrewes: Essays on Style and Order* (1928), as 'classicist in literature, royalist in politics, and anglo-catholic in religion'. He establishes himself as a spokesman for a very different aesthetic and philosophical standpoint from that of *The Sacred Wood* (1920) and *Homage to John Dryden* (1923).

The demands of his professional life as writer and editor become ever more complex and exacting. The celebrated but financially pressed periodical he has been editing since 1922 – *The Criterion: A Literary Review* – switches from being a quarterly to a monthly. 'I am harried and worried to death,' he writes. Lady Rothermere, his patron and founder of *The Criterion*, loses faith in the magazine (which she reckons to be 'dull'), and withdraws her much-needed capital; and the fledgling house of Faber & Gwyer rescues him by taking over the full responsibility.

In addition to writing numerous essays and editorials, reviews, introductions and prefaces – his output includes an introduction to Wilkie Collins's *The Moonstone* and an introduction, 'A Dialogue on Dramatic Poetry', to Dryden's *Of Dramatic Poesie* – and to involving himself wholeheartedly in the business of his new career as a publisher, Eliot refashions himself from the poet of *The Waste Land* into the Christian poet and intellectual he was to remain. In 1926 he delivers the Clark Lectures at Cambridge on the subject of the Metaphysical poetry of the seventeenth century. The Ariel poems, beginning with *Journey of the Magi* (1927), establish an entirely new manner and vision for the poet of *The Waste*

*Land* and 'The Hollow Men'. These short poems enabled him, he said, to release the 'blocked-up stream' of his poetry, and that release allowed him to write the sequence *Ash-Wednesday* (1930). In addition, he struggles to translate the remarkable work *Anabase*, by St-John Perse (nom de plume of the diplomat Alexis St-Léger Léger) – *Anabasis: A Poem* would finally be published in 1931 – which was to be a signal influence upon Eliot's own later poetry.

He publishes also two sections of an exhilaratingly funny, savage, jazz-influenced play-in-verse – 'Fragment of a Prologue' and 'Fragment of an Agon: From *Wanna Go Home, Baby?*' – which are brought together as *Sweeney Agonistes* (1932).

His correspondence with his mother and brother, and with friends and associates including Conrad Aiken, Richard Aldington, Bonamy Dobrée, Geoffrey Faber, Lord Halifax, Thomas McGreevy, Harold Monro, T. Sturge Moore, John Middleton Murry, Herbert Read, I. A. Richards, Robert Sencourt and William Force Stead, documents all the stages of his career. In France, he cultivates writers associated with the *Action Française* including Henri Massis and Charles Maurras.

These critical years in Eliot's career inaugurate a dramatically different public role and poetic voice. But the public persona masks a personal life of frightful torment. During a visit to Paris, his wife Vivien begins manifesting symptoms of severe mental distress: she feels persecuted and has hallucinations. She hears voices, and has suicidal spells; and she states that she has taken poison. She is hospitalised in the Sanatorium de la Malmaison, where she remains in care for many months. Eliot reports: 'She has had to have continuous guarding, night and day, and a special room for suicidal cases.' Later, Eliot and his wife will stay for a while at Divonne-les-Bains, a convalescent resort in the mountains near the Swiss frontier. The anxiety and misery of his private life are unremitting, even as he becomes a famous public figure.

This comprehensive gathering of Eliot's correspondence from the period 1926–7 includes all of the major letters, and covers every aspect of his life and work, friendships and contacts. To keep the edition to a relatively manageable length, a number of minor letters have been left out of the printed text: all them will be made available in due course on the Faber and Faber website.

VALERIE ELIOT
JOHN HAFFENDEN
2012

# BIOGRAPHICAL COMMENTARY
# 1926–1927

1926 JANUARY – TSE returns to London after two months in the south of France. Having gone on doctor's orders for a rest cure to the Alpes Maritimes, he had also made a visit to Ezra Pound in Rapallo. While abroad he has drafted three of the Clark Lectures to be given at Trinity College, Cambridge. Vivien is back in London, with her servant Ellen Kellond and a nurse. TSE employs in addition an elderly man-of-all-work named William Leonard Janes, a retired policeman. Faber & Gwyer relaunches *The Criterion* as *The New Criterion*. TSE publishes in vol. 4, no. 1, a manifesto, 'The Idea of a Literary Review', plus pieces by Virginia Woolf ('On Being Ill'), Aldous Huxley ('The Monocle') and D. H. Lawrence ('The Woman Who Rode Away – II'). In discussion with the publishers Routledge, TSE agrees to become involved in a new series of book-length volumes entitled 'The Republic of Letters'. But he also develops at Faber & Gwyer a 'rival' series to be called 'The Poets on the Poets'. (TSE's brief monograph *Dante* is to appear in the latter series in 1929.) By mid-February, TSE reports: 'Routledge's will confine themselves to literary artists, novelists, poets, etcetera, while our series will probably cover those writers such as Renan and Schopenhauer who have literary importance but who are primarily philosophers, historians, etcetera.' TSE publishes 'The Fifteenth of November', by Gertrude Stein, in *The New Criterion*. He is ostensibly collaborating (since Oct. 1925) with Robert Graves on a book to be called *Untraditional Elements in Modern Poetry*; by March 1926, his part in that joint venture is taken over by Laura Riding Gottschalk – much to TSE's relief. The collaboration between TSE and Graves is duly superseded by *A Survey of Modernist Poetry* (1927), co-authored by Riding and Graves. 26 JANUARY – TSE delivers the first of his eight weekly Clark lectures – the series being entitled 'On the metaphysical poetry of the seventeenth century with special reference to Donne, Crashaw and Cowley' – having been nominated by his predecessor and friend John Middleton Murry. This commitment requires him to spend two days a week in Cambridge, for almost two months; he has a sick wife at home, in addition to all the same considerable demands put upon him by the editorial work of *The Criterion*. 'I am harried and worried to death at present,' he tells a friend. The stipend for his lecturing (£200) is paid only at the end of the course. FEBRUARY – TSE relates to Murry that Vivien is 'too ill to be left alone with our servant only'. (A young man named Jack McAlpin lodges with them, to help out.) 'You are in some sort of purgatory,' TSE tells Murry, 'I am perhaps thoroughly damned. But that's one reason why I want to see you. And I always feel with you "mon semblable – mon frère".' He institutes a series of regular dinners for the principal *Criterion* contributors: the 'Criterion Club'. MARCH – Henry Eliot and his new wife Theresa visit TSE and Vivien in London. TSE is delighted to notice that Theresa seems to have a 'tonic effect' on Vivien. The Eliots move from their flat at 9 Clarence Gate Gardens, near Regent's Park, to a compact house at 57 Chester Terrace (now Chester Row), London S.W.1. With a two-year lease still to run at 9 Clarence Gate Gardens, they sublet the flat on a furnished basis for several months. But the new house proves unsatisfactory in all sorts of ways. Vivien will later lament, in 1928: 'I am so very very lonely over here in *Chester Terrace*.' 8 MARCH – TSE arranges for Richard Cobden-Sanderson (printer of *The Criterion*) to publish *Savonarola: A Dramatic Poem*, by Charlotte Eliot, with an Introduction by TSE (300 copies): TSE's mother meets the printing bill of £55 10s 6d. MARCH – Eliot's final Clark Lecture in Cambridge is attended by Henry and by Theresa (who makes a drawing of TSE at the podium). Later the same month, VHE suffers from shingles and temporarily retreats from visitors (including her parents) to the flat at Clarence Gate Gardens. Ellen Kellond leaves the Eliots' employ to get married. Vivien writes of Ellen, 'She has been my greatest – best – almost only friend for 9 years.' TSE and Vivien are witnesses at the wedding at Paddington Register Office, and take the bride and groom out to lunch at Frascasti's. Vivien will go on lamenting: 'I miss *Ellen* . . . – & of course *she* can never be replaced.' Mrs Minnie Grant becomes Vivien's maid (though they will feel obliged to let her go, for financial reasons, during their extended stay on the Continent during April and May). APRIL – The *New Criterion* includes pieces by E. M. Forster ('The Novels of Virginia Woolf') and W. B. Yeats ('Our Need for Religious Sincerity'). 1 APRIL – Henry Eliot and his wife travel to Paris to continue their honeymoon; at their invitation, TSE and Vivien follow them there a week later. 23 APRIL – TSE and Vivien, with Henry and Theresa, take the night train to Rome. In Rome, TSE and Vivien stay at the Pensione Fray, near the Borghese Gardens. Vivien's brother Maurice Haigh-Wood, who is working in Rome, stays at the same pension. According to Theresa Eliot's later signed testimony, they go together to visit St Peter's Basilica; and it is there that Theresa witnesses TSE fall to his knees before Michelangelo's *Pietà*. They propose to stay for two weeks in Rome, roughly coinciding with the period of the General Strike in England, 3–12 May. Ezra Pound visits them in Rome, travelling all the way from Rapallo. They prolong their stay, and eventually remain in Rome until nearly mid-May. Back in England, Geoffrey Faber puts TSE up for a Research Fellowship at All Souls, Oxford (of which Faber is a Fellow and Bursar), with warm testimonials from Charles Whibley and Bruce Richmond (editor of the *TLS*). 12–24 MAY – TSE and Vivien remove from Rome to Freiburg in Germany – to consult with Dr Karl Martin (whom Vivien had consulted in an earlier year, much to her distress, and whose treatments combined starvation dieting, psychoanalysis and injections of milk) – and end up spending over a week there. Geoffrey Faber reports that unhappily TSE has not been elected to a fellowship at All Souls: certain of his Oxford colleagues blocked the election on account of their expressed shock at Eliot's poetry. By 29 May, TSE is back in London, having returned for a brief while from Germany to Paris, and having left Vivien with the Pounds there. Vivien begins manifesting symptoms of severe mental distress: she feels persecuted and has hallucinations. Among her most alarming symptoms, she says she hears voices; and she has felt so terrified that she sleeps on the floor of the Pounds' hotel room. She also has suicidal spells, and later states that she even took poison in Paris. At some point during this period, Vivien writes to Osbert Sitwell, and separately to Edith Sitwell, saying that she has been involved in some sort of scandal and asking for their imperative help. The 'scandal' presumably refers to her attempted suicide in Paris: there is no evidence that she became involved in any other form of scandal. Vivien is admitted to the Sanatorium de la Malmaison, 4 Place Bergère, Rueil (Seine-et-Oise), under the supervision of Henri

Claude, Professor of Psychiatry at the Sorbonne, at a cost of 300 francs a day. The Pounds wire TSE to tell him of the situation and he hastens back to Paris; he tells his brother on 3 June, 'She has had to have continuous guarding, night and day, & a special room for suicidal cases.' In July, Vivien will try to explain herself to John Middleton Murry: 'I have been in hell here, but it is a good place, & the doctors are good, & *absolutely kind* . . . *IF* I had stayed in Rome, *where I was happy*, – if I had stayed there, & let Tom go back to England & his brother & sister-in-law (with whom we are travelling, *a most awful nightmare*) go on with their honeymoon, I think I should have been allright. But Tom's brother's wife persecuted me, & I felt I had to *justify my condition* by going straight from Rome to Freiburg. I had 9 days there, with T., under Dr M[artin] & I left there completely destroyed. I had a perfect horror & loathing of Dr M.' Also in the summer Vivien looks back on the awfulness of what she has been through: 'It was *within* a week of leaving Freiburg that I took poison in Paris.' JUNE – the *New Criterion* includes a piece by D. H. Lawrence ('Mornings in Mexico'). 7 JUNE – TSE comes home to London, and almost immediately returns to Paris for a few days, 15–20 June. In Paris, he is a guest at a grand dinner – 'the most exquisite dinner I have ever tasted' – thrown by the *Action Française*: those in attendance include Charles Maurras, Léon Daudet, Henri Massis, Jacques Maritain and Jacques Bainville. The following day, he goes to the theatre to see *Orphée* by 'my friend Jean Cocteau'. On another day, he attends the grand premiere of George Antheil's *Ballet Mécanique* at the Théâtre des Champs-Élysées. Formally dressed, complete with top hat, TSE is Lady Rothermere's escort for the evening. Others in attendance include Sylvia Beach, Adrienne Monnier, James Joyce and his family, Ezra Pound, Sergei Diaghilev, Koussevitsky and Brancusi. Some of the audience barrack the music, and the evening ends with a riot. Of Vivien's conduct at Malmaison, TSE tells his brother on 24 June: 'She is very affectionate and gentle, and her regrets and self-accusations are terribly pathetic . . . she has not made any attempt on her life for over a fortnight.' By the last week of June, he returns to London: it is a short-lived respite, for on 26 June he goes back to Paris for a week. On 29 June he is in the audience at the Salle Pleyel for a performance of *Paroles de Villon: Airs and Fragments from an Opera Le Testament*, written by Ezra Pound, with Pound's mistress

Olga Rudge (1895–1996) on the violin. 6 JULY – Vivien writes to Middleton Murry, from Malmaison: 'Something awful has happened to me. I can't help myself & I can't ask God to help me. I don't ask Tom to help me now. I am quite alone & I have nothing at all inside . . .' Meanwhile, when he is briefly back in London, TSE goes on a march, in company with Bonamy Dobrée, to help to save the City churches. He is back in Paris again by the middle of the month. Vivien writes, in another letter (July) to Murry: 'for 6 or 8 months I HAVE known that I am absolutely alone, & I *have* known that I do not understand Tom. His presence, still always terribly longed for, gives me a feeling of such utter isolation. *I can't tell you* . . . Mind, I think he feels *exactly as lonely* with me. But is it the same? No. He is free. I am not. O I know I am utterly worthless, a sparrow. I know it does not *matter* what becomes of me. But I am in pain, in pain. I have been in gilded cages 11 years. One cage after another. I have never *grown up*. I don't know anything. Can't you tell Tom it is *nicer* to see birds free than in cages?' Murry offers her the use of a cottage in the West Country, but she is unable to take it on grounds of her health. 29 JULY – TSE tells his brother about Vivien: 'the doctors agree that of insanity, that is of *mental* disease proper, there is no trace. The trouble is wholly emotional . . . I should be very glad if you and Theresa would write to her, merely to express affection . . . You see she still believes that you and T. particularly disapprove of her, and at her worst she imagined that you were plotting to annul our marriage . . . She is still inclined to suppose that anyone who is my friend and wishes me well *must* be her enemy.' 6 AUGUST – TSE lunches in London with Aldous Huxley, who reports to their mutual friend Mary Hutchinson that TSE 'looked terribly grey-green, drank no less than five gins with his meal, told me he was going to join Vivien in her Paris nursing home to break himself of his addictions to tobacco and alcohol, and was eloquent about Parisian luncheons with resoundingly titled duchesses. In the intervals we had a very pleasant and friendly talk about books.' In the second week of August TSE joins Vivien at the Sanatorium de la Malmaison for a 'rest cure' ending on 25 Aug. 22 AUGUST – TSE's sister Charlotte – Mrs George Lawrence Smith – dies of peritonitis: 'a great shock . . . a tragedy,' mourns TSE. From 31 August, TSE and Vivien are due to stay for a month at the Grand Hotel, Divonne-les-Bains – a convalescent resort near the

Swiss frontier – where they will attend a clinic for nervous disorders. But their departure from Malmaison is delayed for a week, until 8 September, because Vivien has contracted bronchitis. In addition, Vivien suffers from peritonitis while at the Grand Hotel. At Divonne, TSE undergoes treatments including the *douche écossaise* (the doctors deprecate drugs and tend to avoid psychoanalysis). 'It is very dull & very expensive,' says TSE. A fellow patient is Robert Esmonde Gordon George (1890–1969), critic, historian, biographer – he is better known under his nom de plume Robert Sencourt – who writes in a later year about his first impressions of Eliot: 'Here was someone extremely approachable and friendly, even confiding, someone to whom one took immediately. One felt that he was sincerity incarnate, the most natural and the most modest of men . . . How well I remember my first glimpse of Vivienne . . .! Her black hair was dank, her white face blotched – owing, no doubt, to the excess of bromide she had been taking. Her dark dress hung loosely over her frail form; her expression was both vague and acutely sad.' TSE himself would later say simply, 'Divonne was dreadful.' TSE has been working on a translation of *Anabase*, by St-John Perse (nom de plume of the diplomat Alexis St-Léger Léger). He writes to his cousin Marguerite Caetani, owner of the Paris-based literary magazine *Commerce*: 'My wife is constantly worrying me to do more on *Anabase*. She is afraid it will never be done. I confess it is more difficult than I thought at first, because the idea (and there decidedly is one) is conveyed by a cumulative succession of images – and one *cannot* simply translate the images.' 23 SEPTEMBER – TSE publishes his essay 'Lancelot Andrewes' in the *TLS*. He examines a Cambridge fellowship dissertation by James Smith. 6 OCTOBER – TSE and VHE rest at the Cecil Hotel, Passy, en route back to England. TSE publishes in *The Criterion* 'Fragment of a Prologue' (part of a play in verse reprinted in due course as the first section of *Sweeney Agonistes*, 1932). NOVEMBER – He puts in hand his intention to become a British citizen; he had meant to take this step much earlier, but the events of the summer held him back. Vivien passes some time at Cannes before returning to London by the end of November. DECEMBER – Vivien returns to Bertrand Russell some jewels he had given her in an earlier year. She writes to Henry Eliot at Christmas-time: 'Tom has been well, increasingly for the last 3 months. It is a long time since I have seen him so well & easy in mind.'

1927 JANUARY – TSE publishes in *The Criterion* 'Fragment of an Agon. From *Wanna Go Home, Baby?*' It will ultimately become the second section of the never-completed *Sweeney Agonistes* (1932). This marks the close of *The New Criterion*; it will appear next in late April as *The Monthly Criterion*. TSE publishes in *The Enemy* (ed. Wyndham Lewis), 'A Note on Poetry and Belief', contesting I. A. Richards's declaration that *The Waste Land* had 'effected a complete severance between poetry and *all* beliefs'. 15 JANUARY – TSE finishes the draft of his translation of *Anabase* (*Anabasis*), and sends it off to St-John Perse for comment and corrections. But he has to wait for many months before a response is finally vouchsafed by the distinguished busy diplomat. In January and February TSE consults a friend, the Revd William Force Stead, about joining the communion of the Church of England; confiding, 'for the moment, it concerns me alone, & not the public – not even those nearest me.' He reassures Stead that as a Unitarian he had been baptised; but Stead correctly argues that by definition, having been brought up as a Unitarian, TSE would not have been baptised 'in the name of the Trinity'. FEBRUARY –TSE submits his introduction to Seneca. He pushes ahead with the process of naturalisation. He and Vivien stay at St Leonards-on-Sea, on the Sussex coast, 'for a week or two', primarily to help to nurse Vivien's father, Charles Haigh-Wood, who is dying of cancer at the Warrior House Hotel. MARCH – TSE writes in *The Dial* that the chief distinction of Man is to glorify God. 11 MARCH – TSE is 'back in town'. He reports to his brother on 15 March: 'V's condition is anything but satisfactory, her delusions are very serious indeed, & quite beyond the point of "severe handling". They are quite genuine.' 18 MARCH – He addresses the Shakespeare Association, London, on the subject of 'Shakespeare and the Stoicism of Seneca'. 25 MARCH – TSE's father-in-law dies. Maurice Haigh-Wood will later remark that at the funeral he believed TSE to have had a 'vision'. TSE has to undertake an extraordinary amount of work as executor (with Rose Haigh-Wood and Maurice Haigh-Wood) of his father-in-law. Since Maurice is now working at a bank in Rome, and since the ageing Mrs Haigh-Wood is badly afflicted by rheumatism, for many months the burden of correspondence with lawyers, accountants and brokers falls entirely upon TSE. Vivien contracts 'severe & tenacious bronchitis' (following her father's death). APRIL – Ernst Robert Curtius publishes a translation of *The Waste Land – Das wüste Land* – in the periodical *Neue Schweizer Rundschau* (Zurich). 28 APRIL is the date of the first appearance of *The Monthly Criterion*, after four years as a quarterly: it will continue as such until March 1928. The next issue is to be published on 26 May. TSE says he has been 'busy and flustered' by the process of turning the magazine into a monthly. To celebrate the relaunch, Eliot takes Geoffrey Faber and his wife Enid to dinner at the Commercio, in Frith Street, and afterwards to enjoy an evening of boxing at the Royal Albert Hall. 3 MAY – TSE delivers his introduction to Wilkie Collins's novel *The Moonstone*, for publication by World's Classics. He publishes an article on Baudelaire, in *The Dial*. 6 MAY – TSE publicises his intention to seek British citizenship, with a formal announcement being placed in two newspapers. 16 MAY – Probate of the will of Charles Haigh-Wood. JUNE–JULY – TSE and Vivien spend some time on a part-holiday in Eastbourne, Sussex, renting a house at 55 Meads Street; TSE commutes to London for up to three days a week. 22 JUNE – TSE returns to Bertrand Russell some debentures, worth £3,500, in a manufacturing firm which Russell had passed on to TSE and VHE during the Great War on grounds of his pacifism (he had assumed the firm would be making armaments). TSE informs Russell, 'I may say that this transfer is now not only satisfactory to Vivien's of course entirely morbid conscience, but, what is in a sense more important, to my own. Her father has recently died, so that she will shortly come into possession of property yielding income almost, if not quite, equal to that she is surrendering. And I [am] myself influenced by the fact . . . that you have heirs, and I have, and shall have, none.' Of Russell's recent pamphlet, *Why I Am Not A Christian*, he tells Russell frankly: 'All the reasons you advance were familiar to me, *I think*, at the age of six or eight; and I confess that your pamphlet seems to me a piece of childish folly. But I was brought up as an Atheist . . . Why don't you stick to mathematics?' 29 JUNE – TSE is baptised by William Force Stead at Holy Trinity Church, Finstock, Oxfordshire. The witnesses are the theologian Canon B. H. Streeter, Fellow of Queen's College, Oxford, and Vere Somerset, History Tutor and Fellow of Worcester College, Oxford. Vivien is not present. TSE was to write in 1932: 'the Christian scheme seemed the only possible scheme which found a place for values which I must maintain or perish (and belief comes first and practice second), the belief, for instance, in holy living and holy dying, in sanctity, chastity, humility, austerity.' He would say also, 'the convert of the intellectual or sensitive type is drawn towards the more Catholic type of worship and doctrine.' On the following day, 30 June, he is confirmed by Thomas Banks Strong, Bishop of Oxford, at the Bishop's Palace in Cuddesdon. He writes *Journey of the Magi*. JULY – TSE publishes 'Archbishop Bramhall' in *Theology*. 27 JULY – He stands as godparent at the christening of Tom Faber (b. 25 Apr. 1927). Three weeks later, TSE gives his godson a pre-publication copy of *Journey of the Magi*, with the inscription: 'for Thomas Erle Faber, / from T. S. Eliot / 17. 8. 27'. He protests against the activities of the American publishing pirate Samuel Roth, who has already 'pilfered and mangled' *Ulysses* and pirates a poem by TSE for the September issue of *Two Worlds Monthly*. During July, TSE and Vivien rest at Eastbourne, driving out to nearby places of interest including Winchelsea, Rye and Battle. When they return to London at the end of July, Vivien's friend Lucy Thayer stays with them. TSE tells his brother, 29 July, with reference to Vivien's state of mental health: 'the letters which I write to [mother] are composed primarily for the purpose of cheering and pleasing her . . . You must not suppose that any letters I write to her are of any value as a statement of facts.' 22 AUGUST – TSE writes to his brother: 'You will realise that it is more difficult for me to get away than most know – it has got to the point where staying here is not a mere matter of sentiment or conscience, but a matter of duty and almost daily anxiety and necessity.' 25 AUGUST – TSE publishes *Journey of the Magi* ('Ariel Poem' no. 8), with illustrations by E. McKnight Kauffer, in an edition of 5,000 copies. It is the best seller of a group of eight volumes in the first series of 'Ariel Poems' (the others include poems by G. K. Chesterton, Thomas Hardy, Siegfried Sassoon and Walter de la Mare). Setting himself to writing the 'Ariel' poems enabled him, as he later said, to release what he had thought the blocked-up 'stream' of poetry, and the release allowed him to write *Ash-Wednesday*. 30 AUGUST – TSE tells Henry: 'So long as Vivien is as she is, I do not see how I can leave . . . We must therefore wait until she either annoys people in the public street (which I am always expecting) or tries to take her own life, before I can do anything about it. Meanwhile I feel that I must not leave her, even for a night, as this sort of thing might happen at any time.' SEPTEMBER – VHE returns voluntarily to Malmaison. TSE accompanies her to Paris for a week from mid-month, and returns to London for his birthday on 26 September. 27 SEPTEMBER, Geoffrey Faber records in his diary: 'Took Eliot to lunch at club. Heard much about his wife, who is now in sanatorium in Paris. E. said "For a long time it has been just as much as I could do to keep going. I'm like a man who can just keep his head above the water by treading water but can't begin to think of swimming."' 22 SEPTEMBER – publication of *Shakespeare and the Stoicism of Seneca*; subsequently reprinted in *Selected Essays 1917-1932* (1932). TSE also publishes his Introduction to *Seneca His Tenne Tragedies* translated into English, ed. Thomas Newton anno 1591 (The Tudor Translations, Second Series, ed. Charles Whibley: 2 vols, London, 1927): 1,025 copies printed. TSE's 'Introduction' is to be reprinted as 'Seneca in Elizabethan Translation' in *Selected Essays*. OCTOBER – VHE continues to reside at Malmaison. 20 OCTOBER – TSE goes to a party thrown by the art critic Clive Bell; other guests include Leonard and Virginia Woolf, and Harold Nicolson. Two days later, Woolf records in her diary: 'Tom, of course, in white waistcoat, much the man of the world; which sets the key & off they go telling stories about "Jean" (Cocteau), about Ada Leverson, Gosse, Valéry, &c. & L. & I feel a little Bloomsburyish perhaps; no, I think this sort of talk is hardly up to the scratch.' 22 OCTOBER – TSE spends the weekend as Faber's guest at All Souls College, Oxford. Presently he visits Lord Halifax – the most eminent Anglican layman in the UK – for a weekend at his residence, Hickleton Hall, near Doncaster, Yorkshire. (He has been introduced to Halifax by Robert Sencourt.) By 25 October he composes his contribution to John Dryden, *Of Dramatic Poesie an essay 1668 . . . Preceded by a Dialogue on Poetic Drama by T. S. Eliot* (London: Frederick Etchells and Hugh Macdonald, 1928); the essay, which debates the merits of verse over prose in dramatic utterance, will be reprinted as 'A Dialogue on Dramatic Poetry' in *SE*. 25 OCTOBER – For the very first time he mentions to his brother that he has applied for naturalisation. 'If this shocks you, I will present you my reasons; in any case, don't tell mother.' But Henry will tell him on 26 November, 'I am afraid the news is out.' At the end of October, TSE visits Kenneth Pickthorn at Corpus Christi College, Cambridge. 2 NOVEMBER – a certificate of naturalisation is granted to TSE, who later explains: 'I don't like being a squatter.

I might as well take the full responsibility.' To Charles Whibley, he writes: 'I expected to be summoned to the Home Office at least, if not before the Throne. Instead I merely had to swear an ordinary oath before an ordinary commissioner, just as one does in ordinary life.' *Time* magazine reports on 28 November: 'Last week a sleek, brilliant citizen of the U.S. became a subject of His Britannic Majesty King George V. He is Thomas Stearns Eliot, relative of the late Charles William Eliot, President Emeritus of Harvard University . . . His many adverse critics, in no wise surprised by his change of nationality, hint that a certain superciliousness toward U.S. letters caused him to feel more at home in England, where neo-literary figures abound profuse as the autumnal leaves.' TSE's new citizenship confirms his sense that he had done exactly the right thing in joining the Church of England: 'It is . . . all right for Britons to be Papists when they have been so since before Henry VIII consecutively. But (except as a consequence of political events which I hope will not occur), I should think it unseemly for a naturalised British subject to support any but the church as by Law established.' TSE examines a Cambridge dissertation by Fr F. J. Yealy SJ on the subject of 'Emerson and the Romantic Revival'. He also comments on the typescript of I. A. Richards's work-in-progress *Practical Criticism*. Briefly in mid-November, TSE returns to Paris to see Vivien again. Back in London, his aged retainer, 'poor old Janes', falls downstairs and injures himself: TSE pays the doctor's bill and visits him daily in hospital. Reviewing the performance and the prospects of the *Criterion*, Geoffrey Faber takes the view that sales have not increased, as a result of making the magazine into a monthly, in proportion to the increase of expenses. The net average sale of *The Monthly Criterion*, including subscribers' copies, is found to be between 700 and 800 copies. For the period from January 1926 to June 1927 the total net loss amounted to £2,315 5s 7d. For the period from June to December 1927 the estimated total net loss was £790 4s 9d. TSE's editor's salary is guaranteed by agreement with F&G: whatever falls out, his salary will be sustained to the end of 1931. Taking all things into consideration, however, TSE volunteers, in the event that the *Criterion* has to be closed down, that he will be content for this sum to be reduced to £250. He is also in receipt of a director's fee from F&G of £400 a year. A Directors' Meeting at F&G, held on 17 November, favours a reversion to the quarterly format, beginning in 1928. But it is acknowledged that since Lady Rothermere is still co-proprietor, her views must be taken into consideration. TSE travels to Switzerland to have an emergency consultation with her: the abrupt upshot is that she withdraws all her capital from the *Criterion*, for which she says she has an intense dislike – and (says TSE) she expresses 'her resentments against me'. TSE reports that 'she was very sick' of it. 'I must say I am thankful to get rid of the Harmsworth connection,' TSE relates to a friend; and in a later year: 'We did not part on the best of terms.' He tells his mother, 'I must say that the connection was always a great strain, as she is not only an eccentric person, but belongs to a world from which we should never choose our friends, a world of millionaires with no social background or traditions and no sense of public responsibility.' Contributors are informed on 6 December that the *Criterion* is suspended henceforth 'owing to differences of opinion between the Proprietors on matters of policy'. However, less than a week later, on 12 December contributors are gratifyingly told that the magazine will after all be able to continue, at least for a while. Looking back over the last couple of years, TSE relates to his mother too: 'One gets very tired in time of doing a job in which oneself is so submerged; fighting other people's battles, and advertising other people's wares. Of course it is pleasant to do something that many people think useful, and to have people depend on you is perhaps the most substantial and solid human relationship, in general, that there is; for you can depend on people's dependence more than on their affection . . .' Of Vivien, he remarks: 'I have not told her anything about *The Criterion* crisis, because she has the *Criterion* so much at heart that it would have distressed her, and she is always terribly inclined to worry, and to convince herself that everything is her fault, and as *The Criterion* is going on for the present there is no need to tell her.' 10 DECEMBER – TSE publishes 'Salutation' – it will form part II of *Ash-Wednesday* (1930) – in *The Saturday Review of Literature* and also in the *Criterion* (Jan. 1928). TSE spends Christmas week in Paris (with his mother-in-law) visiting Vivien; he is back in London on the 28th.

# ABBREVIATIONS AND SOURCES

PUBLISHED WORKS

| | |
|---|---|
| *ASG* | *After Strange Gods* (London: Faber & Faber, 1934) |
| *AVP* | *Ara Vos Prec* (London: The Ovid Press, 1920) |
| *CP* | *The Cocktail Party* (London: Faber & Faber, 1950) |
| *CPP* | *The Complete Poems and Plays of T. S. Eliot* (London: Faber & Faber, 1969) |
| *EE* | *Elizabethan Essays* (London: Faber & Faber, 1934) |
| *FLA* | *For Lancelot Andrewes: Essays on Style and Order* London: Faber & Gwyer, 1928) |
| *FR* | *The Family Reunion* (London: Faber & Faber, 1939) |
| Gallup | Donald Gallup, *T. S. Eliot: A Bibliography* (London: Faber & Faber, 1969) |
| *HJD* | *Homage to John Dryden: Three Essays on Poetry of the Seventeenth Century* (London: The Hogarth Press, 1924) |
| *IMH* | *Inventions of the March Hare: Poems 1909–1917, ed Christopher Ricks* (London: Faber & Faber, 1996) |
| *KEPB* | *Knowledge and Experience in the Philosophy of F. H. Bradley* (London: Faber & Faber, 1964; New York: Farrar, Straus & company, 1964) |
| *L* | *Letters of T. S. Eliot* (London: Faber & Faber, Vol 1 [rev. edn], 2009; Vol. 2, 2009) |
| *MiC* | *Murder in the Cathedral* (London: Faber & Faber, 1935) |
| *NTDC* | *Notes towards the Definition of a Culture* |
| *OPP* | *On Poetry and Poets* (London: Faber & Faber, 1957; New York: Farrar, Straus & Cudahy, 1957) |
| *P* | *Poems* (London: The Hogarth Press, 1919) |
| *P 1909–1925* | *Poems 1909–1925* (London: Faber & Gwyer, |

| | |
|---|---|
| | 1925) |
| *POO* | *Prufrock and Other Observations* (London: The Egoist Press, 1917) |
| *SA* | *Sweeney Agonistes: Fragments of an Aristophanic Melodrama* (London: Faber & Faber, 1932) |
| *SE* | *Selected Essays: 1917–1932* (London: Faber & Faber, 1932; 3rd English edn., London and Boston: Faber & Faber, 1951) |
| *SW* | *The Sacred Wood: Essays on Poetry and Criticism* (London: Methuen & Co., 1920) |
| *TCC* | *To Criticise the Critic* (London: Faber & Faber, 1965; New York: Farrar, Straus & Giroux, 1965) |
| *TUPUC* | *The Use of Poetry and the Use of Criticism: Studies in the Relation of Criticism to Poetry in England* (London: Faber & Faber, 1933) |
| *TWL* | *The Waste Land* (1922, 1923) |
| *TWL: Facs* | *The Waste Land: A Facsimile and Transcript of the Original Drafts*, ed. Valerie Eliot (London: Faber & Faber, 1971; New York: Harcourt, Brace Jovanovich, 1971) |
| *VMP* | *The Varieties of Metaphysical Poetry*, ed. Ronald Schuchard (London: Faber & Faber, 1993; New York: Harcourt Brace, 1994) |

PERIODICALS AND PUBLISHERS

| | |
|---|---|
| *A.* | *The Athenaeum* (see also *N&A*) |
| *C.* | *The Criterion* |
| F&F | Faber & Faber (publishers) |
| F&G | Faber & Gwyer (publishers) |
| *MC* | *The Monthly Criterion* |
| *N.* | *The Nation* |
| *N&A* | *The Nation & The Athenaeum* |
| *NC* | *New Criterion* |
| *NRF* | *La Nouvelle Revue Française* |
| *NS* | *New Statesman* |
| *TLS* | *Times Literary Supplement* |

PERSONS

| | |
|---|---|
| CA | Conrad Aiken |
| RA | Richard Aldington |

| | |
|---|---|
| RC-S | Richard Cobden-Sanderson |
| BD | Bonamy Dobrée |
| CWE | Charlotte Ware Eliot (TSE's mother) |
| EVE | (Esmé) Valerie Eliot |
| HWE | Henry Ware Eliot (TSE's brother) |
| TSE | T. S. Eliot |
| VHE | Vivien (Haigh-Wood) Eliot |
| GCF | Geoffrey (Cust) Faber |
| IPF | Irene Pearl Fassett (TSE's secretary) |
| JDH | John Davy Hayward |
| MH | Mary Hutchinson |
| AH | Aldous Huxley |
| JJ | James Joyce |
| DHL | D. H. Lawrence |
| FRL | F. R. Leavis |
| WL | Wyndham Lewis |
| FVM | Frank Vigor Morley |
| OM | Ottoline Morrell |
| JMM | John Middleton Murry |
| EP | Ezra Pound |
| HR | Herbert Read |
| IAR | I. A. Richards |
| BLR | Bruce Richmond |
| ALR | A. L. Rowse |
| BR | Bertrand Russell |
| ES | Edith Sitwell |
| WFS | William Force Stead |
| CW | Charles Whibley |
| OW | Orlo Williams |
| LW | Leonard Woolf |
| VW | Virginia Woolf |
| WBY | W. B. Yeats |

ARCHIVE COLLECTIONS

| | |
|---|---|
| Adamson | Donald Adamson Collection |
| American Jewish Archives | Jacob Rader Center of American Jewish Archives, Cincinnati, Ohio |
| Archives Nationales | Archives Nationales, Paris |
| Arkansas | Special Collections, University Libraries, University of Arkansas |

| | |
|---|---|
| BL | British Library, London |
| Beinecke | The Beinecke Rare Book and Manuscript Library, Yale University |
| Berg | Henry W. and Albert A. Berg Collection of English and American Literature, the New York Public Library |
| Bodleian | The Bodleian Library, Oxford University |
| Bonn | Universitäts und Landesbibliothek, Bonn University |
| Brotherton | The Brotherton Collection, Leeds University Library |
| Butler | Rare Books and Manuscripts Division, Butler Library, Columbia University, New York |
| Caetani | Fondazione Camillo Caetani |
| Cambridge | Cambridge University Library |
| Cornell | Department of Rare Books, Olin Library, Cornell University |
| Durham | Special Collections, University Library, Durham University |
| Exeter | Exeter University Library |
| Faber | Faber & Faber Archive, London |
| Guggenheim | Guggenheim Foundation, New York |
| Harvard | University Archives, Harvard University |
| Herrick | Herrick Memorial Library, Alfred University, New York |
| Houghton | The Houghton Library, Harvard University |
| House of Books | House of Books, New York |
| Huntington | Huntington Library, California |
| King's | Modern Archive Centre, King's College, Cambridge |
| Lilly | Lilly Library, Indiana University, Bloomington |
| McFarlin | McFarlin Library, University of Tulsa, Oklahoma |
| McMaster | Mills Memorial Library, McMaster University. Hamilton, Ontario |
| Magdalene | Old Library, Magdalene College, Cambridge |
| Morris | Morris Library, Southern Illinois University at Carbondale |
| National Library of Scotland | National Library of Scotland, Edinburgh |
| Northwestern | Special Collections, Northwestern University |

| | |
|---|---|
| | Library, Evanston, Illinois |
| OUP Archive | Oxford University Press Archive |
| Fondation Saint-John Perse | Fondation Saint-John Perse, Aix-en-Provence |
| Pierpont Morgan Library | Pierpont Morgan Library, New York |
| Princeton | Department of Rare Books and Special Collections, Princeton University Library |
| Private Buyer | Sold to an unknown private buyer at a book auction |
| Reading | Reading University Library |
| Rosenbach | Rosenbach Museum and Library, Philadelphia, PA |
| Sussex | Manuscript Collections, University of Sussex Library |
| Syracuse | Syracuse University Library |
| TCD | The Library, Trinity College, Dublin |
| Texas | The Harry Ransom Humanities Research Center, University of Texas at Austin |
| Tulsa | Department of Special Collections, McFarlin Library, University of Tulsa, Oklahoma |
| UCLA | University of California at Los Angeles |
| VE Papers | Vivien Eliot Papers, Bodleian Library, Oxford |
| Victoria | Special Collections, McPherson Library, University of Victoria, British Columbia |
| Virginia | Alderman Library, University of Virginia Library |

# CHRONOLOGY OF THE *CRITERION*

*The Criterion*

Vol. 1. No. 1. 1–103, Oct. 1922; No. 2. 105–201, Jan. 1923; No. 3. 203–313, Apr. 1923; No. 4. 315–427, July 1923.

Vol. 2. No. 5. 1–113, Oct. 1923; No. 6. 115–229, Feb. 1924; No. 7 231–369, Apr. 1924; No. 8 371–503, July 1924.

Vol. 3. No. 9. 1–159, Oct. 1924; No. 10. 161–340, Jan. 1925; No. 11 341–483, Apr. 1925; No. 12. 485–606, July 1925.

*The New Criterion*

Vol. 4. No. 1. 1–220, Jan. 1926; No. 2. 221–415, Apr. 1926; No. 3. 417–626, June 1926; No. 4. 627–814, Oct. 1926.

Vol. 5. No. 1. 1–186, Jan. 1927.

*The Monthly Criterion*

Vol. 5. No. 2. 187–282, May 1927; No. 3. 283–374, June 1927.

Vol. 6. No. 1. 1–96, July 1927; No. 2. 97–192, Aug. 1927; No. 3. 193–288, Sept. 1927; No. 4. 289–384, Oct. 1927; No. 5. 385–480, Nov. 1927; No. 6. 481–584, Dec. 1927.

Vol. 7. No. 1. 1–96, Jan. 1928; No. 2. 97–192, Feb. 1928; No. 3. 193–288, Mar. 1928; No. 4. 289–464, June 1928.

*The Criterion*

Vol. 8. No. 30. 1–185, Sept. 1928; No. 31. 185–376, Dec. 1928; No. 32. 374–574, Apr. 1929; No. 33. 575–773, July 1929.

# EDITORIAL NOTES

The source of each letter is indicated at the top right. CC indicates a carbon copy. Where no other source is shown it may be assumed that the original or carbon copy is in the Valerie Eliot collection or at the Faber and Faber Archive.

*del.* deleted

MS manuscript

n. d. no date

PC postcard

*sc.* *scilicet*: namely

ts typescript

< > indicates a word or words brought in from another part of the letter.

Place of publication is London, unless otherwise stated.

Some obvious typing or manuscript errors have been silently corrected.

Dates have been standardised.

Some words and figures which were abbreviated have been expanded.

Punctuation has been occasionally adjusted.

Editorial insertions are indicated by square brackets.

Words both italicised and underlined signify double underlining in the original copy.

Where possible a biographical note accompanies the first letter to or from a correspondent. Where appropriate this brief initial note will also refer the reader to the Biographical Register at the end of the text.

Vivienne Eliot liked her husband and friends to spell her name Vivien; but as there is no consistency it is printed as written.

'Not in Gallup' means that the item in question is not recorded in Donald Gallup, *T. S. Eliot: A Bibliography* (1970).

# THE LETTERS
## 1926–1927

# 1926

## *Vivien Eliot*[1] TO *Dr Hubert Higgins* MS Valerie Eliot

2 January [1926] The Stanboroughs, Watford

Dear Dr Higgins

When you came to see me at this place on Wed. Dec. 1st had you then offered me the *choice* of a place abroad, to go to with your nurse, *or*, suggested I went to a place where I had friends or relatives, *I shd have agreed at once & stuck to my agreement*. My previous distrust of you wd have disappeared & I shd have believed you were acting in my interests as well as my husbands. As it was, the offer you made me seemed intended to penalize me as well as to put as great a distance as possible between me & my husband.

*As I have said before, I understand* your desire to protect my husband, but you are going the wrong way to work. I think you are over zealous & guided largely by emotion. This makes me distrust you. If you were more judicial & tried to give me the kind of life in which it wd be most easy for me to *make* a life without my husband; if, instead of isolating me you gave me the chance of depending on other people for my mental life & physical well being, you wd be playing yr cards much better in my *husband's interest*. Will you consider this point?

Yrs.
V. H. Eliot

If you had not over-reached yourself in trying to make me as uncomfortable as you could, I should now probably have been going abroad, & it wd probably have been the best thing for my husband, & for me.

It is you yourself who are driving me to worry my husband. If you leave me alone, I shall leave him alone. If you interfere with me, I shall have to let him interfere in my affairs the whole time. *Leave me alone*, & you can get yr information through the nurse about me & as to whether I am *persecuting my husband*.

1 – Vivien Eliot, née Haigh-Wood (1888–1947), see Biographical Register.

When I have let Clarence Gate for him, & finished my work there, you & he can discuss my next move. But if it isn't London, it will have to be Rome, Rapallo, or Paris.

You like plain speaking. By coming to see me you will defeat yr own ends.

I have *not anything* I can say to you. Please do not come to see me. If you do – I don't know what will happen.

Yrs.
V. H. E.

The reason I reject Brighton is that it is not good enough for either of us. My husband will go up & down to see me, spending time & money, & I shall not have sufficient diversion *in the place* to be independent of him, & to get well.

## TO *Leonard Woolf*[1] — TS Berg

4 January 1926 — *The New Criterion*, 24 Russell Square, W.C.1

Dear Leonard,

There were many things I wanted to talk to you about which somehow seemed impossible on our first meeting after such a long time. I wonder if you would lunch with me soon, any day you choose. If so I should be glad if you cared to pick me up here so that I could show you the establishment.[2]

Yours ever
T. S. E.

## *Vivien Eliot* TO *T. S. Eliot* — MS Valerie Eliot

5 January [1926]

Dear Tom

Do you wish your wife to be the boon companion of your masseur. I shd like an answer.

1 – Leonard Woolf (1880–1969), writer and publisher: see Biographical Register.

2 – VW told Vita Sackville-West on 7 Jan.: 'Leonard is lunching with Tom Eliot' (*Letters* III, 226). The chief topic of conversation was VHE's state of health, and the advisability of various treatments: LW had so counselled TSE at earlier meetings.

The nurse suggests today that 'Mr Williams' wd like to 'run us about & take us round in his car'. What could I say?

If I went to Brighton, your masseur wd come to stay the night – for weekends for surprise visits – *& I shd be helpless.* You, innocently in London, wd never know. *I shd be powerless in the hands of the 2 of them.* I am trembling all over. I am doomed. Even Molly sees the danger. Is this how I am to be pushed in the gutter? You *know* Higgins wants to make out I am *common*, & *beneath you.* You *know* Lady R. will believe anything he says. O Tom, where are yr eyes? You, the grand Eliot are to be protected from your *common* wife, by a cunning plot to surround her with common people, to make her so isolated, so powerless, that bit by bit I am *forced to agree to be this* companion (or they wd *persecute* me) they *could*, & they *would* persecute me in every cunning way. Then when I am down to their level, Higgins can *prove* my commonness by telling Lady R. that I am great '*pals*' with the masseur & his fiancée.

This line was indicated to me long ago by his rudely telling me, at Watford, that the 'nurse-*companion*' was to be a '*pal*' to me, for *several years.* At Southampton, they taunted me all the time with my *commonness*, my *lowness*, my *hoarse* voice, my unfitedness [*sic*] to be the wife of a decent man. They told all this to Higgins, who, *knowing* it to be really untrue, yet used it & is using it for his own purposes. The net is being drawn bit by bit, so stealthily, so *cunningly* round me. You, with your head in the air, in your splendid isolation are leaving yr wife to be most vilely & cunningly ruined

I appeal to you once more. Will you protect me, or will you not?

If you *cannot, then return me to* Watford, where, at the least, I am treated as a gentlewoman.

Would this kind of thing happen to *Nancy*? Why can't I even have the freedom & respect which is accorded to Nancy the *real* tart?[1]

[Unfinished]

1 – Probably Nancy Cunard (1896–1965), writer, journalist and political activist; see TSE's letter to her, 2 June 1927, below.

## TO *C. P. Hawkes*[1] CC

5 January 1926 [*The New Criterion*]

Dear Sir,

I have just returned from abroad and find your two letters of the 11th November and the 30th December. I very much regret the inconvenience to which you, as well as a number of other contributors, have been put. The explanation is that the negotiations for the transfer of the publication of *The Criterion* from Mr Cobden-Sanderson to Messrs Faber & Gwyer Limited could not be completed in time for any autumn number to be published at all. As a matter of fact these negotiations were further delayed by my own ill health and the preparations for the January number had to be made at very short notice when I was summarily ordered abroad by my doctor. I was under the impression that your book containing 'Cherrero' was to appear before Christmas and I therefore omitted 'Cherrero' from the January number which went to press in November. In normal circumstances I should have written to you to this effect and it was only owing to haste and great pressure of work necessitated by my departure that I failed to do so.[2]

I am very sorry indeed that this has happened and can only say that I hope that you will again have something to offer us. And if your book contains much material as interesting as this essay and of the same type I should be very glad if we might have the opportunity of reviewing it.

Yours faithfully,
[T. S. Eliot]

1–Lt.-Col. C. P. Hawkes (1877–1956) served in the regular army, 1900–20. A lawyer, he was Registrar in the Supreme Court (Probate, Divorce and Admiralty Division), 1925–50. He contributed to newspapers and periodicals; and his writings included *The London Comedy* (1925) and *Mauresques, with Some Basque and Spanish Cameos* (1926).

2–Hawkes wrote (18 Jan.) that Methuen was in no hurry to publish the book, *Mauresques*, in which his article 'Cherrero' was to feature; it appeared in *NC* 4 (Apr. 1926), 297–305.

## TO *E. M. Forster*[1] CC

5 January 1926 [London]

Dear Forster,

I should like very much to see your essay on Virginia Woolf as soon as you can let me have it.[2] It is merely a question of whether I can squeeze it into the April number or not, and I will let you know as quickly as possible. Who is publishing it in America?

Sincerely yours
[T. S. Eliot]

## TO *S. S. Koteliansky*[3] TS Berg

5 January 1926 *The New Criterion*

Dear Koteliansky,

I have just got back from abroad and find your letter of the 11th November. I owe you many apologies. The fact is that the negotiations for the transfer to the publication of *The Criterion*, which were protracted by my own ill health, made it impossible to issue any October number at all. Furthermore, the January number had to be made up under very considerable difficulties exactly at the moment when I was ordered abroad for two months by my doctor and had only a few days in which to clear up all my business. I should like to hear from you exactly how much you have suffered by this unfortunate delay. I hope that I can use the contribution in the April *Criterion* and in any case I shall take the matter up with my principals with a view to securing you an immediate payment for it.[4]

Also, now that I am back in London I should very much like to see you.

Sincerely yours,
T. S. Eliot

1–E. M. Forster (1879–1970), novelist and essayist: see Biographical Register.
2–On 2 Jan. Forster had submitted his article 'The Novels of Virginia Woolf' (3,500 words). He wrote again on 7 Jan. to say the piece would be appearing in the *Yale Review* on 20 March. He had shown it to VW – 'and am glad to say that she found the interpretation of *Mrs Dalloway* correct'. See *NC* 4 (Apr. 1926), 277–86.
3–Samuel S. Koteliansky (1881–1955), Ukrainian émigré, translated works by Tolstoy and Dostoevsky, some in collaboration with VW and LW.
4–See Koteliansky's translation of letters by F. M. Dostoevsky to N. A. Liubimov, 'Dostoevsky on "The Brothers Karamasov"', *NC* 4 (June 1926), 552–62.

## TO *Edwin Muir*[1] CC

5 January 1926 [*The New Criterion*]

Dear Mr Muir,

As I do not know where you are at present I am writing to this address. Will you let me know how soon you are likely to be in town as I want very much to see you and can arrange a time at your convenience. Meanwhile, there is no hurry about the Hauptmann because it is probable that we shall not be able to start publication of our series[2] until the autumn and we may be obliged to modify it in some respects.

Sincerely yours
[T. S. Eliot]

## TO *Wyndham Lewis*[3] TS Cornell

9 January 1926 *The New Criterion*

Dear Lewis

I have been back in London since Christmas day but have been too busy to write and thank you for your letter[4] which was forwarded to me in France. It is the only really intelligent comment upon my book which I have had either in print or out. Of course I agree with you about the footman[5] and indeed about most [of] the early stuff. But the intellectual critics of the day have already made up their minds what to say about me and to say it unanimously, and they would say the same thing whatever I included or omitted. The correct phrase is 'The sordidness of reality'. This will satisfy their requirements for many years to come. But I wanted to collect all my stuff and get rid of it in one volume so as to get it out of my own way and make a fresh start. I observe that no one but yourself has made any comment on the last part of the volume, so I take it that everyone is waiting for everyone else to decide whether any notice need be taken of it or not.

1–Edwin Muir (1887–1959), Scottish poet, novelist, critic; and translator (with his wife Willa) of Franz Kafka: see Biographical Register.
2–The 'Poets on the Poets' series.
3–Wyndham Lewis (1882–1957), painter, novelist, philosopher, critic: see Biographical Register.
4–Not preserved. WL had written about *Poems 1909–1925*.
5–'And I have seen the eternal Footman hold my coat, and snicker' ('The Love Song of J. Alfred Prufrock', l. 86).

This is my address and I am often accessible on the telephone in the afternoon. I wish you would write here or ring up, and have lunch with me one day next week.

Yours ever
T. S. Eliot

## TO *J. M. Robertson*[1] CC

9 January 1926 [London]

Dear Mr Robertson,

I have been abroad for my health for about two months and have just returned. I am making your *Mr Shaw and the 'Maid'* the occasion for writing to you. I found it here on my return and fell upon it at once with joy. I congratulate you upon it and congratulate myself on once more finding myself fighting in your ranks. I have been attacking this play myself and you will find one acid reference to it in my introductory note for *The New Criterion*.[2] I shall review your book myself in the April number.[3]

I should like to remind you again of the essay on Turgenev which I hope may be somewhat nearer to existence than it was when I wrote to you last.[4]

Sincerely yours,
[T. S. Eliot]

1–J. M. Robertson (1856–1933), author, journalist, politician: see Biographical Register.

2–In 'The Idea of a Literary Review', *NC* 4 (Jan. 1926), TSE wrote, on the appearance of *Saint Joan*: 'at two points, if not more, in his long series of plays Mr Shaw reveals himself as the artist whose development was checked at puberty'.

3–'Books of the Quarter', *NC* 4 (Apr. 1926), 389–90: 'what issues most clearly from a reading of Mr Robertson's book is Mr Shaw's utter inability to devote himself wholeheartedly to *any* cause. To Mr Shaw, truth and falsehood (we speak without prejudice) do not seem to have the same meaning as to ordinary people. Hence the danger, with his "St. Joan", of his deluding the numberless crowd of sentimentally religious people who are incapable of following any argument to a conclusion. Such people will be misled until they can be made to understand that the potent ju-ju of the Life Force is a gross superstition; and that (in particular) Mr Shaw's "St. Joan" is one of the most superstitious of the effigies which have been erected to that remarkable woman.' TSE later wrote to Prof. Thomas Dawes Eliot, 26 Jan. 1953, of Shaw: 'I don't think any man of letters in my lifetime has ever fooled more of the people more of the time.'

4–Robertson replied (10 Jan.), 'I had meant to work out the (begun) Turgenev essay in my two months holiday in Wales . . . And behold, I did two booklets instead.'

## TO *Ezra Pound*[1] CC

9 January 1926 [London]

Dear Ezra,

This is purely a business letter. I will write personally later. Meanwhile yours of the 3rd received with a one lira stamp on it and three halfpence to pay. If Italian postage has gone up, please take note.

Re. Moretti.[2] I feel that the conference between you and myself followed by the conference between Mussolini and Austen at the same address ought to result in the Anglo-Italian *entente* and that we should do well to print some dago at the earliest opportunity.[3] While I am getting hold of Flint[4] can you start some process by which Flint shall get the official right to translate, and we the official right to print. This is, from the point of view of an editor, of the utmost importance.

Re. Bird, M'Almon [*sic*], etc. etc., I have so far had nothing and therefore, as God knows there has been enough else to think about, I am not mentioning the matter to my principals until I have something more to go upon.

Best wishes for the musical season.

Yours,
[T.]

## TO *Charles Whibley*[5] CC

9 January 1926 [London]

My dear Whibley,

I have been back in London for some days but have been in too rapid a whirlpool of business and personal preoccupations to write any letters at all. Your last letter arrived at La Turbie after my departure for Rapallo and I therefore found it in London on my return. But I am writing to my bookseller in Paris and will include the book which you ask for.

I did not stop in Paris but came straight through from Rapallo, so that I did not have the opportunity of using your name in calling upon Daudet;[6]

1–Ezra Pound (1885–1972), American poet and critic: see Biographical Register.
2–Marino Moretti (1885–1979), Italian poet and novelist.
3–In a letter ('26 del '26'), Moretti gave permission to translate 'mia novella "Di Sopra".'
4–F. S. Flint (1885–1960), English poet, translator, civil servant: see Biographical Register.
5–Charles Whibley (1859–1930), journalist and author: see Biographical Register.
6–Léon Daudet (1868–1942), right-wing journalist and novelist, critic of the Third Republic;

I hope to get over to Paris for a few days in a month or so and shall then try to see all the people I wanted to see, whether they are in gaol or not.

This is simply a note to tell you that I am back and should very much like to come down for a night or weekend whenever convenient to you.

And meanwhile I should be glad to have news of you. I will reserve all my own personal views until we meet, either at Brickhill[1] or in London.

Yours affectionately,
[T. S. Eliot]

P.S. Our firm is publishing sometime in the spring what is expected to be a definitive edition of Burke's letters in several volumes.[2] I should be more than delighted if you cared to have these volumes and make them the occasion for an essay on Burke.

## TO *E. M. Forster* CC

11 January 1926 [London]

Dear Forster,

I have received your essay on Virginia Woolf and like it extremely. I make no difficulty of its appearance in the *Yale Review* on March 20th because I assume that to be in the April number[3] and I do not suppose that more than a negligible number of our readers will read it in the *Yale Review* before they see the *Criterion*. The only difficulty is the price. *The New Criterion* is for the moment in no position to pay even favoured contributors at higher rates than was the old *Criterion*. I hope that it may soon be in a firm enough position to be able to increase its rates all

---

co-founder, with Charles Maurras, of the royalist *L'Action Française*. In 1927, when F&G was offered a book by Daudet, *Le Stupide XIXe siècle*, TSE wrote in his reader's report on 11 Oct.: 'I think that this book would be worth doing. It is extremely lively and capable of interesting a fairly wide public, and fairly bristles with violence and highly contentious statements. It is certainly anything but dull and is fairly typical of Daudet's writing. Daudet's style, however, is a peculiar one and requires an extremely competent translator. If badly translated, it might sound either flat or grotesque. In any case I do not think that we ought to commit ourselves to taking sheets of a translation without having seen the translation; unless we are assured that the translation were to be supervised by some real authority. If we took it, I should certainly suggest that a preface by Charles Whibley, who is a very old friend of Daudet's, would be desirable, and I think I could get it' (Faber).

1–Whibley lived at Great Brickhill, Bletchley, Oxfordshire.

2–*The Correspondence of Edmund Burke*, ed. Lewis Melville, was advertised by F&G in Spring 1926 as 'forthcoming'; the autumn 1926 catalogue noted, 'It is hoped to publish in the Spring, 1927, at a price of about six guineas per set.' But the project was abandoned owing to editorial problems.

3–Forster's essay came out in *Yale Review* 15 (Apr. 1926), 505–14.

round, or at least exercise a certain discrimination; and I presume that the prosperity of the *New Criterion* will affect the payment to contributors before it affects the salary of the Editor. However I cannot at present offer more than our former rates of £10 per five thousand words; the best I can do is in this case commit myself to £10 for your essay although it falls short of that number of words.[1]

I should very much like to publish the essay and take the liberty of holding it until I hear from you again.

Yours sincerely,
[T. S. Eliot]

## TO *Richard Aldington*[2] CC

11 January 1926 [London]

My dear Richard

I should have written to you two or three days ago but have been working under great pressure. I was going to let you know at once the tentative conclusions to which we have come about 'The Republic of Letters',[3] as I should like to see you before taking the matter up again with Stallybrass.[4]

If it is possible for you to come up to town one date this week, and if after reading this letter you think that the occasion justifies your taking that trouble, please send me a wire *here* and I will rearrange my other appointments to fit.

1–Forster had suggested a fee of £20 but accepted TSE's offer.

2–Richard Aldington (1892–1962), poet critic, translator, biographer, novelist: see Biographical Register.

3–See Norman T. Gates, *Richard Aldington: An Autobiography in Letters* (1992), 76: 'In 1923, Routledge had asked RA to collaborate in a series of critical biographies to be edited by William Rose [Lecturer in German, King's College, London] and to be called "The Republic of Letters". RA invited Herbert Read and T. S. Eliot to contribute, but both refused. Then, Eliot, as a director of Faber & Gwyer, initiated a similar scheme called "The Poets on the Poets", and Routledge, after consulting RA, proposed to combine the two series under the joint imprint of the two publishing houses and the joint editorship of Rose and Eliot. Although Routledge tried to ease the situation by making RA editor of the French section of their Broadway Translations, RA resented the "set-back" in his efforts to lift himself "out of the mire of journalism and poverty" and blamed Eliot's about-face. (See 'Richard Aldington's Letters to Herbert Read', ed. David S. Thatcher, *Malahat Review*, July 1970, pp. 7–8.)'

4–William Swan Stallybrass (1855–1927), publisher at Routledge.

I have thrashed the matter out with Herbert[1] and with Bruce[2] and have discussed it again with Faber. There is a pretty close consensus of opinion now that it would be better for everybody if Faber & Gwyer altered their programme to retain an independent series, but a series which need not conflict and might co-operate with that of Routledge. It would be too long a matter to go into all the reasons and considerations advanced by one person or another against the unification of the two series. I should like an opportunity to give you these in conversation: I will only repeat now that both Herbert and Bruce were strongly of the same opinion. I asked Richmond to look at it from my point of view, from Faber & Gwyer's, from Routledge's and from his own point of view both as Editor and as a member of the purchasing public, and from every point of view he came to the same conclusion. May I add that although I was myself influenced by the hope that a separation of the two series might be advantageous to you, I did not mention this aspect to anyone else; so you may feel sure that the discussion is quite impersonal.

What I now propose is that we should have another conference with Stallybrass at which I should outline the nature of a separate, and of course much shorter, series to be undertaken by us, and at which we might draw up some preliminary protocol by which any overlapping might be avoided. Though I think I can draw my lines in such a way that conflict is unlikely. But I should like to have some assurance of occasional conference with Stallybrass or Rose so that we might always know each other's programme in advance.

You will understand that I am very anxious to see you before taking the matter up again with Routledge. Part of the concessions which I should ask from them in return for our not poaching on their property might be that they should take over the book on Rimbaud which Fletcher has undertaken with great enthusiasm, and which is really more suitable for their series than for what I had in view.[3] In any case I must not let Fletcher

1–Herbert Read (1893–1968), poet, literary and art critic: see Biographical Register.

2–Bruce Richmond (1871–1964), editor of the *TLS*: see Biographical Register.

3–RA replied (18 Jan.), 'I have written Stallybrass about the Rimbaud–Fletcher book and he has promised to let me have his decision immediately . . . As soon as [I] hear definitely I will let you know. If you will then explain the situation to Fletcher and ask him to communicate with me, the affair will be off your hands.' But he wrote again on 3 Feb., 'I'm having a very devil of a time with that Fletcher–Rimbaud book. Routledge are sore because Fletcher's Parables was a failure . . . Fletcher is sore with Routledge because they've turned down a long poem of his . . . I have soothed him a bit by giving him a translation to do. I am being very pertinacious over the Rimbaud book, because Routledge ought to do it – they ought to afford the inevitable loss!' (Fletcher had agreed in Sept. 1925 to write a volume on Rimbaud for TSE at F&G.)

down. We might want to do a few authors who would nominally be included in such a series as Routledge's, but they are not, I think, authors whom Routledge would be likely to include for the next few years.

What I have generally in view as a result of my discussions is a library of biographical essays on masters of philosophy and criticism. What I want is a category which would include a number of people rather on the frontiers of literature, and this classification would include your *Rémy de Gourmont* which I am anxious to get.[1] I should like to find, however, a shorter and more alluring title for the series.

One reason for seeing you first is to decide on the method of approach to Routledge in order to make the alteration as attractive to them as possible, and as advantageous as possible to us personally. I want to do it in such a way that they will realize that the negotiations have been in the end to their advantage and in such a way that it will fortify our own position there.

I will have Read's book[2] sent to you. I have just lent it to Faber who is very much interested in it and I will send it on as soon as he returns it to me.

Whether you telegraph or not, I hope you will let me hear from you and give me your own opinions at once.

Ever yours affectionately,
[Tom]

1 – *A Modern Man of Letters* (Seattle, 1928). Rémy de Gourmont (1858–1915) was a novelist and critic whom TSE regarded (in his early criticism) as 'the critical consciousness of a generation (*SW*, 44); as 'the great critic' (*SW*, 139). TSE quoted in *SW* from both *Le Problème de Style* (1902) and *Lettres à l'Amazone* (1914), and wrote in his Preface to the second edition of *SW* (1928) that he had been 'much stimulated and much helped by the critical writings of Rémy de Gourmont. I acknowledge that influence, and am grateful for it; and I by no means disown it by having passed on to another problem not touched upon in this book: that of the relation of poetry to the spiritual life of its time and of other times' (viii).

2 – *In Retreat* is an account of the retreat of the British Fifth Army from St Quentin in March 1918. Written in 1919, it was published by the Hogarth Press in 1925 and reissued by F&F in 1930. TSE said that HR had a 'claim to distinction' as a 'master of English prose': '*In Retreat* is in its kind one of the few masterpieces that our period will leave behind' ('Views and Reviews', *The New English Weekly*, 20 June 1935).

## TO *J. Kessel*[1] CC

12 Janvier 1926 [London]

Cher Monsieur Kessel,

Après quelques mois de mauvaise santé j'ai repris la direction des affaires du *Criterion*. Je vous écris pour vous rappeler votre excellente chronique et de vous demander si vous voulez bien donner à nos lecteurs le plaisir de vous lire dans *The New Criterion* d'Avril. Je serai enchanté si vous pouvez nous préparer une chronique, si vous serez si aimable, aussitôt que possible afin que nous ayons le loisir d'en faire une bonne traduction. Je n'ai pas besoin de vous donner aucune indication de ce que nous exigeons; vous n'avez que prendre votre première chronique comme modèle.

En attendant de vos nouvelles avec impatience, et espérant vous revoir à Paris au mois de Février.

Je suis,
Cordialement votre,
[T. S. Eliot][2]

## TO *F. S. Flint*[3] CC

12 January 1926 [*The New Criterion*]

My dear Flint,

I am back in town and should very much like to see you. If lunch in this neighbourhood is inconvenient for you I could easily come to some restaurant named by you. This is my best address at present and I am usually accessible on the telephone here after 2.30. There are various things to talk about but meanwhile I hear from the new printers that they

1–Joseph Kessel (1898–1979), French journalist and novelist, won fame with novels of heroism including *L'Équipage* (1923) and *Les Captifs* (1926) – awarded the Grand Prix du roman de l'Académie Française. *Belle de jour* (1928) was filmed in 1967 by Luis Buñuel.

2–*Translation*: Dear Mr Kessel, After some months of poor health, I have once again resumed the editing of the *Criterion*. I am writing to remind you of your excellent chronicle and to ask if you would give our readers the pleasure of reading you in the April edition of *The New Criterion*. I shall be delighted if you would be so kind as to prepare a Chronicle, and as soon as possible so we may have plenty of time to make a good translation of it. I don't need to give you any indication of what we require; you only have to use your first chronicle as an example.

In anticipation of receiving news from you soon and in the hope of seeing you in Paris in February, I am, Yours cordially, [T. S. Eliot].

3–F. S. Flint (1885–1960), poet, translator, civil servant: see Biographical Register.

are anxious to have the copy by the 1st February. Is it possible for you to let us have your notes by then?[1]

I hope that you are in much better health. We want to revive the fortnightly meetings in the form of a dinner rather than those hurried and disturbing lunches. Will this be possible for you?

Ever yours,
[T. S. Eliot]

## TO *Humbert Wolfe*[2] CC

12 January 1926 [London]

Dear Wolfe,

I am back again in London and smothered in work. But I should like to see you. If you are not away on one of your too frequent Diplomatic pilgrimages will you drop me a line or ring me up any afternoon after 2.30.? And is this neighbourhood too remote for you to come and lunch with me? If so, I could meet you in some part of town more convenient for yourself, as I am no longer forced to inflict my own luncheon neighbourhood on other people.

By the time I see you I shall have got the *Criterion* material into enough order to be able to tell you how soon I could use your essay which is in my possession. I have a lot of books of poetry for you but I forbear sending them on until I hear that you are in town and willing to receive them.[3] I hope that we may meet soon.

Yours ever
[T. S. E.]

## TO *Edith Sitwell*[4] CC

12 January 1926 [London]

Dear Edith

I am back in London and this is the first opportunity I have had to thank you for your letter of the 9th December. I hope that you received

1–FSF covered periodicals in French, Italian, Danish, Spanish (*NC* 4 [Apr. 1926]).
2–Humbert Wolfe (1885–1940), poet, satirist, critic, civil servant: see Biographical Register.
3–Wolfe reviewed books of verse by Thomas Hardy (*Human Shows*), George Rylands (*Russet & Taffeta*) and Barrington Gates (*Poems*), *NC* 4 (Apr. 1926), 384–8. See too 'English Bards and French Reviewers', *NC* 5 (Jan. 1927), 57–73.
4–Edith Sitwell (1887–1964), poet, biographer, novelist: see Biographical Register.

my book which I sent off from La Turbie as soon as I got a few copies from London.[1]

I have since seen the review that you mention. It was kind of you to write to *The Times* about it but I am not surprised that it was not published. But we shall be able to deal properly with J.C.S.[2] sooner or later when Sir Edmund[3] is safely interred in the Abbey.

I was very pleased to hear about Robert Graves. I found a letter from him here mentioning his appointment. I hope that they will both be better in health for it.[4]

By the way, I am printing a short thing by Gertrude Stein in the *Criterion* which will be out next week; so that if there is an outcry I hope that you will stand by me.[5] Would you be willing to do a short review of her

1–Sitwell replied ('Thurs' [n.d.] 'I did receive the book [*P 1909–1925*], and it is quite impossible for me to thank you enough for it, or to tell you how magnificent I feel it is.'

2–In fact, the review of *Poems 1909–1925* of which Sitwell complained did not appear in *The Times* (which explains why her letter of protest was not published by *The Times*); it was an anonymous piece (though published alongside a review by J. C. Squire) headed 'The Case of Mr Eliot', *The Observer*, 6 Dec. 1925, 4, including the following remarks: 'The *Poems* of 1920 contained some dreadfully false stuff, and then came *The Waste Land* with its parade of easy learning, its trick of impasted quotation, and its echoes of modern prose-writers. In these later poems Mr Eliot has completely abandoned that theory of art which insists that a poem should be a unity . . . If Mr Eliot's earlier verse is . . . inchoate, his later is really protoplasmic. There is no reason why *The Waste Land* should begin where it does, go on as it does, or end when it does . . . Mr Eliot himself treats his poem with portentous solemnity . . . [T]he main impression left by this volume is one of accident: occasionally, in the earlier and the frivolous pieces, of a happy accident, but generally of an accident to the processes of imagination and thought, an accident in which poetry has been wounded to death.' ES wrote to TSE again on 14 Jan.: 'I am determined that Squire shall be punished *now*, – if he isn't, we shall have him teaching the Archangel Gabriel how to play his trumpet in Heaven, – and as I'm not allowed to punish him in England, I'm going to do it in an American paper!' J. C. Squire had attacked *The Waste Land* in 'Poetry', *London Mercury* 8 (Oct. 1923), 655–6; and would scoff at his poetry again in *London Mercury* 13 (Mar. 1926), 547–8.

3–Sir Edmund Gosse (1849–1928): poet, editor, critic of art; translator (with William Archer) of Ibsen; chief librarian of the House of Lords, 1904–14. His works include studies of Sir Thomas Browne, William Congreve and Thomas Gray; *Life and Letters of Dr John Donne, Dean of St Paul's* (1899); and *Father and Son* (1907).

4–ES (14 Jan.) wrote of Graves, who had just been appointed Professor of English Literature at the University of Cairo: 'Robert has always been a bit of a Pilgrim Father, – the only fault in an otherwise perfect character, – and his departure from England had rather too much of that kind of thing about it. For I understand that he took with him, not only Nancy and all the children, which of course was quite right, but also Miss Laura Gottschalk [Laura Riding, 1901–91], – whose poems I think are the biggest bore, and I hope you agree; but Robert is encouraging her recklessly.'

5–'The Fifteenth of November', *NC* 4 (Jan. 1926), 71–5. Sitwell already knew the subject of Stein's 'short thing', as she wrote in her reply to TSE: 'She showed me the portrait of you when I was in Paris. What fun it will be when it appears.' Lady Rothermere wrote to TSE on 2 Mar.: 'The number is a very good one and I'm amused at the newspaper commentaries re G Stein!! Personally I hope it's the first & last to appear in the Criterion – !! It's so much

enormous book *The Making of Americans* for the April number? It would be difficult to get in a long review because so many books have come out before Christmas from which I must choose the few that we review; but I should very much like to have something about it.[1]

This is merely a business letter so please take note of my new address where I am to be found most of the time. And I will write again soon.

Yours ever,
[T. S. E.]

## TO *Antonio Marichalar*[2] TS Real Academia de la Historia

Le 12 Janvier 1926 *The New Criterion*

Mon cher Ami,

Après quelques mois de convalescence aux Alpes Maritimes me voici encore dans la chaire de directeur de revue. Faites bonne note, je vous en prie, de la nouvelle addresse.

Maintenant je vais [vous] demander quelque chose. Nous avons commencé à donner à nos lecteurs dans chaque numéro de notre revue trimestielle quelques chroniques étrangères pour les renseigner sur les courants littéraires et artistiques de l'Europe. Nous avons confié la Chronique Française à Monsieur Kessel de *La Nouvelle Revue Française* et la Chronique Américaine à Monsieur Seldes du *New York Dial*. Vous

---

nonsense – but it was a good thing to publish it once.' TSE told Donald Gallup (22 July 1952): 'I believe I really was interested in her work, though to have said I was interested in *everything* she wrote was perhaps excessive. I understood later that "The Fifteenth of November" was supposed to be a portrait of myself. The title certainly commemorated the date on which the first Lady Rothermere took me to see Miss Stein. That was the only occasion on which we met. I thought Miss Stein rather inclined to make sweeping statements for immediate effect – the only one I can remember was her assertion that Trollope was the only English novelist of his period who could write good English.'

1–Sitwell hailed Stein's work (*NC* 4: 2 [Apr. 1926], 390–2) as 'the product of one of the richest, and at the same time most subtle, minds of our time . . . [T]he wisdom, the rich loamy life, the vitality, and the insight contained in this book are of an astounding order.' ES wrote to Stein in Apr. 1926: 'It is not a long review, because the space doesn't permit of it, but as everything in the *New Criterion* is regarded as a newer and more important Apocalypse, I hope it will help. I needn't tell you the review is a most enthusiastic one' (*Selected Letters of Edith Sitwell*, ed. Richard Greene [1997; revised edn, 1998], 66).

2–Antonio Marichalar, Marquis of Montesa (1893–1973): Spanish author, critic, biographer and journalist; contributor to the newspaper *El Sol* and the periodical *Revista de Occidente* (on subjects including Claudel, Joyce, Valéry, and Virginia Woolf). His books include *Mentira desnuda*: 'The Naked Lie' (essays on European and American culture, 1933); *Riesgo y ventura del duque de Osuna* (1932): *The Perils and Fortune of the Duke of Osuna*, trans. H. de Onís; *Julián Romero* (1952).

voici appelé à être notre correspondant de Madrid. Je serai enchanté si vous accepterez de nous envoyer une petite chronique de temps en temps, qui sera payée comme toutes contributions.

Il s'agit d'une chronique qui réléverait les faits d'actualité les plus intéressants de litérature, d'art, de théâtre ou de philosophie générale. La chronique ne devrait pas dépasser 1500 ou 2000 mots. Naturellement dans une chronique d'une étendue si restreinte on n'attend pas à avoir un compte rendu de tous les évènements de quelque mois. Il s'agit simplement d'en choisir ceux qui vous paraissent les plus significatifs. Parfois un chroniqueur peut se limiter presque à un seul livre, une seule pièce ou une seule question du jour. L'important c'est de rendre aux lecteurs étrangers l'impression, la sensation même, de l'actualité de la vie intellectuelle de votre pays.

En outre, je vous serai reconnaissant de me donner de temps en temps votre conseil sur les auteurs espagnols que vous nous recommandez pour traduction dans *The New Criterion* et naturellement, à part votre chronique, de collaborer plus largement dans notre revue.

En espérant que vous soyez disposé à nous donner votre appui,[1]

Je suis,
Cher ami,
Cordialement votre
[T. S. Eliot][2]

1 – Marichalar agreed on 16 Jan. to contribute a regular Spanish chronicle.

2 – *Translation*: My dear Friend, After some months of convalescence in the Alpes Maritimes, here I am again in my editorial chair. Please make a careful note of our new address.

I am now going to ask you something. We have begun offering our readers, in each number of our quarterly, letters from abroad so as to keep them informed of literary and artistic trends in Europe. The Letter from France has been entrusted to Monsieur Kessel of *La Nouvelle Revue Française* and the Letter from America to Mr Seldes of *The New York Dial*. You are hereby called upon to be our correspondent in Madrid. I shall be delighted if you would agree to send us a short letter from time to time; the fee will be as for all contributions.

The letter should pick out the most interesting topical developments in literature, the arts, the theatre and general philosophy. It should not exceed 1500 or 2000 words. Of course, in such a limited space we don't expect an account of all the events occurring over a period of months. It is simply a matter of choosing those which seem to you most significant. Occasionally it may be possible to restrict yourself to a single book, or a single play or a single topical event. The important thing is to give foreign readers the impression, the sensation of what is actually happening in the intellectual life of your country.

In addition, I would be grateful if you could advise me from time to time about Spanish authors whom you would recommend for translation in *The New Criterion*, and also, of course, if in addition to your chronicle, you yourself contributed more frequently to our review.

## TO *His Mother*  TS Houghton

12 January 1926  *The New Criterion*

Dearest Mother,

This is primarily a business letter, to tell you that all the proof has been passed for printing.[1] In order to save time, I decided on a plain black cloth binding which is not very expensive, and a white paper label at the back somewhat similar to that on my poems, with black lettering. The paper label in my opinion looks better than having white letters directly printed on the cloth, and is considerably cheaper. We decided on 300 copies. We shall have 100 bound up to begin with. Cobden is in communication with American publishers: if one of them buys some of the books, he will take it in the form of 'sheets', print a new title page, bind the book himself and print his own wrappers.

I am accordingly designing a wrapper for the English edition solely. The style of wrappers is somewhat different here from that usual in America; they do not put on so much letterpress. I am therefore choosing the testimonies of Norton[2] and Grandgent,[3] as these two opinions will carry more weight here by themselves than if we added those of Soldan and Hosmer, who are unknown. I shall also give their titles, viz.: The late Charles Eliot Norton, translator of Dante and Professor of Fine Arts in Harvard University; and Charles Grandgent, Professor of Romance Languages in Harvard University. The book ought to be ready by March; and I will have review copies sent to various British periodicals and will send free copies to several important people here. The American distribution you will deal with yourself; before approaching any booksellers there we

---

In the hope that you will feel able to give us your support, I am, dear friend, Yours cordially, [T. S. Eliot]

1–*Savonarola*.

2–Charles Eliot Norton (1827–1908): cousin of Charles William Eliot, president of Harvard; author, editor, translator of Dante; editor of *North American Review*; friend of James Russell Lowell, Henry Wadsworth Longfellow, Thomas Carlyle, Edward FitzGerald, Leslie Stephen and John Ruskin (of whom he was literary executor); first Professor of the History of Art at Harvard, 1875–98. His publications include *Letters of Carlyle and Emerson* (1883); *Carlyle's Letters and Reminiscences* (1886–8); and *Notes of Travel and Study in Italy* (1859). He is commemorated by the Charles Eliot Norton Lectures, which TSE was to deliver in 1933. See James C. Turner, *The Liberal Education of Charles Eliot Norton* (1999); Linda Dowling, *Charles Eliot Norton: The Art of Reform in Nineteenth-Century America* (2007).

3–Charles Hall Grandgent (1862–1939): linguist; scholar of Dante; Harvard Professor, 1896–1932; author of *Introduction to Vulgar Latin* (1907), and *From Latin to Italian: An Historical Outline of the Phonology and Morphology of the Italian Language* (1927). TSE's library holds a copy of Grandgent's *Dante* (1920).

will wait to see if we get an American publisher. The total cost will be well under £100, which I think was your limit.

I have asked Cobden to send you a copy of the preface direct. It was difficult to write, as I felt perhaps an excessive diffidence about referring to the poem itself, and I am not quite satisfied with it. It is not so eulogistic, therefore, as my own feelings. The comparison with Shaw is perhaps a little misleading; I wanted only to introduce some bright and controversial matter into my remarks, rather to stimulate curiosity in the poem than to tell the reader anything about it.[1] But I do not suppose that I should have been satisfied with anything I could have done. I have put in the dedication 'TO MY CHILDREN'.

I am very happy and contented in this office and my new work. I have a good deal to do with the general business as well as with the *New Criterion*, and enjoy it. I have been very busy – I have written (i.e. dictated) 50 business letters in the last three days. I am getting to work on my lectures, of which I had written only three abroad; I begin at Cambridge on the 26th.[2] And I have reviewing for the *Times*, and a preface to write, and multifarious other work to do.

1 – TSE opens his Introduction to *Savonarola* by arguing that 'a work of historical fiction is much more a document on its own time than on the time portrayed' (vii). With that argument in mind, he praises his mother's 'dramatic poem' in comparison with the work of a famous contemporary: 'Whatever documentary value pertains to the following series of scenes of the life of Savonarola is due to its rendering of a state of mind contemporary with the author (and such rendering is always shown by the choice of subject as well as by the treatment). The same is true of Mr Bernard Shaw's *St Joan*. This Savonarola is a disciple of Schleiermacher, Emerson, Channing and Herbert Spencer; this St Joan is a disciple of Niezsche, Butler and every chaotic and immature intellectual enthusiasm of the later nineteenth century. Savonarola has escaped from the cloister to the parsonage; St Joan has escaped from the parsonage to a studio in Chelsea, and pretends to be one of the People . . . In both is perceptible a certain opposition to ecclesiasticism; the author of *Savonarola* opposes it directly by exhibiting the beauty of a character which was certainly above fanaticism, and which was not without moral grandeur, in conflict with the hierarchy of its place and time. Mr Shaw opposes the Church by the more insidious method of defending it, and thereby creating the illusion of tolerance and broadmindedness, which will deceive many, no doubt, but will not deceive the Muse of History' (ix–x) As to the achievement of *Savonarola* in terms of 'dramatic form', however, TSE feels obliged in his peroration to laud his ('fastidious') mother merely for recognising her limitations in choosing a form that could definitely never be staged: 'those fastidious persons who preserve a regard for the decencies of verse do well to incorporate their dramatic ideas in forms which are frankly impossible for the stage. The term "closet drama" is only a form of reproach when applied to plays – like those of Tennyson, Browning and Swinburne – about which there hovers some ambiguity as to whether their authors really thought that they could possibly be acted or not. A closet drama should never allow the reader to doubt that it was intended for reading or for declamation and not for acting. Such was the intention of the author of the following scenes from the life of Girolamo Savonarola' (xii).

2 – TSE was to deliver the first of his eight weekly Clark lectures, entitled 'On the metaphysical

I am however very much better in health. So is Vivien, she is back in Clarence Gate with a nurse to help her, and Ellen; as there is hardly any room, and in order to keep a strict routine – my working hours are long and late. But I see her every day.

Write to me here at 24 Russell Square, then I get it more quickly.

Very very much love from
Tom.

Your letters have given Vivien *very* much pleasure & happiness.

## TO *Herbert Read*[1] CC

13 January 1926 [*The New Criterion*]

My dear Read,

I am rather annoyed at hearing from the printers that they want to have the copy for the April number by the 1st February. Is this possible for you? I am buried in correspondence and consequently a letter which I dictated to you several days ago is now out of date before it could be typed. So I will rewrite it in a day or two and hope to arrange another meeting with you next week.

Many thanks for reading Massis' article.[2] In my letter to you I had made some observations about it similar to your own, but I do think that the article is worth publishing if we include an editorial note intimating that this is merely a statement of one aspect of the question. I should very much like to read the books of Maritain[3] and I think an article on Stryzgowski[4] would

---

poetry of the seventeenth century with special reference to Donne, Crashaw and Cowley', at Trinity College, Cambridge, on 26 Jan. He had been nominated by his predecessor John Middleton Murry, who lectured in 1924–5 on 'Keats and Shakespeare'; and the College Council had resolved on 6 Mar. 1925 to invite TSE. The stipend of £200 would be paid only at the end of the course. For a full account of TSE's tenure of the Clark Lectureship, see Ronald Schuchard's 'Editor's Introduction' in TSE, *The Varieties of Metaphysical Poetry* (1993), 1–31.

1–Herbert Read (1893–1968), poet, literary and art critic.

2–Henri Massis, 'Defence of the West', for *NC* 4 (Apr. & June 1926).

3–Jacques Maritain (1882–1973), French philosopher and neo-Thomist, converted from Protestantism to Catholicism in 1906. Early works included *La philosophie bergsonienne* (1914) and *Art et scolastique* (1920). TSE met him in July 1926.

4–Josef Strzygowski (1862–1941): art historian and polemicist; Professor of the History of Art at the University of Vienna, 1909–33; author of *The Orient or Rome: Contributions to the history of late antique and early Christian art* (1901), *The visual art of the future* (1907) and *The Architecture of the Armenians and Europe* (1918). An ardent pan-Germanist, he would later support Hitler and the Nazis.

be capital if Braunholtz[1] is competent to do it. I think we can probably put a good deal of work into Flint's hands sooner or later if he will undertake it, and I am writing to ask him when I can see him. I have got to see Murry[2] tomorrow and will let you know the result. He wants to publish the essay in the *Adelphi*, where it will perhaps do less harm than anywhere else.[3]

Yours ever
[T. S. E.]

## TO *Nancy R. Pearn*[4] CC

13 January 1926 [*The New Criterion*]

Dear Miss Pearn,

I have now returned from France and am settled at this new address of which I beg you to take note for future correspondence and manuscripts. I have considered carefully the question of Mr Lawrence's 'Mornings in

1–H. J. Braunholtz worked in the Department of Oriental Languages and Ethnography, British Museum. He translated (with O. M. Dalton) Strzygowski's *Origin of Christian Church Art* (1923). No article by him appeared in the *Criterion*.

2–John Middleton Murry (1889–1957), writer and critic: see Biographical Register.

3–3–JMM – in 'The "Classical" Revival', *The Adelphi* 3 (Feb. 1926), 585–95; (Mar.), 648–53 – offered this evaluation of TSE's professed classicism: 'in the peculiar case of Mr T. S. Eliot . . . a serious classicism at the present time is self-contradictory and sterile': there was a 'striking discrepancy between his critical professions and his creative practice'. Mr Eliot was far from 'superficial', JMM went on. 'Nevertheless, Mr Eliot, in the most significant part of him, is typical of "the modern mind". He *is* completely sceptical and antinomian. He differs from the Augustans because his sceptical and antinomian condition is a torment to him . . . The intellectual part of him desiderates an ordered universe, an ordered experience, and an ordered society; the living, emotional, creative part of him goes its own disordered way . . .

'There's the rub. Mr Eliot has no spiritual superior. The apostle of authority has no authority to submit to . . .

'How is Humpty-Dumpty to be mended? There seem to be but two ways. The one more obviously indicated is that he should make a blind act of faith and join the Catholic Church: there he will find an authority and a tradition . . . The Poet Laureate today is an avowed disciple of Milton. But Mr Eliot is a Puritan by descent, and it is precisely against Puritanism that he has been struggling all his life. The classicism he desires is more august and more flexible – it is a Catholic classicism.

'There is no such classicism in English literature . . . Chaucer's work, as surely as Dante's, was made possible by the theology of mediaeval Catholicism . . . Dante could trust his own intellectualism because he believed in that supra-intellectual reality which he used it to articulate. His theology was, so to speak, a metaphysic *of which he was certain* . . . The modern trouble is not to accept (or to invent) a theology, but to believe in God . . . Mr Eliot, as his poems amply reveal, is in a Godless condition . . . To be without a knowledge of God is an agony to him.'

4–Nancy Pearn was head of the Serial Rights Department of Curtis Brown literary agency.

Mexico'. I should very much like to publish it, as indeed I should be glad to publish almost anything by Mr Lawrence, but I am afraid that I cannot commit myself to definite publication before the July issue of *The New Criterion* (which remains a Quarterly). The difficulty is due to the fact that Mr Lawrence's 'The Woman who Rode Away' is so long that we had to publish it in two parts, one in the number of last July and the second part in the number of January 15th which is about to appear. The difficulty is aggravated by the fact that owing to reorganization of publishing we were unable to produce an October issue, so that the forthcoming January issue is the first since that of last July. I do not feel that I can afford in a Quarterly to publish work by any one author, however eminent, in three consecutive numbers.

If, therefore, you have made or wish to make arrangements for American publication before July, I will regretfully return the manuscript; if it does not appear elsewhere earlier than July, I shall be glad to publish it in the July number.[1]

Yours faithfully,
[T. S. Eliot]

## TO *H. P. Collins*[2]

TS Maryland

13 January 1926 *The New Criterion*

Dear Mr Collins,

I am glad to hear from you although sorry indeed to hear that you have had such a prolonged illness. I rather imagined that you are impenitent because I understand that you have not published my little note.[3] I am

1–'Mornings in Mexico', *NC* 4 (June 1926), 467–75.

2–TSE wrote in a testimonial (6 Sept. 1946): 'I have known Mr H. P. Collins for many years and Mr. Collins frequently reviewed books for *The Criterion*, which I edited, from very early in the career of that review. I have always regarded him as a very sound and reliable reviewer and critic with a wide knowledge of English literature and of varied interests. My impressions derived from Mr Collins' writing are confirmed by my knowledge of Mr Collins and my conversations with him. I am very glad to have the opportunity of recommending him for the post of lecturer at any training college for teachers. I may mention that part of the value of Mr. Collins' literary criticism was derived from his interest in and knowledge of political and social history.'

3–TSE had written a review of a critical volume by Collins which was accepted for *The Adelphi* but not published: not found. Collins had thanked TSE (17 Dec. 1925) 'for your very just criticism of my book. I'm afraid I'm rather impenitent about my sins of omission because the scope of the book is less than you seem to assume: I said in it that I had virtually to confine myself to poetry in the English tradition.'

very firm in my opinion and should be glad to discuss it with you here one afternoon. Will you not write to me here, or telephone here any afternoon after 2.30., suggesting a day next week, or better a choice of two days, when you could look in between 3 and 5?

Sincerely yours,
[T. S. Eliot]

I hope your health is enough improved to allow you to come?[1]

## TO *Robert Graves*[2] CC

13 January 1926 [*The New Criterion*]

Dear Graves,

I heard while I was away of your election to the Chair at Cairo and have only been waiting for the opportunity to write and congratulate you.[3] I know nothing about conditions at either Liverpool or Cairo but personally I think I should much prefer Cairo. The climate, if tactfully dealt with, ought to be very good. I am only afraid that this letter will not reach you, so if it is properly forwarded I hope you will let me hear from you at once.

I am relieved to hear that you do not intend to abandon this very interesting scheme and hope you will let me know from time to time how you are getting on.[4]

1–Collins replied (15 Jan.) that he felt too unwell to come into town. He went on: 'No, I have no ignoble idea of suppressing the review of my book. The Adelphi has been reduced, and my reviews are in arrears and chaos. A more lengthy review of your poems will also appear in the course of time. We have no editorial office, and things get scattered, though Middleton Murry did come over here a fortnight ago.'

2–Robert Graves (1895–1985), poet and novelist: see Biographical Register.

3–Graves wrote (undated): 'I have got this English Chair at Cairo & sail on Jan 8th on a 3 year contract. I shall get on with my share of our projected volume & if I find that it's getting on too fast I shall possibly finish it myself. But not without giving you fair warning & a chance to collaborate. I enclose some criticism sent me by Laura Gottschalk. If you would like it for the *Criterion* . . .' (*In Broken Images: Selected Letters of Robert Graves 1914–1946*, ed. Paul O'Prey [1982], 161–2).

4–Graves had adumbrated, in a letter to GCF (?Oct. 1925), what he called a 'scheme for some sort of critical survey of that part of modern poetry which has, so to speak, "gone round the corner": to traditionalists this movement has meant complete disappearance, to liberals a misguided straying, to others a natural (and once that leap has been made) quite obvious entry into a hitherto unsuspected thoroughfare. I see T. S. Eliot is one of your authors & hear that he is also in some advisory or directing capacity. I wonder whether he would consent to cooperate with me in a work of this sort – I know his distrust of anthologies, which I cordially share but this would be more than an anthology – and whether if so, you would like to publish. There has been no adequate review of this round-

I have not yet had a moment in which to read the manuscript you enclose but I am very glad to have it because I have seen a little of her verse which is interesting and want to see more. Whether I can use it or not I will write and tell you what I think of it and will in any case keep the manuscript until I know your address.

Meanwhile all my most cordial good wishes for your success in Cairo.[1]

Yours ever,
[T. S. Eliot]

## TO *Mario Praz*[2] CC

13 January 1926 [London]

Dear Mr Praz,

I have quite recently returned to London and from now on am always accessible at this address. This is the first opportunity I have had to thank you for your two kind letters which gave me much pleasure. I am very glad if my review makes your book any better known to the people in England who ought to know it.

I should be extremely interested to see an essay from you on Chaucer's debt to Italy.[3] Far too little has been written about Chaucer in this country and there are very few scholars, I fear, capable of dealing with this subject. Five thousand words equals approximately fourteen to fifteen pages in the *Criterion*. In such an essay it seems to me that you cannot help quoting extensively the Italian texts, and quoting them in Italian. For although such an essay should, as you say, not be a *Quellenforschung*[4] one does not intend it for the illiterate, and the educated English reader ought to know that he is expected to be able to read Italian whether he does or not. But in the case of any passage which might be in the least difficult of

---

the-corner stuff; there is a great deal of undirected popular interest in it; and I believe from a short conversation and correspondence with Eliot that we are interested in the same poets. Will you ask him, if you approve?' (Faber E3/1/8 [B95]). GCF had responded (14 Oct.), 'The critical survey which you suggest interests me very much indeed, and would, I think, be extraordinarily worth while doing' (CC in Faber Archive). TSE had felt willing to collaborate on a book – he 'should be honoured', he told Graves on 27 Oct. 1925 – to be provisionally entitled *Untraditional Elements in Modern Poetry*.

1 – Graves replied to this letter (undated): 'This job is just a joke but well paid . . .'

2 – Mario Praz (1896–1982), scholar of English literature: see Biographical Register. At the time of this letter, he was Senior Lecturer in Italian, Liverpool University, 1924–32.

3 – 'Chaucer and the Great Italian Writers of the Trecento', C. 6 (July 1927), 18–39; and (Aug. 1927), 131–57.

4 – 'Original Research'.

interpretation I think that you ought to give an English translation in a footnote.

Many thanks for your pamphlet on Ayres etcetera[1] which will be very useful to me.

I have noted the name of your new Italian Weekly[2] and think that we might like to include it in our exchange list for notice in the *Criterion*. If so I will ask you to arrange the exchange for me.

If ever you should happen to be in London I hope you would write or telephone to me here so that we may meet.

With very many thanks for your flattering remarks.

Yours sincerely,
[T. S. Eliot]

## TO *C. K. Scott-Moncrieff*[3] CC

14 January 1926 [London]

Dear Scott-Moncrieff,

I am again in town and now permanently at this address and picking up the threads of correspondence. I will answer the most important question by saying that I propose to use 'Cousin Fanny', or the first section of it, in the number of April 15th.[4] The rest will appear in the summer number.

About Pirandello, I should like to hold off for the present because Pirandello has been appearing in several places as well as once already in *The Criterion* and I should like to be able to introduce a few other Italians before using another of his stories. Meanwhile I should be interested in any suggestions of Italian authors.

The next *Criterion* will be out on the 15th. It is too big – that is the most obvious criticism of it. I should be interested to hear what you think of the number as a whole when you have looked it over.

With best wishes for the New Year,

Yours sincerely,
[T. S. Eliot]

1 – 'Stanley, Sherburne and Ayres as Translators and Imitators of Italian, French and Spanish Poets', *Modern Language Review*, July 1925, 280–94; Oct. 1925, 419–31.

2 – *La Fiera Letteraria*, an illustrated Milan weekly for which Praz was English correspondent. He had already published in the periodical 'Giovani poeti inglesi: T. S. Eliot', 31 Jan. and 21 Feb. 1926. See also Praz's Italian translation of *The Waste Land*, V – *La Terra Desolata* – in *La Fiera Letteraria*, II: 8 (21 Feb. 1926), 5.

3 – C. K. Scott Moncrieff (1889–1930), British translator of Proust and Pirandello.

4 – Scott Moncrieff, 'Cousin Fanny and Cousin Annie', C. 4 (April & July 1926).

## TO *Jean Cocteau*[1] CC

Le 15 Janvier 1926 [*The New Criterion*]

Mon Cher Cocteau,

Voilà ce qui se passe. J'avais l'idée que vos charmants 'Scandales' se trouveraient dans le volume *Rappel à l'Ordre* et je croyais que ce volume allait paraitre chez Stock au mois de décembre. Donc, je ne croyais pas pouvoir l'insérer dans *The New Criterion* de janvier. Au dernier moment, au commencement de novembre, quand j'allais partir pour la Côte d'Azur sous les directions de mon médecin, j'ai compris que 'Scandales' restait inédit. Puisqu'il n'y avait plus le temps de faire traduire cet article vous le trouverez dans *The New Criterion* de janvier en français.[2]

Maintenant vous direz que nous aurions dû vous envoyer des bonnes feuilles. Ces feuilles, on les a envoyé, mais précisément à une adresse surannée. Dans mon absence il n'avait personne au bureau qui savait l'adresse 10 rue d'Anjou. Alors, on m'a télégraphé à La Turbie et j'ai corrigé à la hâte les épreuves qu'on m'avait envoyé. Mais je n'avais pas votre texte, qui accomplissait probablement un pélérinage à travers Paris pour vous trouver. Vous aurez maintenant la préscience de quelques fautes impardonnables qui restent. Quand même je nous félicite.

Et probablement étiez vous à côte de moi à Villefranche.

En espérant de vos nouvelles et des nouvelles de Myers,

Je suis toujours votre
[T. S. Eliot][3]

1–Jean Cocteau (1889–1963), playwright, poet, librettist, novelist, film-maker, artist, designer: see Biographical Register.

2–'Scandales', *NC* 4 (Jan. 1926), 125–37. Rollo Myers had told TSE on 3 Nov. 1925 that Cocteau asked him to say that 'Scandales' was 'an "*inédit*" – intended specially for the *Criterion* – & will not form part of "Le Rappel".'

3–*Translation:* My dear Cocteau, This is what has happened. I assumed that your charming 'Scandals' would be included in *Recall to Order*, and I understood that Stock was bringing the book out in December. Consequently, I felt unable to put it in the January number of *The New Criterion*. At the last moment, at the beginning of November, as I was about to leave for the Côte d'Azur on my doctor's instructions, I realised that 'Scandals' was not being published. Since there was no longer time to have the article translated, you will find it, in French, in *The New Criterion* for January.

You will now say that we ought to have sent you the page proofs. We did, in fact, send them, but, as it happens, to an obsolete address. In my absence, there was no one in the office who knew the address: 10 rue d'Anjou. They therefore telegraphed to La Turbie and I hastily corrected the proofs which had been sent to me. But I was without your original, which was probably on its pilgrimage through Paris in search of you. You will now have the foreboding that a number of unforgivable mistakes remain. Nevertheless, I congratulate us.

And you were probably just next door to me in Villefranche.

Hoping to have news of yourself and of Myers. Yours ever [T. S. Eliot]

## TO *Henri Massis*[1] CC

Le 16 janvier 1926 [London]

Monsieur,

J'ai étudié, avec une appréciation croisante, vos divers études littéraires et vos livres de critique. Mais j'ai été surtout frappé dernièrement par votre 'Défense de l'Occident' qui est parue dans *La Revue Universelle* le 15 octobre passé. Voilà un article qui aborde d'une façon magistrale un problème d'une grande importance pour toute l'Europe, et un sujet qui jusqu' ici a échappé à l'attention des littérateurs anglais.

Voici mon affaire.

Je vais vous demander permission de faire traduire cet article et le publier dans le prochain numéro du *New Criterion*. Si vous m'accordez cette permission, l'article sera payé à notre cours fixé, c'est à dire £10 les 5000 mots, moyennant les frais de traduction.

En général nous ne publions que des inédits: par exemple nous avons publié des choses inédites de Marcel Proust, de Jacques Rivière[,] de Jean Cocteau et d'autres français. Mais puisque je tiens à poser ce problème de l'Occident à nos lecteurs anglais et puisque je trouve dans votre article la meilleure constatation de ce problème que j'aie vu, je voudrais pour cette fois faire exception.

Je vous envoie, sous pli separé, un exemplaire de notre numéro de janvier. Si vous me ferez l'honneur de l'examiner vous pourez vous assurer que les buts et les idées de notre revue sont plus apparentés aux vôtres que ceux d'aucune autre revue anglaise.

En attendant avec impatience de vos nouvelles, et en espérant avoir une réponse favorable, je vous prie, Monsieur, de recevoir l'expression de mes sentiments les plus distingués.[2]

[T. S. Eliot][3]

1–Henri Massis (1886–1970): right-wing Roman Catholic critic; contributor to *L'Action Française*; co-founder and editor of *La Revue Universelle*: see Biographical Register.

2–Massis replied in French on 17 Jan. that he would be pleased for a translation of '*La Défense de l'Occident*' to appear in *The Criterion*. He had considerable additions to make – 'une grande partie *inédite*' – but he would be happy for TSE to arrange for a translation of the initial extract from *La Revue universelle*. See *NC* 4: 2 & 3 (Apr. & June 1926). *La Défense de l'Occident* came out in full in 1928.

3–*Translation*: Dear Sir, I have studied, with growing appreciation, your various literary studies and critical works. But I was particularly impressed recently by your 'Defence of the West' which appeared in *La Revue Universelle* on the 15th October last. It is an article which deals most authoritatively with a problem of great importance for the whole of Europe, and a subject which has so far escaped the attention of English men of letters.

Coming now to the point of this letter, I would like to ask your permission to have the article translated and to publish it in the next issue of *The New Criterion*. If you grant

## TO *F. W. Bain*[1] CC

16 January 1926 [London]

My dear Bain,

I am deeply distressed by your letter of yesterday.[2] I had been abroad for over two months on a holiday enforced by my doctor and was obliged during that time to separate myself almost altogether from the affairs of *The Criterion*. It was consequently necessary that many things should be done without my knowledge and when finally I did return there was inevitably an enormous mass of correspondence and other affairs awaiting me. I have been, and am still, rather handicapped by the fact that I am not supposed to do more than a limited amount of work each day.

I was very much pleased to find your first letter and ought to have reciprocated at once. But I found that the best I could do was to arrange all my letters in order of urgency and I felt obliged to deal with the more public and business correspondence first. At the present moment I am still about twenty letters behind in addition to the daily business correspondence. I should certainly have written to you in two or three days but I am extremely sorry for the delay.

---

permission, the fee payable will be at the fixed rate of £10 per 5000 words, minus the cost of the translation.

As a rule, we take only previously unpublished texts: for instance we have brought out unpublished texts by Marcel Proust, Jacques Rivière, Jean Cocteau and other Frenchmen. But as I am keen to put the problem of the West to our readers, and your article is the best formulation of it I have come across, I would like, on this one occasion, to make an exception.

I am sending you, under separate cover, a copy of our January number. If you will do me the honour of looking at it, you will be able to assure yourself that the aims and ideas of our review are more closely related to yours than are those of any other English review.

I await your reply with impatience, and in the hope that it will be favourable. Yours sincerely [T. S. Eliot]

1–F. W. Bain (1863–1940): author and scholar; educated at Christ Church, Oxford; Fellow of All Souls College, 1889–97; Professor of History and Political Economy at the Deccan College at Poona, India, where he was esteemed 'not only as a professor but also as a prophet and a philosopher', 1892–1919. An old-style High Tory, enthused by the writings of Bolingbroke and Disraeli, his works include *The English Monarchy and its Revolutions* (1894), *On the Realisation of the Possible and the Spirit of Aristotle* (1897), and a series of 'Hindu love stories' purportedly translated from Sanskrit originals. See K. Mutalik, *Francis William Bain* (Bombay, 1963).

2–Bain was hurt by TSE's failure to answer a letter he had sent in Jan.; also, he said, his name had been left off a *TLS* advertisement (14 Jan. 1926) listing contributors to *C.* In fact, the quarter-page advertisement for the first number of the new series under the title *The New Criterion* had included F. W. Bain in a starburst of the 80 'names of those who had contributed to *The Criterion* during the years 1922–1925'.

The omission of your name from the list of contributors is quite an independent accident of which I had no knowledge and by which I am very annoyed. I saw and passed the advertisement for the *Times Literary Supplement* in which were included the names of all the contributors during the last three years. And I knew that a smaller advertisement was being prepared in which only a select list of contributors could be given. It did not for a moment occur to me that any name as important as yours would be omitted. I have this [carbon copy incomplete].

## TO *Richard Cobden-Sanderson*[1] CC

16 January 1926 [London]

Dear Cobden-Sanderson,

I have now written to Lady Rothermere stating that I now no longer need for editorial purposes the office at 23 Adelphi Terrace House which she engaged in her own name by an agreement with Miss Harriet Weaver terminable at three months' notice on either side. I have reminded her that this agreement can of course be cancelled only by a letter from herself to Miss Weaver.[2]

Messrs Faber & Gwyer as publishers of *The New Criterion* have no responsibility for the rent and rates of 23 Adelphi Terrace House. I therefore wish to pay the enclosed application for rent and also the sum of £1. 11. 0. for cleaning and fires (payable to the housekeeper, W. Read) for one quarter due Christmas 1925 out of the credit balance of *The Criterion* account at Barclay's Bank. If you will kindly draw cheques for these payments I will sign them and return them to you.

I am immediately notifying Lady Rothermere that we are settling her liabilities in this way and that we shall continue to do so out of the balance of the old *Criterion* account until up to the date on which she will have terminated the tenancy.

Yrs ever
[T. S. Eliot]

1–Richard Cobden-Sanderson (1884–1964): printer; publisher of *The Criterion*, 1922–5: see Biographical Register.
2–TSE was to give up the room at 23 Adelphi Terrace House on March quarter day.

## TO *Jean Paulhan*[1] CC

Le 16 janvier 1926 [*The New Criterion*]

Cher Monsieur,

Un petit mot pour vous souhaiter la bonne année et pour vous dire que je n'ai pas pu m'arrêter à Paris, ayant été rapellé inopinément à Londres. Mais j'espère revenir à Paris pour quelques jours au mois de février.

Je vous préparerai ma chronique sur le roman contemporain en Angleterre aussitôt que possible. Puis je vous demander la bonté de m'envoyer pour m'aider dans la préparation de cette chronique un exemplaire du *Roman Contemporain Anglais* d'Abel Chevalley qui est parut chez Gallimard. Je sais que ce livre n'est pas tout à fait d'actualité mais on me l'a loué et je ne veux pas écrire sur un sujet pareil sans faire attention à ses opinions.

Je voudrais savoir aussi si M. Gallimard serait disposé a nous envoyer de temps en temps, et sur commande seulement, des livres nouveaux de sa librairie pour que nous puissions en faire des notes dans *The New Criterion*. Je crois que le public du *New Criterion* est à peu près le même public anglais qui achète et s'intéresse à la littérature contemporaine française.[2]

Je suis, cher Monsieur, très cordialment votre

[T. S. Eliot][3]

1–Jean Paulhan (1884–1968), editor of *Nouvelle Revue Française* (in succession to Jacques Rivière), 1925–40, 1946–68. He was active in the French Resistance during WW2. Publications include *Entretiens sur des fait-divers* (1930), *Les Fleurs de Tarbes, ou, La Terreur dans les lettres* (1936), and *On Poetry and Politics*, ed. Jennifer Bajorek *et al* (2010). See William Marx, 'Two Modernisms: T. S. Eliot and *La Nouvelle Revue Française*', in *The International Reception of T. S. Eliot*, ed. Elisabeth Däumer and Shyamal Bagchee (2007), 25–33.

2–Paulhan wrote on 21 Jan. that he was sorry not to have seen TSE; he had already posted the Chevalley book; and he would happily supply any books TSE desired from the '*éditions de la N.R.F*'. He looked forward to seeing TSE's chronicle.

3–*Translation*: Dear Mr Paulhan, Just a note to wish you a Happy New Year and to say that I was not able to break my journey in Paris, having been called back unexpectedly to London. But I hope to return to Paris for a few days in February.

## TO *Leonard Woolf* MS Berg

17 January 1926 24 Russell Square, W.C.1

Dear Leonard

This is merely to tell you – as I have been waiting to do for several days – that your counsel & general information the other day was & is of great help and use to me. This, because I did not express my appreciation at the time, & I believe it cost you something.

I may well need your advice again, but it will be more on points of detail in my present case.

Yours ever
T. S. E.

## TO *Lady Rothermere*[1] CC

18 January 1926 [London]

Dear Lady Rothermere,

There are two or three points which I ought to mention to you at once.

One is about the payment of the rent for the office at 23 Adelphi Terrace House. In my last letter I told you that so far as I was concerned I was quite ready to give up this expense of twenty odd pounds a year which now seems superfluous. But even if you notify Miss Weaver at once, there will be the rent and rates to pay up to the end of March, amounting to something over ten pounds. As Cobden-Sanderson has now paid all the debts of the old *Criterion* and there is still a balance on the *Criterion* account at the bank, I am arranging with him that we shall pay these expenses out of that account and that he shall eventually withdraw the balance and pay it over in a cheque to you. This seems to me much the

---

I will have my article on the contemporary English novel ready as soon as possible. Can I ask you to be so kind as to help me in its preparation by sending me a copy of *Le Roman contemporain anglais* by Abel Chevalley, which is published by Gallimard. I know that the book is not very recent, but I have heard it well spoken of, and I don't want to write about the subject without taking Chevalley's opinions into account.

I would also like to know if M. Gallimard would be prepared to send us from time to time, but only at our request, certain of the newly published books, so that we can notice them in *The New Criterion*. I think *The New Criterion* public is more or less the same English public as is interested in contemporary French literature.

With best wishes [T. S. Eliot]

1 – Mary Lilian Rothermere, née Share, Viscountess Rothermere: proprietor of *The Criterion*: see Biographical Register.

simplest way of settling the matter and the way in which you will be given the least trouble.[1]

Before I went away, and indeed while I was in France, I had some correspondence with a young man in Paris named Stewart[2] who appears to be a friend and adjutant of Paul Valéry.[3] Stewart and Madame Bussy (Lytton Strachey's sister) were preparing translations of some of Valéry's prose works, especially the dialogues.[4] Stewart approached me with a view to getting us to do another volume like *The Serpent*.[5] I told him frankly that you had certain other books in preparation for special editions by

1 – 'I am *very annoyed* with C.S.,' wrote Lady Rothermere (21 Jan.). 'He has treated Miss Beach very badly indeed – I hope Faber & Gwyer will put things right with her.'

2 – William McC. Stewart was teaching at the École Normale Supérieure, Paris V.

3 – Paul Valéry (1871–1945), poet, essayist and literary theoretician, was born near Marseilles (his father was French, his mother Italian) and educated at the University of Montpellier, where he read law. After settling in Paris in 1894, he developed friendships with André Gide and Stéphane Mallarmé. For many years, he worked for Edouard Lebey, director of the Press Association and Havas news agency; and he co-edited the review *Commerce*, 1924–32. His reputation was built on his symbolist poems and some reviews, supplemented by two prose studies, *Introduction à la méthode de Léonard de Vinci* (1895), and *La Soirée avec Monsieur Teste* (1896) – an abstract, rational figure in search of quintessences. After a delay of nearly twenty years, he published a poem, *La Jeune Parque* (1917), and a volume entitled *Charmes* ('Incantations', 1922) which gathered up his poems of the period 1913–1922, and which included his celebrated work, 'Le Cimitière Marin' ('The Graveyard by the Sea'), a symbolical, classically strict, modulated meditation upon the essence of death and life. In 1925 he was elected an *académicien*, and from 1937 he held the post of Professor of Poetry at the Collège de France. Later writings include elegantly composed essays distilled from the pages of the vast number of *Cahiers* that he filled out – over a period of almost 40 years – with reflections upon literary theory and philosophy. Works translated into English include *Le Serpent* – for which TSE wrote the preface (1924). TSE, who came to know Valéry from 1923, later said that his '"philosophy" lays itself open to the accusation of being only an elaborate game. Precisely, but to be able to play this game, to be able to take aesthetic delight in it, is one of the manifestations of civilised man . . . His was, I think, a profoundly destructive mind, even nihilistic. This cannot, one way or the other, alter our opinion of the poetry; it can neither abate nor magnify the pleasure or the admiration. But it should, I think, increase our admiration of the man who wrote the poetry. For the *agony* of creation, for a mind like Valéry's, must be very great . . . It is strange, but my intimacy with his poetry has been largely due to my study of what he has written about poetry. Of all poets, Valéry has been the most completely conscious (perhaps I should say the most nearly conscious) of what he was doing . . . [I]t is he who will remain for posterity the representative poet, the symbol of the poet, of the first half of the twentieth century – not Yeats, not Rilke, not anyone else' ('Paul Valéry', *Quarterly Review of Literature* 3, 1946).

4 – Dorothy Strachey (1865–1960), eldest of the Stracheys, was married to the French artist Simon Bussy and lived in France, where she was friendly with Matisse and Gide. She had recently completed a translation of *L'Âme et la Danse*.

5 – Stewart had written to TSE on 8 Nov. 1925 that Valéry 'much prefers the idea of a separate limited edition of each of the dialogues as far as possible in the form of *The Serpent* (with a similarly suitable emblem on the cover in each case: he very much liked the serpent biting his tail in red).

the Criterion Press, that everything had been very much held up by the transfer from Cobden-Sanderson to Faber & Gwyer, that *The Serpent* itself was hardly likely to do more than pay expenses and that I could not honestly advise you to take on more of Valéry's work at the present time. I do not think that the idea of turning the Criterion Press into an advertising medium for Valéry will appeal to you any more strongly than it did to me – great as is my admiration for Valéry's work.[1] I suggested as an alternative that Faber & Gwyer might be willing to publish a bigger book of Valéry's prose works if Valéry would contribute a new introduction, but even this would hardly be what one could call a commercial proposition. The latter idea, however, did not appeal to Valéry who seems infatuated with the notion of limited editions of particular works. So there the matter rests.[2]

I tell you all this to give you the opportunity of taking the matter up if it appeals to you; but I do not recommend it. The last point I ought to mention is about La Bluette. I expect Madame de Sanoît[3] has let you know about the two people who were after it when I was there; one an English woman who wanted to take it furnished as it is for the winter months, the other a man from Nice who would like to buy it. Whatever you have in mind for the future I felt that it would be a good thing for you to let it in the winter whenever possible. I think you would find it too cold in the winter for yourself, and although it seems well built and was in surprisingly good condition, I noticed a few damp patches on the walls, and I think that it would keep in much better condition if occupied more often.

In haste,
Yours always sincerely,
[T. S. Eliot]

---

'A subsequent publication of selected prose works in a one-volume unlimited edition, with possibly a new foreword by himself and an introduction by some English man of letters, such as yourself or Mr Whibley, he would certainly welcome if you think it would find a publisher.'

1–TSE was later to affirm of Mark Wardle's translation of *Le Serpent* that it was 'a very good translation' (letter to Miss Cecily Mackworth, 2 Dec. 1943). But when he reread his own preface, he had to 'confess that after such a lapse of time I am rather ashamed of it. Such a preface written when Valéry's work was still comparatively little known in this country is not such as I would write today. Of course, the fact that I know much more of Valéry's work than I did then, and also the fact that the picture of Valéry is somewhat altered in view of his subsequent work, make the whole thing rather out of date' (letter to Yves-Gérard le Dantec, 11 Oct. 1946).

2–'I quite agree: re Valéry,' said Lady Rothermere.

3–Alice de Sanoît.

## TO *John Shand*[1] CC

18 January 1926 [London]

Dear Mr Shand,

As I supposed that the matter was pressing I have read you[r] manuscript and return it at once together with Murry's letter.[2]

I think that your short article is clever and well written, though if Mr Murry considers it the best thing of yours that he has seen then he cannot have seen very much. This is no disparagement to your article; it is as good as the subject matter permits. It does not seem to me that the subject matter is of sufficient importance to justify *The Criterion* in recognizing the existence of Mr Michael Arlen;[3] and therefore I return it.

I cannot at the moment think of any other likely quarter for this article. It is too short for some purposes, too long for others. In the weekly papers reviews have to be very much reviews and this is probably too much of an article and too little of a review for their purposes. And if it were accepted by a Quarterly, some other Quarterly than the *Criterion*, which again is doubtful owing to the unimportance of Mr Arlen, you would probably suffer from having to wait a long time before it appeared, and from the fact that nobody would read it, because nobody reads quarterly reviews. On the whole I think that I should advise you to let the *Adelphi* have it, and write something more saleable.

I hope that the Lubbock book will prove to be worth your pains.[4]

Yours sincerely,
[T. S. Eliot]

## TO *Harriet Shaw Weaver*[5] CC

19 January 1926 [*The Criterion*]

Dear Miss Weaver,

I certainly told Lady Rothermere that I was writing to you, and should have done so already but for pressure of work.[6] It is quite true that I no

1–John Shand (b. 1901) was an occasional contributor to the *Criterion*. He was later to write 'Around *Little Gidding*', *Nineteenth Century* 136 (Sept. 1944).
2–JMM wanted to print Shand's MS in *The Adelphi*; Shand hoped TSE might take it.
3–Michael Arlen (1895–1956): Hungarian-born novelist; author of *The Green Hat* (1924).
4–Shand contributed to *NC* 'The Region Cloud', a review of the book by Percy Lubbock.
5–Harriet Shaw Weaver (1876–1961), editor and publisher: see Biographical Register.
6–Lady Rothermere had told Weaver she did not require the office at 23 Adelphi Terrace House beyond the present quarter; Weaver wished to hear from TSE himself.

longer need the office at 23 Adelphi Terrace House which has, however, been so very useful in the past and for which I am very grateful to you. I have been abroad for my health and was unable to attend to the matter before now. I think that the notice required is three months but I am not sure. I thought, however, that as the place seems to be so sought after that the landlords might be glad to accept cancellation at less than three months' notice. I am very sorry to give you the trouble of enquiring into this. If you find that it is now too late to give up the office on Quarter Day the 25th March and that it is necessary to keep it on until June 25th, please let me know.

There is another small matter which I am afraid I have neglected and for which I owe humble apologies. I know that there was some arrangement between us that we should take over and pay for the furniture in that office. Of course I no longer require this furniture and I think that if I can I will find out whether the following tenants would like to have it, but in any case I know that a certain sum of money, I have forgotten how much, is owing to you for it. I had completely forgotten the matter and I will make this right after I hear from you.

With most cordial good wishes from my wife and myself,

Yours sincerely,
[T. S. Eliot]

## TO *J. F. Holms*[1] CC

19 January 1926 [London]

Dear Sir,

I have read with great interest two reviews by you in *The Calendar*,[2] one on the work of Virginia Woolf and another on the work of David Garnett.[3] They seem to me the best pieces of criticism that I have recently

1–John Holms (1897–1934): gifted British talker and unproductive writer; lover of Peggy Guggenheim, collector of modern art. See Guggenheim, *Out of This Century: Confessions of an Art Addict* (1979); Mary V. Dearborn, *Peggy Guggenheim: Mistress of Modernism* (2004); Edwin Muir, *An Autobiography* (1954): 'Holms was the most remarkable man I ever met . . . [His mind] had the quality which Joubert attributes to Plato's mind: you could live in it, walk about in it, take your ease in it.'

2–*The Calendar of Modern Letters*, ed. Edgell Rickword and Douglas Garman, ran from Mar. 1925 to July 1927.

3–Holms's reviews were mostly 'dismissive: he admitted . . . to finding *Mrs. Dalloway* to be Virginia Woolf's best book thus far, but rejected it as "aesthetically worthless", and . . . he found David Garnett's *The Sailor's Return* "without aesthetic life"' (Dearborn, *Peggy Guggenheim*, 79).

seen on these authors. I should very much like you to review also for *The New Criterion* if you care to do so. Our only condition would be – a condition in which I expect the Editor of *The Calendar* would cordially concur – that you do not review the same books for both. But there need be no difficulty about this, for I could easily find other books for you.

I should be very glad to hear from you or should be glad if you would call on me here, if you could telephone any day after 2.30 to arrange an appointment.

Yours faithfully
[T. S. Eliot]

## TO *James Smith*[1] CC

19 January 1926 [London]

Dear Mr Smith,

You have no need to waste half a sheet of paper in recalling yourself to someone who remembers you perfectly well and a very pleasant dinner with you at the Union.[2] I shall be very pleased to lunch with you one day in Cambridge if you will do me the same honour when you are next in London. May we make it the day after my third lecture? I am not quite sure when that is but I think it must be the 9th February as I begin on the 26th and the lectures are on the same day every week. Does this suit you?

I am writing as quickly as possible without yet having read your poem; I am glad that you have sent it to me and will let you know exactly what I think of it as soon as I can.[3]

Yours sincerely,
[T. S. Eliot]

1–James Smith (1904–72), critic and educator: see Biographical Register. At this time he was reading English and Modern Languages at Trinity College, Cambridge.
2–Smith had invited TSE to address the Cam Literary Club in 1924.
3–Smith's poem (title now unknown) was not to appear in the *Criterion*.

## TO *I. A. Richards*[1] CC

19 January 1926 [London]

My dear Richards,

I am hoping to see you frequently during this term as I am coming down every week to lecture. My lectures begin on the 26th and are weekly thereafter.[2] Could we arrange a meeting the second week either on the Tuesday or the Wednesday?

I have just received from Kegan Paul John B. Watson's *Behaviourism* which I ordered for the purpose of asking you to review it for *The Criterion*. I shall be very happy if you will, because there are very few people competent to tackle this book which seems to me an important one. Only I should have to ask you to let me have the review by the 15th February. May I send you the book?[3]

Sincerely yours,
[pp T.S. Eliot – I.P.F.]

## TO *Edwin Muir* CC

20 January 1926 [London]

Dear Mr Muir,

Thank you for your letter of the 8th. Do let me know as soon as you are sure of the date of your arrival in London and I will save the time.

1 – I. A. Richards (1893–1979): educator and theorist of literature, education and communication studies; College Lecturer in English and Moral Sciences, Magdalene College, Cambridge, 1922–30: see Biographical Register.

2 – TSE's Clark Lectures were delivered at Trinity College every Tues. afternoon, 26 Jan.–9 Mar. IAR attended all eight of them. On the relations between TSE and IAR, see 'Introduction: I. A. Richards and his Critics', in *I. A. Richards and his Critics*, ed. John Constable (2001), x–li (*I. A. Richards: Selected Works 1919–1938*, vol. 10).

3 – 'I'll do Watson,' said IAR (25 Jan.). 'I know the book well & to consider it again fits in fairly well with what I'm thinking about just now.' See IAR's review in *NC* 4 (Apr. 1926), 372–8. He wrote too: 'I'm looking forward to the Lectures. You will have an interested and rather good audience. Trinity [College] is too big a place, of course, for the purpose. No group less than 1000 could form in it. So you won't feel at all what *they* (it) are (is) doing & feeling. And there is a certain 5.0 o'clock committee somnolence to fight against. Murry was too soporific – didn't work people up enough (if even by pauses) also he brought a Chapel feeling with him.

'There will probably (there always is) be a preponderance of women. The general feeling is very friendly mixed with a lively curiosity. I'm always being asked what your views are, and skepticism as to their interest and importance is very rare.'

I hope that you can come and lunch with me. I should like to talk to you about Nietzsche.[1]

Yours sincerely
[T. S. Eliot]

## TO *Marianne Moore*[2]

MS Beinecke

21 January 1926 *The New Criterion*

Dear Miss Moore,

This is to introduce to you a valued contributor to the *Criterion* – Mr T. MacGreevy ('L. St. Senan')[3], & a friend of Mr Yeats.

Sincerely yours
T. S. Eliot

## TO *Ramon Fernandez*[4]

CC

21 January 1926 [*The New Criterion*]

My dear Fernandez,

I am delighted at last to hear from you.[5] I cannot understand why you received none of my letters but I am glad to hear that my book reached you duly. At the same moment as hearing from you I have a letter from Madame Salmon[6] sending me tickets for your lecture on the 30th which I shall not fail to attend. If you receive this letter in time will you send me a wire to let me know whether you can lunch or dine with me on that day or lunch with me on the following day, and which time you prefer. I wish that we had longer notice of your coming because there are many people whom I should like to invite to your lecture.

1–Friedrich Wilhelm Nietzsche (1844–1900): German philosopher; author of *Thus Spake Zarathustra*.

2–Marianne Moore (1887–1972), poet and critic: see Biographical Register.

3–McGreevy took his pseudonym from St Senan (d. 560), founder of several monasteries in north Kerry, Ireland.

4–Ramon Fernandez (1894–1944), philosopher, essayist, novelist, was Mexican by birth but educated in France, where he contributed to *NRF*, 1923–43. His works include *Messages* (1926) – which included an essay entitled 'Le classicism de T. S. Eliot' – *De la personnalité* (1928), and *L'Homme est-il humain?* (1936). In the 1930s, he was a fierce anti-fascist, but during WW2 he became a collaborationist.

5–Fernandez claimed on 19 Jan. not to have heard from TSE (though TSE's book had reached him in Italy); he wondered whether TSE still wanted him to write on T. E. Hulme. He was giving some lectures in England, finishing in London on 30 Jan.

6–Yvonne Salmon, Secretary of the *Alliance Française*, London.

In haste,
Yours sincerely,
[T. S. Eliot]

P.S. Yes of course I want the essay on Hulme[1] very much indeed or if not that something else. And one thing that I was going to write to you about is this, that Frederic Manning has written a reply to your essay on Newman which has appeared in our last number. I should like very much to have a short reply from you on Manning's criticism, either a short article or perhaps just in the form of an 'open letter' which would be paid for at regular rates.[2]

1–T. E. Hulme (1883–1917): Imagist poet and philosophical critic; killed in action in WW1. TSE called him in 1926 'the most *fertile* mind of my generation' (*VMP*, 82); and said of his posthumous essays, *Speculations*, ed. Herbert Read (1924), in *C.* 2 (Apr. 1924): 'With its peculiar merits, this book is most unlikely to meet with the slightest comprehension from the usual reviewer: with all its defects – it is an outline of work to be done, and not an accomplished philosophy – it is a book of very great significance . . . In this volume he appears as the forerunner of a new attitude of mind, which should be the twentieth-century mind, if the twentieth century is to have a mind of its own. Hulme is classical, reactionary, and revolutionary; he is the antipodes of the eclectic, tolerant, and democratic mind of the end of the last century' (231–2). Fernandez's essay was not forthcoming. Later, TSE wrote to Patric Dickinson (29 Sept. 1955): 'I never met Hulme, and therefore have no personal impressions of the man . . . Hulme's work . . . is fragmentary. It is also tentative and not altogether mature. There are many germinal ideas present in the fragments, but they could not all, if developed, be maintained by the same mind. I regard Hulme as having been a stimulating writer for men of my generation, and a little younger, but I should think that his work was of historical rather than of actual importance.

'The picture you give of Hulme, is that of a rather brutal and aggressive type, such as would have been attracted by one or another form of totalitarianism. I do not know whether this is a true picture or not, but it does seem to me that if you are to give such an impression, it should be more fully substantiated . . . The possibility that quite incompatible attitudes may be traced to Hulme, or associated with him, is instanced by your collocation of Mr Pound's fascism and my Anglo-Catholicism, though I cannot see why these two "isms" should be called complementary.'

See further Robert Ferguson, *The Short Sharp Life of T. E. Hulme* (2002); Ronald Schuchard, 'Did Eliot Know Hulme? Final Answer', *Journal of Modern Literature*, 27 (2004), 63–9.

2–Manning would write on 17 Feb: 'I was not satisfied by my Newman article. I saw too many aspects of the subject to do more than suggest some of them. But I am glad Ramon Fernandez is returning to the question because I admire both his literary ability, and his insight into the psychological problem.

'It occurred to me that I might add a short note to his reply: but only if he were willing. I do not want to indulge in any controversy. My point is this, that in Newman's life, the development of his action diverges from the development of his thought, his action is based on faith (i.e. on a *real* assent), his thought is based on faith (i.e. a notional assent). In his writings he seeks to find a common measure with the minds of other men, and he used invariably the *argumentum ad hominem* as the chief weapon of the proselytiser. In the light of his own life his writings lose most of their value: except as almost perfect examples of

## TO *W. McC. Stewart*[1] CC

21 January 1926 [London]

Dear Mr Stewart,

I am now back in London at this address and beginning to pick up the various threads of business which have either been dropped or tangled during my absence. Could you let me know exactly what the present situation is concerning Valéry's prose? I am waiting to hear from Lady Rothermere about it but I am afraid that if Valéry still prefers a series of limited editions rather than one larger volume of selected prose the matter will, so far as we are concerned, have to wait over for some time.[2]

I shall be writing to Valéry but I shall not attempt to go into the various details which I have explained to you.

With all best wishes,
Sincerely yours,
[T. S. Eliot]

## TO *George Rylands*[3] MS King's

22 January 1926 9 Clarence Gate Gardens, N.W.1.

Dear Rylands

Please forgive my delay – I have been away in Bedfordshire for two or three days. Very many thanks for your invitation, but my wife has just

---

style and method. But if faith be the vital motive of action, then Newman's action has a greater validity than his thought as that is exhibited in the Sermons, the Essay, and the Grammar of Assent. We cannot put aside his catholicism.'

Fernandez sent 'Réponse à M. Frederic Manning' in May: 'The Experience of Newman: A Response to Frederic Manning', *NC* 4 (Oct. 1926), 645–58.

1–William McCausland Stewart (1900–89) was born in Dublin and educated at Trinity College, Dublin. Resident Lecteur d'Anglais at the École Normale Supérieure, Paris, 1923–6 (while studying at the Sorbonne), he taught too at the École des Hautes Études. He was Lecturer in French, University of Sheffield, 1927–8, and taught at St Andrews and Dundee before becoming Professor of French at Bristol, 1945–68. He was elected Chevalier de la Légion d'Honneur, 1950; Officier des Palmes Académiques, 1950; Commandeur, 1966. His works include translations of Paul Valéry's *Eupalinos* (1932) and *Dialogues* (Bollingen Series XLV, 1956).

2–Stewart replied (25 Jan.) that Valéry 'prefers complete editions of the dialogues, which cannot, he holds, bear cutting . . . As for the "Crise de l'Esprit", he pointed out that it had appeared first in English in the *Athenaeum*; but it could, I suppose, appear in a volume of selected prose . . .' Lady Rothermere told TSE on 28 Jan.: 'I see no objection at all to your proposals – do just as you like.'

3–George Rylands (1902–99), scholar and theatre director: see Biographical Register.

rejoined me in London, & also Wednesday is I fear an impossible day. I may not be back from Cambridge till late in the evening. When I get back I will suggest a day & hope you will lunch with me.

Sincerely yours
T. S. Eliot

## TO *Jean de Menasce*[1] CC

22 January 1926 [London]

Dear Menasce,

I am glad to hear from you at last.[2] I have heard vaguely of you from several people but have not yet been long back. I am looking forward to seeing your translation of *The Waste Land* in print. I did not know that *Philosophies* had changed its title or its form but I hope that it will continue and succeed because it seemed to me one of the most interesting of the Paris reviews.

You do not mention your own poem.[3] I have been waiting for that also and hope that it will soon appear.

Have you been doing any translations of Stefan George[4] and have you considered translating any into English? I should be interested to see anything you do in this way.

But this is primarily to let you know that I am settled in London again and that you will find me here whenever you come.

Yours ever,
[T. S. Eliot]

1–Jean de Menasce (1902–73), theologian, orientalist, Dominican priest: see Biographical Register.

2–Menasce wrote on 18 Jan. that his translation of *TWL* 'will come out in *L'Esprit* (the new form of *Philosophies*) early this year'. See *La Terre mise a nu – 'revue et approuvée par l'auteur' – Esprit* 1 [May 1926], 174–94; repr. in *Philosophies* as *La Terra gaste* – the revised title being warmly approved by TSE. Menasce went on: 'I am getting more and more "in to" Stefan George . . . There is no doubt, I feel, that he belongs to the Dante Shakespeare Baudelaire family.'

3–Not identified.

4–Stefan George (1868–1933), German lyric poet and translator associated with Stéphane Mallarmé and Paul Verlaine. Classicist and élitist (his disciples called him the 'Master'), his works include *Hymnen, Pilgerfahrten, and Algabal* (1900), *Der Krieg* ('The War', 1917) and *Das neue Reich* ('The New Empire', 1928).

## TO *E. R. Curtius*[1] CC

22 January 1926 [London]

My dear Curtius,

This letter is a very long delayed one. In the summer I was in very poor health and all of my affairs fell into arrears; I was then obliged to go to the south of France for several weeks for my health and I am only now beginning to pick up the threads of my correspondence.

I hope that you received a copy of my poems which I had sent to you during my absence from England direct from the publishers. If you have not received it, please let me know.

But I should like first of all to thank you for sending me a copy of your book – *Französischer Geist im Neuen Europa*.[2] I have only just begun to read it so I cannot yet pass any intelligent criticism upon this particular book, but I think that the work that you are doing is one of great importance for the uniting of Europe and it inspires me with two wishes, one that we had someone in England who could interpret any foreign literature to us as well as you interpret France to Germany, and second that you might undertake some work on contemporary English literature parallel to your work on French literature. Such criticism of yours is not merely valuable to the compatriots of the critic but has its own value for each other nationality – that is to say it interprets the French to themselves and also to a third nationality such as the English.

Now that I am able to take up my work again you shall hear from me later about your Balzac.[3] I think that the English edition would be well worth doing although I imagine that for English publication it ought to be somewhat reduced in size.

There are two questions that I have to ask you at the moment. One is this: the German periodicals which come to *The New Criterion* for review go direct to the member of the staff who deals with them and I do not see them. I feel that I ought to try, now that I have more time, to keep in closer touch with foreign literature myself and I should like to subscribe for my own use to one German literary periodical. Which one would you advise me to choose? And could you at the same time tell me the price of the annual subscription and the address of the publisher.

1 – Ernst Robert Curtius (1886–1956), German scholar of philology and Romance literature: see Biographical Register.

2 – *Französischer Geist im neuen Europa* (1925).

3 – *Balzac* (1923).

The second question is this: apart from any essays which you care to send us from time to time I am anxious to have a brief half-yearly 'chronicle' of the current literary, artistic and theatrical life in Germany. I am aiming to have one correspondent in each country. In the number of *The New Criterion* which I am sending to you you will find the New York chronicle which is very much on the lines required. That is to say, the chronicler has considerable liberty; he is not required in such a small space to cover all the events of three months but can if he likes devote most of his space to one thing – a book, a play, a problem of the day, etcetera, which seems to him particularly important or interesting.

Would you be willing to undertake such a regular chronicle for Germany yourself? Or if not could you recommend someone whom you think competent and likely to undertake it?

With all best wishes,
Sincerely yours,
[T. S. Eliot]

## TO *Conrad Aiken*[1] TS Huntington

22 January 1926 *The New Criterion*

Dear Conrad,

I am very sorry to hear about your relapses and backslidings but you seem to be all right for all essential purposes except to produce literature.[2]

1 – Conrad Aiken (1889–1973), American poet and critic: see Biographical Register.

2 – Aiken had written to TSE on 21 Jan.: 'after a relapse, haemorrhage (purulent offensive discharge) and vivid nightmare of Op. 3, I am now recovering again and can manage a pub-crawl at moderate speed . . . A page more of dialogue in my novel, every second day, about all I can rise to.' (The letter is printed in *Selected Letters of Conrad Aiken*, 111). Shortly beforehand, TSE had sent him a copy of *Poems 1909–1925* (published on 23 Nov. 1925). Aiken acknowledged the gift from a London hospital where he was undergoing an operation for an anal fistula: 'with his head full of ether,' as he was to relate in his idiosyncratic autobiography *Ushant: An Essay* (1952); he praised TSE's work with a 'kind of drunken fulsomeness', to which TSE had responded 'with a printed page torn out of *The Midwives' Gazette*, on which he had underlined in ink certain words and phrases – *Blood – mucous – shreds of mucous – purulent offensive discharge*. That was all – no comment or signature' (133). (Aiken had first referred to the incident to another friend on 4 Jan. 1926: see *Selected Letters*, 109–10; and he seems to have been so disturbed by it that he put it on record even in an obituary essay, 'T. S. Eliot', in *Life*, 15 Jan. 1965, 93.) Aiken had an exact memory for the text (if not for the title of the journal): 'model answers' for the nurses' examinations on the subject of 'Vaginal Discharges' had featured in *The Nursing Mirror and Midwives' Journal*, 28 Nov. 1925, 190. TSE did not have to look far for his cutting: F&G had just taken over publication of that periodical, so recent issues were to be found at their new offices at 24

The Wharton book is arriving by the ordinary postal means.[1] There is either a great hurry or none at all, i.e. if you let me have the review by the 15th February it will probably be printed in the April number and if you let me have it after that date it will appear in the July number. As the delay is not likely to make all the difference for you between solvency and bankruptcy I cannot feel justified in the circumstances for pressing for an early reply.

The answer to paragraph 3 of your letter is that I did not think it was good enough and that it did not seem to fit in very well with the rest.[2]

Your remarks about *The Criterion* are noted with satisfaction. If you are suffering from the disease you mention I think I can use any amount of your stuff.[3]

Ezra's address is – via Marsala 12 int. 5, Rapallo, Italy. If you should be going there walk straight up to the seventh floor and knock, because the lift doesn't work and the bell is out of order, but he has a very nice roof garden overlooking the harbour. As for the price of the Outline of History, I suppose it is designed to keep it out of the hands of blokes like ourselves.[4]

Yours ever,
[T. S. E.]

---

Russell Square. TSE, in response to a copy of *Ushant* that Aiken sent him on publication, would write on 7 Nov. 1952: 'I was, as a matter of fact, somewhat shocked to find myself described as having a streak of sadism in my nature. I haven't the faintest recollection of the two incidents on which you base this diagnosis, but if it was like that, then it seems to me I must have behaved very badly. I hope in that case you have forgiven me.'

1–Aiken promptly considered (31 Jan.) *The Writing of Fiction* by Edith Wharton to be 'very meagre', and he disposed of the copy so it was not to be reviewed in *C*.

2–CA repeated his request to know why TSE had omitted the verses 'this is my affliction' ('Eyes that last I saw Tears') from *Poems 1909–1925*.

3–CA wrote (21 Jan.): 'The new crit. is damned good: don't again take a compliment amiss: but I have in my possession a document written by a dementia praecox patient which outgertrudes Gertrude [Stein].'

4–CA asked why EP presented his 'universal history' at such a prohibitive price. *A Draft of XVI Cantos* had just been published in Paris by the Three Mountains Press in an edition limited to 70 copies at a price ranging from 400 to 1600 francs.

## *Vivien Eliot* TO *Mary Hutchinson*[1] MS Texas

22 January 1926 9 Clarence Gate Gardens, N.W.1.

Dear Mary,

I was so glad to have a letter from you.

I am really well! But *not* going abroad until April or May.

I am afraid the rumour that Tom has a studio in Marseilles is false. That he is lecturing at Cambridge is true. That he has a new suit is false – but he *has* a new overcoat, & a smart one.

Tom & I have not disappeared. I mean we did disappear but we are coming to light again.

I am delighted you remember the Spring day at [?Hanover] Row, & Ezra Pound & Tom looking out of the window. I never forget it.

On Sunday week (31st) Tom is giving a tea party in honour of a gentleman[2] from France, one connected with the *N. R. F*.- & very handsome, so Tom says. *Will you come?* You are invited. Please come. At 4.30. And Jack[3] too? If he wd not be bored. I want it to be the beginning of a new series of spring days. We are moving from here, in March.

With love
Vivien

## TO *Lady Rothermere* CC

23 January 1926 [London]

Dear Lady Rothermere,

Thank you for replying about 23 Adelphi Terrace House. I am in communication with Miss Weaver and endeavouring to obtain release by the end of March.

About Cobden-Sanderson, versions vary. I understand here that while I was away they had great trouble in obtaining information from him because he was always out and very busy and never available. Faber & Gwyer are writing at once to Miss Beach about it. They intend to make efforts to obtain a larger distribution in Paris, but for the present number propose to go on with Miss Beach as before. There has been a great deal to do and I must say that matters were extremely difficult for

1–Mary Hutchinson (1889–1977): a half-cousin of Lytton Strachey; prominent hostess, author: see Biographical Register.

2–Ramon Fernandez.

3–St John ('Jack') Hutchinson (1884–1942), barrister-at-law; Mary's husband.

them, handling a new publication in my absence. I am asking them to communicate with Galignani.[1] The copy for the announcement was duly sent to *La Nouvelle Revue Française* and we shall find out whether they are using it on the 1st February. If not, it is their own fault. But I think that it is better that the announcement should appear on the 1st February rather than the 1st January because if people enquire for a review on the strength of an advertisement and find that it has not yet appeared they are apt to be annoyed. On the other hand, if it is stated in the advertisement that the periodical will not appear for another fortnight, they are apt to forget about it. So I hope that the 1st February is settled.

About the chalet, I enclose a letter written to me just before I left La Turbie by the lady who wanted to take it for the winter months. Her name appears to be Mavor. Madame de Sanoît has the address of the man in Nice who wanted to buy it, and I understand from her that she knew him personally or at any rate knew a great deal about him.

I hope you will enjoy Palermo. Both my wife and I are getting steadily better.

Yours ever sincerely,
[T. S. Eliot]

## TO *Henri Massis* CC

Le 23 janvier 1926 [*The New Criterion*]

Monsieur,

Je vous remercie de vos deux lettres de l'envoi du manuscript complet.[2] Je trouve votre orthographie parfaitement lisible et je l'ai aujourd'hui donné à traduire.

Je me félicite beaucoup de votre permission de publier cet article et aussi d'en avoir quelques feuilles encores inédites.

Je m'aperçois qu'en dictant ma lettre de l'autre jour j'ai mit 'moyennant les frais de traduction' au lieu de 'moins les frais de traduction'. Mais

1 – Galignani: the oldest English-language bookshop in Paris.

2 – Massis had sent (19 Jan) 'a considerably extended' text of his article: '*j'ai surtout ajouté des textes, des faits, des citations de documents, afin de lui donner un ton moins abstrait*' ('the main change is that I have added texts, facts and quotations from documents, in order to make the tone less abstract'). He was writing another ten pages or so about '*les principes* spirituels *de l'Asie et de l'Europe*' ('the *spiritual* principles of Asia and Europe'). He hoped the translator would be able to read his handwriting. On 20 Jan. he sent the final pages, with a brief conclusion touching on 'the ideological side of the problem'. He would be in London on 20 Mar., he added.

naturellement je tiendrai ma parole et vous aurez le prix nommé dans ma lettre.

Je suis enchanté de croire que vous allez visiter l'Angleterre et je vous engage de me prevenir lors du moment quand la date soit fixée afin que vous puissiez au moins dîner ou déjeuner chez moi.

Je vous prie, Monsieur, d'agréer l'expression de mes sentiments les plus distingués.

[T. S. Eliot][1]

## TO *Jose Ortega y Gasset*[2] CC

25 January 1926 [*The New Criterion*]

Dear Sir,

Thank you for your letter of the 20th January. We shall be very pleased indeed to exchange with your review.[3] As a matter of fact I was under the impression that your review was already on our exchange list and am surprised to find that it is not, as I have formed a very high opinion indeed of it.

Will you be so kind as to send the *Revista de Occidente* regularly direct to:

F. S. Flint, Esquire,
The Ministry of Labour,

1–*Translation*: Dear Sir I thank you for your two letters, and for sending the completed manuscript. I find your handwritten script perfectly legible and have today sent it off for translation.

I am pleased to have your permission to publish this article, and also to have a few, so far unpublished, pages.

I notice that, in dictating my letter of a few days ago, I said 'in consideration of the translation costs' instead of 'minus the translation costs'. But I shall naturally keep my word, and you will receive the fee mentioned in my letter.

I am delighted to think that you are about to visit England, and I insist that you give me due warning when the date has been fixed, so that you can at least dine or lunch at my house. Yours faithfully [T. S. Eliot].

2–José Ortega y Gasset (1883–1955), Spanish liberal philosopher and essayist, educated in Spain and Germany, was appointed (1910) Professor of Metaphysics at the Complutense University of Madrid. In 1917 he began contributing to *El Sol*; and in 1923 founded *Revista de Occidente*, which he directed until 1936. For ten years from the outbreak of the Civil War he exiled himself in Argentina and Portugal; but in 1948 he returned to Madrid where he founded the Institute of Humanities. Works include *España invertebrada* (*Invertebrate Spain*, 1921) and *La rebelión de las mases* (*The Revolt of the Masses*, 1930) – TSE called the latter a 'remarkable book' (Leslie Paul, 'A Conversation with T. S. Eliot', *Kenyon Review* 27 [1965], 14).

3–*Revista de Occidente* (Madrid).

(Room 21, 2nd Floor East)
Queen Anne's Chambers,
Tothill Street,
London, S.W.

as this gentleman reviews in our pages the Spanish literary periodicals.[1]

I will have *The New Criterion* sent to your offices.

A long time ago I wrote to you asking you whether you would care to contribute an essay to our pages. I received no answer, but on hearing from you again I cannot forbear renewing my suggestion and saying that we should be highly honoured if we could publish some *inédit* by you. If you are willing to contribute I hope that you will let me hear from you.

Yours very truly,
[T. S. Eliot]

## TO *Richard Cobden-Sanderson* CC

29 January 1926 [London]

Dear Cobden-Sanderson,

I return to you herewith the dummy for *Savonarola*[2] which seems to me excellent in every way. I should only suggest that the lettering on the paper label ought to be in black instead of red because my mother was very keen on having the cover entirely black and white. About compressing the lettering, I will leave that entirely to your judgment. If you think it can be compressed with advantage, do so. I will try to send you the wrapper copy by Monday.

About the delivery of Lady Rothermere's copies. It seemed to me that the best thing would be to have them delivered to 58 Circus Road. I am almost certain that the housekeeper is there (Hampstead 2076) and as

1–See David Callahan, 'The Early Reception of Ortega y Gasset in England, 1920–1939', *Forum for Modern Language Studies* 26: 1 (1990), 75–87: 'In 1923 F. S. Flint, a central figure in the development of English modernism, wrote an appraisal of the first issue of the *Revista de Occidente* in T. S. Eliot's *Criterion* comparing the two journals' internationalism and seriousness. When he next came to review the journal in 1926 [*NC* 4 (Apr. 1926), 413–14] he expressed regret that he had not been able to get hold of any issues in the intervening years (suggesting a tardiness on the part of the *Revista*'s circulation department rather than anything else)' (76).

2–*Savonarola: A Dramatic Poem*, by Charlotte Eliot – a 'closet drama' about the Dominican friar, religious enthusiast and moral reformer Girolamo Savonarola (1452–98) – with Intro. by TSE, was to be published by Cobden-Sanderson on 8 Mar. 1926 in an edition of 300 copies. TSE's mother, Charlotte Champe Stearns Eliot (1843–1929) – see Biographical Register – met the costs of the printing.

Lady Rothermere has not replied, I think it is really up to her to arrange for their distribution. But if you prefer they can delivered here.

It is now arranged that 23 Adelphi Terrace House shall be given up on Lady Day. I think you sent me by hand a cheque to sign for the housekeeper's charges of £1. 11. 0. Can you confirm this? I remember signing two cheques a week or so ago and returning them to Burnett. The reason I ask is that Miss Fassett has the housekeeper's account book here, and if the bill has been paid she will return the book to the housekeeper to be receipted.

There is another point which I had forgotten for a very long time. When we took over the office I undertook to buy from Miss Weaver the office fittings which she valued at something under four pounds. I have just realised that this payment was never made to her. Have you enough money of Lady Rothermere's on hand to pay the rent and rates to Lady Day and enough then to pay this debt of something under four pounds to Miss Weaver? If so that is the best way to settle the matter, and if I sell the furniture then to the next tenant I will hand over the proceeds to Lady Rothermere.

In haste,
Yours ever,
[T. S. Eliot]

## TO *I. A. Richards* CC

30 January 1926 [London]

My dear Richards,

I think it would be best if you could arrange definitely to have breakfast with me on Wednesday. That will give us more time and a quiet place in which to talk. Could you leave a note for me at Trinity on Tuesday saying at what time I can expect you? (As far as I am concerned, as early as possible.) As you spoke so ascetically about breakfast, please let me know what you might perhaps eat or drink if anything.

Yours ever,
[T. S. Eliot]

## TO *Bonamy Dobrée*[1] CC

30 January 1926 [*The New Criterion*]

My dear Dobrée,

I and a few of the inner circle of contributors to the old *Criterion* are reviving our fortnightly meetings. We propose to do this hereafter in the form of an informal dinner once a fortnight, as far as possible on the same evening and at the same place. We should be greatly pleased if you would come to these meetings as often as you can. We propose to meet for the first time on Friday evening at seven o'clock at the *Etoile* in Charlotte Street, just off the Tottenham Court Road. Will you come? Read, Flint, Harold Monro and myself will be present. I do not think there will be anyone else.

This is the first opportunity I have had to replying to your letter of the 17th and I should like to make an appointment for us to dine privately a little later.[2]

Yours sincerely,
[T. S. Eliot]

## TO *Dr William Rose*[3] CC

30 January 1926 [London]

Dear Rose,

I am sending you separately the two books of Curtius which you were interested to see. There is no hurry about returning them.

I think you will agree that the Balzac book is a little too long either for your purposes or for general publication in this country. If you use it, I think that he would be willing to alter and adapt it to your needs. I confess that I have only glanced at it.

1 – Bonamy Dobrée (1891–1974), scholar, critic, editor: see Biographical Register.

2 – BD had written, 'I should like to see you again – especially to hear more about this series – & what sort of thing, if any, is expected of me.'

3 – William Rose (1894–1961): Lecturer in German, King's College, London; later Reader in German, 1927–35; Sir Ernest Cassel Reader in German, University of London; Head of the Department of Modern Languages, London School of Economics, 1935–49; and Professor of German Language and Literature, University of London, from 1949. Publications included *From Goethe to Byron* (1924) and *Men, Myths and Movements in German Literature* (1931). General Editor of Routledge's 'Republic of Letters' series.

I enjoyed my lunch with you and I am looking forward to your coming to lunch with me in about a fortnight.

Sincerely yours,
[T. S. Eliot]

## TO *Herbert Read* TS Victoria

30 January 1926 *The New Criterion*

My dear Read,

This is just a hasty note in case I do not see you at the lecture or do not have time to speak to you if you are there. I think that the Bagehot article is quite first rate and also that it ought to be extremely interesting to anybody. I should like to talk to you about your remarks on Conservatism. In the article I think you were wise to take it to that point and no further. I shall speak of the article to Richmond and, with your permission, I shall suggest to him that the same author ought to do a leader on Sir Henry Maine![1]

I am glad that Friday next suits you for dinner. I have taken the liberty of asking Dobrée to come. Otherwise there will only be Flint, Monro and ourselves. Have you any objection to Orlo Williams?[2] He is a little dull but he has a tendency towards the light and I think would help to give a kind of balance and proportion. I do not think that Harold is enthusiastic about him, but then they have never met.

I think that the new title for your book is excellent.[3] I had come round again to 'Sic et Non' but I think that the one you have chosen is much better from the point of view of the market.

Yours ever,
T. S. E.

1 – Sir Henry Maine (1822–88): jurist; a founding editor in 1855 of *Saturday Review*; author of the best-selling *Ancient Law* (1862).

2 – Orlando (Orlo) Williams (1883–1967): Clerk to the House of Commons, scholar and critic; contributor to *TLS*: see Biographical Register.

3 – *Reason and Romanticism: Essays in Literary Criticism* (F&G, 1926).

## TO *T. Sturge Moore*[1]

TS Texas

1 February 1926 *The New Criterion*

Dear Mr Sturge Moore,

I understand from my secretary that she has already sent you back your essays. I hope it is not troubling you too much to ask you to let me have the first of them again as soon as you can, and in any case before the 15th of this month, as we go to press on that date. Of course there is no hurry about returning the second essay as that will appear in the June number.[2]

I have read Part III and been considerably tempted.[3] If the *Criterion* were a monthly review I should have no hesitation in accepting it, especially because of my admiration for your poetry. But as we are only a Quarterly I have to keep the idea of diversity of contents before me; it is an exception for the *Criterion* to continue contributions over two numbers and I am afraid that it is impossible to publish contributions by the same author, however admirable they are, in three consecutive numbers. But if your book should not appear for a year or so, may I have another opportunity?

I like the whole series immensely.

With many thanks,
Yours sincerely
T. S. Eliot

## TO *Bruce Richmond*[4]

CC

1 February 1926 [London]

My dear Richmond,

I am sorry that this letter should follow so closely my last letter to you; but this is not concerned with my private affairs at all and is purely for the public good. There is a young Irishman named M'Greevy, a friend

1–Thomas Sturge Moore (1870–1944): English poet, playwright, critic, artist; brother of the philosopher G. E. Moore: see Biographical Register.

2–Moore had written three articles under the collective title 'A Poet and His Technique'; but only one (on Valéry) appeared in the *NC* 4 (June 1926), 421–35. See further Michael Tilby, 'An Early English Admirer of Paul Valéry: Thomas Sturge Moore', *The Modern Language Review* 84: 3 (July 1989), 565–86.

3–Part III of his work on Paul Valéry, 'The Poet and His Technique'.

4–Bruce Richmond (1871–1964), editor of the *TLS*: see Biographical Register.

of Yeats and of Lennox Robinson,[1] who, owing to certain local literary activities which brought him into collision with the Jesuit powers in Dublin, has come to London in the hope of picking up a living here. He has done some work for me under the name of L. St. Senan which I have liked very well indeed, and is to do more. Some months ago I gave him an introduction to Leonard Woolf from whom he has had a considerable amount of reviewing. I promised him that when he had more specimens of his work to exhibit I would give him an introduction to you.

At the moment, in order the less to embarrass either you or him I refrain from giving him the introduction but send you with this letter several reviews of his out of *The Nation*. I like the man, and his work seems to me both intelligent and educated. If you could find any use for him I should be very glad; but in any case I hope you may keep an eye on his future work.

Yours ever,
[T. S. Eliot]

## TO *J. B. de V. Payen-Payne*[2] CC

2 February 1926 [*The New Criterion*]

Dear Sir,

In reply to your letter of the 27th January I have to inform you that *The New Criterion* is open to correspondence when such correspondence is pertinent to the other contents. Whether I am able to use your enclosed communication will be a question of the exigencies of space. I am glad to hear that *The New Criterion* interested you but I think that you have misinterpreted my preliminary remarks. If you will glance over the list of contributors past and present and ascertain their dates, I think you will find that the majority of the contributors including myself were born a good many years before 1900.[3]

With regard to your enclosed communication I may assure you in private that there is every reason for believing that Mrs Leverson was in

1–Lennox Robinson (1886–1958): Irish dramatist and director; served on the Board of the Abbey Theatre, Dublin, from 1923; author of *The Whiteheaded Boy* (1916).

2–James Bertrand de Vincheles Payen-Payne (1866–1945): Principal of Kensington Coaching College, 1898–1936; his works include school editions of French authors.

3–Payen-Payne complained: 'I am sorry to note from your preliminary words that anyone born before 1900 is not welcomed as a contributor. Even the Yellow Book printed Henry James but then it lasted only 13 quarters – may you go on increasing.'

1895 of an age to have attended the first night of *The Importance of Being Earnest*.[1] The other questions I am not competent to decide; I was myself absent from England on that occasion.[2]

Yours very truly,
[T. S. Eliot]

## TO *Rollo H. Myers*[3] CC

2 February 1926 [London]

Dear Myers,

The arrangements for the Cocteau book are going forward and are now out of my hands. There is just one point, however, on which I have been asked to write to you; I should have enquired about it from Miss Harriet Weaver but I understand that she is now in Paris herself. It has been decided that the best frontispiece for the book will be the same reproduction of the Picasso drawing which was used in the *Egoist* edition

1–Ada Leverson, née Beddington (1862–1933): notable salonière (her friends included Beardsley and Beerbohm); novelist and contributor to the *Yellow Book* and *Punch*. She was an intimate friend of Oscar Wilde, who called her 'The Sphinx' and saluted her as 'the wittiest woman in the world', and she was loyal to him in his trials. TSE's friend Sydney Schiff was her brother-in-law. See Violet Wyndham, *The Sphinx and her Circle: A Biographical Sketch of Ada Leverson 1862–1933* (1963); Julie Speedie, *Wonderful Sphinx: The Biography of Ada Leverson* (1993).

2–Payen-Payne's dubiously gallant letter complained of Leverson's article 'The Last First Night', *NC* 4 (Jan. 1926), 148–53: 'Surely Miss Ada Leverson is too young to have been at the first night of *The Importance of Being Earnest* in 1895. My memory of the night has remained very clear because of the *débâcle* that so soon followed. I think I am right in saying that the author's words when he took his call were: "I have enjoyed my evening immensely." His looks had sadly deteriorated since the first night of *The Ideal Husband* at the Haymarket, when he shocked all the critics by appearing with a cigarette in his mouth. He looked like a combination of George IV in his latter years and one of the viler busts of the Emperor Nero.

'My memories may be different from those of Miss Leverson as I did not have the advantage of seeing the play from a box but from the front row of the pit.

'And was it Oscar Wilde who lay on Mrs. Langtry's doorstep half the night or, as most memoir-writers tell us, the less romantic figure of Mr. Abington Baird? Or did one of them plagiarise the other? / Your obedient Servant / Old Playgoer.'

3–Rollo Myers (1892–1985) wrote on music for *The Times* and the *Daily Telegraph*, 1920–34. His translation of Cocteau's *Rappel à l'ordre – A Call to Order . . . written between the years 1918 and 1926 and including* 'Cock and Harlequin', 'Professional Secrets' *and other critical essays* – was to be published by F&G in July 1926. Other writings include studies of Satie and Debussy. As Schuchard notes, the blurb for *A Call to Order* was probably written by TSE (*VMP*, 210 n. 12).

of *The Cock and the Harlequin.*[1] Can you tell us, or find out for us, whether the block from which these reproductions were printed is still in existence and how we can get hold of it, or at the worst whether we can have the loan of the original portrait in order to have a new block made. We should much prefer to have the original block if it is still in existence. Possibly the block was made in this country and is still in this country.[2] But I should be very much obliged if you could find out for me. If no one knows about it except Miss Weaver, I should be grateful if you could ask her. I understand that her address is –

Hotel de Bourgogne et Montana,
rue de Bourgogne,
Paris

Sincerely yours,
[T. S. Eliot]

## TO *Rev. W. F. Sorsbie* CC

2 February 1926 [London]

My dear Sir,

I have read your letter of the 19th January with great interest.[3] The essay you suggest is somewhat outside of the scope of *The New Criterion* but at the same time if it has a distinct literary interest I should be very glad to consider it.

*The New Criterion* is not averse to contributions of Biblical history and scholarship, but also it is distinctly not the place for any controversial matter on theological subjects, and of course not for any matter which might have any sectarian or non-sectarian bias whatever. Meanwhile I should be very glad to read your essay with attention and a disposition in its favour, but I cannot make any promises, and perhaps you do not care to complete your work until you are assured of the place of publication.

Yours faithfully
[T. S. Eliot]

1 – 'Cock and Harlequin', trans. Rollo H. Myers, with a portrait of the author . . . by Pablo Picasso (1921). 'On n'a pas retrouvé le bloc de Picasso,' wrote Cocteau (Mar. 1926). 'Je vous envoie un dessin de moi. S'il vous plaît – mettez le en tête.'

2 – Myers said (13 Feb.) he could not find out anything about the Picasso block.

3 – Revd W. F. Sorsbie (Coleby Vicarage, Lincoln) was writing an article on the *Acts of the Apostles* from a literary-critical point of view: 'My view is that it is a work of *high art*, admirably constructed and finished absolutely as it was intended to be.'

## TO *S. S. Koteliansky* TS BL

3 February 1926 *The New Criterion*

Dear Koteliansky,

Thank you for your letter of the 1st. I should very much like to publish the Tolstoy story if you are fairly certain that it has never been published in English.[1] I do not think, however, that I could use two in the same number. What I should like to do is this. I should like to have the Tolstoy now for publication in June and as you have already been the victim of such delays I would undertake to pay for the Tolstoy story on receipt. I am assuming, of course, that it is not of greater length than our usual fiction; Lawrence's 'The Woman who Rode Away' was much too long, and I think it is a great pity to have to break things up and put them in two numbers instead of one.

Will you let me know whether this arrangement suits you? If you will let me use the Tolstoy story I shall use it instead of the Dostoevsky; *otherwise* the Dostoevsky will be used and you shall be paid for *that* at once.

Yours ever,
[T. S. Eliot]

## TO *A. E. Taylor*[2] CC

3 February 1926 [*The New Criterion*]

Sir,

I take the liberty of writing to you on behalf of *The New Criterion* of which I send you enclosed a circular giving the names of previous contributors. I have for many years been interested in your work and have much desired to obtain a contribution from you. Some time ago Professor Burnet[3] signified his willingness to let me have an essay when his health permitted, but as I have since heard indirectly that his health has not been good I have refrained from troubling him again.

*The Criterion* is primarily a literary Quarterly but aims to include besides literary criticism and a minimum of fiction and verse serious contributions

1–Koteliansky offered Tolstoy's 'Notes of a Madman' (*c.*5000 words), though he had yet to check whether it had already been published. It did not appear in *NC*.
2–A. E. Taylor (1869–1945): Professor of Moral Philosophy, St Andrews, 1908–24; Edinburgh, 1924–41; President of the Aristotelian Society, 1928–9. Works include *St Thomas Aquinas as a Philosopher* (1924); *Plato, the Man and his Work* (1927).
3–John Burnet (1863–1928), clacissist, had been a colleague of Taylor's at St Andrews.

on any subject which concerns the public of literary interests and general culture. It is not in any sense a popular review and desires only to present the best thought of the best minds.

What I have had particularly in my head in writing to you is some subject connected with mediaeval philosophy and particularly with St Thomas. This is already a subject in which I am very much interested, my interest having been much stimulated within the last two years by the activities of some of my French friends. In the circumstances of course it would be necessary to treat such a subject from a philosophic point of view without disturbance of either Catholic or Anglican theology. I should very much like to have something from you on this subject, more particularly because I do not know anyone else in Britain who is competent to deal with it; but you may be assured that almost any other contribution from your hand would be equally welcome.

I remain, Sir,
Your obedient servant,
[T. S. Eliot]

## TO *Lewis S. Benjamin*[1] CC

5 February 1926 [*The New Criterion*]

Dear Sir,

I have now read *through* the transcript of Thackeray's review of *Godolphin*.[2] It is, as you say, extremely interesting. I think, however, that it is a little too long for the purposes of the *Criterion* and that the effect of the whole could be given by a considerable amount of quotation. What I should suggest for the *Criterion* is this: that if you could write a short essay on Thackeray's literary opinions, on his reviewing in general, on the class of fiction which he attacked, on the periodical which he edited and on the reasons for attributing this review to him, the review in question would suit the *Criterion* admirably.[3] On the other hand you may prefer

1–Lewis S. Benjamin (1874–1932), English author (pen name 'Lewis Melville') whose publications included an edition of Thackeray's works in 20 vols (1901–7).

2–Benjamin wrote on 22 Jan.: 'In a little weekly owned and edited . . . by Thackeray, there is an article on Lytton's "Godolphin", which though, like all the other articles unsigned, is unmistakably his. It is a vigorous onslaught on Lytton's work of that period, and I think it might be reprinted . . . Thackeray was . . . given to attacking those novels of Lytton and Ainsworth in which the hero is a murderer or a seducer or a highwayman and the heroine rather worse than she should be.'

3–'On an Unreprinted Article by Thackeray', *NC* 4 (Oct. 1926), 700–12.

to reprint the review entire and in that case I do not dissimulate the probability that any of the elder quarterly reviews would be glad to have it. It is therefore for you to choose, but if you prefer the latter course I shall regret the loss.

With many thanks for allowing me to see the manuscript,

I am,
Yours very truly,
[T. S. Eliot]

## TO *Geoffrey Faber*[1] TS Valerie Eliot

5 February 1926 *The New Criterion*

My dear Faber,

I return herewith the typescript of Professor Fraser-Harris' lecture on 'Biology in Shakespeare'. I think that it contains the material for a very interesting essay if it were rewritten and much condensed. The lecture form would have to be entirely removed. Professor Harris includes a great many minor and trivial instances which on the printed page would be tedious. I think that he should rewrite it completely and reduce it very much, perhaps to about a half of its present size. What is particularly interesting is his own remarks about the state of science in Shakespeare's time.

Even as a lecture it seems to me impossibly long. Unless his rate of delivery is about twice as fast as that of the ordinary lecturer, I should think that it would take about two hours to read this paper aloud to an audience.[2]

Yours ever,
T. S. E.

1 – Geoffrey Faber (1889–1961), publisher and poet: see Biographical Register.

2 – GCF promptly wrote to Harris: 'I return you herewith the typescript of your essay *Biology in Shakespeare*. I think you will be interested to read what the editor of *The New Criterion* says, and at the risk of being too frank, I enclose a copy of his letter to me' (5 Feb. 1926; Faber Letter Book no. 4). Harris replied on 6 Feb., 'I wish [TSE] had marked in the margin what he considered as "trivial"; I cannot myself discover any instances in Shakespeare which exactly fit that description.'

## TO *I. A. Richards* CC

6 February 1926 [London]

My dear Richards,

I rather hope that you will be able to come to my lecture on Tuesday and to breakfast the next morning as you did last week because the next lecture contains, of course in a very sketchy form, some of the notions about Dante's and Donne's development which I was discussing with you. I do hope this is not too much to ask.

If you can get copies of your own book without paying for them I wish you could send one to Ramon Fernandez, 44 rue du Bac, Paris.[1] He has been in London[2] and I told him that he ought to meet you at some future time if it is ever possible. I shall ask him to send you his book on personality[3] as soon as it appears. I think he is one of the most intelligent men in Paris.

Yours ever,
[T. S. E.]

P.S. I have just ordered your book on Meaning.[4]

1–IAR (8 Feb.): 'I shall send a copy of Principles to Fernandez . . . I get them cheap' (*Selected Letters of I. A. Richards, CH*, ed. John Constable [1990], 41).

2–GCF noted in his diary, 4 Feb.: 'Went w. Enid to tea with the Eliots – Edith Sitwell, a satisfying person in a dark cloak with bright coloured collar-flap & cuffs, & a great long nose. She talked of her hatred of suffering, & of herself as "useless". Mrs [Brigit] Patmore. Ramon Fernandez. A rather "choked" little party' (Faber).

3–Fernandez, *De la personnalité* (1928).

4–IAR (8 Feb.): 'I should be grateful if you would mark some of the passages which offend you in *The Meaning of M.* & let me see your copy later. There are plenty which offend me. I doubt if I can get them out though!' IAR asked too, 'I find myself writing an Essay on your poetry for the New Statesman. Could you bear to have it read to you? I send it in at the end of the week. It would be so interesting to find out whether all my notions about it are erroneous as I suspect. But if you had rather not see it before it is printed, I shall understand.' 'Mr Eliot's Poems', *NS*, 20, Feb. 1926, 584–5; repr. App. B of the 1926 edn of *Principles of Literary Criticism*.

## TO *Terence Prentis*[1] CC

6 February 1926 [London]

Dear Prentis,

As I was away from England when I wrote to you I did not expect you to write, but I am very glad to hear from you.[2] I only deprecate your discouraged tone. You certainly ought to go on writing and I am sure from what I have seen of your work that if you do keep it up you will arrive at something quite definite in the end. I am sorry to hear that you are so very busy although I suppose that from another point of view it is very encouraging; but I know that nevertheless you can, if you will, find time for a little practice in writing. And remember that it is not merely the time you spend with pen and paper but is as much, or more in fact, that you always keep a corner of your mind working on poetry, more or less unconsciously, (a sort of continuous chemical process of transformation of sensations, emotions and ideas into poetical material) that makes all the difference. You have my most cordial good wishes and constant interest.

Sincerely yours,
[T. S. Eliot]

## TO *Mary Hutchinson* TS Texas

7 February 1926 *The Criterion*

Dear Mary,

I am indeed glad to hear from you, and to learn that you are recovering. I should love to come and dine as soon as possible, but for the next fortnight, until I have finished my Cambridge lectures, I am anxious to avoid evening engagements (John's birthday was of course an inevitable exception) and also your Saturday night is going to be a Party – so, unless

1–Terence Prentis's works include *Music-Hall Memories*, ed., with intro. by Sir Harry Lauder, (1927).

2–Prentis wrote in an undated letter: 'I most certainly ought to have written to you before thanking you for the extreme kindness you showed in criticising my three poems. I have been ruminating about the advice proffered me and am prepared to abide very much by what you say. Certainly if I even attempt to write again it will be to embody at least that much of your counsel as I am able to apprehend.

'At the moment however my other work – that of poster designing – is absorbing all my energies. I do not think I shall be much loss to literature.

'I am very conscious of the care and interest which you displayed and wish only that I had it within me to merit a prolongation of such interest.'

you are to be away, might I see you more quietly one evening after the 24th?

Affectionately
Tom

## FROM *F. Scott Fitzgerald*[1]

MS Valerie Eliot

[early February 1926]

c/o Guarantee Trust Co,
1 Rue des Italiens, Paris, France

Dear Mr Elliot,

I can't express just how good your letter made me feel – it was easily the nicest thing that's happened to me in connection with *Gatsby*.[2] Thank you.

It might interest you to know how I first became aware of your work – the moment in which I first came under the spell of it was simultaneous. John Bishop,[3] who was in my class at Princeton, introduced me to Keats and Shelley (by way of Swinburne) and to the 'new poetry movement' which among other mediocrities and monstrosities produced, you'll remember, the Henderson-Monroe anthology. I realized immediately that, with the exception of some school recitations by Masefield, *The Portrait of a Lady* was the only poem with a new spiritual rhythm in it. John liked it but didn't share my enthusiasm, as I remember.

After the war I'd hear no more of you and, altho it was my favorite modern poem, I'd begun to feel that inspite of your personality, of that indescribable glow that emanates from the work of all first rate men, you were probably an Ernest Dowson. Then one day Edmund Wilson,

1 – F. Scott Fitzgerald (1896–1940): American novelist and short story writer; author of *The Great Gatsby* (1925), *Tender is the Night* (1934), *The Last Tycoon* (1941).

2 – Fitzgerald wrote in response to TSE's letter of 31 Dec. 1925 extolling *The Great Gatsby*: 'it has interested and excited me more than any new novel I have seen, either English or American, for a number of years . . . In fact it seems to me to be the first step that American fiction has taken since Henry James.' Fifteen years later, when Edmund Wilson sought permission to publish TSE's letter (it would appear in *The Crack-Up* [New York, 1945], 310), TSE replied on 13 Nov. 1941, 'I haven't the least objection to <your printing> anything I said to him at the time about *The Great Gatsby*. I still think it a very remarkable work and I am ready to say so again . . . I should certainly like to read his last book and if it is published here I shall get a copy.'

3 – John Peale Bishop (1892–1944), poet and man of letters, was the original of the character Thomas Parke D'Invilliers in Fitzgerald's first novel *This Side of Paradise*. His publications include *Green Fruit* (poetry, 1917); *Act of Darkness* (novel, 1935); *Selected Poems* (1941); and *The Collected Essays of John Peale Bishop* (1948).

also an old Princeton friend, phoned me that he had the *Dial* proofs of a new long poem. I'll never forget that afternoon. Since I first read *Youth* I'd had no such elation. I discovered that Knopf had issued your other poems. I confess, ~~almost~~ without shame, that at least twice in *Gatsby* I have unconsciously used your rhythms (see the bottom p. 141 – compare with *Waste Land*.[1] Also p. 217 'pondered in whispers' for 'picked his bones in whispers'. There's another place but I can't find it.) (Excuse this tear – I'm out of paper.)

I like your work so much that I even get a vicarious pleasure from imitations of it – for example Archie Mcliesh's *Pot of Earth* [1925].[2] I read the essays last summer for the first time and liked them enormously, except two. I have been waiting eagerly and anxiously for the projected sonnets.

I'm sorry to say that *Gatsby*'s in the hands of Chatto and Windus. It will appear in England on the eleventh of this month. Would previous American publication bar a story from *The Criterion*? I have a fine short story which you might have if you like it – one of the only three decent ones of the many I've written. (I lead a double literary life.)

We are in the Pyrenees for a month *en route* to Nice. I don't dare hope that you'll be on the Riviera again this summer.

With many thanks and best wishes, that are entirely selfish, for whatever you are now writing, I am

Yours Gratefully and Humbly
F. Scott Fitzgerald

## TO *I. A. Richards* CC

11 February 1926 [London]

My dear Richards,

I will keep Tuesday evening for you and we can meet either at your rooms or at Trinity as you prefer. But my room is very comfortable as you know and should be a very good place to meet after dinner about nine

1 – '"What'll we do with ourselves this afternoon?" cried Daisy, "and the day after that, and the next thirty years?"' (*The Great Gatsby*): '"What shall we do tomorrow? / What shall we ever do?"' (*The Waste Land*, II 'A Game of Chess', 133–4).

2 – Archibald MacLeish, in a letter to TSE (21 Feb. 1926) regretting that he had never yet met his hero, admitted the degree of his indebtedness: 'It isn't because I think that I could tell you better verbally than I have already done in ink how much I owe you (indeed you must be only too painfully conscious of it if you ever happen on my *Pot of Earth*). It is simply that you're becoming legendary and I have a very human desire to look at you.'

o'clock and I shall expect you there unless I hear to the contrary; also anyone whom you wished to bring.[1]

Yours ever
[T. S. E.]

## TO *James Smith* CC

11 February 1926 [London]

Dear Smith,

Will you please tell your charming friend whose name I never caught but whom I hope I may see as well as yourself after breakfast next Wednesday that the address of Henry Massis is '*La Revue Universelle', 157 Boulevard St. Germain, Paris (6)*. I find, however, that he is going to speak in London on the 20th March.[2] It is quite possible that he may be in England for a week or so before that and might be able to come to Cambridge earlier than the 20th. But I am not sure that it would not be too near the end of the term for you in any case. However, if he writes to Massis he had better mention my name and say that I hope he will be able to accept.

I enjoyed your lunch party and meeting you and your friends very much indeed.

Sincerely yours
[T. S. Eliot]

P.S. It is possible that Charles du Bos[3] is coming to England before that date. He is quite a good critic and I think he would be able to speak in English if necessary. Would you care to have him?

1–IAR responded (15 Feb.), 'I have some hopes that you will show me the pieces you spoke of. I am very *very* curious about them. I improved, I think, my notes for the *New Statesman* ['Mr Eliot's Poems'] before sending them in. Many thanks for letting me read them to you.' He suggested too that TSE might like to meet Margaret Gardiner, 'who has, I think, *very* good natural judgement in poetry besides being intelligent & attractive.' Also, perhaps later, 'the remainder of the English lecturers (Faculty folk) e.g. [E. M. W.] Tillyard, [Aubrey] Attwater, [Mansfield] Forbes. The last is amusing, the others dullish . . .'
2–Massis was to lecture on 'Orient et Occident'.
3–Charles du Bos (1832–1939), French critic of French and English literature.

## TO *Lady Rothermere* CC

11 February 1926 [London]

Dear Lady Rothermere,

I have today received the following telegram[1] which I interpret as coming from you.

> VESEED NOT RECEIVED ORITERIN PLUSE FORWARD
> COPIES EXCELSIOR NAPLES

This seems all the more likely because I made enquiries and find that no copies appear to have been sent to you. This is very annoying indeed but I am afraid that it is partly my fault because I should have remembered to give instructions to this effect. The six copies are being sent to you today and I hope you will accept my apologies.

By the way, I understand from Cobden-Sanderson that he has delivered to 58 Circus Road twenty-four bound copies of volume 3.

In haste,
Yours ever sincerely
[T. S. E.]

## TO *Virginia Woolf*[2] MS Berg

11 February 1926 *The New Criterion*

Dear Virginia,

I understand from the Manager that you questioned the rate of payment – I had completely forgotten the special rates, which, as a matter of fact, had never been applied to anyone but Joyce and yourself. *The New Criterion*, having an editor (which the Old didn't) has to pay all contributors at the uniform rate; but you were never warned, & I know your essay[3] was written at considerable cost to yourself, so please accept my apologies for this informal way of doing [business] – I should be greatly distressed that you should suffer by my negligence!

Yours ever
T. S. E.

1 – Dated 9 Feb.
2 – Virginia Woolf (1882–1941), novelist and essayist: see Biographical Register.
3 – 'On Being Ill', *NC* 1 (Jan. 1926); later published by the Hogarth Press, 1930.

*When* can we come to tea? Tuesdays & Wednesdays are the only quite impossible days for me – and Sats. & Sundays I have to work – so Thursday, Friday & Monday are the best?Thank you for sending the MS (Dalgleish?) to us. I am looking out for it.

## TO *Hugh Fraser Stewart*[1] CC

12 February 1926 [London]

Dear Dr Stewart,

I have looked over my engagements immediately on coming back and find that the nights on which I have no engagement are the 16th February and the 5th March. I am also free on the 9th March but if either the 16th February or the 5th March were possible for you, either is a better date for me.

It is very kind of you to ask me to stay with you on one of my visits and I most cordially hope that one of these nights will be convenient.

Yours very sincerely,
[T. S. Eliot]

1–Hugh Fraser Stewart, DD (1863–1948) was a Fellow of Trinity College, Cambridge from 1918. Ordained in 1894, he gained his DD in 1916. He taught at Marlborough College; was Vice-Principal of Salisbury Theological College, 1895–9; and was a Fellow and Dean of St John's College, Cambridge, 1907–18. An authority on the works of Pascal, his publications include a posthumous bilingual edition of the *Pensées*. TSE reviewed Stewart's *The Secret of Pascal* in 'The Great Layman', *Cambridge Review*, 29 Nov. 1941: 'French critics have analysed and criticised [Pascal's] famous style, but an explanation of it for English readers can best be given by an English critic, and no one is better qualified, first, by his knowledge of theology and erudition in French literature, and, second – what is equally important – by a lifelong devotion to Pascal, than is Dr Stewart.' (Not in Gallup.)

## TO *F. L. Lucas*[1] CC

12 February 1926 [Trinity College, Cambridge]

Dear Lucas,

Your men all turned up and I liked them all very much indeed.[2] I only hope that they enjoyed themselves enough to induce them to come again. They are a very attractive lot. As they all arrived together, no doubt out

1–F. L. ('Peter') Lucas (1894–1967): poet, novelist, playwright, scholar; Fellow and Librarian of King's College, Cambridge. Author of *Seneca and Elizabethan Tragedy* (1922) and *Euripides and his Influence* (1924), he was to be praised for his edition of the *Complete Works of John Webster* (4 vols, 1927) – TSE considered him 'the perfect annotator'. Lucas had published an unfavourable review of *The Waste Land* in the *NS* (3 Nov. 1923); and he attacked TSE in *The Decline and Fall of the Romantic Ideal* (1936). In a later year, as E. M. W. Tillyard would report, Lucas was to become 'openly hostile' to TSE (*The Muse Unchained: An Intimate Account of the Revolution in English Studies at Cambridge* [1958], 98); and T. E. B. Howarth gossiped that matters were to become so rancorous that Lucas 'would not even allow Eliot's work to be bought for the [Trinity College] library' (*Cambridge Between Two Wars* [1978], 166). VW noted down Lucas's mischievous report of TSE as Clark Lecturer: 'Tom has been down lecturing, & not creating a good impression at Cambridge, I fancy. He tells the young men, in private, how they cook fish in Paris: his damned selfconsciousness again, I suppose' (*The Diary of Virginia Woolf*, III, 65).

2–Lucas wrote to TSE, in an undated letter: 'I have arranged with about half-a-dozen of the most intelligent undergraduates I know, to visit you in the guest-room . . . on Wed. I thought it might help, if I told you a little about them. George Barnes is Mary Hutchinson's half-brother, and you may have met him: he is in some ways the nicest, I think, though not the cleverest of them. George Thomson is the admirer you met at lunch here: I hope he won't be too consistent in his role of "gracious silence". He is Celtic and twilit and interested in mysticism, which is our perpetual bone of friendly contention. John Hayward is an ex-pupil of mine who edited, aged 20 or something, the Nonesuch Rochester: he is slightly paralysed, which may distress one for a moment; and he is doing French now – which might provide you with an opening for talk, if needed. Clutton-Brock is the son of his father; nice, quite clever, and *much* improved since he came up, when he was the silliest young man I've ever seen. Dennis Procter is a friend of George Barnes and sent partly because so inseparable. T. R. Barnes is a clever poor young man, with some sort of Trade Union exhibition or the like, but v. promising in his own way. Will talk to any length on the Maddermarket Theatre at Norwich where he has acted.'

George Thomson (1903–87) took firsts in the classical tripos at King's, where he would be elected to a fellowship in 1927. A distinguished classical scholar, and from 1933 a Marxist and Communist, he taught at University College, Galway, for three years from 1931; and he was Professor of Greek at Birmingham, 1938–70. His publications include *Greek Lyric Metre* (1929), *Aeschylus and Athens* (1941), *The First Philosophers* (1955), *The Greek Language* (1960), *From Marx to Mao* (1972), *Capitalism and After* (1973); editions of Aeschylus' *Prometheus Bound* (1932) and the *Oresteia* (1938); and a beautiful translation from the Irish of his friend Muiris (Maurice) O'Sullivan's memoir of his years on the Blasket Islands of Ireland, *Twenty Years a-Growing* [1933]. In 1934 he married the musician Katharine Stewart, daughter of TSE's friend Hugh Fraser Stewart. John Hayward [1905–1965], editor and bibliographer: see Biographical Register. Alan Clutton-Brock,

of a strong self-protective instinct, and all left together with the exception of Hayward, I did not have the opportunity of talking to any of them individually, but if they will continue coming that will no doubt be possible later.

One of them looked like you and unless my ear deceived me gave his name as Lucas. Have you a younger brother?

It proved to be just about as large a number as I could comfortably cope with.[1]

With many thanks,

Yours sincerely,
[T. S. Eliot]

---

born in 1904, was to become art critic of *The Times* and Slade Professor of Fine Art at Cambridge. Dennis Proctor, later Sir Dennis [1905–83] took firsts in the classical tripos at King's, 1924–8; a Cambridge Apostle, a Marxist, and a close friend of Guy Burgess and Anthony Blunt, he was to become a distinguished civil servant: he ended up as permanent secretary at the Ministry of Power, 1958–62; and chairman of the Tate Gallery, 1953–9; his publications include *Hannibal's March in History* [1971] and an unexpurgated edition of *The Autobiography of Goldsworthy Lowes Dickinson* [1973].)

1–TSE 'was prepared to receive undergraduates after breakfast on [Wednesdays]', William Empson was to recall years later. According to George Watson's account of TSE's appearances in Cambridge, Empson (who attended the coffee parties but not the lectures) remained 'impressed to the end of his life by the seriousness with which [TSE] listened to questions and arguments, and the earnestness of his answers' (George Watson, 'The Cambridge Lectures of T. S. Eliot', *Sewanee Review* [Fall 1991]; repr. as 'Eliot in Cambridge', in Watson, *Never Ones for Theory? England and the War of Ideas* [Cambridge: The Lutterworth Press, 2000], 46). Empson noted that TSE recommended the students to read the sermons of Lancelot Andrews. Empson was to record too, in 1957: 'As a young man I snatched at any chance to hear wisdom drop from Mr T. S. Eliot, and he once remarked that the test of a true poet is that he writes about experiences before they have happened to him' ('Donne the Space Man' [1957], *Essays on Renaissance Literature*, I, 127). More substantively, a memoir by Empson reports some of the awkwardness of TSE's audiences: 'At the first of these awed gatherings [John Hayward] asked him what he thought of Proust. "I have not read Proust," was the deliberate reply. How the conversation was picked up again is beyond conjecture, but no one cared to plumb into the motives of his abstinence. It was felt to be a rather impressive trait in this powerful character. Next week a new member of the group asked what he thought of the translation of Proust by Scott Moncrieff, and Eliot delivered a very weighty, and rather long, tribute to that work. It was not enough, he said, to say that it was better than the original in many single passages; it was his impression that the translation was at no point inferior to the original (which, to be sure, was often careless French), either in accuracy of detail or in the general impression of the whole. We were startled by so much loquacity from the silent master rather than by any disagreement with what he had said before; in fact it seemed quite clear to me what Eliot meant – he did not consider he had "read" a book unless he had written copious notes about it and so on. I no longer feel sure that this was what he meant, but I am still quite sure that he was not merely lying to impress the children; maybe at the earlier meeting he hadn't bothered to listen to what they were saying' ('The Style of the Master', *T. S. Eliot: A Symposium*, ed. Richard March and Tambimuttu [1948], 36–7). However, Schuchard comments on Empson's account: 'Empson evidently misheard

## TO *John Middleton Murry*[1] MS Valerie Eliot

12 February [1926] 9 Clarence Gate Gardens, N.W.1

My dear John,

I had been going to ask if we could have tea together tomorrow (Saturday) but Vivien is too ill to be left alone with our servant only, and the young man MacAlpin who lives with us wants to have tea with his aunt tomorrow on her 69th birthday, so I must stay at home. (You know we both have a preference for male nurses.) So *perhaps* I can manage Monday or Tuesday (if you can). But you will find me a burden, I warn you. You are in some sort of purgatory, I am perhaps thoroughly damned. But that's one reason why I want to see you. And I always feel with you 'mon semblable – mon frère'.[2] Neither your friends nor mine could understand this.

Yrs.
T.

## TO *Bonamy Dobrée* MS Brotherton

12 February 1926 *The New Criterion*

My dear Dobrée

I did not have time to write to you after I saw Stallybrass. I saw him on Tuesday morning and had to leave for Cambridge almost immediately and only got back last night.

The point about the demarcation of the two series is that Routledge's are to do men who can be treated as primarily literary artists and we are to control men who are primarily something else but incidentally great men of letters.[3] The tentative scheme which I have drawn up includes three sections. 1. Philosophers and Theologians, 2. Historians and Politicians, 3. Critics and Moralists. Of course there may be some difficulty in individual cases in connection with section 3, as Routledge's may want to

---

or misremembered the dialogue: Eliot may not have read "the last volume" of Proust, but he had certainly read and formed an impression of earlier work before the Cambridge visit' ('Editor's Introduction', *VMP*, 14).

1–John Middleton Murry (1889–1957), writer, critic, editor: see Biographical Register.

2–Baudelaire's 'Au Lecteur' (*Les Fleurs du Mal*) is quoted too in *TWL*, l. 76.

3–BD had written on 9 Feb.: 'I gather I am to do Burke for you & Ibsen for [Stallybrass] . . . I am not altogether happy about the exchange: I don't really see a big book on Ibsen, and I am a little bit frightened about the philosophical implications of your series. I am no philosopher.'

do some authors who would fall naturally into this section. But I did not think there will be any difficulty about sections 1 and 2; they will be pretty distinctly outside of Routledge's territory.

In the circumstances it was obvious that Ibsen was a prize that I should have to surrender. On the other hand we should be very glad to do Burke, specially from the commercial point of view because we are about to publish his collected correspondence. If the scheme goes through as I have outlined it – and this may be settled before I have an opportunity of seeing you again – we should be delighted to have you do a Burke. <You *might* prefer someone else – we will see.>

I am not worried by your professed inability to deal with the philosophical aspect. You would have plenty of time to do the book and I hope that we should have plenty of opportunities to discuss any difficulties either real or imaginary.

It is true that I am frightfully rushed at present because, having to spend two days a week in Cambridge, a great deal has to be crowded into other days. I am afraid that I can make no appointment until after the next *Criterion* dinner tomorrow week. But as there is another matter which I should to speak to you about privately would it be possible for us to meet by ourselves either here or at the restaurant before dinner? If you would pick me up here at 6.30. on that evening it would suit me very well.

Yours sincerely
T. S. Eliot

## TO *Richard Aldington* TS Texas

12 February 1926 *The New Criterion*

My dear Richard

The *Chartreuse de Parme* will be ordered and sent to you on receipt. I shall be very glad if you will do it. The Cambridge lecture was not at all boring to me but I cannot speak for the audience.[1]

I shall send you a tentative list of my borderline men of letters in a few days.

1 – Among those who attended the lectures were a number of the younger dons of the English School including IAR, E. M. W. Tillyard, Basil Willey, Mansfield Forbes and F. R. Leavis; plus a full turnout from the women's colleges, Newnham and Girton. Also in support, at least at the last, were TSE's brother Henry and his new wife Theresa – who did an expressive sketch of TSE in the course of the last lecture.

I never acknowledged the draft of your prospectus of the Library of Eighteenth Century French Literature. The prospectus seems to me *excellent* and you have got a brilliant list of editors. Does this mean that in all of these cases the same person is translating and writing an introduction? And by the way I have heard that Brigit Patmore[1] is translating some French book for Routledge's and is getting £65 for it. Is this credible and is it true? I did not know that she was a French scholar and should hardly have thought that she was up to the standard although I have no knowledge to the contrary.

If you turn up on Friday week (today week) we shall all be delighted. Meanwhile I hope that you will think over the question of Sainte-Beuve and Gourmont. There is another point that occurs to me. If Stallybrass (whose name I hear, I do not know on how good authority, was originally Sonnenschein[2]) gives you special rates for your books in his series, it seems to me that we ought to give you the same rates for any books you do for our series. For you will have been as instrumental to its success and will have taken almost as much trouble over it as over the Republic of Letters.

Affectionately,
T. S. E.

## TO *Gilbert Seldes*[3] CC

12 February 1926 [London]

My dear Seldes,

Thank you for your letter.[4] I wish that it had arrived a few days sooner because your copy of *The New Criterion*, and I believe your cheque, have been sent to the New York address.

1–Brigit Patmore, née Ethel Elizabeth Morrison-Scott (1882–1965), Irish author who married John Deighton Patmore (grandson of the poet Coventry Patmore), and became a popular hostess in London. Her friends included EP, RA and H.D. Her memoir *My Friends When Young* (1968) affords a sympathetic picture of VHE.

2–Stallybrass was a Sonnenschein by birth; he and his son had assumed the name Stallybrass (his mother's maiden name) in 1917.

3–Gilbert Seldes (1893–1970), journalist and critic: see Biographical Register.

4–Seldes wrote, in an undated letter, that he had gone to Paris (having experienced 'an evil time in New York'), where he had been absorbed in a play that flopped. Since he did not feel able for a while to write a 'light and varied' Chronicle like the most recent one (*NC* 4: (Jan. 1926), he recommended Edmund Wilson of the *New Republic*: 'I think he has an admirable equipment and his integrity I would vouch for.' Seldes's next New York Chronicle appeared in *NC* 4 (Oct. 1926), 733–40.

I know Edmund Wilson's[1] work and I think he is a good critic although like yourself I might not always agree with him. But as I should not want another American Chronicle until the summer in any case, I think that I should prefer to let it slide for another three months and have one from you. That is to say, can you promise me a chronicle some time during the month of July? Even if you have not been back to New York before then it will not matter. You are perfectly competent to write a New York Chronicle even from the interior of China, so do not allege this excuse.

I hope that you may pay a visit to London before you go home.

Sincerely yours
[T. S. Eliot]

## TO *Ezra Pound* — MS Beinecke

12 February 1926 — *The Criterion*, 9 Clarence Gate Gdns

Dear Rabbit,

Occupation of yr flat in Rapallo (+ expenses for wear & tear but wd be careful) for 2 w. or 1 mo. from date of yr departure still desired.

Is it possible?

Is it convenient?

What is probable date?

In haste
Possum.

## TO *Wyndham Lewis* — MS Cornell

12 February 1926 — *The New Criterion*

Dear Lewis,

Thanks for your note and for the circular of Chatto and Windus. The advertisement of your book is all right. Will you ask them to send us a review copy as soon as it is out.[2] Unfortunately neither Tuesday nor

1 – Edmund Wilson (1895–1972), literary critic and cultural commentator: see Biographical Register.

2 – TSE praised *The Art of Being Ruled* in his 'Commentary' (*NC* 4 [June 1926], 419–20) as 'significant of the tendency of contemporary thought . . . [I]t is enough to observe that Mr Lewis's observations of contemporary society tend toward similar conclusions to those of such critics as Benda, Babbitt, or Maritain, whose approach is very different.' See review by W. A Thorpe: *NC* 4 (Oct. 1926), 758–64

Wednesday is ever possible for me during the next two months because I go down to Cambridge early on Tuesday and return late on Wednesday. I could manage lunch on Monday if you had the manuscript ready by then and could drop me a line to let me know. Meanwhile, I will keep Monday lunch open.

Yours ever,
T. S. E.

P.S. *Can* you let me have the *Criterion* notes as well as the 'Politics', on Monday or by Tuesday?[1]

## TO *S. S. Koteliansky* TS BL

12 February 1926 *The New Criterion*

Dear Koteliansky,

I have your letter of the 11th. The cheque for four guineas was intended to be the advance payment for the Dostoevsky on a rough estimate of the number of words, but even on our rough estimate it seems to have been incorrectly computed. Our guess was twenty eight hundred words and our cheque should therefore have been for five pounds twelve shillings. When the document is set up in type our printers will count the number of words exactly and the payment will of course be rectified.

I am afraid that I did not make myself clear.[2] What I meant was that I found it impossible to get the Dostoevsky into the April number and would use it in the June; but that if you meanwhile offered us the Tolstoy story I should prefer that instead and would print it instead of the Dostoevsky in June. But if you can hold up American publication of the Dostoevsky until June I shall be quite satisfied and in the meantime do not wish to hamper your other American negotiations in any way. So go ahead with the Tolstoy and if it should happen that it was not to be published in America before June I should be glad to consider substituting it for the Dostoevsky in that number.

I wish that you would come in and have lunch or tea with me one day.

1–WL replied on 19 Feb., 'I am sorry to say that I can't do an Art-Note, because I can think of nothing to say for the moment. It may be that as I have not been able for some time to have a studio and practise my delightful calling that, since I am prevented from doing it, I do not care to *write* about it' (*The Letters of Wyndham Lewis*, ed. W. K. Rose [1963], 164). WL wrote just two 'Art Chronicles' for C: 2 (July 1924), 477–82; 3 (Oct. 1924), 107–13.

2–Koteliansky hoped TSE would not mind if he offered the Tolstoy story elsewhere: 'I should like it to be published before June.'

Next week I have no time for tea but would be free for lunch on Friday if you cared to call for me here at one o'clock. Otherwise I am free for tea on Monday or Friday of the *following* week.

Sincerely yours
T. S. Eliot

## TO *Denis Saurat*[1] CC

12 February 1926 [London]

Dear Mr Saurat,

Thank you very much for your letter of the 8th.[2] I am afraid that we are both very much booked up at present and I find that I am already engaged on Monday the 15th. My first free days are Friday the 19th and Monday the 22nd. Would it be possible for you to come and have tea with me here on either of those dates?

Yours very sincerely,
[T. S. Eliot]

## TO *Margaret Storm Jameson*[3] TS Valerie Eliot

13 February 1926 Faber & Gwyer Ltd

Dear Miss Storm Jameson

Thank you for your letter of the 9th. I should be glad to publish a complete edition of my poems in America, and so far as the English rights go it is quite possible.[4] I think it simply depends first on whether Mr

1–Denis Saurat (1890–1958): Anglo-French scholar; Professor of French Language and Literature, King's College, London, 1926–50; *Directeur du l'Institut français du Royaume Uni*, 1924–45. His works include *La Pensée de Milton* (1920; *Milton: Man and Thinker*, 1925) and *Blake and Modern Thought* (1929).

2–Saurat asked to meet TSE; their friend Sidney Schiff had often spoken of him.

3–Margaret Storm Jameson (1891–1986), novelist and journalist. Daughter of a master-mariner, she was educated at Leeds University (the first woman to graduate in English, and with a first-class degree) and at King's College, London, where she held a research fellowship. Her MA thesis was published as *Modern Drama in Europe* (1920). Her novels include *Cousin Honoré* (1940), *Cloudless May* (1944), *The Journal of Mary Hervey* (1945) and her *summa*, the 2-volume *Journey from the North* (1969–70). See Jennifer Birkett, *Margaret Storm Jameson: A Life* (2009). Margaret Storm Jameson was the first female President of PEN, and acted as President from 1938 to 1944, some of the most tumultuous and important years in PEN's history.

4–Jameson wrote as UK representative of Knopf: 'We would very much like to make a collected edition of your poems, similar to that issued by Faber and Gwyer.'

Knopf[1] and Mr Liveright[2] can agree, and second on the sort of contract that Mr Knopf is prepared to give. I had not been informed that *The Waste Land* had gone out of print in America. Can you confirm this fact?[3]

Sincerely yours,
T. S. Eliot

## TO *William King*[4] CC

13 February 1926 [London]

Dear King,

I have been meaning to write to you for some time to ask if you would ever care to do any reviewing for *The New Criterion*. We only review a small number of books and when the book is worth more than a short paragraph a thousand to fifteen hundred words is the usual length. I want a good longish review for the June number of Richard Aldington's *Voltaire*. Would you care to do this?[5]

Yours sincerely
T. S. E.

1–Alfred A. Knopf (1892–1984) founded Alfred A. Knopf Inc. in 1915. He was responsible for publishing in the USA many important European authors, and he brought out not only TSE's *Ezra Pound: His Metric and Poetry* (1917) but also *Poems* (1920) and *The Sacred Wood: Essays on Poetry and Criticism* (1921).

2–Horace Liveright (1884–1933), publisher and (later) stage producer. With Albert Boni, he founded Boni & Liveright in 1917, which published not only *The Waste Land* (1922) but Ezra Pound's *Instigations* (1920) and *Poems 1918–21* (1921), and works by Ernest Hemingway, Theodore Dreiser, Djuna Barnes, Bertrand Russell and Hart Crane. He was a strong campaigner against censorship. EP called him 'a jewel of a publisher'. See Tom Dardis, *Firebrand: The Life of Horace Liveright* (1995).

3–Jameson replied on 16 Feb.: 'Mr Knopf's letter to me reads: "Liveright published the WASTE LAND but seems to have permitted it to go out of print early." That is not exactly confirmation, which I think I could get for you, but which you could probably get yourself more certainly.' She wrote further on 1 Mar.: 'I hear from the Knopfs that the Liveright edition of *The Waste Land* is definitely out of print, so that I cannot imagine that he would need to be considered in this question of a collected edition; but your agreement ought to settle this once and for all.'

4–William King (1894–1958), educated at Balliol College, Oxford, had worked since 1914 at the Victoria & Albert Museum, first in the Department of Ceramics and then in the Department of Woodwork. In 1926 he moved over to the Department of Ceramics and Ethnography at the British Museum, and he was ultimately to become Deputy Keeper of the Department of British and Medieval Antiquities (until retirement in 1954): his areas of expertise being British and European glass and ceramics. His works include a catalogue of the Jones Collection at the V & A (1922), *Chelsea Porcelain* (1922), *English Porcelain Figures of the Eighteenth Century* (1925) and *Memoirs of Sarah Duchess of Marlborough* (1930).

5–See King, untitled review of RA's *Voltaire* (1925): *NC* 4 (June 1926), 587–89.

## TO *Frederic Manning*[1] CC

13 February 1926 [*The New Criterion*]

My dear Manning,

I am very glad to hear from you and to have an address at which to write.[2] Your cheque will be sent to the same address as this letter; your copy of the *Criterion* had already gone to the Australian Bank of Commerce.

I was very sorry that you were not in London a week ago because Ramon Fernandez was here for a few days lecturing and I should have liked you to meet him. He read your essay and is going to write a short reply for the June number, chiefly, I think, to point out the difference between his own critical approach and yours. He was disappointed not to meet you but if there is any point on which he wants elucidation he may write to you.

I should be very glad to have the short notice you suggest though it will be too late for the April number which has gone to press. Nevertheless, I should like to have it as soon as convenient.[3]

I wonder if you would care to write down any impressions of Ireland or whether your impressions are such that it might be unwise for you to publish them.

Many thanks for the probable subscriptions. Do let me know when there is any prospect of your coming to London.

Yours very sincerely,
[T. S. Eliot]

## TO *F. Scott Fitzgerald* TS Princeton

13 February 1926 *The New Criterion*

Dear Mr Scott Fitzgerald,

In spite of the fact that you persist in misspelling my name your letter gave me very much pleasure and shall be preserved as a testimonial to posterity.

I am of course very disappointed to hear that *The Great Gatsby* is already arranged for;[4] in fact, on the day after receiving your letter I spoke

1–Frederic Manning (1882–1935), Australian who found fame with *The Middle Parts of Fortune* (1929), a novel about the Western Front: see Biographical Register.
2–Manning was in Dublin.
3–See Manning's review of two works by Albert Houtin – *Un Prêtre Symboliste: Marcel Hébert*; *Une Vie de Prêtre: Mon Expérience* – NC 4 (June 1926), 590–3.
4–It had appeared on 11 Feb.

to someone who had already seen an advance copy. <Have just seen the book.> Let me hope, however, to publish some future work.

Could you let me know in what periodical in America appeared the story which you suggest sending to me? It all depends upon that. Otherwise I should of course jump at the opportunity because I like your book so much. I should be glad to reprint your story if it has not appeared in any of the magazines which some of our readers are likely to have seen.

I am not likely to be abroad again until May; but I hope that there may be some prospect of our meeting then?

Yours ever cordially,
T. S. Eliot

## TO *Humbert Wolfe* CC

15 February 1926 [London]

My dear Wolfe,

Many thanks for your letter of the 12th and for the admirable review of Hardy which arrived this morning.[1] I should like very much to be able to come to the dinner of The Omar Khayyam club,[2] but I am so extremely busy that I am afraid that I must decline all engagements of pure pleasure until after the middle of March.

The *Criterion* will dine on Friday next at the *Etoile* restaurant in Charlotte Street, where we lunched, and I should be very glad if you could come.

For how long are you in England?

Yours ever,
[T. S. E.]

## TO *E. R. Curtius* TS Bonn

15 February 1926 *The New Criterion*

My dear Curtius,

Very many thanks for your kind letter. What you say about my poems gives me great pleasure.[3] I have sent a subscription to *Die Literarische Welt*

1–Review of Hardy, *Human Shows: Far Fantasies*, *NC* 4 (Apr. 1926), 384–8.

2–Wolfe had invited TSE to dine at Pagani's on 11 Mar.

3–Curtius said (24 Jan.): 'Thank you first of all for your poems. I have read them often, and let myself be carried away [*lit.* pervaded] by their atmosphere. These verses are strange, sad,

on the strength of your recommendation and two interesting numbers which you sent me.

Thank you for giving me the name of Dr Rychner.[1] I am considering his name with several others which have been given to me. I presume that although he is at present in Zurich he is a German? I hardly expected that you would be able to find time to do it yourself, but whenever you can send us anything be sure that it will be welcome.

I have been very much interested in the speech of Max Scheler which you sent me and may mention it in *The Criterion.*[2]

I ought to tell you what I have done about your Balzac. An important London publishing house, Routledge and Sons, are publishing a series of critical biographies of men of letters of every nationality, under the editorship of Professor Rose of London University. I have been in communication with Dr Rose because my own firm, Faber & Gwyer, are proposing to publish a series of short biographies themselves. We have had, therefore, to define our territories so that the two publishing houses should not conflict with each other in any way; the result is that Routledge's will confine themselves to literary artists, novelists, poets, etcetera, while our series will probably cover those writers such as Renan and Schopenhauer who have literary importance but who are primarily philosophers, historians, etcetera. Dr Rose was considering including Balzac in his series and I therefore drew his attention to your book, and have sent it to him to read, and suggested at the same time that it ought perhaps to be somewhat abbreviated and modified for English readers.[3] He seemed very favourably disposed, and when I hear his decision, whether to ask you to allow your Balzac to be translated, or whether he prefers to order a new book from some English writer, I will let you know.

exciting, strong like paintings by Breughel. Your work has impressed me deeply. It seems to me one of the most important, one of the few important [works] that are produced today.' (original in German; trans. Iman Javadi).

1 – Curtius recommended Max Rychner, editor of the *Neue Schweizer Rundschau.*

2 – Max Scheler had written a book on Sympathy – *Wesen und Formen der Sympathie* (Bonn, 1923) – and a short address entitled *Die Formen des Wissens und die Bildung*. TSE, in his next 'Commentary' (*NC* 4 [Apr. 1926], 221–3), drew attention to the significance of Scheler's address to the Lessing-Akademie in Berlin in lamenting the many instances of censorship and suppression in Russia, Italy and Spain. 'Herr Scheler continues in the same strain concerning the dangers, coming from both Socialism and the Church, to freedom of opinion in the German universities. It is notable that in this list neither France nor England is included. We do not vouch for his accuracy, we pass no opinion; but it is a matter for sober reflection, rather than for premature jubilation, that he appears by implication to consider that in England and in France the culture of ideas has still as much liberty as, let us say, in the Sorbonne in the XIIIth century' (223).

3 – Curtius replied (24 Jan.) that he would agree to 'considerable abridgements'.

Meanwhile I shall consider the possibility of your Barrès[1] fitting into our series, although I am afraid it will be a considerable time before the idea of the series has taken enough form for me to be able to decide.

With most cordial good wishes,
Yours ever sincerely,
T. S. Eliot

## TO *Messrs A. P. Watt & Sons* CC

15 February 1926 [London]

Dear Sirs,

I have your letter of the 12th instant and confirm the arrangement for publishing Mr W. B. Yeats' essay, 'The Need for Audacity of Thought', in our April number at our usual rates of £2 per thousand words for the British serial rights.[2]

Yours faithfully,
[T. S. Eliot]

## FROM *Dr Reginald Miller* TS Valerie Eliot

16 February 1926 110 Harley Street, London, W.1

Dear Mr Eliot,

I saw Mrs Eliot and the nurse the other day and have waited a little while in the hope that, before hearing from me, you would be able to find some improvement. Your last letter was a sad one.

I do not feel worried about Mrs Eliot's fears: they are not dominant and should soon cease to mean much. I have exhorted her to get on with the settling of the new house, to get in there with you, and have the proposed holiday abroad with you.

She has the idea that she is temperamentally very dependable [*sic*] on you; that she likes to be a sort of dressed up doll. This I did not allow at all. I said that in so far as such feelings were real they were not temperamental. Were they so, they would show themselves by extreme unselfishness.

1 – *Maurice Barrès und die geistigen Grundlagen des französischen Nationalismus* (Bonn: Cohen, 1921). Barrès (1862–1923): novelist, journalist, and politician who declared for nationalism and anti-Semitism. In the 1890s he was a vocal Anti-Dreyfusard.
2 – Published as 'Our Need for Religious Sincerity', *NC* 4 (Apr. 1926), 306–11.

That when, as she says, she is selfish about your time and other matters, it shows that the sense of depending [on] you is a morbid and not an inborn sense.

I feel still very strongly that there are two things wrong in the atmosphere and regime. They depend upon each other. One is that there is perpetually in her mind that she must dominate you, or you will dominate her. The other is the cause of it but is difficult to express. I feel that there is an attempt on both of your parts to make the two circles of your lives too coincident. That her sphere is far too closely superimposed on yours. I think that far greater happiness would be reached if the two circles overlapped to a much less extent. That your sphere should include much of your work outside her sphere and that she should have many activities, chiefly physical rather than intellectual, outside your sphere. Thus your two lives would overlap to a less extent but where they do overlap, there would be peace and happiness. I express all this clumsily, but I got Mrs Eliot to see what I was after.

The nurse told me about the telephone episodes, at which I was shocked. I said it must certainly stop. Do not take her too seriously: so much is put on, and if you are not deceived by it or upset, it will cease. On the other hand there is a lot of great admiration and love for you, if you could only 'tap' them, as it were.

I was very glad to hear that Mrs Eliot was paying visits to her friends again: and I hope for better times for you with all my heart.

Sincerely yours,
Reginald Miller.

## TO *Richard Cobden-Sanderson* CC

17 February 1926 [London]

Dear Cobden-Sanderson,

SAVONAROLA

I return the wrapper for *Savonarola* with many thanks. I have only one alteration to make myself, as you will see, and there is the alteration of a small p to a capital P. As for the initial T, I also agree with you that it ought to be reduced in size to the same type as the title.

I am harried and worried to death at present because I find that lecturing at Cambridge takes so much time. Delivering the lectures takes practically two days out of every week and preparing the remaining lectures takes the weekend and most evenings and leaves me only three days a week in which to do all my other business.

Yours ever,
[T. S. E.]

## TO *Richard Aldington* TS Texas

18 February 1926 *The New Criterion*

My dear Richard,

I send you herewith a copy of a tentative list which I have drawn up for our series. I am aware that some of the names are unpractical, at least at the beginning, but I want to make the list as comprehensive as possible so as to make matters clear between myself and Rose. You will see that I have put down both Gourmont and Sainte-Beuve, but if you were so inclined I should be very glad <for you> to do the Sainte-Beuve first. There may be other people who could do Gourmont, though I don't know who they are, but there is certainly no one else who could do Sainte-Beuve. I am seeing Dobrée separately for a little time tomorrow and will find out what he is up to. Burke certainly fits into my programme as it is at present. I sent a copy of this list to Richmond but have not heard from him except an acknowledgement.

We shall all be sorry not to see you tomorrow night and I am very sorry about the present circumstances. If when our series is settled you could consider starting on a book for it, I would try to get an advance before delivery of the manuscript. I should also try to get you the same terms as Routledge gives. It is sad to think that you do not have time for any of the things you really want to do.

I quite understand the difficulties you are in with the Patmore case and think that you behaved with great magnanimity, but I cannot feel that your obligations to her, whatever they are, are as great as you imagine. I say this because my wife was present at a conversation in which Brigit mentioned having got this work from Routledge's and was apparently fishing about for suggestions of names for the introduction. Middleton Murry who was present, I dare say in order to protect himself from being invited to write the introduction, asked her why she did not try to get you to do it. She seems to [have] evaded this question and said that she had not seen you for a long time. It struck me on reading your letter that she had behaved very shabbily in not mentioning to the audience the fact that she had only received this work through your kindness, especially as your name had been introduced into the conversation by someone else. As for the financial distress, of course that is hardly possible to disprove.

Would you care to cut up Sandburg[1] for the June *Criterion*. I feel that what reputation he has in this country ought to be exploded, and I have pointed out to several English people who seem not to trust their own judgments in the matter of American poetry how second rate his work is, and also how great is his unacknowledged debt to Ezra Pound. Still, this work of demolition may not interest you and I hesitate to suggest it to a man whose time is so occupied. If you did it you might deal with Amy Lowell in the same review.[2]

Remember also that I always want an essay of some sort from you or some verse, but that I should be more importunate only if the *Criterion* paid better.

Yours ever,
Tom.

## TO *Ramon Fernandez* CC

18 February 1926 [London]

My dear Fernandez,

I am sending you a copy of the relevant part of a letter from Frederic Manning which I thought might interest you. I look forward to your note, and my secretary will let you know later the latest possible date for the June number.

I asked I. A. Richards, a Fellow of Magdalene College Cambridge, to send you his last book, and I hope that you will let him see your book on Personality when it appears. He is one of the most intelligent men in Cambridge and he is at present engaged on problems related to those in which you are interested, and at some time I hope that you will meet. I hope that in some way or another we may get you to Cambridge within a

1–Carl Sandburg (1878–1967), poet, biographer, editor, writer for children. A proud mid-westerner, he grew up in Illinois and left school at the age of 13 in order to take up a series of labouring jobs, before becoming a reporter for the *Chicago Daily News*. In his mature years he produced many works in prose including a Pulitzer Prize-winning biography of Abraham Lincoln, and popular works for children rooted in the local culture including *Rootabaga Stories* (1922); collections of folk songs; and volumes of poetry including *Chicago Poems* (1916), *Corn Huskers* (1918), *Smoke and Steel* (1920) and *Collected Poems* (1950).
2–It was not done.

reasonable time. I enjoyed immensely seeing you in London and my wife joins me in sending kindest regards.

Yours always sincerely
[T. S. Eliot]

## TO *Jean Cocteau* CC

Le 18 février 1926 [London]

Cher Cocteau,

Votre lettre sans date reçue. Je suis ému par votre inquiétude et je ferai ce que je peux pour vous appuyer. Le notice de Myers est déjà supprimé.[1] Quant au texte – je vous envoie sous pli separé les bonnes feuilles du livre; je vous prie de les examiner et de les montrer aux amis loyaux les écrivains anglais et americains desquels vous parlez. Je relirai le texte moi même et je ferai ce que je peux mais vous savez que [illegible] affaire délicate pour un éditeur d'intervenir entre un auteur et son traducteur. Mais tout ce que je peux, sans me martyriser, je le ferai.

Fraternellement vôtre,
[T. S. Eliot][2]

## TO *T. Sturge Moore* CC

18 February 1926 [*The New Criterion*]

Dear Mr Sturge Moore,

I wired to you three days ago at your address but was subsequently informed by the Post Office that the wire could not be delivered as you

1 – Cocteau wrote (undated): '*Le notice de Myers est détestable, dangereuse etc.*' Myers wrote to TSE (13 Feb.), 'With regard to the *Introduction* I wrote for the "Call to Order", as I now learn that Cocteau is *particularly anxious* that there should be *no notice of any kind* about himself or his works in the book, I want to withdraw it.'

2 – *Translation*: Dear Cocteau, I have received your undated letter. I am deeply moved by your anxiety, and I shall do all I can to help you. Myers' comments have already been dropped. As for the text, I am sending you under separate cover the proofs of the book; I beg you to examine them and to show them to our loyal English and American friends and writers whom you mention. I shall re-read the text myself, and I shall do whatever I can; but you know that for an editor to intervene between an author and his translator is always a most delicate task. Still, whatever can be done, without having myself turned into a martyr, will be done.

With brotherly affection, [T. S. Eliot]

were away.[1] Meanwhile I have your corrected proof so that I assume that letters are being forwarded to you and am therefore writing to your usual address. I wired to say that it had proved practically impossible to include the first part of your essay in the April number, and I wanted to know whether, if we put the first part in the June number, we should still be able to use the second part in the October number before the book appears.[2] I gathered from previous correspondence that you had not expected to have the book ready for publication for another nine months or so, and I therefore hope that this is all right.

The confusion is due to a combination of circumstances: the amount of material accepted during the last year and the fact that no October number was published at all. These circumstances combined with the packers' strike. Before Christmas I had promised to use a number of things before books in which they were to be included were published; and as several of these books were delayed by the strike I found myself compelled to fulfil these promises. I was confident up to the last moment that a certain accepted contribution could not be published because I understood from the author that the book would appear in March: but I now learn from him that the book will not appear until May or June and I am therefore obliged to use his article.

I want you to know that in any other circumstances I should certainly have given the preference to your essay over other things which I am now obliged to publish first. I hope that this will not inconvenience you and that it will still be possible for you to let me use both of the two first parts of your essay which I am very keen to do.

Yours sincerely,
[T. S. Eliot]

## TO *Denys Winstanley*[3] CC

19 February 1926 [London]

Dear Winstanley,

I should have been delighted to dine with you on the 2nd March but I find that I have promised to visit the Queens' College Literary Society that

1–TSE wired (15 Feb.): 'Owing congestion old material find impossible print part one till June wish use both will book be out before November deep regrets please write Eliot.'

2–'A Poet and His Technique', *NC* 4 (June 1926), 421–35; (Oct. 1926), 680–93.

3–Denys Winstanley (1877–1947), historian, was a Fellow of Trinity College, Cambridge; Senior Tutor, 1925–31; Vice-Master from 1935.

evening. I wish I had not done so. I am up again on the following Friday, but I have promised to stay that night with Dr Stewart.[1] That only leaves the 9th which I have kept free, and which of course is my last visit.

So if it is possible for you to arrange another meeting I shall be free on the 9th, or, what is perhaps better, I could come to lunch any Wednesday, the day after my lecture, or on Saturday the 6th. I am very much disappointed that I cannot come on the 2nd.

Yours sincerely
[T. S. Eliot]

## TO *Bruce Richmond* CC

19 February 1926 [London]

Dear Richmond,

Thank you very much indeed for your letter. I hope to get the Dekker done in a week or so, but I want to re-read Defoe first.[2]

I should like very much to see you as soon as possible. The first day I have is Thursday, the 25th, and I could either pick you up for lunch or meet you or come to rather late tea that day. I think you told me that tea suited you best. If it falls out so, I could probably meet you in Kensington by 5.30. I have a Directors' Meeting at 2.30 but I think it will be over by that time and if not I could leave before the end. So I shall come to you on Thursday the 25th at 5.30 unless I hear to the contrary.

Yours ever
[T. S. Eliot]

P.S. I am sorry to trouble you at such a time about M'Greevy whose reviews I sent you.[3] There is no immediate hurry for the next month or so. I want to show you a very good review of George Moore's last book which he has done for me. The review justifies the principle of setting an Irishman to criticise an Irishman.[4]

1 – The Revd Hugh Fraser Stewart, Trinity College, Cambridge.

2 – 'Plague Pamphlets' – *The Plague Pamphlets of Thomas Dekker*, ed. F. P. Wilson – *TLS*, 5 Aug. 1926, 522. 'The review of Dekker need not be hurried,' said BLR (18 Feb.), 'as long as your Cambridge lectures are on.'

3 – 'I will look at your Irishman's things, and will try him if I can; but the queue is dreadfully long – Edwin Muir, Bonamy Dobrée and several others about whom I have been approached and whom I have not yet had any opportunity to try – but I will if I can.'

4 – 'L. St. Senan' (Thomas McGreevy) reviewed George Moore's *Héloïse and Abélard* in *NC* 4 (Apr. 1926), 368–73.

## TO *Wyndham Lewis* TS Cornell

22 February 1926 *The New Criterion*

Dear Lewis,

I quite understand your inability to do anything in the way of a regular art chronicle or even any occasional writing about matters connected with art at the present time. Please believe that the matter will be left entirely open until the subject is raised between us in conversation. And if there is any likelihood of your being able at some future date to contribute an art chronicle, and if it is at all likely that you would care to do so, I should much prefer to wait for you. I only regret that I understood from you when I saw you last that your notes for this number had been written, and were in the hands of a typist. Such misunderstandings are undesirable, and I hope unnecessary, between you and myself.

Sincerely yours
T. S. Eliot

## TO *T. Sturge Moore* CC

23 February 1926 [*The New Criterion*]

Dear Mr Sturge Moore,

Thank you very much for your kind letter of the 20th. I shall be very much relieved if it is possible for us to publish the second chapter of your book before the book appears. Our October number, in which I shall use it comes out on the 15th of the month. But even so, I shall still suffer from editorial exasperation in that I realize that there is very little in my April number of the same rank as your postponed contribution.[1]

With many thanks,
Sincerely yours,
[T. S. Eliot]

1 – The first part of 'A Poet and His Technique' appeared in *NC* 4 (June 1926), 421–35; the second in *NC* 4 (Oct. 1926), 680–93.

## TO *Bonamy Dobrée* CC

25 February 1926 [*The New Criterion*]

My dear Dobrée,

I am returning herewith the Etherege dialogue which we were talking about the other evening.[1] I am returning it entirely and regretfully on the grounds mentioned. You spoke of another dialogue which is under way. May I ask whether there is any possibility that it may be completed in a short time so that it would be available for the June *Criterion*?

Yours ever,
[T. S. Eliot]

'Denham' just arrived and gone to printers! Proof in due course.[2]

## TO *Yvonne Salmon* CC

26 February 1926 [London]

Dear Madame Salmon,

I have your letter of the 25th about Monsieur Massis and should like to do what I can. I understand his vacant days are Friday the 5th, Saturday the 6th and Sunday the 7th. Saturday and Sunday are not, I think, very good days for lectures in Oxford or Cambridge, and unfortunately I am lecturing myself in Cambridge on the 5th; I say unfortunately only because I am afraid that we should divide the audience which is none too large at best. But I am writing to an undergraduate who is active in a literary society in Cambridge and I shall also write to a member of the Faculty and see what can be done. Have you tried Oxford or made any arrangements for him there? At the present time I am much more in touch with Cambridge than Oxford.

Yours sincerely,
[T. S. Eliot]

1–'John Wilmot, Earl of Rochester: A Conversation between Sir George Etherege and Mr FitzJames, at a House in the Street of the Envoys at Ratisbon. Summer, 1686' was included in Dobrée, *As Their Friends Saw Them: Biographical Conversations* (1933), 33–62.

2–'Sir John Denham: A Conversation between Bishop Henry King and Edmund Waller; at The Palace, Chichester, March 1669', *NC* 4 (June 1926), 454–64; repr. in *As Their Friends Saw Them*, 13–30.

## TO *James Smith* CC

27 February 1926 [London]

Dear Smith,

When I lunched with you a fortnight ago there was some conversation about the French writer, Henri Massis, and I wrote to you afterward to let your friend know that Massis was coming to London on the 20th. I now hear that he is coming to England next week and that the *Alliance Française* would be glad to make any engagements for him on the 5th, 6th, or 7th of March. If it could possibly be arranged, I think it would be a very good thing to get him to come to Cambridge, and the lecture would be very interesting although of course in French. I understand from the Secretary that it could be arranged without the necessity of providing travelling expenses. If you, or your friend who arranges these matters, are interested you should write at once to

Madame Salmon,
14, Morgan Road,
Reading

mentioning my name.

I hope I may see you again next week,

Yours in haste,
[T. S. Eliot]

## TO *Jean Loiseau*[1] CC

27 February 1926 [London]

Dear Mr Loiseau,

I hear from Madame Salmon, the Secretary of the *Alliance Française*, that Henri Massis is coming for a lecture tour next week and that he has a few vacant dates on any of which she would be pleased to arrange a lecture from him anywhere. I gather that the *Alliance Française* would pay expenses. The free dates are the 5th, 6th and 7th March. Madame Salmon says that she wrote to Professor Prior, whom I do not know, about this. But if you are interested and think that it would be possible to arrange a lecture in Cambridge, I should like to ask you to propose it to the proper authorities. I do not know whom I should approach on such a matter.

1–Jean Loiseau (Trinity College, Cambridge), author of *Abraham Cowley: Sa vie, son œuvre* (1931) and *Abraham Cowley's Reputation in England* (1931).

If they are favourable they should write at once to

Madame Salmon,
14 Morgan Road,
Reading.

I look forward to seeing you again on Tuesday.

Amitiés cordiales,
[T. S. Eliot]

## TO *George Rylands*

TS King's

27 February 1926 *The New Criterion*

Dear Rylands

Many thanks for your review which seems to me excellent.[1] In some ways it is like your poetry (which, by the way, has been favourably reviewed for the same number) in that it is learned, allusive and indirect, rather too much so perhaps for a critical review, in which directer if sometimes cruder methods, though always according to the Queensberry rules, are more effective. But we will try to find some more substantial material next time and I hope you will suggest something yourself. As to your postscript, I am not wholly insensible myself to the quality of the composition to which you refer.[2] These weaknesses can be remedied in time!

Sincerely yours,
T. S. Eliot

## TO *Herbert Read*

TS Victoria

27 February 1926 *The New Criterion*

My dear Read,

Thank you very much indeed for your long letter about the series of biographies. I find that for the first time I am compelled with some diffidence to dissent in several particulars. First, do you think it worthwhile

1–Review of Noël Coward's *Three Plays*, *NC* 4 (Apr. 1926), 392–4.

2–Violet Ray, 'The Theatre', *NC* 4 (Jan. 1926), 161–9. Rylands said in his letter (22 Feb.), 'I nearly wrote to express my horror and disgust at an article on the stage in the first number – but asked Peter Lucas to tackle you on it instead. He was equally shocked. If this article bears any resemblance to that, destroy it. I refuse to be tarred with the same brush!'

to include Croce[1] or anyone else for the purpose of exploding him? I question whether such a series is quite the place for a campaign against the subject of the book, and no doubt you will agree that it is better to omit Croce altogether than to publish a book by someone who would favour him. I doubt whether either Ellis, Santayana, Dewey, Royce or Schiller is worth the trouble. Emerson might well be included much as I dislike him, Mill also. Some of the Germans you mention might be included later.

I think it is hopeless to endeavour to give the series too much unity. It seems to me that the contemporary interest of any dead writer big enough to be the subject of a book at all depends very much on what the author of the book manages to make of it. Macaulay I am inclined to withdraw.

I had thought of trying to start off with you on Bagehot or Henry Maine, with Dobrée on Burke, with Aldington on Sainte-Beuve, possibly with Muir on Lessing or some other German. I believe that H. P. Collins might like to do a Joubert if you think he is up to it.[2] I think Sullivan is quite good enough to deal with some scientific writer, with Darwin or Huxley. Renan and Taine are big subjects and I do not know who is competent or would care to tackle either of them. I should rather like to deal with Hooker[3] myself if he were included. It is difficult to think of just the man for Nietzsche.

I see something in your alternative idea and before I come to a possible conclusion I will try to think of a list of writers who could be so dealt with. Contemporaries would probably have to be excluded for copyright reasons unless they were foreigners whose works had not yet been translated. I think that the scheme might have a larger sale; on the other hand, Faber does not appear to consider it such a good advertisement for the firm and it is questionable whether the expenses would not be as large or larger than for the series of critical biographies.

1–Benedetto Croce (1866–1952): Italian philosopher and critic; author of *The Philosophy of the Spirit* (4 vols, 1902–17) and *The Poetry of Dante* (1922). TSE had published an English translation of 'On the Nature of Allegory' in *C* 3 (Apr. 1925).

2–Collins wrote on 16 Apr., as from *The Adelphi*: 'We have come to an arrangement [with Aldington] for a full-sized Joubert book.' Collins later translated *Pensées and Letters of Joseph Joubert* (1928).

3–TSE wrote at the foot of a page of the second of his Clark Lectures, '[Donne and the Middle Ages]': 'I believe that Hooker's philosophy was much more "mediaeval" than Donne's; but I shall deal with this elsewhere' (Schuchard, *VMP*, 68).

I will write to you again. Meanwhile, I have received the second Calverton article[1] and I will deal with him direct about both. I return herewith, with some relief, the letter from him to you.

Ever yours,
T. S. E.

## *Henry Eliot*[2] TO *His Mother* MS Houghton

2 March 1926 [London]

[Extract]

We have been at the Stafford [Hotel] for 3 days . . . We went to tea at Tom's the day after our arrival, and Vivien was very pleased and got along finely with Theresa, and both of them liked and admired her very much. We had a nice time; I gave Tom news of the family, and Tom played the phonograph. I am glad to discern a firmer attitude on Tom's part, in that he insisted in playing the phonograph when Vivien objected slightly, and that he maintained that she was in excellent health, in contradiction of her faint protests. Tom looks to me very well indeed. The next night he dropped in to the Stafford to have dinner with me and Vivien, looking very well in a new suit. He is very lovely and so nice and pleasant to Theresa.[3]

. . . Bertrand Russell has invited us to tea Friday.

1–The one article by V. F. Calverton pertained to 'New American Literature'; the other cannot be identified.

2–Henry Ware Eliot (1879–1947), TSE's elder brother: see Biographical Register.

3–Henry Eliot had married Theresa Anne Garrett (1884–1981) on 15 Feb. 1926. The couple travelled to Europe on honeymoon. E. W. F. Tomlin took note in a later year of TSE's conversational remark 'that it was people like Theresa, originally from [Louisville,] Kentucky, who had enlivened his Puritanical New England family. "They warmed us up", he said, followed by his chuckle. The phrase pleased him so much that he repeated it' (*T. S. Eliot: A Friendship* [1988], 227).

On 28 March 1970, Theresa Eliot wrote this memo: 'Henry, my husband, sent money to Tom for some years, but Tom never said anything to his family about Vivienne's ill health and the doctor's bills. It was only in 1926 that on our honeymoon in England Vivienne asked us to go to see her doctor about her health, as she couldn't tell us herself. The Doctor said she took drugs, and had started at 16 under some doctor's orders' (Houghton: *AC9. E1464 Zzx Box II, envelope 13).

## TO *Edwin Muir* CC

3 March 1926 [*The New Criterion*]

Dear Mr Muir,

I am very distressed that your arrival in London falls out as it does because I am afraid that both of those dates are quite impracticable for me.[1] I shall have to be in Cambridge. If there is any possibility of your being able to stay over Monday could you let me know at once, and I should be delighted if you could lunch with me. If this is impossible will you at least let me have some address abroad at which I could write to you, and let me know when you are likely to be returning, when I sincerely hope that I shall be in London.

Yours sincerely,
T. S. Eliot

## TO *Thomas McGreevy*[2] TS TCD

3 March 1926 *The New Criterion*

My dear M'Greevy,

I am returning to you herewith your reviews from *The Nation*. I have spoken to Mr Richmond about you and it appears that there is a considerable waiting list for *The Times Literary Supplement*, but that if you are willing to begin by doing some small bits instead of columns Richmond would like you to call on him. I do hope that you will ring him up at *The Times* offices, mentioning my name and reminding him that I showed him some of your reviews, and ask for an appointment.

Yours sincerely,
T. S. Eliot

1 – Muir and his wife were arriving the following weekend, en route for France.

2 – Thomas McGreevy (1893–1967) otherwise known as L. St. Senan: poet, critic of literature and art, and museum curator: see Biographical Register.

## TO *Robert Graves* CC

3 March [1926] [*The New Criterion*]

Dear Graves,

I am very glad to hear from you again.[1] I hope that your comic opera university has really provided you with rest, health and unearned income, though I suspect that you are doing more work than is necessary. If it gives you a good climate and opportunity to do your own writing we shall all be delighted.

I am glad to hear that Miss Gottschalk is sending a new manuscript because, to tell the truth, the other was so illegible that I have postponed reading it as long as possible. I shall look forward to receiving the new copies.

I cannot see any objection to her collaborating with you and she might be very useful on the American side. It suits me very well to come in on the job at the end of the year, though I expect to find by that time that my intervention will be unnecessary. I have forgotten what names I picked for myself but I hope that you will at least reserve Ezra Pound for me because I do think that I understand his poetry better than most people.

My present pressure of work and the picture you draw of Cairo would make me very inclined to join you there if I could.

Yours ever,
[T. S. Eliot]

1 – Graves had written on 11 Feb.: 'Egypt is not to be despised as a resort, but the University is a beautifully constructed farce in the best French style and dangerous if taken in the slightest degree seriously. My rather serious nature has to be closely guarded against a conscientious explosion: the heavy pay and impossibility of getting any work done with students makes me rather ashamed of myself. Anyhow there's opportunity for my own work here. Laura Gottschalk is with us . . . & I have a message for you from her: that a clean and revised copy of the *H. D. Legend* I sent you is to be forwarded to you from our agent Pinker. He also has two critical essays of hers, *Criticism & the Poet* and *Genius & Disaster*. One of these I can't remember which, I sent you a rather messy copy of: Pinker now has copies of both & in proper shape & will send you them.

'I am going on with the proposed *Untraditional Elements in Poetry*. Have you any objection to her collaborating in this business after what you have seen of her work? She is far more in touch with the American side than I am and is anxious to get ahead with it. She suggests that at the end of a year – until which you could promise nothing – you might come in as arbiter between our contributions. Please tell me how you feel about this. Her list of poets corresponded exactly with yours; and her critical detachment is certainly greater than mine.

'I think the University will soon have to be reconstituted with English speaking professors instead of Frenchmen as it is at present in the Faculty of Letters. The students speak no French & very little English. If this happens & you are in want of a holiday, it would be fine for you.' (*In Broken Images*, ed. O'Prey, 163–4)

## *Vivien Eliot* TO *Mary Hutchinson* MS Texas

4 March [1926] 9 Clarence Gate Gardens, N.W.1.

My dear Mary

I was very sorry about Tuesday. Tom's brother & his new wife are a bother. I am trying to move in a week, & Ellen is going to be married, which is rather a blow.

I want to see you very much indeed, but I have to go to Cambridge once more, & so it may be the end of next week before I can ring you up, but if I have a time free unexpectedly I shall find out if you can see me.

With love
Vivien

## TO *Herbert Read* CC

8 March 1926 [*The New Criterion*]

My dear Read,

Very many thanks for reading and recommending Vivante's article.[1] I have merely glanced at it but it struck me as excellent, and on a cursory reading even in paragraph 4 I do not find any cause for personal disagreement.

I shall hope to see you in any case on Friday week, but if possible I should like to arrange a private meeting before then.

Yours ever,
[T. S. E.]

P.S. Would you like to review Dostoevsky (portrayed by his wife), edited and translated by Koteliansky? If not, who is the best man to do it?[2]

1–Leone Vivante, 'The Misleading Comparison between Art and Dreams', *NC* 4 (June 1926), 436–53. HR had written on 5 Mar.: 'I feel quite sure of Vivante's article. It deals with a point that very much needs treatment, & he does it admirably. The expression – perhaps inevitably, in a translation – is a bit clumsy, & might be simpler. But that is a small consideration in view of the importance of the material. I think I entirely agree with all he says, but I found myself wondering whether you would altogether agree with all he said in notably § 4 .'

2–HR was 'not very keen' (12 Apr.) on Dostoevsky; he recommended Prince D. S. Mirsky (who was resident in London).

## TO *Juan Carlos Figari*[1] CC

8 March 1926 [London]

My dear Sir,

I am shocked to find how long ago you wrote to me.[2] I should have written to you before but have been very overworked and have had to be in Cambridge for a large part of the time. I should very much like to see you if you are still in London. I shall be away again for most of this week, but if you could drop me a line here I should be delighted to arrange an appointment at the beginning of next week.

Sincerely yours,
[T. S. Eliot]

## TO *Wyndham Lewis* MS Cornell

8 March 1926 *The New Criterion*

Dear Lewis –

Here is MS.[3] What I have read I like exceedingly. *If* you will return it by Wednesday night, I shall have read it all by Monday; and on Friday next (even before I have read it all[)] I will discuss it with Faber. If you are likely to lose your other chance by waiting 10 days, try the other people first, & then let me have it again as soon as possible.[4]

Please reply.

I can see you any day next week, I think

Yrs ever
T. S. E.

1–Juan Carlos Figari was a son of the Uruguayan painter Pedro Figari; friend of writers including Paul Valéry, Valery Larbaud, Paul Claudel, and Alexis St Léger-Léger.

2–Figari, who was visiting London, had written to TSE on 12 Feb. 1926; he had an introduction dated 7 Feb. from Adrienne Monnier at *La Maison des Amis des Livres*.

3–Either *Time and Western Man* or *The Lion and the Fox*. WL had been agitating for a decision or a prompt return of his MS: another publisher had expressed interest.

4–WL responded on 8 March: 'I am very glad to hear that you like the MSS . . . All I wished to make sure of was that I should not be left in uncertainty of the issue for an indefinite period, owing to your great press of work . . . The enquiry from another publisher does not require an immediate response: it is only I, unfortunately, who am in a hurry, somewhat.'

## TO *Richard Aldington* CC

8 March 1926 [London]

My dear Richard,

Thank you very much for your letter of the 5th. I am in complete agreement with you on every point. There is really no more to be said. When I next see Herbert I shall take the liberty of letting him know that I have laid his arguments before you and that we are in agreement about them. That is unless you object to his knowing that I referred them to you.[1]

I shall now see Rose again as soon as I can and arrange to appropriate all of these authors and possibly some others. After that I think that I might get some *undated* contracts drawn up and send you a couple for the Sainte-Beuve and the Gourmont. Of course I realize how much other work you have to do before you could start on either. Also before I send you the contracts I shall take up the question of giving you better terms than the other contributors in consideration of the part you have played in the negotiations and your special terms with Routledge.

I am very busy this week as I am again to lecture twice. It will be a great relief to me to finish this course and have more freedom.[2] Perhaps before I start to work turning the lectures into a book I will show you some of them as they are and get your criticism and advice.

Yours in haste,
[Tom]

P. S. Routledge's have sent in F. A. Wright's complete translation of Catullus in the Broadway Translations. About half of the book is introduction. The translation seems to me very poor and I suppose that you yourself, in the circumstances, would prefer not to deal with it. If so, who is the best man? A complete translation of *Catullus* seems to me to deserve notice whether it is good or bad.[3]

1–RA replied (9 Mar.): 'By all means tell Herbert [Read] that I disagree with his plan. I am pleased that you thought I was right.'

2–'I too shall be very glad when your Cambridge "chore" is over, for I hope it may be possible to spend some time together either here or in town.'

3–'Wright's Catullus might perhaps go to Fred Manning, who will deal faithfully and competently with it.' *Catullus: The Complete Poems*, trans. and ed. by F. A. Wright, was reviewed by 'F.M.' in *NC* 4 (June 1926), 603–5.

## TO *Messrs John Lane The Bodley Head* TS Herrick

8 March 1926 *The New Criterion*

Dear Sirs

*Leone Vivante*[1]

Referring to your letter of the 22nd ultimo I find Signor Vivante's essay extremely interesting and should like if possible to publish it in June.[2] Could you inform me meanwhile whether you have full rights to negotiate for the author and to receive payment for him, or whether I ought to communicate with him direct. Our rates are ten pounds per five thousand words, and where there is any payment to be made to a translator, this payment has to be deducted from the author's fees.

I am now making up the June number of *The New Criterion* and should be able to let you know in a short time whether I can make use of this valuable essay.

Yours faithfully,
T. S. Eliot

## TO *I. A. Richards* TS Magdalene

8 March 1926 *The New Criterion*

My dear Richards,

If you are going to be extremely busy please let me know as I do not wish to be a nuisance, but I should like to get as much copy out of you as I can before you disappear indefinitely. Do you read Italian easily? I have a book which I think is decidedly in your line, by an Italian named Leone Vivante. It is called *Note Sopra La Originalità Del Pensiero*. I have not

1–On 15 Aug. 1951 TSE would write to Prof. John U. Nef (Committee on Social Thought, University of Chicago) on behalf of Leone Vivante: 'I have . . . a high opinion of Vivante, whom I have known off and on for some years, and who in the old days contributed to *The Criterion*. The book to which I wrote a preface [*English Poetry and its Contribution to the Knowledge of a Creative Principle* (F & F, 1950)] seems to me not only interesting as criticism of English poetry by a foreigner, but for the very interesting theory of poetics which the author advances. I should myself recommend Vivante strongly. He is a very nice fellow, and very much at home in the English language . . . I believe that he is of Jewish extraction, and found it necessary to absent himself from Italy after the promulgation of the anti-Semitic legislation which was enacted there under Mussolini, under Hitler's influence.'

2–John Lane The Bodley Head wrote on 5 Feb. to announce *Note Sopra La Originalità del Pensiero*, in an English translation by Prof. A. Brodrick-Bullock; Vivante had made a 'special extract of an essay from his book' – 'The Misleading Comparison between Art and Dreams' – to appear in *NC* 4 (June 1926), 436–53.

read this book, but what I have seen of his work impresses me favourably and I have an essay which I may use in June. I cannot think of anyone but yourself who could deal with such a book properly, so if you are interested and if there is any possibility of your being able to do a note on it before you go away, may I send it to you?[1]

I shall try to see you again on Tuesday or Wednesday if I can.

Yours ever,
T. S. Eliot

## TO *George Rylands* CC

8 March 1926 [*The New Criterion*]

Dear Rylands,

I have deciphered most of the calligraphy on your post-card[2] and will you come in and see me here one day next week? If you would ring me up here say on Monday after eleven we could arrange a meeting.

Yours sincerely
[T. S. Eliot]

## TO *Nancy Pearn* CC

9 March 1926 [London]

Dear Miss Pearn,

I have read D. H. Lawrence's story, 'Sun', which you left with me and I am returning it herewith. I am afraid I do not like it at all: it seems to me to have some of Lawrence's characteristic vices and absurdities without many of his virtues. So I shall stick to 'Mornings in Mexico' which I think I can use in June, and if not will certainly use in September; but I am now making up the June number and will let you know definitely in a short time.[3]

1 – Vivante's tome would not be reviewed in *NC*.

2 – 'Very relieved about the review,' wrote Rylands (pc, ? Mar.). 'Apologies for being impertinent about the theatre notes – but such work is so hard to get, so coveted, and one resents the success of the uneducated.' He asked to do a poetry review – 'perhaps Humbert Wolfe's new poems.'

3 – 'Mornings in Mexico' appeared in *NC* 4 (June 1926), 467–75. 'The Man who Loved Islands', by DHL, was to be returned by TSE to Pearn in Oct. 1926.

I was glad to see you the other day and I hope that we can be of mutual advantage.

Yours sincerely
[T. S. Eliot]

## *Henry Eliot* TO *His Mother* — MS Houghton

9 March 1926[1] — [Lion Hotel, Cambridge]

[Extract]

Tom came in [to his lecture] with A. E. Housman as escort . . . Vivien is coming up tomorrow to hear the last of the lectures . . .

Tom looks very nice and I think Vivien is well and cheerful . . . He says he is working on a play now – I understood that it was a play of modern life . . .[2] We are going to take Tom's flat next week, furnished, as they are taking a small house and subletting 9 Clarence Gate 'as an investment', Tom says. They have a long lease and rents have gone up there. We shall occupy it while they are advertising it.

## *Vivien Eliot* TO *Ottoline Morrell*[3] — MS Texas

10 March [1926] — Cambridge

Dearest Ottoline

Thank you *ever* so much for your very kind letter. You have no idea how much we enjoyed seeing you.[4] You have no idea how much we have both *always* clung to the thought of you, as being perhaps the only real friend, & the only *real person* we know. I really think that you & I & Tom have rather a special understanding of one another, don't we!

1–HWE and his wife attended TSE's penultimate Clark lecture at Trinity College, Cambridge. Sadly, Henry suffered from severe deafness and could hear but little.

2–*Sweeney Agonistes*.

3–Lady Ottoline Morrell (1873–1938), patron of the arts: see Biographical Register.

4–'When Ottoline dined on 3 March, she noticed that Tom was watching Vivien all the time. The couple seemed more cheerful than normal, and Vivien in particular appeared oddly elated, smoking and eating chocolates. Afterwards Ottoline heard from Bertie Russell that Vivien was threatening to sue her husband for putting her away, although Ottoline remembered indignantly that Vivien had herself told Ottoline earlier how happy she had been in the "home"' (Seymour-Jones, *Painted Shadow*, 416–17; citing OM's Journal, 3 Mar. 1926, from the Goodman Papers).

You were very sweet to the Henry Eliots & I was grateful to you for it.[1]

Thank you *very much* for the invitation for the 20th. Tom will add a line to this to say he has got another marvellous Frenchman[2] coming over that weekend who he promised to see many weeks ago, and I am afraid it will prevent me coming to you on that date. I am *dreadfully* sorry. It was so like you to invite my dogs as well. I *must* bring them one day. I long to see them in your gardens. But can you arrange another weekend? If not – But please, please *do*. Tom is writing. In haste

With very much love
*Affectionately*
*Vivien*

## TO *Ottoline Morrell* MS Texas

10 March [1926] Trinity College, Cambridge

My dear Ottoline,

Many thanks for your letter which gave me great pleasure. *I* enjoyed the evening immensely – we were very happy having you.

I should have *loved* to come on the 20th – but an unfortunate complication – a Frenchman named Henri Massis is coming to lecture in London on that afternoon – and as I was largely responsible for getting him here, we *must* go to his lecture & see him afterwards at dinner.

*Will* you please invite us any weekend after that? We are both very disappointed, and should love to look forward to a visit.

With much love,
Yrs aff.
Tom

1–'On 13 March 1926 Ottoline dined with Bertrand Russell and his new wife Dora, and that evening the Eliots' "troubles" were the main topic of conversation; the Henry Eliots were also present, and Theresa blamed Vivien for her possessiveness. Vivien was vampire, Tom martyr, in this version of events, in which Henry, in his letters home to his mother, compared Tom to Job; Vivien's "vampiring" drained "poor Tom" of his vitality, they all agreed' (Seymour-Jones, *Painted Shadow*, 424).
2–Henri Massis.

## TO *I. A. Richards* CC

11 March 1926 [London]

Dear Richards,

Thank you very much indeed for your letter and for thinking of me in this connection.[1] Even assuming that there were any likelihood of its coming off, I am afraid that Liverpool is of no use to me. I am hoping to see you soon and will explain more in detail when we meet.

With many thanks,
Ever yours,
[T. S. Eliot]

## FROM *Rev. F. J. Yealy*[2] MS Valerie Eliot

13 March 1926 St Edmund's House, Cambridge

Dear Sir, –

I hope you will pardon my taking the liberty of pointing out an apparent inaccuracy in one of the early lectures of your course on the metaphysical poets just completed at Trinity College. I think you were understood to quote a certain meditation on death as occurring in the text of the *Spiritual Exercises of St Ignatius* and as being the work of St Ignatius himself.[3] As a matter of fact, no such meditation occurs in

1–IAR wrote in an undated letter: 'I have just heard that Liverpool University can't find a suitable successor to [William] Elton for their chair of English Literature. The appointment has to be made by next term. I've just had it suggested to me much to my surprise. So I thought I would pass it on to you doubtless as an equal surprise.'

2–Fr. F. J. Yealy, SJ (1888–1977), an American Jesuit from the St Stanislaw Seminary, Florissant, Missouri, was pursuing a doctoral degree on the subject of 'Emerson and the Romantic Revival' at Christ's College, Cambridge – in the event, TSE was to be one of the examiners of Yealy's thesis in 1927 – and he went to TSE's Clark Lectures. In a later year he was to be author of *The Story of Missouri's Oldest Settlement* (Sainte Genevieve: The Bicentennial Historical Committee, 1935).

3–St Ignatius Loyola, the sixteenth-century Spanish mystic, founded the Society of Jesus. TSE quoted in his third lecture from the 'Second Exercise on Death', from *Manresa: Or the Spiritual Exercises of St Ignatius, for General Use* (London, 1881) – 'Contemplate – (1) Your apartment faintly lighted by the last rays of day, or the feeble light of a lamp; your bed which you will never leave except to be laid in your coffin; all the objects which surround you and seem to say, You leave us for ever! (2) The persons who will surround you: your servants, sad and silent; a weeping family, bidding you a last adieu; the minister of religion, praying near you and suggesting pious affections to you. (3) Yourself stretched on a bed of pain, losing by degrees your senses and the free use of your faculties, struggling violently against death, which comes to tear your soul from the body and drag it before the tribunal of God. (4) At your side the devils, who redouble their efforts, to destroy you; your good

the authentic text. The Exercises, as you probably know, are a series of outlines of considerations which are supposed to be developed somewhat by a director and thus presented to a person making a spiritual retreat. Directors who are pleased with their work do sometimes publish their developments; perhaps without always making clear in just what relation their work stands to that of St Ignatius. The meditation quoted must have originated in some such way. The authentic Latin version of the *Exercises* states that the director may add other meditations on death, etc. (cf. *The Spiritual Exercises of St Ignatius of Loyola*. Ed. by Longridge, p. 306) – I think you will find St Ignatius' own thought as austere and straightforward in its way as that of Richard of St Victor. May I add that I did not think your comparison especially happy? Richard's treatise on contemplation is analytical and discursive. The Exercises, besides dealing primarily with the different though related business of asceticism, are not a treatise at all but a series of fairly obvious working principles whose virtue is supposed to lie partly in their arrangement and partly in being assimilated in the most intimate and practical manner possible by personal effort. –

Let me thank you heartily for the great pleasure and stimulation I had from your lectures.

Sincerely & respectfully yours
F. J. Yealy, SJ[1]

## TO *Wyndham Lewis* — TS Cornell

15 March 1926 — *The New Criterion*

Dear Lewis,

Your manuscript received and I am reading it. Your book[2] having just arrived from Chatto and Windus, I think it is desirable that I should read a great part of that also in order to strengthen my position before carrying the matter on. Hence a few more days' delay may be necessary.

Yours ever
T. S. E.

---

angel, who assists you for the last time with his holy inspirations' – and said of it: 'Is this not a spiritual haschisch, a drugging of the emotions, rather than, as with Richard of St Victor, an intellectual preparation for spiritual contemplation?' (*VMP*, 105–6).

1 – For TSE's reply, see 16 Mar. below.

2 – *The Art of Being Ruled*.

## TO *Messrs Small, Maynard & Company* CC

15 March 1926 [London]

Dear Sirs,

I should be very much obliged if you could send me two copies of Ezra Pound's *Sonnets and Ballate of Guido Cavalcanti* which you published some years ago.[1] If you will send me the invoice immediately, I will send a money-order. If the book is out of stock, I should be very much obliged if you would let me know.

Yours faithfully
[T. S. Eliot]

## TO *Ezra Pound* CC

15 March 1926 [London]

Dear Rabbit,

Should be glad to see serious study of work of Stein mentioned in your previous[2] and regret to say owing to pressure of work etcetera have so far failed to write to Small and Maynard but have written by this same post.[3] Meanwhile will forward to you copy you gave me and send you one of other two subsequently. If you could ever pick up a copy of some Italian edition of which you approve I should be glad to have it and would pay for it.

[T.]

1 – *The Sonnets and Ballate of Guido Cavalcanti* (Boston: Small, Maynard, 1912).

2 – EP wrote on 5 Mar. (with Lady Rothermere in mind): 'I onnerstan that some of your hypocrites lecteuses are annoyed with you for printink Miss G. Stein.

'I haff chust recd. a article about the lady [Stein], somewhat personal, in fact somewhat in the young American tone; but readable, and alas
TOO true.

'D[orothy] says its amusing and that it wd amuse her mother. I pussnly dont quite see it in the Criterion, (as I remember that August and orderly publication, which, as reported, I have not seen for some years), but if you think it wd amuse you I will submit it to yr editorial acumen.'

3 – EP wrote on 11 Mar. about his 1912 edition of Guido Cavalcanti (c. 1255–1300): 'It wd of course fall that for the first time in my life I get into a argymint with a native, starting with a flagrant life of Dante by some scholastic, in which G Cs character is rammed by journalese method, i, e, neglect of the man's work.

'I don't mean its the first time I have tried to get a eyetalian to recognize the dif. Bet. G[uido] C[avalcanti] an let us say Petrarch . . . But still . . . copy of my text wd save time, So if you havent writ S. Maynard will you please go to it.'

## TO *Jack Isaacs*[1] CC

15 March 1926 [London]

Dear Isaacs,

Thank you for your letter of the 12th. I shall be delighted to come to your lecture if I can manage it.[2] But I am afraid that it is hardly possible because I have an appointment here at 6.30 and I should be obliged to leave before your lecture was finished which I should very much dislike to do. Is there any likelihood of your paper being published soon?

Sincerely yours,
[T. S. Eliot]

## TO *Rev. Francis Yealy* CC

16 March 1926 [London]

Dear Sir,

I am very much obliged to you for your letter of the 13th instant. I am very anxious to have my facts accurate before I revise my lectures for publication in book form.

I should like to ask you a further favour. Could you let me know what is considered the authentic text of the original Exercises of St Ignatius, together with the name of the publisher, as well as any English translation which recognises the difference between St Ignatius' own words and subsequent additions? This would be a great help to me. In the final preparation of my lectures I was obliged to depend on the resources of the

1–Jacob ('Jack') Isaacs (1896–1973), English literary scholar, educationist and film critic, saw active service in France in WW1 in the Royal Garrison Artillery before going up to Exeter College, Oxford, to take his degree in English Language and Literature. In 1924 he became an Assistant Lecturer in English at King's College, London, and a Lecturer from 1928. A founding member of the Film Society (1925–38), he performed in Eisenstein's *Lost*. Later he was the first Montefiore Professor of English at the Hebrew University of Jerusalem, 1942–5; then Professor of English Language and Literature at Queen Mary College, London, 1952–64. Famed for his enthralling lectures, and with redoubtable skills as textual editor, bibliographer, theatre historian and radio broadcaster, his writings included *Coleridge's Critical Terminology* (English Association, 1936), *An Assessment of Twentieth-Century Literature* (1951) and *The Background of Modern Poetry* (1951). He edited, with William Rose, *Contemporary Movements in European Literature* (1928). The circumstances of his first meeting with TSE are not known, but they quickly became firm friends.

2–Isaacs was to lecture 'on Shakespeare as a possible producer and practical wielder of theatrecraft'. This lecture was ultimately published as *Production and Stage-Management at the Blackfriars Theatre* (Shakespeare Association, 1935).

London Library. As you are probably aware, I chose the exercise which I quoted because of the striking similarity of imagery to that of Donne, and I am still of the opinion that Donne's mind is partly Jesuit and partly Calvinist.

I was certainly under the misapprehension that I was quoting from St Ignatius himself, although I was of course aware that the Exercises were, and are, used by directors who have considerable scope in the handling of their own patients.

I confess that I maintain my prejudice in favour of the methods and frame of mind of the thirteenth century. You have no doubt gathered that my criticisms were not directed against your church but against the seventeenth century and against the weaknesses of that century which I believe to be revealed in both Roman and Protestant churches of the time. I was more concerned with the similarities between Jesuism, Lutheranism and Calvinism and their common differences from the thirteenth century than with the similarities between Catholicism and the two centuries as against Protestantism. In other words my division is historical and not sectarian. In the same way I associated Cardinal Newman with Coleridge on the one hand and Walter Pater on the other as representatives of the nineteenth century, instead of contrasting the religious and heterodox movements within the century.

Until you persuade me to the contrary I remain in sympathy with the Dominican tradition in contrast to the Jesuit tradition. I have perhaps expressed myself with some prolixity in order to make the simple point that I am not so much interested in the opposition between Catholicism and Protestantism as I am in what I believe to be differences within the Catholic church.

With many thanks,
I remain,
Yours faithfully,
[T. S. Eliot]

## TO *Owen Barfield*[1] CC

16 March 1926 [London]

Dear Mr Barfield,

I am returning with regret two manuscripts. One I should have been glad to use before now but for a vast accumulation; and now that your book has appeared it is too late; the other interests me very much and seems to be working along a new line for you. I do not feel that you have quite reached the necessary point, though I hardly know why. But will you let me see some more of your work soon?

With all best wishes,
Sincerely yours,
[T. S. Eliot]

## TO *Michael Bolloten* CC

16 March 1926 [London]

Dear Mr Bolloten,

I have your letter and am extremely sorry to hear that so much effort has been expended with so little result.[2] I cannot at the moment think of any other avenue to explore.

I should, however, like to see you again before you make up your mind what to do. I am extremely busy throughout this week, but I could see you

1–Owen Barfield (1898–1997), writer, philosopher, anthroposophist, studied at Wadham College, Oxford, where he took a first in English Language and Literature, 1921. (At Oxford he and C. S. Lewis – whom he later called 'the most unforgettable friend – part of the furniture of my existence' – became founder-members, with J. R. R. Tolkien, Charles Williams and Lord David Cecil, of the Inklings: see *Owen Barfield on C. S. Lewis*, ed. G. B. Tennyson, 1989.) From 1929 to 1959 he worked as a solicitor in his father's law firm. His publications include *History in English Words* (1926), *Poetic Diction: A Study in Meaning* (1928), *Romanticism Comes of Age* (1944), *Worlds Apart* (1963), *Unancestral Voice* (1965), *What Coleridge Thought* (1971) and *The Rediscovery of Meaning* (1979). TSE was to tell Richard de la Mare on 15 July 1962: 'I feel very strongly that Barfield is an author too valuable to let go. Of course he is difficult to sell but I think he will make his mark in the long run. I myself have a high regard for his work and I think you have also.'

2–Michael Bolloten had been desperately trying to secure a job; his home life was 'growing terrible', he said, and he hoped to work in a magazine or publishing office: 'correcting MSS, etc. would be something, and I can also type a bit, though I can't do shorthand' (15 Mar.). However, he was 'good at remembering the frocks worn in theatrical shows', and could design things. 'Any more – at least, another fortnight, – of this will drive me frantic . . . I'm tired to death of tracing the streets of London in looking for a job and then having to suffer mental agonies at the table each night.'

here next Monday afternoon if you would write and name a time from 3 o'clock. I might be able to see you sooner and if you wish to see me this week I should suggest your ringing up this number, during the afternoon, to find out whether I am here.

Yours sincerely,
[T. S. Eliot]

## TO *Allen Tate*[1] CC

16 March 1926 [London]

Dear Mr Tate,

I am returning your essay on Marianne Moore because Miss Moore's work is not yet well enough known here to have reached the point at which such analyses are possible for the British Public. But I was very much struck by some of your incidental observations and wondered whether you could not turn this essay inside out, or write another one, making the modern attitude of people like More and Babbitt towards past ages the principal theme. If such a notion appeals to you, please let me know.[2] I should like to keep your poems for the present: I think I may be able to use some of them.[3]

Yours sincerely
[T. S. Eliot]

1–Allen Tate (1899–1979), American poet, critic, editor and educator: see Biographical Register.

2–Tate (26 March) did not wish just then to rewrite his piece on Moore but he was interested in doing an essay on Paul Elmer More – 'a moralist . . . developing his viewpoint through literature' – whom he thought 'a superior critic' to Irving Babbitt. Professor of French at Harvard, Babbitt had been one of TSE's most influential teachers: see 'The Humanism of Irving Babbitt' (1928); *SE* (1932). Babbitt had written to Dean B. R. Briggs of Harvard on 27 Feb. 1914: 'I understand that Mr. Thomas S. Eliot is a candidate for a Sheldon Fellowship. He did unusually good work for me a few years ago in French 17. From my knowledge of him both in the classroom and outside of it, I have no hesitation in recommending him as a man of both intellectual and personal distinction.' In due course, Tate contributed 'The Fallacy of Humanism', C. 8 (July 1929), 661–81, which also appeared in *The Hound & Horn* 3 (Jan.–Mar. 1930), 234–57; repr. as 'Humanism and Naturalism' in *Reactionary Essays on Poetry and Ideas* (1936).

3–Tate had submitted three (unidentified) poems on 28 Feb.

## TO *Messrs John Grant* CC

16 March 1926 [London]

YOUR CATALOGUE FOR MARCH NO. 1357a

Dear Sirs,

I was very disappointed to find that the fifteen volumes set of the works of Saint Augustine which you have sent me is merely an English translation without the Latin text. What I particularly wanted was a Latin edition, and I would point out that in your catalogue it is stated merely that this edition is 'edited' by Marcus Dods but not that it is translated.[1] As this edition is of no use to me, I should be obliged if you would receive it back. I will gladly pay you the full amount of the invoice on hearing from you, if you will credit me with the price of this set against future purchases.

I should be glad to know if you would let me know whenever a complete Latin text of the works of Saint Augustine falls into your hands. I am also anxious to pick up odd volumes of the Migne *Patrologia Latina*. The volumes which I should particularly like to obtain are those containing the works of the following:

Richard of Saint Victor
Hugh of Saint Victor
Saint Anselm
Saint Thomas
Saint Bonaventura
John of Salisbury
Erigena and Dionysius
Saint Bernard

I await your reply. When I return the Saint Augustine to you I shall be glad if you will send me the set of Hawthorne mentioned in previous correspondence.[2]

1–Marcus Dods, *The Works of Aurelius Augustine, Bishop of Hippo: A New Translation* (1872–6).

2–The set of Hawthorne (Walter Scott Ltd) supplied by the Edinburgh booksellers remains in TSE's library, though one volume is missing. TSE was to write to Ezra Pound on 8/10 Dec. 1933: 'My great-grandfather was on same witch jury with Nat Hawthorne's great-grandfather; and I naturally smell out witches etc.' To Geoffrey Curtis, TSE wrote on 20 Oct. 1943: 'Hawthorne is, I think, about the best prose writer America produced. In my own opinion, *The House of the Seven Gables* is a greater book than *The Scarlet Letter* and I think the best that he ever wrote. Perhaps I am not a fair judge. It must mean more to me for traditional reasons than it would to an English reader. Hawthorne's background is so much the same as mine both in physical and theological environment. As a matter of fact, his first ancestor in America and mine both engaged in the pursuit of hanging witches in Salem.'

Yours faithfully,
[T. S. Eliot]

P.S. My secretary will see that the set of Saint Augustine is dispatched to you tomorrow.

## TO *Sydney E. Hooper*[1] CC

16 March 1926 [London]

Dear Sir,

I thank you for your letter of the 15th instant concerning a possible course of lectures on Aesthetics to be delivered at your Institute during the summer of next year.

I am considerably flattered by your invitation, but I must with regret acquaint you with the fact that I am quite unqualified to lecture on such a subject as Aesthetics. I am only a writer of verse and a literary critic.

With many thanks,
Yours faithfully,
[T. S. Eliot]

## TO *Richard Aldington* TS Texas

17 March 1926 *The New Criterion*

My dear Richard,

Very many thanks for your letter of the 15th.[2] The series interests me very much and I know enough about Rougier[3] to believe him to be absolutely reliable and really one of the first rate minds in France.

1 – Sydney E. Hooper (1880–1966): Director of Studies at the British Institute of Philosophical Studies; editor of *Philosophy*.

2 – 'I enclose the prospectus of a French series of 15 books, dealing with the opponents of Christianity. The editor, Rougier, is an admirable fellow and a type dans le genre de Renan. I have a sort of option to deal with the English and American rights, which Routledge have refused to take up . . . Would you be inclined to consider it . . .? . . . If Faber and Gwyer would do the series, I would undertake to arrange the English translations and to act as English editor, on the same terms as for Routledge, viz. a small overhead royalty on each copy, the exact percentage to depend on the published price of the book (. . . it would be 3% on a 7/6 book and 4% on a 10/6 book).'

3 – Louis Rougier (1889–1982), philosopher, taught at the University of Besançon, 1925–48; noted for his work in epistemology, inc. *Les Paralogismes du rationalisme: essai sur la théorie de la connaissance* (1920), and for his opposition to Christianity in *La Scolastique et le thomisme* (1924) and *Celse contre les chrétiens* (1925).

I have discussed the matter of translating the series and we have come to the following conclusions which I set down in a rather haphazard manner. From the point of view of British sale, we think that a different title ought to be given to the series, and that the series really falls into two parts one of which would be much more valuable than the other. The first six or seven volumes appear to me extremely valuable and might have a great deal of interest for the more intelligent clericals of this country. The first seven volumes will be really important documents in the study of the history of Christianity. But the volumes from VIII to XV are more sporadic studies in the history of anti-Christianity which is quite a different matter, and, in a way, cannot be said to be history at all. The Nietzsche and the Gourmont (although any books by Gaultier[1] or Rougier must be interesting) would conflict with our own series; and after your *Voltaire* what sale could there be for *Voltaire* written from such a special point of view? Furthermore, I think that to emphasise editorially the anti-Christian character of the work of such men as Bruno,[2] Spinoza[3] or Valla[4] is just the way to kill it with the British Public.

As, therefore, it seemed to me that the series fell definitely into two parts and that the second part really injured the first, I recommended Faber to consider taking over the first seven. For several reasons he is not inclined at the moment to launch into a programme which would involve the outlay of perhaps a couple of thousand pounds. We are assuming that we should have to pay about fifty pounds to any good translator; the volumes would be of a good size and would not be cheap to produce; and of course many people would buy the French edition with which we could not possibly compete in price.

1–Jules de Gaultier (1858–1942): French philosopher; advocate of Nietzsche, as in *De Kant à Nietzsche* (1900), and famous for propounding the concept of Bovarysme (based on the novel by Flaubert) – *Le Bovarysme: essai sur le pouvoir d'imaginer* (1902), which argued for the continual capacity of humans to deceive themselves.

2–Giordano Bruno (1548–1600): Italian Dominican friar, philosopher, mathematician and cosmologist; infamous as a proponent of the conception of an infinity of worlds. Condemned by the Roman Inquisition, he was burned to death.

3–Baruch de Spinoza (1632–77), Dutch philosopher most famous for his *Ethica Ordine Geometrico Demonstrata* (1677), usually known by the simple title *Ethics*. His works were to be placed for some time on the Index Librorum Prohibitorum.

4–Lorenzo Valla (1406–57), Italian humanist, rhetorician, philologist, controversialist, wrote under the protection of Alfonso V of Aragon. He was renowned for his eloquent defence of Epicureanism in his dialogue *De Voluptate*, and for his critique of the post-Classical corruptions of Latin prose style, *De elegantia linguae latinae* (1444); famous too for exposing a hoax: *De falso credita et ementita Constantini Donatione declamatio*.

I should, however, be very much inclined to undertake the first volume which has already appeared, without committing ourselves to any of the subsequent volumes until we had seen them. Even so, I do not think that we would consider volumes VIII to XV.[1]

If Rougier would consider our publishing a translation of Volume I, I should be very glad to hear. And if we did arrange to publish the first volume, we should certainly like to have an option on the other six. Would he send us a copy to examine?

If we came to an agreement in this form, I should certainly like to have you act as English editor, on the general terms you outline.

If you are in touch with Rougier, I should very much like to get a contribution to the *Criterion* from him.[2]

With very many thanks,

Yours ever,
Tom.

## *Henry Eliot* TO *His Mother*

MS Houghton

17 March 1926 [London]

[Extract]

Tom & Vivien are well and are moving into their house. I have not seen the house, but they say it is somewhere back of Buckingham Palace. Tom's work seems to me not very heavy: although he has numerous engagements. He is not in his office a great deal of the time. It is a very pleasant office in a fine big house newly done over, in a fine big square just back of the British Museum.[3]

1–RA replied on 19 Mar.: 'Do you think F. & G. would make a definite offer for Rougier's Celsus and take up an option on the whole series? In answer to your objection about stressing the anti-Christian bias of Spinoza, Bruno and Valla, *nota bene* that Rougier says he has "aucun caractère polémique" . . . I feel that an offer for half the series or rather for one book and an option on six others is too timid.'

2–RA (19 Mar.): 'will you see if the introduction to Celsus would do as an article. If not, I will send you the Rationalisme book as soon as I get it . . .'

3–24 Russell Square.

## *Henry Eliot* TO *His Mother*

MS Houghton

21 March 1926 57 Chester Terrace, S.W.1.

[Extract]

Lady O.[1] expressed so much affection for Tom and thought he was the greatest poet of the period, but berated Vivien a good deal for being hysterical over her health and making Tom cancel many engagements at the last minute. She thought Vivien jealous of Tom's many friendships and recognition, and altogether too touchy. She said that Tom never admitted Vivien's faults but that people understood his problems.

## *Vivien Eliot* TO *Mary Hutchinson*

MS Texas

[Postmarked 25 March 1926] 57 Chester Terrace, S.W.1.

My dear Mary

I have been wishing to see you before you go away. You don't know how much I want to see you. We began to move here before I quite got over having influenza so that I was more than commonly inefficient. You know what moving from one end of London to another feels like, but your move was towards civilization[2] & our move *feels* – at present – like a plunge into the outer suburbs. We have put Tom's brother & his new wife into Clarence Gate, which we left as neat as a pin for them. Whenever we go there now, or think of them there we are in a rage.

I sit here in the middle of the most frightful chaos. It is a terrible house. The workmen have all had to come back as the paint never dried & we were covered with it.[3] They have now removed it all & are starting again. Ellen is leaving on Saturday (to be married!) & then I shall only have a mad ex-policeman aged 70, to help.[4] I am trying very hard to get straight before she goes & to get someone in her place. I don't think I shall ever

1–OM had entertained Henry and Theresa Eliot to 'early tea' at her home, Garsington Manor, Oxfordshire, on 20 Mar.

2–The Hutchinsons had moved from Hammersmith to 3 Albert Road, Regent's Park.

3–TSE would write to his brother on 3 May 1932 that he had taken the house at 57 Chester Terrace 'because I thought Vivienne wanted it and then finding that she did not like it – it was about the worst small house in London'. He would recall too, in a letter to John Hayward, 21 Dec. 1944: 'It was not until after I had had that house in Chester Terrace for some months that I discovered that the River Westbourne ran (after passing through a tube over the railway line at Sloane Sq. station) directly under it, causing fungus on the basement walls.'

4–William Leonard Janes, an ex-policeman who had worked for TSE since 1924.

see any of my friends again! If you were not going away I shd certainly have come over to see you some dark night next week. But there are only 3 days left this week & I dare not leave the house. I promise to have it clean & tidy by the time you come back & then after I have come to see you I will ask you to visit us & inspect.

Meanwhile we send our love.

Yr
Vivien

I suppose you do not know of a hard-working woman, or girl, or a man & wife?

I hope you will enjoy your holiday.

## TO *Dorothy Todd*[1] CC

25 March 1926 [London]

Dear Miss Todd,

This letter is to introduce to you Mr Michael Bolloten who is very anxious to get work either in the reviewing of plays and novels or in the designing of dresses. He has already had some experience, I understand, in the latter profession, and tells me that a design of his has just been accepted by one of the Sunday newspapers. As unfortunately I had no work in the way of reviewing to give him because the scope of *The New Criterion* is so limited and the number of regular contributors so large, I thought that possibly he might be able to do some designing for *Vogue*, and therefore take the liberty of sending him to call on you with this letter of introduction.

Yours sincerely
[T. S. Eliot]

1 – Dorothy Todd was editor, 1922–6, of British *Vogue*, which she sought to make increasingly literary (Aldous Huxley and Raymond Mortimer were on the staff for a time, and Todd developed friendships with other writers including VW, Rebecca West and Ivy Compton-Burnett). When Todd was sacked in 1926, VW was to gossip to her sister Vanessa Bell: 'It is said that Condé Nast threatened to reveal Todds private sins, if she sued them, so she is taking £1,000, and does not bring an action' (*Letters* III, 295). Todd's later publications include *The New Interior Decoration* (with Raymond Mortimer, 1929). See N. Luckhurst, *Bloomsbury in Vogue* (1998); and Anne Pender, '"Modernist Madonnas": Dorothy Todd, Madge Garland and Virginia Woolf', *Women's History Review* 16: 4 (Sept. 2007), 519–33.

## TO *Michael Bolloten* CC

26 March 1926 [London]

Dear Mr Bolloten,

I am sorry that private circumstances have prevented my attending at my office for several days, but I enclose herewith the introduction to the Editress of *Vogue* which I promised you.[1] I hope that something may come of it, and I shall be interested to hear the result.

Sincerely yours
[T. S. Eliot]
(IPF)

Dictated by Mr Eliot and signed by his secretary after he had left the office.

## *Vivien Eliot* TO *Ottoline Morrell* MS Texas

27 March [1926] 57 Chester Terrace, S.W.1.

Dearest Ottoline

Please forgive me for not writing before. Tom wrote to you that I had influenza – that was after I had been to Cambridge. On top of that my family arrived from Rome, & my brother only for 3 days so that I had to

1–TSE had two interviews with Bolloten: he had no work for him, but promised to introduce him to *Vogue*. Bolloten wrote to TSE on 24 Mar. with the news that his father was threatening to send him out of the house if he went on 'doing nothing'. 'Couldn't you just try me with a play-review?' he begged TSE. 'You can't imagine the agony I have to go through, and yesterday was a vile disappointment, – all the more so, because you mentioned in our first interview that, even if you did not find my specimens suitable, you would yet try me with the review of a play. I can now only assume that either my personality or my work must have grated on you.' He thereupon posted off a further long letter of the same date, lamenting that he was so 'unpractical, self-conscious, morbid, changeable and temperamental'. He recalled that TSE had said to him, only the day before: 'Surely a boy who can criticize the drama ought to be businesslike, too.' Bolloten reflected on TSE's words: 'That's just the funny thing about me. I have always been the same.' He was useless at the practical things of life; he had always loved Shakespeare, plays and the opera, but he felt quite unlike other boys: he was hopeless at sports – he was not 'able even to cane a ball'. He went on: 'Pardon me for writing confidentially, but – I am sure it is not a delusion on my part – you seem as if you might be interested in me. Oh, believe me, it's hateful feeling that everybody thinks I'm worthless when I know too well what beautiful things are inside me . . . Yes, I am sure you must be thinking I'm a little bit hysterical. Yet I am sure you sympathize. I need someone so badly to appreciate me a little . . . Everything happens inside me, I can never reveal myself to anybody. I hope you will see me again. I should like to see you often, but I daren't hope for such a favour on your part. Besides, I am so much younger.'

get up rather soon. Then we had to move, & to put the Henry Eliots into the flat (where they are now).

I have been wanting to write to you all this time. You are *always* in my thoughts. It is *so* good of you to invite us to Garsington. When I saw you I forgot to mention to you my greatest trouble. Ellen[1] (Sarah) is being married again. She has been engaged for a year & a half & never told me until 3 weeks ago, because she wd never leave me until she felt I was better, & more or less settled & 'safe'. She has been my greatest – best – almost only friend for 9 years. She left today & has just gone. She has worked like a slave to get us settled in this house & to leave it all clean & perfect & has been hunting everywhere to find me someone else, herself. She has done all the interviewing & going about. I *believe* she has found us a good woman who will come on Monday. So now you see what has been happening. I gave Ellen yr invitation! which delighted her. She always thought more of you than of anyone we ever knew. You, *& Bertie*! Well, before I leave this subject, as Ellen is being married next Saturday, *will* you, please, I beg, send her a few flowers? She would be so *fear*fully *proud*. Forgive my asking it, I hope you understand.

The house is very lonely after a flat. And hard work – stairs & muddles. And so strange being in this neighbourhood – rather cut off & isolated.

I was wondering if it wd not be better if you could find us 2 rooms in the village for when we come for the weekend? Might it not be better? I could then see you as much as you cared to see *me*, & I shd not be in the way or worry your family, I am so exceedingly dull at present, & although I know you will bear with me out of your friendship & yr goodness of heart, I cannot hope that other people would. I do hope that you will see what I mean by this, & by no means be offended with me. You see things are not what they were. One gets old, & life looks different. I long to talk to you. And I thought perhaps that wd be the best way. Any weekend after April 10. Do say you are coming to London this summer. I hope so above all things. With my love, Excuse this dreadful letter,

Ever yours
Vivian

1 – Ellen Kellond married William Sollory, who lived in Bushey, Hertfordshire, and worked in the metal industry.

## TO *His Mother* TS Houghton

29 March 1926 *The New Criterion*

Dearest Mother,

This is merely a business letter to enclose Cobden-Sanderson's bill[1] and a copy of the contract for you to sign. It seems to me perfectly fair, and if you will sign it and return it to me I will exchange it against the copy which he will sign and will forward the copy signed by him to you.

We are still waiting to hear whether any American publisher will take a certain number of unbound copies. If not, we shall of course try some of the principal booksellers in Boston and New York. Fifty or sixty copies have already been sold and a good many have been distributed for review by Cobden-Sanderson or as presentation copies by myself. I am hopeful that a certain number may be sold in America, even if no American publisher takes it up.

Your loving son
Tom.

## TO *Richard Aldington* TS Texas

29 March 1926 *The New Criterion*

My dear Richard,

First, I am suggesting to the members[2] that we should now alter one *Criterion* dinner from Fridays to Tuesdays. When they were originally arranged, Tuesdays were impossible for me because I had to be in Cambridge, but my impression is that I was the only person affected by that day of the week. Will you let me know whether there is any more likelihood of your being able to come if we hold them on Tuesdays? It struck me that Tuesdays would suit your business arrangements very much better.

I think that it is now quite definite that we do not want to risk either Rougier's series or even his *Celsus* alone.[3] The subject is interesting

1–The bill of £55 10s. 6d. was for the printing of 300 copies of *Savonarola*.

2–Members of the 'Criterion Club'.

3–Louis Rougier, *Celse contra les chrétiens* (1925). The Greek Epicurean philosopher Celsus had assailed Christianity in his (now lost) treatise *Discours véritable*, otherwise known as *Discours contre les chrétiens*. RA replied on 30 Mar.: 'I am glad to have a definite decision in the case of Rougier's series. Will you let me have by return the copy of his "Celse" and the correspondence and leaflets I sent you? I liked the tone and views of Rougier's preface so much that I shall make every effort to place the series for him.'

and important and I do not question Rougier's scholarship. But the introduction struck me as somewhat too anti-clerical in tone, as well as being a tissue of dubious generalities.[1] Another difficulty is that in order to make the book really substantial we should have to go to the trouble and expense of getting a competent person to translate *Celsus* direct from Greek into English, as well as another to translate Rougier.

On the other hand I am very keen about publishing Rougier's *Paralogismes*.[2] Do not bother to send me the book, I have it. It would be a big thing to do and we should want an expert opinion. This will take a little time as the universities are in vacation and we should try to get some mathematical-philosophical authority to pronounce upon it. If you are in correspondence with Rougier, will you let him know the possibility and tell him that we consider very favourably this translation and are only awaiting the expert opinion? I should also be grateful if you would tell him that I should be very glad to have for the *Criterion* some unpublished contribution by him.[3] I will send him a copy. I am extremely sorry that I could not connect with you on Saturday and I apologise for not having wired you to that effect, but I have been moving and this has prevented me from attending to anything else. Please note our new private address:

57 Chester Terrace,
Eaton Square,
S.W.1.

If I get over to Paris this spring I should certainly like to see Rougier, and, as you say, that would be much more satisfactory. Meanwhile, we thank you very much for your kindness in letting us have this opportunity. I think that we can bring the *Paralogismes* book off unless Rougier settles with somebody else first.

Yours ever,
Tom.

1 – 'As to the Celsus and Rougier's preface,' said RA (7 Apr.), 'I am . . . not competent to decide whether it is made up of "dubious generalities" but its implicit defence of Hellenic good sense and balance, and of Roman tolerance, pleased me very much.'

2 – *Les Paralogismes du rationalisme: essai sur la théorie de la connaissance* (1920) set out a conventionalist epistemology allied to the logical positivism of the Vienna Circle.

3 – 'I hope you will not mind', wrote RA, 'if I also try to place his Paralogismes elsewhere . . . I feel that your offer is too general and vague to make any basis for discussion. I also feel that it would be better for him to have all his books issued by one publisher . . . With regard to articles – I will certainly inform Rougier that you wish to have unpublished work from him . . . I will let you have first refusal of any unpublished work he sends me.'

## TO *Bruce Richmond* CC

29 March 1926 [London]

Dear Richmond,

Yes. The Cambridge lectures are over. Many thanks for your kind letter which I have left unanswered for a week.[1] The fact is that I have been moving and have had other responsibilities at the same time, such as a brother and sister-in-law both in a nursing home. Of course I am, as always, very much tempted by your suggestion, but I look at the three books which you have given me and which weigh very much on my conscience, and I am determined to refuse even the most tempting suggestion until they are done. I still want to keep my nose down to column reviews for you for several months consecutively before facing a leader.

May I suggest that Bonamy Dobrée knows Otway very well and I imagine would be delighted to have the opportunity of writing a leader about him and would do it as competently as anybody.[2] In fact he would probably do it in a way more satisfactory to the general public than mine, because I should probably make it only an occasion for an essay on the development of the eighteenth century mind. Though I should have liked to try to convert you, because I really enjoy Otway.

When I have cleared my name by reviewing these three books I shall write to you again.

Sincerely yours,
[T. S. Eliot]

1 – 'Are the Cambridge lectures over?' BLR had asked on 17 Mar. 'If so, I should be very glad of something from you for the Supplements of April 1 and 8.'

2 – 'I see the Nonesuch Press are publishing a complete Otway – a good deal of whom I read last summer with immense boredom. Do you feel inclined to write us a leader on him and (incidentally) convert me?'

## TO *T. O. Beachcroft*[1] CC

29 March 1926 [London]

Dear Beachcroft,

I am very glad to hear from you; I had feared that we had lost contact altogether. I am glad to hear that you are in London.[2] You do not say whether your occupation restricts your liberty within certain hours, but would it be possible for you to have lunch or tea with me one day, say the latter part of next week. If you have not the time to call here for me, I might be able to meet you in some part of town near your work.

Sincerely yours,
[T. S. Eliot]

## *Henry Eliot* TO *His Mother* MS Houghton

[postmarked 31 March 1926] 57, Chester Terrace

Dear Mother –

I am writing a note at Tom's, while waiting to have dinner with him. Vivien is meanwhile having dinner with Theresa. We had tea at Tom's day before yesterday, and admired the house very much. It is on a charming little street, full of little houses in a row, all much alike, with iron fences in front of each and pretty doors. There is a little living room on the first floor and a bedroom back of it. Below (in the basement) is a neat and light kitchen. You go out of the kitchen into a back yard which is below the level of the street. The back yard is paved with old flagstones with a garden bed running around three sides, and a brick wall also. All the houses in the row have such back yards. Tom says that in June he is going to give a garden party in the back yard. Upstairs is a large bedroom and another room. I do not know what other rooms there are but the house, while small, is ample for them and very comfortable. Tom said Vivien had been discouraged about the house but was much cheered up by Theresa's and my enthusiasm over it. It is clean and bright and needs only more

1–Thomas Owen Beachcroft (1902–88), author. In a testimonial addressed to the Overseas Establishment Officer of the BBC, TSE would write on 12 June 1941: 'I have known Mr T. O. Beachcroft for many years and . . . I have a high opinion of him . . . His background is excellent, he is a man of culture and charm and, I believe, of unexceptional character.'

2–Beachcroft sent some more of his poetry on 24 Mar. He was working as an advertising copywriter (Paul E. Derrick Advertising Agency). 'I have perpetrated a series of children's stories which Heinemann are sufficiently misguided to think that they may do something with. This is not certain but hopeful.'

furniture and pictures. But I believe they have some other furniture – some at Tom's old office (Faber & Gwyer's I suppose). I understand from the Haigh-Woods[1] that they had a summer house – where I do not know – and have sold it. They do not own this house but rent it. Tom's rent at 9 Clarence Gate is £150 or $750 a year and he has a lease for two years more. He says rents are going up in that neighborhood and that he can profitably sub-let their flat furnished, as they have this other furniture from the summer house.

I will send with this some photographs taken at Oxford & Warwick. I took some of Tom today, inside and outside his office, and hope they will be good. This afternoon Theresa & I went to Hampstead Heath. This morning to the Victoria & Albert (Kensington) Museum, which Theresa enjoyed immensely.

Later:–

Had a most pleasant dinner with Tom. The dining room is downstairs, next to the kitchen and is small but cosy. We talked about all of you and about books and about Vivien and Theresa. Tom says V. is perfectly well now though subject to querulous moods occasionally. Both Tom and V. like Theresa immensely and Tom thinks Theresa has a tonic effect and it is good for V. to be with her. Tom says V. has taken a strong liking to Theresa.

I will put in photos tomorrow and mail this. We leave for France early day after tomorrow morning.

Affectionately
Henry.

Your 2 letters received (one forwarded back from Paris) very glad to get them & showed 1 to Tom.

1–Charles Haigh-Wood (1854–1927), TSE's father-in-law. Born in Bury, Lancashire, he attended Manchester Art College and (from 1873) the Royal Academy School in London: he exhibited in the Academy three years later. He became a member of the RA and pursued a career as a portrait and genre painter. On his mother's death, he inherited properties in Ireland – the portfolio comprised 1, 3, 4 & 5 Haigh Terrace, Dun Laoghaire, Dublin; 1 to 10 Eglinton Park; Eglington Park House, Spencer Hill, Tivoli Road (Dublin 6th District): the Irish property was valued in Dec. 1927 as £6,390 – and was thus well supported by the rental income. He and his wife Rose Esther moved to West Hampstead in 1891, settling at 3 Compayne Gardens. According to TSE (Oct. 1920), Vivien was 'particularly fond of her father; she takes more after him and his side of the family, and understands him better than the others do.' Maurice Haigh-Wood advised Robert Sencourt on 6 Oct. 1968: 'My father was a kindly & simple man & my mother a very loving mother & both very quickly recognised Tom's sincerity & high character & they took him to their hearts as a son-in-law' (Donald Adamson Papers).

## *Vivien Eliot* TO *Ottoline Morrell* MS Texas

[?early April] 1926 (Temporarily) 9 Clarence Gate Gardens. N.W.1

My dearest Ottoline

Thank you *so* much for your charming & affectionate letter. It was the greatest pleasure to hear from you. Especially as when one is ill for a very long time one begins to feel that one has no friends left – a fearful feeling of isolation. It is indeed *awful* that you have been in London for months & that I have never seen you. It is a dreadful catastrophe, because you so seldom settle in London for any length of time. *Of course,* I have seen *no one*. Only a lot of miserable doctors. I *was* much better, & we had moved to the house in Chester Terrace, where I was looking forward to being your neighbour for a time, when suddenly my parents arrived in England, (when all the worst was over!) & bore down on me & settled down in a hotel with nothing on earth to do but interfere with me & shout advice in my ears & sit over me & make my life a hell. I very soon got shingles then, owing I believe, to the extra dose of misery, & as we had *great* difficulty with servants there, the only thing was to rush back to cover in this flat. We had, & do intend to let this flat furnished as it wd be a dead loss to *give it up*. (We have a fairly long lease, & they let furnished very well). To continue this boring tale of afflictions, I have been laid up with shingles ever since & am all stuck up with bandages & ointments & loathsomeness. My father & mother are still sitting over me & driving me to desperation but they are leaving on Monday. But *you* are leaving on Sunday. I might have seen you at the last minute but I am too involved in parental toils to call a moment my own. Isn't it *horrible*? Being helpless I can do nothing. They come *every* day, or *twice* a day. If I live till Monday I shall be surprised.

All the same I feel too degraded & bandaged & in a mess (with my hair about 3 inches down my back) even to see *you* with satisfaction. One of the worst features of this complaint is that you may not have a bath. You can scarcely *wash*, & to move is intolerable.

Yes, Tom is learning at a motor school, altho' we shall never be able to afford a car. My one, my only remaining ambition is to have a car & drive to Garsington to see you!

With ever ever so much love, dearest Ottoline, & the most bitter regrets – (I can hardly say how I have felt it)

Your affectionate old friend
Vivien

No. I have not lived in a wonderful world of my own. I was soon dragged out of that. I have lived in a world of unpleasant unrealities. I have read nothing interesting – only Law, statistics, Constitutional history, & I may yet turn into a barrister.

Tom felt I needed some very *hard* food for my mind, & I have always hankered after the Law, so he turned me onto it – it really *is*, to me, fascinating.

## TO *Sydney E. Hooper* CC

1 April 1926 [*The Monthly Criterion*]

Dear Sir,

I am greatly flattered by your taking the trouble to write to me again, but I must state firmly that I think I know my own limitations and that I am convinced of my incompetence.[1] My only theory of aesthetics is the theory of the difference between aesthetics and literary criticism, and my theory implies that I know something of literary criticism but nothing of aesthetics.

Yours faithfully,
[T. S. Eliot]

1 – Hooper had written again on 17 Mar. in the 'hope' that it was only 'modesty' that caused TSE to say he was unqualified to lecture on Aesthetics. Might he reconsider?

## TO *A. E. Housman*[1] CC

1 April 1926 [London]

Dear Mr Housman,

It has been one of my ambitions since becoming an editor to publish a really authoritative and final essay on Wilkie Collins. Several people have intimated to me that it is a subject about which you know everything, and that if I could induce you to write a paper on Wilkie Collins I should be performing a public service and proving my own editorial ability.

I write, therefore, without the slightest ray of hope, but if you should hold out to me any prospect of your considering such a task, I should, during an indefinite future, refuse any other contributions on that subject.[2]

Yours sincerely,
[T. S. Eliot]

1–A. E. Housman (1859–1936): poet and classical scholar; Fellow of Trinity College, Cambridge. He had attended TSE's Clark Lectures, having declined to give the series himself – though it has been reported that TSE observed (from the lectern) that Housman assumed 'a face so impassive that he had no idea whether or not Housman had approved' (Hugh Lloyd Jones, *London Review of Books*, 22 Nov. 1979). According to George Watson, all the evidence points to the conclusion that Housman, who held a romantic view of poetry, disliked Eliot's arguments ('Eliot in Cambridge', *Never Ones for Theory?*, 46–9). Two years later, Housman was ready to criticise what he called 'the ignorance of Mr Eliot' concerning the meaning of Shelley's 'Ode to a Skylark': 'the silver sphere is the Morning Star, the planet Venus; and Shelley is giving a true description and using an apt comparison' (letter to the Editor of *The Times*, *c*.13 Dec, 1928; *The Letters of A. E. Housman*, ed. Archie Burnett (2007), II, 97). TSE seemed to take no offence: he was to send Housman an advance copy of *Journey of the Magi* inscribed 'A. E. Housman respectful homage of T. S. Eliot 17. 8. 27': see Schuchard, 'Editor's Introduction', *VMP*, 29–30. When Muriel St Clare Byrne proposed in 1931 to submit to *C.* an article that was critical of *A Shropshire Lad*, TSE responded: 'Housman was certainly a great influence twenty or thirty years ago, and I only just escaped his influence myself, but at the present day I feel that so far as *The Criterion* is concerned, he ought to be left to as tranquil an old age as he is capable of enjoying in the cloisters of Trinity. I hope I am not unduly affected by the fact that he has always been very pleasant to me and that I have found him a delightful person in conversation, but I do feel that it would be rather going out of our way to criticize him now' (7 Apr. 1931.

2–Housman replied on 2 Apr. that he was 'much flattered', but that his knowledge of Collins was not what TSE had been led to believe; and he had neither the talent nor – 'fortunately' – any inclination for literary criticism. He was glad TSE took an interest in the works of a novelist which he would like to see revived in a similarly successful way to those of Trollope – 'whose merit, whatever may be thought of their competitive value, was of a much less singular and original sort'.

## TO *Ezra Pound* TS Beinecke

1 April 1926 [*The New Criterion*]

Dear Ezra,

Yours of the 21st acknowledged. I like the enclosure which is the best criticism of Gertrude Stein that I have seen. Cannot yet decide whether possible to use it. Until decision made I do not enquire name of author, but should like to know later whether it would have to be published anonymously.[1]

Re. May. If you have any chance of letting flat, don't lose it for our sake. We shall not be able to decide positively until the eleventh hour. Am very grateful for trouble you have taken.

Re. Derek.[2] Have seen the boy and quite like him, but attempt has already been made here and it is not in my power to do more. Will communicate with you shortly.

Yrs.
T.

1–EP, who sent this letter on to Robert McAlmon (1896–1956), author of 'Gertrude Stein', typed at the foot: 'Dear R: So that's that. These things move with majestic slowness; so different from our own febrile tempo' (McAlmon, *Being Geniuses Together 1920–1930*, 228). EP told TSE he found the 'Portrait' 'TOO true' but did not 'quite see it' in *C.* TSE did not use it, and EP printed it in *The Exile* 4 (Autumn 1928), 70–4. It is reprinted, entitled 'Portrait', in *Being Geniuses Together*, 229–30.

2–Derek Patmore (1908–72), elder son of Brigit Patmore, was looking for a job in publishing. He was to become a playwright, travel writer and biographer; and he edited Coventry Patmore's poems and also his mother's memoirs, *My Friends when Young* (1968). In 'T. S. Eliot as a young man' (unpub. memoir, 1970), he recalled: 'I was anxious to work in publishing and follow a literary career. So one day [TSE] invited me to dine with him at Pagani's Restaurant, near the flat off Baker Street where he and Vivienne were living at the time. I was flattered and excited that he should ask me out alone, and my only fear [was] that I might bore – after all, I was only nineteen, and even in those days T. S. Eliot had a formidable reputation. We agreed that I should pick him up at his mansion flat. When I arrived and entered the living room, I stood for a moment rather shyly in the door. To my surprise, Tom turned to his wife Vivienne and exclaimed:

'"Isn't Derek beautiful?"

'It is true I was very tall and handsome at this age, and this remark, which I have never published before, confirmed a secret suspicion which I have always believed that T. S. Eliot had a hidden streak of homosexuality in his nature. It comes out at times in his poetry but he was very Puritan and careful to hide his real feelings.' (Father K. G. Schroeder, English Dept., Loras College, Dubuque, Iowa).

## TO *Ramon Fernandez* CC

1 April 1926 [London]

My dear Fernandez,

I was very glad to get your letter. Will it be possible for you to let us have your contributions by the 30th April? The summer number of *The Criterion* is to appear on June 15th instead of July 16th, so that we are rather pressed. I very much hope that you will be able to finish your notes on Newman by then, and should also be delighted if you would write me a note on the book of Prévost which you mentioned.[1] In fact I should be most happy if you could review some important book in the same way every quarter.

I am glad that you are interested in Richards's book.[2] I must warn you that it is not very well written and that it is badly arranged. This makes it difficult reading. I think that his next book will be much better written; he contributed an article to the *Criterion* last year which I think shows more development than anything in his book, and I am sending you a copy.[3]

If Gallimard thinks well of having a translation made, will you ask him to write to I. A. Richards at Magdalene College Cambridge of which he is a Fellow?[4] Richards will probably not reply very promptly because he will have left for a long voyage to America and China.

My wife asks to be remembered to you and we both look forward very keenly to our next meeting with you, whether in London or Paris.

Yours always sincerely
[T. S. Eliot]

1–'The Experience of Newman: Reply to Frederic Manning', *NC* 4 (Oct. 1926), 630–58. Fernandez asked (25 Mar.) to review *Plaisir des Sports*, by Jean Prévost.

2–I. A. Richards, *Science and Poetry* (1926).

3–I. A. Richards, 'A background for Contemporary Poetry', *C.* 3 (July 1925), 511–28. TSE's remarks are confusing, since IAR's *Criterion* article had already turned into chs. 5–7 of *Science and Poetry*: his 'next book' was *Practical Criticism* (1929).

4–Fernandez thought he could arrange to have IAR's book translated for Gallimard's new series *Collection dialogique*.

## TO *Alec Randall*[1]

TS Tulsa

1 April 1926 [*The New Criterion*]

Dear Randall,

Thank you for your letter of the 18th. Yes, I had ordered *Die Literarische Welt* and *Die Weltbühne* to be sent to you, and if you hear of any new periodicals which you would like to receive, I will get them for you.

We miss your presence at the fortnightly meetings which are now much more satisfactory than before, having been converted into dinners. The atmosphere of greater leisure has a beneficial effect on the conversation. I hope that we can arrange to have one of these dinners coincident with your next visit to England.

About *Nietzsche*, I am sorry to say that your suggestion had completely slipped from my mind. During the last six months I have been trying to organize a kind of series of critical biographies, which should cover some ground not already appropriated, such as The English Men of Letters. We originally intended it to be The Foreign Men of Letters, but discovered that such a series would almost inevitably conflict with Routledge's Republic of Letters. I am therefore trying to construct a Borderline of Letters series dealing with men who were primarily philosophers, moralists, historians, politicians, etcetera, but whose work has great literary value. Thus Nietzsche did fall into my series, but unfortunately I have offered that subject as well as Schopenhauer to Edwin Muir. Herewith is a tentative list of the series. I do not suppose that there is any name on the list which would interest you so much as Nietzsche, but it may suggest to your mind some other important writer, German or not, whom you would like to tackle. I hope this may be so and that I shall hear from you about it.

I envy you in Rome now and hope you are enjoying the life there thoroughly.

Yours ever
T. S. Eliot

1–Alec Randall (1892–1977), diplomat and writer: see Biographical Register.

## TO *Ottoline Morrell* MS Texas

5 April 1926 57 Chester Terrace

My dear Ottoline,

This is to thank you for your persistent kindness in inviting us. I want to ask you whether we could come one weekend in May – *any* weekend after the first. The reason is that we are going to Paris on Sunday next, at the invitation of my brother and sister in law, who are there. We *may* stay only a week, but we are going as their guests, and if they stay on, we may remain a fortnight. This would bring it up to the 24th, so that we dare not accept an invitation for that weekend.

We are *very* anxious to come. *Would the 8th or 15th be possible?*

We have been having very difficult times indeed. We had to start preparing for Ellen's wedding *at the same time* as moving in here – and you know how devoted & attached to Ellen Vivien is – she would not leave anything undone – buying presents etc. at the same time as engaging a new maid, & all sorts of things had to be put right about the house too – it is not really fit to live in yet. We went to the wedding as *witnesses*, at Paddington Registry Office, & that was a great strain, & then we had the bride & groom to a lunch at Frascati's[1] afterwards. This was very painful – we both felt that Ellen's husband was suspicious & jealous of us, & not nearly good enough for her: he has just lost his job as well – was very depressed – not *at all* friendly – and we are very worried about Ellen's future with him – doubt whether he will be good to her – and she has to look after his children. So we found the whole business exceedingly mournful & V. was quite knocked out.

Ellen was *delighted* with your flowers, and proud as punch, & wore them during the ceremony – (and what a wretched ceremony!)

On top of this, the ex-nurse who has been living with us to help V. with massage etc. is getting married on Saturday *next*, & I have let myself in for giving her away. I am cursing myself for a fool, as otherwise we could have gone to Paris *this week* in comfort. And Vivien is taking a lot of trouble over this too – she *will* take so much responsibility for other people – even when there is no occasion whatever.

1 – Frascati's, occupying a large gold-framed frontage at 32 Oxford Street, London, was a sumptuous restaurant decorated throughout in gold and silver. Opened in 1893, it featured a huge glass-domed dining-ballroom called the Winter Garden as well as smaller rooms for private functions; in the 1920s the head chef was a Belgian named Jules Matagne, who had been chef to the late King Leopold of the Belgians.

This is just to give you a superficial idea of the life we are living – but the difficulties are very great – much more than even you can imagine – and more than I can put in a hurried letter.

But know that you have given us support and help by your loyalty & kindness!

Very affectionately
Tom.

You gave my brother & sister a very happy afternoon. Thank you.

## *Henry Eliot* TO *His Mother*

MS Houghton

6 April 1926

Tuileries Hotel,
10 Rue Saint-Hyacinthe, Paris, 1er

[Extract]

We have been here Saturday, Sunday and Monday, all three days being holidays here, and so could not get letters from the American Express Company until this morning. Then I was much distressed to hear from you that you had not been so well, and to think that I had put upon you all that work of buying Tom's bonds . . . Do not think of it again. We have sold the stock and Tom can now write the Old Colony to invest it, and you will have no more responsibility.

I wrote you about Oxford and about Tom's comfortable circumstances. I took some pictures of Tom and hoped to have them today but they were not ready. On the last evening that we were in London Tom and Vivien and Theresa and I went to a hotel in Kensington to dinner and had such a jolly time. We then danced a while, Vivien was in fine humor and very nice. It seems she has taken a great fancy to Theresa. We stayed over four days in London principally to see them, as they had been so busy before, moving into their house on Chester Terrace, which as I wrote you is small but attractive and comfortable. Tom is so much pleased that Vivien likes Theresa and likes her so much himself, and was so grateful to us for I do not know what. But I believe it has done both Tom and Vivien a great deal of good to have us in London. It has toned Vivien up to make a new friend and it has brightened Tom up. Tom says he is writing a play of modern life, in which some of the characters of his poems appear again. Tom's office is easy to reach from Chester Terrace, by the Tube.

## TO *George Rylands* CC

8 April 1926 [*The New Criterion*]

Dear Rylands,

Please ring up here as soon as you are in London to find out whether I am in London too. It is possible that I may have to be in Paris for a week; but if not I should like you to lunch with me early in the week. I shall certainly be in London the following week and hope that you may prolong your visit.

Lucas's book has already been assigned.[1] Would you care to do the Nicolson *Swinburne* and the Garrod *Keats* as one review, i.e. as a comparative study of biographical criticism of poets. If so, write to my secretary and she will order the books for you.

Yours sincerely,
[T. S. Eliot]

## TO *Bonamy Dobrée* MS Brotherton

Thursday [?April 1926] 57, Chester Terrace, London

My dear Dobrée,

I am worried about the book, because it *was* the Daniel.[2] I brought it to give to you, put it on the piano, & forgot all about it. I went in the Comercio today, found the private room converted into a laundry, everything in disorder, & no sign of Daniel. But Madame promised to interrogate our waitress, who was out; so the enquiry is not quite finished. I cannot think that such a book could be mislaid. The last reveller may have spied it and taken it. But if after 'exploring every avenue' the book is not found, I shall of course advertise for another copy for you. (By the way, those *plays* ought to be reprinted.)

Meanwhile, I apologise humbly.

Trend's address is

10, New Quebec Street, W.1

but in writing to him please don't call it a *Criterion* but merely your invitation. This is on account of (not Wolfe but) Williams,[3] who has been very good in doing *N.C.* work & I like him, & don't want to hurt

1–Rylands had asked (4 Apr.) to review F. L. Lucas's *Authors Alive and Dead*.

2–An edition of the works of Samuel Daniel (1562–1619), poet and playwright.

3–Orlo Williams.

his feelings by letting him think he has been left out of an *N.C.* dinner. You see, he came before regularly, & on the last occasion Trend saw him afterwards & mentioned the dinner.

I had a frightful attack of rheumatism the next day. I'm afraid I sang too much.

By the way, as I left in a hurry, the lady would not let me pay for my booze. How much do I owe, & whom?

Yrs
T. S. E.

You failed to find it, because it is under *R* (ristorante)!

T. S. E.

## TO *Richard Aldington* TS Texas

9 April 1926 *The New Criterion*

My dear Richard,

I am sorry that Faber's illness and various preoccupations which have kept me away from the office – moving into a small house, arranging the wedding of an old servant, etc. – have delayed the return of the *Celsus* and the Rougier correspondence. I want to get hold of the book on St Thomas.[1] If we go to Paris for a few days next week, which we may do, at my brother's invitation, I shall try to get a copy there. If I have time, I should also like to call upon Rougier, giving your name, but of course I shall not discuss any questions of English publication with him unless it be concerning some article for the *Criterion*.

I wish we might have the opportunity soon to discuss the rest of your letter.[2] I agree with you about Christ and I do not disagree with anything

1 – Rougier, *La Scolastique et le thomisme* (1924).

2 – RA had written (7 Apr.): 'I respect and admire the Roman Church – she alone among the Churches is august and venerable – but I distrust a system which needs support by a hundred sophisms and then must appeal to the secular arm for aid. To you in confidence I can say that if I could join the Church I think I would, but my temperament and what little ability to think I have are both violently opposed to it. Moreover, I don't really like the gospels, and I don't much like Christ. I really think Paul was more interesting. He appears to have been a man; I have suspected that Courchod is right and that Christ is an invention.

'Perhaps I am influenced by the fact that I have recently been "reviewing" Gibbon (as he would say) . . . Confess, Tom, that perfect lucidity and self-control are extraordinarily seductive. I have never quite forgiven you for calling Gibbon's prose "dessicated" – I find the Decline and Fall irresistible – a sort of stupendous funeral oration over the Roman Empire, with all the factitious grandeur required of that form of art.' (In 'The Local Flavour', *Athenaeum*, 12 Dec. 1919, 1332–3, TSE had referred to 'the dessication in the classic prose of both languages, in Voltaire and Gibbon'.)

else. Gibbon is, as you say, irresistible, and I do not think that the word 'dessicated' is at all appropriate. I should now use a very different word about him, namely 'narcotic'. I find that a chapter of Gibbon acts on me like a very powerful drug.

Ever affectionately,
Tom

## TO *Richard Aldington* CC

9 April 1926 [London]

My dear Richard,

Is anything wrong?[1] Of course I don't mind a bit when you are unable to do reviews, because it is understood that you are only to review for the *Criterion* when you have time enough to afford the luxury of reviewing a book which you would not otherwise review at all or of saying something you would rather say in the *Criterion* than elsewhere. But your letter to Miss Fassett rather suggests that you do not feel able to review for the *Criterion* at any time. I hope this is not what you meant and I hope that I have not inadvertently offended you in any way. Remember that I always want anything that you care to give us at any time.

Yours, in haste,
[Tom]

---

'Apropos the Church,' RA went on, 'have you considered the monstrous indecency of making a saint of Sister Theresa of the Infant Jesus? I have her book – the most loathsome effusion of religious sentimentality and insipid devotion I have ever seen; and her soi-disant miracles would be laughed at by a cretin.'

1 – RA had told IPF (8 Apr.), 'I am returning the two volumes of Scott Moncrieff's Stendhal. I shall not have time to do them. I will let Mr Eliot know if I have time to do any more reviews.'

In response to this letter from TSE, RA explained on 12 Apr. that he had committed himself to too much reviewing. 'I will confess that . . . I am in some danger of neglecting my essential stand-by the T. L. S. . . . It is very good of you to suggest other contributions to the Criterion, but I have nothing in hand, have no leisure to begin anything and, in any case, distrust my power to live up to the Criterion standard.'

## TO *Rev. Francis Yealy* CC

9 April 1926 [London]

My dear Sir,

I must apologise for not having answered your letter or having thanked you for your very kind presentation of an authentic text of St Ignatius.[1] This will be very useful to me in preparing my book and I shall read it attentively.

I have at the moment, owing to confusion in moving, mislaid your letter which I should like to answer in detail as soon as I find it. But there is one point which remains in my memory. I do not want to give the impression that I think The Society of Jesus to be the cause of the seventeenth century state of mind. In such a complex subject as the history of mind it is hardly safe to talk about causes at all. No phenomenon which one mentioned could play more than a small part when the number of causes is so limitless. I consider The Society of Jesus rather as a representative of an aspect of the seventeenth century mind. I could not rightly either praise or blame it. I am quite aware of the necessities of the time which you indicate; it could have been no other than what it was, and one can only say that the necessity for the existence of a polemical or militant body was in itself a deplorable necessity. What I really regret, therefore, is the intellectual break up of Europe and the rise of Protestantism. Whether Protestantism in any of its forms is today desirable, tolerable, indifferent or noxious is another question which I do not attempt to answer. One might approve of the maintenance of The Church of England in our time and yet deplore its origin.[2]

Again with many thanks,

Yours faithfully
[T. S. Eliot]

1–Fr Yealy had sent TSE a copy of *The Text of the Spiritual Exercises*, 4th edn revised, trans. John Morris and others, from the original Spanish (London, 1923).

2–In reply, Yealy rehearsed the letter TSE had mislaid, in an undated letter in which he called into question 'the supposed Mohammedan inspiration of the Society of Jesus. May I again refer you to the Month of November 1899 pp. 517–26 where this view is discussed? I feel sure that further acquaintance with the Society is eventually going to make you consider the idea really a little bit fantastic and a disfigurement of your book. – If you are interested in looking at Father Rickaby's English and Spanish text of the Exercises you will find it at Dr. Williams' Library at 14 Gordon Square . . . I hope my persistence does not annoy you.'

## TO *Herbert Read* TS Victoria

9 April 1926 *The New Criterion*

My dear Read,

Many thanks for your letter.[1] *Savonarola* was written by my mother many years ago; an unexpected small bequest made it possible to get it published; I am very glad to have been able to do it. She was very anxious to have a preface by myself. I am pleased to find that although the book has not been advertised and has been very little noticed, a number of copies have already been sold.

I may be obliged to go to Paris for a week on Monday. If not, I shall be at the dinner and would like to lunch with you in the latter part of the week. If I do go, I should like to lunch with you early the following week, say Wednesday.

I have seen the proof of your essays and I think they look very well indeed. Faber is enthusiastic about the book.

I knew Matthew Prichard many years ago and am in many ways deeply indebted to him, but I should prefer not to see him again. I do not think that you need to worry about his connection with Bergson.[2] Of course, Prichard's philosophy may have very much developed since I knew him. But my belief is that his own aesthetics, based as they are on experiences of a very remarkable sensibility, have an independent value, and that Bergson provided him much more with a valuable emotional stimulant

1–HR admired *Savonarola*. RC-S had 'produced a very attractive book,' he wrote (7 Apr.). 'Perhaps when we meet again you will tell me something of the author.'

2–Matthew Prichard (1865–1936), English aesthete who had served as Assistant Director of the Boston Museum of Fine Arts, 1904–7. A devotee of Henri Bergson, he advocated a non-representational theory of aesthetics, and while living in Paris (1908–14) introduced Henri Matisse to Byzantine art. HWE had given TSE an introduction to Prichard. HR said he had found much to agree with in the aesthetics of Prichard, but was 'not a little startled to discover they were based on B's philosophy'. Bergson (1859–1941), French philosopher whose works influenced the young TSE, taught at the Collège de France from 1900, being Professor of Modern Philosophy, 1904–20; he was elected to the Académie Française in 1914. His extensive writings include *Essai sur les données immédiates de la conscience* (*Time and Free Will*, 1889); *Matière et mémoire* (*Matter and Memory*, 1896) – a book that TSE said he found important for himself and his generation ('Lettre d'Angleterre', *NRF*) – *Le Rire* (*Laughter*, 1900); *L'Evolution créatrice* (*Creative Evolution*, 1907); and *Les Deux Sources de la morale et de la religion* (*The Two Sources of Morality and Religion*, 1932). TSE would write to E. J. H. Greene, on 18 Apr. 1940: 'So far as I can see, Bergson had no influence on either my verse or my prose. It was only during the years 1910 and 11 that I was greatly impressed by his work.'

than with an intellectual structure.[1] And of course Prichard's personality is so strong, and his conviction (I might say his fanaticism) so intense, that his conversation has an almost hypnotic influence. You will need all your intellect to resist it. In any case, his sensibility to art is greater than that of anyone I have ever met, and also you will find him an interesting psychological case.

I wish I could join you at Richard's, but I hope that we may have a weekend there together later in the year. My new address is

57 Chester Terrace,
Eaton Square,
S.W.1.

Yours ever,
T. S. E.

## TO *Thomas McGreevy* TS TCD

9 April 1926 *The New Criterion*

Dear McGreevy,

I have heard from Miss Moore of *The Dial* who writes rather vaguely as follows:

'We are happy that you should have us in mind and do very seriously like the work of Mr T. McGreevy. At present we are not seeking verse, but certain of these poems almost tempt us to disregard that fact.'[2]

I hope you are getting on with *The Times*. Would you care to do rather a short note on The Ballet for the next number of *The New Criterion*? Of course, nothing has happened to justify such a chronicle, but I should like to keep it up and I thought you might use Margaret Morris's book as a peg to hang some general observations upon. If you would like to do this, I will have the book sent to you; I only hope that you will cut it up thoroughly.[3] I should have to ask you to let me have your notes by the 30th of this month.

Yours always sincerely
T. S. Eliot

1 – Over twenty years later, TSE was to say of himself: 'My only conversion by the deliberate influence of any individual, was a temporary conversion to Bergsonism' (*A Sermon preached in Magdalene College Chapel* [1948], 5).
2 – Marianne Moore's letter to TSE is dated 25 Mar. 1926.
3 – L. St Senan, 'The Ballet' – a review of *Margaret Morris Dancing*, by Margaret Morris and Fred Daniels – *NC* 4 (June 1926), 570–3.

## TO *Max Rychner*[1] CC

9 April 1926 [London]

Dear Sir,

I have asked my friend Dr Ernst Robert Curtius to suggest to me the name of some German writer, closely in contact with current literature, drama, philosophy and ideas in Germany, who might be willing to contribute to *The New Criterion* short chronicles of recent literary events of international importance. Our French chronicle is undertaken by Monsieur Kessell of *La Nouvelle Revue Française*, our American chronicle by Mr Gilbert Seldes of the New York *Dial*. I should be delighted if you would be our German correspondent and would send us chronicles from time to time, which would be paid for at our usual rates, namely two pounds per thousand words less the translator's fee.

Such a chronicle should not be more than fifteen hundred or two thousand words in length. Naturally, with this restriction it is impossible to give account of all the interesting events of several months, and it would rest with you to select those which seemed to you the most significant. Sometimes a chronicler will report on a single book, play or question of the day. The main point is to give to our readers an impression of the contemporary movement of ideas in your country.

I am sending you under separate cover a copy of *The New Criterion* containing a chronicle from New York. *If you would care to undertake German chronicles, could you let me have one by the 30th of this month*? I may add that *The New Criterion* is the leading literary periodical of this country.[2]

Yours faithfully,
[T. S. Eliot]

1–Max Rychner (1897–1965): writer and critic; editor of *Neue Schweizer Rundschau*, Zurich, Switzerland.

2–Rychner said (15 Apr.) he would be happy to contribute on TSE's terms.

## TO *G. B. Angioletti*[1] CC

Le 9 Avril 1926[2] [London]

Monsieur,

Je vous écris sur le conseil de notre ami M. Orlo Williams qui m'a montré des morceaux de critique que vous avez donné à *L'Esarmé* qui m'ont vivement interessé.

Je vous envoie, sous pli separé, un exemplaire de *The New Criterion*. Nous avons commencé à donner à nos lecteurs dans chaque numéro de notre revue trimestielle quelques chroniques étrangères pour les renseigner sur les courants littéraires et artistiques de l'Europe. Nous avons confié la chronique française à M. Kessel de *La Nouvelle Revue Française* et la chronique americaine à M. Gilbert Seldes du *New York Dial*. Je serai enchanté si vous accepterez de nous envoyer une petite chronique d'Italie de temps en temps, qui sera payée comme toutes contributions.

Il s'agit d'une chronique qui relèverait les faits d'actualité les plus intéressants de littérature, d'art, de théâtre ou de philosophie générale. La chronique ne devrait pas dépasser 1500 ou 2000 mots. Naturellement dans une chronique d'une étendue si restreinte on n'attend pas à avoir un compte rendu de tous les évènements de quelques mois. Il s'agit simplement d'en choisir ceux qui vous paraissent les plus significatifs. Parfois un chroniqueur peut se limiter presque à un seul livre, une seule pièce ou une seule question du jour. L'important c'est de rendre aux lecteurs étrangers l'impression, la sensation même, de l'actualité de la vie intellectuelle de votre pays.

En outre, je vous serai reconnaissant de me donner de temps en temps votre conseil sur les auteurs italiens que vous nous recommendez pour traduction dans *The New Criterion*, et naturellement, à part votre chronique, de collaborer plus largement dans notre revue.

Si vous accepterez, pourriez vous bien nous donner une chronique ou quelques notes avant le trente avril, afin que nous ayons le temps pour le faire traduire pour notre numéro de juin?

1–Giovanni Battista Angioletti (1896–1961): novelist and journalist; editor from 1929 of *Italia letteraria*; correspondent for *Corriere della Sera*; founder-editor of the literary review *Trifalco*, 1930. Novels include *Il giorno del giudizio* (1928, Bagutta Prize); *La memoria* (1949; Strega Prize); *I grandi ospiti* (1960; Viareggio Prize). He was to be founder and chairman of the European Community of Writers.

2–This letter was addressed c/o the magazine *L'Esarmé*, Milan; a copy was sent on 12 Apr. to a different address.

En espérant que vous soyez disposé à nous donner votre appui, je vous prie, Monsieur, d'agréer l'expression de ma haute considération.[1]

Pour *The New Criterion*
[T. S. Eliot][2]

## *Geoffrey Faber* TO *The Warden, All Souls College, Oxford*

Text printed for the Selection Committee

11 April 1926[3]

All Souls College, Oxford

Dear Mr Warden,

MR T. S. ELIOT

In view of the approaching meeting of the Research Fellowship Committee, of which you have been good enough to notify me, I have pleasure in re-stating what I know of Mr Eliot, and in collecting what I can of his

1 – Angioletti (13 Apr.) admired a piece by Mario Praz in an Italian periodical that included a translation of a poem by TSE (*La Terra Desolata*, in *La Fiera Letteraria* 2: 8 [21 Feb. 1926], 5); he would be delighted to write a chronicle.

2 – *Translation*: Dear Sir, I am writing to you on the advice of our friend M. Orlo Williams who has shown me some samples of criticism that you have given *L'Esarmé* and that interested me greatly.

I am sending you under separate cover, an edition of *The New Criterion*. We have begun offering our readers, in each number of our quarterly review, chronicles from abroad so as to keep them informed of literary and artistic trends in Europe. The chronicle from France has been entrusted to Monsieur Kessel of *La Nouvelle Revue Française* and the chronicle from America to Mr Gilbert Seldes of the *New York Dial*. I shall be delighted if you would agree to send us a short chronicle from Italy from time to time, for which the fee will be the same as for all contributions.

The chronicle should pick out the most interesting topical developments in literature, the arts, the theatre and general philosophy. It should not exceed 1500 or 2000 words. Of course in such a limited space we don't expect an account of all the events occurring over a period of months. It is simply a matter of choosing those which seem to you most significant. Occasionally a chronicler may restrict himself to a single book, or a single play or a single topical event. The important thing is to give foreign readers the impression, the sensation of what is actually happening in the intellectual life of your country.

In addition I would be grateful if you could advise me from time to time about Italian authors whom you would recommend for translation in *The New Criterion*, and also of course in addition to your chronicle, I trust that you will contribute more frequently to our review.

If you would agree, could you give us a chronicle or a few notes before the thirtieth of April, so that we have plenty of time to have it translated for our June edition?

In the hope that you will feel able to give us your support, please accept my kindest regards.

3 – GCF wrote in his diary on 11 Apr.: 'Wrote an "apology for Eliot", wh. took me most of the day.' He noted too, the previous day: 'Read Eliot's Clark Lectures – v. good, I think – pessimistic.' And on 23 May: 'Re-read Eliot's lectures.'

*dossier*. For the convenience of the Committee I propose to have several copies made of this letter and of the attached documents.

I will begin by resuming the facts stated in my letter to you of October 24, 1925.

Mr Thomas Stearns Eliot belongs to the same family as the *emeritus* President Eliot of Harvard University. He is an American by birth, but has lived in England for the last twelve or thirteen years. He has applied for permission to naturalise himself as an English subject.[1] He is thirty-seven years of age. He took his MA degree at Harvard, and subsequently studied at the Sorbonne, returning to America to continue his studies in Philosophy and Indian Languages. He obtained one of the Harvard Annual Fellowships; and from 1913 to 1914 he went into residence at Merton College, Oxford. During his Oxford period he was working upon Aristotle, under H. H. Joachim. He wrote a thesis for the PhD degree at Harvard on 'Meinong's Theory of Objects and Bradlley's Theory of Knowledge', which was accepted. But owing to his marriage in this country he did not return to America to take his degree.

For some time after leaving Oxford Mr Eliot was a master at Highgate School; and he also lectured as an Oxford University Extension Lecturer on Modern French Thought and Literature and as a London University Extension Lecturer on English Literature of the seventeenth and nineteenth centuries. From 1917 to 1925 he was at the head of the Foreign Trade Intelligence Department of Lloyds Bank – a post for which his considerable knowledge of modern languages especially qualified him.

In 1925 he became the Editor of *The New Criterion*, a quarterly literary review, upon terms which enabled him to resign his business appointment and devote his time to literature and critical journalism. He had, for three years, been the unofficial (and unpaid) Editor of *The Criterion*. The publication of *The New Criterion* was, at the end of 1925, taken over by the firm of Faber & Gwyer, Ltd, of which I am the Chairman; and Mr Eliot was, by virtue of his Editorship, appointed a Director of the Company. It is desirable that I should explain that this Directorship is not a Managing Directorship; it involves little more than formal duties, and is only worth seventy-five pounds a year to Mr Eliot.

Mr Eliot has recently delivered (during the Hilary Term of the present year) the series of eight lectures at Trinity College, Cambridge, known as the Clark Lectures. His subject was 'The Metaphysical Poetry of the

1 – TSE's father-in-law, C. H. Haigh-Wood, was one of those who made a Declaration in support of TSE's bid for citizenship.

Seventeenth Century, with special reference to Donne, Crashaw and Cowley'.[1]

During the last ten years Mr Eliot has laid the foundations of a growing reputation both as a poet and critic, though the limited leisure at his disposal and the deliberate avoidance of hasty generalisation, by which all his work is marked, have combined to restrict his published output. He has contributed a good deal to such periodicals as *The Times Literary Supplement*, and, of course, *The Criterion*. In 1920 he collected some of his critical essays in *The Sacred Wood* (Methuen); followed in 1924 by *Homage to John Dryden* (Hogarth Press). In 1925 he published his *Poems 1909–1925* (Faber & Gwyer), which is on the point of going into a second edition – an unusual distinction in these days. He is, at present, writing a monograph on *Dante* for Routledge's *Republic of Letters*. His lectures on 'Metaphysical Poetry' are to be rewritten and largely expanded for publication in book form.

It is as a literary critic, but a literary critic of a very special kind, that he comes before the College as a candidate for a Research Fellowship. The interest of his criticism is not solely, or even primarily, in the literary form – diction, versification, and so forth – of the objects of criticism; it is in their intellectual content, and in the ideas of the age which they exemplify; and, beyond that, in the identifications and differences between the ideas of different ages, including our own. I venture to draw the attention of the Committee to this characteristic of Mr Eliot's work – particularly manifest in his lectures on the 'Metaphysical Poetry of the Seventeenth Century', which he compares and contrasts with the Florentine Poetry of the Trecento, and the School of Baudelaire – because it brings him definitely into the category of 'history' as well as of 'literature'. The history of ideas is, I suppose, in one sense history *par excellence*. Statute III. Clause 9 empowers the College to elect to a Research Fellowship for the purpose of 'some literary or scientific' piece of work. But it is natural that the College should *ceteris paribus* incline to encourage a form of research closely allied to its special studies. Mr Eliot's work is, I venture to urge, so allied; and, further, as I pointed out in my letter of October 24, it is, in its union of history and literature, in the tradition associated with the College by W. P. Ker.

1 – Robert Graves had written to GCF on 15 Oct. (?1925): 'Admirable idea, Eliot running for an All Souls fellowship. I was glad recently to be able to commend him for the Cambridge lectureship he has got, assuring them of his social qualities and unimpeachable character' (Faber E3/1/8).

The subject of Mr Eliot's research (should he be elected) may be briefly described as 'The Mind of the Elizabethan Age'. In the foreword to his Lectures he has explained that the Lectures, as rewritten and greatly expanded by detailed consideration of the work of other poets besides Donne, Crashaw and Cowley, will form a single volume on *The School of Donne*. He adds 'It is intended as one volume of a trilogy under the general title of "The Disintegration of the Intellect"; the other two volumes will deal with *Elizabethan Drama*, its technical development, its versification, and its intellectual background of general ideas; and with *The Sons of Ben* – the development of humanism, its relation to Anglican thought, and the emergence of Hobbes and Hyde. The three together will constitute a criticism of the English Renaissance.'

In a previous letter to me, dated January 24, 1926 (which I attach), Mr Eliot developed his ideas at greater length. It is, of course, at once apparent that the scale is that of a man's life-work; and Mr Eliot has since estimated the time needed for its execution as certainly not less than fourteen years, and the number of volumes needed to embody it as certainly more than three. The letter of January 24 is therefore to be taken as a statement of Mr Eliot's ultimate aims, rather than of his immediate programme. The latter is contained in the quotation I have made above. But the immediate programme, to be seen in its proper perspective, should be read in the light of the longer statement.

It is possible that the letter of January 24 may be thought to outline altogether too ambitious a task; and Mr Eliot's modesty of statement about his own qualifications may appear to support such a view. As such a doubt has been privately expressed to me by one member of the Committee, perhaps I may give my own reasons for dissenting very strongly from it. Mr Eliot is no 'light skirmisher', unaccustomed to laborious study, and designing no more than 'a brilliant attack upon received views from the point of view of a modern mind'. (I quote from the letter written to me by a member of the Committee.) On the contrary, he is an unusually well-equipped scholar, at home in Sanskrit, Greek, Latin, and the chief modern languages of Europe, familiar as few men are with their literatures, deeply read in philosophy, and much more than merely well-informed on a great variety of other matters. Even more to the point is the temper of his mind, which is patient, analytical, painstaking almost to excess. The letters from Mr Whibley and Mr Richmond bear witness to both these statements. It is the unusual combination of these qualities with independence of vision and creative power, which fits him to undertake the task he has outlined for himself. I speak here of the complete task, which, if it is carried out, may well count among the great achievements of English letters. But even if the complete task is never fulfilled, the shorter programme is surely capable of fulfilment, and would in itself amply justify election to a Research Fellowship.

Besides Mr Eliot's letter I also attach some letters in which Mr Charles Whibley and Mr Bruce Richmond express their confidence in Mr Eliot's suitability as a candidate for a Research Fellowship.

Mr Eliot has also 'put in' the Lectures, referred to, as part of the evidence in the case; but he is anxious to make it clear that they are deliberately popular in form, and will be almost completely rewritten.

I think it is relevant to add that Mr Eliot cannot hope to execute any considerable part of his intention, unless he is assisted by a Research Fellowship, or in some similar way. He would have been unable to write the Lectures, if it had not been for the Clark Foundation.

I am, Mr Warden,
Yours sincerely,
Geoffrey C. Faber.

## (1) FROM *T. S. Eliot*

24 January 1926.

My dear Faber,

The purpose of this letter is to explain, in more detail than I have done, the nature of the rather extended work which I wish to undertake. As it lies in an unexplored territory where the frontiers of philosophy, history, literature and the technique of verse meet, the work can perhaps most easily be made intelligible by some account of its origins in my mind.

The genesis is in certain passing remarks in my book of essays *The Sacred Wood*, which led Mr B. L. Richmond to suggest to me that I should write a series of several leaders for *The Times Literary Supplement* on the development of blank verse from Marlowe and Kyd to Milton and perhaps further. In meditating these essays I conceived another series of 'Four Elizabethan Dramatists' (Webster, Tourneur, Middleton and Chapman), inspired partly by dissatisfaction with all of the existing criticism of these authors, in which I purposed to expose the connexion between their versification and dramatic form and the underlying philosophy of the age (such as it was) neither of which seem to me to have been properly dealt with. Neither of these series has ever been written: but whether I write them or not, my field of enquiry has widened between and after these conceptions, so that the two series have become merely parerga; and what I wish now to do will never, I fear, be possible in the form of articles in periodicals – the only form of writing sufficiently remunerative to justify my occupying myself with it.

I did in fact write and publish, in *The Criterion*, the first essay in the series of 'Four Elizabethan Dramatists'; and the last paragraphs of this essay adumbrate the point of view of the work I have in mind.[1]

For a long time, at any rate since the age of Lamb and Coleridge, the criticism and consequently the production of English literature has been largely determined by the opinions held concerning Shakespeare and his age. Any revaluation of literature is therefore dependent upon a revaluation of the literature of this age. This is what I wish to attempt; but it is manifest that any attempt at such a large reorganisation must exceed the borders of 'literature'. It is a study, focused upon a definite point, of the temper and mind of the period from Henry VIII to Cromwell, and must take account of influences and interests political, philosophical, theological and social. And it involves comparison with other periods, which requires further study.

While, accordingly, such a piece of work implies primarily an examination of the versification, dramatic form, and mental equipment of the Elizabethan dramatists, it implies further a study, more comprehensive than has yet been made, of the origins of the whole period; of the extent to which the dramatists are representative of the whole period; of the relation between various types of interest – such as the humanist and the theologian; of the extent and directions of such influences as Seneca (both dramatist and 'morale'), Plutarch, Machiavelli, Montaigne; the effects of humanism on popular literature; the effects of current political and theological controversy upon general ideas; the influence of St Theresa and St Ignatius, of Calvin and Luther; the emergence, in England, of the 'Renaissance' out of the 'Mediaeval'. But its focus upon literary criticism will give it, I hope, more precision and point than, for instance, that which I can attribute to Mr H. Osborn Taylor's *Mediaeval Mind* and *Renaissance Mind*.

1–'A Preface', C. 2 (Feb. 1924), 122–3: 'Even the philosophical basis, the general attitude toward life of the Elizabethan, is one of anarchism, of dissolution, of decay . . . The Elizabethans are in fact a part of the movement of progress or deterioration which has culminated in Sir Arthur Pinero and in the present regiment of Europe . . . The case of John Webster . . . will provide an interesting example of a very great literary and dramatic genius directed toward chaos.'

The book requires, as you may have observed, two lines of preparation: one, a more minute study of the Elizabethan literature with which I am acquainted, and two, a study of a very considerable amount of literature, philosophy and history with which I have some acquaintance, but in respect of which I cannot at all profess to be an expert: such as the Trecento, Aquinas, and a great mass of theology.

Some of the ground will be covered in the Introduction which I am writing for the *Ten Plays of Seneca* in the 'Tudor Translation Series'; and some in my Cambridge lectures in which I shall contrast the literature of the XVII century with that of the XIII in Italy; but these studies must be too fragmentary or too popular to serve me as a final statement. It is hardly desirable that I should attempt here to propound my own theory about the course of literature from the XIII century to the XX century.

Part of the work which I have outlined may appear to demand another equipment than that of a man of letters or a student of English literature. The only subject on which I have the right to assert myself to be an authority is of course Versification and the history of English Prosody. But I spent some years in preparing to become a professor of philosophy – in fact a thesis on 'Meinong's Theory of Objects and Bradley's Theory of Knowledge' was accepted at Harvard for the doctorate of philosophy which I never returned to take – and it is an interest which I have never abandoned!

But I feel that my account of the projected work is much more vague than the scheme in my mind, and if you would like me to attempt a further elucidation, I will try to give you something more satisfactory.

Sincerely yours,
T. S. Eliot.

## (2) FROM *Charles Whibley*

7 February 1926

Broomhill House, Great Brickhill,
Bletchley

My dear Faber,

I have much pleasure in telling you what I know and think of T. S. Eliot. I have been intimate with him for some years and have had many opportunities of judging his literary and historical gifts. He is very apt for research both by habit and temperament. To all that he studies he brings the cool, analytical talent of the scholar. He is by no means limited in his interest to pure literature. He is deeply read in history, especially in the history of the Elizabethan period, and has a clear understanding of political philosophy. I have not the smallest doubt that, were he elected to a Research Fellowship, he would do excellent work and do credit to the College. I might add that his knowledge is not confined to one period or to one literature. He knows many languages, and can illustrate, as few can, the intellectual movement of one country and one century by the movement of another country and other centuries.

He is, also, as you know, a most agreeable companion. He is an admirable talker, and knows how to share with others his knowledge and his interests.

I am, my dear Faber,
Yours always sincerely,
Charles Whibley.

## (3) FROM *B. L. Richmond*

18 February 1926 3 Sumner Place, S.W.7

Dear Mr Faber,

This has turned out to be, perhaps, not at all what you want. It came out like this – and it *is* true that the desire to get everything in and to link everything up has always been his way – and what looks in my testimonial like a journalistic shortcoming is really, and is meant to look like, an A1 qualification for a Fellowship.

I hope I haven't muddled it all. Please let me know.

Yours etc.,
B. L. Richmond.

## (4) FROM *B. L. Richmond*

18 February 1926 3 Sumner Place, S.W.7

Dear Mr Faber,

I am very glad to hear of the proposal of Mr T. S. Eliot for a research fellowship. I have already written to you the high opinion I have of him as a critic: but I should like to add a little to what I wrote then, because I do think he is peculiarly a person to put a research fellowship to admirable use; and the reasons for my thinking so are based quite as much on what he has not written for us as on what he has. May I give three instances?

(1) The three essays in *Homage to John Dryden* are, as the preface shows, three of a contemplated historical series of literary studies – a series abandoned for want of leisure for study.

(2) Three years ago I suggested to Mr Eliot that some remarks of his on Blank Verse in a review should be expanded into a leader – this, on discussion, expanded into three or four projected leaders – and finally I agreed to publish in the course of a year six leaders to form the skeleton of a historical survey of English blank verse from the start to Tennyson.

Want of leisure for study and want of health have prevented this.

(3) Last year, Mr Eliot was to have written for the *Literary Supplement* the tercentenary article on John Fletcher. Again the expanding historical background prevented it. The article had to be abandoned. Mr Eliot was already deep in the study of the Elizabethans which is now his proposed subject of research: Fletcher could not be isolated and compressed into journalistic limits.

Forgive my going into this domestic detail. But Mr Eliot's critical output of books has been small. And I want to press the point that, while a strong historical sense is plainly felt in his criticism, it is also the desire to be always widening and widening historically the scope of his subject that has restricted his output, and has led so many of my suggestions for articles to end in (at present) unwritten books.

If a research fellowship should lead to those books being ultimately written, I think All Souls will be willing to sponsor the result.

Bruce L. Richmond

## TO *Henry Eliot*

TS Houghton

Telegram 15 April 1926 [London]

URGENT = HENRY ELIOT HOTEL DU QUAI VOLTAIRE PARIS = COME LONDON IMMEDIATELY IF ONLY FOR ONE NIGHT MUST SEE YOU AT ONCE YOU CAN SLEEP CLARENCE CABLE REPLY AND TRAIN CHESTER TERRACE URGENT = TOM =

## TO *Henry Eliot*

TS Houghton

Telegram 16 April 1926 London

COME AT ONCE REAL DANGER BRING OR LEAVE THERESA CLARENCE GATE READY FOR YOU = TOM =

## *Vivien Eliot* TO *Ottoline Morrell* MS Texas

16 April [1926] 57 Chester Terrace, London

Dearest Ottoline

Forgive me for not writing all this time. Thank you for all yr kindness – *thank you.* I am in great trouble. I have not been to Paris. T. went just for 2 days. I am in great trouble, do not know what to do. In great fear. I wish I could see you.[1]

I will write again. Dear Ottoline. Do keep in touch with me.

Ever yrs.
Vivien

## TO *Virginia Woolf* PC Berg

22 April 1926[2] Postmarked Paris 23. IV. 1926

We are stirring about Europe in a caravan, on a secret errand to the Pope, of high philosophical & political importance. We wish you were with us, but want to show you the little house if you will come to tea with us on our return.

Yrs ever
Tom

## TO *I. P. Fassett* Valerie Eliot

Telegram, stamped 23 Apr. 1926

GO CHESTER NINE EVENING TELL JANES[3] RETURNING ANY DAY URGENT BUSINESS DONT MENTION ITALY USE CHESTER OR GO CONSTANTLY

1–See TSE's letter to Osbert Sitwell, 13 Oct. 1927.
2–On 20 Apr. TSE had gone to a private preview of a Walt Whitman exhibition (first editions, MSS, photos) put on by Sylvia Beach and Adrienne Monnier at Shakespeare & Co.; other visitors included James and Nora Joyce, Paul Valéry, Natalie Barney, Valery Larbaud, EP, Hemingway, and Harry and Caresse Crosby.
3–W. L. Janes (1854–1939), ex-policeman who acted as handyman for the Eliots at 57 Chester Terrace. 'If I ever write my reminiscences, which I shan't,' TSE reminisced to Mary Trevelyan on 2 Apr. 1951, 'Janes would have a great part in them' ('The Pope of Russell Square': courtesy of the late Humphrey Carpenter). TSE later wrote to Adam Roberts, 12 Dec. 1955: 'I . . . knew a retired police officer, who at one period had to snoop in plain clothes in the General Post Office in Newgate Street – he caught several culprits, he said' (Adam Roberts).

## *Henry Eliot* TO *His Mother*

MS Houghton

[Extracts]

[PC 23 April 1926]

. . . tonight take the Rome Express – Vivien, Theresa, Tom and I. V. and Tom will be with us in Rome for two weeks – Maurice is also there.[1] We are having a jolly time . . . Tom & Vivien are very well and we are delighted that they are going with us – it will be the best part of our trip.

[Letter begun in Paris on 22 April; posted in Rome, 24 April]

This letter has been written at odd moments, and we are now on the Rome Express, with Tom and Vivien, who going to spend two weeks with us in Rome. Maurice of course will be there. We are delighted to have them go with us. The holiday will be a splendid thing for them, and it makes our trip to Rome a regular picnic. It will be delightful. It is such a relief not to have to try to understand the jabbering porters and the unfamiliar routine of railway travel, for Tom is our courier . . .[2]

We left Paris at 10.20 p.m., and have had our first night on the train . . .

You will be glad to know of Tom's and Vivien's holiday, it is just what they need, and we shall all enjoy it. Vivien adores Theresa and I am so delighted to see something of Tom.

Much, much love. I will wire you and I hope you are quite well.

Much love to all.

Your affectionate son
Henry

7 May 1926 Rome

As I cabled you, it looks as we would not be back much before June 15. Previously I expected to be back about the end of May. Our trip has been delayed a good deal at various times by Tom and Vivien, who express so great desire to see all they can of us that we have yielded to their pleadings. Vivien seems to have formed a great attachment for Theresa, and Tom seems to crave some one of his own family constantly. We have been in

1 – Maurice Haigh-Wood was working at the Banca Italo-Brittanica, Rome.

2 – They stayed in Rome at the Pensione Prey, near the Hotel Boston. 'Tom & Vivien's room overlooks a beautiful villa,' wrote HWE to his mother (4 May).

Rome two weeks, though we intended to leave earlier.[1] We want to see Venice and Florence, and I think then will have to come back, though we had originally intended to see old towns in Italy and France. Now the strike in England[2] complicates things a little, as Tom cannot get back very well, and two trunks of ours are in Tom's house. I have written Buchen, and Tom says he is not needed at his office for a while, as the *Criterion* has just gone to press, and it is doubtful whether it can be distributed anyway. Tom and Vivien want to go on to Florence with us, which I think they might as well do, as it is in the line of their return home, and it is as cheap there as here. At this *pensione* we pay 40 lire apiece a day (about $1.70) which includes all three meals.

Ezra Pound has come to Rome to see Tom, and we are just awaiting his arrival to go out to dinner. I met him this morning in the waiting room, in my dressing gown, and I recognized him from his pictures and he evidently recognized me from family resemblance, so we introduced one another. He is an extremely pleasant and kindly fellow, stalwart though not especially tall, with a mop of blonde hair and a pointed reddish beard. He has rather wide cheekbones and a small narrow chin, which makes his face unusual. He has a pleasant, rather diffident manner, which surprises me in view of the violence of his style in literary arguments in print . . .

Your affectionate son
Henry

16 May 1926 Florence, 26, Via Montebello

We left Tom and Vivien in Rome, having prolonged our stay there to nearly 2½ weeks at their urging, and we shall see them again in Verona . . . Ezra Pound came down to Rome just before we left, a ten hour trip from Rapallo (near Genoa) where he has a flat with 'fairy casements opening on the sea'. Apparently he came solely to see Tom, who had wired him, although it seems Pound has many friends in Rome and wanted to go to some concerts there. He plays the bassoon (!) and the clavichord himself

1 – George Every (1909–2003) – whom TSE knew from 1933 as a lay brother at the Society of the Sacred Mission, Kelham, Notts. – wrote in an unpublished paper 'Eliot as a Friend and a Man of Prayer' that Theresa Eliot would remember 'when they all together entered St Peter's, Rome. Vivien, who wasn't really impressed, said something like "It's very fine", and then they suddenly saw that Tom was on his knees praying . . . It was the first hint that his brother and sister-in-law had that his conversion was imminent, and they naturally misunderstood it. They thought he was going to Rome, and perhaps he thought so himself' (cited in Barry Spurr, *'Anglo-Catholic in Religion': T. S. Eliot and Christianity* [2010], 43).
2 – The General Strike, 3–12 May.

and is much interested in modern music. We all had dinner, with Pound, one evening and went afterward to a very good concert in a small hall called the Sgambati Hall.[1] Pound is an extremely pleasant fellow and a loyal and warm friend of both Tom & Vivien. Vivien gets along finely with him and behaves well. (One thing she needs is much company – she is by nature social.) Pound is unmistakeably American; you would take him for a professor in some Western college. He is a reddish blonde of slightly Scandinavian appearance, with a mob of marcelled hair like a middle western football hero, and a pointed blond beard – ruddy, wide cheeks and a small pointed chin which is emphasized by his pointed beard. Aside from that there is nothing remarkable in his appearance except that he wears a blue 'sport shirt' with a wide collar which he wears outside of his coat collar, and for overcoat, a sort of heavy reefer something like what is worn by Michigan lumberjacks. He interested me particularly because, instead of the cocky and self-assertive person that I expected (from the belligerent tone of all his critical writings and from his many fierce literary quarrels) he appeared constantly uneasy and embarrassed and constantly trying to laugh away his embarrassment. He is quite candid in his opinions and apparently he adopts this conciliatory manner to temper the effect of his frequently severe judgments.

Pound is very anxious for Tom and Vivien to live in Italy, because it is so cheap, so delightful, and so cheerful. He says he has added 10 years to his life by coming to Italy to live. He says that Tom's duties on the *Criterion* necessitate his presence in London only four times a year. I think there is much to be said for this on the score of Tom's and Vivien's general health and happiness. Vivien is keen to do it, but it is a matter requiring thought and re-arrangement of their affairs. It is very good for Tom to have Pound for company. He needs the moral support of some member of his family or else some good friend.[2] . . .

1 – The concert, on Wednesday 7 May, was in honour of Mrs Elizabeth F. Coolidge, wife of the US President.

2 – Maurice Haigh-Wood would recall, in a letter to Robert Sencourt (13 Oct. 1968), that 'Ezra & Dorothy Pound came to Rome from Rapallo & we all had some highly enjoyable meetings' (Adamson).

FROM *Geoffrey Faber* MS Valerie Eliot

28 April 1926

Buckley Arms Hotel,
Dinas Mawddwy, Cemmaes Road,
Montgomeryshire

[Extract]
My dear Eliot
[. . .]

I enclose, for your interest, a copy of the print which is going (has gone) to the Committee, about you.[1] I hope it doesn't state the case too high! & isn't demonstrably inaccurate. The thing lies now on the knees of the gods. Gordon[2] will report on your lectures, I suppose, & the Committee will probably make their report in a week or two. The affair will be decided at the Whitsun meeting.

I much enjoyed Massis in the N. C.[3] Curzon I thought not quite up to standard.[4] I am a little afraid I may have stressed too much the importance of bringing in the N. C. within the ordinary man's scope. It wld never do to do that by putting in too solid ballast! May I also say that I endorse Read's criticism of Viola Tree?[5] I really do not think her adequate. Forgive these impertinences; I do not mean to put my finger in the difficult editorial pie – but you wld rather, I know, that I said what I thought. I should like it, if you could definitely contribute an article over your name to every no. – do you think you can? [. . .]

Yrs. ever
G. C. F.

1 – See GCF's letter of 11 Apr. above.
2 – George Stuart Gordon (1881–1942): Merton Professor of Engish Literature at Oxford University, 1922–8; later Vice-Chancellor, 1938–41. On 2 Jan. 1926 GCF had written in his diary, mysteriously: 'Letter from Warden enclosing a chit from Gordon about Eliot. Speaks warmly, but is afraid of "research". Phoned E & wrote Warden: I think we can get over this all right.' And on 31 Jan., 'Warden asks me to withdraw Eliot – or at least postpone. . . . Long late night talk with Woodward.'
3 – Massis, 'Defence of the West' (trans. F. S Flint), *NC* 4 (Apr. 1926), 224–43.
4 – Desmond Chapman-Huston, 'Lord Curzon the Orator and the Man', 313–28.
5 – Viola Tree, 'The Theatre', 350–6. See TSE's letter to Tree, 29 May, below.

TO *Pearl Fassett* MS Faber

29 April 1926

c/o M H Haigh-Wood Esq,
Banca Italo-Britannica, Rome

Dear Pearl

As I am not yet certain how long we shall stay here or where we shall go next, will you please do the following for me.

1. I send under separate cover the key of the cupboard next [to] the window in front ground floor room of Chester. Please borrow key of Chester from Mrs Haigh-Wood, and take from cupboard a bundle of papers. Some of these I want, & as they are all mixed up please take them all and make a *parcel* ready to send by *registered post* as soon as you hear from me where to send them. Keep parcel at office till I let you know.

If you do not get key at same time or say 2 days after this letter, *wire me here*.

2. Please collect all letters from Clarence and Chester and send them with any at Russell Sq. (chosen at discretion) *when you hear from me where to send them*.

3. If Commentary is too *long* cut out last section but one leaving in the remarks about Lewis. But it is more likely to be too short.

4. You will have to get keys (Yale and *double* lock) of Clarence from Janes (101 Lumley Bdgs, Pimlico Road). I enclose note to him. *<Keep C.P.P. double locked.> Keep them* till you hear from me again, so that you can fetch letters. Get two post office (readdress) forms to send to me when you hear from me again.

5. Enclosed is cheque: 25/- for Minnie and 25/- for Janes. If you cannot find Minnie at the end of the afternoon at Chester, you will have to send her a P.O. to her address: Mrs Minnie Grant, 13 Rosetta St., South Lambeth Road, S.W.8 enclosed p.c. to yourself for acknowledgement.

Yours
T. S. E.

Do not have any conversation with Janes about my affairs or Saigie's[1] or give any information. Answer evasively and keep to the point.

1 – A nickname for VHE: derivation unknown.

## TO *Henry Eliot*

MS Houghton

Wednesday [12 May 1926] [Rome]

Dear Henry

1. I instructed Amer. Express to forward letter to Via Montebello 36 [Florence] till the 16th, then to Am. Ex. Co. Venice.

2. Wire came from Elizabeth[1] saying had reserved room.

3. No one knows anything about hot water bottle, I am sorry to say.

4. We leave tomorrow night.[2] Please *do not* give our address to anyone in Europe, and *if* you should write to the Haighwoods (not that I suppose you will) *do not mention that we are going to Germany*. We have not written to them about it, it would be too long to explain to them in advance. *This is important. Nobody but you is to know where we are for the next 10 days. Please make this clear to Theresa.*

Will write from Germany.

Yours affy
Tom.

## TO *Pearl Fassett*

MS Valerie Eliot

13 May 1926 [Rome]

Dear Pearl

I am enclosing cheque to pay Janes and Minnie. There is an extra week's pay for Minnie instead of notice. Her address is 13 Rosetta St. South Lambeth Road S.W.8 as you know. *Please go* to see her, give her the money, take this letter, and read out to her as follows:-

'As Mr & Mrs Eliot are not certain when they are returning, or what their plans will be, they cannot afford to keep on a maid servant indefinitely, and therefore send you a week's wages instead of notice. They are very sorry, as they were quite satisfied, & should have liked to keep you.'[3]

*If* you have not yet got the key from her, please get it at the same time. Please give the enclosed letter to Janes with his pay.

*Schedule over.*

1 – Elizabeth Wentworth, an Eliot family friend.

2 – In fact they delayed their departure until Monday, 17 May.

3 – IPF replied on 19 May: 'I saw Minnie last night, gave her her money, obtained a receipt and read out the appropriate portion of your letter. She took it all with perfect good humour and seemed very satisfied.'

| | |
|---|---|
| Minnie: last week | 1. 5. – |
| this ” | 1. 5. – |
| week's notice | 1. 5. – |
| Janes: last week | 1. |
| this ” | 1. |
| | £5. 15. – |

Enter into no discussion, be very formal & cold. Do not say where we are or what we are going to do.

I will write you my next address, *strictly private*, so that you may send out papers.

T. S. E.

## *Vivien Eliot* TO *John Middleton Murry* MS Valerie Eliot

16 May [1926] Rome

Dear John

I have been here about two weeks. Left suddenly. You wrote & asked me to tea. Since getting away from England I have seen so much. Never seen before. I believe you saw before anyone – & always saw right, I remember, years ago. But I never understood you. I understand now. You advised me right twice before. Advise me, please, once more. What shall I do, where go. What *can* I do. Please, altho' you know how much I have spoken against you & been malicious and dishonest with you. Because you know, advise me now.

Write to –

C/o Eq. Sig. M. HaighWood
Banca Italo Brittanica
Piazza Colonna
Rome/

as *soon* as possible, if you will. Please do.

Yrs. ever
Vivien

## TO *Pearl Fassett*

MS Faber

Sunday, 16 May [1926]

Dear Pearl,

I should be very much obliged if you would go out to Driver's, see the dogs,[1] and get from him a bill to date – or for the first 4 weeks, to send to me when I have an address.

It would do just as well, at your discretion, if you asked your brother to do this (if he is in London, and if you think he could report adequately on the dogs' condition).

Yours
T. S. E.

Please address enclosed envelope (X) to the Lady Ottoline Morrell, The Manor, Garsington, near Oxford, and post it (and any other letters I send you to post) *with your own hand*.

## *Vivien Eliot* TO *Henry Eliot*

MS Houghton

18? [May 1926]

Kurhaus Hoven [Hansastrasse 9]
Freiburg im Breisgau [Baden]

Dear Henry

Tom has showed me your letter[2] & I hasten to write to tell you how heartily I agree. Your psychology could go deeper, but you don't intend it to, or wish it to & so on the face of it you are perfectly right. I may say I expected just such a letter from you ever since we parted. All you say is so true that I just want to point out to you that of *all* the 'rôles' a woman enjoys & delights in, that of the browbeaten wife is the most delicious. Every woman hankers for it and thrives on it. There is no length to which an egoist will not go to enforce on her husband the reaction of a bully. My mother has striven all her life to impose on my father the character of a savage & bullying husband. She has succeeded in making him a helpless invalid dependent on her for every thing in life. I know many cases – so do you. The mastered wife is the happy wife. Dr Miller knows all this as you say.

1 – Lulu and Henry were reported to be in good condition while staying with a Mr Driver of 11 Heath Street, Hampstead.
2 – Not found.

I wd like to add, & Tom will witness it – not that the signature of such a 'poor whipped dog' signifies anything – that within the last 3 months I have implored Tom to throw his boots at me, to shout at me, & to demand every possible & impossible thing of me.

I don't *think* any woman really enjoys mastering her husband. It humiliates her extremely, it's a great strain on the character & the health.

Anyhow, unless Tom had had that something so intensely delicate & rare in him he wd never have been so shattered. And anyhow I am at the end of my tether, & I knew it before we went away with you, & I shall just hang up somewhere & keep out of his way now.

Yrs.
*V. H. E*

## TO *Marguerite Caetani*[1] MS Caetani

19 May 1926 c/o M. Haighwood [*sic*] Esq,
Banco Italo-Britannica, Rome

Dear Cousin,

I must apologise humbly – we have been taking a holiday on the continent and nothing has been forwarded. I shall probably be in London in a few weeks, but am writing you a hurried note of apology first. Most important – about *Anabase*.[2] Circumstances have been *most* adverse and complicated – I have got no farther – & it is unlikely that I can even touch it for a couple of months. In the circumstances, & as I have tried your patience so long, it has occurred to me that my friend F. S. Flint is the man. He is a *brilliant* translator, knows French intimately, is most conscientious, and *also* is a poet himself: and finally, I believe he needs the money. I am sure he would do it as well as, or better. If you are in a hurry, do write to him c/o *The New Criterion* – or, if you would rather discuss it further, I shall be in London in two or three weeks – if there were time to stop over in Paris I would do so.

I am more grieved than you will ever believe about this.

Yours always sincerely
T. S. Eliot

1–Marguerite Caetani (1880–1963): Princesse de Bassiano, Duchesse de Sermoneta; a cousin of TSE; proprietor of the magazine *Commerce*: see Biographical Register.
2–Caetani had invited TSE to translate the poem *Anabase*, by St-John Perse (pseud. of Alexis St Léger Léger), poet and diplomat, for publication in *Commerce*.

FROM *Geoffrey Faber* MS Valerie Eliot

Whit Monday 1926 All Souls College, Oxford

My dear Eliot

I grieve to say that you have *not* been elected, and it is small consolation that none of your 3 rivals were elected either. The College was evenly divided, & the 2/3 majority necessary was not to be obtained. But I should like you to know that you had *very* warm support from the more enlightened half of the College, including the Warden. What did you in was alas! your Poems, which had shocked some professorial old women; there was also the narrow angular opposition of the academic historians to any kind of research other than that which they themselves understand.[1]

1 – The Committee appointed to consider candidates for Research Fellowships at All Souls comprised the Warden (Francis W. Pember), the sub-Warden (the Revd Arthur Johnson, Chaplain of the College), Sir Charles Oman (Chichele Professor of Modern History), C. G. Robertson (historian), A. F. Pollard (historian), E. L. Woodward (historian) and J. L. Brierly (Chichele Professor of International Law). Two meetings were held, the first on 25 Apr. when D. B. (later Lord) Somervell was co-opted as a temporary member of the body, and the second on 16 May when Pollard was absent. The sub-Warden 'did not feel prepared to express an opinion one way or another' and as the Committee was equally divided as to whether to recommend TSE, the decision was left to the College, thirty-six members of which were present at the General Meeting on 24 May. Before reading the report on TSE's candidature the College amended its By-Law, making a two-thirds majority, instead of a simple one, essential for election.

Apparently the Warden, Robertson and Somervell were in favour of TSE for the following reasons:–

'1. We are satisfied that, on the evidence submitted (including the typescript draft of certain public lectures recently delivered by him) Mr T. S. Eliot is a candidate of first rate ability and has the necessary equipment as a scholar to undertake the subject which he proposes.

'Objections to the soundness of some of his general ideas, even if accepted, do not, in our view, affect our main conclusion that Mr Eliot may produce work that will be a real contribution to literary and historical criticism. We were impressed with the fact that no member of the Committee disputed the ability shown by Mr Eliot.

'Mr Eliot is of the age when the financial help and recognition implied in our Research Fellowships will be of the greatest assistance to him in undertaking a serious and prolonged piece of original work; and, in our view, this is the right principle on which the College should act in awarding these Fellowships.

'We feel, also, that Mr Eliot and his work will benefit by being brought into close touch with historians in Oxford and particularly in this College.'

Oman, Woodward and Brierly, 'while agreeing that [TSE] was a poet and critic of distinction', felt unable to support him because:–

'a. They think that the subject of research as interpreted by Mr Eliot himself, is far too wide for any one man to undertake, and must lead to generalisations, the value of which must be doubtful, since the foundation of knowledge on which they are based must frequently be inadequate.

'They have had an opportunity of examining cursorily the recently delivered lectures, which he regards as the prolegomena to his subject. While they do not venture to criticise his

I send you the enclosed letter from Grant Robertson, the Principal of Birmingham University, who was one of your strongest supporters.[1] It will, I think, give you some pleasure to read; & you may possibly some day be able to make use of his offer. Will you let me have it back again? & will you treat his remarks upon the shallow character of the unintelligent opposition which turned the scale — as confidential.

On those who are best qualified to judge your Clark Lectures, in spite of some inaccuracies & roughnesses, due no doubt to the circumstances of their composition, made a very profound impression. I hope that fortune

---

purely literary examination of certain seventeenth-century poets, they cannot find evidence of a depth of knowledge sufficient to justify his philosophical and historical conclusions. This deficiency, which would be less important in a younger man, must be a serious handicap for a man of thirty-seven undertaking a work of such magnitude.'

Following a protracted discussion the meeting adjourned to the Common Room. Later it was announced that none of the four candidates had been elected.

GCF wrote in his diary, 24 May: 'A dreadfully long meeting. Eliot not elected. He only got 14 out of 35 votes. A very hard disappointment; unforgiveable attacks by Lucas, Adams & Macgregor on his poetry as obscene & blasphemous!!' (Faber Archive)

A. L. Rowse lamented in his diary for 28 May: 'Here at All Souls at our last meeting we turned down T. S. Eliot, for a Research Fellowship. Now that is irreparable, and unforgivable. The spectacle in Hall was a sight to see. The two bishops were anxious only for a theological Fellow, Headlam [Bishop of Gloucester] consumed with impatience, and gnawing not only his knuckles but his whole hand. Several sensible speeches in favour of Eliot from Grant Robertson, [Sir Dougal] Malcolm and [Lord] Brand. Then came a thunderbolt from the blue, just when one might have thought Eliot had a chance to win in spite of his poetry. Doddering old Sir Charles Lucas [retired civil servant and historian] got up and said he'd never heard of Eliot before his name was brought before the College; that he'd read two poems the night before, and he thought them indecent, obscene and blasphemous; why such a man should be regarded with approval, or rather singled out for high honour he didn't know, and he hoped he had not lived to see the College make such an election. This obviously shook the Archbishop. The fat was in the fire over this. There got up in a row three high-minded and narrow-minded Scots, Lucas, Adams and Macgregor, none of whom had read any of Eliot's work until that weekend, when they singled out a few of the more comprehensible but questionable poems as a text for moral denunciation. After that, there could be no doubt' (*The Diaries of A. L. Rowse*, ed. Richard Ollard [2003], 22–3).

In a memoir published during his lifetime, *All Souls in My Time* (1993), Rowse admitted in addition: 'For the non-election of T. S. Eliot I was partly responsible. He was proposed for a research Fellowship by Faber, on the basis of his typescript Elizabethan Essays. As a junior Fellow, known to write poetry and an admirer of Eliot, I was the only person to possess his Poems, and was asked to lend them around. Ingenuous as ever, it never occurred to me that others might hold them against him. However, when a couple of Scottish Presbyterian professors, Macgregor and Adams, encountered the amenities of "Lune de Miel":

A l'aise entre deux draps, chez deux centaines de punaises,
La sueur aestivale, et une forte odeur de chienne . . .

(what Eliot elsewhere calls "the good old female stench"), these sons of the manse were shocked and voted him down' (22).

1–Not found.

will place the means in your hands of executing the invaluable work you want to carry out.

My own personal disappointment is very great; & I blame myself for having been the cause of your entertaining hopes which have not been realised.[1]

Yours ever
Geoffrey C. Faber

P. S. I shall be in chains again at R. Square on Wednesday.

## TO *Messrs A. P. Watt & Sons* CC

29 May 1926 [London]

For Mr Walker.

Dear Sirs,

I must apologise for having retained Mr Guy Morton's sketches for such a long time, but I have only just had the opportunity of considering them carefully.[2]

I think that Mr Morton's work, especially that part of it which might be termed 'Dolly Dialogues',[3] is extremely clever and amusing. It is difficult to make any suggestions, because it is not due to any defects that the work seems to me unsuitable for *The New Criterion*; for on the contrary, the work is quite accomplished. It is because Mr Morton's sketches seem to be of a kind which should be extremely acceptable to many magazines which pay very much higher rates than *The New Criterion*, that I am returning them. Mr Morton's work seems to me so good of its kind, that I must say that it is more to his interest to continue and to perfect it than to attempt some other type of fiction which might be acceptable to *The New Criterion* and nowhere else. It is difficult to formulate in a few words the

1–TSE was to say in his eulogy for GCF, 'Only those who are aware of Faber's intense devotion to the College will realise what a great honour he wished to do me, and what generous feeling inspired him. It was a distinction for which my qualifications were not obvious either to myself or to the College. I am happy to say that the College was spared the ignominy of electing an unscholarly member and I was spared the waste of energy involved in pretending to a scholarship which I did not possess' (*Geoffrey Faber 1889–1961* [1961], 15). Enid Faber wrote to TSE on 11 May 1961: 'How well I remember the efforts over All Souls. Ernest Woodward removed *The Waste Land* from the Common Room, as he thought it might spoil yr chances. G[eoffrey] was furious.'

2–The stories by Guy Morton (Peter Traill) that had been submitted by A. P. Watt & Son were 'Backbone' and 'Can Such Things Be?'

3–The Hungarian-born Dolly Sisters (b. 1892) comprised a successful singing act.

kind of fiction which does interest us; all that I can say is that we wish to publish short stories of conspicuous merit which would not easily find a market among the more popular reviews.

I should, however, be quite pleased to read with special care anything further that Mr Morton may care to submit.

Yours faithfully
[T. S. Eliot]

## TO *Viola Tree*[1] CC

29 May 1926 [London]

Dear Miss Tree,

I have only just returned from the Continent where I have been moving about too rapidly and uncertainly either to communicate or be communicated with, and it is therefore some weeks since I have attended to any business or even any private correspondence.

On taking up my work again I find it obvious that, owing to the effects of the strike and related causes, *The New Criterion* must hereafter be somewhat reduced in size. We have had to increase it in some respects, in consequence of what appears to be the popular taste, and especially in the department of book reviews, the length of which cannot possibly be curtailed without damaging the importance and interest. I have therefore decided with great regret that we must for the present dispense with regular dramatic criticism, even your own. For that part of the public which is interested in the subject, I am sure that your criticism is as valuable as any part of the quarterly, but this interest is somewhat confined to persons who are either able to see a few at least of the performances criticized, or who have enough interest in the art of the theatre to enjoy and benefit by criticisms of plays that they have not seen. I have been very perplexed in deciding in what way I ought to effect this reduction of *The New Criterion*; and I have come to the conclusion that I must waive my personal preferences and, adopting a commercial standpoint, consider it from the interest of the majority of our readers who are outside of London.

I very much regret this necessity and I hope that you will, on the other hand, be inclined to let me have, from time to time, occasional articles, notes or reviews, and that you will suggest any subject that occurs to you.

1–Viola Tree (1884–1938), eldest daughter of the actor-manager Sir Herbert Beerbohm Tree, had trained as a singer. She wrote occasional pieces on the theatre for *The Criterion*.

If you are in London at the moment, I should be delighted if you would care to have tea with me one day in my office which is not far from your house.[1]

Yours very sincerely,
[T. S. Eliot]

## TO *Henry Eliot*

MS Houghton

Thursday, 3 June[2] [1926] Hotel Restaurant Foyot, Paris

My dear brother

So much has happened that I have had no time to write. We *intended* to join you in Milan.

The German doctor took a very serious view. But I think things had already gone too far for his methods to avail. Her ideas of persecution grew rapidly. When we got back to Basel she was in such a state that I encouraged her to believe that the best thing was to go straight to England. We got as far as Paris, to this hotel where the Pounds are living. P. took her in hand & I left for England in the hope that she might pick up without me. In 3 days the Pounds were at the end of their resources & wired for me. The hallucinations (voices etc.) had got worse etc. She had been sleeping on the floor of their room, in terror. I intended to take her back to London but she was too ill. Thanks very much to Pound's great help I got her out to a home near Paris – I believe the best in France – & she is being cared for under the direction of Claude, the Professor of Psychiatry at the Sorbonne.[3]

I do not know when or whether she will come out. Meanwhile I shall tell mother merely that she has had to go to another home for a time, owing to her system not having been thoroughly restored at the last.

I have not seen her since. It costs 300 fr[ancs] a day, but in a few days, when the crisis is over, they will put her in a cheaper room – 200 fr. It

1 – Tree responded on 1 June: 'I am very sorry you feel you have to chuck me – . . . [P]erhaps the last article wasn't comprehensive enough. Perhaps you feel you want someone who'll go to every play – or are you really chucking the dramatic notes? . . . I seem to be difficult to get off your hands! but frankly I hate losing the kudos of being on your paper.' She offered to contribute signed articles. 'If it's because you want someone *else*, and I'm just a drag, say so, but if it's me you want cheaper, or different, think it over. Your letter was most kind – so I couldn't judge how meant.'

2 – Misdated May.

3 – Henri Claude (1869–1946) was elected to the Académie de Médicine in 1927. He would look after Zelda Fitzgerald during her brief stay at the Sanatorium de la Malmaison in 1930.

would be at least as costly, probably *more* so, in any place of the same standing in England. She has had to have continuous guarding, night and day, & a special room for suicidal cases.

If all goes well I return on Monday to London, & come over from time to time. I shall try to settle down & earn money.

I want you and Theresa to know that she was desperately unhappy, up to the end, at the idea that she would not see you again – she is very deeply attached to both of you.

She was very pathetic.

Of course, it is possible that she will recover. If so, I shall try to take her to Rapallo, & keep her out of England for a long time.

Very much love to both of you. I shall miss you very much indeed.

Tom.

[P. S. on envelope] I wish the photograph of you was better. You have had much better ones.

## TO *Charles Whibley* CC

7 June 1926 [London]

My dear Whibley,

I have had to be abroad again and have just returned this morning. I must go away again from the 15th to the 20th. After that, I hope to be in London for some time continuously. But I should like very much to see you if possible before my next disappearance, that is to say during the present week. If you are coming to town within that time, I hope you will keep a little time for me; if you are at Brickhill and alone, and if it is convenient, I should very much like to come down for one night. I have much more to say than I could possibly get into a letter, but if you cannot see me this time, I shall hope that we may meet after the 20th.

Yours ever affectionately,

[T. S. Eliot]

## TO *W. S. Stallybrass*[1] CC

7 June 1926 [London]

Dear Mr Stallybrass,

I have just returned from abroad and find your letter of the 27th ultimo. I apologise for having kept you waiting for the answer to such a simple but important question. I have no objection whatever to your settling with Professor Ashton for the book on Molière. On the contrary, as I think I told you, the subject is outside of the direct line of my work at present, and therefore to do a book on Molière at any time within the next ten years would be only a nuisance to me.[2]

I find I never completed the Dante contract. Here it is. Will you let me have the counterpart?

With many thanks for your courtesy.

Sincerely yours,
[T. S. Eliot]

## TO *Eric Partridge*[3] CC

7 June 1926 [London]

Dear Mr Partridge,

I must apologise for having kept your article on the origins of drama for such a very long time. The idea is a very interesting one, but I think that its expression is much too fugitive and that you could much better make an essay of four thousand words than one of eight hundred words. Of course such a long essay would require supporting your thesis by extensive use of fact and reference, as well as discussions of contrary opinions. But if

1–W. S. Stallybrass (1855–1927), Managing Director of George Routledge and Sons Ltd.

2–TSE had hoped to contribute a study of Molière to Routledge's 'Republic of Letters' series, and it was understood that they would await his convenience 'unless a really good author' (as Stallybrass put it) came forward. Now Professor H. Ashton (Univ. of British Columbia), an authority on seventeenth- and eighteenth-century France who had recently completed a textbook for Longmans (*A Preface to Molière*, 1927), had offered to write the volume. His *Molière* was to be published in 1930.

3–Born in New Zealand, Eric Partridge (1894–1979), lexicographer, etymologist, philologist, studied at the University of Queensland, Australia, and at Oxford, where he took his MA and BLitt. At the time of this letter, he was a lecturer in English Literature at East London College. His works include *Slang Today and Yesterday* (1933), *A Dictionary of Slang and Unconventional English* (1937), *Shakespeare's Bawdy* (1947), and *Usage and Abusage* (1942). See also *Eric Partridge in His Own Words*, ed. David Crystal (1980).

you think such a task worthwhile, I should be very much interested to see the result.

Yours faithfully,
[T. S. Eliot]

## TO *Max Rychner* CC

8 June 1926 [London]

Dear Sir,

I have just returned to London and thank you for your letter of the 25th April and confirm my secretary's letter of the 10th May.

I have read your chronicle with great interest and can say that it is exactly the sort of thing that I hoped from you. I much regret that we were unable to include it in the June number, but perhaps it is even more suitable that it should appear, as it will, in the October number, after Monsieur Massis has completed the statement of his case.[1]

With very grateful thanks,

Yours faithfully,
[T. S. Eliot]

## TO *Henri Massis* CC

8 June 1926 [Le 8. Juin, 1926] [London]

Cher Monsieur,

Me voici revenu à Londres d'où je m'empresse de vous écrire avec votre lettre du premier courant sous ma main.

J'attends avec beaucoup de plaisir le dîner auquel Monsieur Maurras[2] me fait l'honneur de m'inviter. Donc je descends à Paris le matin du quinze à six heures. Je descendrai à l'hotel Foyot, rue de Tournon. Voulez vous bien m'envoyer à cette adresse un petit mot pour dire où la réunion aura lieu et à quelle heure et comment s'habiller? J'espère que Monsieur Maritain aussi peut venir.

1 – Rychner's chronicle in part took issue – '*amicalement*' – with Henri Massis on the subject of the Defence of the West: '*bienque ses remarques sur l'esprit allemand et l'Est ne soient pas d'une portée générale. Mais cela, vous le savez bien; notre ami Curtius est un des représants parmi les défenseurs allemands de l'Ouest.*'

2 – Charles Maurras (1868–1952): poet, critic, political philosopher, polemical journalist; founding editor of *L'Action Française*: see Biographical Register.

Je vous ai confirmé dans la Place Ste. Sulpice que vos idées au sujet de l'honoraire sont exactes. Vous permettrez que nous ajoutons la somme soustraite en erreur au chèque qu'on vous enverra bientôt pour la deuxième partie de votre article? Cela serait beaucoup plus simple et pratique, d'envoyer deux chèques au lieu de trois.

Dans l'attente de vous revoir, croyez cher Monsieur à ma sympathie fidèle.

[T. S. Eliot][1]

## TO *Conrad Aiken*

TS Huntington

8 June 1926 *The New Criterion*

Dear Conrad,

Are you back in Rye or not? Please let me know also whether there is any chance of seeing you in London. I shall be away again for most of next week, but if you have spent all your money in Spain and cannot think of visiting London, I might after that be persuaded, without much difficulty, to come down and spend a night with you.

Also is there any possibility of getting a longish review out of you for the October number. I should like one of your most corrosive. What do you say to doing the Great American Novel? You can be supplied with the works of Scott Fitzgerald, Ring Lardner and a delightful book called *Gentlemen Prefer Blondes*.[2] Or if you are feeling liverish, there is the

1 – *Translation*: Dear Sir, I am now back in London and hasten to write to you, with your letter of 1st June in front of me.

I look forward with great pleasure to the dinner, to which Monsieur Maurras has done me the honour of inviting me. I am due to arrive in Paris on the morning of the 15th at six o'clock. I shall be staying at the Hotel Foyot in the Rue de Tournon. Would you be so kind as to send a note to that address, saying where the meeting will take place, and at what time and how one should dress? I hope that Monsieur Maritain will be able to be present.

I confirmed in the Place Ste Sulpice that your view about the fee is correct. Will you allow us to add the amount deducted in error to the cheque that will be sent to you shortly for the second part of your article? It would be simpler and more practical to send two cheques rather than three.

I look forward to seeing you again and assure you of my warmest regards.

2 – CA concurred (9 June): 'Anita Loos is delightful – liebfraumilch.'

Herman Melville biography in the 'English Men of Letters'.[1] Is there any chance of your coming to London for another operation?

Yours ever,
T. S. E.

## TO *J. M. Robertson* CC

8 June 1926 [*The New Criterion*]

My dear Robertson,

I have returned from abroad and found your letter of the 26th April together with your essay on Poe which I sat down and read through.[2] I have always wanted to publish something substantial about Poe and here it is: the only question that arises is whether you will allow me enough time. I shall have to publish it in two consecutive numbers and could not begin it until April of next year, or January at the very earliest. Meanwhile, you would be losing the opportunity of disposing of it in America. I like it very much indeed, and now it is entirely your decision whether I am to publish or not.

In any case, I very sincerely hope that it will grow into a book.

Yours sincerely
[T. S. Eliot]

## TO *Messrs A. P. Watt & Son* CC

8 June 1926 [*The New Criterion*]

Dear Sirs,

I am returning to you with regrets the play by Mr Yeats which you sent with your letter of the 1st March.[3] I find that on account of other engagements I should be unable to make use of it until long after the time

1 – 'I should like, extremely, to do the Melville, but for two very good reasons – one, that I don't much care for [Jon] Freeman's treatment of the subject, and do greatly care for Freeman himself; and two, that it would be a long job, would entail reading a lot of Melville . . .' The 'other suggestion' – the Great American Novel – 'attracts me more,' he went on, 'as it seems to carry less responsibility. Could Dreiser's new magnissimum opus [*An American Tragedy*] be added to the lot?'

2 – Robertson sent an article of over 10,000 words on 'The Genius of Poe', taking off from a discussion of recent works on Poe. 'You know I was a Poe-champion in my youth when there weren't many. I am soberer now, but still a bit Poe-itic.'

3 – *The Resurrection*.

when I suppose it is likely to appear in America. If, however, it should not be published in America within the next two months, I should be very glad if you would let me have another opportunity.

I regret the delay which is due to the fact that I have had to be abroad for a very long time. In ordinary circumstances I should endeavour to give you an immediate decision in the case of work of any writer so important as Mr Yeats.

Yours faithfully,
[T. S. Eliot]

## TO *Francis Musgrave* CC

8 June 1926 [*The New Criterion*]

Dear Sir,

I have to thank you for your letter received in my absence which was answered by my secretary on the 11th May.[1] While the idea of a Prague chronicle is a very tempting one – I know that there is specially great dramatic activity in that capital – I am afraid that we must for the present confine our chronicles to the five countries already covered. We have to consider limitations of space and we are at present able to include chronicles of these five countries only twice a year each. We cannot afford more space, and we cannot have our chronicles appear less frequently than every six months. So I am afraid that for the present I must decline your interesting offer. Were this review a monthly, the position would be very different.

Yours faithfully
[T. S. Eliot]

## TO *Allen Tate* Princeton

8 June 1926 [London]

Dear Mr Tate,

I find your essay, 'Poetry and the Absolute', very interesting. I am almost certain that I could use it [in] one of the next three numbers. Will you allow me to keep it, or do you intend to publish it in some conspicuous

1 – Francis Musgrave, who had recently returned from a two-year stay in Czecho-Slovakia, volunteered (in an undated letter) a 'Prague Chronicle'.

magazine in America very shortly? I should very much appreciate it if you could hold it back for me. I may be able to use it in January.[1]

Excuse the brevity of this letter. I have just come back from abroad and have an enormous mass of correspondence to deal with. I shall be writing to you again about your poetry.

Yours sincerely
[T. S. Eliot]

## TO *H. J. C. Grierson*[2]

TS National Library of Scotland

8 June 1926 *The New Criterion*

Dear Sir,

My secretary has just shown me your undated letter.[3] She is quite right in her statement to you that I have so far been able to include very little correspondence, but I am writing to say that I wish if possible to print your letter in our October issue. I regret that our June issue had already gone to press before your letter was received. Meanwhile, you may possibly hear from the author of the review.

May I take this opportunity of expressing my own very great personal indebtedness to you as an authority on the literature of the seventeenth century? During the past winter, I delivered a series of lectures at Trinity College Cambridge on the metaphysical poetry of that century, and in preparing these lectures I found that you were the only writer whose authority both in scholarship and taste I could never question.[4] When my other labours permit, I intend to rewrite these lectures for publication, and I had thought of venturing to ask your permission to submit to you certain parts before they went to press.[5]

Yours very truly,
T. S. Eliot

1–'The Fallacy of Humanism', C. 8 (July 1929), 661–81.
2–H. J. C. Grierson (1866–1960), Regius Professor of Rhetoric and English Literature, University of Edinburgh, 1915–35: see Biographical Register.
3–Grierson's letter – published in *NC* 4 (Oct. 1928), 748 – took issue with HR's review of his edn of *The Poems of John Milton*, *NC* 4 (Apr. 1926), 396–8.
4–See TSE's review of *Metaphysical Lyrics and Poems of the 17th Century: Donne to Butler*, ed. Grierson: 'The Metaphysical Poets', *TLS*, 20 Oct. 1921, 669–70.
5–Grierson responded on 11 June: 'I am very much gratified by your kind words though they make me feel a little shy as I know the defects of my work very well. These critical questions are problems which one attacks again & again and never comes off quite victorious, &

## TO *H. P. Collins* TS Maryland

8 June 1926 *The New Criterion*

Dear Mr Collins,

Your essay on Coleridge is very interesting and makes some excellent points and I should like to use it. The only difficulty is that (with a view to varying the contents of *The New Criterion*) it falls closely within the same category as several other essays which had already been accepted before yours arrived and which therefore take precedence. I think, however, that I might be able to arrange things so as to use your essay in January.[1]

On the other hand, if you prefer to use this essay elsewhere, would you care to review H. A. Fausset's new book on Coleridge? I have not the slightest doubt that it is a very bad book, but if so, it ought to be thoroughly torn to pieces, and would at any rate give you another opportunity of stating your views on the subject.[2]

Sincerely yours,
T. S. Eliot

## TO *Alec Randall* CC

8 June 1926 [London]

My dear Randall,

I left Rome two days after I saw you and owing to unforeseen circumstances have been abroad most of the time since but was unable to return to Rome as I had hoped. I am only now answering your letter of the 26th April. Many thanks for your fidelity in writing your admirable reviews in the midst of your other work. Please reassure me that you will

---

I am apt to make still impulsive errors. But the quest is always interesting & I like best myself to read criticisms that are in the nature of quests, not *ex cathedra dicta*, that is why I have enjoyed reading your *The Sacred Wood* and *Homage to [John] Dryden*. I am far from agreeing with all your critical conclusions but they always interest me & make me think. I will not, however, be a hypocrite & profess that I have yet come to understand & appreciate *Waste Land* but on that & Mr Ivor Richards' critical theories I hope, when I have time, to have something to say. He is very interesting.'

1–'The Criticism of Coleridge', *NC* 5 (Jan. 1927), 45–56.

2–Collins had already written a note for *The Adelphi* on Hugh I'Anson Fausset's *Samuel Taylor Coleridge*, and replied to TSE (9 June): 'I may be able to persuade you that it neither requires reviewing very urgently, nor really requires to be slaughtered. Why, if he goes on like this, he will be invited to contribute to the English Men of Letters series.'

be able to continue these reviews for us and that your official work is not likely to crowd them out.

Would you care to take anything up to four pages of small print in the October number (the June number being already printed) for reviewing any important German book or books? I should be most interested in the article you mention, only it would have to be for the January number as the main body of the October number is practically full.[1] So I hope you can let me have a good review for the October number in any case.

I shall write to you again about the series later. Aquinas would certainly be a very interesting subject for a book in English, but he does not quite fit in to my present scheme.[2] But if we can do nothing with him, we must find you something else.

I hope that you may get back to England for a few weeks during the summer.

Yours ever
[T. S. Eliot]

## TO *F. Scott Fitzgerald* TS Princeton

8 June 1926 *The New Criterion*

Dear Mr Scott Fitzgerald,

I have had to be a good deal abroad myself for some weeks and have had no time for correspondence and have just returned and am looking at your undated letter and find that you give this address only until the middle of June.[3] So I now hasten to reply. Thank you very much for sending me *All the Sad Young Men* which I very much enjoyed reading although it does not seem to me up to the form of *The Great Gatsby*. I am afraid, however, that neither of the stories you mention will do.[4] It is not merely that I am staggered by the number of dollars you have received, but that it would rather damage our prestige in America to publish *anything* by *anybody* which had already appeared in a book in

1–Randall had asked, 'How would a general article, which I should like to call "The German Literary Crisis", be considered?'

2–'I should much like to attempt St Thomas Aquinas, whom I am, in this very suitable atmosphere [at the Holy See], reading hard.' St Thomas Aquinas (*c.*1225–74): philosopher and theologian; author of *Summa Theologica* (printed 1485).

3–Fitzgerald was staying at Juan-les-Pins, France.

4–FSF offered 'The Rich Boy' or 'Absolution' (the others being 'trash') from his collection *All the Sad Young Men* (New York, 1926). Both had been published separately in the USA: for the former he was paid $3,500, for the latter $116.

that country. I should be tempted by anything which had only appeared in a periodical there unless it was one of three or four which are more or less read over here – though even *that* is against our principles. I can only rest in the hope that you may, sooner or later, have something which you can let drop into my hands – at our usual rates.

If you are to be in Paris at all this summer, do let me know. I shall be there off and on.

Sincerely yours,
T. S. Eliot

## TO *Peter Monro Jack*[1] CC

8 June 1926 [London]

Dear Mr Jack,

I have just seen your letter of the 3rd instant which gives me much pleasure.[2] I am afraid that you overrate my knowledge of Pater, but I sympathise with your attempt because I feel sure that he has been much misunderstood. I am not quite sure that I know how much is implied by 'supervise', but I shall be very glad to do anything I can to help you. So please let me know when you are ready to see me and we will arrange a meeting. Should you be in London, you might come to see me here during the Long Vacation. When the time comes, I suggest also that you should

1–Peter Monro Jack (1896–1944), born in Scotland, graduated from Aberdeen University before becoming (at the time of this letter) a doctoral research student at Trinity Hall, Cambridge, where E. M. W. Tillyard was to supervise his thesis on the 'Aesthetic teaching of Walter Pater'. He edited *The Gownsman*, and in 1926–7 was 'Skipper' (Literary Editor) of *The Granta*. In the late 1920s he taught at Michigan University before moving in 1930 to New York, where he became a lecturer and freelance writer. He was a regular reviewer for the *New York Times Book Review*.

2–Jack regretted that he was making little progress with his research on Walter Pater: 'with the exception of Mr [Mansfield] Forbes there's no one here (now that Richards has gone down) who will take me in hand and drastically abuse me either for saying wrong things about Pater, or for saying nothing at all.' Jack proposed to argue in his thesis that Pater 'is a quite important critic in the direct modern line; that his critical approach to literature is by way of intellectual analysis of the feelings, which seems to mark him as a psychological critic, however inadequate his psychological technique, as against the philosophical dogma of Arnold. He is transitional, leading into the 20th century . . . [C]ertainly I'll only get further by contact with one who has a psychological, or broadly a scientific, attitude towards literature . . . [Forbes] said, what I knew, that you were preeminently so; he said, what I always suspected, that you had the mid and later 19th century, especially the criticism, at your finger tips; but he added, what was a great surprise, that *possibly* you may care to take some supervising next term . . . Might it be possible?'

ask Forbes to write to me about the work you have already done and the work you have in mind.

Yours sincerely
[T. S. Eliot]

## TO *Orlo Williams* CC

9 June 1926 [*The New Criterion*]

Dear Williams,

I have got back to England but have been having a very busy week. Next week I must be away again, but I should be very glad to know that you are to be in London after that and should like to see you as soon as I get back.

'Capitaine Ensorceleur' has gone to the printers for the October number and you will receive proof in due course.[1]

In your letter of 20th April, which I never acknowledged and have only this week seen, you mentioned seeing a good criticism of Miss Stein by Robert M'Almon.[2] Now I have in hand a very good criticism of her indeed by the same Robert M'Almon which I was intending to use, and I should very much like to know whether it is the same which you have presumably seen in print. Could you let me know where you saw it or even let me see a copy if you have one? I am asking because if this criticism appeared in any conspicuous place in America I should hardly care to use it, but if it appeared more obscurely I should still use it.

I think Angioletti's chronicle is very good.[3] He writes suggesting the

1–*NC* 4 (Oct. 1926), 659–72.

2–'The reviews, as usual, are extremely good though I entirely refuse to admit that Edith Sitwell is a trustworthy critic,' wrote Williams (20 Apr.). 'Much the best review of Miss Stein that I have seen was Robert McAlmon's, & in which, with all approval, he pointed out that [Stein] was anything but exciting, having the peculiar merits of primeval mud.' On 11 June he repeated that he felt sure McAlmon's review had been 'in the *Nation & Athenaeum* shortly before I wrote to you. Certainly in one of the London weeklies.' He must have been shown it privately, since it ultimately appeared in EP's *The Exile* no. 4 (Aut. 1928), 70–4.

3–Angioletti had submitted his first chronicle on 28 Apr., with the request that it be translated by Orlo Williams who had good Italian. OW responded to this letter from TSE on 11 June: 'I am glad you have Angioletti. Italian is a damned difficult language to translate in to decent English. Every phrase goes the wrong way round, & I don't flatter myself that I could make much of it. But Angioletti was gratified that I did it. If you get Bacchelli & Baldini, I warn you they will make a great point of my translating them.'

names of two Italian authors, Riccardo Bacchelli[1] and Antonio Baldini.[2] Before I reply, I should like to know if these people are known to you, and if so what you think of their work.

Sincerely yours,
[T. S. Eliot]

## TO *Mrs Hugh Fraser Stewart* CC

9 June 1926 [London]

Dear Mrs Stewart,

You did not write to the wrong address but to the right one and it was on the contrary your letter of the 1st which went to what is now a wrong address.[3] The reason why you had no answer to either of your previous letters and why the answer to your last one is so long delayed is that I have been for some weeks abroad without any address. It is extremely kind of you to renew your invitation and I very much wish that I could accept. But I only arrived from London on Monday and private business compels me to go abroad again on Monday for at least a week, and I suppose that by the following week the term will be over and you and your family will have disappeared from Cambridge. May I express the hope that you will ask me again either in or out of term and if I am in London I shall come.

1–Riccardo Bacchelli (1891–1985): journalist, novelist, dramatist; co-founder of the magazine *La Ronda*, 1919–23. Following *Il filo meravigliosi di Ludovico Clo* (1911), he became prolific, his best-known work being a historical epic, *Il mulino del Po* (1938–40). Many years later, TSE wrote an unsolicited letter to the Swedish Academy with his suggestions for possible Nobel laureates: 'I should myself rejoice, for several reasons, if an Italian author were chosen. The name that will at once occur to every mind is that of Benedetto Croce; but if a creative, rather than a philosophic and critical writer were to be chosen, I should like to mention Riccardo Bacchelli. My personal acquaintance with Signor Bacchelli is slight; and I must admit that I know only his reputation, and not his work. (I believe that *Il Mulino del Po* has been published in a Swedish translation.) The fact that he is a member of both the Accademia dei Lincei and of the Accademia della Crusca testifies to his standing in his own country; and I should have thought that his reputation was sufficiently established in Europe' (letter to Dr Oesterling, 6 Jan. 1949).

2–Antonio Baldini (1889–1962): journalist, novelist, dramatist, poet; co-founder with Bacchelli *et al.* of *La Ronda*; columnist for *Corriere della Sera*. Early works include *Pazienze e impazienze di Mastro Pastoso* (1914), *Nostro Purgatorio: Fatti personali delle guerra italiana, 1915–1917* (1918), and *Michelaccio* (novella, 1929).

3–Jessie Stewart wrote on 28 May, and again on 1 June, (i) to invite TSE to visit them in Cambridge (they proposed to organise an outing to Little Gidding); and (ii) to enquire whether Denis Arundell might have the option to produce TSE's play – *SA* – at the ADC Theatre (to be presented on behalf of a local charity).

The only difficulty about my play is the tense. It is true that I am going to write it, it is partly true that I have partly written it and it is wholly untrue to say that it is written. Were the whole play in existence, I should have had no hesitation; it would be the ADC who would hesitate. But two or three unfinished scenes are of no use to anybody.

With very many thanks and best wishes to Doctor Stewart and yourself,

I am,
Sincerely yours,
[T. S. Eliot]

## TO *Denys Winstanley* CC

9 June 1926 [London]

My dear Winstanley,

I have just returned from abroad in a state of indigence and therefore take the liberty of writing to you privately to ask you whether you can give me any idea when the college is likely to pay me for my lectures.[1] I am sorry to bother you, but it really is of importance to me to know. And your petitioner will humbly pray, etcetera.

I had looked forward to sponging on your hospitality once more during this term, but all my plans have been unsettled. I have been abroad for a long time and of the time that is still left during this term I shall have to spend a part in Paris and the rest in hard work in London. So Cambridge is safe at least until the autumn.

If you spend any time in London after the end of term, I do hope you will let me know and come to dine with me.

Sincerely yours,
[T. S. Eliot]

## TO *F. S. Flint* CC

9 June 1926 [*The New Criterion*]

My dear Flint,

I returned to London on Monday, have been very busy, am going away again next week but shall be back again the week after. If you should feel disposed to lunch with me this week before Sunday, please ring up here. If not, I shall write to you again the week after next.

1 – Winstanley said (10 June) that TSE ought to receive a cheque 'in a day or two'.

We accept your suggestion about payment for translations, i.e. that payment shall be made on receipt of the manuscript translation from you.[1] As the printers are the final arbiters of the numbers of words, payment will be subject to adjustment on receipt of proof, but that is not likely to be of any importance.

We therefore owe you for the second part of the Massis article. Meanwhile I should be extremely grateful if you would undertake, on the terms above and as soon as possible, the following:

Max Rychner – German chronicle
Another article by Fernandez in reply to Manning

both for the October number.

By the way, I saw Fernandez in Paris and he spoke of your remarks about him and accepted without demur your criticism of his style.

I should be very glad to send you these two things as soon as I hear from you, and also the cheque for the Massis.

Yours ever,
[T. S. Eliot]

## TO *Conrad Aiken* CC

10 June 1926 [*The New Criterion*]

Dear Conrad,

Thanks for yours. We are shipping you all the documents in our possession on the Great American Novel and I have ordered the rest. But if you want Dreiser's book, kindly give us a title as I am not yet able to trace.[2]

I will send you a wire week after next and arrive with or without bathing suit and flannels.

Yours ever,
[T. S. E.]

1 – Flint had argued to IPF (26 May): 'A translation is a job – and a plaguy uninteresting one at that – and properly it should be paid for when the ms is delivered.'

2 – CA reviewed F. Scott Fitzgerald, Ring Lardner and Anita Loos, in *NC* 4 (Oct. 1926), 773–6.

## TO *W. A. Thorpe*[1] CC

10 June 1926 [*The New Criterion*]

Dear Mr Thorpe,

Your letter seems to have crossed one which my secretary wrote to you yesterday (addressed to Ross). I am using the 'Thucydides' in the form of an article, not in the form of a review, and it occurred to me that for that purpose you might find a more attractive title than merely 'Thucydides'. Will you try to think of one?[2]

I should be glad if you would devote a considerable space to Lewis's book and Graham Wallas's together. Say fifteen hundred or sixteen hundred words. It seemed to me that Lewis's book should be considered primarily as political philosophy. I wonder if you would be willing to mention in the same review two books which I have had on hand for several months and which I am sending you under separate cover. *Contemporary Political Thought in England* contains a chapter on Graham Wallas and is therefore quite to the point. The other book, *The History of Political Science*, is a rather dull and formless treatise and probably deserves only the barest mention.[3]

The Lewis book and the Wallas book will follow when we have obtained them.

Yours sincerely,
[T. S. Eliot]

## TO *J. M. Robertson* CC

10 June 1926 [*The New Criterion*]

My dear Robertson,

Thank you for your letter of the 9th. I return your Poe essay herewith, but very regretfully. If you *don't* place it in America meantime, I wish you would let me have it back early next year.

As you say you have written a book on the Shakespeare sonnets – to

1 – W. A. Thorpe worked at the Victoria & Albert Museum, Kensington, London.

2 – Thorpe replied (15 June): 'I suggest for a title (1) Thucydides and the discipline of detachment. Or (2) The mind and method of Thucydides.' (The piece had begun as a review of G. F. Abbott, *Thucydides: A Study in Historical Reality*.) See 'Thucydides and the Discipline of Detachment', *NC* 4 (Oct. 1926), 630–44.

3 – See Thorpe's untitled review of WL, *The Art of Being Ruled*; Graham Wallas, *The Art of Thought*; Lewis Rockow, *Contemporary Political Thought in England*; R. H. Murray, *The History of Political Science from Plato to the Present*, in *NC* 4 (Oct. 1926), 757–64.

which I look forward with great interest – I am taking the liberty of sending you herewith an essay which has been submitted to me on that subject, and on which I should like your opinion.[1] It may be unfair and a gross imposition to do this, but I cannot resist the temptation. I do not want to bother you more than necessary in returning this to me. I suggest that when you have read it, or if you refuse to read it, you should get a district messenger boy to return it here and we will pay him at this end.

Yours ever,
[T. S. Eliot]

## TO *Messrs J. B. Pinker and Son* CC

11 June 1926 [London]

Dear Sirs,

In reply to your letter of the 7th instant, I have had time to examine carefully the three essays of Miss Laura Gottschalk.[2] While they are all extremely interesting, I regret that none of them seems particularly appropriate to the next few numbers of *The New Criterion* and I am returning them with thanks.

I am interested to see any of Miss Gottschalk's verse.

Yours faithfully,
[T. S. Eliot]

1–The essay was by Robert L. Eagle (1888–1977), an amateur scholar who had joined the Bacon Society in 1912. He published *New Light on the Enigma of Shakespeare's Sonnets* (1916), *Shakespeare: New Views for Old* (1930) and *The Secrets of the Shakespeare Sonnets* (1965). Robertson thought the writer 'a harmless lunatic': 'He puts, in fact, a theory that has, I think, been seven times advanced in various forms – that S. in the Sonnets is addressing "his own genius" . . . To that thesis Mr Eagle conjoins the other, that the Sonnets were really written by Bacon addressing his genius as "beauteous & lovely youth". Bacon would, wouldn't he?'

2–James B. Pinker & Sons (Literary, Dramatic & Film Agents) had submitted in mid-March three articles by Laura Riding Gottschalk: 'Genius and Normality', 'Criticism and the Poet', and 'The H. D. Legend'.

## TO *Gertrude Stein*[1] TS Beinecke

11 June 1926 [London]

Dear Miss Stein,

Many thanks for your letter.[2] I am indeed sorry to have been absent from England and unable to swell your triumphant progress, but I hope that we may meet again in Paris. I should be most interested to see your Oxford and Cambridge lecture, although I am afraid it would be impossible to use it in *The New Criterion* at any rate for the next six months. But I hope that you will let me have the pleasure of reading it.

Yours very sincerely,
[T. S. Eliot]

## TO *Herbert Read* CC

11 June 1926 [*The New Criterion*]

My dear Read,

Will you please send me the poems as soon as you can?[3]

I think I might be able to do all that is necessary for Cocteau by weaving it in as one small thread in the fabric of the article I spoke to you about. So feel no obligation if the task is uncongenial. Only I should like *something* substantial from you. If you think of nothing better, I shall offer you a book on the Romantic Theory of Poetry for which I have sent.[4]

1–Gertrude Stein (1874–1946), American writer; author of *The Making of Americans* (1911) and other experimental essays in prose and drama; famous for her Paris salon and association with artists and writers including Picasso and F. Scott Fitzgerald.

2–Stein wrote (undated) that she would be very pleased for her 'Cambridge and Oxford' lecture to appear in *C. Composition as Explanation* (Hogarth Press, 1927) was to be given a brief anonymous review in *NC* 5 (Jan. 1927), 162, by someone who had seen her perform and perhaps talked with her: 'She was met with respect and a humble desire for enlightenment; as a writer she is unquestionably sincere. As a person, on the other hand, Miss Stein equally resents agreement and curiosity, any attitude in fact except one of devotion and faith. Cross-question her on the subject of her style and she retires at once into her shell, like our grandparents when doubt was cast upon the literal truth of *Genesis* or the belief in personal immortality.'

3–HR's submission included (20 June) 'Ritz', 'Cranach', 'The White Isle of Leuce'. 'The Lament of Saint Denis' (12 parts) appeared in *NC* 4 (Oct. 1926), 673–9.

4–A. E. Powell (Mrs E. R. Dodds), *The Romantic Theory of Poetry*, was briefly and anonymously noticed in *NC* 4 (Oct. 1926), 790–1. H. P. Collins reviewed *Romanticism*, by Lascelles Abercrombie, in *NC* 5 (Jan. 1927), 137–9.

I will ring you up as soon as I get back.

Yours ever,
[T. S. E.]

## TO *W. Matthew Norgate*[1] CC

11 June 1926 [London]

Dear Mr Norgate,

I regret very much that I have had to be away from England for such a long time, especially since I find several letters from the PHOENIX awaiting me. I enclose a cheque for the sum which I promised to contribute to the PHOENIX, and am sorry that you could not have had it a month ago.[2]

Unfortunately it is necessary for me to leave England again on Monday next for about a week. As I have had to be absent from several meetings and as I am unable to attend the next meeting, I feel that I ought to offer the Directorate my resignation from the body, and I should be obliged if you would convey this message to them on Tuesday next. Please make it clear to the Board that I merely wish to give them the opportunity of replacing a member who cannot pretend to have been very useful; and assure them that in any case I shall wish to do everything in my power to assist their work if they will call upon me.[3]

Sincerely yours
[T. S. Eliot]

1–W. Matthew Norgate: Secretary of The Phoenix Ltd., a company dedicated to the production of old plays.

2–The eight members of the Directorate of The Phoenix (including TSE) agreed at a meeting on 6 May to contribute £5 each in order to settle a printing account.

3–Norgate said (16 June) that the Directorate 'very much hope that you will not resign from the Board, as they consider your presence on it, even if it is in name only, to be of the utmost value to the Society'. TSE, in his next 'Commentary' (*NC* 4 [June 1926], 417–19), expressed scepticism towards 'the project of a national theatre, at which all masterpieces shall be performed in rotation, is one that makes us quail. We have no confidence in any combination of persons which might rise to power; in any commissions, boards, committees or directors who might be elected to choose and produce the repertoire.' Yet he maintained too: 'it would be a very great pity if, in the meantime, The Phoenix were incinerated for ever . . . [I]ts greatest value, among all the societies, is this: that the plays which it has presented, constitute an assertion of *literary* values on the stage . . . The modern tendency is opposed to Sophocles, Racine and Shakespeare; the performances of the Phoenix, where we may hear dramatic poetry which we have never heard, but only read, are of inestimable value in maintaining the importance of the literary element in drama.'

## TO *Mrs George Caffrey* CC

11 June 1926 [London]

Dear Madam,

I apologise for the delay in settling the point raised in your letter of April 28th, but I have myself been away from England for reasons of health and my office were not in touch with me.

We have estimated Mr Caffrey's essay at about two thousand words, and at our invariable rates of payment the fee for this is £4, for which I enclose our cheque. I am sorry that we are unable to offer more generous terms.

Mr Caffrey's essay will appear in the October number of *The New Criterion*. I am very sorry indeed to hear of your difficulties but hope that the conditions may soon improve.[1]

With all sympathy,
Yours very sincerely,
[T. S. Eliot]

## TO *W. E. Süskind* CC

11 June 1926[2] [*The New Criterion*]

Dear Sir,

I owe you many apologies for the delay in replying to your letter of the 15th April.[3] I have myself been away for reasons of health, and my

1–Daisy Caffrey wrote further (from Locarno) on 28 June: 'Life is truly cruel and though many have forgotten the dreadful war, yet we must always feel it – and in every direction – The saddest part naturally being my husband's continual suffering – and being *forced* to work at an occupation at present which naturally is using up what little strength he has left. I *dare* not think what is in store. And all this is the result of *civil* internment.' In a memo of 10 June TSE wrote of George Caffrey: 'This man, who I understand is very poor, sent me some time ago an essay which I have accepted and intend to publish in October. Attached is a letter from Mrs Caffrey. I should be very glad to oblige her if you can see your way to drawing the cheque at once. The essay is short – about two thousand words – so that the sum should be approximately four pounds (£4.)' 'Rudolf Borchardt', which Caffrey had submitted in May 1925, would appear in *NC* 5 (Jan. 1927), 81–7.

2–This letter was first printed, mistakenly, in vol. 2 of *Letters* (as of 11 June 1925).

3–W. E. Süskind glossed his article 'Die Tänzerische Generation' (*Neue Merkur*, Apr. 1925): 'it gives the problem of the younger generation in the post-war Germany quite correctly, if rather out of the usual way. I don't know, however, whether the problems are alike or similar in your country; at any rate my article . . . deals amply with the "Western" mind, as far as I could perceive it from English and French books, and from the impressions I got in your country.'

office was not for a long time in touch with me. I read with great interest your essay on the 'Tänzerische Generation' which I took abroad with me. I confess that I was very much tempted, but our policy has always been to print only inedited matter or at any rate to print simultaneously with some foreign periodicals, and I feel that it would be a dangerous precedent for us to republish an essay from so well known a periodical as the *Neue Merkur*. We recently, however, modified this principle so far as to publish an essay by Monsieur Henri Massis, a part of which had already appeared in *La Revue Universelle*; but Monsieur Massis modified and extended this essay for us so as to give it new value.[1] If it interested you to write for us another essay similar to the one you sent me, I should be very happy indeed; and I should also be very glad to see more of your work.[2]

With many thanks,

Yours sincerely,
[T. S. Eliot]

## TO *Viola Tree* CC

11 June 1926 [London]

My dear Miss Tree,

Please do not give me the pain of probing into my letter for any significance beyond what you find on the surface. What I have said is, alas! literally true, and the reasons I have given you apply just as well, I am afraid, to the Cinema.

I hope that we may continue to have you as an occasional contributor under your own name. It was always a matter of regret to me that you insisted on remaining in the shadow of a pseudonym. I am going abroad on Monday for about a week, but I expect to be in London the following week and will let you know on my return in the hope that you will come to tea with me here.

Yours sincerely,
[T. S. Eliot]

1–Henri Massis, 'Defence of the West', *NC* 4 (Apr. & June 1926).

2–Süskind replied on 20 June that he hoped to submit a similar article 'ere long'; 'also some short story of mine'. On 9 May 1927 he was to submit a story he had published in *Berliner Tageblatt*, but TSE found it 'unsuitable' (24 May 1927).

## TO *P. N. Rowe* CC

12 June 1926 [London]

Dear Mr Rowe,

Many thanks for your pleasant letter of the 10th instant.[1] One so often feels that the work of editing a literary review is quite useless and makes no difference in the world whatever beyond providing the editor with a salary and distracting him from other work, that it is extremely agreeable to receive such a letter. I remember your previous letter to which I did not have time to reply.[2] It is extremely difficult to choose appropriate contents for a literary review without falling into the mistake of becoming too narrowly and aridly literary.

I cannot provide you with a complete bibliography of Gertrude Stein. So far as I know, none of her books has been published in this country. *Geography and Plays*, the book which Miss Sitwell particularly admires, is published by the Four Seas Company, Boston, U.S.A. Miss Stein's enormous novel, *The Making of Americans*, was published by the Contact Publishing Company and is to be obtained, I believe, from Three Mountains Press, 29, Quai d'Anjou, Paris. I do not know the price of either of these books. I think that all Joyce's works, with the exception of *Ulysses*, are now published by Jonathan Cape. If you do not know his little book of songs, *Chamber Music*, it is well worth buying.

With many thanks,

Yours very truly,
[T. S. Eliot]

1–Rowe wrote in praise of the Apr. issue of the *NC*: 'some of us are prepared to regard the New Criterion as a beacon-light shining through the darkness . . .'

2–Rowe had written on 3 Feb.: 'It surely cannot be that our Tory Prime Minister has found a positive political ally in the New Criterion, and yet after reading Mr Dalway Turnbull's outburst vide Aristotle ['Aristotle on Democracy and Socialism', *NC* 4 (Jan. 1926), 7–18] one was led to say: "Was T. S. E. just leg pulling when at the end of his somewhat aloof discourse – The Idea of a Literary Review – he wrote: "Must protect its disinterestedness, must avoid the temptation ever to appeal to any social, political or theological prejudices." Well, what is Dalway Turnbull doing if he isn't appealing to political prejudice? . . . Frankly, sir, some of us are keen on being loyal to you in your professed desire to make known the true basis of culture.' Rowe urged that readers should not 'be treated to any more anti-communist propaganda.'

## TO *Herbert Read*

CC

12 June 1926 [*The New Criterion*]

My dear Read,

I am sorry about the dinner. I am afraid that seven o'clock Monday evening is cutting things too close for me, as I leave at 8.20, but I expect to be back in a week.

Of course it was very stupid of me. After sending you the letter I remembered that you had reviewed the Oxford book in the *TLS*.[1] About the Cocteau business, I am sending you first the A. E. Powell book on the Romantic Theory of Poetry. After you have looked at it you can decide which you prefer.[2] If you don't like this, I will send you on the Cocteau books and the Maritain correspondence.

Yours ever,
[T. S. E.]

## TO *Richard Le Gallienne*[3]

CC

12 June 1926 [London]

My dear le Gallienne,

This is very distressing.[4] You arrive again in London on Monday: I leave again for Paris Monday evening. I return to London probably on the following Sunday. I exhort you to remain in London for ten days or to go away and return to London. Surely after all this time you will not depart during the week and deprive me of the pleasure which I promised myself. Do let me have a word here which I shall find on my return.

1–'English Prose' – on *The Oxford Book of English Prose*, ed. Sir Arthur Quiller-Couch (1925) – *TLS*, 4 Mar. 1926, 149–50.

2–HR considered Powell's *The Romantic Theory of Poetry* 'a bit jejune' (20 June).

3–Richard Le Gallienne (1866–1947), English author and journalist, lived in New York. His writings include *George Meredith* (1890); *Robert Louis Stevenson and Other Poems* (1895); *The Quest of the Golden Girl* (1896); and *The Life Romantic* (1900).

4–Le Gallienne (8 June) wrote, 'as I feared, we do not reach London till Friday evg – when we will lodge, as we said, at the Thackeray Hotel. From Saturday aftn. to Monday we will be staying with friends in Surrey.

'Then we shall be free to study the humanities of the Halls with you, as you so kindly suggested.

'It was a great pleasure to meet you, and, may I say? to find you so human a human being! I sometimes think that there are not many left; but, doubtless, that comes of living so long in the Catskills instead of in Paris.'

May I reciprocate the compliment by expressing my appreciation of your own humanity. It is a great pleasure to meet anyone who, besides possessing other qualities, is a person who one would not be ashamed to introduce into one's favourite public house.

With kindest regards to Mrs le Gallienne and the hope of seeing you week after next,

Sincerely yours,
[T. S. Eliot]

## TO *John Middleton Murry* — TS Northwestern

12 June 1926 — 57 Chester Terrace, S.W.1.

Dear John,

Some weeks ago I addressed for Vivien the envelope of a letter which she wrote to you from Rome. I registered this letter. She never heard from you. I should very much like to know whether you ever received it or not.

Yours ever
T. S. E.

My best address is 24, Russell Square, W.C.1

## TO *H. J. C. Grierson* — TS National Library of Scotland

12 June 1926 — *The New Criterion*

My dear Sir,

I thank you extremely for your kind letter, although I perceive that it is evasive of the matter I had most at heart. But the compliments that it contains are very grateful to me from such a source.

I return the enclosed letter which has also given me great pleasure.[1]

Yours sincerely,
T. S. Eliot

1–Grierson had enclosed with his letter of 11 June a letter written in 1925 by 'one of my younger lecturers' in appreciation of TSE – 'w. no thought of your seeing it'.

## TO *Orlo Willliams* CC

12 June 1926 [*The New Criterion*]

Dear Williams,

Many thanks for your letter. How does Thursday the 24th, dinner, suit you? If that is all right, I will communicate with you on my return as to when and where to meet.

I am aware that by using the 'Captain' in October I am sacrificing 'Tom Jones'.[1] I must plead the exigencies of editorial combination. Good stories are much more scarce than essays: or rather, a story has to be very good in order to pass muster, whereas an essay is possible if it is good in parts. That is to say, I am chronically hard up for fiction. It may be that my tastes in fiction are very, very limited, but when I look at that in even the best of the other periodicals, even *The Calendar* and *The Dial*, I am never interested.[2]

Thanks for your useful information about Bacchelli and Baldini. They both sound rather slight.[3] Would you mind my asking Angioletti to submit a few things to you first? If I kept turning things down, he might become discouraged, whereas you could indicate to him better than I could what was wrong.

Yours always sincerely,
[T. S. Eliot]

1 – Williams wrote on 11 June: 'I am very pleased to learn that "Capitaine Ensorceleur" has gone to the printers, for the October number, *but* I can't help reminding you . . . that "Tom Jones" will be in a book to be published this autumn . . .'

2 – TSE was to tell Delmore Schwartz on 26 Oct. 1939: 'As for the fiction, I was always at a loss where to turn for good stories; what were offered were usually appalling; and I didn't like to beg from people who could command a higher price elsewhere' (Beinecke).

3 – Williams had written on 11 June: 'I know some of Bacchelli's work. He wrote a very entertaining & witty story called "La Sa & Tonno", about a young tunnyfish's adventures – a satire on modern society – which he is dying for me to translate. So I would, if I could get an American publisher, but Secker, who wants the book, offers me terms I couldn't possibly accept. Bacchelli also writes in the Convegno, & has been doing dramatic criticism in the literary weekly *La Fiera Letteraria*.

'Baldini's work I only know from occasional articles in the *Corriere della Sera*, but Linati told me that he is the best "essayist" in Italy. I should inquire rather closely into the subject, I think, in either case, before commissioning contributions. Some of the modern Italian work, judged by our standards, is rather wanting in pep & point.'

## TO *Terence Prentis* CC

12 June 1926 [London]

Dear Prentis,

I have your letter long unanswered, but have been away from England for a very long time.[1] I quite like the poem you enclosed. It seems to me a distinct improvement in simplification and directness over the ones I have seen before. I question the rhyme of *Arcades* and *Facades*. The one word being more fully assimilated into the language than the other, and I do not quite grasp the grammatical construction of the second stanza. It also seems to me a little violent to present flowers as both crisp and carnal (fleshy) and as setting fire to tinder. But the poem, though slight, does seem to me, I repeat, to make an advance in simplification and movement, and I hope that you will soon have something more substantial to show me.

About novel jackets, I have mentioned the matter and I suggest that you submit a few specimens of your work to Mr Geoffrey Faber. I might indicate that from a commercial point of view the more realistic type of design is more useful than the abstract or purely decorative.

With all best wishes,
Sincerely yours,
[T. S. Eliot]

## TO *Henry Eliot* TS Houghton

13 June 1926 24 Russell Square London

My dear brother,

I was very grateful for your wires and your and T.'s kind letters. V. is I believe in the best nursing home in France for such cases, and I have been very favourably impressed with the intelligence of the French doctors,

1 – Prentis wrote (undated): 'it is really very heartening to realize that one's abortive attempts at writing can attain any significance in others' eyes. From you especially the slightest word of encouragement would amount to a command if poetry were a thing to be commanded. That, for me, is where the trouble lies. I hope that I shall be able to write again sometime and to find that I have benefited by my, for however short or long, abstention. I am enclosing the only thing I have written lately. Please do not trouble to return it or feel obliged to furnish any comments.

'Would it be straining your kindliness too far if I were to ask you to mention my name to the production manager of "Faber & Gwyer", should you be able to, as a potential designer of novel jackets etc.'

and their apparent humanity.[1] It has turned out, in some ways, for the best; that is, she would obviously have had to go somewhere, and if it had not come so suddenly she would have come back to England. And I think it is easier both for the present <and the future> that this should have happened abroad; she seems to take more kindly to this place than she probably would have done to any in England. Apparently she has not distrusted the people there, but has been devoured by self-accusations to the point that she has had to be watched day and night. The most worrying thing is perhaps the voices which she still hears constantly. The doctors do not allow me to be very optimistic. Mr and Mrs Haigh-Wood are in Paris, but neither they nor I have been allowed to see V. and she does not write or receive letters. I am going over tomorrow for about a week. Of course I have been very busy here trying to put my affairs into some sort of order. I was very grateful for the two hundred dollars, but you must not send any more. I think I can manage: and now I shall be able to work and add to my income. The cost (the franc being fortunately so low) is about ten pounds a week at the sanatorium, but of course I can now economise in other ways, and it is a relief to have one big definite expense rather than innumerable petty and wasteful ones. I am merely saying to friends that V. has not been at all well and is staying abroad for a rest cure. I shall not say much more than that to mother, to whom I am writing today. So please instruct Theresa accordingly.

It was a great joy to her as well as to myself to have as much time as we did have with you and Theresa, and I know she remains very fond of you both. You both wrote very sweet letters to her and it is a pity she could not see them, but when and if she gets better I know you will both write again.

I shall miss you both very keenly – you leave a great vacuum in London, and I feel very isolated. But *whichever* way things turn out, it does seem to me more likely that I can get to America within a year.

Write when you can. Very much love.

Tom

1–The Sanatorium de la Malmaison, housed in a mansion in Rueil, 10 kilometres west of Paris, was built in the early 19th century (the Empress Josephine had died there); in 1911 it was transformed into a sanatorium specialising in '*des affections du système nerveux*'. The dramatist Georges Feydeau (1862–1921) died there; and Zelda Fitzgerald was to pass a few days there following a nervous breakdown in Apr. 1930 (Kendall Taylor, *Sometimes Madness Is Wisdom: Zelda and Scott Fitzgerald: A Marriage*, 2002). Since 1965 it has been the headquarters of the Institut Française du Pétrole. See M. de Brunhoff, *Le Sanatorium de la Malmaison* (1913).

## TO *His Mother*

TS Houghton

13 June 1926

57 Chester Terrace, Eaton Square, S.W.1. BEST ADDRESS is always 24 Russell Square as heretofore.

My dearest mother,

You will perhaps have heard from Henry – I understand that he is stopping with you for a few days – that Vivien has not been very well and that I left her behind, as she did not want to return to London until she was strong enough to keep house etc. and I think she has done wisely to put herself under a French doctor, for they are, the best of them, the cleverest in Europe. She will probably stay for some weeks and then we may go down to Rapallo for August or September, where it is hot and sunny and there is good bathing. I have been back for a week and very busy indeed with all sorts of matters that I could not attend to from a distance. Our little garden is doing well, the rosebushes and lupins and larkspur will soon be in flower, and I wish Vivien was here to see them. But it has been a backward rainy season.

We enjoyed immensely our time with Henry and Theresa, and I hope that they did. We both took a very strong fancy to Theresa, she is very sweet and very sane, and we hated to part with them. I know that Henry has written long letters to tell you of all that we saw. Rome is delightful; I want to go back there some day. Italy is delightful to live in; less of a mental strain than France, more cheerful than either France or Germany; and extremely well governed. I found it a good country to work in; the people are restful, the climate very good, and intellectual distractions few. The Italians are distinguished by being, physically and mentally, the healthiest race in Europe; and if they are therefore a little less interesting they are all the better to live among.

*The Criterion* is going on fairly well, though the publishing season in general has been very bad. The publishing business in England depends upon two seasons, from October to Christmas, and from March to June. The autumn season was injured by a packers' strike, and the spring season by the general strike. It has affected us all alike, of course, but the lighter class of book the most; accordingly my poems have proved to be one of the most successful of Faber & Gwyer's books – about 1400 copies have sold so far and they have printed a second edition.[1] *The Criterion* has

1 – The first edition had almost sold out: *Poems 1909–1925* was published on 23 Nov. 1925 in an edition of 1,460 copies. (The Publication Manager's Report for Dec. 1925 recorded

increased its sales to about 1100, and I hope to see it up to 1500 in a year. It is also reaching the point where it takes less time – otherwise I could hardly have staid away so long consecutively. And I think it is being read more and more for the regular features – the reviews, the chronicles, etc. – which makes things easier for me – I do not have to worry about famous names or 'star' articles in every number. One of my editorial advantages is that I am more closely in touch, both directly and through my adjutants, with foreign literature than anyone else in England or indeed in America. But the whole merit of an editor is to choose the right people and then let them write almost anything they wish to write – and I think that most of the men who write for the *Criterion* do their best work for it.

The article by Henri Massis proved to be the most popular in the last number. He is one of the royalist and neo-catholic group as are in fact most of my friends in Paris. The more one sees of the disorganisation and bad government of the republic since the war, its corruption and lack of continuous policy and the utter selfishness of so many politicians, the growing power of socialists under Russian influence, the more one sympathises with the movement which aims to replace the republic by the kingship. And since the Russian revolution socialism has come to mean more and more definitely not only anti-clericalism but anti-religion. The 'foreign agitator', sometimes Russian and often Jew, is no longer confined to America; he is conspicuous in England and still more so in France. But France is in a far worse way than England. Here the administration of justice has never been impugned. In France, several of my friends (of the royalist party) might at any time be shot at by some communist fanatic, and even in case of death, the chances are 100 to 1 that the assassin would escape with a light punishment. They are, for that matter, also in risk of being put into gaol themselves, for some nominal infraction of the law. When I go back to Paris, in a few days,[1] to see how Vivien is getting on, I am attending a small dinner of some of the heads of the party – Charles Maurras, Massis, Maritain, Bainville[2] etc. – partly because they want to have English politics explained to them. I am afraid I am not in close enough touch with events here to explain, but at least I can try to explain some of the differences in mentality which make England saner than France, and politics less interesting.

---

that the volume had sold 623 copies up to 12 Dec. 1925.)

1 – GCF noted in his diary on Mon., 14 June: 'Eliot goes to Paris.'

2 – Jacques Bainville (1879–1936): historian, journalist, royalist, follower of Charles Maurras; co-founder of *Action Française*; editor of *Le Revue Universelle*; author of *Histoire de deux peuples* (1915) and *Les Conséquences politiques de la paix* (1920).

Politics are, in fact, too interesting in France, they absorb literature. A detached point of view, even a detached passion for literature, is impossible; all their criticism is tainted with party, and all their art with politics. On the other hand, they have reached the point of realising the importance of issues to which people in England are not yet awake. The Bernard Shaw or the Wells type is much more vigorously attacked in France than here.

You will like to know that I met Margaret de Bassiano and her husband while I was in Paris for a few days. She is a nice unpretentious woman of about forty, I should say; her husband is a person of considerable charm, more like an Englishman than an Italian (I imagine he is partly English or has British blood, he spoke of Lord Crawford[1] as if he were a relative) speaking both English and French without the slightest trace of an Italian accent – and it is very rare that an Italian speaks any language without an Italian accent. I shall go out and see them at Versailles when I go back.

Ezra Pound and his wife are in Paris for the summer, and have again been very very kind to both of us. Mr and Mrs Haigh-Wood are there for a few days, and are going on to Aix where Mrs Haigh-Wood has to go every year for the arthritis. She is so crippled by it that at times she can hardly use her hands at all; that is why her writing is so illegible. And Mr Haigh-Wood is not at all well, his lungs give him difficulty. In the circumstances, it was extremely good of Mrs H-W to let our flat for us; she took an immense amount of trouble getting it ready and advertising it and interviewing prospective tenants; and at the same time, in spite of her own health and her husband's, she was looking for good lodgings for Theodora,[2] which she has found.

I have been bitterly sorry that in the circumstances I have been unable to do anything further about *Savonarola*. But I shall see Cobden-Sanderson either tomorrow or as soon as I get back from Paris, and arrange the autumn campaign in America. Professor Rand's letter pleased me very much. Oddly enough, *The Times* have sent me a book of his to review.[3]

My friend (a younger friend) Herbert Read has just brought out with us a volume of essays, which is very good and which I think I will send to you. I will send with it his little book *In Retreat*, which is a very impressive account of part of his war experiences. Although a very quiet and retiring

1–David Lindsay, 27th Earl of Crawford (1871–1940): politician; art connoisseur; diarist.

2–Theodora Eliot Smith (b. 1904) – TSE's niece; daughter of Charlotte (Mrs George Lawrence Smith) – was visiting Europe for some months.

3–TSE, 'The Latin Tradition' – on Edward Kennard Rand, *The Latin Tradition* – *TLS*, 14 Mar. 1929, 200.

man, he received two decorations and was several times mentioned for gallantry in action, and got his captaincy, so he knows what he is talking about. He is more important to me than any of the other men connected with the *Criterion*.

I will write often now. I long for news of you; and I wish you would give me news of the rest of the family. I thought Henry in capital health, and he seemed very happy. Now I am looking forward to my next travels being to America, in the winter or spring. When I have cleared off this summer's work (The Seneca is not for Faber & Gwyer, but for Charles Whibley) and Vivien is strong again, I shall have much more freedom of movement.

With very much love
Tom

## TO *Theodora Bosanquet*[1] — TS Houghton

21 June 1926 — *The New Criterion*

Dear Madam,

I am returning your interesting manuscript only after considerable hesitation.[2] But I cannot feel that the activities of *surréalistes*, or of super-realists as we perhaps ought to call them – perhaps it would be better not to say their activities inasmuch as some of the products are of interest, but rather their theories – I cannot feel that the theories of the *surréalistes* are of sufficient importance to justify us in treating them with so much care.

May I hope that you will find occasion to send me some other essay in which the subject is worthy of the author.

Yours very truly,
T. S. Eliot

1–Theodora Bosanquet (1880–1961) had been Henry James's secretary, 1907–16: her memoir *Henry James at Work* (1924) was no. 3 of The Hogarth Essays. A graduate of University College, London, she was Executive Secretary of the International Federation of University Women, 1920–35; literary editor of *Time and Tide*, 1935–43. Works include *Harriet Martineau* (1927) and *Paul Valéry* (1933).

2–Bosanquet had submitted her article on the Surrealists on 7 Feb. 1926.

## TO *James Smith* CC

21 June 1926 [London]

Dear Smith,

Forgive me if you can for my long silence with regard to your manuscript. I have long ago read it, but lacked the energy, time and wit to compose the critical letter which it requires. Please accept these hurried comments in lieu of criticism.

The desire to imitate or emulate Pope is itself rare and commendable. To imitate Pope is in itself highly useful for anyone who wishes to write poetry. I have done it myself, not so very long ago either, and with the exception of one or two lines I do not think that my verses were any better than yours, and perhaps not so evenly good. I destroyed mine[1] and recommend you to do the same. Nothing in this style of verse is of any value except as an exercise: and this for the reason that it has already been done literally to perfection. You cannot improve on Pope, nor can you get anywhere by burlesquing him or ragging him because there is just sufficient element of burlesque in Pope himself to render him immune. So there you are. Send me something else and drop me a line if you are ever in London. I suppose you are now in Caledonia.

Sincerely yours,
[T. S. Eliot]

## TO *H. J. C. Grierson* TS National Library of Scotland

21 June 1926 *The New Criterion*

Dear Professor Grierson,

Thank you extremely for your very kind letter.[2] As you speak of preparing a course of lectures in America, I suppose that you will be absent from Britain during part of next year and therefore I might as well send you some of my material in its present form. I have lent the manuscript to a friend in London for his opinion, but will profit by your kind permission to send you some parts as soon as he returns it.

1 – See early drafts of 'The Fire Sermon', *TWL: Facs*, 22–3, 26–7, 38–41.

2 – Grierson had replied on 18 June to TSE's letter of 12 June: 'I did not understand what . . . you meant by my evasion until yesterday I happened to pick up your letter again & found in it the request about your proofs . . . It is a great compliment to be asked & I shd much like to read your proofs . . . I am preparing a course of lectures for America & shd probably be helped by comparing my ideas w. yours.'

At the same time, I must say emphatically that I *dread* your inspection of my manuscript in its present form. It represents lectures as they were delivered and most of it was written in circumstances of great difficulty; it is full of hasty generalisations, unsubstantiated statements and unverified references; there are great gaps in my knowledge which ought to be filled; and the style is abominable.

I have indeed read Mario Praz's book – in fact I reviewed it for *The Times*, and made great use of it and I hope sufficient acknowledgment of my indebtedness [appears] in my lectures.[1]

With many thanks for your courtesy,

Believe me,
Sincerely yours,
T. S. Eliot

## TO *Allen Tate*

CC

22 June 1926 [London]

Dear Mr Tate

I am now returning the poems which you sent me. I should have been tempted to keep them longer but I hope that my returning them will incite you before long to send me some more recent and more perfected work. Much of your poetry seems to me suggestive of the influence of Baudelaire, which is interesting and good.[2] It seems to err, if I may be allowed to express my opinion, chiefly by a certain stridency and over-emphasis. This is to say, the emphases occur too frequently; you are tempted to look for the strongest word in every place; whereas the strong word ought to be led up to and followed by words which do not demand so much attention. This effort for exactness is good, but the result goes beyond exactness and overreaches itself. In consequence you never arrive at the rhythm

1–Grierson enquired, 'Have you read Signor Mario Praz's book . . .?' *Secentismo e Marinismo in Inghilterra: John Donne – Richard Crashaw* (1925), was in part the inspiration for TSE's Clark Lectures. TSE had identified his cue in his review (*TLS*, 17 Dec. 1925, 878): 'No one is more aware than [Praz] of the world of difference between the religion of the seventeenth century and that of the thirteenth. It is the difference between psychology and metaphysics. Here Signor Praz is able to supply what has been a conspicuous defect of English criticism of Donne: a comparison between Donne and the metaphysical poets of the age of Dante. This is a point upon which he touches lightly, and which we wish he might examine in greater detail.'

2–Charles Baudelaire (1821–67): author of *Les Fleurs du mal* (1857) and the posthumous *Le Spleen de Paris* (1869); a speaking presence in *The Waste Land*.

and harmony of Baudelaire, or at his often astonishing amalgamation of sublimity and conversational simplicity. On the other hand (if I am right in attributing so much importance to his influence over you) Baudelaire has been too strong an influence to permit your developing any different kind of rhythm. But it is a poetry in whose future I am most interested.[1]

I am hoping to hear from you in reply to my last letter about your essay.[2] Later on, I should be very much interested to see something by you about Paul More.

Sincerely yours,
[T. S. Eliot]

## TO *F. S. Flint* CC

23 June 1926 [*The New Criterion*]

My dear Flint,

This is a question which the excitement of the evening put out of my mind. Would you be willing to do a note on J. B. Trend's book for the October number? Trend being a colleague, we ought to take notice of his book, and I dare say it is a very good book too. It is a collection of essays,

1–It is likely to have been this letter to which Tate refers in 'Homage to T. S. Eliot' (1966): 'There had been some formal correspondence as early as 1923 concerning some of my early poems which he had declined to publish in *The Criterion*. Years later, in 1956, when he was my guest in Minneapolis, I showed him his first letter to me in which he said that I ought to try to "simplify" myself – advice I was never able to take, try as I would. When he had finished reading the letter, with that sober attention that he always gave to the most trivial request of a friend, looking over his spectacles, he said: "It seems awfully pompous and condescending"; and then he laughed. His laugh was never hearty; it was something between a chuckle and a giggle; and now he was laughing both at himself and at me – at me for what he evidently considered the absurdity of keeping a letter of his all those years' (90).
2–Tate would thank TSE (13 July) for his 'excellent brief review . . . [I]t gives me a certain pleasure to agree with your analysis of my style because the agreement tends to confirm the terms of my own criticism. I should say (eliminating the real approval I have of some of my work) that the poems are rather synopses of effects than sustained compositions. Hiatuses in pattern, due to rejection of all but the pivotal significations, do of course make these key significations unduly complex: for a very good reason I have avoided an explicit rendition of the content of my ideas, the result being a strained implication of meaning in telescoped images. I do not hesitate to confess that this method has been due to the philosophical incertitude of the mind which the poems represent. I have not been willing to risk the explicit assertion of a rational attitude in a context derivative of sensations, with which it might not fuse. So far as the problem exceeds the special limits of my own personality (and all problems exceed personality) I suppose this bifurcation of the intelligence is characteristic of those minds of the age which covet the unusual integrity of being actually contemporary. Pardon me if this is defensive.'

mostly about Spanish literature which I am incompetent to criticise, but covering all periods of Spanish literature up to the present, and you could pick out any part that you are interested in to write about. It might be amusing to make some observation à propos of the essay which he has included on Gongora. In any case I hope you will do the book.[1]

Yours ever,
[T. S. Eliot]

## TO *Bonamy Dobrée*

TS Brotherton

23 June 1926 *The New Criterion*

My dear Dobrée,

I enclose an invitation to Pound's concert next Tuesday evening.[2] I should be very glad if you and your wife could come.

I dare say that your time in Paris will be very fully occupied, but if you would care to do so I should be delighted if you would go to see Cocteau's little play, *Orphée*, at the *Théâtre des Arts* on the *boulevard des Batignolles*. I have seen it myself and think it is well worth the trouble, although not altogether successful. If you would care to see it with a view to writing a note about it for the October number, let me know on Friday morning and I will write to Cocteau and try to get him to send you press tickets. I suggested to Read that he should do something about Cocteau in the October *Criterion* à propos of the English translation of *Rappel à l'Ordre* which we are publishing shortly. But Read is not very keen about the subject and I am inclined to think myself that it is perhaps premature to commit ourselves to a complete opinion concerning this

1 – Flint replied (24 June), 'if you are incompetent to criticize a book about Spanish literature, how much more so am I?! I know practically nothing about it, and it would not be fair to Trend to give it to me to do.' See the anonymous review – probably by CA – of *Alfonso the Sage and Other Essays*, *NC* 4 (Oct. 1926), 789–90.

2 – *Paroles de Villon: Airs and Fragments from an Opera Le Testament*, by EP, was performed at the Salle Pleyel, Paris, on 29 June, with Olga Rudge (1895–1996) – EP's mistress, who had borne his first child, Mary, in 1925 – playing the violin. Robert McAlmon would recount in his memoirs (written in the 1930s): 'Ezra's opera was given in a small hall . . . but still a sizeable audience arrived on time and waited patiently for the performance to begin. I was with Jane Heap, Djuna Barnes, Mina Loy, and Kitty Cannell, and all around us were people we knew well. As the opera got under way I saw T. S. Eliot slip into a seat in the back row. Mina Loy and Jane Heap said that they would like to meet him, and I thought surely he would remain to go behind and greet Ezra, but before the performance was ended he slipped away as he had come' (*Being Geniuses Together 1920–1930*; revised, and with supplementary chapters and New Afterword by Kay Boyle [London, 1984], 196).

enigmatic Middleton Murry of France. Also I think that the one side of Cocteau's work which so far has shown itself to be of incontestable value and interest is his theatrical side, and about this you, of course, are the most suitable person to express an opinion for us.

The *Rappel à l'Ordre* is not occupied with the Theatre alone, but I thought if you took this and the novels and the *Potomak* and the recent verse (all of which I can send you) and saw the play, you could do a most interesting review with special attention to his dramatic talent and (what is still more certain) his theatrical talent. For me this would kill several birds with one stone: it would partly fill our theatrical gap which I mentioned to you and would avoid the necessity of mentioning Cocteau's recent and notorious *Lettre à Jacques Maritain*.

Let me know what you think about all this on Friday. And for Heaven's sake do not forget my ticket for the 9.20 to Newhaven on Saturday night. I forgot to explain that you cannot reserve ordinary seats on the Victoria–Newhaven train, but that what I want to do if agreeable to you is to reserve seats in the 2nd class *Pulman* where the dinner is, according to English railway standards, extremely good. And the distance from London to Newhaven allows just comfortable time to dine without haste.

Yours ever
T. S. Eliot

I much enjoyed your hospitality.

## TO *Herbert Read* CC

23 June 1926 [*The New Criterion*]

My dear Read,

Here are one or two things I forgot to mention yesterday. 1. Have you had time to look at that sketch by Salinas.[1] 2. It has occurred to me that we might dispose of the Cocteau matter by turning it on to Dobrée and getting him to emphasise the dramatic side. This would relieve you altogether and would avoid the necessity of expressing an opinion about the letter to Maritain. I have just written to Dobrée about this.[2] 3. The poetry book failing, I have two other books, one Henry Bett's *Erigena*[3]

1–Pedro Salinas (1891–1951), Spanish poet, playwright and critic. HR wrote (24 June): 'The sketch by Salinas has already been published in La Revista de Occidente'; it 'must be extremely well translated to be effective'.

2–BD tackled all of the recent Cocteau creations in *NC* 4 (Oct. 1926), 764–8.

3–Henry Bett, *Johannes Scotus Erigena: A Study in Mediaeval Philosophy* (1926), was to be reviewed by HR in *NC* 4 (Oct. 1926), 776–82.

(Cambridge University Press) which I think you ought to have, and the other the *Year's Work in English Studies* which would probably be merely a good pretext for original observations.

Yours in haste
[T. S. E.]

## TO *Jean de Menasce*

CC

23 June 1926 [Paris ]

My dear de Menasce,

If you are in Paris will you come to this concert on Tuesday evening? If you can come, I want to introduce you to Madame de Bassiano.

Even if you cannot come, I wish you would drop me a line to the Hotel Foyot and let me know when we can meet. I should like to see you and in particular I want you to undertake, if you will, to translate into French some verses which I will show you.

Yours ever
[T. S. Eliot]

## TO *G. B. Angioletti*

CC

23 June 1926 [London]

Dear Mr Angioletti,

I do not think that I have ever written to you personally to acknowledge your letter of the 28th April and thank you for your most successful and interesting chronicle.[1] I hope that you can let me have another one for *The New Criterion* of next January and will write to you again to give you due warning.

I should have written to you before but during most of the spring and summer I have been out of England. For a considerable time I was in Italy and had it been possible for me to stop in Milan I should have attempted to see you.

I have spoken of your letter to Orlo Williams and I should be very glad if you would send direct to him any manuscript which you think might be suitable for translation for *The New Criterion*. In each case, of course, I have to consider not only the intrinsic merit of the writer

1 – Angioletti's 'Italian Chronicle' – *NC* 4 (June 1926) – had included a sceptical review of Italo Svevo's *La Coscienza di Zeno* (1923).

but the possibility of conveying his qualities through the medium of an English translation, and in criticising contributions from this point of view Mr Williams has kindly consented to help me. We particularly wish to secure *inédits*, although there is no objection to their appearing in Italy immediately afterwards.

I await also the contribution of your own which you mention in the last paragraph of your letter, and beg you to send it to me, at this address.[1]

With very many thanks and sincere appreciation of your interest,

I am,
Yours very sincerely,
[T. S. Eliot]

## TO *Max Clauss* CC

23 June 1926 [London]

Dear Sir,

I apologise for not having thanked you for your letter of the 13th April. I have had to be a great deal abroad during the last three months and have been obliged to neglect many matters of importance.

I appreciate the honour of being invited to contribute to your review, a copy of which I have perused with great interest.[2] For some time to come I am afraid that my other engagements are too numerous to permit my writing anything worthy of your review, but I should like to hope that a contribution from myself would be acceptable at a later time.

We should be glad to exchange with your review, and upon hearing from you that you have received this letter we will send you the latest number. I should be obliged if you would send the *Europäische Revue* regularly *not* to this address but *direct* to my colleague who has charge of the department of German literature for *The New Criterion*, namely:

A. W. G. Randall, Esq
C/o the British Legation of the Holy See,
67, Via S. Nicolo da tolentino
Rome (5), Italy.

With many thanks,

Yours very truly,
[T. S. Eliot]

1 – Angioletti assured TSE (2 July) he would send the article within a few days.
2 – *Europäische Revue.*

## TO *His Mother*

TS Houghton

24 June 1926 *The Criterion*

My dearest mother,

I have at last seen Cobden-Sanderson, and cleared matters up with him. It appears that I never gave him the copy of agreement signed by you, and I handed it to him yesterday, and he is sending you the copy signed by him direct. I am very disappointed that he was unable to place any copies in America; but he is a very small publisher, and has no agent in America for sales, and that makes a great deal of difference. And I am afraid that the 150 copies he sent you arrived too late for the spring and summer season. I should try the booksellers again [in] the autumn. Several friends – Whibley and Robertson – have expressed warm appreciation of the poem, but we have fared badly in press notices.

I had a very interesting dinner with the 'Action Française' – they did very well by me – a private room in one of the best restaurants – fifteen people – and the most exquisite dinner I have ever tasted – everything done in the best French taste.[1] All the leaders of the party were present, including Léon Daudet and his wife – the latter a very charming woman of about sixty, rather tragic (I think I mentioned the frightful scandal of a few years ago, when their son Philippe was killed, a boy of fourteen, apparently by communists.)[2] Charles Maurras himself is deaf as a post, so that one only communicates with him through someone who knows how to scream at the right pitch. He is a prodigious worker, left about 10.30 for his newspaper office, where he works every night till about five in the morning. Briand having just resigned,[3] the party was rather excited, but no good was expected; and indeed the situation in France at this moment gives cause for considerable anxiety. The following evening, dined at the Bassianos at Versailles; they have a beautiful villa and garden there, and

1–TSE would remember this dinner party as one of the finest of his life – 'It was a very good dinner,' he told E. J. H. Greene (19 Apr. 1940), 'and I remember the canard aux oranges with permanent pleasure' – and only exceeded in his first sixty years by a Shrove Tuesday dinner that was to be hosted by Ashley Dukes in 1948.

2–Philippe Daudet (1909–23), son of the writer and Royalist Léon Daudet, had run away from home and was presently discovered to have shot himself in the head in a taxi; but the family Daudet, with the support of *Action Française*, fostered the conviction that the boy had been murdered by anarchists or Republicans.

3–Aristide Briand (1862–1932), socialist politician, served ten times as Prime Minister of France, having been elected for the first time in 1909. Briand's eighth government, in which he was President of the Council and Minister of Foreign Affairs, ran from 9 Mar. to 23 June 1926. He was awarded the Nobel Peace Prize, 1926.

two quite attractive children. The next day, spent afternoon with Jacques Maritain discussing theology;[1] in the evening went to see the new play of my friend Cocteau.[2] Did not like it overmuch; too many angels in it, he having been recently re-converted to the Church; but I like to see everything new in the drama, for my own purposes. Another evening with Ramon Fernandez, my brilliant Mexican, and Charles Du Bos, and André Gide, and a German professor, and a duchess of something; these evenings are tiring, as they keep on talking till 1 or 2 in the morning. One afternoon to George Antheil's concert, very modern music, very much to my taste, but not to that of all of the audience, some of whom demonstrated; Ezra (who is Antheil's champion) got very excited, and rushed about in high glee.[3] All this will show you that Paris is not restful,

1–TSE told E. J. H. Greene on 19 Apr. 1940, 'I think that I first heard of Maritain about 1925, when I think I came across *Art et Scolastique* [1925], but it may have been some other of his books available at that time. I certainly had not heard his name very long before then, and think that I first came across it in the *Action Française*, with which he was at that time very friendly. I first met him in July 1926 at a dinner given by Léon Daudet at that restaurant where the Académie Goncourt used to meet . . . There were present the Daudets, Maurras, the Bainvilles, the Massis, Pujo and myself, and Maritain came in after dinner. I daresay that was the last formal occasion on which he met them, because you will remember that the letter of Cardinal Andrieu against the *Action Française* which eventually led to the Vatican condemnation appeared in that year.' (See further Maritain, *Une opinion sur Charles Maurras et le devoir des catholiques*, 1926.) In 'The Idealism of Julien Benda' (*New Republic*, 12 Dec. 1928), TSE declared: 'The influence of Bergson . . . as well as that of [Charles] Péguy and the ecstatic Léon Bloy, is strong upon the leader of the Catholic rationalists, M. Jacques Maritain. I have a warm personal admiration for M. Maritain, as much for his saintly character as for his intelligence; but I have never seen a more romantic classicist, or a Thomist whose methods of thought were less like those of Aquinas. His occasional intemperance of language, and his occasional sentiment, hardly qualify him for the philosophical crown which M. Benda is waiting to bestow upon someone.' On 24 Oct. 1951, TSE told Canon B. Iddings Bell: 'I have always been fond of Maritain personally, but I must admit that he seems to me, in recent years, to have less and less of importance to say.' E. W. F. Tomlin remarked of TSE that 'although he much liked Maritain as a person . . . he felt that the French post-Bergsonian intellectual approach, even if called "Neo-scholastique", differed markedly from that of S. Thomas himself: it was the difference between a hovering darting kestrel and a "dumb ox" pawing the ground' (*T. S. Eliot: A Friendship*, 73); and again: 'He commented . . . that while he found Maritain a most charming man, his philosophical work, though claiming to reflect at every point Thomist orthodoxy, was in spirit quite unlike that of St Thomas' (94).
2–*Orphée*, a one-act tragedy (1925).
3–George Antheil (1900–59), child of German immigrants, was an American avant-garde composer (and from 1936 a successful film composer in Hollywood), pianist, critic and author, who had studied music in Philadelphia and New York before sailing for Europe in 1922. Taken up in Paris by Sylvia Beach, who enabled Antheil and his Hungarian wife Boski Markus to live over the bookshop Shakespeare & Company, he became acquainted with Beach's friends including James Joyce (with whom Antheil talked of collaborating on an opera), and EP – who celebrated the prodigy in *Antheil and the Treatise on Harmony*

or a good place in which to work; since returning to London I have been extremely busy, but it is peace itself in comparison. Paris is not favourable to independent thinking either: it is so clearly divided into groups and parties, each of which is provided with its own unshakeable convictions and prejudices, and a complete set of derogatory anecdotes about the others; the whole atmosphere is highly polemical; and politics, religion and art are inextricable. This makes for some excitement and interest, but not, as I said, for complete independence of judgement.

The Haigh-Woods were in Paris, on their way to Aix, and I took at least one meal with them every day. They were very good. I have been rather anxious about them, neither is very well, and I was glad to see them off to Aix, where Mrs Haigh-Wood is to have treatment for her arthritis. Her hands are dreadfully crippled, and at times she can hardly use them at all – that is why her handwriting is so bad.

Vivien is much better, and is enjoying being in France. She finds the doctors very intelligent, and everyone connected with the place is very kind and friendly, and the whole atmosphere is much more *cheerful* than anywhere in England. And it is a beautiful place. Another advantage is that in French medical or health institutions you see not one but several doctors everyday; they work together, and you are not dependent on the judgement or the personality of one man. She sends you her love.

I must stop now. I am eagerly awaiting your news.

Your devoted son
Tom.

(1924). TSE attended the grand premiere of Antheil's *Ballet Mécanique* – a percussive and dissonant work originally scored for synchronised player pianos, grand pianos, electronic bells, xylophones, bass drums, a siren and three aeroplane propellers, but in the event (the technical problems having proved overwhelming) performed on just one pianola and a parade of pianos – at the Théâtre des Champs-Élysées. Formally dressed, complete with top hat, TSE escorted Lady Rothermere. Others in attendance included Beach, Adrienne Monnier, JJ and family, EP, Diaghilev, Koussevitsky and Brancusi. Some of the audience barracked the music, and the occasion ended with a riot in the streets. See Antheil's memoirs, *Bad Boy of Music* (1945); Carol Oja, 'George Antheil's Ballet Mécanique and Transatlantic Modernism', in *A Modern Mosaic: Art and Modernism in the United States*, ed. Townsend Ludington (2000); N. R. Fitch, *Sylvia Beach and the Lost Generation*, 237–40.

## TO *Henry Eliot* TS Houghton

24 June 1926 *The Criterion*

My dear brother,

I have just returned from Paris, where I had a very busy and tiring week. I shall go soon again. Apart from my own reasons for being there, I have unfortunately a very large acquaintance in Paris, whom, or some of whom, I have to see – one would meet them on the street anyhow: I am much more protected in London, and it is a real rest to be here, however busy one is. I like the little house, and there are flowers in the garden now, lupins and violas and a few roses. And it is premature to give it up yet. V. may be able to live in it again. I don't know. The signs are not very encouraging. She is very affectionate and gentle, and her regrets and self-accusations are terribly pathetic; she is very grateful to everyone in the home, and says they are very good to her. She does not want to leave, so far; the worry will begin when she does. Her beliefs in persecution are unshaken, and she still hears voices. But she has not made any attempt on her life for over a fortnight.

I don't know whether I thanked you for the money. It was very useful. I am gradually clearing up the mess. The Haigh-Woods have been very good and very helpful; but they are both infirm, and I found them, in Paris, something of a responsibility themselves. The doctors have not yet ventured on any prophecy. If she has to remain there, or somewhere, indefinitely, it will mean something like £500 a year. Of course, if I eventually get rid of this house, which I am loath to do, I can live quite inexpensively by myself. What seems likely is that in September, I shall try to let it for the winter; if V. is at large we could spend the winter at Rapallo, and I could make periodical visits to England; for in any case I think she had better stay out of England for a year or so.

What I am telling mother, and people generally, is that V. got very run down on our travels, had a touch of influenza, did not want to start again in England until she was quite fit to keep house, and decided to go into a country sanatorium in France to get fit. I have not mentioned the address to *anyone*: it is so well known that the word "Malmaison" is almost synonymous with insanity.

I shall rejoice when I get the first letter from you.

Ever your affectionate brother
Tom

I would write to Theresa if I knew her address. She wrote a sweet letter to V. but as I said it was undesirable to give it to her.

## TO *Harold Monro*[1] TS Beinecke

24 June 1926 *The Criterion*

My dear Monro,

The next day after I saw you, I received a telegram from Madame de Bassiano asking me to try the Hogarth Press for the *Commerce* agency. So, as I was seeing Leonard Woolf today in any case, I put it up to him. The Woolfs seem fairly favourable, in fact, rather more favourable than you did. We shall see. Had you seemed at all keen to undertake it, I should have let you know first; but I got the impression that you felt no enthusiasm – which I certainly should not have done, myself. It is simply a question, however, of who wants it most, or, of who is least disinclined to assume the burden. If you still care about it, let me know.[2] If the Woolfs decide that they want it, or if they decide that they don't want it, I shall let you know. It makes no difference to me whatever. I shall offer *my* £20 p.a. (as 'British correspondent') to whoever take it on.

I hope to see you next Tuesday week, and I hope that your eyes will improve rapidly, and let you finish that article.

Yours ever,
T. S. Eliot

## TO *Ottoline Morrell* TS Texas

24 June 1926 best address:
24 Russell Square, W.C.1

Dearest Ottoline –

I got back to London on Monday, and have been hoping to send you a wire to propose myself for one night. But I have had everything to keep me in London – immense arrears – and I leave again for Paris on Saturday. But I must see you before you leave (on the 10th?) and expect to return to London on Monday week, and will wire you then in the hope that you can find a night for me.

The circumstances are too many to explain in a letter. V. is in France, in a sanatorium, and likes the place. I saw the Woolfs today; this is all that I told them, and therefore all that you need to know officially – they

1–Harold Monro (1879–1932), poet, editor and publisher: see Biographical Register.

2–Monro said (28 June) he had not intended 'to appear unenthusiastic': it would be 'interesting and advantageous' for the Poetry Bookshop to 'take up the agency'.

said they were going to Garsington on Saturday. I am having lunch with Leonard tomorrow and shall tell him more, as I have in the past found his experience and advice helpful – and he is a good man; but, for various reasons, it is not, I think, advisable that Virginia should know more than I have told her, and than I have said above.

It was very interesting to learn that you are coming to London in the autumn; it would be more interesting if I were sure that we should be here. Of course I don't know till I see you, why you are coming, but the news is, *prima facie,* delightful.

You wrote me a very kind letter some time ago. But I am afraid I see myself too clearly to be even flattered or pleased by what you said!

Remember that when I see you I shall speak frankly to you – if to anybody.

Ever yours
T. S. E.

## TO *F. Sobieniowski* CC

25 June 1926 [London]

Dear Mr Sobieniowski,

I have your two letters and was extremely sorry that I could not be here this morning to see you when you called.[1] I am very sorry to hear of your difficulties, and would be glad to do anything possible. We occasionally pay for contributions on receipt and acceptance, in very special circumstances, but this case is rather different. I did not have time to look over the manuscript which you left yesterday and which you took away this morning and it was unnecessary for me to do so because it was obviously of such a length that it could only be published in book form. As Editor I have no control over the finances of *The New Criterion*, and

1 – Floryan Sobieniowski asked to meet TSE in connection with a book he was working on: *English Literature 1900–1925*. In addition, he had completed a draft of a translation of a long essay by the painter, sculptor, poet and dramatist, Stanislaw Wyspianksi (1868–1907) – *The Tragicall Historie of Hamlet, Prince of Denmarke, by William Shakespeare*, published as a book (1905) – 'the most profound book on *Hamlet*' – which Sobieniowski was convinced had solved all the key problems of the play. He would leave the manuscript at Faber & Gwyer for TSE to look at. Sobieniowski found himself 'in urgent need' of £8 10s 0d, and hoped TSE could advance him at least £6 10s 0d to meet his immediate debts. 'You have no idea how hard I have to fight for a bare existence,' he pleaded. He had not paid his rent for three weeks – it was all a 'nightmare'. In 1927 Sobieniowski would translate (with E. H. G. Pearson) Wyspianski's *Wesele* (1901) as *The Wedding*.

as I say, it is only when I have definitely accepted a manuscript and have it in my hands for publication in the next issue that I can approach my principals with a request for advance payment to the author.

I shall be very pleased to examine as quickly as possible any work you submit which is suitable for *The New Criterion* and not too long.

I am afraid, therefore, that I cannot do anything for your immediate predicament, but I hope that you will soon have something to offer us and that it will prove suitable.

Yours very truly,
[T. S. Eliot]

## TO *Gertrude Stein* — TS Beinecke

25 June 1926 *The New Criterion*

Dear Miss Stein,

I am returning to you with many regrets the manuscript which you sent me. I should have been very glad to use it but, as I think I told you, it would not have been possible before January. I now learn from Mr Leonard Woolf that The Hogarth Press are publishing it as a pamphlet[1] in the autumn which I am sorry to say renders it impossible for us.

With many regrets,
Yours very sincerely
T. S. Eliot

I like it.[2]

1–Published in Nov. 1926, *Composition as Explanation* (Hogarth Essays, Second Series, No. 1) was to be reviewed by TSE: 'her work is not improving, it is not amusing, it is not interesting, it is not good for one's mind. But its rhythms have a peculiar hypnotic power not met with before. It has a kinship with the saxaphone' ('Charleston, Hey! Hey!' *Nation and Athenaeum*, 40: 17 [29 Jan. 1927], 595).

2–Stein responded (26 June): 'I am glad you like it. I was about to ask you whether it should appear in the New Criterion now that the Hogarth Press is publishing it. Would you want to print "A Saint in Seven" which interested the two audiences the most perhaps of the things I read them, it has never been printed.'

## TO *Edwin Muir* 

CC

25 June 1926 [*The New Criterion*]

My dear Muir,

The firm has received a communication from Mr B. W. Huebsch[1] proposing that we should come to some arrangement about your future book on Nietzsche. It is not quite clear from Mr Huebsch's letter exactly what your contract with him is, but apparently you have assigned him some rights of priority in your next book. Mr Huebsch is himself travelling on the Continent somewhere. Would you mind telling me – in strictest confidence if you like – exactly what rights you have given him and whether they are universal rights or American rights only, so that I can reply in due course to his letter intelligently?

I hope that you are still enjoying the South of France, but that you will not remain away from Britain altogether.

Yours sincerely,
[T. S. Eliot]

## TO *J. B. Trend*

CC

25 June 1926 [*The New Criterion*]

My dear Trend,

I have ordered and received your *Alfonso*[2] but am having a certain amount of difficulty with it because all the people I know feel that you know so much more about Spain than anyone else in England that they are terrified to tackle it. If the man to whom I have just proposed it declines on the same grounds, can you suggest anyone yourself who would be competent?

I have had to be a great deal out of England myself for the last few months and have not had time to write to you; and indeed most of the time have not known where you were. But I think it is time that I expressed my appreciation and conveyed to you the sense of the numerous compliments *The New Criterion* has received on your Music Chronicles. They are so very good and so uniformly good that it is to be hoped that they will not

1–The publisher B. W. Huebsch (1876–1964) wrote to GCF (19 June) that the Viking Press, New York, held a contract with Muir 'for future work' and therefore had an interest in the arrangements that F&G had made for the publication of Muir's book on Nietzsche. The Viking Press was to approve of Muir's arrangements with F&G in Sept. 1926.

2–*Alfonso the Sage and Other Essays* was reviewed in *NC* 4 (Oct. 1926), 789–90.

be allowed to perish but will at least make the material for a book, which, if you make it, I should be delighted to urge upon my own firm. But apart from that, your chronicles contribute immensely to the strength of *The New Criterions* – much more than you can imagine – and I hope that you will continue them as long at least as I continue to be its Editor.

I am not at present in a position to reproach, but it is a matter of regret to many people, and especially to our other regular collaborators of *The New Criterion*, that you are so seldom in this country.

Sincerely yours,
[T. S. Eliot]

## TO *Conrad Aiken*

TS Huntington

25 June 1926 *The New Criterion*

Dear Conrad,

I have been very rushed this week and am going to Paris tomorrow but hope to be back in a week's time and shall propose myself at the first opportunity. Meanwhile, would you be willing as a favour to do a shortish note for the October number on a new book by our colleague J. B. Trend? It is a collection of essays on subjects chosen from various periods of Spanish literature, and I want it to be reviewed by somebody – because Trend is a very regular contributor and a very good one. I do not think that it would be difficult, but it ought to be handled by someone with at least a respectable acquaintance with Spanish and a little Spanish literature. I am not competent myself. Would you be willing?[1]

Yours in haste,
T.

P.S. I have also received El Artista Adolescente by James Joyce with an introduction by Antonio Marichalar, if that would interest you.[2]

But don't let anything distract you from the Great American Novel.

1–CA replied on 28 June, 'My acquaintance with Spanish literature is pretty scanty – I regard the Trend book with the feelings of a gambler. I *might* be able to do it without giving myself away – provided that I played very safe.'

2–'Thumbs down on the Italian Joyce,' answered CA. The Spanish translation of JJ's *Portrait* was reviewed in brief, and anonymously, in *NC* 5 (Jan. 1927), 158.

## TO *F. S. Flint* CC

25 June 1926 [London]

My dear Flint,

Your modesty is no doubt a very engaging quality but it is constantly causing me annoyance. As the point in question is a minor one, however, I shall give way.

Do not forget, however, that you are reviewing Robert Bridges' book for the October number.[1]

I enclose a sketch by Salinas about which Marichalar is very enthusiastic.[2] Would you mind reading it and letting me know whether you think it is good enough for translation for the October *Criterion*. If you think it *is* good enough and will tackle it yourself, I am willing to let you off either the Fernandez or the Rychner, although of course I should much prefer that these should be done by you. Rychner, at any rate, ought not to give you much trouble.

Yours in haste,
[T. S. Eliot]

P.S. I am arranging for exchange with L'Italiano of which I enclose an advertisement. If you do not begin to receive this within a fortnight, please let Miss Fassett know. I am hoping to see you on Tuesday week.

## TO *Harold Monro* TS Beinecke

Friday [2 July 1926] Hotel Foyot, Paris

My dear Monro,

This is to remind you that I shall go to the Oxford in Wardour[3] on Tuesday evening (no other place having been arranged) but I shall be at my office on Tuesday afternoon in case you telephone any change of plans. As my secretary is away, I wonder if you would mind reminding Read and Flint and Dobrée?

I have owed you a letter for some time. Have had no time. About the *Commerce* – I ought to explain: after I discussed it with you I thought that you were very hesitant, and that on the whole you thought it not

1 – See Flint's review of Bridges's *New Verse* in *NC* 4 (Oct. 1926), 768–72. Flint had written to IPF on 8 Apr.: 'I want to put up a serious argument on Bridges.'

2 – On 25 Jan. Marichalar had sent some work by Pedro Salinas, whom he thought popular with the youth of Spain.

3 – The Oxford Restaurant, Wardour Street, London.

worthwhile. Meanwhile Madame de Bassiano wired me suggesting the Hogarth, so as I was seeing the Woolfs the next day I put it to them. They were keener than I should have expected anybody to be – frankly I did not see why anyone in England should take it up – and have got into communication direct with Madame de Bassiano, and I understand from her that it is almost settled. If I had thought that you were really interested I could have stopped it at the outset, but after that it was out of my hands, and she wanted to arrange something as quickly as possible. My only interest in the matter was, that as she had appealed to me to find somebody, I wanted to do what I could with as little trouble to myself as possible.

Please don't think that I was in the least offended the other evening; I tried to show that I was not. There was nothing you said that you did not have every right to say at any time; I was only (I confess) a little grieved that you should have formed a theory about my behaviour and attitude which I, of course, believe to be wholly mistaken

On thinking the whole matter over, I don't see how certain people can be excluded from anything called a '*Criterion* dinner' – I mean the people who have been before, and, for my part, I should like to have Fletcher, and even Conrad Aiken on the rare occasions when he [is] in town. What might be possible is to make the dinners *monthly*, but have fortnightly informals chosen somewhat differently – smaller – at the Poetry Bookshop. Only, in that case, it would have to be arranged that everyone should contribute something to drink: I consumed an unjust quantity of your excellent whisky the last time.

If Tuesday night does not suit please ring me up Tuesday P.M. at Russell Square, or Tuesday morning at Sloane 3184.

Yours ever
T. S. E.

## TO *The Warden, The Helena Residential Club* CC

5 July 1926 [London]

CONFIDENTIAL

Dear Madam,

I have only today seen your letter of the 24th June as I have been out of England for the past week and have had no correspondence forwarded. Miss Theodora Eliot Smith is my niece and her standing and position are therefore in every way the same as mine. I have no hesitation in making myself responsible for her and I am sure that you will find her in every way a desirable member. She is a quiet studious girl and very well educated.

Should you have any need to communicate with me further about her, I am at your disposal.

I am, dear Madam,
Yours faithfully,
[T. S. Eliot]

## *Vivien Eliot* TO *John Middleton Murry* — MS Valerie Eliot

6 July [1926] — Sanatorium de la Malmaison,
4 Place Bergère, Rueil, Paris S&O

My dear John,

Thank you. I do appreciate you. I understand about the letter. But *don't forget*. You have something to do with me. I can wait, but you *will* help. You sent me the necessary words. 'Keep calm & quiet'.

I managed to for that day, but you know, I *can't*. Something awful has happened to me. I can't help myself & I can't ask God to help me. I don't ask Tom to help me now. I am quite alone & I have nothing at all inside. It is absolutely dark. I must speak to you honestly, for there is no one else who wd at the same time understand & not be *hurt* by it.

I can't keep calm & quiet John. It's no use. Why does Tom love me? You know I love Tom in a way that destroys us both. And it is *all* my life. Nothing remains.

'*The annihilation of personality*'. That you shd have written that has knocked me out. *I have known* this for several months. One's personality has got to go. Everyone is so angry about it. They think you can keep it & still arrive at something.

Write again *when you can*, & forgive me if I often write to you.

Vivien

## TO *George Rylands* — CC

6 July 1926 — [*The New Criterion*]

My dear Rylands,

I have just got back from Paris and am very sorry to learn that you have left London for the rest of the summer. I hope that you will let me know as soon as you are back in town, but meanwhile would you care to do a note on Walter de la Mare for the October number?[1] About the length of your review of Noel Coward. Only I do not know whether you have ever read any of de la Mare's prose – the books which I have for review are all prose – or what you think of it. My opinion is that although he is over-rated he has certain original and valuable qualities, especially in *The Memoirs of a Midget*, and I do not think it is worthwhile for anyone to tackle him who does not care for what he has to give. One must be critical of course, but I do not think it is necessary to be quite so harsh as was Leonard Woolf in the last *Nation*. Or rather, I think that what Leonard said was all perfectly true, but there are other things in de la Mare's work worth praise.[2]

I shall be away for a week from Saturday next, so that it would really be better if you waited a day or two and wrote to me at the Hotel Foyot, 33 rue de Tournon, Paris (6), where I shall be for the whole of next week.

Yours sincerely,
[T. S. Eliot]

## TO *Bruce Richmond* CC

6 July 1926 [London]

Dear Richmond,

Very many thanks for your letter and for the new book which looks very satisfactory. I have by no means forgotten Andrewes; as a matter of fact this article[3] will be a pretty serious matter for me as I shall have to clear up my mind and try to come to conclusions, in connection with Bishop Andrewes, affecting my whole position.

I am only sorry to hear that your troubles are not yet over.[4] All that I can say is that there is a world of difference between trouble which appears likely to end and that which appears likely to be endless, and I trust that yours is on the right side.

1–Untitled review of four works by Walter de la Mare – *Henry Brocken*; *The Return*; *Memoirs of a Midget*; *The Connoisseur* – *NC* 4 (Oct. 1926), 785–7.

2–LW alleged that de la Mare's work suffered from what he called 'queerishness', and 'his queerishness defeats him as an artist'. As for de la Mare's artistic capability: 'The intenser sound of song will be found but rarely to enter into Mr de la Mare's poetry; his prose is practically destitute of rhythm, or at least of significant or subtle rhythms' ('Queerish Talk in the Circumstances', *N&A* 39 [3 July 1926], 386).

3–'Lancelot Andrewes', *TLS*, 23 Sept. 1926, 621–2.

4–BLR wrote on 1 July: 'We've had a beastly time: and though my wife is going on splendidly, there will be further (but, it is hoped, not serious) surgical trouble in the early autumn. I can now realise better what your long anxieties have been.'

In the circumstances, I do not want to press my company on you. I am leaving for Paris on Saturday for a week and expect to be in London from the 19th. If then you have any freedom I shall be delighted.

Ever yours,
[T. S. Eliot]

P.S. I was relieved to see that my review of Spingarn was not printed in my absence, as it gave me the opportunity to correct in the proof what seemed to me an error of taste.[1]

## TO *P. M. Jack* CC

7 July 1926 [London]

Dear Mr Jack,

I have your letter of the 28th June.[2] I had not realised that this was such a complicated business, as I was under the impression that it consisted only in a private and informal arrangement between you and myself, nor did I realise that any fees were involved.[3] I shall be very glad to see you as

1 – 'Creative Criticism' – on J. E. Spingarn, *Creative Criticism: Essays on the Unity of Genius and Taste* – *TLS*, 12 Aug. 1926, 535. TSE was dismissive of Spingarn's use of the term 'The New Criticism', which he thought 'a misnomer': 'It implies that this is the creed of the youngest critics of importance, which is far from being the case. The younger critics, or some of them – witness Mr Ramón Fernandez in France and Mr Herbert Read in this country – have by no means done with "all moral judgment of literature"; on the contrary, they seem to be resuscitating it to a new and different life.' Subsequently, the publisher Alfred Harcourt wrote to complain on behalf of Spingarn (1875–1939), who was Professor of Comparative Literature, Columbia University: 'Will you permit us, in fairness to Mr Spingarn, to point out that his "Creative Criticism" first appeared in America in 1917, and that the English edition which you reviewed in your issue of August 12 is merely a reprint without change of the edition of 1917? All the essays in the volume were written between 1910 and 1913. It is obviously unjust to review the book as an expression of Mr Spingarn's latest thought' (published in *TLS*, 9 Sept. 1926, 596). BLR reassured TSE on 17 Sept.: 'Don't bother about Spingarn. The publishers have written to complain, and we have published their complaint; and the only person to complain is myself for not recognizing a book on which we had written four or five years ago. All we wanted from you was just a line to say whether there is any sign on the book of its being a reprint; because if there is not, although I am still wrong, I have at any rate ground for writing an abusive letter to the publishers.'

2 – Jack reported on the progress of the proposal that TSE might undertake to be his supervisor: 'I have seen Mr Forbes, Mr Tillyard and Mr Priestley, the Assistant Registrar, and they promise to put it through the Board of Research Studies, as far as it is in their power . . . I shall come to London once or twice during the term, and read you what I have written. At the end of term I suppose a short report is sent by the supervisor to the Board. Forbes will tell later about all that, and about the fees.'

3 – Jack sought to reassure TSE on 8 July 'that it will not really be complicated, or at least, though the Board will no doubt complicate itself as usual in its own way, there will actually

often as possible, but I hope that you will let me know as long beforehand as possible the times when you propose being in London.

Sincerely yours,
[T. S. Eliot]

## TO *Richard Aldington*

CC

9 July 1926 [London]

My dear Richard,

This is just to tell you that for the present I am in London only every other week and am spending the alternate week in Paris. I therefore find my time very overcrowded while I am in London; and more particularly this week on account of an overwhelming affluence of American relatives including a niece for whom I am responsible. When I get back I will drop you a line, and I shall be glad to know 1. whether you could come to a *Criterion* dinner on Tuesday the 20th and 2. whether you would have accommodation for me one night at Padworth.[1]

Meanwhile, can you answer a business question? We have been offered a translation of a novel called *Theofi: The Story of a Greek Odalisque* by the Abbé Prévost. I am quite ignorant, knowing nothing whatever about the Abbé beyond having read *Manon Lescaut*.[2] Do you know this book and do you think it is worth handling? Personally I am rather inclined to leave such things to Routledge's and other people who have such series. In any case, Faber is only inclined to accept the book if you could be induced to write a preface. Needless to say, that would make all the difference to

---

be little difference between the informal arrangement that you had so generously considered and the arrangement that has to be officially sanctioned.' A profile of P. M. Jack published a year later in *The Granta* ('Those in Obscurity', May Week Double Number, 10 June 1927, 517) joked about the fact that TSE had been retained to advise on his thesis: 'It is said that they keep [Jack] in Cambridge because he is vaguely supposed to be private supervisor to Mr T. S. Eliot . . . [W]hen he does come to write his book on Walter Pater, we expect it to be worth reading.'

1–RA replied that he and his wife would be 'glad to see' TSE; but since a number of visitors were due in the near future, including the painter E. McKnight Kauffer and D. H. Lawrence and his wife, it would be best for TSE to send a wire.

2–Antoine François Prévost (1697–1763), author and Benedictine monk – the Abbé Prévost – is best known for *Manon Lescaut* (1731), excerpted from a novel in seven volumes, *Mémoires et aventures d'un homme de qualité qui s'est retiré du monde*.

my own opinion, but of course I do not know whether your commitments elsewhere would prevent your doing this.[1]

Yours ever affectionately,
[Tom]

## TO *P. W. Robertson* CC

9 July 1926 [London]

Dear Mr Robertson,

Thank you very much for your letter of the 26th May. It is the sort of letter which any writer like myself ought to be very glad to get and I only wish that I might receive more such criticisms.[2]

The essay in which the offending statement occurs was written, I believe, in 1918. I have changed my mind on many points since the book appeared, but on none more definitely than on the use of scientific

1–RA had rejected the translation of *Théofi*, he replied (22 July). 'It is not bad, but not quite good enough. Even if Faber decided to do it, I should find it awkward to write the introduction to it, after having strongly advised Stallybrass not to print it!'

2–Robertson reproached TSE (letter not found) for the remarkable passage in 'Tradition and the Individual Talent' – taking off from a parody of Walter Pater's dictum 'All art consciously aspires toward the condition of music' (1919) – 'There remains to define this process of depersonalization and its relation to the sense of tradition. It is in this depersonalization that art may be said to approach the condition of science. I therefore invite you to consider, as a suggestive analogy, the action which takes place when a bit of finely filiated platinum is introduced into a chamber containing oxygen and sulphur dioxide . . . When the two gases . . . are mixed in the presence of platinum, they form sulphurous acid. This combination takes place only if the platinum is present; nevertheless the newly formed acid contains no trace of platinum, and the platinum itself is apparently unaffected: has remained inert, neutral, and unchanged. The mind of the poet is the shred of platinum. It may partly or exclusively operate upon the experience of the man himself; but, the more perfect the artist, the more completely separate in him will be the man who suffers and the mind which creates; the more perfectly will the mind digest and transmute the passions which are its material' (*SE*, 1932, 17–18). TSE published in C. 12 (Oct. 1932) an anonymous notice of his *Selected Essays 1917–1932* that he possibly wrote himself: 'It is a pity that Mr Eliot, in revising some of the earlier of these essays for this volume, did not consult a professional chemist – or even some friend with an elementary knowledge of chemistry. On p. 17, line 25, he takes oxygen and sulphur dioxide, and on p. 18, lines 9–11, he produces sulphur*ous* acid from them! $O_2$ + 2 $CO_2$ do *not* equal 2 $H_2So_3$ but only 2 $SO_3$, which *in the presence of water*, gives $SO_3 + H_2O = H_2SO_4$, sulphur*ic* acid. There is, of course, a catalytic reaction involving platinum and one of the sulphur gases, but the present writer is separated from his library and cannot quote the exact terms and conditions, which however can be found in any text-book of inorganic chemistry.

'Whether the theory of poetic creation which Mr Eliot supports by this celebrated metaphor remains valid, is a more difficult question to decide.'

analogies. They convey to the hasty or ignorant reader an impression of precision which is misleading and even meretricious. My analogy suffers, it is true, by the fact that it is false and reveals, as you point out, an ignorance of chemistry. But I should go further than yourself and say that a scientific analogy, when one is dealing with a question of aesthetics of this sort, is just as objectionable when it is scientifically sound as when it is scientifically false; and from my present point of view I should avoid even such an analogy as that which you suggest yourself. There is of course an exact Aristotelian analogy, but that is not what either you or I used. I hold that an analogy such as those I used myself is merely a method of making intelligible a concept in unfamiliar material by the use of a parallel concept in more familiar material. The illustration, that is, ought to be drawn from a field familiar to the reader; it ought not to be used to mystify or to overawe; furthermore, it is always apt to lead to confusion in the mind of a reader who may think such an illustration is tantamount to a demonstration. And of course it demonstrates nothing.

I accept your criticism gratefully and I hope that you will accept mine. If I should ever prepare another edition of my book, I should like very much to make use of your letter.

Yours very truly,
[T. S. Eliot]

## TO *Messrs A. P. Watt & Sons* CC

9 July 1926 [London]

For the attention of Mr Walker
Dear Sirs,

I have your letter of the 7th instant.[1] While I shall always be very happy to consider any short stories by Mr Morton for publication in *The New Criterion* I am afraid that serial publication is impossible. We did on one occasion attempt publishing a novel serially but the experiment was not a great success owing to the wide interval of time between consecutive numbers of *The New Criterion* and the fact that a novel is almost certain to be ready for publication in book form long before we could publish the whole of it. For your general information I will say that we still publish long articles when they can be divided into not more than two parts, but

1–Walker (A. P. Watt) offered TSE the opportunity to run *The Stranger in the House*, by Guy Morton (Peter Traill), as a serial in *NC*; it was to be published by F.&G. in 1927.

I much prefer to have all the contents of each number complete within that number.

Yours very truly,
[T. S. Eliot]

## TO *Kurt L. Wagenseil*[1] CC

9 July 1926 [London]

Dear Sir,

I have your letter of the 3rd instant, the first part of which is receiving attention from our General Office. With regard to your manuscript, I should be glad to consider any of your brother's stories, which I presume he could let me see in the German text, if they were sent to this address.[2] If I considered any of the stories suitable for publication in *The New Criterion* it would be paid for at our usual rates which are £10. per 5000 words less the translator's fee of fifteen shillings per 1000 words, and of course we should not expect you to purchase any copies except what you desire.

Yours faithfully,
[T. S. Eliot]

## TO *Egmont Arens*[3] CC

9 July 1926 [London]

Dear Mr Arens,

Thank you for your letter of the 18th instant. I am sorry to hear that the Post Office suppressed your May issue on account of alleged obscenity. From the inspection of the numbers you so kindly send me, that is almost the only ground on which, were I the Post Office, I should not suppress it. I am always on the side of tolerance. But I am afraid that *The New Masses* is not the right place for my own work such as it is.

[T. S. Eliot]

1–Kurt Wagenseil (1904–88) lived in Munich.

2–Hans B. Wagenseil published in the *Neue Rundschau* in 1929 a translation of VW's story 'An Unwritten Word'.

3–Egmont Arens was an editor of *New Masses* (New York) – a 1926 revival of *The Liberator*, a radical American weekly magazine affiliated to the Communist Party which had been suspended in 1924.

## TO *S. S. Koteliansky* CC

23 July 1926 [*The New Criterion*]

Dear Koteliansky,

I am returning herewith the Rosanov which does not seem to me quite suitable for *The New Criterion*, but I should like very much to learn more about him from you and to see you.[1] I am going away again for a few days but will drop you a line on my return and hope that you can come in and have tea with me.

Yours always sincerely
[T. S. Eliot]

## TO *Aldous Huxley*[2] CC

23 July 1926 [London]

My dear Aldous,

I also had heard that you were in London but I did not know where or for how long.[3] I am going away tomorrow until next Wednesday, and I should be delighted if you could lunch or tea with me when I come back. Could you drop me a line here, or still better ring me up here on Wednesday afternoon, so that we can arrange it?[4]

I shall probably be in France again continuously during most of August. So if we cannot manage to meet while we are in London please write to me here and let me know when and where you are to be in Paris. It is also likely that you would be able to get news of me when in Paris at the Hotel Foyot.

1–On 28 June Koteliansky had submitted a few chapters from Rosanov's last book, *Apocalypse*, written in 1917–18 after the advent of the Bolsheviks. *Uedinennoe* (1912), by Vasilii Rozanov (1856–1919), was translated by Koteliansky as *Solitaria* (London, 1927): this edition included excerpts from 'The Apocalypse of Our Time'.

2–Aldous Huxley (1894–1963), novelist, poet, essayist: see Biographical Register.

3–Huxley had written to renew contact on 12 July.

4–Huxley was to write to Mary Hutchinson on Fri., 6 Aug.: 'I lunched with Tom, who looked terribly grey-green, drank no less than five gins with his meal, told me he was going to join Vivien in her Paris nursing home to break himself of his addictions to tobacco and alcohol, and was eloquent about Parisian luncheons with resoundingly titled duchesses. In the intervals we had a very pleasant and friendly talk about books' (Texas; *Selected Letters*, ed. James Sexton [2007], 179).

Vivien is very much better and we may be taking a holiday at the sea or in the mountains in the latter part of August.

Ever yours,
[T. S. E.]

## TO *Ada Leverson* CC

23 July 1926 [*The New Criterion*]

My dear Miss Leverson,

It is very nice to hear from you[1] and I am so sorry on my irregular and very crowded visits to London I have so far been unable to call on you. I am glad to hear, however, that you are likely to be in London for some time.

I am afraid that I have not the equipment, especially in the summer months when there is always a part of the staff on holiday, to undertake to deal with the American periodicals for you, much as I should like to have the pleasure of placing 'The Importance of Being Oscar' in America. May I suggest that the best way is to get one of the good agents here to do it for you? I think that Curtis Brown or Watt or Heath would be very satisfactory. In writing to them I think you might suggest that they should try not only *The Dial* but *The Yale Review, The North American Reviews, Scribner's, Harper's* and *The Century.* All of these would be better than *The Saturday Review* which perhaps does not publish anything that is not purely criticism. If you enclose the letters, I should recommend enclosing a copy of the letter from Vivian Holland giving you permission to print.

I do hope you are well and enjoying life, and I look forward very much to seeing you as soon as I can. Vivien and I are probably going for a holiday in Switzerland during September.

Very sincerely yours,
[T. S. Eliot]

1–Leverson asked TSE (21 July) to place her essays on Oscar Wilde with *The Dial* or *Saturday Review* or 'any American paper you think suitable, and if it were accepted I should naturally insist on going halves on any remuneration'. Also, she had a letter of permission to publish Wilde's letters to her which were now in an American university.

## TO *Bruce Richmond* CC

23 July 1926 [London]

Dear Richmond,

Thank you very much for your encouraging letter; I am not well pleased with any of the last things I have sent you and am anxious to make another attempt. I imagine the translation of Montaigne you mention is one published by the Harvard Press and made in fact by a relative of mine, one Grace or Sarah Norton, I have forgotten which.[1] I am certainly not prepared to tackle a long review about Montaigne, but it might be interesting to compare her with Florio. I confess, however, that the book on Troilus attracts me more and I should like to do that.[2]

I shall be going away on Monday next, but if that is your best day I should be very glad to look in on you on the following Monday if you will let me.

I hope matters are now going well with you.

Sincerely yours,
[T. S. E.]

## TO *Arundel del Re*[3] CC

23 July 1926 [London]

Dear Mr del Re,

Please forgive me for having left your letter of the 9th May unanswered. I have been abroad and have only been able to pay one or two flying visits to England and have therefore, I am afraid, been obliged to neglect a great deal of correspondence.

Thank you for having written to Mr Susskind. He sent me something which I liked but was unable to use for the reason that it had already been

1–TSE's cousin Grace Norton had published *Studies in Montaigne* in 1904. BLR asked on 22 July whether TSE might like to review 'an enormous five-volume translation of Montaigne, by an American lady, published by the Oxford Press'.
2–TSE, 'Chaucer's "Troilus"' – on *The Book of Troilus and Criseyde, by Geoffrey Chaucer*, by Robert Kilburn Root – *TLS*, 19 Aug. 1926, 547.
3–Arundel del Re (1892–1974) – half Italian, half Anglo-Irish – worked with Harold Monro in launching *Poetry Review* in 1910, and was to become a professor of English Literature at Tokyo University, 1927–30. He later taught in Formosa (Taiwan), 1930–43. At the time of this exchange he was working for *The Oxford Magazine*.

published in Germany.[1] I have been in correspondence with him and he will, I believe, submit something else.

It is a pleasure to receive the *Oxford Magazine* and I hope you will kindly continue to send it. I trust that the difficulties you mention in your letter came to an end with the conclusion of the strike.

Do let me see your essay on Florio if it is actually written.[2]

With many thanks,
Sincerely yours,
[T. S. Eliot]

## TO *J. B. Trend* CC

23 July 1926 [*The New Criterion*]

Dear Trend,

I am going away tomorrow till the middle of next week but I should like very much to see you when I come back if you are still in London. Please drop me a line here and let me know if that is possible.

There is one small matter I should like to explain to you now. It is understood that any manuscripts dealing with musical matters, which I am inclined to accept, be submitted to you for approval. During the last month there have been several concerts in Paris for the work of George Antheil. I am very much interested myself in this composer. Ezra Pound, who has been largely instrumental in arranging these concerts for him, has written a short note about him which I should like to print both on account of my interest in Antheil and my friendship for Pound.[3] It is not highly technical, or contentious. In order to save time, I am having it set up at once, but I will send you a proof copy as soon as it comes in and should then like to know how it strikes you.[4]

Sincerely yours,
[T. S. Eliot]

1–W. E. Süskind, 'Die Tänzerische Generation', *Neue Merkur*, Apr. 1925.

2–'I suppose you would not be interested in an article on John Florio, about whom little is known, and who occupied an important position under Queen Anne of Denmark.'

3–EP, 'Antheil, 1924–1926' (primarily on *Ballet Mécanique*), *NC* 4 (Oct. 1926), 694–9. EP had already contributed 'George Antheil', *C.* 2 (Apr. 1924), 321–31.

4–Trend said (11 Aug.) he found EP's article 'very interesting'.

## TO *Richard Aldington*

CC

23 July 1926 [London]

My dear Richard,

Thanks very much for your letter. I will, as you suggest, send you a wire and hope that we can arrange it somehow. Of course I should prefer to come down when you were alone. On the other hand, rather than miss seeing you altogether for a considerable length of time, I should be glad to come and put up at the inn, if I were not wholly unsuitable for the company you might be having at the time. And in the circumstances it might be more convenient for you and Dorothy[1] if I put up at the inn in any case. Many thanks for your hint about *Theofi*. I think that settles it. King's review[2] is fairly good, but I confess I was a little disappointed in it and regretted that I had not done better by you, but I am very glad to hear that the book has been doing so well.

Ever yours affectionately,
[Tom]

## TO *John Middleton Murry*

CC

23 July 1926 [London]

My dear John,

Thank you very much for your letter. I should like very much to come down to spend a night with you at the first possible moment after I get back. Would Thursday next suit you? And if so, could you let me know something about the trains late in the afternoon and trains back to London the next afternoon? I have been so little in London that when I am here every minute is crowded, but I should like very much to come even if only for a night and a morning. I do not even know how long a journey it is.

In haste,
Ever yours
[T. S. E.]

1 – Arabella (Dorothy) Yorke: RA's lover, 1920–8.
2 – William King's review of RA's *Voltaire*, *NC* 4 (June 1926), 587–9

## TO *The Secretary, The Board of Research Studies, Registry of the University, Cambridge* CC

23 July 1926 [London]

Dear Sir,

I return herewith a cheque for two guineas which I have received from you this morning with the statement that it is the fee for supervision of the studies of Mr P. A. M. Jack during the Easter term 1926. I think that this cheque has been sent to me under a misapprehension. I have done nothing whatever for Mr Jack during the Easter term except to undertake to supervise certain of his studies during the Michaelmas term next. I accordingly beg to return this cheque with thanks.

I am,
Yours faithfully,
[T. S. Eliot]

## TO *Wyndham Lewis* TS Cornell

23 July 1926 *The New Criterion*

Dear Lewis,

I am glad to hear from you.[1] *The Art of Being Ruled* is being reviewed at some length by a young man who seems to be very keen about it and who is not, so far as I know, personally connected with anyone with whom he should not be connected. He is an acquaintance of Herbert Read's.[2] Of course I shall look over it carefully, but one has to give people a fairly free hand. I wanted Read to do it himself, but he did not have time to tackle such a big job.

I should like to see you next week when I am back in town – after Wednesday. Of course I should be very glad to help with your review in any way possible, though I doubt whether I should be able to undertake to write anything before the late autumn.[3]

Yours ever
T. S. E.

1 – WL had urged that – since *The Art of Being Ruled* was a political book and driven much less by a person than an impersonal principle – he ventured 'to hope that . . . you will find a suitable reviewer for it – not anyone that is personally acquainted with me (and very likely disposed therefore to attack *me* in *it*)' (undated).

2 – W. A. Thorpe, in *NC* 4 (Oct. 1926), 758–64

3 – WL was proposing to launch a review, *The Enemy*, in Sept. TSE would contribute 'A Note on Poetry and Belief', *The Enemy* 1 (Jan. 1927), 15–17.

## TO *Paul Rosenfeld*[1]

TS Virginia

24 July 1926 — *The New Criterion*

Dear Mr Rosenfeld,

Thank you very much for your letter of the 1st instant, and for your kind invitation to join the *American Caravan*. It sounds a very interesting venture indeed and I wish you all success. At present I have very little leisure and am trying to work off several very long-standing commissions, but I shall certainly keep the *Caravan* in mind as it seems to have a place of its own and to be suitable for very long things which one could not use elsewhere.

I gather that you only want contributors of American nationality, but within that limit I shall be glad to turn in your direction any manuscript that strikes me as suitable.

Yours ever sincerely,
T. S. Eliot

## *Vivien Eliot* TO *John Middleton Murry*

MS Valerie Eliot

Sunday, [?25 July 1926] — Sanatorium de la Malmaison,
4 Place Bergère, Rueil

Dear John

I got your letter this morning.[2] I *ought not* to have written to you like that. I felt ashamed when I read your letter. You have your work. But it is so *good* of you to bother with me, & I cannot help being thankful that you will.

I think Tom will be in London from *Wednesday, until Aug. 4th*. I hope he will come to see you. But in any case I want to tell you something more than I did. I must. But if I cld only see you, it wd be so much better. I can't write anything *shortly*.

About being here. It had to be, & it is a *good* place. I have been in hell here, but it is a good place, & the doctors are good, & *absolutely kind*. Not only that but they are clever. For some time *before* what I told you about happened in Paris I had hallucinations, & I must have been in a

1–Paul Rosenfeld (1890–1946): music critic of *The Dial*, 1920–7; author of *Musical Chronicle* (1923); and co-editor (with Alfred Kreymborg and Lewis Mumford) of *The American Caravan*, a yearbook of American literature – the first edition was to appear in New York in Sept. 1927.

2–None of JMM's letters to VHE from this period has survived.

very bad state. Tom left me in Paris with the Pounds, hoping I shd be able to pull up, but it was much too late & in 4 days I was completely out of my mind. *IF* I had stayed in Rome, *where I was happy*, – if I had stayed there, & let Tom go back to England & his brother & sister-in-law (with whom we are travelling, *a most awful nightmare*) go on with their honeymoon, I think I should have been allright. But Tom's brother's wife persecuted me, & I felt I had to *justify my condition* by going straight from Rome to Freiburg. I had 9 days there, with T., under Dr M[artin][1] & I left there completely destroyed. I had a perfect horror & loathing of Dr M. and wd not have stayed even if he had not been just leaving for England. It was *within* a week of leaving Freiburg that I took poison in Paris. To go back to when I saw you in London, in the spring, at Mrs Patmore's. I was extremely unhappy then, desperately so, and I should have liked to talk to you but you seemed to me so cold & distant that I was very much disappointed & I felt it was no use following up that meeting. At that time I was living at Clarence Gate Gardens alone with a nurse. A dreadful little woman who

[incomplete]

1–Dr Karl Bernhard Martin lived at Dorfstrasse 15, Freiburg-Günthersthal, Germany, and ran a clinic called Sanatorium Hoven, Lengenhardstrasse. The treatments he meted out combined starvation dieting with psychoanalysis. One of his most socially prominent English patients was Lady Ottoline Morrell, who chose to submit herself to his ministrations for several years. Lytton Strachey, who met Martin at Morrell's country house, Garsington, thought him 'a miserable German doctor – a "psycho-analyst" of Freiburg' (letter to Dora Carrington, 3 June 1923). According to Miranda Seymour, Morrell's biographer, 'It was as a doctor, not as an analyst, that Marten [*sic*] was an unfortunate choice. "He thinks he has found out my trouble – some old germ left from typhoid years ago," Ottoline reported to Bertie [Russell] in November 1923, "and now he is injecting me with all sorts of injections of milk and other things in advance of England." The milk injections did her no good; Marten's belief in starvation diets, dutifully followed by Ottoline over the next ten years whenever she felt ill, did her considerable harm. No woman of her age and complicated medical history should have expected an improvement in health from fortnightly régimes of fruit and water which left her so weak that she could scarcely sit up, but that was Dr Marten's panacea for all ailments' (*Ottoline Morrell: Life on the Grand Scale* [1992, 1998], 448–9). In due time, Virginia Woolf too would encourage Roger Fry to consult Dr Martin. Another such sorry patient was Edward Sackville-West (novelist, music critic, patron of the arts; heir to Knole House), who spent some weeks in Freiburg under Martin's orders in the hope of getting a 'cure' for his homosexuality. Strachey mocked his efforts, in a letter to Carrington: 'After 4 months and an expenditure of £200 he found he could just bear the thought of going to bed with a woman' (Michael De-la-Noy, *Eddie: The Life of Edward Sackville-West* (1988, 1999), 87). In Jan. 1926, analysis proved that Dr Martin, who was a charlatan, had been injecting Morrell merely with milk.

## *Vivien Eliot* TO *John Middleton Murry* MS Valerie Eliot

Sunday [1926] Sanatorium de la Malmaison

Dear John

I got your letter of the 21st today. I have been writing to you all day, but it was no good. If I could talk to you, if only I could speak to you.

I felt ashamed when I read yr letter. I ought not to have bothered you, I ought not to have shocked you.

You have your work. Ought I to let you trouble with me? I don't know. I want help, God knows, & I want the help I believe *only you* can give me.

You are so good, John. You are so really great & big & important that one almost turns to you as if you were John the Baptist. I was going to say Christ.

I must write to you frankly, & you *must* let me. Just to let me do that is a great big Help & a great thing for you to do. Don't be shocked at anything I say, & don't laugh. I am always sincere & I want to speak to you. Just to be able to write down things as they come to my mind. I started to tell you *facts* – but that was no good.

It is my fear of Tom. Now help me. About Tom. You said, in another letter that I should know what it is to be absolutely alone, & that I shd come to know that I did not *understand* Tom, & to be absolutely apart. John, believe me please – for 6 or 8 months I HAVE known that I am absolutely alone, & I *have* known that I do not understand Tom. His presence, still always terribly longed for, gives me a feeling of such utter isolation. *I can't tell you.* Each time I see him it is a shock.

And whenever he speaks to me, about himself, & his interests, work, thoughts, desires, I know so frightfully that *I simply do not understand* him, that sometimes, when I am tired or overwrought, it gives me the sensation that he is mad. Sometimes that he is mad or else that he is most *frightfully* & subtly *wicked* and *dangerous*. That he is a terrible *menace*. That I must either somehow cut free & run, run, run to somewhere where there is a clear sky & open fields & *air*. Or else that I shall be stifled, that I must sink down, down into a heavy vapour, & so gradually be stifled to death.

You know he is fond of me. Very very fond. I don't think he ever was fond of me until he got me, somehow, under. Don't mistake me. I am not being cruel, I am not bitter & venomous, now. I love him, & I want to see him happy & successful in the way he sees, because there is no other way for him my dear John. But O my dear, I want air.

But if I have air, will he love me, or will it spoil everything for him? To lose me, would, I believe make him bitter. I don't mean really lose me. But I don't know. You see I simply don't understand him, it's no good. I got to the point when I felt the only thing I could do was to get out of his life in that way. A sort of sacrifice.

Mind, I think he feels *exactly as lonely* with me. But is it the same? No. He is free. I am not.

O I know I am utterly worthless, a sparrow. I know it does not *matter* what becomes of me.

But I am in pain, in pain. I have been in gilded cages 11 years. One cage after another. I have never *grown up*. I don't know anything. Can't you tell Tom it is *nicer* to see birds free than in cages?[1] People have always said to me, but why *don't* you go away & do what you like? John, I never *dared*. First, it meant losing Tom. (*Losing my hold* on Tom). Now, it means hurting Tom, & *losing myself, doesn't it*?[2]

What is my duty?

What shall I do?

Tell me, please.

Thank you for the photo of dear Egg.[3] I love her.

Vivien

1–Cf. 'Letters of the Moment – I', which appeared above VHE's most secret by-line 'F. M.' in *C.* 2 (Feb. 1924), 220–2: 'Now one begins to beat against the bars of the cage: the typewriter and the telephone, and the sight of one's face in the glass. One's soul stirs stiffly out of the dead endurance of the winter – but toward what spring?' VHE's image of beating 'against the bars of the cage' derives from Stravinsky's *The Firebird* – as is made clear by the typescript draft of a letter from VHE to IPF: 'Do you remember in the first act, after the bird is captured, it tries to fly, over and over again, wings beating' (Bodleian: MS. Eng. misc. c. 624, fol. $25^r$).

2–Some years later, VHE would note in her diary (31 July 1935; Bodleian): 'I see now the significance of the French word *dédoublé*. It was used a *great* deal when I was at the Sanat. de la Malmaison. So, as Edith Lawrence always said, I seem mad, but *am right* – I presume that back in 1926 they were faking up a double for T. S. Eliot.' *Dédoublement* – now known as multiple personality – was first discussed in 1875 by Eugène Azam: see Ian Hacking, *Rewriting the Soul: Multiple Personality and the Science of Memory* (1995), 159–70. In a *Criterion* commentary dating from Apr. 1933 TSE noted the use of irony '(as by Jules Laforgue) to express a *dédoublement* of the personality against which the subject struggles'.

3–JMM's daughter Katherine Middleton Murry, b. 19 Apr. 1925. VHE must have misheard the child's nickname, which was actually 'Weg'.

## TO *F. S. Flint*

CC

26 July 1926 [London]

My dear Flint,

Faber and Gwyer are inclined to accept for publication a book called *5,000* (récit sportif) by Dominique Braga if they can get it translated.[1] It is very short – 186 small pages sprinkled with a small quantity of type – and quite amusing. It is merely the account of a five thousand metre race from the point of view of one of the runners from beginning to end. Do you think you might be willing to tackle it? Faber asked me to ask you. I very much hope that you will, but I don't ask it in any way as a favour. It is for the publishing house and not for the *Criterion*. If you are at all favourably disposed, we will discuss terms when we next meet.[2]

Yours ever,
[T. S. Eliot]

## TO *Orlo Williams*

CC

28 July 1926 [London]

Dear Williams,

Thank you for your card about Angioletti. I am glad to know, although there is no hurry about his article. I suppose that you will not be settled in town again until October. I expect to be abroad on holiday during most of September myself and in the circumstances do not propose to resume the *Criterion* dinners regularly until some time in October. Those who are in town occasionally meet, and if you are in London next Monday evening, I and two or three others, I do not know exactly who, will probably be dining at the Oxford in Wardour Street and should be very glad of your company.

Yours ever
[T. S. E.]

1–Dominique Braga, *5,000* (Paris: NRF, 1924).
2–Flint said (29 July) he was 'inclined to it' – though 'translating is ten times as hard as original writing, and the pay! O my Gawd!'

## TO *Hugh Fraser Stewart* CC

28 July 1926 [London]

Dear Dr Stewart,

I have just got back from Paris this morning and find your letter of the 27th.[1] I shall be very glad to give you my opinion for what it is worth on Smith's dissertation – with or without a fee. The only question is this: in September, and perhaps for the whole of September, my address will be The Grand Hotel, Divonne-les-Bains, Ain, France.[2] If it suits you to send the thesis out to me there I will read it and report on it and send it back registered. Will you let me know whether to expect it? I should be glad if Smith could get a fellowship as he is a very likeable and intelligent boy, but my report will be quite impartial.

Will you please tell Mrs Stewart how very sorry I am that I have been obliged to be out of England most of this spring and summer. I have made several flying visits to London but they have all been packed with work and interviews and at no time have I been here over a weekend. I had been looking forward to proposing myself to spend another night with you and I hope that the invitation will not be cancelled before the autumn. Tell her also that she will be well advised to withdraw her kind proposal to urge my play (when finished) upon the A.D.C., as she will have the opportunity of seeing a couple of fragments of it in successive numbers of *The Criterion*. The inspection of these fragments may lead her to think better of her suggestion!

With all best wishes,
Sincerely yours,
[T. S. Eliot]

1 – Stewart invited TSE to give 'a second opinion', for 'a small fee', on a Fellowship dissertation by James Smith entitled 'The use and meaning of character in dramatic criticism'. Smith 'will have to present a convincing case to get elected; but he is a serious candidate of Fellowship calibre, so far as I have seen his work. I hope the interest which you evidently feel in this young man will lead you to consent to lend a hand.'

2 – Divonne, a commune in the Ain department in eastern France, abuts French-speaking Switzerland (Geneva); forming part of the Rhône-Alpes region, it lies between the Jura mountains and Mont Blanc. The Grand Hotel, which was built in the 19th century, was to become a centre for the treatment of nervous ailments.

## TO *Leonard Woolf*

CC

28 July 1926 [London]

Dear Leonard,

I have just got back this morning and find your letter of the 24th. I knew you would be going away about this time but had hoped just to catch you in London before your departure. I am very sorry.

I am very glad that you have settled about *Commerce*. I saw the princess for a few moments in Paris and she referred to my offering to help to draft a circular.[1] I made the suggestion to her before the arrangement with The Hogarth Press was contemplated, and I have told her that it seems to me now that my intervention would be impertinence. You can probably draft a better circular than I could but if I can be of any use let me know. I understand that copies of the *Criterion* circular have been procured for you. I don't suppose that I know very much about *Commerce* that you do not know yourself. It is largely under the influence of an inner circle of the *N.R.F.* including Paulhan but not particularly Gide. I suppose that in a circular you would lay some emphasis on its cosmopolitan character. I think their principle of printing verse in the original language with a French translation is a good one. I really cannot think at the moment of any aspects for special emphasis but if I do I will let you know.

Yours ever,
[T. S. E.]

## TO *W. S. Kennedy*[2]

CC

28 July 1926 [London]

Dear Mr Kennedy,

Thank you very much for taking the trouble to answer the letter which I addressed to Norgate. I am very sorry to hear that matters are still so unsatisfactory, but I hardly expected that it could be otherwise. It is very hard that the founders of the society (with of course one exception) should be hit in this way and I am sure that all the rest of us will want to do anything we can at least so that the society can be wound up without anyone's suffering financially. Therefore I hope that the autumn

1 – LW wrote (24 July 1926), 'We have taken over COMMERCE and the Princess [Bassiano] says that you will help me in drafting a circular.'
2 – W. S. Kennedy worked for the Incorporate Stage Society.

performance can be managed. I should like to have been of more use to 'The Phoenix' than merely serving as one of the pall bearers.

Sincerely yours,
[T. S. Eliot]

## TO *Henry Eliot*

TS Houghton

29 July 1926

24 Russell Square, W.C.1

My dear brother

I have your letter of the 17th this morning, and was very glad, as it had seemed to me a very long time since I heard from you. Your news, what there is of it, seems good. When you have settled down you will write and tell me how you find married life. It has only just begun.

I am quite satisfied with your telling Charlotte[1] about my affairs, provided that you warned her, as you seem to have done, that none other of the family knew or was to know anything about it except what I tell mother. Unitarianism is a bad preparation for brass tacks like birth, copulation, death,[2] hell, heaven and insanity: they all fall within the classification of Bad Form. It often seems to me very bizarre that a person of my antecedents should have had a life like a bad Russian novel.

Vivien is now very much better. Of course she need[s] a long period of physical building up and nutrition; and it is quite possible that she may have a similar attack in a few years time. But the doctors agree that of insanity, that is of *mental* disease proper, there is no trace. The trouble is wholly emotional. The delusions are not fundamental, but are projections of a state of emotional anguish. At present they have wholly disappeared, though she is still inclined to believe that everyone disapproves of her.

1–Charlotte Eliot (1874–1926), TSE's third eldest sister, married George Lawrence Smith, an architect, in 1903. She studied art in St Louis and then in Boston.

2–Cf. 'Fragment of an Agon' (from *Sweeney Agonistes*):

SWEENEY: Birth, and copulation, and death.
That's all, that's all, that's all, that's all,
Birth, and copulation, and death.
DORIS: I'd be bored.
SWEENEY: You'd be bored.
Birth, and copulation, and death.
DORIS: I'd be bored.
SWEENEY: You'd be bored.
Birth, and copulation, and death.
That's all the facts when you come to brass tacks:
Birth, and copulation, and death.

I should be very glad if you and Theresa would write to her, merely to express affection etc. without alluding to the exact nature of her illness (I have asked Charlotte also). You see she still believes that you and T. particularly disapprove of her, and at her worst she imagined that you were plotting to annul our marriage, kidnap me to America etc. Her assumption was that she had ruined my life, and that therefore you would inevitably try to save me from her. She is still inclined to suppose that anyone who is my friend and wishes me well *must* be her enemy. But she came in to Paris yesterday with a nurse; we sent the nurse away and I took her out to tea etc.; and although the circumstances were trying – there was a thunderstorm in the street, and I was leaving for London the same evening, she surprised me by her calmness and stability. I think that in many ways she is better than she has been for a long time.

I have confided details to a *few* friends in England – mostly friends who have had experience of similar cases, being married to them.

I am going on Wednesday to the Sanatorium de la Malmaison, 4 Place Bergère, RUEIL (Seine-et-Oise) France, which is where Vivien is. I shall stay for 3 weeks for a rest cure. It is a splendid institution. Also the doctors will be able to observe the effect on her. Or course I shall be in a separate house etc. Then we go to the Grand Hotel, DIVONNE-LES-BAINS (Ain) which is in France near Geneva, in the mountains. We shall there be in an hotel, but she will be under the charge of a doctor there who is in relations with her present doctors. I hope she will stay abroad the whole winter; I shall come back to London for a good deal of the winter to attend to affairs. But if she wishes she shall come back too.

I don't know what to say 'what change this has made['] in my life. I have been freer to see more of certain friends and acquaintances of more or less 'political' importance, but of course have avoided all 'social' life in general. I have strengthened my position in Paris, and have been able to consolidate a little my group of younger men in London. I attach some importance to this: to forming a group of men which will hold together, and persist in the same direction, after I am gone. It is very indirect, and imperceptible action; but such a group of young men might have considerable influence on even the political future of England. There is a change, perceptible in a few, in the last five years. But one must not try to gain or keep 'disciples': that is a house of cards, and is only vanity and pride anyway. One must efface oneself as much as possible, to have any genuine influence. But as for 'lasting sort of happiness' . . . I don't know. One realises that one never arrives at anything, but must just go on fighting every day as long as the strength lasts.

The Haigh-Woods have been good and have given what financial help they can. I am just about to review my financial position before returning to France.

I do feel that as between you and me the trip abroad was of very great value. I shall always probably speak and write to you more frankly than I should otherwise have done, and more than to anyone else in the world.

Always your affectionate brother,
Tom

Write whenever you can.

## TO *Doris N. Dalglish* CC

30 July 1926 [*The New Criterion*]

Dear Madam,

I am returning with regret your interesting essay on the work of Mr Middleton Murry. Criticism of contemporaries is always a difficult task: and some contemporaries can, owing to the nature of their work, be dealt with more adequately and justly than others. I cannot feel that the moment has arrived when any of us can either interpret or judge Mr Murry's work as a whole; all that we can do is to accept or reject different parts or aspects and give our reasons. I am sure that his philosophy is still in process of development and that its exposition must for the present be left to Mr Murry himself. I have thought it worthwhile to try to explain to you why I think this manuscript is unsuitable and to encourage you to submit something else.

Yours very truly,
[T. S. Eliot]

## TO *D. Fraser-Harris*[1] CC

30 July 1926 [London]

Dear Sir,

I am returning to you herewith your essay on the Hermaphrodite Character of the Human Mind for the reason that it is not quite suitable for the character of *The New Criterion*. I am retaining, however, your

1–David Fraser Fraser-Harris (1867–1937), British academic and author, researched physiological physics and the history of physiology: he had been Professor of Physiology, Dalhousie University, 1911–24; President of the Nova Scotia Institute of Science; Halifax Medical Society; and the Medical Society of Nova Scotia. Publications include *Life And*

essay on Shakespeare's Perception of the Functional Importance of the Brain which I have found very interesting and which I shall be pleased to accept for *The New Criterion* if you will not be too exigent about the date. As *The New Criterion* is a Quarterly, long periods must necessarily elapse between acceptance and publication: the October and January numbers are already filled and I should therefore use your essay probably, but not at this moment with absolute certainty, in the April number. I should be glad to hear from you if you can agree to this condition.[1]

Yours very truly,
[T. S. Eliot]

## TO *Laura Riding Gottschalk*[2] CC

30 July 1926 [*The New Criterion*]

Dear Miss Gottschalk,

It had slipped my mind that the poems you sent me would not be available after this summer and I am very sorry for that as there were two which I might well have used.[3] I am returning them to you herewith. The other poems I am going to re-read carefully and you shall hear from me again. Meanwhile I have taken note that both you and Mr Graves would be willing to do reviews and notes for *The New Criterion*. I am very glad to hear this though I must warn you that the rates which we can afford to pay are not very high; the maximum is £3 for the longest reviews of two thousand words, and we can only print a few reviews of this length in each number. But if you are willing to do shorter notices also it will be easier as we hope to have more of these in the future. The reviewing for the October number was already settled when you wrote to me but I will keep you in mind for January.

Yours sincerely,
[T. S. Eliot]

---

*Science* (1923), *Nerves, Master-System of the Body* (1927) and *Morpheus, or the Future of Sleep* (1928). At the time of this letter he was general editor of a series published by F&G called 'The Modern Health Books'.

1 – Harris's essay did not ultimately appear in the *Criterion*.

2 – Laura Riding (1901–91), American poet and essayist: see Biographical Register.

3 – Graves wrote on 24 June, 'About Laura Riding Gottschalk's poems. The ones sent you from Egypt will be out shortly in a book so are not available . . . Have you any books to review for L.R.G. & myself' (*In Broken Images*, 166–7). Riding stated on 3 Apr.: 'There are five of the unprinted poems in the volume [*The Close Chaplet*, 1926] to be brought out simultaneously in England and America this summer, probably, by the Hogarth Press and the Adelphi Press respectively.'

## TO *Edwin Muir* CC

30 July 1926 [*The New Criterion*]

Dear Muir,

I like the poems of Trask although they are very rough and not accomplished. One or two I am quite likely to use and I am writing to him.[1] I am very much obliged to you for letting me see them. Excuse this note which is written in great haste just before leaving England.

Sincerely yours,
[T. S. Eliot]

P.S. I am having this letter duplicated and sending a copy to France and a copy to Scotland.

## TO *Elmer E. Stoll*[2] CC

30 July 1926 [*The New Criterion*]

Dear Professor Stoll,

I am glad to have at last an excuse for writing to one whose work I respect so highly as I do your own. Your essay, I am sorry to say, is not quite suitable for the *Criterion*. This is not in any way a criticism of its quality but rather of its type. *The New Criterion* is obliged to restrict its contents and to publish work of a type for which there is little place elsewhere, and a meditative essay on travel has less point in the *Criterion* and more point elsewhere than any other kind of writing. I hope, however, that once having begun you will let me see other essays.

I had not seen your essay in the January *Edinburgh*,[3] but I will try to obtain it; nor did I see – what would very much have interested me – your reply to Clutton Brock.[4] Needless to say, that controversy is one in connection with which I have not changed my mind during the five years; and I hope that you have not materially altered your own position, expounded in that admirable monograph.[5] I did not feel myself that there was anything to be gained by engaging in polemic against such a

1 – Sherwood Trask, 'A Footnote of History' (poem), *NC* 5 (Jan. 1927), 43–4.

2 – Elmer Edgar Stoll (1874–1959): Shakespearean scholar; Professor of English, University of Minnesota, 1915–42.

3 – 'The Fruits of Prohibition', *Edinburgh Review* 243.495 (Jan. 1926), 102–22.

4 – Arthur Clutton-Brock, 'The Case against "Hamlet"' (*Shakespeare's 'Hamlet'* [1922], 14–32), took issue with TSE's finding ('Hamlet' [1919], *SE*) that the play was an artistic failure.

5 – *Hamlet: An Historical and Comparative Study* (1919).

confused mind as that of the late Mr Clutton Brock; and the fact that he had quite distorted one or two of my remarks (no doubt unconsciously) while pretending to quote them accurately made me all the more satisfied to keep my peace. My friend Robertson was not so reserved: he produced an excellent little book: but my own opinion is that if people cannot see by inspection the difference between clear thinking and prejudice there is no use arguing with them.

With all best wishes and appreciation of your work,

Sincerely yours,
[T. S. Eliot]

## TO *R. P. Blackmur*[1] TS Princeton

30 July 1926 *The New Criterion*

Dear Mr Blackmur,

I am returning herewith a long poem[2] which you sent me nearly a year ago. The reason that I have kept it for so long is that I was enough interested in it to want to repay you by some sort of critical comment and I have not had time to do so. It is all the more difficult because this poem is not one which can be re-written: it is too good for that. No criticism of detail would matter very much. What I think is that it is too thoughtful. That is to say, the harder you think and the longer you think the better: but in turning thought into poetry it has to be fused into a more definite pattern of immediately apprehensible imagery, imagery which shall have its own validity and be immediately the equivalent of, and indeed identical with, the thought behind it. A great many very good poems just miss reaching this point. The result is something which we have to *think* instead of immediately apprehending.[3] The more thought that is turned into poetry the better; only it must be, in the final form, *felt* thought.

1–R. P. Blackmur (1904–1965), American literary critic and educator. In 1935 he published his first book, *The Double Agent: Essays in Craft and Elucidation*; and on the recommendation of Allen Tate he taught from 1940 at Princeton, where he ran the Creative Arts Program. He was a Hodder Fellow; a member of the American Academy of Arts and Sciences; Vice-President of the National Institute of Arts and Letters; Fellow in American Letters at the Library of Congress; Pitt Professor of American History and Institutions at Cambridge University. He was to publish three volumes of poetry.

2–'A Funeral for a Few Sticks'.

3–Cf. TSE's earlier formulation, in 'Hamlet' (1919): 'The only way of expressing emotion in the form of art is by finding an "objective correlative"; in other words, a set of objects, a situation, a chain of events which shall be the formula of that *particular* emotion; such that when the external facts, which must terminate in sensory experience, are given, the emotion is immediately evoked' (*SE* [1932], 145).

I express myself very badly on a difficult matter, but I hope that you will take this letter as intended encouragement and send me something more. I should be very glad to see your essay on Pound's *Cantos*.[1]

Yours very truly,
T. S. Eliot

## TO *Charles Norman*[2] CC

30 July 1926 [London]

Dear Mr Norman,

I am so sorry that I was out of England and therefore unable to see you when you were in London in the spring. Your poem[3] would have attracted my attention even without the recommendation of Estlin Cummings[4] and Walter Shaw, and I like it so well that I want to tell you why I think it is still unfinished. The general feeling and tone seems to me right, but when I take it to pieces I find a good many phrases which seem to me just not right. The whole thing seems to be just a turn of the screw out of focus. For instance in the first line neither of the adjectives 'sombre' and 'hushed' seems right. Stones are not sombre, because they are merely elements in a landscape the whole of which may be sombre, because a landscape as a whole cannot be detached from the state of mind of the perceiving consciousness: on the other hand the concrete elements in a landscape are merely objects. I cannot see why stones should be 'hushed' unless there has been some question of their making a noise. It is not clear why the stones should *continue* to make a magnificence or why the magnificence should be 'wan'. On the next page you employ again this adjective 'wan, which is once too many in a short poem, and you employ it in application to the mouths of houses. It is not clear what feature of the buildings resembles a mouth and therefore one does not know why the mouths should be wan. To say that the mouths utter flowers seems to me a confusion for which there is no justification, and I do not know what unblossomed fruit means unless it means fruit which has been produced without the natural process of previous flowers. There are very few actual

1–Blackmur published 'Masks of Ezra Pound' in *The Double Agent* (1935), 30–67.

2–Charles Norman (1904–96), Russian-born poet and biographer (his parents emigrated to the USA in 1910), made a name for himself as poet and journalist. After WW2 he taught for a time at New York University and went on to become better known for his biographies of Samuel Johnson (1951), E. E. Cummings (1958), Ezra Pound (1960) and Christopher Marlowe (1971). His poetic output includes *The Far Harbor* (1924) and *Poems* (1929).

3–'Dead Men Under Buildings', revised, is in *Poems* (New York, 1929), 20–2.

4–Edward Estlin Cummings (1894–1962), poet, novelist, painter, playwright.

birds which can rightly be described as 'silver' – you may be thinking, of course, of the snow bunting or something of that sort but this seems to be an excursion into debased modern baroque for which there is no excuse.

But the fact that three out of every ten words of a poem are not the right words does not mean that the poem is a complete failure or that it could not be made into a good poem.

And when I criticise other people's poetry I refuse to accept any objections based on reference to my own verse. I have made a great number of mistakes myself.

If you get this letter, do send me something more soon.

Yours very truly,
[T. S. Eliot]

## TO *V. F. Calverton*[1]

CC

30 July 1926 [London]

Dear Mr Calverton,

After long consideration I am returning to you the two interesting manuscripts which Mr Read so kindly obtained for me to see. For various reasons neither of these is quite suitable for *The New Criterion* but I am certain that I want something from you sooner or later. I think that your article on 'The New American Literature' contains references to rather more quantity of unknown literature than our public is able to digest at once, but something implying less knowledge of the material on the part of the reader might be extremely useful. In any case I hope that you will soon have something more to send me.[2]

Yours every truly,
[T. S. Eliot]

1–V. F. Calverton (1900–40) – born George Goetz – American Marxist critic; founder-editor of *The Modern Quarterly*, 1923–40. See Leonard Wilcox, *V. F. Calverton: Radical in the American Grain* (1992); and Haim Genizi, 'V. F. Calverton, A Radical Magazinist for Black Intellectuals, 1920–1940', *The Journal of Negro History* 57: 3 (July 1972), 241–53.
2–HR had told Calverton on 6 Mar. 1926: 'I don't think it is any use disguising the fact that there is a fundamental opposition between your point of view and Eliot's. You stand for a proletarian spirit which he simply does not accept in any way, or regard as anything but the contrary of the cultural values he believes in. You will have your own reaction to that, but as a fact you must accept it. I too have had my doubts of your position, though I don't think they are so fundamental as Eliot's. But when you make a statement, such as that vers libre is a direct reflex of bourgeois society (and it is some such statement that you do make towards the conclusion of one of the essays) then I feel that your conception of a sociological criticism has run away with itself and involved you in absurdities' ('A transatlantic correspondence', ed. Eric Homberger, *TLS*, 22 May 1981, 586).

## TO *F. L. Lucas* CC

31 July 1926 [London]

My dear Lucas,

I am applying to you to know whether you have any pupil or ex-pupil who would care to undertake a tutoring job from about the end of August. It is for an Italian boy aged ten who speaks English perfectly as he is more than half English.[1] The family is a wealthy one and the position would be, I believe, at Deauville and afterwards at Paris, more or less as a member of the family. What is wanted is a personable young man who could teach the usual subjects to a boy of ten who is eventually going to Oxford. I do not yet know what the terms would be – I suppose that would be a matter of arrangement – but it might be an interesting experience for anyone who had no immediate prospects of anything permanent. I don't think that an intimate knowledge of French or any other foreign language would be expected: what is wanted is an English University man who knows the rudiments of tennis, etcetera.

I shall be leaving England again in a few days, but letters will be forwarded. I have been very little in England during the last term, otherwise I should have tried to pay a visit to Cambridge; but I hope that I may see you in the autumn.

Please give my kindest regards to your wife,

Yours sincerely
[T. S. Eliot]

## TO *George Rylands* CC

31 July 1926 [London]

My dear Rylands,

In your last letter you mentioned that you were out of a job. Would you care, as a stop-gap, to take a position tutoring an Italian boy in France? It could probably be arranged either merely for the rest of the summer near Deauville or for a longer period, the winter to be spent probably in Paris, though there might be a certain amount of travel in Italy and Germany. Camillo is ten, and speaks English perfectly, his father being half English and his mother American. He is going to Oxford later. It might at any rate be amusing as the family are wealthy and know a great many people.

1 – Camillo Caetani, son of his cousin Marguerite, Princess of Bassiano.

I have no details about terms, etcetera, as I only heard from the family this morning. If you are interested or if you have any friend who might be interested do let me know at once.

Yours ever,
[T. S. Eliot]

## TO *Marguerite Caetani*

TS Caetani

31 July 1926

As from Sanatorium de la Malmaison

Dear Cousin,

I have written to Denys Winstanley and Peter Lucas, at Cambridge, to ask about any pupils of theirs; I do not know where either of them is at the moment. I have also written to a young friend of mine, George Rylands, who has nothing to do at present, and would suit admirably if he would care to undertake it: he taught at Eton for a time. I am rather out of touch with Oxford, but I will ask Geoffrey Faber if he can make any suggestion.

It is not the best time of year, and you give short notice. It is a pity that I shall not be in England, as I could interview applicants myself. You *might* also write to Gabbitas & Thring, who are the best scholastic agency; at 36 Sackville Street W. 1. I have one or two boys in mind, but I do not know where they are or what they are doing, and it would take too long to find out. If I hear of anyone who seems *prima facie* suitable, I will put him in touch with you, and you can take up references etc.

I will write about *Commerce* later. This is in great haste.

Yours always sincerely
T. S. Eliot

## *Vivien Eliot* TO *John Middleton Murry* MS Houghton

Monday [? 2 August 1926] [Sanatorium de la Malmaison]

Dear John,

This is a letter I *began*, & did not send. However, I think I will send it. Things have changed since I wrote.

1) I am so much better that I am allowed to go *out*, with relations, friends or a nurse.

2) Tom has arranged to come here himself, for a fortnight or so, on August 4th. He is very *very* tired indeed. I urged him to come, & I am so glad. He won't be in the same 'Pavillon' as I am. I rather trust these doctors, they are cunning fellows, & I think our *both* being here will be a good thing – for us both.

3) The Paris specialist I have wishes me to go, when I leave here, to a resort for convalescents in the mountains, near Chamonix. *I think I am to go*. It may not be bad. I *believe* one is *free*.

After that I want my liberty – I mean my *equality*, with Tom. Help me to get it, *& to keep it*. By the way Bertrand Russell is the *only other* person I write to in England. He is very good to me – & always has been. He will help, I think. I don't know if you know him, or dislike him.

Thank you John for what you have done. I mean written, *& thought*. You help me & you strengthen me.

Yrs.
Vivien

## TO *Ada Leverson* CC

3 August 1926 [*The New Criterion*]

Dear Mrs Leverson,

I have only been in town for a week and I am so sorry that I have not had a moment to spare even to drop you a line until today, and I am leaving town tonight. It is a pity that our visits to London could not coincide, but I hope that we will have better fortune in the winter; unless you withdraw to Italy altogether.

The October number is already made up and the January number more or less so, but I will certainly keep in mind that you are willing to do notes or reviews and thank you very much indeed for the suggestion.[1]

With all best wishes, and hoping to see you on my return in October,

Sincerely yours,
[T. S. Eliot]

## TO *Thomas McGreevy* TS TCD

3 August 1926 *The New Criterion*

Dear McGreevy,

To yours of the 26th. The Herbert Read book isn't available because I have done a notice of it myself.[2] I shall keep you in mind for the Edith Sitwell book when it appears though I cannot say definitely at the moment as there are other people to be considered. So I should be glad to have a few more suggestions from you, both for longer reviews and short notices – indicating if possible which books you think suitable for which. There is no hurry about this, nor need it all be done at once. Just drop me a line here (or preferably to my secretary) whenever anything appears that interests you. I am going abroad tonight for some weeks, but hope to find you here on my return.

Do you think that the introduction to the Spanish edition of Joyce's *Portrait* is interesting enough to merit a half page notice?[3]

Sincerely yours,
T. S. Eliot

## TO *Antonio Marichalar* CC

3 August 1926 [London]

My dear Marichalar,

I have not written to you for a long time but that is partly because I have been waiting to report on one or two things. I have been so much

1 – Leverson asked (28 July) to review 'a few books . . . either for October or January . . . (For years I did it for the Saturday Review here unsigned.) . . . It is not for money but for fun. I'd like to!'

2 – TSE, review of HR's *Reason and Romanticism*, *NC* 4 (Oct. 1926), 751–7.

3 – *El Artista Adolescente*, trans. Alfonso Donado, with introduction by Antonio Marichalar, was briefly noticed in *NC* 5 (Jan. 1927), 158.

out of England during the last few months and have been so busy when here that I cannot remember whether I ever wrote to you to thank you for your admirable chronicle. I hope that you will consider it a model for your future chronicles.

I am returning to you the piece of *Salinas* for two reasons. One is that I understand that it has now appeared in a book, and the other that we decided in consultation that it was rather a particularly difficult piece to translate without losing most of the flavour of the original. We are considering a very attractive little play by Bergamin which he gave to Herbert Read who I think met Bergamin through yourself.[1] And I should be glad to hear of other things also.

Furthermore, we are interested in getting opinions from various quarters on the question of 'The Defence of the Occident' raised by the article of Henri Massis which seems to have excited a good deal of interest. A German colleague, Max Rychner, is dealing with the subject briefly and from rather a limited point of view in the October number, and I am also expecting one or two letters on the subject from English collaborators. I should rather like to have a Spanish opinion and our friend J. B. Trend who knows Ortega y Gasset well suggested that the point of view of the latter would be a particularly interesting one. Do you think that Ortega y Gasset would be inclined to write something for us on this general question? Of course, Massis's article was much longer than the space we ordinarily assign and we cannot, with the space at our disposal, continue to discuss at the same length. But if Ortega were willing to do anything we should be overjoyed. I hope that you will let me have your opinion about this.[2]

Ever yours sincerely,
[T. S. Eliot]

## TO *Ronald Finlayson* CC

3 August 1926 [London]

Dear Sir,

Your letter of the 15th June has been faithfully forwarded to me by Messrs Beaumont. I think that you are probably confusing some poem

1–F. S. Flint later adjudged (29 Nov.), 'it seems an amusing metaphysical skit.' Nothing by Bergamin appeared in *NC*.
2–Ortega y Gasset did not ultimately contribute to the debate over Massis's article.

of mine with a poem by another author. I am certainly the patentee of the character named Sweeney, but it is possible that other Sweeneys exist. I cannot prevent that. At any rate I can assure you that I have never introduced Sweeney or any other character into an aeroplane, nor has any of my puppets ever disembarked at New York, nor has any of these ever performed any action (I cannot decipher the verb in your letter) which has any relation to *Monna Lisa*.[1] I will refer you to the collected edition of my poems by Messrs Faber and Gwyer.

With many thanks for your kind sentiments,

Believe me,
Yours very truly,
[T. S. Eliot]

## *Theodora Eliot Smith* TO *Her Mother* — MS Houghton

6 August 1926 — St Cloud S et O

[Extract]

Now to the main point of interest. Wednesday I had lunch with the Haigh-Woods, the whole family, including Uncle Tom & they were good enough to include me in the family as a sort of in-law. Both Maurice & Vivien were there and there was a sort of feeling of suppressed jubilation on account of her health. They were all so glad to have her back that at times they could hardly say anything but we had a jolly time all the same and nobody could say enough for French doctors. They have done wonders and I gather that she is her old self again, at least that is what her father said to her. That is to say she is better now than she has been for years & getting better all the time. She looks rather badly of course but she is much calmer than I had expected though when a thing is to be done she wants it done at once without delay.

I tried to make myself a[s] small & inconspicuous as possible and not butt into the family party, perhaps I made it easier, I don't know. I was so awfully glad to meet them all that it didn't matter and I was so glad to see with my eyes, for Uncle Tom's sake, that Aunt Vivien was better. This seems an involved sentence.

1 – Finlayson wrote from Adelaide, Australia: 'For some time I have had a line running in my head which I feel sure comes from one of your poems. It relates to someone Sweeney I think taking flight & disembarking at New York "smiling like Monna Lisa".' Could TSE please identify the source in his work?

I like Maurice very much too but he didn't say much and was quiet most of the time.

I think Aunt Vivien liked me a bit too at any rate I am going out to see her at Malmaison on Tuesday afternoon and we are going to have tea together. This is partly because of you & partly because I was so *désolée* at the thought of not seeing her again and anyway I'm thrilled at the prospect and I shall probably write Granny[1] a letter about that and not you as Uncle Tom will be there too, if he is rested by then, and I shall have only good news to give her so that is my chance to cheer her up about them.

After Uncle Tom & Aunt Vivien had left to go shopping Maurice took me to the American Express Co (vile place!) and it was a funny trip for I didn't have anything of any account to say, naturally, but my only consolation is that he didn't say anything of any account either, so we were both dumb, which is just like me . . .

Lots of love to you all
From Dodo.

Mr & Mrs Haigh-Wood are to be in London when I am, just on the other side of the park from me. And I expect to see them a good deal.

## TO *John Middleton Murry* — TS Northwestern

Tuesday, 10 August [1926] — Sanatorium de la Malmaison

My dear John,

It was quite true that I could not have taken the time to come to see you without neglecting important practical matters. As it was, I needed another fortnight in London; but I had promised to be here on a certain date.

And then, I reflected, that probably no good could have been done by my seeing you expressly on this subject. Vivien would have known, and I dislike concealment. I could not have reported the whole conversations, as she would have wished me to. And from experience I know that it might merely have resulted in your losing what influence you have. Had you subsequently said anything unpalatable to her, she would have been quite likely to attribute it to my intervention, and my prejudicing you. You see I am speaking quite frankly.

I do not know what can be done, or at what point she can be helped. I think that it is just as likely that you can help her acting as you must be

1 – Charlotte Eliot, TSE's mother.

more or less in the dark, than if you had the whole miserable history in your hands.

I have not found religion of any use to her, either mine or anybody else's. I am oppressed by a sense of doom, against which I struggle.

Ever affectionately
Tom

We are here till the 25th. After that, we go to Divonne together. While here, I get my letters separately, and you can write freely.

## TO *Bonamy Dobrée*

TS Brotherton

11 August 1926 Sanatorium de la Malmaison

My dear Dobrée,

I return your broadsheet with my compliments.[1] I have racked my brains to think of any criticism, but cannot. It seems to me admirable. As for borrowing from my paragraph, you have borrowed only the one thing in it worth borrowing, i.e. the contrast of visible and invisible church,[2] which I think is a good one and you must keep it. The only disadvantage

1–BD recalled, in 'T. S. Eliot: A Personal Reminiscence' (1966): 'in the summer of 1926 the City churches were largely threatened with destruction, as the Church wished to raise funds for better-attended places of worship. Eliot was deeply opposed to this, as indeed I was, though not altogether for the same reasons. At all events I agreed to write a broadsheet for sale or distribution in the City (I have lost all trace of this, and even the memory of it), of which Eliot approved . . . So one Saturday afternoon my wife and I accompanied Eliot at the head of a protest procession through the City, at intervals chanting "Onward, Christian Soldiers" and other hymns. The churches were saved.'

2–TSE, in 'A Commentary', *NC* 4 (Oct. 1926), challenged the decision of the National Assembly of the Church of England (*The Union of Benefices and Disposal of Churches (Metropolis) Measure*, 1926) to permit the selective demolition of churches: 'A visible church, whether it assembles five hundred worshippers or only one passing penitent who has saved a few minutes from his lunch hour, is still a church: in this it differs from a theatre, which if it cannot attract large enough audiences to pay, is not better than a barn. The destruction of a church which has the added consecration of antiquity and even a little beauty, is a movement towards the destruction of the Church, with Disestablishment on the way. Possibly some reflections of this nature might give our Shepherds pause: we shall cease to appeal in the name of Christopher Wren and his school, and appeal in the name of [Archbishop] Laud and the *beauty of holiness*' (629). Cf. *FLA*, 18: 'the voice of [Lancelot] Andrewes is the voice of a man who has a formed visible Church behind him, who speaks with the old authority and the new culture'; 'Parliament and the New Prayer Book' (letter), *The New Adelphi*, June 1928, 346: 'The Church of England is not a visible Church of communicants, but a wholly invisible Church of shy schoolboys'; 'Choruses from *The Rock*' IX, *CPP*, 165: 'Visible and invisible, two worlds meet in Man; / Visible and invisible must meet in His Temple; / You must not deny the body . . . // Light / Light / The visible reminder of Invisible Light.'

that I can see is that just this point might make some reader of both think that the broadside was written by me, and the only disadvantage of that is that the authority of 'Some Men of London' (a good signature) might be diminished if it were thought that this imposing menace concealed merely T. S. Eliot. I throw out this suggestion for what it is worth; it may not signify.

Of course the audience that I had in mind is chiefly the city clerk type; I don't think the broadside is too highbrow for them. The two important points are, of course, the street distribution and the obtaining [of] some measure of newspaper comment.

Ask Read to discuss with you a question about which he wrote to me: that of turning the *New Criterion* into a monthly. I am wholly in sympathy with the principle, and so is everyone connected with the paper; but I have written Read a letter putting forward the difficulties at the moment. It might profitably be discussed at the next dinner, from which I shall be absent. *Mais le coeur y est.*[1]

I hope you won't go to Egypt, but I can't think of any grave obstacle to impose in your way. Graves told me that the climate did not agree with his children, that his colleagues were mostly Belgians, and that the whole tuition was virtually a farce. Also that the position was a complete sinecure. But that is not enough to dissuade you from accepting and assuring yourself £1100 for ten months residence.[2]

Ever yours
T. S. E.

Let me know how the broadsheet progresses.

1–'But the heart is there'.

2–Robert Graves had written on 24 June, 'I have left Egypt: because the climate didn't suit the children & the University was just comic opera. If you want a sinecure at £1170 free of income tax between Oct 1 & June 1st (passage paid) I daresay I could get it you. The students are noisy: the other professors are mostly Belgians. You do about 2 hours a week. Nothing but elementary school, say 6th standard. Cairo is about the only possible sequel to *The Hollow Men*.' Graves had finally quit Egypt in July 1926, after less than six months in post at the university.

## TO *Herbert Read*

TS Victoria

11 August 1926 Sanatorium de la Malmaison

My dear Read,

Thank you very much for your letter of the 5th.[1] I very highly appreciate the thought that you have devoted to this matter.

1–HR wrote: 'I have been thinking a good deal about the New Criterion since our talk the other day, & I enclose a few observations on "quarterlies" in general which show the trend of my ideas. I can't judge about the possibilities of organisation, the amount of time involved, & particularly of the financial aspects. I am merely looking at the question from the outside, which is, however, a useful viewpoint. I can't help feeling that there is a danger of frustration. Faber's suggestion of a cloth-bound journal at 10/6 is desperate. I am convinced that the direction should be quite opposite – lower costs of production and wider distribution. I personally would like to see a 1/- monthly, printed more or less in the style of the N.R.F. & thoroughly organised for distribution and advertisement. But I can see that this would involve the use of capital with a considerable element of risk. But I doubt whether, starting with this idea, you would have needed more than you have already expended.

'The Adelphi's circulation went up to 17,000 or more. Perhaps the causes of this leap into popularity are not to be emulated. But there should be a fairly solid public of 10,000. Cf. Ford's *English Review*.

'I imagine a monthly Criterion very much on the same lines as the present one, and not absorbing, in three months, more than twice the material of the present quarter. The make-up might run to:

Comments........................ 2 pages
(3) Main articles............ 40 pages
(2) Chronicles ................. 8 pages
Reviews......................... 20 pages
......................... 70

That as a minimum. But a monthly can with advantage run a serial, & perhaps Faber could arrange for some of his novels to run this way prior to publication in book form. I realise that his novels are not quite in tune with the Criterion, but he might find some that were. And in any case, I think you could sacrifice principles for circulation in this case. It is a curious fact, which has only just occurred to me, that none of the regular contributors to the Criterion ever write novels. How do you account for this?

'These ideas are in the main shared by one or two other people – Flint certainly, & perhaps Dobrée. We feel there is a certain lack of life about the Criterion as at present constituted, & my own opinion, which has become much more definite in the last day or two, is that such lifelessness is inherent in the very nature of a quarterly.

'But I realise that there are many more considerations than these rather abstract ones.'

He attached a page of summary observations headed 'The "Quarterly"':

'The quarterly is an obsolete form of journal. It belongs to an age of leisurely communications, the three-volumed novel, and a general atmosphere of patience.

'It belongs to a pre-journalistic age, using "journalistic" to cover the shift of influence from the journals proper to the "press".

'There is now such a multiplicity of appeals to the literary public that it is difficult to create *a continuity of interest* at intervals of three months.

'The public interest in a new book, even if it is a popular success, rarely lasts as long as three months. This may be a bad sign, but a quarterly is not going to make any difference

I think that everything you say, about the advantages of a monthly over a quarterly, and the antiquation of the quarterly principle altogether, is perfectly sound. Many of these reflexions had already occurred to us. It might certainly have been better if the *Criterion* had begun as a monthly. This, as you know, was out of the question: what was originally intended was no more than Art and Letters: and Lady Rothermere would not have been disposed in the beginning to provide enough money, nor could I, unless I had been paid a salary, have given enough time, to run a monthly. Anyway, the question is only that of changing now. We did consider this last autumn. The difficulties are of two kinds.

1. Money. It would certainly require considerably more capital to launch it as a monthly. It is *possible* that Lady R. would be willing to put down her share at any time, for she was very favourably inclined to the change, and indeed suggested it. But I think that for F. & G. it would be at the moment out of the question; and the money required would have to be put down in equal parts, so that the control of the paper should remain equably divided as at present. Remember that F. & G. had already started a new and expensive venture (*The Nursery World*) before they took on the *Criterion*; and this is not yet on a paying basis. And there have been two bad seasons at the very beginning of the whole enterprise. In another year, if all goes well, they might look at it differently. We are all therefore – I, Lady R., Faber and yourself – agreed in principle: but for F. & G. the only

---

to the fact. By the time a quarterly can publish a review of a book, it is forgotten – or at any rate, stale.

'But any periodical must depend for its circulation on the stimulation of critical interests. Opinions, not "literature", are the only (and the proper) life of journals. You can make your opinions carry literature along with them; but opinions must form the main energy or drive of a journal.

'A "quarterly" inevitably tends to be bulky; otherwise it does not look solid enough, or important enough, for the kind of role a quarterly is (or rather *was*) meant to fill. A bulky volume means a bulky price. Five shillings, or even 3/6, is a bulky price where journals are concerned. Journals are bought casually, as a rule; they are "picked up" off bookstalls & counters. They should not entail deliberation on the score of cost.

'The psychology of prices. A man will spend 6d a week on a weekly paper, but not 13 x 6 = 6/6 on a quarterly. He will give 2/6 for a journal because half-a-crown is a unit, a single coin in his pocket. He will more easily spend four separate shillings than one half-crown. Four people will much more easily each spend one shilling than one person will spend half-a-crown.

'Therefore: 2/6 is the highest psychological price that you can put on a casual article like a journal. 1/- is a better price because you can make it yield a higher aggregate return.

'The present quarterlies which are priced at 5/-, 7/6 or 10/- exist on a traditional circulation, confined in the main to institutions; they could not begin all over again. They have been carried over into this age by a momentum gained in a previous age.'

possible course at the moment is to nurse the thing along, reduce expenses in every way possible, and await a more prosperous moment.

2. There is the question of time. I don't say that it would occupy three times as much editorial time; but however exactly one worked it out, even making each number exactly one third of the present number, I am sure that it would take considerably more of my time, and would also require a part time assistant editor or *remplaçant* (as some editor ought to be on the spot month in month out) or at least a more highly paid secretary. I should want more salary for more time. But I confess that personally less time and less salary suits me better at present. That is partly immediate conditions (which are hardly to be considered, as the change could not be made before another year, for the reasons above) and partly that I am getting on in years, that I have accomplished very little, that I am growing lazy and tired, and that I want to get a few more things done before I am too old.

My policy is frankly a waiting one. If I can keep expenses within tolerable compass for the next year, we shall revise the situation then; and if the general position in publishing and in our business is brilliant enough, I should certainly recommend the change. Of course I am sure that in the end a monthly would pay much better: it is only the first year or two that would be more costly. But certainly, by that time – by the time that the change was feasible, I should – if I had enough income in other ways, which I cannot foresee – try to put a younger man in my place.

I shall send your summary on to Faber in a day or two. I have not at all meant that all consideration of the change must be shelved; on the contrary, I think that the more it is considered and discussed among ourselves the more likely it is of eventual realisation.

Ever yours,
T. S. E.

## TO *Pearl Fassett*

TS Faber

11 August 1926

Sanatorium de la Malmaison

Dear P.,

Enclosed

1. Corrected proof of commentary.
2. Yr review with alterations. Put it in.[1]

1–IPF had sent a note on *Dostoevsky portrayed by his Wife*, ed. S. S. Koteliansky, saying:

3. Communication from Read which please hand to Mr Faber on his return.

4. Fraser-Harris correspondence. Please write to Harris and say that this question is outside my domain but I have referred it to the Chairman. Then give it to Mr F. and ask him to deal with it as he thinks fit.

A. Please estimate length of Flint translations (if they are all in) as closely as possible and ask Mr F. to authorise payment on this basis. If the sum is a large one ask Delamare to check your figures.

B. I should like to see galleys of all reviews which I have not seen (have seen Read, Cocteau and Flint), and of Fletcher (and Porter) letters.

C. Please send me

Hooker's Ecclesiastical Polity, 2 vol. Everyman, blue.
Selections of Donne's Sermons Oxford
Latimer's Sermons 1 vol. blue, Everyman[1]
Baedeker's Northern France & Switzerland.

The first two are in the open shelves in the office; the others are I think in the glass shelves in the office.

Allright about Rylands.[2]

Yours
T. S. E.

## TO *V. B. Metta* CC

12 August 1926 [*The New Criterion*]

Dear Mr Metta,

I am abroad and apologise for the delay in answering your letter of the 1st August.

First, for your story, I should be glad if you could leave the decision till about the 1st October. The choice of fiction is very difficult, we have so much to choose from and publish so little.

---

'I have enjoyed what I have read re Dostoevsky, but I cannot swing any more onto the old lady's diary and reminiscences. The second paragraph could well be omitted if you think it undesirable.' See her review, *NC* 4 (Oct. 1926), 791–2.

1–In 'Lancelot Andrewes' (1926) TSE dubs Latimer 'merely a Protestant', as against Andrewes who had 'a formed visible Church behind him, who speaks with the old authority and the new culture. It is the difference of negative and positive; Andrewes is the first great preacher of the English Catholic Church' (*FLA*, 15).

2–IPF had mislaid a letter from Rylands: 'he thanked you very much indeed for your suggestion [apropos the tutoring of Camillo Caetani] but had already arranged to go abroad for the rest of the summer.'

About the 'East and West'. Some of the points you mention are good, for instance the influence of Arab philosophy. But that is rather a complicated tangle to get into, as Arabic philosophy itself is largely Greek in origin. I am inclined to think that the most interesting thing you could do would be, as you suggest it, a 'Defence of the East', but certainly with some allusion to Massis. Only one must avoid Massis's own difficulties – i.e. he covers far too much ground, for him the East is now Russia (which is largely a product of European-Jewish influence in its present condition) now India, now China; all of which are as different from each other in many ways as 'Europe' and 'Asia'. One must stick to what one knows: you might very well limit it to India.[1]

Your last suggestion interests me very much – the reaction of an Oriental (or say an Indian) to English literature.[2] I hope you will do that in any case: the essay you showed me in the *Freeman* leads me to believe that you would do it very well.

I return to England early in October.

Yours very truly,
[T. S. Eliot]

## *Theodora Eliot Smith* TO *Her Mother* MS Houghton

13 August 1926 [Helena Club] 82 Lancaster Gate,
London W2 (!!!!)[3]

[Extract]

Yesterday afternoon I had a very jolly time, at Malmaison, of course. Tuesday afternoon when I arrived Aunt Vivien said that our cousin the

1–Metta had re-read Massis on the Defence of the West – 'So far as I can make out he is against the German & Russian groups for being pro-Oriental & non-Latin' – and he wanted advice. 'I could refer to the fact that Europe has been always influenced by Asia: (1) All European races originally came from the East . . . (2) Egyptian & other Oriental influences on Greco-Roman art, & philosophy. (3) Christian influence is Oriental. (4) The Arab influence on European philosophy . . . Also that it is better that the East & West should continue to fuse their cultures – in the hope that a more universal culture might spring from the fusion. The bondage of Greco-Roman culture, I feel, has been a misfortune for Europe, since it has limited her horizon. Massis' idea of "Oriental anarchy" is absurd, since Indian & Chinese civilizations are very highly organized.' See 'In Defence of the East' (letter), *NC* 5 (Jan. 1927), 100–5.

2–'I could write something if it interests you of what an Oriental thinks & feels about English literature.' See his 'Bias in History', *NC* 6 (Nov. 1927), 418–25.

3–Theodora ('Dodo') had stayed at the Helena Club on a previous visit to London.

Italian princess (née Chapin)[1] had telephoned that she was coming out & so Aunt Vivien said it was an awful pity to have our afternoon spoiled by the Princess & couldn't I come again on Thursday & I said I certainly could & would. Well, the Princess woman never came at all & we missed our tea on account of her but we three had a good time sitting in the garden together & talking & for the first time I felt that I was getting to know Uncle Tom to say nothing of Aunt Vivien whom I like better every time I see her. She is a dear & so absolutely wide awake & very bright. I don't see why they made such a row when Uncle Tom married her, I can remember at the time getting the impression that she was rather xxxx [*sic*].

Mrs Haigh Wood just called up at this point to know how I was & how the trip was & I am going to tea there tomorrow at 4 o'clock!! Quick work that & typical of Mrs Haigh Wood. I never knew anyone so kind & thoughtful in all my life, it makes you want to do everything for her but there doesn't seem to be anything I can do except give her good news of Aunt Vivien which I shall do, & take the place of her children (as best I can) for she does like having young people about that's evident.

To continue with the tea party yesterday when I arrived Uncle Tom told me that a friend of theirs was passing through Paris & was coming out to tea too, so I didn't have them to myself but I managed to survive. Jack —— (I can't remember his other name)[2] was very nice & not so awfully English except that when excited he would say 'I say, I say, I say' half a dozen times. Aunt Vivien had seen 4 doctors a masseuse & a chiropodist all that day & had a right to be tired but even with all that she is steadily getting better, I think. I have only seen her 3 times in all but each time she seemed better than the time before. We all four went out for a walk & had tea in a little garden back of a café & I can assure you that having tea meant sitting there most of the afternoon. Uncle Tom beats them all at tea drinking. I only had three cups but he keeps right on until it must be only cold slops that he is drinking but he doesn't seem to mind. During the course of the tea drinking Aunt Vivien & I reached a formal agreement that she should adopt me & I consented. In what capacity I don't know, for she doesn't want me as a niece & therefore I should think a daughter would be much worse but at any rate we have adopted each other, so 'That, said John, is that'. The Dolly sisters were staying at Malmaison while she was there & you ought to hear her describe them, may be you

1 – Marguerite Caetani.
2 – Probably the Eliots' friend Jack Culpin.

don't know who they are but they are American at any rate (meaning that they were born there, though their parents were probably not) . . .[1]

Lots of love to you all
from Dodo.

[P.S.] As I was going to say, to go back a paragraph, even at my tender age I got the impression that the family in general felt that Uncle Tom had been caught & that he ought to have known better & certainly ought not to have married. This may be all my imagination but at any rate people ought to wait till they know the facts before they kick up a row & they ought always to expect their children to act strangely & then perhaps they won't. This oration is not aimed at you or Uncle Henry but at the rest of the family in general (Eliots) & their clan attitude. I seem to be wandering but what I mean is that I don't really think anyone need regret that Uncle T married Aunt Vivien because I am beginning to think that she has probably done a lot more for him than people think, not omitting the illnesses which have no doubt served their purpose.

If you make any sense out of this you will be doing well but there is a meaning there if you can find it.

## TO *Pearl Fassett*

TS Faber

14 August 1926 Malmaison

Dear P.,

I return herewith the Pound–Trend correspondence. The corrections are too slight to bother about; make the alterations that Trend suggests and return the proof.

I enclose cheque for two pounds. One pound is for Janes for tomorrow (the 15th) and the other for Janes for the following Sunday. When you have used up all of my money let me know.

Will you please get Driver to send his bill to you, and when you get it simply give me the total & I will send you cheque for him. Do not send me on his bill. The doctor advised me not to tell V. the news yet: I don't know whether that is right, but I could not make up my own mind on the matter.

1–The 'Dolly Sisters' – twins Rosika (Rose) and Jansci (Jenny) Deutsch, born in Hungary in 1892 and brought to the USA in 1910 – was a highly successful dance duo, performing in vaudeville, appearing in movies, and touring the theatres and dance halls of Europe. Jenny commited suicide in 1941; Rose survived until 1970.

Will you please send me Lecture VII (Crashaw)[1] taking a copy NOT out of the bound book of the text which you made for me, but one of my own original typings in the green pocket folder.

I think the only job remaining for me for October is to give titles to the reviews for the cover.

Yours in haste
T. S. E.

## TO *Kurt L. Wagenseil* CC

14 August 1926 [Sanatorium de la Malmaison]

Dear Sir,

I have to thank you for your letter of 20th July. Of the two short stories which you sent, I return 'Verkommenes Subjekt', because we never publish contributions which have already appeared elsewhere, unless we can be practically certain that none of our readers will have seen them, or for some other exceptional reason.[2] The other, 'Die Schlagende Stunde', I should like to retain for a time and submit to the colleague who has special jurisdiction over German contributions.

As for the review you suggest, we are able only to review a very small number of foreign books, and those should be chosen among the most important books of the moment in their own country. We should always of course welcome suggestions. The book you mention does not seem from your account to be of sufficient importance, but if your [brother] cares to submit a notice, it will certainly be carefully considered. I mean, that we should ordinarily review foreign books only of the importance of let us say, the work of Spengler.[3]

With many thanks.

[Yours sincerely,
T. S. Eliot]

1 – TSE meant to ask for Lecture VI.

2 – The story had already appeared in French in *Revue Européenne*, and in Swedish.

3 – Allen & Unwin had recently published a translation of *Der Untergang des Abendlandes: Umrisse einer Morphologie der Weltgeschichte* (2 vols, 1918–22), by Oswald Spengler (1890–1936) – which had sold 90,000 copies in Germany – under the title *The Decline of the West*. During TSE's absence abroad, H. L. A. Hart had volunteered to review it for *NC*, but for some reason the offer was not taken up.

## TO *Bonamy Dobrée* TS Brotherton

15 August 1926 Sanat. de la Malmaison

My dear Dobrée,

That is very annoying.[1] In a business like this people cannot make material objections or alterations or the whole thing falls through. Unless Dent[2] has something obviously much better to suggest, the question is merely how many people will support the venture in virtually its present form? The next step is (unless you are yourself tired) to find out what it will cost to print, and how and at what expense it can be distributed (peddled). Then get the money out of the others before there is too much discussion and go ahead. It is sometimes desirable to be arbitrary and present *faits accomplis*. But to do that you must know how much money is needed and get it. My pound is ready when you want it.

Thanks for the sight of these two letters. The Railway is an amusing swindler. I confess I rather sympathise with Maurras; perhaps he hopes that the tram and gasometers may help to get rid of the artists. In any case, I don't understand Read's letter, nor the relevance of this *contretemps* to the City Churches.[3] What does he mean by 'a bit uncertain' and why 'advocatus episcopi'! I don't understand.

I have written to Fernandez twice without a reply, but if he responds I will ask him,[4] and if I am anywhere near the Bvd. Raspail I will certainly enquire for you.[5] I have not been in to Paris at all, and am only going in this week to buy tickets to Divonne, we leave here on the 25th.

I haven't looked at Chamfort[6] (or Rivarol[7]) for years and years. My

1–BD wrote on 13 Aug.: 'I see the Broadside [on the City churches] is going to fizzle out. Dent doesn't like the form – & everybody will dislike something, and metaphysical doubts will creep in, and no one will want to commit themselves, and some will be afraid of looking silly. Unless there can be some degree of unanimity there is no point in going on, as I don't propose to be landed with the whole expense.'

2–J. M. Dent & Sons (est. 1888), publishers; directed after the death of J. M. Dent (1849–1926) by his sons Hugh and Jack Dent, and by Jack's son F. J. Martin Dent.

3–'Read's parallel . . . won't do. We are not concerned to preserve the "picturesque" and "quaint" from a natural healthy development, but the finished product of a civilization, the work of a great artist, from an attempt to bolster up a decaying institution. Read, I suppose, objects to the Velasquez in the Prado being painted over to make advertisements for Dentol.'

4–'If you see Fernandez, ask him if he got a book I sent him.'

5–Dobrée asked TSE to call at a bookshop to ask after an order he had placed.

6–BD had been reviewing Sébastien-Roch-Nicols Chamfort (1740?–1794) – *The Maxims and Considerations of Chamfort*, trans. with an intro. by E. Powys Mathers (2 vols, 1926) – and found him 'better than I supposed'. 'The Maxims of Chamfort', *TLS*, 9 Sept. 1926, 592.

7–Antoine de Rivarol (1753–1801): French writer and epigrammatist; Royalist. See Bernard Fay, *Rivarol et la Révolution* (1976).

recollection is that I thought Chamfort the better, but a very long way behind Vauvenargues.[1]

We are getting on well, and shall be sorry to leave here. If you ever want to rest under supervision this is the place to which to come.

Yours ever,
T. S. E.

I quite agree about the distinction between the picturesque and the monument of a civilisation. And I make the further point that to destroy these churches is to accelerate the decay of the church – it is not party funds that makes a church prosperous. Though it seems to be almost inevitable that Canterbury should eventually be superseded by Rome in any case. It is their own fault.

## *Vivien Eliot* TO *John Middleton Murry* MS Valerie Eliot

16 August [1926] Sanatorium de la Malmaison

Dear John

I have not written because I have been in a horrible state of mind. It is frightfully hot here, & I am not at all well just now.

I will just write briefly now. The enclosure you sent, of Katherine's, was extraordinary. And extraordinary of you to send it, to know. It touched me immensely, although I had guessed she thought all that.

It is *Exactly* what I have thought, for myself, for ages. It is just where I am. O dear, Katherine is always so near to me. You don't know.

Thank you John, thank you.

About the cottage. I want it. But I can't *take* it until next March. I don't know what you want for it. Is it to let, or for sale? Please write, at once, & tell me exactly the details, & if I could take it *from next March*. Because they won't let me return to England at all until next spring. I don't *think* I can afford to take it until March, & not be in it. I have to be in Italy or Switzerland. Tom would like it, too. He is here now. Please write at once.

I shd *so like* to be near you. You are the only person in England I feel I want to know. But I *yearn* for the English country.

Yrs ever,
Vivien

Give my love to Egg.

1–Luc de Clapiers, Marquis de Vauvenargues (1715–47). See Herbert Read's essay 'Vauvenargues' (1929), in *Collected Essays in Literary Criticism* (1938), 220–33.

## TO *John Middleton Murry* TS Valerie Eliot

16 August 1926 Sanatorium de la Malmaison

My dear John,

Thank you very much for your letter. I wanted you to know that, even had I not had enough business in London to prevent my taking 24 hours with you, there was still an obstacle in my mind. I am convinced that my intervention, between Vivien and anyone with whom she wants communication, is, even when (as it often is) at her own request, undesirable. But I should like you to know that nevertheless I was disappointed at not seeing you.

Your point of view is so much your own, and my own spiritual steps so tentative, and so obscure and doubtful even to myself, that I must await more illumination, both from you and from myself, before I can respond to what you say about religion. In such a wilderness or desert, one can learn from others, one may even inadvertently do good (or harm) to others, but there can be no question of intellectual association or cooperation. What makes intellectual association possible is a practical end, an external action, something concrete where minds touch in action, a common aim of minds which have come, and so far as they have come, to a common conclusion however indefinable. But the purpose is deformed and the aims are diffused and adulterated, in the process of execution, and the end like the beginning is solitude. And the difficulty in the end is to keep one's solitude in humility and not in pride.

But I am quite aware of the solitude in which you live, and of its difference from mine. My constant desire is to recognise at every moment the limitations of 'association', so that it may not become a drug, or a flattery of ephemeral and illusory power.

Thank you very much for your letter. You must know that it is with great regret that I think best to destroy it. Meanwhile I hope you will keep in communication with V. as and when you can.

yours ever affectionately,
Tom.

## TO *Alec Randall* CC

20 August 1926 [24 Russell Square, London]

My dear Randall,

Many thanks for your letter of the 11th August. I am abroad in France at present, but as I shall be moving next week the address above is best at present. I have some hope of getting to Rome again this winter; my wife's family will be there, and it is thought that the climate there would suit my wife for this winter better than in England or France. If I do, I shall certainly not fail to find you this time.

I am delighted that you have at last done some German books for us. As it is rather short notice, and as at this moment we are trying to keep down the size of the *New Criterion* (which was made up for October before I heard from you) it may be necessary this time to hold them over for January. This does not matter so much in the case of foreign books, but I am sorry.

I am glad the Massis interested you, and I should be glad if you could contribute something on it for January or April. Will you do this? It has aroused considerable interest. In the October number we have an indifferent expression of a German point of view by Max Rychner,[1] but I think there is a great deal more that you could say better. There is also a capital letter about it from J. G. Fletcher. A hindu wants to write a Defence of the East,[2] and we are trying to get Ortega y Gasset to say how it strikes a Spaniard.

Do you know anything about a German named Wagenseil? I have been pestered with letters from his brother, who wants me to publish something. I have said that I must refer the matter to our editor for German affairs, so here is a short thing: will you be so good as to give me your opinion on it? I have refrained from reading it until I know what you think of it.

We miss you at the *Criterion* reunions, which at present consist of Read, Dobrée, Flint, Monro, Fletcher, Williams, and occasionally Wolfe.[3] It is agreed that the *N.C.* ought to be turned into a (smaller) monthly, that it is too big and too expensive, and that nobody wants to read a quarterly nowadays anyway? What do you think? The capital and organisation

1–'German Chronicle', *NC* 4 (Oct. 1926), 726–32.
2–V. B. Metta, 'In Defence of the East' (letter), *NC* 5 (Jan. 1927), 100–5.
3–John Gould Fletcher would remember the *Criterion* lunches and dinners: 'Harold Monro, now graying and aging, as taciturn in his own way as [Herbert] Read . . . F. S. Flint, getting even vaguer and more ineffectual with the falling years; . . . [and] the tolerant, witty, and friendly Bonamy Dobrée' (*Life Is My Song* [1937], 309).

for a monthly are however at present lacking. The publishing year has been a bad one, and we are trying to keep it down to about 180 pages, to economise.

With many thanks,

Yours ever
[T. S. Eliot]

From the 30th my address will be the Grand Hotel, Divonne-les-Bains, (Ain) France.

## TO *Pearl Fassett*

TS Faber

20 August 1926 Sanatorium de la Malmaison

Dear P.,

Letter of 16, 17 and 18 received. Also books. Also lecture. I find I asked you for the wrong one: I want Lecture VI (Crashaw); it was VII that I asked for and you sent. May I have this.

Please send Pound proof to Hotel Foyot.

I am writing to Wolfe.

Only photographs in existence are that of Hoppé, and later ones by Maurice Beck.[1] Perhaps latter would suit better. I have none.

Have paid Peter Jones.

Return milk bill with cheque for £2. Will you please pay milk bill by p.o. and use £1 for Janes NEXT week, unless you are out of money yourself.

I enclose letters with which I have dealt. Please write for me to the University College Literary Society to say that I am obliged to them for the invitation, but that I am at present not in a position to make engagements for next term, as I do not know what my movements will be, but if they care to write again during the winter I will see what I can do.

On separate sheet cover titles for reviews.

When you give me complete contents will tell you what to leave out (BESIDES Wolfe).

1–Harold Monro had asked for a photograph of TSE, to whom IPF wrote: 'It seems that he would never *dream* of making a practice of bothering other people or himself in such matters, but a very nice Canadian man has asked him where he can obtain a photograph of you as he admires your work so much. He doesn't want it signed or any fuss' (17 Aug.). Emil Otto Hoppé (1878–1972) – the best-known photographer of the Edwardian era, later a photojournalist – had taken photographs of TSE in Dec. 1919. Maurice Beck (1886–1960) was the chief photographer for *Vogue* (London).

Yrs ever
T. S. E.

We leave here on the 30th for Divonne. Please look up address of Vanity Fair New York & forward enclosed letter to Crowninshield.[1]

## TO *Herbert Read* TS Victoria

21 August 1926 Sanatorium de la Malmaison

My dear Read,

Don't worry about worrying me – I am glad to be worried about these matters.[2] Practically (to reply to one of your points) I think that Miss F. could quite well handle all of the extra *routine* work. The only other person who could be of any use would be, not one of the young about the office, but someone who could quite well step into my shoes if necessary. Because I think a review ought to look as if the editor himself had devoted thought to every item in it, and had planned everything for its place and its purpose.

We will thrash this out (and with Faber) when I get back.

I should be very glad if Watson inspired you to something.[3] It struck me as an enormously fertile idea to apply history morals and religion and the theory of knowledge (assent). But you will have to put much more of yourself into anything you write about it than if Richards had not already

1–Frank Crowninshield (1872–1947), scion of a Boston Brahmin family, was editor of *Vanity Fair*. 'Crownie', who was hired by his friend Condé Nast, published many of the leading writers of the era including TSE, Aldous Huxley, Gertrude Stein, F. Scott Fitzgerald and Dorothy Parker; he also cultivated many contemporary artists. TSE's 'enclosure', whether letter or contribition to *Vanity Fair*, has not been found.

2–HR wrote on 14 Aug.: 'I am afraid my outbreak on Quarterlies was a bit unnecessary. I wrote without much premeditation & I might have realised . . . that you had probably traversed most of the ground yourself in the last year or two. But I am glad to find you agree in principle & of course I fully realise all the difficulties in the way. I was considering the matter rather impersonally – a monthly as against a quarterly – & all this was apart from the question of personnel. I am the last person to want to see you involved in more administrative work & wouldn't like to see the change made without some provision for relieving you in some way of the additional burden . . . The general feeling I have is that The Criterion provides material for a wider & more active instrument than the present 5/- quarterly format can possibly give us. Between the material & the potential public there is a reach – a scope – a coincidence – which you will never fully explore or discover with the magazine as it is at present constituted or organised.

'But it is a shame to make you worry over these questions when you should be having a quiet rest.'

3–'I have been reading [John B. Watson's] *Behaviourism* [1925] with increasing respect. I think it is enormously important, though not so adequate as it pretends to be.'

reviewed it for us (a review which seemed to me inadequate at the time).

Ever yours,
T. S. E.

## TO *Humbert Wolfe*

CC

21 August 1926 [Sanatorium de la Malmaison]

My dear Wolfe,

No, I am not in London, and you are never in London when I am. I have had your office rung up once a fortnight during the whole summer (I wanted to get you to write a longish review of De la Mare; but when it seemed that your return could not be depended upon, I passed it on to Rylands.[1]) My secretary has instructions to ship you all the poetry on hand as it comes in, for January; but would you also care to look at Robert Graves's and Vernon Lee's latest pamphlets on Poetry in the Hogarth series?

I shall not be back in England now until the beginning of October. On the 30th August we leave here for the Grand Hotel, Divonne-les-Baines (Ain); that is quite near to Geneva, and it occurred to me that if you were in Geneva at any time during September we could easily arrange to meet. Is there any possibility?

The present *Criterion* position is this: printing costs have ascended, the coal strike continues, we are desirous of ultimately reducing the price (five shillings is too much, and at the same time we give too much for the price). It is agreed on all hands that the *Criterion* is too big; i.e. that the people who will pay five shillings for it will just as readily pay five shillings for something smaller, say by fifteen or twenty pages. We have decided to keep it down to about 184 pages, with a view to eventually cutting the price, then turning it into a relatively somewhat larger *monthly*.[2] In cutting it down, we shall rather increase the number of reviews (this an idea strongly urged by Monro) as people seem to like reviews, and we

1–Rylands on Walter de la Mare, *NC* 4 (Oct. 1926), 785–7.

2–At some point over the next few weeks Wolfe dined with TSE to discuss the future of the *Criterion*; he told his wife: 'It is being converted from a quarterly into a monthly, though I can't believe it will survive many months . . .' Of TSE himself, he went on: 'I can't understand how a body so thin and white goes on living. My word if he were your husband you'd have cause to worry. I look positively robust and coarse beside him. He's had pneumonia twice, and my belief is that he has consumption. However, he's very bright and cheerful about "The Monthly Criterion" as it is now to be called' (quoted in Philip Bagguley, *Harlequin in Whitehall: A Life of Humbert Wolfe, Poet & Civil Servant, 1885–1940* [1997], 239).

have already done rather particularly brilliantly with reviews. In this way I think that we shall be able, early next year, slightly to increase the very poor rates of payment for long reviews. For the moment, in this geddesaxeing,[1] the Bards[2] (as your secretary suspected) have suffered: they have been promoted to the rank of Senior Contribution for the January number. Against seniority there is no appeal, and therefore the Bards are inevitable for the January number; the other two contributions cut out of this number must wait until April. At all events, I am not spreading our best butter too thick: I am afraid that there is a certain proportion of marge in October.

Let me know (1) about books for January (2) if you are to be in Geneva.

Ever yours
[T. S. Eliot]

## TO *Marguerite Caetani* TS Caetani

21 August 1926 Sanatorium de la Malmaison

Dear Cousin,

How very good of you – and most considerate, as this is more particularly useful at the present time. Incidentally, there is no question of rate adjustment; I should have had to cash some money this week before leaving for Divonne, and as the rate at which I should have had it is 170, the balance is on the other side. And it probably makes the performance of the translation more certain.

We were very disappointed not to see you again, but I knew that you would probably be too busy on the Friday before your departure to come to Malmaison.

About the lecture – I expect to receive the one I thought would suit *Commerce* best, in a day or two.[3] I sent for it at once, but the wrong one came. As Menasce has not yet started translating, I will look over both and decide then which is best for *Commerce*, and give you that one. I have not got on with my Hymn to the Virgin[4] so that is of no use for the present. It does not matter which lecture goes to which but the one I had in mind is more literary, the other more philosophical.

1 – In 1921 Sir Eric Geddes (1875–1937) had chaired a committee on government expenditure which urged severe cuts affecting every section of the economy.
2 – Wolfe, 'English Bards and French Reviewers', *NC* 5 (Jan. 1927), 57–73.
3 – 'Crashaw', no. 6 of the Clark Lectures.
4 – The several verses that would ultimately comprise *Ash-Wednesday* (1930).

I am not very much impressed by the poems you sent. I will send them back as soon as I can get an envelope. But if you want poetry, I think I can let you have something better when I get back to London. I am not anxious to 'dump' (as you did with the *Navire*) but putting my own pseudo-dramatic verse into the *Criterion* means that for the next two numbers I can use so much the less of other people;[1] and I have two or three Americans on hand who are really quite interesting. I think Laura Gottschalk has some merit. Robert Graves is sometimes pretty good (for an Englishman) and I am sure I could get something from him.

I hope that Salzburg is a great success. Thank you again very much for the cheque.

Ever yours sincerely
T. S. E.

## TO *Bonamy Dobrée*

TS Brotherton

21 August 1926 Sanatorium de la Malmaison

My dear Dobrée,

Many thanks for your diverting letter. I am delighted to hear that matters are straightening out. I did think the style just a shade too archaic, but considered it a captious criticism. Did you have Dent at the dinner?[2]

I rather wonder whether H M is practical enough for the purpose.[3] You want someone very practical indeed, and the sheet should be distributed not by Louis XV shepherdesses but by rough and tumble hawkers with hoarse voices and a financial interest in the sale.

We will pursue the discussion of the monthly when I get back.[4] I have sent on Read's report to Faber who is however trout fishing. When we get a bit farther we might have a round table with Faber present.

Interim, to consider (a) whether the character of the contribution should be altered at all for a monthly, and (b) lengths and proportions of the several kinds of matter. Read has already drawn up a suggested distribution for 70 pages per month.

1–'Fragment of a Prologue', *NC* 4 (Oct. 1926); 'Fragment of an Agon', 5 (Jan. 1927) – i.e., *Sweeney Agonistes: Fragments of an Aristophanic Melodrama* (1932).
2–BD wrote on 19 Aug.: 'The affair [City churches] is looking more cheerful. I replied to Read . . . and at the last dinner he came round completely. Dent, whom I met, was very helpful, and the phrasing is improved, all archaic taint being removed.'
3–Harold Monro had agreed to distribute the broadsheets – and yet, said BD, 'I can't altogether trust H. M. but tell it not in Russell St.'
4–'I discussed a monthly Criterion with Read. It seems to me an excellent idea – indeed salvation. The only objection of any weight is that of your time . . .'

I do not expect that Canterbury will EVER embrace Rome or vice versa. What I meant was that after Disestablishment the Church of England will lose its whole reason for existence; and that its more serious members will gradually go over to Rome. Some will fall into nonconformity; the majority will content itself with civil marriages and individual Gods (my God for my dog, my pipe, my golf-tools and my allotment garden, your god for yours) but Rome will very slowly become stronger.

Yours ever
T. S. E.

## TO *Pearl Fassett* — TS Valerie Eliot

21 August 1926 — Sanatorium de la Malmaison

Dear P.,

Enclosed cheque for £18:6:- for Driver.

Times received this morning. Please order the following:

| | | |
|---|---|---|
| *Political Ideals of the English Romanticists* | | Milford |
| *Can we then Believe?* | Bishop Gore | Murray |
| *Cosmic Evolution.* | Boodin. | Macmillan |
| *English Speech Today.* | Macdonald | Allen & Unwin |

I should be obliged if you would also send a *Times*[1] regularly to my mother. (Mrs Eliot, 24 Concord Avenue, Cambridge Mass U.S.A.) I would subscribe for her but I want the things I have written to be marked for her to read. This one has a review of 'Troilus' to mark;[2] the next thing of mine will be a review of *The Outlook for American Prose*;[3] and I will always let you know in advance. The one before this had only 'Creative Criticism'.[4]

I don't think it likely that the Trace de Dieu has been arranged for in England.[5] When you have read it you can recommend it. It did not

1 – *The Times Literary Supplement.*

2 – 'Chaucer's "Troilus"' – on *The Book of Troilus and Criseyde, by Geoffrey Chaucer*, ed. Robert Kilburn Root – *TLS*, 19 Aug. 1926, 547.

3 – 'American Prose' – on works by Joseph Warren Beach, Otto Jespersen and Fred Newton Scott – *TLS*, 2 Sept. 1926, 577.

4 – 'Creative Criticism' – on *Creative Criticism: Essays on the Unity of Genius and Taste*, by J. E. Spingarn) – *TLS*, 12 Aug. 1926, 535.

5 – IPF had asked on 19 Aug.: 'Has anyone bought the English rights of Jacques Rivière's book (*À la trace de Dieu*)? If not, do you think it could be suggested to F & G? If there is any possibility of the rights being obtainable in a satisfactory way, I should like very much to report on the book to the firm with the suggestion that they negotiate. This is just the sort of

impress me very much, but I was not considering its saleability. But I imagine that the Correspondence de J. Rivière avec Paul Claudel (Plon[1]) is better, and before recommending Trace it would be best to examine this. Please write to Plon for me and ask them to send it for review. Then report on both to Faber by all means.

I am sending *Les Amants de Venise*,[2] which I have already mentioned to him. You can look at this yourself, but in reporting on it please mention that I suggest that the introduction should appear in any translation as an appendix instead, so as not to frighten the frivolous reader. The last chapter of the book is very fine.

Yours
T. S. E.

FROM *Geoffrey Faber* MS Valerie Eliot

26 August 1926 Faber & Gwyer Ltd.

My dear Eliot,

I have just got back from Scotland, where I have had a very good time, and feel very much the better for my holiday. I am glad to hear the same of you.

I have read Read's comments on Quarterlies v Monthlies with interest and much agreement. I think he considerably overestimates the possibilities of circulation even for a monthly version of *The New Criterion*. It cannot be compared with either Middleton Murry's[3] or Squire's[4] ventures, because it does not make, and does not pretend to make, any sort

---

thing to go down really well. I think it would find a large and heterogeneous public. It is far more likely to achieve success than such a book as *Sous le Soleil* [*Sous la soleil de Satan*, by Georges Bernanos (1888–1948)] – chiefly because the most Anglo-Saxon person born could not suspect that his leg was being pulled. At the time when this could appear in English, the English public would be *ripe* for it. I have as yet only read a little of it straight through, but my impression was immediate and unlooked for . . . All this is provided I do not find some terrible snag in the middle of the book.'

1 – Librairie Plon, publishers.

2 – Charles Maurras, *Les Amants de Venise: George Sand et Musset* (1926).

3 – *The Adelphi.*

4 – J. C. Squire (1884–1958), poet, essayist, journalist and parodist, was literary editor of *The New Statesman* and founder-editor, 1919–34, of *London Mercury* – in which he showed himself to be utterly out of sympathy with modernism; he sniffed at *The Waste Land*: 'it is a pity that a man who can write as well as Mr Eliot does in this poem should be so bored (not passionately disgusted) with existence that he doesn't mind what comes next, or who understands it' (23 Oct. 1922). Evelyn Waugh delighted in mocking him – in the person of 'Jack Spire', editor of the *London Hercules* – in *Decline and Fall* (1928).

of popular appeal. If it did it would lose its character. Nevertheless I think it quite possible that as a monthly it might considerably increase its circulation. It is worth remembering that *The Calendar of Modern Letters began* as a monthly and then became a quarterly. At any rate your reply to Read that the present moment is not an opportune one for such a change is true.

I think too that Read, like most men without practical experience of the book trade, exaggerates what can be done in the way of organization and wider distribution. It is difficult to see how we can do very much more than we are at present doing. I took up your suggestion that copies might be supplied to booksellers on sale or return, on condition that they were displayed in a prominent position. But this is far from being the simple proposition which it sounds. Book space in a bookseller's shop is valuable, and no one has a higher sense of that value than the bookseller. Impossible, except in those rare cases where the bookseller is himself a judge of good literature, to get him to treat a periodical like the *Criterion* in that way. He may take the copies on sale or return, but they will in nine cases out of ten lie unseen at the back of his shop. There is no money in it for him, and he will not bother. Short of spending very large sums of money on advertising, there is nothing more to be done than we are at present doing; and I am afraid we must depend on a gradual extension of interest on the part of the small intelligent public for any increase in sales. I confess that this is all a good deal clearer to me now than it was when I originally planned to take joint responsibility for the paper. Please don't think from this sentence that I in any way regret the connection of Faber & Gwyer with *The New Criterion*. I have always believed, and I still believe, that the connection will in the long run prove to have been a profitable one for my firm. But the profit is not going to be a direct profit I am afraid. I will keep Read's letter and enclosure, unless you would like me to send them to you. Please give my regards to your wife.

Yours ever,
Geoffrey Faber.

## FROM *Harold Monro* TS Valerie Eliot

30 August 1926 [London]

My dear Eliot,[1]

Herbert Read, Bonamy Dobrée and F. S. Flint had supper with me on the evening of the 30th August. After the first exchanges, pleasantries, glasses and hors d'oeuvres, Herbert Read suggested that, while we were still sober, it might be worthwhile and of some service to you if we discussed the future of *The New Criterion*; whereupon the company emptied their glasses, opened another bottle, and proceeded. For brevity, the results are given below in the form of resolutions, though of course we recognise that they are no more than suggestions for your consideration.

(1) Resolved that *The New Criterion* shall be transformed from a quarterly into a monthly review, since it was the unanimous opinion of the company that the 'quarterly idea' is one that no longer evokes response from present-day society.

(2) Resolved that *The New Criterion*, as a monthly review, shall bear the name of the editor prominently on the cover.

(3) Resolved that, in principle, the bulk of *The New Criterion* shall be 68 pages.

(4) Resolved that the 'Commentary' shall be a permanent, prominent and vital feature of the review, to which all regular contributors (hereinafter referred to as 'associate editors') shall be invited to contribute, the editor retaining of course full powers of rejection and *remaniement*.

(5) Resolved that the make-up of the *The New Criterion* shall be all or any of the following:

(1) Commentary
(2) Two critical articles
(3) A poem (possibly)
(4) A story or instalment of a serial
(5) One foreign chronicle
(6) Dramatic chronicle
(7) Art chronicle
(8) Music chronicle
(9) Reviews of books
(10) Divers and various

(6) Resolved that advertisements shall be accepted and solicited.

1–Dominic Hibberd notes, 'HM wrote the paper, Flint typed it, making a copy for HM to sign and send to Eliot' (*Harold Monro: Poet of the New Age* [2001], 286).

(7) Resolved that Messrs Faber & Gwyer shall provide a business manager, if the review is worth providing a business manager for.

(8) Resolved that for the first two or three months of the publication of *The New Criterion* as a monthly no money shall be spent on newspaper advertising, but that the money which would be otherwise so spent shall be used to defray the cost of extra copies of the review, to be distributed for advertising purposes in such a way as commends itself to the editor or to an editorial committee, if the editor decide[s] to appoint such a committee.

(9) Resolved that *The New Criterion* shall distinguish itself as the most trenchant publication for the reviewing of books in a short and pithy manner; that, for this purpose, eight pages of the review shall be devoted each month to the criticism of sixteen selected books, half a page to each; and that these reviews shall be the best short reviews in Great Britain of philosophy, poetry, history, art, religion, criticism, aesthetics, science, etc., etc.

(10) Resolved that a private gathering of associate editors of *The New Criterion* shall meet each first fortnight of the month (a) at six o'clock p.m. at the offices of *The New Criterion* to discuss business and policy with the editor, (b) afterwards at a restaurant to be chosen which is open until 11 p.m.

(11) Resolved that in the second fortnight of the month the editor and associate editors shall dine together, at the selected restaurant, or separately as they please, with their guests, and that they with their guests shall afterwards adjourn to The Poetry Bookshop or elsewhere.[1]

(12) Resolved that whatever the venue of the adjourned meeting referred to under (11) may be, the editor and associate editors shall provide for the entertainment of their own guests, but that wine or other refreshment thus bought to the place of congregation shall be dispensed in common.

1 – BD was to recall: 'The dinners were enormously stimulating, but more so were the small evening gatherings which dovetailed with and eventually took the place of the dinners, at Harold Monro's above his book shop opposite the British Museum. These consisted of Monro himself, of course, Frank Flint, Herbert Read, [Frank] Morley – and later [Montgomery] Belgion. The conversations there were equally gay, but more useful. There we really did discuss policy and contributions. Sometimes the conversation tended to the deeply serious, but Eliot did not like too ready a mixture of the serious and the convivial. ("I hate mixing things" – in a letter they were separated.) On one occasion, when someone began to intrude a religious issue, Eliot put a stop to it by saying, "The only two things I care for are dancing and brandy." Monro was horrified. "O Tom! You mustn't say things like that!"' ('T. S. Eliot: A Personal Reminiscence')

We put forward these suggestions to you because we think *The New Criterion* is the only review appearing in England that is worthy of serious consideration, and because we wish it a successful career.

Yours sincerely,
Harold Monro

## *Vivien Eliot* TO *John Middleton Murry* MS Valerie Eliot

30 August [1926] Sanatorium de la Malmaison

My dear John

I shd have written *long* before, to thank you. Don't think I am not grateful, I know exactly how big a thing you are offering me, & all it means. Perhaps *no one else* wd offer this to me. No, I am *sure no one would*. First I thought a great deal. Then I consulted various doctors. Then I began to make a translation of that thing of Katherine's you sent me, & I have nearly finished it. It is such an important document.

Then, we were to have *left* here last Thursday, & gone to Divonne. I wasn't very well & enfin I got a bad attack of bronchitis, really bad. I have been in bed for a week. I could not write until today.

Now, you see. *I do want your cottage, & I can't say just what I think of you for offering it to me*. There is only one detail you left out, which I feel is important. I must know. Who inhabits the 4th cottage? All depends on that. I gather you inhabit 2, you offer me one, & you say there are 4. Therefore, who is X?

In such a position I need not explain to you that it is an important point. All the rest sounds *delightful*, & quite in order. I take it the water is drinkable. You don't say how many rooms but I suppose about 2. What I need is *sun*, & air. Chiefly sun. I take it I can get plenty if there is any about.

Dear John. You are a saint. Knowing all, you offer me this.

You understand I could never be there *absolutely alone*. I am sure it is *possible* in the winter, for odd times if one cld get anyone to go with one.

About furniture. I suppose it is unfurnished, & it is always more amusing to furnish one's own cottage. I like it better. So now please write here at once & say who has the 4th cottage. That is all I want to know.

O yes, & how far from the nearest station – Weymouth, or Dorset?

You still believe one should *stay still* somewhere. I am going by you. *I don't know*. All these doctors here want me to wander about Europe all the *winter*. But yes, I do see what you mean. One must stay still. About

Tom, I don't know. He never seems to really *like* the country, or to know what to do with it. But I have got to live, I suppose, and I do thank you for offering me this chance. I rang the Adelphi in Paris.

We can't leave here not until Sept. 8. So please write here.

My love,
V.

## TO *Pearl Fassett*

MS Faber

30 August 1926 Malmaison

V. ill with serious bronchitis here – cannot leave for 10 days – communicate with me *here* all this week.

In haste.
T. S. E.

## TO *John Middleton Murry*

TS Valerie Eliot

31 August 1926 [London]

Dear John,

This is merely a line to tell you that I very highly appreciate your offer of a cottage to Vivien. I doubt whether she will accept it, because it is very difficult for her to make her mind up on anything; and if she does take it I doubt whether she will use it. However, I should be glad if she would take it, though I shall not urge her. The less I have to do with the matter the better it is for her. But I certainly should not expect to live there six months of the year myself. It is not so easy for me to absent myself from London for long periods; and I have unfortunately to make as much money in one way or another as I can, which is not a very great deal; past expenses and present liabilities are heavy. And I do not suppose for a moment that it would be possible for me to do much good work under such conditions – not that I have any objection to the country *per se*. And it would be undoubtedly better for her to achieve a little more independence and not to be with me the whole time.

One question is, would it be possible for her to obtain provisions, get to a doctor if necessary, etc. in this place? She has thought that she would have to have a small car as well; that would of course be a good thing, when it can be afforded, and if she can master it herself.

No need to acknowledge this letter in any way.

Ever affectionately,
Tom

## TO *Marguerite Caetani*

TS Caetani

3 September 1926

Sanatorium de la Malmaison

Dear Cousin,

Your letter reached me, because we have been delayed here; my wife has been in bed with a bad attack of bronchitis for a week. We are actually leaving on Wednesday the 8th September; and the address is the Grand Hotel, Divonne-les-Bains, (Ain).

I had already posted to you to Benarville the MSS. of a lecture, somewhat chopped about to make it possible for publication, and the poems. As for my lecture, you will read it and decide whether you think it suitable. If not, destroy it. If so, I think it would be much quicker if someone in France could translate it. Larbaud[1] of course is one of the best, but the Fry essay[2] was very well done, I thought, though I have not seen the original. The quotations could be left in the original languages, with a prose translation after, or as a footnote.

I should hardly give the authoress of the poems very much encouragement – though it is too much responsibility to *dis*courage her! She writes English deadly, it has no life to it, only a dead fluffiness.

I will see about verse when I get to London. But I shall not try to palm off second-rate stuff, or the work of friends etc!

We shall be at Divonne for about a month. I will write from there, and we shall also hope to see you in Paris in October. Many thanks for your kind letter.

Ever sincerely,
T. S. E.

1 – Valery Larbaud (1881–1957): poet, novelist, essayist; of independent means and with erudition and taste. He translated, *inter alia*, JJ's *Ulysses*. Pseudonymous author of *Poèmes par un riche amateur* (1908) and *Le Journal intime de A. O. Barnabooth* (1913). In a letter of 20 Mar. 1922, TSE called him 'a great poet and prose author'. Larbaud's lecture-essay 'The Ulysses of James Joyce' had appeared in C. 1 (Oct. 1922).

2 – Not found.

## TO *Herbert Read* TS Victoria

3 September 1926 Rueil

My dear Read,

We leave on the 8th for the Grand Hotel, Divonne-les-Bains, (Ain) France.

I have heard nothing from Dobrée about the quarterly question.[1] Many thanks for your suggestions. I should think that he probably is a very good journalist indeed, and certainly worth getting into touch with.[2] The first question really would be, when the time came, whether we could offer a salary that would be acceptable to such an experienced man: I imagine that what he really wants is a paper of his own. But we will keep him in mind. The name of Hamish Miles I seem to have heard.[3] We must arrange to meet him. I wonder if any evidence can be collected about him? Bates I have never heard of before.[4] The review does not impress me very much – the first long passage that he quotes with praise from the book – I return the cutting – seems to me very conventional and not wholly true – certainly misleading. But I liked very much his reply to the author. Have you seen anything else of his that is interesting?

I shall indeed be sorry if Dobrée takes the job in Cairo; but it is well paid.[5] But this sort of thing is always likely to happen, and we must as you suggest be always on the lookout for new personnel.

I think that Thorpe, within his limitations (and a certain humourlessness) has done pretty well with Lewis.[6]

Many thanks. How are you getting on with Watson? Fernandez came out here one day and read us parts of his book on personality which is

1–HR wrote (22 Aug.): 'Dobrée & I had a talk about the Quarterly question & I think he is writing to you about it.' It was in fact HM who had written on 30 Aug.

2–At the prompting of FVM, HR suggested that TSE might recruit Phillip Tomlinson (who had worked successfully on *The Adelphi*, and now had 'an interim job as editor of the weekly edition of the *Times*') as 'business editor' of *C*. HR and FVM had taken the occasion to talk with Tomlinson, though without mentioning *C*. HR would later (4 June 1927) call Tomlinson 'a hard-working journalist'.

3–'Do you know anything of a man called Hamish Miles? He has been a publisher (with Guy Chapman) but has withdrawn & is said to be "the kind of man the Criterion ought to get hold of" (Morley) as a reviewer.' Miles (1894–1937) was an author and translator.

4–'The enclosed clippings might amuse you. I don't want them back. E. S. Bates is an American whom I have noted several times as being on the right scent.'

5–'Dobrée's presence among us was, I imagine, becoming rather a comfort to you & his absence, if he takes on the Cairo job, will be our loss even if it is only for three years.'

6–W. A. Thorpe's review of Wyndham Lewis, *The Art of Being Ruled* (and of three books by other authors), *NC* 4 (Oct. 1926), 758–64.

coming out in November; I got the impression that there is a good deal of bunkum in it.

Yours ever,
T. S. E.

## TO *Pearl Fassett*

TS Faber

3 September [1926] Sanatorium de la Malmaison

Dear P.,

We are leaving on Wednesday the 8th and arrive at Divonne on Thursday morning. So do not write again here after receipt of this. I have your letter with copy of letter sent to Divonne.

Have received the Smith Dissertation.

No initials on short notes.

M'Greevy can have the books he wants.[1] Only half page on the Huxley travel book, but it ought to be mentioned. Long review of Barren Leaves precludes notice of this.

Include Randall review as last of signed as you suggested.

You can send Metta on to Divonne.

I return Seldes cut. It is still much too long. I therefore enclose letter which you can send on to him.

Reviews are all right. Ballet better printed as it is.

I enclose slip of Canada Life Assurance Co., signed. Will you please witness my signature and forward to my brother H. W. Eliot at 1018 North State Street, Chicago? This is important as it concerns a refund of insurance premiums. Please date it from London. This is irregular but there is no English speaking person here.

Yours
T. S. E.

Cheque £3 enclosed. *Please* pay Janes.
<Can you send me to Divonne a Remington portable black ribbon?>
<Omit Caffrey.>

1 – IPF had written on 30 Aug.: 'Mr M'Greevy approached me on the subject of books he would like to review . . . He would still like Edith Sitwell's poems, he would like to do a brief note on a sixpenny book by Gilbert Murray (gather he wants to have a slap at him) and is keen to do Aldous Huxley's letters from India when they appear. As he asked me what I thought, I mentioned that Conrad Aiken had done Aldous Huxley up to date when *Those Barren Leaves* appeared and so I thought it *possible* that you might not want him rounded up again so soon . . . He was in a good mood. What a pity that both his work and his demeanour are so uneven. I think there is a lot of good stuff in him really. In one way I think he is genuinely unsophisticated – and this is why his freshness is sometimes so stimulating.'

## TO *Geoffrey Faber*

TS Faber

4 September 1926 — Sanatorium de la Malmaison

My dear Faber

Many thanks for your letter and for copies of the two letters sent to Divonne. My wife has nearly recovered from her bronchitis, and we are leaving for Divonne on the 8th.

I quite agree about Fraser-Harris.[1] I liked the essay, but set no great store by it, and I very much object to paying for contributions before publication, unless they are likely to improve the sales. And the individual contribution which will make a material difference to the sales is a very rare one indeed.

I am very glad to know about Woodruff[2] and Adams[3] (there is something familiar about the former name). Adams is an oddity, I imagine an autodidact, but with the freshness of interest of autodidacts, and seems to have read a great deal. If he wants to write about Bolingbroke[4] it is because he has something to say. There is no good book on Bolingbroke (there is rather a bad one on the lowest open shelf in my room). De Toqueville[5] I must confess I know little about. I will drop a line to both of these men, tell them I expect to be back in about a month, and would like to see them: – on second thoughts I will wait until I hear from you before writing to them.

1–GCF wrote (2 Sept.) that Dr Fraser-Harris, author of an 'article on Shakespeare's appreciation of the something-or-other of the brain' – 'Shakespeare's Perception of the Functional Importance of the Brain' – had asked for payment in advance of publication. When GCF declined, Harris had 'elected' to take back the article.

2–Douglas Woodruff (1897–1978), Catholic journalist – who had won a first in Modern History at New College, Oxford in 1923 – was Colonial Editor of *The Times*, 1926–36; Editor of *The Tablet*, 1936–67; Deputy Chairman of the publishers Burns and Oates, 1948–62; Director of Hollis and Carter, 1948–62; and Chairman of Associated Catholic Newspapers, 1953–70; author of *Plato's American Republic* (1926); *Talking at Random* (1941); and *The Tichborne Claimant* (1957). Woodward of All Souls had told GCF that Woodruff had written a book on de Tocqueville; but Woodruff told GCF he could not afford to undertake such a commission. Still (GCF suggested), de Tocqueville 'might perhaps find a place in your contemplated series'?

3–John J. Adams, author of *The Tower of Babel*, was keen to write on Bolingbroke.

4–Henry St John Bolingbroke: 1st Viscount (1678–1751), Tory politician and philosopher; his *Collected Works* were published in 1754. See TSE, 'Augustan Age Tories', *TLS*, 15 Nov. 1928, 846. TSE later criticised his friend Whibley for having 'somewhat overpraised the virtues, and too much extenuated the faults, of Bolingbroke as a statesman, because of the brilliance and vigour of Bolingbroke's style, and the great attraction of his personality' (*SE*, 458, 496).

5–Alexis de Tocqueville (1805–1858): political thinker and historian; author of *Democracy in America* (1835, 1840); *The Old Régime and the Revolution* (1856).

The suggestion of these two men seems to give a new impulse to the series. Before I left I had outlined and discussed with Read a scheme for another series, of much smaller books at half a crown, on contemporary men of letters and thought, for which I had about a dozen names of subjects and authors (that would be quite enough); I had intended to propose it as a scheme which would cost much less, both in royalties and printing, than the other; especially if you wished to postpone the more elaborate series to a favourable opportunity. But you were very busy, and also I came to the opinion that every such scheme had best be postponed until the conclusion of the strike, if it ever is concluded.

About the Monthly, I am inclined, as you are, to discount the profits of the conversion. In any case, I shall feel more assured of the possibility of making money out of a monthly when we have proved that it is not necessary to lose so much out of a quarterly; and we have ample time to make the tests of restriction of size and modification of contents which we have discussed. I think that something can be done by emphasising the element of 'discussion', even to the extent of including a larger amount of correspondence; the 'Defence of the West' has had a success of this kind exceeding its merits; it is a subject about which everyone thinks he has something to say.

I see the autumn list is in *The Times*; it looks promising, with the exception of one or two very expensive books. Clayton[1] seems to have had a good press. Massis is turning his *Defence* into a book for this winter; we might have a look at it with a view to translation. I have sent Miss Fassett the *Amants de Venise* to give you, she might read it first.

About Léger. I am afraid that the arrangement in our conversation, and subsequently in conversation between myself and Madame de Bassiano, was that she should pay the author and should pay me for the translation, and cost of publishing to be borne by the publishers. But this was purely verbal. The book is a small one; the French text is 41 pages not wholly covered, so that it might be as well to include the preface by Valery Larbaud which does not appear in the French edition but was written for the Russian translation. That is 5 pages.[2] But if there is a misunderstanding, let me have an estimate of the cost of printing etc. and I will take the matter up with her and come to an arrangement. I should

1–Joseph Clayton, *The Rise and Descent of Socialism* (1926).

2–Larbaud's 'Préface pour une traduction russe d'*Anabasis*' (a Russian translation by Guéorgui Ivanoff and Anamovitch), *NRF* 147 (Jan. 1926), 64–7, was to be reprinted, in English, in St-John Perse, *Anabasis*, trans. TSE (3rd edn revised and corrected: New York, 1949), 101–4.

suggest a small book, almost a pamphlet, like some of the Hogarth Press, and a printing of 500.

I hope that everything is going well with you, and that you enjoyed the fishing in Scotland. The weather here has been superb until the last day or two, but the summer climate near Paris is insupportably heavy and humid, and we have been exasperated by this delay in getting to the mountains.

Yours ever,
T. S. E.

## FROM *Henry Eliot* — CC Houghton

5 September 1926 — 1018 North State Street, Chicago

My dear Tom:

In your last letter to me you speak more optimistically regarding the likelihood of Vivien's recovery, and in a letter to Charlotte, which she forwarded to me, and I returned to her, before her death[1] (though I think she died without having seen my last letter to her) you spoke still more optimistically, with expectation that Vivien would again live with you. According to your last letter to me you and Vivien are now at Divonne-les-Bains, for how long I do not know. About a week ago I received a letter from Theodora, which I sent on to Theresa (who is still at Haddam) and which she forwarded to Mother, and which, when I get it back, I will mail to you, as in it she speaks with so much affection of Vivien and all the Haigh-Woods, and with so much delight of the meetings you had in Paris or at Rueil. It was written, of course, before Charlotte's death.

I share with you a considerable degree of optimism about Vivien, and return to my previous skepticism about the nature of her illness, which was shaken only for a while after receiving your first letter written after we left Italy. In other words, I share the view of Dr Miller, not that I believe his opinion authoritative on mental disturbances, but that I believe him a shrewd judge of human nature, and in this case, about right. The doctors of Paris agree that there is no trace of mental disease proper, and that the delusions are projections of a state of emotional anguish. To this I would add, as my opinion, that the state of emotional anguish is self-induced, voluntarily and deliberately. It is not melancholia, which is something more involuntary. It is something which Vivien herself could

1–TSE's sister Charlotte – Mrs George Smith – had died of peritonitis on 22 Aug. 1926.

put a stop to at any moment, by an effort of will; that is, so far as one is able to break any bad habit by an effort of will. My observation (and I think the theory is upheld today) is that the will is not autonomous, but is at least to a considerable extent under the sway of the emotions, which in turn are reactions to external circumstances. The will, however, is responsive to auto-suggestion as well as external suggestion. I am not inclined to a censorious attitude, however, since I have several bad habits of my own which I am not, in my present environment at least, able to break. On the other hand, the suggestion that the will is impotent is an exceedingly bad one to make to any person who is lacking in self-control.

Analysis is intriguing, and, for the patient herself at least, not only futile but aggravating to the trouble. It seems to me that the secret of a cure lies in as completely as possible forgetting the whole business, in wiping the slate clean, obliterating the past. That is easier said than done. Some new and absorbing interest, such as a new talent discovered, the exercise of which might bring some recognition and satisfy the ego (the teaching of dancing?) would do it. A new environment – a new social environment particularly – might do it. Vivien is naturally social, and for such types (vide Margaret) deprivation of social activities induces melancholia.[1]

I think her social life is one of the origins of her state of mind, one of the causes of what the doctor calls her 'mental anguish'. Naturally egotistical, she finds herself completely eclipsed intellectually and socially by you. An inferiority complex consequent upon this causes her to hate all those who admire you and respect your accomplishments. This is probably aggravated by the notion that she is inalienably entitled to the right of a certain amount of condescension due any American. It is also aggravated by the supercilious attitude which is a characteristic of most literary and artistic circles. Consequently she picks up friends (I judge from insufficient evidence) of a very ordinary type, much inferior to her, for the comfort she derives from a feeling of superiority to them. What she needs is company composed of persons of intelligence and education, capable of literary and artistic appreciation, but without sophistication or great learning. An interest in dancing (which I detest) is desirable. But to furnish her with a completely new milieu, made to order, is a difficult task.

The individual is swayed to and fro by two sets of impulses, one set of which may be called robust and healthy, the other set morbid and diseased; the one set beneficent, the other malignant. To desire to cut a pitiful and

1 – TSE was later to say of his sister Margaret Dawes Eliot (b. 1871) that she was 'a somewhat eccentric recluse' (letter to G. F. Higginson, solicitor, 22 Mar. 1950).

pathetic figure in the world is morbid; to desire success and admiration is healthy. Baffled in the attempt to secure the latter, one is likely to attempt the former. The recent attacks followed soon after Vivien's attempts to emulate Katherine Mansfield.[1] To prefer excuses for non-success to success is morbid. To prefer cherishing a bitter grievance to cherishing affection is a common form of this state of mind; it is characteristic of the type of person known as quarrelsome, and such persons undoubtedly derive an intense though torturing pleasure in fomenting their bitterness. An excess of sentimentality is morbid as well as almost purely selfish; Vivien seems to cling to a school-girl ideal of marital affection, which expresses itself in cloying affections, pinning flowers in your coat, drowning you in solicitude, and then harassing you with fictitious alarms concerning herself.

Of all the harassing things that a wife may do, the worst is self-accusation. If one's wife bores one, it is tolerable; but when she asks constantly, 'Do I bore you?' the situation becomes intolerable, because no protestations to the contrary, however severe they may be, can be made to sound sincere. The accusation, made to put one on the defensive, puts her in the grateful position of being injured and the husband in the uncomfortable position of being delinquent. Vivien's self-accusations are wholly insincere, though it is quite possible that she does not realize this fact herself. Having committed some act which causes you pain (gratifying one malignant impulse) she then seeks by elaborate confession to evoke sympathy and solicitude for her contrition (gratifying another morbid desire).

As for her alarms, her delusions of voices and plots, I believe implicitly that these are self-propagated purely for the effect on you and on such other audience as she may have. Having no longer physical ailments, at least none so definite as before, by means of which to secure for herself the notoriety and attention which is meat and drink to her, she has resorted to an attempt to undermine her sanity, at least to produce a not too dangerous mental condition which will, even more than physical illness, arouse concern, alarm and solicitude. There is a decided satisfaction to be derived from being sensationally ill; there are few people who do not enjoy the notoriety of having had a serious operation. The climax of her

1 – Katherine Mansfield (1888–1923), New Zealand-born short story writer. Her early stories were collected in *In a German Pension* (1911). She met JMM in 1911 (marrying in 1918), and became involved with other writers including D. H. Lawrence and his wife Frieda, and VW (who published *Prelude* in 1918). She published *Bliss* (1920) and *The Garden Party* (1922). After her death from tuberculosis at the Gurdjieff Institute, Fontainebleau, JMM published two collections of stories; her *Journal* (1927); and *Letters* (1928).

satisfaction would be to suffer some fate, not extinction, and not too painful, which would be incontestably dramatic. I do not believe for an instant that any of her attempts at suicide were genuine, although it is possible that in her ardor to make the attempt to appear genuine she might injure herself or even succeed. I do believe that to a slight extent she has succeeded in producing a neurotic condition, and that from feigning fear she has come to feel actual fear, that she has been able to work herself up to a pitch of emotion by the same methods as are employed by emotional actresses. I read in the papers that Pola Negri, a popular film actress, fainted twice at the bier of Rudolph Valentino, another film favourite. I do not think that this indicates that she was fonder of the actor than my mother was of my father.

My belief is that these fears and delusions would immediately disappear with the removal of any audience to behold them. For that reason you are the worst person in the world for Vivien to be with, because you have cultivated in yourself what I consider in itself a harmless and charming, but in her case a very harmful habit – the habit of polite and interested solicitude. The habit in you is now fixed, automatic and unalterable unless by a continuous effort of will. It has become a mannerism which reacts upon you in the manner described by psychologists; you become anxious because you look anxious. It has become more and more exaggerated as Vivien's demands for sympathetic and anguished consternation on your part have grown. She has reveled in her power to keep you in a state of quivering attention. During intervals of relief from her presence your natural elasticity restores your poise. It is a result that could have been accomplished only by years of pinpricks.

The peculiar part of this is that I believe Vivien would herself experience great nervous relief if you adopted exactly the opposite attitude – one of complete self-possession and healthy indifference to her state of mind or body, of disbelief in her complaints, of contempt for her qualms. It should be made apparent to her that every pose of hers is completely transparent to you, that there is not one in her bag of tricks that is not absurdly obvious, that the only impression they make on you is that of utter silliness and puerility. Thus her audience would be eliminated and the motive for her actions reduced to impotence. That she would prefer this attitude is shown by her enthusiasm for Dr Miller, whose attitude is skeptical and amused.

Vivien is introspective, analytical, and a shrewd judge of human nature, including her own. That she acts with her tongue in her cheek much of the time I am certain from a gleam that I have occasionally caught in her eye.

Nothing interests her more than a discussion of her own faults; they are her precious little offspring, they are interesting, they distinguish her from the crowd, they are indicative of a sensitive and complex organization. As a matter of fact, they are not pathological, they are not interesting, they are simply self-exaggerations of tendencies to be found in the majority of human beings, developed in her by giving rein to all self-control. They are the perversities of a spoiled child.

That she would rejoice in any calamity to you that exalted her in some way in public esteem is one of the more malignant phases of her state of mind. For this reason suicide, with the implication that you had in some way driven her to it, would be deliciously satisfying to her, but for the inconvenient fact that she could not enjoy the aftermath of it. A public disgrace for you, a torrent of abuse for you from the press, would afford her delight – mixed, however, with normal emotions, not yet extinct, of affection and sorrow. A bitter jealousy is one of the most serious of her complexes. An unsatisfied ego is another. Whether there is any way to satisfy it I do not know.

As I say, however, I feel a certain degree of optimism. I think she may be cured simply by wearying of that particular pose. She may try a new role; and it might conceivably be a sweet, forgiving, noble role. Such things do happen. She has now attained the notoriety of having been confined in an insane asylum, and of having attempted, according to reports, suicide. That accomplishment may satisfy her desires in that direction. At any rate, the other pose is now 'old hat'. She may take a notion to surprise people, to show them that they are unable to guess her next move. At any rate, I think there will be a change, and it is likely that she will want the change to be as surprising as possible.

I am much encouraged by Theodora's letter, from which it would seem that there is a decided change for the better. I believe that there is a tendency, a vis medicatrix naturae, for things to heal themselves, to 'run their course'. Usually this takes place just at the time when things seem most hopeless, at the point which physicians call the crisis. I know that after my ear had suppurated for seven years (which it had never done before) and a doctor advised operating, it suddenly ceased; at least I have had no trouble for over a year. A wart on my foot, which had grown to larger and larger dimensions, and which had been treated unsuccessfully with x-rays, became apparently worse on my travels, and suddenly went away, so quickly that I did not notice until it had gone. The body, its cells, its molecules, and its atoms and even electrons, think, act and feel independently of the collocation of them which we call the mind.

My final advice, with regard to the whole matter, is simply, *forget*. The elasticity of your nature will tend to pull you back to the norm. Do not be too much together, mix with people, and relax and regain strength – you as well as she.

Affectionately,
[Henry]

## TO *Henry Eliot*

TS Houghton

7 September 1926

Sanatorium de la Malmaison

My dear brother,

We leave here tomorrow for the Grand Hotel, Divonne-les-Bains, Ain, France, for a month. It is a convalescent resort in the mountains near the Swiss frontier, where Vivien will be under a doctor who is in touch with Professor Claude and with the doctors here. She is very much better, but needs mountain air. Her lungs are weak (she has just recovered from a bad attack of pleurisy here; the climate here is moist and sultry) and she needs principally building up. After that I am not sure whether she will come back to England with me or spend the winter abroad.

Thank you for your letter with receipt to sign. I have signed it and sent on to my secretary in London to witness; this is irregular, but I see no reason why the insurance company should know anything about it. I shall be very glad to [have] the money, but it is really yours, and an extra present.

I should be glad to hear from you something more personal, and about your married life, of which you say little. When Theresa's charming letter to Vivien arrived V. was not able to receive letters, and then it got mislaid and I think destroyed, so V. never saw it. I should be very much obliged if you and Theresa could write her a short line. This is the more desirable, because she thinks from your silence that you are offended with her, or expressing disapproval.

Charlotte's death came as a great shock. I have had a letter from mother giving some details, and showing that it was a very serious and dangerous operation indeed for anyone so weakened as Charlotte. Mother seemed to be quite self-possessed, but I should be glad to hear from you how it has affected her. It is a tragedy for the children, and especially Theodora.

Write to me as soon as you can.

always affectionately,
Tom

## TO *Herbert Read* MS Victoria

14 September 1926 Grand Hotel, Divonne-les-Bains

My dear Read,

Yr letter gave me much pleasure. Of course I take the 'resolutions' in good part.[1] I am very grateful. Some of them could be realised at once. I shall type out a reply to send round.

I shall be very keen to see the results of your reading of Watson. I want to go through the book carefully myself when I return. By all means try the American market at once.[2]

Vauvenargues is very good, I think.[3]

I am very disturbed at having let Monro down. I am afraid it was largely distraction, having other affairs on my mind, but I had not realised that his party would be so early as the 30th, or that all his other supports would fail.[4] I had rather it were almost anyone than Monro, because he is sensitive to the point of suspicion, & I am afraid he will take it very hard. And the worst is that I do not know him intimately enough to be quite frank in explaining the reasons for my delayed return. If you see him please find out for me how he feels. I am hoping that he can postpone his party for a couple of weeks.

1–HR had written on 10 Sept.: 'You will have received from Monro a set of resolutions which I hope you took in good part. I was a little afraid at one time that we had gone beyond the limits of pertinent suggestions.'

2–'I have finished Watson; also another, more technical but slightly earlier book . . . If you want it, all right [but] I would like to see if there is any American market for it: I shall be in desperate need of money in the next year . . .'

3–HR had been reading WL – 'So much is the outcome of personal irritations and tastes. So much of it is mere petulant reaction to environment. I don't feel that he ever gets above his subject . . . But there is a right ideal behind it all, and I only wish there was a little more grace and sympathy in the expression of it' – and thought to apply to WL remarks by Luc de Clapiers, Marquis de Vauvenargues (1715–47), whose work he had just read: '*Le duc de La Rochefoucauld a saisi admirablement le côté faible de l'esprit humain; peut-être n'en a-t-il pas ignoré la force; peut-être n'a-t-il contesté le mérite de tant d'actions éblouissantes, que pour démasquer la fausse sagesse. Quelles qu'aient été ses intentions, l'effet m'en paraît pernicieux; son livre, rempli d'invectives contre l'hypocrisie, détourne, encore aujourd'hui, les hommes de la vertu, en leur persuadant qu'il n'y en a point de véritable.*'

4–Monro had implored TSE (6 Sept.) to 'deliver a short address at the formal opening' of the new Poetry Bookshop premises at 38 Great Russell Street, London. 'PLEASE REALISE, as I am sure you do, THAT I AM ABSOLUTELY RELYING ON YOU: relying upon your keeping the promise which was so kindly and readily given and so gladly received.' According to George Sims, in 'Alida Monro and the Poetry Bookshop' (*Antiquarian Book Monthly Review*, July 1982, 265), TSE wired back 'Absolutely impossible to return in time grievously distressed if postponement impossible can I send something to be read.'

There is one Gordon George here, quite pleasant, the author of that leader we discussed.[1] He is very much interested by your Descartes, which I like very much, & hope to discuss with you later.[2]

Ever yours
T. S. E.

## TO *John Middleton Murry*

MS Valerie Eliot

19 September 1926 Grand Hotel, Divonne les Bains

My dear John

This is a hasty line as Vivien is not able to write. She has not been at all well since we got here, and it is more & more certain that it is *impossible* to make *any* plans for next year: the doctor here wishes her to await the effect of the stay here and then consult the specialists in Paris about the *climate* which she ought to have. So now everything is in suspense. So *don't* keep your cottage empty on our account. She thanks you for the wonderful offer you have made. It is simply that she is now so unwell that we dare not look *one inch* ahead.

Affectionately
Tom

1–Robert Esmonde Gordon George (1890–1969), critic, historian and biographer, would presently take the nom de plume Robert Sencourt: see Biographical Register under 'Robert Sencourt'. He was much later to reveal, in *T. S. Eliot: A Memoir* (posthumously published, 1971), that in mid-September 1926 he too had been a patient at the clinic for nervous disorders at Divonne-les-Bains: 'What were my own first impressions of meeting Eliot? Here was someone extremely approachable and friendly, even confiding, someone to whom one took immediately. One felt that he was sincerity incarnate, the most natural and the most modest of men . . .

'How well I remember my first glimpse of Vivienne as she walked almost as though in a trance along a wooded path! Her black hair was dank, her white face blotched – owing, no doubt, to the excess of bromide she had been taking. Her dark dress hung loosely over her frail form; her expression was both vague and acutely sad . . .

'The treatment at Divonne which the Eliots and I took and from which Tom profited more than Vivienne, was a variant of the douche écossaise in which strong gushes of hot, alternating with icy cold, water were played on the naked body. The doctors on the whole deprecated drugs and avoided psychoanalysis. Their idea was that once they had gained a patient's confidence, he would soon divulge the reasons for his strain. It was evident that the strain from which my new friends were suffering was that they no longer lived together in deepest unity' (102–3).

2–'The Dethronement of Descartes' – on Alfred Espinas, *Descartes et la Morale*; Jacques Maritain, *Trois Reformateurs: Luther, Descartes, Rousseau*; and *Correspondence of Descartes and Constantyn Huygens, 1635–1647* – *TLS*, 9 Sept. 1926, 585–6.

## TO *Marguerite Caetani* MS Caetani

27 September 1926 Grand Hôtel, Divonne les Bains

Dear Cousin

Very many thanks for your kind letter and for your cheque, which you should not have sent until you could use the essay, if you ever can. Of course I don't mind, and in any case it will probably be a year before I can make the lectures into a book if then, so you have plenty of time. If meanwhile I can do anything that wd suit you better you are welcome to it. It is almost too easy to promise you my next verses because I am not likely to produce any for some time!

My wife is constantly worrying me to do more on *Anabase*. She is afraid it will never be done. I confess it is more difficult than I thought at first, because the idea (and there decidedly is one) is conveyed by a cumulative succession of images – and one *cannot* simply translate the images. One must find equivalents – that cannot be done bit by bit, but by finding an English *key* to the combination.[1]

We wish indeed that we had elected the sand & sun of Deauville instead of taking the medical advice to come to a small French semi-alpine spa. There has not been much sun, my wife is not allowed the treatment, such as it is, on account of her lungs, it is very dull & very expensive! We shall in fact be glad to get back to Paris, which may be at any time now, and hope to find you there.

With many thanks
Affectionately yours
T. S. Eliot

## TO *H. F. Stewart* TS Cambridge (Add. MS 9613)

29 September 1926 Grand Hotel, Divonne Les Bains

Dear Dr Stewart,

I enclose my report on Smith's dissertation. I do not know whether it is too long or too short; whether it covers the points which interest the examiners or not; I am very much in the dark as to what you want. On

1 – TSE was to write to St-John Perse on 3 Feb. 1958: 'I think that the first requirement for a translator is to realise that he does not know French as well as he should and the second qualification is that he should realise that he does not know his own language as well as he should. I experienced both these realisations when translating *Anabase*' (Fondation Saint-John Perse).

the other hand it may be more illuminating for you to have a report from someone like myself who *is* in the dark as to what is wanted. The Gull in wintertime! The bull is unintentional! If there is any doubt, and you want something else from me, do not hesitate to let me know. My intention is favourable: I should say Yes. Some of my comments have been included with a view to the possibility that you examine candidates orally, and are meant to suggest questions to be put. The essays seem to me serious. There is no nonsense about him; he is a sound fellow.

We are probably leaving here for Paris – on the way to London, where I may arrive shortly after the middle of the month – so that the best address for me is always 24, Russell Square.

With best wishes to Mrs Stewart and yourself, and the hope of seeing you both during the term,

Very sincerely yours,
T. S. Eliot

I retain the dissertation, with your permission, in case you want a further report from me. T. S. E.

29 September 1926 — 24 Russell Square, London, W.C.1.

Report On Two Essays By James Smith
(dissertation submitted to Trinity College)

These two essays are thoughtful and well-written, and show evidence both of wide and intelligent reading and of original reflexion. I find that the author has almost always my sympathy; in essentials, he seems to me to hold the right end of the stick. While his tendencies accord with modern directions, he seems to arrive at his conclusions independently.

As a completed piece of work, the second essay is the more satisfactory. The first essay shows a certain immaturity, chiefly in defect of form. It suffers from a defect common to undergraduate and postgraduate compositions, that is to say it attempts to deal with too much material and does not cover it adequately. It is very much in Mr Smith's favour that the best part of it should be the treatment of Aristotle: where he differs from Zeller, and from other commentators, I think that he is usually right. Mr Smith has at least grasped something that most people never learn: that is the fallacy of interpreting Greek philosophy through modern prejudices and conventions (chiefly German); so that though one may cavil at his interpretations of ἦθος ἕξις etc., one feels a confidence that he will arrive at an interesting and valuable conclusion in the end.

His essay would have been a more satisfactory whole if he had confined himself to Aristotle and his commentators. His survey of German theory and practice in the Romantic Age is interesting and acute: it suffers from two defects. It should have been supplemented by an examination of French theory and practice, at least from the prefaces of Corneille, from La Harpe and Voltaire etc. to Hugo and to the actual successes of the modern French stage; and I should have been glad if he had paid more attention to Rymer etc. But this is merely to say that the emphasis on the German tradition is disproportionate, except so far as it can be proved that Coleridge propagated German standards in English criticism. The *influence* of Coleridge remains a little vague.

I am not sure to what extent Mr Smith realises that he challenges (as it ought to be challenged) the whole modern conception—vague as it is, but leading to grave consequences—of Personality, and that his position implies a theory of Personality.

An important omission is the lack of a discussion of the relative position of plot and character in tragedy versus comedy; and still more (what might I think have served the author's turn very well) the lack of a discussion of the nature of caricature and farce.

I think too that at the end he somewhat too hastily marshals in his ranks contemporary authors of very different degrees of importance; and I cannot think that the sudden comparison of various arts (e.g. Picasso) is very sound. But such examples as his analysis of *The Cherry Orchard* are both original and perceptive.

I am reporting on this dissertation without knowing whether competitive essays are being submitted, and without knowing what qualities, in the selection, seem to the College of the highest importance. And I am not considering the thesis as a completed work (for it should not be *published* in this form). I take into account the circumstances of its writing. When I say that it is a work of great promise, I mean nothing vague: I mean that Mr Smith seems to me to have already a considerable reading for his age, and to have understanding of what he has read; I mean that he shows a very valuable clairvoyance and skepticism; I mean that (after discounting everything adventitious) he shows an instinctive sympathy with what I believe to be the tendencies of the best minds of the age; and I mean that with greater maturity and years of reading and thought, he will be capable of work which will be neither pedantic nor flashy <and which wd certainly be worthy of the College>. So far as I understand the requirements, I do not hesitate to recommend Mr Smith for the dignity for which he is a candidate.

T. S. Eliot

## TO *Frederic Manning* CC

1 October 1926 [*The New Criterion*]

My dear Manning,

I have just returned to London[1] and am more than sorry that I have again missed you through my absence from England since early in August. On my return I have found many omissions to correct: incidentally I have written to accept definitely one of Mrs Clarke's stories for *The New Criterion*.[2]

I will look out for the *Epicurus's Morals* with interest and will try to do justice by it, although it is likely that we cannot say anything about it in the January number.[3] So far as book reviewing goes, the January number is always the most difficult to arrange, owing to the nuisance of the bulk of publication occurring in the autumn.

Your remarks about Fernandez are very interesting and I am tempted to ask you whether you would care to embody them in a letter for publication in the January *Criterion*.[4] There is one other suggestion which I should like to make: would you be willing to review Frazer's *The Worship of Nature* for the *April* number? <Or wd you make the book a *peg* for an essay on Frazer?> If Volume 2 appeared I would send it along in due course. This is the first time we have had occasion to review Frazer in the *Criterion* and I want to get something substantial on him to lead off the April reviews.

Always yours sincerely,
[T. S. Eliot]

1–This letter must have been written in anticipation of an immediate return to London, where it would be posted; in fact, the Eliots returned only some days later.
2–TSE had accepted a story by Lia Clarke, 'Darling Daudey'; but it did not appear.
3–Manning had written an introduction to a new edition of *Epicurus, His Morals*, ed. Walter Charleton (1619–1707). He urged TSE on 26 Oct.: 'Charleton deserves to be rescued from the comparative obscurity in which he survives.'
4–Manning replied on 2 Oct.: 'With regard to Fernandez I am indifferent . . . if you wish for a short letter I could of course let you have one; but I am inclined to doubt that it would sufficiently interest your readers.'

## TO *Bonamy Dobrée* MS Brotherton

1 October 1926 Grand Hotel, Divonne-les-Bains

My dear Dobrée,

This is not an answer to yr letter which gave me much pleasure – it is merely to say

1. Have ordered Secretary to send you *Inge* – two books on hand, another ordered. Am very pleased you care to tackle this. I ordered the books thinking they *ought* to be done, & fearing that I shd have to do them myself!

In a *Criterion* of 1925 I have already expressed my opinion of Inge. If you have not this copy, please ask my sec'y to find it & send to you. *NOT* that I wish yr views to fit mine, but it is just as well you shd know what has been said in *Criterion* already. My opinion is that as a theologian Inge is an heretic, & as a social philosopher (*Evening Standard* standards) a humbug.[1] But I may be – barring his newspaper vociferations – quite mistaken, & if so, shd be glad to know it. Please make it an important review!

2. I take it that Egypt is settled – for which I am very sorry – we shall miss you in London much more than you can possibly realise. But you must spend your holidays with us – I have as much reason as you to say '*come over and help us*'![2]

1–TSE castigated Dean W. R. Inge for his attacks on culture, made on the occasion of the Byron centenary: 'Dean Inge attacks culture [. . .] by violent and unmeasured statements on literary matters in his occasional essays in an evening newspaper . . . It is not merely that Dean Inge says nothing about Byron of any novelty or interest, or that he makes a statement about Byron which is manifestly untrue: his assertion that Byron had no ear . . . What is more important and more dangerous to culture, is the violence of Dean Inge's abuse on hearsay . . . But the most remarkable combination of violence, prejudice, ignorance, and confusion is found in the following sentence: "But I venture [. . .] to think that Greek sculpture is absolutely beautiful, while Cubist art is intrinsically and objectively hideous." To what period of Greek sculpture does the Dean refer? What does he mean by *absolute* beauty? And what particular works of art does he include under the term Cubist?' ('Commentary', C. 2 [Apr. 1924], 233–4). Four years later, TSE wrote a brief review of Dean Inge's *The Church in the World*: 'This book is neither good nor bad. When the Dean of St Paul's drops his favourite hobby of Papist-baiting and when he forgets his attitude of omniscience (which has perhaps been aggravated by his devotion to popular journalism) he is often sound and sensible. The chief weakness of this book is that it is a collection of previously published essays, reviews, addresses, and an Introduction; and several of these papers are too pedestrian to justify reprinting' (*MC* 7 [Mar. 1928], 286–7).

2–BD had written on 21 Sept.: 'I hope your extra stay will do you & your wife good – but I also hope you will soon dream of someone calling to you "Come over & help us".' The allusion is to Acts 16.9: 'Come over into Macedonia, and help us.'

3. We shall probably be here a week or two longer. Write to me & incidentally tell me whether you think I have offended H. M. mortally. I particularly don't want to – & I know quite well how sensitive he is.[1]

4. In the circumstances, I don't urge you to go on with the broadsheet (being absent myself) but perhaps I shall ask you to do an editorial on the subject for January *Criterion,* if the situation remains the same.[2] Personally, I see large & dangerous implications for the future of England – is this my own nightmare?

Yours ever
T. S. E.

## TO *Marguerite Caetani*

MS Caetani

6 October 1926

Cecil Hotel, 30 rue St. Didier XVI,
Passy 49.44

Dear Cousin

Very many thanks for your charming letter, which reached me at Divonne – we were in the middle of preparations for departure and I did not have time to write from there. We arrived in Paris very tired, but are very thankful to be here, & feel very much stronger and more cheerful here. Divonne was dreadful. And Divonne was poisoned by the news of the death of my favorite sister from peritonitis. This was a great shock in itself and has considerably affected our plans, as my sister's daughter who was here at the time was going to spend the winter with my wife in Italy. She had to return to Boston at once. It was a great disappointment, as she is a most intelligent and sympathetic girl; if you had come to see us on that day when you didn't come you would have met her.

1–BD was to write further, on 4 Oct.: 'I don't think H[arold] M[onro] is mortally offended. In fact he was worried and annoyed rather than offended; he had a crisis in which he felt everybody was deserting him, except the office boy. I will not conceal the fact that I saw the correspondence. Only hideously jangled nerves could produce that letter he wrote you. It was meant to be a lasso which would drag you over willyou nillyou, but I told him that if anything would harden your resolution to stay away it would be that. I fear he has very little sense of humour, sense of proportion: his sensitiveness is extreme because it is so egotistical. Poetry for him is the Poetry Book Shop. However, the meeting went off very well, and crowds of people came in the expectation of hearing you; most stayed.'

2–BD had thanked TSE for his 'corrections to the Broadside': 'Rest easy, you will not be asked to carry millstones or milestones in your old kit bag . . . Harold Monro advises me to drop it, & everyone seems very half-hearted. Besides, all the work will fall on me, which I shouldn't mind if I thought it was certain to do good.'

I am very glad to think that *Commerce* is in good hands in London, & to hear that Virginia will give you a part of her new book. They are great friends of ours, and I am sure you would like them.

My wife sends you her best remembrances and says she wants very much to 'be on your side' and is happy to think you are on hers. I believe she has various doctors and friends to visit this week but I could come out to see you before you go to Cannes either *Friday* or *Sunday*, for tea, if either suited you. If so, will you *telephone* or wire to me here.

Yours ever sincerely
T. S. Eliot

## TO *Geoffrey Faber*

MS Valerie Eliot

8 October 1926 Hotel Cecil, Paris

My dear Faber

I wrote to you a few days ago – this is just in reply to your suggestion – I think Muir's book will certainly be a good thing to have, series or no series.[1]

Personally, I am relieved that Graves's book has fallen through – I don't think it wd be a money maker.[2]

1 – Muir's putative book on Nietzsche. 'I think we shall have to discuss the series very carefully when you come back . . .', said Faber (1 Oct.). 'I have been wondering myself whether a deliberate re-evaluation of literary reputations by "modern" critics, and covering the ground already covered in the good old Morley manner in the English Men of Letters Series, might not have something to be said for it.'

2 – Graves had written to GCF in an undated letter (?Sept. 1926): 'I am afraid I have rather let you down on this "Round the Corner" business. Laura Gottschalk a very brilliant young American poet collaborated with me in doing a commissioned book for Heinemann on a similar but not identical subject [*A Survey of Modernist Poetry* 1927], and now it is nearly finished we find that we have used up so much material that the other book intended is hardly worth doing. What happened was that the book we intended for Heinemann was to be very elementary but has turned out too good. I am so sorry to have let you down.

'But we have nearly completed a book which we would like to offer you – about 30–40,000 words (the first book of its kind) written in very lively style about Anthologies: a sort of Anthology-pathology. Intended both for England & America. We are calling it "Anthologies against Poetry". It treats of at least 60 anthologies & is mostly scurrilous & all very carefully true. Begins with Meleager & Agathias Scholasticus: pauses at Tottel & Company & finally cuts up rough with Palgrave & the Oxford Book of English Verse & others. Constructive suggestions at the close' (Faber E3/1/8).

GFC replied to Graves on 20 Sept.: 'I quite understand about the "Round-the-Corner Poetry" business. Anyhow we had no claim upon you for the book, though I should have been glad to do it. More glad than the anthology book, which sounds exactly what anthologies deserve, but not very much like what the public will buy! But I dare say that I am wrong there, and in any case I should very much like to see it . . .'

I understand that *The Times* are sending me the Brimley Johnson book to review.[1]

The weather keeps quite heavenly, and we have a room with a sunny balcony on the top floor of a little hotel in one of the highest & healthiest parts of Paris.

Ever yours
T. S. E.

## FROM *Geoffrey Faber*

TS Valerie Eliot

9 October 1926 Faber & Gwyer Ltd

My dear Eliot,

Many thanks for your letter. I hope it will be possible for you to be back for our October Board Meeting which is on Friday the 29th. I should like to write you a long letter, but I have not the time. Things have moved rapidly here lately; we have found it necessary to dismiss our Advertisement Manager, Mr Smithers, summarily, for what we considered to be, and were advised by Counsel was, a serious breach of his agreement. Fortunately we have been able to obtain the services of an absolutely first-class man in Mr Wynne Williams, who until recently was Advertisement Manager to *The Times*. He is actually at work here now. We find an extraordinary absence of organisation in Smithers's office, and

---

On 1 Dec. 1926 TSE was to write in his F&G reader's report on 'Anthologies Against Poetry'): 'This book has an original subject and the subject is in itself a good one, but it seems to me much more suitable for condensation into a review article than for expansion into a book. I cannot see what the public for such a book would be. The people who like anthologies will go on liking anthologies and will not read this book; the people who do not like anthologies are not interested enough to read a long attack on anthologies. Therefore the only people who could be interested would be those who feel a deep resentment or violent fury against anthologies, so that they would enjoy reading somebody who is himself violently furious against anthologies. I do not know just how much circulation Robert Graves has, but my impression is that he is writing more little books and pamphlets about poetry than the market will absorb. The only reason for accepting this book would be to have Robert Graves's name on our list, and I suggest that the best thing would be to decline this book in very flattering terms and try to get a book of verse out of him (*not* by Robert Graves and Laura Riding Gottschalk, but by Robert Graves alone).' (Faber Misc. 5/1)

In due course, *A Pamphlet Against Anthologies* (Jonathan Cape, 1928) levelled this charge against TSE: 'The high-brow success of the *Waste Land* [*sic*] brought T. S. Eliot into the anthologies with *Conversation Galante* and other ingratiating early pieces . . . And now, captured by general fame, he is busy wiping out his waste years with poems like *Journey of the Magi*, pursuing his anthology career in earnest' (162).

1 – *Poetry and the Poets: Essays on the Art of Poetry by Six Great English Poets*, ed. with intro. by R. Brimley Johnson (London: F&G, 1926), was not reviewed by TSE.

Wynne Williams will have his work cut out for some time in getting things straight.

As for the general publishing, of course the continuance of the coal strike is having its inevitable effect. It is too early yet to say whether the season will be up to our expectations. September has not quite come up to them, but I don't think we have any reason for serious anxiety. All otherwise is well. The coal strike appears to be gradually failing. There are now about twenty to twenty-five per cent of the men back at work. But it will certainly be a considerable time yet before normal conditions are restored. Please give my kindest regards to your wife.

Yours ever,
G. C. F.

## TO *W. L. Janes* CC

20 October 1926 [London]

Dear Janes,

I enclose one pound in payment for your work up to Sunday last (October 17th). I was not able to get to Chester Terrace yesterday as I have been ill and have been staying indoors. Will you please be at No. 57 on Friday between 5 & 6 pm, as I hope to get round then. If I do not come then by any chance, will you please be there again on Monday at that time?

Yours truly,
[T. S. Eliot]

## FROM *Henry Massis* MS Valerie Eliot

Le 25 Octobre 1926

*La revue universelle,*
157, Boulevard Saint-Germain,
Paris VI$^{e}$

Cher Monsieur Eliot,

Je viens de recevoir le numéro d'Octobre du *New Criterion*. J'ai lu la lettre du M. Fletcher et je suis navré d'avoir y répondre par celle que je mis adressé ici. Mais c'est indispensable.[1]

1 – John Gould Fletcher's letter in response to Massis came out in *NC* 4 (Oct. 1926), 746–50. Massis's reply to Fletcher appeared in *NC* 5 (Jan. 1927), 106–7.

Avez-vous quitté Paris? Y reviendrez vous bientôt? Jean de Menasce m'a envoyé la traduction de votre essai.[1] Je crois qu'il en vous en a adressé une copie. Si vous avez quelque changement à y faire, ne tardez pas trop, car nous allons devoir envoyer les manuscripts à l'imprimerie.

Croyez-mois bien cordialement votre

Henri Massis[2]

## TO *Henri Massis*

CC

Le 1 novembre 1926 [*The Monthly Criterion*]

Cher Monsieur Massis,

Je vous remercie de votre lettre du 25 octobre et de la lettre formelle en réponse à Mr Fletcher. Soyez sûr que la dernière paraîtra dans le numéro de janvier qui sera bientôt sous presse. Malheureusement, M. Fletcher est parti pour l'Amérique et nous devons attendre longtemps sa réponse s'il en a.

J'ai été désolé de quitter Paris sans vous revoir. Après quelques jours tous occupés par des affaires personelles j'ai partir en province et puis rentrer aussitôt que possible à Londres. Mais j'espère revenir passer quelques jours à Paris de temp en temps pendant l'hiver, et je ne manquerai point de vous prevenir.

Je serais interessé de savoir à quelle époque paraîtra *Le Roseau d'Or* avec mon petit article,[3] et surtout n'oubliez pas de m'envoyer *La Défense de l'Occident*.

Rapellez moi à Maritain duquel j'ai attendu un article qui n'est pas parvenu, et croyez moi toujours bien loyalement

Vôtre

[T. S. Eliot][4]

1–TSE, 'Deux attitudes mystiques: Dante et Donne' (lecture), trans. Jean de Menasce, *Chroniques du Roseau d'Or*, 14 (1927), 149–73. See *VMP*, 309–18.

2–*Translation*: Dear Mr Eliot, I have just received the October number of the *New Criterion*. I have read Mr Fletcher's letter, and am distressed to have to make the enclosed reply, which is however essential.

Have you left Paris? Will you return soon? Jean de Menasce has sent me the translation of your essay. I believe he has posted a copy to you. If you have any changes to make, do not delay, because we are about to send the manuscripts to the printer. With all best wishes, Henri Massis.

3–'Deux attitudes mystiques: Dante et Donne'.

4–*Translation*: Dear Mr Massis, I wish to thank you for your letter dated 25th October and for the formal letter in response to Mr Fletcher. You can be sure that the latter will be published in the January edition, which will go to press shortly. Unfortunately Mr Fletcher

## TO *Robert Graves* CC

1 November 1926 [London]

Dear Graves,

I got back to England two days ago and asked my secretary to write to you about a book which I hope you may care to review.[1] Subsequently I find that I have not acknowledged your letter of the 18th September. Needless to say I am very sorry that we cannot have the book to which I looked forward, but I quite understand how it has happened.[2] I hope that you will remember us and write to me or to Faber as soon as you have another book of any kind ready or in view.

Yours always sincerely,
[T. S. Eliot]

## TO *Wyndham Lewis* TS Cornell

1 November 1926 *The New Criterion*

Dear Lewis,

I have just returned from abroad. I have not been able to get anything done while away, but am writing to say that if it is not too late let me know and I will try to do something for you for your review. But I should

---

has left for America and we will have to wait a while for his answer if there is one.

I was saddened to leave Paris without seeing you again. After a few days all busy with personal affairs, I left for the country and then went back to London as soon as possible. But I hope to come back and spend a few days in Paris from time to time during the winter and I will make sure to let you know.

I would be interested in finding out in what edition *Le Roseau d'Or* with my little article will be published and moreover do not forget to send me *La Défense de l'Occident*.

Remember me to Maritain from whom I have expected an article which never arrived and believe me as always faithfully yours [T. S. Eliot]

1–Graves had been asked to review *Psychology and Ethnology*, by W. H. R. Rivers; and *Crime and Custom in Savage Society* and *Myth in Primitive Psychology*, by B. Malinowski. See *MC* 5 (May 1927), 247–52.

2–'I have just written to Faber to apologise about that suggested critical book of modern poetry. What happened was that Laura Gottschalk & I undertook a commission for Heinemann to write a book on a similar but not identical subject [*A Survey of Modernist Poetry*]. Now we are nearly done we find that it has covered too much of the other ground, so much as to make it imposs. to write the other book. The only satisfaction we have with regard to you is that we are now permitted to discuss your poems: & without your work a discussion of modernist poetry is *Hamlet* without well . . . at least . . . the Gravediggers & the Ghost. There is no Prince of Denmark obviously discoverable. We hope you'll forgive us in this . . . The book for Heinemann is supposed to be "Modernist poetry explained to the Plain Man" but it is rather more elaborate than that we fear' (*In Broken Images*, 168–9).

be very glad, also, if you happen to have any manuscript on hand that you could let me publish in the *Criterion*. I should like it if we could have lunch together one day soon.

Yours,
T. S. Eliot

## TO *Alfred Sperber*[1]

CC

1 November 1926 [London]

Dear Sir,

I have been abroad the whole summer and have only just returned to London. It is true that your letter of the 18th August, together with your translation of *The Waste Land*, was forwarded to me,[2] but I delayed reply[ing] in the expectation of seeing some one of my German acquaintances who are also thoroughly conversant with English literature in order that I might ask their opinion of one or two passages. However, I was not favoured by fortune, as on the one occasion on which I met someone who fulfilled these qualifications I was temporarily separated from my luggage in which your translation was contained. I have therefore no right to retain it any longer and return it herewith with my compliments.

So far as I am competent to judge, the translation is admirable and supports my theory that this poem would translate better into German than into any other language. I think that I have found only two passages to question. I do not understand why, at the beginning, you translate my phrase 'at the Archduke's' by 'im Erzbischof'. The other point occurs on page 9 of your manuscript, where you translate only two of the speeches of the three Thames daughters. I do not know whether the latter was intentional or whether it is a scribal oversight. Otherwise I must say that I like your translation very much and I have no objection to your publishing it in any periodical in Germany or Austria that you think fit. In the case of foreign translations I only insist as a rule on retaining *book*

1–Alfred Margul-Sperber (1898–1967): German-Romanian poet, translator and anthologist; lived in New York, 1921–4, later in Bucharest. See *Anthology of Contemporary Romanian Poetry*, ed. Roy MacGregor-Hastie (1969).

2–Sperber, who wrote from Bucovina, Romania, anticipated that his translation of *TWL* would be published in *Die Neue Rundschau*.

rights of publication as the subject of special agreements between myself and foreign publishers.

I am, dear Sir,
Yours sincerely,
[T. S. Eliot]

## TO *H. F. Stewart* CC

1 November 1926 [London]

Dear Dr Stewart,

I have just returned to England. Meanwhile I have received the probably undeserved honorarium for reporting on Smith's Dissertation, but I should be very glad to know from you that you received this report which I sent to you from Divonne, whether you found it of any use and of course whether Smith has been chosen or not.[1]

I hope that you and Mrs Stewart are well.

Yours very sincerely,
[T. S. Eliot]

## TO *Orlo Williams* CC

1 November 1926 [*The New Criterion*]

Dear Williams,

I intended to write to you from abroad a month ago but was moving about and became more and more lazy in my correspondence. I have just returned and should like it if we could lunch together soon.

Many thanks for your letter about the Italians.[2] Having just returned I have not had time to read the manuscripts, which I hope to do before we meet, but I have no doubt I shall follow your advice on that matter.

Your book came out some time before my return and I therefore had it sent to Herbert Read who was interested instead of holding it to do

1–Stewart wrote on 3 Nov.: 'Yes, I had your most useful report & read it to the electors. There were only 2 vacancies & Smith had to stand down but the promise of his work augurs well for another time. I have had a heart to heart talk with him & conveyed your criticisms to him (without a name). He asks for his dissertation back, as he wants to scribble on it. I have already returned him one copy, but since he wants the other would you mind letting me have it, if you can lay your hands on it?' TSE posted it by return.

2–On 28 Sept. Williams had forwarded two articles by Angioletti and one by Bacchelli.

myself.[1] I should have liked to have reviewed it but I am afraid that with all I have to do at present, and also as I am by no means an authority on the subject of the Novel, I should not have done you justice. The book has left the office without my having seen it, but I shall get hold of a copy later and will at least let you have my private criticism for what it is worth.

Yours always sincerely,
[T. S. Eliot]

P.S. Would you care to have Blanchard's huge book on Fielding sent to you? It looks at least a very thorough performance. If you would like to have it and if you find it worthwhile, let me know if you would care to do a note on it for the April number.[2]

## TO *Charles Whibley* CC

1 November 1926 [London]

My dear Whibley,

This is just a line to tell you that I am finally back in London and that I hope you will let me see you on the next occasion of your coming to town. I should have thanked you for your very kind letter of the 6th September, but I can only say that I did not have the opportunity for correspondence. I hope to get well on with the 'Seneca' at once. I was very sorry to learn that you have had a painful time again and hope that you can let me have good news of your last month. The report of your health discourages me because I was going to remind you that you had promised to let me have something for my January number, and you suggested that you might write on the subject of Thomas Rymer.[3] Is this impossible for you, or is my reminder too late? Needless to say that I was very anxious to have something from you again long before now but did not like to press you, knowing how busy you have been. But I should be extremely grateful if you had anything however short which you could let me have, with which to lead off the first number of the New Year.

[Yours ever affectionately
T. S. Eliot]

1 – Orlo Williams, *Some Great English Novelists: Studies in the Art of Fiction*, was reviewed by HR, in *NC* 5 (Jan. 1927), 117–20.

2 – Anon. notice of Frederic T. Blanchard, *Fielding the Novelist: A Study in Literary Reputation*, *NC* 5 (Jan. 1927), 157.

3 – Whibley replied (10 Nov.): 'My head is still worrying me. But I am at work, & I would gladly write you something on Rymer.' The essay was not forthcoming.

## TO *Bruce Richmond* CC

1 November 1926 [London]

Dear Richmond,

I am just back a day or two ago and have sent you separately a review of the Hearnshaw book.[1] You also sent me a book by Brimley Johnson containing essays by poets on poetry, but I learn that this book has been withdrawn from publication. Therefore I have written nothing about it. So I am ready for anything else. I shall get on quickly to the Davies book and should be glad to know the date for which you want it.[2]

I find I have not answered your letter of the 12th October addressed to me in Paris containing the essay by Mr H. O. White on The Reverend Thomas Purney.[3] Faber is away today but I expect to see him tomorrow and will discuss the matter with him and let you know.

I hope everything is well with you, and if so I hope that you will let me see you soon.

Yours ever,
[T. S. E.]

1 – *The Social and Political Ideas of Some Great Thinkers of the Sixteenth and Seventeenth Centuries*, ed. F. J. C. Hearnshaw – lectures by various authorities on Bodin, Hooker, Suarez, James I, Grotius, Hobbes, Harrington and Spinoza, delivered at King's College, London, during 1925–6. TSE concluded in his review ('Hooker, Hobbes and Others', *TLS*, 11 Nov. 1926, 789): 'Perhaps the final problem for historical students is a problem of imagination – that is, to reconstruct for ourselves so fully the mind of the Renaissance, and the mind of the pre-Renaissance, that neither of them shall be dead for us – that is to say, unconscious parts of our own mind – but shall be conscious and therefore utilizable for our future development.'

2 – 'December 8th is the anniversary of the death of Sir John Davies,' BLR had ventured on 17 Aug. 'I should like to have something about him, if only because the last two stanzas of "Humane Knowledge" have stuck in my head since I was a boy. Would you care to let us have either a leader or perhaps two columns for the middle page . . .?' See 'Sir John Davies', *TLS*, 9 Dec. 1926, 906; repr. in *OPP*.

3 – Not found.

## TO *Geoffrey Gorer*[1]

CC

1 November 1926 [London]

Dear Mr Gorer,

I must apologise for leaving unanswered your letter of the 12th October as I was abroad at the time. I know quite well the name of René Crevel although I do not know his work.[2] I have been trying to think what I can recommend but my acquaintance with literary societies is not very wide. The only club in Oxford at all similar to the 'Cam' is one called 'The Ordinary'; I spoke to them three or four years ago. I have since lost touch with them and I do not know the name or address of the present secretary; but if you have any friends in Oxford who could help you to find out, I should think that this was the best Society for the purpose. When I met the Society there were a number of very keen critics in it. I am sorry that I cannot think of any other suggestion.

With all best wishes,
Yours sincerely
[T. S. Eliot]

## TO *Jean de Menasce*

CC

2 November 1926 [London]

My dear de Menasce,

Many thanks for your letters of the 9th and 15th October. I have not heard from M. Pierre Legouis but if I do, I shall be very glad to be of any use to him that I can.[3] I also thank you for your earlier letter about my manuscript which was very gratifying. Of course my aim has been to alter

1–Geoffrey Gorer (1905–85), writer and social anthropologist, was reading classics and modern languages at Jesus College, Cambridge. His first book was *The Revolutionary Ideas of the Marquis de Sade* (1934), but he won a reputation as an anthropologist (associated with his friends Margaret Mead and Ruth Benedict), with works including *Africa Dances* (1935), *Himalayan Village* (1938) and *Exploring English Character* (1955).

2–Gorer had asked for advice concerning the writer and surrealist René Crevel (1900–35), author of *Mon Corps et Moi* (1925) and *La Mort Difficile* (1926), who was due to read a paper to the Cam Literary Club on 18 Nov.: could TSE please recommend any other university societies which Crevel might also address?

3–De Menasce wrote (9 Oct.), 'I am referring to you a M. Pierre Legouis . . . on the suggestion of Praz, about a thesis he is writing on Marvell and a short study of Donne's style.' He had told Legouis that 'most of what is to be said [about Donne] has now been said by Praz and by you . . . Perhaps you will let him share in the good fortune of reading the "premier état" of your book, which you so kindly granted me.'

and develop the book very much as it seems to you should be done.[1] I am very much obliged to you for reading it. When you have done with it would you mind registering it back to me here?

I approve of the alterations which you have made and am very pleased indeed with your translation, for which I thank you.[2] I wish I were equally certain that all of my ideas in that essay were just. I have heard from Massis that he has received the other copy from you.

Having just returned I am overwhelmed with work but hope to write to you at more leisure. Are you settled for the winter in your delightful climate or is there any possibility of your visiting Paris or London?

Yours ever,
[T. S. Eliot]

## TO *Louis Untermeyer*[3] CC

3 November 1926 [London]

Dear Untermeyer,

When you wrote to me I was in the depths of the country in France and not even anywhere near Paris, so that a meeting was quite hopeless. I am very sorry to have missed you, but if by chance you happen to be still in Europe do let me know.

1–In his letter of 18 Sept., de Menasce offered a learned and perceptive critique of the manuscript of TSE's study of metaphysical poetry, which he saluted as 'the germ of a very great, important and beautiful work'. He suggested that when TSE came to revise the work, he ought to show 'that the transitional period produced a sort of bastard of the two. The metaphysicals were surely not conscious of the change, nor was the XVIIth century as a whole; people were still convinced that they were dealing more with reality than with the modes of its apprehension; their psychologism slowly penetrated through their ontological form . . . It is not till late in the XVIIIth century that people began to *think* psychologically . . . Now I incline to think that the metaphysicals (Donne) and what you call the Spanish mystics . . . are just half-way between Dante and 1926 . . . Thus Dr Johnson's, or still better Taine's hostility towards Donne, could be accounted for by the fact that they were not quite sure *what* Donne was talking about, and categorically denied that *he* knew what he [was] talking about; the latter assumption being, on the whole, deeper than *they* could realize.' He remarked too, *inter alia*, 'that whereas you quite rightly reject Middleton Murry's identification of St John of the Cross' "dark night" with your "dark night" (I am not satisfied that you *have* a dark night at all) you seem to imply that the dark night is identical with Mr D. H. Lawrence's God'.

2–De Menasce had been working on a translation of TSE's essay for *Roseau d'Or*.

3–Louis Untermeyer (1885–1977): poet, editor, translator, parodist, anthologist; co-founder and contributing editor of *Seven Arts* magazine; Poet Laureate Consultant to the Library of Congress, 1961–3; author of *Collected Parodies* (1926) and *Long Feud: Selected Poems* (1962).

On the contrary, is there any reason why your *Miscellany* should stop? I should certainly encourage you to go on with it, but beyond that point I should hesitate to advise whom to include. I do not know the work of Jeffers but I certainly approve of MacLeish.[1]

Yours ever sincerely,
[T. S. Eliot]

## TO *Richard Cobden-Sanderson* MS Texas

3 November 1926 *The New Criterion*

Dear Cobden-Sanderson,

I have only been back in England since a few days, most of which I have spent in bed with a cold – and only just learn through an evening paper of your mother's death. Allow me to express my sincere & cordial sympathy to you, joined to my regret at never having met a woman who must have been a very unusual personality & a parent to be very proud of.

It must be a satisfaction to you at least that she should have seen your father's diaries in print,[2] & known of the book's success. I am reading it now – I congratulate you upon it.

With best wishes

Ever yours
T. S. Eliot

## TO *Walter Hanks Shaw* CC

3 November 1926 [London]

Dear Mr Shaw,

I am sorry that having been abroad until recently I have not hitherto acknowledged your letter myself. In any case, as my secretary will have

1–Robinson Jeffers (1887–1962), American poet and ecocritic *avant la lettre*, lived, relished and wrote about coastal California, urging the concept of inhumanism – the theory that mankind has become too self-engrossed and solipsistic and had better attend to the 'astonishing beauty' of natural things. Publications include *Roan Stallion, Tamar and Other Poems* (1925), *The Women at Point Sur* (1927) and *Dear Judas and Other Poems* (1929).

Archibald MacLeish (1892–1982), American poet (whose early work is considered in part to be derivative from TSE's and EP's), as well as playwright, essayist, editor and lawyer.

2–T. J. Cobden Sanderson (1840–1922): bookbinder; associated with William Morris and the Arts and Crafts movement; founder in 1900 of the Doves Press. *The Journals of Thomas James Cobden-Sanderson, 1879–1922* (2 vols, 1926).

informed you, your contribution would then have been too late for the autumn number, and I am afraid that the January number would be too full to admit of any more chronicles. If there is an interesting season this winter I should be very glad to have one from you for the *April* number. I should suggest for the next time making more of such theatrical and other productions as are not likely to come to England, and minimizing the Diaghileff ballet. The reason for this is that the Diaghileff ballet is usually dealt with here after it has been in London and I want to avoid any risk of repetition. But of course mention anything that is entirely new.

If you have any other suggestions I should be glad to hear from you.

Yours very truly,
[T. S. Eliot]

## TO *George Rylands* CC

4 November 1926 [London]

Dear Rylands,

I am glad to hear that you are in town and should very much like to see you. Would it suit you to come in and have tea with me here on Monday afternoon? If not, suggest another day at your convenience. Meanwhile, here is a modest suggestion. We intend, beginning with the January number, to have in each number several pages of half page notes of books as well as the longer reviews. A half page note would be about two hundred words, and what we want – it is not so easy to find people who can do it and who will enter into the spirit of the thing – is to avoid the perfunctory *notice* and have each note or paragraph contain some definite critical point. It is not very easy to write such notes and it is only worthwhile when one is more or less interested in the book. I want to get a few people who would care to do this sort of thing. To each one I would give the opportunity of noticing three or four books in each number so as to make the occupation slightly more remunerative, though the five or seven shillings which we should be able to offer for each note is not very much of an inducement in itself. I hope that you will have some book in mind on which you might care to do a long review for the April number, but meanwhile would you be interested in doing a few short notes immediately for the January number on any of the following or possibly any other which occur to you?

*The Close Chaplet* by Laura Gottschalk
*Composition as Explanation* by Gertrude Stein

*Rochester* by Bonamy Dobrée
*Catchwords and Claptrap* by Rose Macaulay
*Collected Poems* by Edward Shanks
*News of the Devil* by Humbert Wolfe
*The Political Ideas of the English Romanticists* by Crane Brinton

But I should like to know at once, as otherwise I shall be making the same proposal to others.[1]

Hoping to see you on Monday,

Sincerely yours,
[T. S. Eliot]

## TO *George Williamson*[2]

MS Mrs M. H. Williamson (Dr Charlotte Williamson)

8 November 1926 *The New Criterion*

Dear Sir,

I am obliged to you for allowing me the pleasure of seeing your essay on the relation of my verse to my prose.[3] I am afraid that its subject matter makes it unsuitable for the review which I edit, inasmuch as I cannot as editor exploit or defend my own work. This objection is insurmountable, but I should like to say also that you seem to me, for what my opinion is worth, to be correct and to express very nearly my own opinion on the matter. If you care to send me other specimens of your work, on other subjects, I shall be glad to consider them with particular attention.

Sincerely yours,
T. S. Eliot

1 – Rylands's contribution was a review of Walter de la Mare – *Henry Brocken*; *The Return*; *Memoirs of a Midget*; *The Connoisseur* – *NC* 4 (Oct. 1926), 785–7.

2 – George Williamson (1898–1968), author and educator, taught at Pomona College, Claremont, California, 1925–7; later at the University of Chicago (1936–68), where he was Professor of English from 1940. Works include *The Talent of T. S. Eliot* (1929), *The Donne Tradition* (1930) and *A Reader's Guide to T. S. Eliot* (1953).

3 – Williamson wrote on 19 Oct.: 'Although the enclosed essay has been damned by an American magazine as too scholarly, I thought it might interest you, though perhaps not to the extent of printing. It at least makes clear a debt of pleasure that I owe to the author of *The Waste Land*.' Arguing for 'the very close relation between Eliot's aesthetic theory and his practice in *The Waste Land*', the essay was to be made use of as part II of Williamson's study *The Talent of T. S. Eliot* (1929), 20–6.

## TO *Charles Norman* CC

8 November 1926 [London]

Dear Mr Norman,

Your letter gives me much pleasure, and also the fact that you should have thought it worth your trouble to let me see the second version of your poem.[1] Whether it is due to my criticism or not, I cannot tell, but in any case I can sincerely assure you that the alterations seem to me to improve the poem very much. I shall look forward with particular interest and great hope to the next piece of work that you think fit to show me.

Sincerely yours,
[T. S. Eliot]

## TO *R. Ellsworth Larsson*[2] CC

8 November 1926 [London]

Dear Mr Larsson,

I am of course flattered by the invitation contained in your letter of the 15th ultimo and I only regret that it is quite impossible for me to accept.[3] I have at present literally nothing whatever which would be possible for publication in any anthology. I am doubtful, as a matter of fact whether anything of mine would ever be particularly suitable for an anthology with the name which you have chosen, but as I have nothing to offer in any case that question does not arise. I can only say that I am extremely grateful that you should have wished me to be included, and I wish you the best of success for the anthology to which I shall look forward with much interest.

I should advise you to publish the enclosed poems in some other review than *The New Criterion*. While they are by no means inferior to those which I had the pleasure of publishing, I should be unable to use them for

1 – 'Dead Men under Buildings' appeared in *Poems* (1929), 20–2; and was radically rewritten, put into rhyming quatrains, for later showing in *Selected Poems* (1962), 3.

2 – Raymond Ellsworth Larsson (b. 1901), American poet and journalist, grew up in Wisconsin and worked in newspapers until journeying in 1926 to Europe, where he visited France (his poetry appeared in the magazine *transition* in 1927), England and Belgium. After returning to the USA in 1929, he worked for a while as an advertising manager. He entered the Roman Catholic Church in 1932.

3 – Larsson invited TSE to contribute an unpublished poem to a volume he was editing, *Montparnasse Anthology* (for E. W. Titus at the Black Manikin Press).

a very considerable time, and the fees paid by *The New Criterion* are, as you suggest, unworthy of your consideration.

Yours very truly,
[T. S. Eliot]

## TO *B. H. Haggin*[1] CC

9 November 1926 [London]

Dear Mr Haggin,

I have read your musical study with great interest but unfortunately the space which *The New Criterion* is able to give to such subjects apart from our regular Musical Chronicle is extremely limited and I am afraid that there would be very little prospect of our being able to use it.[2] But if I have the opportunity I shall follow your work with much interest.

Yours very truly,
[T. S. Eliot]

## TO *The Under Secretary of State, The Home Office*[3] CC

9 November 1926 [London]

Reference 412,614/2

Sir,

I have to acknowledge your form letter of the 6th instant. In reply I refer to your previous letter in which you stated that there was nothing to be done until I returned from my sojourn in France. While away, therefore, I left the matter in abeyance and have only returned to London a few days since. The matter shall now, of course, receive my immediate attention.

I have the honour to be, Sir,
Your obedient, humble servant
[T. S. Eliot]

1 – B. H. Haggin (1900–87), American critic of music. A graduate of the Juilliard School, New York, he wrote for the *New Republic* and was music and ballet critic of *The Nation*, 1936–57. His works include *A Book of the Symphony* (1937), *Music on Records* (1938) and *Conversations with Toscanini* (1959).

2 – Haggin had been told by Mark van Doren (*The Nation*) that his essays were reminiscent of *SW*; Haggin therefore submitted to TSE (16 Oct.) his introduction to a set of articles on music and music criticism, in the hope that it might be published in *NC*.

3 – This letter is the earliest known evidence of TSE's desire to take British citizenship.

## TO *Messrs Methuen & Co Ltd* CC

11 November 1926 [London]

Dear Sirs,

With reference to our contract of the 20th April 1920 for the publication of *The Sacred Wood*, it is quite clear that your rights do not apply in general to translations of this book or parts of this book, for which I have the sole right to negotiate. But I have just been asked for permission to translate one essay from this book – that on *Hamlet* – into Urdu,[1] and as Urdu falls within the British Empire I am not quite sure whether this permission should be obtained from me or from you. Please note that in this case there is no question of translating the book as a whole, but merely one essay. I should be obliged if you would let me know your opinion on this point so that I may reply to my Indian petitioner. As to myself, I have no objection to this translation being made.[2]

Yours faithfully,
[T. S. Eliot]

## TO *Charles Whibley* CC

11 November 1926 [*The New Criterion*]

My dear Whibley,

I am very glad to hear from you. I suspected that you might be at Cambridge, but was half afraid that you might already have driven south for the winter, which would have distressed me greatly. I am more sorry than I can say to hear that your head is still troublesome and in any case you must not feel bound to write anything for me until you are quite well. Of course I should have liked your essay particularly for the January number, but as I should have had to ask you for it by the 15th November, it is evidently quite out of the question. So I hope that circumstances will allow you to let me have it by the end of the year, in time for the following number.

1 – TSE had been approached by M. M. Aslam Khan, c/o M. M. Din, Editor, *The Sufi*, Punjab, India.

2 – Methuen & Co. replied (16 Nov.) that even though they had the 'sole right of publication of *The Sacred Wood* in the British Empire and elsewhere', they would be happy to permit a translation of the single essay as detailed in TSE's letter.

I look forward impatiently to your next visit to town.

Yours always affectionately,
[T. S. Eliot]

## TO *D. S. Mirsky*[1]

CC

12 November 1926 [London]

Dear Sir,

I should be delighted to consider the essays you suggest or any other.[2] As a matter of fact I was on the point of writing to you to ask you whether you had anything which you could offer us.

Yours very truly,
[T. S. Eliot]

1–Prince D. S. Mirsky (1890–1939), Russian scholar, was the son of Prince P. D. Svyatopolk-Mirsky, army officer and civil servant (on his mother's side he was descended from an illegitimate son of Catherine the Great). Educated at the University of St Petersburg, where he read oriental languages and classics, he served for several years as an officer in the army, and was wounded during WW1 while fighting on the German front; later he was to serve in the White Army. In 1921, he was appointed lecturer in Russian at the School of Slavonic Studies, London (under Sir Bernard Pares), where his cultivation and command of languages brought him to the attention of a wide literary circle: he became acquainted with TSE, E. M. Forster and Leonard and Virginia Woolf. He published several books, including *Contemporary Russian Literature* (2 vols, 1926) and *A History of Russian Literature from the Earliest Times to the Death of Dostoevsky, 1881* (1927), and articles on literature, culture and history. In 1931 he joined the Communist Party of Great Britain (see 'Why I became a Marxist', *Daily Worker*, 30 June 1931), and in 1932 returned to Russia where he worked as a literary critic (and incidentally became acquainted with Edmund Wilson and Malcolm Muggeridge). In 1937 he was arrested in the Stalinist purge, found guilty of 'suspected espionage', and sentenced to eight years of correctional labour: he died in a labour camp in Siberia. See G. S. Smith, *D. S. Mirsky: A Russian–English Life, 1890–1939* (2000).

2–Mirsky said he was preparing two articles: one on 'Chekhov and the English'; the other on the 'Present State of the Russian Mind and its relations to the "Occident"'. His first contribution was 'Chekhov and the English', *MC* 6 (Oct. 1927), 292–304.

## TO *W. Force Stead*[1] CC

13 November 1926 [*The New Criterion*]

Dear Stead,

Thank you very much for your kind letter of the 14th October and for sending me your book which you may be sure I shall read with great interest.[2] It is quite true that when I last saw Gordon George I expected to be back in England much sooner; in fact I expected to be here when he was here himself. It was very pleasant having his company for a short time in France and I was interested to learn from him that he was also a friend of yours.

I shall certainly look you up if I come to Oxford, but as there is no immediate likelihood of that I would impress upon you that I should very much like to see you at any time when you were in London.

Yours sincerely
[T. S. Eliot]

P.S. I was very sorry to see in the paper a notice of the death of Cobden-Sanderson's mother. I immediately wrote to him but do not know whether he is in London or not.

## TO *R. Gordon George (Robert Sencourt)* CC

13 November 1926 [London]

My dear George,

Many thanks for your kind letter from Tours which I was unable to answer in time to reach you at that address, being engrossed by work and engagements which I found awaiting me. Flattery is always welcome even when one is convinced that it is undeserved and it is pleasant to have your second opinion on the Andrewes although I cannot agree with it.[3] It will be a pleasure to me to put myself into communication with Gordon

1–Willliam Force Stead (1884–1967), poet, critic, diplomat, clergyman: see Biographical Register.

2–WFS, who had first met TSE at a lunch in 1923 (through their mutual friend RC-S), had sent a copy of *The Shadow of Mount Carmel* [1926] – 'as I hear from R. Gordon George [Robert Sencourt] that you are in England at present'. He invited TSE to look him up in Oxford. WFS informed TSE's secretary (19 Oct.) that Gordon George 'had been seeing a good deal of Mr Eliot on the Riviera recently'.

3–George wrote (undated letter) of TSE's article 'Lancelot Andrewes', *TLS*, 23 Sept. 1926, 621–2): 'I read Andrewes again with great care when it came out, and felt a full admiration for it. It is an extraordinarily delicate and penetrating piece.'

Selwyn as soon as I have time – that is to say as soon as I have read the *Essays Catholic and Critical* which looks very interesting. As for Lord Halifax, I do not think that the time is yet ripe but I will write to you later about this.[1]

I have sent to you to Tours a book on de Maupassant which you mentioned, thinking that if you considered it worth mentioning you might care to do a note on it for the April *Criterion*.[2] I should be glad to hear from you about this. I should like very much to see either your essay on Comedy or the one on Maritain's 'Philosophy of Beauty'.[3] Your paper on the 'Genesis of Fine Art' has arrived today without any explanatory letter and I am wondering whether it is a possible contribution to the *Criterion* or an essay written for some other periodical which you are giving me the privilege of reading before publication. Will you explain? In either case I shall read it with much interest. But if it is offered to the *Criterion* I must say in advance that I could not use either this or your proposed article on Maritain in the immediate future for the plain reason that I have now in the press an essay by Maritain himself on the same subject which will run in the January and April numbers.[4] It is impossible in a quarterly to publish simultaneously two essays so nearly related, and therefore it would not be available before the number of next July. I therefore hope that you will also send me the essay on Comedy.

It is a little unsatisfactory writing to anyone so elusive as yourself. I can only address this to Hyères and hope that in the course of weeks or months I may receive a reply.

Ever yours,
[T. S. Eliot]

1 – George urged TSE to contact Gordon Selwyn and to 'suggest a contribution' to *Theology*. 'If I know more of your plans, I could arrange introductions to Lord Halifax or the Archbishop of Canterbury, or the Dean of Winchester.'

2 – George did not review the book in question, but he later contributed 'Guy de Maupassant', *C.* 9 (July 1930), 618–30.

3 – 'And now I am going to send you a thing for the Criterion on comedy, and if you will care to look at another on Maritain's philosophy of beauty.'

4 – 'Poetry and Religion', *NC* 5 (Jan. 1927), 7–22; 5 (May 1927), 214–30.

## TO *Antonio Marichalar* CC

13 November 1926 [*The New Criterion*]

My dear Marichalar,

Thank you very much for sending your chronicle so promptly: it shall appear in the January number.[1] I am sorry to have bothered you unnecessarily with my telegram. Owing to the shortness of time I have had to send the chronicle off for translation without having read it, but I look forward with great interest to reading the translation.

I am very much obliged to you for having spoken to Ortega y Gasset on the subject I mentioned to you.[2] We should be delighted to have him among our contributors and I hope that he will let me have something for the following number. I shall be writing to him shortly, but hope that he will have written to me in any case.

With very many thanks,
Yours ever sincerely,
[T. S. Eliot]

## TO *Bonamy Dobrée* TS Brotherton

13 November 1926 *The New Criterion*

My dear Dobrée,

Your review of Kipling has gone to the printers.[3] I like it very much. When we meet on Tuesday we will consider the question of cutting it down. It would be a pity to do so, but on the other hand in view of the number of reviews scheduled for the next number, and also in view of your future essay on Kipling, it is worth considering. Something turns on the point of how early in the series your essay comes. Personally I should like it to be fairly early. It is rather an important essay for the reason that obviously Kipling is almost the only edifice of which much will be left standing after our examination is completed.[4]

1–'Madrid Chronicle', *NC* 5 (Jan. 1927), 94–9.

2–Marichalar reported (6 Nov.) that Ortega y Gasset would be happy to contribute a piece in response to Massis's article on the defence of the West: but he did not do so.

3–Review of Rudyard Kipling, *Debts and Credits*, *NC* 5 (Jan. 1927), 149–51.

4–'Certain of the regular contributors to *The New Criterion* have agreed to provide . . . a series of essays on the more important figures of the previous generation, having the character of an *inquest*, in the French and perhaps also slightly in the English sense of the word. Each contributor will deal separately with one figure of the elder generation, and will be solely responsible for his own opinions. He may or may not modify these opinions in

I have the feeling that there are one or two other authors of that generation who ought to be included, but talk of that on Tuesday.

Incidentally, you make several quotations in your review and also in *The Nation* review (which I herewith return) which interested me to the point of wishing to identify and look them up. What is the source of the two sentences quoted at the bottom of the first column of *The Nation* review?[1]

I believe that you are being rather unjust to Henley,[2] but I don't really know enough about him to speak with authority.

I certainly propose to mention the series beforehand.

Yours ever,
T. S. E.

Don't worry over Cocteau![3] There's no pleasing people like that, & I have too much experience of offending people to care. I shall write & rebuke him & point out the English view of such matters.

---

consequence of the criticism which his essay will have received before publication. How far a common judgement will emerge is unknown to the contributors themselves. The figures to be examined are Wells, Shaw, Kipling, Chesterton and Belloc (together), and Ford Madox Hueffer (Ford). Possibly a few others will be added' (TSE's 'Commentary', Jan. 1927, 2).

1 – 'There is much virtue in a creed or a law, but when all is prayed and suffered, drink is the only thing that will clear all a man's deeds in his own eyes . . . Then Tom took more drink till his drunkenness rolled back and stood off from him as a wave rolls back and stands off the wreck it will swamp' ('The Record of Badalia Herodsfoot', *Many Inventions* [1893]).

2 – W. E. Henley (1849–1903) is not mentioned in the published version of either article.

3 – Cocteau had taken exception to BD's review of *Orphée* – at the Théâtre des Arts, Paris – in *NC* 4 (Oct. 1926), 764–8. 'Assuming that all art is symbol,' wrote BD, 'you cannot on the stage present the symbol, and leave aside the stuff of which it is made. Yet this is precisely what M. Cocteau seems to be trying to do. Thus his Orpheus and Eurydice remain symbols . . . Perhaps it was the realization of this which led M. Cocteau into his greatest dramatic mistake, the direct statement . . . Still . . . one cannot but applaud the delicacy and grace of his piece, its beautiful phrasing.' Cocteau, added BD, seemed to be moving towards 'a new apprehension of life, a development of sensibility, which would seem to be in the direction of relating the sense of miracle to normal actuality . . . To the English mind his very gaiety, his lightness of touch, may suggest shallowness: but his light-heartedness is that of seriousness' (767–8). Cocteau told TSE (Nov. 1926): 'De mon immense effort, de cette longue agonie, de cette opération chirurgicale à chaud qui est mon oeuvre, *rien n'est vu ni même entrevu.* Mais chez vous, cela me peine plus que partout. [P. S.] Il n'y a pas un symbole dans *Orphée.* C'est 12 ans de drame jetés <cachés> là.' Francis Steegmuller translates Cocteau's letter: 'Of my tremendous effort, of the long agony, the emergency surgery that my book is, *nothing* is seen or even glimpsed. Coming from close to you, this hurts me particularly . . . There is not a single symbol in *Orphée*. Twelve dramatic years are projected, hidden, in it' (*Cocteau: A Biography* [1970], 381). BD would later say, 'on rereading my effusion it seems to me generous and fairly understanding' ('T. S. Eliot: A Personal Reminiscence', in *T. S. Eliot: The Man and His Work*, ed. Allen Tate [1966], 72).

## TO *Eric Partridge* CC

15 November 1926 [*The New Criterion*]

Dear Sir,

I have your letter of the 12th instant. I should be very glad to try your reviewing work as I formed a favourable opinion of several contributions which you offered me but which I was unable to use.[1] The reviewing for the January number of *The New Criterion* has all been arranged, but I am sending you a book – *The Political Ideas of the English Romanticists* [–] which I should be glad if you would examine with a view to a notice for the April number.

I am unable to examine thoroughly the books which I send out for review and what I ask of all reviewers for *The New Criterion* is this: if in your opinion any book sent is undeserving of notice in *The New Criterion*, which owing to limitations of space can only notice what it believes to be the most important books of the quarter, will you please let me know at once and some other book will be found. I am also glad to have the majority of notices as short as possible, either two hundred words (half a page) or four hundred words (a page). I doubt whether the present book deserves more, but probably we can find something more interesting for you before the April number goes to press.

I must warn you that the reviewing which any one person can do for *The New Criterion* in a year will add very little to his income; the chief inducement, to be quite frank with you, is that reviews in the *Criterion* are read and observed by other editors who have more patronage to give than I have.

Yours very truly,
[T. S. Eliot]

## TO *T. Sturge Moore* TS Texas

15 November 1926 *The New Criterion*

Dear Mr Sturge Moore,

On this occasion I am writing to you primarily on behalf of a French literary quarterly called *Commerce* (circular enclosed). I have a sort of informal, personal relation with this review and the editors have asked me to approach you for an unpublished poem. I hope that you will have something you can give them: you will appear in pretty respectable

1 – Partridge asked to be a reviewer, but nothing by him appeared in *The Criterion*.

company, they take great pains with translation and they will also publish your English text on the opposite page which is an additional safeguard. And finally, they pay extremely well. I must add that it will increase their estimation of myself if you yield to my solicitations.

But please do not let them have all your best poems, but save something for *The New Criterion.*

Yours every sincerely,
T. S. Eliot

## TO *J. M. Robertson*

CC

15 November 1926 [London]

My dear Robertson,

Very many thanks for your letter and let me hasten first of all to congratulate you on your birthday party which I should not have suspected.[1] But I also am frequently supposed to be much younger than I am. Could you lunch with me on the 22nd, that is to say today week? I also am very busy at the moment, although all of my labours put together seem less than any of the three you enumerate. If I had, as you suggest, been striking oil in America, I might have felt in a position to sneer at *John Bull*,[2] but the state of my finances does not allow me to feel anything but awe for its contributors and their cheques, and in fact I do not imagine myself to be respectable enough for that company. I will keep your essay as a hostage if the efforts which I intend to make to pry the Turgenev or the Arnold out of you fail, but I am very persistent.[3] If Monday does not suit you please suggest another day.

Yours very sincerely,
[T. S. Eliot]

1–Robertson announced to TSE on 9 Nov. that he was to turn 70 on 14 Nov.

2–For financial reasons Robertson had undertaken to write 'miscellaneous articles' for *John Bull*, 'which was toning up its columns and roping in professors and D.Ds'. Two hours' work would earn him more than he could get for an essay on which he had spent a week or a month; he cited Tennyson: 'the jingling of the guinea helps the hurt that Honour feels' ('Locksley Hall', 105). *John Bull* was a popular weekly periodical specialising in financial and other scandals. Founded in May 1906 by Horatio Bottomley (1860–1933), who edited it for sixteen years until he went to prison for fraudulent conversion, it was discontinued in 1960 after amalgamation with *Illustrated Weekly*.

3–An essay entitled 'Creation'. 'Alas, Turgenev is still in the far background . . .' On 16 Nov. he allowed: 'There will be no difficulty about the Arnold paper, when I get a day's leisure. But you can't use it before April can you? As to Turgenev, as the country parson said in his sermon, "When that will be, God knows; that is to say, nobody knows!"'

TO *H. J. C. Grierson* TS National Library of Scotland

15 November 1926 *The New Criterion*

Dear Professor Grierson,

I am pleased that you should have thought of *The New Criterion* for the review by Professor Entwistle.[1] By a curious and unfortunate coincidence we already have in the press for the January number a review of this same book by J. B. Trend who writes our music chronicle and who, as you perhaps know, reviews most of the Spanish books noticed by *The Times Literary Supplement*. But I should be very glad if you would tell Professor Entwistle that I should like to have his future collaboration and should be glad to see essays or to entertain suggestions for reviewing books if he cares to do so.

But to tell the truth what would please me much more, and what I hoped for when I saw a letter in your handwriting with a manuscript attached, would be to have something from yourself. And this is not solely an enthusiasm of my own, because two of my colleagues have independently said that I ought to make a serious effort to obtain something from you. Possibly you have a manuscript of a lecture which you might allow to be published, or if not I hope that you will give me at least a vague promise. And if I hear nothing from you I shall renew my appeals periodically.

Yours very sincerely,
T. S. Eliot

P.S. I note that your way of spelling my name is, from a Scot, a compliment.[2] But at the same time I must point out that my variation of the name is pure Somerset and that I must remain a despised Southron![3]

1 – Grierson had enclosed with his letter a review by W. J. Entwistle, Professor of Spanish at Glasgow (and an old pupil of Grierson's), of Edward Dent's *Terpander, or Music and the Future*. 'It is not well written & is too condensed & obscure for an audience unfamiliar with the whole subject,' said Grierson; but perhaps *The Criterion* might be able to make use of 'a better and clearer' version?

2 – Grierson addressed TSE as 'Elliott'.

3 – A Southerner, an Englishman (by analogy with Briton and Saxon).

## TO *Mary MacCarthy*[1]

CC

15 November 1926 [London]

Dear Mrs MacCarthy,

I ought to have answered your kind note before and have just realised that the invitation is for tomorrow afternoon.[2] I wish so much that I could come and hear M. Crevel who I have never met and it would have been a great pleasure to renew my acquaintance with yourself and your husband, but unfortunately someone is coming up from the country to see me whom I cannot very well put off and therefore I can only hope for another opportunity.

With all best wishes,
Sincerely yours,
[T. S. Eliot]

## TO *V. B. Metta*

CC

16 November 1926 [*The New Criterion*]

Dear Mr Metta,

I wish to publish your essay on 'The Defence of the East' but owing to pressure of other matter previously accepted I find it impossible to include it in the main body of contributions. But as I should particularly like to print it in this next number while the interest excited by M. Massis' article is still alive, I am including it with the correspondence (there is a letter also from M. Massis himself).[3] Of course I shall consider it as a contribution and you will naturally receive the regular payment for it.

Sincerely yours,
[T. S. Eliot]

1–Wife of Desmond MacCarthy (1877–1952), literary and drama critic, associated with the Bloomsbury Group. Literary editor of the *New Statesman* 1920–7; editor of *Life and Letters*, 1928–33; he moved in 1928 to the *Sunday Times*, where he stayed until his death.

2–Mary MacCarthy invited TSE (Nov. 8) to a lecture by René Crevel, 'L'Esprit contre la Raison', at the MacCarthys' home, 25 Wellington Square, Chelsea, on 16 Nov. 'He is a friend of Raymond Mortimer's. I think his gospel is "Sur-Réalisme" which I hope he will expound to us.'

3–Metta's essay appeared as a letter, 'In Defence of the East', *NC* 5 (Jan. 1927), 100–5; and Massis's reply to a letter from John Gould Fletcher on 106–7.

## TO *Marguerite Caetani* TS Caetani

18 November 1926 *The New Criterion*

Dear Cousin,

Thank you very much for your letter of last Saturday. I enclose herewith a small contribution which I have got from Sturge Moore for you. I do not know why I had not thought of him before as I have a very high opinion of his verse. I cannot say that I think these stanzas particularly good poetry, but they are fairly typical and exhibit his usual scrupulousness and care. He explained that everything he had been doing lately seemed much too long, and this, therefore, is merely a part of a longer poem which he thinks might be printed separately.[1] He also says that his wife (who is French) has translated other things, including a book of Tagore's,[2] into French prose: and I have no doubt that under his direction she would make a very good translation indeed, if you have no one else in mind who could translate it into something like verse.

But if you do not like this at all, let me have it back, as I like it well enough to use in the *Criterion*.

I would have written to you before, but that since returning I have been buried in work. I have had to put aside *Anabase* in order to rush through my long Introduction to Seneca's Plays which is two years overdue. I will send you a copy of the book, in the Tudor Translation Series, when it comes out, but I do not suppose it will be until early in the spring. As soon as I have finished this, I shall return to polishing my *Anabasis* and expect to send you a copy well before Christmas. The book, however, can hardly appear in any case before March.

I am so pleased that you like my 'Mallarmé' which is merely a few hurried and incoherent notes,[3] but I shall probably develop the idea in my book on Donne next year. I have not yet seen the Woolfs, but will give them your message. I am very glad that Virginia has given you a good bit of her novel.

Possibly you might like better than Robert Graves's verse some of the work of his American friend, Laura Gottschalk. I will send you her book[4] presently so that you may judge for yourself.

Vivien did not find that Cannes suited her very well and so she is now back in London and is really much happier looking after her ménage and

1 – T. Sturge Moore sent (17 Nov.) what he called 'two detachable stanzas'.
2 – *Crescent Moon*.
3 – 'Note sur Mallarmé et Poe', trans. Ramon Fernandez, *NRF* 158 (1 Nov. 1926), 524–6.
4 – *The Close Chaplet* (1926).

setting her house in order than she was in continental hotels, and I am sure she has done the wisest thing. She sent you her warmest regards. I believe, however, that you will find what you want at Cannes; Vivien found it in some ways very lovely.

By the way, I have been in communication with Mirsky and intend to ask him to lunch with me as soon as I have time. I have not yet received the new *Commerce*.

Ever yours affectionately,
Tom

P.S. I forgot to say that Sturge Moore's address is:
T. Sturge Moore. Esqre., Hillcroft, Steep, Petersfield, Hants. England.

## TO *Wyndham Lewis* CC

19 November 1926 [London]

Dear Lewis,

This is the best I can do in the circumstances.[1] If there had been more time I might have done something better. If you don't want it, let me have it back.

Yours,
[T. S. E.]

## TO *Alexis St Léger Léger*[2] TS Fondation Saint-John Perse

19 November 1926 *The New Criterion*

Cher Monsieur,

Je vous fais toutes mes excuses. En rentrant à Londres j'ai trouvé tant d'affaires qui attendaient mon attention que j'ai été tous les jours à quatre chemins. Mais en somme j'ai posé vos conditions à l'Administration et je crois que nous sommes d'accord. Je suis invité à vous demander si nous pourrions nous entendre pour une édition de 2,000 exemplaires. C'est à dire nous ferions un premier tirage de probablement moins de 1,000 exemplaires et si le premier tirage se vend,[3] nous continuerons de faire

1–'A Note on Poetry and Belief', *The Enemy*, 1 (Jan. 1927), 15–17.
2–Alexis St Léger Léger (1887–1975) – St.-John Perse – poet and diplomat; Nobel Laureate, 1960: see Biographical Register.
3–The authorised French edition of the TSE–SJP correspondence corrects TSE's usage to '*inférieur a 1000 examplaires et que, s'il vendait*' (*Letters atlantiques: Saint-John Perse, T. S. Eliot, Allen Tate: 1926–1970*, trans. and ed. Carol Rigolot [Gallimard, 2006], 32).

d'autres tirages jusqu'au chiffre total de 2,000. Après un tirage de 2,000, tous les droits reviendront à l'auteur.

Si vous êtes d'accord, veuillez renvoyer le contrat et nous y mettrons le clause convenable.

J'ai été désolé de ne pas pouvoir vous revoir à Paris, mais j'espère pouvoir faire une visite à Paris pendant[1] l'hiver quand j'espère avoir une entrevue à plus grande loisir.

Reçevez, cher Monsieur, l'expression de mes sentiments d'admiration et d'amitié.

T. S. Eliot[2]

## TO *T. Sturge Moore* — Photocopy of TS

18 November 1926 — *The New Criterion*

Dear Mr Sturge Moore,

I appreciate immensely your kindness in replying so quickly to my request and have forwarded your manuscript today. I have also suggested your wife as a translator, but it is possible that they may wish Valery Larbaud or St Léger Léger to translate the poem into verse. I have given them your address so that they may correspond direct.

I hope that you will remember *The Criterion* as soon as you have anything else that you care to print. I also should like some verse the next time.

With many thanks,
Yours very sincerely
T. S. Eliot

1 – '*y retourner*' (*Lettres atlantiques*, 33).

2 – *Translation*: Dear Sir, Please accept my apologies. On my return to London, I found so many matters needing my attention that I have been constantly running this way and that. But basically I have explained your conditions to the administration and I think we are in agreement. I have been commissioned to ask you if we can settle for an edition of 2,000 copies. That is to say we shall bring out a first run of probably less than 1,000 copies, and if this first batch sells, we shall continue to bring out others, up to a total of 2,000 copies. Beyond 2,000, all rights will revert to the author.

If you are in agreement, please return the contract and we will insert an appropriate clause.

I was very sorry not to see you in Paris, but I hope to be able to visit Paris during the winter, when I hope we can meet in more leisurely circumstances. Allow me to assure you of my admiration and friendship. T. S. Eliot

## TO *Lady Rothermere*

CC

19 November 1926 [London]

Dear L. R.,

I have been meaning to write to you for the last fortnight ever since I have been back in England, but have been scrambling about the whole of the time making up arrears. Your last letter about delay in receiving copies I took to be purely impersonal![1] And therefore I did no more than make enquiries and ascertain that an endeavour had been made in my absence to repair the fault. But when the next number comes out, I shall ask my secretary to send you a letter on the same day on which the copies are supposed to be dispatched to you, and if they do not reach you within a day after the letter please let me know at once. I understand that hereafter they are to be sent to you care of Miss Beach.

For the last three months, until a fortnight ago, I had not been in England at all. The advertisement which you dislike was just as much of a surprise to me and I have expressed my dislike of it; as a matter of fact, Faber mentioned it to me even before I had time to complain of it; apparently it was the result of the energy of the Advertisements Manager who has now been censored. I do not suppose it had occurred to anyone but himself that manufacturers of shirts and similar products would care to advertise in the *Criterion* at all. I do not think that it will occur again.[2]

1–Lady R had written to GCF on 21 Oct., from Cap Ferret (Gironde): 'I find the new volume which has *at last* arrived – (surely you can arrange for the review to be in the shops in Paris *at the same time* as London. Or at least within a day or two?

'It is an exceedingly good number – but I am disappointed to find a very ordinary page of advertisements *immediately* facing the first page. This is indeed a mistake & will not I hope be repeated. I am also sorry to see an add: on the back of cover! I should have thought also that it was fairly easy to get "adds" of highclass schools Hydros etc. . . . Such adds suit a quarterly; & is it impossible to get publisher notices? I am sorry I shall not be in London again this year as I should like to see you re these questions.

'Is T. S. in Paris? Please tell him I shall be in Paris all November. I hope very much to see him.'.

2–GCF replied to Lady Rothermere's letter on 26 Oct.: 'I am glad you think the October number of The New Criterion a good one. I am entirely at one with you on the matter of the advertisement which greets the eye as one opens the number. I had already refused to allow the appearance of the same advertisement with a half-tone block, and our Advertisement Manager (I really think out of malice) slipped this advertisement in with a line block in place of the half-tone block at the last moment, without my knowing that he had done so. Since then he has had the sack, and we have engaged a first-class man to take his place, who will, I hope, be able to do rather better for The New Criterion in the way of advertisements. But to secure advertisements for a quarterly with a small circulation is a very difficult proposition indeed. Personally I do not object to an advertisement on the back, and it is very important that we should use every possible source of revenue if the magazine is to

I must say that you are almost as bad a correspondent as I am. Why do you never write to me and express your opinion of the numbers or make any suggestions? It seems as if you had completely forgotten the *Criterion*!

Are you going to be in Paris much of the time this winter? I have so recently returned from France – I was very little in Paris and most of the time in the country – that I cannot afford to leave things to look after themselves for a long time, but I hope to run over for a visit some time in the new year. I should like to know something of your plans if possible, and how you are.

Ever yours sincerely,
[T. S. E.]

P.S. Did the copy sent to Fribourg ever reach you?

## TO *H. J. C. Grierson* CC

22 November 1926 [*The New Criterion*]

Dear Professor Grierson,

Thank you for your kind reply. You are tantalisingly vague, but it is a great deal even to extract a general promise from you and the particular subject which you suggest is one that would interest us very much. So I shall continue to remind you from time to time.[1]

Thank you for calling my attention to the misprints.[2] I apologise particularly for the misprint in your own letter. I was abroad at the time and the working staff were rather short handed.

With many thanks,
Yours sincerely,
[T. S. Eliot]

---

live out its appointed span. Nor do I think that we can possibly avoid advertisements facing the front page, if we are to have advertisements at all. I do not myself object to any of the advertisements in the present issue, with the single exception of the Luvisca advertisement, which is altogether impossible.' (CC)

There were in fact three pages of advertisements in the prelims – for John & Edward Bumpus, booksellers; 'Luvisca' shirts; and voyages to India or Ceylon by P&O at reduced midwinter fares of one hundred guineas return, first saloon – and the back cover was filled by an advertisement for Player's No. 3 Virginia Cigarettes.

1–'I have an idea', said Grierson (17 Nov.), 'that some day when I have studied it a little more I should like to write on Mr Richards' theory of poetry.'

2–In Grierson's letter, 'wasted' had become 'rested'; 'cognoscit' appeared as 'cogniscit'.

## TO *Alec Randall*

TS McFarlin

22 November 1926 *The New Criterion*

My dear Randall,

Thank you very much for your letter of the 16th. Your copy is indeed in time and has gone to the printers. If I find we have too much material for this number, I shall hold over the review of Schickele, but I hope that it will be able to appear.

As for the periodicals, it is rather for you to say whether there are any others that you want. If so, you have only to let me know and I will try to arrange an exchange.

Many thanks for your kindness in reporting on that little story.[1] You confirm my own hasty opinion. If you ever come across a particularly brilliant German short story, which you think would also translate well, I should be glad to know. As a rule I believe that we do best if we can stick to the English product in fiction and choose foreign writers rather among essayists. That is to say that thought is generally more importable than sensibility. But good English stories are hard to find and there must be a few foreign writers who could usefully fill gaps.

I am interested to find that you also are decidedly in favour of the monthly versus quarterly publication.[2] Everybody, in fact, is now in favour of a monthly and the only barrier is the financial one, but we may overcome that eventually. For the present no change.

Yours ever,
T. S. Eliot

1–Randall said of Wagenseil's story: 'It is not worth publishing. If ever you want a German short story for publication, I could suggest a hundred suitable ones.'

2–'What a pity . . . you can't get out every month, return to the original *English Review* kind of publication . . . You have a programme, and a better one, in my opinion, than the young Ford Madox Hueffer. But I still feel enthusiasm when I think of the early *English Review*, and if only the *Criterion* came more frequently it would get much more notice. I suppose, however, it would be necessary to find another Sir Alfred Mond. The money would be well spent. The "European tradition" on the Continent tends to run to crankiness, and to have a sane exponent of it appearing in England once a month would be a real help to English intellectual prestige.'

## TO *Maurice Marston*[1] CC

22 November 1926 [London]

Dear Sir,

I have your letters of the 21st October and 15th November and I must apologise for the fact that having but recently returned from abroad I had in pressure of business overlooked your first letter. I highly appreciate your invitation to deliver a lecture for the Council and I wish that I could conscientiously accept, but I have several long-standing obligations which will take most of my time for the next six months so that I have been obliged to refuse all lecturing engagements for about that period. I should like to say, however, that I am keenly interested in the aims of the National Book Council, and if you should be attempting any lectures in a subsequent season I hope very much that I might be of use to you. I should also be glad to co-operate in any other way possible, and meanwhile you have my most cordial good wishes for the coming season.

With very many thanks,
I am,
Yours faithfully,
[T. S. Eliot]

## TO *John Dover Wilson*[2] TS National Library of Scotland

23 November 1926 *The New Criterion*

Sir,

I take the liberty of writing to you to ask whether you would be willing to do me the great favour of reviewing for *The New Criterion* Mr J. M. Robertson's recent book, *The Problem of the Shakespeare Sonnets*. It could be reviewed at any length you thought fit up to 2,000 words which is our maximum. It is not a matter of haste, as the January number (the

1 – Maurice Marston, Organising Secretary, National Book Council, was putting on a series of five lectures at the Mortimer Hall in Feb.–Mar. 1927, under such headings as 'Reading and Architecture' and 'Poetry and Travel'. He invited TSE to talk on 'Reading and Poetry'.

2 – John Dover Wilson (1881–1969): literary and textual scholar; Professor of Education, King's College, London, 1924–35; Regius Professor of Rhetoric and English Literature, Edinburgh University, 1935–45. Renowned as editor of the New Cambridge Shakespeare, 1921–66; author of critical studies including *Shakespeare's Hand in the Play of 'Sir Thomas More'* (1923); *The Manuscripts of Shakespeare's 'Hamlet'* (1934); *The Essential Shakespeare* (1932); *The Fortunes of Falstaff* (1943); and *Shakespeare's Happy Comedies* (1962).

review is a quarterly) is already in the press; therefore I am anxious to have a review of this book by the 24th January for inclusion in April.

I presume that both myself and the review which I edit are unknown to you and I am sending you a copy of the last number in order to reassure you. I should not ordinarily have written to you without an introduction from a mutual friend or acquaintance, but I am anxious that this book should be reviewed by the most competent person possible and there is, I think, no one whose knowledge or opinions on the subject I should accept so absolutely as I should yours.

I am, Sir,
Your obedient servant,
T. S. Eliot

## *Vivien Eliot* TO *Ottoline Morrell* MS Texas

Wednesday [24 November 1926] 57 Chester Terrace, S.W.1

Dearest Ottoline

I had been looking forward to seeing you very much indeed.

I think it was good of you to come here, & I most fully appreciated it. Directly I saw you some sort of subconscious hope that I had not known that I still had, went out. I felt then that I must at least show you that I see, or perhaps I can say only that I have begun to see. I'm trying to show you that I was aware, & that I saw, I think my manner was dull & unpleasant. I did not want it to be that, but it is all new. I hope to get used to it in time.

Anyhow please try to believe that I was very very glad to see you, & as much as I was aware of today you have been trying to show me for years & years – very patiently.

I am glad you thought Tom looks a little better. He is an extraordinary analyst isn't he?

I[t] was good of you to have suggested a visit to Garsington. I *had* forgotten the letter, & I quite see why you withdrew it.

With affectionate remembrances

Yrs. Ever
V. H. E.

## TO *Leonard Woolf* CC

25 November 1926 [London]

Dear Leonard,

Very many thanks for the book on Whitman of which you shall have a review by the date set.[1] I shall be glad to review anything else that you care to send me.

Also I thank you for your letter which I have been considering carefully.[2] I should very much like to do it if I could. Here is my present position. Apart from reviewing and the *Criterion* work I am at present occupied with a long introduction to Seneca's plays and with the translation of a long French poem, which jobs will certainly take all of my time till the end of the year. After that I must set to work on rewriting and expanding my Cambridge lectures for book form as I have promised it for the summer. This rewriting involves also a good deal of supplementary reading and I am not now sure that I can get the book ready for publication before next autumn. In the circumstances, and as I am a very slow and costive writer, I do not see how I could possibly promise a book by the end of next year, and it would be impossible to put aside the other work to do this first. As you know, Faber & Gwyer have the first refusal according to our contract of any books that I write, and if for any reason I want to do a book for another publisher I must get their permission. I don't feel that I can ask for this until I have done at least one pretty substantial book for them. That is why I am not in a position to make any definite promise.

I should rather like to have a talk with you; we might be able to arrive at an understanding. Could you lunch with me one day next week? I should like to see you. I have only been in London for a few weeks, during which I have been toiling to make up arrears. Otherwise I should have given some hint of my presence. Please give Virginia my love and say that I should like to come and see her soon. I hope you are both well.

[T. S. E.]

1–'Whitman and Tennyson', *Nation & Athenaeum* 40 (18 Dec. 1926), 418 (on Emory Holloway, *Whitman: an Interpretation in Narrative*).

2–LW invited TSE (18 Nov.) to contribute to a new Hogarth series (to be edited by LW and George Rylands) entitled 'Lectures in English Literature'. 'Modern Poetry and Poetical Tradition' was suggested as a possible subject for TSE, with a length of between 30,000 and 35,000 words, and with a delivery date of the end of 1927. (Other essayists were to include H. J. C. Grierson on 'Nineteenth Century Lyric'; F. L. Lucas on Tragedy; VW on 'Perspective in the Novel'.)

## TO *J. M. Robertson* CC

25 November 1926 [London]

My dear Robertson

In spite of your terrifying list of works which you are engaged upon I cannot resist the temptation to ask your advice on a particular point. I am doing a preface for the 'Tudor' translation of Seneca's plays.[1] In my preface or introduction I am discussing such of the points about Seneca's influence as seem to me never to have been thoroughly dealt with. I particularly do not want merely to re-hash the results of scholarship but only to deal with things that have been neglected or ill-treated in literary criticism. One of the points I am taking is Seneca's supposed bad influence on 'The Tragedy of Blood', i.e. I think that the extent to which the taste for horrors is supposed to be due to imitation of Seneca has been grossly exaggerated.[2]

One of the plays I want to touch upon is *Titus Andronicus*. My *Shakespeare Canon*, or what there yet is of it, is unfortunately among the books which were left in a flat which I have let and I cannot at the moment lay my hands on it. Have you discussed *Titus Andronicus* there or elsewhere, and if not can you tell me what is the best existing discussion of the authorship and origin of this play?

I have just read *Titus Andronicus* again and it seems to me almost the worst play of the whole epoch.[3]

If you have time to drop me a line I should be extremely grateful. I ought to have raised this question at our lunch, but the other subjects discussed were too interesting.

Yours ever sincerely,
[T. S. Eliot]

1–Vol. 1 of *Seneca His Tenne Tragedies* (1927) contained TSE's 'Introduction', v–liv; repr. as 'Seneca in Elizabethan Translation', *SE* (1932).

2–In reply (26 Nov.), Robertson recommended J. W. Cunliffe's *Influence of Seneca on Elizabethan Tragedy* (1893) as the 'most important book' on the subject.

3–Robertson declared: 'You are quite right about *Titus*: not one scene of it, not a single entire speech, is by Shakespeare.' He would ask his publisher to send TSE a copy of his *Introduction to the Study of the Shakespeare Canon* (1924), in which he had 'greatly expanded (threefold)' his original book on that 'odious play'. He volunteered too: 'Perhaps the Prolegomena may interest you? I had to pulp Sir (then Mr) E. K. Chambers, who is a forty-horse-power Ass; and [George] Saintsbury, who is a ten-horse-power Ditto.'

## TO *Herbert Read* CC

26 November 1926 [*The New Criterion*]

My dear Read,

I have read Worringer[1] with much interest. It also seems to me extremely readable and the sort of thing that would catch the public interest. I think of writing to him and asking him to let us publish it if he will reduce it to a suitable length (a great deal of the beginning could be cut out). Do you approve, or have you come across anything else of his that you think more suitable? If you agree, you can give me his address on Monday, when I shall come to your Italian restaurant in South Kensington at one o'clock.

Yours ever
[T. S. E.]

## TO *George Rylands* CC

26 November 1926 [*The New Criterion*]

Dear Rylands,

Many thanks for the two notes you have sent.[2] I should like to know, however, whether you are silent about the other three books because you think they are not worth reviewing or merely because you have not had time to do them. I should particularly like to know your opinion of Sacheverell's book. Of course it is too late to do anything about it now, but if in your opinion it is good enough for a notice, we might have something about it in the following number.

I meant to ask you also, have you done any poetry that you could let me see?

Sincerely yours,
[T. S. Eliot]

1–Wilhelm Worringer, 'Art Questions of the Day', *MC* 6 (Aug. 1927), 101–17.
2–Rylands had written (22 Nov.): 'Humbert Wolfe & G. Stein will follow tomorrow but I should like to do 400 on S. Sitwell for the next number.'

## TO *F. S. Flint*

CC

30 November 1926 [Faber & Gwyer Ltd]

Dear Sir,

I have to confirm the arrangement which I made with you over the telephone on behalf of Faber & Gwyer Limited for you to translate for us the Life of Beethoven by Hévesy which I sent you: the complete translation to be handed to us before January 1st 1927; in consideration of the said translation being provided by the said date, you to receive from us the sum of thirty five pounds (£35) on delivery of the manuscript. I should be obliged for the favour of your confirmation.[1]

I have also to remind you that we should be glad to receive the translation as soon before that date as possible, and we should very highly appreciate your diligence in this respect as we have no doubt of the quality. We are extremely glad that you can undertake this piece of work.

I should be greatly obliged if you would be so kind as to telephone to Mr Richard de la Mare at this office tomorrow and let him have what you consider the best title for the book in English, as he wishes to prepare the advertisement of it immediately.

Yours faithfully,
For Faber & Gwyer Limited,
[T. S. Eliot]
Director.

## TO *John Dover Wilson*

CC

30 November 1926 [*The New Criterion*]

Dear Sir,

I thank you cordially for your letter of the 27th instant. Of course I regret that you are unable to undertake this review for us for the April number. But I was quite prepared to find that you were too busy; and as *The New Criterion*, being a quarterly, cannot be very punctual in reviewing books in any case, and as therefore I aim rather at having books reviewed by the most suitable persons than at having them reviewed quickly, I shall consider it a favour if you will review Mr Robertson's book for the number which appears on *June* 15th. Copy for this number should be received here by the 15th April.

1 – André de Hévesy, *Beethoven: The Man*, trans F. S. Flint (F&G, 1927).

I shall be sending you a copy of the book.[1]

With many thanks,
Yours faithfully,
[T. S. Eliot]

## TO *Messrs Macmillan & Company* CC

30 November 1926 [London]

Dear Sirs,

If you can do so I should be greatly obliged if you send us for review a complete set of the cloth bound pocket edition of the works of Mr Kipling. This is for the purpose of aiding the preparation of a long study of Kipling which Mr Bonamy Dobrée is writing for *The New Criterion*.[2] Possibly it is contrary to your policy to send out full sets for review.

Yours faithfully,
[T. S. Eliot]

## TO *H. C. Crofton*[3] CC

1 December 1926 [London]

My dear Crofton,[4]

This is to welcome you back to the horrors of city life in December, but I wish that you could have had three months more tennis on the Riviera first. As soon as I make my next expedition to E.C.4. I shall certainly try to secure you for lunch.

Yours ever,
[T. S. Eliot]

1–Dover Wilson reviewed Robertson, *The Problems of the Shakespeare Sonnets*, in *MC* 6 (Aug. 1927), 162.
2–'Rudyard Kipling', *MC* 6 (Dec. 1927), 499–515.
3–Henry Crofton had been a colleague of TSE's in the Colonial & Foreign Department of Lloyds Bank Ltd., 80 Gracechurch Street, London, EC3.
4–Crofton wrote on 26 Nov., in response to a (now lost) enquiry from TSE: 'I have been at Aldeburgh for the last six weeks playing strenuous hard court tennis and feeling like a two year old. Am going back to work on Dec 1st and hope that at long last my health problems are over. Ring me up when you are coming citywards and we will have lunch together.'

## TO *Wilhelm Worringer*[1] CC

1 December 1926 [*The New Criterion*]

Sir,

Our friend Mr Herbert Read has lent me your two pamphlets, *Kunstlerische Zeitfragen* and *Deutsche Jugend und Ostlicher Geist*, both of which have interested me very much. I should be very glad if we might use either of these (especially the former) for publication in *The New Criterion*, a quarterly review which I edit and which I believe Mr Read has mentioned to you. In the case of foreign contributions for which we have the expense of translation, our rates are twenty five shillings per thousand words, the cost of translation being high. The only difficulty from our point of view is that limits of space make it undesirable to publish contributions of much more than five or six thousand words. We are from time to time forced to publish long essays in two instalments, but I avoid doing so when possible as the interval of time elapsing between the two parts of the essay is a disadvantage.

If you will give your consent to publication I should be glad if you could find it possible to abbreviate the *Kunstlerische Zeitfragen*. As the essay was originally an address, it seems to me that a certain amount of compression, especially at the beginning, is possible. If you agree, I suggest that you should send me a copy, marking the omissions which you think might be made.[2]

The subject of this essay is one especially suitable to *The New Criterion*, which aims at treating subjects of European importance. I think that it might excite writers in England and in other continental countries to a discussion in our pages which would be of great interest. Earlier in the year we published an essay by Mons. Henri Massis on the cultural relations of contemporary Europe with the Orient, which provided a subject of great interest both to our readers and colleagues in every country. Your *Deutsche Jugend und Ostlicher Geist* is a contribution to the same problem, but of the two I should prefer the *Kunstlerische Zeitfragen*, in the expectation of arousing another discussion.

1–Wilhelm Worringer (1881–1965): influential art historian and theoretician; author of *Abstraktion und Einfühlung: ein Beitrag zur Stilspsychologie* (*Abstraction and Empathy: A Contribution to the Psychology of Style*, 1908) – on the relation between 'primitive' abstract art and mimetic 'empathy' – *Formprobleme der Gotik* (*Form in the Gothic*, 1911); *Ägyptische Kunst: Probleme ihre Werte* (*Egyptian Art*, 1927).

2–'Art Questions of the Day' (the substance of an address given by Worringer to the Munich branch of the Goethe Fellowship), *MC* 6 (Aug. 1927), 101–17.

I am sending you a specimen copy of our last issue.

I am, Sir,
Your obedient servant,
[T. S. Eliot]

## TO *Orlo Williams* CC

2 December 1926 [*The New Criterion*]

Dear Williams,

I am very sorry indeed to hear that you cannot come on Tuesday next because I had meanwhile issued notices to some of the others for that date. As you cannot come, I think the best thing is not to count it as a regular meeting and I will try to arrange a first one for a week or a fortnight later, calling it our Yule Tide festival. Perhaps a fortnight thence is the best time and I will send you a formal notice in good time.

I am returning to you the *Chevalley* manuscript, although it is interesting stuff. You want to publish it somewhere for him and it is doubtful whether I could get it into *The New Criterion* until next autumn. The trouble is that I already have, or have been promised, more foreign stuff than I can use, and I think that you will agree that if we have more than a cautious proportion of foreign contributions in any one number it may do more harm than good; people may even think that we publish foreigners because we can't get anyone here to contribute. The *Maritain* thing which we listed for January has turned out so long that it will spill over into April; I have also had for some time a thing by Claudel which I have promised to publish; there is Angioletti for April or June (besides his chronicle); there are two Germans and there is Ortega y Gasset who has promised something which may turn up at any time. All this stuff must be tactfully spread out.

(What I should particularly like to get from abroad is good short stories as these are so very scarce everywhere.)

I have read your 'Ambassadors' with great interest; that is a very different matter and provokes me to a discussion. I shall drop you a line in a week or so and ask you to come and lunch with me if you will.

Yours,
[T. S. Eliot]

## TO *Richard Aldington* TS Texas

2 December 1926 *The New Criterion*

My dear Richard,

I should very much like to have a word to know that you are alive and what you are doing, as I can get no very recent news of you from anybody. I am myself settled in London for some time to come.

I am also writing to urge you to try to get up to London as soon as possible to one of our every-other-Tuesday dinners which take place at 7.15 at *Commercio* in Frith Street. There will be a small and select meeting on Tuesday next at which we should especially like to have your company, and a fortnight later there will a larger, Yule-Tide festival. I know that everyone else is as anxious as I am that you should appear at one or both.

Ever yours,
Tom

## TO *William King* CC

2 December 1926 [London]

Dear King,

I am very glad to hear from you.[1] Your idea is a good one. I had intended to take some notice of the *Gay* but I am not sure whether we should be able to give it a length that would make it worth your while. I try to pick out all the most important books of every quarter, but our limits of space make it necessary to lay down some rules of selection and my rule has been not to give very much room to books which are only reprints or new editions of classics – however valuable the edition may be. But in any case the review would be for the April number as the January number is already in the press, and it is difficult to tell so far ahead. I should be very glad to send you the book on the condition that you would be willing to do quite a short note about it if I find that there are too many new books which require reviewing at length. Perhaps in that case there is some other

1–King wished (30 Nov.) to review GCF's edition of Gay in the Oxford Poets series. See *MC* 5 (May 1927), 276: 'all true lovers of the eighteenth century will be grateful to Mr Faber for this edition of Gay's poems and the majority of his plays. Mr Faber has directed upon the text of Gay all the careful scholarship which editors of Greek and Latin writers are accustomed to devote to their authors, with none of the unhappy misuse of emendation that so often disfigures the patient toil of years. Not only is his introduction explaining his method a model of sensible and lucid argument, but even his *apparatus criticus* makes interesting and instructive reading.'

book within our scope which you would do at more length. We could discuss this over a lunch. Can you lunch with me on Thursday or Friday of next week?

Yours,
[T. S. Eliot]

## TO *G. B. Harrison*[1] CC

[November/December 1926] [London]

Dear Sir,

I am highly honoured by your invitation to address the Shakespeare Association and shall be very glad to do so if we can agree upon a subject suited both to my capacities and to the interests of the members. So far as I can tell, your date the 25th March, at 5.30. p.m. will suit me very well.

Could you give me some idea of the type of subject upon which members of the Association would be most willing to hear me?[2]

Yours very truly,
[T. S. Eliot]

## TO *M. A. A. M. Stols* CC

Le 3 décembre 1926 [London]

Monsieur,

Je vous remercie de votre aimable lettre du 30 novembre.[3] Je suis extrêmement flatté par votre invitation de collaborer au recueil d'hommage à Paul Valéry. Je vous donnerais volontiers mon appui, mais pour moi c'est une question de temps puisque je me trouve à present accablé par mes devoirs de routine. Cependant je vous prie de m'envoyer un mot pour

1–G. B. Harrison (1894–1991), literary scholar, wrote numerous studies of Shakespeare and his contemporaries, and would become renowned as general editor of several series of inexpensive, popular editions of Shakespeare. Having been taught at Queens' College, Cambridge, by E. M. W. Tillyard, Mansfield Forbes and I. A. Richards (he was proud to have been Richards's first pupil in the English Tripos), he was at the time of this letter Assistant Lecturer in English at King's College, London, and Honorary Secretary of the Shakespeare Association.

2–*Shakespeare and the Stoicism of Seneca* (1927): address given on 18 Mar. 1927.

3–Stols (*Analecta ex MSS Pauli Valerii*, Bussum, Holland) invited TSE to contribute to a Europe-wide volume of essays in honour of Paul Valéry on the occasion of his election to the Académie Française.

me dire la dernière date possible pour l'envoi d'un manuscrit. Et je ferai tout ce que je peux.

Je vous prie, Monsieur, de recevoir l'expression de mes sentiments distingués et de ma haute considération.

[T. S. Eliot][1]

## TO *The Editor of* The Nation & The Athenaeum[2]

6 December 1926 — 24 Russell Square, London W.C.1

Sir, –

I was not aware of 'Kappa's' contribution to Mr J. M. Robertson's birthday party until I read Mr Middleton Murry's letter in *The Nation* of December 4th.[3] If it is not too late to intervene, I should be glad to

1–*Translation*: Dear Sir, I wish to thank you for your kind letter dated 30th November. I am extremely flattered by your invitation to contribute to the volume of essays in honour of Paul Valéry. I would willingly give you my support but for me it is a question of time as I find myself currently burdened by my routine duties. However I wish you would send me word of the latest date possible for the submission of a manuscript. And I will do all I can.

Please receive, dear sir, the expression of my kindest regards. Yours faithfully, [T. S. Eliot]

2–Published as 'Mr. J. M. Robertson and Shakespeare', *N&A*, 18 Dec. 1926, 418.

3–'Kappa', in his *N&A* column 'Life and Politics', lamented the scholarship of J. M. Robertson: 'Few of Mr J. M. Robertson's vast output of books have come my way. I do not derive much pleasure from rationalist propaganda . . . He is austere, a little bleak, even a little forbidding, and tremendously competent. One recent development of his multifarious activities is his remorseless "disintegration" of Shakespeare. Mr Robertson loves Shakespeare so much that he would free him of all the accretions of inferior stuff that have crept into the Canon. I wish myself that Mr Robertson had left Shakespeare alone. We can never know, so why unsettle our faith and make the reading of the plays an uneasy delight. I will cling to the skirts of Sir Edmund Chambers and stop my ears to the harsh Scottish voice that rationalizes Shakespeare into fragments' (20 Nov. 1926, 261). JMM protested: 'I am no rationalist – far from it – but I feel it is someone's duty to protest against "Kappa's" facile dismissal of the work of Mr J. M. Robertson. The only part of it with which I am familiar is his Shakespeare criticism; but with that I am familiar, and I am quite certain that is the most valuable single contribution to Shakespeare criticism that has been made in my time . . . Kappa's feeble "We can never know" is the merest obscurantism. If it is true, then we can never know anything of the faintest importance . . . But those who believe they can know, and know what Mr Robertson has done to help them know, will share my irritation at seeing his work peremptorily described as "rationalizing Shakespeare into fragments"' (*N&A*, 4 Dec. 1926, 333). 'Kappa' replied on the same page to JMM's protest: 'The remarks which Mr Murry so much dislikes expressed my own feeling that the disintegration of Shakespeare – the attempt to break up the mass of plays called Shakespeare's works and to allot authors to scenes and passages of the composite plays – is a hopeless as it is certainly a confusing and profoundly disturbing business . . . I am as far as possible from admitting the charge which Murry makes by implication that I am ready to swallow the canon as 100 per cent Shakespeare. Of course not; there are

express my cordial agreement with Mr Murry's protest. 'Kappa's' original comment appears to have been in indifferent taste in the choice of an occasion: but he now carries the controversy beyond the limits of his sneer at Mr Robertson. The 'Kappa' programme, in fact, seems to comprehend a sweeping out of the temple of Shakespeare of such insignificant insects as Professor Pollard,[1] and Professor Dover Wilson, and anyone who has attempted to clear up any of the problems of that bewildering epoch.

No more than 'Kappa' do I profess 'to have an expert's acquaintance', but at least I have studied these problems. I write as a literary critic who has, like Mr Murry, paid some attention to this period of English literature; and I am convinced that no literary critic who is concerned with this period today can afford to neglect the work of such scholars as those I have mentioned. 'Kappa' is, on the other hand, a true Conservative: he likes things to be left as they are. That is to say, since we cannot *prove* to his satisfaction who is responsible for *Titus Andronicus*, we should continue to dishonour the name of Shakespeare with the ascription. 'Kappa' may have reason to be satisfied with his own 'aesthetic instinct'. I refuse to surrender myself to the mercy of the 'aesthetic instinct' of Coleridge, who can talk glibly about *Richard II* and *Richard III* without mentioning the name of Marlowe.[2]

I am, Sir,
Your obliged, obedient servant
T. S. Eliot[3]

---

masses of non-Shakespearean matter in the canon; it is the greatest of literary tragedies that Shakespeare did not sort out and edit his plays for posterity. In the circumstances one is left to one's aesthetic instinct, if that is the right phrase; the instinct which the greatest of all Shakespeare critics, Coleridge, possessed pre-eminently.'

1–A. W. Pollard (1859–1944): eminent Shakespearean scholar, 'new bibliographer' and textual critic; author of editions and studies including *Shakespeare Folios and Quartos: A Study in the Bibliography of Shakespeare's Plays, 1594–1685* (1909); *Shakespeare's Fight with the Pirates and the Problems of the Transmission of his Text* (1917); and *Shakespeare's Hand in the Play of 'Sir Thomas More'* (ed., 1923)

2–Robertson wrote (1 Dec.): 'We are substantially at one on *R.2* and *R.3* but with one or two deviations. Both plays are mainly Marlowe, with some piecing by S.'

3–Robertson told TSE on 13 Dec.: 'It was very good of you to write to the *Nation*, though "Kappa" isn't worth powder & shot. And it was very generous of Murry to do it. I have felt impelled to thank him. Now I can never review his Life of Jesus!'

But 'Kappa' still had the last word, though it was only to put the blame for the whole situation on Shakespeare himself: 'I see that Mr T. S. Eliot has joined Mr Middleton Murry in deploring my alleged indifference to Mr Robertson's work on the text of Shakespeare. Really now, cannot a humble diarist be allowed to express his own – possibly benighted – preference for reading Shakespeare by the light of the despised "aesthetic instinct" without all this learned acrimony . . . I suggest that my critics should expend a little indignation on Shakespeare himself. I shall never cease to lament the carelessness or indifference which

## TO *The Editor of* The Times Literary Supplement

6 December 1926[1] London

Sir,

I must apologise to Dr Reed for having mistaken a Junius who was only a name in an obscure corner of my memory for a Junius with whom I am on more intimate terms.[2] I presume that I was misled by the juxtaposition of the name Junius with that of Dryden, these being as I supposed the names of two masters of English prose. Such an error, coming from a scholar of Dr Reed's accuracy, astonished me very much; but I should have realised that it was an error of which Dr Reed was incapable.

At the same time, I must insist that the last paragraph of Dr Reed's letter surprises me not a little. To a plain man of letters it is certainly a reversal of values to learn that the scholar of the seventeenth century is 'the great Junius' and that the author of the Letters is merely 'an anonymous politician of the eighteenth century'.

Another point occurs to me. Has Dr Reed unwittingly provided a clue to the identity of the Junius he despises? Was Sir Philip Francis also acquainted with the fame of 'Francis Junius'?

I am, Sir,
The Reviewer

## *Vivien Eliot* TO *Bertrand Russell*[3] MS McMaster

6 Dec[ember 1926] 57 Chester Terrace, S.W.1

Dear Bertie,

I shall have to ask you to believe me that I became conscious, during the time I was in France, that I had stolen a part of this jewellery from you. Since getting back to England I have not had the courage to come to

---

allowed him to neglect the job of straightening out his own text and giving us a decent edition of his own plays. If Ben Jonson could do it, why not Shakespeare?' (*N&A*, 24 Dec. 1926, 447)

1–The text is taken from the *TLS*, 9 Dec. 1926, 913. The third paragraph was probably added at proof stage as it does not appear in the carbon copy of the letter.

2–Reviewing (anonymously) *Early Tudor Drama* by A. W. Reed (*TLS*, 2 Dec. 1926, 880), TSE had expressed amazement 'at learning that Junius and Dryden belong to the same generation. Has Dr Reed brought to light evidence which antedates Junius a hundred years?' Dr Reed replied that he was referring to Francis Junius (1589–1677), philologist and antiquary.

3–Bertrand Russell (1872–1970), philosopher: see Biographical Register.

your house & to give it to you. Which is what I ought to do. So now I am asking Tom to hand you the packet, & as it is nothing to do with him I hope you will not speak of it together, it wd be very painful to him. I am not showing this letter to him, or anyone. I shall not ask you to forgive me because you cannot.[1]

As to the money,[2] that being in Tom's name, & our not yet having been able to agree about it, I must leave it till he sees it as I do. I shd have to get him to do the transferring. You see I have not had the courage to live alone.

Please do not answer this letter in any way.

Yours ever sincerely
V. H. Eliot

I gave one ring with turquoises in it to Ellen Kellond, whose name is now Sollery.

## *Vivien Eliot* TO *Ottoline Morrell* — MS Texas

8 December [1926] — 57 Chester Terrace, S.W.1

Dearest Ottoline

I was very delighted to get yr letter yesterday morning. Thank you indeed for *both* your letters.

It is extraordinarily kind of you to have invited Tom & me to Garsington. I have shown yr letter to Tom & he is very much touched.

So far as I am concerned although I am happy to have been invited I know I am not ready for visiting anyone, & I can't possibly impose myself on people at present. I am altogether too dull & depressing, for more than a *very* short time.

1–On 20 Apr. 1936, VHE recalled in her diary that Russell had given her 'all his jewellery which I returned but he made me keep one valuable pendant which has been stolen. I wish I could get back the pendant which BR made me keep. It was one large pearl in a dark blue enamel setting and a thick solid gold chain' (Bodleian). Maurice Haigh-Wood was to venture on 28 Jan. 1980, in conversation with the playwright Michael Hastings: 'Russell gave Vivie dresses, then Russell family heirlooms. Russell's family asked Vivie for a ring back . . . Mummy made her give back the jewels' (cited in Seymour-Jones, *Painted Shadow*, 447–8).
2–In 1968 Russell wrote: 'I held some debentures nominally worth £3,000, in an engineering firm (Plenty & Son, Newbury), which during the War naturally took to making munitions. I was much puzzled in my conscience as to what to do with these debentures, and at last I gave them to Eliot. Years afterwards [in 1927], when the War was finished and he was no longer poor, he gave them back to me' (*Autobiography* II [1968], 9–10).

But I do hope, very much indeed, that I may see you whenever you come next to London, if you will. I shd really love it. I shall try & go to see *The Magic Flute* thank you for telling me about it.

Again thanking you for yr invitation & for both your letters, & with much love to you,

Always affectionately
*Vivien*

## TO *Charles Whibley*

CC

9 December 1926 [*The New Criterion*]

My dear Whibley,

I am very sorry indeed to hear your news. It was good of you to write at all in the circumstances. I remember your mentioning to me a year or two ago that your sister had been very ill, but I am very sorry to hear of such protracted agony. There are indeed cases in which one is glad for the sufferer to die.[1] My own sister died this summer but only after a very short illness, and while distance makes these things more painful at some moments it makes them easier in others. It was hardest on my niece who was just hoping to spend a year at Oxford or Cambridge.

If you do get up to London before Christmas I shall be very happy. I expect to have my final section[2] ready for you early next week.

Affectionately yours,
[T. S. Eliot]

## TO *Wilhelm Worringer*

CC

9 December 1926 [*The New Criterion*]

Dear Professor Worringer,

Thank you very much for your kind letter of the 7th December and for the copy of *Kunstlerische Zeitfragen* which arrived with it.[3] I shall take

1 – Whibley had reported from Basingstoke (8 Dec.) that he was staying with a niece 'for the funeral of my sister, who died on Sunday. Death came to her, poor thing, as a release from months of pain. But that makes the shock no less.'

2 – TSE's introduction to *Seneca His Tenne Tragedies* (1927).

3 – Worringer gave permission for his pamphlet *Kunstlerische Zeitfragen* to be published in translation in *MC*, though he had reservations: it was written in 1921, he explained, and 'today I see certain aspects differently'; all the same, he enclosed a copy marked with suggested cuts and authorised TSE to make further cuts if necessary. He was pleased to

advantage of your permission and make light of your modesty for which there is no occasion. If you wish, however, we will publish a note at the beginning mentioning the date 1921, but it seems to me that the questions you raise have in no way been answered or altered in the intervening years. I congratulate myself on being able to present this essay to English readers. I will have it translated with great care and shall publish it in April, or more likely in June.

Of course if meanwhile you have anything else which you would prefer us to publish I shall be delighted to receive it, but you will find it difficult to dissuade me from publishing the *Kunstlerische Zeitfragen* in any case.

With very many thanks,
Believe me,
Yours very truly,
[T. S. Eliot]

## TO *E. G. Selwyn*[1] CC

9 December 1926 [London]

My dear Sir,

Thank you for your letter of the 8th December.[2] Mr Gordon George talked to me about you when I met him in France this summer; and in consequence of our conversations I have just procured a copy of *Theology* which I had not read before. I should be very happy to contribute if we can find a subject on which I am competent and if you will allow me sufficient time. At the present moment I am very busy, but should probably be able to write something during the winter if the subject fitted in with my general programme.

---

know 'that the European spirit in the best sense [of the word] has on English soil such a sound and wisely looked-after place [as *The Criterion*].' See *MC* 6 (Aug. 1927), 101–17.

1–The Revd Edward Gordon Selwyn (1885–1959), editor of *Theology: A Monthly Journal of Historic Christianity*, 1920–33. Educated at Eton and King's College, Cambridge (Newcastle Scholar; Porson Scholar and Prizeman; Waddington Scholar; Browne's Medallist; 2nd Chancellor's Medallist), he was Rector of Redhill, Havant, 1919–30; and Provost in Convocation, 1921–31. He was ultimately to be Dean of Winchester, 1931–58. Publications include *The Teaching of Christ*; *The Approach to Christianity*; *Thoughts on Worship and Prayer*; and *The First Epistle of St Peter*.

2–Inspired by TSE's *TLS* leader on Lancelot Andrewes, Selwyn invited TSE to write for *Theology*. TSE's first contribution would be 'Archbishop Bramhall' (rev. of W. J. Sparrow-Simpson, *Archbishop Bramhall*), *Theology* 15 (July 1927), 11–17; repr. as 'John Bramhall' (*FLA*).

I am not sure that I am competent to review the books you mentioned for such a periodical as *Theology*, although I should be interested to do it. Two persons whom I have in mind to write about (with a view to a volume in which the essay on Andrewes would be included) are Hooker and Laud.

With many thanks for your invitation and your kind appreciation of my article.

I am, dear Sir,
Yours very truly,
[T. S. Eliot]

## TO *Jose Ortega y Gasset* CC

14 December 1926 [*The New Criterion*]

Sir,

I think that you are probably acquainted with *The New Criterion* of which I am the Editor. Since this paper was founded I have been anxious to secure your collaboration; you may not remember that I wrote to you very early in the history of my review – three or four years ago – but received no reply. I am now, however, making another attempt; it would be a great pleasure to me to introduce something of yours in this country. I have already mentioned the matter to our friend Señor Marichalar who promised to intercede with you; and to another friend and collaborator Mr J. B. Trend.

One suggestion was that it would be of very great interest to our readers to have your views as a representative of Spain on the problems discussed by Mons. Massis in his *Défense de l'Occident*. This would please me very much, but if you would prefer to be represented by something else, almost anything else would be equally welcome. Permit me at the same time to express my respect and admiration for the *Revista de Occidente*.

I am, Sir,
Your obedient humble servant,
[T. S. Eliot]

## TO *Rollo H. Myers* CC

14 December 1926 [London]

My dear Myers,

I must apologise for not writing to you sooner about your essay, but I have hesitated a long time in the hope that I should be able to make use of it.[1] But my present position is that a great deal of material has accumulated for the last year so that I must accept the minimum, and as *The New Criterion* is not primarily concerned with Music I do not think that I can during the next year accept any more Musical Articles than those provided by our regular critic. But I should always be interested to see anything you wrote.

With many thanks and best wishes,

Sincerely yours,
[T. S. Eliot]

## TO *Messrs Longmans, Green & Co.* CC

14 December 1926 [London]

Dear Sirs,

In reply to your enquiry of the 13th instant I am sending you (under separate cover) a copy of the October number of *The New Criterion*. I will point out, however, that you have already sent us a book for which we asked, namely *Science and Ultimate Truth* by Dean Inge, which forms part of the subject of a very long review to be included in the January number. I would also point out that we receive all of the books for which we ask from Messrs Macmillan, Methuen, Routledge, Constable and the Oxford and Cambridge University Presses and from all of the publishers to whom we have applied.

*The New Criterion* does not encourage publishers to send books *unsolicited* except when publishers are thoroughly familiar with the interests of this quarterly review.

Yours faithfully,
[T. S. Eliot]

1 – Myers submitted 'The Possibilities of Musical Criticism' in mid-Oct. TSE had shown it to J. B. Trend, who advised on 10 Dec.: 'Myers is not brilliant (to judge by this article). I don't consider that either his ideas or his treatment of them is up to your standard.'

## TO *Rudolf Kassner*[1] CC

14 December 1926 [London]

Dear Dr Kassner,

I have been very tardy in acknowledging your letter of the 16th November but I wanted to read your essay on Sterne before replying and found myself obliged to put it off from day to day.[2] I have found it extremely interesting and it gives me several ideas about Sterne which I think are quite new. We shall be very glad if you will allow us to have the essay translated and published in *The New Criterion*. I am not quite sure for what number this would be – the review appears only quarterly – but it would be during the year 1927.[3]

With many thanks and my compliments,

Sincerely yours,
[T. S. Eliot]

## TO *Walter Hanks Shaw* CC

14 December 1926 [London]

My dear Mr Shaw,

I am very glad to hear that you will be able to write for our April number a chronicle similar to those you have given us before and shall look forward to it with much interest.

About the use of the title 'Paris Correspondent', I see that it would be helpful to you in obtaining access to theatres etcetera and personally I should be very glad indeed to fall in with the suggestion.[4] But there is a difficulty which at present I see no way to overcome. If we give this authorisation to you, we should be obliged to do so with all of our other

1–Dr Rudolf Kassner (1873–1959), cultural philosopher, was a close friend of Rilke, Hofmannsthal, Gide and Valéry. Publications include *Die Moral der Musik* (1904); *Die Chaimäre* (1914); *Zahl und Gericht* (1919); *Die Grundlagen der Physiognomik* (1922); and *Sämtliche Werke*, ed. E. Zinn (from 1969). TSE contributed 'Thomas Stearns Eliot Gratulation' to *Rudolf Kassner . . . Gedenbuch* (Switzerland, 1952).

2–Kassner wrote, 'I like the idea of a very very distant relation of Sterne reading it.'

3–In the event, Kassner's Sterne was not used; his sole contribution was to be 'Concerning Vanity', *C.* 10 (Oct. 1930), 35–54.

4–Shaw wrote (30 Nov.), 'I wanted to ask you permission to use the title, "Paris Correspondent of The New Criterion", on my business cards. The benefit to me would be purely commercial – such as getting free theatre tickets and other advantages which would facilitate my writing the article. Would you object to my doing so?'

correspondents; and this, in certain cases, I am not anxious to allow. There is the added complication in the case of Paris, where we have also a French correspondent – Kessel – who is supposed to notice more particular literary events about twice a year. I hope that you will see my difficulty and realise that there is no adverse personal discrimination.

With all best wishes,
Yours very sincerely,
[T. S. Eliot]

## TO *I. A. Richards* CC

15 December 1926 [London]

My dear Richards,

I do not suppose that you are anywhere within five thousand miles of Cambridge but as I have no news of you from any source I am writing on the remote chance of this letter reaching you. I have just been reading and reviewing for *The Dial* your *Poetry and Science* and I should have liked to show you my review and to discuss it with you before publication, especially as there are several points on which I may have misunderstood you.[1]

1 – TSE's review of *Science and Poetry* was commissioned on 6 Oct. by Marianne Moore, who was keen to run a substantial review by TSE: she wrote further on 16 Nov., 'Two Dial pages – i.e. about eight hundred words – would seem to us very short; ten pages would not be too many.' See 'Literature, Science, and Dogma', *The Dial* 82: 3 (Mar. 1927), 239–43. IAR's view, noted TSE, is 'that science (restricted though it be) has squashed the religious, ritual, or magical view of nature upon which poetry has always depended'. The key to IAR's theory of value – since IAR is apt only to give 'merely a scientific answer' to 'a supra-scientific question' – is that value is 'organisation': 'The goal is the avoidance of "conflict" and the attainment of "equilibrium" . . .' TSE then commented, 'I am not so unsophisticated as to assert that Mr Richards' theory is *false*. It is probably quite true. Nevertheless it is only one aspect; it is a psychological theory of value, but we must also have a moral theory of value. The two are incompatible, but both must be held, and that is just the problem. If I believe, as I do believe, that the chief distinction of man is to glorify God and enjoy Him for ever, Mr Richards' theory of value is inadequate: my advantage is that I can believe my own and his too, whereas he is limited to his own . . . Poetry "is capable of saving us," he says; it is like saying that the wall-paper will save us when the walls have crumbled. It is a revised version of [Matthew Arnold's] Literature and Dogma.' Moore told TSE (28 Dec.) on receipt of his essay: 'our happiness in it is very great. Its emphasis and firmness are most gratifying, as obviously not the outcome of a dogmatic mechanics and your neatness of expression does make conclusive a theme which is in any case, persuasive. Your figure of walls versus wall paper is surely memorable.' IAR later answered him (1 Oct. 1927) that 'a good deal of misunderstanding *had* occurred. My fault – I am not very successful as an active communicator in writing' (*Selected Letters*, 43).

In any case I hope to hear from you as soon as you return to England, if you ever return.

Yours ever,
[T. S. Eliot]

## TO *Sylvia Beach*[1]

CC

15 December 1926 [*The New Criterion*]

Dear Miss Beach,

I have your letter of the 13th this morning and send you at once my signed copy of the protest.[2] I had already taken note of the marked newspaper you sent me. Unfortunately the January number of *The New Criterion* had gone to press, so that I cannot mention the matter in that issue; but I will ask you to keep me in touch with any developments so that I may give an up to date account of the matter in the Editorial column of the April number.

1–Sylvia Beach (1887–1962), American expatriate who in Nov. 1919 opened (with Adrienne Monnier) Shakespeare & Company, a bookshop and lending library, at 8 rue Dupuytren, Paris, moving two years later to 12 rue de l'Odéon. Her customers included JJ (she published *Ulysses*), Gide, Maurois, Valéry, EP, Hemingway and Gertrude Stein. Beach wrote of TSE after their first meeting in 1923: 'He is such a charming fellow and so interesting, the old fashioned sort of American and very good looking. I only wish he lived in Paris. He is our only modern writer I like after Joyce . . . Everyone that he was exhibited to was carried away by Eliot' (Noel Riley Fitch, *Sylvia Beach and the Lost Generation: A History of Literary Paris in the Twenties and Thirties* [1984], 158). Beach and Monnier published their translation of 'The Love Song of J. Alfred Prufrock' in the first issue of their magazine *Le Navire d'Argent* ('The Silver Ship'), June 1925 – 'we never heard any reproaches from our victim,' said Beach. TSE was grateful to them for introducing his verse to French readers: to follow the *Times* obituary (11 Oct. 1962), he wrote in tribute ('Miss Sylvia Beach', *The Times*, 13 Oct. 1962): 'I made the acquaintance of Sylvia Beach, and . . . Adrienne Monnier, on a visit to Paris early in the 1920s, and thereafter saw them frequently during that decade. Only the scattered survivors of the Franco-Anglo-American world of Paris of that period, and a few others like myself who made frequent excursions across the Channel, know how important a part these two women played in the artistic and intellectual life of those years.'

2–Samuel Roth was pirating *Ulysses* in his magazine *Two Worlds*, and had announced the publication of work by TSE. Beach was sending round a protest. See also 'Pirate Publisher Of Fake "Ulysses" Is Exposed By Miss Sylvia Beach', *Chicago Tribune*, 20 Nov. 1926; 'Miss Beach Plans to Sue Mutilator of Joyce's Work', *Chicago Tribune*, 23 Nov. 1926; and 'Publisher Claims Book Is "Pirated"', *New York Herald*, 24 Nov. 1926. A legal injunction against Roth's piracy was granted on 27 Dec. 1926: *Letters of James Joyce*, ed. Richard Ellmann, III (1966), 185–6; and TSE was one of numerous signatories to a statement regarding the piracy issued on 2 Feb. 1927: ibid., 151–3; *Ulysses*, 1st unlimited edn (Bodley Head, 1937), App. A, 743–6. See also *Pound/Joyce: The Letters of Ezra Pound to James Joyce, with Pound's Essays on Joyce*, ed. Forrest Read (1967), 224–9.

I was quite unaware that Samuel Roth either had published or was intending to publish anything by myself. To the best of my memory I have never had any correspondence with Mr Roth and have certainly never met him. All that I know of his magazine is the advertisement which appeared in one or two papers in this country, I believe a year or so ago. I should be very grateful if you could let me have any newspaper cuttings or other documents showing that Mr Roth either has published or proposes to publish anything by myself.

So far as I know, nothing that I have written has been excluded from the mails or officially suppressed or reproved in any other way in America; the question of piracy can only arise with regard to a number of occasional articles and a little verse published in reviews in England and Europe which have never appeared in America.

I should be glad to join in any concerted movement by the other writers of whose work or of whose names Mr Roth has made use.

With many thanks,
Yours sincerely
[T. S. Eliot]

## TO *Ezra Pound* TS Beinecke

15 December 1926 *The New Criterion*

Cher E.,

For God's sake don't start another review unless you are likely to get at least £250 a year out of it and not a great deal of work.[1] All reviews are worse than useless and my only excuse is that I derive the larger part of my income from this source.

Having thus relieved myself and given a piece of advice which you certainly will not take (by the way, I understand that D. H. Lawrence is going to start an independent review and I had the impression that

1–EP had written on 4 Dec. about his plan to launch a review called *The Exile*: 'There seems to be a certain desire (M. Walsh being dead) that an extreme left review shd. exist. Also the means for its existence, and a certain amount of stuff that cd not be used in the Criterion.

'I dont see that it can do the Criterion any harm; it wont go to, or come from the same strata of life, though the two publics may overlap.

'If there are any authors whom you wish to reserve for your pussnl. use, you might let me know. I shan't pay 'em as well as you do, in any case, so they wd. be very unlikely to give me anything you haven't already refused. In fact I have thought of making it a condition of acceptance that all mss. must either have been refused by, or obviously impossible for, you and several other editorial confreres.'

Hueffer was also going to start an independent review) I am perfectly amiable and wish you godspeed. I don't imagine that your review is likely to do the *Criterion* the slightest harm and I see no necessity for any trade conventions. I do not want to take advantage of your kind suggestion that I might wish to reserve any authors for my personal use. If you want to make your review a paying concern I hope you will have the sense not to take the sort of thing I publish in the *Criterion*; if on the other hand you simply want to make it the ideal review I feel quite confident that you wouldn't accept the sort of stuff I publish at any price. So go ahead.

As soon as you have time, you might write me a letter giving the main facts regarding D[orothy], the child and yourself as given in your previous letter and even in slightly more detail.[1] Your previous letter, with its mysterious allusions to the other letter which I certainly shall not introduce into my home, is, you will understand, useless from this point of view.[2] A prompt reply would be appreciated.

I hope and trust that your physical health and spiritual energy are unabated and improved. Farewell.

T.

1 – EP had written on 26 Nov. about the birth of his son, named Omar (b. 10 Sept. 1926): 'Infant male . . . Infant not a Hercules, but don't think you need feel worried about it . . . D[orothy] very well, and had, I understand, extremely easy time, as these things go.' In response to this letter, he wrote (21 Dec.): 'I went out to play tennis, came back to hotel and found she had gone to hospital, phoned to hospital; they said: "yes, she is here, but out walking in garden, she has apparently made a mistake, but will keep her here till morning." I went out at three and infant had arrived. Apparently she had her lunch in comfort at about one o'clock . . . I spent a week in hospital, am now recovered. Saluti.' He said again on 21 Dec.: 'Infant no Hercules, but said to be sound in wind and limb.'

2 – In his previous letter (26 Nov.), EP said he had sent TSE some thoughts about his personal problems, which (by implication) should not be read by VHE at home: 'As you will gather from yesterday's note; I had been thinking in your direction, and trying to elucidate various matters. If this is forwarded to you, !! you will, or shd. find the other at F. and G's as it is labled strongly NOT to be forwarded.' The 'other' letter (24 Nov.) reached TSE in due course: 'I think you are "under a curse" but not a kind that I have come up against before. I knew a "doom of the house" once, but it proceeded from a known cause. I have also seen people "in danger"; but from the "powers of the air" or some sort of chaotic wind or torrent or unformed energy. Against which one cd. interpose a simple block of will; and make it effective.

'In your case I think you have got to find your own clue <comprehension not volition>. I mean you probably <naturally> have more data to go on than I have; despite everything. I don't believe there is anything outside yourself that can intervene; or offer any more "clue" or sort of thread to the labyrinth, save the sort that I am now dangling.

'I don't think I cd. have articulated ANYTHING two months ago. Save determination NOT at any price, in state of mental muddle and weakened volition, to give consent to, or say yes to, anything whatever.

'Or to accept any kind of jurisdiction, ab exteriore. so ist es.'

P.S. I forgot to mention that Wyndham Lewis has started another independent review.[1]

## TO *A. L. Hutchinson* CC

15 December 1926 [London]

Dear Sir,

I am deeply honoured by your invitation to take part in a debate at the Union and I should be very happy if I could do so, but I am afraid that it is impossible for me to make any definite engagement to come down to Cambridge at present.[2] Perhaps you will let me come on a later occasion as a mere auditor.

If I were able to be present I should certainly protest against the pestilential word 'modernist' for which I can see no excuse. What on earth is 'modernist verse'? The word is almost as hopeless as 'Futurist'. The word itself seems to me to obstruct any sensible criticism because its effect is to associate a number of writers who may have very little in common and merely to marshal two hostile groups of prejudices against each other. Surely what critics need is to be taught to discriminate between one contemporary writer and another. If versifiers apply the term 'modernist' to themselves, then I think my sympathies are rather with the critics. The term 'Modernist' is a good ten years out of date.

With very many thanks for your kind invitation and my most cordial expression of regret to the Society.

I am,
Yours very truly,
[T. S. Eliot]

## TO *D. S. Mirsky* CC

15 December 1926 [London]

Dear Sir,

I thank you for sending me your essay on 'Chekhov and the English' which I shall have much pleasure in using in *The New Criterion*. At the

1 – *The Enemy*.

2 – A. L. Hutchinson, President of the Cambridge Union Society, invited TSE on 13 Dec. to take part in a debate on the motion 'This House sympathises with the critics rather than with the writers of modernist verse', to be held on 18 Jan. 1927.

moment I cannot tell you in what number; I can only say that it will be as soon as possible and during the course of 1927.

Until Christmas I am extremely pushed for time, but I have been looking forward to asking you if you will lunch with me one day, and I hope that you will be able to do so early in the new year.[1] I believe that we have a number of common acquaintances, and especially Madame de Bassiano has often spoken of you to me.

With many thanks,
Yours very truly,
[T. S. Eliot]

## TO *Wyndham Lewis*

TS Cornell

17 December 1926 *The New Criterion*

Dear Lewis,

I am highly pleased and flattered at having the advance copy of your book with inscription,[2] and intend to read it during the Christmas holidays. I should like to arrange to meet you soon after that.

With many thanks,
Yours ever,
T. S. Eliot

## *Orlo Williams* TO *J. B. Trend*

CC

17 December 1926 [London]

Mr Orlo Williams, Master of Ceremonies of the New Criterion dinner, presents his compliments to the Musical Director of that occasion, Mr J. B. Trend, and submits a roundelay to be performed as part of the evening's ceremony.

17 December

Mr T. S. Eliot presents his compliments to the Master of Ceremonies and begs to inform him that the roundelay which he so kindly prepared has

1–Mirsky replied (16 Dec.): 'I have been hoping to meet you for a long time & shall be exceedingly glad to have lunch with you as you suggest.' He would be returning from a visit to the Continent on about 12 Jan. 1927.

2–*The Lion and the Fox: The Role of the Hero in the Plays of Shakespeare* (1927), inscribed 'To T.S. Eliot from his devoted friend, the author of the Lion & the Fox. Dec 15. 1926.'

been given into the hands of the Choir Master, Mr J. B. Trend, who will take charge of the Sunday rehearsal.[1]

## TO *Stanley Rice*[2] CC

19 December 1926 [London]

Dear Mr Rice,

I am returning with many regrets your essay on Women in Heroic Literature with apologies for having kept it so long. I am afraid that it would be impossible for me to use it in the near future and I think that you ought to have the opportunity of submitting it elsewhere. I have such an accumulation of accepted and promised manuscripts that I feel that for the moment I must stick to subjects directly within our scope and as far as possible outside the scope of other periodicals.

I have been for some time exceedingly busy, but I hope that after the new year we may be able to meet again.

Yours sincerely,
[T. S. Eliot]

1–Dobrée relished the 'constant parties' associated with the *Criterion*, especially: 'the dinners which used to take place in a reserved room in a Soho restaurant [*The Commercio*, an Italian restaurant on Frith Street]. These were by no means cold or high-brow gatherings. We naturally discussed literature more than anything else, but the atmosphere was entirely gay. There were Herbert Read, Harold Monro, J. G. Fletcher, F. S. Flint, T. O. Beachcroft, Frank Morley, Montgomery Belgion and J. B. Trend, among the twenty or so people gathered there. One night, I remember, we sang a catch, written (words and music) by Orlo Williams, for three voices.

First Voice. Sweeney said to Misses Porter
Pretty bit of po'try about you and me.
Second Voice. Who's this Eliot any way?
Well, from all I hear, he's a personal sort of beggar.
Third Voice. I like young Eliot, he's got style
But, I ask you, is it po'try?

'This went well. Eliot was hugely amused. When he liked he could be the soul of gaiety. Very little of the conversations at these dinners remains in mind, but I remember one little interchange. Someone – let us call him X – mentioned the *Bhagavad Gita*, to which Eliot, with great interest: "Oh, have you read the *Bhagavad Gita*?" "Er, well," X answered, "I can't say I have in the original – but in translation I've studied it, and though of course in translation . . ." Then Morley broke in: "It's all right, X. You're among gentlemen here."' ('T. S. Eliot: A Personal Reminiscence', 80)

2–Stanley Rice worked for The East India Association, Westminster, London.

## TO *John Middleton Murry* CC

20 December 1926 [London]

My dear John,

Thank you for the MS.[1] I am not sure that I shall be willing and ready to return it to you by Wednesday and I hope that you will let me keep it a little longer. I should like to use it in the April number but I have already for that number about twice as much material as I can use. Do you think that it would suffer by being held over until June? I do not want to cramp your space in any way.

In any case, would you be willing to review A. E. Taylor's *Plato* for the April number?[2] I should be very happy if you would. Taylor is a very good man you know, and his book deserves a serious review; it is the only competent book on the subject since Burnet's *Greek Philosophy*, vol. I., appeared in 1914. There is also a new book on the Cambridge Platonists which I have looked at but I do not think that the Cambridge Platonists have much to do with Plato.

Yours ever,
[Tom]

## TO *Sylvia Beach* CC

23 December 1926 [London]

Dear Miss Beach,

I return to you at once, under separate cover, the two periodicals you kindly sent me.[3] I am interested to see that what they propose to print of myself is an old sketch which originally appeared in *The Little Review*, and it occurs to me that this appearance in *The Little Review* ought to make it copyright in America. Is this not so? I propose to write to Miss Anderson and ask her if she would be good enough to protest on behalf of *The Little Review* against his reprinting.

With many thanks,
Yours sincerely
[T. S. Eliot]

1 – 'Towards a Synthesis'.

2 – After examining the work, JMM decided he was 'not *competent* to do it' and had no time in which to prepare himself by 'a long re-reading of the Greek' (14 Jan.).

3 – Beach had sent TSE (17 Dec.) copies of *The Saturday Review of Literature* (New York) and *The Nation*, both of which advertised Roth's piratical plans via-à-vis TSE.

## TO *Ada Leverson* CC

29 December 1926 [*The New Criterion*]

Dear Mrs Leverson,

It is delightful to hear from you again and to have an address to which I can write to send you our most cordial good wishes for the New Year.[1] I have been meaning to write to you for a long time and now of course when I am in London and have the opportunity I find that you have flown to Italy. But I envy you as the London Christmas has been wrapped in the usual fogs and glooms. It is interesting to know that you have disposed of your flat and I hope that the new address will be your permanent one in London; for Half Moon Street seems exactly where one would like to think of you!

Do let me know how you find Italy, and send from time to time anything that you may think suitable for *The New Criterion.*

With very best wishes from Vivienne and myself,

Sincerely yours,
[T. S. Eliot]

## TO *Ottoline Morrell* MS Texas

30 December 1926 *The New Criterion*

My dear Ottoline,

I was very much pleased & touched to get the charming diary. I had been carrying & using, up to the same day, the diary you gave me a year ago, & I was very happy to be able to substitute for it another from the same person & with the same remembrances. It is something I make use of daily & never without remembering from whom it came.

I am looking forward to your final arrival in London. Don't postpone it on any account.

Ever yours affectionately
Tom

1 – Leverson was living at 36 Half Moon Street, London, W.1.

## TO *G. B. Harrison*

CC

30 December 1926 [London]

Dear Mr Harrison,

When you came to see me a few weeks ago I suggested a title for my paper on March 18th and said at the same time that if another subject occurred to me which I would prefer to substitute I would let you know before the end of the year. What I find I should really like to talk about is 'Shakespeare and the Stoicism of Seneca'. This subject is connected with that on which I have recently been working for my Introduction to *Seneca's Tenne Tragedies* but will not in any way be covered by anything that I have said in that Introduction: it is rather a subject suggested by the work that I have been doing.

But if you think best, I am quite willing to stick to my original suggestion of a comparison between the versification of Shakespeare and Marlowe.

Yours sincerely,
[T. S. Eliot]

## TO *Bruce Richmond*

CC

30 December 1926 [*The New Criterion*]

Dear Richmond,

Thank you very much for your letter. I hope it indicates that your cold is distinctly on the mend; at any rate it suggests that you are in possession of a fair amount of your usual but singular energy. No, the Newton and the Beethoven are certainly not in my line: I think I know whose business they are. But Middleton I should be very glad to tackle; not the Reverend Conyers's Middleton, of course, but the original Thomas.[1] Yes this is a good subject because there is nothing very final about him. As for our old project, I am greatly pleased that you still have it in mind and I should like to perpend (as John Murry would say) the subject.[2] It is only that having for some time been thinking about other things, I must get my mind back

1–BR had been 'centenary-hunting for 1927', he wrote ('Late December'): 'Newton & Beethoven are not particularly your pigeons, I imagine. But how about Middleton who died in July 1627? Will you do a leader on him, and convert me to him?' (At Harvard in 1909 George Pierce Baker had set TSE to editing Middleton's *Michaelmas Term*, which he found 'a profitless task', he told EVE.) See [TSE], 'Thomas Middleton', *TLS*, 30 June 1927, 445–6.

2–'And is there any chance of your getting back to our old project of three or four leaders on the growth of blank verse?' BLR had proposed the project after reading TSE's 'Some Notes on the Blank Verse of Christopher Marlowe', *Art & Letters* 2 (Aut. 1919), 194–9.

to thinking about this before I can tell you whether I believe that I have anything to say; but on principle, I should like to have a shot at it.

Your interference with a leader on my behalf overwhelms me.[1] Needless to say that I am fully appreciative and that I am filled with curiosity to see the leader itself. It is possible that I have already divined the name of the author but I will not divulge it to you.

I am glad to hear that you are to have a holiday if that is what it is. I shall be glad to have the Bodley Head plays; meanwhile I have Jespersen and the book you have just sent me,[2] and I have just turned in a short review of *The Phoenix Nest*.[3] I did not think that the last of these required more than half a column.

I hope I may see you when you return to London.

Yours ever,
[T. S. Eliot]

## *Vivien Eliot* TO *Henry Eliot* — MS Houghton

30 December 1926 — 57 Chester Terrace, S.W.1.

Dear Henry

I was so astonished to get your presents. I had, of course, thought about sending things to you and Theresa, but I did not think you would care to get anything from me. I shall give myself the pleasure of sending you something before, let's say, St Valentine's day. Meanwhile I must tell you how very much I like & appreciate the things you have sent. The pillow is a good idea, & I like it very much. The jumper or sweater is also particularly nice. Please thank Theresa for me, & accept my thanks.

Theodora also sent me a charming gift, at which I was surprised. My family have all been in London for this season & we had two family parties. Also a quiet Xmas here together with Lucy Thayer, of whom you have heard much. She is at present staying here & we both find in her a friend. She is sensible, good-tempered, unselfish, & we have great cause to be grateful to her.[4]

1–Disliking vague references, BLR had noted in a draft *TLS* leader the phrase 'A recent critic praising Dryden' and replaced it with a mention of TSE and the title *Homage to John Dryden* ('Imagination and Intellect', *TLS*, 30 Dec. 1926, 953–4).
2–In all, three books – Otto Jespersen, *S. P. E. Tract no. XXIV: Notes on Relative Clauses*; Joseph Warren Beach, *The Outlook for American Prose*; Fred Newton Scott, *American Slang* – were reviewed by TSE in 'American Prose', *TLS*, 2 Sept. 1926, 577.
3–'The Phoenix Nest', *TLS*, 20 Jan. 1927, 41.
4–VHE would record in her diary for 5 Apr. 1935 (Bodleian) that she remembered living 'in

Tom has been well, increasingly for the last 3 months. It is a long time since I have seen him so well & easy in mind & I think you wd be pleased at that, in any case.

With a great many thanks. Your photographs of your house are delightful, you have beautiful things.

Yrs.
V.H.E.

## TO *The Postmaster, South Western District Office* CC

30 December 1926 [London]

Dear Sir,

I should be greatly obliged if you would kindly rescind my order to send all letters addressed to me at 57 Chester Terrace, S.W.1. to my office at 24 Russell Square, W.C.1 instead. As I am now in residence at 57 Chester Terrace I should be glad to have letters to that address delivered to that address. I am writing this letter instead of filling in one of your order forms because I particularly wish to avoid confusion. I do *not* wish that letters addressed to me at 24 Russell Square should be forwarded to 57 Chester Terrace but *only* such letters as are originally addressed to 57 Chester Terrace to be sent to that address.

With apologies for troubling you,

I am, dear Sir,
Yours faithfully,
[T. S. Eliot]

## TO *H. M. Kallen*[1] CC

30 December 1926 [London]

Dear Kallen,

When your letter arrived I was in a remote place in France.[2] I am very sorry indeed to have missed you and hope that we may have better luck

*a happy mess* at 57 Chester Terrace' with Lucy Thayer.

1–Horace Meyer Kallen (1882–1974): German-born philosopher; co-founder in 1918 of the New School for Social Research, New York: see Biographical Register.

2–Kallen had asked TSE to lunch (26 Aug).

next time, as I should have liked to see you again. The next time you come to London, do let me know in advance if you can.

Yours always sincerely,
[T. S. Eliot]

## TO *Laura Riding Gottschalk* CC

30 December 1926 [*The New Criterion*]

Dear Miss Gottschalk,

I am returning your poems to you as you require them, though with much regret. I have been guilty of holding them longer than I should have done because I had been hoping for the necessary space to print 'The Tiger', but it is very seldom that we have the opportunity to print anything of that length.

May I express the hope that you will have something else, shorter than this, which you can soon let me see?

With all best wishes,
Yours sincerely,
[T. S. Eliot]

## TO *Ezra Pound* CC

31 December 1926 [London]

Cher E.,

Thank for your letter of the 28th instant.[1] I don't want to rob you of any good stuff and it may be that these things require the institution of a new review and would be more suitable for yours than for mine: *The New Criterion* does not, you know, represent the finest siftings of my own taste, *but* if you choose to let me see any stuff it shall have immediate consideration and an immediate answer; on the other hand, even when I accept stuff I cannot by any means promise immediate publication. So I

1–EP said he had 'had two months fun out of the prospect' of editing a new review. But a questionnaire he had sent out had 'elicited ONE mss. that I want to see in print' – a piece by a man named Guy Hickock (Paris correspondent of the *Brooklyn Eagle*), who had published 'an amusing thing' in the *Transatlantic*. Would TSE like to use the Hickock piece? 'And if you care to put 'em in the next Criterion I shall be inclined to drop the idea of yet another review.' Koteliansky had translated 'some Rosanov, a bit too diffuse for my intended purposes, but which you might as well see. I dare say Rosanov has to be considerably weeded: I hear the bit in the Calendar is about the top of his speed.'

leave it to you. Having already expressed my opinion of reviews in general I have relieved myself of all responsibility, and if you choose to start one I shall be glad to do anything in my power to aid it, or perhaps you will prefer me to say I will do anything in my power not to obstruct it.

Have seen the Rosanov stuff in *The Calendar* and have seen more that Koteliansky showed me a year ago. I thought it was rubbish. All about suffering christs and that sort of thing.

[T]

P.S. Thanks for specimen letter received and exhibited.

# 1927

## TO *Bonamy Dobrée* MS Brotherton

Sunday [? January 1927] 57 Chester Terrace, S.W.1.

To wish you God speed. If you can, find out about the Ostridge (does he run backwards to keep the sand out of his eyes, & has he haemmorrhoids in consequence?)

Hope to see you in June.
T. S. E.

## TO *John Gould Fletcher*[1] CC

2 January 1927 [London]

My dear Fletcher,

I am returning herewith your cheque made out to *The Monthly Criterion* and will ask you whether you will be so kind as to cancel this cheque and make out a new one to the order of F. V. Morley. The reason is that for the present we think it much safer that no moneys pass through the *Criterion* account and consequently that no cheques be endorsed on behalf of the *Criterion*. The arrangement is that Morley will collect the money and will then make out a cheque to Faber & Gwyer Limited who will pay contributors, etcetera out of it. In view of the attitude taken up by Lady Rothermere, we think it is best to adopt every precaution.

You might, if you will, send the new cheque to F. V. Morley, c/o The Century Company, 10 Essex Street, W.C.2.

You need not be so punctilious as you are about returning books so quickly. Many thanks, however, for the *Stained Glass*[2] which reached me this morning. I have one or two new French books which may interest you.

1–John Gould Fletcher (1886–1950), American poet and critic: see Biographical Register.
2–Herbert Read, *English Stained Glass* (1926).

I hope you can turn up for lunch on Thursday. We had a very small party last week.

With very many thanks,

Yours always,
[T. S. Eliot]

Cheque enclosed T. S. E.

## TO *Henry Eliot*

MS Houghton

2 January 1927 *The New Criterion*

Dear Henry,

This is just to thank you for your cheque and also for the wonderful pencils – just what I wanted & the best I have ever had, the leads just the right softness. I shall always carry one or the other.

Altogether we are overwhelmed by your and Theresa's kindness to us this Christmas. Vivien was delighted with the jumper, which is a beauty, and the pillow.

We are going on very happily here, & I have done a great deal of work in the last 3 months. I am going to subscribe to the *Times Literary Supplement* for you. I'll write again when I have more time, but am very rushed with writing commissions at the moment. Ever your affectionate brother.

Love to Theresa.
Tom.

## TO *John Middleton Murry*

CC

3 January 1927 [London]

My dear John,

I should very much like to have your note on Saintsbury's book though if you have not done one I do not to press you to do it. If the March number comes out, as I hope, I shall want your note; but you have a great many other things to think about and I don't want to urge you to waste time on something which possibly will never appear and in that case could not be paid for.[1]

1 – JMM did not contribute a review of any book by George Saintsbury.

I should be very glad to have any news about your own affairs. I hope that you are in less anxiety.

Yours ever,
[T. S. E.]

## TO *Charles Whibley*

CC

3 January 1927 [London]

My dear Whibley,

Thank you for your letter. As for sending the Introduction[1] to the printers, I leave that to your discretion. So far as I know, and subject to your own opinion, the only alterations I have to make in the second and third parts are such as could easily be made in the proof; and the only important alteration which to my knowledge must be made in the first part is the one which you yourself indicated, viz: that I should make clear that the distinction between Greek tragedy and that of Seneca is not the distinction between non-declamatory and declamatory verse. So far as I can see this does not mean altering more than a few sentences and perhaps inserting a few. It would certainly suit me to have the thing in proof as I can get a much more objective impression of my own work from the printed page than from the typed.

I have a full copy of the printers' proof but I have not the original text. I have not seen it since I sent it back to you to send to Constable for setting up.

Will you let me know if you wish to undertake the duty of correcting the proof of the plays themselves? If so, I shall have the text back and it would certainly take me a full week. I do not suppose that there is any need to collate the *Tenne Tragedies* text with the original texts of the separate plays? But I shall in any case examine the first editions at the Museum.

In haste,
Ever yours affectionately,
[T. S. Eliot]

1 – TSE's Introduction to *Seneca His Tenne Tragedies* (London: Constable & Co.; New York: Alfred A. Knopf, 1927).

## TO *R. Cobden-Sanderson*

CC

5 January 1927 [London]

Dear Cobden

In accordance with our conversation of today I am returning to you herewith the copy of the Revenue Account and Balance Sheet in reference to *The Criterion* for the two years ending October 15th 1926 which you sent me with your letter of the 15th ultimo. I am also sending you herewith the list of unexpired subscriptions which you provided showing that copies of *The New Criterion* have been and are to be sent out to the equivalent of £34. 7. 2. I say 'equivalent' for the sake of exactness, inasmuch as the nominal value is greater; for, as I said, we decided to complete unexpired subscriptions to *The Criterion* without taking any notice of the rise in price.

We should be extremely grateful if you would ask your auditors to draw up another Balance Sheet showing this debt of Lady Rothermere as proprietor of *The Criterion Ltd* on account of unexpired subscriptions. The new Balance Sheet will of course show the debit excess.

This one change as agreed upon in our conversation this morning will be sufficient for our needs.

When this is settled I understand that you and I will draw a cheque upon the old *Criterion* account to pay the auditors. I hope that we may be able to arrange with Lady Rothermere that she shall pay the difference direct to *The New Criterion Ltd* and that you and I shall then draw the balance of the old *Criterion* account in favour of *The New Criterion Limited*.

Yours ever,
[T. S. E.]

## FROM *Geoffrey Faber*

TS Faber

6 January 1927 Faber & Gwyer Ltd

My dear Eliot,[1]

The enclosed letter, and further enclosures, came from our mutual friend[2] this morning. I attach a copy of my reply – which I will not send till I have seen you.

1 – GCF noted in his diary, Thurs., 6 Jan.: 'Wrote to Eliot about the New Criterion, & the possibility of dropping it.'
2 – Lady Rothermere.

As you know, I have perceived more and more clearly that we are in a cul-de-sac. And if Lady R. could be persuaded to cut her losses – as she is evidently losing interest – and relieve us of our guarantee, or the major part of it, I think it might be best.

What I should propose, in that case, would be that, in place of your editorship, you should (a) take a rather more active part in the direction of F. & G. (b) concentrate on producing a book or books. Later on, if and when the financial position is improved, we might either buy or start a monthly. But that would have to wait on the knees of the gods for a time.

I realise that you will feel unhappy about this, and its possible consequences; but I also think you will probably agree that we can't go on as we are. Do come and talk to me about it this weekend. Could you take a meal or a walk at Hampstead any time Saturday or Sunday? (Ann has been having a mild go of German Measles, but you wouldn't run any risk. Or does your hygienic spirit revolt?)

Yours ever,
G. C. F.

## TO *G. T. Browne* CC

7 January 1927 [London]

Dear Sir,

Thank you for your letter of the 6th instant.[1] I am interested to know that you possess a copy of the eighteenth century engraving of the arms of Edward Eliot. I think that it must be the same that I already possess myself: there could hardly be two of exactly that epoch. The copy which I own is coloured and the arms are not quite correctly given.

I thank you very much for your offer and suggest that there are numerous other members of the Eliot family some of whom might be glad to possess your copy, and if I have any enquiries I will refer them to you.[2]

Yours faithfully,
[T. S. Eliot]

1 – G. T. Browne wrote from Frinsted Rectory, Sittingbourne, Kent (6 Jan.), that he possessed 'an 18th century engraving of the Arms of Edward Eliot, Baron Eliot'. Would TSE care to see it, and perhaps even to buy it for 25/-?

2 – Browne returned on 8 Jan.: 'The print of which I wrote you is not a coloured one, but perhaps what is of greater interest is the pedigree. I do not think the Eliot family is a very numerous one but of course you should know better than I do.'

## TO *Mario Praz*

CC

7 January 1927 [London]

My dear Mr Praz,

I was extremely unhappy that I was obliged to fail yesterday and am very sorry that you were so sceptical of my ability to appear today. I managed to get out this morning and feel none the worse for it. I got your message at about twelve o'clock and would have called for you at the Museum but unfortunately I have had no ticket for the library for several years as during that time I have never had the leisure to be able to make use of it. I was therefore unable to penetrate the sanctuary in which you had concealed yourself. I can only say that I am extremely disappointed and it will be a great pleasure to me if you do stay over the weekend and consent to lunch with me on Monday.

Incidentally, I have wanted to extract from you before you left London some definite promise of your Chaucer essay.

Yours sincerely,
[T. S. Eliot]

## TO *William Force Stead*

TS Beinecke

7 January 1927 *The New Criterion*

Dear Stead,

Thank you for your letter of 5th January.[1] The only thing that mattered was to clear up my position in your own mind; I thought it was quite

1 – WFS apologised for the possibility that he might have told OM that TSE had 'repudiated' his early work (as WFS had gathered from Gordon George). 'My impression was that you had changed your point of view; that you were dissatisfied with both the form and mood of the Waste Land and that you are now working in more strict stanza form and from an outlook on life based not upon doubt and negation but upon a theistic philosophy . . .

'I should be most interested to know if I was right in the strongest impression that I derived from my talk with Gordon George – that you had conquered your sceptical mood and were going to come out clearly on the side of theism. I hope you will not laugh at my simplicity when I say that this roused me to such delight and enthusiasm that I couldn't sleep all night for thinking about it! I foresaw a great fluttering of the dove-cotes, or rather the bats and owls of agnosticism and Freudian sensualism.

'The reason that most literary people don't believe anything is not because they are learned in philosophy but because they believe – and this is about as much as they believe – that the people whose judgment they respect have sound reasons for not believing anything. Most of us are cowards. We have not strength enough within us to stand up and make a great affirmation in the face of almost universal denials. We are afraid that if we confess a faith in God, or anyway in the God of Xtian theology, we "compromise our intellects". And so

possible that Lady Ottoline might have misunderstood you because she seemed to think that you had seen me quite lately which of course was not true. One may change one's ideas, sentiments and point of view from time to time; one would be rather atrophied if one did not; but change of mind is a very different thing from repudiation. Certainly I am 'dissatisfied' with everything I have done; but that also is a very different thing from repudiation. I do not see why one should 'repudiate' anything that one has written provided that one continues to believe that the thing written was a sincere expression at the time of writing. One might as well repudiate infancy and childhood. As for your other impressions, they are mainly correct, though I should qualify them with the remark that 'conquer' is too positive a word and that this word should be reserved for a later date. And in any case I am not at the moment interested in fluttering dovecotes or any form of publicity. As for the rest of your letter, I find it extremely sympathetic and thank you for it. I hope that you will be relieved at finding that your more important impressions were correct.

When you come to town again there is one matter in which I might ask you to be of use to me.[1]

Yours very sincerely,
T. S. Eliot

---

while being shy of the word we are practically atheists because we are afraid to affirm that there is a supreme reality and that it is supremely good and true and beautiful. Yet atheism is not the latest advance in knowledge. Plato in the Laws said of the atheists of his day "many before our time have suffered from this disease." And I found in the time of my utter and practical atheism that it really is a kind of disease – a state of internal sickness, weakness and sourness – an impoverishment of one's whole being in which one can only say that nothing means anything and nothing matters. This is especially prevalent now because there's an impression abroad that it is the intelligent view.

'But you are looked upon as the leader of the younger generation of intellectuals, and so I felt that if you came out strongly on the side of Christian theism, the old sickness from which literature has suffered since the days of Swinburne would take an immense leap forward toward health and strength again. I certainly got the impression from Gordon George that you had worked your way round to a well reasoned belief in something very much like the theology of the Church of England. I was astonished and delighted – I foresaw a wonderful Renaissance of the Faith! Absurd maybe – yet I hope it's true.'

1 – TSE had made a resolution to join the Church of England.

## TO *E. R. Curtius*

CC

7 January 1927 [London]

My dear Curtius,

Thank you very much for your kind letter after this long silence. I have thought of you often in the interval.

I cannot tell you how pleased and honoured I feel at your caring to translate *The Waste Land* into German.[1] I should like nothing better. Unfortunately there is one difficulty in the way which I will place before you exactly as it is. About six months ago a man who is completely unknown to me, named Alfred Sperber, wrote to me suddenly from Storojineti, Bucovina, enclosed a translation of *The Waste Land* which he had made, asked for my criticism and begged me for permission to publish his German translations in some German review. I had always wanted to see *The Waste Land* in German because I felt that it could be rendered more adequately into German than into any other language; no one else had ever offered to make such a translation; his rendering seemed to me pretty good and I therefore wrote to him, making several suggestions and authorising him to submit the translation to some German review. He intimated that he would submit it first to *Die Neue Rundschau* and then if rejected to *Die Europäische Revue*. The last I heard from him was on 10th November and I do not know what has become of his translation.[2]

I do not know why there should not be two translations, but that depends partly on German copyright law of which I am ignorant, and Mr Sperber certainly has my authority to translate *The Waste Land* for a periodical, though *not* of course to present that or any other of my poems in book form. I think that I had better write to him and find out what has happened, but in the meantime I hasten to let you know the circumstances and perhaps you can make some suggestion.

I should much like to know how you are occupied at present and whether there is any chance of your contributing again before very long to *The New Criterion*. It is true that I was in Paris for a few days in October,

1 – Curtius wrote on 29 Dec. 1926 that he was translating *TWL*; he enclosed a 'sample' – his version of 'The Burial of the Dead'. 'Please let me know if you find it satisfactory. I have tried particularly hard to reproduce properly the rhythm and the variations of rhythm.' '*Das wüste Land*', *Neue Schweizer Rundschau* (Apr. 1927), 362 ff.; reprinted in *Das wüste Land* (Wiesbaden, 1957; Frankfurt, 1975). See Earl Jeffrey Richards, *Modernism, Medievalism and Humanism: A Research Bibliography on the Reception of the Works of Ernst Robert Curtius* (Tübingen: Niermeyer, 1983).

2 – Margul-Sperber's translation, 'Ödland', would appear only posthumously in his collection *Weltstimmen: Nachdichtungen* (Bucharest: Literaturverlag, 1968), 74–86.

but I hardly saw anyone while I was there; if I missed an opportunity of meeting you I very much regret it.

Ever yours,
[T. S. Eliot]

## TO *E. G. Selwyn* CC

7 January 1927 [London]

My dear Sir,

Thank you for your letter of the 5th January. I should be glad to review the book you mention at the length you suggest, referring of course to other books in the series. Whether I should care to avail myself of your kind offer to write two successive articles, one on Hooker and one on Bramhall, would depend on my opinion of the book which I have not seen.

If you will send me the book, I will think the matter over and let you know whether I should like to submit two essays or only one.[1]

With many thanks,
I am
Yours very truly
[T. S. Eliot]

## TO *Alec Randall* CC

8 January 1927 [*The New Criterion*]

My dear Randall,

Many thanks for your New Year wishes which I cordially reciprocate. I do not suppose that I am likely to be in Rome again this spring, but I hope that you will have a long holiday in England at some time during the year when I am in London.

There is one point about which I should like to hear from you. Would you care to undertake any more Dutch periodicals? We have practically nothing at present and if you cared to make notes of them I would be very pleased to beat some of them up. I have lately been in correspondence

1–'Archbishop Bramhall' (review of *Archbishop Bramhall*, by W. J. Sparrow-Simpson), *Theology* 15 (July 1927), 11–17; repr. as 'John Bramhall', *FLA*.

with a friendly Dutchman named den Doolaard[1] who appears to be one of the regular collaborators of a not uninteresting literary paper called *Den Gulden Winckel*. Here are the names of some other Dutch literary papers an exchange which I think he could arrange:

*De Vriye Bladen*
*De Gemeenschap*
*De Stem*
*De Gids*
*De Witte Mier*

I should be glad if you would let me know if you care for any or all of these or any others. Thank you for the notice of *Die Schöne Literatur*. We have written to them as you suggested.

Ever yours,
[T. S. Eliot]

## TO *R. Gordon George* CC

8 January 1927 [London]

My dear George,

I am glad to hear from you at last.[2] I am afraid I have been rather dilatory about reading the essays[3] which you so kindly sent me, but for this delay your own mode of life gives me the excuse. I have had a great deal of work to do and a great many manuscripts to consider immediately and as you disappeared leaving behind you such vague and uncertain addresses I felt that haste on my part might be premature. But I can answer one paragraph in your letter at once. I will look out for the book on Maupassant and have it sent to you. The other book did not indeed look very promising to me. About Read's book on stained glass. It is rather out of our line, and Read's other books – his essays and poems

1–A. Den Doolaard, pen name of C. Spoelstra (1901–94), journalist, novelist and campaigner, who was to contribute regular Dutch chronicles to C.

2–George wrote from Cap Martin Hotel, France, on 3 Jan. to request a review copy of a new book on Maupassant to be published by Knopf on 12 Jan.; he also wished to write on HR's *English Stained Glass*. He added, 'I hardly expect to be in England before June.' See Robert Sencourt, 'Guy de Maupassant', C. 8 (July 1929), 580–91.

3–In an undated letter George mentions having sent 'The Genesis of Fine Art' – 'of all the things I had by me, it came closest to what we had been saying together' – and that he would send an essay on comedy. In addition, he has in hand 'another paper on Religion and the Arts in relation to Ruskin, and another to Michelangelo'. See Sencourt, 'The Æsthetic of Michelangelo', C. 8 (July 1929), 580–91.

– will have received pretty adequate attention from *The New Criterion*. But a rather short notice would not come amiss and if he can get his publishers to send a copy (it is an expensive book) for this purpose you shall have it. I expect to see him in a few days and will ask him whether a copy is sent to *The XIXth Century*. If so, and if you get this copy, we might waive asking for another copy for *The New Criterion*.

I am sorry to know that it will be such a long time before you are again in England and the prospects of coming across you on the continent are extremely remote, but I shall look forward to renewing our acquaintance in June.

Yours ever,
[T. S. Eliot]

## TO *Marianne Moore*

TS Beinecke

8 January 1927 *The New Criterion*

Dear Miss Moore,

Thank you for your letter of the 28th ultimo.[1] I am glad if my review is satisfactory. I cannot think of any other better title than that of the book itself.

I understand from the second paragraph of your letter that you are making two suggestions, one that I should write a paper on the criticism of poetry and the other that I should review Arthur Symons' book on Baudelaire. If I am correct, then I would say that I should like to think over the first suggestion as it is rather a big subject and I ought to be sure that I have something to say about it before undertaking to say anything. As for the second, it would please me very much to review this book if you would send it to me.[2] There are two new editions of Baudelaire in progress to one of which I have subscribed and I think the time is ripe for re-opening this subject.

With many thanks,
Yours sincerely,
T. S. Eliot

1 – Acknowledging on 28 Dec. 1926 TSE's review of I. A. Richards's *Science and Poetry*, Moore asked 'will you be so good as to give us a title?' In addition, she asked for both 'an article upon the criticism of poetry' and 'a review of Arthur Symons' Baudelaire'.

2 – 'Poet and Saint . . .' (*Baudelaire: Prose and Poetry*, trans. Arthur Symons), *Dial* 82 (May 1927), 424–31; repr. with revisions as 'Baudelaire in Our Time' (*FLA*).

## TO *Humbert Wolfe*

CC

11 January 1927 [London]

*Private & Confidential*

Dear Humbert,

I am sending you a copy of the rough figures of production and income for one number of the *Criterion*. You will observe that for the sake of caution we have kept the income down to the very minimum, actually lower than the actual sales of any monthly number. At any rate, it is safe to say from these figures that the usual loss on a single number is well under a hundred pounds. The only figures omitted are those of minor expenses such as stationery which are very small and our own advertisements which have been limited to one insertion in the *Times Literary Supplement*. We have also disregarded, to be on the safe side, the small income from advertisements in the *Criterion* itself.

Yours ever,
[T. S. E.]

## TO *Conrad Aiken*

CC

11 January 1927 [London]

Dear Conrad,

In reply to yours of the 6th. In view of your approaching departure I thought it best to push things forward as fast as possible and try to get a decision.[1] I am practically certain that I shall be able to let you know by this post tomorrow. I am sorry it could not be managed sooner. Is there any chance of seeing you, even for a short time, in town before you leave? I am free on Friday afternoon if you should be here.

Yours ever,
T.

1 – CA's first novel, *Blue Voyage*.

## TO *Conrad Aiken* CC

12 January 1927 [London]

Dear Conrad,

I am returning your manuscript tonight by registered post. As I told you, I rushed through it to get an official opinion before you left. I was not hopeful *a priori* because I know that as the result of the past season and present commitments the policy is at the moment to turn down everything that does not at least give the illusion of being a sure seller. That is precisely what happened. I collected several admiring opinions but general doubt about the advisability of tackling what they thought was a book for a select public. I am sorry about this; I think myself that the chances of anything like this would be much better six months hence. It is a remarkable book, there has been no doubt about that.[1]

If there is any chance of seeing you before you sail, please write, wire or ring up here and I will do my best. Otherwise, can I have an address to which to write to you, and how long do you expect to be away?

Yours ever,
[T.]

## TO *G. F. Williams*[2] CC

12 January 1927 [London]

Dear Mr Williams,

I hope that this letter will reach you before you return to Cambridge.[3] I did not write immediately as I hesitated a good deal and waited to see if I could possibly fit in a visit and a paper. Unfortunately, owing to matters which only arose during December, I am now busier than ever, and furthermore I have made two provisional engagements to go to Oxford during the term if I can find time. I only was tempted to make these promises on the understanding that it was merely to meet members of certain societies informally and not to read a paper. But I am well aware

1 – Aiken responded on 13 Jan., saying of *Blue Voyage*, 'I'm sorry – but not, to tell the truth, greatly surprised. For I have no illusions about the book's saleability. Very many thanks, however, for your efforts' (*Selected Letters of Conrad Aiken*, 132). The novel would be published in due course by Gerald Howe (1927).

2 – Gwilym Ffrangcon Williams (1902–69) was to become Vice-Chairman of the National Savings Committee. He would be knighted in 1960.

3 – Williams had invited TSE on 3 Jan. to read a paper to the 'Heretics' at Cambridge.

that the Heretics want not only a paper but one's best, so I am afraid I must say that it is impossible during this term.

I can say again that I should like to come down in the summer term if it could be arranged, although I know that that is a very crowded time in both universities. By that time I shall probably have ready an Introduction which I am going to write for a volume based on my Clark lectures. The Introduction will of course be much more general and speculative than the lectures themselves. But has that subject perhaps lost its interest in Cambridge?

Yours sincerely
[T. S. Eliot]

## TO *F. S. Flint*

CC

12 January 1927 [*The Monthly Criterion*]

Dear F. S.,

I should be glad to have the rest of the *Maritain* translation as soon as you can bring yourself to do it.[1] Not that it is absolutely pressing; a month hence would do; but the earlier I have it the more convenient for me.

By the way, there is a small point which I should have mentioned to you if you had turned up at Dobrée's the other night. I hear from a tiny bird that Orlo Williams would not be averse to doing the Italian periodicals if at any time you wished to chuck them. I have no desire to make any change, as I hardly need to assure you; at the same time I felt it my duty to pass on this whisper to you in case you might be thankful to get rid of the Italians.

I hope to see you tomorrow night at Monro's.

Yours ever,
[T. S. E.]

1 – 'Poetry and Religion', *NC* 5 (Jan. 1927), 7–22; *MC* 5 (May 1927), 214–30.

## TO *Ezra Pound* CC

12 January 1927 [London]

Cher E.,

Thanks for yours of the 9th instant. In reply to the second part of your letter, I understand Spengler has done very well in this country. There is even a book about him recently published by Constable called *Civilisation or Civilisations*.[1] Can't say whether refutation would be marketable but should think that there is enough interest. I believe there has been a lot written about him in Germany, both periodical and books.[2]

Yours,
[T.]

## TO *Alfred Kreymborg*[3] TS Virginia

13 January 1927 *The New Criterion*

Dear Kreymbourg [*sic*],

Many thanks for your letter of the 8th December. I wish that I had something to offer you but I cannot find that I have anything which I care to print or reprint. I have no verse that I care to publish in America – especially in such a conspicuous place – and I should not care to be represented by heavy and rather inefficient prose. I should not like to offer you anything

1 – E. H. Goddard *et al.*, *Civilisation or Civilisations: An Essay on the Spenglerian Philosophy of History* (1926).

2 – EP asked: 'Has this damn book of Spengler's "Decline of the Untergang of the Eveninglands. Even in glands. Abendlands.*

'Had enough sale, or created enough friction to make it a commercial proposition to write a refutation.

'For the first time in years I feel extremely erudite, and quite ready to shoot Mr S. full of bullets both on fact and on his boschische induktions . . . If Richmond weren't such a puffling shit, one might demand a few front pages of the Slimes Slit Subpoooplement . . .

'Do you know anything about the alledged German "literature" on Spengler, supposed laurels and cacti ??????'

* EP is alluding to *Der Untergang des Abendlandes* (2 vols, 1922), by Oswald Spengler.

3 – Alfred Kreymborg (1883–1966), poet, playwright, puppeteer (who also supported himself for some years as a chess-player). His works include *Puppet Plays* (1923) – which TSE found fascinating – and *Lima Beans* (1925); and *Troubador* (1925), which includes an account of his meetings with TSE in London. In 1915–19 he edited *Others* (which took TSE's 'Portrait of a Lady') – see Suzanne Churchill, *The Little Magazine Others and the Renovation of American Poetry* (2006) – and he was to be co-editor, with Van Wyck Brooks, Lewis Munford and Paul Rosenfeld, of *American Caravan*, an annual anthology of new writing.

which would look as if it had been dug out, and I simply have no time to write anything specially for *The Caravan* as I should like to do.

All I can offer you are my best wishes and the hope of being invited to contribute to the next year-book.

When are you bringing your puppets back to England?

Ever yours,
T. S. Eliot

## TO *Lady Rothermere*

CC

13 January 1927 [London]

Dear L.R.,

Faber has just shown me some correspondence he has recently had with you. I should like, if you don't mind, to take the matter up myself and try to express my own views.[1]

I quite agree with you about the advertisements in the *Criterion* as at present produced: I would go even farther and say that I do not take kindly to an advertisement of Player's cigarettes on the back. And it does seem certain that it is impossible for a quarterly review so young as ours to get enough advertisements to cut any ice. As a quarterly I should much prefer the *Criterion* without any advertisements unless one admitted a few publishers' advertisements at the end. I should think that the profit on a few advertisements that a quarterly can get is negligible. But, as Editor, I am not in a position to object so long as advertisements bring in any money at all. What I could suggest, however, is this: that if you and Faber and Gwyer agree to cut out advertisements altogether, I should be ready to make future numbers of the *Criterion* a little shorter so as to save on production what we lose from these advertisements.

I have just looked at the last number of the *Mercury* and of the *Adelphi* and I find that they have exactly the same 'P. & O.' advertisement in exactly the same place as ours. The *Calendar*[2] also have an advertisement

1–Lady Rothermere had written in an undated letter to TSE: 'Why this silence! Since F & G took over the publication of our review it seems no longer necessary to include me in any consultation etc! I feel completely out of touch with the whole thing . . .

'Please write to me & if you are in Paris come & see me . . .

'P.S. I *strongly object* to an add. being placed *directly* facing first page – .'

2–*The Calendar of Modern Letters*, ed. Edgell Rickword with assistance from Douglas Garman and Bertram Higgins (Mar. 1925–July 1927), published contributions from authors including William Gerhardi, Liam O'Flaherty, Pirandello, Chekhov, Aldous Huxley, Wyndham Lewis, Robert Graves, Laura Gottschalk, Hart Crane, John Crowe Ransom and Allen Tate. See *Towards Standards of Criticism*, ed. F. R. Leavis (1933), and Bernard

facing the first page, though it is merely *The Mask* which I suspect is not paid for.

I should like to know what you think of my suggestion.

Now about the question of making the *Criterion* into a monthly, which, you will remember, we touched upon at the time of the change of publishers. I have been going into the matter lately and taking opinions. I had not reached the point at which I felt it was worthwhile to lay the matter before you, as I wished to be quite certain that the project was practical; but in view of your correspondence with Faber I am mentioning it now.[1]

First of all, there can be no question of increasing your liability. That could not be done without a whole business of raising the capital, for which your approval would naturally be necessary. I have therefore been working on the possibilities of making this change with our present means; and I have been encouraged to pursue the calculations by remembering that it was originally your own idea.

You believed that a monthly would be much more effective and would interest many more people than a quarterly, and my enquiries show that everyone else is of your opinion. I have come round to this opinion within the last year; and I find that the people who write more or less regularly for the *Criterion* would all prefer to write for a monthly. A year ago it was primarily myself who stood in the way of the change. My reasons were severely practical: I did not wish to give the extra time and toil involved in bringing out a periodical twelve times a year instead of four times, without a larger salary, and this was out of the question. It is still out of the question, but as opinion seems to be so unanimous in favour of monthly publication I should be ready to waive this objection. After all, I have in the past put enough of my best energies into the *Criterion* to be willing to make some sacrifice for its future success.

If I found that the *Criterion* could be produced in a monthly form – of course as a monthly it would be much smaller, no one would want a monthly so bulky as the present *Criterion* and in fact I believe that its bulk puts off a good many timid readers – would you now be averse to the change?

It appears that 'the trade', as the booksellers and newsagents are called, would welcome the change, and I am assured unofficially but directly that

---

Bergonzi, 'The Calendar of Modern Letters', *The Yearbook of English Studies* 16: *Literary Periodicals Special Number* (1986), 150–63.

1 – GCF wrote in his diary on 13 Jan.: 'Examined monthly Criterion figures with de la Mare & they seemed to show a chance of improvement, if we made the change.'

we might expect W. H. Smith to order a thousand copies instead of the present two or three hundred. It also appears certain that as a monthly we could go in for advertisements on a really paying scale.

Of course if you and Faber and Gwyer should decide, now or at any time, that you prefer to close down the *Criterion*, then there is nothing for me to say about it. But I should very much like to know from you privately what you think of my suggestions.

I hope that your being in Paris means that you no longer have any need for doctors in Switzerland, or anywhere, and that you are enjoying the winter there.

Ever yours sincerely,
[T. S. E.]

## TO *Ferris Greenslet*[1] CC

15 January 1927 [London]

Dear Mr Greenslet,

Thank you very much for your letter of the 2nd December. I have only just lately been able to take the time to read *Streets in the Moon*[2] carefully. I have already shown my interest in Mr MacLeish's poetry and I think that this volume does him credit. Also, I compliment the Houghton Mifflin company on an admirable piece of book making.

I like the poems so much that I am now submitting your kind suggestion to my principals and will let you know our decision as soon as possible.

With many thanks,
Yours faithfully,
[T. S. Eliot]

## TO *Louis Untermeyer* CC

15 January 1927 [London]

Dear Untermeyer,

I must apologise for my delay in answering your letter of the 8th December. I am very glad that the *Miscellany* is going on. I am afraid that

1–Ferris Greenslet (1875–1959): literary adviser; director of Houghton Mifflin Co, Boston. His books include *James Russell Lowell: His Life and Work* (1905), *Under the Bridge: An Autobiography* (1943), *The Lowells and Their Seven Worlds* (1946).
2–Archibald MacLeish, *Streets in the Moon* (1926).

I have nothing whatever that seems to me fit for publication. It is not that I intend to publish anything anywhere else. I have nothing whatever except the 'Fragments' of which you speak and I really do not feel that these are suitable and I should prefer not to publish any of them in America at all for the present; until they have taken a more substantial and very much revised form. I am very sorry about this, and once having contributed I should like to continue to contribute. I can only say that if I have anything suitable in a year's time you shall have it.

With best wishes and hoping to see you again next year,

Sincerely yours,
[T. S. Eliot]

TO *Alexis St Léger Léger* TS Fondation Saint-John Perse

15 janvier 1927 57 Chester Terrace, S.W.1.

Cher monsieur Léger,[1]

Je vous envoie ci-inclus la traduction complète d'*Anabase*.[2] J'y ai ajouté quelques notes. Je vous prie de lire attentivement traduction et notes (qui

1–This letter was reproduced in *Honneur a Saint-John Perse*, ed. J. Paulhan (Paris, 1965), 419. See also E. J. H. Greene, *T. S. Eliot et la France* (Paris, 1951), 135.

2–Invited by Jean Paulhan (21 Oct. 1949) to contribute a reminiscence to a memorial issue of *NRF*, TSE wrote on 7 Dec. 1949: 'Nearly twenty-five years ago I made the acquaintance of *Éloges* and *Anabase*, and set myself to translate the latter work into English. I am proud of the fact that my translation of *Anabase* – imperfect as it was, though improved, I think, in later editions – was the first presentation of St J. Perse to the English and American public. It appeared with the French text and English translation en regard, and will never, I hope, be printed by itself: for its sole purpose was to introduce a new and important poet to a foreign audience, and to facilitate the understanding of his work.

'Certainly, a quarter of a century ago, St J. Perse was to be considered a difficult poet. He fitted in to no category, he had no obvious literary ancestry or consanguinity: a great part of the difficulty was that his poem could not be explained in terms of anything but itself. I myself should have a far more imperfect understanding of *Anabase* if I had not set myself to the task of translating it. It was beyond my resouces to do it justice: I came to think that not only my command of French but my command of English was inadequate. But its influence appears in some of the poems which I wrote after completing this translation: influence of the imagery and perhaps also of the rhythm. Critics of my later work may find that this influence still persists.

'So it is with the credentials of the first translator into English that I present myself; but I take the opportunity of acknowledging a personal debt. There is much else that I should say about the work of St J. Perse, could I arrange and develop ideas; under pressure of time, I confine my homage to the poet to the words: "I have learned something from you".' TSE's letter is reproduced in full, in a French translation by Dominique Aury, in *Hommage a Saint-John Perse*, 18–19.

sont des questions que je vous pose), et de me donner le profit de vos idées avant que j'envoie la traduction aux imprimeurs.

J'espère que vous pouvez me répondre dans quelques semaines, ou peut-être un mois. Je voudrais faire paraître le volume au mois de mars ou avril.

J'ai lu les critiques de Larbaud[1] et de Fargue,[2] et je crois que je pourrais écrire une petite préface que présenterait mieux votre poème aux lecteurs anglais.

J'espère que vous renverrez bientôt le contrat, afin que nous puissions y insérer la clause que vous désirez.

Je voudrais en même temps vous exprimer un peu de mon admiration pour *Anabase*. Le poème me semble un des plus grands et plus singuliers des temps modernes, et si je peux parvenir à faire une traduction qui soit presque digne d'un tel chef d'oeuvre, je serai tout à fait content.

J'ai l'intention de faire imprimer le titre en caractères grècques *ΑΝΑΒΑΣΙΣ*.

Recevez, cher monsieur Léger, l'expression de mes hommages empressés et de mon amitié loyale.

T. S. Eliot

Autre chose: dans ma préface, peux-je dire que St. J. Perse et St. Léger Léger, l'auteur d'*Anabase* et l'auteur d'*Éloges*, sont identiques, ou voulez-vous garder votre anonymat fragile?

T. S. E.[3]

---

Roger Little remarks, in 'Preface to a new Translation of Anabase', *The Arlington Review* 2: 4 (Autumn 1970), 111: 'In a letter to an Israeli scholar, Perse has written concerning Eliot: "Malgré l'amitié personnelle que nous avons pu partager, tout nous opposait au fond, dans nos conceptions du principe poétique et [de] la création littéraire aussi bien que du comportement humain face à la vie elle-meme ou face au seuil métaphysique'. (Little's source is S. Ebbaz, 'La représentation symbolique dans les premières oeuvres de T. S. Eliot et Saint-John Perse', unpub. Master's thesis, Jerusalem [1966], 5.)

1 – Valery Larbaud, 'Préface pour une édition russe d'*Anabase*', *NRF* 148 (Jan. 1926).

2 – TSE names the poet and critic Léon-Paul Fargue, who was a close friend of SJP—SJP would write the preface to Fargue's *Poésies* (Paris, 1963) — but it is more likely that he meant to cite Lucien Fabre, whose essay '*Publication d'*ANABASE', *Les Nouvelles Littéraires* (Aug. 1924; repr. in *Honneur à Saint-John Perse: hommages et témoignages littéraires*, 406–11) is credited by TSE in the Preface to his translation of *Anabase*.

3 – *Translation*: Dear Monsieur Léger, I am sending you herewith the complete translation of *Anabase*. I have added a few notes. I beg you to read both translation and notes carefully (the latter are questions that I put to you) and to give me the benefit of your ideas before I send the translation to the printers.

I hope you can reply within a few weeks, or perhaps a month. I would like to bring out the volume in March or April.

## TO *Frederick N. Sard*[1] CC

15 January 1927 [*The New Criterion*]

My dear Sir,

I thank you for your letter of the 4th December and for your flattering invitation. I should be quite willing that my name should be included in a committee of the persons you mention provided that I was not expected to subscribe without my previous sanction to any action purporting to be made by the said committee. On these terms you are welcome to my name if it has any value for you. I should hesitate, however, as an outsider to commit myself to any expression of criticism of so great a musician as Beethoven. I am completely incompetent to do so. Of course I am familiar as an ordinary listener with a great deal of his work, but I have no special knowledge of his chamber music or of his later work.

Your offer of the Beethoven records is an extremely tempting one and did I think myself competent to offer the opinion for which you ask I should not hesitate to take advantage of it. But I feel that any public statement by myself in the way of a criticism of Beethoven would be only an impertinence.

With all best wishes for your Centennial,

Yours very truly,
[T. S. Eliot]

---

I have read the critical articles by Larbaud and Fargue, and I think I could write a short preface which would make your poem more accessible to English readers.

I hope you will return the contract soon, so that we can insert the clause you have asked for.

I would at the same time like to express to you a little of my admiration for *Anabase*. I look upon it as one of the greatest and most unusual poems of recent times, and if I can succeed in producing a translation which is almost worthy of the original, I shall be extremely pleased.

I intend to have the title printed in Greek characters: *ΑΝΑΒΑΣΙΣ*.

Rest assured, dear Monsieur Léger, of my respectful admiration and loyal friendship. T. S. Eliot

A further point: may I say in my preface that St J. Perse and St Léger Léger, the author of *Anabase* and the author of *Éloges* are identical, or do you wish to preserve your fragile anonymity?

1 – Frederick N. Sard: Executive Director, Beethoven Centennial, 20–6 Mar. 1927.

## TO *Ramon Fernandez*

CC

18 January 1927 [*The New Criterion*]

My dear Fernandez,

I wonder whether it is carelessness or caution which prevents you from signing your letters whenever they are typed. In this case, however, you addressed the envelope yourself and I do not suppose that you will disown your letter of the 15th January.

I am very glad to hear from you, particularly because I learn that you did not receive the *Criterion*; and on enquiry I find that you have not cashed your cheque for the 'Reply to Manning'; so I wish you would let me know at once if you have not received it. Both the *Criterion* and the cheque were sent to the Hotel Pont-Royal, 37 rue du Bac. If the cheque has not yet reached you we will have it cancelled upon hearing from you and issue a new one.

I am glad that you like my remarks about your book but I am afraid (as I have already said to Read) that they are very superficial; they can hardly pretend to do more than advertise the two books discussed.[1] As I said, however, I felt that it was premature to try to get at the roots of your work until the appearance of your book on Personality which is eagerly awaited. My own criticism of psychologism is something which I have got to work out with more detail and more cogency in the immediate future.[2]

Thank you for your suggestions. I think the first two would be the most suitable and particularly the essay on George Eliot.[3] Is it already written? I hope that you will let me see it as soon as you can spare a copy.

I am glad to hear you are coming to England. I am writing to Stewart who is the only person I know in the French department of Cambridge and will of course let you know if anything comes of it.[4]

1–TSE's review of *Reason and Romanticism*, by HR, and *Messages*, by Ramon Fernandez, *NC* 4 (Oct. 1926), 751–7.

2–Fernandez had written: 'I thank you heartily for your review . . . nothing more accurate and more profound has been written yet on my work. "An idealist without ideals", this may very well be my fate, for all I know . . . All I can say, though I understand, and even up to a certain point accept, your criticism with regard to psychologism, for my part I cannot think of any other language than that of psychology. The rational and moral frame I try to build for our age, though it is a pattern very similar to the one you admire, I cannot but build it with psychological material; and as I am the contrary of a Pragmatist, I can see no other alternative to my actual creed than hopeless anarchy.'

3–Fernandez proposed (i) an essay on George Eliot, 'from a French point of view'; (ii) a piece on 'Shaftesbury's philosophy of life'.

4–Fernandez was to be in England, 13 Feb.–8 Mar., and hoped to lecture at Cambridge.

Please tell your wife that it is hoped that she will come to England with you and that we shall try to give her a favourable impression of the country.[1]

Sincerely yours,
[T. S. Eliot]

## TO *H. F. Stewart* CC

18 January 1927 [London]

Dear Dr Stewart,

I am taking the liberty of writing to you about Ramon Fernandez. I have just heard from him and also from Miss Salmon of the Alliance Française. It appears that Fernandez is coming to England to lecture from the 13th February to the 8th March and that he is free on the following dates: February 20th, 26th, 27th, 28th. I know that he would like to lecture in Cambridge. He has already lectured in Oxford but has never visited Cambridge. You have met him at Pontigny[2] and probably know as well as I do that he could lecture in English almost as well as in French. I do not know whether you have ever heard him speak but I know myself that he is an extremely good lecturer and I think he is certainly one of the most interesting of the younger Frenchmen. Do you think that it would be possible to arrange any lecture for him under the auspices of the University of the Foreign Language School? If so, I should be very glad. I think that I might write to one or two undergraduates who might be glad to get him to speak to undergraduate societies, but if it is not too much trouble I should like to hear from you first.

Please forgive me for worrying you. I hope that you will remember me most kindly to Mrs Stewart and that you are both very well.

Yours very sincerely,
[T. S. Eliot]

1 – Fernandez, who married on 1 Dec. 1926, wished to introduce his wife to TSE.
2 – For the years 1910–14, 1922–39, the philosopher Paul Desjardins (1859–1940) set up at the Abbey of Pontigny (originally a Cistercian monastery founded in 1114), near Auxerre in Burgundy, colloquia he styled 'Decades of Pontigny' (each conference went on for ten days), where leading intellectuals from all over Europe would gather to discuss issues of literature, arts, politics and society. The theme for 1927 was classicism and romanticism.

## TO *Yvonne Salmon*[1]

CC

18 January 1927 [London]

Dear Miss Salmon,

Thank you very much for your letter of the 17th instant. I doubt whether it will be possible for me to attend your lecture on Saturday but if I am in London I shall make a special effort to try to come.

I have heard from Fernandez and am writing to the only man I know in the French department at Cambridge on his behalf and will let you know if anything comes of it.

I have been meaning to write to you for several weeks about Claudel.[2] You will see that his article has not appeared in the January *Criterion*. The reason is that the essay by Jacques Maritain which I had commissioned turned up unexpectedly and I had to fulfil my undertaking to him.[3] I felt that it would be imprudent to expect our British public to assimilate both Maritain and Claudel at once, but I shall publish the Claudel essay very soon.[4] I must apologise for not explaining this point to you several weeks ago.

In any case I am afraid that it would be impossible for me to attend your dinner on Sunday,[5] but I thank you very much and I hope that I may have the pleasure of seeing you again before very long.

With very many thanks,

Yours very sincerely,
[T. S. Eliot]

## TO *Herbert Read*

MS Victoria

18 January 1927 57 Chester Terrace, S.W.1.

My dear Read

The point I forgot is this – you speak of the 'Americanisation' of Russia (I quite agree) but a few lines further on say that 'Russia is turning to the East' (or words to that effect). The two statements, as put there, seem

1 – Yvonne Salmon was Secretary of the Alliance Française, London.
2 – Paul Claudel (1868–1955), Catholic writer.
3 – 'Poetry and Religion', trans. F. S. Flint: [i], *NC* 5 (Jan. 1927), 7–22; [ii], *MC* 5 (May 1927), 214–30. Gallup says (p. 214) this was actually translated by TSE.
4 – The essay by Claudel was never to be published in the *Criterion*.
5 – A dinner in honour of Claudel.

contradictory. I should also like to know what you have in mind in the second.[1]

That is the only criticism I have to make. It seems to me first rate. I only feel that H.J. is especially difficult because to me he seems *not wholly conscious*. There is something bigger there, of which he is hardly aware, than 'civilisation' & its 'complexities'. In some ways he seems to me, as a conscious person, a child: which is perhaps why I like some of his poorer stuff better than his best; in his poorer stuff something bigger appears without his knowing it – e.g. I like especially 'The Altar of the Dead' & 'The Friends of the Friends'. But I imagine that it is impossible for a person in my position to be any more detached about H.J. than, from an opposite point of view, is Van Wyck Brooks.[2]

I hope yr Sterne will be ready soon, for I think it is important, for impressing B.R., that you shd have in soon something which his public can *understand*.[3]

I had not realised, till I saw Squire's review, that *Stained Glass* was anything but a special treatise.[4] Now I am reading it, & there are points which I much want to discuss on Monday – e.g. Byzantine & Gothic.

Yrs ever
T. S. E.

1–HR responded (19 Jan.): 'I think I mean something sensible by "Russia returning to the East" . . . I think of East and West as on each side of a line between Danzig & Odessa . . . Up to the time of Peter the Great, or Catherine, Russia kept pretty well to the East of the Danzig–Odessa line . . . Then during the 18th & 19th century there was a deliberate "orientation" to the west of it. It was probably an unnatural tension: at any rate, after the Revolution, I see Russia as rebounding & once more keeping to the East . . .

'Russia did not in reality return to anything positive, but only to barbarism, *from* which the only outlet (in which the only organization is:) the rational civilization & mechanistic logic of that order of life we agree to describe as Americanization. That is all I meant & I wonder if you can now agree?'

2–'I know that feeling, or doubt, that H[enry] J[ames] was not wholly conscious. But I have simply – perhaps too simply – dismissed it as inconceivable. Could he possibly have kept it up so long? Wouldn't there have been, as Van Wyck Brooks argues, an actual decline in its integrity, instead of a progressive increase & depth of feeling & intelligence? "Understanding" is perhaps the right word to describe his particular faculty, & understanding implies a less conscious attitude than say "intelligence" or "reason".'

3–'Sterne cannot appear before Feb. 14th the date of my lecture – & won't indeed, be ready before then. But I am conscious that I have overstepped the limits of B[ruce] R[ichmond]'s tolerance, & must now play to the gallery a little.'

4–HR's *English Stained Glass* had been published in Oct. 1926.

## TO *Marguerite Caetani* TS Howard

18 January 1927 *The New Criterion*

Dear Marguerite,

Very many thanks for your New Year's letter and every good wish for you and the health of your family for another year. I delayed answering it until I could produce the necessary proof of my existence which is the complete translation of *Anabase* enclosed herewith. I have sent another copy to Léger together with thirty or forty notes of passages on which I want his opinion, and if, as I expect, I have no reply from him within two or three months I shall ask you to use strong pressure. I should like to get the book out in March or April but that will not be possible without his collaboration. As soon as he answers all my questions it will be a matter of only a few days to repair the translation. I then propose to write a short introduction myself, which I can do because I now like the poem immensely. I only hope that the translation will produce a fraction of the impression which the original has made on me.

I have not yet found a way of expressing 'fasting sky' in English;[1] if I don't I shall commit myself to the mistranslation in a footnote.

Allow me to say that I was not in the least 'cross' with you; my temper is, I admit, irascible, but I have never been in a sweeter mood than when I wrote to you. No, as Whistler used to say, 'I was only telling you'.[2]

It was certainly a disappointment to both of us not to be at Cannes for Christmas when you were there; but after all, you don't seem from your address to be at Cannes yourself. In that case, we have very little to regret by being in England. It is very good of you to suggest Dr Chauvet. When we come to Paris again we will think about him, but meanwhile we are getting on very well.

I gather that there is no immediate hurry about the tutor and that you would rather wait until April and be sure of having what you want.[3] I will organise a *battue* of young men before Bassiano arrives. (Incidentally is there not every reason why, for everybody's sake, you should come to England yourself in April?) I have seen one or two young men who I think would be glad of such a post but whom I am not satisfied with.

1–TSE translated 'au fond du ciel à jeun' as 'at the end of the fasting sky' (*Anabasis* [1930], 75). See also Roger Little, 'T. S. Eliot and Saint-John Perse', *The Arlington Quarterly* 2: 2 (Autumn 1969), 5–17.
2–'I am not arguing with you – I am telling you' (James McNeill Whistler, *The Gentle Art of Making Enemies*, 1890).
3–Marguerite Caetani was looking for an English tutor for her son Camillo.

Certainly that is a good time to look at candidates because it is then that young men who are going down from the universities in the summer will be wondering what they are going to do next.

I have a letter from *Les Feuilles Libres* asking me for an homage to Fargue.[1] I should have been very glad to give it on your account but I must confess that I know almost nothing of his poetry, and as they seem to want a contribution almost immediately I have declined. I have of course declined not on the ground of ignorance which would be impolite, but on the ground of lack of time. Perhaps you will tell me some time what I ought to read of his work.

Always affectionately,
Tom.

## TO *The Director, Les Feuilles Libres* CC

19 janvier 1927 [London]

Monsieur et Cher confrère,

Je vous remercie de votre lettre flatteuse du 30 décembre.[2] Vous me faites un grand honneur en m'invitant à collaborer au numéro des *Feuilles Libres* consacré à l'illustre Fargue. Je voudrais bien vous donner mon appui et exprimer mon admiration pour ce poète. Mais à ce moment je suis encombré d'affaires et entravé de promesses et il me faudrait au moins deux mois pour vous donner quelque chose qui fût digne d'un tel sujet.

Je voudrais, cher Monsieur, exprimer mon appréciation de la haute qualité de la revue que vous dirigez, en vous offrant l'expression de mes sentiments les plus loyaux.

[T. S. Eliot][3]

1 – See next letter.

2 – The editor of *les feuilles libres* announced he was to dedicate the next number to the poet Léon-Paul Fargue (1876–1947), and asked for a contribution from TSE.

3 – *Translation*: Dear Sir and colleague, I wish to thank you for your flattering letter dated 30th December. You do me a great honour by inviting me to contribute to the edition of *Les Feuilles Libres* dedicated to the illustrious Fargue. I would like to give you my support and express my admiration for this poet. But at this time I am burdened by business and tied by promises and I would need at least two months to give you something worthy of such a subject.

I would like, dear Sir, to express my appreciation of the high quality of the review you direct, by offering the expression of my most loyal feelings (by being yours faithfully), [T. S. Eliot]

## TO *P. N. Rowe*

CC

19 January 1927 [London]

Dear Mr Rowe,

Thank you very much for your kind letter of the 17th.[1] It is a great pleasure to me to receive such a letter. You have certainly apprehended my aims and intentions and I am aware how far performance falls short – and I only wish that all our readers understood our purposes as clearly as you do.

I agree with you in your opinion of the work of Dean Inge and in your appreciation of Mr Dobrée's review, and I shall not fail to let Mr Dobrée know of your appreciation.[2]

Yours very truly,
[T. S. Eliot]

## TO *Alfred Sperber*

CC

19 January 1927 [London]

Dear Mr Sperber,

Within the last fortnight I have received from my friend, Professor Ernst Robert Curtius of Heidelberg, a translation which he has made without my knowledge of *The Waste Land*. He intimated that he was about to offer it to *Die Neue Rundschau*. I immediately wrote to him telling him of my understanding with you. I now hear from him saying that he sees no reason why both translations should not be published, and cites as a precedent that he and Rilke made simultaneous translations of some of M. Valéry's poems. He says that both his and Rilke's versions were

1–Rowe wrote, 'your January issue has proved a veritable tonic to one at least of your subscribers. I believe I understand aright when I say that you are not out for the separation of literature from life, but to show that literature is a part of life, not to speak merely to the aristocrat, the "high brow", the cynic, the "intellectual"; but to create a love of culture, as Matthew Arnold understood it, in society as a whole. I don't put the case very well, but if I did not think the *New Criterion* stood for something akin to the foregoing I should have to turn away, more in sorrow than in anger!

'I am specially glad that your reviewer has been able to "place" Dean Inge. It was high time for this to be done & done with good temper, knowledge & firmness. If I were to stray into controversy I should express the view that the famous Dean is an even bigger danger than the socialists he decries.'

2–BD's review of three works by the Dean of St Paul's, *NC* 5 (Jan. 1927), 109–14.

published and that there is nothing in German copyright law to prevent such duplication.

I cannot very well ask Professor Curtius to withhold the translation which he has made, but at least I can write to notify you of its existence. I should be very glad to hear from you whether you have succeeded in getting your translation accepted by some periodical. In any case I do not suppose that Professor Curtius's translation will be quite ready to offer to a publisher for some little time; so that yours, which I consider extremely good, has meantime the advantage.

With all best wishes,
I remain,
Sincerely yours,
[T. S. Eliot]

P.S. I hope that you received the copy of *The Sacred Wood* which I sent you.

## TO *Humbert Wolfe* CC

19 January 1927 [London]

My dear Wolfe,

It is very tiresome of you to go away just now. I was hoping that we might meet in a few days privately and less boisterously than the last time. When will you be back?

About the books, will you not send word of anything you would like and let us forward it to Geneva for you (if that is where you are going)? Alternatively, do you not think that Quennell perhaps deserves a longish notice? Personally I am not in favour of trying to review half a dozen books of verse together in one review unless they have a great deal in common – which is seldom the case; the only common quality of verse is usually its mediocrity. What I like is to notice at some length any one book which deserves it, and deal with any others in paragraphs by themselves. Of course it is for you to decide how you like to organise your reviews; but it is a point I had wanted to talk about.[1]

Anyway I should like to get one longish notice out of you and a few paragraphs.

Do let me know your address and how long you expect to be away.

1–John Gould Fletcher reviewed Peter Quennell's *Poems* (1926), and works by eight others (inc. Barfield, Yeats, Monro, Townsend Warner and Plomer), C. 8 (Sept. 1928), 128–34.

Ever yours,
[T. S. Eliot]

P.S. 'English Bards and French Reviewers' appears to be very popular.

## TO *P. M. Jack*

CC

19 January 1927 [London]

Dear Jack,

Thank you for your letter. You are quite right about the comma.[1] It is one of the misprints that I had noted. I think that you would find that it is not in the previous editions. There are two or three other mistakes of the same kind. On page 79 line 308 there are two commas to be deleted and I intended the four 'burnings' to be printed with double spacing between each. On page 66 there ought to be a double space to isolate the quotation line 42 like the quotation above. Besides the misprint of 'pervigilium',[2] the word 'thrush' on the previous page is printed as "thrust".[3] I think that these are all the errors which I have so far noticed but I should be grateful if you came across any others.

The contradiction you mention in *The Sacred Wood* is one which I am very glad to have pointed out to me.[4] There are several inconsistencies in the book which are due to this being a collection of essays subsequently revised, but written for various occasions. The contradiction you mention,

1–Jack had queried the punctuation, in *Poems 1909–1925*, of TSE's 'Gerontion' –

These with a thousand small deliberations
Protract the profit, of their chilled delirium,

– 'I should like the comma after "profit" deleted. Or, if the reader should thereby miss the rhythm, then a semi-colon after "delirium" and after "sauces" – so yielding a version punctuated thus:

These with a thousand small deliberations
Protract the profit, of their chilled delirium;
Excite the membrane, when the sense has cooled.
With pungent sauces; multiply variety
In a wilderness of mirrors.

'But naturally,' Jack recommended, 'I read the second line without the comma.'

2–'On page 92 of the Collected Poems, *Perviglium Veneris* should be *Pervigilium*?'

3–Jack would write in reply to this letter from TSE, on 20 Jan.: 'You have forgotten that I had mentioned the *thrust* . . . when you were up.'

4–'On p. 14 of The Sacred Wood, "The poetic critic is criticising poetry *in order to* create poetry" . . . "It is fatuous to say that criticism is *for the sake of* creation" . . .

'The seeming contradiction is probably merely verbal.

'I should say you have now said, by way of the review on Read and Fernandez (p. 753 . . . the recognition of value is of utmost importance . . .), that criticism is for the sake of creating values.'

however, is not one of this sort but is pure carelessness of expression. I do not now assert, as at any rate I appear to do there, that the only criticism of poetry worth noticing is that of poets. In the main, I still think it is true but one ought to be more careful not to mix up assertions which are, so to speak, on different levels. Theoretically, it does not matter at all whether the critic is a poet or not; it is merely true in experience that most of the best critics of poetry have been poets themselves. I do not believe that I had then quite made up my mind what criticism was for. I certainly believe now that there is no more need to ask this question than there is to ask what poetry is 'for' or what philosophy is 'for'. I should certainly hesitate to say that criticism is 'for the sake of creating values'. I should not say that values were created by thought although thought certainly enters into the creation of value. In dealing with values one has to assume that they exist already and that thought is merely *discovering* them.

I am waiting for your notes, however tentative, on Pater.[1] Thank you for the *Granta*. I have read your reviews with interest and mostly with agreement. I like particularly your note on Keats.[2] I think that you have rather dodged Miss Stein, but what you say about Miss Macaulay, especially the last sentence, is, I think all that there is to be said about that author.[3]

Sincerely yours,
[T. S. Eliot]

1–Jack had confessed on 14 Dec. 1927 that, on account of the demands of his work as literary editor of *The Granta* ('a great deal of pleasant though aimless reading'): 'I find it difficult to find a starting point for Pater.' His thesis was never to be written.

2–In a review of H. W. Garrod's *Keats* (1926), Jack considered Garrod's thesis that 'Keats is by nature a purely sensuous poet' inadequate: 'what seems to me not to have been made clear . . . is the fact of Keats's youth . . . The matter cannot be decided simply on the merits of the finished poems: the question is not What has been well done? but What is the tendency? Of that there is no doubt. It is towards a more informed understanding of human affairs, allowing a larger sympathy and a deeper penetration into the heart of tragedy. The world was no longer a haven for thoughtlessly sleeping away the days. It was a challenge to immerse himself in the stream of life' ('Eulogy in Dead Fashion', *The Granta*, 3 Dec. 1926, 175).

3–Jack regarded Gertrude Stein's *Composition as Explanation* as 'perfectly easy to understand, and though it offers no passe-partout to her work, it does very definitely give the evidence of her integrity and intelligence'. Rose Macaulay's essay *Catchwords and Claptrap* he found 'mainly trite and often untrue. She restates the fact that people use emotive language rather than symbolistic, without realising the validity of such writing. It has always been Miss Macaulay's misfortune to see very clearly what is going on, but never to understand why. It is stupid to suppose, as she does, that if labour journalists were better educated they would write accurately and sensibly. The truth is, if journalists were other than emotive and rhetorical, their power over the people would be at an end. The remedy lies in the reader, not the writer . . . In her timorous desire for exactitude, Miss Macaulay is driven into clumsy pedantry' ('Steinography and Rosewater', *The Granta*, 26 Nov. 1926, 139).

## TO *Ezra Pound*

TS Beinecke

19 January 1927 *The New Criterion*

Cher E.,

I have read Mr Hickock's essay[1] with interest and sympathy. I think that it is rather out of the line of *The New Criterion*; it is not what either the English or the American readers expect from us. I think that it would make much more impression on English readers if it could appear in one of the more conventional English papers or even in a weekly – i.e. it should appear either in an English paper which is not supposed to have any American connections or else in *The American Mercury* which has some circulation here. I think that in *The New Criterion* it would fall flat. What shall I do with it? Shall I return it to you or to the lady from whom I received it, or would you like me to try *The Nation*, or do you prefer to print it yourself?[2]

Do you want any poetry for your review? I get quantities of it. On the whole I prefer not to publish imitations of you or of myself unless there are strong reasons.[3]

Ever yours,
T.

1–Guy Hickock, 'Or those synthetic states'. EP wrote on 28 Dec., of Hickock: 'He did an amusing thing for Ford (transatlantic) entitled "With Herriot in the States". Always swears he cant write, is mere journalist etc.

'I saw him in Sept. . . . and on his reemergence I demanded the results.

'I have read him them with considerable pleasure.'

2–EP, in a letter of the same date, said he would have to print Hickock's essay in his review *The Exile* (which had apparently been announced without his knowledge): it appeared in *The Exile*, no. 1 (Spring 1927), 7–21.

3–EP responded: 'you fair tyke the woids outer me mouf. I keep, as you say, turning away reflections of our two so dissimilar talents. If you find any verse NOT obviously inspired by either of our collected works, I shd be delighted to look at the same . . . Send me the outlaws and goalboids, if there are any. Les méchants, les nihilists, etc. . . . In shot, de TOUGH and de NIGGUHS . . . I mean I am not a eelemosinary institute for the mewling. Not fer the infantile, but for the stubborn wot wont larn tew be good.' (21 Jan.)

## TO *E. R. Curtius* TS Bonn

19 January 1927 *The New Criterion*

My dear Curtius,

I am very glad to get your letter of the 12th January. I have read over your translation[1] once and like it very much. At the first reading I could not find myself competent to make any suggestions, but I shall read it again and return it to you in a few days. Certainly I hope that you will be able to get it published, and I can hardly doubt the acceptance by any important periodical of anything for which you are responsible. I have written to Mr Sperber to notify him of the existence of your translation, as I felt bound to do; but even apart from the merits of the work, I am quite aware that it would be immensely more to my advantage to have your translation appear, backed by your reputation and prestige, than a translation by another hand. In fact there is no one by whom I should prefer to be sponsored in Germany rather than yourself.

By the way, I see from the *New Criterion* that you have recently published in Germany an article on our friend Maritain. I do not see the German periodicals which come to the *New Criterion* for review as they are sent direct to my colleague Randall, in Rome (he is secretary of the British legation to the Holy See), who has always dealt with them.[2] I should be extremely grateful if you could let me have a copy of this essay?

I await your book[3] with double impatience: first to read the book itself; and second, to know that you will be free to write something for the *New Criterion*. It is too long a time since you last appeared in our review.

Always cordially,
T. S. Eliot

1–'*Das wüste Land*'.

2–Randall wrote (*NC* 5 [Jan. 1927], 178): 'Dr Curtius shows [in *Die Literatur*, Oct. 1926] how the intransigent Thomism of Maritain . . . corresponds to the needs of the Roman Catholic Church and, for the matter of that, of the world generally.'

3–Curtius said in his letter of 12 Jan. that he was working on 'An Introduction to French Culture' – this was presumably 'Die natürlichen Grundlagen der französischen Kultur', *Nord und Süd*, Oct. 1927; or else possibly *Die Französische Kultur* (1931), trans. by Olive Wyon as *The Civilization of France* (1932).

## TO *Herbert Read*

MS Victoria

Thursday [20? January 1927] 57 Chester Terrace, S.W.1.

My dear Read,

Thank you for your elucidation.[1] Yes, I was merely pointing out what seemed a defect in expression. But I think you will have to make it clearer still. Massis' propaganda is a good icebreaker to move ahead of us, but there are plenty of difficulties behind. The point is to be made clear that the 'occident' is a bad term if it includes both Europe & America. In some ways America is more like Asia than it is like Europe: at any rate the world can no longer be divided into 'East & West', there is a third position now. It does not seem to me that much of what is worth preserving in the 'occident' exists in America.

I speak with diffidence about James. I mean partly that he directed to the intensification of social values feeling which is properly religious, so that part of his work has to be interpreted & given a sense he would not [have] admitted himself. I feel that the *Vita Nuova* is more 'conscious' than 'The Friends of the Friends' or 'The Altar of the Dead'. But what I have never done is to read the works straight through chronologically. I should be glad to be persuaded, though I should think no less of him if I was right!

1.15 Monday.
Yrs ever
T. S. E.

I want to show you O.W.'s essay on *The Ambassadors*[2] and J.M.M. on St Thomas.[3]

I am reading 'The Nature of Metaphysical Poetry'[4] carefully (for my own vile purposes).

Why do you think that (p. 44)

'the philosophical spirit in both Donne & Chapman was I think derived *directly* from Dante and the early Italian poets?'[5] italics mine!

1 – See HR's comments quoted in footnotes to TSE's letter of 18 Jan. above.
2 – Orlo Williams, 'The Ambassadors', *C.* 8 (Sept. 1928), 47–64.
3 – JMM, 'Towards a Synthesis', *MC* 5 (June 1927), 294–313.
4 – 'The Nature of Metaphysical Poetry', *Collected Essays in Literary Criticism* (1938), 69–88.
5 – Ibid., 78.

I shd have thought Chapman's was 'derived' largely by *lifting* passages from Ficino (see the *T.L.S.* next week)[1] & is there any evidence that either C. or D. studied Dante and *l'un e l'altro* Guido carefully?

## TO *Humbert Wolfe* CC

21 January 1927 [London]

My dear Wolfe,

I have your letter saying that you are leaving on Saturday. This letter is a test to find out whether, when you leave for one of your continental junkets, you visit your office before leaving. If I should hear from you soon, I shall assume that you have visited the Ministry and reviewed your staff before leaving, if not I shall believe that you started your holiday in advance. I am having *Genesis* and Sarah Teasdale looked up (they do not sound particularly inspiring)[2] and if they arrive within the next few days I will have them sent to Montagu House. If not, they must await your return. In the momentary poetry famine I had hoped that you would suggest some prose books.

The 'inquest' originated partly in Dobrée's desire to write about Kipling and therefore Kipling is unfortunately the personality which is most definitely collared.[3] Is there not any other contemporary about whom you might be inspired to write a Dialogue? I like the idea of a Dialogue about some contemporary. Is there anybody you particularly detest and would

1–[TSE], 'The Phoenix Nest' – on *The Phoenix Nest. Reprinted from the Original Edition of 1593* (The Haslewood Books) – *TLS*, 20 Jan. 1927, 41.

2–HW, who was going to Geneva and possibly Italy, had asked (20 Jan.), 'I rather agree that to group a great number of books together is a mistake. But I cannot think that either Quennell or Vines deserve half a longish notice. Perhaps if you could throw in Lady Wellesley's *Genesis* and Sarah Teasdale's new book of verse, that would do.' HW reviewed Sarah Teasdale, *Dark of the Moon*; Sherard Vines, *The Pyramid*; Dorothy Wellesley, *Genesis*; John Freeman, *Solomon and Balkis*, in *MC* 5 (June 1927), 347–50.

3–'A Commentary'. *NC* 5 (Jan. 1927), 2: 'We said a year ago: "editor and collaborators may freely express their individual opinions and ideas, so long as there is a residue of common tendency, in the light of which many occasional contributors, otherwise irrelevant or antagonistic, may take their place and counteract any narrow sectarianism." . . . Having in mind this responsibility of opinion, and this notion of common tendency, certain of the regular contributors to *The New Criterion* have agreed to provide in the current year and the following year, a series of essays on the more important figures of the previous generation, having the character of an inquest, in the French and perhaps also slightly in the English sense of the word.' Wolfe noted: 'I should rather have liked to have attempted another dialogue on Rudyard Kipling.' See BD, 'Rudyard Kipling', *MC* 6 (Dec. 1927), 499–515.

be particularly malicious about? Please make a suggestion. It would be welcome.

Let me know as soon as you get back so that we can meet.

Yours ever,
[T. S. Eliot]

## TO *Harold Joachim*[1]

CC

21 January 1927 [London]

Dear Mr Joachim,

I receive your letter with regret but without surprise.[2] Thank you for letting me know. You will probably have a more intelligent public than

1–Harold H. Joachim (1868–1938): Fellow and Tutor in Philosophy at Merton College, Oxford, 1897–1919; British Idealist philosopher and follower of F. H. Bradley; author of *The Nature of Truth* (1906), an influential account of the 'coherence theory' of truth. TSE recalled buying *The Nature of Truth* at Harvard, and taking it with him in 1914 to Oxford, where Joachim was his tutor. According to Brand Blanshard, it was claimed that 'if you started any sentence in the *Nicomachean Ethics* of Aristotle, Joachim could complete it for you, of course in Greek' ('Eliot at Oxford', in *T.S. Eliot: Essays from the Southern Review*, ed. James Olney, 1988). TSE wrote an obituary letter in *The Times* (4 Aug. 1938), and also paid tribute to Joachim in the introduction to *Knowledge and Experience in the Philosophy of F. H. Bradley* (1964). In a late letter, he said 'he taught me more about how to write good prose than any other teacher I have ever had' as well as revealing 'the importance of punctuation in the interpretation of a text such as that of the *Posterior Analytics*' (24 June 1963: ts Merton College). Aurelia Hodgson, wife of the poet Ralph Hodgson, took a few notes from talks with TSE in Jan.–July 1932; her jottings include this anecdote: 'Once he was reading aloud a paper of his, to his tutor. Joachim sat in silence, smoking. Presently he removed his pipe and only commented: "Why do you use metaphors?" The inflection dropped in the middle of the question – as Eliot imitated it – most effectively. The lesson did not need repeating.' (EVE) TSE's systematic notes on Joachim's lectures on Aristotle's *Nicomachean Ethics* at Oxford 1914–15 are at Houghton (MSAM1691.14 (17). On 6 July 1915 Joachim had penned this testimonial: 'Mr. T. S. Eliot spent last year (Oct. 1914 – June 1915) in working at Philosophy at Merton College, Oxford. During that time, he was my pupil, & brought me Essays (partly on modern Logic & Metaphysics, but mainly on the philosophy of Plato & Aristotle) every week. I was greatly impressed with his ability & enthusiasm for the subject, & also with his conscientiousness & patient endeavour to master the details in every piece of work. From what I have seen of him & of his work, I am quite sure that he would make a most successful teacher: & that he would deserve & win the affection, as well as the respect, of his pupils' (photocopy with EVE).

2–Joachim wrote on 16 Jan.: 'some years ago, at your request, I sent you a paper on "the attempt to conceive the Absolute as a spiritual life". As you did not publish it in the *Criterion*, and as I have heard no more from you since January 1924 on the subject, I thought myself at liberty to publish it elsewhere. Accordingly, I offered it a few days ago to the editor of a philosophical journal, who had asked me for a paper, & he has accepted it. I am writing to let you know of this, in order to prevent any misunderstanding, as I believe you still have a copy of the MS. in your possession.'

mine. I have been somewhat at the mercy of circumstances but I had hoped to have the honour of printing your essay eventually. I shall at some time appeal to you again.[1]

Please remember me kindly to Mrs Joachim.

Yours sincerely,
[T. S. Eliot]

P.S. I enclose the manuscript herewith.

## TO *Thomas McGreevy* MS TCD

21 January 1927 *The New Criterion*

I have pleasure in recommending Mr Thomas M'Greevy very warmly for the post of *Lecteur* in English Literature. I have known him for several years, during which he has written for the Review which I edit. I have a very high opinion both of his abilities and of his scholarship. He has both knowledge and good taste. He is a regular Contributor to my Review.

T. S. Eliot M.A.

## *I. P. Fassett* TO *Eugene Jolas*[2] CC

21 January 1927 [*The Monthly Criterion*]

Dear Sir,

In reply to your letter of the 16th January Mr T. S. Eliot wishes me to say that the matter of remuneration in connection with foreign translations of his work is not important to him, but before giving his assent to your using any of his poems he would be glad to know the names of some of the 125 poets to be included as this seems to him rather a large number,

1 – Professor Joachim was never to be a contributor to *The Criterion*.

2 – Eugene Jolas (1894–1952), poet, editor and translator, was born in the USA (his father was French, his mother German) but educated until the age of 15 in France. Back in the USA, he was employed as a newspaperman, and in the 1920s he returned to France, working for a while for the Paris edition of the *Chicago Tribune*, for which he wrote a literary column (in succession to Ford Madox Ford) and got to know leading writers and artists. An ally of JJ, he promoted the interests of the work that became *Finnegans Wake*. In 1927 Jolas co-founded (with his wife and Elliot Paul) the avante-garde magazine *Transition*. Other publications include *Secession in Astropolis* (1929) and his posthumous memoirs, *Man from Babel*, ed. Andreas Kramer and Rainer Rumold (1998).

and particularly he would like to have the opportunity to revise any translation of work of his which you propose to include.[1]

Yours faithfully,
[I. P. Fassett]
Secretary.

## TO *Hart Crane*[2]

TS Robert Craft

24 January 1927 *The New Criterion*

Dear Mr Crane,

I must apologise for having kept the enclosed manuscript for so long.[3] I am very sorry that I cannot make use of it, but I should like it very much if you would occasionally let me see other things, as I should like to have you appear in *The New Criterion*.

Yours every truly,
T. S. Eliot

## TO *Frederic Manning*

CC

24 January 1927 [London]

My dear Manning,

I am very glad to hear from you though sorry to learn that you are so far away.[4] We never seem to be in London at the same time.

1–Jolas had announced to TSE (16 Jan.) that he had translated into French poems by '125 other poets' for inclusion in an anthology of modern American poetry to be published by Simon Kra; he proposed to include also two poems by TSE, 'Prelude' and 'Portrait of a Lady'. He added: 'It is best perhaps, to say right here that it will be impossible for me to pay for this inclusion as neither I nor the publisher expect a penny's profit on the book.' (A letter from Mrs Jolas on 31 Jan. sent the draft translation of 'Portrait of a Lady', and listed some of the poets to be represented in the anthology: they included Hart Crane, E. E. Cummings, Ezra Pound, Wallace Stevens, Allen Tate, and William Carlos Williams.)
2–Hart Crane (1899–1932): American poet; author of *White Buildings* (1926) and *The Bridge* (1930). See Hart Crane: *Complete Poems and Selected Letters*, ed. Langdon Hammer (1997), and Lee Oser, *T. S. Eliot and American Poetry* (1998).
3–Crane had submitted (17 Oct. 1925) two poems, 'Passage' and 'The Wine Menagerie', which were to be published in *White Buildings* (1926): see *Complete Poems and Selected Letters*, ed. Langdon Hammer (1997), 15–16. Hammer notes: 'Marianne Moore accepts Crane's "The Wine Menagerie" for *The Dial*, but cuts and revises it drastically, much to his chagrin, publishing it as "Again" in May 1926' (749).
4–Manning was visiting Rome.

On receipt of your letter I have had Macmillans rung up and they say that they do not know when the second volume of Frazer's book will be ready. In the circumstances, and as you express some willingness to go into the subject more thoroughly if you are given time, I should really prefer to give this time and to ask you to make a leading article of it: that is to say, would you care to write from 3,000 to 5,000 words about Frazer with special reference to this book? If so, let us fix publication for June. I mean I could give you till April 1st. Do you agree?[1]

I think that I agree with you about Frazer.[2] It is perhaps premature to say what his influence will be; as you suggest, he can be used in more than one way. But I do not think that there is any doubt that his influence will not have been very great, certainly as great an influence, and perhaps wider and more enduring, as that of Freud. I have always felt the existence of the weaknesses which you point out: the difficulty of testing the evidence in detail where there is so much, so indirect and so varied.

Yours always sincerely,
[T. S. Eliot]

1 – Manning, 'A Note on Sir James Frazer', *MC* 6 (Sept. 1927), 197–205.

2 – Manning had written (19 Jan.): 'My own prepossessions with regard to Frazer can be stated very simply. Except for Tylor [*Primitive Culture*] and Robertson-Smith [*Religion of the Semites*], he has had the field to himself . . . For this reason, he may be said to have influenced all that body of opinion, which approaches the study of religion along the lines which he first traced. Without directly attacking "revealed" religion, he has shown that it possesses no characteristics which it does not share with "natural" religion, and revelation thus appears as a superfluous claim. On the other hand, he shows how general to humanity are the ideas of God, of immortality, of sin, and of atonement; and from our point of view he may be held to have established the validity of these ideas, as natural and necessary assumptions . . .

'His generalizations often strike me as being far too sweeping; as when he says that Christianity and Islam were "created, at a blow" by a single mind . . . The religion of Israel is . . . like Christianity itself not a simple but a composite fact. Its development is not different from that of the religion of any other gifted or fortunate race.

'Again: Frazer's work is mainly a compilation from an immense variety of sources; and how are we to test with regard to any particular detail, the credibility of the evidence. He relies on the account of some traveller, who may have been quite incompetent to understand the mind of the savage, while the savage himself may have been at considerable pains to mislead his questioner, or, worse, to gratify him to approximate to his interpretation . . .

'I conclude that Fraser's work is scientific in so far as it deals with the structure of religion, that is to say, broadly, with ritual.'

## TO *John Maynard Keynes*[1]

MS King's

25 January 1927

57 Chester Terrace, S.W.1.

Dear Keynes

Very many thanks for your letter.[2] I *hope* that you mean my quasi-verse contribution;[3] but whether you mean that or another, the compliment, from this source, gives me great pleasure.

I should like to see you very much. I seldom dine out – except very informally & domestically – & my wife not at all: but I should be delighted to look in, on that evening, or almost any evening, when you are in London, after dinner; or to tea. So just let me know when you care to have me come.

Sincerely yours,
T. S. Eliot

## TO *Herbert Read*

MS Victoria

28 January 1927

57 Chester Terrace, S.W.1.

My dear Read,

You are a Rock. I can give *you* (in confidence) till *Feb. 28*.[4] Your suggestions are admirable.

Smith Perry and Ellis can wait.

Collingwood – a good suggestion. I will try him. I went to his lectures on the *De Anima* when at Oxford, & liked them. But I don't think he is much older than I am.[5]

1–John Maynard Keynes (1883–1946): influential economist and theorist of money (expert on macroeconomics); pamphleteer; patron of the arts (begetter and financier of the Arts Theatre, Cambridge), government adviser and negotiator; editor of *The Economic Journal*, 1912–45; columnist for the *Nation and Athenaeum* (of which he was chairman from 1923); intimate of the Bloomsbury circle; Trustee of the National Gallery; author of *Indian Currency and Finance* (1913), *A Treatise on Probability* (1921), *The Economic Consequences of the Peace* (1919), *A Treatise on Money* (2 vols, 1930) and *The General Theory of Employment, Interest and Money* (1936). He married in 1925 the ballet dancer Lydia Lopokova (1892–1981).

2–'How *excellent* your contribution is in the last *Criterion*' (23 Jan.). 'Yes – I meant the quasi-verse of course. Yours is the *only* modern poetry in my opinion.' (28 Jan.).

3–'Fragment of an Agon', *NC* 5 (Jan. 1927), 74–80.

4–HR asked (27 Jan.) for an extension to his deadline until the week ending 19 Feb.: he promised to send five pieces, including reviews of Whitehead and Calverton, and of Stanley Unwin's *The Truth about Publishing*. HR reviewed *Religion in the Making* by Alfred North Whitehead, and *Reality: A New Correlation of Science and Religion* by Burnett Hillman Streeter, in *MC* 5 (May 1927), 259–63.

5–For a reviewer of Taylor's Plato, HR suggested R. G. Collingwood – 'of whom I know

Wahl is a good suggestion, but the machinery of giving reviews to foreigners is more difficult.[1]

I remember Wheen.[2] I should be glad to try him out.

Specialists in biology – I don't *think* we want Julian Huxley? – Who else is there? Yes, I think Orlo's essay will do more good than harm. And I think every reference to Hulme is valuable – more valuable, in a sense, than Hulme himself.[3]

There is one undoubted reference or rather allusion by Donne to the *Commedia*.[4] But I think his indebtedness is small, his similarity non-existent. Both Donne & Chapman have certainly more relation to Italy than to Spain, (in contrast to Crashaw) but I should question both their knowledge & their sympathy with the Guidos & Cino etc. & with Dante himself. And it is just this 'philosophical spirit' in Donne & Chapman & Shakespeare! that I am at present bothered about![5]

Yours ever
T. S. E.

---

nothing, but who wrote a very intelligent paper in Mind on Plato's theory of Poetry'. Collingwood (1889–1943), philosopher and historian (who was six months younger than TSE) had gone up to University College, Oxford, to read Literae Humaniores in 1910.

1 – Jean Wahl (1888–1974), philosopher; a professor at the University of Besançon (later at the Sorbonne, 1936–67); author of *Etudes sur le Parménide de Platon*; *Pluralist Philosophers of England and America*; *Le Malheur de la conscience dans la philosophie de Hegel* (1929), and *Etudes Kierkegaardiennes* (1938).

2 – HR had written: 'Emerson. This wants a fresh point of view. If you approve I will ask Wheen, who is now back from Australia (you will remember meeting him at the Grove, & the story of his experience as a spy in the German trenches). He has a lot in him, if only he can be dragooned a little.' See 12 Sept. 1927 below for TSE's letter to Arthur Wheen (1897–1971).

3 – 'I am sending O[rlo] W[illiams]'s [essay on The] Ambassadors now. It has its good points, but it doesn't become at all exciting until he begins to quote Hulme on p. 23. I dislike the pre-war post-war basis on which he opens. It is quite false. I read most of Henry James in the trenches, & found it more tolerable than other "bedside" books. And there is no difference now. But that is merely personal – at any rate, a minority movement. Orlo may be in the swim, but he swims round & round & never gets to the centre. But it would do no harm to publish it: as a temperate statement it might do good.'

4 – Edmund Gosse, in *The Life and Letters of John Donne* (1899), I, 41, identified in Donne's *Fourth Satire* one of 'the very rare Elizabethan references' to Dante: 'At home in wholesome solitarinesse / My precious soule began, the wretchednesse / Of suiters at court to mourne, and a trance / Like his, who dreamt he saw hell, did advance / It selfe on mee, Such men as he saw there, / I saw at court, and worse, and more.' See *VMP*, 72.

5 – HR had picked up (27 Jan.) on a point made in conversation by TSE: 'your query about the passage on p. 44 of "The Nature of Metaphysical Poetry". The passage in question was a reaction to some statement of Gosse's, I think, but as Dante doesn't appear in the index of his *Life*, I can't trace it. I seem to remember one direct reference to Dante by Donne. But otherwise I was merely writing with my nose – not an infallible organ – and I shouldn't really

## TO *John Maynard Keynes* MS King's

31 January 1927 57 Chester Terrace, S.W.1.

Dear Keynes

Many thanks for your letter and patience. I should have liked to come & to see Garnett & Fry but as any evening this week turns out to be very inconvenient for me – and as you have left it open – I should much like it if you would ask me next week, or at your convenience, with the same, or similar, or no company at all. It would really be a great pleasure to see you again.[1]

Let me say again how much pleasure your approval of my Fragment has given me. I did not expect that *anyone* would like it – still less those who like my previous work – and so far you are the first person to say anything for it. Judge then of my pleasure.

Hoping to see you soon

Sincerely yours
T. S. Eliot

## TO *H. S. Milford*[2] MS OUP

31 January 1927 57 Chester Terrace, S.W.1.

Dear Sir,

Thank you for your letter of today, which I have just received.[3] Nothing would please me better than to write a preface to *The Moonstone*: I

---

like to say anything now about Chapman's origins. But I did then feel (& I think still do) that there is a "philosophical spirit" in both Donne and Chapman that is more akin to their Italian precursors than to their Spanish ditto.'.

1–Keynes wrote on 28 Jan: 'Next Wednesday is not a formal dinner party at all – no-one except Bunny Garnett and perhaps Roger Fry. So do come to dinner if you can (8 p.m.). But if you'd rather come another day *solus*, let me know.'

2–TSE, who could not make out the signature, addressed his letter to 'H. S. M. Ifar'. H. S. Milford (1877–1952) was Manager of the London office of Oxford University Press and Publisher to the University of Oxford, 1913–45. President of the Publishers Association, 1919–21, he would be knighted in 1936. In 1928 he was to be responsible for the publication of the first edition of the *Oxford English Dictionary*. See Nicolas Barker, *The Oxford University Press and the Spread of Learning, 1478–1978* (1978).

3–Having just read TSE's praise of *The Moonstone* – 'the great book which contains the whole of English detective fiction in embryo . . .; every detective story, so far as it is a good detective story, observes the detective laws to be drawn from this book' (*NC* 5 [Jan. 1927], 140) – Milford invited him to write an introduction to an edition for the World's Classics list (which OUP had bought from Grant Richards in 1906). 'It remains so much the greatest of detective novels that someone ought to do it justice among the populace.'

am engaged on a long article on Collins for the *Times* (but with special attention to his less known work) so that it would fit in well.[1] I must first get the formal approval of my principals (Faber & Gwyer Ltd) as I have undertaken to give them the option on all my non-periodical work, but I think there will be no difficulty. I will therefore write to you again in the course of a few days.

Yours very truly
T. S. Eliot

I have been under the impression that you already had *The Moonstone*. It certainly deserves a place in your series. *I* think that *Armadale*[2] also is worth your consideration. It is a favourite of that admirable writer, A. E. Housman.

## TO *Herbert Read* — MS Victoria

1 February 1927 — 57 Chester Terrace, S.W.1

My dear Read

I think it is a certainty that we become a monthly, and from April 15.[3]

1. Can I have your *Behaviourism* essay, as soon as needed.

2. I think it would be a pity to ask Trend to write *monthly* notes. The whole point of his present work is that he can digest what has happened in a quarter. *Monthly* notes on music, art or drama would tend to scrappiness. Working from this idea about Trend, my notion is

> to have 1 foreign chronicle each
> month – each f.c. to appear twice a
> year. 6 f.c. in all.
> to have *quarterly* notes on *music*,
> *art*, drama – *one* each month.

If we had all – music, art, drama, – *each* month, they would be scrappy notes – for we could not allow more than 3 pp. each.

It is more interesting for the chronicles.

As you know, I had wanted Dobrée for drama. But he is in Egypt for 3 years. And Flint is doing drama in *Vogue*. I have suggested it to him, & he is not averse. I think he is the right person.

1 – 'Wilkie Collins and Dickens', *TLS*, 4 Aug. 1927, 525–6.
2 – Wilkie Collins, *Armadale* (1866).
3 – The first issue of *The Monthly Criterion* (5: 2) would appear in May 1927.

But who for *Art*? Lewis refused, some time ago, and anyway he can not be trusted to produce his copy in time. Shall I try Clive Bell? or even Fry? – It might be better to get some more humble person who could be trusted to provide copy in time? But can you think of anyone else? I shd like your advice.

Ever yours
T. S. E.

Dinner today *week* – & we *lunch* certainly on *Monday next*??

## TO *John Middleton Murry* MS Northwestern

1 February 1927 *The New Criterion*

My dear John,

Thank you for your letter. You have my sympathy for the flu.[1]

Of course, John, I will do everything I can.[2] I am not sure that it is much. My own 'prosperity' is a stucco façade, & I never feel sure that I shall not be cast out at any moment. With your approval, I will

1. Write to Marianne Moore, re *The Dial*.
2. See Leonard Woolf next week about the *Nation*
3. Write to Mark Van Doren (who is under some obligation to me for receiving his poems) about the N.Y. *Nation*.

I can also try the *N.Y. Saturday Review*, Canby,[3] but perhaps you know them better than I do.

These are all the places that I know. The London Sunday papers are not friendly to me. I *may* be able to get hold of some Chicago papers. I ignore, of course, European periodicals, which pay badly.

Couldn't you get hold of work writing introductions? There is the Oxford World's Classics. If I can think of anything for F. & G. (a book) I will suggest it, or you might. It is not much trouble writing an introduction.

I wish you would review for the *New Criterion*, though there is very little money in it. Can you suggest any book? Will you take on the Swinburne *Hyperion* when it comes out?[4]

1–JMM (28 Jan.) had been in bed for a fortnight.

2–JMM needed work. 'If you can put me in the way of a little honest journalism, I shall be grateful . . . I rather badly need to make an extra £150–£200 a year.'

3–Henry S. Canby, editor of the *Saturday Review of Literature*.

4–Georges Lafourcade, *Swinburne's Hyperion and other Poems: With an Essay on Swinburne and Keats* (F&G, 1927). JMM replied on 2 Feb.: 'What I chiefly need is to be able to break through the inhibition that prevents me from asking for work: if you will help me in the ways you suggest, I am sure I shall manage it. During the last four years a

I have written very heavily about *The Life of Jesus*.[1] You may not be pleased, but you know I take theology seriously, as you do.

Ever aff.
Tom.

My present circumstances prevent my doing anything very punctually.

## TO *T. M. Taylor* CC

1 February 1927 [*The New Criterion*]

My dear Taylor,

Faber has shown me your letter of the 25th and as I learn from it that I am not likely to see you for several weeks I am taking the liberty of replying myself.

I had already observed the errors to which you call attention as well as several others.[2] It is largely my own fault. When the proof of the article appeared, de la Mare called my attention to several obvious mistakes and I said that I would look up the quotation in my *Teubner*. I did so, but unfortunately at the time I was very much pressed by other affairs and I only looked through *Ennead* I. 8. very hastily and failed to find the quotation.[3] De la Mare therefore made one or two corrections and I made another, but when the final copy appeared there seemed to be a wholly new crop of errors. I certainly did not pass ἔχεῖ ! or φίλην without an accent. It is rather a disaster in a periodical like the *Criterion* which should be especially careful about Latin and Greek quotations. But there is always so much difficulty with printers in Greek quotations that it seems as though it would be better to adopt the practice of Schopenhauer and omit Greek accents altogether. Our former printers, Hazell, Watson and Viney, were much more accurate in these matters, but they were also much more expensive.

You say that I would feel uncomfortable if I saw a French quotation misquoted. Well, there are two conspicuous French quotations in the present number and they are both misprinted. One gives 'catalouges' instead of 'catalogues'[4] and the other gives 'galere' instead of 'galère' and

strange mixture of shyness & pride has slowly taken control of me, & I find it very hard to overcome.'

1–TSE reviewed *The Life of Jesus*, by JMM, in *MC* 5 (May 1927), 253–9.

2–Jacques Maritain, 'Poetry and Religion', *NC* 5 (Jan. 1927), 7–22.

3–A quotation from Plotinus, *Enneads* I,8, was used as epigraph to the Maritain essay.

4–A quotation from Arthur Rimbaud, 'Une saison en enfer', given on p. 17.

puts a senseless full stop at the end of the second line instead of a comma.[1] As a matter of fact, however, I am less humiliated by misprints in French than in Greek: the former are probably attributed to carelessness; the latter might be attributed to ignorance.

It seems that I shall have to pay special attention myself to every quotation from any foreign language – at any rate those foreign languages which the ordinary person may be expected to know.

Yours sincerely,
[T. S. Eliot]

## TO *Ramon Fernandez* CC

2 February 1927 [London]

My dear Fernandez,

I am afraid that the trouble is the same as always: that the *Alliance Française* programmes are never arranged long enough in advance to make it possible for us to arrange University lectures at Oxford or Cambridge. I am going to try to see whether the *Alliance* cannot co-operate better with the Universities, because as it is, Oxford and Cambridge seem to miss all the best foreign lecturers through shortness of notice.

Stewart suggests that one or two of the Undergraduates' literary societies might be delighted to have you address them. Would you be able to do so and would you if necessary speak in English – as you perfectly well can?[2] Mrs Stewart also desires me to say that if you would care to attend the performance of *Electra* (see enclosed cutting) she would be very glad if you would stay with them. She has asked me also, but I am afraid that I cannot get down to Cambridge during this month.

Yours in haste,
[T. S. Eliot]

1 – A quotation from a sonnet by José-Maria de Hérédia, cited in Humbert Wolfe, 'English Bards and French Reviewers', 71.

2 – Fernandez lectured to the French Society on 17 Feb.; writing to TSE in an undated letter ('Monday'): 'Yesterday, I lectured in English for the first time in my life. The result was better than I had anticipated. And I met I. A. Richards, who appeals to me very much.'

## TO *Bruce Richmond* CC

2 February 1927 [London]

Dear Richmond,

I am very glad to hear that you are back and hope that your holiday has been successful. I am plodding away on Jespersen, having got his book on Language from *The Times* in your absence, but I shall be very glad to do a column on Harrington for you immediately.[1] He is a person who interests me though I hardly know his epigrams. I will let you have this some time next week.

Of course I am delighted to do Middleton and Machiavelli.[2] I see that their birthdays occur both in the middle of the year – I think in June and July respectively. I accept Middleton because I think I can do him as well as anybody; I take Machiavelli because I should like to write about him, although I know perfectly well that there are a thousand people more competent than I.

Let me know next week when you could see me. I could look in at your office or I could come to tea at your house, and I should like it still better if you would lunch with me somewhere convenient to Printing House Square.

Yours sincerely,
[T. S. E.]

P.S. On looking up my note I find that Machiavelli died on the 22nd June. So far as I can find out, Middleton died in 'midsummer'. Perhaps you will let me know in due course whether it is convenient to you to interpret 'midsummer' as May or July. There is rumour that he was buried on the 4th July, so I should suggest that the first or second fortnight in July would do. It is a little inconvenient that they died so near together although a hundred years apart.

1 – On 2 Feb. BLR sent Harington's *Epigrams*: TSE did not review it.

2 – BLR had written, 'I hope it is all right about Middleton and Machiavelli – you accepted the first. If I remember right, you hesitated over the second. Don't hesitate any more.' 'Nicolo Machiavelli', *TLS*, 16 June 1927, 413–14; 'Thomas Middleton', *TLS*, 30 June 1927, 445–6.

## TO *George Rylands* CC

2 February 1927 [*The New Criterion*]

Dear Rylands,

It would do quite well; not for the next number because there isn't room, but as soon after as possible.[1] The only thing I don't like is this Marcia; she reminds me too much of *Chrome Yellow* [*sic*] and the general Aldous Huxley type of love affair. Would be you prepared to do anything about Marcia or not?

Could you come and see me next week?

Yours ever,
[T. S. Eliot]

## TO *J. B. Trend* CC

2 February 1927 [London]

My dear Trend,

Are you in London and will you be able to come to a *Criterion* dinner on Tuesday next?

There are two points I want to mention. One is about the Spanish periodicals, such as they are. Orlo Williams has now taken over from Flint the Italian periodicals, and Flint has suggested that it would be most fitting if you could and would do the Spanish periodicals in his stead. I hope that you will. I do not think it would give you very much trouble, as there are not very many Spanish literary periodicals, and you would not be obliged to produce the notes very regularly, only when enough material had accumulated to make some comment worthwhile. I think that the only one we have at present is the *Revista de Occidente* which I will have sent to you, although I suppose that you get it in any case. Any others that you wanted we would try to get. Of course you would be the ideal person as you know and are in touch with the people who are writing in Spain, but don't bother if it seems to you too much of a burden.

*The New Criterion* is probably on the point of becoming a monthly. In this case, I have been wondering how I ought to arrange the Chronicles, and I should like to have your opinion. The monthly *Criterion* would be about half the size of the present quarterly. As I have worked out the form of it, there would be room each month for two Chronicles of the same length as our present Chronicles, that is one foreign Chronicle and one

1 – In the event, Rylands's 'Lost Identity' was not published.

other. It would be obviously too much of a burden to ask you to produce Music Chronicles of the same kind and quality as often as once a month, and I should not like the Music Chronicle to be altered in any way. My idea therefore is that we should have an Art Chronicle and a Dramatic Chronicle as well, formed on the model of your Music Chronicle; that each of these Chronicles should be quarterly and that therefore there would be one Chronicle, Music, Art or Dramatic, every month.

Such an arrangement would of course not affect you at all; you would continue to give us your quarterly Chronicle. But before fixing it I should like to have your opinion of this way of arranging matters. If we do the Music, the Art and the Dramatic Chronicles every month, it will mean that none of the Chronicles will be more than snippet notes on current events. One can read that sort of thing anywhere; even with the *Criterion* a monthly, I should like to preserve the character of Chronicles as being not so much a report as an essay on that particular art by someone who has had the time and has the ability to express his own ideas about that art, with reference of course to any recent events which illustrate what he wants to say.

By the way, I wrote some little time ago to Ortega y Gasset to ask him for a contribution and have had no reply. Whenever it is convenient I should be grateful if you would put in a word yourself. This is the second time I have written to him without avail.[1]

Ever yours,
[T. S. E.]

1–Trend replied on 5 Feb.: 'I think you are quite right about keeping the chronicles at their present length, and (if the New Criterion becomes monthly) letting them recur at regular intervals. (Readers will be told?) I have thought it over; in fact I began a long letter to you about it, but destroyed it.

'Of course, in a weekly, and even in the [*London*] *Mercury*, musical people do resent the fact that there's always drama, and art, & films etc: and music only now and then – and you never know when it will be. But I agree absolutely, that snippets are out of place in The New Criterion: and incidentally, I couldn't undertake to do them. (I do appreciate, very much indeed, your having given me complete liberty of choice. Having sacrificed everything to beable to travel, I don't want to settle down just yet; and regular musical criticism is to the last degree demoralizing!)

'Flint has done the Spanish periodicals extraordinarily well, I think; and it is a great advantage that they should be done by someone who reads other periodicals as well as Spanish ones. I would really rather not; & one reason is that you may find some young & brilliant person who will, perhaps, more or less pick up the language as he reads them. The "profession" (teachers, etc.) are, for the most part, *hopeless* – at least those I know of. The *Occidente* is by far the best, but there may be others which from time to time have something. What purports to be a sort of *Times Lit. Supp.* has been started in Spain; but I haven't seen it.

'As to Ortega, I *did* write, begging him to do the article you asked for.'

## TO *The Director, The Library of the British Museum* CC

3 February 1927 [24 Russell Square, London]

Dear Sir,

I beg to apply for a card of admission to the Reading Room of the Library. I have had a card, or rather successive cards, in previous years – I think the first card was granted me in 1914. But my admission lapsed six or seven years ago and I have lost the card which I had at that time.

The address above is my business address. My private address is 57 Chester Terrace, Eaton Square, S.W.1.

I am,
Yours faithfully,
[T. S. Eliot]

## TO *John Middleton Murry* CC

3 February 1927 [London]

My dear John,

I am most awfully sorry to hear that it has been pneumonia and I hope that you will take good care of yourself and nurse your strength for a long time to come as there is nothing more weakening. You really ought to go away from London for a time as soon as you are strong enough, but I suppose that Dorset is too inclement at this time of year. I am very sorry for you.

I will let you know of any results and perhaps I shall be able to think of something else. I have one or two ideas.

Affectionately yours,
[T.]

## TO *W. Force Stead* MS Beinecke

[?3] February 1927 24 Russell Square, London W.C.1

My dear Stead,

I was very sorry to miss you – but your notice was *very* short! and at the weekend too![1]

1–WFS had hoped (1 Jan.) to see TSE by 3 Jan.: 'This is short notice I know – but my comings and goings are not only unknown to my friends but even to myself – I am the wind, if not of inspiration, then of vanity. But I'd like to blow across you if possible.'

I shall probably be going shortly to the country for 2 or 3 weeks. But I shd like to see you as soon as you can arrange – I will let you know when I get back. What I want to see you about is this: I want your advice, information & your practical assistance in getting Confirmation with the Anglican Church.[1] I am sure you will be glad to help me. But meanwhile I rely upon you not to mention this to anyone. I do not want any publicity or notoriety – for the moment, it concerns me alone, & not the public – not even those nearest me. I *hate* spectacular 'conversions'.

By the way, I was born & bred in the very heart of Boston Unitarianism.

Sincerely
T. S. Eliot

If you reply (*to 24 Russell Square*) please mark the envelope *Personal & Private*.[2]

1–WFS wrote in a memoir of TSE (written in the mid-1950s, this piece was reviewed and corrected by TSE himself): 'I can claim no credit for his conversion. But I did set up one milestone along his way – I baptised him . . . We had been having tea in London, and when I was leaving he said, after a moment's hesitation,

'"By the way, there is something you might do for me."

'He paused, with a suggestion of shyness.

'After a few days he wrote to me, saying he would like to know how he could be "confirmed into the Church of England," a quaint phrase, not exactly ecclesiastical. He had been brought up a Unitarian, so the first step was baptism' ('Mr Stead Presents An Old Friend', *Trinity College Alumni Bulletin*, 38: 2 [Winter 1965]).

2–WFS replied on 4 Feb.: 'Your letter offers me the very opportunity I had been hoping for. You may be sure that I shall take the greatest pleasure in helping you, and that I shall make it a point of honour not to mention this to anyone. Later on perhaps you will give me permission to tell a few people like Streeter and Rawlinson both of whom have worked round to their position as Anglican theologians after some years of agnosticism. But they will not – nor will I – write you up in the papers. The Church of England has no publicity department and suffers itself to appear a fool when it really contains some wise men; modesty is a chaste virtue, but I think it is a pity when a first rate man like A. E. Taylor enters the Anglican Church and hardly anyone hears of it. – However to come to practical points, forgive me if I ask whether you have been baptized? My idea of Unitarians is of austere people who abstain from baptism as well as communion. Perhaps I do them an injustice. Anyway one must be baptized before being confirmed, tho' it is not necessary that one should receive Anglican baptism. It is different with confirmation where everything depends upon the Apostolic succession.

'Recently I had a similar opportunity for a friend who was anxious to avoid publicity, so I took him out to Littlemore Church, locked the door and baptized him in private. Later we went to Cuddesdon and the Bishop of Oxford confirmed him in his private chapel. The advantage of this is that the absence of a crowd enables one to concentrate on the service. Would you like me to make some arrangements for you? The whole thing would take only a couple of hours, but I ought to have a week or two notice in advance. As soon as you can give me an approximate date I'll write to the Bishop. I'll have to mention your name to him but you can be sure that he won't betray your confidence.'

## TO *Lady Rothermere* CC

3 February 1927 [London]

Dear L.R.,

Many thanks for your letter.[1] I feel fairly hopeful about the prospects; anyway I am delighted to have a shot at it and I think we can make it go. I hope to produce a monthly number in April – if we are going to change it would be merely a waste of money to bring out another quarterly number. I will give you more details later. I am delighted to hear that you are well, and I suppose in the sunshine. Cannes is a nice place and there would be no excuse for your not being well or for your not enjoying yourself there. I envy you very much; there is no inducement in London at the present moment.

If I can possibly get over to Paris this season I shall certainly let you know in the hope of finding you there. But I don't suppose you will want to leave the South for the next two months.

Ever yours sincerely,
[T. S. E.]

## TO *Marianne Moore* TS Rosenbach

3 February 1927 *The New Criterion*

Dear Miss Moore,

I have received the *Baudelaire*. I thought it was to be a book about Baudelaire and was surprised to find that it is a series of translations. But I think I can make a pretty good long review out of it. I shall have to pitch into the publishers for the effrontery in calling it *Baudelaire Complete*. There are about fifteen volumes of Baudelaire and Symons hasn't even translated the whole of *Les Fleurs du Mal*.[2]

While I am writing I should like to suggest earnestly that you ought to get some reviewing from Middleton Murry. He is certainly as good a reviewer as anybody and his name carries weight. I am sure that he would be glad to do it and I think that he needs the money. I should be highly delighted myself to see him among your reviewers: it would in fact be a personal favour to myself. His address, in case you have not got it, is *1a, the Gables, Vale of Health, Hampstead, London, N.W.3*.

1 – Not found.
2 – 'Poet and Saint . . .' – on *Baudelaire: Prose and Poetry*, trans. Arthur Symons – *Dial* 82: 5 (May 1927), 424–31; repr. with revisions as 'Baudelaire in Our Time' (*FLA*).

Allow me to compliment you on the quality and interest of the last few numbers of *The Dial*. It has certainly lost nothing under your direction.

Sincerely yours,
T. S. Eliot[1]

## TO *Charles Whibley* CC

3 February 1927 [London]

My dear Whibley,

Many thanks for your letter which evidently crossed a second letter from me which I hope you have received. I am delighted to hear that the operation appears to be successful.[2]

I am afraid Monday night is impossible for me but I can certainly manage to come in to the United Universities at 5.30 on Monday with the proof, and shall look forward to seeing you.[3]

Ever yours affectionately,
[T. S. E.]

## TO *Henri Massis* CC

4 février 1927 [*The Monthly Criterion*]

Cher Ami,

Je vous remercie beaucoup pour l'envoi de votre petit livre sur *L'Art du Roman*. Je l'ai déjà lu, et avec le plus grand intérêt. Vous avez fait quelque chose de très beau et de très solide. Votre examen de l'oeuvre de Radiguet m'a bien impressionné et m'a bien éclairci l'importance de cet auteur qui a exprimé un point de vue assez profond dans un style qui est parfois décevant dans sa simplicité. Mais j'attribue le plus d'importance au

1–Moore responded on 16 Feb.: 'I am sorry to have been inexplicit in my description of the Baudelaire and value your willingness to take it as you find it. Of course one must be courageous in recognizing faults, but we honour your implication that it is more congenial to speak well of a book than to speak ill of it.' Of TSE's compliment: 'That you should feel that The Dial has not retrograded is an encouragement and an incentive.'

2–Whibley's symptoms had included pain in the head.

3–Whibley (2 Feb.): 'I want very much to go through the proofs of the Seneca with you. Could you dine with me on Monday next at the University Club at 8? . . . If this won't do, could you come to the club at 5.30 o'clock on Monday, & read them before dinner.'

dernier chapitre de votre livre. J'ai prêté le livre à Mons. Herbert Read qui nous fera peut être une note intéressante là dessus.[1]

Quant va paraître *Défense de l'Occident*? Je l'attends avec impatience. J'ai plusieurs idées dans la tête que je vous communiquerai plus tard.

Avec mes amitiés loyales,
[T. S. Eliot][2]

## TO *E R Curtius* CC

4 February 1927 [London]

My dear Curtius,

Very many thanks for your letter of the 21st January. I am very much pleased with your translation. There are only three small suggestions I have to make. One is about the printing of the line from Ariel's song in Shakespeare's *Tempest* – 'Those are pearls that were his eyes'. Another is that 'staves' (plural of staff) is, I suppose 'staben'. The last is that I note that you have translated 'with a little patience' by the imperative. Is this right? I meant that we were dying patiently but without any great struggle or revolt, and therefore not much patience was necessary. It is intended to convey a state of torpor or exhaustion after a great or overwhelming event; not as an exhortation. But I have nothing but compliments and appreciation to offer. It will be a very great pleasure to me to see your translation in print. I am glad to hear that you have arranged with the *Neue Schweize Rundschau*. I am also very grateful to you for insisting on publishing the thing as a whole, because I think that any selections from the poem would give a very poor impression of it.[3]

1 – HR's review of Massis, *Réflexions sur l'Art du Roman*, *MC* 6 (Aug. 1927), 175.

2 – *Translation*: Dear friend, I wish to thank you very much for sending me your little book on *The Art of the Novel*. I have already read it and with the greatest interest. You have done something very beautiful and very reliable. Your study of [Raymond] Radiguet has impressed me a lot and has enlightened me on the importance of this author, who has expressed with depth his point of view in a style which is sometimes disappointing in its simplicity. But I give most importance to the last chapter of your book. I have lent it to Mr Herbert Read who will perhaps do us an interesting note on the subject.

When will *Defence of the West* be published? I am waiting for it with anticipation. I have several ideas in mind that I will communicate to you later. Your loyal friend. [T. S. Eliot]

3 – 'T. S. Eliot', *Neue Schweizer Rundschau* 32 (Apr. 1927), 348–61. Curtius's essay has been reprinted in English as the first part of 'T. S. Eliot', in his *Essays on European Literature* (*Kritische Essays zur europäischen Literatur*), trans. Michael Kowal (1973), 355–71.

Thank you very much for your essay on Maritain which I have read with the greatest interest and consider perfectly fair.[1] I have passed it on to Mr Herbert Read.

It is true that the *Roseau d'Or* are publishing shortly an essay of mine on 'La Mystique de Dante et la Mystique de Donne' and I shall not fail to have a copy sent you.[2] It is a sketch for a chapter in a book which I am writing on 'The Metaphysical Poetry of the Seventeenth Century' – chiefly in England.

I share the wish and hope of our meeting.[3] It is indeed strange to me to think that we have never actually seen each other. All that I can do is to let you know beforehand of my next visit to the Continent, whether to France or to Germany, and hope that we might be able to meet. If I could pay a visit to Germany I should make a point of coming to Heidelberg to find you.

By the way, I have heard nothing more from Mr Sperber of Bucovina, and the *Europäische Revue* does not appear to have heard from him either. So I suppose you need not concern yourself about his translation.

Yours ever
[T. S. Eliot]

## TO *The Editor of* Europäische Revue — CC

4 February 1927 [London]

My dear Sir,

Many thanks for your letter of the 22nd January and for the two copies which you have sent me personally. I am very glad to have these as the review copies go direct to Mr Randall and I do not see them here. These are very interesting numbers indeed and I congratulate you.

I understand perfectly the difficulties which you mention as I am always struggling with the same difficulties myself. As an Editor one is unfortunately obliged to do what one can to interest the public, and the public is not interested in general ideas or *Prinzipiendiscussion*. In order

1 – Curtius had declared in his letter that he could not accept the Thomist position.
2 – Henri Massis had advised Curtius that an abbreviated version of TSE's third Clark lecture, on Donne and the *Trecento*, was being translated by Jean de Menasce for the third number of *Le Roseau d'Or* (1927). '*Deux Attitudes Mystiques: Dante et Donne*' – a translation TSE approved – is reprinted as Appendix 1 of *VMP*, 309–18.
3 – 'I have a great wish that we should meet one day. Through your work and your magazine you have enriched and stimulated [lit. fertilised/pollinated] me. But many of these shoots could only blossom in the living contact of being together.'

to have influence one has to insinuate ideas gently; but the great difficulty, as you say, is to find other material which is both light and readable and at the same time of really high literary quality.

I have not forgotten my promise to contribute to your review, but unfortunately I have been and am very heavily burdened by pressing local commissions, and am struggling in the midst of editorial duties to write a book. I can only say that I shall continue to keep the *Europäische Revue* in mind.

It is curious that you should have heard nothing from Herr Sperber. He evidently took a great deal of trouble in translating my poem and I have not heard from him again since I wrote to him in November. I wrote to him again a fortnight or more ago and told him what our friend Professor Curtius was doing, but I have had no reply. You will understand that Herr Sperber sent me his translation which he had already made before consulting me, long before I had any idea that Curtius thought of doing it. I made a few corrections in the translation, and gave Herr Sperber my consent to his offering it to the *Neue Rundschau* or to you. Apparently the *Neue Rundschau* has not heard from him either. Meanwhile, Curtius has completed his translation, but I understand from him that he has made some engagement with the *Neue Schweizer Rundschau*. In any case I should be quite willing to have any other of my verse translated and as soon as possible should be glad to offer you a piece of prose. I could not do so without breaking other promises of very long standing.

With cordial good wishes,
I am,
Yours sincerely,
[T. S. Eliot]

## TO *T. Sturge Moore* CC

4 February 1927 [London]

Dear Mr Sturge Moore,

I quite understand your annoyance.[1] I do not know whether I explained to you in my last letter that I had written quite strongly to the lady on the subject and pointed out that I must decline to do any more soliciting unless my judgment was to be accepted as final. I shall never

1 – TSE had sent Princess Bassiano a translation by Sturge Moore of a poem by Valéry, 'The Torrent'; but for a number of reasons, Sturge Moore begged for it to be withdrawn.

again attempt to oblige in this way a publication over which I have no official control.

I believe that your typescript has been returned to you with the proof. I can of course only accept with regret your decision not to publish the stanzas in this form and will substitute something else.

I would only say that my keeping the stanzas did not appear in my own eyes as in any way an act of kindness or compensation, and that I regretted from the beginning that I had not obtained them for *The New Criterion* instead of for *Commerce*.

Yours very sincerely,
[T. S. Eliot]

## TO *G. C. Robertson* — CC

7 February 1927 — [London]

Dear Mr Robertson,

Thank you for your letter of the 4th.[1] I had been expecting to hear from you again and should have written myself to enquire your wishes but that I have been very busy.

It is rather difficult to come to any definite conclusion at the moment because I am probably leaving tomorrow for two or three weeks' absence.

But I did understand from your telephone message that you only wanted to take the flat on until some time in June so that your new proposition finds me somewhat unprepared. I would say, however, that it suits me better than the first. I should not have wanted the flat for my own use in June in any case. So that I can say definitely now that I am quite willing to let you keep it on for at least six months at the same rent. I should be disposed to agree to a year's tenancy. As for nine months, you will understand that it makes a good deal of difference to the landlord of the flat at what time of year it becomes vacant. The best times for letting are the early spring and the autumn; so that if the flat became vacant in November I should possibly be unable to let it again for two or three months. I should be inclined to say, therefore, either six months or a year.

At the moment you will understand that I am unable to take any steps myself about redecoration. If you are so inclined, I should suggest that you get detailed estimates of what you want done from two or three

1 – Robertson and his wife, tenants at 9 Clarence Gate Gardens, wished to stay on for nine months or a year. They wanted rooms to be redecorated, excess furniture to be removed.

decorators and I will call upon you as soon as I return. Two firms which have done good work for me in the past are William H. Lambert & Son, Park Road, Regent's Park, N.W.1 and Minter's (I forget the address – they are in the telephone book). I should be glad to meet you in this matter, but of course neither of us can speak definitely until we know what the operations are likely to cost.

I cannot at the moment give you any address, but any correspondence sent here will be forwarded at once.

Yours very truly,
[T. S. Eliot]

## TO *J. B. Trend* CC

7 February 1927 [London]

Dear Trend,

Thank you very much for your letter. I am very glad that you agree with me in principle on the method of running our Chronicles. I am very glad to think that you are willing to continue your own invaluable Chronicles in the same way as before. As for the Spanish periodicals, I will not bother you with them. If Flint is willing to continue, very well; if not, we will try your friend with the astonishing name.[1] You might discuss the point with Flint tomorrow night.

Is there any chance of ever getting a book out of you or of inducing you to work up your *Criterion* Chronicles into a book now or at some time in the future?

Ever yours,
[T. S. Eliot]

## TO *Ottoline Morrell* TS Texas

7 February 1927 *The New Criterion*

My dear Ottoline,

Forgive me for my delay in answering your letter. I confess that I am quite unable to answer your question. I am not very strong on

1 – Trend recommended (5 Feb.) Ali Ilhami: 'He is really an Englishman; & I can answer for his *Spanish*, as we travelled together in Spain. At present he is (I think) writing a novel about Constantinople – from the point of view of someone who has become a Muhammadan (technically at least) though he drinks wine and limits his seraglio to one.'

Commentaries and am especially weak about the Canzoni.[1] I am glad that you like them and if I can find out I will let you know. I will try.

I have been wondering why you have been silent for so long and am sorry to learn that it is 'flu. When are you coming to London? That is what we want to know. I think that Whitehead's book is very fine though I have not yet read it thoroughly.[2] Lewis's book[3] is tremendously interesting and I should like to talk to you about it. Will you not be in London soon?

Much love from both,
Tom

## TO *William Force Stead*

MS Beinecke

7 February 1927

24 Russell Square

Dear Stead,

Very many thanks for your kind letter. I can reassure you on one point. There *is* a form of baptism, a ritual with water, in Unitarianism. I cannot of course swear that I was baptised! I don't remember – is a certificate needed? But my people considered that they were identical with the Unitarian church – their position in Boston Unitarianism is like that of the Borgias in the Papacy! – and I have seen younger members of the family baptised, very formally; and I have in short not the *slightest doubt* of my Baptism.

By the way, Unitarians have a kind of Communion Service – once a month, also. I never communicated; my parents did, regularly; but they did not bother about me.

I shall not be able to avail myself of your kind offer for some weeks, but I will give you due notice. But do I have to prepare myself to answer any set questions? or any examination?

Yours with many thanks.
T. S. Eliot

1 – OM wanted to know (29 Jan.) of a commentary on Dante's Canzoni, which (she said) 'have taken such a hold of me & are so extraordinarily beautiful . . . but I don't really understand them or know whether they are addressed mostly to a Spiritual Conception or to a lady of flesh & blood – etc.'

2 – OM: 'I have always wondered if you read Whitehead's Science and The Modern World – & if so if you approved of p. 266 to 268. It seems to me well put. Indeed the last two chapters seem to me *very* fine.'

3 – Wyndham Lewis, *The Lion and the Fox*.

I am acquainted with the Prayerbook form of confirmation – but I don't know it by heart.

## TO *Mansfield Forbes*[1]

CC

7 February 1927 [*The New Criterion*]

My dear Forbes,

I am hastening to reply to your letter. I do not as a rule come to my office on a Saturday, otherwise you would have received a reply this morning.

Last year, before I finished my lectures at Cambridge, I had a talk with Winstanley on the question of next year's lecturer.[2] This statement is, like your letter, confidential. It was before I knew that the appointment of Morgan Forster was in the wind. I suggested several names. One of them was Bonamy Dobrée whom you mention yourself; another was Herbert Read. I had not thought of Edwin Muir. I should myself at the present moment recommend Bonamy Dobrée particularly; I think that he would be a good lecturer and I think that anything he had to say would be interesting and valuable. But he has recently gone out to Cairo as Professor of English at the university there. He told me that he had made a contract for three years. In any case I do not suppose that he would be available for next year. If he were, I should be as keen for his appointment as anybody.

Edwin Muir is certainly a good man. My chief objection to him hitherto has been that I have thought he needed time to educate himself. He is a dour Scot from the North (not from your part of Scotland but I think from the Hebrides) whose education apart from what he has received in Scotland has been chiefly teutonic. So much so that I have found his ideas always limited by his education. He was, and is still as far as I know, very

1 – Mansfield Forbes (1890–1936), Fellow in English, Clare College, Cambridge. See Hugh Carey, *Mansfield Forbes and his Cambridge* (1984).

2 – Forbes had approached TSE on 2 Feb.: 'The authorities at Trinity are looking out for next year's (1928's) appointment for the Clark Lectureship, and the mention of a certain name as a possible has caused me to intervene with H. F. Stewart, and suggest others. The names that immediately occur'd to me were those of *Bonamy Dobrée*, who, I know, can lecture well – and *Edwin Muir*. Personally, I slightly favour the latter, if he can & does lecture. I should be very greatly obliged if you can give me any information on this point, and also as to whether there are others you would be disposed to recommend.

'The appointment must take place by the 18th of this month, so the matter is fairly urgent, as appointers have generally to be put in touch with works of the possible appointees, & otherwise coached & cajoled a little.'

much under the influence of Germanic valuations[;] i.e. he knows all about Ibsen and Nietzsche and Schopenhauer and has very good ideas about some of the Russians; but I think that for absolute opinions his defect of classical and Latin culture is still apparent. His recent book, *Transition*, is good, honest, serious and independent criticism, but I feel that even there his lack of tradition makes him take the ephemeral present too seriously. I am speaking quite frankly. You could get many worse men and are not likely to get many better. Still, I feel that as a guide for the young he is not altogether a safe one. But whether I, in your place, pushed his candidacy or not would depend entirely on what one was likely to get in his place.

One of the other men I mentioned to Winstanley was Herbert Read. He has developed a good deal since his recent book, *Reason and Romanticism* which expresses unsatisfactorily rather his process of development than its conclusion. If you consider him at all, get hold of his book called *English Stained Glass* (which is published by Putnam) and examine the philosophy of history which he outlines in that book. I do not altogether agree with his conclusions, and it is by no means true that he and I have identical views on everything.

I also know two distinguished French writers, both of whom have an intimate knowledge of English literature and could lecture perfectly well in English – Ramon Fernandez and Charles du Bos: but I imagine that the appointment of a Frenchman would be impossible.

I am only answering this part of your letter which I take to be urgent. I want to write to you presently in reply to the rest of this very interesting letter.[1]

As to Jack, I cannot yet speak positively because he has not yet shown me any of his writing or notes upon Pater.[2] In conversation with him and from one or two of his reviews in *The Granta* which he has shown me, I have been very favourably impressed with him; but we have not yet got far enough for me to form any strong opinion. I have pressed him to send me some notes on the subject of his thesis as soon as possible.

I had not heard that Richards was married though I have always expected that he would get married.[3] I have missed him very much and shall be very glad when he decides to return to England.

Yours always sincerely,
[T. S. Eliot]

1 – Forbes had indulged himself with his views on 'the Romantic-Classic *impasse*'.
2 – 'What . . . do you think of P. M. Jack, the Trinity Hall researcher on W. Pater?'
3 – 'As to Richards,' remarked Forbes, 'I hear he has married his climbing-partner, Miss Pilly [Dorothea Pilley], at Honolulu, & is on his lengthy homeward way.'

## TO *Herbert Read*

MS Victoria

Monday [? Feb. 1927] 57 Chester Terrace, S.W.1.

One point I particularly wanted to mention. I have suggested your name quite informally (I have only been consulted personally & privately) for the Clark Lectureship for next year. I don't suppose my word will carry much weight – only – *if* it would be *im*possible for you to give them, please let me know. So that I can urge somebody else. But *if* it comes off, I hope you can – it means lecturing in the late afternoon 6 or 8 times in a term – once a week. Surely the Museum would let you off once a week for 8 weeks?

I say I don't believe my word carries much weight, because last year, as there was a small movement in favour of Dobrée, I backed him – with the result that Forster was chosen. But *you* have much more published work to your credit than you had a year ago.

It is well paid – £25 per lecture – you give 6 to 10 lectures, as you choose – & you get a book out of it.[1]

Yours ever
T. S. E.

## TO *John Middleton Murry*

MS Northwestern

8 February 1927 57 Chester Terrace, S.W.1.

My dear John,

I am returning your Essay, together with some notes by Read. Could you prepare a final draft in time for publication in May[2] – That is to say, I should like to have it by *March 15* at the latest, preferably before. If you cannot do this, please let me know *at once*, at 24 Russell Sq. as otherwise I shall depend upon you. I should press this, but do not know how much work you are able to do at present.

1–HR replied on 9 Feb. 1927: 'It is good of you to think of me for the job, & I think if I were asked I should make a special effort to accept. Do you mean for 1928? Presumably, since Forster must be this year. The lectures would enable me to fulfil my promise of a book for Woolf's series. But I quite understand how tentative the whole thing is, & I won't build up any hopes about the business.' Ultimately, HR was to write to TSE on 11 Mar. 1929: 'An invitation has arrived from Trinity Lodge: your kind offices have borne fruit. Before I accept, I would very much like to see you & find out more exactly what it involves. I am fairly free all this week & will try & fit in with any arrangement convenient to you.' HR was to give the Clark Lectures, on Wordsworth, in 1930.

2–'Towards a Synthesis', *MC* 5 (June 1927), 294–313.

I agree with most of Read's objections. Where I am more on your side than his is in the assumption that T.'s[1] theology must be, in essentials, accepted exactly as far as his philosophy is accepted. Where I chiefly differ from you on points not raised by Read, is that I think your whole philosophy of history implies a pragmatist or relativist attitude of a type that I cannot accept. You *assume* a progress in the Renaissance – I admit progress within very narrow limits only. Your assumption, based on unconscious popular Darwinism, has got to be defended. You assume that Truth changes – you accept as inevitable what appears to me to be within our own power. I am, in a way, a much more thoroughgoing pragmatist – but so thoroughgoing that I am sure there is nothing for it but to assume that there are fixed meanings, and that Truth is always the same. I cannot perceive that *you* admit any objective restraint upon translating any feeling into a belief, & I think this can only lead to non-conformist individual chaos.

It is on the point of Evolutionism & pragmatism that I should attack you.

Ever affectionately,
Tom.

## FROM *John Middleton Murry* — MS Valerie Eliot

9 February 1927 — 1a The Gables, Hampstead N.W.3

My dear Tom,

I am out of bed – lackadaisical, but back or back coming back into life. Yes, I think I can promise to return the essay revised by March 15, and I will try for March 10. I didn't tell you – perhaps I shouldn't now – that your poem[2] in the last N.C. depressed me frightfully. (That sounds as though I were trying to blame you for my pneumonia.)

No, I suppose that *au fond* I am a reprehensible non-conformist individualist. I can't help it. The only thing that gives me profound satisfaction is the contemplation of individuals. Institutions fill me with horror – a reverential adhorrence. I dislike humanity in the mass; and when it is controlled (as it ought to be) I don't dislike it less. I am an impossibilist – and in my heart of hearts I suspect that you are too.

1–St Thomas Aquinas.
2–'Fragment of an Agon'.

Perhaps I am guilty of cheap Darwinism – I don't know. I shouldn't have thought it. I don't think mankind improves. I simply believe that it is (on the whole and in the long run) prevented from degeneration by individuals – individualists if you like. Institutions, aggregates always degenerate; until they are galvanized by individuals. I am an unashamed hero-worshipper.

And yet – to be quite honest – I suppose I do believe that things gradually improve. Whenever I dive into the middle ages, or classical times, I am horrified by the sheer cruelty of life: I say to myself: 'They didn't feel it as cruel, & I, had I lived then shouldn't have done', but that doesn't convince me. I am glad that I didn't live then; – but I mistrust my feeling on the point. On the whole – my moments of illumination, or self-deception apart – I feel that things have always been, as Katherine once said, 'mush of a mushness'.

As for Truth – I don't much believe in it. The permanent truths are the unpleasant ones – e.g. that mankind is a herd. Dynamic truth interests me more – e.g. that a man who has the strength to follow his own star makes a good end – is satisfying to contemplate. To be a hero without heroic illusions – if that is possible – is my ideal: and I can't live up to it.

Something too much of this.[1]

Ever affectionately
John

Please give my love & good wishes to Vivien.

## TO *James Smith*

CC

16 February 1927 [London]

Dear Smith,

That is quite all right.[2] You can rely upon me if I am approached for an opinion. I very much hope that you will get it.

1–*Hamlet*, 3. ii. 64.

2–Smith had written on 15 Feb.: 'Today I have just discovered is the last day for the entering of applications for a University Scholarship of which I stand in need if I am to spend a further year in Cambridge before burying myself in Whitehall or in a Secondary School. It is of the value of £200 per annum, and is awarded for research in Classics, Literature, Music or Moral Sciences. For the last two years I have been studying the philosophical implications of dramatic criticism, and the influence of current philosophical ideas upon the dramatic criticism of their day. I would like to complete this, or at least to carry it further. So I have sent in an application for the Scholarship, and without consulting you, given your name as one of my three referees.

I do not know whether it is irregular to mention the fact, but I *did* read your thesis, and in any case I consider that I have quite enough knowledge to be able to speak strongly. I await a letter from the Authorities. And I hope that you will let me know if ever you are in London.

With all best wishes,
Yours very sincerely,
[T. S. Eliot]

## TO *Mansfield Forbes* CC

17 February 1927 [*The New Criterion*]

My dear Forbes,

I am at present in the country for a week or two but came up to London for the day and hasten to reply to your letter of the 14th. With regard to your suggestion of Wyndham Lewis for the lectureship.[1] If you find that there is enough support for him to make it worthwhile pushing his nomination I would gladly support it, for anything that my support is worth, and if you like would approach him myself on the subject. My hesitation is due to 1. Ignorance of local politics. If it is important to keep out a certain anonymous horror to whom you allude, then the question must be decided on political grounds, i.e. which one of the candidates suggested would enlist the strongest support against the candidate whom you oppose. 2. is the one you mention yourself, that Lewis is not a very dependable person. I think, however, that if he accepted the post he would actually give the lectures.

I am interested to hear that you disagree with me categorically and you must admit that such an admission implies the obligation on your part to write to me fully in the matter; and I await the letter with impatience.[2] There

---

'I was emboldened to this by the memory of your constant goodwill to me; but chiefly by a message you sent me by Peter Jack, that you hoped I should gain a Fellowship. As I cannot recollect having spoken to you within recent years of my academic ambitions, I assumed that you must have been condemned to read the sketch of a thesis I sent to the Fellowship Electors last October.'

1 – Forbes had written: 'Personally I favour Wyndham Lewis more than anyone these days as inspiring disturber, & blaster of inhibitions & des-, or ab, -integrating academic & quasi-academic "scrupulousness" – His introduction, for instance, to The Lion & The Fox is miraculously, to my mind, pregnant – But he is hopelessly unreliable as a lecturer, & in relation to punctilio, is he not?'

2 – Forbes said in his letter, in response to a second (now lost) letter from TSE: 'to be candid, I utterly disagree'.

are other terms which I should like to get rid of as well as Romanticism-Classicism: for instance, Aesthetics, Art and *possibly* Literature. But it is no use writing any more about this until I can write at great length, and meanwhile I hope to hear from you.

By the way, as I shall be out of town for a week or so, I should be glad if you would address any letter to this office instead of to my home so that it may be forwarded.

Yours every sincerely,
[T. S. Eliot]

## TO *William Rose* CC

17 February 1927 [London]

My dear Rose,

I must apologise for my long silence and the delay in giving an opinion about the books by Hans Heinz Ewers which you kindly showed me.[1] We went into the matter pretty carefully; I read some of the stories myself and had others read by a reader. They certainly have unusual merit, but the consensus of opinion was that there is no sale whatever in this country for volumes of short stories; and probably a volume of short stories translated from another language would be even less popular. But I thank you very much for letting me see them. I am returning them to you under separate cover.

I expect to be out of town for a week or so, but when I get back I will drop you a line and hope that you will come and lunch with me. I trust that the Republic of Letters is flourishing.

Yours sincerely
[T. S. Eliot]

1–Hans Heinz Ewers (1871–1943),: German author and short story writer who was to become best known for his trilogy of novels on the subject of one Frank Braun (who stands more or less for Ewers himself). During WW1 Ewers was active in the USA as a German propagandist, and was subsequently interned as an enemy alien. He is considered a seminal figure in the modern revival of fantasy and horror literature, and his works include *Der Zauberlehrling* ('The Sorcerer's Apprentice', 1910), *Alraune* (1911), *Vampyr* (1921?) and *Der Geisterseher* (1922), as well as a number of film scripts.

## TO *J. M. Robertson* CC

17 February 1927 [London]

My dear Robertson,

I am delighted to have your letter of the 10th, enclosing the Burns typescript.[1] I have read the essay with great pleasure and general agreement. I am not competent to express any opinion of Henley's opinion of Burns because I have not read Henley himself on the subject; but as you put it, I certainly agree with you. On the other hand, I am very glad to have justice done to Henley's verse, especially 'In Hospital' which I have always admired. Of course Henley wrote a fair amount of versified rubbish as well, jingles about kings in Babylon and what not, but I have never changed my opinion about 'In Hospital' and some other of 'London Voluntaries'.[2]

Are you in a hurry to get the Burns published? The alteration of *The Criterion* from a quarterly to a monthly is requiring some painful adjustments in the editorial mind, and I find it difficult to realise how little a monthly will contain. In any case, of course, the Burns will have to be serialised into two parts. Would it suit you if I began it in May or in June? I am very anxious to publish it and I hope that you will give me a little leeway.[3]

With many thanks,
Yours ever,
[T. S. Eliot]

1–Robertson, in his covering letter, deprecated his Burns lecture: 'I quite definitely and disgustedly realised its merely popular quality – of which, remember, I warned you.'

2–W. E. Henley wrote a sequence 'In Hospital' while a long-term patient at the Royal Infirmary, Edinburgh, 1873–5. 'London Voluntaries IV: Out of the Poisonous East' figures the 'Wind-Fiend, the abominable – / The Hangman Wind that tortures temper and light' settling down 'To the grim job of throttling London Town'. 'I was a King in Babylon' finds the king lamenting in age the 'Christian . . . Virgin Slave' whom he bent and broke and killed despite the fact that she is reported to have loved him. 'London Voluntaries' was dedicated to Charles Whibley. See W. E. Henley, *Poems* (1898).

3–'Burns and his Race', *MC* 7 (Jan. 1928), 33–46; (Feb. 1928), 154–68.

## TO *Mario Praz*

CC

17 February 1927 [*The New Criterion*]

Dear Praz,

I am sorry that we did not meet yesterday. I hoped that you might call in time to have lunch with me, and when I went out I left word where to find me. But I must look forward to your next visit to London.

Thank you for returning the lectures and for your invaluable letter.[1] It is the most useful comment that I have so far had, and be sure that when I

1–Praz wrote on 13 Feb., after reading TSE's Clark Lectures: 'You are the best critic of yourself; and I could only repeat in a less intelligent way what you have known all this time. My only wonder is, whether you will be able to give a more detailed and eindringlich illustration of your theory about the disintegration of the intellect. Will the suggested theory, which looks very convincing in your lectures, hold good after you will have tried to test it case by case? Trimming and compromising will do only in so far as you confine yourself to a synthetical survey, as you have done in your lectures, but the more detailed your examination will be, the more arbitrary many of your assumptions are bound to seem, under the microscope of analysis. You know how unreal a penetrating remark may be caused to appear, when worked into any consistent system: I am thinking for instance of Spengler's famous book. A little inaccuracy of interpretation, which remains unnoticed when slurred over in the course of a lecture, may wreck the whole work, when insisted upon and magnified in a book. I am not sure, for instance, about what you are saying in your III lect., p. 19 on the trecentisti having no idea of a dichotomy between soul and body. I have not gone very far into the question myself; but, before coming to any conclusions concerning Dante, for inst., I would examine carefully all the passages of his work bearing on the subject – a task rendered very easy to us by the admirable index raisonnée appended to the Testo Critico of Dante's Works, Bonporad 1921. I daresay you are familiar with it. Lect. II, p 11: Is really the Soc. of Jesus so different from the Orders of the M. Ages in so far as its chief purpose was to combat heresy? What about the Dominican Order? As for S. Teresa, have you read what Unamuno, no mean authority for the interpretation of Spanish mysticism, writes of her in Ensayos (Madrid 1916) I, 163? 'Santa Teresa no quería que sus hermanas fuesen mujeres en nada, ni lo pareciesen,' 'sino varones Fuertes' y tan varoniles, que 'espanten a los hombres'. Obviously the real S. Teresa is a very different creature from Crashaw's and Marino's fainting Saint: her works, says Unamuno – p. 152 – 'son autobiografies psicológicas de un realismo de dibujo vigoroso y preciso, sin psicologiquería alguna.' The truth is that too often in our affirmations we rely on second-hand authorities; we start from other people's interpretations accepting them as sound premises. Thus, the inaccuracies grow in a geometric proportion the more one gets further from the sources, until one is speaking of ghosts, trattando l'ombre come cosa salda. Is R[emy] de Gourmont a sound authority on Dante and provencal literature? Are you right in including S. Philip Neri among Spanish mystics? (Lect. II p. 19, IV 19). But I needn't warn you any longer in this pedantic strain, because, as I was saying, I am sure you are aware of those as well as of many other objections. Another remark, a very secondary one, on what you say about the opening lines of Donne's *Ecstasy* (III, 14). Of course the image of the bed and the pillow is preposterous, and the languour of the violet seems conventional, but Freud, perhaps, might find the poet's mood on that occasion mirrored even in an apparently superfluous detail like that one: it is a nuptial simile in a nuptial poem, and in so far it has its *raison d'être*. What I liked best are Lectures V, VII, VIII: they throw light on your own verse, apart from the

am putting the book in order I shall follow up all the lines of enquiry that you have suggested. But your letter increases my sense of the enormous gap between the lectures in the form you have seen them and any possible book; I feel now that it may be years before I can present the book, and possibly by that time I shall be too disgusted with what I have written to re-write it at all.[1]

With many thanks, and looking forward to your next visit,

---

interest of the theories as such. I am very much looking forward to your trilogy: it will be a book of criticism which will read like fiction, perhaps, and so much the better for it, if it does: history is, after all as somebody said, always contemporary history, and in writing your book, you will be writing the history of your own mind. And your mind, I am afraid, interests me even more than Donne, Crashaw and all the dead worthies.'

TSE declared in the typescript of his Clark Lectures that he was proposing to rewrite them as a book, *The School of Donne*: 'It is intended as one volume of a trilogy under the general title of "The Disintegration of the Intellect": the other two volumes will deal with *Elizabethan Drama*, its technical development, its versification, and its intellectual background of general ideas; and with *The Sons of Ben* – the development of humanism, its relation to Anglican thought, and the emergency of Hobbes and Hyde. The three together will constitute a criticism of the English Renaissance' (*VMP*, 41). As the years moved on, this 'trilogy' was abandoned: and even as early as 1931 he made public his judgement that, since so much had recently been published on the Metaphysicals, there was 'no possible justification of turning my lectures into a book' ('Donne in Our Time', in *A Garland for John Donne*, ed. Theodore Spencer [1931]).

1 – Praz replied on 18 Feb.: 'Probably you are right in thinking that the writing of *the whole* of your trilogy would be a matter of years: but the lectures could, even in the present form, make a stimulating book. If I were you, I would not try to press too much the suggestions contained there: in so far as they remain such, they are true, as paths and tracks which are visible only from an aeroplane, and seem to disappear as soon as one gets too close to the ground. If I were you, I would publish as soon as possible the lectures: it would help very much the development of your thoughts on the subject, through the discussions that might ensue. But, of course, if you brood over them a long time, you will get sick of them. Besides, you have more important things to do than to work in the British Museum!' (MS VE) On 19 June 1935, TSE would write to Praz: 'I never republished my Clark Lectures at Cambridge, and I have no intention of doing so. I may have changed my mind on many points, and I am certainly conscious of having written outside of my actual knowledge . . . The point is that to rewrite the Clark Lectures in any form which would be now acceptable to me would be an immense labour and I am now more interested in doing other things and writing about other subjects' (Galleria Nazionale d'Arte Moderna, Rome). On 7 Oct. 1948 TSE was to write to Elizabeth Drew, who was seeking to quote from the Clark lectures in a forthcoming book: 'I should explain about the Clark lectures that I never had any intention of publishing them and have always regarded them on the whole as a pretentious and rather poor piece of work. Indeed, I should have destroyed the manuscript long ago but kept it thinking that there might be things in it which I could incorporate into something better later. Then when the war came there was an auction of manuscripts and first editions on behalf of the Red Cross. Hugh Walpole wrote and asked me to contribute, and having nothing else I gave them this typescript which was auctioned and subsequently acquired by Harvard University. I have never ceased to regret it' (CC VE).

I am,
Yours very sincerely,
[T. S. Eliot]

### TO *Richard Aldington* TS Texas

24 February 1927 24 Russell Square

My dear Richard,

Very glad indeed to get your letter of the 10th. I have had no time hitherto to answer it properly, and even this may seem to you merely a scrap, though to me it will seem a long epistle. I was pleased that you should identify, and approve, my note on the Chapman book. That is certainly a point which I want to hammer as much as I can.[1]

Well here goes into the deep cold water.[2] I DONT think that philosophy should be 'based' on science. It seems to me something quite different. I agree that a philosopher should be as well informed about science as possible, but philosophy by scientists is as bad as science by philosophers: even Whitehead flounders. Then there are many people neither fish flesh fowl nor herring, some of them very clever too, who seem to me to mix up everything appallingly: look at our friend Richards, who is a most brilliant chap; if you read his little book on Poetry and Science[3] you will find that he can be quite good on Poetry, and I dare say quite good on Science, at any rate quite glib on Psychology; but the two don't fit in the least, his right and his left hand function quite independently, though he thinks they work together.[4] But when I say that a philosopher ought to know

1 – RA wrote, 'Your very clear statement about the necessary connection between scholarship and literary criticism ought to be valuable as a help towards making our amateur criticism a little less amateur . . . I do hope you will continue hammering on this line.' In a later letter (26 Feb.), RA disclosed: 'It was not *very* clever of me to detect your hand in the Chapman review, since I had sent the book to B. L. R. with a suggestion that it was exactly your subject.'

2 – RA had challenged TSE: 'It is generally agreed that philosophy must be based upon science . . . Well, if that is so, is not medieval philosophy absolutely invalidated? Whatever its dialectical skill, whatever its perfection of method, is it not pure waste from the absurdity of its premises and the inadequacy of its knowledge? . . . In other words can one really separate the method of your great namesake [St Thomas Aquinas] from his theology (which is fabulous) and his science, which is equally fabulous? . . . The 11th, 12th, 13th, 14th centuries were highly successful in the imaginative arts and architecture . . . but their science was null and worse than null. Consequently, their philosophy must be null, because it is founded on the sands of theology and fabulous science.'

3 – *Science and Poetry*.

4 – See TSE, 'Literature, Science, and Dogma', *Dial* 82: 3 (Mar. 1927), 239–43.

as much science as possible (and FAR more than I do – I can never be a philosopher) I mean, because, unless you know a good deal about science, you don't know enough to AVOID it. There is a lot of talk in philosophy manuals about the gradual emancipation (since Thales[1]) of science from philosophy; but there is less said about the equally difficult and important, and much farther-off event, the emancipation of philosophy from science. The middle ages didn't get anywhere near it; their bad science discredits their good philosophy, but it is their own fault. <And damned difficult to disentangle 'em.> But the present age is equally dark; read any of the more recent philosophical works of Bertrand Russell, and see what a dark age of gross superstition we still live in. The middle ages were a period of scientific superstition, this is an age of philosophic superstition. But if you are going to prove that my great namesake's theology is fabulous, waal, you got a tough job before breakfast. I don't say that the Church cannot be too strong, that's a different matter: Atheism should always be encouraged (i.e. rationalistic not emotional atheism) for the sake of the Faith: a distinction is to be drawn between people like Leonard Woolf and J. M. Robertson (and I hope yourself) who are Good (or White) Atheists, and people like Russell and Murry who are Bad (or Red) Atheists, otherwise heretics.

To come down to brass tacks, I don't believe that the study of Science is going to help one to write better poetry. Anyway, I can't bother. What do you think? Though I am often saying to myself, When I have TIME, I shall get a block of paper, a pencil, a text book, and really take up algebra.[2]

Ever thine
Tom

1–Thales of Miletus (*c.*620 – *c.*546 BC): pre-Socratic Greek philosopher; founder of the school of natural philosophy, eschewing mythological explanations of the universe.

2–RA answered on 26 Feb.: 'May I be allowed to express some surprise at your statement about philosophy and science? Are you not making philosophy entirely a matter of metaphysics? . . . Is not metaphysics a set of hypotheses about the unknown? . . . The emancipation of philosophy from science seems to me most dangerous as an idea . . . You shock me – "don't believe the study of Science is going to help one to write Poetry"!!!! Tom!! Sir, will you compare the mere embellishment of fictions with the pure light of truth, with the intense joy of contemplating ultimate realities which do not exist?'

## TO *Bruce Richmond* CC

25 February 1927 [London]

My dear Richmond,

I posted to you this morning before seeing your letter my review of the Marlowe book. It is rather long, but I think that the book deserves it.[1]

It is very kind of you to send me Lewis's book, and particularly the book on *Restoration Comedy*, which will certainly be very useful to me.

I return herewith the two letters you enclosed. I have taken note of Schoell's address, and will write to him.[2] Meanwhile I suppose you are publishing a note about his nationality. My suggestion was superfluous, but when a man's christian name is Frank and he is stated to be a professor at the University of California is it not natural to assume that he is an American?

I am afraid that I cannot answer the other letter. And I can only suggest that Mr Plomer[3] write to Dr McClure himself. I admit that I am not acquainted directly with Harrington's letters. All I know is that Dr McClure quotes some of them, which quotations are very agreeable, and that he speaks himself of them as if they might make better reading than the Epigrams.

I should have suggested another meeting, but at present we are, for a few weeks, at the seaside, and I only come up two or three days a week. As soon as I am settled again in London I will let you know.

Yours ever,
[T. S. E.]

1–'A Study of Marlowe' – on *Christopher Marlowe*, by U. M. Ellis-Fermor – *TLS*, 3 Mar. 1927, 140.

2–'I enclose two letters,' wrote BLR (22 Feb.), 'one from Mr Schoell, who desires to make your acquaintance and also desires us to state that he is not an American but a Frenchman, and another asking for information.' Schoell's letter was in response to TSE's review 'The Sources of Chapman' – on Frank L. Schoell, *Études sur l'Humanisme Continental en Angleterre à la fin de la Renaissance* (Paris, 1926) – TLS, 10 Feb. 1927, 88 (not in Gallup). See TSE's letter to Schoell, 7 Mar.

3–William Plomer.

## TO *Virginia Woolf* TS Texas

25 February 1927 *The New Criterion*

My dear Virginia,

We are present for a few weeks at the seaside, and I am only up in town by the day; hence the delay in replying to your letter.

I have not the ghost of an idea who E. A. Abbott[1] may be, or what his address is. The other question I am sorry to say I must answer in the affirmative: the money was received and was spent.[2]

The only possible recipient of whom I can think for the fund is one which appeals to me, but which perhaps would not be likely to appeal to many other contributors. But in any case a donation of this sort would involve so much labour and correspondence for you and so many enquiries from the contributors that I should hardly put forward any suggestion very urgently. But what I have in mind is the Poetry Book-Shop which has fallen on hard times and which I know (in strict confidence) is urgently in need of support. It has done good work and filled a certain role in the past, and I should be sorry to see it disappear. I know that Harold Monro was anxious if possible to get people to invest in it, and even to form a limited share company if sufficient capital could be found. I merely put this forward tentatively.

Our last meeting was certainly very unsatisfactory to me, although it gave me the opportunity to admire your brilliance and self-possession in a dazzling company which has reduced me to a very small corner. I should like to come to tea on Monday. The only difficulty is, that as I only come up for the day I have a great deal to get through in the time. But if it should happen that I was to spend a night in town on Monday I should

1–E. A. Abbott (1838–1926): teacher, writer, theologian; headmaster of the City of London School (where his pupils included the future prime minister H. H. Asquith), 1865–89; Hulsean Lecturer at Cambridge (his *alma mater*) in 1876. Writings include *Shakespearean Grammar* (1870); *Bacon and Essex* (1877); *Philochristus* (1878); *The Anglican Career of Cardinal Newman* (2 vols, 1892); *St Thomas of Canterbury, his Death and Miracles* (1898); and *Flatland: A Romance of Many Dimensions* (1884), a socio-religious satire set in two dimensions. Whether or not the money he gave to the Eliot relief fund was returned to his family is not known.

2–VW was seeking (Feb. 1927) to wind up 'that cursed fund, which your admirers subscribed': 'Ottoline, Aldington & I are agreed that it is best to return the money with thanks to the donors. There seems to be no candidate acceptable, if you retire.

'The only questions now are; who is E. A. Abbott – & what is his address: & did you return, or did you, as I hope, spend, a cheque for £50 which was, I see, paid to you out of the fund in January 1923?'

take the liberty of ringing you up on Monday morning and finding out whether the invitation was still open.

Ever yours,
Tom

We are at St. Leonards for a week or two.

## TO *Charles Whibley*

CC

25 February 1927 [24 Russell Square]

My dear Whibley,

I have registered to you this morning the final proof of my *Seneca*. I should be very grateful if you would run through it once more, noticing my alterations and additions, and if you find anything to question, either alter it or let me know. Otherwise, I have now nothing to change.

I am now asking you to fulfil your promise as you will see from the enclosed documents. What you have to do is to complete and declare before a Commissioner for Oaths the form which you will find on top; and at the same time to get the Commissioner for Oaths to write in on the back of the other form, which I have marked with an X in blue pencil, a statement similar to this on the front.[1]

As I told you, Sydney Waterlow's[2] testimony is no longer valid because he has gone to Siam.

There is no great hurry about this, and you can keep it until it is convenient for you to see a Commissioner for Oaths. And I have got to send it afterward to Harry Crofton to re-declare before I deliver it at the Home Office.

1–CW responded on 26 Feb.: 'I will, with the greatest pleasure, sign the necessary papers & discover a commissioner of oaths somewhere in this town on Monday. I shall rejoice to see you an Englishman in name, as you are already in heart & genius. As a reward you must promise to dine with me on the day that you are naturalized.'

2–Sydney Waterlow (1878–1944), diplomat and writer. Educated at Eton and Trinity College, Cambridge, he joined the diplomatic service in 1900 and served as attaché and third secretary in Washington. TSE met him in 1915, when Waterlow invited him to review for the *International Journal of Ethics* (Waterlow was a member of the editorial committee). In 1919 Waterlow served at the Paris Peace Conference (helping to negotiate the Treaty of Versailles), and in 1920 he was reappointed to the Foreign Office, later serving as Minister to Bangkok, 1926–8; Athens, 1933–9. In Jan. 1920, Eliot told his mother he was 'fond of Sydney', who had been 'kind'. On 10 Dec. 1944 he wrote in a letter of condolence to Waterlow's widow: 'Sydney was one of my oldest friends, and one to whom I was indebted. For it was owing to his kindness, in 1915, that I had my first opportunity as a reviewer . . . I don't think I have many friends who will more often recur to my thoughts.' See further Sarah M. Head, *Before Leonard: The Early Suitors of Virginia Woolf* (2006).

I shall be very grateful to you, and I cannot tell you how deeply I appreciate the honour.

When you next write to me, please write to 24 Russell Square. We are at present at St Leonards; I come up every few days to this office, but I do not frequently go to my house.

I hope that you have still reason to congratulate yourself on the results of the operation, but I should be glad to know from yourself how you are.

Yours affectionately,
[T. S. E.]

## TO *William Force Stead* CC

28 February 1927 [London]

Dear Stead,

I am awfully sorry to say that I am at present at the seaside and only in London for the day, and Thursday is impossible for me. The first day that I could manage would be next Monday.

I must apologise for not having answered your kind letter sooner. I do not think that there is any need for you to consult the Bishop on the point you mention: Baptism is obviously necessary. I have, and shall read, one or two of the books you mention; and the others I can get hold of.[1] I shall let you know as soon as I am settled in town again, and shall not fail to write to you before very long.

1 – WFS had written on 8 Feb.: 'I have a profound respect for you not only as a man of letters, but by your own account as one of the Borgias of Unitarianism. And then I pause and wonder, – did your zeal, or the zeal of your house, really lead you to poison the heretics who indulged in such detestable enormities as reciting the Athanasian Creed? . . .

'Now to be serious, it seems to me that the Unitarian baptism is the only exception to the general rule which I mentioned in my last letter, namely that any baptism whether episcopal or not is recognised as valid, for the one essential is baptism in the name of the Trinity, and that I infer could not be expected in the Unitarian Church. I will bring this up with the Bishop when the time comes for making an appointment.

'About an examination, the Bishop puts no questions to you other than those in the confirmation service. But he will not accept any one without the priests's assurance that the candidate has been duly instructed . . . But I think in your case if you can write such an excellent review of Bishop Lancelot Andrewes, you are already above the average in your knowledge of Anglican theology. You know I presume the Catechism and 30 Articles – these you may take with due allowance for the age and points at issue when they were written. The Church of England is always trying to hold the essentials of the faith once delivered to the saints but to express it in the terms and according to the issues of the current age, and therefore its teaching is Catholic but not inflexible. Have you time for any reading? – I would suggest Temple's *Christus Veritas* – Streeter's *Reality* and *Essays Catholic and Critical* – Let me hear again.'

With very many thanks,

Sincerely yours,
[T. S. Eliot]

Richmond is in London & I shall write to him about you.[1]

## TO *H. F. Stewart*

CC

28 February 1927

[Warrior House Hotel, Warrior Square, St Leonards-on-Sea]

Dear Mr Stewart,

I have your letter of the 27th, and will reply quite freely and confidentially.[2] In my letter to Forbes I did not mean to cast any doubts on the social qualifications of Muir; in two or three meetings I have found him quite an agreeable Hebridean; though at the same time I cannot quite imagine him hitting it off with Winstanley. From this point of view Dobrée would certainly have been the best, but I assume that he is out of the calculation for next year.

I think that Fernandez would do extremely well, and I am certainly ready to back his unwritten as well as his written works. I imagine that he first learnt English either in America, which he knows pretty well, or in contact with Americans. His accent, which has a very slight trace of foreign origin, is not American, but I must admit that it is very slightly common. I should perhaps add that I have known Fernandez to make a very poor impression on several women who were otherwise quite qualified to recognise his abilities, on account of what they all, and without collusion, termed a certain cock-sureness of manner. He is certainly more lively and more likely to stimulate undergraduates than Du Bos. It is rather a toss-up how he would impress people in Cambridge.

1–WFS desired an introduction to Bruce Richmond in the hope of being commissioned to write some reviews for the *TLS*.

2–Stewart asked for advice on candidates for the Clark lectureship: Edwin Muir, Herbert Read, Charles du Bos, Ramon Fernandez. 'My own inclination is divided between Read & Fernandez,' he disclosed. 'The "dourness" wh. you hint at in Muir [in TSE's letter to Mansfield Forbes] gives me pause, not so much for my own sake or the lecture room as for Winstanley's, who as Senior Tutor is destined to see a good deal of the lecturer . . .

'Suppose we offered the job to Read what sort of subject wd he treat? Is he very metaphysical, in the non-poetic sense? . . .

'Someone said that F[ernandez]'s English was not particularly good, nor his accent. I know Dubos, & I shd prefer F. for this business, tho' D. is of course a very nice person – perhaps a trifle heavy for our purpose. N'est-ce pas? F. is so very much alive.'

Read is a very safe person; he is a Yorkshireman, and very quiet and retiring, but quite well-bred, and has a sense of humour. His tendency is certainly to squeeze facts into theories; if he were chosen I should myself warn him against being too philosophical. I am afraid there is no time now for me to find out what subject he would treat. He can't take the Metaphysical Poets, because I did; and he can't take the English Novel because Forster has done that.[1] I think that he might be very good either on Pope and the Augustinian point of view (joining up Pope with Locke etc) or on the Romantic Movement in the nineteenth century.* The only danger would be that he might want to be too philosophical and psychological, and I think that I could mitigate that.

It is very difficult to decide among people so different and with different qualities and defects. Of all those considered, Fernandez seems to me the most 'alive' as you say. But I should definitely prefer Read to Muir at this stage. I think that Muir needs several years more ripening (I did not mean to make a pun on his name), and I do not think that he is yet sufficiently well-educated or well-balanced to be the right man to talk to undergraduates.

I am at present at the sea-side and only in London by the day. It is hardly likely that you will want to consult me again before Friday, but if you do, my address is Warrior House Hotel, Warrior Square, St Leonards-on-Sea.

Yours very sincerely,
[T. S. Eliot]

* But I think he would take some idea of development & trace it through English Poetry.

## TO *R. Gordon George* CC

28 February 1927 [London]

My dear George,

Many thanks for your two reviews of the Maupassant books and Read's *Stained Glass*.[2] They shall be used as quickly as possible; that is all I can say, because there is at present a certain indigestion of review copy owing to the alteration of the *Criterion* from a quarterly to a rather smaller monthly, which takes place at the end of April. Eventually this will give us much more scope.

1–E. M. Forster, *Aspects of the Novel* (1927).
2–Unsigned review of HR's *English Stained Glass*, *MC* 6 (Nov. 1927), 474–5.

I am inclined to judge Read's books much more favourably than you do. Nevertheless your strictures seem to me perfectly fair. As a matter of fact I have already had one or two discussions with him about what seems to me his tendency to dragoon a great many phenomena into a rather narrow and arbitrary framework. I cannot agree that because the thirteenth century is supreme in philosophy it also manifests the highest forms of art.

Please keep me in touch with your movements and addresses. Many thanks for reminding me about Lord Halifax; there are however two or three matters which I must deal with before there is any point in my seeing him. But when the time comes I shall not fail to remind you.

Ever yours,
[T. S. Eliot]

## TO *Bonamy Dobrée* TS Brotherton

28 February 1927 *The New Criterion*

My dear Dobrée,

I was greatly cheered to receive a letter from you after such a long silence, but sorry to observe from the date of your letter that the postal facilities between Cairo and London are not what they should be. I am very grateful to you for your useful information about the ostrich, and I am tempted to impose on your good nature further by asking you if you would kindly look into the matter of the crocodile and his supposed responsibility for the Pyramids.[1]

No one who is struggling with existence in the English climate of February is qualified to advise you how to remove yourself from the horns of your dilemma.[2] I rather imagine that the Egyptian climate will, in the

1–BD wrote (14 Feb.): 'I made enquiries about the esterych, and beg to report as follows. He does not run backwards to keep the dust out of his eyes (a theologian such as you are should have known that he [illegible word] hides his head in the sand). Nor does he have haemmorhoids from so doing. He suffers from them because he believes the legend that he can digest anything, and they are the cause, not the effect, of his running backwards. The hind pressure on the afflicted parts gives him a perverse pleasure. And that is all I have been able to gather about the esterych, which does not inhabit these parts. You may incorporate this information in your next Commentary, without acknowledgement.'

2–'I am on the horns of a dilemma – either I can say, in the proper Egyptian manner, "never mind, tomorrow", do no work worth speaking of, & relapse into cynical indifference: or, & I fear my Protestant upbringing is forcing me to this, I can cry "Reform" & expend my energies in trying to change the face of the immemorial East.'

course of time, have such a demoralising effect upon your character that the dilemma will disappear, and you will leave your native students to that career of idleness for which after all they are best fitted. Remember that if they responded to your exhortations to industry, they would probably begin making mischief, speeches, manifestations and other supposed subversive activities; so that it is really the duty of an Empire-builder like yourself to encourage their native indolence.

Many thanks for your reviews. Have I told you that *The New Criterion* is definitely committed to a monthly from the 25th of April? As I have gathered as if for a quarterly I shall hold your review of Lewis over for the June number.[1] I like your Lewis very much: and he is a very difficult man to review. Has he sent you a copy of his new periodical? If not I will ask him to.

Of course the success of a monthly depends very largely on the regular support of a few most valued contributors, and I hardly need to tell you how much importance I attach to getting regular work from yourself. This is another reason why I would discourage your taking too much interest in the Egyptian students. Any books you want you have only to ask for, and anything else you would write you have only to suggest.

When Kipling turns up I shall use it as soon as possible.[2] June or July would suit me very well, but if you find you need more time you must take it. I don't want any of this series to be hurried.

In speaking of series, and in connection with the change to monthly form, it has occurred to me that we might, instead of using your Munro [*sic*] as a review, make it the first of a series of notes on contemporary dramatists by yourself. How does this idea appeal to you? It depends of course on whether you think there are enough other dramatists of this generation to be worth notice. On the other hand certain people whom we rejected for the other series might fit in very well to a series on contemporary drama: I am thinking of Barrie and Galsworthy. Do write again soon.

Yours ever,
T. S. E.

1–Review of WL, *The Lion and the Fox*, *MC* 5 (June 1927), 339–43.
2–'I am steeped in Kipling, & hope to begin writing next week.'

## TO *Jane Harrison* CC

28 February 1927 [London]

Dear Miss Harrison,

I am greatly flattered and honoured by receiving a letter from you.[1] I wonder if you remember that I wrote to you long ago when you were living in Paris to say that I should like to have you as a contributor to *The Criterion*.[2] I have not changed my mind since then.

At present I am established at the sea-side, and only in London for the day, so that it is impossible for me to go out to tea and also catch my train. But I will take you literally, and if I am in town for the night any time before March 12th – and I have every expectation that I shall be – I shall try to press myself upon you, even at the risk of disturbing your convenience.

With very many thanks from one who has been for many years indebted to your work.

I am,
Yours sincerely
[T. S. Eliot]

## TO *Alec Randall* TS Tulsa

28 February 1927 *The New Criterion*

My dear Randall,

Thank you for your card of the 14th. I am very sorry to hear of your domestic difficulties with influenza, although it is a consolation to anyone who is obliged to support the English climate in February to know that

1–Jane Ellen Harrison (1850–1928) invited TSE (27 Feb.) to take tea with her and Hope Mirrlees on a day between 6 and 12 Mar. She hoped he would 'pardon this request from a very old woman who does not go out but still likes to keep in touch with what is finest & youngest in literature'. Educated at Newnham College, Cambridge, where she became a research fellow in 1898, Harrison was author of *Prolegomena to the Study of Greek Religion* (1903), *Themis* (1912) and *Epilegomena to Greek Religion* (1921). Mirrlees (1887–1978), daughter of a businessman, studied under Harrison. She and Harrison lived at the American University Women's Club in Paris, 1922–5, then at Mecklenburgh Street, London. Mirrlees published three novels, *Madeleine, one of Love's Jansenists* (1919), *The Counterplot* (1924; translated into French as *Le Choc en retour*, with an afterword by Charles du Bos, 1929) and *Lud-in-the-Mist* (1926). But her enduring claim to fame may prove to be *Paris* (the fifth publication of the Hogarth Press, 1920), a 600–line minor modernist masterpiece. TSE was to become a close friend of Hope and her mother.

2–No article appeared.

even in Rome hygienic happiness is not certain. But I hope that by this time your whole family is completely cured and inoculated.

Your German Periodicals and your review[1] are most welcome. In the next number, which is the first monthly number, I expect to include your notice of Schickele.[2] The Rilke has occasioned me a good deal of worry.[3] I liked it very much, but unfortunately and unexpectedly, although I should have expected it, our German correspondent, Rychner, has sent in simultaneously his German Chronicle, due to appear in the next number, which also is entirely concerned with Rilke.[4] I cannot very well refuse it, as he is commissioned to do a chronicle every three months, because I did not warn him that anyone else was going to write about Rilke. He does not say the same things as you do; but I do not feel that it is possible to expect our public to absorb two essays simultaneously about a man of whom they know nothing. So I hope you will forgive me if I withhold your own essay. Of the two I should have preferred it, but you see how I am placed. It is of course my own fault for not having foreseen what would happen; at the same time I could hardly ask our German correspondent to avoid a subject of so much importance to Germans at the present moment.

I am really very annoyed about this, and hope you will forgive me.

Yours ever
T. S. Eliot

I shall write to you soon about the Monthly, in [which] I hope to get you to collaborate rather more than you have done.

## TO *John Middleton Murry* — TS Northwestern

28 February 1927 — *The New Criterion*

My dear John,

I am relieved to hear that you are out of danger; but I hope that you will get, or have got, away for a holiday; and that you will take extremely good care of yourself thereafter, for pneumonia is a treacherous disease.

1–Review of *Paulus unter den Juden*, by the dramatist Franz Werfel, and *Franz Werfel: Versuch einer Zeitspiegelung*, by Richard Specht: *MC* 5 (June 1927), 350–3.

2–This review did not appear.

3–Randall had submitted an obituary of the poet and art critic Rainer Maria Rilke (b. 1875) – author of *Duineser Elegien* (1922), *Sonette an Orpheus* (1922) and *Die Aufzeichnungen des Malte Laurids Brigge* (1910) – who had died on 29 Dec. 1926.

4–*MC* 5 (May 1927), 241–6.

I should have sent you ere now a copy of my review of *The Life of Jesus*.[1] But I made so many alterations, and again in the first proof, that I am waiting for the second proof to send you. If it offends you, tell me so at once, and why. It is not meant so; it is merely that I think this an important book to have an opinion on; and I take these matters seriously; and if a man disagrees with you about Jesus I think he ought to go for you hard. But it is not meant to be at all personal. But I find that most people do not separate their opinions and their personal friendships as clearly as I do, and I have given offence in the past. So I want to be sure of my ground.

*Hyperion*[2] is not yet out, and in any case I wish you would suggest something else yourself. At any rate, you cannot say everything you need to say, to the *Adelphi* public, and the *Criterion* is open.

I want to answer your letter[3] at more leisure. I suppose our attitude towards 'humanity' is much the same; and I also believe in a sense that 'things' improve. There is no past age that does not horrify me, in comparison with my own; but is not every normal person better fitted to deal with the faults of his own age than those of any other? It is quite possible that later ages would horrify me as much as past ones. One MUST like one's own time best. It is like 'liking' one's own people better than 'foreigners'.

To be a hero without illusion is a TURRIBLE high ideal, and I wish I could get near it. The only two human values that seem to be supreme are heroism and sanctity. But I can't agree that one can be even human unless one has super- and extra- human values as well as human ones, and institutions seem to me an attempt to capture these. The crowd, of course, *except* as crowd, is despicable. 'Society' (of which I see less and less, and regret not at all) offers merely the choice (at best) between brutality (at the top), vulgarity (in the middle, and including the 'intelligentsia') and bestiality (at the bottom).

Ever affectionately
Tom

1–TSE, untitled review of *The Life of Jesus*, by JMM, *MC* 5 (May 1927), 253–9.
2–Lafourcade, *Swinburne's Hyperion and other Poems*.
3–JMM's letter of 9 Feb.

## TO *Richard Aldington* MS Texas

[March 1927] [London]

In re philosophy – anyway I agree and applaud everything you say about Wm Blake.[1] Blake is a chapter in the History of Heresy (my great underwritten work in 15 vols. qto).

– In your last letter you ask such inconvenient questions that a Cove can't answer, that I have postponed replying till more leisure. But I have just realised that you also ask one or two praktisch questions which shall be answered directly.

– You and Gosse have come together at last! And I have been invited to lunch by Israel Gollancz. It will be kinder to conceal these events from Ezra. Have you seen the *Exile*?[2] Vell!!!

Ever yours aff.
Tom.

How are you in health, spirits; + purse?

## TO *Francis Schoell* CC

7 March 1927 [London]

My dear Sir,

The editor of *The Times* has shown me your kind letter, to which I hasten to reply. It gives me great pleasure to know that my review of your book[3] was satisfactory to you, and I will add that the book seems to me to have great importance, that it will in the future be of great use to myself, and that I look forward impatiently to your complete study of the work of Tchachman. Having said so much, I fear that I must disabuse you. I am by no means an authority on the work of Tchachman; but merely a literary critic who has devoted special attention for many years to this period.

I must apologise for having rather gratuitously assumed that you were an American. If you are at any time in London I shall hope that you will let me know, and that I may have the pleasure of making your acquaintance.

Yours very truly,
[T. S. Eliot]

1 – RA's letter prompting these remarks is now lost. See Ronald Schuchard, *Eliot's Dark Angel: Intersections of Life and Art* (1999), 138, 244 n. 17.

2 – EP's literary review *Exile* ran for four issues, from Spring 1927 to Aut. 1928.

3 – 'The Sources of Chapman' – on Frank L. Schoell, *Études sur l'humanisme continental en Angleterre à la fin de la Renaissance* (1926) – *TLS*, 10 Feb. 1927, 88.

## TO *William Force Stead*

TS Beinecke

7 March 1927 *The New Criterion*

Dear Stead,

Again I am in town only for the day, and am writing in great haste. At present I am slowly working over the *Essays Catholic and Critical*. When I have done with that I shall get hold of Streeter's book.[1] I have rather an unreasonable prejudice against Temple, but will buy his book on your recommendation.[2] Very many thanks for your invitation to stay the night in Oxford. When I find it possible for me to come to Oxford I will take the liberty of letting you know whether I can accept your invitation.

Yours very sincerely,
T. S. Eliot

## TO *Harold Stein*

CC

7 March 1927 [London]

Dear Sir,

Thank you for your letter of the 24th February, and for your kindness in commenting on my informal reading.[3] You will understand that in a hurried reading of forty minutes one cannot make very many qualifications, but can merely point to a few things which seem to need emphasis. I agree

1–B. H. Streeter, *Reality: A New Correlation of Science and Religion* (1926)..

2–William Temple, *Personal Religion and the Life of Fellowship* (1926). Temple (1881–1944) – son of Frederick Temple (1821–1902), Archbishop of Canterbury – taught Classics at Oxford University; was ordained in 1908; served as Headmaster of Repton School, Derbyshire, 1910–14; and was (at the time of this letter by TSE) Bishop of Manchester, whence he was translated in 1929 to the Archbishopric of York. After thirteen years at York, he became Archbishop of Canterbury in 1942. His writings include *Christus Veritas* (1924), *Nature, Man and God* (1934) and *Christianity and Social Order* (1942). In the 1920s he won authority as a leader of the movement for international ecumenism – 'this world-wide Christian fellowship,' as he invoked it.

3–Harold Stein had been interested to note that, at a recent poetry reading, TSE had juxtaposed Poe and Hood – 'because I had noticed the same thing'. And yet, he went on, 'The use of the short couplets [by Poe] might be due to Shelley, [as in] e.g. The Sensitive Plant, which Poe admired.' However, 'while the metrical arrangement [in Shelley] may have affected Poe . . . his rhythm seems to owe nothing to Shelley.' Still more notably, he wrote: 'I do not think you stress the Byronic strain strongly enough; it can hardly be overestimated in any poet of the first half of the 19th century . . . I can not help feeling that the character of the man, and the locale of The Assignation were affected by Byron and his career in Venice. Perhaps it would be fairer to say that having chosen a Venetian scene Poe inevitably had to paint a man who had some of the Byronic characteristics'. In addition, TSE had apparently remarked upon Byron's 'vulgarity'. See further TSE's 'Byron' (1937), in *SE*.

that there is some influence by Shelley; but it would take considerable space to make clear the extent and limitations of this influence. You are quite right in thinking that I emphasised the influence of Hood out of proportion; and in thinking that I passed rather lightly over the influence of Byron. In referring to the 'assignation' however, I intended, however indirectly, to emphasise the Byronic influence. One must also take account of the considerable influence of More.

Had I had more time I should have read 'The Raven' and probably 'Asrafel'. I think that would have been all.

Yours very truly,
[T. S. Eliot]

## TO *Philippe Soupault*[1] CC

7 March 1927 [London]

My dear Sir,

I beg to acknowledge your letter of 15th February.[2] I am very glad to be able to contribute to your American Anthology with regard to which I have had some correspondence with Mr Jolas. I am quite willing to have Mr Jolas' translation of the poems which he has sent me published in this anthology, and I do not expect to receive remuneration of any kind beyond one copy of the anthology. But I must protest against the expectation that contributors to this anthology should subsidise it to the extent of five copies. It is not of the slightest interest to me that my poems should be translated and, especially considering the claims of many local charities in which I am interested, I have not preferred to subsidise the translations to the extent of a guinea or so. If the group of readers to which such a book

1–Philippe Soupault (b. 1897), poet and novelist (in the 1920s he was a *surréaliste*), and literary director of the firm of Kra. His works include *Rose des vents* (poetry, 1920) and *Les Dernières Nuits de Paris* (novel, 1920). In Mar. 1919 he founded, with André Breton and Louis Aragon, the review *Littérature*. He assisted with the French translation of the 'Anna Livia Plurabelle' section of JJ's *Work in Progress*. See Soupault, 'A Propos de la traduction d'Anna Livia Plurabelle', *NRF* 36: 212 (1 May 1931), 633–6; Soupault, *Souvenirs de James Joyce* (Algiers: Editions Fontaine, 1943); and *A James Joyce Yearbook*, ed. Maria Jolas (Paris: Transition Press, 1949), which reprints Soupault's memoir of JJ.

2–Soupault sent details of the forthcoming anthology of modern American poetry (inc. poems by TSE), to be translated into French by Eugene Jolas. He expressed the hope that TSE would purchase 'at least five copies' at a cost of $1.25 a copy.

appeals is too special to allow the book any commercial value, I should question the desirability of publishing it at all.

I am Sir, your obedient servant,
[T. S. Eliot]

## TO *Charles Whibley* CC

7 March 1927 [London]

My dear Whibley,

Thank you very much for your letter of the 3rd, and for signing the documents which appear to be quite in order.[1]

I look forward to seeing you very soon.

Yours ever affectionately,
[T. S. E.]

## TO *Mario Praz* CC

10 March 1927 [London]

Dear Praz,

Thank you for your card. I have sent you the book on Chaucer and leave it entirely to your discretion whether you mention it in your essay or in a separate notice, or if you think the book negligible, not at all. I have hardly glanced at it. I am delighted to hear that your essay is so far forward. Yes, I think the bibliography would be well worth having. If your essay turns out to be a very long one I shall simply have to spread it over two numbers; if therefore it appears to you to be more than six thousand words I should be grateful if you could indicate a possible point of division.[2]

Many thanks for the additional biography.[3] You may be sure that I shall examine everything you suggest. Perhaps I did not make clear that

1–Whibley wrote on 3 Mar., 'I am up in town for the day, & I have taken the chance of going to a commissioner of oaths. I think you will find it all right.'

2–Praz, 'Chaucer and the Great Italian Writers of the Trecento' [I], *MC* 6 (July 1927), 18–31; [II], *MC* 6 (Aug. 1927), 131–57; III: 'Bibliography', *MC* 6 (Sept. 1927), 238–42.

3–Praz had sent TSE a note (8 Mar.) to say that he would find 'considerable support' for his views in *Saggio Critico sul Petrarca* (new edn, 1921), by Francesco de Sanctis (1817–83); and he appended a list of recommended books and articles on Donne and the other metaphysical poets (King's). On Praz's continuing absorption with TSE's work on Donne and the metaphysicals, see Schuchard, 'Editor's Introduction', *VMP*, 19–21.

I am substantially in agreement with all of your criticisms in your first letter, and with your general suggestions in the second. There are many statements in the lectures which I shall have to retract.

Sincerely yours,
[T. S. Eliot]

P.S. I shall certainly read your essay on Sidney.

## TO *Michel Licht*[1]

TS Syracuse

11 March 1927 [London]

My dear Sir,

In reply to your letter of the 12th ultimo, I have not the slightest objection to your translating into Yiddish and printing in your periodical the two essays from *The Sacred Wood* which you mention.[2] In giving my permission it is understood first that this permission is for these two essays only, and for publication in the periodical in question only, and also that you have the full permission of Alfred A. Knopf Incorporated. I shall expect no remuneration.

I shall be very glad to see a copy of the magazine in which the essays appear, although I regret that I shall be unable to read it. With all best wishes for your venture,

Yours very truly,
T. S. Eliot

1–Michel Licht (1893–1953), Russian-born Yiddish poet and translator resident in USA.
2–Licht asked permission to translate into Yiddish 'The Perfect Critic' and 'Tradition and the Individual Talent'.

## TO *Jacques Maritain*[1]

CC

Le onze mars 1927 [*The New Criterion*]

Cher Monsieur Maritain,

J'ai reçu la lettre du 23 février qui me fait part des corrections que vous avez faîtes dans le texte français de 'Poésie et Religion'. Le texte anglais est déjà sous presse pour notre numéro d'avril; mais si vous m'envoyez immédiatement le nouveau texte c'est probable que je peux insérer les corrections les plus importantes.[2]

Je veux vous signaler que le public le plus averti d'ici a montré un grand interêt dans la première partie, et que je me félicite d'avoir eu l'honneur de la publier dans le *New Criterion*.[3]

J'attend le plaisir de vous revoir chez vous à ma prochaine visite à Paris, et je vous prie, cher Monsieur Maritain, d'agréer l'expression de mes sentiments dévoués.

[T. S. Eliot][4]

## TO *H. F. Stewart*

CC

11 March 1927 [London]

Dear Dr Stewart,

I am now writing to you confidentially about our friend James Smith. He asked my permission to use my name as a reference in his application for a certain scholarship at Trinity. This permission I was very glad to

1–Jacques Maritain (1882–1973), philosopher and littérateur. At first a disciple of Bergson, he revoked that allegiance (*L'Evolutionnisme de M. Bergson*, 1911; *La Philosophie bergsonienne*, 1914), and became a Roman Catholic and foremost exponent of Neo-Thomism. For a while in the 1920s he was associated with *Action Française*, but the connection ended in 1926. His works include *Art et scholastique* (1920); *Saint Thomas d'Aquin apôtre des temps modernes* (1923); *Réflexions sur l'intelligence* (1924); *Trois Réformateurs* (1925); *Frontière de la poésie* (1926); *Primauté du spirituel* (1927).

2–Maritain, 'Poetry and Religion' [II], *MC* 5 (May 1927), 214–30.

3–'Poetry and Religion' [I], *NC* 5 (Jan. 1927), 7–22.

4–*Translation*: Dear Monsieur Maritain, I have received the letter of the 23rd February telling me about the corrections you have made to the French text of "Poetry and Religion". The English version has already gone to press for our April number; but if you can send me the new text as soon as possible, I can probably insert the most important corrections.

I am eager to inform you that the first part has aroused great interest among the most enlightened readers here, and I am delighted to have had the honour of publishing it in the *New Criterion*.

I look forward to the pleasure of calling on you when I am next in Paris. Yours sincerely [T. S. Eliot]

give. I saw him in London a few days ago, and told him that I had had no enquiry from the relevant authorities, and assured him that I was very willing to take any step possible for me on his behalf. He suggests that I should write to the electors. I do not know who the electors are, or whether it is fitting that I should write to them; so I am taking the liberty of writing to you for information. I do not wish, as an outsider, to intrude in this affair; at the same time I should be sorry to leave undone anything that I could do on behalf of a young man of whose abilities I have so high an opinion.

Forgive me for troubling you. Needless to say I am waiting with great curiosity and detached interest to know the result of the election to the Clark lectureship.

With all good wishes and kindest regards to Mrs Stewart.

Yours very sincerely,
[T. S. Eliot]

## TO *Bruce Richmond* CC

11 March 1927 [London]

Dear Richmond,

I am back in town and should be very happy to see you at your convenience next week, or as soon as you have time.

I expect to have the Wilkie Collins ready very soon, and the Jespersen will not take me much longer. I have also just received the Spinoza book, so that I have plenty to do.[1] Many thanks.

I hope that you will not consider it impertinent if I write on behalf of two people who would like to get work for the *Supplement*. They do not belong to the same category. One is a young man who took his degree at Trinity College Cambridge last year, and who has, I believe, a very good chance for a fellowship there. I know his capacities pretty well, and was asked to read a dissertation which he submitted. He is very competent in English literature, literary criticism, and in philosophy, and is a fair classical scholar. He is a very intelligent Scotchman, has never done any journalism outside of Cambridge, but would be willing to begin with quite short and humble notices if there were any chance of preferment. I intend to give him some reviewing myself as soon as there is space. I may

1 – 'Spinoza' – *The Oldest Biography of Spinoza*, ed. A. Wolf – *TLS*, 21 Apr. 1927, 275.

T. S. Eliot at his desk in the Faber & Gwyer offices, 24 Russell Square, in a photograph taken by Henry Ware Eliot.

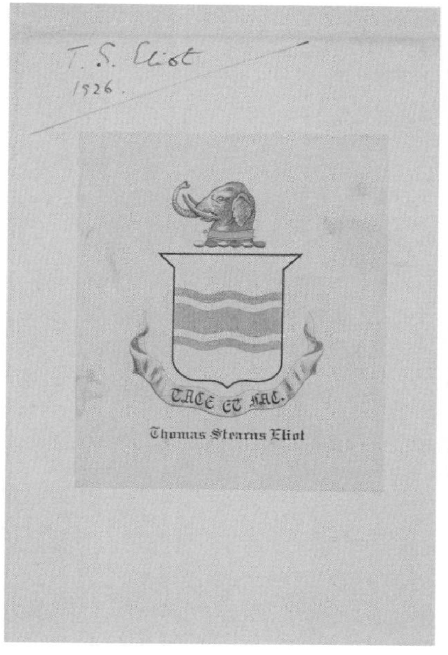


Eliot's bookplate, with the family motto, '*Tace et fac*'.

Cover of the first edition of *Journey of the Magi* (1927).

Eliot delivering the final Clark Lecture at Trinity College, Cambridge, 9 March 1926. Graphite drawing by Theresa Garrett Eliot, 1926.

From left, Maurice Haigh-Wood, T. S. Eliot, Henry Eliot and Vivien against a backdrop of trees, Rome, 1926.

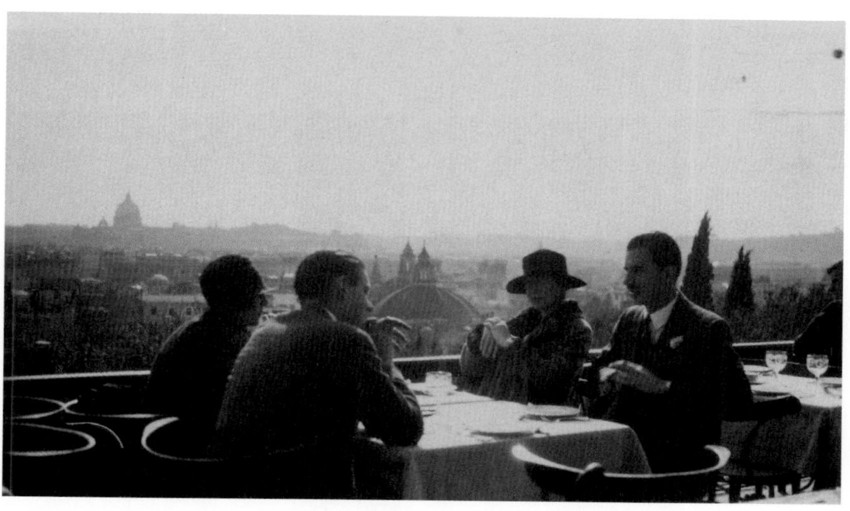

From left, Vivien, T. S. Eliot, Theresa Garrett Eliot and Maurice Haigh-Wood on a terrace in Rome, 1926.

John Middleton Murry at Menton in the south of France. Photograph by Ida Baker, 1920.

William Force Stead. Detail of a group at Garsington. Photograph by Lady Ottoline Morrell, 1922.

Henry Ware Eliot, profile portrait, c.1920s.

Geoffrey Faber, studio portrait in Eliot's possession, c. early 1930s.

Herbert Read. Photograph by Elliott & Fry, c.1925.

Bonamy Dobrée. Photographer unknown, late 1920s.

Virginia Woolf. A snapshot by Lady Ottoline Morrell, June 1926

Eliot with Maurice Haigh-Wood on the Janiculum, Rome, 1926.

Grand Hotel
Divonne les Bains
19.9.26.

My dear John

This is a hasty line as Vivien is not able to write. She has not been at all well since we got here, and it is more + more certain that it is impossible to make any plans for next year: the doctor here wishes her to await the effect of the stay here and then consult the specialist in Paris about the climate which she ought to have. So now everything is in suspense. So don't keep your cottage empty on our account. She thanks you for the wonderful offer you have made. It is simply that she is now so unwell that we dare not look one inch ahead.

Affectionately
Tom.

Letter from Eliot to John Middleton Murry, sent from the Grand Hotel, Divonne les Bains, 19 September 1926.

A pensive Eliot in his study.

1

This Passport contains
32 pages.
Ce passeport contient
32 pages.

PASSPORT.
PASSEPORT.

UNITED KINGDOM OF GREAT BRITAIN AND NORTHERN IRELAND.
ROYAUME-UNI DE GRANDE-BRETAGNE ET D'IRLANDE DU NORD.

No. of PASSPORT / No. du PASSEPORT: 812031

NAME OF BEARER / NOM DU TITULAIRE: MR. THOMAS STEARNS ELIOT.

ACCOMPANIED BY HIS WIFE (Maiden name) / ACCOMPAGNÉ DE SA FEMME (Née)

and by / et de — children / enfants

NATIONAL STATUS — NATIONALITÉ

BRITISH SUBJECT BY NATURALISATION
IMPERIAL CERTIFICATE No. A 15337
DATED LONDON 2 NOVEMBER 1927.
See page 5.

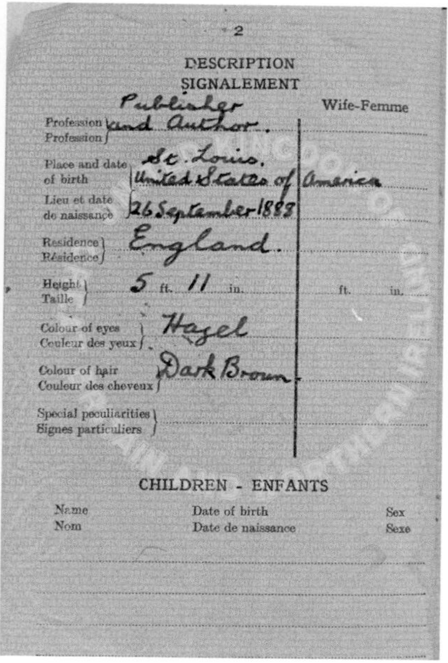

2

DESCRIPTION
SIGNALEMENT

| | | Wife-Femme |
| --- | --- | --- |
| Profession / Profession | Publisher and Author. | |
| Place and date of birth / Lieu et date de naissance | St. Louis, United States of America 26 September 1888 | |
| Residence / Résidence | England. | |
| Height / Taille | 5 ft. 11 in. | ft. in. |
| Colour of eyes / Couleur des yeux | Hazel | |
| Colour of hair / Couleur des cheveux | Dark Brown | |
| Special peculiarities / Signes particuliers | | |

CHILDREN - ENFANTS

| Name / Nom | Date of birth / Date de naissance | Sex / Sexe |
| --- | --- | --- |

Two pages from Eliot's British passport, 2 November 1927.

Portrait head of Eliot. Pencil drawing by Powys Evans, late 1927.

add, what has perhaps a certain significance, that the idea of his writing for *The Times* emanated from me, and not from himself.

The other person is a clergyman at Oxford, who expressed a desire to write for you. I am under a certain obligation to him, but I think nevertheless that he might be a very safe person; neither too high nor too low; nor too broad nor too new for current theological literature. Though I imagine that you have swarms of clergy at your command, when you want them.

I won't bother you with further details about either of these men unless you want to have them.

Ever yours,
[T. S. E.]

## TO *F. S. Flint*

CC

11 March 1927 [London]

My dear Flint,

I am back in town at present and should like to suggest lunch together in the immediate future. Will you suggest a day next week, except Monday or Tuesday. I suppose the usual place is the best.

I should be rather pleased if you would take on for review Edith Sitwell's *Rustic Elegies*. I don't know that you will consider it a particularly original task, but I simply cannot think of anyone else whom I would trust to do it. Anyway will you be willing to have a look at it? There is a preposterous book just published called *The Three Sitwells* by R. L. Mégroz which might go with it. Mr Mégroz will not worry you very much. Incidentally he is not aware that Paul Valéry and Valery Larbaud are two different people.

Ever yours,
[T. S. E.]

## TO *Jean Cocteau* CC

Le onze mars, 1927 [London]

Cher Jean,

Je vous remerçie infiniment pour l'envoi d'Orphée avec le dédicace charmant.[1] Je crois que j'ai déjà témoigné ma grande admiration pour votre oeuvre; et vous devez savoir combien de plaisir et de contentement j'ai reçu en regardant la répresentation d'Orphée par les Pitoeffs.[2] Vous savez que je comprends bien que c'est une belle oeuvre ce que vous avez fait, et que j'attend de vous, comme attendant tous vos amis, des chefs d'oeuvre de théâtre plus angéliques encore.

Je suis toujours votre dévoué,
[T. S. Eliot][3]

## TO *Lia Clarke*[4] CC

11 March 1927 [*The New Criterion*]

Dear Madam,

I have the honour of sending you herewith enclosed our cheque for £4. 12, being payment at our customary rate of £2 per thousand words, for your story 'Darling Daudet'.

1 – Cocteau's *Orphée* had been reviewed by BD, *C*. 4 (Oct. 1926).

2 – George Pitoëff (1884–1939), Armenian-born, Paris-based actor, director, designer and translator, worked during the 1920s on numerous productions at the Théâtre des Arts.

3 – *Translation*: Dear Jean, I thank you most sincerely for having sent me Orphée and for your charming dedication. I believe I have already expressed to you my great admiration for your work; and I am glad to tell you how much I enjoyed Pitoëffs' production of Orphée. I am all too aware of the fact that this is a great work, and I and all your friends expect from you even more exalted dramatic masterpieces.

I am always your devoted, [T. S. Eliot]

4 – Cornelia Clarke, née Cummins (1889–1943), Irish short-story writer, poet and journalist of private means, was married to the poet Austin Clarke (1896–1974). An habituée of Dublin literary and theosophical circles, she was known to W. B Yeats and Maud Gonne MacBride; and the writer George Russell (*AE*) made a pencil sketch of her *c*.1920. 'A well-educated older woman with a small private income who had lived abroad, Cummins established a career as a journalist who also published short stories and poor-quality verse under the pseudonym Margaret Lyster. She was considered eccentric, even mad; violently anti-Semitic, she harboured strong Nazi sympathies in later life. She and Clarke married secretly in a register office in Dublin on 31 December 1920, but the union was probably unconsummated and lasted less than a fortnight' (*ODNB*). See *Best Short Stories* (1925), p. 400, for biographical note on Lia Clarke; and p. 299 for mention of stories.

*The New Criterion* is about to be converted into a monthly magazine from the next issue. In effecting this conversion we are somewhat altering the character of the review, in order to make it have a more general appeal. Consequently we have been obliged to reconsider all of the contributions in hand submitted to *The New Criterion* as a quarterly. Much of the material which was suitable to the *Criterion* as a quarterly is no longer appropriate for the monthly magazine into which it is to be converted. We therefore find ourselves obliged to return a certain number of contributions, with payment, which we cannot use. We have not altered our opinion of the story 'Darling Daudet', but it falls within the category of contributions which are likely to appeal only to a rather small and select audience. Especially at the moment of affecting the change we feel that it is necessary for us to emphasise our in future somewhat more popular character in the fiction which we publish.

You are, of course, quite at liberty to publish 'Darling Daudet' elsewhere, and we beg to express our regret at being now unable to publish such a remarkable study. I should of course be very happy to see more of your work; and had I foreseen the change in the policy of the Review, I should probably have been more inclined to accept the other story instead of the story which you sent.[1]

Yours very truly,
[T. S. Eliot]

1–Clarke responded (13 Mar.) by re-submitting her other story 'One of the Twelve'. On 19 Apr. she submitted a new story, 'The Merry Go Round'; adding, 'I am glad you are still retaining the Judas story. I showed it when I first sent it to you to Mr W. B. Yeats who liked it best of my work.'

## TO *Ray Strachey*[1] CC

14 March 1927 [London]

Dear Mrs Strachey,

Thank you for your letter of the 10th.[2] I was as a matter of fact under the impression that we had met, but I see from your letter that I must be wrong.

Do by all means send me your manuscript. I cannot say that the company accepts whatever I recommend, but I can assure you that your book will be most carefully read, and that you shall have an opinion within two or three weeks. As one of the joint authors of that admirable detective story you have a very strong claim upon us.[3]

Sincerely yours,
[T. S. Eliot]

1–Rachel (Ray) Strachey, née Pearsall Conn ((1887–1940), was a feminist and writer. Her mother, Mary Pearsall Smith, sister of the writer Logan Pearsall Smith, eloped from her marriage with the art historian Bernard Berenson when Ray was just four years of age. Educated at Cambridge, Bryn Mawr College, Pennsylvania, and Oxford University, Ray married in 1911 the musician and mathematician Oliver Strachey (1874–1960), brother of Lytton Strachey (1880–1932), and committed herself to the cause of women's suffrage and employment rights. She was Parliamentary Secretary of the National Union of Women's Suffrage Societies; Chair (during WW1) of the Women's Service Employment Committee; head of the Women's Service Bureau; co-founder of the Women's Employment Federation; and Chair of the Cambridge University Women's Employment Board, 1930–9. Works include *Frances Willard: Her Life and Work* (1912), *A Quaker Grandmother* (1914), *The Cause: A Short History of the Women's Movement in Great Britain* (1928) and *Millicent Garrett Fawcett* (biog., 1931).

2–'I am writing to ask whether you would like me to send you a rather serious & peculiar novel I have written . . . It deals with religious fanaticism as it broke out in U.S.A. about 1830–40, & it is perhaps rather an unpleasant book in some ways, but at any rate unique! I hoped that Harcourt Brace, who published my other American novel "Marching On" would take it; but they said they thought it would offend American feelings too much . . .' See *Shaken by the Wind: A Story of Fanaticism* (F&G, 1927). Strachey told TSE too: 'I possess also some very remarkable (& very indecent) papers on the same subject left me by my grandmother . . . All you know of my writing so far, no doubt, is that I am one of the four authors of that frivolous detective story which Faber & Gwyer have just taken!' This too was to be published, as *Religious Fanaticism: Extracts from the Papers of Hannah Whitall Smith*, ed. Ray Strachey (F&G, 1928).

3–Ray Strachey's sister-in-law Marjorie Strachey had submitted a story entitled 'The Mystery of the Training College', disguising the authorship as by 'Marks'. TSE wrote in his reader's report, dated 28 Feb. 1927: 'This detective story was written by Marjorie Strachey and three other people, and she sent it to me at my request. It seems to me really a first-rate detective story, and I recommend publication, though no doubt you will desire to get another opinion. My only doubt is about the title. I am not sure that the general public knows clearly enough what a Training College is, to be able to feel an immediate thrill on hearing that there has been a mystery there' (Faber Misc 5/3).

## TO *Henry Eliot*

MS Houghton

15 March 1927 57 Chester Terrace, S.W.1.

My dear Henry

The Old Colony has just advised me that a Bond (Solvery & Co.) has been called, & that consequently they hold $2150 00 for me. I now want to ask you – could you please recommend them a *bond to buy for me* with the proceeds? Especially with my present preoccupations, I am quite out of touch with the N.Y. Bond market.

I am writing to tell them to take your instructions, so *please* write to them.

My hands are full: apart from my work, Mr Haigh-Wood seems to be dying (V. does not know yet how serious it is) and I shall have the Executorship on my hands.[1] And V's condition is anything but satisfactory, her delusions are very serious indeed, & quite beyond the point of 'severe handling'. They are quite genuine.

I am distressed that Mother thinks that Vivien will 'prevent' me coming to America. V. is far beyond preventing or encouraging. At the same time

---

The novel, published as *Midnight*, by 'Mark Strange' (F&G), included this challenging 'Author's Note': 'This story was the work of four people, M., A., R., and K. The method adopted was simple and can be recommended to those readers who feel sure that they themselves could write a detective story if it was not so much trouble. M., A., and K. discussed the plot and then wrote alternate chapters until the book was complete in outline. R. was then called upon and inserted 10,000 additional words distributed evenly among the different parts. The authors defy the public to trace their separate hands or to locate the padding' (p. 5). The jacket copy, which may well have been written by TSE, stresses a private joke, teasing the reader with hints as to the primary author's real name: 'Owing to the sustained demand for detective fiction, and its consequent multiplication, there is coming to be a technique of the genre as distinct and almost as exacting as that of the Sonnet. This technique may be said to consist of actually *deepening* the darkness of mystery by adding ray after ray of light. Judged by such standards, *Midnight* by Mark Strange may be said to deserve its title; its whole construction is a triumph of this difficult technique. Information reaches the reader as soon as it does the investigator, and the two sleuthing processes, those of reader and detective, proceed *pari passu* throughout. Ray after ray of light is forever being skilfully handled, and yet the original pitchy darkness of mystery is maintained until almost the last page.'

1–TSE was to be co-executor with his mother-in-law Rose Esther Haigh-Wood and his brother-in-law Maurice. Charles Haigh-Wood wrote in 'Notes & Instructions for my Executors' that his executors were 'entitled to their expences but as they are members of the family I don't leave any legacy except that I should like Tom to have a personal gift of £25 to compensate him for the loss of time etc. or rather I should say in recognition of it.' In practice, because MH-W was living in Rome – working for the Banca Italo-Britannica – the bulk of the correspondence, interviews with solicitors etc. fell upon TSE's shoulders.

I dare not explain to mother how ill V. is; so it is difficult to explain. At the moment, I put it onto Mr Haigh-Wood's illness.

Love to Theresa. I have very much missed all news from you.

Ever aff.
Tom.

## TO *A. Den Doolaard*[1] CC

16 March 1927 [London]

Dear Mr Den Doolaard,

Thank you very much for your letter of the 5th which gave me such pleasure. I have read with very great interest the translation you so kindly made, and realise how much of it escaped me when I attempted to read it in the original.[2] It is not I suppose for myself to offer anything except my best thanks; a writer is hardly expected to be the best critic of his own critics; but I must say that several points which you made gave me great pleasure, as for instance your remark on the violent change of technique in the later poems, which has escaped the notice of most English critics. If you have not had the two numbers of the *New Criterion* which contain certain recent fragments of mine, I shall be very happy to send them to you, in order to have the benefit of your opinion.

I look forward to meeting you at Christmas of next year, as there is no hope of seeing you before then.[3] You have no need to apologise for your delay in writing, so long as I may count on receiving your Dutch Chronicle in time. May I count upon it for publication in the July number which will appear on June 25? For this number I should be glad to have it about the first of May. I hope you can write and confirm this, as otherwise I ought to make arrangements for some other foreign chronicle.

Thank you for your full information about Dutch periodicals. I will, as you suggest, write to these periodicals, and on hearing from *De Witte Mier* I will have the exchange copies for that periodical sent direct to you.

With many thanks,
Yours every sincerely,
[T. S. Eliot]

1–A. Den Doolaard (pen name of C. Spoelstra) contributed Dutch Chronicles to C.
2–Den Doolaard had translated an article about *Poems 1909–1925* that appeared in the periodical *Den Gulden Minckel*.
3–TSE misread Den Doolaard, who had written that he was 'already looking forward to our meeting Xmas 1927'.

P.S. I have just observed that you ask for the January number, and am having it sent to you. I assume that you have seen the April number.
P.P.S. I see you do not give the address of De Witte Mier. Am I to understand that this will be sent to us without any request on my part?

## TO *H. F. Stewart*

CC

16 March 1927 [London]

Dear Dr Stewart,

Thank you very much for letting me know.[1] I am delighted to hear of Smith's good fortune. Of course I must admit that I am a little disappointed that Maurois should have been the successful candidate, as he seems to me distinctly a light-weight.[2] But I dare say he is a very good lecturer!

Sincerely yours,
[T. S. Eliot]

## TO *James Smith*

CC

16 March 1927 [London]

Dear Smith,

Dr Stewart has written to tell me of your success, and I drop you this line merely to say that I am delighted. I shall reply to your letter fully as soon as I have a little more time.

Yours ever,
[T. S. Eliot]

1–Stewart wrote (14 Mar.) that James Smith had been offered the Allen Scholarship ('a University not a College affair'); and that the Vice-Chancellor had 'implied that your name carried the weight it deserved with the electors'. In addition, he passed on to TSE the news that André Maurois had been appointed Clark Lecturer for the next academic session; adding, 'H. Read & Fernandez will both, I hope, have their turn in due course.'
2–André Maurois (1885–1967) was the nom de plume of Emile Herzog, French author, biographer and historian who legally changed his name to Maurois only in 1947. His works include *Les Silences de Colonel Bramble* (1918), *La Hausse et la baisse* (1922) and *Ariel; ou, La Vie de Shelley* (1923), as well as studies of writers including Byron and Dickens.

## TO *John Middleton Murry* CC

16 March 1927 [London]

Dear John,

Thank you very much for sending me the essay.[1] I have not yet read the revisions, but I think that I will send it direct to press and let you have an early proof. I should probably be able to use it in the June number which will appear on May 25.

It is curious that I should have thought of you when I saw the review of Alison Peers' book in *The Times*. I shall send for it, and accept with pleasure your suggestion of doing the two books together.[2]

I enclose herewith my review.[3] It seems to me very poor stuff. But I am coming to the conclusion that I am only capable of reviewing books in which I am not interested. I can turn out a column for *The Times* with the greatest ease; but when it comes to reviewing for the *Criterion* I pick out books I want to read; and it is quite impossible, within the limits of a review, to say what one wants to say about any book worth the trouble.

Ever yours,
[T. S. E.]

## FROM *John Middleton Murry* MS Valerie Eliot

18 March 1927 1a The Gables, Hampstead, N.W.3

Dear Tom,

My wife now has pneumonia: but we believe the crisis is safely past.

I once promised Valéry that if ever 'La Soirée avec M. Teste' was translated into English I wd write an introduction. Now the lady who translated it, Natalie Clifford Barney, has approached me through an emissary, to say that she (and Valéry) desire that her translation shd be published in book form over here, and ask that I shd redeem my promise, which I am quite willing to do. I am also appealed to to help find a publisher, which was not in the bargain. However, it seems to me that F. & G. might like to make a small expensive brochure of it. The translation, wh. appeared in the Dial, was good; and I wd try to write a tolerable essay. Wd you let me know what the prospects are?

1 – JMM, 'Towards a Synthesis', *MC* 5 (June 1927), 294–313.

2 – 'Seven Spanish Mystics' – on Allison Peers, *Studies in the Spanish Mystics* – *TLS*, 10 Mar. 1927, 154. JMM suggested (14 March) reviewing Peers's book alongside Radhakrishnan's *The Hindu View of Life*.

3 – Review of JMM, *The Life of Jesus*, *MC* 5 May 1927) 253–9.

Thank you for the review.[1] There is nothing at all offensive in it: and much that is truly friendly. I don't know that I quite like the spectacle of myself <(1)> *leading my disciples into the wilderness* to the accompaniment of <(2)> *a titter of derision from civilised Europe.* (1) is fair criticism, to be received in meekness: but whither, O Tom, have you led *your* disciples? quite as numerous, and a good deal more affluent than mine? As for (2) is it *true*? I didn't know that my activities had excited the attention of 'civilised Europe'. No doubt it would titter with derision if it observed me. But, on second thoughts, would it? Is a titter of derision the geste of '*civilised* Europe'? I don't know. But then I don't know much about 'civilised Europe'. The titter, aforesaid, *is* the gesture of Bloomsbury: but I don't accept their claim to be 'civilised Europe'. If you will forgive me for saying so, this strikes me as one of those *obiter dicta* which slip rather too easily from your pen, and are unworthy of you. But perhaps I have missed the real intention.

Of the substance of the review I have but one *criticism* to make: it concerns the quotation & your comment on it, on the 3rd page. And, of course, as ever, it cuts down to fundamentals. For I completely deny that Jesus' teaching, as I represent it, or as it was, 'is the familiar gospel of Rousseau'. I think, moreover, that it is *very* hard, if not impossible, for you (standing where you do) to appreciate the difference. As things are, you think that there is no tertium quid between the doctrine of original sin, – & Rousseauism. (So did I, once: *vide* the essay 'Flaubert & Flaubart' written in 1921). But nevertheless, there is. And the discovery of this, first in experience, then slowly & with no small pains ratified by appeal to the history of religions, poetical, & mystical experience, is the underlying theme of all my writing since March 1923, when the discovery came to me.

The doctrine of Jesus is the doctrine of rebirth, of actual spiritual reintegration, as experience. And, unless this is either an actual or imaginative reality of anyone, I believe my book must be finally meaningless. And, on this specific point, it strikes me as strange to criticise my account of Jesus' teaching because it implies a denial of original sin. The question is whether it is a true account or not. I believe it is. But to call it Rousseauism is a spiritual solecism. (Of course, your implication may be that I am trying to 'Rousseauize' Jesus; but in that case you wd have to show where, explicit or implicit, is the doctrine of original sin in any recorded words of Jesus.)

1–TSE's review of *The Life of Jesus* was to appear in *MC* 5 (May 1927), 253–9.

On a slightly less important point—but still important—you charge me with [using the term] 'Son of God' as though it had a precise meaning. No, I don't do that. I use it as though it had a *real* meaning. It had a real meaning for Jesus — sonship was the condition which supervened under rebirth. Precise meaning it cannot have. I know you believe that there is no meaning which is not precise. But you are mistaken.

Of course you are at liberty to believe it is 'a wholly vague metaphor'. But you must make your criticism of Jesus, not of me. Probably you would. I don't think you can realise that 'son of God' is a description of a religious experience & condition, not a theological statement.

So, when you ask me for a theology, my reply is that I haven't got one; and the reason why I don't even try to get one is that the men of religious experience (of whom Jesus is to me the highest example) didn't have, or want one. They knew, what I too know, having learned it from them, that theologies are unnecessary to misleading. Tell me what theology you can get out of St Paul – or the sayings of the Buddha in the Pali canon.

You may turn these men down: I revere them.

And so, when you make (perfectly legitimate) fun of me for saying that we must be sons of God, and we must be God, and say the metaphors cancel out, and that the 'idea is incomprehensible', I can only say that it is not an *idea* at all. If the wisdom of Jesus had been an 'idea' you would have absorbed it long ago: because it is not, it eludes you. But there is no contradiction between these two metaphors. (It is not the habit of metaphors to contradict, or cancel one another: metaphors, you know as well as I, are not logical statements.) To be son of God is simply an experience of a blessed & quasi-filial relation between ourselves and 'the power not ourselves which makes for righteousness' – 'to be God' is an experience of identification with that power. These two conditions are the same condition really. And Matt. Arnold's phrase will not really do. It should be: 'the power not ourselves, and yet ourselves, which makes for righteousness'. Not ourselves & yet ourselves. How incomprehensible! I am sorry. I would make it plainer if I could; but I can't. And if I seem to you to be maintaining 'the rosy' tradition of Rousseau & Wells, it doesn't matter.

Yours affectionately
John.[1]

1–See TSE's response to this letter, 28 Mar. below.

## TO *Wyndham Lewis* TS Cornell

21 March 1927 *The New Criterion*

Dear Wyndham,

I have just read *The Enemy*[1] and beg to give you my warmest compliments upon it.

*The New Criterion* is about to be transformed into a monthly of smaller size. *The Lion and the Fox* is being reviewed by Bonamy Dobrée for the number which will appear in May.[2] I wish that we could have published this review earlier, but the change from quarterly to monthly publication somewhat retards our reviewing for the next two to three months. I shall try to publish a serious consideration of *The Enemy* in an early issue.

If you are in London, could you manage to lunch with me one day next week? Please drop me a line here, and mention a day that would suit you.

Ever yours,
T. S. E.

## TO *Henri Massis* CC

21 March 1927 [London]

Cher ami,

Je suis enchanté de reçevoir enfin une lettre de vous, et de savoir que je reçevrai bientôt des bonnes feuilles de la *Défense de l'Occident*. Puisque j'ai déjà eu le bonheur d'en faire paraître un morceau en Angleterre, je tiens beaucoup à l'espoir de pouvoir présenter le livre complet. Je trouve excellente votre idée d'une préface de Chesterton, et je la proposerai a mes collègues de notre maison.[3]

Quant à vos scrupules, ou plutôt vos solicitudes au sujet de Catholicisme de votre ouvrage, je ne peux pas, naturellement, parler définitivement avant d'avoir vu le texte complet; mais je n'y vois d'avance aucun obstacle. Je crois que votre point de vu est plus près au mien que vous ne pensez. Il n'y a pas grande différence entre votre Catholicisme et notre Anglo-Catholicisme, parceque je devine en votre Catholicisme une certaine partie inévitable de Gallicanisme. Est ce que j'ai tout à fait tort? Je crois

1–The first number of WL's periodical *The Enemy: A review of art and literature* had appeared in Jan. 1927.

2–It appeared in the June number, 339–43.

3–Henri Massis, *Defence of the West*, trans. F. S. Flint, with a preface by G. K. Chesterton (F&G, 1927).

qu'une politique pareille doit s'allier avec une théologie pareille.

Vous avez toute ma sympathie dans le situation agonisante qu'on traverse à ce moment; donnez, je vous prie, l'expression de ma sympathie également à Maurras et à Daudet.

J'ai beaucoup de choses à vous dire; j'attends une conversation à loisir; j'espère visiter Paris avant l'été, mais je ne peux pas encore fixer une date.

Croyez moi, mon cher, toujours votre dévoué.

[T. S. Eliot][1]

## TO *William Force Stead* — TS Beinecke

21 March 1927 — *The New Criterion*

Dear Stead,

Thank you very much for your letter of the 18th.[2] It is good of you to give me these hints, and they are useful. As for the English Society, I am

1 – *Translation*: Dear Friend, I am delighted to have at last received a letter from you, and to know that I shall soon have the page proofs of *La Défense de l'Occident*. Having already had the pleasure of publishing an extract from it in England, I earnestly hope to be able to bring out the complete text. I think your idea of a preface by Chesterton is excellent, and I shall put it to my colleagues in the firm.

As for your scruples, or rather concern, about the Catholicism of your book, naturally I cannot say anything definitive until I have seen the complete text; but I do not foresee any obstacle. I believe that your point of view is nearer to mine than you think. There is not a great difference between your Catholicism and our Anglo-Catholicism, because, in your Catholicism, I sense an inevitable element of Gallicanism. Am I completely wrong? I believe that similar political views must be allied to similar theological attitudes.

You have all my sympathy in the agonising situation we are going through at the moment; please convey my sympathy also to Maurras and Daudet.

I have a great many things to tell you; I look forward to a leisurely conversation; I hope to visit Paris before the summer, but cannot yet fix a date.

Your ever devoted friend, [T. S. Eliot]

2 – WFS wrote: 'I was very glad to hear you are reading Essays Catholic and Critical – It is a very good book and not only does it show how one can accept the best conclusions of modern thought while remaining a High Anglican, but also, – and this gives me no small comfort – it has fluttered and flustered the Modernists who for a long time have complacently assumed they had *all* the brains in the Church. Perhaps you saw the review in which Dean Inge rather peevishly complained that the Anglo-Catholics seem to have more than their due share of brains!

'But don't trouble about reading Temple. You know his point of view already and as his type of mind does not help you it would be better to try something else . . .

'I was reading a paper to the English Society the other day and they said you would be reading a paper to them next term. Of course I said nothing about the affair on foot between us but I thought that if you were coming to Oxford for this purpose we might achieve several things at the same time. What do you think? and have you any sort of approximate date for your paper? I would like you to dine in Hall with me and see the Bishop also, if possible.

afraid that they took my provisional refusal as future consent. I think that when they asked me to address them I merely made the mild suggestion that they should call upon me again in the next term, and I would then see what was possible. I cannot yet be certain about next term. I hope very much that I can get down for a night on your kind invitation, and meet a few of your friends in Oxford, but I hate to complicate it by any engagement to speak, which is always very tiring. As for dining with you at Worcester and meeting the Bishop, that would please me very much. Your suggestions are delightful, and you may be sure that if I can get away, giving you a couple of weeks warning, I shall not fail to do so.

I am very glad to hear that you have finally settled in a house. I have written some days ago about you to Richmond. I have just heard from him that he has been very busy with private affairs,[1] but I hope to see him within a week or two.

Ever yours,
T. S. Eliot

## TO *Sirdar Ikbal Ali Shah*[2] CC

21 March 1927 [London]

The Editor of *The New Criterion* presents his compliments to the Sirdar Ikbal Ali Shah.[3] He is interested in the contribution sent by the Sirdar

---

We would be delighted to put you up out here or I could probably get you a room in college through my friend Vere Somerset of Worcester.

'Now that I have taken a house I am so desperately broke that by hook or crook I must get some hack work and earn a bit extra: it would be a help if the Times Lit could give me some reviewing.'

1 – Richmond's wife was unwell.

2 – Sirdar Ikbal Ali Khan (1894–1969) – the title 'Sirdar' designates a military leader – Indian-Afghan author and diplomat. Scion of a family of Musavi Sayyids (descendants of the Prophet Muhammad), he travelled widely (publishing narratives of his visits to Middle Eastern and Central Asian countries), and became the friend and publicist of statesmen including Kemal Atatürk and the Aga Khan, and King Abdullah of Jordan and the royal family of Afghanistan; he undertook assignments for the British Foreign Office, and worked in collaboration with the League of Nations. His articles appeared in the *Edinburgh Review*, *Fortnightly Review*, *Journal of the Royal Asiatic Society of Great Britain and Ireland*, and *The Times*. An advocate of Islamic modernisation, he laboured to promote Islamic unity, and to interpret East to West, as well as Europe to Asia; he also pioneered the study of Sufi philosophy as a bridge between East and West (a project that was greatly advanced by his son, Idries Shah, writer and teacher of Sufism). He wrote over twenty books in English including *Afghanistan of the Aghans* (1928), *Westward to Mecca* (1928) and *Islamic Sufism* (1933).

3 – The Sirdar Ikbal Ali Shah had submitted on 22 Mar. 'The Meeting of the East and the West', an essay originally written for a prize at the University of Edinburgh.

Ikbal Ali Shah and considers that it might be possible to use it in *The New Criterion* if it could be considerably abbreviated, as its length is in excess of the usual *New Criterion* contributions. He suggests that if the Sirdar Ikbal Ali Shah is willing to consider an abbreviated version, that the manuscript might be considerably shortened in the parts which deal with the work of Shelley, Wordsworth and other English poets. The first part of the manuscript he thinks extremely interesting. He returns the manuscript herewith, and would be glad to hear from the author.

## TO *Peter Quennell*[1] CC

22 March 1927 [London]

Dear Mr Quennell,

I should be very glad if you could call here and see me one day next week. I have been much interested by what I have seen of your poetry. It is difficult for me to be sure in advance on what days I shall be free, but I think that I should be free any afternoon except Wednesday or Thursday. I should be glad if you would drop me a line or if you would telephone to my secretary here and make an appointment.

Yours very truly,
[T. S. Eliot]

## TO *Wyndham Lewis* MS Cornell

23 March 1927 57 Chester Terrace, S.W.1.

Dear Wyndham

I shall be glad to fix next *Tuesday*. Call for me at 24 Russell Square, or write there if you prefer to choose another place of meeting. Say 1 o'cl.

1–Peter Quennell (1905–93), biographer, essayist, journal editor. Though rusticated from Balliol College, Oxford, he went on to become a man of letters (encouraged by figures including Harold Monro, Edward Marsh and Edith Sitwell). His publications include *Baudelaire and the Symbolists* (1929); *Four Portraits* (1945); *Alexander Pope: The Education of Genius 1688–1728* (1968); *Samuel Johnson: His Friends and Enemies* (1972); and works of autobiography including *The Marble Foot* (1976) and *The Wanton Chase* (1980). He edited *The Cornhill Magazine*, 1944–51; co-edited (with Alan Hodge) *History Today*, 1951–79.

I must add that I cannot at the moment be *absolutely* certain of keeping any engagement, as my father in law is dying, within a week or next few hours.

Yours ever
T. S. E.

## TO *Wyndham Lewis*

MS Cornell

25 March 1927 57 Chester Terrace, S.W.1.

Dear Wyndham.

Referring to my last: my father-in-law died this morning, and on Tuesday I shall have to go to Eastbourne for the funeral.

I shd like to see you as soon as possible afterwards. If I am back on Wednesday I have promised to lunch with Trend, who is leaving for Spain – Anyway, I think I can safely say *Friday* (same time & place). Is that possible for you?

Yours ever,
T. S. E.

## TO *Valentine Dobrée*[1]

Brotherton

25 March 1927 57 Chester Terrace, S.W. 1

Dear Mrs Dobrée,

I admit that I postponed reading your novel[2] as long as possible. I have had enough experience in reading books, when I know the author, to dread it. But now I have read it, and can, to my great relief, say that I like yours *immensely*. I feel myself quite incompetent to judge novels, and I profess a complete ignorance of human 'psychology'. Outside of detective stories, I regard 'fiction' simply from the point of view of a verse maker. That is, what impresses me is something I call 'tone' or atmosphere. I find it in the novelists I like – Turgenev, & Tolstoy, & Flaubert, & Dickens. I

1–Valentine Dobrée (1894–1974) – née Gladys May Mabel Brooke-Pechell, daughter of Sir Augustus Brooke-Pechel, 7th Baronet – was a well-regarded artist, novelist and short story writer. In addition to *Your Cuckoo Sings by Kind* (1927), she published one further novel, *The Emperor's Tigers* (1929); a collection of stories, *To Blush Unseen* (1935); and a volume of verse, *This Green Tide* (Faber, 1965). She married Bonamy Dobrée in 1913. See further *Valentine Dobrée 1894–1974* (The University Gallery Leeds, 2000).

2–See anonymous review of *Your Cuckoo Sings by Kind*, in *MC* 5 (June 1927), 363.

think your novel has this 'tone'. I get a 'feeling' about Christina from the beginning, which belongs to her and to no one else whom I have known – and that is the main thing. And it seems to me one of the saddest books I have read. I should like to forget it, but can't.

Yours very sincerely
T. S. Eliot

## TO *Henry Eliot* MS Houghton

27 March 1927 57 Chester Terrace, S.W.1.

My dear Henry

This is a line in haste to tell you that Mr Haigh-Wood died on Friday, at Hastings. He will be buried at Eastbourne on Tuesday.

If you or Theresa wrote to Mrs Haigh-Wood[1] I know she would be very appreciative. Letters, either here or to 3 Compayne Gardens, N.W.6 wd be forwarded.

He had a kind of tumour on the lung. It had been known for a long time that it would finally kill him. There was no tuberculosis or consumption of any kind.

In great haste

Always affectionately
Your brother
Tom.

## TO *John Middleton Murry* MS Northwestern

28 March 1927 *The New Criterion*

Dear John

My answer to your letter[2] has been delayed by three things: Vivien has been ill with bronchitis – almost pneumonia, my father-in-law has died, involving visits by myself to the country, & much legal business only beginning, and I mislaid your letter. I found that I had put it to mark the passage from Arnold in question.

First, about Valéry. I was not in a strong position to recommend this to F. & G. for the following reasons. Lady Rothermere, with my

1 – Rose Esther Haigh-Wood.
2 – See WL's letter of 18 Mar. above.

support, published the *Serpent*, in a limited edition, at 10/6. I wrote an introduction. The translation, by Wardle, was a very good translation.[1] The edition so far has come within £10 of paying expenses, but what we gave Valéry & Wardle was negligible. Then Valéry, whose mind is set on expensive editions, wanted us to do a series of his other works in the same way. I put this both to Lady R. and to F. & G. but at the same time expressed my disapproval. I said they would never sell, & they would not. At the same time, I suggested to Valéry that an ordinary edition, a book of his selected prose works, 300 or more pages, at 7/6 or 10/6, with a new introduction or preface by himself, and a preface by an English author, would be a possible proposition. F. & G. would have done it, but Valéry would not. I put your proposal before F. & G. but I could not go back on what I said before. So their decision is the same: separate short works, NO: but if Valéry would allow a bigger book, of whole or selected prose, to be done at a reasonable price, that could be considered.

Now, I have removed the especially offensive phrase. It was, of course, a quotation from Arnold: still, Arnold was speaking of England, not of one individual. About disciples, I must protest on my own acct. Does the relative affluence of 'my' disciples make any difference? Are you not insinuating an irrelevance? Do you not include those persons without thought or imagination, who plagiarise me, & use me, for their own ends, without acknowledgement and even with a sneer for me? Do you not include also those Gadarene swine, who merely garble my text in order to prove by distortion that they are right to go in the direction in which they are determined to go? Have I *any* disciples, any people who are anxious to know my attitude on the whole, not merely to snatch some sentence in their support? O John, I have not got to the point where I should consider myself strong enough to bear a disciple – but if I have any *real* disciples already, I doubt if they are on the whole more 'affluent' than yours. I think that the sneer was undeserved.

And must you be so respectful of 'Bloomsbury' as to maintain that it can copyright the '*titter*'? Could not one titter at Bloomsbury also?

Two points:

1) if one has no theology, should not one try to get one? They *are* misleading, but to have *no* theology is to be still worse mislead [misled].
2) *Metaphors*

[Incomplete.]

1 – Valéry, *Le Serpent*, trans. by Mark Wardle, with an introduction by TSE (1924).

## *I. P. Fassett* TO *Louis Zukofsky*[1] CC

30 March 1927 [London]

Dear Sir,

The Editor has been interested in your manuscript 'A Preface and 18 Poems to the Future' but regrets that he cannot make use of it.[2] I accordingly return it to you herewith.

Yours faithfully,
For the Editor of the *New Criterion*

## TO The New Criterion *Subscribers*

31 March 1927

Faber and Gwyer Ltd.
24 Russell Square, London W.C.1

'THE NEW CRITERION' IMPORTANT NOTICE TO SUBSCRIBERS

Dear Sir (or Madam),

We beg respectfully to inform you that *The New Criterion* which has hitherto been published quarterly, will in future appear monthly as *The Monthly Criterion*. The price of the Review will be reduced from Five shillings to Half-a-crown.[3]

Mr T. S. Eliot will continue to edit the Review, which will maintain its distinctive character. A rather larger portion of its space will be given to the Book Reviews. In this department a Monthly has obvious advantages

1–Louis Zukofsky (1904–78), American poet, son of Lithuanian Jewish parents, grew up speaking Yiddish and was educated at Columbia University (where he studied under Mark van Doren and John Dewey). In 1927 he sent to Ezra Pound 'Poem Beginning "The"' – a parody of *TWL* – which was received with enthusiasm and published by EP in his review *The Exile*, no. 3 (Spring 1928), 7–27. Zukofsky worked for the Works Projects Administration, 1934–42, and as an instructor in the English Dept. of the Polytechnic Institute of Brooklyn, 1947–66. A leader of the 'Objectivist' group of poets (associates included William Carlos Williams), his writings include *'A'* (a poem begun in 1927 amd published in full in 1978), *Prepositions: The Collected Critical Essays of Louis Zukofsky* (1968), *All: The Collected Short Poems, 1923–1964* (1971) and *Autobiography* (1970). See also *Selected Letters of Ezra Pound and Louis Zukofsky*, ed. Barry Ahearn (1987), and Mark Scroggins, *The Poem of a Life: A Biography of Louis Zukofsky* (2007).

2–Zukofsky had submitted his manuscript in Nov. 1926. Two poems by Zukofsky were to be published in C. 8 (Apr. 1929), 420–1 – possibly at EP's prompting.

3–This notice anticipated the formal transformation of the periodical from *New* to *Monthly* agreed at an Extraordinary Meeting of The New Criterion Ltd on 21 Apr.

over a Quarterly. The more frequent appearance of the magazine will also much increase the value of the various 'Chronicles'.

The first number of *The Monthly Criterion* will be dated May, and will be published on Thursday April 28th. In order to preserve continuity it will be numbered 'Volume V, Number 2', and will take the place of the quarterly issue, which would have appeared on April 15th.

The monthly issue will appear regularly either on the last Thursday, or the last Thursday but one, preceding the month of issue. They will be in precisely the same *format* as the quarterly issues (which will be discontinued), but will be less bulky. The white cover, which has been found unsuitable for bookstall handling, will be replaced by a coloured cover.

The subscription rate for *THE MONTHLY CRITERION* is thirty shillings for a year, post free to any address, and for periods of six or three months, *pro rata*.

As a subscriber to *THE NEW CRITERION* you have the option of terminating your subscription or of transferring it to *THE MONTHLY CRITERION*. The amount of your subscription unexpired is 15/- which is sufficient to cover 6 issues of *THE MONTHLY CRITERION*. If you wish to terminate your subscription, and will notify us to that effect not later than April 15th*, a remittance to the value of 15/- will be sent to you. Otherwise we shall assume that you wish your subscription to be transferred.

We venture to express the hope that you will continue to support the Review, and we shall be grateful for your assistance in making this new departure generally known.

We are,<br>Yours faithfully,<br>FABER & GWYER LTD.

* Subscribers abroad are asked to let us have this information as soon after this date as possible.

Where subscriptions are paid through Agents, kindly apply to the Agent if refund is required.

## TO *F. S. Flint*

CC

4 April 1927 [London]

My dear Flint,

I have three questions for your consideration.

(1) I *am counting* upon some sort of dramatic essay from you for the June issue to be published May 25.[1] I shall therefore need it by the 15th of this month. It does not need to be very long, and I hope it will not give you very much trouble. About the same length as Trend's music stuff will be all right.

(2) Are you willing to translate an essay in German by Read's friend, Worringer, for the following *Criterion* [del: June 25]? I hope you can squeeze it in, and if so will you let me know and I will send it at once. Fortunately it is a pamphlet already in print and is in Latin type.[2]

(3) In as much as you translated Massis's essay for the *Criterion*, would you be willing to translate for F. & G. the book which is an expansion of that essay? I should have asked you in any case, but also Massis himself has written to say that he hopes that we can get you to do it, as he was very much pleased with your translation of the essay. The book, which has the same title, is 280 pages, and I could send it to you at once. We should consider of course that it was entirely a fresh translation; i.e. we should not dream of making any deduction on account of the part which you have already translated. You know his style, and I do not think it would give you very much trouble. Chesterton has agreed to contribute a preface. I am ready to undertake all negotiations with you myself. If you agree in principle I will proceed to settle a price with you. I very much hope that you can do this, and if you agree I should like to have some idea as to how long it would take you, because I do not know whether you have finished that German book, or whether you have any other engagements at present.[3]

I shall come to South Kensington to lunch on Thursday if possible, but I have an engagement in the morning and I am not sure whether I can get there on time. If not, I shall suggest a lunch next week.

Yours ever,
[T. S. Eliot]

1–'Dramatic Chronicle', *MC* 5 (June 1927), 334–8.

2–'Art Questions of the Day', *MC* 6 (Aug. 1927), 101–17.

3–*Defence of the West*, trans. F. S. Flint, with preface by G. K. Chesterton (1927).

## TO *Frank Griffiths*

CC

5 April 1927 [London]

Dear Sir,

*In re C. H. Haigh-Wood Dec'd.*

Mr Maurice Haigh-Wood, who has just left for Rome, has handed me your letter of the 30th ultimo. The three Executors of the Estate are Mrs Haigh-Wood, the widow, Mr Maurice Haigh-Wood, and myself. In Mr Maurice Haigh-Wood's absence I am taking up the matters which he began. I should be very glad if you could arrange to call on me at your early convenience.

If you can make an appointment during the day I should be glad to see you at this address. I shall be free during Friday next, but should prefer an appointment in the afternoon if possible. I could I think arrange an appointment for the latter part of Thursday afternoon. If it is only convenient to you to call in the evening, please let me know, and I will arrange an evening appointment with you at my private address, 57 Chester Terrace, Eaton Square S.W.1.

I might add that I should be glad to consult you concerning my own Income Tax Returns, as I have to make a return including the property of my wife, Mr Haigh-Wood's daughter; and I wish to make my return for the Irish Property, for 1926-7, conform to that of my father-in-law.

Yours faithfully,
[T. S. Eliot]
Executor of C. H. Haigh-Wood Dec'd

## TO *A. E. James*[1] CC

5 April 1927 [London]

Dear Mr James,

*In re Charles H. Haigh-Wood Dec'd.*

I have today called upon Mr Haigh-Wood's Brokers, and on the District Bank Limited, and I thought it best to let you know the result of my enquiries.

I understand that the District Bank have written to you today; that they have given you the quotation for Southport & Cheshire Extens. Rwy. Co. Ordinary Stock; that they have informed you that British Cellulose, under the new name of British Celanese Limited (8, Waterloo Place) is quoted in the Official Intelligence; that the Stock of the Newcastle & Gateshead Water Co. *is* the 1876 Stock.

As to your other queries. No address can be found for the Pavilion Gardens (Kingstown) Ltd., but I have written tonight (and will post tomorrow *registered*) a letter to the Secretary of that company, addressing it merely Dun Laoghaire (Kingstown), Dublin, Ireland. I have also written to the Secretary of the East Lancashire Paper Mills Company Ltd., Radcliffe, Lancs., for a quotation for the 25th March 1927.

With regard to the Southport & Cheshire Rwy. Stock above mentioned, there is no further evidence, but it would seem that this was part of Mr Haigh-Wood's Estate. I do not know why it was in both names.

With regard to the Queensland 5% Stock 1940–60 £180, this has been with the District Bank since 1917 (it therefore can have nothing to do with the Estate of Emily Spencer Wood,[2] who died later). It appears to be registered in the names of 'Charles Haigh HAIGH-WOOD and Lewis Emmanuel Emmet' (verbatim). *All* Dividends have been paid regularly to the Bank for Mr Haigh-Wood's account, and there are no contra entries in his account to show that it was for any one else's benefit. Is this enough to prove ownership, or must we enquire further? Mr Emmet, of course, is living, and I understand is a Solicitor in Sheffield. You are fully acquainted with the details of a law-suit, some years ago, between him and Mr Haigh-Wood, concerning the estate of a common relative, Mrs Agnes Emmet.[3]

1–Charles Haigh-Wood, in his last will and testament dated 3 Jan. 1920, specified: 'As Messrs James & James proved my sister Emily's Will & know practically all about my affairs I wish them to undertake the probate of my Will, with a <u>*strong*</u> request that Mr [Alfred E.] James will *personally* supervise the matter.'

2–Haigh-Wood's sister (one of three), who predeceased him and left 'all her property to [her brother] for life with remainder to Vivienne & Maurice in equal parts'.

3–A cousin of Charles Haigh-Wood.

It is quite certain that the securities standing in the name of Mrs Rose E. Haigh-Wood are actually the sole property of Mrs Haigh-Wood. I have seen the Certificates at the Bank, which are in her name solely, and I find that the dividends have been paid regularly into her separate account. Mrs Haigh-Wood knew that her husband from time to time bought securities for her, and he had frequently expressed to her his desire that she should have an independent income.

I think that this covers all of your queries. I have now a question concerning the

*Estate of Emily Spencer Wood Dec'd.*

Is it necessary that the Misses Evans should make themselves responsible for the *division* of the property, or could they merely transfer the securities to Maurice and Vivien jointly, leaving them to divide equally? It seems desirable, from every point of view, that the Misses Evans, who have no interest in the matter, should have as little trouble as possible.

What I should like to suggest is, that every investment that can be divided equally, should be divided equally. This is the majority. Then, that where the holding is a small one, it should go to whichever of the two already has a holding. (For instance, Maurice has some Newcastle & Gateshead, Vivien has none.) Third, that certain securities, of small and inconvenient amounts (i.e. some of the railway stock) should be sold, and the proceeds divided). It would I think be much more convenient for everyone if the Misses Evans did not have to meddle themselves with these calculations . . . There would probably remain, as a few years ago in the other Wood estate, a small balance to be paid by Maurice to Vivien, or vice versa, to adjust matters.

Finally, does this division have to await the Probate, and does Death Duty have to be paid out of the E. S. Wood Estate first?

I shall inform you immediately I hear from Dublin and from the Paper Company, and we shall communicate the result of the assessment of the personal property in the house, which is to be taken on Friday.

Yours sincerely,
[T. S. Eliot]

## TO *C. Henry Warren*[1] CC

8 April 1927 [*The Monthly Criterion*]

Dear Mr Warren,

I am afraid I have made a muddle, partly owing to preoccupation with private affairs.[2] When the Mégroz book arrived I quite forgot that I had promised it to you, and I merely added it as a kind of post-script to Edith Sitwell's last volume of poems[3] which had also just arrived, and which I was sending to F. S. Flint. I am very sorry for this oversight, but I think it may be for the best. I looked at the Mégroz book, and it seemed to me a poor piece of work, and deserving only of a short notice; in any case I could not have devoted much space at the same time to Edith Sitwell's book and to a book about the Sitwells. So that I should have had to ask you to write only a short notice. I should like to send you something with which you could deal at greater length. In the case of novels it is very rarely that one novel is worth a long review, but there are a number of authors who might be treated at some length a propos of their most recent novel. Do you for instance know anything about Sinclair Lewis, and does he interest you?

Yours sincerely
[T. S. Eliot]

1–C. Henry Warren (1895–1966), author, broadcaster, reviewer, worked as an English teacher; as a lecturer for the National Portrait Gallery, 1927; and for the BBC, 1929–33.

2–Warren asked (25 Mar.) to review Mégroz's book on the Sitwells. 'I've seen it, & it isn't any too good – but it would provide a peg on which to hang something.'

3–*Rustic Elegies*.

## TO *Basil Bunting*[1] CC

8 April 1927 [London]

Dear Mr Bunting,

I must apologise for not having written to you sooner, but my time has lately been engrossed by certain private affairs.[2] I am returning to you herewith your manuscript, as I understand that you want to use some of it at once, and you do not specify which. It is however enough to assure me that I should like you to review for *The Criterion*, and as soon as the congestion of the next two months is reduced I shall hope to have something to send you. I should very much like to see more of your original work, such as 'The Salad Basket'.

Yours very truly,
[T. S. Eliot]

## TO *Thomas McGreevy* TS TCD

8 April 1927 *The New Criterion*

My dear MacGreevy,

I hope that you are getting on comfortably at the École Normale and find the life agreeable. I should be happy if you would write and let me know how you like it.

I have a tentative suggestion to put to you. We are considering producing a book to be called *The Story of the Russian Ballet* or something similar. That is to say it should be an explanatory introduction to the Russian

1–Basil Bunting (1900–85), Northumberland-born poet, became known to the literary world when he lived in Paris in the early 1920s, working for Ford Madox Ford at the *Transatlantic Review*. Subsequently he was mentored by Ezra Pound, whom he followed to Rapallo, Italy, in 1924. In the 1930s he would work as an assistant to EP and Olga Rudge (1895–1996); and it was through EP that he became acquainted with JJ, Zukofsky and Yeats. EP published his work in *Active Anthology* (1933); but his enduring fame came about in the post-war years with the publication of his poem *Briggflatts* (1966). *Collected Poems* appeared in 1968. See R. Caddel and A. Flowers, *Basil Bunting: A Northern Life* (1997).

2–Bunting wrote on 4 Apr.: 'You will remember that I called on you in the autumn, introducing myself with Pound's name, and that subsequently, by your request, I sent you samples of the kind of journalism I was then doing, together with two or three of my poems, the bad as well as those I think good. I have not heard from you since.

'Could you let me have my roll of typescript back? Pound has asked me to send him something for Exile, and I think I sent you my only copy of a story which might serve his purpose, called "The Salad Basket"

'I suppose I may take it, from your silence, that there is no prospect of my being allowed to do a few reviews for the Criterion?'

Ballet for the person who goes to see it without any previous knowledge. It should be a description and explanation of the principal ballets at present produced by Diaghilev, with something about the music and the scenery of both; and possibly, if the author liked, some mention of the dancers who have in the past been starred in each ballet. The book would be accompanied by photographs of some of the most important scenery which we should obtain.

Would it interest you to write such a book? Once published it might have to be brought up to date from time to time when any important new ballets were added to the repertoire. If you are interested in principle and have the time to do it, we will discuss details and terms. I think that you could do it as well as anybody![1]

Yours ever,
T. S. Eliot

## TO *Harold Monro* CC

8 April 1927 [London]

My dear Monro,

This is just an advance note to tell you that I took the liberty a little time ago of mentioning the Poetry Book-Shop to Virginia Woolf, who is in touch with some rich people. I had a letter from her a few days ago just before she left for Spain saying that she had been in communication with some rich person whose name she did not mention, who she thought would be inclined to invest money in the shop. I have not been able to reply to her or get any details as she had left England before I got her letter; and in any case she said that she would not be able to resume negotiations with this person until the beginning of May.[2] I hope that you will be back before then.

Yours ever,
[T. S. E.]

1 – McGreevy said (13 Apr.) he would be interested in principle. The book was not written.
2 – VW wrote to TSE on 27 March, 'I was writing to a very rich woman, who wants to waste a little money on literature, & put the case of the poetry book shop before her. If they would allow her some control & work I think she might pay for it.'

## TO *R. N. Rowe* CC

8 April 1927 [*The Monthly Criterion*]

Dear Mr Rowe,

In reply to your letter of the 3rd instant.[1] It is quite true that only two numbers of *The Tyro* ever appeared. You do not seem to be quite up-to-date about Mr Wyndham Lewis. Besides the book which you mention he has recently published *The Lion & the Fox* (Grant Richards) which is a study of Shakespeare and a very interesting book. I should particularly recommend you, however, to get hold of *The Enemy*, a new pamphlet or periodical of which Mr Lewis has produced one number, and most of which he has written himself. It can be obtained from The Arthur Press, 113a Westbourne Grove, W.2. I think that this last would interest you particularly. If you read that essay you will find that Mr Lewis makes it quite clear that he is not the Wyndham Lewis of the *Daily Mail*, who is quite a different sort of person.[2] I imagine that the reason why Mr Lewis is not painting at present is that he is too busy writing books.

Sincerely yours,
[T. S. Eliot]

1–Rowe asked (3 Apr.) what had happened to Wyndham Lewis after the appearance of the two issues of *The Tyro*. *The Art of Being Ruled*, recently published, seemed to be merely 'the sociological response of a dispossessed artist'; it did 'not strike the vital note which one found in what Mr Lewis wrote in the days of the ill-fated *Tyro*'. Also, could TSE confirm that D. Wyndham Lewis of the *Daily Mail* was a different person? 'And is it true that Lewis is so utterly dispossessed that he will not paint or draw any more?'

2–D. B. Wyndham-Lewis (1891–1969), British author, journalist, humorist, wrote in the 1920s a regular column for the *Daily Mail* headed 'At the Sign of the Blue Moon': his pieces were collected in *At the Sign of the Blue Moon* (1924) and *At the Blue Moon Again* (1925); he wrote too for the *News Chronicle*, and had been the first contributor to write as 'Beachcomber' in the 'By the Way' column at the *Daily Express*. He wrote biographies of figures including François Villon, Ronsard, Rabelais, Molière, Boswell and the Emperor Charles V; and with Charles Lee he edited the best-selling and perennially popular anthology of bad verse, *The Stuffed Owl* (1930, 1948). With Charles Bennett he wrote the screenplay of Alfred Hitchcock's movie *The Man Who Knew Too Much* (1934).

## TO *Frances Gregg*[1] *Wilkinson* CC

8 April 1927 [*The Monthly Criterion*]

Dear Madam,

I am returning to you herewith your two stories 'The Cry' and 'Lombard Street', neither of which I find quite suitable for *The New Criterion*, but I should very much like to see more of your work.

Yours very truly,
[T. S. Eliot]

## TO *Maurice Haigh-Wood*[2] CC

9 April 1927 [London]

Dear Maurice,

I wrote to James about the distribution of the E. S. Wood Estate, and here is the relevant part of his letter:

'The Misses Evans are as trustees responsible for the Duties payable on the testator's death and have their instructions to prepare the necessary account but if Maurice and Vivien request them to transfer the investments in any particular way instead of selling them and dividing the money they are bound to comply with that request, and I will see that nothing is done until the two concerned have arranged how the division is to be met. Some investment will of course have to be sold to pay the death duties. The division cannot be made until these death duties have been satisfied but this and the Probate application can proceed simultaneously.'

I suggest that, beyond the sale to cover duties, it would be more satisfactory for you and Vivien to arrange the distribution and take affairs out of the hands of the Misses Evans as early as possible. I should think the Misses Evans would prefer it too.

1–Frances Gregg (1884–1941), American writer, was brought up in Philadelphia. Friend of EP and intimate of H.D. (Gregg wrote in her diary: 'Two girls in love with each other, and each in love with the same man. Hilda, Ezra, Frances'), she married in 1912 the writer Louis Wilkinson ('Louis Marlow') after breaking with H.D. (and she divorced him in 1923). She contributed poems to *The Egoist* and *Others*. See Gregg, *The Mystic Leeway*, ed. Ben Jones (1995), which includes an account of Gregg by her son Oliver Wilkinson; *The Letters of John Cowper Powys to Frances Gregg*, vol. 1, ed. Oliver Marlow Wilkinson (1994); and Richard Perceval Graves, *The Brothers Powys* (1983). Gregg's career is rehearsed by Helen Carr in *The Verse Revolutionaries: Ezra Pound, H.D. and The Imagists* (2009).

2–Maurice Haigh-Wood (1896–1980), TSE's brother-in-law: see Biographical Register.

After a discussion with Marshall, it seems to me that the best thing then would be to divide equally all stuff that can be divided equally, which is the majority (I showed him the list). Where one of you has a small holding of something already and the other none, I suggest that your aunt's holding of that stock should go to the one who already has some. I believe there are one or two cases. Finally, there is a mixed lot of small holdings of railway stock, which Marshall thought it would be best to sell before the division, and divide the proceeds.

I dare say that you will be in England again before this point is reached, but we ought to have your views on this subject at once. I wish you would let me know, and also drop a line to James about it.

I shall write again in a few days.

In haste,
Affectionately,
[Tom]

## TO *A. E. James* CC

9 April 1927 [London]

Dear Mr James,

Mrs Haigh-Wood has handed me your letter of the 7th instant.

With regard to the Rates paid, £23:5:6d., I presume that these are for the ensuing half year. But I presume also that they should be paid out of the Executors' Account, and not by Mrs Haigh-Wood personally?

The Rent due from the Sub-Tenant has just been paid by the Agent, by cheque in favour of the Executors. It is stated by the Agent that the sum paid is for the period Apr. 5 – May 31st, so that from what you say it should *not* be included in the Account to the Revenue Authorities. But I am not clear to what account it should go. Should it be handed over to Mrs Haigh-Wood at once, or held in the Executors' Account to be delivered to her after the Probate is granted?

I presume that the Rent paid to the owners of the house is for the preceding quarter, and therefore a debt due by the Estate. But perhaps it would be as well if I confirmed this from the Landlord's Agent.

I have not been able to find anything about Income Tax paid last year, and no papers connected with it appear to have been found. I have an appointment with the man who looked after his Income Tax Returns, and he may be able to throw some light on the matter.

I have not yet heard from the Pavilion Gardens.

Sincerely yours,
[T. S. Eliot]

## TO *Ottoline Morrell* MS Texas

Sunday [?10 April 1927] 57 Chester Terrace, S.W.1

My dear Ottoline,

We were both very glad to hear from you, having wondered for some time what had been happening to you. We are sorry to know you have not been well, but are looking forward to having you in London.

It is very kind of you to ask us down. But just at present Vivien has been in bed for a week with severe & tenacious bronchitis – and so far no further engagements can be made. I wish I could see you and talk to you, and you have been constantly in my mind – much more than you imagine. There are more & more things that I should like to talk to you about.

Vivien was really *very pleased* by your letter. Thank you.

Ever affectionately
Tom

## TO *Mario Praz* CC

11 April 1927 [*The New Criterion*]

My dear Praz,

Thank you very much for your Chaucer essay which I read immediately with great interest. Certainly I think that it ought to be published without abbreviation, and the bibliography should be published with the first part, as it is obvious that for *The Criterion* it would have to be divided. I think I can start it about Midsummer; but of course if you found the occasion for publishing it more advantageously I hope that you would let me know. I should certainly use it as soon as possible, and I am greatly pleased to have it.[1] I am sending this to Liverpool, as I fear missing you at the Hague, but I hope that you may have an hour or so in London, and catch me before you return.

Sincerely yours,
[T. S. Eliot]

1 – 'Chaucer and the Great Italian Writers of the Trecento' [I], *MC* 6: 1 (July 1927), 18–31; [II], 6: 2 (Aug. 1927), 131–57; III: 'Bibliography', *MC* 6: 3 (Sept. 1927), 238–42.

## TO *Antonio Marichalar* CC

11 avril 1927 [*The New Criterion*]

Mon Cher Ami,

Je vous fais toutes mes excuses. Je vous prie de me pardonner. J'ai eu tout mon temps accaparé par des affaires personelles. Soyez sûr que j'accepte avec grand plaisir votre témoignage d'amitié.[1] Je suis honoré au delà de mes mérites. Monsieur Stols m'avait demandé quelquechose pour ce même album, et j'ai été navré de ne pas pouvoir y montrer mon admiration et mon amitié pour Valéry. Mais je n'ai eu que très peu de loisir pendant ces derniers mois, et je ne voulais pas envoyer quelque chose qui ne fut pas digne.

Vous saurez déjà que le *Criterion* paraîtra désormais mensuellement, donc je vous préviens que j'espère recevoir votre chronique pour le numéro de septembre. C'est à dire que nous devrions recevoir le manuscrit avant le premier août. Est-ce-que je peux compter sur vous?

Toujours votre dévoué,
[T. S. Eliot][2]

## TO *Bonamy Dobrée* TS Brotherton

11 April 1927 *The New Criterion*

My dear Dobrée,

Replying to your first letter first I will inform you that I have sent for the translation of Diehl's book, and if it arrives I shall send it to your friend in Cairo with a letter asking him to write about it. The suggestion is welcome, and I should be glad to have something authoritative; I attended

1–On 16 Feb. Marichalar had sent TSE a proof of his article 'Sima (Introducción al Método de M. Teste)' – for *Hommage des Écrivains Étrangers à Paul Valéry*, ed. and pub. A. A. M. Stols (Paris, 1927) – with the request that he might dedicate it to TSE.

2–*Translation*: My dear friend, Please receive all my apologies. I wish you would forgive me. All of my time has been taken by personal business. Be sure that I accept with great pleasure our profession of friendship. I am honoured beyond what I deserve. Mr Stols had asked me for something for the same compilation and I was sorry not to have been able to show my admiration and friendship for Valéry. But I have had very little spare time in the last few months and I did not want to send something that was unworthy.

You will already know that the *Criterion* will be published monthly from now on, so I warn you that I hope to receive your chronicle for the September issue. This is to say we should receive the manuscript before 1 August. Can I count on you?

Yours truly as always, [T. S. Eliot]

Diehl's lectures years ago, and have read a couple of his books. Do you know his *Manual*? It has a lot of interesting illustrations.[1]

Replying to your second letter second, I must express my regret at finding my Egyptian correspondent so careless and inaccurate. You have sent under date of the 15th March a great deal of information about the Camel, but if you will refer to my letter, you will find my enquiry concerned the Crocodile.[2] The only thing I want to know about the camel is whether, as American authorities assert, it is always necessary to walk a mile for one. I shall have to give you in detail my information about the crocodile, which is derived from Herodotus and from Pliny the Elder.

The monthly promises well, and the first number ought to be out in about a fortnight. Your review of Lewis will lead off the reviews in the following number, which I am now making up. I should always be glad of news about the Kipling, and the dialogue suggested would be very welcome.

I liked your Otway in the *Times* very much indeed.[3] I do not know Otway very well, and I found nothing in the article to question. It had the advantage of comparison with Squire's perfunctory essay in the *Observer* a few days later.[4]

I finally found time to read *Your Cuckoo*, and wrote to your wife about it; I think she got my letter just before leaving England. I may not have expressed myself very well, but I was very much impressed and moved by the book, and I look forward to her next work. I hope, by the way, that her next book will not be a continuation of Christina in the way that Miss Richardson goes on about successive phases in the life of one heroine.[5] One of the things that I especially liked about your wife's book was a certain objectivity; I mean an interest in the way things look, and a cutting

1–Charles Diehl (1859–1944), French historian specialising in Byzantine art and history, taught classes at the Sorbonne. His works include *Manuel d'art byzantin* (1910; 2nd edn, 1926) and *Histoire de l'empire byzantine* (1920). BD suggested in his letter of 10 Mar. that Diehl's *Figures Byzantines* (1906, 1908) – trans. by Harold Bell as *Byzantine Portraits* – should be sent to Henri Grégoire, Professor of Greek and Dean of the Faculty of Letters at Cairo University, who was fluent in English.

2–BD explained at length (15 Mar.) why the camel was not responsible for the pyramids.

3–BD, 'Thomas Otway' – on *The Complete Works of Thomas Otway* (3 vols), ed. Montague Summers – *TLS*, 3 Mar. 1927, 133–4.

4–J. C. Squire, in 'Tender Otway' (*Observer*, 6 Mar. 1927, 6) was enthused by the editor's 'unfailing gusto and pugnacity' – 'Mr Summers's enthusiasm and raciness are such that he could impart life to a time table' – but had little time for Otway's oeuvre: 'A hundred editions will not bring Otway back to the stage.'

5–Dorothy Richardson (1873–1957): English novelist; putative pioneer of the 'stream of consciousness' technique; author of a series of novels under the joint title *Pilgrimage* – the first being *Pointed Roofs* (1915) – that would ultimately run to 11 volumes by 1935.

out of superfluous detail about the way they feel. Mr and Mrs Harris had a kind of reality which has been disappearing from English fiction within the last fifty years. This leads me to think that she could invent and imagine objectively outside what might be called her own experience. This sticking to one's own experience by novelists seems to me to narrow the field of experience itself. Let me hear from you soon.

Ever yours,
T. S. E.

## TO *H. S. Milford*

CC

11 April 1927 [24 Russell Square]

Dear Mr Milford,

Thank you for sending me the proofs, as I have found to my surprise that it is difficult to procure a copy of *The Moonstone*, and I have been dependent on the London Library.[1] I think I can let you have the introduction in three or four weeks if you want it. But if you do not want it within that time I should be glad to know.

Yours sincerely
[T. S. Eliot]

## TO *Virginia Woolf*

TS Berg

11 April 1927 *The New Criterion*

My dear Virginia,

I do not know whether this letter will follow you, but if not, let it wait in Tavistock Square to ask you to let me know when you get back so that I may come and see you. I was very sorry to learn that you had left. It is true that I was up and down between London and the sea-side during the whole time. Vivien's father died there just before you left and I have been engrossed in executorial responsibilities.

I envy you in Rome at this time of year. I know what it is like now.

Ever yours,
Tom.

P.S. Harold Monro also is abroad, so that matter can wait. Very many thanks.

1 – Milford had begun sending the proofs of the novel on 4 Apr.

## TO *Frances Dublin* CC

11 April 1927 [London]

Dear Madam,

I have your letter of the 17th ultimo.[1] I am not quite sure that I understand your question, but I should like to suggest that I may not have made my own meaning clear. I should distinguish between what may be called 'Poetry of Doubt' and what may be called 'Poetry of Unbelief' in Mr Richards's sense. Poetry of doubt or unbelief such as that of Mr Hardy does not seem to me to fall within Mr Richards's category of poetry of unbelief. I mean that Hardy's unbelief, like that of Matthew Arnold, is essentially parasitical. It depends upon the fact that other people have believed things, and his whole point of view is determined by other people's beliefs. I imagine that Mr Richards is envisaging a type of poetry quite different from this, and that he is using the terms 'belief' and 'unbelief' in a much profounder sense. My point was that there is no sign of such a type of poetry coming into existence; or, alternatively, if it is coming into existence it has always existed.[2]

Yours very truly,
[T. S. Eliot]

1–Frances Dublin wrote from New York (17 Mar.): 'In your review of "Poetry and Belief" by I. A. Richards (*The Dial*: March, 1927) you question the emotional value of the poetry of unbelief, so-called. If, from your interpretation, I rightly gather Mr. Richards' meaning, I should venture to say that Mr. Hardy's verse, in large measure, falls in with such a division. The cry, "O, doth a bird deprived of wings go earthbound willfully?" expresses more than a passing mood; is, in fact, in feeling, at the very centre of his poetic thought: and which no loyalty, no ultimate acceptance, ever completely assuages. Thus, as an integral mode, it cannot be ignored in a total estimate of Mr. Hardy's poetry; and further, as to its emotional value, it clearly reaches a high level of excellence. The conditions here then (that is, considering that portion of the poetry which bears this stamp of "unbelief") fit in with what Mr. Richards predicates; therefore your question, if I have grasped your meaning, is already answered: a poetry of unbelief *can* yield rich emotional values.' She wrote again on 27 May, 'I think your definition of a true poetry of "unbelief" is no more existent than that which is to be found in Hardy's verse. That is to say, can anything, and particularly a product of the imagination, exist apart from outside influences? Are not all things tangential to other things, whether in great or small measure?'
2–Cf. TSE's remark, in 'A Note on Poetry and Belief' (*The Enemy*, no. 1 [Jan. 1927], 15–17), *contra* IAR's comments on *TWL* ('A Background for Contemporary Poetry', *C.*, July 1925) – that IAR 'looks forward to a possible development of the human mind in which sensibility and intellect will in some way be separated, in which "belief" will consist in the provisional assent given to tenable scientific hypotheses . . . But I cannot see that poetry can ever be separated from something which I should call belief, and to which I cannot see any reason for refusing the name of belief . . . It takes application, and a kind of genius, to

## TO *F. J. Powicke*[1]

CC

12 April 1927 [*The New Criterion*]

Sir,

I have read with great interest your book on the Cambridge Platonists and your contribution to *The Legacy of the Middle Ages*. Both of these we expect to notice as soon as possible in this review. I am writing to say that I should feel greatly honoured if you would consider contributing to *The New Criterion* on one of the subjects on which you write with such distinction. I have wondered whether you would agree to publishing anything either on the Victorines or one or more of the Spanish mystics.[2]

In making this suggestion I regret only that our terms cannot be more generous: We offer £2 per thousand words, and articles should not exceed six thousand words.

If you are not acquainted with the character of this Review I shall be glad to send you a copy of the next issue, which will appear on the 25th instant. The Review has heretofore been a quarterly, but from the next issue will be published monthly.

I have the honour to be, Sir,
Your obedient Servant,
[T. S. Eliot]

---

believe anything, and to believe *anything* . . . will probably become more and more difficult as time goes on . . . We await, in fact (as Mr Richards is awaiting the future poet), the great genius who shall triumphantly succeed in believing *something*. For those of us who are higher than the mob, and lower than the man of inspiration, there is always *doubt*; and in doubt we are living parasitically (which is better than not living at all) on the minds of the men of genius who have believed something' (*I. A. Richards and His Critics: Selected Reviews and Critical Articles*, ed. John Constable [2001], 59–62).

1–TSE had confused the Revd F. J. Powicke (1854–1935), Congregational minister and historian of seventeenth-century Puritanism, with his son Frederick Maurice Powicke (1879–1963), whose interests lay in medieval history. While F. J. Powicke wrote *The Cambridge Platonists*, his son had an illustrious career as Professor of Medieval History at Manchester, 1919–28; Regius Professor of Modern History, Oxford, 1928–48. He was elected FBA in 1927; became President of the Royal Historical Society in 1933; and was knighted in 1946. His works include *Christian Life in the Middle Ages* (1926), *King Henry III and the Lord Edward* (1947) and *Modern Historians and the Study of History* (1955).

2–HR had written on 9 Feb.: 'There is a man called F. M. Powicke, Professor of Mediaeval History at Manchester, who writes an extremely good chapter on "The Christian Life" in that book on the Middle Ages which you gave me to review . . . I think he might be interesting on the Victorines or Meister Eckhart.' 'Victorines' denotes the School of philosophers and mystics based at the Augustinian Abbey of St Victor in Paris, founded in the twelfth century by William of Champeaux. Prominent members included the mystic Hugh of St Victor and his disciple, the theologian Richard of St Victor (a Scot), who is mentioned in the *Paradiso* X: 130).

## TO *Gilbert Seldes* TS Timothy and Marian Seldes

12 April 1927 *The New Criterion*

My dear Seldes,

I was glad to get your letter of the 31st March, and particularly because it clears up the mystery of your mystery stories.[1] It is needless to say that I had read 'The Victory Murders' within 24 hours of receipt, and had been speculating on the identity of the author without success. I have enjoyed the book very much; my only criticism is that according to my private canons it is not a pure detective story, but a mixed detective and adventure story. That is to say, in a pure detective story there are no adventures after the first chapter; the book is entirely concerned with the accumulation, selection and construction of evidence about something which has already happened. In your story things keep happening. This is by no means a disadvantage; it is merely a nice point of definition. I am perfectly willing to admit that the pure detective story is extremely rare; the most austere example of the type is of course *The Case of Marie Roget*.[2]

You say that you have already written another.[3] If you have not arranged for publication in this country, is there any chance of our being allowed to see it and make an offer for it?

I do not know whether the news has yet reached you of the conversion of *The New Criterion* into a monthly. The first monthly number will appear about the moment when you receive this letter. I propose to continue the foreign chronicles, and to have each foreign chronicle regularly twice a year. As things fall out your next chronicle should fall due for the October number; that is to say I should want to have your manuscript before the 1st of September and another one exactly 6 months later. Do these dates suit you? If not we may be able to re-adjust them later. Of course there will be very little to report for 2 or 3 months before, but I think that your chronicle of this season would not be amiss at the beginning of next season. Besides, it is not an advantage to appear in July, August or September, because during those months people read chronicles with much less attention. So I hope you will be willing to appear in the October number, and send me your chronicle as long before the 1st of September

1–On 31 Mar., after reading 'with extreme interest' TSE's review of nine recent detective novels (*NC* 5: Jan. 1927, 139–43), Seldes sent a copy of *The Victory Murders*, published under the pseudonym Foster Johns. See Michael Kammen, *The Lively Arts* (1996), 152–3.
2–Edgar Allan Poe, *The Case of Marie Roget* (1842–3).
3–*The Square Emerald*.

as is convenient. As for what you are to include, I think that I ought to leave this entirely to your own preference.

Yours ever,
T. S. Eliot

## TO *Orlo Williams*

CC

12 April 1927 [Faber & Gwyer Ltd]

My dear Williams,

I am beginning to worry about my mental condition, having just discovered that I had forgotten an important telephone message at 3 p.m. today, I received the message that you had rung up having expected me to lunch. I am really forgetting everything of late. I find I made a note of it in my diary, but unfortunately I have two diaries, one in my pocket and one on my desk, and the one I consulted was on my desk. I am truly humble and apologetic. It is all the more annoying because it would have been extremely convenient as well as agreeable to have lunched with you today; but I had a solitary chop in my usual chop-house.

Now what are your movements, and when will you be back? Can you suggest a date now, or will you drop me a line the moment you return. I think in the circumstances that you must come and lunch with me.

I was going to mention to you a suggestion, which I must now make in writing instead. The question of reviewing novels is always a difficult one for *The New Criterion*. There are very few that are worth long reviews; but on the other hand I find that the subject matter of the long reviews tends to become heavier and heavier. I had thought that we might sometimes have a long review by making some recent novel the occasion for an examination of the whole work of some well-known novelist. Do any names occur to you that you would be interested to examine when suitable novels appear?[1]

1–Williams replied (15 Apr.): 'As regards the reviewing of novels, I think yours is quite a good idea. I only point out that the consideration of a prolific novelist's whole work is a terrific task – e.g. Wells, Bennett, Hardy – and one almost impossible to conduct in a small space. Names of novelists whose work seems to promise permanence are extraordinarily few but authors of high talent and many merits are innumerable. Virginia Woolf would be worth doing, & one must keep an eye on Sackville West, Percy Lubbock, Storm Jameson, ok, and many others. But when I look for importance and a more than passing significance I am at a loss. Is there really any successor to Hardy?'

Do write to me at once and say you forgive me, and will come and lunch with me as soon as you are in town again.

Ever yours,
[T. S. Eliot]

## TO *Rose Esther Haigh-Wood* CC

12 April 1927 [London]

Dear M.,[1]

Just a line to say that I have heard from Mr James this morning that the rent (the cheque you got from Match's) must be paid first into the Executors Account, and then transferred to your personal account as soon as Probate is granted. I expect the Bank will have done this anyway, if you have already paid it in, but I can find out.

I suppose you have given, or will give Mr James as soon as Grant has let you have it, the Appraisal. Mr James has all the other figures he needs, so I expect the Probate should be given in about a week.

Affectionately,
[Tom]

## TO *The Income Tax Adjustment Agency Limited* CC

13 April 1927 [57 Chester Terrace, London, S.W.1]

Dear Sirs,

*Your reference BA*

I am one of the Executors of the late Charles Haigh-Wood Esq., of 3, Compayne Gardens, N.W.6., who died on the 25th March last. I understand from certain correspondence in my possession (the last letter from you dated February 1st 1927) that you had been making Mr Haigh-Wood's Reclaims of Income Tax.

I should be greatly obliged if you could inform me, at your very earliest convenience, of the amount re-claimed for Mr Haigh-Wood for the fiscal year 1925–1926. These figures are required for our estimate of amount to be reclaimed for 1926–1927, to be included as an item in the Application for Grant of Probate. If you reclaimed for him separately on account of British and on account of Irish Income Tax, I should be grateful for both figures.

1 – TSE often addressed Rose Haigh-Wood as 'Mother-in-Law', or 'M.i.l'.

I enclose stamped envelope for reply.

Yours faithfully,
[T. S. Eliot]

## TO *Arundel del Re*

CC

15 April 1927 [London]

Dear Mr del Re,

Thank you for your letter of a few days ago.[1] I should be very glad to support in any way possible, both by writing and by suggesting others to write, your Golden Cockerel project, if it does not in any way conflict with something that Faber & Gwyer are doing. We intend to reprint the First Folio, with short scholarly prefaces by one man, play by play, at a popular price. Your edition should appeal to quite a different public – ours will not be a 'specimen of fine book-making' – and the introductions of a different type; and no doubt your volumes will be much more expensive. So I should like to suggest that you use some other edition than the First Folio; in that case I think there will be no conflict at all. A conflict would only mean that we should divide the public, and both lose money. But if the two editions are quite different, I should be very glad to be of use to you. This letter, like yours, is confidential.

Sincerely yours,
[T. S. Eliot]

I await the Florio patiently.

## TO *F. M. Powicke*

CC

Good Friday [15 April] 1927 [London]

Dear Sir,

I apologise for my blunder, but I hope that it means that I may have two contributors instead of one.[2] I shall write to your father – I imagine that

1 – Arundell del Re invited TSE to introduce one of the plays of Shakespeare to be published in a series of fine editions by The Golden Cockerel Press.

2 – F. M. Powicke's letter of 13 Apr. was in reply to TSE's of 12 Apr.: 'I doubt if either my father or I could deal adequately with any of the subjects you mention; but you may like to secure his help in other directions . . . If you ask him, you should remember that, as a retired dissenting minister, he may take a line which is not altogether consistent with the main tendency of your periodical; but he would be sure to appreciate and act upon any hints which you might care to give him on this; so far as his convictions allowed.'

any differences of opinion might be easily adjusted – but as I have already entered upon correspondence with you, may I say that I should be very happy if and when you found time to give me an essay on something to do with mediaeval thought, even if you are unwilling to tackle the Victorines. Will you consider, or at least hold out some hope for a remoter future?

With many thanks,
I am,
Yours very truly,
[T. S. Eliot]

## TO *John Dover Wilson* CC

Good Friday [15 April] 1927 [*The New Criterion*]

Dear Dover Wilson,

Success to your tramp, and may you not have to read this letter until you return. I am very glad we are both suited about the date of the review. But don't disappoint me; and make it any length you like up to a maximum of 2500 words – most of our longs are 1500 to 2000.

I am very happy to know that we are likely to have your support in our First Folio. It made all the difference, to myself approving the scheme. But the idea of a First Folio, at a reasonable price, not a luxury for bibliophiles but a necessity for scholars and students, appeals to me very strongly under such auspices.[1]

I appreciate your compliments on my paper, but they make me all the more fearful of printing it. I fear that when you see it in cold print, you will find that the charm has evaporated, and nothing left but a series of unsubstantiated generalisations.

With all best wishes,
Sincerely yours,
[T. S. Eliot]

1 – *Facsimiles of the First Folio Text*, introd. John Dover Wilson (1928): ten titles.

## TO *His Mother*

TS Houghton

Good Friday [15 April] 1927 *The New Criterion*

Dearest Mother,

Thank you for your letter of April 4th. A letter for Vivien and one for Mrs Haigh-Wood arrived from you by the same post. I thought I had explained that Vivien and I had already returned to London, and it was immediately on returning here that Vivien got bronchitis. She had a very bad attack indeed, and the doctor said that if she got up and went down to Hastings she would very likely get pneumonia, so there was no question about it. Mrs Haigh-Wood is now in London in an hotel, and Maurice, who arrived in time and stayed for about three weeks, had to go back to Rome. It is very lonely for Mrs Haigh-Wood, but I must say that she is very plucky and independent, and proves extremely competent in looking after her affairs – fortunately she has had a great deal to do – and she has a very sound old lawyer who has been the family lawyer for a generation.

I have been very busy over the monthly *Criterion*, especially as my secretary has been away ill for a month, and will only return next week. But the first number is now quite ready, and the second is nearly ready, and I think I can always keep a month ahead.

About my letters. For heaven's sake don't send them to me. If there is one thing more depressing than reading other people's old letters it is reading one's own. What I suggest, even beg, is that you keep all or any that you want to keep, but leave instructions that they be destroyed after your death. I do not want my biography, if it is ever written – and I hope it won't – to have anything private in it. I don't like reading other people's private correspondence in print, and I do not want other people to read mine.

I do not know how many books I have at home. There are probably some that I should like to have, others that I have since duplicated, and many that would be useless. If there are not many, I should like a list; if there are many, I shall let you give them to other members of the family, or to anyone you see fit. I want to save you trouble over them.

I have just sent you a copy of the March *Dial*, with something of mine,[1] and a copy of the *Neue Schweizer Rundschau*, with an essay about me, and a translation of *The Waste Land*, by my friend Professor Curtius of Heidelberg.[2] He is the most conspicuous critic of foreign literature – English and French and Italian and Spanish – in Germany; so I hope,

1 – 'Literature, Science and Dogma', *Dial*, 82: 3 (Mar. 1927), 239–43.
2 – *Das Wüste Land*, *Neue Schweizer Rundschau*, 20: 4 (1 Apr. 1927), 362–77.

as this review has considerable circulation in Germany, that his article will stimulate demand there for both my poems and the *Criterion*. I understand that the Germans buy a good many foreign books now that they have a stable currency.

I must stop now. It is Good Friday, four days holiday, and I have brought a lot of work home.

Your very loving son
Tom

## TO *Richard Cobden-Sanderson* cc

Good Friday [15 April] 1927 [London]

Dear Cobden-Sanderson,

I am writing just a line to explain to you the delay in settling the accounts. It does not appear to be the fault of Faber & Gwyer; you understand that we must get the authority of Lady Rothermere before you and I can deal with the small balance. The simplest way for us would be of course to draw a cheque to her for the balance, and let her settle with F. & G. for the unexpired subscriptions. But we thought that the simplest way for her – which as you know is the simplest for everybody in the end! – was to get Horne's[1] approval for our paying the balance to F. & G. and perhaps wash out the rest. But the devil is that all this time we cannot get any instructions from either Lady R. or Horne. The uncrowned king of cement (as the papers call him) seems to be cementing his interests abroad. As soon as we can get hold of either of them we hope to get a decision.

Yours ever,
[T. S. E.]

## TO *G. B. Harrison*[2] cc

15 April 1927 [London]

Dear Harrison,

I am rather diffident about the Shakespeare-Seneca paper which I promised, and perhaps Sir Israel[3] made the suggestion in an expansive

1 – H. S. Horne: Company Secretary, Faber & Gwyer Ltd.

2 – G. B. Harrison (1894–1991), Hon. Secretary of the Shakespeare Association.

3 – Sir Israel Gollancz (1863–1930): Professor of English Language and Literature, King's College, London, 1903–30; a founder, Fellow and Secretary of the British Academy.

moment which he might later regret. It seems to me to need complete re-writing before it is presentable in print; but if you care to take the trouble I will gladly send it to you, as it is, not for immediate publication but for your opinion.[1]

I am enthusiastic about the Marston, and my people are very favourably disposed towards it. I think that if it is not a question of publication this year, they will probably jump at it; but they have undertaken two rather costly productions of the same type for the immediate future, and we cannot put all our eggs at one moment in one sort of basket.[2]

Sincerely yours,
[T. S. Eliot]

## TO *Bruce Richmond*

CC

19 April 1927 [London]

My dear Richmond,

It has just occurred to me that there are two forthcoming books which I should very much like to review. One is a Biography of Laud which is to appear in a series of British Churchmen edited by Sidney Dark[3] and published by Macmillan. The other is the reprint of Bradley's *Ethical Studies* which the Clarendon Press are to bring out.[4]

These suggestions, like any that I make, are with the understanding that you are likely to have at your disposal specialists who are much better qualified and more and better entitled to review the books than am I. But I should like to review them myself if they would otherwise be reviewed by someone equally incompetent. I have lately been reading some of Laud with a view to certain other work, and want eventually to write a long essay on him.[5]

1–TSE's *Shakespeare and the Stoicism of Seneca* was to be published for the Shakespeare Association on 22 Sept. 1927; and it would be included in *SE* (1932). Harrison answered TSE's diffidence on 2 May: 'Sir Israel Gollancz and I have discussed your paper again and we should very much like to print it as it stands. We propose to issue it first as a brochure and later to include it in a volume of papers.'

2–Harrison replied (16 Apr.) that he would be glad to read TSE's paper; his edition of Marston would not be ready before 1928–9.

3–Sidney Dark (1872–1947), editor of the Anglo-Catholic *Church Times*, 1924–41. Works include *Archbishop Davidson and the English Church* (1929), *The Lambeth Conferences, their History and their Significance* (1930), *The Folly of Anti-Semitism* (1939), *The Church Impotent or Triumphant* (1941), and *Not such a Bad Life* 1941).

4–[TSE], 'Bradley's "Ethical Studies"', *TLS*, 29 Dec. 1927, 981–2; repr. as 'Francis Herbert Bradley', *FLA*.

5–William Laud (1573–1645): Archbishop of Canterbury from 1633; leader of the High

My final question is to ask when you could lunch with me. This week is a short week for me, as I have on two days meetings early in the afternoon which render lunch engagements impossible; but I am at present free next week any day but Thursday. I would suggest the Cock or the Cheshire Cheese or some ordinary convenient for you.

Yours ever,
[T. S. Eliot]
Personal

## TO *Rev. E. G. Selwyn* CC

20 April 1927 [London]

Dear Mr Selwyn,

I must apologise for not having replied to you before, and I am very sorry to learn that I failed to acknowledge the receipt of the Bramhall. I have been working upon the article with many interruptions. If possible I should prefer to let you have it for your July number rather than the June number. In that case I suppose you would want it by June 7th at the latest. I have found it necessary to do a great deal of reading both of Bramhall himself and of Laud, and I am at present re-reading certain parts of Hobbes.

I am taking the liberty of sending you the forthcoming number of my review which has now become a Monthly. I apologise for the colour of the cover which is not my own choice, but I hope that some of the contents may interest you, especially a contribution of my friend Maritain.

Yours sincerely,
[T. S. Eliot]

Anglican party. In 'Lancelot Andrewes', TSE said that the bishop's prayers 'illustrate the devotion to private prayer . . . and to public ritual which Andrewes bequeathed to William Laud' (*FLA*, 18). Laud was a passionate advocate for the powers and rights of the established Church in harmony with the monarchy. He was opposed to Puritanism and nonconformism, insisting that ecclesiastical uniformity was the necessary correlative of order in the state. His conviction as to the catholicity of the Church of England led to suspicions of popery. TSE said of Richard Hooker, in *VMP*, 164: 'it is no wonder that before he joined the Church of Rome he found the church of Archbishop Laud the most sympathetic, of Laud who took his stand for the liturgy and "the beauty of holiness" . . .'.

TO *Geoffrey Faber* TS Valerie Eliot

20 April 1927 *The New Criterion*

My dear Faber,

It is rather easier, in both the circumstances, to reply to your letter by letter than verbally; since we are never able to meet at present except between other interviews, and to discuss the price of a book, or the colour of a periodical, or such trifles.

I am glad if my letter had any value.[1] It was written upon instinct. There is only one thing I want to say. I don't think you need to worry about yourself. Your absorption in the business is partly, I think, a transference of your worry about the business so far as it affects your family. And I find myself, when I am tired, that I become more absorbed in administrative work. I have found, for some time past, that when I should have been thinking about what I was going to write myself, I was making little schemes in my head for arranging other people's writings, and getting new reviewers, and making this or that combination. I find reading just as difficult as you do, and I never want to write anything myself. Sometimes I wonder, if I found myself suddenly with no occupation but with complete leisure for thinking, whether I should have anything to think about.

But I hope that in some ways you will feel lighter in heart after ten days or so.[2]

Yours ever,
T. S. E.

1–The letter to which this refers has not been found, but evidently GCF had spoken of his professional anxieties. On 26 July 1926, he wrote in his diary: 'The position is a somewhat anxious one, & I find it hard to justify my buoyant self-confidence of last year. If this proves another failure I shall not again try to take on a big responsible job, for it will have proved me deficient in the qualities necessary for commercial success. Meantime I hope that is not so. Much hangs on the Coal Strike – & that is not in my control; but I ought, I think, to have foreseen trouble & gone more cautiously.' On 7 Jan. 1927: 'Things are now looking at their most difficult for me . . . May God help me to win through, for all our sakes: as I trust, with such help, I shall.' On 18 May 1927: 'In all this period, I feel life is not worth living: the business seems to present insuperable obstacles – anxieties become acute – the burden is too great to be carried much longer.' Through all such times of worry and strain, TSE and GCF were strengths and stays to one another; and GCF came to depend on TSE's advice. All the same, not every day was dark: they would often talk over subjects of positive mutual interest; as on 11 Aug. 1927: 'Lunched with Eliot, & had an interesting if rather (on my part) incoherent talk, chiefly about the poetic impulse & its different characters.'

2–Perhaps by way of celebrating the *Monthly Criterion*, TSE laid on a treat – as GCF recorded in his diary on 4 May: 'Dined, as Eliot's guest at the Commercio restaurant in Frith Street, & we went on to the Albert Hall, where as Lady R's guests we sat in a Grand Tier box & watched boxing. Amazing sight – crowd, lighting, organ, & the supple bodies of the boxers. Teddy Baldock beating Bell.'

## TO *J. Moore, Assessor of Taxes* CC

25 April 1927 [London]

Sir,

*Your ref. 1501: C. H. Haigh-Wood Esq. Dec'd.*

I have received your application for Income Tax Return of Mr Charles Haigh-Wood for the year 1927–28. I have to inform you that Mr Haigh-Wood died on the 25th March last, and that the Executors, of whom I am one, are now preparing the Application for Probate, which we expect to lodge within the next fortnight. Should you desire any further information, or evidence of death, I shall be glad if you will apply to me.

I am, Sir,
Yours faithfully,
T. S. Eliot
Joint Executor.

## TO *C. Henry Warren* CC

27 April 1927 [*The Monthly Criterion*]

Dear Mr Warren,

I am so sorry I was not in this morning to explain what has happened as my secretary knew nothing about it. I found that I should just have room in the next number for a short note about *Elmer Gantry* by reviewing it together with *Nigger Heaven*. As I have rather encouraged the publishers to believe that current fiction would be reviewed punctually I wrote the note myself and sent it off.[1] I was going to write to tell you this and suggest to you the alternative of a long review of Lewis's work as a whole

1–Unsigned review of *Elmer Gantry*, by Sinclair Lewis, and *Nigger Heaven*, by Carl van Vechten, *MC* 5 (June 1927), 364–5. Of *Nigger Heaven*: 'All the negroes in the book are either prigs or debauchees. The more priggish ones hold long discussions about the colour question. The rest spend their time in drinking, drugging and dancing; but, though we are several times reminded of the negro love of excitement, the narrative itself is anything but exciting.' Of Sinclair Lewis's novel: '[W]hat makes *Elmer Gantry* a finer book than *Babbitt* is the much greater violence of his hatred for his bestial, bullying, rapacious hero . . . If Mr Lewis wishes to write a better book than *Elmer Gantry* he will have to generalise his human beings so as to make them representative of humanity and not merely of local conditions . . . *Mantrap* is so far much his best piece of fiction. It contains four distinct and interesting characters, and the relations of these characters are handled with great insight. It is well constructed, and has – for instance, in its description of the American Indians – a power of humour which is elsewhere rather suppressed.'

several months later, or a long review of somebody else, turning upon some quite recent novel, in the next number but one which is the first in which in any case there would have been room for it. The only difficulty is, with the kind of review which [you] propose, that is not always easy to get review copies of the earlier work of the more copious novelists. If you would like to stick to Lewis I will try to get the other books for you as well as *Elmer Gantry*, only the review cannot appear so promptly. If there is anyone else whom you are interested in, please let me know. I see that a new novel by May Sinclair is about to appear; I do not know whether this would appeal to you and I admit that it is difficult to find anything to say about the whole work of a writer so voluminous and various. But I should very much like to have a long review about her and if you have already read a few of her novels of different periods I should be very happy if you would do it. I might be able to get some of her older novels if you wanted them as I would write to her and ask her to ask her publishers to send them.

Sincerely yours,
[T. S. Eliot]

## TO *Messrs A. P. Watt & Son*

CC

29 April 1927 [London]

Dear Sirs,

Before telephoning to you today I looked carefully over the manuscripts in my possession, and also consulted our manager concerning the date of publication. With great regret I came to the conclusion that (1) if we postponed Mr Yeats's poem we should have to delay publication of the next number, and that (2) if we postponed his poem I should have to fill up the space with inferior matter.

Mr Yeats's poem took seven pages of the *Criterion*.[1] Seven pages is a space difficult to fill: there is almost no other poet except Mr Yeats whom I would print to the length of seven pages; and I have no prose contribution accepted on hand which would fill less than twice that space. The number has entirely gone to press, with the exception of the final proof of Mr Yeats's poem; every page is numbered. It is very exceptional that I publish so long a poem; and accordingly the rest of the number had been arranged around his poem; in order to make another satisfactory

1–'The Tower', *MC* 5 (June 1927), 287–93.

number now I should have to choose quite different material; and it is now too late.

Please understand that I sympathise with Mr Yeats in the injustice which he suffers due to the present state of American copyright law. If I were in a position to consider only my personal regard and admiration for Mr Yeats I should gladly accede to a postponement; but I am obliged as editor to put the interests of my review first. Had the *Criterion* been longer in existence as a Monthly, the production of an inferior number would matter less; at this moment, it is of crucial importance; and I am responsible to my employers for producing the best possible.

I should be glad if you would suggest to Mr Yeats that I should be very glad if he would write a note of any length (provided we receive it in time) for the following number, explaining, or expressing a protest against the American law. Such a note, coming from an author of so loyal an American public as has Mr Yeats, might carry much weight in America; and incidentally, might frighten possible pirates. In any case, I propose to include in the same number as Mr Yeats's poem, an editorial note, explaining the loss to which he is subject.

Yours very truly,
[T. S. Eliot]

## TO *Roger Chitty* CC

29 April 1927 [London]

Dear Sir,

I am writing immediately to acknowledge your letter of the 27th instant, as it was the first of those which I have already received in response to my note.[1] Your suggestion seems to me a very good one. I should explain that I did not consider that the essay on Babbitt which I published was adequate; but it was sent in involuntarily, and as I considered that Babbitt had never received his due, I was glad to publish anything about him. I ought to know, as I was once his pupil.[2] I have had in suspense in my mind an essay

1 – In response to a note asking readers to nominate books for review, Roger Chitty remarked upon 'the marked kinship between the work of Irving Babbitt and Dean Inge'. While Babbitt had in fact been the subject of a *Criterion* article, Chitty considered that effort 'neither original nor profound'; and BD, in 'The World of Dean Inge' (Jan. 1927), had to all intents and purposes discountenanced Inge's work. Chitty argued that there was 'a very strong resemblance between Babbitt's doctrines of authority and Control and Inge's semi-Platonic outlook'.

2 – Gorham B. Munson, 'The Socratic Virtues of Irving Babbitt', *NC* 4 (June 1926), 494–503.

pointing out Babbitt's (unconscious) relation to orthodox Christianity: his doctrine of Grace, in *Democracy and Leadership*, is singularly near to Christianity, and in my opinion cannot be made acceptable without Christianity.[1] As for Inge,[2] I am quite aware that only half of him has been considered: it is the half which is most conspicuous at this moment, and which I think is wholly reprehensible. His relation to neo-Platonism, and also his relation to Christianity, are yet to be considered. On the occasion of a new book of the right kind by either Professor Babbitt or Dean Inge, I have had in mind to treat either of them differently; but I owe to you the idea, which had not occurred to me, of treating them together.

I might add that a Review is always handicapped in dealing with any writer who has arrived at a certain degree of celebrity. If we praise a particular work, it is taken as approbation of everything the man has written; similarly if we attack a work, that is taken as reprobation of everything he has written. I by no means fail to admire some of the work of such persons as Shaw or Wells; but I attack them as symbolical figures.

Yours very truly
[T. S. Eliot]

## TO *Arnold Bennett*[3]

TS Beinecke

30 April 1927 — *The New Criterion*

Dear Mr Bennett,

I enclose a copy of a letter which I have had the fancy of writing to *The Standard*. But they might not print it, and in any case, as it is really addressed to yourself, I prefer to send it to you first.[4] I wish that it might bring forth the right response.

I was very much pleased that you found the *Enemy* interesting.

1–See TSE, 'The Humanism of Irving Babbitt', *Forum*, 80: 1 (July 1928), 37–44; and 'A Commentary', *C.* 13 (Oct. 1933), 115–20, developed in *Irving Babbitt: Man and Teacher*, ed. Frederick Manchester and Odell Shepard (1941), 101–4.

2–BD reviewed three books by the Dean of St Paul's – *Lay Thoughts of a Dean*; *England*; *Science and Ultimate Truth* – in *NC* 5 (Jan. 1927), 109–14. 'The comfortable householder, who, as Dr Inge justly remarks, reads to save himself the trouble of thinking, will find his own prejudices flattered at every turn, his dislike of Roman Catholicism, his fear of labour, his instinctive hatred of things he does not understand: on every point he will be assured of his right-mindedness . . . The need of the moment is for a man with a power of analysis, tolerance of judgment, and formative ideas. Dr Inge has none of these qualifications.'

3–Arnold Bennett (1867–1931), author and journalist: see Biographical Register.

4–Bennett's secretary replied (3 May) that Bennett was away on a yachting cruise.

Yours very sincerely,
T. S. Eliot

I don't think I shall send this to *The Standard*, but I am impelled to send it to you.

## TO *The Editor of* The Evening Standard CC

29 April 1927

Sir,

In his very interesting and appreciative notice of Mr Wyndham Lewis's *The Enemy* in *The Standard* of April 28th, Mr Arnold Bennett says that 'we want more (quarterlies). And we want some monthlies.' He then asks: 'But who is to pay for them?'

I should like to tell Mr Bennett, in reply, exactly how such periodicals as he likes are at present paid for. There are four 'payments', and of these the smallest payment is that made by the person who buys a copy. The people who pay are the enlightened patron of intellect, who pays in money; the enterprising publisher, who pays in labour and worry, and perhaps in money too; and finally the contributors, who 'pay' by being underpaid. An intelligent review must rely upon three classes of contributors. There are the young men who find it to their advantage to write in order that their work may be commended to other editors who can pay better. There are the benevolent authors of established reputation who are sufficiently flourishing to be able occasionally to bestow, for what to them is trifling payment, a contribution; and finally there are the men, neither very young nor of world-wide reputation, each of whom is doing *two men's work*. That is to say, they are supporting themselves and their families in the Civil Service, or in museums, or in universities, or in banks and commercial houses; and are thus able to think, and read, and write independently of a livelihood. They must provide much of the substance, and most of the continuity and personality, of any good serious review; they get no credit and little thanks for arduous lives.

Mr Bennett himself belongs to the second class of contributor. I would remind him that I have more than once asked him, and that he once gave me a sort of promise to contribute to *The Criterion*. If he would contribute, it would certainly be easier to get the ordinary public to pay.

I am, Sir,
Your obliged obedient servant,
[T. S. Eliot]

## TO *H. S. Milford*

CC

1 May 1927 24 Russell Square

Dear Mr Milford,

I enclose my introduction to *The Moonstone*. It is possible that I may want to add another paragraph to round it off; I hope that you can let me see galley proof.

I am afraid that you may find it rather short for your purpose. But I found that if said more in a general way, about Collins or about this form of fiction, it seemed to cease to be an Introduction to this book; and if I said more particularly about this book, I was telling the new reader more than he wanted to know in advance. It is difficult to write a long introduction to a single novel, and I doubt whether many readers want it.

Mr B. L. Richmond has hoped to publish my leading article on Collins before the book appeared; on the other hand he had intended to use my article in August for holiday reading.[1] I should be glad if you could come to an understanding about it, although of course he cannot in the circumstances use the book as the occasion for my article.

Yours very truly,
[T. S. Eliot]

## TO *E. R. Curtius*

CC

2 May 1927 [London]

My dear Curtius,

I have been so busy for the last month with the preparations for the transformation of the *Criterion* into a monthly that I have had no time to write and thank you for your great kindness to me. It would be an impertinence for me to criticise your translation of *The Waste Land*, but in any case I should have no criticisms to offer. It seems to me the most admirable piece of work, and I flatter myself and you by thinking that it still reads like poetry in translation. And I must say that it seems to translate better into German than into any other language. And for your very generous essay, it would again be an impertinence for me to criticise your criticism, and there is no subject on which I am less qualified to

1–'Wilkie Collins and Dickens', *TLS*, 4 Aug. 1927, 525–6; used as 'Introduction' to the Oxford World's Classics edition of *The Moonstone*, v–xii, published on 1 Mar. 1928; repr., as 'Wilkie Collins and Dickens', in *SE* (1932).

judge than on myself. But I appreciate fully the care and fullness with which you have written and there is nothing in it which seems to me to distort or misinterpret my meaning in any way. I could not be happier in my introduction to the German public, both in the translation and the preceding article, and I thank you again.

I hope that you will approve the *Criterion* in this new form and that as soon as you have leisure to do so will let me have a contribution. It is too long since anything of yours has appeared in this country.

Yours very cordially,
[T. S. Eliot]

## TO *A. E. Coppard*[1]

CC

2 May 1927 — *The Monthly Criterion*

Dear Mr Coppard,

You may remember that two years ago the *Criterion* published your story 'The Field of Mustard' which I very much admired. Since then I have not had the pleasure of receiving any ms from you, but I hope that you will again consider the *Criterion* as a vehicle. It has now been converted into a monthly and will publish one piece of fiction in every number so that I am particularly anxious to secure stories of that quality.[2]

Yours very truly,
[T. S. Eliot]

## TO *Richard Aldington*

TS Texas

2 May 1927 — Faber & Gwyer Ltd

My dear Richard,

During the last two months I have been more than usually busy. Besides the labour involved in converting the *Criterion* from a quarterly to a

1–A. E. Coppard (1878–1957), short-story writer and poet. After a hard childhood, he laboured as salesman, artisan and confidential clerk, before publishing *Adam and Eve and Pinch Me* in 1921; this was followed by a regular series including *Clorinda Walks in Heaven* (1922), *Fishmonger's Fiddle* (1925) and *The Field of Mustard* (1926) – of which TSE had published the title story in C. (Apr. 1925).

2–Coppard replied on 5 May, 'I don't think there is anything available at the moment but I will get my agent A. D. Peters to show you my next story, which I think will be ready in about a fortnight.'

monthly, I have had a great deal of work as executor of my father-in-law who died at the end of March.

So I do not know whether I have answered even your purely practical questions in your last letter.[1] If not, please forgive me. Of course there is no reason whatever why you should not reprint your translations from the Poets' Translation Series. I do not think that we should have any legal grounds for refusing consent and in any case we should not want to; and I consider that the chief value of the stock which we possess has its value as a first edition. So go ahead by all means.

Do let me have a line to know how you are going on. Would it be possible for you to spend a night in town before long? If so and if I had a few days' notice we should like to arrange a dinner. The dinners have rather fallen into desuetude lately, partly because I have been very busy and also our small numbers are diminished by the absence of Dobrée, Monro and Trend.

Also, is it likely that you will have the leisure to be able to afford to write anything again in the *Criterion*? Remember that if I have not pressed you it is entirely out of consideration for your time and pocket book.

Ever yours affectionately,
Tom.

3 May 1927
The letter herewith was dictated yesterday. It answers one of your questions but not the other. I am having a copy of the January number sent to you, as I ought to have done at the time, containing Frank's notice. I should have liked to have given it longer notice but there were so many books to choose from that I felt that new editions and also translations could not be given much space. I have given out to Willie King the three first volumes of your new series for a long notice in June or July. I think he will do it better than he did your Voltaire as I have talked it over with him.

Do let me see your essay on Lawrence as soon as you can. I am immensely interested and would like to see it. I am also sending a copy of the new monthly number and am anxious to have your comments.

Tom

1 – RA asked in a letter of 2 May. (1) 'Have you thought about the question of the copyrights of my translations in the P. T. S. [Poets' Translation Series]?' (2) 'At the request of an American university I have written a 7000 word pamphlet on D. H. Lawrence [*D. H. Lawrence: An Indiscretion*]. It is loose, "romantic", and rather harum-scarum, but I think not unamusing, if only for its truculence. Would you care to look at it for the Criterion?'

## TO *David Garnett*[1] TS Texas

2 May 1927 *The Monthly Criterion*

Dear Garnett,

I have heard a rumour that you have written some stories much shorter than any of those which have been published as books. If this is so, I hope I may appeal to you for some for the *Criterion*. As you know, the *Criterion* is now a monthly and I am faced with the problem of finding twelve pieces of fiction per annum. Your kind of thing is just what we want and I hope that you will try to let me have something.

Yours sincerely,
T. S. Eliot

## TO *Henri Massis* CC

Le 3 Mai 1927 [*The Monthly Criterion*]

Cher Ami,

Vous savez sans doute que nos maisons ont entamé des discussions au sujet de la *Défense de l'Occident*. Nous tenons beaucoup, M. Faber et moi, à publier le livre ici, et nous serions navrés si les pourparlers n'aboutissent à rien. Quand il s'agit d'une traduction nous devons soigner nos chiffres; il y a des frais pour le préface de Chesterton (que nous avons déjà obtenue), des frais de traduction qui sont assez chers et au delà des frais des droits. Nous avons fait des calculs assez exacts et nous avons conclu que nous ne pouvons pas accepter le prix cité sans avoir les droits pour l'Amérique aussi. J'espère que vous joindrez vos efforts aux miens afin que nous puissions venir à bout et peut-être aussi former des liens permanents entre les deux maisons.

Avec toute ma sympathie,
Votre dévoué
[T. S. Eliot][2]

1 – David Garnett (1892–1981) won the Hawthornden and the James Tait Black Prizes for *Lady into Fox* (1923). Later works include *The Sailor's Return* (1928), *The Grasshoppers Come* (1931), *Beany-Eye* (1935) and *Aspects of Love* (1955).

2 – *Translation*: Dear Friend, You no doubt know that our two publishing houses have entered into discussions about the *Défense de l'Occident*. Mr Faber and I are very keen to publish the book here, and would be extremely sorry if the negotiations came to nothing. In the case of a translation, we have to look at the figures very carefully; there is the expense of the preface by Chesterton (which is already to hand), as well as translation costs which are

## TO *Bonamy Dobrée* TS Brotherton

3 May 1927 *The Monthly Criterion*

My dear Dobrée,

This is just a hurried line to say that of course I like the Congreve very much but that if there is a real hope of getting the Kipling in time for the August number, I should prefer to keep this as you suggest for the anniversary.[1] Anyway I shall not let go of it unless you want to use it somewhere else at once.

Do you see the *Times Literary Supplement*? If so, I hope you will drop me a line whenever there is any book you care to do for *The Criterion*. Also, I am hoping to hear from you soon in criticism of the first monthly number which you must by now have received.

Yours ever,
T. S. E.

## TO *H. M. Tomlinson*[2] CC

3 May 1927 [*The Monthly Criterion*]

Dear Mr Tomlinson,

I do not know whether you will remember that we have met once or twice, though only in a brief and casual way.

I very much admire some of your writing and I venture to hope that you will keep the *Criterion* in mind – especially now that it appears monthly – as a possible vehicle. Anything that you wrote would be of interest to

---

quite high and additional to the copyright payment. After fairly precise calculations we have concluded that we cannot accept the figure quoted, unless we also hold the American rights. I hope that you will combine your efforts with mine so that we can find a solution and thus perhaps establish a permanent link between our two firms.

With all good wishes, Yours ever, [T. S. Eliot]

1–BD said (14 Apr.) he had not finished his Kipling. He offered a piece on Congreve, but thought it might be best to keep it for the bicentenary in 1928. 'William Congreve: a Conversation between Swift and Gay . . . 1730', *MC* 7 (June 1928), 295–305, repr. in *As Their Friends Saw Them*, 75–92. 'Rudyard Kipling', *MC* 6 (Dec. 1927), 499–515.

2–H. M. Tomlinson (1873–1958), journalist and novelist – son of a foreman at the East India Dock in London – had gone to work at the age of 13 as a shipping office clerk. From 1904 he was a journalist for the *Morning Leader* (later incorporated into the *Daily News*), while also contributing to the *English Review* under Ford Madox Hueffer (Ford); and from 1918 to 1923 he was Assistant Editor of the *Nation*. He built his reputation on exotic travel sketches (based on his experiences of seagoing). His first book was *The Sea and the Jungle* (1912); later works include *London River* (1921), *Gallions Reach* (1927) and *A Mingled Yarn: Autobiographical Sketches* (1953).

our readers, but if you had any short stories or nature studies I should be more than delighted.

Sincerely yours,
[T. S. Eliot]

## TO *Peter Quennell* CC

4 May 1927 [London]

Dear Quennell,

I am returning to you herewith the translation from Laforgue which you sent me. It seems to me a very good translation and you are specially successful in catching the tone of the little scraps of verse which is hard to do. But I have been cogitating whether I ought to advise you to go on with the whole book or not. It is a good thing to do, and yet I cannot feel that there is likely to be any sale for the book. I imagine that the small public that there is for Laforgue is likely to have read him, or pretended to have read him, in French. Rimbaud would probably have a better sale, but then Rimbaud has been rather overdone. I think that a useful thing would be a book doing for these people, including Corbière, what Symons did for them for his own time in the symbolist movement in French poetry. Such a book ought, I think, to deal with poets only and include much fuller translations from their work. In such a book, also, you would have no difficulties, I think, about French copyright.

If you like the idea, I wish you would come and see me about it at some time.[1]

Sincerely yours,
[T. S. Eliot]

1–Quennell related, in *The Marble Foot: An Autobiography 1905–1938* (1976), how TSE prompted him to write his book *Baudelaire and the Symbolists* (1929): 'To meet the poet of *The Waste Land* was an historic privilege. He still wore the short black coat and pin-striped trousers of an old-fashioned City gentleman, had a long sallow face, sympathetic brown eyes and a slightly twisted smile. His manner of speaking was quiet and precise, and his whole appearance '*un peu clergyman et correct*', as Gustave Kahn said of Jules Laforgue, when he first encountered him. Under my arm I had my translations of Laforgue's *Moralités Légendaires*; and Eliot shrewdly suggested that, instead of trying to translate these almost untranslatable tales, I should endeavour to write a book on the Symbolist Movement and its adventurous protagonists. No such book, he remarked, had been published in English since Arthur Symons's famous study [*The Symbolist Movement in Literature*, 1899], which had come out over a quarter of a century earlier, and was written very much from the point of view of a late-Victorian "decadent". His authoritative advice encouraged me; and I immediately adopted it' (160). Quennell contributed 'Notes on a Reading of Jules Laforgue' to *MC* 7 (Mar. 1928), 219–31.

## TO *James Smith* CC

4 May 1927 [*The Monthly Criterion*]

Dear Smith,

I have spoken to Richmond about you and he is very encouraging. He asked me to suggest that you should write to him when you can come to London and he will be glad to make an appointment to see you. Better mention my name and remind him that I told him about you. I hope you can run up to town soon.

I wish you would do a few short notices for me and have sent you a couple of books. I hope in the early autumn to have space for a longer review, so please keep it in mind in case you have any suggestions to offer.

Yours sincerely,
[T. S. Eliot]

## TO *J. B. Trend* CC

5 May 1927 [*The Monthly Criterion*]

My dear Trend,

Thank you very much for your letter. The copies of the *Criterion* have been sent to the addresses you give. Ordinarily we should sell numbers to contributors at trade rates, but there is no question of your paying for copies sent which may benefit the *Criterion*.

I have arranged matters so that I shall want your next chronicle for the September number, that is to say I shall want the copy about the 15th July. If that does not give you enough time please let me know at once and I will re-arrange again; but I should naturally like to have it as soon after the festival as possible.[1]

I envy you your journey to Portugal but earnestly hope that you will be cautious and not run into any danger from bandits or revolutionists or anti-revolutionists. Do you wish to make public your views on the Truth about Portugal?[2]

1–Trend, 'Music', *MC* 6 (Sept. 1927), 243–9.

2–Trend was anticipating (8 Apr.) 'the prospect of a yoyage to Portugal with some Catalans; whereby I hope to get a point of view entirely different from the average English one. A Catalan has the advantage of having none of the traditional Spanish scorn for Portuguese things, while this particular Catalan (Eugenio d'Ors) knows various writers – the few people of intelligence who remain in the country. The last revolution, I hear, (and not only from Ors) was not "Bolshevik" as English papers said; but was made chiefly by the staffs of the

Thank you very much for speaking to Ortega. Tell him that I look forward very keenly to meeting him in October.[1] I hope that we shall have some common language in which we can communicate.

Yours ever,
[T. S. Eliot]

## TO *Henry Furst* CC

5 May 1927 [*The Monthly Criterion*]

My dear Furst,

I remember you perfectly well and have wondered from time to time what had become of you.[2] I am glad at least to have an address for you.

I like the story that you sent me but I do think that it is too slight for a magazine which only publishes one piece of fiction in every number, so I am returning it to you herewith. But I should be very glad to see other things from time to time or to receive suggestions, especially as the *Criterion* is now a monthly. Of course I have heard of Bontempelli, which means that he is very well known indeed. I have also heard well of *900*. As a matter of fact I wrote to them some time ago and suggested that they should exchange with the *Criterion*, which might be to their advantage as we have regular reviews of foreign periodicals, but I have not had a reply. If you are in touch with them I should be very grateful if you would stir them up. I have not seen Earp for a very long time. I should like to see him but he is a very elusive person.

Sincerely yours,
[T. S. Eliot]

Museums & the National Library, who are now begging their bread in Madrid – if they were not caught & shot . . .'

1–'I saw Ortega, and pressed your petition for an article; he is disposed to do it, and will eventually. When – I don't know: but he may be coming to London in October, in which case (for he very much wants to meet you) something might be arranged.'

2–Henry Furst, whom TSE had met in 1914 – Furst was at Exeter College, Oxford, TSE at Merton, and they had a mutual friend in the art critic T. W. Earp – sent from Rome on 5 Mar. a 'short story' by Massimo Bontempelli, chief editor of *900* (a new Italian quarterly published in French): it was a section from *La Donna dei Miei Sogni*, much of which had been published in *NRF*. Earp hosted the undergraduate society 'The Coterie' at his rooms in Beaumont Street where TSE gave the first public reading of 'The Love Song of J. Alfred Prufrock'.

## TO *C. Henry Warren* CC

5 May 1927 [*The Monthly Criterion*]

Dear Mr Warren,

I am very disappointed that you do not feel inclined to tackle May Sinclair as I had been congratulating myself upon the suggestion. Failing May Sinclair I should still like to thrash about for someone similar and I am not sure that T. F. Powys is as yet of sufficient importance to treat at that length.[1] I will let you know as soon as I have thought of some happy combination. Meanwhile I am taking you at your word and sending a novel for a 200 word notice.[2] I shall no doubt have more from you very soon.

Whereas the long reviews are always of books which I am certain are important, in the case of the short notices I am obliged to leave very much more to the discretion of the reviewer. Therefore the position of a 'small' reviewer is much more confidential than that of a long reviewer. They are very often books that I know nothing about and therefore if in your opinion any book sent is not really deserving of notice at all (considering the ground that we cover) just drop me a line and we will cancel it.

Yours sincerely,
[T. S. Eliot]

## TO *Thomas McGreevy* TS TCD

5 May 1927 Faber & Gwyer Ltd

Dear McGreevy,

Yours of the 29th received. We ordered the Baty book[3] for you at the time but it has never turned up. I will enquire about the Palmer book for you, but unless it is pretty recent we shall have to dispense with it.[4]

1–T. F. Powys (1875–1953) had enjoyed reasonable success as an author. *Mr Weston's Good Wine* was to appear in a limited edition on 21 Nov. 1927. Warren had written (28 Apr.), 'I don't think I could do May Sinclair – her work somehow hasn't come my way much. As an alternative I suggest the work of T. F. Powys, who interests me very much.' Warren ultimately contributed a round-up review of eight recent titles by Powys, including *Mr Weston's Good Wine* (1927), to *MC* 7 (June 1928), 422–5.

2–Unidentified.

3–Gaston Baty, *Le Masque et l'Encensoir*. Baty was director of the Studio des Champs-Elysées.

4–McGreevy had asked to review John Palmer's *Studies in the Contemporary Theatre* – 'a lamentable work'.

Now that the *Criterion* is a monthly we must try to get the reviews out as quickly after the appearance of the books as possible. Meanwhile I am sending you a few things for short notes; or rather, two things: *The French Poets of the Twentieth Century* on which I should like a page (400 words) and *The Marionette* by Edwin Muir on which I should like half a page (200 words).[1] The books are being sent under separate cover. I will look out for something for a long review to appear in the autumn.

We have had to defer the project of a book on the Ballet as our calculations do not seem to show that it is an economic venture at the present moment. If we revise our opinion later, I will take it up again with you.

Shall you be over in England during the summer? If not, I hope that I may be in Paris and see you there.

Yours sincerely,
T. S. Eliot

P.S. Yes, I am afraid it is too late for Gide's Dostoevsky.[2] But keep your eye on his publications as I suppose the Congo journal[3] will be out soon.

## TO *Herbert Read* CC

5 May 1927 [*The Monthly Criterion*]

Dear Read,

Thank you for your criticisms.[4] I was aware of that objection and I have cut the thing about which improves it considerably though the

1–Unsigned notice of Muir, *The Marionette*, *MC* 6 (Sept. 1927), 284–5.
2–'Is it too late to do Gide's *Dostoevsky*? Or has it been done? I haven't read it . . .' *Dostoevsky* had been published in London (J. M. Dent & Sons) in 1925.
3–André Gide, *Voyage au Congo; Carnets de Route* (Paris: Gallimard, 1927).
4–TSE had shown HR a draft of his 'Commentary' for the June issue of the *Criterion* which opened with a reply to a 'semi-editorial article' in *The Calendar* (April 1927) that had criticised what it designated 'neo-classicism . . . the literary version of a reactionary Latin philosophy which is being adapted, in one or two English reviews, into a repressive instrument of literary criticism'. By implication, the *Criterion* was accused of purveying this 'instrument of literary criticism'. But in what way, queried TSE, is 'neo-classicism' (a term he disdained) 'repressive'? TSE's commentary continued, in draft: 'If this reproach is addressed to us – and at whom else can it be levelled? – it reads more like the cry of a muddled neo-communist against what he believes to be, to adopt his own jargon, a form of neo-fascism. We feel that the reproach of "repression" is cruelly undeserved.'

HR commented (3 May): 'I am afraid it will please the Calendar to have so much notice taken of them. But it enables you to say some things worth saying. I query the phrase "cruelly undeserved": isn't it what a politician says when someone has called him a liar?' See final text in *MC* 5 (June 1927), 284, which omits the sentence in question.

fundamental objection is not disposed of. As for 'cruelly undeserved', I was actually using this in an ironic sense, but if you thought that I intended it to be good English probably many other people will and I have therefore cut it out. But the problem of editorial subjects throughout the year is one I should like to discuss with you again to see if we cannot get at some general lines that could be taken up again and again.

Here is Bonamy's essay.[1] I wish you would read it before Monday, and I want to find out whether any of the criticisms that immediately occurred to me will occur to you also.

Yours ever,
[T. S. E.]

## TO *Alida Klemantaski*[2] — TS UCLA

5 May 1927 — *The Monthly Criterion*

Dear Miss Klemantaski,

Some time ago Mr Monro gave me two lots of poems which he was considering for a possible *Chap Book*. He told me that he would be glad if I cared to use either of them in the *Criterion*. One lot I am still keeping. It consists of two poems by Miss Stella Gibbons which I shall probably use.[3] The other consists of two poems by Rupert Croft-Cooke that I do not think that we want. I thought it better to return them to you to deal with, as possibly Mr Croft-Cooke might not be very pleased if he got his poems back unexpectedly from another source.

I hope that Mr Monro is making progress in Switzerland and should very much like to hear from him.

Sincerely yours,
T. S. Eliot

1–BD, 'Rudyard Kipling', *MC* 6 (Dec. 1927), 499–515.

2–The Polish-born Alida Klemantaski (1892–1969) had married Harold Monro, founder of The Poetry Bookship, as his second wife on 27 Mar. 1920. Her publications include *Twentieth Century Poetry: An Anthology* (1929) and *Recent Poetry 1923–1933* (1933)

3–Stella Gibbons, 'The Giraffes' and 'The Cunning Huntress' (which Harold Monro had accepted for the 'problematical' *The Chapbook*), *MC* 6 (Sept. 1927), 236–7.

## TO *Allen Tate* CC

6 May 1927 [*The Monthly Criterion*]

Dear Mr Tate,

I like this stuff very much in some respects but it seems to me, if I may say so, that you are a little tied up in your own tail at present, but I am sure that it will get straightened out in time. Do continue to let me see things from time to time.

Yours sincerely,
[T. S. Eliot]

## TO *J. T. Gordon Macleod*[1] CC

6 May 1927 [*The Monthly Criterion*]

Dear Mr MacLeod,

I am now returning your poem though with considerable regret. In any case, of course, it is too long for the *Criterion* but also I think that your own criticism of it is just – that the idea is beyond the instrument.[2] But I

1–Joseph Todd Gordon Macleod (1903–84), poet, playwright, actor, theatre director, historian and BBC Newsreader, was educated at Balliol College, Oxford (where he was friends with Graham Greene), and in 1927 joined the Cambridge Festival Theatre, of which he became director, 1933–6 (his productions included Ibsen's *The Seagull* and Ezra Pound's Noh plays, as well as five of his own plays). In 1938 he joined the BBC as announcer and newsreader, retiring to Florence in 1955: it was during the BBC period that the poetry he produced under the pseudonym 'Adam Drinan' became sought-after by editors in Britain and the USA; and he was admired by writers including Basil Bunting and Edwin Muir. His first book of poems, *The Ecliptic* (1930), was to be published by TSE at Faber & Faber. His plays included *Overture to Cambridge* (1933) and *A Woman Turned to Stone* (1934). See also James Fountain, 'To a group of nurses: The newsreading and documentary poems of Joseph Macleod', *TLS*, 12 Feb. 2010, 14–15.

2–Macleod had submitted (27 Jan.) what he called 'my last play' – "Eclogue in the Future Tense" – 'sadly though I realise how little it carries my meaning. Very probably when you were my age, Sir, (which is 23) you also found that your ideas outstripped your instrument. At any rate I comfort myself that they must have done so. It is a melancholy experience for the intellect to be young . . . I am aware, Sir, that this play, or as I have called it, this Eclogue can hardly be published in the *New Criterion* – I fear it is too long in any case – but more than publication I would judge welcome your criticism of it or a suggestion from you where I have gone off the rails . . . P.S. On account of the ineffable crassness of theatrical managers I have never had any plays publicly produced. An old complaint. Do I make myself ridiculous?'

should like to see more of your work and if you are in town some time I hope you will call to see me.

Yours very truly,
[T. S. Eliot]

## TO *R. G. Collingwood*[1] CC

9 May 1927 [*The Monthly Criterion*]

Dear Mr Collingwood,

Very many thanks for sending your review in such good time.[2] It is a great help to a busy editor who is always worrying whether his more important reviewers will have their material ready when it is wanted.

You need have no doubts about the manner of treatment. It is exactly the way that the *Criterion* wants things handled; the other type of review is more suitable for the technical journals of scholarship.

I answer your letter in haste and hope to write to you before very long.

With many thanks,
Yours truly,
[T. S. Eliot]

## TO *The Under Secretary of State, The Home Office* CC

9 May 1927 [London]

Sir,

Your Reference 412614/2

I am directed by Mr T. S. Eliot to enclose herewith the relevant pages of *The Morning Post* of Friday May 6th 1927 and *The Westminster and Pimlico News* of the same date, in both of which he has marked the notice which he has had inserted in connection with his application for naturalization.[3] He trusts that the necessary formalities are hereby fulfilled.

1–R. G. Collingwood (1889–1943), philosopher and historian: see Biographical Register.

2–Review of A. E. Taylor, *Plato, The Man and his Work*, and Jean Wahl, *Étude sur le Parménide to Platon*, MC 6 (July 1927), 65–8. Collingwood wrote (8 May): 'I decided to devote the review to the central problem – the question of the relation of Plato to Socrates – and let everything else slide. Of course one can't review even the main points of the evidence, on so complex a question, in so few words . . .'

3–'NOTICE IS HEREBY GIVEN that THOMAS STEARNS ELIOT of 57, Chester-terrace, Eaton-Square, S.W.1, has APPLIED to the Home Secretary for NATURALISATION, and that any person

Mr Eliot thinks that he ought to notify you that his father-in-law who made the primary declaration on his behalf died on the 25th March 1927 at St. Leonards-on-Sea. As his statements were perfectly in order and attested, Mr Eliot trusts that this circumstance will not interfere in any way with the progress of his application.

I have the honour to be, Sir,
Your obedient servant,
[I. P. Fassett]
Secretary

## TO *The Editor of* The Saturday Review CC

9 May 1927 [*The Monthly Criterion*]

Dear Sir,

In thanking you for your courtesy in noticing the first issue of *The Monthly Criterion* may I point out for the benefit of your readers that your paragraph contains four errors.[1] The name of the periodical is not *The Modern Criterion* but *The Monthly Criterion*. It has been in existence as a quarterly not for two years but for four years. It has not 'reverted' to the monthly form, inasmuch as it began as a quarterly and has been for four years a quarterly and its appearance as a monthly is wholly an innovation. And finally, my name is not T. S. Elliott but T. S. Eliot.

It is of minor importance if I suggest to your reviewer of periodicals that the verb "go for" is a strong and perhaps misleading phrase when applied to serious reviews like those of Mr Robert Graves and myself.

I am Sir,
Your obliged, obedient servant,
[T. S. Eliot]

---

who knows any reason why naturalisation should not be granted should send a written and signed statement of the facts to the Under Secretary of State, Home Office, London, S.W.1' (*The Morning Post*, 6 May 1927, 1).

1–A note about *MC* had appeared in *The Saturday Review* (London), 7 May 1927. The editor Gerald Barry apologised to TSE by letter on 16 May.

## TO *G. Herbert Thring*[1]

CC

9 May 1927 [London]

Dear Sir,

Mr T. S. Eliot has asked me to acknowledge your letter of the 2nd instant and to enclose herewith his cheque for thirty four shillings and sixpence, this being his annual subscription to the Society and his subscription to *The Author*. I should be obliged by the favour of acknowledgement of receipt.

Yours faithfully,
[I. P. F.]
Secretary

## TO *Orlo Williams*

CC

10 May 1927 [London]

Dear Williams,

Many thanks for your suggestion.[2] It wants a bit of thinking out and I must get the opinion of my people here. It has a good deal to recommend it and I should like to see you again soon and talk it over with you. Incidentally, would you mind letting me know again which nights you are in London? I should like to arrange a small *Criterion* dinner next week if possible.

Would you mind looking over the enclosed and telling me whether you recommend the exchange asked for. If you think it advisable, whether you want a periodical or not, will you return the letter so that I may write to them?[3]

1 – TSE was elected to the Society of Authors on 2 May 1927: he had been invited to become a member on 23 March. Thring was Secretary of the Society.

2 – Williams wrote: 'I believe it out of place in a monthly to have any short notes on novels at all. Notes on other books may be unavoidable, but two or three notes on novels, seeing the multitude of them, produces a scrappy effect without any advantage that I can see. Novelists get plenty of reviews of that kind and it just looks as if the Criterion reviewed one or two because it happened to have received them, not because it selected them. My feeling is that you would score much more heavily by giving some space to one, or two, novelists each month, sometimes to none, & having the thing more or less conclusively done; even if this meant asking publishers not to submit novels unless requested.

'I make the suggestion without any idea of annexing the novels for myself. Whoever does them, I hold to it. The novel reviews in the current number do not strike me as adding to its prestige: rather the reverse. All your reviewing, I think, should be up to the level of your very good best' (6 May).

3 – Williams responded (11 May): 'If you feel inclined to help an obviously worthy institution,

I have stirred up *L'Italiano*. Nothing seems to have been heard from *900*. I have written to a man in Rome who seems to be in touch with that paper.

You should receive proof of your Italian notes in a few days.

Yours ever,
[T. S. E.]

## TO *William Force Stead*

MS Beinecke

10 May [1927] 57 Chester Terrace, S.W.1.

Dear Stead

You had been in my mind for two or three days. – Nothing would please me better.[1] Could it be done (inc. bapt. – conf.) between Sat-Mon? If not, I will arrange to come for a night in the middle of the week instead.

I should like very much to meet Streeter,[2] of whom I have a very high opinion, as well as the Bishop. Rawlinson[3] I shd like to know too. As for the undergraduates, I leave that to you! But when I do come, I want to get the real ceremonies accomplished, & the rest is whatever is possible.

Tell me how you got on with Richmond, if you saw him – I had a talk to him about you.

Ever yours,
T. S. Eliot

I should certainly send the *Criterion* to the Cultura d'Arte, which seems to have aims of the Polytechnic kind.'

1–This is in answer to a (now lost) letter from WFS.

2–Burnett Hillman Streeter (1874–1937): New Testament scholar; Fellow of Queen's College, Oxford (where in due course he became Chaplain and then Provost); Canon in Hereford Cathedral. His works include *Studies in the Synoptic Problem* (1911), *The Four Gospels: A Study of Origins* (1924), *Reality: A New Correlation of Science and Religion* (1926) and *The Buddha and The Christ* (Bampton Lectures, 1932).

3–The Revd A. E. J. (Jack) Rawlinson, DD (1884–1960): theologian; Student and Tutor at Christ Church, Oxford, 1914–29; Bishop of Derby, 1936–59; lecturer and preacher; author of *Authority and Freedom* (1923); a textual commentary on St Mark (1925); and *The New Testament Doctrine of Christ* (Bampton Lectures, 1926).

## TO *Bonamy Dobrée* TS Brotherton

10 May 1927
This Day of St. Isidore. *The New Criterion*

My dear Bomany Dobrée,

Yours to hand and contents noted.[1] I regret to find that you are so completely inefficient. Your confusion of the Crocodile and the Camel recalls the behaviour of the primitive inhabitants of Bolovia. A notoriously lazy race. They had two Gods, named respectively Wux and Wux. They observed that the carving of Idols out of ebony was hard work; therefore they carved only one Idol. In the Forenoon, they worshipped it as Wux, from the front; in the Afternoon, they worshipped it from Behind as Wux. (Hence the Black Bottom.) Those who worshipped in front were called Modernists; those who worshipped from behind were called Fundamentalists.[2]

Yours respectfully,
Thos. Eliot

P.S. I will give you one more chance. Can you obtain any information about (1) the Native Cat (2) the Edible Dog (3) the proper pronunciation of the word ARAB. Is it A-rab, or Arrub, or Eye-rab? And (4) do they fold their tents, and if so in how many folds, and if so is it always in the same folds like a napkin or serviette (as called in seaside hotels)?

<See *Grillparzer: Kultus und Sittenlehre des Bolovianer,* passim.>

1–BD had sent his Kipling essay on 26 Apr. Apropos TSE's further enquiries, he added only: 'I apologise humbly for having confused the camel with the camel: as regards my camel the facts are as stated. As regards your camel, I do not know whether you have to go a mile to find one, but you may have to run two miles to escape one. For further information as to this interesting (if improper) beast, please apply to your correspondent in the Yemen, where he is more frequent, and less tainted with civilization.'

2–BD recalled, in 'T. S. Eliot: A Personal Reminiscence' (1966), TSE's 'elaborated joke, nurtured through years. It is about some primitive people called the Bolovians, who wore bowler hats, and had square wheels to their chariots. This invention he apparently began to toy with when he was at Harvard, there figuring King Bolo and his Queen. He did not tell me much about those characters – though he sent me a drawing of them – but I was given portions of a Bolovian Epic (not always very decorous) and something about their religion. This latter was in part an amiable satire on the way people, anthropologists especially, talk about the religion of others. One piece of sheer fantasy concerned the name of their two gods, both called Wux, and how to pronounce the name.' TSE was to write to Clive Bell on 3 Jan. 1941 that his praise of *East Coker* might inspire him to complete the work of *Four Quartets*. 'I may even take in hand the long neglected task of putting in order the epical ballad on the life of Chris Columbo (the famous Portuguese navigator) and his friends King Bolo and his Big Black Queen.' For early examples of Bolovian verses, see *Inventions of the March Hare: Poems 1909–1917*, ed. Christopher Ricks (1996), App. A, 315–21.

## TO *E. G. Selwyn*

MS Beinecke

11 May 1927

57 Chester Terrace, S.W.1.

Dear Mr Selwyn,

Thank you for your kind letter.[1] It is tempting of you to suggest that I should let you have the suppressed passages. If the indiscretion affected only myself I would let you have it, but I consider that the passage in question would be anything but helpful to my French friends. It is one thing for me to tell them, as I do, that the *Action Française* is necessarily committed to an extreme Gallicanism, and is therefore bound to come into conflict with the Vatican (I anticipated this long before the present dust up), but it is another thing to say that about them publicly. It is a pity, however, not to say these things, because the whole of the present situation between the Vatican and the Catholic Royalist party in France is one that ought to be both interesting and instructive to Anglicans; and very little attention has been paid to it in this country.

If you should at any time be coming to London I hope that you will give me the opportunity of a meeting.

Yours very truly,
[T. S. Eliot]

## TO *Messrs Romeike & Curtice Ltd*[2]

CC

11 May 1927

[London]

Dear Sirs,

As you already supply me with my personal cuttings, and with those concerning *The Criterion*, I should be obliged if you could obtain for me the following.

Within a few days Probate will probably be granted in the Estate of Charles Haigh Haigh-Wood Deceased of 3, Compayne Gardens, Hampstead, N.W.6. As the Executor, I should be obliged if you would supply me with cuttings from any newspapers mentioning this fact.

1–Selwyn, in acknowledging receipt by *Theology* of TSE's article on Bramhall, remarked (10 May): 'Your secretary says that you have deleted a passage discussing ecclesiastical politics in France at that time, as it seemed to you rather indiscreet. But indiscreet things have a way of being very interesting; so that, if it is still available, I should like to see it.' He hoped too to see an article on Hooker by Oct. or Nov., but it was not written.

2–Press Clipping Bureau, Ludgate Circus, London.

I should be glad if you would let me know if you will do this, and what your charges will be.

Yours faithfully,
[T. S. Eliot]

## TO *Maurice Haigh-Wood* CC

11 May 1927 [London]

Dear Maurice,

I have from James another list of your Aunt Emily's investments. As he says he has sent you a copy also, I presume that he has written you much the same letter.

As you and V. both hold Bucknell, East Lancs Paper, and Neuchatel, I suggest that these be divided equally. As V. already holds some Anglo-Arg. Pref., Canadian Northern Debs., and Lanarkshire C.C., I suggest that she take these – unless you happen to have any yourself, in which case divide again. I suggest that the Tadcaster Breweries be sold, and all of the Southern Railway, unless there are any items you would like. As an approximate contra to the Anglo-Arg., Can. Northern and Lanarks. will you pick out any things you would like? (The value at date for probate is about £441.) If you don't want anything particularly, of course you could take it in cash out of the sales.

I will get Marshall's opinion about what is best to sell for Duties. Nearly everything can be divided, except the shares of Manchester & County would have to be 13 to 12. I suggest that the Newcastle & Gateshead is rather small for division, and perhaps you would like to take that.

Let me know your opinion on these points.

Yours ever aff.
[Tom]

## TO *Mario Praz* CC

12 May 1927 [*The Monthly Criterion*]

My dear Praz,

Here is the proof of your Chaucer entire. I am rather worried by the length. I had allowed for twenty pages which is more than double the length of any of the other contributions I am fitting in with it; and I find that with the Bibliography the first part runs to twenty seven pages. I am much more strictly limited in number of pages with a monthly than with a quarterly. Do you think that you could possibly reduce the first part by about five pages, making twenty-two? If not, I am afraid we shall simply have to cut the paper up into three parts instead of two which will be a pity. If you cannot reduce it will you try to indicate as closely as possible a division into three parts? I am very sorry indeed, but you see how I am placed.

Yours always sincerely,
[T. S. Eliot]

## TO *Conrad Aiken* CC

13 May 1927 [London]

My dear Conrad,

I am sorry to trouble you first of all about a small matter of business. I have received from Knopf a cheque for twenty five dollars, being my share of payment for selected rights from the book of poems which they published used by you in your anthology. They say that they received fifty dollars from the Modern Library Inc. for the right to republish in that anthology. Can you tell me if this is O.K.? Don't think I am grumbling about the price because I didn't expect much anyway and I am quite satisfied with this, only I should like to check up on Knopf. Can you illuminate me on another point? With my consent you published in this anthology 'The Hollow Men'. I am not worrying about royalty on this, which is nothing to do with Knopf; but I should like to know: one or two sections of 'The Hollow Men' were never printed in America before. They were printed in England over a year ago. Does this printing in America in your anthology secure copyright in America for those parts of the poem? Excuse me for troubling you, but American copyright is so puzzling that I need information.

I wish that I might hear from you occasionally. I have just seen Fletcher who tells me that you are about to become a don at Harvard. Will your pedagogic duties allow you any time for reviewing for the *Criterion*? I shall be writing to you later about your poem, but the truth is that I have been so busy and flustered turning the *Criterion* into a monthly that I have not yet had time to read it.[1]

Yours ever,
[T.]

1–Aiken, 'From "Changing Mind"', *MC* 6 (Dec. 1927), 523.

## TO *Richard Aldington* CC

13 May 1927 [London]

My dear Richard,

I am sorry about Manning as I shall now have to tackle him myself, but I quite understand and rather anticipated your refusal.[1] I have sent you another book in which you may or may not be interested; but if you are not interested, for Heaven's sake do not draw on your time to review it, merely out of friendship.

I am returning your essay on Lawrence.[2] I have read it very carefully; but, candidly, Richard, I do not think that it falls in with the general position of the *Criterion*. And I am not speaking merely of my personal position, which in several details differs from that of anyone else; I am speaking of the general position, which I always try to keep in mind, which is arrived at by pooling the points of view of the more important contributors including yourself: in other words I am putting myself at the point of view of what I conceive would be the consensus of opinion of the people who attend the *Criterion* dinners. I might even say that I could publish this were it signed by J. Middleton Murry: for when we publish anything by him it must be more or less recognised by him or by any one of several others that we are publishing something which does not represent the *Criterion* point of view – in fact, in the next number, I am publishing an essay by Murry which represents almost the antithesis of the *Criterion* point of view.[3] But anything signed by you will be taken, and should be taken, as representing the *Criterion* view: it will be assumed by that small part of the public which knows anything about it – and that part will communicate its impressions to other parts – that you and I and Read and Flint and perhaps a few other people adopt substantially this attitude.

You see, I try to be very careful – I do not say that I always succeed – not to express in the *Criterion* any opinions of my own with which others of our more important colleagues would be in real opposition. If I want to say such things, I try to say them elsewhere; even in *The Times* I can say things which I would not say in the *Criterion*. And it seems to me only fair to ask the same of my colleagues; and when I say things myself in the *Criterion* which do not represent the consensus of opinion I want them

1–RA had sent a postcard declining TSE's invitation to review Manning.

2–RA had sent his article on D. H. Lawrence on 4 May. 'It is purely an impression, dashed off in two sittings; but perhaps it was an appropriate way of dealing with the subject.'

3–JMM, 'Towards a Synthesis', *MC* 5 (June 1927), 294–313.

to criticise me for it. For I am aware that even when I write things signed by my own name, if I print them in the *Criterion* it will be assumed that they represent not only my own personal views but the official views of the paper.

I am not criticising your essay in detail: it is both interesting and brilliant. But I think that Lawrence is one of the men on whom the *Criterion* ought to express itself with most care; and I think that if I printed this it would seem to the public to be the judgment of a party as well as of an individual.

But I must add that the *Criterion* has missed being able to show any evidence of your adhesion: and I should very much like to have something by you, either an essay, a poem or a review, however brief, during the present year, the first year of the monthly.

Yours ever affectionately,
[T.]

## TO *Herbert Read* CC

13 May 1927 [*The New Criterion*]

My dear Read,

I have got rather tied up with Wyndham Lewis who for some reason unknown to me wants to see me immediately and have inadvertently promised to lunch with him on Monday. I am very sorry, but could you lunch on Tuesday instead, of if not on Wednesday? Tuesday best. Please accept my apologies, I was rather muddled.

I saw Flint yesterday and learn to my relief that he had already seen Richard's essay on Lawrence and did not like it.[1] So I have sent it back to Richard today with a long letter telling him frankly that it does not seem consistent with the *Criterion* position, and pointing out in the most flattering way possible that anything by him in the *Criterion* would seem to the public to arrive with the approval of the rest of us. I hope he will not mind, but god knows how Richard will take a thing like this, especially as he seems to have gone completely off his head about Lawrence.[2]

Yours ever,
[T. S. E.]

1 – *D. H. Lawrence: An Indiscretion* was published as a University of Washington Chapbook, no. 6 (1927); then as *D. H. Lawrence* (London: Chatto & Windus, 1927).
2 – HR had written (9 May): 'Richard is vulgar & unconvincing. I don't see that you can possibly do anything with it, & I only wish I could invent a tactful excuse for you.'

## TO *Virginia Woolf*

TS Berg

13 May 1927 Faber & Gwyer Ltd

My dear Virginia,

If you are back in London, as I hear from George Rylands, and if and when convenient, I think you might invite me to tea. If so, I shall bring you a new gramophone record.

Yours ever,
Tom

## TO *W B Yeats*[1]

CC

13 May 1927 [*The Monthly Criterion*]

Dear Mr Yeats,

I am more sorry than I can tell you about the difficulty over the copyright in 'The Tower' over here and in America and I am therefore writing you a line to extenuate my action in publishing it in our next number.[2]

The notification from Messrs Watts only arrived after the whole of my next monthly number had been set up. Indeed, everything but 'The Tower' and a few notes at the end was already in page proof. In the conversion of the *Criterion* from a quarterly to a monthly, I have a particular responsibility to the proprietors to make the first few numbers saleable and interesting; for if the *Criterion* cannot succeed as a monthly it will have to be abandoned altogether. Your poem was my star feature. Nevertheless I should have been willing to postpone it had I had anything else on hand acceptable which would have filled approximately the same number of pages. I am held down to a maximum of ninety six pages. Your poem filled seven pages; and seven to eleven pages is a very difficult space to fill. I had no poetry on hand, either by one or several contributors,

1–William Butler Yeats (1865–1939), poet and playwright. According to TSE, he was 'one of those few whose history is the history of their own time, who are part of the consciousness of an age' (*On Poetry and Poets*). TSE met Yeats soon after arriving in London; but despite their mutual admiration of Pound, they had little contact until late 1922, when TSE told Ottoline Morrell that Yeats was 'one of a very small number of people with whom one can talk profitably of poetry'. In his review of *Amor Silentia Lunae*, TSE said, 'One is never weary of the voice, though the accents are strange' ('A Foreign Mind', *Athenaeum*, 4 July 1919). Yeats was instinctively opposed to TSE's work, but discussed it at length in the Introduction to *Oxford Book of Modern Verse* (1936), and declared after the publication of *The Waste Land* that he found it 'very beautiful' (Jan. 1923).
2–*MC* 5 (June 1927), 287–93.

which could have filled this space. There is hardly anyone else of whom I would publish so long a poem, and I had already arranged the rest of the number to fit the length of your poem. On the other hand, I had no prose contribution short enough to fill the right number of pages. I was therefore faced with the alternative of injuring you or of injuring my proprietors, the future of the paper, and incidentally of course myself.

The American copyright law is of course monstrous in respect of people resident in England, and seems to be still more monstrous in respect of persons resident in Ireland. I suggested to Watts and suggest again to yourself that I should be very glad to publish any statement that you might care to make about this subject. I should like *The Criterion*, furthermore, to be your organ in this country for every purpose within its scope.

It is possible that I may have to come to Dublin on business during the summer and if so I hope very much that I may find you there.

Yours sincerely,
[T. S. Eliot]

## TO *T. Sturge Moore* TS Texas

13 May 1927 *The Monthly Criterion*

Dear Mr Sturge Moore,

Thank you very much for your letter of the 11th and for sending me your very interesting letter about Father Brown's book.[1] I should like very much to print it, but I must explain to you first what the situation is. The book is being reviewed for us, not at very great length, by Mr Herbert Read who was interested in it.[2] I have not yet seen his review, and I therefore cannot tell whether your letter would quite do in its present form. I therefore suggest that I should send you a proof of Mr Read's review as soon as it is received and that you should make any necessary alterations in your letter so that it could be printed in the *following* number, after Mr Read's review. Of course I have not the slightest idea who wrote the *Times* review or in what particulars Mr Read will agree or disagree with that review.

1–Sturge Moore had written a letter to the *TLS* in response to a review 'The World of Imagery' – on Stephen J. Brown, SJ, *The World of Imagery* – in *TLS*, 28 Apr. 1927, 294. But BLR would not print it (for lack of space, he said). Sturge Moore therefore asked TSE to use the letter, suitably rewritten, as a review in *MC*.
2–*MC* 6 (July 1927), 89.

Meanwhile I am retaining your letter which I should very much like to publish. But as your letter is addressed to the *Times* in connection with its review and would obviously have to undergo slight alterations in any case, I hope that you will accept my suggestion.

With best wishes,

Yours very sincerely,
T. S. Eliot

## TO *Virginia Woolf*

TS Berg

16 May 1927 Faber & Gwyer Ltd

My dear Virginia,

If I am in London, and I probably shall be <will telephone> in London, I shall be delighted to come to tea with you on the 23rd. If you are then still in domestic difficulties, remember that I shall be very glad to come without any tea, or rather having had tea before I arrive; so you need not bother about refreshments.[1]

My only information about the Poetry Bookshop is that Harold Monro is said to be resident in Geneva having treatment for his eyesight; that I wrote to him about the Poetry Bookshop, when I first heard from you, to tell him vaguely that there was some prospect of getting support; that I have since written to Miss Klemontaski, or whatever her name is,[2] and that I have had no reply. However, I have not at present any more information about Mrs Woolf than I have about the Poetry Bookshop.

I look forward to Monday.

Yours ever aff.
Tom.

## TO *J. M. Robertson*

CC

16 May 1927 [London]

My dear Robertson,

Thank you for your letter of the 13th. I am sending you Volume IV although you don't want it. I don't think that your having reviewed the

1 – VW wrote on ?15 May 1927: 'We have been without a meal in the house – cook ill – or I should have asked you before. Will you come to tea on Monday 23rd, at 4.30?' She did give tea to TSE on 23 May: 'Tom – so glad to gossip with me off handedly over a cup – no 6 cups – of tea; then he played the gramophone' (*Diary*, III, 137).
2 – Alida Klementaski, Monro's wife.

volumes separately disqualifies you in the least; if you review the work as a whole you will simply talk about anything you like at length.[1]

Yes, I thought Murry 'did you well'; but I reflected at the time that it is rather tiresome to be done well by a person whose point of view is so alien![2]

Ever yours,
[T. S. Eliot]

## TO *Bertrand Russell*

TS McMaster

16 May 1927

57 Chester Terrace, S.W.1.

Dear Bertie,

I shall shortly be transferring to you, at Vivien's request, Debentures £3500 of Plenty & Son Ltd. of Newbury.[3] There is no reason for you to demur. We both wish that this should be done without delay. I want to ask you however if you will write me a letter to say that you and yr heirs or assigns will hold my estate harmless against any payment that might be due, in the event of my death within three years from the transfer, by my estate to the Inland Revenue of Great Britain, owing to the inclusion of these securities within my estate. As you are aware, any 'gift' made by anyone within three years of his death is included in his estate for purposes of death duties, and I do not want to leave my affairs buggered up if I should die suddenly. I have however no expectation or intention of dying within three years.

Yours ever affectionately,
T. S. Eliot

1–D. A. Wilson, *Carlyle* (6 vols). Robertson had reviewed each volume to date, and expressed an anxiety that 'perhaps my reviewing them all singly may be a disqualification for reviewing the whole set?'

2–'Murry "did me well" in the *T.L.S.* – front page – but Murry really hasn't studied the subject.'

3–See note to VHE to BR, 6 Dec. 1926, above.

## TO *Richard Aldington* TS Texas

16 May 1927 Faber & Gwyer Ltd

My dear Richard, –

And I write at once to say that I appreciate your generous attitude.[1] As for the English heretic, and what your typing machine correctly calls the

1–RA wrote on 14 May: 'I write at once to say that I perfectly understand your position about the Lawrence article, and that I was more than half prepared for you to reject it . . .

'I sympathise with your desire [letter to RA, 13 May] to infuse some discipline into your platoon of francs-tireurs. You and Herbert [Read] have much in common – Thomas Augustus and Herbert Caesar, as I once called you to Bonamy [Dobrée] – but how do you include the others? Frank [Flint] is a Socialist, affiliated to the Labour Party; Harold [Monro] is intellectual Labour; Bonamy is more or less a Gallio in these matters, though he was impressed by Wyndham Lewis "Art of Being Ruled" – a bad book, I thought; then you have Trend, who is an amiable and learned dilettante; and you have me, a wayward soul of distinctly heretical tendencies; and you have [Frederic] Manning, a relic of the nineties. What are we supposed to agree about? Except that we all admire and love you. Alas, I believe you will find that it's the man is followed, not the doctrine.

'As to my nice Lorenzo [*D. H. Lawrence: An Indiscretion*], I am bound to say I quite disagree with your notes in the N.R.F. Merely in the matter of style, I think Lawrence at his best, superior to any novelist we have.'

TSE, in his article on the contemporary English novel (*NRF* 28 [1 May 1927], 669–75) adjudged – the following quotation is taken from TSE's unpublished original in English (EVE Archive), since the version published in French was by an unknown translator – 'Mr Lawrence, it would seem, is serious if anybody is, is intently occupied with the most "fundamental" problems. No one, at any rate, would seem to have probed deeper into the problem of sex – the one problem which our contemporaries unanimously agree to be serious. No line of humour, mirth or flippancy ever invades Mr Lawrence's work; no distraction of politics, theology or art is allowed to entertain us. In the series of splendid and extremely ill-written novels – each one hurled from the press before we have finished reading the last – nothing relieves the monotony of the "dark passions" which make his Males and Females rend themselves and each other; nothing sustains us except the convincing sincerity of the author. Mr Lawrence is a demoniac, a natural and unsophisticated demoniac with a gospel. When his characters make love – or perform Mr Lawrence's equivalent for love-making – and they do nothing else – they not only lose all the amenities, refinements and graces which many centuries have built up in order to make love-making tolerable; they seem to reascend the metamorphoses of evolution, passing backward beyond ape and fish to some hideous coition of protoplasm. This search for an explanation of the civilized by the primitive, of the advanced by the retrograde, of the surface by the "depths" is a modern phenomenon. (I am assuming that Mr Lawrence's studies are correct, and not merely a projection of Mr Lawrence's own peculiar form of self-consciousness). But it remains questionable whether the order of genesis, either psychological or biological, is necessarily, for the civilized man, the order of truth. Mr Lawrence, it is true, has neither faith nor interest in the civilized man, you do not have him there; he has proceeded many paces beyond Rousseau. But even if one is not antagonized by the appalling monotony of Mr Lawrence's theme, under all its splendid variations, one still turns away with the judgement: "this is not my world, either as it is, or as I should wish it to be".

'Indeed, from the point of view which I have indicated, Mr Lawrence's series of novels mark, from the early (and I think the best) *Sons and Lovers*, a progressive degeneration in

'inner vooice' – oh well, are *all* English people heretics? You are better qualified to speak than I; but I cling to some alternative to Bellochesterton which I do not like,[1] and I cling to my martyr'd archbishop, Wm. Laud. These be matters to be discussed in a long evening over unlimited port. Shall that ever happen?

As for the Diversity of Creatures, that must be admitted; the one thing universally accepted seems to be the Empire; and I don't believe that any of us can smoke Empire Tobacco: *I* have tried and failed. But do you think it is hopeless to distil any common quality, more than such a common

---

humanity. This degeneration is masked, and to some extent relieved, by Mr Lawrence's extraordinary gifts of sensibility. Mr Lawrence has a descriptive genius second to no writer living; he can reproduce for you not only the sound, the colour and form, the light and shade, the smell, but all the finer thrills of sensation. What is more, of *detached* and unrelated feelings, in themselves and so far as they go feelings of importance, he has often the most amazing insight . . . And this is one of the directions in which psychology – not psychology for the psychologists, but that is a science with the right to go where it likes, but psychology in its popular inferences – may have misled the novelist: in suggesting that momentary or partial experience is the standard of reality, that *intensity* is the *only* criterion.'

RA remarked too, in his letter to TSE of 14 May: 'I confess to you that I have found it difficult to write for the Criterion, precisely because I found myself in a slightly false position. In the Times [*TLS*] an air of scholarly dullness gives one a perfect solidarity with most of the other contributors. But at heart I am the English heretic, and any sense that I am trying to conform to something which is not an immediate and spontaneous impulse, leaves me horribly embarrassed. This is why I have not been able to do anything for you for some time. It is J.M.M.'s "inner vooice" [*sic*]! Lament, my dear Tom, most of the English are like that – a peculiar and exasperating race.'

1–Building on encyclicals by Pope Leo XIII (*Rerum Novarum*, 1891) and Pope Pius XI (*Quadragesimo Anno*, 1931), G. K. Chesterton and Hilaire Belloc advocated the economic philosophy of Distributism: a decentralisation of the means of production based on an organic and artisan view of economic order and culture. Distributism seeks to put productive property directly into the hands of families and local communities (as against control by the State, big business or a few wealthy individuals). Notable texts include Chesterton's *What's Wrong with the World* (1910). In a review of two other key works, *The Outline of Sanity* by G. K. Chesterton and *The Servile State* (1912; 3rd edn 1927) by Hilaire Belloc; and *The Conditions of Industrial Peace* by J. A. Hobson, TSE noted: 'One has much sympathy with the Belloc–Chesterton gospel of Distributive Property. It is a fertile idea; and in the form of exposition which they have chosen there is material for one excellent essay. But in full books we expect more than that: we expect some indication of a "way", answers to some of the objections that occur to us, and an admission that the problem is simplified for expository purposes . . . There could be no greater contrast than that between Mr Belloc and Mr J. A. Hobson [who] is a serious economist of the old school . . . [H]e knows his subject matter in detail . . . On the nature of Capitalism, he is at one point far more illuminating than Belloc. He observes, in effect, that the "evils" of capitalism are not primarily due to the concentration of ownership, and are therefore not mitigated by the multiplication of owners. On the contrary, the multiplication of small security-holders places more power in the hands of the few directors who have the knowledge; diffusion of ownership diffuses their responsibility. The "Capitalist" is this director or manager' (*MC* 6 [July 1927], 72–3).

quality of mediocrity and dullness as reeks from the *Mercury*? – And while we are puzzling over such grave matters, little newspaper reviewers are whispering that the *Criterion* is merely an organ for the mutual adulation of a small clique! Seriously, I should love to talk to you about the ideal of impersonality I hinted at in my last letter.

As to Lorenzo, I have a strong suspicion that he is the sort of person about whom posterity will accept neither your, nor my nor any contemporary opinion of. Posterity will be pretty busy with him anyway.

I am glad of one thing, that the books I sent are not unpleasing; as I chose them for you out of a welter. May I venture to pick out in future anything that seems particularly yours?

But you must make time to come to London soon. It is a common complaint among your friends.

Ever yours affectionately
Tom

## TO *J. M. Robertson* CC

18 May 1927 [London]

My dear Robertson,

Thank you for your letter. I have just heard from Routledge that the *Carlyle* will not be completed for at least a twelvemonth, so you will have plenty of time. 2500 words would not be too much for a book of this size.[1]

I think myself that it would be better if the *Times* front page articles never pretended to be reviews at all. I should rather myself have a book of mine reviewed well in one column inside than have it used as the pretext for a literary essay on the cover. Let me hear more about your masterpiece. Why did you disclose only one title when you say you have three?[2]

Ever yours,
[T. S. Eliot]

1–Robertson wrote on *The Two Carlyles*, by Osbert Burdett, *C.* 10 (Jan. 1931), 363.
2–Following his study of the Shakespeare sonnets, Robertson published two books in 1927, *Modern Humanists Reconsidered* and *Jesus and Judas: A Textual and Historical Investigation*; he also introduced a 2-vol. edition of *The Essays of Montaigne* (1927).

## TO *Laura Riding* CC

19 May 1927 [*The Monthly Criterion*]

Dear Miss Riding,

I am returning with much regret the chapter from your and Mr Graves's book.[1] The subject is a capital one and I look forward with great interest to the appearance of the book. But in choosing essays for the *Criterion* I try to keep to subject matter which no other periodical of the sort has yet got on to, and the fact that another chapter has already appeared in *The Calendar* would rather take the gilt off the gingerbread.

With many thanks,
Yours sincerely,
[T. S. Eliot]

## TO *The Under Secretary of State, The Home Office* CC

20 May 1927 [London]

Sir,

I have received with some chagrin your letter of the 18th instant, reference 412614/2. Before troubling another sponsor with this matter I should be obliged if you would let me know precisely whether there are any further qualifications necessary other than that the person must be a male native born British subject resident in this country. Also whether there are any other disqualifications than those of which you have advised me.

I presume that Mr Sydney Waterlow having been disqualified as accessory sponsor on the ground of being British minister to Siam is equally disqualified as primary sponsor? What I should like to know more particularly is this: whether any other civil servant – *not* in the Home Office – is also disqualified by reason of being a civil servant, although resident in this country.

I have the honour to be, Sir,
Your obliged, obedient servant,
[T. S. Eliot]

1–Laura Riding and Robert Graves had sent (3 Apr.) 'a chapter from a book we have written together (*Anthologies Against Poetry*). Perhaps you could use it in *The Criterion*. It may be cut if necessary.' The letter was signed by both Riding and Robert Graves.

## TO *J. M. Robertson* CC

20 May 1927 [London]

My dear Robertson,

Certainly. *The Secret Vice* is by far the best of your titles and ought to sell thousands of copies. But I cannot commit myself to an opinion about the propriety of the title until I have had the pleasure of reading the masterpiece. I hope I may see it soon. But don't bother about my Jewess: I think that her bloom has already faded.[1]

I should be delighted to have the Last Word on Shelley if it is unpopular enough.[2] I will admit in advance to certain prejudices against the author who seems to me one of the dullest of the Great English Poets; and my prejudices have only been strengthened recently by reading Professor Whitehead's praise of that author in his *Science and the Modern World*.[3] If Shelley is science, then science is one of my lost illusions.

I will not go so far as to say that you will outlive *The Criterion*, for it is my duty to be optimistic about the latter; but I am willing to bet you five shillings that you will outlive me. In any case, if you do not work yourself to death in the next few months, burst a blood vessel on some Thursday morning after reading *The Times Literary Supplement*, you are likely to see your 'Burns' in print.

I cannot answer your question about Murry;[4] but I am told that Selfridge's Information Department can answer most questions if you ring up Gerrard 1234.

Yours ever,
[T. S. Eliot]

1–Robertson wrote on 19 May: 'Why this sudden craving for titles? The others are "Veritas Vini", and "The Secret Vice" . . . But the point is that it is to be a piece of *prose* that will leave Sir Thomas Browne skinned, and make your Jewess shut up abashed.'

2–'I am cogitating a Last Word on Shelley; *not* popular. If I thought you might print it before I am dead – which seems unlikely – I might start on it soon.'

3–Alfred North Whitehead enthused in *Science and the Modern World* (1926), 122–3: 'Shelley's attitude to science was at the opposite pole to that of Wordsworth. He loved it, and is never tired of expressing in poetry the thoughts which it suggests. It symbolized to him joy, and peace, and illumination. What the hills were to the youth of Wordsworth, a chemical laboratory was to Shelley.'

4–Having just finished a book entitled *Jesus and Judas* – 'in which, incidentally, I deal quite gently with Murry' – Robertson asked: 'Poor Murry, will he ever do a sane book?'

## TO *Richard Aldington* CC

20 May 1927 [London]

My dear Richard,

Yours of the 30th Floréal[1] to hand and contents noted with many thanks for same. I put pen to paper in great haste as I am just going out to buy a packet of Empire cigarettes for which I shall hold you responsible.

As for the *Criterion* being more imaginative and artistic, Good Lord, my dear Richard, don't you think I should like to see it so?[2] The *Criterion* is, I insist, widely open to all the efforts of *les jeunes*: only, it seems necessary to attach a rather fine strainer to the opening. If you know of any of *les jeunes* who don't get into the *Criterion* and who are any good at all, all I need say is, lead me to it. I will put on my roller skates, as the old song says, for that purpose. After all, one can't show specimens of what should be done until it is done; for a specimen is an *is* and not a *should*. I agree that England is sterile, but quality as well as fecundity is valuable, and one cannot encourage the feeble-minded to breed.

Your 'Naples' has gone to press.[3]

Ever yours affectionately,
[T.]

1 – Floréal was the eighth month in the French Republican calendar; it ran from 20 Apr. to 19/20 May. RA's letter is lost, but '30th Floreal' was probably 19 May.

2 – 'Honestly I think les jeunes are afraid of you,' wrote RA on 21 May. He regretted the extravagances and cameraderie of pre-war days: 'Then, the faults of les jeunes were too much optimism, towering self-conceit, a sublime disposition to dethrone the gods; you have to struggle with the sterility of cynicism and disillusion which the war has left us.' In his letter dated '30 Floreal': 'But the Criterion . . . is unsympathetic to me because it is too intellectual and philosophical, not sufficiently imaginative and artistic. I see a purely critical journal on the lines of the old Quarterly; but my ideal journal is the paper which opens itself freely to all the efforts of les jeunes – painters, poets, sculptors, musicians, architects, all that is really imaginative and creative. I've got tired of hearing about what ought not to be done and where Homer nods; I want to see lots of specimens of what should be done. An editor's ability consists not in finding fault but in finding talent.

'This is very impertinent, but represents a real desire to see something created, much created. But England is sterile as an old hag with drained breasts.'

3 – Untitled review of Cecil Headlam, *The Story of Naples*: *MC* 6 (Aug. 1927), 172–5.

## TO *Henri Massis* TS (photocopy)

20 May 1927 [London]

Mon cher ami,

Merci beaucoup de votre lettre dont je suis fort touché. Je suis bien content d'apprendre que l'affaire de la *Défense de l'Occident* est réglée. Donc j'ai arrangé avec M. Flint de préparer la traduction aussitôt que possible. Et je peux vous assurer que le livre paraîtra dans l'automne. Les choses dont vous traitez tombent si bien à propos des affaires actuelles anglo-soviétiques et anglo-chinoises que nous voulons l'avancer aussitôt que possible.

J'ai lu dans *La Revue Universelle* pour le 15 Mai l'intéressant Prologue de Charles Maurras. Croyez vous qu'il serait disposé à nous permettre de publier une traduction dans le *Criterion*? Et est-ce que je peux vous demander de lui en parler?

Malheureusement je ne sais pas encore à quelle date il sera possible de venir à Paris, mais je ne manquerai point de vous avertir.

Bien affectueusement,
[T. S. E.][1]

## TO *Bonamy Dobrée* TS Brotherton

23 May 1927 *The New Criterion*

My dear Bungamy Dobrée,

Have returned your Kiplin under sep. cover.[2] General opinion: needs concentration. Flint thinks you were 'too close to the object[']; thinks you ought to get farther away from him and not worry about dealing with everything or being too just or accurate. Thinks you need a period

1 – *Translation*: My dear friend, Many thanks for your letter by which I was greatly touched. I am very pleased to hear that the question of *La Défense de l'Occident* has been settled. I have therefore arranged with Mr Flint to have the translation ready as soon as possible. And I can assure you that the book will appear in the autumn. The matters you discuss are so highly relevant to current Anglo-Soviet and Anglo-Chinese relations that we wish to bring the book forward as soon as possible.

I have read the interesting Prologue by Charles Maurras in *La Revue Universelle* of 15 May. Do you think he would be willing to let us publish a translation in *The Criterion*? And can I ask you to speak to him about this?

Unfortunately, I am still not sure at what date it will be possible for me to come to Paris, but I will not fail to let you know. Yours affectionately, [T. S. E.]

2 – BD's essay was to appear as 'Rudyard Kipling', *MC* 6 (Dec. 1927), 499–515.

of digestion and forgetting what Kiplin wrote. Read thinks much as I do: that you get all the real strong punches into the first part, and the 2nd part about his poetry gives [the] impression of a postscript 'for the sake of completeness'. *I* suggest that anything you have to say about poetry you incorporate into [the] body of it, to give more unity and damn completeness; your main and good point is his Empire vision etc. There are brilliant things in it; but in such a series one must give one impression of each author, even if not all-rounded. If you are coming home on June 20 as advertised we can discuss, as I want it certain for October number. I think only trouble you have been too conscientious: your *Criterion* and *Nation* reviews when you weren't worrying were admirable.

If not too late will you obtain most recent information re camelopard stop does he change his spots query stops stop or does he ever stop stop when once started.

Yours ever
T. S. E.

Does he change after starting or only during stops stop how many changes has he stop

## TO *A. E. James* CC

23 May 1927 [London]

Dear Mr James,

In reply to your letter of the 20th instant I enclose herewith the authority to the District Bank to hand you as and when required any of the certificates held in the name of the late Mr Charles Haigh-Wood, for re-registration and return to the District Bank.

Maurice has returned to England a few days ago; but as he has been away for the weekend, and as his signature is unnecessary, we are sending you the form signed by myself and by Mrs Haigh-Wood.

We are very much obliged to you for your successful efforts in keeping the statement of Probate out of the newspapers.

Yours sincerely,
[T. S. Eliot]

## TO *H. V. Routh*[1]

CC

24 May 1927 [*The Monthly Criterion*]

Sir,

I have inspected with great interest your book *God, Man and Epic Poetry*.[2] I should be honoured if you would occasionally be willing to contribute and to review for *The Criterion*; and I should be glad if you had any suggestions to make or if you were willing to receive suggestions from me.

I am, Sir,
Your obedient servant,
[T. S. Eliot]

## TO *Mrs Rose Bartlett*

CC

24 May 1927 [*The Monthly Criterion*]

Dear Mrs Bartlett,

I must apologise for not having answered your letter sooner.[3] It took me some time to identify you under your change of name. Since I saw you last the *Criterion* has considerably changed and has become a monthly magazine requiring the whole of my time. And of course, I have a regular secretary who works for me during the day. I am no longer compelled to edit it in the evenings.

I am very sorry therefore that I have no need for any supplementary secretarial assistance. I shall be very glad, however, to let you know as soon as I hear of anyone who requires assistance of the kind that you are in a position to give; particularly as I remember the exceptional efficiency of your work and your unfailing good humour under trying conditions.

Yours very truly,
[T. S. Eliot]

1–H. V. Routh (1878–1951): University Reader in English, London University, 1919–37; first Byron Professor of English Literature and Institutions, University of Athens, 1937; founder and director of first Institute of English Studies in Greece, 1938–9. His works include *Money, Morals and Manners* (1935) and *Towards the Twentieth Century* (1937).

2–Routh's 2-vol. study was reviewed by Peter Quennell: *MC* 6 (Nov. 1927), 455–7.

3–Mrs Bartlett, who had worked in a part-time secretarial capacity at the *Criterion* in 1923, asked TSE on 13 May whether he had any further part-time work available.

## TO *H. P. Collins* CC

24 May 1927 [London]

Dear Mr Collins,

After reading your letter of the 23rd. I am sorry to find, on looking up my files, that I never answered your question about Mrs Gregg's volume of stories. I did not find either of the two stories submitted quite suitable for the *Criterion* but I should be glad to see more of her work. As for the volume, we should be very glad to consider it if you will send it on here. But I must admit that the opinion of the firm, and I think of most publishing firms in London at present, [is] that volumes of short stories sell very badly; and unless they are of obviously very remarkable genius or unless there is some other reason for considering them, it is the universal opinion that the public will not buy books of short stories. So I cannot offer any great hope; nevertheless, I will see that the book is seriously considered on its merits.[1]

If you ever think of any book you would particularly like to review I wish you would let me know. Do you know anything about James Hogg? If so, would you care to do a short review on *The Ettrick Shepherd* by Edith C. Bathe (A Critical Study of the Life and Writings of James Hogg)?[2]

Yours sincerely
[T. S. Eliot]

## TO *Alice L. Jones*[3] CC

24 May 1927 [London]

Dear Madam,

I return Mr McNulty's letter with this and a reply from myself. It is quite a matter of indifference to me, and I leave it entirely to the discretion of the Editor, whether this correspondence is worth publishing. My only

1–Collins wrote on 23 May, 'the delay is on my conscience, because she is not only in circumstances of rather severe poverty, but is also in the earlier stages of cancer, which will, I understand, not allow her more than about eighteen months more of life.' Collins had submitted a piece by Frances Gregg, plus a volume of stories by her, on 8 Mar. TSE published one story by Gregg, 'Locust Street': *MC* 6 (Sept. 1927), 206–9.

2–Collins replied (25 May): 'I know almost nothing about the Ettrick Shepherd . . . The Study of Landor by Earle Welby . . . might seem to you worth a short notice.'

3–Alice L. Jones was Secretary of *The Nation & Athenaeum*.

request is that if you publish Mr McNulty's letter you should publish my reply.

Yours sincerely,
[T. S. Eliot]

## TO *The Editor of* The Nation & The Athenaeum[1] CC

24 May 1927 [London]

Sir,

Mr McNulty expresses surprise at my comparison of Whitman and Tennyson. May I assure him that I intended this comparison to be quite serious; and if he will look back at the earlier number of *The Nation* in which I reviewed a recent biography of Whitman he will see that I have made the same assertion at more length. I would remind him first of Whitman's almost boundless admiration for Tennyson, and second I would say again that Whitman's and Tennyson's respective attitudes towards the society which they inhabited are closely parallel. I quite agree that Tennyson's verse is 'perfect'; but I would assert that Whitman's gifts were of exactly the same kind. He was, in my opinion, a great master of versification, though much less reliable than Tennyson. It is in fact as a verse maker that he deserves to be remembered; for his intellect was decidedly inferior to that of Tennyson. His political, social, religious and moral ideas are negligible.[2]

I have the honour to be, Sir,
Your obliged, obedient servant,
[T. S. Eliot]

1–This letter appeared in *N&A*, 4 June 1927, 302, in reply to the following letter by J. H. McNulty, dated 20 May and published under the title 'Tennyson and Whitman': 'In Mr T. S. Eliot's review of *Israfel: The Life and Times of Edgar Allan Poe* [*N&A*, 21 May 1927, 219], there is a phrase which requires a little elucidation. He writes: "In England the romantic cult was transformed by the enormous prestige of Tennyson; in America by Tennyson also and later by Whitman, the American Tennyson." The last four words are certainly amazing, and almost call for Russel Lowell's delightful reply to those who called Bryant the American Wordsworth.

'What is there in common between the perfect verse of Tennyson and the wild formless writing, neither verse nor prose, of the American? May I ask if the phrase is a slip, or a joke, or whether your reviewer can give the slightest reason for it? I ask this in simple bewilderment.'

2–TSE was later to remark, in a letter to Alexander Reid: 'I think [Whitman] is a very undesirable model, even more dangerous than Gerard Hopkins. When Whitman is successful he is, of course, quite first-rate, but then his style and rhythm cannot be adapted to any other

## TO *Herbert Read* CC

24 May 1927 [London]

My dear Read,

I owe you many apologies for not turning up yesterday. The fact simply is that I had made my plans to go to the country for a few days and was under the impression that I had notified you. Then I postponed my departure until tomorrow and still thought until this morning that I had notified you. I am very sorry.

Methuen's have sent in a book about whaling which I imagine is written by your friend Morley (F. V. Morley & J. S. Hodgson). I think it would be pleasant to review the book. It looks interesting and has good photographs and I should like to do it to please Morley. Can you think of anyone who would tackle it, or would you care for it yourself?[1] We could not of course review such a book at any length. There is an interesting photograph of Shackleton's grave[2] and all the photographs are good. It really seems a serious book about the subject.

I will let you know as soon as I am back. It will not be next Monday, and I am not certain whether I shall be back for dinner on Tuesday. I will

---

purpose because it is completely identified with the content of the particular poem. In order to write successfully like Whitman you would have to be as original as Whitman himself and as Whitman's poetry is already in existence that is almost impossible. When Whitman drops below his best he is thoroughly verbose, rhetorical and second-rate' (28 Mar. 1945). Several years later again, he would write in a letter of 20 Aug. 1964 to Cyril Connolly: 'I may be very conceited, but *Little Gidding* strikes me as one of the best patriotic poems in the language and I think goes a good deal deeper than Tennyson on the Revenge or even Walt Whitman on John Paul Jones, which seems to me better than Tennyson.' (McFarlin Library, Oklahoma.)

1–See unsigned review, by Herbert Read, of F. V. Morley and J. S. Hodgson's *Whaling North and South*: *MC* 6 (Nov. 1927), 473–4. HR told TSE on 16 Aug. that the review was 'perhaps a bit facetious, but it seemed to be the only way to tackle it'. HR wrote of his friend's contribution to the volume, an account of whaling in northern seas: 'Mr Morley is full of nonsense. Metaphysical nonsense . . . And a heap of scientific nonsense, and then some statistical nonsense, and "old man of the sea" nonsense. In short, Mr Morley is not as unromantic as he would appear; but this being a disillusioned age, he gives his subject an unromantic gloss. Fairly makes you sick, he does, as he takes you down the flensing-stage and rubs your nose in the blubber. Such is the nonsense. But what really matters is a delightful essay on the Whale in Legend and Myth, and a vivid narrative of the Whale Hunt . . . We imagine Mr Morley to be a city clerk with a feeble physique and a masculine protest – the sort of man who won the V. C. in the war.' In fact, within two years, the robust and portly Morley was to become a director of Faber & Faber.

2–The Antarctic explorer Sir Ernest Shackleton (1874–1922), who died of a heart attack on his last voyage, is buried in the Norwegian cemetery at Grytviken, South Georgia.

drop postcards in a few days and if not, I hope that the company will not mind postponing the dinner for another week.

Yours ever
[T. S. E.]

## TO *Alec Randall*

CC

24 May 1927 [London]

My dear Randall,

Your letter of the 20th arrived just as I am leaving for the country and I am glad to be able to answer it before I go. I am sorry that you did not get the first copy of the monthly *Criterion* and am having one sent to you. You shall, as a chronicler, receive it regularly in future.

I should like to keep the spaces for the various items exactly the same as they were before. That is to say, as you will see from the first two numbers, I do not want little bits of scrappy notes about the periodicals of every country in every number. I hope that each chronicler will prepare his material at the same leisure and with the same fullness, and I shall include only one or two countries in each number. I have not yet fixed any definite time table for the notes on foreign periodicals as I have had such an accumulation of material, but you may reckon that I shall want just the same sort of article as before and at intervals of three months.

As you will see, I have included your review of Werfel;[1] and I should be very glad of notes from time to time on any important German books.

The only difficulty in reviewing German books is of course to avoid duplication with Rychner. I shall also try to print in each number notes *not* on periodicals of the same country as the foreign chronicle in the same number. For your guidance I can tell you that Rychner's German chronicle should appear in the May and November number of each year (each foreign chronicle is to appear twice a year). As therefore your latest German notes are in the June number I should like to have another report in good time for the September number, and the following for December. Notes for September should be received here not later than July 15th.

I hope that all this is clear. I am following the same policy with the other chronicles. I felt, and Trend quite agreed with me, that his music articles would lose their character if he had to shorten them and produce them

1–Untitled review of Richard Specht, *Franz Werfel: Versuch einer Zeitspiegelung*, and Werfel, *Paulus unter den Juden*: *MC* 5 (June 1927), 350–3.

every month. He is therefore doing a music chronicle every three months exactly as before; and this will alternate with a dramatic chronicle by Flint and an art chronicle by Roger Hinks.

I should always be glad of any comments or criticism on the numbers as a whole. I was very sorry to miss you when you were in London and hope that you will be coming again this summer: we should all be glad to have you at the dinners.

Yours ever,
[T. S. Eliot]

P.S. As for the Dutch periodicals, I wish you would send me some notes as soon as you have enough material and I will fit them in as soon as possible. Until the monthly has been going a little longer it is very difficult to arrange definite dates for these things.

## TO *Donald S. Friede*[1] CC

24 May 1927 [London]

Dear Mr Friede,

I am going away tomorrow for a week but I expect to be back in London by Wednesday night and should be very glad to see you on Thursday at 3.30.[2] If by some unforeseen accident I should have been detained in the country I hope that you will come and see our Manager, Mr Stewart, in any case.

Yours very truly,
[T. S. Eliot]

1–Donald S. Friede (1901–65), publisher and literary agent – his father was a Russian immigrant who represented Ford Motor Company in Tsarist Russia, with the happy consequence that the young Friede was very well travelled and well connected, and could speak four languages – was expelled from three universities (Harvard, Yale, Princeton) and worked in various capacities before taking a position as stock clerk for Alfred A. Knopf. He joined Boni & Liveright in 1923, and invested in the firm: he became its first Vice-President in 1925. He was to leave Boni & Liveright in 1928, and joined up with Pascal Covici in the publishing house of Covici, Friede, Inc. (the firm survived for just under a decade). In later years he worked for a while for AFG Literary Agency before becoming Senior Editor at Prentice-Hall, and then Senior Editor, Doubleday & Company.

2–Friede, who was visiting London, wanted to discuss 'general publishing matters'.

## TO *F. S. Flint*

CC

24 May 1927 [London]

Dear F. S.,

Yes, as a matter of fact I had been meaning to get hold of that book and will do so.[1] It was Wyndham Lewis who recommended it to me very strongly some time ago. I am afraid it may be too late to get a review copy, but if so I shall buy it. I think that something might be done about Soddy but one has to tread carefully in these matters and I want to read [the] book first myself.

I half agree with your second paragraph. That is to say, I am not ready to admit that there is any time when it is wholly futile to discuss what you call aesthetic problems; but on the other hand it seems to me very much our business to link up these aesthetic problems with the others, the importance of which we are all agreed upon. I think that the time for a definite aestheticism, as of Ezra and his present disciples in Paris, has passed by; and I think that the whole Ezra point of view about art is as out of date as the Yellow Book. And I agree that in whatever direction you go nowadays you buck up in the end against economics and religion.

Ever yours,
[T. S.]

1–Flint urged TSE (23 May) to review *Wealth, Virtual Wealth and Debt: The Solution of the Economic Paradox* (1926) – by the Nobel Prize-winning radiochemist Frederick Soddy (1877–1956) – which Flint considered 'the most important book in English published since the War'. 'It seems the last degree of futility to be discussing art and aesthetic problems when Europe, in all probability, is being hustled by the usurers, for their temporary profit and their and our ultimate destruction, into a catastrophe before which the late War will dwindle into the dimensions of a Bermondsey street fight.

'More: Worringer shows in his essay that art lacks a vital impulse – a religion if you like. There is one lying there for it; but it is the work of man to create the conditions for its recognition – a religion of life as the [? search] of the human spirit, of the collectivity of nations safeguarding the precious essence of individuals and their individuality.

'What is it that stands in the way of this religion? Usury, the worst, I believe, of the old deadly sins, and many is the uncrowned king of this country. That same spirit which, Worringer says, has transferred from art to science has, in Soddy, invaded economics. No intelligent review can afford to ignore his conclusions.'

Soddy's book was to be reviewed by J. McAlpine: *MC* 7 (June 1928), 429–32.

## *I. P. Fassett* TO *Messrs A. & C. Black Ltd.* CC

24 May 1927 [*The Monthly Criterion*]

Dear Sirs,

I am directed by the Editor of *The Criterion* to write to you concerning the entry relating to that periodical in your *Writers' and Artists' Year Book* for 1927.

*The Criterion* is now issued monthly instead of quarterly and is known as THE (monthly) CRITERION instead of THE NEW CRITERION. It is priced at 2/6d per number instead of 5/- per number, the yearly subscription being 30/- instead of £1. The name of the Editor, T. S. Eliot, now appears on the cover. The Editor suggests that it should be entered in your book under 'C'—CRITERION, THE (Monthly), with a reference under 'N' (NEW CRITERION, THE) pointing out the change to monthly publication. The description of the material published should remain the same.[1]

Yours faithfully,
[IPF]
Secretary.

## TO *R. Ellsworth Larsson* CC

25 May 1927 [*The Monthly Criterion*]

Dear Larsson,

If you have any verse at any time, will you give me an option on it for the *Criterion*?

Also, will you, when you have an inspiration, suggest some books or books for a long review (1000 to 1600 words)? When I have a longish review of yours I may be able to get you into two or three other papers.[2]

I should like it if you could come to tea or lunch in about ten days' time.

Yours sincerely,
[T. S. Eliot]

1–'New Criterion, The: Fiction, verse and literary criticism of the highest quality. Also essays concerned with general ideas and informative articles on any subject of human interest, with the exception of Economics and contemporary Politics. Between three and five thousand words preferred. The average rate of payment is £2 per thousand words. No illustrations used' (*The Writer's and Artist's Year Book 1927*, ed. Agnes Herbert [London, 1927], 58).
2–Larsson did not contribute anything further to C.

## TO *E. R. Curtius*

CC

25 May 1927 [London]

My dear Curtius

I am sending you *The Art of Being Ruled* and *The Enemy* by my friend Wyndham Lewis. If you are interested in contemporary English literature I think that Wyndham Lewis is one of the writers with whom you should be acquainted.[1]

I should like to know again how long it is likely to be before I can print something of yours in *The Criterion*?

Meanwhile, I should be grateful for any suggestions of German writers whom I ought to introduce to England. In July I am printing a very interesting essay by Worringer.[2] Do you recommend Scheler,[3] and if so could you tell me his proper address? I am particularly interested to get hold of things of the type of Massis' 'Défense de l'Occident' and this thing of Worringer's on modern art: i.e. discussions of important questions of interest to Europe as a whole, from whatever point of view.

I hope for news of you soon.

Ever yours cordially,
[T. S. Eliot]

1–Curtius responded on 4 June: 'The first impression of the thick book [*The Art of Being Ruled*] is one of confusion. But that's something one always has to accept nowadays. Our moderns no longer know [how to show] politeness towards the reader, or rather they don't want to know. But your recommendation is enough for me: I will read the book, though not right now. The overproduction of the present time is of course discouraging, and arouses the – dangerous – wish to read only the classics.' On 6 Oct. 1927, IPF was to post to Curtius a copy of WL's *Time and Western Man*. 'This is sent to you at Mr Lewis's request and with his compliments.'

2–Wilhelm Worringer, 'Art Questions of the Day', *MC* 6 (Aug. 1927), 101–17.

3–Max Scheler (1874–1928), philosopher, taught at the University of Cologne.

## TO *Archibald MacLeish*[1] CC

25 May 1927 [London]

Dear MacLeish,

I do not know whether I am betraying a trade secret, but I see no harm in it. And you may know already that Houghton Mifflin offered us (Faber & Gwyer) sheets of *Streets in the Moon*. We finally refused them, entirely for economic reasons; the book was a $5.00 limited, and we could not pay according and hope to do anything with it; for conditions in England are different from America, and we should have had to make it unlimited and cheap.

But I want to say that we should like to have you on our list; and whenever you can make up a volume independently of your engagement with Houghton Mifflin, so that it can be printed in this country, and sold at a price that Britons will pay, I can probably force my firm to take it. But of course you will have to look out for your American copyright.

Congratulations on the poem I am publishing.[2] It suggested to me that you ought to like the work of Léger; do you know *Anabase* which I have just translated?

Yours always sincerely,
[T. S. E.]

## *I. P. Fassett* TO *Nancy Pearn* CC

25 May 1927 [*The Monthly Criterion*]

Dear Miss Pearn,

Mr Eliot has asked me to return the enclosed contributions of Mr Lawrence and to explain that he does not find either of them quite suitable for the *Criterion*. The story is not of quite the right type for us

1–Archibald MacLeish (1892–1982), American poet and playwright, studied at Yale and Harvard (where he took a degree in law), and then lived in France for a while in the 1920s. His poem *Conquistador* (1933) won a Pulitzer prize; and for his *Collected Poems, 1917–1952* (1953) he won three awards: a second Pulitzer prize, the Bollingen Prize and the National Book Award. His verse play *J.B.* (1957) won the Pulitzer Prize for Drama and a Tony Award. During WWII, at President Roosevelt's bidding, he was Librarian of Congress, and he served with the United Nations Educational, Scientific and Cultural Organization. He was Boylston Professor of Rhetoric and Oratory at Harvard, 1949–62. TSE wrote on 29 June 1932 to Ferris Greenslet at Houghton Mifflin Co., 'There is no living poet in America who seems to me to have greater technical accomplishment than MacLeish.'

2–'Land's End', *MC* 6 (July 1927), 14–17.

and the review of Rosanov though extremely interesting is not quite from the *Criterion* point of view. Mr Eliot wishes me to add that he hopes you will not think that his admiration of Mr Lawrence's work is in any way diminished.

Yours sincerely,
[I. P. Fassett]
Secretary.

Enclosed: 'The Escaped Cock'[1]
Review of *Solitaria*

## TO *James F. Muirhead*[2]

CC

2 June 1927 [*The Monthly Criterion*]

Dear Sir,

I have just seen your letter of the 26th ultimo. As my secretary informed you we have had a copy of your book and I have sent it to my colleague who is an authority on modern German literature. He told me that he was interested to see the book and he will probably do a review on it.[3] But as he is a very busy diplomat in Rome, I do not like to hurry him about it. I sincerely hope that he will review the book at some length and favourably, but of course I have to leave my colleagues complete liberty, especially on subjects on which they know better than I do.

By the way, if you and Miss Mayne do any verse translations from Spitteler I should always be interested to see them with a view to publishing a few in the *Criterion*.

Yours very truly,
[T. S. Eliot]

1–Written in Apr. 1927, the first part of D. H. Lawrence's story 'The Escaped Cock' – rejected by TSE – would be published in *Forum* 79 (Feb. 1928), 286–96; the second part was written in June/July 1928. The finished work was published as a novella, *The Escaped Cock* (Paris, 1928); and as *The Man Who Died* (London and New York, 1931).

2–James F. Muirhead (1853–1934) was for over 35 years editor of the English editions of Baedeker's Handbooks, writing (in particular) the volumes on London, Great Britain, the USA and Canada. An inveterate traveller, he published other books including *A Wayfarer in Switzerland* (1926). For some years he made translations from the German of the Swiss poet Carl Spitteler (1845–1924) – Nobel Laureate, 1919 – including *Selected Poems* (with Ethel Colburn Mayne, 1928) and *Prometheus and Epimetheus* (1931).

3–A. W. G. Randall, anonymous notice of Carl Spitteler, *Laughing Truths*, trans. James F. Muirhead: *MC* 6 (Oct. 1927), 376–7.

## TO *Kenneth Pickthorn*[1] CC

2 June 1927 [*The Monthly Criterion*]

Sir,

I am taking the liberty of approaching you at the suggestion of my friend Mr Charles Whibley.[2]

I am sending you at the same time a copy of the last number of the *Criterion*. The *Criterion* prides itself particularly on its reviews of books and I believe it is largely on account of these reviews that the *Criterion* is read, and by means of them that it acquires its influence. Hitherto I have not had reviews of many books concerned with modern history on account of the difficulty of finding historical reviewers who are neither dilettantes nor pedants. Furthermore I did not wish for such book reviewers representing either definite Liberal or Labour views or the feebler sort of Conservatism. When I say this I must add that the *Criterion* does not touch ephemeral political questions and it certainly does not associate itself with any existing political party. At the same time, it has I think a definite character in the world of ideas.

I should, for instance, have had Mr Guedalla's *Palmerston* reviewed, and perhaps several recent books about Disraeli, had I known of anyone to whom to entrust the task. I should like to deal with Mr Guedalla on the occasion of his next book, and I do not doubt that so facile a writer will soon have another ready. Meanwhile I have Ludwig's *Napoleon* on which I should like to get a review of 1,500 to 2,000 words as soon as possible;[3] also Marriott's *Mechanism of the Modern State* for which, however, I should only want a much shorter notice. And I should be glad if you had any suggestions for other books.

If you agree in principle and would care to review for the *Criterion* I should be very glad to hear from you.

I am, Sir,
Your obedient servant,
[T. S. Eliot]

1–Kenneth Pickthorn (1892–1975), historian and politician; Fellow of Corpus Christi College, Cambridge: see Biographical Register.
2–Whibley had written (25 May): 'Pickthorn is a sound historian with sound views.'
3–Pickthorn reviewed Emil Ludwig's *Napoleon* in *MC* 6 (Sept. 1927), 267.

## TO *F. S. Flint*

CC

2 June 1927 [London]

Dear F. S.,

Good. Thank you for your letter.[1] Soddy's book has arrived but I want to look at it myself before doing anything further about it. I hope to have some notions of the subject by the time we meet. I am counting upon you for the dinner today week in any case. At present we are more or less settled in Sussex for a month or two, during which time I intend to come up to town for three or four days a week.

Re Spanish periodicals. I do not respect your scruples but I respect your time. I suppose they had better be left until I can get someone else to do them; fortunately they are few and irregular. I had, as you know, and at your request, proposed the job to Trend; and found him disinclined to take it on; partly because he was so nomadic and partly because he said you did it so well yourself. By the way, I see that the *Nottingham Guardian* is pleased with your dramatic criticism. Let me know how the theatres treat your applications.

Ever yours affectionately,
[T. S.]

1 – Flint had written on 25 May: 'I went further than I thought if I said it was futile to discuss aesthetic questions at the present juncture. What I meant was that it is futile to discuss them without correlating them with both the religious and the economic trends of our time: and by religious I mean something differing, at least in form, from what Mm. Maritain and Massis understand; and by economic, I mean something differing entirely in content from what, say, Keynes or the orthodox economists understand: something that Ruskin (*Unto This Last*) nearly said; something that Soddy seems to say: though on more sober reading he appears to be so charged with his own matter that it comes out occasionally thick and coagulated, when what we need is a clear stream. I welcomed therefore Worringer's statement . . . What I wished to indicate in my letter is that that transfer of the centre of gravity from art to science seems, in Soddy, to have travelled into economics, and, if so, we ought to sit up and take notice. You appear to agree. I am glad. But, as you say, one must tread warily, and examine Soddy's propositions.'

## TO *Max Scheler*[1] CC

2 June 1927 [*The Monthly Criterion*]

Sir,

I am taking the liberty of addressing you with the introduction of our friend Professor E. R. Curtius of Heidelberg who is an occasional and most valued contributor to my review. I should be highly honoured if you would allow the *Criterion* to publish some of your work. If possible, I should prefer something hitherto unpublished, possibly an extract from your work in progress, *Philosophischen Anthropologie*.[2] But if you considered that you had nothing quite suitable unpublished, I should be glad to reprint something which has already appeared in German but not in English, if it could be reduced to the proper length.

The usual length for essays in the *Criterion* is 5,000 to 6,000 words. Our rates of payment are £2 per 1,000 words less cost of translation which is 15/- per 1,000 words.

I am sending you a copy of the last number of the *Criterion*. The *Criterion* likes to publish essays by the most distinguished thinkers and writers of the whole of Europe dealing with some subject of European or universal importance at the present time. I am convinced that you ought to be represented in the *Criterion* as soon as possible.

Expressing my admiration for your work and my desire to introduce it to a larger public in this country,[3]

I am, Sir,
Your obedient servant,
[T. S. Eliot]

1–Max Scheler (1874–1928): German philosopher specialising in ethics, value theory, phenomenology, philosophical anthropology; Professor of Philosophy and Sociology at the University of Cologne, 1919–28; notable influence on Karol Wojtyla, the future Pope John Paul II, who wrote his *Habilitation* (1954) on Christian ethics in the light of Scheler.

2–E. R. Curtius urged TSE (27 May) to request a section of this work-in-progress by Scheler. 'He is a bad correspondent, but a supreme intellect. Even though he is a friend of mine, he is one of the 3 or 4 most important thinkers of modern Europe.'

3–Scheler, 'Future of Man', trans. Howard Becker, *MC* 7 (Feb. 1928), 100–19.

## TO *H. V. Routh*

CC

2 June 1927 [Faber & Gwyer Ltd]

Dear Mr Routh,

I remember perfectly well meeting you at Jepson's[1] but it is so long ago that I was not quite sure that you were the same person. I recently complimented a man about his book and found that it was written by his father, so that I have become very careful.

I still wish that you might make a few suggestions yourself, more particularly because I do not seem to have anything on hand that would be likely to interest you. I have a critical book about Euripides (*Euripides the Idealist* by R. V. Appleton) which I want to get reviewed and would be glad to send it to you if you are interested. Do you care to tackle books on classical literature, as well as medieval literature?

If you see Jepson please tell him that although we have not met for a long time I always remember him and hope to renew our acquaintance.

Sincerely yours,
[T. S. Eliot]

## TO *Herbert Read*

CC

2 June 1927 [*The Monthly Criterion*]

My dear Read,

I am very sorry about last Tuesday. We have been making arrangements to settle at the seaside for the next two months and I propose to be in town about four days a week. We shall meet on Thursday evening but I should like if possible to see you before. I shall be up on Tuesday but I rather gathered from Miss Fassett's conversation with you that you will be away. When will you be back?

I am sorry to bother you again with MSS. The enclosed story[2] was sent by Flint. I am not particularly struck by it myself but as you know, I have

1–Edgar Jepson (1863–1938): English novelist and journalist; author of two volumes of autobiography, *Memoirs of a Victorian* (1933) and *Memoirs of an Edwardian* (1937). He studied Greats at Oxford, under Benjamin Jowett (1817–93), taught for a while in Barbados, and in the absence of Frank Harris edited *Vanity Fair* for six months. He wrote detective stories, fantastic fictions, and children's stories including *The second Pollyooly book* (1914). He was a champion of EP and TSE, and in 'Recent United States Poetry' (*The English Review*, 26 May 1918, 419–28) praised their work at the expense of their American contemporaries.

2–Unidentified.

not very much confidence in my own judgment of fiction. We can let Flint know that I have shown it to you, or not, just as you prefer; but I do not see any reason why I should not take your opinion on it. I wish you would also tell me what you think of the enclosed poem.

I hope you have managed to settle the Purley affair; it must be a great burden to you.

Ever yours,
[T. S. E.]

P.S. I quite agree that Tomlinson would be the best person for the book on whaling, but I wrote to him two or three weeks ago to ask in general if he would contribute but have had no answer. Do you know of any way of getting hold of him? I wrote to an address in Croydon.

## TO *Virginia Woolf* TS Berg

2 June 1927 *The Monthly Criterion*

My dear Virginia,

I think you are rather unkind. I do not pretend that I have read everything that you have written but I have read a great deal more than you imagine; and I am very much better acquainted with your work than with that of Mr Bennett, or Mr Galsworthy, or Mr Wells, or Mr Walpole, or even Miss May Sinclair. But for a person who specialises in detective fiction and ecclesiastical history I think I have done pretty well.[1]

I am sending you *pour votre gouverne* a copy of Mr Williams's little note, and I hope you will agree that he is a gentleman and a cricketer.[2]

At present we are more or less settled at Eastbourne for a month or two. I am going down again tomorrow afternoon and expect to be back

1 – VW had replied (25 May) to a letter from TSE (now lost): 'Many thanks for . . . writing with such discernment. I suspect you have never read a word I've written; so that it is all the more to your credit that you make it sound so interesting. I'm surprised by Conrad; it had never struck me. But what a devilish good critic you are!'

2 – Orlo Williams's review of *To the Lighthouse*: *MC* 6 (July 1927), 74–8. 'Mrs Woolf is not an inventive writer,' Williams opened, 'but then – what time or need has she for inventing, when she cannot overtake all that she sees and feels and observes that other people see and feel? . . . Mrs Woolf's art . . . is intensely personal in its stamp, especially now that she has abandoned the solidly constructive method of narration for her uniquely reflective impressionism . . . For imaginative prose of this kind there ought to be another name, since it is a thing different from the novel, verging at its most exalted moments on poetry . . . Her mastery increases with each book, but, I fear, will always fall short of her vision.'

VW remarked: 'I look forward with mild resignation to Orlo Williams. The only time I saw him he struck me as a gentlemanly man, who would never insult a lady.'

on Tuesday, and thereafter three or four days a week. I am free for tea on Wednesday or Thursday or for dinner on Wednesday. And if any of those times suited you I should be very glad to show you what little I know about the Grizzly Bear,[1] or the Chicken Strut. I should not dare to bring you any more records without being sure that you have not got them already, but have you got The Memphis Shake?[2]

Ever yours affectionately,
T. S. E.[3]

## TO *William Force Stead*

CC

2 June 1927 [London]

Dear Stead,

Thank you for your two letters which I have just received having been out of town. First about the theological books.[4] The two I have in mind and which I am sending you I had kept for some little time because I hankered to read them myself. It is a great temptation when books arrive that one wants to read; but I was obliged to confess to myself that I was

1–The Grizzly Bear was a dance craze from the 1900s. See 'Grizzly Bear': words by Irving Berlin; music by George Botsford (1910): 'Out in San Francisco where the weather's fair, / They have a dance out there, / They call the "Grizzly Bear" / All your other lovin' dances don't compare, / Not so coony, / But a little more than spoony, / Talk about yo' bears that Teddy Roosevelt shot, / They couldn't class with what / Old San Francisco's got / Listen my honey, do, / And I will show to you / The dance of the grizzly Bear.' Cf. 'That Shakespearian Rag': words by Gene Buck and Herman Ruby; music by David Stamper (1912)—which TSE cites in *TWL*, 128–30 —'Bill Shakespeare never knew / Of rag-time in his days, / But the high-browed rhymes, / Of his syncopated lines, / You'll admit, surely fit, / any song that's now a hit, / So this rag, I submit, — / That Shakespearian rag, / most intelligent, very elegant, / That old classical drag, / Has the proper stuff, / The line "Lay on Macduff", / Desdemona was a pampered pet, / Romeo loved his Juliet, / And they were some lovers, you can bet, and yet, / I know if they were here to-day, / They'd Grizzly Bear in a diff'rent way. / And you'd hear old Hamlet say, / "To be or not to be", / That Shakespearian Rag.'

2–VW: 'I shall pin you down to dinner. I enjoyed my tea party the other day very much, and think it should be repeated. We might dance.'

3–VW responded to this letter ('Sunday'): 'Yes – Orlo is a gentleman, as you say: what's odd is that he makes me feel a perfect lady – not Mayfair alas – South Kensington. But I don't & won't & shan't accept maternity for his style: slovenly I am I admit, but not quite to the extent of Orlo's ragbag. But he is very very kind . . .

'Did I ever, even with a headache on me, say that I expected you to read all of me? Have I read all of you, or of Aldous, Joyce, Lawrence &c &c? No, I've not. My phrase, about contemporary authors, is, "I'm beginning on the 1st of August" – that day soon passes. We know our contemporaries without reading them – such is my convenient theory.'

4–WFS agreed on 27 May to try his hand at reviewing: he tackled first of all *The Original Jerusalem Gospel*, *MC* 6 (Nov. 1927), 457.

wholly incompetent to write even short notes; and I have too many other things to do to be able ever to become anything of an authority. What I want for books like these is short notices of half a page to a page; and I know that in order to write a short notice it is necessary to know more about the subject than for writing a long notice. I should be grateful if you thought it worth your while to do short notes on these books. And if not, could you think of someone else to pass them on to who would care to do them?

The trouble with poetry is that there are so many people with claims on the *Criterion* who like to write about poetry. God knows why; it seems to me the dullest subject going. As for art, we don't have much space and I leave that almost entirely to my art editor. As for politics, there is an idea, so long as we do not deal with the ephemeral questions of the moment. Have you any suggestions?

It is quite all right about the 19th.[1] As a matter of fact we are now settled in Sussex for a month or two and I come up to town for three or four days a week, so that it is going to be rather more difficult to get to Oxford this term than I thought. Anyway don't trouble to keep week-ends open for me; but I might possibly be able to arrange matters so as to come down the following weekend, the 26th; but I am afraid that would be too late for my purpose, would it not?[2]

Yours ever,
[T. S. Eliot]

1 – WFS said in an undated note that RC-S and Wardle wanted to visit him at Oxford for the weekend of 19 June: he hoped that would not inconvenience TSE.

2 – WFS was to write (13 June), apropos the arrangements for TSE's baptism and confirmation in the Church of England: 'The Bishop of Oxford is booked up for the weekend June 25–27 . . . But if you can come, let me know and I'm sure to manage it through either the Bp. of Buckingham, or Bp. Shaw [and] his two suffragans.

'I have seen Streeter and he thinks he will be free and able to join you for the week end here. This will give you an opportunity for a good thorough talk with him; he is delightful, keen and very much to the point on serious subjects and continually bubbling over with a rich sense of humour . . .

'The new service of baptism for adults is a great improvement on the old – I will use the new form if you approve. Godparents are only required for children & have to carry the burden of the children's sins until they come to years of discretion. As you are presumed to have reached that age – (which to be sure few of us ever do reach) – I am afraid you will have to be responsible for your actions and Godparents will therefore not be required . . .'

For unknown reasons, it was difficult to settle upon a day in June when all parties would be available for the brief ceremonials. WFS wrote again on 16 June, 'As briefly suggested in my wire I think Wednesday 22nd or 29th will be all right. With three Bishops to turn to, we ought to manage the Confirmation any way . . . [Y]our telegram seems to suggest that you could come at any time on Wednesday the 22nd or 29th.

## TO *Nancy Cunard*[1]

CC

2 June 1927 [London]

Dear Nancy,

Your letter was forwarded to me in the country but by the time it reached me it was too late to let you know.[2] I am so sorry to have missed you, but at any rate I now have your address in Paris and hope to use it. But when I do get to Paris you will probably be in Spain or Turkey or somewhere.

Yours ever
[T. S. Eliot]

## TO *E. R. Curtius*

CC

2 June 1927 [London]

My dear Curtius,

Many thanks for your cordial letter. I am very grateful for what you say about Scheler and have written to him today. Should you see him or be writing to him I hope you will say that I am extremely keen to get a specimen of his work.

---

'Acting on this last inference I am writing the Bishop to know if he has a spare half hour on either of those days. There is not much time between now & the 22nd – but it is just possible that with two dates before him, one or the other will be feasable [*sic*].

'However, it is most important to know the approximate hour of your arrival. It will take say ¾ hr from the station to [The Palace,] Cuddesdon – but then we ought to allow more time, for Baptism on the way – say at Littlemore.

'Therefore since the hour is all important, will you most kindly wire me immediately on receipt of this saying "Could arrive Oxford such & such an hour" . . .'

1–Nancy Cunard (1896–1965): writer, journalist and political activist; daughter of Sir Bache Cunard, heir to the Cunard Line shipping business, and of an American heiress named Maud Alice Burke, who flourished as a London hostess under the name Emerald Lady Cunard. She cultivated lovers and friends including Michael Arlen, Aldous Huxley and Louis Aragon. In 1920 she moved to Normandy where she ran the Hours Press (successor to Three Mountains Press), 1928–34: her productions included works by Pound and Beckett. Her own publications include *Black Man and White Ladyship* (1931); *Negro: An Anthology* (1934); *Authors Take Sides on the Spanish War* (1937) – a pamphlet sponsored by *Left Review* – and *These Were the Hours: Memories of My Hours Press, Réanville and Paris, 1928–1932* (1969). See *Nancy Cunard: Brave Poet, Indomitable Rebel*, ed. Hugh Ford (1968); Anne Chisholm, *Nancy Cunard* (1981); and Shari Benstock, *Women of the Left Bank: Paris, 1900–1940* (1986). Lois G. Gordon, *Nancy Cunard: Heiress, Muse, Political Activist* (2007), surmises an affair with TSE.

2–Cunard wrote from 1 Percy St. on 25 May to ask TSE to dine one night during her visit. Otherwise, when he next visits Paris, he must dine at 2 Rue le Regrathier.

I should be grateful at any time for any other suggestions from you. I was very disappointed to hear nothing from Bertrand [*sc.* Bertram] whose book on Nietzsche I admired so much.[1] And keep in mind that I await impatiently the leisure which will allow you to write something yourself.

Ever yours cordially,
[T. S. Eliot]

## TO *John Gould Fletcher* CC

2 June 1927 [London]

Dear Fletcher,

I got back to town last night. Many thanks for your letter and for the poem.[2] I am afraid it is too late for the July number but I should like to use it in the August number which appears on July 28th if that suits you. Is that all right?

I should be very glad if you would sometimes review poetry.[3] Wolfe has been doing most of it, but he is out of town and anyway, without prejudice, I think it is better to vary reviewers. Do you think you could let me have some poetry review by the 16th of this month? I have not got a copy of Laura Gottschalk's book as I sent it to Wolfe and he never did anything with it. I should be very interested to know what you think of her; my own conclusion was that it was a variety of Jewish cleverness making a neat compound of Gertrude Stein and Marianne Moore.[4] I am sending you also two things which have just come in, one by Ruth Manning Sanders and one by Sacheverell Sitwell, on neither of which I have an opinion of any kind. If you can do something by that date I should be very glad to know at once. I am ordering from Knopf the Ransom book.[5] I have been

1–Ernst Bertram, *Nietzsche: Versuch einer Mythologie* (Bonn: Bouvier, 1918); trans. as *Nietzsche: Attempt at a Mythology*.

2–'Transatlantic', *MC* 6 (Aug. 1927),128–30

3–Fletcher had volunteered to review John Crowe Ransom's *Two Gentlemen in Bonds* (Knopf) and Laura Gottschalk's *The Close Chaplet* (Hogarth Press).

4–F. S. Flint, to whom TSE had sent a batch of poems submitted by Riding, belatedly gave his opinion in mid-July: 'I don't think Laura Riding comes off. She leaves me completely untouched. A discursive mind examining its own operations but not a poetic mind summing them up in a synthesis having the body and spirit of imagination.' (Riding had written to TSE in the meantime, in an undated letter, 'May I have those poems back if you do not intend using them?' TSE noted on her letter, for the attention of IPF: 'Write to *Flint* & say she is clamouring. Could he return with his opinion.')

5–Fletcher reviewed Sacheverell Sitwell, John Crowe Ransom, Laura Riding Gottschalk and Ruth Manning Sanders in *MC* 6 (Aug. 1927), 168–72.

thinking over what you say about the Arcos raid and should like to put it to the meeting next Thursday.[1] My own feeling is that this is too much a matter of the moment for the *Criterion* to take up. If we are going to take up politics at all I think we ought to take a very long view and hammer on essential points and not on heated questions of the hour. I am rather shy of dealing with questions of the day in reply to which anyone might say 'Ah but don't you know all the facts'; there is another difficulty in this particular question which I will explain when we meet.

I am now in town for three or four days every week. I count upon seeing you on Thursday evening in any case. Let me have your essay on Spengler when it is ready.[2]

Ever yours,
[T. S. Eliot]

## TO *Roger Hinks*[3] CC

2 June 1927 [London]

Dear Hinks,

At present I am living in Sussex and coming up for three or four days a week. Tomorrow is no good as I have had to pack so much into this short

1 – On 12 May 1927 the police raided the offices of the All-Russian Co-operative Society (ARCOS), the British-registered Soviet trading company, on suspicion – in the wake of the General Strike – that it was a front for Communist subversion. While no evidence of such activity was found, the incident caused a breach in diplomatic relations with the USSR which was only to be repaired by the government of Ramsay MacDonald in Oct. 1929. Fletcher urged TSE to 'comment editorially on the Arcos raid . . . I am not concerned whether England will gain or lose by forfeiting its trade with Russia; I am concerned with the bad moral effects of a government which hasn't principle enough to openly oppose the Bolsheviks, but which nevertheless is prepared to use force majeure against them, when it finds its own half-hearted compromise falling through. I don't know whether you agree or not . . .'

2 – Fletcher was preparing a paper on the subject of 'Marx vs. Spengler'. His next contribution was to be 'East and West', *MC* 7 (June 1928), 306–24.

3 – Roger Hinks (1903–1963) – son of Arthur Hinks (Secretary of the Royal Astronomical Society and Gresham Lecturer in Astronomy) – was educated at Trinity College, Cambridge, and at the British School in Rome. From 1926 to 1939 he was Assistant Keeper in the Department of Greek and Roman Antiquities, British Museum, from which he resigned in consequence of a scandal caused by his arrangements for deep-cleaning the Elgin Marbles. He later worked at the Warburg Institute, at the British Legation in Stockholm, and for the British Council (Rome, The Netherlands, Greece, Paris). His writings include *Carolingian Art* (1935), *Myth and Allegory in Ancient Art* (1939) and *Caravaggio: His Life – His Legend – His Works* (1953). See also 'Roger Hinks', *Burlington Magazine* 105: 4738 (Sept. 1964), 423–34; and *The Gymnasium of the Mind: The Journals of Roger Hinks, 1933–1963*, ed. John Goldsmith (1984).

week. I shall be up again on Tuesday and suggest Wednesday or Thursday for lunch. Let me know if either of these days suits you.

I think it would be very interesting indeed if you would tackle Blake next time.[1] And let me know whenever there are any art books that you want.

Sincerely yours,
[T. S. Eliot]

## TO *Herbert Read* CC

3 June 1927 [*The Monthly Criterion*]

My dear Read,

There is another important point which I have had in mind and have kept forgetting to mention. Now that you have had the June number with Murry's article in it are you disposed to write a short reply from your own point of view.[2] I leave this entirely to your discretion and in fact should be very glad of your considered opinion whether you think it desirable that I should do so myself or not. One Charles Mauron has just sent me a short reply to Murry from *his* point of view,[3] and if you think it suitable we might publish all three together. I would of course show you mine before printing it but the three, and any others, would be quite independent. Let me know as soon as you can.[4] I am leaving town this afternoon but expect to be back again on Tuesday.

Yours ever,
[T. S. E.]

1–Hinks's next Chronicle was 'The Centenary of William Blake', *MC* 6 (Nov. 1927), 431–6.
2–JMM, 'Towards a Synthesis', *MC* 5 (June 1927), 294–313.
3–Charles Mauron, 'Concerning "Intuition"' (trans. TSE), *MC* 6 (Sept. 1927), 229–35; letter by Mauron in *MC* 7 (Mar. 1928), 263–5.
4–HR replied on 4 June: 'I think Murry's article ought to be replied to. It is a first class issue & one that ought to attract spectators. But it will not be easy. At any rate, my own feeling is that I would like to see you taking the field first.'

## TO *Jean Paulhan*

CC

3 Juin 1927 [*The Monthly Criterion*]

Mon cher ami,

Je vous remercie de votre aimable lettre et du numéro de *La Nouvelle Revue Française* où vous avez fait imprimer ma chronique.[1] Pendant les derniers mois j'ai été toujours à quatre chemins, surtout à cause de *Criterion* qui commence à paraître mensuellement. Je voudrais bien vous envoyer une autre chronique pendant l'été; je propose comme sujet ou 'L'Histoire et la Biographie Actuelle' ou 'Le Roman Américain et la Littérature Anglo-Américaine de Montparnasse'.[2]

Je n'ai aucun espoir de passer à Paris avant le mois de septembre. Est-ce que vous serez en vacances à ce moment là, car je tiens beaucoup à vous voir?

Toujours votre dévoué
[T. S. Eliot][3]

## TO *Edmund Wilson*

CC

3 June 1927 [London]

Dear Mr Wilson,

Thank you for your two letters of May 17th and May 18th.

First of all about the Greenberg scheme.[4] I have read Greenberg's letter to which Mr Stewart, our Manager, is replying. Personally, I could not

1 – 'Le roman anglais contemporain', *NRF* 28: 164 (1 May 1927), 669–75.

2 – Paulhan replied (20 June) that while he preferred 'L'Histoire et la biographie', he would be delighted to receive either piece.

3 – *Translation*: My dear friend, I wish to thank you for your kind letter and the issue of *La Nouvelle Revue Française* where you have had my chronicle printed. During the last few months, I have been here and everywhere, mainly because of the *Criterion* which is becoming a monthly. I would very much like to send you another chronicle during the summer; I suggest for a subject 'History and contemporary biography' or 'The American novel and the Anglo-American literature of Montparnasse'.

I have no hope of coming to Paris before September. Will you be on holiday then, as I am anxious to see you? Yours truly as always, [T. S. Eliot]

4 – Wilson wrote on 17 May: 'The American publisher, Greenberg, has asked Allen Tate, Mark Van Doren and me to edit a series of modern American poets. We hope to get for the coming season volumes by Allen Tate, Hart Crane, Léonie Adams and one or two others. We wanted . . . to ask . . . whether you would care to make recommendations of any British poets with volumes not yet published in America who could be included in the series. The publishers want to include some British poets, and they would accept any recommendations that you might make . . . Greenberg has written to Faber and Gwyer about the possibility of bringing out the American volumes in England.'

advise the firm to make any comprehensive engagement, and I do not think that any other English publishers would do so. You must remember that poetry does not sell in England anything like as well as it does in America. In any case we should be introducing in England several American poets whom we should have to run at a loss for at least five years before they became established. I never expect that we can make any money out of poetry but I am anxious to see that what poetry the firm publishes should be the best obtainable; but I cannot ask them to commit themselves to an indefinite number of dead losses for the immediate future. I do not know anything about Greenberg, but the fact that you and Allen Tate and Mark van Doren constitute the committee would be quite sufficient guarantee of getting the right stuff. My only anxiety is that my firm should not be loaded with too much good, and consequently unsaleable, stuff at once. But if it were possible to make an arrangement so that we could select from your list and publish a little at a time I should urge my people to take it up. As for my personal collaboration in this venture, I should be very glad to assist you in any way possible, by making recommendations and so far as possible negotiating with people here, even without any remuneration. There is, to tell the truth, not much that I can recommend. Faber and Gwyer have published, at my recommendation, Herbert Read's *Poems*[1] and John Gould Fletcher's *Branches of Adam*;[2] and I should like to see these published in America. There are one or two younger people whom I might persuade to get together a volume for publication. I assume that you do not want stuff like the Sitwells, etc.

Third, about my chronicles in the *Nouvelle Revue Française*.[3] I am quite willing to let you reproduce in *The New Republic* these chronicles within a month after their publication in French, as I have the general consent of the *Nouvelle Revue Française* to do this. If you want to publish my last letter about the English Novel, you are quite welcome to do so. In a few days I will send you a copy of the original English text. I am not keen about introducing the word 'psychoanalysis' into the title and I suggest that a more modest title would be 'Four English Novelists' or something of that sort. But if you keep the word 'psychoanalysis' out of it you can give it what title you please.[4]

1 – *Collected Poems 1913–25* (1926).

2 – John Gould Fletcher, *Branches of Adam* (1926).

3 – Wilson asked permission (17 May) for the *New Republic* to reprint TSE's 'letter', 'Le roman anglais contemporain'.

4 – Wilson wrote (18 May): 'I think your article in the *N.R.F.*, if you let us have it, ought to have a different title – something about the modern English novel and psychoanalysis, perhaps.'

With regard to what you said about Garnett.[1] It is quite possible that the superficial allegory is present. But whatever Garnett thinks he meant I am sure that this curious approximation of the human and animal is a real inspiration. The best part of *The Man in the Zoo* is the account of the affection of the man for his tiger cat; his feeling towards the lady is tame and conventional but his feeling for the cat is really inspired. *The Sailor's Return* is a book I have only glanced at; but I suspect that the human-animal relation is there replaced by the curiosity of a white man-negress relation. Mind you, I am not thinking what Garnett 'intends' but what he accomplishes. I am not, however, really satisfied with my account of Garnett in the French chronicle. I doubt whether he is really so settled and secure as I intimated.[2] From what I know of him it is quite likely that he is very doubtful and worried and that the superficial security represents merely the effort to keep himself together.

Finally, you suggested that my book reviews from the *Criterion* might be printed simultaneously in an American magazine. So far as my pocket book is concerned I should like this very much indeed as I do not pay myself for these reviews; but I think that I must decline on principle. I do not like the idea of people publishing the same book review in more than one paper; I do not want to set a bad example; I think that book

1 – 'I am surprised at what you say about *Lady into Fox* [by David Garnett],' wrote Wilson (18 May). 'I had always supposed that it was simply a story of a lively and fickle girl married to a very steady and sober-minded man, to whom she is unfaithful. I thought the animal part was merely a metaphor for his point of view about her – as being a creature belonging to an entirely different race. Are you sure that Garnett intends the animal–human situation to be taken literally?'

2 – TSE's remarks about Garnett were published in French translation (by another hand) in 'Le roman anglais contemporain', 674–5; the relevant passage in his English original, 'The Contemporary Novel', reads: 'Mr [Aldous] Huxley is tormented; Mr David Garnett, a far more accomplished writer, is secure. Mr Garnett is one of the more interesting examples of psychologism. His intention, *prima facie*, is to revive the simple and direct narrative in a "tale of wonder". He is said to admire Defoe, whose style he sometimes adopts with astonishing virtuosity. There is no prose writer of the day who displays more pure technical skill in "writing". But if we examine his first two tales, *Lady into Fox*, and *A Man in the Zoo*, with a little care, we find the inspiration to be wholly unlike that of Defoe. The "simple narrative" is a façade; the two tales are post-Balzac, and exactly as much post-Balzac as the time between the dates of birth of Balzac and Mr Garnett. For the theme is that of "*Une Passion dans le Désert*": the abnormal, or at any rate peculiar relations possible between man and beast. To these possibilities Mr Garnett has a very rare and exquisite sensibility. Only, while Balzac gives this relation, in his story, a real moral significance – the story is a miracle of humanisation – Mr Garnett withdraws it: the theme is reversed, the human is assimilated, with every trick of ingenuity, to the beast. And accordingly Balzac's story is dramatic, and Mr Garnett's is not. Conrad's, in spite of some appearances, are not dramatic. And the contemporary novel is not dramatic.'

reviews, especially the book reviews in the *Criterion*, ought to represent the interest of the writer in the magazine for which he is writing.

Yours very sincerely,
[T. S. Eliot]

## TO *Conrad Aiken* CC

8 June 1927 [London]

Dear Conrad,

I have been trying to see how I could squeeze in 'Changing Mind'. I was already booked up with verse to the September number when I got it, so that the only chance of using it would be in September or October. The prose things which I have got to use in those numbers will not leave room for the whole of the poem which is a pity. Now, if you want me to try Squire or anyone else with it in the hope that somebody might be able to print the thing entire before October, let me know and I will do my best. The only part which it seems to me possible to detach and use separately is the short Part IV which, it seems to me, might be quite effective by itself. If therefore you do not print the whole thing somewhere else in England during the summer, I should very much like to use Part IV by itself in the September or October number. Please let me know as soon as you can what I should do.[1]

Don't bother about payment for 'The Hollow Men'. You are quite welcome to it.

Between the lines of your letters I read something like a horror of contemporary American life and God knows I should jump at any chance of getting you back to England, and if anything turned up I would cable. I wish that the *Criterion* had a circulation of ten or fifteen thousand. If it ever reached that point I should want a colleague. At present, getting out a number every month is a bloody sweat; it is not that it takes so much more of my time when I am in London as that I have to be in London more of the time; and if I am to get away at all this summer there will probably be more worry than holiday about it.

Ever yours,
[Tom]

P.S. I should think that the best shot would be if you could get a job like Frank Morley who is settled over here as representative of the Century Company. I am rather sceptical about American publishing firms establishing

1 – 'From "Changing Mind"', *MC* 6 (Dec. 1927), 523.

offices over here and competing with English firms, as Harper does, but the Century arrangement seems to me to be very sensible. Could you not persuade Houghton Mifflin to give you a similar job. They ought to have over here an American representative who knows England well and who could get in touch with the right authors and the right publishers for the purpose of steering American copyrights of English books in their direction.

## TO *Kathleen Nott*[1] CC

9 June 1927 [London]

Dear Madam,

I have read your poems with interest and I should like to see some more in a year's time.[2] I think that by that time you ought to have got on a good deal farther. What your present verse seems to me to lack is concreteness. I do not mean that poems should be decorated with images; and in fact metaphors are to be avoided as much as possible; but I mean that the idea ought to be realised as a kind of perception, or even hallucination if you will. I feel after reading a number of your poems that I am in a world of abstractions. It is probably this abstractness which makes them seem to be descriptions of feelings rather than statements, and which gives them a kind of monotony. But it seems to me that you are trying to express something of your own and that is why I am writing.

Some of the poems in free verse have interesting rhythms here and there and I hope you will go on practising both regular and irregular forms of metre.

Yours sincerely,
[T. S. Eliot]

1–Kathleen Nott (1905–99), poet, novelist, critic, editor and philosopher. At the time of this letter she was an Open Exhibitioner, studying first English and then PPE (Philosophy, Politics and Economics) at Somerville College, Oxford. In later years she published many book reviews and essays; she was editor for 27 years (1960–88) of the *Pen Bulletin of Selected Books* (later *Pen International*), and she was President of PEN for a year in 1975. She published her first novel, *Mile End*, in 1938; and a first volume of poetry, *Landscapes and Departures*, in 1947. A dedicated atheist and humanist – those who sought to disagree with her were dismissed as 'nincompoops' – she published in 1953 *The Emperor's Clothes: an attack on the dogmatic orthodoxy of T. S. Eliot, Graham Greene, Dorothy Sayers, C. S. Lewis and others*. She was President of the Progressive League, 1959–61; and an Hon. Associate of the Rationalist Press Association, 1979–99.

2–Nott had written in her undated letter that she had no '"view to publication" at least not at present, but I do badly need the sympathy of another poet & his point of view about them'. On 16 Nov. 1990 she wrote to Valerie Eliot, with reference to this letter of 9 June 1927: 'I thought Eliot's letter was mostly disparaging and perhaps bored. Now I see how thoughtful & helpful, even encouraging it was – as well as generous and kind.'

## TO *Bruce Richmond* CC

10 June 1927 [Eastbourne]

Dear Richmond,

I enclose my essay on Machiavelli[1] with apologies. Owing to my misunderstanding and the consequent rush to finish it, I am not very well satisfied with it myself. I only hope, however, that you will not find in it any statements contrary to the policy of *The Times*. But of course you can suppress or alter anything without consulting me. If *The Times* can send me proof on Saturday so as to reach me on Monday or even Tuesday morning they should be sent to me at

55 Meads Street,
Meads,
Eastbourne.

Yours sincerely,
[T. S. E.]

## TO *Herbert Read* CC

15 June 1927 [*The Monthly Criterion*]

My dear Read,

The enclosed Jesuit seems to me rather interesting though long,[2] and I should be very grateful if you would let me have your opinion some time next week. I suppose you are very busy now getting settled and so I shall not expect an immediate reply.[3]

Yours ever,
[T. S. E.]

1–'Nicolo Machiavelli (1469–1527)', *TLS*, 16 June 1927, 413–14. 'Last week's leader was extremely interesting,' wrote Richmond. 'I had a sort of feeling that it would make it look a little less ambitious, and would also give the gist of the article better, if I had called it Machiavelli and "Machiavellian"; but I hate doing these things without the writer's consent' (21 June).

2–M. C. D'Arcy, 'The Thomistic Synthesis and Intelligence', *MC* 6 (Sept. 1927), 210–28.

3–HR replied on 22 June: 'This is excellent, and almost does the job for us. It is a complete answer to Murry and I do not myself feel that there is much else to be said . . . This, I think, is better than Mauron, but Mauron is from another point of view, and still useful . . . I don't think you should let D'Arcy exempt you from an onslaught, but perhaps you will reserve your fire. Who is D'Arcy? He should be good for other things.' TSE printed his own reply to JMM in 'Mr Middleton Murry's Synthesis', *MC* 6 (Oct. 1927), 340–7 –

## TO *Arnold Bennett*

TS Beinecke

15 June 1927 *The Monthly Criterion*

Dear Mr Bennett,

Very many thanks for your kind letter of the 3rd which I would have answered sooner but that I have been very little in town during the last three weeks. I am rather glad that I did not send the letter to *The Standard*, and am quite satisfied by having shown it to you and by hearing from you that you do not disapprove.[1]

If you are in London I should very much like to see you. I am now up in town from Tuesday evening to Friday every week. It would be a great pleasure to see you again, and I should endeavour to break down your perfectly unreasonable modesty. Do you actually suppose that I myself have any exact knowledge of any subject on earth?[2] The only subject on which I pretend to know anything is English versification; and you know how to write novels which is at least as difficult.

Sincerely yours,
T. S. E.

---

about which HR wrote by letter on 16 Aug.: 'I have no criticisms to offer on "Mr Murry's Synthesis". I think it will do admirably & it will be amusing to see how (if at all) he wriggles out of the uncomfortable corner you have put him in. And he may begin to feel that your attack is getting rather savage, but perhaps you don't mind that.'

1–Bennett wrote that he was sorry TSE had not sent the letter [29 Apr. above] to the newspaper [*The Evening Standard*] 'as it was full of sense', but the right moment had passed.

2–'I would like to send you a contribution, but I am really afraid of doing so. I should have to take so much care over it! My articles, especially those about books, are rather slapdash. I am also handicapped by an intense ignorance. Indeed my life-long regret is that I have no exact knowledge on any subject on earth. I always envy scholars.' (*Letters of Arnold Bennett* III, ed. James Hepburn [1970], 286)

TO *Richard Aldington* CC

15 June 1927 [London]

My dear Richard,

I owe you many thanks for your criticism of Partridge's essay.[1] You have really taken infinitely more trouble over it than I should have dreamt of asking of you. Your erudition on this subject staggers me. I am completely ignorant of all this matter. In fact, as you ought to know, I have a smattering of a great many subjects and periods but an exact knowledge of none. I am trying to make myself rather more solid in England in the seventeenth century, in all the ramifications of literature, politics, philosophy and theology; but it will be a very long time before I can talk even of that subject and look anyone squarely in the face. My own feeling is that Classicism and Romanticism are terms which slip through our fingers like sand if one attempts to apply them like footrules to literature. They seem to me in a sense to be terms of political rather than critical or philosophical value; using the word 'political' in the widest possible sense. I think that there are, in a not very definite sense, classical and romantical points of view in general; but that one cannot use these terms of literature except when one is considering literature in all of its widest relations. If one uses them purely as aesthetic criteria, it is so apt to come down merely to distinction between good writing and bad writing, or honest writing and dishonest writing; and if so it is much better to call things by these names than to call them classic or romantic. Romance, on the other hand, seems to me to represent something definite and I like your distinction.

And when, if ever, are you likely to come to London?

Ever yours affectionately,
[Tom]

P.S. I almost forgot to mention something important. Your reviews are highly appreciated and I should be grateful for everything that you care to do. But our rates of payment are so poor that I only ask that you should review from time to time books that you really want to read and have not got from elsewhere. So I hope that you will occasionally be willing to make suggestions.

1–RA (10 June) thought Partridge's piece on the 'classiques attardés' too specialised. 'Romance (as distinct from Romanticism) is eternal in European literature, particularly French . . . Romanticism I am inclined to define as a more or less artificial revival of Romance, and so far from its beginning with Chateaubriand, one can trace it back before Rousseau to the earlier part of the century . . . Fundamentally, Classic and Romantic are points of view, and I doubt whether they have much meaning outside France.'

## TO *Orlo Williams*

CC

15 June 1927 [Eastbourne]

Dear Williams,

I trust that you have now returned to London. We were sorry you could not be present the other evening. I should like to know whether tomorrow week (the 23rd) is a possible date for you for dinner. If not, please let me know and we will try to change it. Thank you for your comments on the June number. I am going to write a short reply to Murry myself and try to get Read to write another; and Charles Mauron has sent in a very interesting rejoinder from his own point of view.[1]

I remember having seen an advertisement of Croce's *Autobiography* and have since been trying to trace it. Can you tell me who published it and I will try to get it for you.[2]

I confess that Angioletti's bookshop[3] had slipped my mind. My memory is that I promised to induce my people to let Angioletti have a dozen copies of each number on sale or return. Is this not it? I will raise the matter and meanwhile should be glad to have the address of the bookshop.

I have just sent you three numbers of *900*. They reached me by the hands of an American named Henry Furst who lives in Rome and seems to be in very close touch with that group, as he told me that he himself would write notices of *The Criterion* in *900*. He is returning to Rome shortly and assured me that he would see that future numbers reached us.

There are two questions I want to ask. One, may I send you Angioletti's *Settentrione* to translate? Two, would you be willing to do another novelist very soon in the same way as you handled Virginia Woolf? There are several fairly conspicuous people who have recently published new novels. Do you think that Edith Wharton is worth a long notice? I have just received a new book by her under the name of *Twilight Sleep*. If you like the subject I will send you the book; otherwise I await suggestions. I am more or less living at Eastbourne for the next month but am in town from Tuesday night to Friday night. Perhaps in any case you could come and lunch with me one day next week?

Ever yours,
[T. S. Eliot]

1 – Williams thought the second number 'good, though a little on the small side. I question whether the chance purchaser wouldn't think he wanted more for his 2/6. Middleton Murry's article seemed to me important, and I think it needs comment from other sources – an admirable basis for a symposium from English & foreign contributors.'

2 – Benedetto Croce, *Autobiography*, trans. R. G. Collingwood (1927).

3 – G. B. Angioletti had opened a bookshop, Libreria di Brera, in Milan.

## TO *Alec Randall* CC

15 June 1927 [*The Monthly Criterion*]

My dear Randall,

Many thanks for your letter of June 11th. You ask two questions. Of course I should be delighted to see anything you approved both by Italian and German writers. The famine of short fiction is dreadful, and I shall be very hard put to it to find twelve pieces of decent fiction per annum unless we can gather in all the best continental story writers as well as the native product. If you have anything in mind, do let me see it as soon as you can.

About the Dutch literature. I should very much like to use your Introduction, but there is the possibility of conflict and I think that we had better wait until you have seen the July number, of which I shall send you a copy as soon as it is available. Unfortunately we have got hold of a Dutchman who has done the Dutch Chronicle in that number; I am afraid he is rather long-winded and not as interesting to English readers as you would be; but there it is; so after you have seen the number you can judge for yourself whether we could use your Introduction as well.

Are you coming to England at all this summer?

Ever yours,
[T. S. Eliot]

## TO *Henry S. Canby*[1] CC

15 June 1927 [London]

Dear Mr Canby,

I must explain that I have been out of town and only read your letter today.[2] I should not have been able to accept your kind invitation in any case, as I had to attend a meeting, but I should very much like to see

1–Henry S. Canby (1878–1961), critic and editor. Having taught for over 20 years at Yale University, where he was the first professor to offer courses in American literature, and where he was assistant editor of the *Yale Review*, 1911–20, he was founder-editor of the *Literary Review* (*New York Evening Post*), 1920–4, and co-founded and edited the *Saturday Review of Literature*, 1924–36. In 1926 he became Chair of the newly founded Book-of-the-Month Club. His publications include *Classic Americans* (1931), *Thoreau: A Biography* (1939), *Walt Whitman, an American: A Study in Biography* (1943), *American Memoir* (1947) and *Turn West, Turn East: Mark Twain and Henry James* (1951); and he was co-editor of the *Literary History of the United States* (1948).

2–Canby had invited TSE to take tea at Rumpelmeyer's on the following Tuesday. IPF jotted on Canby's letter, 'thought it best to do nothing about this'.

you while you are in London. At present I am in town every week from Tuesday night to Friday night and if you are to be in London next week I wish you would let me know and we will see if we can arrange a meeting.

Yours sincerely,
[T. S. Eliot]

## TO *Abel Chevalley*[1] CC

16 June 1927 [London]

My dear Sir,

I was very much pleased to receive your letter of the 22nd May and I thank you for the gracious manner in which you accept my dissent.[2] We have many common friends and I cherish the hope of meeting you either in London or in Paris sooner or later. I am not likely to come to Paris this summer but it is possible that I may be there for a moment in September, or in the early autumn. If so, I shall endeavour to arrange a meeting with you and hope to find you there.

Yours very sincerely,
[T. S. Eliot]

1–Abel Chevalley (1868–1934): French writer and critic, based in Paris; author of *The Modern English Novel* (New York, 1925).

2–Chevalley wrote on 22 May: 'J'ai été fort sensible à la façon courtoise dont vous différez avec moi dans la *N. R. F.* C'est plaisir d'être ainsi contredit.' TSE claimed, in 'Le roman anglais contemporain' (*NRF* 164 [1927], 670), that contemporary novels seemed to lack what Henry James had praised in his book on Nathaniel Hawthorne, and which James himself 'so preeminently' possessed: the 'deeper psychology' and the 'moral interest': 'I am aware . . . that in my opinion of Henry James I come into conflict with so distinguished an authority as M. Abel Chevalley. Were M. Chevalley alone in his opinion, I should consider it great temerity to disagree with him. Not only is M. Chevalley as thoroughly documented as any English critic; but a foreign critic with so much knowledge of the language and literature, and with the acumen and judgment which M. Chevalley displays elsewhere, is quite likely to have perceptions, and a line of reasoning starting from a new angle of vision, which will render him decidedly formidable. But in this case M. Chevalley's opinion happens to be, in general, the opinion of that of most English and American critics of Henry James; so that he raises no objection for which I am unprepared.'

## TO *Orlo Williams* CC

16 June 1927 [*The Monthly Criterion*]

Dear Williams,

Thank you for your letter. Unfortunately I am engaged for lunch on the 22nd and may be going down to Oxford for the night. I will send you a line or a wire next week. However, I shall try to change the date of the dinner from the 23rd to the 30th and hope that you will keep that date open.

I am sending you the Angioletti MS and will communicate with him as soon as you can let me have his address.[1]

About Edith Wharton. I should like if possible to have either that or some novel review from you for the September number, that is to say by July 16th. Perhaps that hardly gives you time to deal with Edith Wharton properly, especially as I suppose that the House will be sitting until the end of the month. Would you like to postpone Mrs Wharton until the late autumn, and meanwhile is there any other novel (or novels) which you could do with less trouble for the September number?[2]

With many thanks,
Ever yours,
[T. S. Eliot]

P.S. I should like to have your next report on periodicals by October 1st, for the December number. Is that all right?

## TO *James Smith* CC

16 June 1927 [*The Monthly Criterion*]

Dear Smith,

Excellent. Your review of Bosanquet is much longer than I expected, but after all Bosanquet is worth it and the review itself is very interesting. I hope to use it in the September number, appearing towards the end of August, but will let you know definitely later.[3] Meanwhile, and for that

1–G. B. Angioletti's *Settentrione*. See 'A Northerner', trans. Orlo Williams, *MC* 6 (Nov. 1927), 426–30.

2–Williams wrote on Romer Wilson's novel *Latterday Symphony*, *MC* 6 (Sept. 1927), 277–81; then on Edith Wharton's *Twilight Sleep*, *MC* 6 (Nov. 1927), 440–5.

3–Untitled review of Bernard Bosanquet, *Science and Philosophy and Other Essays*, *MC* 6 (Nov. 1927), 445–8.

purpose, please let me know what your address will be when you leave Cambridge.

Sincerely yours,
[T. S. Eliot]

## TO *Laura Riding*

CC

16 June 1927 [*The Monthly Criterion*]

Dear Miss Riding,

I am returning your interesting prose essays with much regret. In the first place they are too long for inclusion in *The Criterion* and it would be a pity to mutilate them for that purpose. And in the second place I am afraid that they are not closely enough in relation to the point of view of *The Criterion* and its principal collaborators. I hope that these essays will take their place, as they ought to do, in a book, and that this book will appear very soon.

Yours sincerely,
[T. S. Eliot]

## TO *Märit Scheler*[1]

CC

16 June 1927 [*The Monthly Criterion*]

My dear Madam,

I have to thank you for your letter of the 13th instant and learn with much pleasure that I may expect from Professor Scheler a part of his *Anthropologie*.[2] I understand that Professor Scheler will have this translated in Cologne and therefore I propose, when it is published, to send him full payment without deduction, and leave it to him to arrange to compensate the translator.

I should like to be able to publish Professor Scheler's essay before the end of 1927 and should therefore be grateful if I might receive it as soon as possible.[3]

1 – Märit Furtwängler, who became Scheler's second wife in 1912, was a sister of the conductor Wilhelm Furtwängler.

2 – Mrs Scheler reported that TSE's approach was opportune, since 'a treatise of "The Future of Man" could easily be excerpted' from her husband's most recent notes on 'anthropology', which had not yet been published. Scheler wished to have the essay (*c.* 5,500–6,000 words) translated by an American 'disciple' in Cologne.

3 – Max Scheler, 'Future of Man', trans. Howard Becker, *MC* 7 (Feb. 1928), 100–19.

With many thanks,
I remain,
Your obedient servant,
[T. S. Eliot]

## TO *Charles Mauron*[1] CC

Le 16 Juin 1927 [London]

Cher Monsieur,

J'ai lu avec un grand intérêt et beaucoup de plaisir vos notes sur L'Intuition. Je serai très heureux de faire paraître une traduction de ces notes dans *The Criterion*. Je propose même d'y publier des notes par plusieurs personnes, y compris Mr Herbert Read et moi-même, des notes qui entameront la question de plusieurs points de vue. Malheureusement les feuilles du *Criterion* sont prises par des contributions longtemps acceptées pendant deux mois; mais j'espère présenter à notre publique les divers reponses à Mr Murry dans le numéro de septembre.[2] Je ne manquerai point de vous écrire plus tard.

En me félicitant sur votre collaboration et en vous exprimant toute ma sympathie, je vous prie, cher Monsieur, d'agréer à l'expression de mes sentiments les plus distingués,

[T. S. Eliot]

P.S. Est-ce que vous revenez à Paris pendant l'été? Il est possible que je passerai à Paris pendant le mois de septembre, et je tiendrai beaucoup à vous faire la connaissance.[3]

1–Charles Mauron (1899–1966) trained as a chemist but suffered from increasingly impaired eyesight. Author of *The Nature of Beauty in Art and Literature*, trans. Roger Fry (Hogarth, 1927), he translated into French VW's *To the Lighthouse* and *Orlando*, and collaborated with Fry on translations from Mallarmé. His later works include *Aesthetics and Psychology* (1935) and *Des métaphores obsédantes au mythe personnel* (1962).

2–'Concerning "Intuition"', trans. TSE – a reply to JMM's 'Towards a Synthesis', *MC* 5 (June 1927), 294–313 – appeared in *MC* 6 (Sept. 1927), 229–35.

3–*Translation*: Dear Sir, I have read your notes on Intuition with great interest and much pleasure. I shall be very happy to publish a translation of these notes in *The Criterion*. In fact, I intend to publish notes by several people, including Mr Herbert Read and myself, notes which will broach the question from several points of view. Unfortunately, during the next two months, all the space in *The Criterion* will be taken up by contributions accepted

## TO *Ferdinando Garibaldi* CC

16 June 1927 [Faber & Gwyer Ltd]

My dear Sir,

I thank you most cordially for your kind and appreciative letter and also for your more than generous notice of my work.[1] If I say no more about it than this, it is because I consider that I am hardly qualified to criticise criticism of my own work; nevertheless, it seems to me that you have grasped perfectly my intention in *The Sacred Wood* and your reservations and criticisms seem to me wholly justified.

I am sending you a copy of the last number of *The Monthly Criterion* and I am trying to obtain for you a copy of the number containing my *Four Elizabethan Dramatists* for which you ask.

Yours very truly,
[T. S. Eliot]

## TO *Charles du Bos*[2] CC

16 June 1927 [*The Monthly Criterion*]

My dear Du Bos,

I am very much touched and flattered by receiving your second *Approximations* with the inscription which gives it a very great personal value to me. I know quite well that your words about my Baudelaire and about my essay on Dante and Donne are excessive; nevertheless, I cannot help feeling deeply gratified by such words coming from yourself. I expect to read the second series with the same interest and excitement with which I read the whole of the first series.

---

some time ago; but I hope to present our public with the various replies to Mr Murry in the September issue. I shall not fail to write to you again later.

I am delighted to have you as a contributor. With warmest regards. Yours sincerely [T. S. Eliot]

P.S. Are you coming up to Paris during the summer? I may be passing through Paris in September and should very much like to make your acquaintance.

1 – Garibaldi had written from Genoa (6 June), enclosing a copy of his review of *The Sacred Wood*: 'T. S. Eliot', *Il Grido d'Italia*, 5 June 1927. 'Ed Eliot e maestro in quest'analisi di lingua, di stile, nel saper indicare per cascun poeta o scrittore il modo particolare di guardar le cose a l'abito di ritrarle.'

2 – Charles du Bos (1882–1939), French critic of French and English literature – his mother was English, and he studied at Oxford – wrote one review for C. in 1935.

This is all very well, but I must take the opportunity of reminding you that you promised me a year ago, when we talked on your balcony, and that you had as a matter of fact promised me several years before that, some critical essay for the *Criterion*. We had in mind an essay on some personage or aspect of English literature which you know so well, but I assure you that any *inédit* of yours would be equally welcome. You are rather a rare author; but after two series of *Approximations* in French can you not let me have one Approximation in English.

With kind regards to Madame Du Bos and yourself,

I am,
Yours sincerely,
[T. S. Eliot]

## TO *H. S. Horne* CC

16 June 1927 [*The Monthly Criterion*]

My dear Horne,

New Criterion Ltd

I wrote to you on March 23rd enclosing a copy of an audit statement which we, acting on behalf of The New Criterion Limited, got from Cobden-Sanderson. Did you ever receive this?

The point is: The New Criterion Ltd took over the liability for unexpired subscriptions to the old *Criterion*. The total amount of these was £34.7.2. In other words *The New Criterion Ltd* was owed this amount by the proprietor of *The Criterion* – namely Lady Rothermere.

The difficulty was to get Cobden-Sanderson to wind up his accounts; and until that was done it was impossible to say how much money was available in the old *Criterion* banking account to discharge this debt.

When I wrote to you on March 23rd it appeared from the audit statement I sent you that the balance due from Lady Rothermere to The New Criterion Ltd., after using up the old *Criterion* balance, was £21.2.7½.

But we have heard from Cobden-Sanderson that his Accountants made an error and included a sum of £6.3.4. in the 'cash at bank' which ought not to have been included; and further that he has spent a further 5/10 on sundry items. And he has sent us cheques totalling £6.15.4. – this being the whole of the amount remaining to the credit of the Old Criterion Account. These we are paying at once into The New Criterion Limited account.

The position then is now: of the £34.7.2. owing to The New Criterion Limited, £6.15.4. has been paid. The balance of £27.11.10 is owing by Lady Rothermere to the New Criterion Limited. This is £6.9.2. more than the figure given in my letter of March 23rd – the difference being made up by the accountant's error of £6.3.4. and Cobden-Sanderson's additional expenditure of 5/10.

I shall be grateful if you can, acting for Lady Rothermere, discharge this account, and enable us to get this troublesome matter out of the way.

Yours ever,
[T. S. Eliot]

P.S. I enclose copies of the 2 letters from Cobden-Sanderson and one letter from the Accountants to C.S. which will explain the matter more fully.

## *I. P. Fassett* TO *H. P. Collins* CC

17 June 1927 [Faber & Gwyer Ltd]

Dear Sir,

Mr Eliot has asked me to write to you about the stories of Mrs Wilkinson which were sent to Messrs Faber and Gwyer for consideration.

The stories were considered with great care and the directors thought them very good and were tempted to accept them for publication; but they finally decided that they must stand by their decision not to publish books of short stories for which there seems to be so little demand. This decision has been communicated to Mrs Wilkinson.

Mr Eliot read the stories himself and found one or two which he would be glad to use in *The Criterion*. He liked particularly 'Lombard [*sc.* Locust] Street' and has written to Mrs Wilkinson to say that he would like to print it during the current year if she will agree to one or two suggestions concerning it. He hopes to hear from her that she will agree to this,[1] and meanwhile the whole MS of the book is retained in this office.

Yours faithfully,
[I. P. Fassett]
Secretary.

1 – Frances Gregg, 'Locust Street', *MC* 6 (Sept. 1927), 206–9.

## TO *Montgomery Belgion*[1] CC

17 June 1927 [*The Monthly Criterion*]

My dear Mr Belgion,

I owe you very many apologies.[2] The matter of Fernandez' book has been constantly in my mind and has as constantly escaped my mind at the moments when I could and should have wired to you. I expect that you will be more than annoyed with me and to such annoyance I can oppose nothing but meekness and humility. I was at the moment far too busy to undertake such a review; but I should have been glad to do it both because Fernandez is my personal friend and because you asked me; I therefore postponed replying for a few days in the hope that I might have more leisure; and so my downfall began. I suppose that it is now too late for me to be of any use in advertising the book in America, and I presume that some other critic has already reviewed it in the paper in question. If you know of any paper in America in which a review of the book would still be useful, I should be glad to do it.

I have probably no need to remind you of Fernandez' forthcoming book on *Personality*. He has read me some parts of that book and I am sure that it will be a more important work than *Messages*.[3] I venture to hope that you may translate it; and I should very much like myself to write a review of it.

I regret very much that I missed you in London and hope for the opportunity of making your acquaintance at a later date.

Yours very truly,
[T. S. Eliot]

<I am returning by money order the 1/8d which you left at the office for a telegram.>

1 – Montgomery ('Monty') Belgion (1892–1973), author: see Biographical Register.

2 – Belgion had asked TSE on 25 Mar. to review Ramon Fernandez's *Messages* (which Belgion had translated) for the *New York Herald-Tribune Books*.

3 – *Messages: première série* (Paris: Gallimard, 1926).

## TO *Virginia Woolf*

TS Berg

Tuesday [21 June 1927] *The Monthly Criterion*]

Dear Virginia,

May I come to Tea with you one day next week?

Yours etc.
T.

P.S. Have just been to see Ernie Lotinga[1] in his new Play at the Islington Empire. Magnificent. He is the greatest living British histrionic Artist, in the purest tradition of British Obscenity.[2] How did I get in? As I heard a Lady say a few days ago at the Kings Arms at 11.25 a.m.: 'I just Ambled in Unconscious.'[3]

## TO *Bonamy Dobrée*

TS Brotherton

22 June 1927 24 Russell Square

Dear Bungamy,

To await yr return Please let me know by Telephone Museum 9543 of your Return Should be glad to see You but I Warn you there is going to be troubble [*sic*] over that Crocodile.

Yours ever,
T. S. Eliot.

P. S. Since I Last Wrote I have much more Information about the theology of the primitive Bolovians (a race of comic Negroes wearing bowler Hats – why did they wear bowler Hats – that I will Tell you – because their

1–Ernie Lotinga (1876–1951), variety artist, was appearing in *Convicts*, a burlesque melodrama by Norman Lee.

2–In 'A Dialogue on Poetic Drama' (1928) TSE's character 'C' claims that 'Restoration comedy . . . is a great tribute to Christian morality. Take the humour of our great English comedian, Ernie Lotinga. It is (if you like) bawdy. But such bawdiness is a tribute to, an acknowledgement of conventional British morality . . . what I was saying is that our suburban drama is morally sound, and out of such soundness poetry may come' (xviii).

Jack Isaacs related: 'Mr Eliot had written his first dramatic piece, *Sweeney Agonistes: Fragments of an Aristophanic Melodrama*. He had had his Comic Purgation, and was feeling good. So the tone of his "Dialogue" seems to imply. Whether this purgation came directly from Aristophanes or indirectly from Ernie Lotinga, who is not only bawdy, but a direct descendant of the phallic comedy of Greece and Rome, I do not know. This I do know, that if I have done nothing else for literature, I did at least take Mr. Eliot to see Mr. Ernie Lotinga at the Islington Empire' (*An Assessment of Twentieth-Century Literature:* Six Lectures Delivered on the BBC Third Programme [1951], 147).

3–TSE uses this locution when he has Mrs Ethelbert say in *The Rock* (1934), when Bert asks how she got into the church: 'Oh, I just ambled in unconscious' (65–6).

Monarch wore a top hat) they were divided into monophysites, duophysites, hecastophysites and heterophysites. (Also I have discovered the text and tune of their National Anthem, which I have learned to Sing.[)]

## TO *Bertrand Russell* TS McMaster

22 June 1927 24 Russell Square

My dear Bertie,

Thank you for your letter and undertaking, which seems to me quite to cover the case. If it makes any difference to you, I may say that this transfer is now not only satisfactory to Vivien's of course entirely morbid conscience, but, what is in a sense more important, to my own. Her father has recently died, so that she will shortly come into possession of property yielding income almost, if not quite, equal to that she is surrendering. And I [am] myself influenced by the fact (whatever you[r] original idea, which I do not know) that you have heirs,[1] and I have, and shall have, none.[2] There are a good many other (if somewhat adulterated) breeds of Eliot. But I do not know of any other actual breeds of Russell. Also, I shall be able to express more freely my opinion of Henry VIII.

The delay is wholly due to the necessity of my finding some £35 to finance the transaction. Any further detail will be due to the same cause.

I have just read your little pamphlet on Christianity.[3] With some sadness. All the reasons you advance were familiar to me, *I think*, at the age of six or eight; and I confess that your pamphlet seems to me a piece of childish folly. But I was brought up as an Atheist, and you were evidently brought up, and in my opinion remain, an Evangelical. Why don't you stick to mathematics?

Believe me,
Ever yours affectionately,
T. S. Eliot

1–John Conrad Russell was born in 1921, Katharine Jane in 1923.

2–TSE told John Hayward on 29 Nov. 1939 that he sometimes felt 'acutely the desire for progeny, which was a very acute one' (King's).

3–See TSE on BR's pamphlet *Why I Am Not a Christian* (1927) – a 'curious, and a pathetic, document' – *MC* 6 (Aug. 1927), 177–9: 'Mr Russell is essentially a low Churchman, and only by caprice can call himself an Atheist . . . Just as Mr Russell's Radicalism in politics is merely a variety of Whiggery, so his Non-Christianity is merely a variety of Low Church sentiment . . . And his pamphlet is undoubtedly one of the curiosities of literature.'

Sencourt noted of TSE: 'He said at another time that he was driven to belief by seeing agnosticism pushed to its limits by Bertrand Russell, who, though so good a friend, was never his guide as a metaphysician' (*T. S. Eliot*, 132–3).

## TO *Archibald MacLeish* CC

23 June 1927 [London]

Dear MacLeish,

I am glad to hear from you.[1] Please send me your poem as soon as it is ready. It would not matter in the least if you made separate arrangements for publication in America, only of course if we published it here it would be as well from every point of view, to arrange publication as nearly simultaneous as possible. I gather that you do not expect to have it ready for several months, so please do not forget.[2]

Thank you for your interest in my translation of *Anabase*. I am glad you like the original. My translation is practically ready and is to be published here as a small book; I dare say that sheets will be sold to some American publishing firm.[3] But it has been held up now for about nine months merely because Léger is too busy even to look at an agreement or to let me have his own criticism of my translation; and I do not wish to publish it without. It is possible that in the meantime I may publish one or two sections of the poem in *The Criterion*.[4] I will see that you get your copies when it appears.[5]

Sincerely yours,
[T. S. Eliot]

## TO *Ramon Fernandez* CC

23 June 1927 [*The Monthly Criterion*]

My dear Fernandez,

I have not heard from you for a long time and I do not think that you answered my last letter, but I understand that you are at the moment in Paris. I should like to know whether all of your previous suggestions for essays have fallen through and also I have another suggestion to make.

1–MacLeish said (4 June) he was working on 'a single poem' (*The Hamlet of Archibald MacLeish*) which he hoped to finish in the fall: he would be happy to offer it to F & G.
2–TSE was to write in his reader's report on *The Hamlet of Archibald MacLeish*, 30 Dec. 1927: 'This poem has on the whole disappointed me after MacLeish's earlier work, and a good deal of it seems to me to be a pastiche of Ezra Pound and myself. But partly for this reason I should like to have another opinion before returning it' (Faber Misc 5/3).
3–Saint-John Perse, *Anabasis: A Poem*, trans. TSE (1930). The first US edition, revised and corrected by TSE, was published by Harcourt, Brace & Company, 1938.
4–'From *Anabase*', trans. TSE, *MC* 7 (Feb. 1928), 137–8.
5–MacLeish, who found Léger 'magnificent', ordered three copies of TSE's translation.

I am collecting a few replies or comments, mostly as brief as possible, on Middleton Murry's article in the June number; and I hope to publish these comments all together. They will not be anything in the nature of a concerted attack but will merely be independent opinions of people with various points of view. As your name occurs rather frequently in that article and as you are quite entitled to feel that your thought has been travestied by me if not by Murry, I should be delighted if you cared to add a few pages yourself to the debate. It is an interesting subject and I am sure that the readers of *The Criterion* will consider themselves defrauded without a contribution from yourself.[1]

Do let me hear from you in any case.

Sincerely yours,
[T. S. Eliot]

P.S. When is the book on Personality coming out?[2]

## TO *R. Gordon George* CC

23 June 1927 [*The Monthly Criterion*]

Dear George,

I am very sorry to be going out of town, particularly as I shall be away for most of the time during the next three weeks and I am not at all certain on what days I shall be in London.[3] I am coming up next week but shall probably go straight to Oxford.[4] I should like to see you, but the best I can do is to wait and try to get hold of you when I know that I shall be in town. Do let me know how long you are to be here. I hope you enjoyed seeing Fernandez and Maritain.

Ever yours,
[T. S. Eliot]

1 – Fernandez said (25 June) he would be delighted to contribute to the debate: see 'A Note on Intelligence and Intuition', trans. TSE, *MC* 6 (Oct. 1927), 332–9.
2 – Fernandez's book had been delayed because of 'technical problems'.
3 – George wrote (21 June) that he was coming to London: would TSE like to have lunch at the Rembrandt Hotel on Tues., 29 June?
4 – To be received into the Church of England: TSE was not telling.

## TO *Rev. M. C. D'Arcy*[1] CC

24 June 1927 [*The Monthly Criterion*]

My dear Sir,

I find your reply to Mr Middleton Murry extremely interesting and hope to be able to publish it in the near future.[2] I am all the more glad to have it as I hope to publish several essays discussing Mr Murry's problems from various points of view.

You shall receive proof in due course.

Yours faithfully,
[T. S. Eliot]

## TO *S. S. Koteliansky* TS BL

24 June 1927 Faber & Gwyer Ltd

My dear Koteliansky,

Your 'Dostoevsky' has been worrying me a good deal and I am afraid that I have lingered an unforgivably long time over it. I am very much tempted but it would be a very difficult matter. I have just realised that you are anxious to get it published in the next few months; owing to one or two controversies which have brought in a great deal of new material which I must print as quickly as possible I find that I could not even begin to use it before the end of the year. And even so, it would, I think, have to be spread over three or four numbers. It seems quite impossible and at any rate it would be a great pity to print part and not the whole, and of course it really ought to be printed as a small book. But I think you have other Dostoevsky material as well, and intended to make a book of the whole. May I suggest such a book to my firm?

I shall hardly be in London at all during the next two weeks, but as soon as I am back with a few clear days ahead I will drop you a line and hope you will come to lunch again.

Sincerely yours,
T. S. Eliot

1–Martin D'Arcy (1888–1976), Jesuit priest and theologian: see Biographical Register.
2–Fr. D'Arcy wrote on 10 June: 'The subject is your own affair really, but I think you may not be averse to a third party joining in.'

## TO *The Under Secretary of State, The Home Office* CC

24 June 1927 [London]

Reference 412614/2

Sir,

Referring to your letter of the 19th May and our subsequent telephone conversation I have the honour to hand you herewith a declaration by Mr F. S. Flint of The Ministry of Labour to supply the previous declaration by Mr Charles Haigh-Wood deceased. I should be glad to know from you whether the matter is now quite in order.

I have the honour to be, Sir,

Your obedient servant,

[T. S. Eliot]

## TO *W. Force Stead* MS Beinecke

1 July 1927 *The Monthly Criterion*

My dear Stead,[1]

Besides my gratitude for the serious business & the perfect way you managed every part of it, I must say how thoroughly I enjoyed my visit to you, and meeting several extremely interesting & delightful people.

1 – WFS noted on this letter: 'Time of Eliot's Confirmation which I arranged privately at the Bishop's Palace Cuddesdon.' TSE was baptised by WFS at Holy Trinity Church on 29 June; the next day, he was confirmed by the Bishop of Oxford at Cuddesdon. WFS wrote in his memoir, 'Mr Stead Presents An Old Friend' – published as 'Some Personal Reminiscences of T. S. Eliot', *Alumni Journal of Trinity College, Washington*, 38: 2 (Winter 1965) – 'I was living then at Finstock, a small village far away in the country, with Wychwood Forest stretching off to the north, and the lonely Cotswold hills all round. Eliot came down from London for a day or two, and I summoned from Oxford Canon B. H. Streeter, Fellow and later Provost of Queen's College, and Vere Somerset, History Tutor and Fellow of Worcester College. These were his Godfathers. It seemed off to have such a large though infant Christian at the baptismal font, so, to avoid embarrassment; we locked the front door of the little parish church and posted the verger on guard in the vestry. My three guests remained for the night, and after dinner we went for a twilight walk through Wychwood, an ancient haunted forest, "savage and enchanted". I can see Eliot pacing under the mighty oaks and pushing his way through hazel thickets attired in a smart suit, a bowler hat, and grey spats. Maybe he was not wearing spats; it was in the summer, but Cotswold evenings can be damp and chilly even in midsummer. Six months later he was confirmed privately in the Palace at Cuddesdon by the Bishop of Oxford.' TSE wrote on Stead's typescript, against the last sentence: 'Here you are quite out. *It was the next morning*! Very lax of Tommy Strong, no doubt. But I have heard of similar goings-on in *your* church too.'

TSE was to write in 1932: 'the Christian scheme seemed the only possible scheme which found a place for values which I must maintain or perish (and belief comes first and practice

The enclosed letter shows warm appreciation of your kindness, I think.[1]

Ever yours most gratefully
T. S. Eliot
(In haste)

## TO *Thomas Sturge Moore* MS Texas

9 July 1927 *The Monthly Criterion*

Dear Mr Sturge Moore,

Very many thanks for your extremely interesting essay.[2] I have been deliberating. In the September number, I am publishing several 'replies' to Murry that have come in. They are rather long, & I feel that I ought to say something myself, as he does not understand my position & I do not understand his (by the way, I wonder if *he* did Fr. Brown in *The Times*). So that no. is quite full. But your essay seems to me more an independent essay merely *suggested* by Murry, so I wonder if you would let me use it a month or two later?

When are you going to publish a book? I wonder if you would let Faber & Gwyer consider it?

Yours very sincerely
T. S. Eliot

---

second), the belief, for instance, in holy living and holy dying, in sanctity, chastity, humility, austerity' ('The Modern Mind', *The Listener*, 16 Mar. 1932, 383). He was alluding to the devotional works of Bishop Jeremy Taylor (1613–67): *The Rule and Exercises of Holy Living* (1650) and *The Rule and Exercises of Holy Dying* (1651). On 6 Dec. 1932 he informed Sister Mary James Power, SSND: 'I am associated with what is called the Catholic movement in [the Church of England], as represented by Viscount Halifax and the English Church Union. I accordingly believe in the Creeds, the invocation of the Blessed Virgin and the Saints, the Sacrament of Penance etc.' And in 1948 he would say: 'the convert – and I think not only of conversion from one form of Christianity to another, but indeed primarily of conversion from indifference to Christian belief and practice – the convert of the intellectual or sensitive type is drawn towards the more Catholic type of worship and doctrine. This attraction . . . may occur before the convert has begun to inform himself about Christianity at all' (*NTDC*, 80). On 20 June 1963 he would write, in some ts notes about Northrop Frye's book on himself: 'I joined the Church of England in 1927, but only became interested in Anglo-Catholic practices and opinion later. One does not *join* an Anglo-Catholic wing!'

VHE was not present at either ceremony. TSE would write to HWE on 1 Jan. 1936: 'I remember quite clearly that when, in 1927, I was received into the Anglican communion, baptised at Finstock and confirmed at Cuddesdon, I made it as secret as possible. It did . . . occur to me (and I was right) that it might provide a fresh reason for domestic persecution.'

1 – This private and personal letter of gratitude has not been traced.

2 – 'Towards Simplicity'.

## TO *Geoffrey Faber* MS Valerie Eliot

Tuesday [12 July 1927] 55 Meads Street, Eastbourne

Dear Geoffrey,

I shall make every effort to be present on the 18th especially as I am now qualified (in status if not in moral worth) for such an office.[1] But will you drop me a line to say exactly where Hmpstd Parish Church is, so that I may not be late. Meanwhile my best wishes to Thomas and his mother.

In haste,
Yours ever
T. S. E.

## TO *Roger Hinks* CC

21 July 1927 [*The Monthly Criterion*]

My dear Hinks,

Here is another heavy book which ought to be saleable in the Charing Cross Road if you don't want it. Many thanks for your note on Roger Fry's book which I shall use.[2] Your short note on Walston's books suggests that they are hardly worth notice.[3] I shall continue to send books as they come in, but please understand that I leave it entirely to your discretion whether they are worth notice at all. Sometimes when there is nothing else to talk about you may be able to use a book or books in your Art Chronicle. Sometimes when they don't fit in they are worth a separate note; but I am afraid the majority should be ignored. This *Cambridge Ancient History* looks as if it was worth a half page notice.[4]

If you are in town next week we might meet for lunch.

Yours ever,
[T. S. E.]

1–TSE was to be a godparent at the christening of Tom Faber (b. 25 Apr. 1927), which ultimately took place on 27 July. GCF noted in his diary: 'Eliot came up afterwards, & Thomas Erle was duly baptized by the Vicar Carnegie, in the Parish Church, present Godfather T. S. Eliot & godmother Frances Duke, the other godfather Eric Beckett being in Geneva. Afterwards a (to me) rather tedious Christening party.'

2–Untitled review of Roger Fry, *Flemish Art*, *MC* 6 (Oct. 1927), 372–4.

3–Not published.

4–Hinks (27th) passed the *Ancient History* to Humfrey Payne; Hinks had already reviewed it, adversely, for *The Observer*.

## TO *Messrs Parnell & Co.*

CC

21 July 1927 [London]

Dear Sirs,

On receiving the bound volumes of *The Criterion* from you yesterday afternoon, I was exceedingly annoyed to find that, contrary to the explicit instructions of my secretary, the original rough edges had been trimmed.

The delay is causing me great inconvenience, but the only thing to be done is for you to have bound, as quickly as possible, the further copies which accompany this note. *Please see that the covers are bound in, and that the edges remain exactly as they are now with rough edges.*

My secretary tells me that she took great trouble to explain exactly how I wished this work to be done, and furthermore that she told you that in the event of any difficulty in carrying out the work she was to be informed before commencement. In the circumstances I cannot understand why my instructions were disregarded.

Please return the copies of which you have had the edges cut to me in due course.

Yours truly,
[T. S. Eliot]

## TO *E. R. Curtius*

CC

22 July 1927 [London]

My dear Curtius,

I have to apologise for the delay about your article. I only got back to town on the 20th and sent you a wire that night but I gather from your card that the wire missed you. I will therefore repeat that I shall be delighted to use your article and have no objection to its simultaneous publication in Germany and Spain;[1] more especially as it is the sort of article which particularly ought to reach an international public. I shall write to Stewart whom I remember meeting a few years ago to ask him to undertake the translation.[2] As far as I can at present foresee I expect to be

1–Curtius, 'Restauration der Vernunft', *Neue Schweizer Rundschau*, Sept. 1927; 'Restauración de la razón', *Revista da Occidente*, Sept. 1927.

2–Curtius said of the article he had just submitted to *The Criterion* 'on a sudden whim' that it would not be easy to translate. 'I would therefore like to entrust it to a translator that I know personally and hold in very high esteem both as a person and as an intellectual. His name is William Stewart, he was an English lector at the École Normale and now teaches French at the University of Sheffield.'

able to print it in the November number, and I will let you know definitely as soon as possible.[1]

I wish that I might be coming to Paris or that you might prolong your travels as far as London.

Ever yours cordially,
[T. S. Eliot]

## TO *Thomas McGreevy* TS TCD

22 July 1927 *The Monthly Criterion*

My dear McGreevy,

I would have answered your letter sooner but I have been away in the country and deliberately neglected all correspondence.

First, I say Yes to the notice of O'Flaherty for some time early next year.[2] Before that I should like to suggest that you do something about Gide. I sent you the *Journal des Faux-Monnayeurs*;[3] the *Faux-Monnayeurs* itself I have not had, but if you can pick up a copy in Paris I should suggest doing a more or less comprehensive study of 1500 words or so on Gide with special reference to his latest work. Let me know what you think of this.

I wonder from your postcard whether you are conducting tourists or are at Grenoble in some other capacity.[4] Had I been able to offer any lucrative American tourist I should have done so at once; you may be sure that if I hear of any I will try to send them in your direction; but the majority of my own American acquaintance is not, when it travels,

1–'Restoration of the Reason', trans. William Stewart, *MC* 6 (Nov. 1927), 389–97: 'We must learn again the art of directing our emotional states by means of a conscious will . . . [N]eo-classicism or neo-Thomism, and such like, are merely specimens of local carpentry . . . But to linger an instant longer over these examples – both these things, neo-classicism and neo-Thomism – become generally useful, applicable and of real moment and actuality if we set aside their peculiar historical forms – their husk as it were – and get at their essence: the organization of the human domain by means of Reason that assigns values, imposes standards, decides and directs . . . Our task is – not to resuscitate these forms artificially, but to revive the spirit which created them, and so to create a form of Reason proper to the 20th century. Only so will we overcome the various types of radicalism (unfruitful as they are, by definition) and attain that objective which is the most important of all to-day: the reconstruction of the European man' (389, 396).

2–McGreevy asked (21 June) whether he might 'do a kind of comprehensive review of Liam O'Flaherty's books . . . like the one that Dobrée did in the *Criterion* some time ago'.

3–André Gide, *Journal des faux-monnayeurs* ('Logbook of the Coiners') (1927).

4–McGreevy answered from the Hotel de l'Europe, Grenoble (8 Aug.), 'Yes, I am touristing here.'

in a position to afford itself the luxury of a dragoman, even with the additional attraction of its being yourself.

I do hope that you will be able to get another year in Paris. I do not suppose that a word from me would carry any weight in that quarter but I am at your disposal. If and when you are passing through London, try to let me know in advance.

Sincerely yours,
T. S. Eliot

## TO *R. L. Mégroz* — TS Reading

25 July 1927 — *The Monthly Criterion*

Dear Mr Mégroz,

Your book on Francis Thompson has not been overlooked and it is specially suitable for review in the *Criterion.*[1] As a matter of fact it has been reviewed and the notice is in type, but owing to the necessities of fitting in material to make not more than 96 pages each month it has had to be postponed. But I hope to use it soon. I hope you will not mind my saying that it seems to me a very much better book indeed than your book on the Sitwells. I hope at some moment of leisure to read it thoroughly myself.[2]

Yours sincerely
T. S. Eliot

## TO *Arnold Bennett* — TS Beinecke

25 July 1927 — [London]

My dear Bennett,

I must apologise for not having answered your letter sooner. I was away in the country; your letter, but not the manuscript, was forwarded

1–R. L. Mégroz's *Francis Thompson: The Poet of Earth in Heaven: A Study in Poetic Mysticism* (F&G, 1927) was reviewed in *MC* 6 (Oct. 1927), 375–6: 'Mr Mégroz has given us a curious mixture of astute and useful criticism with much trite generalization . . . The critic is indignant that Thompson should be regarded as an artist of arrested development, and insists on his being judged as a complete man delivering a masculine and detached judgment . . . But . . . when he forgets his special pleading and gives himself to pure enjoyment of Thompson's powerful but narcotic genius, then indeed he speaks with real insight.'

2–Mégroz replied, 'what you say of the impression you yourself have of the book is one of the best of rewards for such unprofitable labour!' (28 July).

to me; and I thought it would be an impertinence to write to you definitely about it until I had read it myself. My reply, however, is the same as it would have been had I written without seeing the manuscript; I am delighted and honoured to have it and should like to publish it in three parts beginning with our October number. Will you allow me to divide it into approximately three equal parts, or would you prefer to indicate the divisions yourself?[1]

I am writing primarily as Editor, congratulating myself on the receipt of something which will add to the prestige of my magazine; but I should like also to say that I very much enjoyed reading *The Journal*.

With many thanks,

Yours sincerely,
T. S. Eliot

## TO *Nancy Pearn* CC

25 July 1927 [*The Monthly Criterion*]

Dear Miss Pearn,

Thank you for sending me the 'Flowery Tuscany' of D. H. Lawrence. I should like very much to use it and it is merely a question of time. It happens unfortunately that it coincides with the receipt of a Florentine Journal from Mr Arnold Bennett which I have undertaken to publish as soon as possible. Both subject and treatment are of course entirely different, but as both contributions are concerned with travels in the same country and as they both more or less take the place of fiction in the numbers in which they would appear, I do not think it feasible to publish them simultaneously. And both MSS would run over two or three numbers. I expect to begin to publish Mr Bennett's Journal in the September or October number. I could probably begin Mr Lawrence's in December or January at the latest.[2]

If, therefore, American publication can be delayed, I shall be glad to accept Mr Lawrence's essay on these terms. If not, I can only return it to you; but if you had something by Mr Lawrence which could definitely be called fiction, I could run it much sooner and would be glad to have it.

1–'Please divide the thing how you like,' replied AB (27 July) on the verso of TSE's letter. 'Florentine Journal' (on AB's visit in Apr.–May 1910) came out in three parts: *MC* 6 (Dec. 1927), 484–98; 7 (Jan. 1928), 16–30; 7 (Feb. 1928), 139–53.

2–'Flowery Tuscany', *MC* 6 (Oct. 1927), 305–10 ; (Nov. 1927), 403–8; (Dec. 1927), 516–22.

You will understand that Mr Lawrence is one of the writers about whom I have to be most careful in connection with American publication because his work usually appears in *The Dial*; and of all the American periodicals, *The Dial* is the one most likely to be read by readers of *The Criterion*.

With many thanks,
Yours very truly,
[T. S. Eliot]

## TO *Max Clauss* CC

25 July 1927 [*The Monthly Criterion*]

My dear Mr Clauss,

I owe you many apologies for not having replied immediately to your letter of the 21st June; I have been on holiday and have therefore neglected my correspondence.

I have thought over your suggestions very carefully and should be more than glad to be able to arrange this sort of co-operation between the two reviews as far as possible. I must explain to you first the conditions on which I accept contributions. *The Criterion* does not ask for its contributors' exclusive periodical rights except for Great Britain and its Colonies. If a contributor wishes to publish any contribution in another country he is quite free to do so at his own terms. The only stipulations that I make are that no contributor shall publish a contribution in America previous to its publication in the *Criterion*. And with regard to our continental contributors, I usually ask that their contributions should be *inédites*: that is to say that they should not publish their contribution in a review in their own or any other European language prior to its publication in the *Criterion*. This is simply, of course, putting English and foreign contributors on exactly the same terms.

You will see therefore that I have no right to negotiate with another review for my contributors. I can merely put these contributors in touch with you and let them make their own arrangements. With regard to stories, the position is specially difficult. The majority of the essays written for the *Criterion* are either offered to me first by the writers, or are even written at my suggestion. Whenever I receive an essay which seems to me particularly suitable for our review, I can suggest immediately to the writer that he should offer it to you at the same time. But the majority of the stories, or fiction, that I print come to me not directly from the author but from a firm of literary agents who can make, and very often have made, arrangements for publication in other countries without consulting me. For instance, I have just published in the August number what seems to me an excellent story of Irish life, by the well-known writer Liam O'Flaherty.[1] This was received from a firm of agents – A. D. Peters, 20 Essex Street, Strand, London, W.C.2 – and if you wanted to publish a translation of this story, you would have to apply to these agents. I can of course send you from time to time proof pages of fiction which we are going to publish, and whenever there is time you would be able to form your own opinion and take the matter up with the author or agents.

You will understand that I, as Editor of the *Criterion*, have no objection to occasional, or even fairly frequent, simultaneous publication, and that the chief difficulty is foreseeing what you would like and notifying you so that you would be able to take the matter up yourself. I should be glad to have any further suggestions from you.

Yours sincerely,
[T. S. Eliot]

P.S. As for myself personally, I hope during the next season to be able to send you something, possibly before using it anywhere else. I have only been withheld by lack of time.

## TO *Ottoline Morrell* CC

26 July 1927 [London]

My dear Ottoline,

I hope to be able to see you very soon though the next few days are rather difficult. I will ring you up one morning later in the week. I am distressed to learn that I have not returned the Ms you sent me.[2] I was strongly under the impression that I had returned it at a moment when, as nearly always, I was in a great rush, saying that I wanted to discuss it with you at leisure. But perhaps I merely put it away in the hope of taking it when I saw you. I will certainly have a hunt for it at once. I am all the more sorry because I liked it very much indeed and, I think, appreciated it.

Forgive me for writing in this letter about another matter. I was under

1–'The Mountain Tavern', *MC* 6 (Aug. 1927), 118–27. O'Flaherty (1896–1984), Irish novelist, short-story writer, Hollywood scriptwriter. His novels include *Thy Neighbour's Wife* (1923), *The Black Soul* (1924), *The Informer* (1925) – a successful thriller that was filmed in 1935 by John Ford – *Skerrett* (1932) and *Famine* (1937).

2–OM had let TSE read a draft version of her memoirs, later pubished as *Ottoline: The Early Memoirs of Lady Ottoline Morrell*, ed. Robert Gathorne-Hardy (1963).

the impression that you told me that you let Garsington through an American agent in London who makes a speciality of letting country houses to American visitors. If I am right I should be very grateful for the name and address of this agent. It is for our friend W. F. Stead. He has a charming house near Charlbury which happens to have a large stable with box stalls. He must either let the house for the autumn and winter or give it up, and he thought that it might be suitable for American visitors who would like hunting in Oxfordshire. This may be chimerical, but I should like to help him if possible.

Yours ever affectionately
[Tom]

## TO *W. Force Stead*

CC

26 July 1927 [*The Monthly Criterion*]

Dear Stead,

I have not yet had the opportunity to see Lady Ottoline but I have written to her to ask the address of this agent and will send it on to you immediately.[1] I do hope that something will come of it for it would be a thousand pities if you had to give up your house altogether. I appreciate your difficulties.

I hope to publish your review *in extenso* in a month or two and will let you know further.[2] I think that I am now in London and hope that you would send me a wire if you came up.

In great haste,
Yours sincerely,
[T. S. Eliot]

1–WFS requested TSE (20 July) to find out from OM the name of the property agent of her acquaintance who was in touch with Americans who wished to rent an English house for a short time. WFS needed to let out Finstock House for the winter.

2–Review of Revd J. M. C. Crum, *The Original Jerusalem Gospel*, *MC* 6 (Nov. 1927), 457–9.

## TO *Ralph de Sola*[1] TS Virginia

26 July 1927 *The Monthly Criterion*

Dear Mr De Sola,

I am sorry that my reference to my little paper has led you into fruitless trouble.[2] As a matter of fact the paper in question was never published, or indeed put into form for publication, and I suppose that I therefore had no right to refer to it. It may still exist among my papers; if so, I will look it over and send you a brief digest of its sense. I am afraid that you are right in saying that there is very little literature on the subject. I have had in mind for years to write something about it myself, but my knowledge is not yet ripe. Have you investigated the voluminous bibliography of Christian Ritual, including especially the Greek Liturgy? I think that there are important books in German on the subject, and you might find something in a work which I have heard highly commended called *Das Gebet* by Friedrich Heiler.[3]

Yours sincerely,
T. S. Eliot

## TO *Bonamy Dobree* TS Brotherton

Tuesday, 26 July [1927] *The Monthly Criterion*

Dear Bungamy:

Can you call and lunch with me on Tuesday or Wednesday of next week? I want to question you about (1) the Native Cat (2) the Edible Dog (3) Rudyard Kipling (4) the Tapir (5) Congreve (6) the removal of the Crocodile (George) in the Zoo to new quarters in a coffin specially constructed; and to inform you of new discoveries in Bolovian Theology. It appears that an unpublished poem by Miss Elizabeth Barrett has been

1–Ralph de Sola (1908–93), author based in New York. His works include *Microfilming* (1944), *Abbreviations Dictionary* (1969), *Worldwide What & Where: Geographical Glossary & Traveller's Guide* (1976) and *Crime Dictionary* (1982).

2–De Sola (30 June) had been working on Aztec Ritual, and on Rituals in general. 'With the possible exception of the works of Dr. Rivers, Dr. Levy-Bruhl, Prof. Bartlett, and Miss Harrisson, I find the literature pertinent to this subject is very scanty.' Thus he wanted to know where he could find a paper by TSE, 'The Interpretation of Primitive Ritual', mentioned in his introduction (viii) to *Savonarola*. This unpublished paper, read by TSE in Josiah Royce's Seminar at Harvard on 9 Dec 1913, is in the John Hayward Bequest at King's.

3–Friedrich Heiler, *Das Gebet: eine religions-geschichtliche und religionspsychologische Untersuchung* (1918).

discovered in Salamanca, suppressed from publication by her husband the flagitious[1] Robt. Browning, which throws new light on the God Wux. The first verse (or stanzo) runs as follows:

What was he doing, the Great God Wux?
    Down in the weeds by the river?
Splashing and paddling with feet of a dux
And washing his sox with a packet of lux
And smashing the vegetable matter that mux
    About on the face of the river?[2]

It is known that Wux was always depicted with duck feet (the images have perished, as the island of Bolovia sank into the sea in the year 1500, doubtless as a protest against the Renaissance, including Pater, Bernard Berenson, Vernon Lee and Middleton Murry). But as Miss Barrett says 'feet of a dux' it may be inferred that she inclined to the Duophysite or alternatively to the Duotheistic party. Four feet means two Gods. This is a serious check to my own opinions, which were that Wux or Wuxes were two Persons and one Substance, or alternatively two Substances and one Person.

Yours etc,
T. S. E.

## TO *J. M. Robertson*

CC

26 July 1927 [London]

My dear Robertson,

Forgive my delay. I assure you that your essay on Burns smells as sweet as ever. At the same time I should very much like to see your essay on Shelley and hope that you will send it to me; as I would at least consider swapping about and printing the Shelley first. I admit that I like Burns's poetry and that I don't like Shelley's, so that unless you go for Shelley my prejudices will probably incline me to stick to the Burns.[3]

1 – 'Guilty of or addicted to atrocious crimes; deeply criminal, extremely wicked' (*OED*).

2 – Cf. 'A Musical Instrument', by Elizabeth Barrett Browning (1806–61):

What was he doing, the great god Pan,
Down in the reeds by the river?
Spreading ruin and scattering ban,
Splashing and paddling with hoofs of a goat,
And breaking the golden lilies afloat
With the dragon-fly on the river.

3 – 'Burns and his Race', *MC* 7 (Jan. 1928), 33–46; (Feb. 1928), 154–68. Robertson had

I should like to know when you expect to be settled in London again after the holidays, if holidays they are. The reason is that the inner circle of regular colleagues and contributors to the *Criterion*, which meets regularly once a fortnight for an informal dinner, desires me to say that it desires your presence as the guest of honour at an informal dinner, the date of which to be fixed. The purpose is to express our recognition of your services to English literature and to British life in general, and you will not be expected to prepare a speech beforehand.

Yours ever,
[T. S. E.]

## TO *The Editor of* The New York Evening Post[1] CC

26 July 1927 [London]

Dear Sir,

Owing to the generous activities of Miss Sylvia Beach and others, the affair of Mr Samuel Roth and his serial publication of *Ulysses* has already received some publicity.[2] But I feel that such a matter can only

intimated on 21 June: 'I am reading my way into "The Shelley Balance Sheet", which will be a lot better than the Burns lecture, s'help me.'

1 – The exchange of letters between TSE and Samuel Roth was to be reprinted in *transition*, no. 9 (Dec. 1927), which prefaced the correspondence with a damning essay by Waverley Lewis Root (a former associate of Roth), 'King of the Jews' (pp. 178–84), as well as an editorial, 'The Case of Samuel Roth' (177), scorning 'such lice as Samuel Roth, who is not only an ignorant blunderer but a liar and sneak thief as well. In the appended first-hand study of this parasite Mr Root observes that to be vilified by Roth is almost infallible evidence that one has at some time been robbed by him. This statement is naively confirmed by Roth himself, as regards his pilfering and mangling of Mr James Joyce's work, in the September issue of *Two Worlds Monthly* and, as regards his pirating of a poem by Mr T. S. Eliot, in the self-explanatory correspondence which follows.

'To readers not already familiar with Roth's literary pocket-picking achievements these documents should be an interesting revelation, and we feel confident that our bitterest enemies will join us as readily as our friends in attempting to rid contemporary literature of this poisonous vermin.'

TSE's letter was reprinted in *Two Worlds Monthly* 3: 4 (Oct. 1927), 237–8.

2 – *The Publishers' Weekly*, 2 Apr. 1927, 1416, ran a story, 'Author of *Ulysses* Sues New York Magazine': 'James Joyce, author of *Ulysses*, filed suit in the Supreme Court of New York on March 23rd against Samuel Roth and the Two Worlds Publishing Company, Inc., of which Roth is the head, to restrain him from making any use of Joyce's name in his magazine. A claim of $500,000 damage is also made. The suit follows publication in the magazine of an expurgated *Ulysses* the complete and authorized edition of which is published in Paris by Sylvia Beach. As the book could not be printed in this country the author has no American copyright. Mr Roth has so far avoided conflict with the government censorship by printing the novel in a condensed form . . .

be effectively dealt with if it is continually kept before the public eye; and I have just seen by the courtesy of Mr James Joyce, a copy of Mr Roth's *Two Worlds Monthly* dated May–June 1927 which gives me every excuse for another protest.[1] This number contains its usual instalment of Ulysses and contains also a piece of verse of my own reprinted from *The Criterion*.[2] It is unnecessary for me to say that this republication is quite unauthorised and that I have received from Mr Roth no offer of payment or communication of any kind. This is all part of Mr Roth's game and calls for no special comment. But I should like the advantage of your columns, and that of any fair-minded American paper which is willing to print this letter, to protest most strongly against the effrontery of Mr Roth's dedication of this number of the *Two Worlds Monthly* to myself. If this is not adding insult to injury I do not know what is. Mr Roth's little epitaph runs as follows:

*I DEDICATE THIS ISSUE OF TWO WORLDS MONTHLY TO*
*T. S. ELIOT*
*Who has given us some excellent verses, several*
*sound critical formulae, and one of the most*
*charming literary personalities of our time.*

'Has given us' is a real stroke of humour; Mr Roth chooses to interpret any gift to the world as a gift to himself.

In the same number Mr Roth has a great deal to say for himself, and states that he offered Mr Joyce a thousand dollars. I did not know this interesting fact, but I am certainly in a position to say that Mr Roth has not offered me a penny. It would appear that the flow of money, if any is to flow, is to be in the opposite direction, for he devotes a page to an advertisement, one sentence of which runs as follows:

'If you have money and wish to invest it in one of the most fascinating of civilised ventures write to Mr Samuel Roth, care of *Two Worlds Monthly*.'

I am, Sir,
Your obedient servant,
T. S. Eliot

---

'It is Mr Roth's claim with regard to Joyce's *Ulysses* that he obtained the rights thru Ezra Pound as Joyce's agent. He offered $1000 but had no answer. Subsequently, he claims, Arthur Garfield Hays approached him about paying for *Ulysses* and he paid $200 cash and $800 in 3 month notes. He also claims that he offered Joyce $2,000 a year to control his output and to be continuing editor.'

1–At JJ's request, Harriet Weaver sent TSE his copy of *Two Worlds Monthly* on 19 July.

2–Roth had reprinted 'Fragment of an Agon' (the second part of *Sweeney Agonistes*, which was originally to have been titled *Wanna Go Home, Baby?*), from *C.* 5 (Jan. 1927), as 'Wanna go home baby? Fragment of an Agon', in *Two Worlds Monthly* 3: 2 (May/June 1927), 149–52.

I am sending this letter also to *The Nation*, *The Evening Post* & *The New Republic.*

## TO *Charles Maurras* CC

Le 26 juillet 1927 [*The Monthly Criterion*]

Cher Monsieur et Maître,

J'ai reçu de notre ami, Massis, le texte de votre Prologue et les nouvelles que vous m'accordez la permission de la traduire pour le *Criterion*. Ayant été en villégiature, je n'ai pas pu vous écrire plus tôt. Je vous remercie infiniment, et je me félicite sur ce succès. Je suis surtout enchanté d'avoir le texte intégral. Je propose de me charger moi même de la traduction. Si vous voulez, je vous enverrai la traduction afin que vous puissiez la corriger.[1]

Je vous prie, cher Monsieur Maurras, de recevoir l'expression de mon admiration et de ma sympathie dévouée

[T. S. Eliot][2]

## TO *Charles du Bos* CC

26 July 1927 [London]

My dear Du Bos,

Your letter of the 13th July which I found recently on returning from the country gave me very much pleasure and I owe you many apologies.

I am delighted to accept your suggestion and hope that something will come of it.[3] I look forward with great interest to the book, for there is nothing really adequate on Pater in English and I do not believe that

1–'Prologue to an Essay on Criticism', trans. TSE: *MC* 7 (Jan. 1928), 5–15; (Mar. 1928), 204–18.

2–*Translation*: Dear Sir, Cher Maître, I have received the text of your Prologue from our friend, Massis, together with the news that you authorise me to translate it for *The Criterion*. Having been on holiday, I was not able to write to you earlier. I am extremely grateful to you, and I am delighted with this successful outcome. I am particularly pleased to have the full text. I propose to undertake the translation myself. If you wish, I shall send you the translation so that you can correct it.

Dear Monsieur Maurras, please accept the assurance of my admiration and devoted fellow-feeling. [T. S. Eliot]

3–Du Bos proposed to write a book entitled *Walter Pater ou l'Ascète de la Beauté*, and wanted to offer a chapter to the *Criterion*. 'I want to study a propos Pater the contemplative act, and also the theme of unworldly . . . yet profane sanctity,' he wrote.

there is anyone living so well qualified as yourself. And what little you say of your idea in the book adds to my interest. So do remember that you have promised definitely to let me have a section of the book before publication, for the *Criterion;* and please keep me in mind also when the whole book is completed, as I should like to be able to propose it to my firm for an English publication.

I wish indeed that I could come to Pontigny this year, especially with your own cordial invitation, and as I have also heard from Fernandez and Dr Stewart about it.[1] I should like very much to meet every one of the persons you mention. But I am doubtful whether I can get abroad during August, and if I do it will be at very short notice. In the latter event, I might send word at the last moment in the hope that room might be found for me.

I shall send you the September and October numbers of the *Criterion* which I think will interest you in connection with Murry's article, and I am sending you a copy of the August number which contains what I think is a very interesting essay by Worringer[2] which you may or may not have seen in the German text. The restrictions of my publishers are slightly inconsistent; they are at present sending out specimen copies, but do not wish me to add to the present permanent free list.

With many thanks,
[T. S. Eliot]

## TO *Henri Massis* CC

Le 26 juillet 1927 [*The Monthly Criterion*]

Mon cher Ami,

Je viens de rentrer à Londres après quelques semaines à la plage et je m'empresse de répondre à vos deux lettres. J'ai écrit tout à l'heure à Maurras pour le remercier de sa permission et de l'envoi du texte intégral. Mais je vous remercie aussi bien cordialement, mon cher ami, pour le succès de vos démarches auprès de Maurras.

*The Defence of the West* va paraître probablement le 20 octobre.[3] C'est le meilleur moment. En Amérique, l'excellente maison de Harcourt Brace and Company la publiera au printemps. Je crois que l'édition

1–Du Bos urged TSE to attend the Pontigny seminar on Romanticism; the delegates were to include Max Scheler, Max Rychner, Ungaretti, Ortega y Gasset and Ramon Fernandez.
2–Wilhelm Worringer, 'Art Questions of the Day', *MC* 6 (Aug. 1927), 101–17.
3–Henri Massis, *Defence of the West*, trans. F. S. Flint (F&G, 1927).

américaine sera assez grande puisque Messrs Harcourt Brace ont élu de le faire imprimer eux mêmes en Amérique au lieu d'acheter des feuilles de l'édition anglaise. Quant à moi, je ne peux pas encore dire à quelle date je serai à Paris. Peut-être en quelques jours; peut-être pas avant quelques mois. Je ne manquerai pas de vous prévenir. En quel moment serez-vous en vacances?

Je trouve que nous avons écrit à *La Revue Universelle* sous date du 19 février 1926 pour proposer les changes des revues, et que mon bureau, n'ayant pas reçu de réponse, n'a jamais envoyé le *Criterion.* Mais puisque je reçois régulièrement et lis avec beaucoup d'intérêt *La Revue Universelle*, je vous fais envoyer tous les numéros du *Monthly Criterion*, et j'ai fait inscrire *La revue Universelle* sur la liste. Si vous pourriez envoyer deux exemplaires de chaque numéro, l'un pour moi et l'autre pour Mr Flint qui se charge des notes sur les périodiques français, je serai bien reconnaissant; si non, je donnerais à Flint les numéros au fur et à mesure que je les reçois.

Bien cordialement vôtre,
[T. S. Eliot][1]

1 – *Translation*: My dear friend, I have just come back to London after a few weeks at the seaside and I am rushing to respond to both your letters. I have just written to Maurras to thank him for his permission and for sending the whole text. But I wish to thank you also, my dear friend, for the success of your intervention with Maurras.

*The Defence of the West* will probably be published on 20 October. It is the best time. In America, the excellent firm Harcourt Brace & Company will publish it in the spring. I think the American edition will be quite large as Messrs Harcourt Brace have decided to print themselves in America rather than buying sheets of the English edition. As for me, I cannot yet say when I will be next in Paris. Maybe a few days, maybe not for a few months. I will make sure I let you know. When will you be on holiday?

I find that we have written to *La Revue Universelle* on 19 February to propose the exchange of reviews and that my office, having not received any answer, has never sent the *Criterion.* But since I receive regularly and read with much interest *La Revue Universelle*, I am sending you all the issues of the *Monthly Criterion* and I have added *La Revue Universelle* to the list. If you could send me two copies of each issue, one for me, the other for Mr Flint who is in charge of the notes about French periodicals, I would be grateful; if not, I will give Mr Flint the issues as I receive them. Cordially yours, [T. S. Eliot]

TO *His Mother* TS Houghton

27 July 1927 *The Monthly Criterion*

Dearest Mother,

I was very much pleased to get your last letter, dictated to Marion,[1] and to hear that you are so much better. I am only now worried by the thought of your being in Cambridge during the rest of the hot weather, and wondering how it can be made supportable for you, and whether you could not get away for the worst of August and September. I remember what Cambridge, with all its trees and dampness, is like during August and September, and have worried especially because I know you are in the midst of tram lines and noise. But it was a very great pleasure and relief to hear from you after such a long time. I had feared that you could not stand the heat and closeness of Cambridge during the summer, and had hoped that somehow you would arrange to be away. Apparently you did not arrange to get away soon enough, so you have paid the penalty of illness. Now I hope that you and Marion and Margaret will get away so as to be fit for the winter.

We have come back from Eastbourne, as we could not keep the house any longer. Of course during most of the time I was in London working during the week; but the last two weeks I staid there the whole time and we drove about a great deal; and I wished that you had been with us, to go to places like Winchelsea and Rye and Battle; and in fact the whole of Sussex from Portsmouth to Dover, and Horsham to Canterbury; there was no part of Sussex that we did not drive over, so we got to know that county very well. We are now in London just as before, and Lucy is with us.

I do not think my essay on Middleton[2] very good, at any rate it is inadequate, and needs a good deal more to be said about his cooperation with other writers. On retrospect I think my essay on Machiavelli[3] the best, especially as I have had an enthusiastic letter about it from F. S. Oliver, the author of a remarkably fine life of Alexander Hamilton.[4] The pleasure of testimonials about one's articles in the *Times* is that no one knows who wrote the article, therefore one feels that the testimony is all

1–Marion Cushing Eliot (1877–1964) was the fourth child of Henry Ware and Charlotte Champe Eliot; TSE's favourite sister, she had travelled with her mother to visit him in London in 1921.

2–'Thomas Middleton', *TLS*, 30 June 1927, 445–6.

3–'Nicolo Machiavelli (1469–1527)', *TLS*, 16 June 1927, 413–14; repr. in *FLA*.

4–F. S. Oliver (1864–1934), businessman, and author of *Alexander Hamilton* (1906), wrote on 7 July: 'I think your N. M. better than any essay I have read for a long time.'

the more sincere. I believe that my leader on Wilkie Collins is coming out in a week or two.[1] I am now trying to get together the material for a book of essays; I cannot bring it out before January, as one of the essays to be included is on F. H. Bradley, which I have not yet written, but which should appear in the *Times* during the autumn.[2]

*The Criterion* is doing fairly well; that is to say that the circulation has increased slowly but steadily from number to number; there is only one other literary periodical left (the *London Mercury*) and we are within a measurable distance of the circulation of that. So I think it is doing as well as possible. And I have just had two contributions from Arnold Bennett, who is always friendly to me, and D. H. Lawrence; and two extremely good things from foreigners, Charles Maurras and Max Scheler. It will be several months still before it is more or less automatic; and then I hope to come and see you. A few weeks ago I saw Horace Kallen, Shef's Jewish friend, whom I like, and he wants me to come to lecture at that School in New York with which he is connected, and which I believe has very intelligent and interesting people.[3] Furthermore he said that he would get me an agent in New York who would arrange a lecture for me.[4] I am not sure about the latter, because when I come I shall want to be several weeks at least in Cambridge quietly with you, and should not have time to be touring about the country, as I doubt whether, during next autumn or winter, I should be able to spend more than eight weeks in America; but if I could give a few lectures in New York, in between making my headquarters with you in Cambridge, it would help pay expenses and perhaps be interesting. Anyway, I hope to come to see you in the autumn or winter.

I wish that you could all get out of Cambridge into the country or to the seaside during August and September, as Cambridge weather is then so oppressive and a change of climate is so bracing then. I do hope you will. I am very glad you have seen something of Henry lately. I shall write to him in a day or two.

When you have time, could you send that essay on English Novelists[5] which I lately sent you – it was the only copy – to

1 – 'Wilkie Collins and Dickens', *TLS*, 4 Aug. 1927, 525–6.

2 – 'Bradley's "Ethical Studies"', *TLS*, 29 Dec. 1927, 981–2.

3 – Horace Kallen (1882–1974), philosopher: see Biographical Register.

4 – Kallen had written on 4 July: 'I will take up with an agent the matter of your lecturing round and about and the extraction of fees . . .'

5 – TSE had at some time posted off to his mother the sole typescript, in English, of the article 'Le roman anglais contemporain', *NRF* 82: 5 (May 1927), 424–31.

Edmund Wilson Jr., The New Republic, 421 West 21st Street, New York City.

He wants to publish it in the *New Republic*, and as the *Nouvelle Revue Française* pays so poorly, I should be glad to make a little money that way.

I will write to Marion and to Margaret in a day or two. With very very much love and longing for more news of you,

Your devoted son,
Tom

## TO *John Gould Fletcher* CC

28 July 1927 [London]

My dear Fletcher,

The enclosed letter from Robert Graves is so violent, personal, and thoroughly unreasonable that I am not sure whether we should print it or not. But before making up my mind I send it to you for your own opinion and advice.[1]

If you are in London, I should very much like to arrange lunch one day next week. And in the same event, would you possibly be able to dine on Tuesday or Thursday if I could scrape together a few of the others?

Yours ever,
[T. S. Eliot]

## TO *Dorothea Varda*[2] CC

29 July 1927 [London]

Dear Madam,

I have not yet seen Mr Dobrée as I have just returned to town, but I have today received the manuscript of your translation of the novel by

1–'In the August issue of the *Criterion* . . . Fletcher reviewed Graves's *Poems 1914–1926*, John Crowe Ransom's *Two Gentlemen in Bonds* and Laura Riding's *The Close Chaplet*. Graves took exception to the "absurd" review of *The Close Chaplet* and Fletcher's assertion that one could "readily distinguish the derivations" of Riding's style (from Marianne Moore, John Crowe Ransom, Graves and Gertrude Stein); he wrote an angry letter to Eliot . . . and asked him to print it as a reply to the review' (O'Prey, *In Broken Images*, 176). See also Ben F. Johnson III, *Fierce Solitude: A Life of John Gould Fletcher* (1994), 156–7.

2–Dorothy (Dorothea) Varda (1900/01–51) was proprietor of the Varda Bookshop at 222 Shaftesbury Avenue, London. Anthony Powell would recall: 'Varda, who had not long before been billed (no misnomer) as "The Beautiful Varda" in one of C. B. Cochran's shows

Raymond Radiguet.[1] I thank you for letting me see this translation, and will submit it to my principals for consideration, and will write to you again later.

Yours truly,
[T. S. Eliot]

## TO *Geoffrey Faber* CC

29 July 1927 [Faber]

I have just received from Professor Max Scheler a manuscript essay for *The Criterion*, in response to an urgent invitation from myself. Scheler is one of the two or three most important philosophers in Germany today, and I have been particularly anxious to get him into the *Criterion*. Professor Scheler has had his manuscript translated by an English pupil of his in Cologne.[2] I have now a letter from Scheler, or rather from his wife, asking whether we could make payment for this essay in advance of publication, for the reason that the pupil who made the translation is rather needy, and they want to pay him for the work. It is possible that Scheler, like many professors in Germany, is not very well off himself, and

at the Pavilion Theatre . . . owed her name to an odd circumstance. She had been married for a short time to a Greek surrealist painter, Jean (Yanko) Varda [1893–1958] . . . As well as beauty, Varda possessed a sharp and witty tongue. "The only woman I know with a male sense of humour", Constant Lambert used to say (*To Keep the Ball Rolling: The Memoirs of Anthony Powell*, I: *Infants of the Spring* [1976], 96). 'Varda was the original of Mrs Mendoza in Powell's novel *Agents and Patients* (1936). Her second husband, whom she would also ultimately divorce, was the art connoisseur Gerald Roberts Reitlinger. In 1936 she married the civil servant Dennis Proctor (1905–82). She committed suicide.

1–Raymond Radiguet (1903–23), French author (teased as '*Monsieur Bébé* on account of his youthful precocity); friend of artists and writers including Picasso and Cocteau, died of typhoid fever. He left two fine, controversial novels: *Le Diable au corps* (1923) and *Le Bal du comte d'Orgel* (1924). TSE wrote of the translation: 'This manuscript is sent me by a lady who is completely unknown to me. It is a translation of the first of the two novels of Raymond Radiguet, a very brilliant French novelist who died a few years ago at the age of about twenty. I know the original, but have not examined this translation. While I have no doubt whatever of Radiguet's abilities, I am rather doubtful whether a translation of one of his novels, even if it were done by Scott Moncrieff or someone much more conspicuous than this lady, would have very much sale in this country. I suggest however that you give it to some reader to examine on its merits, as Radiguet is still so little known in England that the prestige of publishing something of his would not count. I notice that the translation does not say whether she has arranged for translation rights with the Radiguet family. Such matters are rather complicated and extremely definite in France' (Faber TSE4/Misc. 5/2). *Le Diable au corps* was to be translated by Kay Boyle as *The Devil in the Flesh* (1932).

2–'Future of Man', trans. Howard Becker.

I should like to make the payment, although I shall not be able to use the essay for two or three months. Will you authorise such a payment after I have found out the number of words in the Ms?[1]

## TO *Eric Partridge* CC

29 July 1927 [*The New Criterion*]

My dear Mr Partridge,

I am highly pleased to have a copy of your beautiful book on Robert Landor, so beautifully printed, and am very much honoured by the inscription which I find in it.[2] I had already received copies of the ordinary edition which have been sent out for review, and now that I have another copy for myself, I shall look forward to reading it with great interest.

With many thanks.

Yours very sincerely,
[T. S. Eliot]

1–TSE wrote in an internal memo to Mr Garnham, 5 Aug. 1927: 'I should be very much obliged if you would draw a cheque on account of *The New Criterion* to the order of Professor Max Scheler for £15 (twelve [*sic*] pounds), as per attached memorandum, countersigned by Mr Faber. The sum of £12 is approximate, and I imagine that there will be a small balance in Professor Scheler's favour when we have obtained the exact number of words in his manuscript. This payment is for a contribution to appear in *The Criterion* at some time during the present year, and will of course be deducted from the payment sheet of *The Criterion* for that month. If you would kindly let me have the cheque on Monday, I and Mr Faber, or I and Mr de la Mare could sign it.' (TSECRI8).

2–*Robert Eyres Landor: A Biographical and Critical Sketch* (1927).

## TO *Julian Green*[1] CC

29 July 1927 [Faber & Gwyer Ltd]

Dear Mr Green,

Thank you for your letter.[2] I had been meaning to write to you to thank you for sending me copies of *Adrienne Mesurat* and *Le Voyage[ur] sur la Terre*, but had delayed until I should have been able to read both books. The idea of having you translated into English had already occurred to me. I am afraid that the objection that *Le Voyage[ur] sur la Terre* is too short is a serious one; but I will write to you again when I have read it. Meanwhile I should be very much obliged if you would let me know whether you have arranged for any English publication of *Adrienne Mesurat*.[3] If not, I should like to bring it up with my firm for consideration.[4]

I hope that when I am next in Paris I may have the pleasure of making your acquaintance.

Yours sincerely,
[T. S. Eliot]

1 – Julian Green (1900–98), American novelist, playwright and prolific diarist (16 vols), was born in Paris, where his wealthy father represented an American cotton company. After studying for three years at the University of Virginia, the bilingual Green, who converted to Catholicism by the age of 17, spent his adult years in Europe, where he wrote most of his works in French. Euan Cameron has written, 'His very first publication, *Pamphlet contre les Catholiques de France*, an impassioned attack on what Green saw as the lukewarm faith of French Catholics, still in print today, was published in 1922 (it is thought to have been translated into English by T. S. Eliot) and caused a minor stir' (*News from the Royal Society of Literature* 1999, 43). However, there appears to be no evidence for Cameron's claim. Green's early novels, including *Adrienne Mesurat* (1927), established his reputation in France; and he would be the first foreigner to be elected to the Académie Française.

2 – At the suggestion of Henri Massis, Green wrote to ask whether F&G might be interested in publishing a translation of his short novel *Le Voyageur sur la Terre*.

3 – *Adrienne Mesurat* was to be published in translation by Harper's (USA).

4 – In a memo on the subject of *Le Voyageur sur la Terre* addressed to the F&G Book Committee (29 Aug. 1927), TSE counselled: 'The author of this book, Julian Green, is a young writer who has had considerable success in Paris during the last year. When he sent me this book he asked whether Faber and Gwyer would consider publishing a translation. I wrote back to him to say that I thought it was rather short for the English public and asked whether his longer novel, which I have not read, was available. He now says that an English translation of the longer book is to be published by Harper's and urges me to consider this one. The story is quite good but I still think that it is too short to be worth considering, especially from an author unknown in this country. Before writing to him finally, however, I wish to submit it to you for your opinion' (Faber).

## TO *W. Force Stead* CC

29 July 1927 [*The Monthly Criterion*]

Dear Stead,

I have just heard from Lady Ottoline that the person you want is Miss Wheeler, 17 Berkeley Street, W.1. She does not add any information about the lady, but as she seems to be slightly annoyed with me at the moment, I am not surprised.

I am reading the Vere Somerset Dialogue, and will write to him.[1] I have not quite made up my mind, but I do not think that it is quite well enough finished for this type of thing. I will however write to him as you suggest and may be able to make some other suggestions to him. He seems to be a person who ought to be encouraged in writing, and I should like to get something out of him.

Sincerely yours,
[T. S. Eliot]

## TO *Bonamy Dobrée* TS Brotherton

29 July 1927 *The Monthly Criterion*

Dear Bungamy,

I am consternated by two recent occurrences.

The first is that since writing to you I have received a letter from Professor Doctor Breitensträter of Giessen which Upsets my hupothe3/8is 3/4 3/4 3/4 -. Prof. Breitensträter says that he has a photograph of a copy of a copy of a genuine Bolovian Image, which shews Wux with four legs and feet, rather like Shiva. Prof. Breitensträter says that owing to the cencorship [*sic*] he dares not send me the Photograph, but he gives an inventory of the God wux according to this photograph as follows:

4 Legs
4 Feet (Duck)
4 Arms
4 testicles
2 Penisses

1–WFS had sent TSE on 27 July a 'composition' by Vere Somerset, Fellow of Worcester College, Oxford – 'an imaginary conversation between Fénelon and his chaplain – typical of Vere in its French 18th Cent graces. I find it quite charming, but am no judge in these matters. If you can't use it, do let me have a nice letter with some soothing phrases to pour over his wounds – or you might as well send it to him direct.' The 'Dialogue' did not appear in *The Criterion*.

1 speedometer
1 clock
1 dash lamp
4 wheel brakes
extra wheel and toolchest

This is very interesting, and completely upsets my theories. What is more, Professor Breitensträter, who as you know is Professor of Physical Culture, says that he is '*nicht geübt zingulären und Haeretisehen Ideen* and *Meinungen zahm und zartlich zu acceptzieren*', that he characterises my theories as '*komischen und affenartigen Verworrenheiten*', and that if I maintain my theories and ever come to Giessen he will [give] me '*die Augen oder Lampen verputzen*' i.e. he will black my eye. Now I long to go to Giessen, and therefore I feel obliged to withdraw all my theories and make a handsome apology to Prof. Dr Breitensträter. I hope you will understand and agree with my firm attitude of retractation. I am now preparing a complete new theory of Bolovian Theology based upon this new discovery, but I still expect to shew a complete Orthodoxy.

2. The other point is that I find, being slightly in confusion, as my secretary (photograph enclosed) is away on holiday, that I had made a priory attachment for Tuesday Lunch with American friends who really exist, name and address can be given on application with stamped envelope. Now I shall problybe free on Thursday or Friday but cannot cannot tell Which, having suggested one day to Leonard Woolf. I am certainly Lunching on Wednesday at the Imperial Restaurant, round the Corner from South kensington Station, on Wednesday at 1:15 with Herbert read at 1:15 round the corner from South kensington Station, the Imperial restuarant at 1:15 precisely. I suggest first that you Be present or call for me at Russell square at 12:45 on wednesDay, and that if Possible you keep Thurs. and Fir. so That I can arrange one of those days with your Privately. If we could arrange thurs. or FriDay I hope you will be able to come Shopping with Me afterWards; I have to buy

1 young talking Parrot in Cage
2 Java Sparrows
2 rosebreasted parrakeets
1 air gun with darts
1 Hornsby [*sic*] LMS train with signals and tunnel
1 small sloop yacht

all in Holborn, and possibly a bull Terrier.

I Remain your obliged obt. Servt.
T. S. Eliot (or Elephant & Castle[)]

## TO *Bonamy Dobrée* TS Brotherton

29 July 1927 *The Monthly Criterion*

Dear Dobrée,

Yes, my meaning was that you should call for me here on Tuesday next at 1 p.m. precisely, and I shall expect you on that date and at that moment.

I am afraid that I cannot accept your Identification with either the Ibex or the Ape.[1] My family tradition is that we are descended from the White Elephant; not the Siamese, but the Indian White Elephant. <'Eliot' is merely a corruption of 'Elephant'.> [2]

Yours ever,
T. S. Eliot

P.S. I cannot answer your last paragraph as your information is not sufficient. Is the person to whom you refer named Harry or Alan?[3]

## TO *H. F. Stewart* CC

29 July 1927 [London]

Dear Doctor Stewart,

I asked my secretary to write to you a few days ago to say that I should be very glad to look at Smith's new fellowship dissertation.[4] I expect to be in London for some time to come, and in any case if you send it to this office I shall receive it and report on it as quickly as possible.

I wish indeed that I could join you at Pontigny. Both Du Bos and Fernandez have written to urge me to come, and the subjects very much

1–BD had written on 28 July: 'Dear Thoth (that, I timorously think, is rather a good one. The god, rather a recent invention I fear, as late as the 7th Dynasty or thereabouts, was depicted alternatively as an Ibex or an Ape. So you may take your choice).' BD wrote in answer to this letter from TSE: 'I am profoundly disappointed that you should reject Thoth as your Totem. Perhaps it is my fault for having written Ibex in mistake for Ibis. Thoth, as you know, was the scribe-god of the Egyptians: he was, in fact, the editor of the Old Criterion . . . and the Father-Confessor of the Serpent of Old Nile.'
2–Walter Graeme Eliot relates: 'The family originally bore arms alike . . . Early in the Sixteenth century, however, the Devonshire and Cornwall families adopted other arms, and in the "Visitation of Devonshire," 1620, we find them thus: Arms – Argent, a fess gules between four cotises wavy azure, a mullet for difference. Crest. – An elephant's head, couped argent' (*A Sketch of the Eliot Family* [1887], 7).
3–BD had closed his letter of 30 July: 'Oh my God! I spent yesterday evening among Bernhard Behrensohnians! Oh Montreal! I take off my hat to the Bolovians.'
4–James Smith was trying once again for a Fellowship at Trinity College, Cambridge; his dissertation this time was entitled 'An enquiry into the meaning of the term "character" in dramatic theory and criticism, from Aristotle onwards'.

attract me;[1] but I am afraid that it will be impossible for me to leave London during August. I look forward in the hope of visiting you and going to Little Gidding in the autumn or winter.[2]

With best wishes to Mrs Stewart and yourself,

Yours very sincerely,
[T. S. Eliot]

## TO *Leonard Woolf* CC

29 July 1927 [London]

Dear Leonard,

On ringing up your house today I have learned that Virginia is away, so that I cannot get at her to express my apologies and regrets about dinner last Friday night. I have only just got settled in London again. If you yourself are going to be in London a little while, could you possibly lunch with me one day, and would next Thursday do?

Yours ever,
[Tom]

## TO *Henry Eliot* TS Houghton

29 July 1927 *The Monthly Criterion*

My dear brother,

This is merely to acknowledge – not to thank you adequately, I shall do that in a letter next week – your two letters, about mother, and return herewith the enclosed letters from Marion; and to *thank* you very briefly for the cheque. I will write to you much more fully soon. I enclose copy of a letter which I have just written to mother. I hope it will do.[3] Of course the letters which I write to her are composed primarily for the purpose of cheering and pleasing her. As to my prospects of coming to see her, you will understand that I am completely in the dark, but that I will come if

1 – Fernandez had told TSE (25 June) that the Pontigny colloquium (21 Aug.–1 Sept.) was to be devoted to 'the "classicism–romanticism" problem'. He added, 'I shall be one of the rare defendants of classicism: would you like to join your forces to mine?'

2 – In the event, TSE was to visit the religious community of Little Gidding in Huntingdonshire for the first time only in 1936. He would write to a friend, Mrs J. C. Perkins, on 10 July 1936: 'The only really lovely day that I remember was a day at the end of May when I was motored over from Cambridge to Little Gidding' (Beinecke).

3 – This may refer to a (now lost) letter explaining TSE's baptism into the Anglican Church.

and when I can; but I thought it best to make her think that it might be quite soon. You must not suppose that any letters I write to her are of any value as a statement of facts.

Very much love from
Tom

I gather that Mother is likely to live about six months or a year? Is this your opinion?

## TO *Kenneth Pickthorn* CC

29 July 1927 [*The Monthly Criterion*]

Dear Mr Pickthorn

I am just writing a line to tell you that I liked your review of Napoleon very much.[1] I have not read the book, but the exaggerated praise which it has received made me rather suspicious of it, and your review seems to be very much to the point. Thank you also for your review of *Burke*, which I shall use a little later.[2] I hope that something will turn up before long which will be more to your taste, and if anything appears, or is announced, that you would like to have, I hope you will let me know and I will get it for you.

Yours sincerely,
[T. S. Eliot]

## TO *Georges Cattaui*[3] CC

29 July 1927 [Faber & Gwyer Ltd]

My dear Sir,

I have a letter from my friend, Jean de Menasce, telling me that you are in London, and it would be a great pleasure to make your acquaintance. Would it be possible for you to lunch with me on Monday, August 8th at

1–Review of Emil Ludwig, *Napoleon*, *MC* 6 (Sept. 1927), 267–73.

2–Review of Bertram Newman, *Edmund Burke*, *MC* 6 (Dec. 1927), 556–9. 'The new life . . . is as unpretentious as possible: this is a virtue which can hardly be, and never is, over-estimated. Mr. Bertram Newman does not claim to have pushed his researches further than the more obvious printed sources, nor does he offer anything very new in the way of interpretation: he has written a very readable account along quite orthodox lines.'

3–Georges Cattaui (1896–1974): Egyptian-born (scion of aristocratic Alexandrian Jews, and a cousin of Jean de Menasce) French diplomat and writer; his publications include *T. S. Eliot* (1958), *Constantine Cavafy* (1964) and *Proust and his metamorphoses* (1973).

1 o'clock? And if so, would it be an inconvenience for you to call for me here? As otherwise I could call at your Legation and ask you to lunch with me somewhere in your neighbourhood.

Yours very truly,
[T. S. Eliot]

## TO *Orlo Williams* CC

2 August 1927 [*The Monthly Criterion*]

Dear Williams,

Many thanks for your cheerful letter. I am taking advantage of your amiability to send you two works by Ernest Hemingway to occupy the superfluity of your rural leisure.[1]

There is one word in your letter which I cannot read, and therefore one sentence which I cannot answer. You say if my . . . something or other has any general conspectus of Thomas Mann etc. you would get it.[2] Anyway, I think I will send for the book, if only to put in a notice to say that we will deal with him seriously later. I have only read two short things by Mann myself, but they inclined me very much in his favour. Have you read *Death in Venice*? That seemed to me first-rate. Many thanks for your kind invitation.[3] I shall take advantage of it with alacrity if I can. But during the present month it will be difficult for me to get out of London, even for a day.

Yours ever,
[T. S. Eliot]

TSE would write to E. R. Curtius on 21 Nov. 1947: 'I received the book by Cattaui [*Trois poètes: Hopkins, Yeats, Eliot* (Paris, 1947)] and must say that I found what he had to say about myself slightly irritating. There are some personal details which are unnecessary and which don't strike me as in the best taste.'

1–In response to a (lost) letter from TSE that included verses playing on Williams's first name, Williams had written on 30 July: 'You must have had an excellent lunch before taking the typewriter so boldly into your hand and treading so heavily on the "cap" key . . . I can give you a better rhyme for Orlo – "swore low".' His further remarks included: 'I have taken all Wharton out of the London Library; & it gives me indigestion to look at, but I will digest it, & send you the result. Well now, as to Hemingway I haven't read a word of him but believe he is good. So we ought to review "Fiesta", I suppose.'

2–Williams wrote: 'I reviewed Mann's *Magic Mountain* in the *Times*, & it is certainly an impressive book. I haven't read his *Buddenbrooks* which has also been translated. But if your Teuton has any general conspectus of Mann to give us, I would get it. He is very German & needs putting in a German background.'

3–Williams had invited TSE to lunch at his home in Newdigate, Surrey.

## TO *John Gould Fletcher* CC

2 August 1927 [London]

Dear Fletcher,

Thank you for your letter. You certainly show much more generosity towards Robert Graves than I should be inclined to do in the same circumstances.[1] I will write to him accordingly, but it is rather difficult to know what to say. To me he seems simply to have gone off his head. I know nothing about the inside of this affair, but I have always thought that it would do him nothing but harm, and his letter seems to be good evidence of what I feared. I will let you know what happens.

I am not certain yet about dinner, except that it cannot be arranged this week, and I have had to fill up all my lunch times this week. In any case could you lunch with me on Wednesday of next week definitely? That is Wednesday 10th August.

Yours ever,
[T. S. Eliot]

## TO *Leonard Woolf* CC

3 August 1927 [London]

Dear Leonard,

I am very sorry indeed to miss you, but that is my misfortune. I should very much like to know whether Virginia is at Rodmell, as I should like to write to her. I did not quite understand from your maid whether she was there or abroad.

Yours ever,
[Tom]

1 – Apropos Graves's letter, Fletcher had advised TSE on 28 July that he should 'not print it – not that I have any objection whatsoever to what he says – but because he is only likely to damage his position severely by appearing in print with such absurd statements. And I really would like to spare him from the humiliation of appearing ridiculous.'

## TO *Robert Graves* TS Morris

3 August 1927 *The Monthly Criterion*

My dear Graves,

I have read over your public letter to *The Criterion* several times, and with considerable misgivings. If you will tolerate such frankness, it seems to me that you express yourself much too warmly on an impersonal matter of criticism; and I do not feel that the publication of your letter would do any good either to you or to the cause which you so generously further. Do not think that I wish to suppress it in favour of one of our reviewers; on the contrary, I will certainly publish it if you wish; but I am taking the liberty of returning it to you for your further consideration. More especially as there is one point in any case which you would have to amend. You refer to Mr Fletcher's long absence from America. As a matter of fact he is only quite recently returned from America, where he spent the whole winter; and he was not merely in one part of America, but in many parts of the country; and I know that he knows John Ransom personally. I do not see any advantage in suggesting that he knows of Marianne Moore through H.D., and of Gertrude Stein through Williams, because I think that he is quite likely to know both these persons in the ordinary way in which I first knew of them myself. I have known Fletcher for some years and I can assert that for a number of these years we both knew of Marianne Moore and Gertrude Stein as a matter of course.

Forgive these remarks. May I take the liberty of suggesting that we should very much like to be able to publish verses as well as correspondence by yourself?

Yours sincerely,
T. S. Eliot

## TO *Edmund Wilson* TS Beinecke

3 August 1927 *The Monthly Criterion*

Dear Mr Wilson,

I must apologise for my delay in answering your letter of June 15th. I have found that the *N.R.F.* article you so kindly asked for has disappeared;[1] that is to say, I find that I sent the only copy of the English text to my mother. I have written to her to ask her to forward it to you if she has

1 – '*Le roman anglais contemporain.*'

read it, but as she has been ill you may not receive it very promptly. In any case you are quite at liberty to reconsider the matter if, when you receive the manuscript, it seems to you out-of-date. But I should not like to have the French text re-translated into English, and so ask you to wait for this. I will send you more promptly the next thing that I write for *The N.R.F.*, but of course it could not be published in English until it has been published in *The N.R.F.*[1]

With many thanks,
Yours very sincerely,
T. S. Eliot

## TO *T. Sturge Moore* TS Texas

3 August 1927 *The Monthly Criterion*

Dear Mr Sturge Moore,

I am sending you back your manuscript as you request.[2] I expect to use it in November, but if it is possible to use it in October I will give you warning. The September number, of course, has already gone to press.

I should be very glad indeed if you cared to review the new *Life of Blake*, still more so as I have met Miss Wilson and thought her very intelligent.[3] I should probably not be able to use the review before the November or December number, but should be certain to use it sooner or later. I should be glad if you would let me know about what length your review is likely to be.

I hope that you will let us see your book as soon as it is ready, but suggest that you have the manuscript addressed to me personally at this address.[4]

Yours sincerely,
T. S. Eliot

I am sending *The Marriage of Heaven & Hell* (Dent) in case you cared to mention it in your review.

1 – TSE's essay, in its original version in English, did not appear in *The New Republic*.
2 – Sturge Moore wanted (28 July) to improve 'Towards Simplicity'.
3 – Sturge Moore reviewed Wilson's *William Blake*, and other books (inc. a facsimile edition of *The Marriage of Heaven and Hell*), *MC* 7 (Mar. 1928), 272–81.
4 – Sturge Moore said he would be submitting to F&G (at TSE's kind suggestion) his book on aesthetics: it would be entitled 'In Defence of Beauty'. He was later to publish *Armour for Aphrodite: An Essay in Aesthetics* (1929).

## TO *John Middleton Murry* TS Northwestern

3 August 1927 *The Monthly Criterion*

My dear John,

In the September number of *The Criterion* will appear two criticisms of your essay on 'The Synthesis'. One by Father D'Arcy, S.J., and the other by Charles Mauron.[1] Needless to say I should be very happy to print any reply you think fit to make, although not of course to the length of the original essay.[2] But as the October number will contain two further criticisms or replies, one by Fernandez and one by myself, I suggest your waiting until the October number is out, so that you can deal with the whole lot. You certainly seem to have the faculty of starting hares which are not electric, but thoroughly alive.

I am hoping to receive your review of 'The Santayana' soon.[3] In any case I should be glad to hear from you where you are and what are your plans. I shall probably be in London throughout August; is there any chance of seeing you?

Ever yours,
[T. S. E.]

## TO *Ramon Fernandez* CC

3 August 1927 [*The Monthly Criterion*]

My dear Fernandez,

Very many thanks for sending me your note, which I shall use in the October number, together with my own note.[4] It interests me very much, though I am not quite sure on a first reading whether I understand you perfectly; at any rate your point of view is quite clearly individual. I shall put a note to my own short essay to say that it was written before I had

1–The Revd M. C. D'Arcy, SJ, 'The Thomistic Synthesis and Intelligence', *MC* 6 (Sept. 1927), 210–28; Mauron, 'Concerning "Intuition"', trans. TSE, 229–35.
2–JMM replied (29 Aug.): 'Three of the criticisms – Mauron's, yours, & Fernandez' – have both interested & stimulated me. D'Arcy's not very much: to my mind, it misses the entire point of the whole business, or at any rate, my point in raising the discussion.'
3–Review of George Santayana, *Platonism and the Spiritual Life*, *MC* 6 (Nov. 1927), 437–40.
4–Fernandez, 'A Note on Intelligence and Intuition', trans. TSE, *MC* 6 (Oct. 1927), 332–9; TSE, 'Mr. Middleton Murry's Synthesis', ibid., 340–7. Both pieces seek to criticise JMM's essay 'Towards a Synthesis' (*MC* 5 [June 1927], 294–313), which was itself written as a critique of TSE's review of books by HR and Fernandez (Oct. 1926).

seen yours; for it is odd that we both criticise, and for somewhat similar reasons, Murry's use of the quotation from Dante.[1]

I am sending you back your précis of the George Eliot essay, and look forward with much pleasure to receiving it in time for the January number. You will probably have to put up with myself as translator of your note of introduction, for Flint is too busy at the present moment, and there is no one else at hand to whom I dare entrust such a piece of work. I will send you a copy of my translation for your criticisms, together with a copy of my own note.

I am very sorry indeed to be unable to come to Pontigny, especially in view of the subjects. But I still hope to be able to come another year.

Yours ever sincerely,
[T. S. Eliot]

## TO *I. A. Richards* CC

3 August 1927 [London]

My dear Richards,

I have been wondering for some time past whether I should ever get in touch with you again. Several months ago I wrote to you at Magdalene, and have had no reply; you are apparently alive somewhere, as I have just read an interesting note of yours in *The Statesman*. I have heard rumours that you intended to settle in America. I hope this is not true. In any case if you get this letter, do let me hear from you.

Yours ever,
[T. S. Eliot]

1–Fernandez expatiated (1 Aug.): 'I hope you will excuse me "pour l'apparence d'impressionisme" of my analysis of "Nessun maggior dolore . . ." [by Dante]. Of course I admit that the import of the verse may be a truth, at least may be implied in a "corps de raison". My point is that the intuition we have is not the intuition of a truth, but of the expression of a truth, or of something that has been stated as, or may become a truth.'

## TO *Dr Max Rychner* CC

3 August 1927 [London]

My dear Mr Rychner,

Your letter of the 29th July gives me much pleasure.[1] Do not suppose however that I meant my remark censoriously, as Curtius could hardly have enlarged his subject within the space of a review article. But I am very glad to accept your suggestion because this is a subject which I have specially at heart, and I think that it is important at the present time to show the community of interest of all European countries. I shall therefore begin to think about an article at once. I can promise you within the next three months such an article; if anything untoward should happen I would get one of my colleagues to do it for me, but it interests me so much that I should prefer to do it myself.

I should very much have liked to come to Pontigny this year, but I am afraid that it will be impossible for me to leave England during August. I regret it very much as all the subjects have my particular interest.

With cordial good wishes,
Yours ever sincerely,
[T. S. Eliot]

## TO *Adrienne Monnier*[2] CC

Le 4 août 1927 [London]

Chère Mademoiselle,

Je vous saurais bien gré si vous pourriez me faire expédier (avec

1–Rychner remarked that in his latest 'Commentary' in *MC*, TSE expressed his regret that E. R. Curtius, in his essay on French and German ideas of culture, had disregarded the English conception of culture. 'Mr Curtius [TSE had written] is chiefly concerned with the relations of France and Germany and the possibility of harmonizing the German idea of Culture with the French idea of Civilization. We regret that his discussion found no place for England, as we believe that there is a British idea of culture and a British idea of civilization, both quite distinct from either French or German' (*MC* 6 [Aug. 1927], 98–9).

Rychner invited TSE to write on the topic for *Die Neue Schweizer Rundschau*. 'I would like to see the English point of view represented in my magazine at some point.'

2–Adrienne Monnier (1892–1955): bookseller, publisher, essayist, translator; founder in 1915 of the bookshop La Maison des Amis des Livres; friend and associate of Sylvia Beach at her English-language bookshop 'Shakespeare & Company'. In June 1925 Monnier launched a magazine, *Le Navire d'Argent* ('The Silver Boat'), featuring a translation by Monnier and Beach of 'The Love Song of J. Alfred Prufrock': the first French translation of any poem by TSE. The magazine, which promoted works by European and American authors, ran for twelve issues. See *The Very Rich Hours of Adrienne Monnier*, memoirs trans. Richard

facture) deux livres par Jacques Bainville, 'Histoire de France'[1] et 'Heur et Malheur des Français' <ou 'de la France?'>; aussi la petite brochure d'Action Française[2] qu'en voici la coupure. Si ces livres sont épuisés, je vous prie de les faire envoyer lors d'une seconde impression.

Recevez, chère Mademoiselle, l'assurance de mes sentiments empressés.

[T. S. Eliot][3]

## TO *Charles Whibley* CC

4 August 1927 [*The Monthly Criterion*]

My dear Whibley,

I wish indeed that I could lunch on Monday. Unfortunately I have promised to lunch with a bore, a man in the Egyptian Legation, who I think will be an utter waste of time, but he is a cousin of my friend Jean de Menasce and I must therefore see him.[4] As I very much want to see you, may I suggest that I could look in at the club at any time either before lunch or after, if you are free?

It is good to know that you like the August number, also that you approve of the Machiavelli in a general way.[5] I should like to have some detailed comment of the latter, if you think of any, before I reprint it in a book.

Yours ever affectionately,
[T. S. Eliot]

McDougall (1976). In response to a request for a contribution to a memorial (8 July 1955), TSE wrote on 31 July 1955 to Françoise Hartmann: 'I wish . . . I could have added my mite to the tribute to be paid to Adrienne Monnier by the *Mercure de France*. My memories of Mlle. Monnier go back to the years immediately after the first world war . . . I have several memories of her and of her bookshop in the period between the wars; and when I revisited Paris in June 1945, I took the first opportunity of returning to that shop, to bring an offering of tea and soap, and to partake of a magnificent cake which Adrienne had baked for the occasion. With the death of Adrienne Monnier another large part of the Paris that I knew has been transferred from the world of actuality to the world of memory.'

1 – *Histoire de France* (Paris, 1924).

2 – *La Presse et la Guerre. L'Action Française. Choix d'articles* (1915).

3 – *Translation*: Dear Miss, I would be delighted if you could send me (with an invoice) two books by Jacques Bainville, 'Histoire de France' and 'Heur et Malheur des Français' <or 'de la France'>, as well as the little pamphlet of Action Française, as per the cutting. If these books are out of print, I wish you would send them to me after the reprint.

Yours faithfully, [T. S. Eliot]

4 – Georges Cattaui.

5 – 'Nicolo Machiavelli (1469–1527)'. Whibley had written on 30 July, 'I am for the moment staying with F. S. Oliver, who praises your article on Machiavelli very highly, & finds a ready echo in me.'

TO *John Middleton Murry* TS Northwestern

4 August 1927 *The Monthly Criterion*

My dear John,

And herewith enclosed is a letter which I wrote to you yesterday, but fortunately did not post before receiving yours this morning. Very many thanks for the review of Santayana, which I shall use in October. It is difficult but valuable. I need hardly say although I have not read the book that obviously Santayana and myself are using the word 'heretic' in quite a different sense. The one point on which we should all perhaps agree is that Dean Inge is a heretic. But you may quite reasonably be able to apply some worse epithet to myself.[1]

Don't bother about the Shakespeare Sonnets; we will find something better. Perhaps you will feel inclined to deal with Santayana more thoroughly at some later time. As soon as this synthesis business is more or less wound up I should like to start a discussion of Classicism and Romanticism; not in order to lay down the law, but to find out if anyone knows, or if any two people agree, on the meaning for these words. I shall certainly depend upon your collaboration.

1 – JMM wrote of Santayana's *Platonism and the Spiritual Life*, 'At the last moment I am overcome by a natural reluctance to criticize this deeply interesting book. On p. 37 of it Mr Santayana asserts that "no one is more unspiritual than a heretic"; and on p. 179 of *The Monthly Criterion* for August, Mr Eliot declares that I am one of the few "genuine heretics" available for examination at the present day. The combination of verdicts seems to disqualify me peremptorily from appreciating Mr Santayana's book.

'On reflection, I have consoled myself by thinking that Mr Santayana and Mr Eliot do not mean precisely the same thing by a heretic; and that, from Mr Eliot's point of view, Mr Santayana is no less a heretic than myself. Mr Santayana would, I am sure, refuse the epithet. He would say, I think, that no one can be judged a heretic by analogy. Because a man's philosophy, or religion, is such that, if he were a member of the Catholic Church, he would be pronounced heretical, it does not follow that he is a heretic. Heresy is not an absolute, but a relative, condition . . .

'Naturally, I think Mr Santayana is right as against Mr Eliot . . . Mr Santayana is, from Mr Eliot's point of view, no less a genuine heretic than myself, and from my point of view, a more competent one.' Murry proceeds to concur with Santayana when he criticises 'Dean Inge's assertion that the chief point common to Platonism and to "spiritual religion" is "a firm belief in absolute and eternal values as the most real things in the universe". The most real things in the Platonic universe are not "values" at all; they are the Ideas which generate . . . being itself . . . It follows that Dean Inge's Platonic Christianity is in danger of making worship, as conceived by traditional Christianity, impossible.' Dean Inge knows only 'dubiously' that 'worship is not really a condition of the spiritual life at all. That element in any religion or philosophy which makes worship possible is superstition . . . Accordingly, Murry avers, Dean Inge '*is* a heretic' (437–9).

Yours ever,
Tom.

I hope yr family are well? Shd be glad of news.

## TO *Charles Maurras* CC

Le 4 août, 1927 [*The Monthly Criterion*]

Cher Monsieur et Mâitre,

Je vous remercie de tout mon coeur de votre lettre du 28 juillet.[1] Je suis bien content d'apprendre que vous m'acceptez comme intermédiaire pour votre prologue. Je vais préparer la traduction aussi vite que possible, (en vue mes autres engagements) et j'espère pouvoir la publier dans notre numéro de décembre au plus tard. Voulez-vous bien me signaler à quel moment on attend l'édition française? Si l'édition française ne paraîtra pas avant la nouvelle année cela me donnera traduction juste.[2]

1–Maurras wrote: '*Je n'ai aucune inquiétude sur l'exactitude et l'élégante sincérité d'une version dont vous serez l'auteur. Mais il est trop certain que j'en serais bien mauvais juge; mes rudiments d'anglais sont si loin! Cependant il me serait très agréable de demander à quelques anglicisants subtils et instruits de mes amis de m'aider à suivre et à comprendre votre effort d'interprétation afin d'en sentir toute l'amitié et le bonheur*' ('I have no worries about the accuracy and the elegant sincerity of a rendering done by you. But it is only too true that I would be a very bad judge of it; my rudimentary knowledge of English was acquired so long ago! However, I would have great pleasure in asking certain subtle and learned English specialists among my friends to help to follow and understand your effort of interpretation, so as to appreciate to the full its friendly and felicitous character').

2–E. J. H. Greene was to ask TSE (15 Apr. 1940): 'Can you tell me exactly when you first read (significantly, from my point of view) Maurras's *Prologue d'un essai sur la critique*? This essay was first published in 1896 in the *Revue encyclopédique Larousse*, and not republished I believe until 1932, when it appeared separately . . . But you translated it and published it in 1928. From all of which I conclude that you attribute, or attributed at one time, a considerable importance to that essay; and I should like to know whether you knew it before or after *The Sacred Wood*, for example.' TSE replied (19 Apr. 1940): 'I think that the text of Maurras's *Prologue* which I translated for the *Criterion* had appeared a few months before in the *Revue de Paris*, which my friend Henri Massis was editing. I don't think I have ever read the 1896 text, and don't know how much the texts differ . . . Certainly I was unacquainted with it before that date [1927], so it obviously has no bearing on *The Sacred Wood*.'

In an earlier letter (10 Mar. 1940), Greene had mentioned that he was getting on with the second part of his graduate thesis on TSE's development. 'In my first chapter I find a good deal, perhaps too much, Rémy de Gourmont, and some Benda and a little Maurras . . . For my second chapter, I find only Maurras who is a real *influence* (perhaps Hulme) and I hope to show this influence in its proper proportions. But I should like to ask you about Rivière and Maritain. On two occasions at least you have mentioned an article by Rivière, "Crisis in the Concept of Literature" . . . Is he otherwise important? And is there any work or works of Maritain that I must study? because I procured a copy of *L'Avenir de l'intelligence*, on

Recevez, cher Monsieur, l'assurance de mes hommages dévoués.
[T. S. Eliot][1]

## TO *Houston Peterson*[2] CC

5 August 1927 [London]

My dear Sir,

Thank you very much for your kind letter of July 25th.[3] I am sorry that I cannot reply in a way that would be useful to you. I have never

---

the faith of an indication in the *Criterion*.' TSE replied on 6 Apr. 1940: 'I should not have thought the influence of Maurras quite so important in my work as your letter suggests; but you may be right, and the evidence is not what I think about it in retrospect, but what you find in the documents. But I think that it decreases after the beginning of the '30s, when perhaps I became more interested in considerations, such as economics, which he ignores, and became more involved with the Christian sociologists. His mind now seems to me to have been lacking in flexibility and capacity for adaptation to new situations: so, like Babbitt, he is a master to whom I am still grateful but from whom I have moved away ... He was a significant figure in his way: a man drawn in two directions by the more powerful forces of Gide and Claudel; and he was a man whom I liked – but an *esprit plutôt flottant*. Not individually important in *my* evolution, I don't think. When you say *L'Avenir de l'intelligence* you mean of course *Réflexions sur l'intelligence* by Maritain; the other is the book by Maurras which affected me strongly as early as 1911. I do think you ought to tackle this early book of Maritain, and you should look also at his *Antimoderne*. Most of his recent books (with the exception of *L'humanisme intégral* which I have read three or four times) I have not had the time to keep up with.'

1 – *Translation*: Dear Sir, Cher Maître, Many thanks indeed for your letter of July 28th. I am very pleased to know that you accept me as your intermediary for your Prologue. I am going to prepare the translation as quickly as possible (given my other commitments) and I hope to be able to publish it in our December number at the latest. Would you be so kind as to tell me when the French edition is due? If it is not coming out before the New Year, I would have a little more time in which to make an accurate translation.

Please accept, dear Sir, the expression of my deepest respect. [T. S. Eliot]

2 – Houston Peterson (1897–1981), Lecturer in Philosophy, Columbia University, New York. Publications included *Great Essays*; *Essays in Philosophy*; *Huxley, Prophet of Science*; and a book on Conrad Aiken entitled *The Melody of Chaos* (1931).

3 – Peterson, who was writing a book – *Havelock Ellis: Philosopher of Love* (1928) – asked if TSE had 'ever commented on [Ellis's] literary or semi-philosophical essays. If you have not done so but are interested in his attitude, would you be willing to set down some of your concrete impressions?' Havelock Ellis (1859–1939), writer and sexologist, was famous for his pioneering descriptive texts about homosexuality – 'inversion' as he preferred to call it – *Studies in the Psychology of Sex* (6 vols, 1897–1910, with vol. 7 in 1928). The first volume in the series, *Sexual Inversion*, was written in collaboration with the poet and critic John Addington Symonds (though published only after his death). A believer in biological determinism, Havelock Ellis was concerned above all to naturalise sex, so that homosexuality should be comprehended as part of the natural order of human behaviour, not as an aspect of perversion. Other works include *The New Spirit* (1890), *The Dance of Life* (1923), *The Psychology of Sex* (1933), *My Life* (1940).

written anything about Havelock Ellis. My friend, Mr Herbert Read, has written a note of his last book, which should appear very soon in *The Criterion*;[1] although I have a great respect for Ellis's work, I have never written anything about it.

As for myself, I hope to publish another volume of essays early next year, and probably they will be published in America as well as here.[2]

Thanking you for your kind comments,

I am,
Very truly yours,
[T. S. Eliot]

## TO *John Cournos* CC

5 August 1927 [*The Monthly Criterion*]

Dear Cournos,

Thank you for your letter of the 24th of July with your notes of Russian periodicals. I must tell you that I not only very much appreciate your punctuality with these reviews, but that I much enjoyed reading the notices themselves, which seem to me extremely good. My only suggestion, after reading the last part, is that I would rather that in these reviews of foreign periodicals nothing about myself should be mentioned.[3]

I will certainly take note to send you in future any books that deal with Russian matters. The last batch of books on these subjects has gone to John Gould Fletcher, who wanted them for a special article, but in future I will see that they go your way.

Should you return to England I hope you will let me know, so that we may meet.

Yours sincerely
[T. S. Eliot]

1 – HR's review did not appear in *MC*.

2 – Peterson added, 'as to my more impersonal motive, there are many of us in New York who would relish another volume of criticism from you, to be compiled from articles scattered through many periodicals in recent years . . .'

3 – Cournos would explain on 20 Aug., 'I thought it would interest you to see what the "wild Russians" were saying about you'.

## TO *John Gould Fletcher* CC

5 August 1927 [*The Monthly Criterion*]

Dear Fletcher,

What my letter said was that I agreed with you, but that I was uncertain of my ability to bring Graves to reason. I have returned his letter to him, and have suggested that he must at least alter his letter, as you have been in America for nearly a year, know what you are talking about, and have only recently returned. When I hear from him again I will let you know. I shall look forward to seeing you here on Wednesday next at any time from 12.45 to 1 o'clock. I wish you would show me your essay on Massis.[1] What I should suggest in advance is that we should use it as soon as possible after Massis's English translation appears.

Yours sincerely,
[T. S. E.]

## TO *Bonamy Dobrée* TS Brotherton

7 August [1927]
Sunday this day of St. Gaetano[2] *The Monthly Criterion*

Dear Bungamy:

Having advanced so far, a Word of caution. At the point which you have reached, in Bolovian Theology, you are likely to imagine that the Subject is much simpler than it really is. This has in fact happened, as shewn by the remark you let drop. I myself, even a few months ago, supposed that the Bolovian Theology was merely a form of Manichaean, Mandaean or Suvermerian dualism; and at one moment I inclined to the thought that this was merely a dualism between the Cosmic and the Comic Principles. But it is infinitely deeper. As you know, there is the God Wux, and the God Wux. But recent researches of mine – and you have no idea how difficult the language itself is, even *I* have only decipher'd the first two verses of the Bolovian National Anthem; and apart from the difficulties of language, the Bolovian theological style is *excessively* terse and roundbottomed – have shewn that there is also Wux, that is the Cosmic or Comic Principle. The Bolovian language has many subtleties and refinements unknown to Ours; but it has also certain Coarsenesses: and one of them is, that there

1 – Fletcher submitted his essay on 10 Aug.: 'I simply had to work off my Protestant gall.'

2 – St Gaetano, better known as St Cajetan (1480–1547), Italian founder of the Theatine Order; canonised in 1671 by Clement X. His feast day is 7 Aug.

is in effect No distinction between Cosmic and Comic. That is where Geo. Meredith gets it in the Neck. You will appreciate this distinction and lack of distinction much more ripely later on.

The fact is, then, to cut a long matter Short, that there Is this Principle Wux, the Cosmic or Comic Principle. With Wux (Modernist) and Wux (Fundamentalist) there is also Wux (C. & C. Principle) the latter being more apprehensible to our minds if we call it the Holy Ghost. These three together make up Wux, the First Principle. When, therefore, Wux is spoken of, you must make sure whether is meant Wux, or Wux, or Wux, or Wux. The chief difference, I think, between this Theology and our own orthodox, is that we think of a Trinity; whereas the subtle Bolovians thought of a Quarternity.

You should now, I think, be prepared to accept the first stanzos of the Boloviad. You must not be impatient, as this great poem – only to be compared to the Odyssey and the Chansong de Roland – moves slowly. The first Stanxo is as follows (in my forthcoming edition there will be 36 pages of commentary to make this stanzo more intelligible):

NOW Chris Columbo lived in Spain –
  Where Doctors are not many:
The only Doctor in his town
  Was a Bastard Jew (named Benny).
To Benny then Columbo went –
  With countenance so Placid:
And Benny filled Columbo's Prick
  With Muriatic Acid.[1]

You may say that that this exordium – magnificent as it is – has nothing to do with Bolovia and the Bolovians. But wait. You must first work through the Catalogue of Ships, the Inventory of Sailors, the Voyage etc. before we bring C. Columbo (Able Seaman) to the western Land of Bolovia. So no more for the Present.

Yours etc.
T. S. E.

The next Stanxo starts –

Columbo and his Caravels
  They set sail from GenOHa,
Queen Isabella was aboard!-
  That famous Spanish HO-AH . . .[2]

1 – This stanza of the Columbo and Bolo saga was drafted more than a decade before this date: see *IMH*, 316.
2 – Cf. *IMH*, 315.

## TO *Alec Randall* CC

9 August 1927 [London]

My dear Randall,

I have taken note of *Abendland* and will try to arrange an exchange; meanwhile we will drop the *Weltbuhne* quietly.

Thomas Mann's *Magic Mountain* has appeared in an English edition and has attracted a certain amount of attention.[1] There is no-one here who knows enough about Mann to be able to review it. It seems to me that Mann is an important writer, from what I know of his work, and I think that we ought to say something about him. Would you be disposed to write a review or notice of some kind about him yourself a propos of the *Magic Mountain*? I do not know the German name of this book or the publishers, but I dare say you do. But of course I leave it entirely to your judgement and discretion whether you think Thomas Mann or this particular book is worth review.

Yours ever sincerely
[T. S. E.]

## TO *Märit Scheler* CC

9 August 1927 [*The Monthly Criterion*]

Dear Madam,

In response to your request I have the honour to enclose a cheque in favour of Professor Scheler for twelve pounds. You will understand that this amount is approximate. Until the manuscript has been returned in proof by the printers we shall not know the exact number of words. I think that probably the sum enclosed is under the final payment; if so the balance will be adjusted later. As soon as Professor Scheler's manuscript has been returned by the printers I shall send him a copy in case he desires to make any further corrections to the proof.

I am glad to say again that I am extremely pleased to obtain for *The Criterion* a contribution of such interest and importance.

I am,
Yours very truly,
[T. S. Eliot]

1–*The Magic Mountain*, trans. H. T. Lowe-Porter (1927), was to become the standard English version of Thomas Mann's *Der Zauberberg*. No review was forthcoming in *MC*.

## TO *Bonamy Dobrée* CC

9 August 1927 [*The Monthly Criterion*]

My dear Dobrée,

I mentioned the other day a Dialogue about Fénelon[1] which I said I would send to you for your opinion. Here it is. It is written by a very worthy and earnest young man named Henry Vere Fitzroy Somerset, a fellow of Worcester College. It seems to me extraordinarily bad but I should be glad of an authoritative opinion before replying to him. Please return it at your earliest convenience.[2]

Yours ever,
[T. S. E.]

P.S. I have some Interesting information for you about the game of Polo as played by the Bolovians. This I will communicate later.

## TO *Ottoline Morrell* CC

9 August 1927 [London]

My dear Ottoline,

I was considerably worried at hearing from you that I had not returned your Ms and I have been looking for it ever since. It shows how deceitful one's memory is; for I was convinced that I had returned it to you, saying that I wanted to talk to you about it. However, I kept on looking and am ashamed and at the same time glad to have discovered it among a lot of private papers locked up in my dispatch case. So here it is. I like it very much, but as I said before I should like to talk to you about it. I agree with part of it but not with all; is it true that you disparage the monastic life?[3]

1–François Fénelon (1651–1715): Catholic theologian, writer, royal mentor; Archbishop of Cambrai under Louis XIV; author of *Les Aventures de Télémaque* (written 1693–4, published 1699), a novel catechising the divine right of kings that became a bestseller throughout Europe; it became, too, the inspiration for Mozart's opera *Idomeneo* (1781).

2–BD considered the dialogue (11 Aug.) 'not worth printing'. It was not published.

3–OM recounts in her memoirs 'how intensely religious' she was in early life: 'It was the centre and ground of my life' (124). She fell under the influence of Mother Julian, the Superior of a Sisterhood, and was enthralled by 'that terrible and beautiful book', *The Imitation of Christ*, by Thomas à Kempis. 'The monkish writer never had a more willing and obedient disciple. In one thing alone I felt I could not follow him: in his command to avoid all human contact' (*Ottoline: The Early Memoirs of Lady Ottoline Morrell*, 84).

I hope to see you before you leave London. I only await a word from you here and should be very happy if you would lunch with me one day; or if that is impossible would come to tea with you.

Ever yours affectionately,
[T. S. E.]

## TO *Robert Graves* TS Morris

9 August 1927 *The Monthly Criterion*

My dear Graves,

I have your last undated letter.[1] Certainly the question whether we print your letter, which you return, rests entirely with yourself; and I should not like you to think either that Fletcher wished the letter to be suppressed, or that I myself wished to suppress it in his interest. I do not think that it makes any difference to Fletcher personally or to myself editorially. The September number has already gone to press; one of my difficulties is that replies to articles in one number are seldom received in time for publication in the next; but I think I can promise to use your letter in the October number.[2]

1–Graves had written in reply to TSE's letter of 3 Aug.: 'I am glad you'll print the letter. My "indiscretion" is my own funeral. My "warmth" is both personal and critical; Fletcher's attack was personal and uncritical.

'Thank you for information about Fletcher's trip to the States. A pity it wasn't indefinitely prolonged. Thank you also for inviting verse-contributions but in the circumstances I do not feel able to offer any for your consideration. It would seem to be approving a popularistic policy in regard to contemporary poetry observable in the last two or three numbers of the *Criterion* with which, frankly, I do not find myself in sympathy. Commercially necessary, I grant, for a monthly: critically indefensible from my point of view.

'I am glad of the opportunity of rewriting the letter to make my point clearer. Please understand that I am "furthering no cause" except that of critical accuracy.

'Forgive these remarks. I have recently come to the point of always saying exactly what I mean in matters concerning poetry: and expect reciprocal activity on the part of those to whom my views are distasteful. When, as will shortly happen, I have no literary friends left, this will provide a natural and graceful end to my literary career,. Miss Riding is as little interested in her literary career as I am in mine, so you need have no misgivings on her behalf any more than on mine' (*In Broken Images*, 177).

2–The revised version of Graves's letter impugning Fletcher's review of Riding Gottschalk's *The Close Chaplet* – which he found 'typical of the sort of false writing that passes for criticism throughout the "advanced" literary press' – appeared in *MC* 6 (Oct. 1927), 357–9. 'What happens is that this sort of reviewer makes a point of knowing the "names" in fashion at the moment as the leaders of the advanced movements in poetry, and of discovering exactly at what price the stock of, say, Gertrude Stein (rising) . . . is being quoted in Bloomsbury, Paris and Greenwich Village. The review then writes itself. (Mr. Fletcher is a

I refrain from making any further comments on your official letter. At the same time I think I am justified in saying that I do not quite understand you. You allude to what you call a 'popularistic' policy in regard to contemporary poetry observable in the last two or three numbers of *The Criterion*. It is not clear to me whether you have in mind reviews by Humbert Wolfe or by F. S. Flint, or by J. G. Fletcher, or altogether. I should have thought myself that the points of view of these three reviewers were sufficiently varied to acquit us of 'a popularistic policy'; and indeed that if we were open to any criticism at all concerning our reviewing of poetry, I should have thought that that criticism would be that we held too many points of view. I really wish that you would, as a favour to me, make this criticism more clear.

As for your prediction that you will soon have no literary friends at all, I am sure that all of us who really care for literature look forward to the same consummation for ourselves.

Yours ever sincerely,
T. S. Eliot

## *Samuel Roth* TO *Robert Potter* (New York Evening Post)

10 August 1927

Two Worlds Publishing Company
Ltd., Five Hundred Fifth Avenue,
New York City

Dear Sir:

I am very much obliged to you for your letter of the eighth and for your considerateness in enclosing a copy of the letter written to you by Mr T. S. Eliot, editor of the *Monthly Criterion*.

As Mr Eliot's action is confessedly a part of the promotion scheme whereby Miss Sylvia Beach has tried to create the impression that my publication of the *Ulysses* was without authorisation I might disregard entirely the matter of Mr Eliot's own poem. But I do not want to entirely

---

little behindhand in the fashions owing to his long absence from the States – his trip last winter was not long enough as a "refresher" course, it seems – or perhaps he would not have committed this professional error with regard to Miss Riding; but that's not the point).' Riding's poems could not be accused of being derivative from the work of Stein, Moore or Ransom, or from Graves himself, he went on: 'The poems which he quotes as derivative from me were written before she had read any poems of mine except some early war-poems . . . [T]hose very "later poems" of mine which Mr Fletcher praises are definitely, though, I trust, not unwholesomely, influenced by Miss Riding's *Close Chaplet* sent me in typescript three years ago by John Ransom with suitable eulogies.'

disregard it. I will merely say that I think it is a very bad poem and that I reprinted it in *Two Worlds Monthly* as an interesting example of the sort of rubbish that is ladled out to us these days as poetry. Naturally there would have been no point in publishing my intention, and it is one of the delicious features of my enterprise that I find this sort of thing taken so seriously. Let Mr Eliot be at peace. At no time has his work ever had commercial value and it certainly was of no commercial value to me, yet as a mere formality I am, under separate cover, sending him a check for $25.00. I assure you that from what I know of Mr Eliot's beggarly past (I once contributed to a fund, instigated by himself towards raising money for him on the plea that he was consumptive and about to die) that I could buy all of his good will and future patronage with less than $25.00, but I fling the money in his teeth. So much for what I think he is worth to me.

As for the matter of *Ulysses*. I have already explained that Mr Ezra Pound, James Joyce's accredited agent in this country, turned over to me all his work which had previously been given to the *Little Review* and which the *Little Review* found impossible to publish. There was never any question, in the correspondence of Mr Pound, which is in my files, of any money to be paid, and certainly the thousand dollars which I offered Mr Joyce is more than he has ever been paid in one lump sum for any work of his, although I was under no obligation to pay him anything. I am proud to say that in spite of the intimidating propaganda of Mr Joyce and his friends, my correspondence coming from every part of the world shows that sentiment in the matter, now that the truth is known, is overwhelmingly in my favour.

Painful though it is, I return to Mr Eliot. It is obvious from his attempt to interpret the phrase 'has given us' as meaning that the things mentioned in my dedication were given to me personally that he is perverting the meaning of the phrase which is that they were given to our generation. Nor can it be true that my offer of a thousand dollars to Mr Joyce was news to Mr Eliot who must have seen my statement in the *New Statesman* of London – a statement about which I have heard from almost every literary man of importance in London.

Well, Mr Eliot has put it over. He has managed to give me something of a feeling of humiliation, for it cannot fail to be humiliating to have one's dedication thrown back at one in that way. I am only faintly consoled by the fact that my esteem for Mr Eliot is only of the lightest. What is more important, I feel duly chastised in myself for having given way so easily in my love of fine phrases. I stand entirely corrected. Mr Eliot if [is] not any of the things indicated in my dedication, and since he has been careful to bring proof of it to the *Evening Post* and two other American papers, I feel entirely free to say that I think he is both a prig and a blackguard.

Very truly yours,
Samuel Roth

## *E. Loewenstein* TO *T. S. Eliot*

10 August 1927

Two Worlds Publishing Company,
Inc., Five Hundred Fifth Avenue,
New York City

Dear Sir:

Mr Roth has asked me to send you the enclosed check in full payment for a poem of yours which he reprinted in an issue of *Two Worlds Monthly*, entitled 'Wanna Go Home, Baby?'

I also beg to enclose a letter which Mr Roth sent to the editor of the New York *Evening Post*. Copies of it have also gone out to the editors of *The Nation* and *The Dial*, to whom your original letter to the New York *Evening Post* [was also] sent.

Very truly yours,
E. Loewenstein
Secretary to Mr Roth

## TO *Jacques Maritain*

CC

10 août 1927

[London]

Cher Monsieur et Ami,

Je dois vous accuser réception de vos deux livres: d'abord de la belle édition d'*Art et Scolastique*[1] dignifiée par votre inscription; et puis de la *Primauté du Spirituel*.[2] Le premier, je l'ai prêté à notre ami et collègue Herbert Read qui s'intéresse au Thomisme, et surtout à vos théories esthétiques. Le second, je suis en train de le lire moi-même; surtout parce que je m'occupe à ce moment avec un livre sur le relation de l'Église et l'État, naturellement d'un point de vue Anglican. Après que j'ai lu votre livre je vous écrirai plus à la longue.

1 – *Art et scolastique* (Paris: Louis Rouart, 1927).
2 – *Primauté du spirituel* (Paris, 1927).

J'ai reçu aussi un avertissement avec votre signature de l'entreprise nouvelle et très intéressante qui s'appelle *Correspondance*. Il parait que vous invitez ma collaboration. Je ne sais pas si mon point de vue s'approche suffisamment au point de vue de vos autres collègues. Vous savez bien que je m'intéresse énormément au Mouvement Thomiste. Mais vous comprendrez que mon point de vue est Anglo-Catholique et pas Catholique de Rome, et qu'il y a certains points sur lesquels nous ne nous entendons pas. Mais si vous voulez la collaboration d'une personne qui souhaite vivement l'union éventuelle du monde chrétien, je serais bien heureux de promettre autant de collaboration que vous voudrez.

Recevez, cher Monsieur et Ami, l'assurance de ma sympathie loyale,

[T. S. Eliot][1]

## TO *Roger Hinks* CC

10 August 1927 [*The Monthly Criterion*]

My dear Hinks,

You ask me in your letter of the 8th instant when I want your next Chronicle. That is not quite so simple a question as it sounds. I can give you two alternatives, owing to the interruption of the cycle which you have noticed. It has been interrupted for several reasons – First, Flint has been away on what he calls official business in Belgium; second, Marichalar's mother has been ill; third, Gilbert Seldes has disappeared; fourth, I am trying to get rid of my French chronicler[2] by letting him lapse. In fact, the cycle is in confusion. If you sent me some sort or any sort of

1 – *Translation*: Dear Sir and Friend, I must acknowledge receipt of your two books: first, the handsome edition of *Art et Scolastique* enhanced by your inscription; and secondly *Primauté du Spirituel*. The first I have lent to our friend and colleague Herbert Read who is interested in Thomism and especially in your aesthetic theories. The second I am in the process of reading myself; especially since I am working at the moment on a book about the relationship between Church and State, naturally from an Anglican point of view. When I have finished reading your book, I shall write to you at greater length.

I have also received an announcement signed by you concerning a new and very interesting enterprise called *Correspondance*. It would seem that you are inviting me to become a contributor. I don't know if my point of view is sufficiently close to that of your other colleagues. As you know, I am extremely interested in the Thomist Movement. But you will understand that my point of view is Anglo-Catholic and not Roman Catholic, and that there are certain points on which we are not in agreement. But if you wish for material from someone who keenly desires the ultimate union of the Christian world, I would be very happy to promise you as many contributions as you may ask for.

Let me assure you, dear Sir and Friend, of my sincere fellow-feeling. [T. S. Eliot]

2 – F. S. Flint.

chronicle before the 15th instant (i.e. the 15th August), it would appear in the October number; and I should be very grateful; if you cannot spur yourself to such an enormous effort, I should be glad to have a chronicle by the 10th September for the following number. Please let me know, at any rate, immediately by postcard whether you think that in the present weather you can goad yourself to doing a chronicle by the 15th of this month.

I have not seen any Art books of particular interest advertised and I have not received any; but if you care to range outside the plastic arts let me know of any books that you would like.

Yours ever,
[T. S. Eliot]

## TO *Bonamy Dobrée* TS Brotherton

10 August 1927 *The Monthly Criterion*

Dear Bungamy:

*Zur Kipling-Forschungen.*

The Kipling in its present form seems to me admirable. I do think, as you suggested yourself, that the last section (technisch) might still be telescoped into the rest if (1) you can keep the Jer-Taylor analogy, which seems to me v. suggestive and fruitful (Murry would say 'pregnant'), and all the quotations.[1] I dont think you have adduced any quotation which is not fruitful (scilicet pregnant). Might we lunch next week and wind up this matter? A first rate essay. I shall have to Go Some (in our crude transatlantic phrase) to deal adequately with Chesbelloc. Should like to consult about that too.

*Zur Bolovischen Ur-Kunde.*

I have just completed, and sent for publication to the Leipziger Akademie fuer Bolowissenschaftslehre (of which I am an Hon. vicepresidaent), a little monograph 'Polemisches gegen Schnitzel', in reply to Prof. Dr Schnitzel of Vienna, of which I shall send you a copy when printed. It

1–BD, 'Rudyard Kipling', *MC* 6 (Dec. 1927), 499–515. BD noted, among other things, 'For the Elizabethans and Jacobeans life gained its glamour largely from its nearness to the plague-pit; its values were determined and heightened by the vigorously expressed dogmas of a church, which, for pulpit purposes at least, believed in hell; the metaphysical void was filled by the sense that life was given to man as a discipline and an adventure: this is still part of Mr. Kipling's belief. Indeed, if one were to have to choose one man from whom he descends . . . one would say it was Jeremy Taylor' (512).

concerns the game of Polo as played by King Bolo. You let drop the other day, whilst immersed in Russian Stout (how good it is) the suggestion that more of modern kulture might be derived from Bolovia than we suppose. Well, one of these is the game of Polo. This is not altogether disputed, but Schnitzel had the impudence to impone that it was not quite the same game. His argument ran, that Bolovian Polo was played with llamas instead of ponies (which is not disputed), that llamas have shorter legs than ponies and heavier bodies, that they do not move so rapidly (which is not disputed), that the mallet was six or seven times the size of the modern mallet (which is not disputed) and that therefore it was a different Game. He goes so far, in disparagement, as to say that the Bolovian game was '*komisch, drollig, und affenartiges*'. In my reply I point out that though the legs of the llama are shorter than those of the powny, the legs of the Boloviam were as long as those of the European, that accordingly in Polo the llama was provided with six legs and could move faster; that if the mallet was six times as big, so was the ball; that the ball was nothing else than a large fresh cabbage; that there is nothing llamas like better than a good cabbage; that therefore they had a stake in the game and a reason for acceleration; that it is certain that the Bolovians knew the game of water-polo, which they practised on occasions of public rejoicing (v. the Boloviad Canto V, v. 352 ff.) and consequently a fortiori they must have known Polo.

Yours etc.
[Unsigned]

## TO *G. B. Harrison* CC

10 August 1927 [London]

Dear Harrison,

Thank you very much. Here is the proof copy of my paper returned.[1] The only important point which I should like to suggest is this: I wish you would put in somewhere, I do not care where, a statement that this was an address read before the Shakespeare Association – otherwise it seems to me much too pretentious; and the fact that it was a paper read aloud may incline readers to pardon certain faults of form and style. So I hope

1–*Shakespeare and the Stoicism of Seneca*, an Address read before the Shakespeare Association, 18th March 1927 (London: Humphrey Milford, Oxford University Press, for The Shakespeare Association, 22 Sept. 1927); repr. in *SE* (1932), 107–20.

that you will do that for me. Otherwise you will find a very small number of corrections.

Yours sincerely,
[T. S. Eliot]

## TO *Lady Rothermere* CC

10 August 1927 [London]

Dear L. R.,

*Seriously*.[1] Very many thanks for your letter as well as for the preceding P.C. which gives me a very positive impression that you are in the very best of health and beauty. I wish that what I have sent you was in a small degree comparable but I know that it is not. I agree with your criticisms.[2] The *Napoleon* is good and I think that this man, Pickthorn, will be useful. I think also that O'Flaherty is good; at any rate I must warn you that I cannot get for every month anything as good as that. If you knew the dozens of second rate and third rate Irish stories that I have read, and the dozens of third rate and fourth rate Russian stories that I have read you would be in the same state of despair about contemporary fiction as I am. So I hope that if you find any inferior fiction in the next few numbers of the *Criterion* you will realise that I accepted it when in a state of absolute despair. I still hope to get something out of Virginia Woolf; I have written to Coppard who has *promised* me his next piece of fiction – which when received will probably (according to my experience) turn out too bad to publish – I have approached David Garnett and Tomlinson neither of whom had anything to offer at the moment, and I am entirely dependent on what fortune and the literary agents send. I have two pieces of near-fiction to use in the near future. One is some travel sketches by D. H. Lawrence and the other a travel diary of Arnold Bennett, but I must admit that I cannot find any first rate fiction.

I agree that our articles are too long. But I assure you that I have to use all of my force of character such as it is and all of my gifts of diplomacy such as they are to keep the articles down to the length which you see. I think that the thing on Chaucer was a mistake: it was much too long and

1–'*Seriously*. Is there any chance of your visiting me in Fribourg this *September*?' Lady Rothermere had asked (undated).

2–'The criticism of Ludwig's *Napoleon* is good. I'm rather tired of Chaucer!!! The short story is good . . . I think some of the articles too long – everything nowadays should be "short & snappy".'

very much too full of notes for our purpose; but I hope not to make that mistake again.

Ever cordially yours,
[T. S. E.]

P.S. Your invitation is in the circumstances an exasperation. There is just a remote possibility, and in that case I would take the liberty of wiring you, if you will keep me in touch with your address. Needless to say, it would be a very keen pleasure.

TSE

## TO *William Rose*[1] CC

10 August 1927 [London]

My dear Rose,

Your letter expressing your wonder whether there is any possibility of my finding time to turn out the book on Dante in the near future arrives just at a time when I am wondering whether there is any possibility of my turning out anything in the near future.[1] To tell the truth, when I agreed to write the book on Dante I allowed myself in imagination about ten years for that task. I find myself at the moment confronted with the preparation of three books which I have undertaken to do as soon as possible; one is a theological work, another is a book of literary essays and the third is the revision of my lectures on Donne. I hope to finish the last by about the end of 1928. I should be very glad to do what I can but I am afraid that at best it would be impossible for me to turn out anything, however unsatisfactory, on Dante before the end of 1929.[2] And if I am to do this work satisfactorily to myself, there is about two years reading in the literature of the 12th and 13th centuries to be done, and I should prefer, before writing the book, to spend a few months acquiring the rudiments of the Provençal language. So I am afraid that this book will be of no immediate use to you.

Meanwhile, however, as Wells would say,[3] are you going to be in London during the rest of the summer, and could you come one day and have a

1 – 'I am wondering whether there is any possibility of your finding time to turn out the book on Dante for the "Republic of Letters" in the more or less near future' (8 Aug.)

2 – TSE's *Dante* was published by F&F on 27 Sept. 1929, as the second volume in a series 'The Poets on the Poets', with a jacket design by Rex Whistler.

3 – TSE is making a joke out of the title of a novel by H. G. Wells, *Meanwhile: The Picture of a Lady* (1927). Cf. TSE's 'Commentary', *MC* 6 (Dec. 1927), 482: 'It is possible, of course,

glass of beer and possibly a Wiener Schnitzel in this neighbourhood? Any time from the latter part of next week would suit me and I should very much like to see you again.

Yours ever sincerely
[T. S. Eliot]

## TO *Robert Graves*

TS Morris

11 August 1927 *The Monthly Criterion*

Dear Graves,

I was pleased to get your letter though not altogether happy about its contents.[1] I mean that I treat your writing to me as a kind of expression of confidence although I am unhappy to learn the surprising deductions you have made from my publication. I do not know Humbert Wolfe very intimately and therefore from your point of view my connection with him is merely a matter of public criticism. But I have known F. S. Flint and John Gould Fletcher for many years, and when you refer to them as 'literary politicians' I can only throw up my hands in despair. Part of my confidence and belief in these two men is exactly my conviction that they are emphatically *not* literary politicians, that neither of them has any axe to grind whatever; and in fact among all the contributors to *The Criterion* I cannot think of any of whose disinterestedness and detachment I am more convinced. As for my own editorials and book notes, they are so various that I cannot reply to such a sweeping

that evolution will bring the human race to such a point of perfection that thinking will no longer be necessary . . . Theology will no doubt become obsolete . . . But in this painful "meanwhile", as Mr Wells would say, during which we are still obliged to think that we think, a great many theological works are being published . . .'

1–Graves had sent an undated reply to TSE's letter of 9 Aug.: 'Please treat the following as a matter not at all for anyone else but ourselves. I have had great respect for you in the past as a man who has really cared for poetry on its own account and conducted himself with dignity in the bad atmosphere of literary politics. Your last sentence about desiring the same consummation for yourself as I expressed for myself reassures me that your principles are the same as in, say, 1914. But then I can only read your editorial consent to reviews by literary poliicians such as Wolfe, Flint and Fletcher as a gesture of complete hopelessness and bankruptcy; and your editorials and book-notes as a humorous ventriloquial entertainment with a journalistic dummy on your knee. All this isn't my business. But you asked me what I meant & this is it. I don't suggest that it would be possible to edit a monthly and sell it except in this way. Nor do I claim that my literary conduct has been above reproach. It hasn't. (It is however only recently that I have realized the extent of my shortcomings and their bad effect on my poetry – but that is by the way). Well, that's enough.' (*In Broken Images*, 177–8)

condemnation unless you will specify details. Of course I want to sell the monthly, but I rather resent your intimation that I have vulgarised it for the purpose of increasing the sales. As for your own literary conduct, I have never supposed or suggested that there was any reproach to be cast upon it.[1]

Yours sincerely,
T. S. Eliot

## TO *Thomas McGreevy* TS TCD

11 August 1927 *The Monthly Criterion*

My dear McGreevy,

In reply to your letter of the 8th instant, I am glad to hear that you think you can tackle Gide.[2] Of course I will allow you all the time you need for it; that is left to you; all that I insist upon is that I must publish your 'Gide'

1 – Graves replied to this letter from TSE, in a further undated letter: 'No insult intended. Only, once a monthly is launched one has to go on with it and if it is not run in a certain way nobody buys it. I would not suggest that you vulgarise the *Criterion* to increase the sales and fill your pockets: obviously you are not that sort of person but I do think that you have compromised about it just as far as was necessary to keep it afloat and I think poetry has been compromised just to that extent. I am saying nothing against Flint, Fletcher & Wolfe whom I do not know well enough to speak against except to say that they are literary politicians as is manifest in their writings; and you are not responsible for this however long you have known them. Wolfe is of course a politician of the more obvious kind. Flint & Fletcher are more missionary politicians, less personally ambitious, less easy in their flattering judgements of successful contemporaries but certainly not detached in the sense that I believe you fundamentally are. Lets stop this correspondence, which perhaps shouldn't have beeen allowed to get as far as this. I am not talking at random about your editorial & other notices, but have no wish to exaggerate the importance either of your editorial activities or my opinion of them. Lets nod and walk on' (*In Broken Images*, 178–9).

Apropos Graves's distaste for the work of Humbert Wolfe: on 30 Oct. 1930, when GCF moved to invite Graves to contribute to the 'Poets on the Poets' series – 'There is a fair field for choice. Dante, Marvell and Tennyson have been impaled. Coleridge, Burns, Christina Rossetti, Wordsworth marked down by others' – Graves responded (undated: Nov. 1930): 'Thank you for inviting me to write a poet on poets, but I can't really, quite apart from having too much work on hand already. A particular reason – I have found it a convenient rule to contribute to no series in which H. Wolfe was making one. A general reason – I think that dead poets should only be critically written about by dead poets and that living poets should only, if at all, write about living ones. With best wishes and congratulations on the success of F. & F.' (Faber E3/1/8).

2 – McGreevy: 'only yesterday I came to the conclusion that I could probably make a hand of it. You will let me have some time? They have not got the Faux Monnayeurs here nor the Dostoevsky and I suppose I ought also to have a look at Si le grain ne meurt.'

before I publish your 'O'Flaherty'. I think you will have to get hold of the *Faux-Monnayeurs* somehow as that is an important step in Gide's recent work. If you find it absolutely impossible to get the *Dostoevsky*, let me know because I think I could at least scrape up in London a copy to lend you. Surely it is possible to get hold of *Si le Grain ne meurt* in Paris. I wish very much that before you write about Gide you would read Henri Massis's essay on him in the second volume of *Jugements.*[1] It expresses a point of view which I imagine is very different from yours and it happens to be very similar to my own: but I confidently expect from you a point of view about Gide different either from that of Gide's Parisian admirers or Gide's Parisian detractors. I admit that I am on the side of the latter, which is one reason why I am giving the review of Gide to someone who, I hope, will have a third and an independent point of view.[2]

I am glad to hear that there is a possibility of your position in the Ecole straightening itself out.[3]

I am afraid that there is little likelihood of my coming to Paris. I should be interested to learn your reactions to the recent *Criterions,* though I cannot promise not to put them on my Index. I am interested and pleased to hear, what I did not know, that Stewart[4] is an Ulsterman, as I have a certain infusion of Ulster ancestry myself. I am not, however, a Calvinist. I hope that you will not allow your sense of obligation either to Stewart or to myself to influence or repress your personal opinions or convictions, if you have *any*. As for the Vatican, I take no responsibility for it and expect

1 – Massis's *Jugements* (Paris, 1923) includes an appendix on André Gide.

2 – McGreevy reviewed *Les Faux-Monnayeurs: Roman* and *Journal des Faux-Monnayeurs, Morceaux Choisis* and *Voyage au Congo: Carnets de Route*, in *MC* 7 (Jan. 1928), 65–9. Attentive to TSE's remarks, he noted *inter alia*: 'Since the death of [Anatole] France, Gide has . . . come to be regarded – outside of his own country especially – as the most representative and considerable of living French novelists.

'Why is it then that Gide has not been elected to the Académie, and that even the idea of his ever being elected is not taken seriously by most interested Frenchmen. Is it that he is in the line of the great nineteenth-century outsiders in whom the spirit of Gothic France was reborn: Balzac, Rimbaud, Mallarmé? Is M. Gide, like them, a pioneer, to be fully justified only in generations to come? He is not reluctant to stake out a claim in the future for himself. He is not greatly troubled by the extent of the present-day hostility to him. He makes no pathetic attempts to force academic doors. He is content to wait. He writes, he believes, "pour les générations à venir".' McGreevy notes that the quotation he had just used 'is taken from an essay on Gide by M. Henri Massis (in *Jugements*), which, though it makes too little allowance for the circumstances that have made M. Gide what he is, is interesting as putting the case against him from the point of view of an implacable neo-Catholic' (65–6).

3 – 'I am venturing to let myself believe that it is getting straight – it's understood that I stay.'

4 – William Stewart.

to be placed on that Index myself.[1] I am sorry to hear that you think of getting married. I cannot quite see the advantage of an Unitarian church over a registry office.[2]

Yours sincerely,
T. S. Eliot

## TO *Messrs The Putnam Syndicate Ltd* CC

12 August 1927 [London]

Dear Sirs,

I am sorry not to have been able to reply before about Mr Williamson's two stories.[3] I am returning to you herewith 'The Drama of the Needles' because nature sketches of this type, however able, are unsuitable for *The Criterion*. I am holding for the moment the second story, 'The Spirit of the Village' as it is possible that I may like to retain this for publication. I will let you know about this as soon as possible.[4]

Yours faithfully,
[T. S. Eliot]

1–'I have been thinking a good deal about all the religious goings on in The Criterion, making notes etc and may venture to send them to you . . . I am hoping for my own sake that if you see Stewart at Pontigny you won't encourage each other any more than you must to take your personal responsibility for the future of Europe more seriously still. He has befriended me, you have too (and in addition were the last hero of my adolescence) so I must listen to him and read you and I'll go mad if I hear much more about what we ought to do about Europe . . . If the Massis, Maritains and Valerys and all the other people who carry their God on one sleeve and their country on the other do succeed in founding a European Academy which is about all they can do it will (for all they be some of them Catholics) only become the Holy Office of the Protestant Papacy at Geneva . . . Stewart had decided to become an M.P. and save Europe (from a seat in the Belfast Parliament) when he is 35 – 7 years from now. Is it any wonder I am concerned?'

2–'I told our Stephen MacKenna (whom I regard as a Cézanne of religion) the other day that I had begun to contemplate matrimony and undertook if it got past contemplation to have the ceremony in a Unitarian Church! He verted to it from Rome two years ago.'

3–Henry Williamson (1895–1977), author of *Tarka the Otter* (1927) and *Salar the Salmon* (1935). In Mar. 1927 the Putnam Syndicate tried to persuade TSE to purchase the first British serial rights in a short nature study by Williamson, *The Race of the Frogs*.

4–Williamson, 'The Village Inns', *MC* 7 (Feb. 1928), 120–36.

## TO *Mrs Richard Church* CC

12 August 1927 [London]

Dear Mrs Church,

I am very sorry indeed to hear your news.[1] Please give your husband my kindest regards and sympathy and tell him to keep the books and review them when he can. I hope that he will improve rapidly, and should very much like him to come and lunch with me as soon as he can get up to town.

Yours sincerely,
[T. S. Eliot]

## TO *John Gould Fletcher* CC

15 August 1927 [London]

My dear Fletcher,

Thank you for the revised copy of 'East and West'. I return herewith the other copy. The essay interests me very much indeed, it deals with fundamental questions and though I by no means agree with the whole of it I certainly think that it ought to be published. But as it may be some little time before I have room for an essay of this length, would you mind doing a very short review of the Fulop-Muller book? Four or five lines would do really, merely to say that it is an important book and to show that we have not overlooked it.[2]

It is possible that the Massis book will be out before I can use this article, and I shall have to have another review of it since you only touch on Massis in passing.

I am rather interested in the approximation of your position to that of Babbit[t]. Have you read *Democracy and Leadership*? I think it is a great book, but I find Babbit like yourself rather more Eastern than I can be.

1–Caroline Church had sent word (10 Aug.) that her husband, the civil servant, writer and critic Richard Church, would 'not be able to do the books you sent him within the three weeks as he is at present at home with a nervous breakdown but hopes to be able to do a little work before very long'.

2–René Fülop-Muller, *The Mind and Face of Bolshevism*, trans. F. S. Flint and D. F. Tair, was reviewed in *MC* 6 (Dec. 1927), 567–8.

Would you be able to come to a dinner on Friday of *next* week?

With many thanks,

Yours ever,

[T. S. Eliot]

P.S. If possible I should like to arrange a lunch with you before you go away because there are two or three points in your article which I should like to discuss. I am certainly, I think, quite in agreement with you about the present policy and tendency of the Vatican.

## TO *Bonamy Dobrée*

TS Brotherton

Monday [15 August 1927] *The Monthly Criterion*

Dear Bungamy:

I shall await you at Russell Square at 12 on Thursday. If you think you can direct Sainsbury[1] to the Grove, do so; the appointment is for 1 o'clock, and the place is a private room engaged by Read: but if you cannot direct him accurately, tell him to come to Russell Square at 12:50. The best way to find the Grove is to walk smartly up Brompton (or is it The Brompton, like The Edgware?) Road to the Bunch of Grapes, and enquire there.

Considering your affliction, I trust that you will take it rather as a preparation of the Mind for the reception of spiritual knowledge, instead of the mere attack of influenza, measles or clap which you may incline to think it.[2] Remember that we should rise on stepping stones etc. to higher things.[3]

Prepare your mind for the reception of higher dogmata of theology by meditation, and try to realise the distinction (v. Murry) between Faith and Reason.

Meanwhile I will treat your Convalescence with literary-historical instead of Philosophico-theological matters, and introduce

1 – Geoffrey Sainsbury: writer; translator of the novels of Georges Simenon.

2 – BD said (11 Aug.) he had been visited 'with a sickness'.

3 – 'I hold it truth, with him who sings
To one clear harp in divers tones,
That men may rise on stepping-stones
Of their dead selves to higher things'
(Tennyson, *In Memoriam A. H. H.* [1850], I, 1–4).

THE CATALOGUE OF SHIPS

The Flagship of Columbo's Fleet
Was call'd THE VIRGIN MARY;
An able vessel fully mann'd
By Seamen brown & hairy.
The other Ships came on behind –
The HOLY GHOST and JESUS;
Well stock'd, to sail o'er perilous seas,
With Ham and Cheddar Cheeses.

THE CATALOGUE OF SHIPMATES

The Cook who serv'd them Pork and Beans
Was known as Careless Cora;
A Dame of Pure Australian Blood –
(With a tincture of Angora).
She wore a Jumper short and red,
Which closely did her shape fit;
And the hair that Lay along her Back
Was Yellow (like ripe ape-shit).

Catalogue of Shipmates to be contined through 25 stanzoes.

What, you will say, has all this to do with Bolovia? Patience. It took Chris. Columbo 3 months to reach Bolovia; can you not wait a fortnight?

Do not worry too much about the Bolovian Heresies. It will comfort you to know that the entire population (before, as I told you, they suffered Complete Immersion from which they have never reappeared) were converted to the Baptist Church.

Yours etc.
T. S. E.

Somerset is a Fellow, *hélas*.[1] But he shall not be discouraged. Many thanks.

1–BD had said he thought Henry Somerset 'worth encouraging' as a writer (11 Aug.) – 'so long, that is, as by fellow of Worcester you mean chap at Worcester and not Fellow of Worcester. If he is the last, the case is hopeless.'

## TO *Richard Aldington* CC

16 August 1927 [London]

My dear Richard,

Your letter has come as a great surprise and has given me a great shock.[1] I hope that it is needless to say that I was ignorant of the circumstances, although I now remember that someone once mentioned to me that Cournos had written a novel in which you and a part of your life had figured.[2] Cournos is almost a stranger to me – in fact I think I have only met him twice in my life, and I took him on originally because I did not then know of anyone else who could do Russian periodicals. At the moment I simply find myself distressed and in a dilemma. *I will write to you further*. I must explain, however, that your admirable review of *The Wandering Scholars* is not only in type but in the next number which is in process of binding and that it would be quite impossible for me to remove it.[3] If I held up that number on this account I should really be committing a default against my employers. I trust that you will understand this point.[4]

Yours ever affectionately,

[T.]

1 – RA wrote (14 Aug.): 'The Russian notes in your last number caused me great surprise. "J. C." must stand for John Cournos. After what that man has done I am shocked that you, a man whom I respect so much, a man with so nice a sense of honour, should employ a creature of that sort. I can only feel that your good-nature has been surprised and that you do not know the base things he has attempted to perform with his novels.

'I feel that it would be humiliating to me to have my work appear in a periodical to which Cournos is (apparently) a regular contributor. In no spirit of hostility to you, but with great regret and respect, I must ask you not to publish anything further in the Criterion while Cournos is writing for it. Strange indeed that I should have to write thus to you, one of my dearest friends; but there are in life some actions which are unpardonable, some people with whom one does not and cannot associate. Cournos is one of them.'

2 – Cournos's *Miranda Masters* (1926) is a *roman à clef* based on his relationship with H. D., Richard Aldington and Ezra Pound.

3 – Review of Helen Waddell, *The Wandering Scholars*, *MC* 6 (Sept. 1927), 274–7.

4 – RA replied (18 Aug.): 'I regret that I left the . . . article so late that my name must again appear in proximity to that *crapule*. Please see that the other articles are destroyed.'

RA told EP on 22 Aug.: 'I have withdrawn from the Criterion on what I consider excellent grounds, i.e. that T.S.E. is employing that Ghetto guttersnipe Cournos. I have told Tom that I won't appear in the same periodical with said C. However, T. and I are still on perfectly friendly terms otherwise' (*Richard Aldington: An Autobiography in Letters*, 81).

## TO *Herbert Read*

TS Victoria

16 August 1927 *The Monthly Criterion*

*Confidential*

My dear Read,

The enclosed letter is of course private and personal but as you also are a friend of Richard's and as I may take it that you are as attached to Richard's interests as I am, I send it to you with the request that you will advise me what to do. I remember a rumour that Cournos had written a novel in which Richard's domestic affairs figured in rather an improper way, but the report did not make very much impression on me. Cournos has been very regular and faithful in his Russian reports and they have seemed to me on the whole quite good; except that, as I have already written to him, a week or two ago, I objected to his dragging my own name too conspicuously into the last report.

I have in the past had experience of Richard's almost morbid sensitiveness, and on one occasion have had to admit that I was in the wrong, though even on that occasion I do not think that a more normal person than Richard would have objected: for indeed on the occasion of our greatest quarrel my only reason for having spoken of Richard as I did was the desire to bring his name into prominence. But on *this* occasion, as I am quite ignorant of the causes and the documents, I feel innocent. Nevertheless, Cournos is quite a stranger to me and I have been associated with Richard for many years. What would you do?

Yours ever in haste,
T. S. E.

I do not know when Cournos' book or novel appeared. But I am strongly under the impression that I arranged with Cournos to do Russian Per[iodicals] *before* I heard about the novel. Will see you Thursday Grove.

## TO *John Gould Fletcher*

CC

16 August 1927 [London]

My dear Fletcher,

Read is arranging a lunch on Thursday. It will be at 1 o'clock at the Grove Tavern in Beauchamp Place, and will be held, I understand, in a private room for which one is to ask. The only way I know of getting to the Grove is this: go to Brompton Road station on the Piccadilly railway, walk up Brompton Road in the direction of Knightsbridge, leave at the right hand a tavern called 'The Bunch of Grapes'. Do not turn down at

'The Bunch of Grapes', but continue beyond and I think that Beauchamp Place is the next turning on the right. Beauchamp Place is not long and the Grove Tavern is somewhere in it. With these directions I think you will be as likely to get there on time as I am and you will be very welcome.

Yours ever,
[T. S. Eliot]

## TO *John Middleton Murry* — TS Northwestern

16 August 1927 — Faber & Gwyer Ltd

My dear John,

I am sending you enclosed a proof copy of my own reply but I must warn you that it may be more or less modified before it appears. Fernandez' reply, which in some respects agrees with mine but is very much more profound, has gone to press. I will send you a copy of the proof immediately upon receipt.

I am afraid that 6–7.30. on any day is no good for me, circumstances being as they are. If it proves possible to meet on Tuesday the 23rd at any time, I am free and can make appointments from about 12 noon to 4. p.m. Try to stay over the night and lunch with me on Tuesday the 23rd.

I hope that your news about your children has not been offset by any bad news about yourself or your wife.[1]

Always affectionately,
Tom.

P.S. Your admirable review of Santayana has gone to press. In it I think you refer to both the religious (or theological) and literary policy of the *Criterion*. When I send you the proof I shall have to ask you to think whether you can modify this statement. The *Criterion* has certainly a literary policy, that is to say a residuum on which half a dozen persons are more or less in agreement, but it has no religious or theological policy. I think you will find that I accept many expressions of views which are not my own and that I never express any religious views in the unsigned editorials. I am responsible as contributor rather than as editor for views which appear over my name. It is as much a policy of the *Criterion* as a paper to express views like yours as to express views like mine.[2]

T.

1 – 'I haven't any good news,' wrote JMM (15 Aug.), 'except that the children are well.'
2 – JMM replied (undated, 'Thursday'): 'I will attend to what you say about my reference to the "policy" of The New Criterion and adjust my remarks accordingly.' He did so.

## TO *Hart Crane* TS Butler

16 August 1927 *The Monthly Criterion*

Dear Mr Crane,

I should like to use your poem 'The Tunnel' in *The Criterion*. At the moment I cannot say definitely in what number I could publish it; possibly November, possibly not until January.[1] I should be very much obliged if you would write to me on receipt of this and let me know whether you have already arranged for publication in America. I never object in the least to simultaneous publication, but as a rule I do not like to publish anything which has already appeared in America.

Yours sincerely,
T. S. Eliot

## TO *Andrew H. Dakers*[2] CC

16 August 1927 [London]

Dear Sir,

With reference to your letter of the 3rd instant, I am retaining the story by Mr Williamson entitled 'Innocence in the Sunlight of a Sinful World' with a view to publication in *The Criterion*. I am not yet able to say for what issue it would go to press but should hope to use it in December or January. I should be glad to hear from you that it would not be published in America previously and would accordingly confirm my acceptance.[3]

Yours very truly,
[T. S. Eliot]

'The Village Inns' and 'The Old Cob Cottage' are returned to you herewith.

1–'The Tunnel' (part VII of *The Bridge*, 1930), *MC* 6 (Nov. 1927), 398–402. Crane wrote to Otto H. Kahn on 12 Sept. 1927: 'I have been especially gratified by the reception accorded me by *The Criterion*, whose director, Mr. T. S. Eliot, is representative of the most exacting literary standards of our times' (*Complete Poems* [2006], 558).
2–Literary agency.
3–It turned out that the story chosen by TSE had already been sold in the UK by Henry Williamson. TSE therefore asked to reconsider the stories he had just returned and chose 'The Village Inns' for publication in *MC* 7 (Feb. 1928), 120–36.

## TO *Powys Evans*[1] CC

17 August 1927 [London]

Sir,

I am flattered by your desiring to do a drawing of me but if your expectation is to publish it in the *Mercury*, I should advise you to make certain first whether Mr Squire cares to publish a drawing of me.[2] I have of course seen many of your drawings and should be very glad to give you the opportunity. At the present time I am extremely busy and before suggesting an appointment I should like to know whether one sitting would do, and if so how long you would wish that sitting to be. If in the meantime you have not changed your mind, and still desire to make what I fear must be, by reason of the subject, a wholly unsaleable drawing, I shall be very glad to arrange with you for a suitable period of time.

I am, Sir,
Your obliged, obedient servant,
[T. S. Eliot]

## TO *Thomas McGreevy* CC

17 August 1927 [*The Monthly Criterion*]

My dear McGreevy,

I am sorry to find that you have worked up a nervous crisis about nothing – although nervous crises usually are about nothing.[3] When you talked in a loose and extravagant way about the theological tendencies

1–Powys Evans (1899–1981), caricaturist and cartoonist known as 'Quiz', contributed to *Saturday Review*, *London Mercury*, and *G. K's Weekly*. He published *Fifty Heads* (1928).

2–Evans applied to TSE on 16 Aug. A sitting took place early in Nov. Evans did two treatments: (i) a water-colour caricature of TSE dressed in pinstripe trousers, black jacket, waistcoat and tie against a background of dark blue wash: TSE sits with a book in his hands and gazes intently into the middle-distance. This caricature is now in the National Portrait Gallery, London. (ii) A pen-and-ink sketch of TSE's head, three-quarter-view, staring into the distance: a good likeness that was to be reproduced in a Supplement to *The Bookman* (London) 78: 463 (Apr. 1930).

3–McGreevy had written on 13 Aug.: 'I do find it difficult to treat Middleton Murry seriously as you suggest one might in this month's *Criterion*. It was the fact of that caused my outbreak for which in so far as it was an outbreak I beg your pardon. Murry is only indecent to me, in his religion, in his criticism and in his personal misfortunes. It's a thing I could if necessary be sorry for, but when it is thriving to the extent that it is – ! The first time I found him in *The Criterion* I was panic stricken and said to somebody in Dublin "Eliot is lost". But it was only panic and later I was able to be more cheerful . . .'

of the *Criterion*, or something to that effect, I had no notion that what you had in mind were the doctrines of Middleton Murry. You had better suspend judgment for a few months until you have read certain criticisms of Middleton Murry made by your co-religionist Father D'Arcy, S.J., Charles Mauron, Ramon Fernandez and myself. You will then know more about Middleton Murry and also about the *Criterion*.

You had better be careful before you drop on Gonzague Truc.[1] He is a good man; furthermore, he is I believe an atheist and has no connection with your religion. If I was, as you suggest, baptised in the Papist Church, I can take no responsibility and accept no consequences.[2]

Ever yours sincerely,
[T. S. Eliot]

## TO *Bonamy Dobrée* TS Brotherton

Wednesday, [17 August 1927] *The Monthly Criterion*

Dear Bungamy:

Reflecting on your recent Illness: it is obviously, manifestly and patently due to your having taken in knowledge of esoteric Bolovian theology too rapidly. On the one hand, I blame myself for not having moderated your Zeal. On the other hand (having done penance for this) I congratulate myself in my selection of a Subject. I am like the Antient Mariner: Intuition (in the Murravian[3] Sense) impels me to fix from time to time One Person with my Eye, and compel him to listen to Bolovian affairs; many are passed over, but One is chosen, and you are among the chosen to pass on the Gospel:

The Wedding Guest Here Beat his Breast
For He Heard the Loud Wuxoon.

For the present, No More, until you are again in Perfect Health. For the present, and as Walls have Ears, and I may not have the Opportunity Tomorrow (Thurs. the 18th inst.) I will tell you merely (this is not Over-Exciting) that I am preparing a little book for Kegan Paul (Psyche Miniature

1–'There was an attack on Gide by Gonzague Truc in Comoedia a little while ago. Except that I was more than ever convinced that the measure of a man's religious faith is too frequently the measure not only of his intolerance but of his moral uncharity I got nothing from it. This idea is true of myself also of course. I have some faiths . . .'

2–'No you are not Ulster, at least not what is perversely called Ulster today. That Irish housemaid [Annie Dunne] if she was worthy of the best traditions of the Irish servant girl in America, and apparently she was, gave you conditional baptism secretly and therefore you are in reality a heretical Irish Catholic!'

3–John Middleton Murry.

Series 2s.6d. net) on THE BOLOVIAN IN OUR MIDST (in Bolovian 'mist' and 'Midst' seem to be much the same). It will shew that many of our most eminent men have Bolovian blood, and it will shew show how to identify Bolovian blood. Obviously manifestly and patently Bolovian blood is only to be found in the most Eminent Men. My Book will tell how to recognise it. I have absolute evidence (On Internal Grounds) that there is a Strong Strain of Bolovian Blood In WINSTON CHURCHILL, CLIVE BELL, and GEORGE ROBEY. You will I am sure agree at once. There are Doubtful Cases. For Instance, GALLOPER SMITH FIRST EARL OF BIRKENHEAD: He has the Bowler and the Cigar, and other evidences, yet I am not sure. What do you think? There are others: such as LLOYD GEORGE, JOYNSON HICKS, and MUSSOLINI, of whom I am doubtful: I am inclined to think that they have strains of inferior neighbouring Blood, such as that of the primitive Wuxamoors or the still more inferior Kickapoos; but I shall not mention them at all, on account of the Law of Libel. But as tomorrow we are about to have Lunch among a large and disorderly assembly of Human Beings, I conjure you to assist me in my work, and keep your Eye Peeled for THE BOLOVIAN IN OUR MIDST.

I shall expect your Presence (Real Presence but not Transsubstantiation) at 12 of the Clock precisely at 24, Russell Square. Remember that the COUNT OF MONTE CHristo, when he had an Engagement at 12 Noon, always appeared on the 12th Stroke of the Clock (it is Assumed that the Clock was Accurate by Greenwich). I Hope that you will appear on or slightly Before the 1st Stroke of the Clock at Noon Tomorrow (Thursday the 18th August).

I have some more Surprises for You about the Crew: including the Boatswain (Bill so-called of Barcelona) and especially the Chaplain (the Reverend Philip Skinner, known familiarly as 'Prick' Skinner) he who converted the Bolovians to Hard-Shell Baptism); the Cook (Mrs Cora Bumpus) and the Cabin-Boy (Orlando (fam. Orlo) K. Putnam).

Yours etc.
T. S. E.

## TO *Nancy Pearn* CC

18 August 1927 [London]

Dear Miss Pearn,

Thank you for your letter of the 17th instant.[1] I regret that it has not yet been possible for the *Criterion* to improve its rates, but I am very much aware that this is the first matter to be attended to when the *Criterion* is in a rather more solid position. I should like to be able to do so at once, but you will understand that until the *Criterion* has been running as a monthly for about another six months it will be impossible for us to take stock of our position and consider this particular matter. I am of the opinion myself that when we raise the rates we ought to do so all round, and I want to take the stand that the *Criterion* must pay for all its contributors at the same rates independently of their position in the outside world. As soon as I am able to increase the rates I shall of course let you know, as I am sure that it will put you into a position to be able to direct more material our way.

I will let you know as soon as possible about the article of Stella Benson which you so kindly sent.[2]

Yours sincerely,
[T. S. Eliot]

## FROM *Herbert Read* MS Valerie Eliot

18 August 1927

Department of Ceramics,
Victoria & Albert Museum,
London, S.W.7

I can't help feeling that Richard [Aldington]'s attitude is entirely unreasonable. He is, in effect, compelling his friends to take up his personal quarrels. There is no analogy between your house & *The Criterion.* The relation between you & Cournos is a business relation & as such a satisfactory one. I cannot see that in your duty as an editor you are called upon to exercise moral judgments. It is just like Richard to make this romantic confusion of values, & it only shows what a mess these people make of life when their only basis is an emotional one. Perhaps this is a high & mighty line & Richard might well say: Wait until you yourself are

1 – Pearn hoped that TSE might be able to pay more than last time.
2 – Benson, 'The Voices of Puppets', did not appear in *MC*.

up against such a situation. But I honestly don't think I should act in such a fashion.

You might think it worthwhile to sacrifice your editorial probity for the sake of Richard's friendship. But I should think twice about the value of that friendship. People like Richard work themselves up into a passion & in that state their professions of affection are of the same value as their resentments.

It is all very difficult, but my advice is that you should attempt to reason with Richard. You know nothing or next to nothing of the Cournos affair (I can't remember the exact date of the publication of the novel, but I think it was before he appeared in *The Criterion* – but perhaps not before you engaged him to appear); you have entered into a contract with Cournos & you cannot break this contract without seeming to interfere in a question of honour to which you are in no sense a party. Cournos may be unscrupulous, but I don't think he is necessarily a scoundrel, or that what he has done is any worse than what other novelists do every day – Richard himself has on a smaller scale done the same thing by making criticisms of Frank [Flint] which were based, not on his work, but on his knowledge of his personality. Although the occasion was a small one, the intimacy that has subsisted between Frank & Richard makes the indiscretion almost equivalent to the Cournos affair. It took Frank a long time to get over it. This is merely to illustrate the unreliability of Richard's own standards, & so to suggest that they do not really deserve *every* consideration.

There is another complication – I mean Richard's undoubted morbidity. I have often discussed this with Frank & we are agreed that he suffers unreasonably but terribly from the sense of his anomalous social position. The Cournos affair must have accentuated this feeling very much. And his way of life gives him every opportunity to brood over his 'tormented soul'. He may, therefore, react violently to any display of reason on your part. But I think you must take that risk.

This has been written hastily & with constant interruptions. It is all muddled & diffuse, but I hope it may be of some help to you. I really don't think it was 'right' of Richard to force such a tiresome dilemma on you.[1]

Yours ever
H. R.

1 – Some time earlier, HR had advised RA (22 Dec. 1925): 'if we link Eliot's brains to a big commercial undertaking, we must have done the trick. We march on to a triumph. But in bickerings, false pride, & mutual mistrust we shall all be lost' (Texas).

## TO *Herbert Read* TS Victoria

Friday [?19 August 1927] *The Monthly Criterion*

Dear Herbert:

Thank you very much for your letter about that matter of R. I shall not discuss it further with anyone. Nor shall I make any further attempts on R. for the moment. I do think my last paragraph was tactless, in view of his reply, as he seems to have taken it just wrong. I think R. is full of 'false' pride, which means, I think, not an instinctive feeling of pride, but a preconception of how a 'proud' man would behave, and a determination to live up to it. However, with all his faults etc. and we hope the same for ourselves. Only, I can't feel that I myself am quite so hysterical as R. I think matters must be left to the healing influences of friends, but not expressly, only when occasion serves.

I find that I have had to arrange to lunch on Monday with Middleton Murry, who is to be in town for the day. Unless I hear from you to the contrary, I shall come to the Grove on Wednesday (I shall avoid the Port, which gave me a fearful Headache), and hope then to arrange a later day for lunch with you.

Yours etc.
T. S. E.

## FROM *Geoffrey Faber* CC

22 August 1927 Chawleigh Rectory, N. Devon

Dear Tom

My pen has just run dry, & I have no ink. Your namesake sends his thanks for the Magi[1] – as do we. And, to descend from the heights, for

1–TSE had sent his godson Tom Faber a pre-publication copy of *Journey of the Magi*, inscribed: 'for Thomas Erle Faber, / from T. S. Eliot / 17. 8. 27'. He would later say: 'I thought my poetry was over after "The Hollow Men" [1925]; and it was only because my publishers had started the series of "Ariel" poems and I let myself promise to contribute, that I began again. And writing the "Ariel" poems released the stream, and led directly to *Ash Wednesday*' (John Lehmann, 'T. S. Eliot Talks About Himself and the Drive to Create', *New York Times Book Review*, 29 Nov. 1953, 5). *Journey of the Magi*, published on 25 Aug. 1927, was Ariel poem no. 8. On 18 Dec. 1948 TSE was to write to C. W. Dilke at the BBC: 'Like my *Song for Simeon* which followed it a year later, [*Journey of the Magi*] asks the question: how fully was the Truth revealed to those who were inspired to recognise Our Lord so soon after the Nativity?'

the Canary Murder Case.[1] I haven't read it yet, but Enid has finished it. My own mind is rather full of Swift; & I am even meditating doing a biographical study myself. At present I am wading through Craik's incredibly stilted Life; & looking forward to Swift's own letters – which I have got here – as to the promised land. S. has always had a strange fascination for me; & I think that of all the 18th Century folk he is the one who most needs repainting in the modern manner. But I expect I shall never get the time. We do hope you will come down here for a few days; & beg you to exercise every effort to that end! It is delicious remote country; & a large & very remote house. Yeoford is our nearest decent station; but Exeter is quite manageable for us.

Do come; & let us know when & for how long to expect you.

Yours ever
G. C. F.

## TO *Orlo Williams* CC

22 August 1927 [*The Monthly Criterion*]

Dear Williams,

I like your review of Edith Wharton very much.[2] I have already wounded my own national susceptibilities to such an extent that no one else could possibly wound them; certainly not an impassionate study like this, with which I am almost entirely in agreement.[3] The only question I raise is whether Hawthorne is right to mention in the same sentence as James and Mrs Wharton. He is, of course, James's spiritual ancestor, but then he seems to me to be James's ancestor precisely on the other side – not in this matter of his preoccupation with American problems but in his preoccupation with general spiritual problems, a share in which is just what makes James a great novelist and prevents him from being merely a chronicler of his time. If you look at it this way, I think that Hawthorne is a much more universal writer not only than Mrs Wharton but also and certainly than James himself. I don't know whether anyone

1 – *The Canary Murder Case*, by S. S. van Dyne, was reviewed (by TSE?) in *MC* 6 (Oct. 1927), 377: 'a book to be recommended to the small, fastidious public which really discriminates between good and bad detective stories.'

2 – OW, review of *Twilight Sleep* by Edith Wharton, *MC* 6 (Nov. 1927), 440–5.

3 – Williams had remarked in his covering letter (21 Aug.): 'I hope nothing in my treatment of her will wound your national susceptibilities, but I rather think you agree with me about the excessive treatment of the "American problem" in fiction.'

agrees with me, but I do think Hawthorne a very much greater writer than James. Hawthorne represents, not so much America in the modern sense, as a particular development of conscience and sensibility which existed everywhere and which merely found its most precise and general realisation in one part of colonial America.

I am sending you Katherine Mansfield's *Journal*. Deal with it at what length you like and when you like.[1] For the point of reviewing such a book depends [on] what he has to say about it.[2]

With many thanks,
Ever yours,
[T. S. E.]

## TO *Sylvia Beach* CC

22 August 1927 [London]

Dear Miss Beach,

I am enclosing copies of certain correspondence which I have had re Mr Samuel Roth, as I thought that it possibly might come in useful to you in continuing your admirable campaign. I don't know whether the *Evening Post* published Sam's letter but I hope very much that it did. In any case you will see that Sam makes certain accusations against Ezra Pound. I have sent Ezra a copy of the letter of course, but possibly James Joyce would be interested as well.

Yours ever sincerely,
[T. S. Eliot]

1–Williams replied on 2 Sept.: 'I have read Katherine Mansfield's journal, which has of course a good deal of personal interest, but it is incomplete as a record of her life and as a record of her personality . . . The journal doesn't show what she gave out, only what she took in, & one wants both.'

2–This sentence has been overtyped, and is not clear.

## TO *Ezra Pound* CC

22 August 1927 [London]

Dear Rabbit

Thank you for your poetical epistle.[1] I am at present considering the poems for inclusion in *The Criterion*. Am glad to know that *Exiles*[2] continues. Do not remember Zukofsky but shall pay attention to the name. I enclose copies of certain correspondence I have had re Mr Sam Roth of New York. This is all in the day's work and I should probably not have bothered you with it except that Mr Sam in his letter of August 10th to Mr R. W. Potter of the *New York Evening Post* makes certain allegations concerning yourself which I must leave you to clear up.

Yours ever obsequiously,

[T.]

P.S. As touching the Persians, are you aware that certain persons allege that the Persian and Arabic poetry of the Sufis is the original inspiration of your Provencal poets in touch with Spain? And are you quite sure about the inversion of Persian poetry? I understand that the Persian poets usually employed the female pronoun.

1–TSE had sent EP a copy of *Journey of the Magi*. By way of thanks, EP wrote out in a letter of 20 Aug. two little squibs, 'The Quatrain that Villon Made' and 'Persicos Odi' – the second of them reading: 'The Persian Buggahs, Joe, / Strike me as a rotten show; / Stinking of nard and musk / Over the whole of their rind and husk; / Wearing their soft-shell clothes / Whichever way the wind blows, / The Persian buggahs, Joe, / Strike me as a rotten show' – which he categorised as 'classic recollections'. He added: 'I was saving 'em for a little anthology in Exile, but as the anthology dont materialize you can have em for the Criterion, or for pussn'l use. I am afraid the second is a little out of the Crit's gen. progm.' He went on to compliment TSE on the appearance in *The Criterion* of one (or perhaps both) of the passages ('Fragment of a Prologue and 'Fragment of an Agon') that would ultimately become *Sweeney Agonistes* – 'I liked your dramatic scene. Dont know ef I dun tole you' – and also to proclaim that he so admired the work of Louis Zukofsky that he wanted to dedicate the third number of *Exile* to his poetry. 'Mr Zukofsky has read us, but has something of his own. I mean he admits he has read us, and begs to differ, or at least to add a few remarks that had not occurred to us, for, racial possibly, reasons.'

2–*The Exile*.

## TO *The Editor of* The Daily Mail[1] CC

22 August 1927 [London]

Dear Sir,

Your admirable photographs of road perils in this morning's *Daily Mail* suggest to my mind a point which I do not think has been mentioned by any of your correspondents.[2]

In speaking of the excessive speed at which charabancs sometimes travel, I have often observed on country roads private motorists cutting in past charabancs. One cannot help having a certain sympathy with such motorists, for I know that it does not add to the pleasures of country motoring to travel for long distances behind a load of charabanc revellers. But the danger of this cutting in is greatly magnified when, as I have often observed in the country, several charabancs follow each other in close succession. They are usually of course one party; very often school children on an outing. But the motorist who passes one of these parties of two or more charabancs is not only endangering himself but also the other innocent motorist who may be slowly passing in the other direction. Would it not be a good thing if charabancs were forbidden to follow each other except at such a distance as would allow a motorist behind to cut in past one of them at a time? Even if such a regulation were not observed, it would at least serve to distribute the responsibility more fairly in case of an accident. One charabanc in a country lane is a risk to private motorists, but two or more in close succession form a great danger.

Yours faithfully,
[T. S. Eliot]

1 – Not published.

2 – The *Daily Mail*, in a front-page story, 'Road Perils', said that its photographer had captured 'many glaring instances' of the 'craze for overtaking, which is increasing to an alarming extent'. One caption read: 'In this picture, the motorist approaching London was forced to pull up dead against the kerb to avoid a collision.' A news article on p. 9, 'A Motoring Nightmare', reproved the 'reckless driving by motorists, who displayed an almost incredible disregard for safety and the courtesies of the road', as witnessed 'on the arterial road between London and Southend, which is becoming known as the "Motorists' Cemetery".' (In 1939 TSE was to feature in *FR* an instance of just such careless driving.)

## TO *The Editor of* The New York Evening Post CC

22 August 1927 [London]

Dear Sir,

With reference to the letter which I recently sent to you concerning Mr Samuel Roth's unauthorised publication of some of my work: I wish to inform you that I have just received from Mr Roth's secretary, one E. Loewenberg [*sic*], a copy of a letter which Mr Roth appears to have directed to you under date of the 10th August 1927. I hope that you have published not only my letter but Mr Roth's reply; inasmuch as Mr Roth's reply constitutes a better reply to himself than any which I could devise.

As Mr Roth has addressed this letter to you, and as I do not wish to have any direct dealings with Mr Roth or his company, I take the liberty of asking you to do me a favour. Mr Roth's secretary, the said E. Loewenberg, has sent me a cheque for twenty five dollars which he says is 'in full payment' for my verses which he pirated. I enclose this cheque, which, as you will observe, is drawn on August 10th 1927 for twenty five dollars to my order by the Two Worlds Publishing Co., Inc, Pauline Roth, treasurer, upon the World Exchange Bank of New York, and is numbered 535. I should be greatly obliged to you if you would kindly return this cheque to the Two Worlds Publishing Co. on my behalf. I do not consider it as payment and I do not propose to accept anything in the form of bribery or hush-money.

I am, Sir,
Your obliged, obedient servant,
[T. S. Eliot]

## TO *His Mother* TS Houghton

22 August 1927 *The Monthly Criterion*

My dearest dear mother:

I had been worrying about you for some time, and was just on the point of cabling when I was delighted to receive a letter apparently from Marion, and was overjoyed to find a real letter from you inside it, in your own dear writing. That makes me very happy, as it is the first real letter that I have had from you for ever so long, and I am so glad that you are better and able to write. I am sending you a copy of my Cambridge Lectures as they were delivered, as it may be another year before I have licked them into shape as a book, and I hope to have two books of essays published first, one directly after Christmas and one in the following summer. I wish that they were already published, as I should like to have something to send you more substantial than any of these things.

I am going to get a little kodak so that I can take some photographs of our house and garden to send you. We have now a little tent in the garden, which Lucy[1] has bought, and we have tea and sometimes supper there every fine afternoon, and some of the flowers have grown beautifully – especially hollyhocks and lupins, and I think we shall have some nice chrysanthemums, and grapes from the vines which old Janes has tended so carefully. And I want to take some pictures of the rooms of the house to send you; the sitting room which has now pictures of you and father and grandpa and grandma and Judge Cranch[2] and Colonel and Mrs Greenleaf and Sir T. and Lady Eliot, and I should like if possible to get pictures of Grandpa and Grandma Faraway and Uncle Oliver and Uncle Asahel.

I don't think that I want to accept any engagements to lecture in New York or elsewhere next winter, for although I should like to visit New York and Chicago etc. I don't suppose that I can come for more than a month, and I want to spend the whole time with you in Cambridge. Perhaps I can make a little money if I can get some lectures to deliver in or about Boston; but although the other lecturing in New York would pay all my expenses I had rather not (this time) spend so much time there, but would prefer to be with you in Cambridge, and just give any lectures I can in the vicinity.

Dearest mother, your letter made me very sad; you speak as if you would perhaps never see me again either here or elsewhere. In the first place I hope to come to America and spend a month with you next winter, and in the second place I have a much more positive conviction than you have that I shall see you in another life. It is rather too soon perhaps to talk of that! but I somehow have a much firmer conviction than you have, and I wish that you felt as I do; for although I am sure of seeing you at least once more in this life, yet as either of us, or anybody, might suddenly be taken away by some accident, I should like to feel that you felt sure as I do of our meeting again. I feel that the 'future life', or our future meetings, may not be in the least like anything that we can imagine; but that if it is different we shall then realise that it is right and shall not then wish it to be like what we can now imagine. After all, any ideas that we can have

1 – Lucy Thayer.

2 – William Cranch (1769–1855) was Judge of the US Circuit Court in Washington, DC, from 1801 till his death.

of the future life can only be right in that such ideas may be more nearly right than any other ideas that we could have. That is what I always feel about the truths of religion: it is not a question of something absolutely true (or false) in so many words; but they are more nearly true than is the contradiction of them. I imagine that many people who think that they will meet 'again' in a future life never meet at all; because I believe that these things will be regulated not by what we consciously think, but by our real affinities. Many people believe that they love each other, and understand each other, who are in reality utterly isolated from each other. But I believe that you and I understand each other and are like each other perhaps more than we know, and that we shall surely meet. And whenever I have done anything that the world has thought good, or that the world is likely to think good for a generation or two after I am dead, I have always felt that it was something that you and I did together, or even something that you had dreamt of and projected before I was born. I often feel that I am merely a continuation of you and Father, and that I am merely doing your work for you. Anyway, you are the finest and greatest woman that I have ever known. I know that you have wanted to do more than anyone could possibly do – not that you have not accomplished more than all but very few people already; but, as I say, I feel when I do anything that it is something you have done, and I should like to think that when I did anything, or that when any of your children did anything, that it was merely a continuation of your own work, and not something separate. I have still – though I know that I am getting old – ambitions of things to be done: I think that I can still do more, that if I am spared to strength and activity I can make a deeper mark on English and European civilisation; but if this is a delusion I am resigned to it.

But I sometimes feel now that I should like to be able to express to you all that I owe you, and all that you have done for me and do for me. It makes me want to do so much more than I have done.

Your very loving son
Tom.

## TO *Henry Eliot*

TS Houghton

22 August 1927 *The Monthly Criterion*

My dear Brother:

Thank you very much for your kind letter, and for sending another letter from Marion. During the last week I had grown increasingly anxious, as I had had no news whatever. Now also I have thankfully a letter in mother's writing, though very shaky.

Thank you also for the portraits, which I shall have framed. As I get older (I might say, Old) I attach myself more and more to such things. There are other portraits I should be glad to have, whenever you come across them: I should like Grandpa and Grandma 'Faraway' and Uncle Asahel and Uncle Oliver, and indeed any family portraits. Your portfolio, which you sent several years ago, is a perpetual source of enjoyment to me. It is strange that one should attach oneself to portraits of ancestors whom one has never known, but one wants to shrink more and more back into one's family as one grows old and sees the future as no more than the past. Thank you also for the copy of the genealogies, which is also a great pleasure to me.

I shall write you privately as soon as I can. I cannot reconcile myself either, and I take it out and try to face it every day, or in the middle of every night. You will realise that it is more difficult for me to get away than most know – it has got to the point where staying here is not a mere matter of sentiment or conscience, but a matter of duty and almost daily anxiety and necessity. When things get *better*, or when they get much *worse*, I can come; meanwhile I must try to put the best face on it I can.

With very great affection
Yours

I am very sorry indeed to hear of Theresa's illness. I know that is a very painful and torturing trouble. I am sure that she bears it with great courage, but try not to be exhausted by it yourself. Give her my love. (In the present delusion stage, you and Theresa are 'great enemies', but not so much so as her brother Maurice and her aunts).

<Tom
Judge how I am torn.>

TO *Walter de la Mare*[1] TS De la Mare Estate

22 August 1927 *The Monthly Criterion*

Dear de la Mare,

Thank you very much for your letter.[2] It gave me more pleasure than I can tell you. First because, having known of and followed your illness, I had not expected nor wished you to acknowledge my small poem; and second because your letter was such as gave me great pleasure. I have not received any comments on that little poem which have given me more pleasure than yours, and I shall treasure your reply among a small collection of autograph letters. I will only say further that as Editor of the *Criterion* there is nothing I more desire than a story, a sketch, a poem, or something from yourself. If I have not been more importunate, it is simply because I am keenly aware that any contribution from a writer of your reputation can hardly be considered as anything but a gift to the *Criterion*. For very young writers I hope that I keep the *Criterion* to such a level as to give them the inducement of the advertisement of contributing to a very fastidious periodical. But to such of the writers of our own generation as I should like to attract (you mention that you were born in 1873; I was born in 1888 and fifteen years does not seem to me enough space to constitute the separation of two generations) I feel that I have nothing to offer; and I can only ask for charity. But please realise that nothing would please me more than to receive a contribution of some kind from yourself.

With very many thanks and sincere good wishes for your complete recovery,

Yours sincerely,
T. S. Eliot

1–Walter de la Mare (1873–1956): poet and writer of short stories for adults and children; author of *Henry Brocken* (1904), *The Return* (1910), *The Listeners* (1912), *Peacock Pie* (1913), *Memoirs of a Midget* (1921) and *Come Hither* (anthology, 1923). See Theresa Whistler, *Imagination of the Heart: The Life of Walter de la Mare* (1993). After de la Mare's death, TSE told his son Richard: 'few poets have done as much of their best work in old age . . . The other remarkable thing is, how quietly & almost imperceptibly he advanced. Forty years ago one thought of him together with several other poets. Now, he is unquestionably far above them – he will remain the poet of a whole literary generation' (22 June 1956).
2–Not found: de la Mare had acknowledged TSE's gift of *Journey of the Magi*.

## TO *Vere Somerset*[1] CC

23 August 1927 [*The Monthly Criterion*]

Dear Somerset,

I have had in mind for some time that I wished to ask you to do something for the *Criterion*. I am very much flattered that you should have cared to offer me this enclosed Ms. I have thought it over carefully, but I do not think that it will quite do. One of my principal reasons is that I think you have got both an important and interesting character, namely Fénelon, and an important and interesting subject, the Nature of Beauty; but I cannot quite see on what historical knowledge I have that these two subjects can fit. If I may say so, it seems to me as if you had been interested in certain problems of aesthetics and were also interested in the interesting personality of Fénelon and had combined the two. I may be ignorant, but the subject of the matter of the dialogue does not seem to me to issue quite spontaneously from what we know of the character.[2]

Whether I am right or wrong, on a subject on which you probably know a great deal more than I, I think, if you will pardon my expressing myself in an editorial way, that you have a real gift for this form of expression and I very much hope that you may have something else for me. If at the moment you have nothing to offer or nothing to propose, may I say that I should be very glad if you would suggest any books that you felt inclined to review at some length? While awaiting a more original contribution, I should be very happy to see your name among our reviewers.

Yours sincerely,
[T. S. Eliot]

## TO *J. D. Aylward* CC

23 August 1927 [London]

My dear Aylward,

It is very good of you to acknowledge my humble offering. I hope that when you do taste it that you will find the flavour to be not of gall and wormwood but, as I should wish, rather that of hot buttered rum.[3]

1–H. Vere Somerset (1898–1965), Fellow of Worcester College, Oxford.

2–Somerset sought to explain on 28 Aug.: 'I am well aware that the Dialogue is imperfect. The reason for Fénelon's appearance was partly, as you say, from favouritism, partly the result of the thought of his interest in Philosophy, & of his own Dialogues.'

3–Aylward acknowledged (20 Aug.) a bottle of rum: 'You do me too much honour in

I have had in mind, with many longings, my promised weekend with you. I wish that it might immediately be realised and that I might accept your very kind invitation for next Saturday which I know would be a weekend of unadulterated pleasure.[1] But I am afraid that at the present time it is impossible for me to leave even for one night. My wife is not very well and my mother in America is very ill indeed, so that I prefer to be on hand to receive immediate telegraphic news.

I gather that your voyage to France was a success and the thought of it fills me with pleasure. I hope that your caravel has been well received by that foreign nation, which I am told is a frog-eating nation, wearing wooden shoes. I should be interested to know whether on your return you smuggled in your booty by means of [runs off the page] near Poole.

Your most respectful chantyman and supercargo,[2]

[T. S. E.]

## TO *Dr. G. C. Govoni* CC

23 August 1927 [Faber & Gwyer Ltd]

Dear Dr Govoni,

I was very glad to receive your letter of the 3rd August. After Haigh-Wood wrote to me I only supposed that you had been delayed in coming to London or else, as often happens, that your transit had been too rapid for you to consider seeing me again.[3] But please remember that I hope you will let me know whenever you come to London and that I in return will try to look you up whenever I am in Paris if only for a few days. I have not been in Paris for nearly a year and do not know whether I shall get there during the present autumn or not.

I have been thinking over your letter and wondering what I could do.[4] Unfortunately I have very little connection with the daily newspapers and have never written myself for any of them. While of course I know Lady

---

offering me a draught from the Pierian spring. It is still untasted. I await the mood.'

1–'You said that you could, perhaps, find a free Saturday and Sunday during August to study the Argonauts in their favourite milieu. Is next Saturday possible to you?'

2–A 'chanty' (pronounced 'shanty') is specifically a working-song on a merchant ship; the chantyman is the soloist or leader of the chorus. The supercargo is an officer who supervises the cargo on a merchant ship, and the business transactions.

3–Maurice Haigh-Wood had notified TSE from Rome on 12 Feb. 1927 that Dr G. C. Govoni, Paris correspondent of *La Sera*, was proposing to visit London in about two or three weeks; he knew that TSE would wish to meet him again.

4–Govoni asked for introductions to newspapers to which he might contribute from Italy.

Rothermere very well, I have never had anything to do with the persons actually in charge of any of the Harmsworth Press. I am afraid that on the point of daily or Sunday newspapers I can be of very little immediate or direct use. I would gladly speak for you to the editors of two or three weekly or monthly papers, but although this might be indirectly useful, I do not believe that there is any money to be made by writing for such papers. I propose to speak to a friend of mine about you who knows the Editor of the *Observer*, but all that I can say at the moment is that if you should get any means of introduction to the editors of any of the daily papers I am quite willing that you should mention my name; although I do not know what weight my name would carry. No doubt it would carry more weight with some editors than with others. But I do not know enough about such people to tell you in advance where it would be useful and where not. I shall presently write to another friend of mine who knows some of the American newspapers in Paris, but I am sorry that I do not know any of them myself. I can only say that if you refer to me I will with pleasure support any application you make.

Yours sincerely,
[T. S. Eliot]

## TO *J. M. Robertson* CC

23 August 1927 [London]

My dear Robertson,

Very many thanks for your letter of the 14th and for the Ms. I must confess that I feared that this MS would be much too long for possible publication.[1] Yet I encouraged you to send it owing, I think, to my private desire to read it. This desire I have indulged and the indulgence has given me great pleasure. It seems to me that you dispose effectively and finally of about nine-tenths of the Shelley legend. May I say without impertinence that your essay aroused in me a desire to dispose of the other tenth? I agree and applaud everything that you have said to demolish the reputation of Shelley. I may be an irresponsible fanatic, but I am almost

1 – Robertson called his essay 'The Shelley Balance Sheet', 'bloated . . . blighted . . . a monstrosity of about 27,000 words. I fancy your most economical plan might be to keep it and the Burns essay till I am dead, & then make a Robertson number of them, with a heliotropic border on the cover.' On 27 July he had said of his article: 'I have a horrible suspicion that it is largely prattle, albeit largely destructive – destructive enough to please you, I think, on that score, though not wholly so, being professedly an eirenicon.'

irresistibly moved to try to demolish what you have left. I admit his gift or facility for versification; and I deny absolutely that the gift or facility for versification is the token of a poet. I was rather sorry that you were so lenient to *The Cenci*. *The Cenci* has always seemed to me a third-rate pastiche of a second-rate Beaumont and Fletcher play; it is often praised by people who would like to be able to say something for Shelley but cannot praise anything else.[1]

Still this is not quite the point. The point is that your Shelley essay is a book in itself and certainly ought to be published as a book. It is far too long for the *Criterion*. Besides, it is a thing which ought to be read straight off: otherwise the ordinary reader may become annoyed with the patient analyses of Shelley's critics, in which I delight. Unless you can detach some part of it for publication by itself, I do not see how I, qua Editor, can possibly use it. So I shall stick to the 'Burns' which I should expect to begin, if not to finish, in the January number as you suggest. But I think that it would be a very great pity if the 'Shelley' remained unpublished; or if, like your 'Poe' it were to be buried in an American periodical. Have you thought of making a small book on Shelley? I like the 'Burns' for very different reasons from the 'Shelley'. I dislike Shelley as you will have perceived, and only reproach you for not disliking him enough. I like Burns, and think even more might be said in his favour than you have said; but no doubt your reserve may be attributed to national modesty.

I hope to arrange our afore-mentioned dinner early in October.

Ever yours,
{T. S. Eliot]

## TO *Herbert Read* — TS Victoria

Wednesday [? 24 August 1927] — *The Monthly Criterion*

Dear Herbert:

I felt positively that I could not honourably get rid of Cournos on this count, and your letter confirmed me. It would make no difference even if Cournos had done a job very badly. What he does anyway isn't essential, and in general I would gladly chuck Cournos to keep Richard. But *qua*

1–Robertson replied (4 Sept.) to this paragraph of TSE's letter: 'you pain me by your *acharnement* against poor Shelley. When you say I have destroyed *only* nine-tenths of the "legend", I suppose you mean the "credit" of Shelley as poet. Go to! Do you want to see removed the last dime of his poetic scalp? Beware, my son, of letting criticism decline to malice. That there is *something* of mastery in Shelley I always maintained.'

editor I don't see that I have the ghost of a justification for chucking Cournos. Of course, if I had known of this business beforehand, I should never have engaged him – but I didn't. And an editor is of no use at all unless everybody is sure that he is absolutely impartial and impersonal, *qua* editor. I don't suppose the job will last more than a year or two more, and I'd like to do it thoroughly.

What I feel more strongly than ever, is that if Richard could take a normal view of things in general he might have taken a more lenient view of this (I still don't know what it's all about, and there is no point in knowing). In my reply I have urged him to come to London for six months. His position is not in the least unique, and anyway nobody is in the least interested except his private friends who know that Richard would like to have children and can't. I hope when you get an opportunity you will try to induce him to this step. He would find that all the people whom he wanted to see would receive him & Dorothy. My own social circle has been considerably restricted in the last year or two, but I would guarantee him the Woolfs and the Morrells, and the Fabers (who are highly respectable) if he liked.

I feel in general that this respectability obsession has spoilt his work: has ruined his verse, and has made him run to these tedious academic scholarly essays and editing. But (except for the children part of it) it is all a delusion; and, apart from that (and I really don't know how much that counts with him) there are plenty of people suffering from much more *real* torments than his own.

I shall be at the Comercio at 7 on Friday night. The others (including by the way Hinks) are summoned for 7:15.

Yours ever
T. S. E.[1]

1–Later, on 31 Aug. 1928, HR would write again in response to a related letter (now lost?) from RA (responding to a letter from TSE that appears also to be lost) that TSE let him see: 'I read this as an admission of the "real rightness" of your letter, and also as a refusal to admit this rightness. I am not sure that there is much else to be done. If you take Frank [Flint] into your confidence, I think his advice will be: "Let time heal the wound. I know Richard & have had these little tiffs with him many a time, & they always blow over. Richard is all right &c. &c." And I think that is about true. His reply to the last paragraph of your letter is very characteristic: it is theatrical & I don't think people are theatrical when they are deeply stirred. I like Richard very much & sympathize with his difficulties. But I can't admire the way he tackles them: he obviously *dramatizes* & is his own hero because he hasn't got a valet, or friends i.e. daily acquaintances who can take the place of a valet.

'Frank, of course, can view the whole business with much fuller knowledge of the circumstances (Richard's circumstances). I think the virtue of your position has been (& still is) that you are ignorant of them. If Richard were wise he would value this lack of curiosity,

## *I. P. Fassett* TO *Orlo Williams* CC

24 August 1927 [*The Monthly Criterion*]

Dear Mr Williams,

Mr Eliot thanks you for your letter of the 23rd and is very sorry that you will be unable to be present on Friday evening.

He asks me to say that he is very anxious that you should read Hawthorne and I am sending you (under separate cover) one volume of Hawthorne which Mr Eliot hopes that you will keep until he sees you. He would be pleased to send you the whole set when you could read it. He suggests that if you are going to read Hawthorne you ought to read also Jonathan Edwards on the Freedom of the Will and *The Institutes of Calvin*, both of which he would be glad to supply.

He thanks you also for your information about Sr. Linati.[1]

Yours faithfully,
[I. P. Fassett]

## TO *Alsina Gwyer*[2] CC

25 August 1927 [London]

My dear Mrs Gwyer,

Thank you very much for your kind letter. I don't expect people to acknowledge trifles of this sort and I was all the more pleased at hearing from you.

It is very kind of you to give such generous hospitality. It would be a very great pleasure to me to be able to talk to you at more leisure than we

---

for it implies respect (or complete indifference, but that is out of the question). It might be difficult to maintain your state of innocence if you went too deep into the question with Frank. This is perhaps fanciful, but my own inclination if I were in your position would be merely to seek confirmation of your own action in the matter, & to avoid at all costs the confidences which Frank would surely feel inclined to shower on you.'

1–Williams had noted in his letter: 'Linati writes that he had been at Rapallo with Ezra Pound, & liked him much as a friend.'

2–Alsina Gwyer (d. 1953), wife of Maurice Gwyer (1878–1952), was the daughter of the philanthropist Sir Henry Burdett, at whose death in 1921 she had inherited the firm that published the *Nursing Mirror*. Mrs Gwyer and her husband (who was a Prize Fellow of All Souls College, Oxford, where Geoffrey Faber was Fellow Bursar), had joined forces with Faber in setting up the general publishing house of Faber & Gwyer. Maurice Gwyer, who was a successful lawyer and civil servant – in turn Treasury Solicitor; first parliamentary counsel to the Treasury; Vice-Chancellor of the University of Delhi, 1938–59 – was knighted in 1928. The Gwyers, who wed in 1906, had a son and two daughters.

have ever had at Russell Square.[1] If I can possibly get away for a night I will let you know, but there are several things which make me uncertain; I may have to go to Paris for a few days at any time, and I am waiting anxiously for news from America where my mother has been very ill. If it proves impossible for me to come down, I hope that I may come to see you later when you are back again.

With many thanks,
Yours very sincerely,
[T. S. Eliot]

## TO *Richard Aldington* CC

25 August 1927 [London]

My dear Richard,

Excuse me for not having written to you again sooner. I wanted time to think over this matter. You say that there is no dilemma from your point of view; but there is a very serious difficulty from mine.

I do not know when Cournos's book appeared or whether its appearance preceded my invitation to him to do the Russian notes for the *Criterion*. And certainly if I had known about his book and known how serious the matter was I should naturally not have invited him to contribute to the *Criterion*. I cannot even say whether I had heard of the book at that time. I remember Flint's mentioning to me that Cournos had written a book in which you were an obvious character. As I remember, Flint mentioned it as a curious instance of human blindness, as I remember it his impression was that Cournos was not aware to what extent he had drawn real people. I cannot verify this until I see Flint which I hope to do in a few days. I do not remember that the book was mentioned as being really insulting to you. In any case, all that I know of Cournos's book was derived from these few comments by Flint. I have never read the book, never seen it, never read any reviews of it and know nothing more about it.

You will see that this affair began by a certain ignorance or unconsciousness on my part unless, as is possible, I first engaged Cournos before the book came out. I have only met Cournos three times in my life. He has never come or been invited to a *Criterion* dinner and there is no reason why he should be. I met him once at your house, once at Garsington; and once he called at this office for a few moments to see me. I neither liked nor disliked him; he was a complete stranger to me. I understood that he

1 – Mrs Gwyer had invited TSE to visit her at The Rosery, West Hoathly, Sussex.

was hard up and suggested that he might now and then review Russian periodicals for the *Criterion.*

As for Cournos's work for the *Criterion*, I have had no fault to find with it except that a few days before hearing from you I had written to him to ask him in future not to mention my name in his writing. So far as I can understand, his reviews have been interesting and intelligent and apparently fair, and he has always been extremely punctual in delivering his material.

Candidly, I do not feel that I can drop Cournos from the *Criterion* on account of a private matter which occurred some time ago and which possibly I ought to have known of but did not know of. I try to keep my private feelings and private life out of the *Criterion*, and I try as far as possible to distinguish clearly my private and my editorial personality. I see your point of view and sympathise with it. So far as personal relations are concerned, I should of course have nothing what ever to do with Cournos now that I know that he has done you wrong. But editorially I do not feel that I should be justified in taking any account of this recent knowledge. It is superfluous, almost to the point of silliness, to say that your collaboration and support are infinitely more important and valuable to me than that of a person like Cournos. I would make any possible sacrifice to gain your support: but I feel that if I got rid of Cournos I should be doing him a wrong quite independent of what I have just learnt. Please do not misunderstand me. I am quite aware that you do not suggest my getting rid of Cournos. And I am quite aware that the *Criterion* as well as myself will suffer.

Now I hope that this matter will not affect your personal feelings towards me, even though it deprives the *Criterion* of your work. And I hope you will forgive my impertinence in speaking to you directly about yourself. Not having read Cournos's book, I am perhaps unqualified to speak, and I speak only from what I know and have observed of you in the last few years. I do feel that you take these matters much too seriously and that one reason why you take them too seriously is that you have lived in isolation in the country and are not in touch with what real people actually think. You have, as you should know, the sympathy not only of your friends but of other people who merely know about you. And there are other people as well who are interested in your work and who would like to know you and are not interested in anything about your private affairs and who would not care one way or another if they did know of them. You are in a situation which makes life difficult I know, and which limits the possibilities of future life. But from the general point of view it is not an important matter. It has happened before and will probably happen many times again. After all, George Eliot was no better off and yet George Eliot lived in London and enjoyed the respect and friendship of the society which she wanted; and what was possible in George Eliot's time is much more possible now. I do feel strongly that you and Dorothy ought to try to spend a winter in London; for I assure you that everybody whom you would care to know in any circumstances would want to see you both. I am not the only person who has expressed regret at your spending your life in the country; I know that all of your friends desire the same thing. And I am convinced that it would be the best thing for both of you. I hope that what I have just said has not offended you as it is only intended in genuine solicitude and affection.

Always yours affectionately,
[T.]

## TO *Geoffrey Faber* — TS Valerie Eliot

Thursday [25? August 1927] — *The Monthly Criterion*

Dear Geoffrey,

Very many thanks for your letter, & Hope that Thomas Enid and the others are flourishing on Devonshire air. Are you hunting with the Stag Hounds, or merely Fly Fishing? I hope that you are Reposing. I am very much interested to hear about the Swift. I never knew that he meant so much to you; he has always been one of the very great men to me;[1] indeed *Gulliver*, and especially the last chapter of the Houhynyms, is to me with *King Lear* as one of the most tragic things ever written.[2] Thackeray's essay is Bad, and no doubt has misled many; but there is one magnificent sentence towards the end of it. It runs something like this: 'so great a man he seems, that the thought of his end is like the end of an empire falling'.[3] I have always felt a particular sympathy and (probably) illusory

1–TSE said in 1926 that he regarded Swift as 'colossal . . . the greatest writer of English prose, and the greatest man who has ever written English prose' (*VMP*, 186).

2–In his introduction to the *Pensées* (1931), TSE would point out that Pascal's 'despair, his disillusion . . . are the analogue of the drought, the dark night, which is an essential stage in the progress of the Christian mystic. A similar despair, when it is arrived at by a diseased character or an impure soul, may issue in the most disastrous consequences though with the most superb manifestations; and thus we get *Gulliver's Travels* . . .'

3–*The English Humourists of the Eighteenth Century*, a series of lectures (1853): 'So great a man he seems to me that thinking of him is like thinking of an empire falling.' See TSE's review of Shane Leslie's *The Soul of Swift* (1928): 'Mr Leslie believes that Swift may have

understanding of Swift in connexion with Stella and Vanessa. There never has been anyone more superbly unpractical; he might have said, like the personage of Villiers de l'Isle Adam: 'as for living – our servants will do that for us!' Did you see, a year or so ago, a fine essay in the *Times L.S.* on the *Journal to Stella*? It was written by Virginia Woolf, not yet, I think, reprinted.[1] There was a touch of her personal experience in it which made it all the more serious.

But I do hope that you will take up this Swift seriously. And soon. For I don't think that publishing is quite enough to satisfy your life; and I do not believe that any, even the fullest or happiest domestic life is enough. And if you don't think you have time now, you never will. At our age one gets easily into a vicious habit of doubting postponement. I should like even to collaborate, to a small extent, on Swift. Do you know the *Drapier's Letters* well? They are magnificent.[2] But I think I could do better justice to the poetry (without vanity) than has yet been done. Swift's obscenity is as little understood as Baudelaire's blasphemy.[3]

I am doubtful about being able to come. My wife would like me to come; but I myself would be rather worried by being away for one or two

---

had a "heart", though no soul. It would really be more plausible to say that Swift had little or no heart, but a soul – and a very sick one . . . And with all Thackeray's prejudice, his is the most memorable phrase that has ever been made about Swift: "So great a man he seems to me that thinking of him is like thinking of an empire falling"' ('The Extempore Exhumation', *N & A*, 43: 14 [7 July 1928], 470, 472). TSE wrote to Roy Morrell on 15 May 1964: 'I am moved to say that I disagree with Thackeray when he was horrified at Swift's writing about a lock of Stella's hair – "Only a woman's hair". To me that was very poignant and expressed his contrition rather than cynicism. Thackeray redeems himself, however, by one magnificent phrase in which Swift's end reminds him of an empire's falling.'

1–24 Sept. 1925; repr. (revised) in *The Common Reader: Second Series* (1932).

2–In *VMP*, TSE ranked *The Drapier's Letters* [1724] with the works of Aristotle, the prose of Richard of St Victor, *The Principles of Logic* [by A. C. Bradley] and vol. I of *Principia Mathematica* [by Bertrand Russell and A. N. Whitehead] as an 'admirable influence [for] the writing of English prose or verse' (106). In 'Charles Whibley' (1931): 'Those persons who are drawn by the powerful attraction of Jonathan Swift read and re-read with enchanted delight *The Drapier's Letters*' (*SE* [1932], 455).

3–Cf. TSE's introduction to Baudelaire's *Intimate Journals*, trans. Christopher Isherwood (1930): 'Baudelaire's Satanism . . . amounts to a dim recognition of a part, but a very important part, of Christianity. Satanism itself, so far as not merely an affectation, was an attempt to get into Chistianity by the back door. Genuine blasphemy, genuine in spirit and not purely verbal, is the product of partial belief . . . The "satanism" of the Black Mass was very much in the air . . . but I would observe that in Baudelaire, as in no one else, it is redeemed by *meaning something else* . . . Baudelaire is concerned, not with demons, black masses, and romantic blasphemy, but with the real problem of good and evil . . . Baudelaire perceived that what really matters is Sin and Redemption. It is a proof of his honesty that he went as far as he could honestly go and no further' (*SE* [1932], 383, 388–9).

nights.[1] And my mother has been very ill, and is not expected to live more than a few months.

Ever yours,
T.

### TO *Peter Quennell* CC

26 August 1927 [London]

Dear Quennell,

I like your essay on Laforgue and shall be glad to use it, though I am afraid that it will be three or four months before I have room.[2] Meanwhile, I shall drop you a line in a week or two and hope that you will come to lunch. I shall be interested to know whether you will consider later a similar essay on Corbière.

Yours sincerely
[T. S. Eliot]

### TO *Frederic Manning* CC

26 August 1927 [*The Monthly Criterion*]

My dear Manning

Thank you for your letter. Today week will suit me as well as any day and I shall look forward to seeing you then. I like your note on Mérimée and will use it as soon as I can.[3] It suggests many points which I should like to discuss with you.

My dispute with Murry, such as it is, is not quite on these grounds. Long ago I wrote an essay on the 'Function of Criticism' <*Criterion* October 1923> which stated in a rough way my disagreement. But my present dispute with him is much more general and concerns his recent essay 'Towards a Synthesis'. There are two replies to that essay in the September number which is just out, and there will be short replies by Fernandez and

1–Later, on 27 Sept., GCF noted in his diary: 'Took Eliot to lunch at club. Heard much about his wife, who is now in sanatorium in Paris. E. said "For a long time it has been just as much as I could do to keep going. I'm like a man who can just keep his head above the water by treading water but can't begin to think of swimming."'

2–'Notes on a Reading of Jules Laforgue', *MC* 7 (Mar. 1928), 219–30.

3–Review-essay on *Carmen, et quelques autres nouvelles de Prosper Mérimée*, intro. by Valery Larbaud, *MC* 6 (Nov. 1927), 448–55.

myself in the October number. I am enclosing a galley proof of these, but you will understand that they will undergo some corrections before they appear.

Yours always sincerely,
[T. S. Eliot]

## FROM *Geoffrey Faber* CC

27 August 1927 Chawleigh, N. Devon

My dear Tom

I am sorry you see so slight a chance of getting away. If circumstances should change at all, I hope you will let us know. We have an extra spare room – the feather-bed variety – which will be available at practically any time.

My sister in law Audrey[1] has formed herself into a Committee, which is to sit upon your poem & report to me this evening when I come back from a day's fishing! Without prejudice to the Report of the Committee, however, I will go so far as to say that it seems to me a singularly beautiful piece. There is a note of serenity there, which your earlier work touches comparatively seldom. Thank you for sending me a copy.

And also for your encouragement in the matter of Swift. It is only during the last few years that I have really come up 'against' Swift, & that happened almost by accident, as I edited his attractive young friend – Gay.[2] That association showed S. in so pleasing an aspect that I began to follow up the road which leads to the real man. A trivial way of approach, perhaps; but it has its advantages. – Your comments leave me with the feeling that it is you who ought to write the book. The temper of the weapon ought to be very well proved! But I think I will go on for my own sake. Your remark about Swift's obscenity interests me greatly; for that is precisely one of the characteristics which most invite my study. To be obscene in Swift's manner is to separate the lees & the wine – is it not?

What is so staggering is the commonplaceness of the minds which have, generally, pontificated about Swift. The present (or late?) Dean of St Patrick's in an introduction to Ball's new edition of the Correspondence writes 'The nastiness of Swift was exceptional, even for the XVIII century'. True, he goes on to admit that S. was never licentious or suggestive, like

1 – Audrey Richards (1899–1984), later a very distinguished social anthropologist.

2 – *The Poetical Works of John Gay*, ed. GCF (1926). Gay (1685–1732) was author of *The Beggar's Opera* (1728) and the verse *Fables* (1727, 1738).

Sterne, & to attribute his [grossness?] to a hatred of shams. This brings him tolerably near the truth; but he ends abruptly 'And this must suffice for a very unpleasant subject'![1]

'The Tale of a Tub' he writes a little further on 'contains many things which no man of reverent mind could have brought himself to write. And his verses 'On the Day of Judgment' provide material for an even graver indictment. For in these verses S. seems to ridicule as unworthy of credit so widespread & fundamental a belief as that of the future judgment of mankind. This is to go much further than the Tale of a Tub.'[2]

That is good, isn't it?

Well, I will at any rate attack the task, & I shall enjoy extracting your help — but not just yet; I am not yet quite at the point when I am ready for an exchange of views.

Yours in haste
G. C. F.

## TO *Donald S. Friede* TS Texas

29 August 1927 *The Monthly Criterion*

Dear Mr Friede,

Thank you very much for your kind letter of the 18th instant.[3] I had been hoping to see you again at more leisure on your return; but it is

1–The Very Rev. J. H. Bernard remarks – in his Introduction to *The Correspondence of Jonathan Swift, D. D.*, ed. F. Elrington Ball, I (1910) – on 'the coarseness of much of Swift's correspondence. His jokes, set down with pen and ink in letters to intimates . . . are apt to be dirty. And not only in letters to men, but even in the Journal to Stella there are nasty jests which (one would think) a decent man of any period would have disdained to make, at any rate to a woman whom he sincerely honoured . . . [W]e must make allowance for the manners of the age . . . But the nastiness of Swift was exceptional, even for the eighteenth century.' He goes on: 'Swift is frequently coarse, dirty, even obscene; but he is never licentious or wantonly suggestive, as Sterne too often is. Sterne may not be as plainspoken as Swift, but his writings are more likely to pollute the mind and inflame the imagination. Swift's coarseness is repulsive, and it makes vice repulsive to the reader, which cannot be said of Sterne . . . His unhappy tendency to dwell in thought and in speech on the bestial side of human nature was not improbably due to a diseased imagination, which was the consequence of the physical infirmities that wrecked his life. It was also, in part, inspired by his hatred of shams . . . But he never wrote a line which would encourage vice. And this must suffice for a very unpleasant subject' (xlviii).

2–Quoted from Bernard, *op. cit.*, xlix.

3–Friede regretted TSE's absence during his 'second flying trip'. 'However, I hope you realize that we want to consider ourselves your publishers at all times. Is there any chance of a new book of verse next Spring? I expect to be over in Europe next Spring . . .'

a pleasure to know that you will be in England again in the spring. I hope that you will not fail to drop me a line both before leaving New York and on your arrival in London so that our next meeting may be less hurried. You have all my best wishes in connection with the trial in Boston.[1] Remember that I asked you to keep me in touch, or at least to let me know what happens.

I am referring the second paragraph of your letter to our management.[2]

Sincerely yours,
T. S. Eliot

## TO *C. S. Stewart* CC

29 August 1927 [London]

Dear Stewart,

I think you have seen this man, and I have seen him.[3] He did not arouse any feeling of friendship in my breast and I have no particular affection for Boni and Liveright, having had experience of them as publishers. His request seems to me quite unreasonable and I can see no reason, as Boni and Liveright are not taking up the *Criterion*, why he should be put on the Free List. In any case, the first volume is impossible as the first two numbers are out of print.

I am writing to him to say that I shall be delighted to see him in the spring and that I am referring the second paragraph of his letter to the management.

T. S. E.

(Friede)

1–In 1927 Friede had been arrested in Boston, Mass., on the charge of selling an obscene book (*Ulysses*) to police agents.

2–'I wonder if you could ask your business department to send me all the numbers of the Criterion starting with #1 (if possible) since its inception, except for the issues of July 1925; January, April and June, 1926; and January, May, June, July and August, 1927. The new numbers I receive as they come out, but if it is possible for me to be placed on your free list, I would be very appreciative.' See next letter for TSE's response.

3–Donald S. Friede.

## TO *William Force Stead* TS Beinecke

29 August 1927 *The Monthly Criterion*

Dear Stead,

Many thanks for your letter. As for myself, I enjoyed the lunch immensely and was very happy to be able to get such a party together. I have just written to Miss Wentworth to pass on your invitation and am quite sure that she or she and her brother will accept it if they possibly can. I know, however, that she has plans for a short visit to Devonshire in the immediate future, so it may not be possible for her.[1]

I have already sent to the people you mention the two copies of the *Criterion* together with a page proof of my own note on the subject which will appear in the October number.[2] I sent Streeter's copies to Queen's College but I suppose that they will eventually reach him?[3]

By the way, as I am inexperienced in such matters, could you tell me how to address the Bishop of Oxford if I should write to him personally?

Thank you also for your final suggestion[4] and very much for your letter as a whole. I hope that we may meet in London again soon.

Sincerely yours
T. S. Eliot

## TO *Elizabeth Wentworth* CC

29 August 1927 [London]

Dear Elizabeth,

I have this morning received a letter from Stead expressing his enjoyment in our lunch party. Among other matters he gives a message which I will report verbatim:

1 – WFS wrote ('Friday') to thank TSE for a lunch party, and to invite Elizabeth Wentworth and her brother to visit himself and his wife in Oxfordshire.

2 – WFS encouraged TSE to send the two issues of the *MC* containing JMM's article and D'Arcy's reply to it, to the Revd Canon B. H. Streeter; the Revd A. E. J. Rawlinson; and Thomas Strong, The Right Revd The Lord Bishop of Oxford.

3 – Streeter, who had a bad throat and was away at the seaside, acknowledged on 10 Sept.

4 – On *Ben Hur*: 'Some things are annoying such as Victorian Church music during the banal Religious Touches; but surely the man's (or eternal boy's) soul is dead who does not respond to the galley-slave and pirate scenes, to say nothing of the chariot race & the Valley of the Lepers. The eye is the keenest of the senses & the senses feed the intellect – it is worth seeing, both as a sight, and as a reminder that Christ has changed the world.'

'Meanwhile will you please assure Miss Wentworth that if she would like a change from London before setting forth we should be delighted to put her up here. Only give us a few days' notice and it is sure to be convenient to us if it suits her. Naturally this applies to her brother and you also – but probably you and he are too much occupied while she might be able to find the time.'

Stead's address is: The Revd W. Force Stead, Finstock House, Finstock, Near Charlbury, Oxford, Oxon. I can tell you that it is a lovely house in the middle of beautiful country. I have not met Mrs Stead as she was away with the children on the one night which I have spent there. Perhaps you would care in any case to drop a line to him. I can assure you from a number of things that he has said to me that he took an immense liking to both of you.

I want to thank you for your kind letter to which I shall not reply except to say that it is rather difficult for me to go out in the evening and I have already made one engagement for this week. Meanwhile I hope you will keep me in touch with your plans, and if I could manage an evening this week or the week after I would let you know as soon as possible.

With very many thanks,
Yours affectionately,
Tom

## TO *Geoffrey Faber* MS Valerie Eliot

29 August 1927 *The Monthly Criterion*

My dear Geoffrey

Thank you very much for your letter, and for your patiently continuing invitation. I shall accept if I can. One never knows.

I shall be very glad to have Miss Richards's comments, but as for you, what you say already is enough & has given much pleasure.

I do *not* want to take any active part in the Swift: I have neither the patience, nor the knowledge of the epoch, nor the scholarly training. I only want to incite you to do it, & should like to have the pleasure of conversing with you about [it] while you do it. You have come to Swift by an unusual & promising route. As you say, there is little of value about him.[1] Whibley's Swift[2] is the political Swift, not the spiritual Swift, which

1–This presumably refers to Elrington Ball's edition of Swift's correspondence.
2–Charles Whibley, *Jonathan Swift* (Leslie Stephen Lecture, 1917).

is what endures. I was indignant some time ago when the wife of an Oxford don said that Dean Inge reminded her of Swift. I suppose because they were both Deans.

I usually deprecate such probing, in literary criticism, & I don't know that I should recommend putting it *into one's book*, but I do think Swift's sexual life ought to be studied carefully & sympathetically, because he is a spiritual type, *not* a mere abnormal.

I *don't* enjoy Sterne – except for the faint aura shed on my mother's family (hence the T. *S*.!)[1] that is a blind spot on the fovea[2] of my appreciative ability.

Ever yours
T. S. E.

## TO *H. W. B. Joseph*[3] CC

30 August 1927 [London]

Sir,

I am writing to ask whether you would be willing to review Mr Bertrand Russell's *Analysis of Matter* for the *Criterion*. In case you are not acquainted with this periodical I am sending you a copy of the latest number.

I am anxious to get an important review of this book of any length up to two thousand words. Our fee would be from three to four guineas according to the length. I have not yet proposed this book to anyone else and the *Criterion* would be greatly honoured if it might have a review

1–TSE's mother C. C. Stearns claimed descent from the novelist Laurence Sterne (1713–68), great-grandson of Richard Sterne (*c*.1596–1683), Archbishop of York. In 1954, however, TSE's cousin Eleanor Hinkley sent him a family tree which disabused him of the idea that the family was (as he put it in a letter of 22 Oct. 1954) 'nearly related to Laurence Sterne. I am sure my mother would not have wanted . . . the rather unsavoury 18th Century parson in her house (she certainly didn't admit Laurence Sterne's works into the library) but she was rather proud of the connexion all the same. But the coat-of-arms that you show is totally different from that in the Sentimental Journey, which we had always supposed to be ours as well . . .' On Sterne's arms, with 'a poor starling' as the crest, see *A Sentimental Journey through France and Italy by Mr Yorick*, ed. Gardner D. Stout, Jr. (1967), 205–6; Michael J. O'Shea, 'Laurence Sterne's Display of Heraldry', *Shandean* 3 (1991), 61–9.

2–'A depression of the retina of the eye; *fovea centralis*, the fovea of the retina' (*OED*).

3–H. W. B. Joseph (1867–1943): philosopher; Fellow of New College, Oxford, from 1891 until his death. His works include *An Introduction to Logic* (1906), *Some Problems in Ethics* (1930) and *Essays in Ancient and Modern Philosophy* (1935). See H. A. Prichard, 'H. W. B. Joseph, 1867–1943', *Mind*, ns 53: 210 (Apr. 1944), 189–91; A. H. Smith, 'Joseph, Horace William Brindley, 1867–1943', *Proceedings of the British Academy* 31 (1945), 375–98.

by you. If you would consider writing such an article, I would not be disposed to press you in the matter of time.[1]

I am, Sir,
Your obedient servant,
[T. S. Eliot]

## TO *Herbert Read* TS Victoria

30 August 1927 *The Monthly Criterion*

Dear Herbert,

As I have introduced you to the first part of this correspondence,[2] I think there is no disloyalty in showing you the consequences. They are very much as we feared. The man is full of false pride. You won't have time to advise me about this when we meet tomorrow so I should be grateful if you would return it with any comments you think of. Although my exhortations may have been tactless, I yet feel that Richard would have replied in a defiant spirit whatever I had written.

I don't propose to acquaint anyone else of this affair, but if you would agree I should like to expose the whole business to Flint and get his advice also. It has really worried me very much.

Ever yours,
T. S. E.

P.S. I have not replied to the enclosed letter and shall not do so until I have heard from you.

## TO *Dorothea Varda* CC

30 August 1927 [London]

Dear Madam,

I have submitted your manuscript to my principals and we have discussed carefully the question of translation. On mature consideration we do not feel that this novel of Radiguet's would have a wide enough appeal to English readers to warrant our publishing a translation. I think myself that of the two books *Le Bal de Comte d'Orgel*[3] would be more

1 – Joseph's review of Russell, *The Analysis of Matter*, *MC* 6 (Dec. 1927), 548–54.
2 – TSE's correspondence with Richard Aldington.
3 – *Le Bal du comte d'Orgel* (1924) was ultimately to be translated by Malcolm Cowley.

interesting to English readers. I am therefore returning you this manuscript with my thanks and regrets.

Yours very truly,
[T. S. Eliot]

## TO *Howard Vincent O'Brien*[1] CC

30 August 1927 [London]

Dear Mr O'Brien,

I am very sorry to have missed you, having heard from Henry that you were coming to London.[2] It is true that I come to Paris occasionally, though usually at short notice, and I cannot be sure whether I shall be there during your stay. If so, I shall not fail to let you know. In any case, I hope that you may be returning by way of London, and that you will write to me in advance so that we may have some prospect of meeting.

Yours sincerely,
[T. S. Eliot]

## TO *Ezra Pound* CC

30 August 1927 [London]

Brer Rabbit,

Thanks for your advice of the 27th instant.[3] I don't intend to have any further communication with the polecat in question. For pussons like

1–Howard Vincent O'Brien (1888–1947) was a colleague of TSE's brother Henry, having worked at David C. Thomas Company (advertising) and at the Buchen Company, Chicago. From 1928 he would work for the *Chicago Daily News*, as literary editor and columnist. Publications include *New Men for Old* (1912), *The Thunderbolt* (1923), *The Green Scarf* (1924), *What a Man Wants* (1925) and *Wine, Women and War* (1926).

2–O'Brien called HWE (26 Aug.) 'the advertising king of the Middle West'.

3–EP had written, with reference to the Samuel Roth affair: 'Brer Possum, you keep away from that polecat.

'I think it is a damn waste of time. After all we have now heard of Ulysses, and nobody that wants the book will buy forty copies of 2 worlds, to get what they can have in one vol. and then not all of it.'

On the same day EP wrote a letter to Robert W. Potter, Editor of the *New York Evening Post* (copied to TSE): 'I am unable to understand why Mr Roth persists in mis-statement even in cases when the real facts are less discreditable to him than those he wrongly alledges. Whether Mr Roth's mendacity contributes to the gaiety of nations I am unable to state . . .

'Mr Roth is indubitably a literary pirate, our national laws encouraging theft of literary composition; and thereby continuing our great anglo-saxon tradition, from which the mother

ourselves it is certainly a damn waste of time. As for *Ulysses*, it can now take care of itself. The only distinction I draw is that this sort of piracy is a kind of advertisement for Mr Joyce, and for pussons like ourselves who have serious occupations it is not only a waste of time but possibly a diminution of royalties.

[T. S. E.]

## TO *Lady Rothermere* CC

30 August 1927 [London]

Dear L.R.,

Thank you for your letter as you need not have acknowledged my small poem at all. I will certainly 'forgive' you for your criticism.[1] The comments which I have received from competent critics on this poem and on the last one are all so completely contradictory – some like one, some the other and some dislike both, and I do not think that anybody *likes* both – that I am wholly bewildered and dependent on my own inspiration to know what to do next.

Did I say that I quite agreed with you about getting more short things into the *Criterion*, but that the difficulty is to get people to write things even as short as they are? However, I have got something from D. H. Lawrence to commence in the October number which cuts up very nicely into short bits[2] and I am hoping to get one or two Italian stories.

It is very sweet of you to mention Switzerland again. I hope that you will be able to get into your house yourself quite soon, and I also hope that you will indeed renew your invitation towards the end of September.[3] I do not know in the least what my situation will be at that time, but I like to think that if there is the opportunity I might have an invitation from yourself. In any case, let me know how your architect gets on.

---

country has, however, more recently departed <in this solitary detail>, in the direction of decency . . .

'Personally I wish to reaffirm my conviction that despite his tendency to levity Mr Roth is intellectually and morally superior to the majority of our 435 members of congress, and to the majority of our fellow citizens who tolerate the personnel of our national legislature; This latter body being responsible for our copyright laws . . .

[P.S.] Mr Roth's statement re/ Mr Eliot appears to me both mendacious and malicious, i.e. libelous and written with intent to do harm.'

1 – Lady Rothermere wrote on 25 Aug.: 'Thank you so much for sending me your latest poem [*Journey of the Magi*]. You must *forgive* me if I am sincere enough to tell you that – it has no meaning for me – as a poem.'

2 – 'Flowery Tuscany'.

3 – Her Swiss home, Brumsberg at Fribourg, was in the hands of builders.

Always yours very sincerely,
[T. S. E.]

P.S. Your invitation is in the circumstances an exasperation. There is just a remote possibility, and in that case I would take the liberty of wiring you, if you will keep me in touch with your address. Needless to say, it would be a very keen pleasure.

## TO *Bonamy Dobrée* TS Brotherton

30 August 1927 *The Monthly Criterion*

Dear Bonamy,

I have two important matters to mention to you. One is the Dialogus.[1] I am writing on the assumption that you are the *Editor* and *Agent*. So far as you are *Agent*, I suggest that you should try to make arrangements in America first, as that is the promised land, let me know immediately, and I will, if possible, publish the Dialogus simultaneously in the *Criterion*; even though it be necessary to postpone Kipling, Congreve, Achigar and the Implications of Behaviourism. But I imagine that you will not be able to arrange for the publication of the Dialogus in America until I have had time to publish it. Anyway go ahead with it in America and I will try to fit in here to accord with American publication.

2. Qua Editor, I have not yet entirely digested the Dialogus, but perhaps that is due to there not being enough mustard. I am very tempted to make one short speech in it myself near the beginning. I should say something to this effect:

| | |
|---|---|
| Interruption by Thomas. | 'Distinguo. You speak of mustard. by<br>But is anyone who asks merely for<br>'Mustard' for a mixed grill capable of<br>talking about Art and Beauty? There are<br>three kinds of mustard. There is<br>Coleman's [*sic*]. There is Estragon. There is Ravigote.<br>Now which kind of mustard do you want? All<br>three are excellent but they have different uses.<br>For myself I should suggest Estragon in a mixed grill.<br>Ravigote for a beef steak or Chateaubriand.<br>Coleman's for a salad or for bacon and eggs' – |

1 – Possibly 'William Congreve: A Conversation between Swift and Gay at the House of the Duke of Queensbury, near London. June 1730', *MC* 7 (June 1928), 295–305.

Yours etc.
T. S. E.

P.S. I had almost forgotten the second (or third) important matter. Here is a letter with which I am helpless but, as Bruce Richmond might say, it seems to me exactly your pigeon. I am sure that information will pour from your mind. Please either answer it yourself, saying that I have sent it to you, or provide me with a reply; whichever is more convenient. T. S. E.

## TO *Ada Leverson* CC

30 August 1927 [*The Monthly Criterion*]

My dear Mrs Leverson,

I was so sorry, too, about your sketch, but you see how it is.[1] An editor has to choose very carefully and try to make his reviews as up to date as possible. I wish that I could definitely promise you Osbert's forthcoming book, but there are three or four people who write pretty regularly reviews of verse for the *Criterion* and I must allow them the first choice if they want to do it. I imagine that the book will not be out before October or November. It will be so interesting also to see Sacheverell's[2] promised book on German Baroque Art which I suppose my Art Editor will want me to get for him.

With all best wishes and kindest regards from both of us,

Believe me, dear Mrs Leverson,
Yours ever,
[T. S. Eliot]

1–Having been informed on 4 Aug. that her notice of Osbert Sitwell's *Before the Bombardment* could not be used, Leverson asked TSE (26 Aug.) if she might write 'a few lines' on Sitwell's forthcoming volume of poetry, *England Reclaimed*.

2–Sacheverell Sitwell (1897–1988): writer, poet and art critic; youngest of the Sitwell trio. T. S. Eliot thought him the 'most important and difficult poet' in the anthology *Wheels* (1918). Reviewing *The People's Palace*, TSE praised its 'distinguished aridity', and said he 'attributed more' to Sacheverell Sitwell than to any poet of his generation (*Egoist* 5: 6, June/July 1918). However, it was not as a poet but as an idiosyncratic writer of books about travel, art and literature, including *Southern Baroque Art* (1924), that Sacheverell Sitwell came to be best known.

## TO *Mona Wilson*[1] CC

30 August 1927 [London]

Dear Miss Wilson,

I owe you very many apologies and very many thanks for your patience, for which a harassed editor is always grateful. I still wish and still hope to print your essay on 'Cressida'. The first result of the change into a monthly has been to excite a flow of contributions of a rather immediately topical nature; and particularly, my projects have been thrown out by the persistence of a discussion initiated by Middleton Murry. There is, therefore, a certain congestion so to speak of main road traffic which has been held up by this cross roads procession. I think I can promise you that if you will leave 'Cressida' with me I could publish it definitely within the next six months. This is even allowing for new 'controversies' that may crop up. I think I shall be obliged, however, to accept your suggestion for shortening it. There are two reasons. One is that I like to have contributions to the *monthly Criterion* as brief as possible, and the other is that I am afraid that the great majority of readers, even of the *Criterion*, are quite unable to follow any quotation in Old French. For me it is difficult: and I imagine that most of our readers would skip such quotations. Would you consider either quoting more briefly in your own translation or else omitting altogether? The majority of the quotations are not only intelligible but necessary.[2]

I have just read with great interest your *Life of Blake* and congratulate you upon it. [3]

Sincerely yours,
[T. S. Eliot]

1 – Mona Wilson (1872–1954), was educated at Newnham College, Cambridge, and became a civil servant (her work took her from the National Insurance Commission to the Ministry of Reconstruction). A close friend of the writer T. Sturge Moore, and a long-time companion to the historian G. M. Young, she published a series of biographical studies on subjects including Sir Philip Sidney and William Blake.

2 – No essay by Wilson appeared in C.

3 – See TSE, 'The Mysticism of Blake', *Nation & Athenaeum* 41: 24 (17 Sept. 1927), 779.

## TO *Henry Eliot*

TS Houghton

30 August 1927 *The Monthly Criterion*

My dear Henry:

I cannot thank you enough for your kindness. I am writing in haste. It is difficult to write at home. It is also difficult to write at my office, as during the part of the day that I am there I have an immense mass of official business to get through, and there never seems to be time for me to borrow the typewriter from my secretary to write a personal letter. I can only say that your gift very much relieved my mind. I have, as a matter of fact, already invested ¼ of it in Imperial Tobacco, which I am told is very good, and hope to invest another ½ of the balance. But with my income tax, and paying off old debts, I feel very much happier to have this balance in hand.

I have had letters from Marion, and a letter from Margaret, exhorting me to come to America to see mother. To Margaret especially, and even to Marion, I shall not be able to explain the circumstances. I must be content to remain in an ungrateful position. But to you (at any moment I may be obliged to cut this letter short) I can explain the quandary. So long as Vivien is as she is, I do not see how I can leave. You will say: kinder to her, and far better for me, to put her away in a Home at once. But that is difficult in England, except when the patient is willing. A few years ago, a man whom every doctor in Harley St. will tell you was a violent lunatic, sued the doctors who had put him away, and actually got damages; such damages that the doctors in question were actually bankrupted to pay him. Since then, every doctor in England is scared pissless about committing people to asylums. There is some hope that the lunacy laws of England may be reformed, so as to give physicians more freedom; but as it is, no doctor will commit anyone to an asylum unless they have either manifestly tried to commit suicide or committed a criminal assault upon someone else. So there is no likelihood of getting Vivien into a Home at present. We must therefore wait until she either annoys people in the public street (which I am always expecting) or tries to take her own life, before I can do anything about it. Meanwhile I feel that I must not leave her, even for a night, as this sort of thing might happen at any time. I hope that you will understand that if I do not come over at once to see Mother, that is the reason; and I hope fervently that she will hang on for six months or a year, until my affairs have really come to a head.

I don't expect even you (and I expect more sympathy and understanding from you, even at this distance, than from anybody) can understand what this life is like.

Yrs. in great haste, very affy.,
T.

## TO *H. J. C. Grierson* TS National Library of Scotland

30 August 1927 *The Monthly Criterion*

Dear Professor Grierson,

Thank you very much indeed for your essay on Milton which I am delighted to have. I should be overjoyed to use it and could begin to do so early in the New Year. I say 'begin to do so' because it is very long for us, and if you are willing that I should print it I should be very grateful if you would indicate possible division into two or three sections. If I can print it in two parts, I will, but I think it more likely that I should want to print it in three parts.[1] I enjoyed the essay very much, as I read it yesterday. Everything that you said about Milton's peculiar theological views interested me and I have been trying to study myself the more complicated theological questions of that particular period. But what particularly interested me is that you quoted two lines which have always stuck in my mind and which always occur to me when I think of Milton and Shakespeare together. One is:

'The expense of Spirit in a waste of shame'

and the other is:

'Eyeless, in Gaza, at the mill with slaves'

When I think of the first, I think how much greater Shakespeare was than Milton; when I think of the second it seems to me that no one has ever surpassed or equalled Milton in his own way.

I have always wanted to meet you and should very much like to lunch with you.[2] Unfortunately, after Friday I am not free for lunch until Wednesday the 7th. On the other hand, I am free on either Friday the 3rd or Wednesday the 7th. If either of these dates should be possible for you I hope you would let me know and I should be more than happy to see you.

With many thanks,
Yours very truly,
T. S. Eliot

1–'John Milton', C. 8 (Sept. 1928), 7–26; (Dec. 1928), 240–57.
2–Grierson invited TSE to lunch at the Junior Athenaeum Club, London, on Sat., 3 Sept.

## TO *John Middleton Murry* CC

30 August 1927 [London]

My dear John

Certainly I shall use what influence I have to arrange reciprocal advertisements.[1] The announcement of *The New Adelphi* interested me very much and I am extremely glad that it is continuing in that form. Apart from my personal feelings, I am really convinced that if several periodicals interested in general ideas can survive at all, they will do each other more good than harm. The very small public that is interested in such things, or capable of being interested in such things, will buy all of them. If I had nothing to compete with except the *Mercury*, I should become extremely discouraged. The main thing is to incite people to think.

I shall expect you here about one o'clock on Monday next.

I don't want to hurry you, and the lapse of a month would not be a serious matter. Please digest all the criticisms carefully and make your reply at leisure. In any case, it is no easy matter to sum up criticisms from such various points of view. I am pleased, however, that these four criticisms of your essay are made from four essentially different points of view.[2]

Yours affectionately,
[T.]

1–JMM asked (29 Aug.) for an exchange of advertisements between C. and *The New Adelphi*. TSE passed on the request: 'Dear de la Mare, I have answered this letter and therefore send it to you. Personally I should be very glad if you could arrange these reciprocal advertisements and I think it would be a good thing.'

2–JMM would write on 22 Sept.: 'When I came to read these criticisms over carefully, and began to write the enclosed, I became more & [more] depressed – and, alas, especially by your own criticism. D'Arcy didn't even interest me. Mauron only moderately. With Fernandez I could come to terms. But with you it is *guerre à outrance*, metaphorically speaking. I understand what you say, but I can't understand why you say it. And all my hopeful feeling when I first undertook that frightful essay has evaporated. It seems that there really is some sort of abyss between us – not humanly thank goodness – but in respect of our ideas & convictions. If I didn't know you, I should suspect you of trying to score debating points – that gives you a notion of the separation I feel at the moment . . .

'I wish you would make some *positive* statement of your position in *The Adelphi.*'

## TO *Bonamy Dobrée*

TS Brotherton

[August/September? 1927] *The Monthly Criterion*

Dear Bungamy:

Re C.C.'s Sense of Smell we have the Following:

One Day Columbo and His Men
  They Took & Went Ashore.
Columbo Sniffed the Banyan Trees
  And Mutter'd: *I* smell Whore!
And when they'd Taken Twenty Steps
  Into the Cubian Jungle,
They Met King Bolo's BIG BLACK QUEEN
  A-scratching of her Bung Hole.[1]

The foregoing is Private and Confidential.

Yours etc.
T. S. E.

Our Next Instalment will be a Description of the Columbian Sport of: Fucking the Tortoise.

THINGS YOU OUGHT TO KNOW:

What is a Wuxuar?
What is a Cuxative?

## TO *Bonamy Dobrée*

TS Brotherton

[September 1927?] *The Monthly Criterion*

Dear Bungamy:

The Stanxo suppressed on Friday (out of respect to Mr Felsinger as a Loyal Son of the Stars & Stripes, and the General Pudicity of Sectarians such as Harold) is as follows: It is called

AMERICA DISCOVER'D
NOW when they'd been 4 months at Sea
  Columbo Slapped his Breaches.
Let someone go Aloft, Said he;
  I'm *Sure* that I Smell Bitches!

1–Cf. *IMH*, 317.

Just then the LOOKOUT man exclaim'd:
  He's spoken like an Oracle!
I see a Big Black KING & QUEEN
  Approaching in a Coracle!

Of Columbo's sense of Smell, there will be more evidence Later. But you will agree that it was Tactful of me not to Recite this Stanzo in the presence of Mr Felainger.

Before acknowledging this Stanzo, await my EPISTLE DEDICATORY to Maister Bomany Dobrée, Tutor In Culture to the Egyptians, Ethiopians and Nubians, and Envoy Extraordinary to the Court of Prester John; and my EPISTLE EXPIATORY to Maister Herbert Read,

yours in haste,
T. S. E.

## TO *Julian Green* CC

2 September 1927 [London]

Dear Mr Green,

I like *Le Voyageur sur la Terre* immensely, but I wish you could produce three or four more of the same type to make a volume.[1] But certainly as you have not yet had anything published in England, not only for the publishers but for yourself, it would be better to bring out a novel first. *Le Voyageur sur la Terre*, about which I have consulted my colleagues, is certainly much too short to be published in English by itself. Meanwhile, I have taken the liberty of making enquiries from Harper's, and we understand from them that they are not publishing *Adrienne Mesurat* here but that the book is being considered by another firm of publishers. If the other firm is not interested we have arranged with Harper's to let us see the book. In any case, I hope that you will keep my firm in mind for your future books. Should anything develop I would let you know.

Yours sincerely,
[T. S. Eliot]

1 – Green (24 Aug.) urged F&G to publish a translation of *Le Voyageur sur la terre* (Paris, 1927). Green replied to this letter (7 Sept.) that regrettably he had no further stories to go with *Le Voyageur*; but he hoped F&G might publish *Adrienne Mesurat*.

## TO *Adeline Moffat*[1] CC

2 September 1927 [London]

Dear Miss Moffat,

It is very nice to hear from you again but I am sorry that you are leaving London immediately.[2] I hope that you will let me know when you return to town, and meanwhile I write to assure you that this address reaches me.

Yours sincerely,
[T. S. Eliot]

## TO *Dorothy Pound*[3] TS Lilly

2 September 1927 *The Monthly Criterion*

My dear Dorothy,

Very many thanks for yours of the 29th. The idea[4] is extremely interesting.

1 – Edward Butscher writes in *Conrad Aiken: Poet of White Horse Vale* (1988) that while at Harvard TSE and CA found 'pleasure in mocking the pretensions of Boston's upper crust [and] located a perfect foil in Adeleine (or Madeleine) Moffat, whose drawing room behind the Boston State House was the frequent locus of tea for acceptable Harvard students. Aiken was harsh on her, "our deplorable friend . . . the *précieuse ridicule* to end all preciosity serving tea so exquisitely among her bric-a-brac," and Ruth McIntyre [. . .] described her as a "tall, flat, arty woman" who "wore long dresses, with long sleeves and wooden beads." In [Aiken's memoir] *Ushant* the verdict is equally sharp but also intent upon [expressing] . . . a critical perception of Eliot in a toadying association with Madeleine, "who, like another Circe, had made strange shapes of . . . the Tsetse" (186). The reference to an early Eliot poem on Circe and to the complex interaction between the shallow lady and the sensitive, reflective young protagonist of "Portrait of a Lady" – based on Moffat . . . – implies that Aiken understood that . . . [Eliot was] drawn to the aristocratic cultivation of the arts she tried so pitifully to emulate' (142). In a much later year, Aiken would gossip to the critic George Watson (6 Nov. 1970), 'I'd have thought the subject of *Portrait of a Lady*, whom we ALL knew at Harvard, and myself, may have influenced him more [than Jean Verdenal], but this is a casual guess. He moved in a mysterious way, let us leave it at that' (Houghton: *2000M – 9F). In his copy of Herbert Howarth's *Notes on Some Figures Behind T. S. Eliot* (1965), TSE made a note on p. 123, which mentions the poem: 'Adeline Moffat!' (TSE Library).

2 – Moffat, who was a friend of TSE's sister Ada, was passing through London on her way to Ireland; she wrote on 31 Aug. that she expected to return in a fortnight. In late Sept. she entertained the Eliots to dinner at the De Vere Hotel in Kensington.

3 – Dorothy Pound, née Shakespear (1886–1973), daughter of Yeats's mistress Olivia Shakespear, married Ezra Pound in 1914 and remained with him for the rest of his long life. Having started, like her father, as a landscape watercolourist, she began to visit Wyndham Lewis's Rebel Art Centre and adopted a Vorticist style. Her 'Snow Scene' appeared in *Blast* 2, and she designed the cover of *The Catholic Anthology* (1915). She was a good friend to TSE and VHE during their years in London.

4 – Apropos EP's projected edition of translations of Cavalcanti.

I don't know whether our humble printers are capable of doing parallel columns, but meanwhile there are two questions from the editorial point of view. What about the copyright? First from the edition of the Talmud from which you quote, and second from that French edition of Confucius. I am not quite clear whether you have yourself translated the Talmud part from some book printed in Italian or some other foreign language, or whether the book itself is in English. In any case, the question of copyright is bound to come up, as these things are extracts. I find foreign publishers in general and French publishers in particular very much on the spot and anxious to hold one up for exorbitant fees, even when the translation is entirely in the interest of advertising the original book. If you can't let me know anything about this, I shall have to make enquiries.

It is very nice to hear from you again. I hope that you and the son are very well. I am sure that Vivien would be very pleased to have a line or a postcard from you whenever you feel disposed to write one. For that purpose our address is 57 Chester Terrace, Eaton Square, London, S.W.1.

Yours ever,
[T. S. Eliot]

Dictated by Mr Eliot and signed in his absence as he was anxious to get the letter off to you. I. P. Fassett. Secretary.

## TO *Bonamy Dobrée* — TS Brotherton

2 September 1927 — *The Monthly Criterion*

Dear Bonamy,

I am pleased to see that you are now having a couple of rounds with that wicked old man Kappa.[1] Middleton Murry and myself fell on him in concert a few months ago, and I think got the best of it. Incidentally, I happen to know that Leonard does not very much like him. You promised to send me Sainsbury's address, but I find that Sainsbury himself sent it several days ago and that the book has been forwarded to him.

I await your news about your party and about Kipling.

Yours ever,
T. S. E.

1–Bonamy Dobrée had published a letter in the *N&A*, 3 Sept. 1927, 716–17, complaining about 'Kappa's' views on the speaking of Shakespeare's dramatic verse: Dobrée, like the actor and director William Poel (1852–1934) – who had worked with the Shakespeare Reading Society and founded (1894) the Elizabethan Stage Society – favoured a natural inflection over the high-declamatory.

Talking Parrot is off. My wife objects – says she has some friends who had 4, & they made conversation impossible. We have compromised on Java Sparrows.

I want to start a Bolovian Club, as I do not feel that either the 'Grove' or the 'Criterion' Club quite covers everything. Morley is to be President, but you shall be a Charter Member, paying *no* entrance fee.[1]

## TO *Bonamy Dobrée*

TS Brotherton

Friday [2 September 1927] *The Monthly Criterion*

Dear Bonmoy:

I forgot one Point in Writing today. Your Point about the Mustard is apparently Sound. But you Forget that Some taverns have mustard and mustard, even in Britain. I think you must specify the GROVE, where there is only one Mustard. The COSMO has two: I.E. they distinguish between Colmans and French, but not between Estragon and Ravigote.

I wish to suggest: is it not worthwhile trying to get a Fee out of Colmans (Mustard Club)? When you say 'mustard' Herbert should say YOU MEAN COLMANS OF COURSE and you will reply COLMANS OF COURSE THAT IS THE ONLY MUSTARD THAT IS MUSTARD TRY IT IN YOUR BATH. You might even give a few slight remarks to the Baron de Beef and Signor Spagetti before proceeding to Beauty. I only suggest this in your own interest.

When appointing Morley President of the newly founded Bolovian Club I think it will be only fair to warn him that as President he will be expected to wear Top Hat and Morning Coat at Dinners (Trowsers facultative). I appoint you Spokesman.

Yours etc.
T. S. E.

1–Frank Morley was to recall, in a letter to TSE on 6 Nov. 1963: 'what I would wish to picture is that a young man ranging about London from Fleet Street (my Fleet Street including Bruce Richmond) discovered nexuses which became intensely interesting. Things proliferated quickly: lunches with [Arthur] Wheen and [Herbert] Read soon meant [F. S.] Flint joining, soon meant meeting you, soon meant The Grove. The Grove, and the Criterion and Geoffrey [Faber] and his problems. Numerous other things were uppermost; but gradually there was a pull exerted toward one who seemed in all that crowded scene as lumen et decus' (Berg).

## TO *His Mother* TS Houghton

Friday 2 September 1927 *The Monthly Criterion*

My dearest Mother:

I have had only one letter from you, and I do not suppose that you can write very often at present, but I should always be grateful for news from Marion or Margaret or anyone in Cambridge. I hope that the weather in Cambridge has not been too hot during August. In London it has been pretty warm, for this climate, but not unpleasant. We have been out of town once, when we went with Lucy in her car on Sunday afternoon last out into Bedfordshire, had tea at a place called Dunstable, near Luton, and got back in time for supper. This week I have been very busy and we have not been away at all. I have just got the October number of *The Criterion* ready, and am preparing the November number. We have had one Criterion Dinner, which was successful. We hope to have another in a fortnight or so, and are waiting to give one for Leon Daudet, the man who recently escaped from political imprisonment in Paris.[1] That should be rather amusing, as Daudet is a very amusing person, besides being one of the leaders of the Royalist Party in France; and I have engaged Charles Whibley and Sir Charles Strachey, (a cousin of Lytton)[2] who are friends of his, to come.

I am just finishing a long review article on William Blake, for the *Nation* (it is Blake's centenary celebration).[3] Leonard and Virginia Woolf are away at their house in Sussex; they asked us to come for a weekend, but it would be difficult.[4] Most people are away from London now; the Fabers are in Devonshire (did I tell you that I am God Father to Faber's younger son Thomas?) but that would be a long journey for us to go for a few days. Meanwhile I have essays to write, one on Hooker, and one on Crashaw for the *Dial*[5] and I have promised to the Saturday Review of New York and to the *Europaeische Revue* of Vienna, and am due for a chronicle for the *Nouvelle Revue Française*. I have just written another

1–Following the unexplained death, presumed suicide, of his son Philippe in a taxicab, Daudet blamed both anarchists and republicans, and even accused the taxi-driver of being implicated in the 'murder'. The driver brought an action for defamation against him, with the result that Daudet was sentenced to five months in prison. But Daudet then fled the country and remained in exile, mostly in Belgium, until 1930, when he was reprieved.

2–Sir Charles Strachey (1862–1942), civil servant and diplomat.

3–'The Mysticism of Blake', *N&A* 41 (17 Sept. 1927), 779.

4–VW invited TSE (24 Aug.) to Monk's House, Rodmell, for the weekend of 24 Sept.

5–'The Poems English Latin and Greek of Richard Crashaw', *Dial* 84: 3 (Mar. 1928), 246–50.

small poem, which I shall offer to *Commerce* (Margaret (Chapin) de Bassiano's review) simultaneously, when I have polished it up, and will send you a copy.[1] The 'Ariel' Poems, of which I sent you a Set, are, I hear, selling like anything; we could get rid of any number of them. It may amuse you to know that the order, in number of copies sold is (1) Hardy (2) De la Mare (3) T. S. Eliot (4) Chesterton (5) Binyon et caetera.[2]

I have just had an amusing fight with a man in New York named Sam Roth, who pirated one of my poems in a periodical of his. I wrote to the *Evening Post* about it, and they have given the matter two columns. What is amusing is that Mr Sam Roth has since sent me a cheque for twenty-five dollars, as he says 'in full Payment' for the poem which he printed without permission; and I have sent this cheque to the *Evening Post* asking them to return it to Mr Roth, saying that I do not accept any form of hush money and do not wish to have anything directly to do with Mr Sam Roth. I will send you the clippings when I have finished with them.

Besides other things, I am trying to get into shape a volume of essays to publish early in the new year. In any case, I should like if possible (though that would of course not affect my movements) to have another prose volume out (since I cannot prepare a full verse volume) before I come to America. Even though I do not propose to go on any lecture tours, but spend all my time with you, I am not unaware of the advertising value of a new volume, especially as I have published so little. But it is really an advantage for any book of mine, that I have published so few.

Now I must stop, but I expect, whether I have any news or not, or any ideas or not, to write to you twice a week.

Hoping and waiting impatiently and eagerly for News,

your devoted son,
Tom

1–'Perch' io non spero', trans. Jean de Menasce, *Commerce* XV (Spring 1928), 5–11.

2–The first series of 'Ariel' poems (Autumn 1927) ran to eight volumes: Thomas Hardy, *Yuletide in a Younger World*; Henry Newbolt, *The Linnet's Nest*; Laurence Binyon, *The Wonder Night*; Walter de la Mare, *Alone*; G. K. Chesterton, *Gloria in Profundis*; Wilfrid Gibson, *The Early Whistler*; Siegfried Sassoon, *Nativity* – and *Journey of the Magi*, with drawings by E. McKnight Kauffer, published on 25 Aug.

## TO *Bonamy Dobrée* CC

5 September 1927 [*The Monthly Criterion*]

My dear Guru,

I have received this morning your 'Rudyard Kipling', neatly typed.[1] Owing to pressure of business, I have not yet read it, but I hope to read it tonight and to report to you upon it tomorrow morning. I shall also return to you tomorrow evening the 'Dialogus Magnus'. I have now read the whole thing. It put me into a very quarrelsome mood. At every speech, I wished to interrupt; and I hope that a second dialogue will be started in which I shall be allowed to speak for the purpose of objecting to both parties. But the 'Dialogue' certainly serves its purpose of arousing thought; and I still await your official reply about it, both as Agent and as Editor.

I hope to see you tomorrow evening. But you still qualify your invitation by saying 'almost'.[2] I hope that you will either write to me tonight or telephone my secretary in the morning to say exactly where, and to say exactly what clothes are to be worn.

[T. S. E.]

## TO *J. M. Robertson* CC

5 September 1927 [London]

My dear Robertson,

Thank you for your rather caustic letter of the 4th instant. I return you, as you request, the essay on Burns. But this is a considerable act of confidence which I should not vouchsafe to ordinary contributors. I am trusting you to return it to me before the 1st of November, so that I may prepare at least half of it for publication in January.[3] This is on my word as an Eliot with one 'l' not two and allows me no opportunity of procrastination. If you will not immediately promise to let me have the essay back by the date mentioned, I must inform my colleagues that I cannot be present at the dinner to be given in your honour.

1 – 'Rudyard Kipling', *MC* 6 (Dec. 1927), 499–515.

2 – BD had written from his home in Hampstead, 'Dinner will almost certainly be here.'

3 – Robertson wished to make a final revision to his Burns essay: 'And if you don't begin to publish it in January I shall become offensive. Remember your past procrastinations.'

About Shelley, I feel rather sad. I see that on this point I am a Radical and you are merely a Liberal. I only wish that I might have had the pleasure of being Shelley's tutor at Oxford.

Yours ever and with many thanks,
[T. S. Eliot]

## TO *Arnold Bennett* TS Beinecke

5 September 1927 *The Monthly Criterion*

My dear Bennett,

Many thanks for your letter. I had meant to write to you to tell you that I have been in communication with Pinker's[1] about your Florentine Journal. I had hoped to start it in our October number, but Pinker's objected as they wanted to arrange for simultaneous publication in America. I have just told them that I have rearranged my matter so as to begin the Florentine Journal in January. But they do not seem to be quite satisfied even with that, and have said that they hope to let me know in a fortnight whether they agree. I do hope that they will: for if I may not be allowed to use it immediately, it would be very nice to be able to begin it in January.

What you say about George Sturt interests me very much.[2] I admit complete ignorance of George Sturt and all his works but I accept your opinion about it; and especially if you would yourself write a short note, even if only one paragraph, to introduce it; and if you would allow me to print this stuff with a rubric, *Introduction by Arnold Bennett*, I will accept it without any question. Please send me anything you can, as soon as you can.

With very many thanks,
Yours sincerely,
T. S. Eliot

1–J. B. Pinker & Sons, London: AB's agent.

2–George Sturt (1863–1927), wheelwright and novelist, wrote under the pseudonym George Bourne. Bennett intended to edit a selection of his old friend's letters to him, which he described as 'fine reading', for publication in *The Criterion,* but he never did. He wrote an introduction to Sturt's posthumous *A Small Boy in the Sixties* (1928), which was unenthusiastically reviewed in the June number of *MC*.

## TO *Sirdar Ikbal Ali Shah* CC

5 September 1927 [London]

Sir,

I am now able to tell you definitely that I should like to publish your essay, 'East and West'.[1] What I should like is to publish it in the same number, or in consecutive numbers, with another essay which I have independently received, with the same title, written by an American of British origin. I think that it would be interesting to publish the two points of view together, inasmuch as you emphasise the likeness in thought between East and West, and my American contributor emphasises the difference, though wholly in favour of the East. The difficulty still is that in spite of the reductions both of the contributions are rather too long for a monthly periodical. I have returned the other contribution and my contributor is trying to reduce the article which is about the same length as yours. Do you think that it would be possible still to make your essay a little shorter? If not, I hope you will say so frankly and I will do my best with it. But if you cannot reduce it, I shall have to produce the two essays in consecutive numbers instead of in the same number. I have your copy, already abbreviated, but presume that you have another copy by you.

With all best wishes,
Yours very truly,
[T. S. Eliot]

## TO *Richard de la Mare*[2] CC

5 September 1927 [London]

Dear de la Mare,

I only wish that Dover Wilson would learn to use a portable typewriter. So far as I can read and understand the enclosed letter, I should say: in

1 – 'The Meeting of the East and the West', *MC* 7 (June 1928), 325–41.

2 – Richard de la Mare (1901–86) – elder son of the poet Walter de la Mare – joined F&G as production manager in 1925 and became a director in 1928; he would rise to become Chairman in 1960, and later President, of F&F. Expert in all aspects of book design and production, which he helped to revolutionise, he commissioned designs and illustrations from artists including Edward Bawden, Rex Whistler and Paul and John Nash; he also introduced to the firm writers including Siegfried Sassoon (a family friend) and David Jones. On 30 May 1941 TSE would write to A. L. Rowse, of de la Mare: 'He is the greatest living producer of books and his word is final and your difficulty will be that if you do not crash against his sense of what is beautiful and suitable in production, you may suffer shipwreck

such a case it is best to follow Dover Wilson's suggestions. His name is going to add a great deal of value to this edition[1] and I think he ought to have as much liberty as possible. It is merely a question of whether his way of doing things will cost more than your way. If not, I should say myself 'Do as he wishes'.

I was not quite sure, however, that I have completely grasped the meaning of Dover Wilson's calligraphy. The first page and the metrical scale completely escapes me.

[T. S. E.]

## TO *Thomas McGreevy* TS TCD

6 September 1927 *The Monthly Criterion*

My dear McGreevy,

In reply to your letter of the 2nd instant.[2] I can't see any reason why you should not contribute to this miscellany if you feel inclined to do so. I cannot say that I think it will do you *very* much good, but I feel fairly certain that it will do you no harm, and if I were you I should make the whole thing depend on what you can get out of them in cash. I never have much faith in royalties unless one can get an advance, and if I were you I should stand out for ten guineas advance on royalties; although I might consider an offer of ten guineas in full payment. I don't know Mr Rickword who was the Editor of the late *Calendar* and I don't know Wishart and Company.[3] Were I in your place, and unless I were

---

on the other rock of his businesss acumen and sense of economy.' A later chairman, Peter du Sautoy, was to write of him: 'He had no use for tricks and quirks that impaired legibility. "For heaven's sake don't show off," was advice he often gave' (*The Bookseller*, 5 Apr. 1986). De la Mare gave the 6th Dent Memorial Lecture, *A Publisher on Book Production*, in 1936.

1–*Facsimiles of the First Folio Text*, introd. John Dover Wilson (F&G, 1928).

2–McGreevy had been invited to contribute to a collection of essays on George Moore, to be published in Wishart's *Scrutinies*.

3–Edgell Rickword (1898–1982), poet, critic, editor and Communist intellectual, fought in WW1 (being awarded the Military Cross); and after a brief period at Oxford went into journalism, writing for the *London Mercury*, *New Statesman* and the *TLS* (for which he reviewed *The Waste Land*). He was founder-editor of the successful but short-lived *Calendar of Modern Letters* (Mar. 1925–July 1927), which was to influence F. R. Leavis in the later review *Scrutiny*. In the 1930s he joined the Communist Party of Great Britain, and became a director of Lawrence & Wishart, official publisher to the CPGB; in addition, he was co-founder of *Left Review*, 1934–8; and editor of *Our Time*, 1944–7. Other works include *Scrutinies By Various Writers* (ed., 1928); *Collected Poems* (1947); *Essays and Opinions, 1: 1921–31*, ed. Alan Young (1978); and *Literature and Society: Essays and Opinions, 2: 1931–1978* (1978). See Bernard Bergonzi, '*The Calendar of Modern Letters*', *The Yearbook*

particularly disinclined to write on this subject, I should make further enquiries and do the article for a suitable advance payment.

Let me know how you get on with Gide.

Yours sincerely,
T. S. Eliot

## TO *Harry Crosby*[1] TS Virginia

8 September 1927 Faber & Gwyer Ltd

Dear Mr Crosby,

I am sorry to have to tell you that I gave away the manuscripts of those two poems some years ago.[2] And of recent years I never have any manuscripts for the reason that I compose on the typewriter and the nearest approach to a manuscript I ever have is the first draft with pencil corrections.

I feel virtually certain that there is no Life of Laforgue in English. In fact, if there is a good biography in French I should be glad to know of it.

I think that *Les chants de Maldoror* were translated and published a few years ago by John Rodker amongst the Casanova Society publications.[3] I daresay that the translation could he obtained from Messrs Routledge and Sons Limited who have taken over the Casanova Society. I believe that it was a rather expensive limited edition.

*of English Studies*, 16: *Literary Periodicals Special Number* (1986), 150–63; and Charles Hobday, *Edgell Rickword: A Poet at War* (1989).

1–Harry Crosby (1898–1929), poet and publisher. Scion of a rich upper-class Boston family and educated at Harvard, he gained the Croix de Guerre as an ambulance driver in France during WW1, then went to work at the Morgan, Harjes et Cie Bank, Paris (he was a nephew of J. P. Morgan), but left to set up, with his wife Polly (who presently changed her name to Caresse), a publishing house, Black Sun Press (it was at first called Editions Narcisse), 1925–36 – the writers they published were to include James Joyce, D. H. Lawrence, Archibald MacLeish, Kay Boyle, Hart Crane and Ezra Pound – and to finance Eugene Jolas's magazine *transition* (of which Crosby was an associate editor). He died in a suicide pact with his married lover: Hart Crane was to discover the bodies. Crosby's works include *Sonnets for Caresse* (1925); *Transit of Venus* (1928; enlarged edition with introd. by TSE, 1929); and *Sleeping Together* (1929). See also George Robert Minkoff, *A Bibliography of the Black Sun Press*, introd. by Caresse Crosby (1970); and Geoffrey Wolff, *Black Sun: The Brief Transit and Violent Eclipse of Harry Crosby* (1977).

2–Crosby had asked to buy the MS of either 'Prufrock' or 'La Figlia che Piange'.

3–*Les Chants de Maldoror* (1868–9), a poem in six cantos by the Comte de Lautréamont (pseud. Isidore Lucien Ducasse); trans. by John Rodker as *The Lay of Maldoror* (1924).

I did not know that *Streets In the Moon* had been given a prize.[1] If so, I am very glad to hear it. I hope that it was *The Dial*.

Sincerely yours,
T. S. Eliot

## TO *Geoffrey Faber* MS Valerie Eliot

8 September 1927 *The Monthly Criterion*

Dear Geoffrey

It has only just occurred to me that the enclosed review of Pollard[2] might be annoying for you. It did not come to my mind until today that he is of course a Fellow of All Souls. If you think best, or if *it embarrasses you in any way*, wire me at once, & I will try to stop it.

Yours in haste
T. S. E.

## TO *Gertrude Stein* TS Beinecke

8 September 1927 *The Monthly Criterion*

Dear Miss Stein,

I am very sorry indeed to return these chapters, but in any case I should not be able to make use of them for a very long time. I have an immense amount of material awaiting publication and some of the writers are getting very impatient. The flow of contributions through *The Criterion*

1 – *Streets in the Moon* had been awarded a Pulitzer prize.

2 – Albert Frederick Pollard (1869–1948) graduated with first-class honours in History from Jesus College, Oxford, in 1887; he was elected a research fellow of All Souls in 1908. Following eight years, 1893–1901, as an assistant editor of the *Dictionary of National Biography*, he became Professor of Constitutional History (a part-time post) at University College, London, 1903–31. In 1906 he was one of the founders of the Historical Association; and in the 1920s he established the Institute of Historical Research (IHR), for which he also set up, and edited for six years, the house journal *Bulletin of the Institute of Historical Research*. His publications include *England under Protector Somerset* (1900), *Henry VIII* (1902), *Factors in Modern History* (1910), *History of England from the Accession of Edward VI to the Death of Elizabeth* (1910), *The Evolution of Parliament* (1920) and *Wolsey* (1929). It is not known which of Pollard's books TSE had reviewed for *MC* – at GCF's request, he did not publish his review, and no copy survives in the archives – but it was likely to have been Pollard's most significant book *The Evolution of Parliament* (1920; 2nd edn, 1926), or *Thomas Cranmer and the English Reformation* (also reissued in 1926).

has lately been very much held up by one or two controversies which, like fire engines, must take precedence.[1]

Yours very sincerely,
T. S. Eliot

## TO *Richard Church*[2] CC

8 September 1927 [London]

Dear Church,

I am glad to hear from you again and to hear that you are going to have a holiday.[3] Thank you very much for the Wordsworth review which I shall use as soon as possible; but I am rather glutted with material at the moment as so many short reviews have turned out rather long ones, and so many long articles have turned out to be very long articles.

If you feel fit when you come back from Paris, ring me up and come to lunch. You ought to make the acquaintance of Ezra Pound but unfortunately he is not in Paris: I have a letter from him this morning from his home in Rapallo. I do not know who is in Paris and who is not,

1–Stein replied (undated card): 'Dear Mr Eliot / Sorry you did not see your way to printing it. Fire engines are important but / Always sincerely yours / Gertrude Stein.'

2–Richard Church (1893–1972), poet, critic, novelist, journalist, autobiographer, worked as a civil servant before becoming in 1933 a full-time writer and journalist. His first book of verse, *Mood without Measure*, was published by TSE at F&G in 1928. Church recalled, in his memoir *The Voyage Home* (1964), TSE's personality in the 1920s: 'its nervous intensity, its deliberate reserve . . . His voice was soft, with no trace of its American origin. The accent indeed was old-fashioned, in the Edwardian mode of such English precisionists as Max Beerbohm and Osbert Sitwell . . . Even though there was a cutting edge to this voice, a hint of merciless satire, I found myself attracted to the personality which it expressed.' Yet Church always harboured a fundamental misgiving about the nature of TSE's work: 'I share Eliot's temperamental attitude towards the demands and function of the art of poetry, both in society and as a discipline in the life of the individual. But I have distrusted the Montparnasse influence in his verse and doctrine, his sponsoring, even out of loyalty, of the writings of Ezra Pound. The dreadful self-consciousness of so many *déraciné* Americans, aping the hyper-civilised European decadents, have always given me the sensation of being in the presence of death' (69–71).

3–Church wrote on 6 Sept.: 'Here is another short notice, of the Wordsworth book, a very good piece of work. I am hoping to let you have the others as soon as possible. At present I am forbidden to work, and am going away tomorrow to Paris with my wife, to try the effect of a change of scene, food, and everything else. I think that probably I have been running in one groove for the last eighteen years, since boyhood, and that the inevitable break has come at last. Strange how feebly we are constructed by the rough-handed gods . . . Ought I to try and make the acquaintance of Ezra Pound while in Paris?'

but if you know of anybody whom you would like to meet and whom I may happen to know, drop me a line.

Sincerely yours,
[T. S. E.]

## TO *Henry S. Canby* CC

9 September 1927 [London]

Dear Mr Canby,

I also was very sorry to have missed you when you were in London, and I am very much pleased to get your letter. I write very little, and it will probably be a year or more before I should have anything that I could call 'A Group of Poems'.[1] I have one poem of forty lines or so which I may publish in my January number and I will send you a copy in a few days.[2] If you do not like it, I wish you would send it back as soon as possible. The January number of *The Criterion* would appear, of course, just after Christmas.

As for the essay you suggest, I should be very pleased to do that too; but I have so much to do at present that I should prefer to write to you again about it in a few months and find out whether you still want it.[3]

With many thanks,
Yours very truly,
[T. S. Eliot]

## TO *Gilbert Seldes* CC

9 September 1927 [*The Monthly Criterion*]

My dear Seldes,

Thank you very much for your letter. Your chronicle does not read at all pedestrianly, but since you have so kindly suggested that if I cared to delay the chronicle you could send me another in November,

1 – Canby wrote on 24 Aug., asking among other things to see 'a group of poems'.
2 – 'Salutation', *MC* 7 (Jan. 1928), 31–2; *Saturday Review of Literature* 4: 20 (10 Dec. 1927), 429.
3 – 'Can I not persuade you to write sometime in the next six months a brief essay on the vital literary endeavour in England as you see it now. My phrasing is purposefully vague for I do not wish to dictate a subject. But I am very desirous of presenting your point of view to American readers who are already interested and I think not as clear as they should be as to its implications.'

I am inclined to take advantage of your suggestion for another reason.[1] This is that your chronicle deals chiefly with several books which have already been extensively reviewed in England. Anyone who is at all interested in these books would be interested in your review, but I am afraid that many people who have seen or read some of the numerous reviews of these books would complain that the chronicle gave them no American news. This is a special difficulty which I am afraid we shall have to take account of in future. American books seem now more and more frequently to appear in England almost simultaneously with their American publication. They can of course be dealt with from America, but in such a chronicle, only, I think, when embedded in some idea or point of view which will strike the Englishman as new to him. American plays don't always get here so quickly, and I think you are pretty safe there. Anyway, it is always interesting to know what America thinks of its plays and books, as very often they are over- or under-rated here. My only objection to the present chronicle is that it rather appears to be introducing books which you assume the English reader does not know. I hope I have made clear what I mean, as otherwise I like your article very much. If you can manage to send me another chronicle in November, I shall be very grateful indeed.[2]

Many thanks for your suggestion to your Agent about your thriller. I hope that it may come to us.

Sincerely yours,
[T. S. Eliot]

## TO *W. H. Auden*[3] CC

9 September 1927 [London]

Dear Sir,

I must apologise for having kept your poems such a long time, but I am very slow to make up my mind. I do not feel that any of the enclosed is quite right, but I should be interested to follow your work. I am afraid that I am much too busy to give you any detailed criticism that would do the poems justice, and I suggest that whenever you happen to be in

1–Seldes sent his 'pedestrian chronicle' on 22 Aug. 'If you should choose to delay your American letter a month or two, I could send you a more entertaining one in November.'

2–'American Chronicle', *MC* 7 (Feb. 1928), 169–75.

3–W. H. Auden (1907–73), poet, playwright, librettist, translator, essayist and editor: see Biographical Register.

London you might let me know and I should be very glad if you cared to come to see me.[1]

Yours very truly,
[T. S. Eliot]

## TO *Julien Benda*[2] CC

Le 9 septembre 1927 [*The Monthly Criterion*]

Cher Monsieur Benda,

J'ai lu avec un grand intérêt vos morceaux dans les derniers deux numéros de *La Nouvelle Revue Française* et j'en attends la suite avec beaucoup d'impatience.[3] L'idée m'est venue de vous demander si vous vous êtes engagé avec un éditeur anglais pour une traduction anglaise du volume complet. Sinon, j'espère que vous voudrez bien vous rappeler que je suis non seulement rédacteur d'une revue, mais aussi un directeur de la maison d'éditions Faber and Gwyer Limited; et que je serais blen content de pouvoir proposer ce livre à mes collègues.

Recevez, cher Monsieur Benda, l'assurance de mes hommages et de ma sympathie cordiale.

[T. S. Eliot][4]

1 – Having been encouraged by Sacheverell Sitwell to submit his work to TSE, Auden wrote of this letter to Christopher Isherwood: 'On the whole coming from Eliot's reserve I think it is really quite complementary' (quoted in *The English Auden*, ed. Edward Mendelson [1977], xiii; Humphrey Carpenter, *W. H. Auden: A Biography* [1981], 70).

2 – Julien Benda (1867–1956), journalist, philosopher: see Biographical Register.

3 – *La Trahison des clercs* was serialised in four parts in *NRF* 29 (1927): Aug., 129–53; Sept., 308–43; Oct., 467–97; Nov. 580–619.

4 – *Translation*: Dear Monsieur Benda, I have read with great interest the extracts of your work in the last two numbers of *La Nouvelle Revue Française*, and I am very impatient to read the sequel. It has occurred to me to ask you if you are committed to any English publisher for the English translation of the volume as a whole. If not, I hope you will kindly remember that I am not only the editor of a review, but also one of the directors of the publishing house of Faber and Gwyer Limited; and that I would be very pleased to be able to suggest this book to my colleagues.

With best wishes, Yours sincerely [T. S. E.]

## TO *Orlo Williams* CC

9 September 1927 [London]

Dear Williams,

A little while ago you suggested that you would be willing to obtain from Linati a story which sounded amusing, and which, I understood from you, was short enough for *The Criterion*. It was a story about a cinema actor. I should very much like to have it. I find that I have practically enough criticism to fill up *The Criterion* till April or May, but the prospect of fiction is rather alarming. I hesitate to ask you, because I should have to ask you at the same time to be so good as to translate it for us. But it would come in very convenient at the end of the year.[1]

What do you think of the idea, which has just occurred to me, to have now and then just a sort of list of fiction recommended? This would take the place of many short reviews. We had already arrived at the conclusion that only first novels should, as a rule, receive short notices, but several people, not without ability, have tried their hand at these short notices, and it does seem to be almost impossible to deal with a book of fiction in less than eight hundred words, unless you deal with it really telegraphically. I do not quite see yet how this list could be done, but you might have some ideas.[2]

I suppose we are not likely to meet again until after your return from Italy; but if you should be in town, do let me know.

Yours ever,
[T. S. Eliot]

1–Carlo Linati, 'One of the Claque: An Improbable Story', trans. Orlo Williams, *MC* 7 (Mar. 1928), 232–6.

2–Williams replied (17 Sept.): 'The novels question is very difficult. The only way to do such a book list is to have some willing person who will devote some time to reading bits of novels in the office. Is it really necessary for the M. C. to give a list of novels, or at least commercially advisable? I should be willing to come & consult with you once a month on the subject, & this, aided by 4 weeks of the *Lit. Supp.* & my general knowledge might suffice to make a bare list. Tabloid reviewing, except as done in the *Times*, is a mistake I am convinced.'

## FROM *Geoffrey Faber* MS Valerie Eliot

10 September 1927 7 Oak Hill Park, Hampstead, N.W.3

My dear Tom,

I write perforce in the gtest haste. It is thoughtful of you about Pollard. I *would* rather the review didn't appear: partly because I see much of P. & partly because I have designs on him as part author of a book. P. has, no doubt, commonplaceness of mind; but he is what they call a 'competent' historian, & has considerable force & energy; & I don't really think quite deserves such a slap in the face!

And is the sentence quoted really so foolish? I confess it adequately expresses my own opinion! The good things are, surely, agreed upon as such by a sufficiently large number of people to warrant the expression, tho' philosophically it is of doubtful value.

Thanks too for the booklet.[1] I would like to tackle it in *The Criterion*: the difficulty is that most of the things I want to say are dangerous for a publisher!

Yr
G. C. F.

## TO *Maurice Haigh-Wood* CC

10 September 1927 [London]

Dear Maurice,

Here is matter about which I should have written to James, and I should be very glad if you would write to him yourself a line, at once, if you agree.

I don't think you have at present any Canadian Pacific Common, & so may not have seen the circular which I enclose. Vivien has 10 shares already, but, as you will remember, we arranged that she should have 12, and you 20, out of your Aunt Emily's estate. I have consulted Marshall about this new issue, and he thinks it is a good thing. Anyway, it is almost certainly better to take up the option rather than let it slide, because if you don't want the shares you can sell the option. On Vivien's *present* holding, she gets option on 1¼ shares (new). I am taking up the 1 share for her, and Birks are selling the option on the fraction.

1 – Unidentified.

It occurred to me that you ought not to let the chance slip on Aunt Emily's shares; so I wrote to James, who replies suggesting that the Evans's should assign the shares to you and V. Strictly speaking, you should have 2½ option shares and V. would have 1½. But these fractions are awkward, because you must either sell them, or buy enough old shares (expensive) to make up a whole. I.e. as you see from the circular, 1 new share is given for every 8 old shares; so you having 20 and V. 12 from your aunt, you would be entitled to buy 2½ and V. 1½ new shares. I suggest that it will be simpler if the Evans assign equally half and half, and the difference can be adjusted later out of cash. Then you can either fork up the money to pay for your two new shares, giving you 22 in all (you see it is payable in 3 instalments, and you would need to provide about 20 guineas at once) or you can sell the option (which would bring in a few pounds) without paying at all. I myself am inclined to take up the two shares for Vivien.

If I have made myself clear, and if you agree, would you write to James confirming my proposal that he should ask the Misses Evans to assign the option on 32 old shares (i.e. option on 4 new shares) option on two new to V. and two new to you? As you see, the whole thing has to get through before September 29th, so there is no time to be lost.

Did you ever get my note asking you to lunch with me last week? You never answered it.

Yrs ever affy.
Tom

## TO *Arthur Wheen*[1] CC

12 September 1927 [*The Monthly Criterion*]

Dear Wheen,

Emerson having proved a washout, would you care to have a look at Professor J. G. Robertson's *Biography of Goethe* in the Republic of Letters series. If the idea bores you, say so; if not, I will send you the book without any obligation on your part. If you find the book isn't interesting

1–Arthur Wheen (1897–1971) grew up in Sydney, Australia, and came to Europe with the Australian Expeditionary Force (receiving the Military Medal for bravery in action). He studied at New College, Oxford, 1920–3, and worked in the Library of the Victoria and Albert Museum, London, becoming Keeper, 1939–62. He translated a number of novels relating to WW1, and became famous for his translation of Erich Maria Remarque's *All Quiet on the Western Front* (1929). See further *We Talked of Other Things: The Life and Letters of Arthur Wheen, 1897–1971*, ed. Tanya Crothers (2011).

enough for you to tackle it yourself, I shan't bother about it at all unless someone else asks for it.[1]

Yours sincerely,
[T. S. Eliot]

## TO *Charles Whibley* CC

12 September 1927 [London]

My dear Whibley,

A note in haste. I have suppressed the first of the enclosed two short notes for obvious reasons, as I have just realised that Pollard is a Fellow of All Souls. Still, I should be very interested to know what you think of the note although it will never be published. It seems to me perfectly fair. I really suppressed it on my own initiative because I was afraid of embarrassing Faber. But I should like you to see it.[2]

In haste,
Yours ever affectionately,
[T. S. Eliot]

P.S. I hope to publish the second note later, and if you have any criticism to make of it, that would be useful.[3] P.S. I particularly enjoyed your

1–Wheen replied (21 Sept.): 'I wish to God I could review a book, but fortunately I know I couldn't . . . I should be very glad to have an opportunity of reading Robertson's *Life*, but . . . I should be glad if you would . . . excuse me for ever from reviewing.' He did review *Literatur-Geschichte als Geisteswissenschaft*, by Herbert Cysarz, *C.* 7 (June 1928), 432–5.

2–Whibley replied (14 Sept.): 'I quite agree with you about Pollard. He has a barren mind. I have wasted many pleasant hours in arguing with him . . . He is merely dogmatic & doesn't understand, as you point out. But I think you are right not to print the note. He is after all a fellow of All Souls.'

3–TSE's other notice was about a book by G. P. Gooch, *English Democratic Ideas in the Seventeenth Century*, first published in 1898 and reissued with supplementary notes and appendices by H. J. Laski. 'It is crammed with information, bibliography and notes; and is still, in fact, useful,' wrote TSE. 'But it is one of those liberal-historical treatises which appear wholly impartial and are in fact extremely biased. It is a good thing that Professor Laski has associated himself with the new edition; for his name will make the tendency of the book more patent. The tendency is Republican, and the author appears to be in sympathy with religious movements in so far as they are rebellious' (*MC* 6 [Nov. 1927], 471). CW commented in his letter: 'As to Messrs Gooch & Laski – they are dangerous men, especially Gooch, who has an appearance of truthfulness & keeps the lie in his soul. He has got his foot into the Foreign Office, where he edits documents, & may do a vast amount of harm. As to Laski, he carries his badge upon him, & warns his readers before he can corrupt them. I agree with all you say in your paragraph . . .' (CW undertook his own thoroughgoing condemnation of Laski and of Soviet Communism in his column 'Musings without Method', *Blackwood's Magazine* 122 [Aug. 1927], 276–81.)

notes in Blackwood's in the last number; about America, and about the Conservative Party, and about French wine. But my own experience is that the wine of Saumur and Angers cannot be transported.[1] [I] may have been unfortunate: but I have found Saumur wine in Paris hardly better than in London. It was only in Saumur that I appreciated it; and I remember in that little village near Saumur where there is an abbey where Couer de Lion or part of him is said to be buried,[2] I struck some really extraordinary Demi-Mousseux in a small tavern. On the other hand, some of the French small wines seem to transport quite well. The Taverne Perigourdine in Paris has an extremely good Montbazaillac. I have never found any book which told one definitely what local wines could only be drunk on the spot and what local wines could be drunk in Paris.

## TO *Geoffrey Faber* TS Valerie Eliot

13 September 1927 *The Monthly Criterion*

My dear Geoffrey,

Thank you for your letter. I am glad that I had the inspiration in time: I have stopped the Pollard review. I quite understand your point of view in the matter; partly because I have already had experience in avoiding attacking Harmsworth policies. I remain, however, unrepentant. Of course, I know nothing whatever about Pollard except this book and a glance or two at a few other things of his. As for the sentence quoted, I should not say exactly that it was foolish; I should rather say that it was immoral. I mean this; I don't think that anybody ought to write about history without having himself a definite *ethics*. When Pollard makes a remark like this, he is simply surrendering to the ethics of the reader, that is, in effect, to the ethics of the mob. I don't think that he has the right to

1–CW, in 'Musings without Method' (*Blackwood's Magazine*, 122 [Sept. 1927], 421–32), writes among other matters in unmitigated praise of a treatise by M. de Cassagnac, *Les Vins de France* (Paris: Hachette), and goes on with gusto: 'Julius Caesar said that all Gaul was divided into three parts, and the wine growers and wine sellers of France have followed the example of Julius Caesar. Against this habit M. de Cassagnac loudly protests, like the patriot that he is. He would render homage to all the wines of France . . . The three regions which produce the finest wines are Bordeaux, Burgundy, and Champagne. They are not the only regions which deserve to be commemorated. There is a continuity of vineyards from Touraine to the south of France, and you may travel as you will and keep the vine always in sight. First, in the valley of the Loire you will find Vouvray and Chinon, and thence, crossing the river you will arrive at Saumur, with its sparkling and generous wines; and from Saumur to Angers is but a step' (427–8).

2–King Richard I (d. 1199) is buried at the Royal Abbey of Fontevraud, near Saumur.

assume a knowledge of the 'good things of life and politics'. That is just what he should tell us. One has not even the right to assume that there *are* any good things of life, and still less to assume that there are any good things of politics! But if I went on like this, I should never stop.

Yours ever,
T. S. E.

I write in haste. I may have to go over to Paris at very short notice. Will let you know as soon as possible.

Cert. enclosed as above.

## TO *F. McEachran*[1]

CC

13 September 1927 [London]

Dear Sir,

I like your essay, 'The Tragic Element of Dante's Commedia', and should like to publish it. It is only fair to tell you that owing to material already accepted I am not likely to have space for it until the numbers of April or May next. If you are content to leave the ms with me I can promise you that it will eventually appear. But if meanwhile you should find an opportunity to publish it elsewhere, you have only to let me know and I will return the Ms.[2]

I may say that I find your point of view extremely sympathetic.

Yours faithfully,
[T. S. Eliot]

1 – Frank McEachran (1900–75), schoolmaster, classicist and author, was to become a friend of TSE and contributor to *The Criterion*. In the 1920s he taught at Gresham's School, Holt, Norfolk (where W. H. Auden was a pupil); subsequently at Shrewsbury School (where Richard Ingrams, editor of *Private Eye*, was a student). Alan Bennett has acknowledged that the eccentric, charismastic schoolmaster Hector, in *The History Boys* (2004), is based on McEachran (Dave Calhoun, 'Alan Bennett: interview', *Time Out*, 2 Oct. 2006). On TSE's recommendation, F&F brought out McEachran's first books, *The Civilized Man* (1930) and *The Destiny of Europe* (1932). His other publications include a study of J. G. Herder (1939), based on his Oxford B.Litt. thesis, and an influential anthology, *Spells* (1955). See John Bridgen, 'Sometime Schoolmasters All: Frank McEachran and T. S. Eliot . . . and a few others', *Journal of the T. S. Eliot Society (UK) 2010*, 21–40.

2 – 'The Tragic Element in Dante's Commedia', C. 8 (Dec. 1928), 220–37.

## TO *Conrad Aiken* CC

13 September 1927 [London]

Dear Conrad,

Many thanks for your letter. I am glad to be more or less in touch with you. Thanks for your compliments about the Christmas poem.[1] I have no illusions about it: I wrote it in three quarters of an hour after church time and before lunch one Sunday morning, with the assistance of half a bottle of Booth's gin. That, incidentally, is one of the reasons why I am anxious to get you back to England. I do not believe that you can get really good gin in Boston. Newbolt, Binyon and Gibson were necessary.

Give my kindest regards to Harry whenever you see him or write to him again. I should like to see him again. Did I tell you that Adeline is at present loose in the British Isles? I had a letter from her a week or two ago, but fortunately she was just departing for Killarney or some remote place in Ireland.[2] So I shall have to dodge her again before she returns to Marlborough Street.

I did not see the article referred to in *The Saturday Review*, but should be glad to see it. On the other hand, I saw somewhere, I think in one of the New York reviews, an admirable, and I thought perfectly fair, article by yourself on Ezra Pound – in spite of certain eulogistic references to myself.[3]

Lewis has now returned from America.[4] He says that the New York police are very fierce.

What about a book or an article or a series of articles by yourself on THE AMERICAN SCENE? Henry James thirty years after, and more intelligent. I think we could deal with it. But I should await your escape from America before publishing it. Anyway, it is something for you to

1–CA thanked TSE (31 Aug.) for sending *Journey of the Magi*: 'Nicely done, and a nice pome, too. I like your reversion to the straight-away, and await developments.'

2–CA noted: 'Harry Wehle . . . called the attention of Sweet Adeline [Moffat] to Portrait of a Lydy before he realized its subject. Her reaction to it gave him insight.'

3–'Vagabondia' – on *Collected Poems of Ezra Pound* – *New Republic*, 51 (22 June 1927), 131–2; repr. in *A Reviewer's ABC* (1961), 323–5.

4–'[Wyndham] Lewis is in this country . . .,' related CA. 'I thought his revolutionary simpleton was damned good fun.'

think about. I dislike *Blue Voyage*[1] extremely; almost more than I dislike *Ulysses*. Anyway, it is an extraordinary book.

Yours ever,
[T. S. E.]

## TO *His Mother* TS House of Books/Robert Craft

14 September 1927 Faber & Gwyer Ltd

Dearest Mother,

I thought it might amuse you to see the enclosed selection of letters from people to whom I sent that last little poem, *The Journey of the Magi*. When you have glanced over the letters, perhaps Marion would like to have them if she is still keeping up her collection of autographs. Some of the autographs should have some value.

I shall write to you in a day or two.

Your very affectionate son,
Tom.

## TO *The Lord Bishop of Oxford*[2] CC

14 September 1927 [London]

My dear Lord Bishop,

I thank your Lordship for your kind letter of the 6th September. I shall take the liberty of sending you the October number of *The Criterion* with two more essays in reply to Middleton Murry. I have not read Dr Harris's book but am very anxious to do so. I imagine that Harris was on the side of Scotus as against Aquinas.[3]

1 – See unsigned review of *Blue Voyage* – perhaps by TSE – in *MC* 6 (Dec. 1927), 565: 'Mr Aiken only reveals his capacities to us intermittently, acting under the influence of Mr. Joyce; to whom he stands in the relation of an actor, with an imperfect knowledge of his part, relying rather too palpably upon the prompter, (Mr. Joyce) whose tones are clearly audible, overlaying the voice we expect to hear . . . Mr Aiken . . . is surely capable of exercising more discrimination and placing less reliance upon borrowed materials.'

2 – Thomas Banks Strong (1861–1944), Dean of Christ Church, Oxford, 1901–20; Bishop of Oxford, 1925–37; author of *Christian Ethics* (1895) and *Manual of Theology* (1892).

3 – C. R. S. Harris, *Duns Scotus* (2 vols, 1927). Strong wrote to TSE: 'I quite think that Fr D'Arcy has quite the best of it in his argument with Middleton Murry. I think he is quite right that Mr Murry's terminology is very loose. I have been reading a good deal about Scholasticism lately, and I have been through this large new book on Duns Scotus, by Dr

You say that you think the scholastic conception of the theory of knowledge is over-elaborated. That is exactly my point against contemporary theories. I admit that I am not primarily a Thomist. I am an Aristotelian and my interest in St Thomas is partly in St Thomas as a reviver of Aristotle. I feel that St Thomas is a witness: if the Aristotelian could be so magnificently revived in the thirteenth century, then I feel that it can be revived again in the twentieth century. People think that what I advocate is a return to St Thomas; but what I really want to see is a revival of Aristotle in the twentieth century analogous to St Thomas's revival of Aristotle in the thirteenth. You say that you cannot see how the scholastic theory can be expressed in terms of recent psychology. The fact that it cannot be expressed in terms of recent psychology is to me a point in its favour. What I am interested to do is to examine the basis of modern psychology, for I think that it rests on wholly unwarranted assumptions. But that is a matter which I cannot explain in a brief letter. But I think that we might find a legitimate point of view from which the shortcomings of modern psychology would be evident. I think that even such writers as Canon Streeter concede far too much to the standpoint of a psychology which, far from being universal, is largely merely the expression of certain teutonic prejudices.

Thanking you again for your kind letter,

I remain,
Your Lordship's obedient servant,
[T. S. Eliot]

---

Harris, of All Souls College; this book, of course, deals at length with the controveries between Scotus and Thomas, and he, of course, argues on the side of Scotus. I cannot deny that the effect of this book has been rather depressing on my mind; it seems to me that much less survives than I expected of the Scholastic Theory; the whole conception of the process of knowledge seems to me to be over elaborated, and I doubt whether it really occurs in the way they describe. Perhaps Fr D'Arcy would say that I too am muddleheaded – and he may be right – but I cannot see my way to expressing the Scholastic Theory in terms of recent psychology.'

## TO *Ezra Pound*

TS Beinecke

14 September 1927 Faber & Gwyer Ltd

Lieber Ezra,

WE are entirely favourable to the idea of Guido.[1] While our officials are estimating the cost of the production, I have one or two points to make and one or two questions to ask:

1. It seems fairly clear that Gabe's text is out of copyright and that we can use it without paying anybody anything. In looking over the Early Italian Poets, I perceive that he has had the misfortune to translate a few poems which you have subsequently translated. For the benefit of the general public which wants as much for its money as possible, I suggest that when the two of you have done the same poem we might include Gabriel's version in an appendix or elsewhere. i.e. that we should include everything that Gabriel has translated.

2. I assume from your letter that Small Maynard's rights are entirely expired and that you have the entire control both of British and American editions. Will you confirm?

3. In that case would you object to our wangling an American edition as well? Would you object to our printing the whole thing rather elaborately and nicely in a *limited* edition in England and America? If we do that, the printing would probably be done in America by the Bruce Rogers people with whom we are in close relations. I assume that you know all about Bruce Rogers, but if you do not I may inform you that he not only does the finest printing work in America but that he is considered one of the

1–EP was planning to publish *The Poems of Guido Cavalcanti* – 'critical edtn. with about 50 collotypes of the extant mss, Italian text and English translations', as he would seek to publicise it in his literary review *The Exile*, no. 4 (Aut. 1928), 109. TSE, in his reader's report, dated 6 Sept. 1927, enthused: 'This book is a translation published by Ezra Pound in America many years ago. I have just heard from him that it is out of print and that the copyright is in his hands. It was never published in England. Guido Cavalcanti is the most important of the contemporaries of Dante. He is a very important poet indeed and I refer to him a number of times in my own forthcoming book "The School of Donne". I think that there will be in a few years' time a greater interest in Cavalcanti. Pound's translation is the only tolerable translation of these poems. What Pound says is this: if Rossetti's translations of other poems of Cavalcanti are not still covered by copyright, he suggests that they should be published in a volume with his translations. When Pound made this volume he omitted the poems already translated by Rossetti because he thought that Rossetti's translations could not be improved upon. Pound's translations are very much in the Rossetti tradition, and I think the two would go very well together.

'Personally, I consider the translations excellent . . . I . . . am in favour of doing this book and think that it would sell slowly but certainly; I think that it would be a much better venture than any of Pound's original work; and that it would benefit not only Pound but the firm which published it.' (Faber Misc. 5/5.)

best printers and producers in the whole world.[1] So that if we do this, you may be sure that the production would be sumptuous and genteel.

4. About Dazzi's job.[2] Would Dazzi require some kind of advance payment? I think that we could at any rate manage to pay Dazzi ten guineas for his job if necessary, as well as allowing you a substantial royalty on the *sales*.

5. I cordially approve any amount of introduction and footnotes and backnotes.

6. Re the three Canzone of doubtful authenticity. I think if possible we ought to get an Italian text even if it is not a very good one. I am particularly fond of the first of the three, about the lady turning the wheel. I think we ought to include these, and if we have the Italian text of everything authentic we ought to do our best to have an Italian text of the doubtful ones as well. If you cannot find a text in your own country, surely I ought to be able to dig out something from the British Museum.

7. When you have time, please look over your Introduction and see if there is anything you would like to alter or embellish or expand before we print it.

I have not yet raised the question of Mediaeval Studies. But I shall certainly do so as soon as Guido is well started.

If we do this book we want to print it rather decently.

Re Dorothy's selections. The question of copyright seems to be satisfactory, and if there is any risk I shall be willing to take it. Will you let her know that I am keeping her Ms and that I should like to use it; but that I am so gummed up with accepted contributions that there is not the slightest likelihood of my being able to use anything new, unless it be poems or fiction, before the next June or July number.

Regards to both,

Yours etc.
T.

1 – Bruce Rogers (1870–1957), typographer, type designer and book designer.

2 – 'What I am doubtful about,' wrote TSE in his Faber report, 'is the establishment of the doubtful and difficult text; and I have heard Pound's Italian text criticised. Pound, however, suggests that he should submit the text to an Italian scholar of Italian literature whom he knows in Italy, named Dazzi, who would provide a proper text. We should then publish the complete Italian text and translations with the Introduction by Pound which I think he would be quite willing to revise if required.' Manlio T. Dazzi (1891–1968), Librarian of the Malatestine Library at Cesena – 'a unique monument to the culture of the best decades of the Renaissance,' as EP would salute it ('Possibilities of Civilization: What the Small Town Can Do', *Delphian Quarterly* [Chicago], July 1936; cited in Noel Stock, *The Life of Ezra Pound* [1970], 318) – helped EP with his edition, which would ultimately be published in Jan. 1932 by Edizioni Marsano as *Guido Cavalcanti Rime*. It was dedicated to Dazzi.

## TO *Sean Ó'Faolain*[1]

CC

14 September 1927 [*The Monthly Criterion*]

Dear Sir,

I have read with interest your essay entitled 'The Cruelty and Beauty of Words'.[2] I should like to publish it, and if you are not in a hurry to arrange publication I can assure you that I will publish it. Only it is slightly longer than most of our essays; and in any case I have already accepted so many critical essays that I cannot promise to publish this essay before May or June of next year. If in the meantime you wish to publish it elsewhere, I should be glad if you would let me know. Until I hear from you I shall keep the essay for publication next year.

My only suggestion is that I think the title might be improved. I like everything that you say about Joyce, but after all you are not talking primarily about Joyce, and he merely occurs as an excellent illustration of a particular point. I think that the original title is a little too sensational. If you agree in principle and are willing to leave the essay with me until such time as I am able to publish it, may we keep open the question of the title?

Personally I consider your essay an extremely valuable contribution to an important subject, and it would be a great pleasure to me to introduce it to the English public.

Yours very truly,
[T. S. Eliot]

1–Seán Ó'Faoláin (1900–91), novelist and short story writer. Brought up in Ireland (where he was born John Francis Whelan), he attended University College, Cork – for a while in the early 1920s he was an ardent nationalist and joined the Irish Volunteers (later the IRA) – and he was at the time of this letter a Commonwealth Fellow at Harvard University, 1926–8. Later founder-editor of the Irish periodical *The Bell*, he also served as Director of the Arts Council of Ireland, 1957–9. Following his first book, *Midsummer Night Madness and Other Stories* (1932), he wrote a wealth of short stories. See *Collected Stories of Seán Ó'Faoláin* (1983).

2–Ó'Faoláin had submitted in May 1927 a story entitled 'Fugue'; and on 18 Aug. he submitted a piece he called 'James Joyce feels the Beauty and Cruelty of Words'.

## TO *Lincoln Kirstein*[1] TS Beinecke

14 September 1927 *The Monthly Criterion*

Dear Mr Kirstein,[2]

Thank you for your undated letter. You need not have troubled in writing to me to appeal to the names of Richard Wood and Bonamy Dobrée, although both these names carry much weight with me.[3]

I am flattered that you should care to publish a bibliography of my work and astonished that such a bibliography should appear to anyone to be worth the trouble. But it seems that you are trying to produce an unconventional type of literary periodical at Harvard and in that you have all my sympathy. It seems to me a hopeless task; but then you must remember that my notions of Harvard and undergraduate interest in intellectual matters are twenty years old; and possibly Harvard has advanced in the last twenty years. I am particularly interested because you say that your series will include Henry Adams, George Santayana and Irving Babbit. These three names, as far as I am concerned, give you all the authority that you need; and I should be more than honoured to be included in a series that included these three honoured names.

As for the bibliography which I return herewith. You seem to know a great deal more about my books and pamphlets than I know myself, and I should not dare to offer any suggestion or criticism. You might, however, if you are going to be so adventurous as to publish a bibliography of

1 – Lincoln Kirstein (1907–96), writer, impresario, connoisseur of art, was born into a wealthy and cultivated Jewish family (his father was chief executive of the Boston department store Filene's). At Harvard he set up, with a contemporary, Varian Fry, the periodical *Hound & Horn: A Harvard Miscellany* – specifically modelling it on *The Criterion* – which ran from 1927 until 1934. Smitten by what he styled 'balletptomaine', he launched in 1933, with his friend M. M. Warburg, the School of American Ballet, and then the American Ballet, which became the resident company of the Metropolitan Opera in New York. In 1946, he founded, with George Balanchine, the Ballet Society, later the New York City Ballet, of which he became General Director, 1946–89. In the 1960s he commissioned and helped to fund the New York State Theater building at the Lincoln Center. He published *Dance: A Short History of Classic Theatrical Dancing* in 1935. See further Martin Duberman, *The Worlds of Lincoln Kirstein* (2007).

2 – This letter was reproduced in Leonard Greenbaum, *The Hound & Horn: The History of a Literary Quarterly* (1966), 35.

3 – Kirstein had written ('September') to announce that *Hound & Horn* proposed to publish a bibliography of TSE's works. 'I have hesitated in writing you about the matter of a bibliography but both Mr. Richard Wood and Mr. Bonamy Dobrée have partially convinced me such a letter as this would not trouble you too much.' Varian Fry's 'A Bibliography of the Writings of Thomas Stearns Eliot' (primary texts) appeared in *The Hound & Horn* in two parts: (I) 1: 3 (Mar. 1928), 214–18; (II) 1: 4 (June 1928), 320–4.

my works, include the two following: first, the lecture on Shakespeare of which I enclose a copy, and second, the edition of Seneca which Constable and Knopf will probably bring out in the autumn. The latter is the last volume (or rather the last two volumes) of the second series of Tudor Translations edited by Charles Whibley. The title is *Seneca His Tenne Tragedies*, Englished by Newton and others, with an Introduction by T. S. Eliot. It is rather a long Introduction, and I flatter myself that it is the most scholarly piece of work that I have done. So I should not like it to be omitted from my bibliography.

I am hoping to bring out two volumes of essays during 1928 but it is rather premature to include their titles in this bibliography.

You have all my best wishes for the success of the *Hound and Horn*, and I hope that you will send me the following numbers. We may be able to notice it in the *Criterion*.

Yours very sincerely,
T. S. Eliot

## FROM *Geoffrey Faber* — MS Valerie Eliot

15 September 1927 — Chawleigh Rectory, N. Devon

My dear Tom,

You are right about P[1] – universally so, at any rate. The unphilosophical historian doesn't stand high on his ladder. P is most certainly no philosopher: & his attitude to moral & other questions is that of the 'ordinary practical man' – rather more so, perhaps. But nobody supposes anything else about him & his work; & while you might legitimately take him as an instance of the failure of academic history, (though, for purely personal reasons, I would rather you chose someone else to be the corpus vile!) I don't think the weight of your attack is well-directed. P isn't responsible for the publisher's blurb – which is as foolish as the blurb so often is. By wisdom I suppose they mean something like common sense. Anyhow, I very much appreciate *your* sense of the situation, though I find myself somewhat uncomfortable in the Northcliffe rôle!

The good things of life have set me thinking: & much upon the part they play in *my* world. A comfortable house, a car, good food, some sport, domestic interests, pleasant companionship, practical curiosities – the list begins at the material end of the scale and lengthens out in the speculative

1 – A. F. Pollard.

direction. We might get to metaphysics in time! Is there any break in kind? Is there any real difference in value between the exercise of the bodily muscles & the more tenuous motions of the mind? I suppose I should, if the question were put to me, reply that there was — but upon what grounds, I am blest if I know. At any rate I do get a deal of satisfaction all along the scale; & those whose minds are neither highly developed nor possessed by complexes & repressions get a great deal of satisfaction at the bottom end. It seems to me right that they should. The child's touch of 'flowers & furs & faces'[1] gives him an immediate pleasure. Should it not do so for us? & are not 'the good things of life' those which give us such direct pleasure – so called because all men are capable of it in this or that manner? I agree of course that the simple pleasure is much perverted by false ideas. The elaborate lady, sinking in her limousine, after a champagne lunch, at (say) the Pass of Llanberis,[2] is an instance of the perversion. But the Chairman of Faber & Gwyer, in his Humber tourer, at the same spot, has the feeling that he is not! Further up the scale no doubt would be a Professor of Geology at the same time on a motor-bicycle in the rain – if Professors ever do ride such machines!

I grow frivolous. The worst of the pursuit of simple pleasures is that simple pains do so get in the way. Here am I, an ardent fisherman, with the run of a deal of first-class water, unable to fish because of this infernal rain, which keeps on & on.

I read your Shakespearian address with a very great deal of pleasure & profit. It is obvious to me that you have the *right* standpoint; & I am delighted by your separation of thinking from poetizing. Murry's nebulous mysticizing is all very tiresome, I think. But S is an enigma, isn't he? I feel in him the supreme combination of the 'ordinary man' with a miraculously gifted craftsman in words. I mean that S enjoyed all the things ordinary folk enjoy – he *was* ordinary in that way. And he had the power of realizing it all – which quite a lot of ordinary people have. And then he had that unanalyzable power over language.

When icicles hang by the wall,  
  And Dick the shepherd blows his nail,  
And Tom bears logs into the hall,  
  And milk comes frozen home in pail,  
When blood is nipp'd & ways be foul,  
  Then nightly sings the staring owl – etc.[3]

1 – Rupert Brooke, 'The Dead', 8: 'Touched flowers and furs and cheeks . . .'  
2 – Gwynedd, North Wales.  
3 – From the song by Winter at the close of *Love's Labour's Lost*, V. ii. 898–903.

Can that be beaten anywhere?

I don't mean that's the whole Shakespeare – it's not the dramatist, or tragedian; but it's the poet, & it's the solid basis of the tragedies. I often wonder how right we are in supposing that S. went through great storm & stress of the soul in order to write Hamlet & Lear. I often suspect that storm & stress exhaust the desire, if not the power, to write greatly; & that an imaginative apprehension of other men's distress, rather than a distressful life of his own, is the real qualification of the great dramatist. But, to be quite truthful, I have never felt overwhelmed by the tragedies. Lear doesn't wring my soul. The speeches are tremendous – but they are exhilarating – like a gale of wind — & the Shakespearian tragedy thrills me much as high weather does – a great exhibition of natural energy, directed to an end, as the wind blows across the compass. Classical tragedy is different, of course – that's oppressive, & humiliating.

I must apologise for throwing these critical crudities at you. Blame the weather, & an idle morning. But as I am in this reckless mood, I am going to indulge myself in a little criticism of you. I am like one of your truthful critics – Henry Warren – who confessed he couldn't understand you, but felt a tide of real bigness in your work. There are great chunks of your poetry of which I simply cannot make head or tail, hard as I have tried. Phrases & pictures flash up; the attitude defines itself & then loses definition like a headland in a drifting mist; the compulsion of your very personal rhythm carries one on and on. But often at the end of a poem, after perhaps a dozen readings, I am left wondering if I have chosen the right interpretation, out of perhaps 3 or 4 which seem equally probable – sometimes, even, at sea altogether. Am I exceptionally dense? I think not; because I am constantly on the defensive (for you) in this matter against intelligent & quick-witted friends. Are you conscious of your own excessive obscurity? Is it an unavoidable element in your poetry? or is it deliberate? Do you, in that case, write only for the intuitively-gifted few? If so, why? Would either the thought behind your poetry, or the quality of its expression, be diminished by a greater effort on your part to meet the reader half-way?

I wish you would answer these questions for me. Meantime, writing now as the professional friend, rather than the critic, I should like to urge you to make the way a little plainer for the earnest reader. You have, as a poet, reached a curiously marked position in contemporary literature. It is the combination of your very modern-seeming obscurity, with sincerity & power, which has done this for you. But unless you now, having achieved your position, set yourself to write less obscurely, you will not go any further. You will remain in literary history – a sort of ossified specimen of genius destroyed by an impossible fashion, which itself created.

I have another criticism to make, which I make with a full sense of my presumption – it is perhaps foolish – you will know. Personally, I grow weary of the no-rhyme, and/or the metre which is an unrevealed law to itself. You spoke once to me of the influence which the drum-tap had on your rhythmic preferences. It tends to monotony? I think you contrasted yourself with Ezra Pound, whose rhythms derived (you said) from the troubadours. Are not both you & he depending too much upon a dead influence – or rather support? The drum-taps, & the plucked strings, are not there. They may be in your mind; they are not in your readers'. English, with its lack of precision in its vowel-sounds & their duration, has always seemed to me to demand a frame, for permanent & effective use in poetry. Not too rigid a frame; but a frame of the sort which the poem carries with it wherever it goes – not one which stays behind in the mood of the poet. Certainly the old frames are dénudés; & if you feel that, cannot you make new ones? Even a strongly personal use of the old ones means that they become, in effect, new: & that is the way our literature has developed, – seldom by the clean break.

Lastly, I will be even more impertinent, & make a personal criticism – one which I feel strongly, but am rather at a loss to phrase. I do think that, for whatever reason, you are putting yourself in some danger by the rigidity of your way of life. It is not right that you should chain yourself to a routine – it will cramp your mind, & ultimately be fatal to you both as poet & critic, if for no other reason than that it will divorce you further & further from the common man. I cannot help at times suspecting that the difficulties are, to some extent, of your own forging. Forgive me if I am being cruelly unjust, out of sheer ignorance. That may be so; & if it is so, wipe these lines out of your memory. But if it is not so, it needs to be said plainly, & I take the risk of error.

Yours always
G. C. F.

P.S. Having delivered myself of so much powder & shot, I think it only right to say that I am quite ready to be shot at myself!

## TO *Geoffrey Faber* TS Valerie Eliot

Sunday night [18 September 1927] Faber & Gwyer Ltd

My dear Geoffrey,

I sit down, with two very difficult letters to write, to say nothing of several reviews and articles, and I find that I prefer to begin – to wind myself up – by writing to you. To put it tropically, I feel impelled to try to pull out a few of the spines that the friendly porpentine has discharged into me. Not all, but just enough to enable me to sit down in comfort.

About the good things of life. As I said, I know nothing of Pollard, and have no prejudice. If I can find a better whipping boy, so much the better. But it seems to me dolorous that a noted pundit of historical scholarship should have such a foggy mind. And yours does not seem to me very clear. You give me a hurried inventory of the good things of life, starting, as you say, from the bottom. Of course one starts from the bottom, but I maintain that one does not know where one is until one has got as near the top as is possible to one's own limitations. You have to go to the top and come down again. If anyone asked me what I take to be the good things of life, I should say, primarily, heroism and saintliness. But of course it is necessary to distinguish between the good *states* of a human being and the good *objects* before that human being – a simple distinction, but one which is not always observed even by professional moralists. I am speaking above of the States. The objects would be, roughly, God, the State (Commonwealth), and Humanity. My own ideal Good Life (state) would be to be such a person that I should, by my nature and without special effort, inspire other persons towards heroism and saintliness.

But I maintain that one's appreciation of the incidental good things of life is modified and in fact increased by one's range, i.e. by the degree of one's highest good. I would even go so far as to say that my own appreciation of the type of good thing that you mention is enhanced by my awareness of God. For instance, if one makes the relation of man to man (or still more to woman) the highest good, I maintain that it turns out a delusion and a cheat. But if two people (say a man and a woman in the greatest intimacy) love God still more than they love each other, then they enjoy greater love of each other than if they did not love God at all. I have found my own love for a woman enhanced, intensified and purified by meditation on the Virgin. But the love of God takes the place of the cynicism which otherwise is inevitable to every rational person; for one's relations to one's friends and lovers, apart from the love of God, always, in my experience, turn out a delusion and cheat. Either they let you down, or you let them down, or both; but no human relation is in itself, satisfactory.

All this may seem to you a fantastical and puritanical catholicism. But I am not preaching abstention from the sort of 'good thing' that you list. Some of the things you mention do not mean much to me personally, but that is an accident: for instance, cars & sport. But that is an accident. I like good food, probably more than you do: I remember a dinner in Bordeaux, two or three dinners in Paris, a certain wine in Fontevrault, and shall never forget them; I remember also minor pleasures of drunkenness and adultery, and of these things, after repentance, I can still say

> it doth min hertes gode
> That I have had my lyf as in my time.[1]

But I do not distinguish between simple and 'complex' pleasures. My pleasures in dining have been pretty complex; it is not a simple matter to remember the pleasure of the *canard aux oranges* and distinguish it in memory from the pleasure of 'the Chambertin with the yellow seal on' as Thackeray would say.[2] (The pleasures of dining well are not transitory, but abide forever). I take pleasure in Adam of St Victor[3] and in Paul Whiteman;[4] in High Mass at the Madeleine[5] and in the Café des Ambassadeurs.[6] Will you still say that I am a Puritan ascetic?

There is another 'good thing of life too, which I have only had in flashes. It is the sudden realisation of being separated from all enjoyment, from all things of this earth, even from Hope; a sudden separation and isolation from *everything*; and at that moment of illumination, a recognition of the fact that one can do without all these things, a joyful recognition

1–'Unto this day it dooth min herte boote [good] / That I have had my world as in my time' (Geoffrey Chaucer, 'The Wife of Bath's Prologue', 472–3).

2–'"Quel vin Monsieur désire-t-il?" / "Tell me a good one." "That I can, sir; / The Chambertin with the yellow seal"' (W. M. Thackeray, 'The Ballad of Bouillabaisse').

3–Adam of St Victor: twelfth-century writer of hymns and liturgical poetry; collected by Léon Gautier in *Oeuvres poétiques d'Adam de St Victor* (1858).

4–Paul Whiteman (1890–1967) – 'King of Jazz' – was the most popular and successful American bandleader and orchestral director of the 1920s. In 1924 he commissioned George Gershwin's *Rhapsody in Blue*, which was premiered by Whiteman's orchestra with Gershwin at the piano. 'Pops' Whiteman recruited many of the best musicians of the age, from Bix Beiderbecke to Bing Crosby (the latter sang first of all in a Whiteman trio called The Rhythm Boys), and his orchestrated jazz band enjoyed numerous hit records – 32 in the period 1920–34 (the final hits including 'Smoke Gets in Your Eyes').

5–The neo-classical Catholic church of Sainte-Marie-Madeleine (1806–42) – 'La Madeleine' – lies to the north of the Place de la Concorde, near the Opéra Garnier.

6–Les Ambassadeurs, in the Hotel de Crillon: a restaurant and nightclub (café-concert) that reached the height of its popularity with artists and the demi-monde in the late 19th century: Edgar Degas and Henri de Toulouse-Lautrec painted its performers and patrons.

of what John of the Cross means when he says that the soul cannot be possessed of the divine union until it has divested itself of the craving for all created beings.[1] And after this one returns (I do anyway) to the *canard aux oranges* or the *moules marinières* or whatever it be with a keener pleasure, because one is less limited to these things.

It seems to me that you have divided the 'good things of life' into material and intellectual. I should say that they were all, according to our capacity, spiritual. If we are rightly directed, a good dinner can lead us towards God, and God can help us to enjoy a good dinner. But the distinction between material and intellectual seems to me less important.

There, I have (I hope) pulled out enough quills for the present, enough to sit down. Besides, Plato has something valuable to say about the theory of value. Remember his oyster.[2]

Ever yours
T. S. E.

## TO *J. D. Aylward* CC

27 September 1927 [London]

Dear Aylward,

I have just returned from a brief visit to the town of Paris and have perused with great pleasure the letter from you which awaited me. I have also been contemplating throughout the morning your photograph which will shortly be removed to the framers and will later decorate my desk together with several other notorious characters. It is an excellent

1–TSE rendered St John of the Cross – '*Hence the soul cannot be possessed of the divine union, until it has divested itself of the love of created beings*' – for one of his epigraphs to *SA* (*CPP*, 115). The reference is in fact to Gonzague Truc's translation of *The Ascent of Mount Carmel*, by St John of the Cross, Bk 1, ch. 4, section 8 – cited in Truc's edition of *Les Mystiques espagnols: Sainte Térèse – Saint Jean de la Croix* (Paris, 1921) – '*Toutes les délices et toutes les douceurs des créatures ne sont que des peines et des amertumes très grandes, lorsqu'on les compare avec les délices et les douceurs de Dieu. Celui-là donc ne mérite que des tourments, qui s'abandonne aux plaisirs du monde*': 'All the sweetness and all the pleasures which all the things of this world furnish to the will are, in comparison with the sweetness and pleasure which is God, supreme pain, torment, and bitterness. He, therefore, who shall set his heart upon them is, in the eyes of God, worthy of pain, torment, and bitterness, and can never attain to those delights with which the Divine union abounds' (trans. David Lewis [London, 1906], 20–1). See further *VMP*, 104.

2–Plato, *Philebus*, 21c: 'If you had no memory you could not even remember that you ever did enjoy pleasure . . . your life would not be that of a man, but of a mollusc or other shell-fish like the oyster.'

photograph and exhibits you in the situation in which I like to think of you.[1]

Having been away for a week, I have an immense mass of material awaiting me, but I am relatively free and should like to get hold of you next week. I could come to the city for lunch, but would like still better to meet you for dinner at the 'Cock' or some other public house which you approve. Will you drop me a line and suggest an evening of next week.[2]

I am, Sir,
Your obliged, obedient servant,
[T. S. Eliot]

## TO *Harry Crosby* — TS Virginia

27 September 1927 — *The Monthly Criterion*

Dear Mr Crosby,

Thank you very much for your letter of the 15th and particularly for sending me the copy of the book on Jules Laforgue of which I had not heard. I shall have great interest in reading it and thank you again for your kindness.

I gather from your letter that Archibald MacLeish has *not* gained a prize. I am very disappointed to hear this. I do not know very much about Leonora Speyer,[3] but I am certainly of the opinion that MacLeish's book deserves a prize as much as any that I have seen for several years. I had hoped from what you said in your first letter that he had got the *Dial* prize as I believe that some of his poems appeared in *The Dial*.

With many thanks,
Yours sincerely,
T. S. Eliot

1 – Aylward had sailed his boat 'Nephele' across the Channel to Calais; a friend had taken photos, of which one was enclosed in a letter of 20 Sept. 'One of these photographs was taken unawares, and it is alleged to represent the Captain anxiously attempting to find the coast of France in the midst of a thick sea-fog and no wind.'

2 – Aylward said (29 Sept.) he looked 'forward to taking a chop with you at the cock, in the style of Major Costigan and Arthur Pendennis . . .'

3 – Leonora Speyer (1872–1956), daughter of Count Ferdinand von Stosch, was born in the USA and became a professional violinist. Her second marriage, to the banker Edgar (later Sir Edgar) Speyer, brought her to London until 1915, when the couple removed to New York. *Fiddler's Farewell*, her first volume of poetry, won the Pulitzer Prize, 1927.

## TO *Messrs Golbie & Green*[1] CC

27 September 1927 [London]

Dear Sirs,

I have your letter of the 15th instant concerning Mr G. C. Robertson who has been my tenant at 9 Clarence Gate Gardens. I know Mr Robertson only as a tenant. However, he has occupied my furnished flat for a year and a half; I have met him several times; and I can say definitely that he has always paid his rent punctually, that he has been a considerate and obliging tenant, and that I have personally a very favourable impression of him. I know nothing of his business or social connections, but my opinion is that he is a wholly desirable tenant. In my flat he has paid five guineas weekly, so that I have no doubt that he is perfectly good for a rental of six guineas weekly.

Yours faithfully,
[T. S. Eliot]

## TO *Edmund Wilson* CC

28 September 1927 [Faber & Gwyer Ltd]

Dear Mr Wilson,

Thank you for your letter of the 14th.[2] There seems to have been rather a muddle. I send copies of all my writings to my mother before they are published. Among them were the English text of my *Nouvelle Revue Française* essay and also the 'Collins and Dickens' which was published in August in *The Times Literary Supplement*. My mother has been ill and I presume that someone of the family sent you the 'Collins and Dickens' by mistake. Ordinarily, I should not have tried to republish anything of mine from *The Times*, but as you have got hold of this and seem to want to use it, I have spoken to the Editor of *The Times Literary Supplement* about it and he has no objection.

I ought, however, to write another chronicle for the *Nouvelle Revue Française* very soon, and will see that the copy of that reaches you direct. If you have no objection to publishing things of mine which may have

1 – Auctioneers, Surveyors, Valuers and Estate Agents.
2 – Wilson had written on 14 Sept.: 'Thanks very much for sending us the Collins and Dickens article, which we shall be very glad to print. No manuscript of the Nouvelle Revue Française article has ever reached us.'

appeared previously either here or on the Continent, I shall always be glad to let you see them.

With many thanks,
Yours sincerely,
[T. S. Eliot]

## TO *Wyndham Lewis*

TS Cornell

28 September 1927 — *The Monthly Criterion*

Dear Wyndham,

Very many thanks for your kind letter and for the presentation copy of your book.[1] I have just returned from Paris and find an enormous amount of work awaiting me, but I hope to have read your book within a fortnight. If convenient to you, however, I should very much like to meet you within that time. Dinner would be just as convenient, and in fact a little more convenient, than lunch. Please ring up or drop me a line and suggest a date.

Yours ever,
T. S. E.

## TO *John Hayward*

TS King's

28 September 1927 — *The Monthly Criterion*

Dear Hayward,

Of course I remember you very well and I should be glad to have some reviews from you.[2] If it is convenient for you, I suggest that it would be

1–TSE had sent him a copy of *Shakespeare and the Stoicism of Seneca*, to which WL responded (undated) in Sept.: 'It seems to me that your "back to the mirror" move is wrong, as you can imagine. You are over modest (as usual) in this case as regards *all* poets, and I do not believe that as a tribe you are so limp. I think some particular doctrine of beauty must be involved in your description. Anyhow, the Senecan Shakespeare is "in character", and your lecture full of valuable things. I wish you would write more.' (WL's letter is printed in full in *The Letters of Wyndham Lewis*, ed. W. K. Rose [1963], 170.) TSE had argued that poets are not philosophers but unconscious interpreters of their times. WL reciprocated by sending TSE an advance copy of *Time and Western Man* (1927); and TSE would write in his next 'Commentary' (*MC* 6, Nov. 1927), with regard to Lewis's new book: 'Mr Lewis is the most remarkable example in England of the actual mutation of the artist into a philosopher of a type hitherto unknown' (387).

2–Prompted by BD, Hayward wrote (undated letter: 'Monday') to ask after the possibility of reviewing for *The Criterion*. 'I have been reviewing for the Nation and the New Statesman. I cannot recommend or condemn myself in any other way.'

simplest if you could come and have tea with me here one day next week. At present, one day is as good as another; please drop me a line and suggest an afternoon, or ring me up here after lunch.

Yours sincerely,
T. S. Eliot

## TO *Jack Isaacs*

Hidehiko Shindo

28 September [1927] *The Monthly Criterion*

Dear Isaacs:

Very many thanks for your monograph.[1] I admire your learning, and I have gained much from reading it. I should have sent you a copy of my address published in the same series, but that I assumed that you would have had a copy already. I can't see that you owe me anything about the Fool; I only said that the Fool was worth noticing; but you have developed the subject quite independently.

If you are about, would you dine with me soon (say at Schmidt's in Charlotte Street) and would you take me afterwards to a Melodrama? Next week?

I have been interested lately in the Film. I have seen one which really astonished me – the HOTEL IMPERIAL[2] – the first part of it is magnificent. Last night I saw METROPOLIS[3] – but that pleased me, and irritated me, exactly as I expected.

Yours ever,
T. S. Eliot

1–Jack Isaacs sent on 20 Sept. a paper on 'Shakespeare as Producer': 'The section on the clown owes not a little to the stimulus of an article by you on the Elizabethan Fool.'

2–*Hotel Imperial* (1927), produced by Erich Pommer, directed by Mauritz Stiller, and starring Pola Negri; based on a Hungarian play (1917) by Lajos Biró. The story concerns an Austrian officer, trapped behind Russian lines during WW1, who falls in love with the chambermaid of a hotel where he has been obliged to seek refuge.

3–*Metropolis* (1927): German expressionist movie directed by Fritz Lang and produced by the UFA (Universum Film Aktiengesellschaft) studio in Berlin, recounting a futuristic dystopia in the mega-city of the title.

## TO *Bonamy Dobrée* TS Brotherton

29 Sept. [1927]
This day of St Michael *The Monthly Criterion*

Dear Buggamy:

I have this day of St Michael sent you a Wire. I have No doubt that meanwhile you have thought of me as what the Bolovians, in their simple, terse and classical tongue call a 'Horse's Arse'. The simple fact is that during over a week preceding I was engrossed with the problem of inducing my poor wife to return to her excellent sanatorium near Paris; which I accomplished; but during the time I neglected every other interest. I returned from Paris myself on Tuesday, with a whoreson rheum. My reference above to Bolovian terminology recalls a Stanzo which you may not know, viz:

DEIPNOSOPHISTIC.[1]

Now while Columbo and his Crew
  Were drinking (Scotch & Soda),
In Burst King Bolo's Big Black Queen
  (That Famous Old Breech-loader).
Just then the COOK produced the Lunch –
  A Dish of Fried Hyeneas;
And Columbo said: 'Will you take Tail?
  Or just a bit of Penis?'

With reference to the Hyena, I should be very much obliged, if, on your next Excursion to the land of Prester John, you would look into the matter, and tell me, What the Hell has the Hyena to laugh at?

Also, about the famous Blue Bottom'd Babboon: Is he *really* the Aristocrat of the Simian World?

I shall shortly begin agin again my instruction in Bolovian Theology. Meanwhile I warn you against one Heresy. Certain authorities (e.g. Schnitzel aus Wien, Holzapfel aus Marburg) think that the Bolovians were the Tenth (lost) Tribe of Israel). This is based on a Corrupt Stanzo, i.e.

Now while King Bolo & his Queen
  Were feasting at the Passover,

1 – Derived from a witty work in Greek. In *The Learned Banquet* (*c.* AD 200), by Athenaeus of Naucratis, the guests at a symposium (some of them being known historical figures) discourse on every possible subject from philosophy to literature, law and medicine. The term *deipnosophist* means a master of the art of dining.

In Burst Columbo and His Men -
In fact Tea-Kettle-Arse-Over.[1]

Now I maintain that this Stanzo is Corrupt (but how lovely it must have been before it was corrupted!) and that it should read

Now the Jewboys of Columbo's Fleet
Were feasting at the Passover:
King Bolo & His Big Black Queen
Rolled In Tea-kettle-arse-over ......

I have written a Monograph to shew that the true Bolovian rhyme is Simple and pure; and whenever we find elaborate rhymes (e.g. Stockings Off – and Hauptbahnhof[2]) we are confronted with a spurious XVII Century addition (Concettismo).

Please Write to say that you forgive me, as I only am the loser by not having seen you again. Please also give my respects to your wife, my thanks for the dinner, my apologies 'which each other eat' for having eaten all of that Excellent lobster; and my apologies to your father in law, who met me as I was dodging out of the Lavabos. He was most kindly, and I salaamed to him as correctly as my equilibrium permitted, but I suspect that he thought me merely one of your drunken & disorderly friends. I believe that he was right; nevertheless, your excellent queer wine was very palatable.

Yrs. fraternally,
T. S. E.

Kip. for Dec.[3]
Please do not address me as Thomarse.

1 – 'Arse over tea-kettle': US slang: an equivalent of 'arse over tip', or 'head over heels'. TSE was to write to John Hayward on 15 Feb. 1938, inviting him to be named literary executor in his will: 'A will is in case I am knocked (as the saying is) arse over tea-kettle by a Buss, or some other unexpected calamity cuts me down like a flower' (King's).

2 – Cf. TSE's letter to EP, 2 Feb. 1915: 'I have corresponded with [Wyndham] Lewis, but his puritanical principles seem to bar my way to Publicity. I fear that King Bolo and his Big Black Kween will never burst into print. I understand that Priapism, Narcissism etc. are not approved of, and even so innocent a rhyme as

. . . pulled her stockings off
With a frightful cry of "Hauptbahnhof!!"

Is considered decadent' (*L* 1, 93–4).

3 – BD, 'Rudyard Kipling', *MC* 6 (Dec. 1927), 499–515.

## TO *Bonamy Dobrée* TS Brotherton

Saint Clelia's[1] Day, 1927 *The Monthly Criterion*

Mr T. S. Eliot, in order to show his Benevolence and Clemency towards the Gentle Ethiopians, wishes to signify to and by the medium of Proffr. B. Dobrée, that he would be pleas'd to present to the University of Ethiopia and Nubia the following works:

*Life of Blake* by Mona Williams.

*The Mysticism of Blake* by Hellen White.

He would simultaneously present to Proffr. Dobrée Max Plowman's *Introduction to Blake*, but not to the University, as he does not consider it suitable reading for the fellaheen undergraudate.

Mr Eliot humbly suggests that the University of Ethiopia and Nubia and the land of Prester John might in return subscribe to one mensual copy of *The Criterion*. It would Do Them Good; and would give Mr Flint a Wider Public for his Imperialistic Doctrine.

If the Offer is accepted by the Proffr. Mr Eliot will Produce the Tomes on Tuesday.

DO YOU KNOW

that King Bolo's Big Black Queen was called the CHOCOLATE CLEOPATRIA?

DO YOU KNOW

that this is due to her words when she first glimps'd C. Columbo, viz.:

Give me my Crown, put on my Robes, I have
Immortal Longings in Me.[2]

DO YOU KNOW that

One day Columbo & the Queen
They fell into a Quarrel.
Columbo shew'd his Disrespect
By farting in a Barrel.
The Queen she call'd him Horse's Arse –
And Blueballed Spanish Loafer:
They arbitrated the Affair
Upon the Cabin Sofa.

1–Possibly a misspelling. Clelia Barbieri (1847–70), founder of the community of Suore Minime dell'Addolorata (1868), was canonised by Pope John Paul II only in 1989.

2–'Give me my robe, put on my crown; I have / Immortal longings in me' (*Antony and Cleopatra*, V. ii. 282–3).

DONT FORGET

To Sport your Bowler among the heathen Tarbouches.

That 'Bowler' is derived partly from 'Bolo'. Why is it called (in France) 'melon'. Because the Melons of Bolovia were perfectly Sperical, and the Hat was moulded upon half a Melon. Why was it called Bowler? For one reason, because the Bolovian game of Bowls was played in the ripe melon season.

## TO *Clive Bell*[1]

TS King's

29 September 1927 *The Monthly Criterion*

My dear Clive,

Hey hey! as we should say in St Louis.[2] I have just returned from Paris & find your letter. Having been out of communication with London for some days, I have a mountain of work to deal with, but will read Miss Mayor's[3] tale as soon as possible. But Length is rather a difficulty. The Viscountess (who is also getting rather bored with Mr Murry's symplexes) likes short & snappy Bits.

I expect to be in London (unless in Paris or America) till the end of October. I should very much like to see you.

Yours ever,
T. S. E.

1 – Clive Bell (1881–1964), writer and art critic, married in 1907 the artist Vanessa Stephen, sister of Virginia Stephen (who in 1912 was to marry Leonard Woolf). From 1915 Vanessa Bell lived with the artist Duncan Grant, while Bell took as his mistress the hostess and patron Mary Hutchinson, who was friends with TSE and VHE. A passionate Francophile, Bell assisted Roger Fry in mounting the first Post-Impressionist Exhibition at the Grafton Galleries, London. His writings include *Art* (1914), *Civilization: An Essay* (1928), *Proust* (1928) and *Old Friends* (1956).

2 – Cf. 'Charleston, Hey! Hey!' – on John Rodker, Gertrude Stein, Basil de Selincourt, Rose Macaulay – *N&A* 40 (29 Jan. 1927), 595. The exclamation 'Charleston, Hey! Hey!' is taken from the lyrics by C. A. Coon and J. L. Sanders of 'I'm Gonna Charleston back to Charleston', recorded in 1925 by the Coon-Sanders Nighthawk Orchestra.

3 – Flora Mayor (1872–1932), novelist and short story writer; author of *The Third Miss Symons* (1913) and *The Rector's Daughter* (1924). Which story Bell offered TSE is not known; but a collection, *The Room Opposite*, was to appear in 1935.

## TO *Eleanor Hinkley*[1] TS Houghton

29 September 1927 [London]

Dear Eleanor:

I have mislaid your letter for the moment, and so cannot answer it exactly, but only from my imperfect memory. I can say however that I was Extremely pleased to have your approbation of my Verses. I am sorry about Sadie; if you accepted, as I do, the doctrine of Original Sin, it might make it easier; but of course I admit that no Dogma can make acceptable a period of imperfect meals. I still have faith in our Mabel, because she won't come on Sunday Morning, as she wants to go to church.

I hope to visit AMERICA before long, and renew our Acquaintance. I hope not to be tarred and feathered there. I have arranged for my Parrakeets to be fed during my absence.

Yours ever
T. S. E.

## TO *Edwin Muir* CC

30 September 1927 [*The Monthly Criterion*]

Dear Muir,

Your poem interests me and I should like to publish it whenever I could.[2] It is hardly possible for me to find room for it before February or March; so that if you would like to sell it more lucratively in America in the meantime, pray do so and let me know when it is likely to appear there.

1 – Eleanor Holmes Hinkley (1891–1971), TSE's cousin, second daughter of Susan Heywood Stearns (1860–1948) – TSE's mother's sister – and Holmes Hinkley (1853–91), a scholar 'of rare modesty and delicacy of temperament' who died shortly before her birth. Eleanor studied at Radcliffe College in Cambridge, Mass. Among the advanced courses she took there was Professor George Baker's 47 Workshop. She went on to act with Baker's group as well as write a number of plays for it (see *Plays of 47 Workshop*, New York: Brentano, 1920). One of these, *Dear Jane*, a comedy in three acts about Jane Austen, was to be produced by Eva Le Gallienne at the Civic Repertory Theater, New York, in 1932. It was through amateur theatricals held at her family home, 1 Berkeley Place, Cambridge, Mass., that TSE met and fell in love with Emily Hale (Biographical Register, *L* 1) in 1912.

2 – Muir submitted 'Tristram Crazed': 'The theme is taken from a couple of pages in Malory which, so far as I know, have not been much used.' It did not appear in *MC*.

I had not heard from you for a long time. If you are settled in England again for a time, I should be very glad if we could meet one day for lunch or dinner.

Yours sincerely,
[T. S. Eliot]

## TO *Mario Praz* CC

30 September 1927 [London]

Dear Praz,

Many thanks for your letter of the 19th. I have been in Paris and hence the delay. I like the poem and the translation.[1] With regard to the points of detail which you mention, we could settle these later. I do not see why you should not say in English 'multitude of dead' just as you would in Italian.[2] I don't think, however, that 'wickers' would do because it does not immediately suggest to us wicker chairs in particular. I will try to think of an alternative.

As I do not think the poem is too long from this point of view, I should rather like to make the experiment of printing it with the Italian text opposite. Do you think that I could get permission to reproduce the Italian text without paying a special fee to the publishers? If the publishers were entitled to a fee and insisted upon it, then I am afraid I could not go to the expense of printing the Italian text.

I think that there are many people in England who can read Italian quite well enough to enjoy following the text with the aid of your translation.

Let me know when you return, and if you pass through London let us try to meet.

Yours ever,
[T. S. Eliot]

1–Eugenio Montale, 'Arsenio', *MC* 7 (June 1928), 342–5. Praz wrote: 'Montale would be immensely pleased to see one of his things printed in yr review. If you find the poem could be edited with a few alterations, you will oblige both of us very much.'
2–'*moltitudine di morti*'.

## TO *A. L. Rowse*[1] TS Exeter

30 September 1927 [*The Monthly Criterion*]

Dear Sir,

I will print your interesting letter with pleasure.[2] I am only sorry that it reached me too late for the November number and will have to go into the December number. As it will appear several months after the review which provoked it, I should suggest making quite clear at the beginning of the letter the subject of the review and the number in which it appeared so that the readers who are interested may turn up the original review. You could do this when you receive proof, in a week or so's time.

I expect to spend a night at All Souls with Geoffrey Faber some time during this month and hope to have the pleasure of meeting you.

Yours very truly,
T. S. Eliot

## TO *John Middleton Murry* TS Northwestern

30 September 1927 *The Monthly Criterion*

My dear John,

I feel after reading your reply at least as baffled as you do. I am quite sure that neither you nor I have yet succeeded in cutting down to the essentials of the difference. I think that our respective attitudes toward psychology have much to do with it; and I quite frankly confess that there

1–A. L. Rowse (1903–97), historian; Fellow of All Souls, Oxford: see Biographical Register.
2–Rowse objected to John Gould Fletcher's untitled review of H. J. Laski's *Communism*, in *MC* 6 (Sept. 1927), 261–7. Rowse's letter reads, in part: 'Here is a book [by Laski], which, despite its failings, is one of the best and most understanding accounts of Marxist theory, from the point of view of an outsider, that have yet appeared . . . [I]n as far as Marx was concerned as a historian to describe as exactly as possible what happened and how it came about, he was not called upon to make judgments of value. And the materialist conception of history is a description of processes, and in itself makes no pronouncement as to values . . . [I]t is important to remark that if it is possible to escape a larger, more universal "materialism", one may fall into a shallow and unworthy materialism. And to impute the whole structure of Marxist theory to the fact that Marx was a Jew, is a particularly unpleasant specimen of the latter kind . . . No one presumably would object more than Mr Fletcher, and rightly, to an attitude of excessive and uncritical adoration of Marx; and it is only to be expected equally that his work should not be subjected to undue depreciation . . . There is the final consideration, that Marxism as a complex of theories in existence and still being added to, is more important even than Marx' (*MC* 6 [Dec. 1927], 542–5).

is a great deal of house cleaning to be done inside my own head on this subject.

I am now quite ready to begin our postcard-chess conversation.[1] The question is what subject to begin with. As we hope that we may wish to publish it afterward in the *Criterion,* I suggest that we should, at the beginning at least, avoid the rocks of Romanticism and Classicism, and indeed approach our central issue – for there is a central issue and our business is exactly to find out what it is – through some other avenue. It seems to me that we might begin either by tackling frankly the theological problem or by discussing the meaning, use and validity of psychological science. In your essay, for instance, you used the word 'psychology' several times on occasions which struck me, and I should like to find out why you used it there and why I myself should not have used it. But I await your suggestions.

I have three books I should very much like you to tackle for the *Criterion*. May I send them to you? One is John Gould Fletcher's translation of Rousseau's *Promeneur Solitaire*.[2] This seems to me just your book. It has a rather long introduction by Fletcher which I should like you to get your teeth into, and I think Fletcher is a man worth your coming to grips with. His point of view is not quite mine and not quite yours, but he is occupied with similar problems and similar material.[3] The other two books only need, I think, short notices; unless you let me know that they ought to be treated at more length. They are new 'Everyman' books. Houghton's *Life of Keats* with an introduction by Lynd, and Renan's *Life of Jesus* with an Introduction by Bishop Gore. As these 'Everyman' editions are the only form in which a good number of important books reach the large public, and as this public may be influenced in reading them by the Introductions, it seems to me that they are worth more critical attention than they usually get. What I should like, if you are willing and have the time, would be a note on each to say whether the introduction is good or bad. However, I will keep these three books aside until I hear from you.

I don't mind your reviewing the same book for the *Adelphi* and the *Criterion* when it is an important book. But I do think that it would be to the interest of both reviews to avoid further duplication as much as

1 – JMM prompted TSE on 8 Sept., 'And don't forget the correspondence game by postcard. I think some good – and certainly some pleasure – may come from it.'

2 – *Rêveries du Promeneur Solitaire.*

3 – 'I like Fletcher,' said JMM (undated), '& it's a very good introduction – but he seems very muddle-headed.'

possible. I note with some regret that Collins has reviewed *The Road to Xanadu* both for you and for me.[1] Of course he was the natural choice in both cases, and in fact you have more right to him than I, but I think that such overlappings ought to be avoided when possible. If you are to be in London this winter, we might occasionally meet and discuss the books which we intend to review. It is very difficult to choose the right books out of such a mass as is published and there would probably be instances in which, if one of us had a good review of a certain book, the other might be glad to eliminate it.

Yours very affectionately,
Tom.

## TO *Laura Riding* CC

30 September 1927 [*The Monthly Criterion*]

Dear Madam,

I have read your letter criticising Mr Fletcher's review with much interest.[2] I am very sorry to say that I am afraid I shall be unable to publish a letter of this length. I have already received, and agreed to publish, another long letter attacking Mr Fletcher's position from much the same point of view as your own.[3] Our space is limited, and except when the author reviewed writes himself to complain of injustice or misstatement, I feel obliged by conditions of space to accept or reject correspondence exactly as if it were ordinary contributions.

Yours very truly,
[T. S. Eliot]

1–John Livingstone Lowes's *The Road to Xanadu: A Study in the Ways of the Imagination* (1927) was reviewed by H. P. Collins both in 'Dubious Approaches', *The New Adelphi* I: 1 (Sept. 1927), 86–9, and in *MC* 6 (Nov. 1927), 465–8.

2–Not found.

3–Robert Graves's letter taking to task John Gould Fletcher's review of Laura Riding Gottschalk's *The Close Chaplet* appeared in *MC* 6 (Oct. 1927), 357–9.

## TO *Ezra Pound* TS

30 September 1927 Faber & Gwyer Ltd

Cher E.,

Your last epistles received and more or less digested. Everything seems O.K., nevertheless I should be glad if you would let me know when you get a reply from Small Maynard's receivers.

Your editorial suggestions are accepted. At the moment our people are making an estimate of costs and the question of publication will come up definitively in a few days, as soon as we have some figures as the cost of production will also depend upon these. I think, however, I could get ten guineas for Dazzi (anyway I am absolutely certain of five and I think we would make it ten) and I feel almost sure that we would give you a sum down in advance of royalties. I will write to you immediately after the final decision is made.

Have just received from Liveright your *Collected Poems*.[1] Seems a good job.

Yours etcetera
T. S.

## TO *Julien Benda* CC

30 September 1927 [London]

Cher Monsieur Benda,

Merci de votre lettre du 14 septembre.[2] Je ne peux pas vous donner quelques idées de nos conditions avant de savoir quelles seraient les conditions de vos éditeurs français. Si vous avez déjà arrangé la publication française, et si ces éditeurs ont acquis les droits pour l'étranger, il s'agit pour nous de savoir les conditions sur lesquelles vos éditeurs nous donneraient les droits pour la Grande Bretagne, les colonies et l'Amérique. Mais si vous n'avez pas encore contracté avec vos éditeurs français, et si vous pourrez réserver pour vous même les droits de traduction, nous pourrons nous entendre avec vous direct.

1 – *Personae: Collected Poems of Ezra Pound.*

2 – Benda was delighted by TSE's suggestion that his book might be published by Faber & Gwyer. While acknowledging that he had as yet written only two sections of the book, he wanted TSE to give him some idea of the 'conditions' that F&G would offer. Edwin Muir, whom TSE consulted over Benda's book, gave his view on 16 Oct.: 'It seems an extraordinarily interesting and good piece of work, and written by a very likeable man.'

À quelle date croyez vous que votre livre sera prêt pour la publication française?

Je vous prie, cher Monsieur Benda, de croire toujours à ma sympathie et à mon appui dévoué.

[T. S. Eliot][1]

## TO *Osbert Burdett*[2] CC

30 September 1927 [London]

My dear Burdett,

I am writing to you about your story.[3] It interests me very much and the reasons which make me hesitate about it have nothing to do with its merit. On the one hand, some readers of the *Criterion* have objected recently to an excessive theological interest in it; on the other hand, I am not quite sure how the theme of your story would be taken by Roman Catholic readers. Unless you are anxious to place it at once, I should like to take another opinion. In any case it would probably be February or March before I had room for another story of this length, so that if you prefer to go straight ahead with America, which after all is infinitely the most lucrative market, please do.

With many thanks,
Yours ever,
[T. S. Eliot]

1 – *Translation*: Dear Monsieur Benda, Thank you for your letter of the 14th September. I cannot give you any idea of our conditions until I know those of your French publishers. If you have already settled with French publishers and they have acquired the foreign rights, we need to know on what terms they would let us have those for Great Britain, the colonies and America. But if you have not entered into any commitment with French publishers, and can retain the translation rights personally, we can arrive directly at an agreement with you.

When do you think you book will be ready for publication in France?

With warmest regards, Yours sincerely, [T. S. Eliot]

2 – Osbert Burdett (1885–1936), author. His works include *The Idea of Coventry Patmore* (1921), *Critical Essays* (1925), *William Blake* (1926), *W. E. Gladstone* (1928), *The Brownings* (1928), *The Two Carlyles* (1930) and *Memory and Imagination* (1935).

3 – Burdett had submitted 'The Last of the Popes', 19 Sept.; it did not appear in C.

## TO *H. W. B. Joseph* CC

30 September 1927 [London]

My dear Sir,

Thank you very much indeed for your highly interesting review of Russell.[1] Not having read the book myself, I suppose I have no right of an opinion, but I am inclined to agree with nearly everything you say.

Your Ms has gone to press and proof will be sent you in a week or so.

With many thanks,
Yours very truly,
[T. S. Eliot]

## TO *Geoffrey Sainsbury* CC

30 September 1927 [London]

Dear Sainsbury,

I have been meaning to write to you for some time, but have been waiting until some book turned up which seemed to be worth your trouble. I doubt whether *Stars and Atoms* is a book quite in our line, but I wish you would let me know whether any conclusions are made in it that would be of general interest. If not, perhaps we need not bother to review it at all.[2] I should like to know whether any of the following would interest you for a long review:

1–Joseph's critique of Bertrand Russell's *The Analysis of Matter* – in *MC* 6 (Dec. 1927), 548–54 – included this observation: 'Mr Russell speaks as if only in perception and by inference did we become aware of anything. By no inference can I pass from consciousness of myself to consciousness of others . . . The question is, why did I come to think of myself as only an instance of that of which there may be other instances? And the only answer is, that it is of the nature of intelligence to do so; and without doing it, I should not come to think of a world, let alone a common world' (553). Writing from Oxford, Joseph had forewarned TSE on 13 Sept., 'It is a book I should in any case read; but, as I expect, with very profound dissent. And I think it only fair to say that.' IPF replied to Joseph (14 Sept.) that TSE 'expected that your point of view would be one of dissent, and asks me to say that it will be all the more interesting to him for that reason'.

2–See review of A. S. Eddington, *Stars and Atoms*, *MC* 6 (Dec. 1927), 569–70: 'Professor Eddington . . . seems to feel that a vein of jocularity must run through his pages to save them from over-seriousness . . . [T]o the more fastidious mind it is not good enough of its kind, and, militating against any real scientific atmosphere or style, it is a slight but continual irritation . . . If Professor Eddington wishes to write a book which will be stimulating to the modern literary mind, let him set his teeth and write something a good deal more grim and forcible, even at the risk of a little uncouthness.'

*Time and Western Man* by Wyndham Lewis
*The Interpreter Geddes* by Amelia Defries
*Theoretical Biology* by J. von Uexkull
*Character and Conduct of Life* by William McDougall

The Geddes book I know nothing about, but you may have heard of it. If you haven't, I think I will send it to you anyway to review or not as you think best.

If you are settled in London, I hope that we may meet again before long.

Yours sincerely
[T. S. Eliot]

## TO *Bonamy Dobrée* 

TS Brotherton

This day of St Gumbolumbo
[?October 1927] Faber & Gwyer Ltd

Dear Buggamy,

On due Reflexion, I consider that you are probably by this time in a fit State to resist influenza, and receive the true Doctrine of the Bolovian Quaternion. In other words, WUX. But before I Impart the Dogma of WUX, it is As Well that you should know something of the Proper pronunciation of the word WUX.

*First, the W.* You will understand that WUX is correctly transliterated, but that the transliteration is quite inadequate to the pronunciation, which is Almost impossible for European Lips. The W, then, is half way between the WH as pronounced in the Gateshead & Newcastle district (sc. as in WHORE in Gateshead) and the HW of Danish (not the corrupt Danish of Jutland and West Friesland, which are affected by High and Low Dutch respectifly, but the Pure Danish of East Friesland) as in *hwilken*. An accurate transliteration would be like this WH but Printers say this is impossible.

*Second, the U.* The U is very long, and might be rendered OOUHOUHUH. There is a slight, a very slight, Caesura in the middle of the U, which is expressed, in Pure Bolovian, by a slight Belch, but no European can render this, *so* do not try.

*Third, the X.* This is a combination of the Greek Ksi and the German *schch*. If you attentively Cough and Sniff at the same time you will get nearer to it.

That is enough for one lesson. You will now realise that the Bolovian tongue is extreamly Subtile,[1] impossible to the European Mouth. You have heard of the Zulu Click, a sound that no Caucasian can make? Well, the Zulu Click is nothing to the Bolovian Fart, by which in that language the most subtle distinctions are rendered. Even our analytic terminology is hopelessly inadequate. Fracastoro, and Cuntarella, in the XVI and XVII centuries respectively, went a little way with their distinctions between the Fart Proper, the Fart Improper, the Farticle, the Gaspop, the Pusspurr and the Butterbreath, but the Bolovian distinctions are comparatively Legion.

At any rate, you should in a week's time, with an Hour's devotions a day, be able to pronounce WUX as well as you ever will.

Yr Brother in Wux
T. S. E.

## TO *I. A. Richards* — TS Magdalene

3 October 1927 — *The Monthly Criterion*

Dear Richards,

It is equally pleasant and unexpected to hear from you and I am delighted to know that the rumour of your settling in America is untrue.[2]

You have been much in my mind lately as I had heard of your essay in the Atlantic[3] but have only this morning obtained a copy and have not yet read it. I certainly expect to be in town when you are up, and will try to keep Friday the 14th (not the 13th) open for either lunch or dinner. But

1–TSE quotes, in *VMP*, from Donne's 'The Funerall' – 'Who ever comes to shroud me, do not harm / Nor question much / That subtile wreath of hair, which crowns my arm; / . . . / For 'tis my outward Soule' – and comments: 'the adjective "subtile" is exact, though its exactness be not to us immediately apparent in the literal sense of the word which has so suffered from the abuse of the kindred word "subtle" . . .'. Schuchard adds this footnote: 'In Donne's usage "subtile" denotes the most delicate sense of "thin", a literal meaning obscured by the accumulated connotations of "subtle" and by the tendency of most modern editions to print the modernized spelling of the word' (*VMP*, 124).

2–IAR, who had returned to England after months in China and the USA, wrote: 'No I haven't settled in America. But have very divided views about that whole thing' (1 Oct.).

3–IAR, 'Nineteen Hundred and Now', *Atlantic Monthly* 140: 3 (Sept. 1927), 311–17. 'Ours is an age of mixed feelings; so is Mr Eliot's poery a poetry of mixed feelings . . . If the signs of the times as revealed in literature point to anything it is this: that no doctrine today has any power to free us . . . Hopes are not so lofty, ideals less in evidence, and faith, if we distinguish this from knowledge, much declined. All this, however, applies to those only who stand out pre-eminently in our literature' (*Collected Shorter Writings 1919–1938*, ed. John Constable [2001], 178–9).

I look forward still more to suggesting myself a little later for a weekend with you in Cambridge where we can really talk properly.

Ever yours,
T. S. Eliot

## TO *Kenneth Pickthorn* CC

3 October 1927 [*The Monthly Criterion*]

Dear Pickthorn,

Thank you very much for your and Mrs Pickthorn's kind letter and invitation. Yes, I am married, but my wife is at present abroad for some little time. I may, toward the latter part of October, go abroad to join her for a time, but in any case I should like very much to come down to spend a weekend with you in Cambridge. My first visit to Cambridge if I can get there will probably have to be to see my old friend Richards of Magdalene who has just returned, but if you will have me I should very much like to come for a weekend with you after that.

With very many thanks,
Yours very sincerely,
[T. S. Eliot]

## TO *R. Gordon George* CC

3 October 1927 [London]

Dear Gordon George,

Very many thanks for your letter.[1] I shall look forward with great pleasure to spending the weekend with Lord Halifax and have written to him.

I should like very much to see you again if possible, and could then give you your Ms and September *Criterion* instead of forwarding them to Paris. I have an engagement for lunch, another for tea and a third for dinner. Therefore the only possible time seems to be here between 3. and 4.; or if you were free at any time in the morning I should be very glad if you would look in on me at my house, 57 Chester Terrace, near Eaton Square.

1 – George wrote (1 Oct.) from Hickleton, Doncaster, to say that Lord Halifax would be delighted if TSE could visit him the following weekend. He asked also if he might see TSE in London on the Tuesday. 'Your presence is full of consolations and joys to me.'

You see, having just come back from abroad, and anticipating having to go abroad again before long, I have had to fill up my time. But if you could manage one or the other of these times, it would be a very great pleasure to me.

Yours ever,
[T. S. Eliot]

## TO *J. M. Robertson* CC

3 October 1927 [London]

My dear Robertson,

Very many thanks for your kind letter.[1] I am particularly pleased to hear that you approve my reply to Murry as I set much store by your opinion.

It may be that I shall have to retract about Spencer, and I believe that I really do not know him well enough to have been entitled to make that remark. Mill, I like very much in spots: the *Autobiography* seems to me a masterpiece, and I think you are also right in defending Mill against those who suppose that Bradley intended to destroy the whole of Mill's logic. Such people have not even read Bradley.

I did not at all mean that I thought that you treated Carlyle from a prejudiced point of view. If I had, I could not have said that your case against Carlyle was almost final. I used the word 'prejudice' in a very loose way, i.e. in the sense in which every human being has his prejudices but that some people's prejudices are exasperating and those of others are not. But it had no connection with what followed in my note.

I agree with your criticism of Fernandez' use of the term 'rationalist'. I am not at all sure what he means by it. As a matter of fact, I am afraid that in spite of the surface of things Fernandez is fundamentally nearer to Murry than he is to myself.

1–In a brief unsigned notice of Robertson's study *Modern Humanists Reconsidered* (*MC* 6 [Oct. 1927], 378), TSE saluted an author 'so voluminous and encyclopaedic and so uniformly interesting and lively'; even Robertson's 'prejudices' were 'pleasant and even exciting; it is equally a pleasure to agree or to disagree with him. This book contains six essays: on Carlyle, Emerson, Ruskin, Arnold, Mill and Spencer. His cases against Carlyle and Emerson seem almost final. He is somewhat less than fair to Ruskin, and his case against Matthew Arnold is incomplete. His destructive criticism of Arnold's literary criticism and theory of criticism is admirable, as also his comments on the element of humbug in Arnold's religious position. To Mill and Spencer he is more than fair.'

In response, Robertson wrote on 30 Sept.: 'Many thanks for your review of my "Humanist's" lectures. It is pleasant, however, to have to report that the last criticism which

Your point about Spencer's remark on mind is well worth making.[1] I ought to know Spencer better. At any rate I think that Professor Whitehead has quite failed to improve on Spencer's theology. A comparison might be interesting.

I don't yet know, and shall not know for another six months whether my review has any economic chances whatever. I only know that, being what I am, if I tried to make it more popular and successful, I should only make a hopeless mess of it. And I had rather that it went down with such laurels as it can gather floating above its head, than succeeded in infamy.

With many thanks,
Yours ever,
[T. S. Eliot]

## TO *Viscount Halifax*[2] CC

3 October 1927 [London]

Dear Lord Halifax,

Mr Gordon George has communicated to me your very kind invitation for this weekend, and I accept with a great deal of pleasure. From what Mr Gordon George says, I gather that the invitation begins on Friday. But as I have an immense amount of work to get through this week, particularly because I may at any moment be obliged to go abroad again, I am really compelled to suggest that I come on Saturday afternoon instead. And as you have never met me, you may quite likely have enough of my

---

reached me was: "Robertson is too hard on Mill." And I fancy some will say the same of my handling of Spencer.

'Incidentally, I think you use "prejudice" exactly. In my teens, & even my early twenties, I was a Carlylean out-and-out. I had no "prejudice": it is all a critical process, whether right or wrong.

'Now, Fernandez is essentially ruled by prejudice – e.g., his account of "*the* rationalist" in the paper you translate ['A Note on Intelligence and Intuition', 332–9]. There is no "*the* rationalist". As an aggregate, rationalists *are* "poets, men of action, dancers" – I have known each kind. Fernandez is in love with his preconceptions. Murry is just Narcissus, pure and simple. His hopeless muddle over "intuition" makes me wince for *the* man of letters. Your article on him ['Mr Middleton Murry's Synthesis', 340–7] is excellent.'

1 – Robertson added to his letter: 'I wish you would rub it into some of these narcissi that the very formulas in which they flaunt their sense of superiority are of the very staple of modern rationalism. Spencer not only said in as many words that "the chief component of mind is feeling", but [?wrought] out the demonstration in his *Principles of Psychology*.'

2 – C. L. Wood, 2nd Viscount Halifax (1839–1934) – eminent Anglo-Catholic ecumenist: President of the English Church Union, 1868–1919, 1927–34 – lived at Hickleton Hall, Doncaster, S. Yorkshire.

company in that time. I should have liked, however, to come on Friday had it been possible.

Please do not trouble to reply to this letter. Unless I hear from you to the contrary, I will take the same train, leaving King's Cross at 4. on Saturday afternoon and descending at Doncaster.

I am,
Your obedient servant,
[T. S. Eliot]

## TO *Virginia Woolf* CC

3 October 1927 [London]

My dear Virginia,

I am glad to learn that you will be back tomorrow. I will inform the police immediately.

And I shall be very happy to dine with you on Wednesday the 12th at 7.45.[1]

Yours ever,
[Tom]

## TO *His Mother* TS Houghton

5 October 1927 Faber & Gwyer Ltd

My own dearest mother:

I am sending you presently my Seneca which is just out. You have already seen the proof, but Constable have produced the book very handsomely, and I want you to have it. My Seneca lecture has aroused a good deal of discussion. I dined last night with Wyndham Lewis, and had a long argument with him – he is a very good friend of mine, and we work together in many ways – and I am seeing Middleton Murry – who in spite of our absolute antagonism on almost every serious matter, is also an intimate friend – tomorrow; I have been gratified by receiving words of approval and support from other and more professional friends, such as Professor Dover Wilson (a great Shakespeare scholar) and Professor Grierson. Whenever I am doubtful about the validity of anything I

1 – VW wrote (2 Oct.) to say they would be home on Thurs. (not Tues, as TSE had understood her to say), and invited him to dinner on 12 Oct. 'without dressing'. 'Not a word about your character from any policeman,' she added by way of a private joke.

write, I like to take the opinion of at least two friends of quite opposite opinions, and if possible, of friends who do not know each other. For instance, my note on Bertie Russell was approved by Middleton Murry and Charles Whibley; who are absolutely at each others' throats on most matters. And my note on Murry (in the Oct. no.) was approved by J. M. Robertson (an Atheist) and by Father D'Arcy (a very intelligent Jesuit). So in both cases I feel pretty safe.

I am also sending you a tiny book which has been of great value to me: Lancelot Andrewes's *Private Devotions*.[1] It may interest you because of the essay I wrote on Andrewes for *The Times* last year; and anything that the great Andrewes wrote is beautifully written. These are the prayers which he wrote for his own use, and which he bequeathed to the man who became Archbishop Laud.[2] I like to turn to them during the night whenever I cannot sleep.

Vivien has I think very wisely decided to go back to her sanatorium in France for a few weeks. She has worked very hard during the winter and summer, and the season was very bad, and she was I thought very run down, so I was thankful that she should have a few weeks rest in this place near Paris which she likes so much; they are good kind people; and she gets on extremely well with the French. So for the moment I am alone here; very lonely, but I have fortunately a great deal to do, and see a great many people. I am going down for the weekend to Yorkshire to stay with Lord Halifax. He is a very saintly man – he is already over *89* – much older than you – but leads a very busy and active life. His son, Lord Irwin, is the Viceroy of India.[3] Next week I must go to stay with dear Charles Whibley, and I have made promises to go to various places if I can: to Cambridge to stay with Kenneth Pickthorn of Corpus, and Richards of Magdalene (who wrote that article about me in the September *Atlantic*.[4]) And the Morrells are now in London, and the Woolfs. And with my reviews and articles, and the *Criterion*, I have enough to keep me busy while Vivien is away.

1 – *Prayers for the Week from the Private Devotions of L. Andrewes* (Edinburgh and London: Oliphant & Co., 1897).

2 – William Laud, Archbishop of Canterbury, edited the sermons of Lancelot Andrewes, whom he hailed in his diary as 'the great light of the Christian world' (*Works*, 3: 196).

3 – E. F. L. Wood, 1st Earl of Halifax (1881–1959), known as Lord Irwin from 1925 until 1934 (being elevated to the peerage after serving as MP for Ripon), would inherit the title of Viscount Halifax on his father's death. He was to have a distinguished career, holding offices including Viceroy of India, 1926–31; Secretary of State for War, 1935; Leader of the House of Lords, 1935–38; Lord Privy Seal, 1935–37; Lord President of the Council, 1937–38; Secretary of State for Foreign Affairs, 1938–40; and Ambassador to the USA, 1941–46. In retirement, he was Chancellor of the University of Sheffield from 1946.

4 – In fact, only the final three paragraphs of IAR's article were 'about' TSE.

Tomorrow I shall try (if sunny) to take some pictures of the garden, and Janes my policeman with George the Cat, and Mabel, to send you.

Devotedly your son
Tom

## TO *H. J. C. Grierson* CC

5 October 1927 [London]

Dear Professor Grierson,

Thank you very much for taking so much notice of my short address on Shakespeare. Like most delivered addresses, it seems to me rather thin on re-reading it in type. I am glad, however, to have so much of your approval as you have given me.[1] What you say about *Othello* is very likely more just

1 – Grierson was interested (2 Oct.) in TSE's *Shakespeare and the Stoicism of Seneca*: 'I am glad to have you with me in the view that I developed in America that even less than his colleagues did Shakespeare give any reading of the universe, any philosophy of life . . . Whatever one may think of *Lear*, Shakespeare says nothing. The pious characters comment piously, the impious impiously . . . But he is certainly not a systematic thinker. He is a dramatist & a poet . . . Donne's interest to me is that he felt acutely the contradictions which the new science was bringing into traditional science & theology . . .

'You say Othello is "cheering himself up", "has ceased to think about Desdemona". In a way he has. He has said his last word over Desdemona . . . It is quite natural that he shd in the reaction turn to consider himself & those who judge him: we can't escape from the thought of ourselves & our social environment. But if he is "cheering himself up" it is in preparation for executing justice upon himself. He says as it were "*You* are not the people to condemn me. I have served you well. It is I who condemn & slay myself." . . . It is a little misleading to say, at foot of p. 9, "Other drama had before existed &c." for *Polyeucte* & *Phèdre* are much later, the former a product of the Catholic recovery, the Counter-Reformation. To me the tragic interest of *Polyeucte* does not centre in the saint – the saint is never tragic, he is passing to glory – but in the reaction of his character on his wife & her lover.

'As to Shakespeare & Dante being no thinkers that is too large a question. You young men are growing very dogmatic in passing sentence on the men of old. It depends on what one means by thinker. Leonard Woolf sweeps Burke aside as no thinker because he resisted the march of triumphant democracy . . . If Burke is not a systematic thinker I know no writer who shows so many penetrating glances into the complexities of human nature and society. You are quarrelling about the meaning of "intuition" so that I hardly like to use the word, but if one may use it as Pascal uses "finesse" to describe the rapid deduction from a number of indefinable premises, as when one judges of a person's character, I should say that Shakespeare has a considerable degree of such power . . . You seem to have in mind a systematic, logical, coherent thinker, Aristotle or Aquinas. Even so I think you set Dante aside too lightly. After all he tackled in his own way the question of . . . the relation between the civil & spiritual authority, and also passed through a phase of religious doubt & philosophical inquiry. If he adopts Aquinas' philosophy as the framework for his great poem, it needs some thinking to assimilate a great intellectual system & clothe it symbolically. But he did not think things out; & loved playing with ideas.'

than what I said myself, but it does not cheer me up any better than I cheered up *Othello*. Your interpretation seems to me to make the whole business even more immoral than mine. But perhaps I am very old fashioned in my attitude to some of the Shakespearian heroes. At any rate what I said was certainly not intended to reflect upon Shakespeare but merely to attribute to Shakespeare a profound knowledge of the imperfections of humanity. I am sorry if my bad writing gave the impression that the mentality in *Polyeucte* and *Phèdre* was pre-Shakespearian. You make a good point about the tragic interest of *Polyeucte* although that at least represents a profound difference from Shakespeare, the mere fact that the tragedy is in the defect of Christianity in the persons surrounding the hero.

I cannot allow you, however, with all respect, to draw any parallel between my remark on Shakespeare and Leonard Woolf's remark on Burke.[1] The latter seems to me merely silly and emphatically untrue. I don't accuse people of not thinking merely because they don't agree with me. Furthermore, you stretch my meaning much wider than I intended. Of course Shakespeare did a lot of hard brain work as a playwright and maker of verses; and his brain was obviously more than first rate. And of course Dante did a tremendous amount of mental work on the Italian language, to say nothing of his political and other theories. I only meant that the poet in writing poetry has his hands quite full if he just writes poetry; and if Shakespeare and Dante had stopped to manufacture philosophies of life they could not have had the time or energy to make their poetry as good as it is. Put this way, perhaps you will agree with what I said. I am ready to admit that in this version my meaning becomes commonplace.

As for Donne, that is a subject which I should very much like to discuss with you at length later, if you ever have time to read my revised lectures on him before they are published. My future book would be greatly indebted to you if you would do this.

Will you let me know how soon you would like to have the typescript of Milton back? What I suggest is that I should have the essay set up as soon as possible, and you could then have galley proof for your convenience, as well as the typescript.

With many thanks,

Yours very sincerely,
[T. S. Eliot]

1–Leonard Woolf, in 'Edmund Burke' (*N&A*, 21 May 1927, 218), asserted: 'Burke's thought is, I am sure, literary and never profoundly philosophical.' Expressing primarily a 'crude and desperate conservatism', Burke was 'a literary genius, not . . . a statesman.'

## TO *Clive Bell*

TS King's

5 October 1927 Faber & Gwyer Ltd

Dear Clive,
I will Roll Up on the date indicated. Meanwhile a line in Haste. You are going to Paris. Try to Meet my dear old friends Jenny and Rosey Dolly (The Dollies & their Collies: address, Casino de Paris). Introduce yourself as a friend of M. Eliot de la Malmaison who was a friend of Johnny Ferguson. They are good Elks and you will appreciate them. If my name don't work, say you are an intimate friend of Arnold Bennett.

In confidence, without prejudice, and with haste,

Yours etc.
T. S. E.

I should very much like you to meet them. It is a very great pleasure to bring old friends together. Rosey is the *better* Elk.

## TO *Bertrand Russell*

TS McMaster

5 October 1927 Faber & Gwyer Ltd

Dear Bertie,

I am today writing to my bank to send the Plenty debentures to the company, and am sending the transfer form to the company, with my cheque for £31. 10. (90% ad valorem, the Secretary's valuation, as the debentures are nowhere quoted). I enclose cheque for the balance of the September payment (£70) i.e. £38. 10. I suppose you will include that half-year in your Income Tax returns, as I shall not include it in mine.

Vivien has, I am glad to say, returned to her sanatorium in Paris. I feel however that this transfer is in accordance with what her wishes would be when she was quite normal; and they were certainly her wishes up to the last; and as the securities are in my name there could be no legal question in any case.

It is generous of you to call it generous; I don't think that it is anything more than honest.

I can see a distinction between theological speculation and progaganda; but even in propaganda I don't see a place for *bad* reasons. But perhaps what I dislike is the smell of the corpse of Protestantism passing down the river.

Ever affectionately,
Tom

What do you think of Soddy? I was much impressed by his *Wealth, Virtual Wealth and Debt*.

## TO *Edmund Wilson* CC

5 October 1927 [*The Monthly Criterion*]

Dear Mr Wilson,

Thank you for your letter of the 25th September and for your kind suggestion of republishing 'The Journey of the Magi'. I am very sorry that I cannot let you have it, but the terms on which the various contributors to that series sold their poems to Faber and Gwyer were exclusive; and as we hope for some sale in America for the pamphlets I naturally must do nothing to interfere with the possibility.

I shall offer you something else as soon as I can.

Yours sincerely,
[T. S. Eliot]

## TO *Wyndham Lewis* TS Cornell

6 October 1927 *The Monthly Criterion*

My dear Lewis,

Thanks for the note.[1] I am sorry that there seems to have been a misunderstanding. I certainly thought you meant that Thorpe was your first choice and Birrell[2] your second. So I wrote at once to Thorpe who accepted eagerly and now has the book.[3] Would you like Birrell to do *The Wild Body*?[4]

I will let Richards know what you say.

In haste,
Yours ever,
T. S. E.

1 – WL's note is missing.
2 – Augustine Birrell (1850–1933): distinguished politician, barrister, academic, witty writer; Chief Secretary for Ireland, 1907–16; works include *Obiter Dicta* (1906) and *The Collected Essays and Addresses of the Rt. Hon. Augustine Birrell, 1880–1920* (1922).
3 – Thorpe's review of *Time and Western Man* appeared in *MC* 7 (Jan. 1928), 70–3.
4 – Wyndham Lewis, *The Wild Body: A Soldier of Humour and Other Stories* (1927).

## TO *I. A. Richards*

TS Magdalene

6 October 1927 *The Monthly Criterion*

My dear Richards,

I am keeping Friday evening, the 14th, open and hope that you can [dine] with me that night.[1]

Wyndham Lewis would like to meet you and asks me to say that when you are in town he would be very glad if you could come to tea with him at 5 o'clock one day. If you can, will you drop him a line at 33 Ossington Street, Bayswater, W.2?

And when are you going to have something for me to print?

I do not think I have congratulated you upon your marriage of which I heard some time ago. I hope that I may have the pleasure of meeting your wife.

Yours ever,
T. S. Eliot

## TO *Rev. M. C. D'Arcy*

CC

6 October 1927 [London]

Dear Father D'Arcy,

Could I persuade you to review for the *Criterion* the new book on Duns Scotus if I can get it for you. It is a very big book (I mean, of course, the book by Harris of All Souls) but I could give you as much time as you needed. I think it would be most interesting if we could have your criticism of this book.[2]

Sincerely yours,
[T. S. Eliot]

1–IAR dined with TSE on the Friday.
2–Untitled review of C. R. S. Harris, *Duns Scotus*, *MC* 7 (Mar. 1928), 266–9.

## TO *Katharine Little*[1] CC

6 October 1927 [London]

Dear Mrs Little (or alternatively, Katharine),

Very many thanks for your kind letter. I have asked them to start sending the *Criterion* to you in Paris; only don't forget to let the *Criterion* know when you return to America.

I should like very much to see some of your work in *Scribner's* and elsewhere, and perhaps when I come to Paris you will show me some.[2] I am certainly likely to be in Paris before you leave, and will certainly look you up.

With many thanks,
Yours sincerely,
[T. S. Eliot]

## TO *William Force Stead* CC

6 October 1927 [*The Monthly Criterion*]

My dear Stead,

You have had for some time a book on Christian mysticism by Dom Butler. As that book is after all only a new edition, I wonder if you would be willing to take two more books and write a much longer review. The two books are: *Man and the Supernatural* by Evelyn Underhill[3] and

1–Katharine D. Andrews had married in 1911 Clarence C. Little (1888–1971) – who had been TSE's contemporary at Harvard – geneticist; cancer and tobacco researcher; President of the University of Maine, 1922–5; President of the University of Michigan, 1925–9; director of Bar Harbor laboratory; managing director of the American Society for the Control of Cancer (later the American Cancer Society); President of the American Eugenics Society; Scientific Director of the Scientific Advisory Board of the Tobacco Industrial Research Committee (later the Council for Tobacco Research), 1954–69.

2–Mrs Little, who was visiting Paris, wrote on 1 Oct.: 'I am . . . especially keen to know what the people who count in present-day poetry are doing. Scribner's is so far the only "good" magazine that has admitted me to its portals, and paid hard cash for so doing.'

3–TSE was to write, in an unpublished memorial piece on Evelyn Underhill: 'I should like to supplement your admirable notice of the late E. U. (Mrs. S. M.) with a word about the side of her activity which is not presented in her published work or known to most of her readers. She concerned herself as much with the practice as with the theory of the devotional life – her studies of the great mystics laid the inspiration not primarily of the scholar or the champion of forgotten genius, but of a consciousness of the grievous need of the contemplative element in the modern world. She gave (with frail strength & constant illness) herself to many, in retreats which she conducted and in the intercourse of daily life – she was always at the disposal of all who called upon her. With a lively and humorous

*Studies in the Psychology of the Mystics* by Joseph Marechal. It seems to me that the three books together would give you an opportunity to say something interesting.[1]

How are you and when are you coming to London again?[2]

Ever yours,
[T. S. Eliot]

## TO *Mr & Mrs Walter Buchen* CC

7 October 1927 [London]

Dear Mr and Mrs Buchen,

I have just had a wire from my brother Henry to say that you are arriving tomorrow.[3] I am going away tomorrow morning for the weekend but expect to be back on Monday and will call at your hotel some time on Monday afternoon or evening in the hope of catching you. If you are not there I should be very much obliged if you would leave a message to say when I could get you on the telephone.

In the hope of seeing you,
Yours very truly,
[T. S. Eliot]

## TO *John Gould Fletcher* CC

7 October 1927 [London]

My dear Fletcher,

Thank you for your letter of the 6th. I like your reply to Graves very much and have sent it to be set up.[4] I shall make every effort to include it in the December number where it certainly ought to be included. I am afraid

---

interest in human beings, especially the young, with shrewdness and simplicity she helped to support the spiritual life of many more than she could in her humility have been aware of aiding. She was at the same time withdrawn and sociable.'

1 – WFS did not review the books mentioned.

2 – WFS replied (8 Oct.) that he had been 'in an extraordinarily run down and nervous state'; but he would soon 'weave together the three books' in a review. He would be in town, chez Cobden-Sanderson, by the Tuesday: they would be lunching with Blunden.

3 – HWE had cabled on 6 Oct.: 'Buchen my partner and wife arrive Piccadilly Hotel Saturday I would appreciate greatly your making brief social call. Henry.'

4 – Fletcher wrote: 'I regret that I have to impose on your space and good-temper in such an instance, but I must defend myself against a charge of literary dishonesty.'

that it is absolutely impossible to print it in the November number. What no one outside this office realises is the length of time ahead by which numbers have to be completely composed. The list is absolutely closed one month before publication, which means that the November number was absolutely completed by the 25th September. This is nobody's fault, nor is it a matter of the convenience of anyone here. It is simply an absolute requirement of the printers. Also I am more and more harassed by the question of space. I can't have more than 96 pages a month: actually the numbers have varied between 92 and 96; this is because I never know in advance how long the reviews are going to be, no matter how carefully I stipulate. Also, I am lately getting more correspondence. This is in itself a good sign, but the more correspondence I put in, the more something else I have to leave out. There will also be in the December number a letter about you by a gentleman named Rowse whom I do not know but who seems to be a champion of Marx. I shall send you the proof within a few days and hope that you will reply to it so that I may print your reply in the January number.[1] But I will also do my best to get your letter into the December number.

Personally, I am glad to hear that you are to be in London for some time. I am going away for the weekend and will drop you a line early next week to suggest an evening for dinner. My wife is abroad at present so I am not doing any housekeeping; but there is a very good little restaurant in Sloane Square, around the corner from me, and we could come back to my house and talk afterwards.

Yours ever
[T. S. Eliot]

P.S. Proof of letter from Rowse herewith.

## TO *Frederic Manning* CC

7 October 1927 [*The Monthly Criterion*]

My dear Manning,

I am sorry that I did not get here in time to speak to you on the telephone. Are you staying in London for a few days? If so, you might drop me a line here and let me know your movements. I am going to Yorkshire for the weekend but expect to be back, and will look in here, on Monday afternoon.

1–ALR, Letter to the Editor, *MC* 6 (Dec. 1927), 542–5. Fletcher's reply appeared in *MC* 7 (Jan. 1928), 62–4.

By all means put that book about Greek religion in the waste paper basket.[1] There are so many books to review that I am thankful always to learn that some book is definitely not worth it. I only regret that it is a bad book because it is always interesting to learn your opinions.

I have sent your letter to be set up. I will make every effort to publish it in the December number, the November number having been absolutely completed for press about ten days ago. I cannot conscientiously swear at the moment that I shall be able to print your letter in December, but I shall if necessary omit a review or two in order to do so. My great problem is always to get everything into the space at my disposal. Unluckily there has been a sudden activity in letter writing of late. John Gould Fletcher has written to reply to Robert Graves and I must print that; and somebody in Oxford has written to attack Fletcher about Marx, and I have promised to print that. But obviously an author who is defending his work against a reviewer has morally the first rights and I shall do my very best to publish your letter in December.

I was not very happy about Collingwood's notice; but your book had waited a long time and I thought it best to print the review as it was.[2]

Do let me hear from you if you are in London.

Always yours sincerely,
[T. S. Eliot]

## TO *Leonard Woolf* — TS Reading

7 October 1927 — *The Monthly Criterion*

Dear Leonard,

Certainly I have no objection whatever to your making any arrangements you like about publishing *Homage to John Dryden* in America. By the

1–Manning wrote on 6 Oct.: '*Later Greek Religion* [by E. R. Bevan] is one of those foolish productions which our grand-parents would have called commonplace books . . . Would you like me to return it to you or shall I put I in the waster-paper basket[?]'

2–In Oct. 1927, R. G. Collingwood had reviewed *Epicurus: The Extant Remains*, ed. Cyril Bailey, and *Epicurus: His Morals*, ed. Walter Charleton, with an introduction by Manning. Verna Coleman notes, in *The Last Exquisite: A Portrait of Frederic Manning* (1990): 'Manning's final break with Eliot's magazine may have followed on the pique he felt at an unfavourable review . . . Collingwood said drily: "the cautious reader will not imagine that Epicurus and Dr Charleton's Epicurus are the same person". Although Manning and the critic seemed in general agreement, Manning took offence, replying with a stiff letter in January 1928, and he wrote no more for the magazine' (155).

way, I am not sure whether you mean all three essays forming the little book, or merely the first, but it does not matter to me.[1]

As for American rights, however, I am afraid the word 'Rights' is legally inexact. My impression is that as the essays were published in England and never printed in America, I have, according to <the flagitious> American law, no rights whatever to sell or give. I think that anybody can print the essays in America without acknowledgment or payment to you or to me. I imagine that you have not seen my recent violent correspondence with Mr Samuel Roth.

I am looking forward to seeing you on Wednesday.

Yours ever,
T. S. E.

## TO *Henry Eliot* — TS Houghton

7 October 1927[2] — *The Monthly Criterion*

My dear Brother,

I have arranged for fifty copies of *The Journey of The Magi* to be sent to you with invoice.[3] I have also ordered that the *Criterion* should continue to be sent to you regularly and that a bill for a new year's subscription should be sent also. It is generous of you to ask to subscribe for five years straight off but I had rather that you did not do this: it really confuses the accounts to have subscriptions for more than a year ahead; and as we do not know positively that the *Criterion* will go on for five years we should prefer to have you subscribe for a year at a time.

I shall be very grateful to you if you can sell any copies of the 'Ariel Poems' to Chicago booksellers. You may tell them that our terms are 9d per copy. They can sell the copies at any price they like. If they order lots of over one hundred copies, we could sell them at 8d per copy. <Retail in England at 1 shilling.> On the other hand, there would be little or nothing in it for very small lots, say ten copies, and we should rather sell one lot of a hundred copies than ten lots of ten. It is worth while pointing out to

1–LW asked (6 Oct.) whether TSE would permit Doubleday, Page & Co. to include 'your essay HOMAGE TO JOHN DRYDEN' in a collection of some of the Hogarth Essays to be published in the USA.

2–On the back of the envelope, TSE noted by hand: 'Change of address to 177 Clarence Gate Gardens NW1.'

3–In addition to the 50 copies sent to his brother in Chicago, TSE ordered 25 copies with invoice to be sent to Mrs H. W. Eliot, 24 Concord Avenue, Cambridge, Mass.

them that this is a series of eight poems and that many people might like to have the complete series. On the other hand, we are perfectly willing to sell lots of any one poem separately. It all depends on the relation of my personal reputation in Chicago to the reputation of the others. But I should think that Hardy and de la Mare would be more popular than myself.

This is a purely business letter and I shall be writing to you privately.

Affectionately
T.

## TO *John Middleton Murry* CC

7 October 1927 [London]

My dear John,

I should like to call your attention for the *Adelphi* to a book which has just appeared called *The Cause of Evil* by I. G. Bartholomew, published by Heath Cranton (6/-).[1] It is not orthodox and I think it is a book which will not get much attention, but I think it is worth looking into. I shall do it myself for the *Criterion* if it is done at all; you will probably want to look at it first yourself, but I suggest that if you don't want to tackle it it is a book which Geoffrey Sainsbury might like to do.[2]

In my next book of essays I want to write a note on Babbitt's *Democracy and Leadership*. I don't want to do it in the *Criterion* because I had a long review of the book at the time by Read and I shall be handling it in a very different way from Read's – though I don't suppose you will find my position any more sympathetic than Read's is. It doesn't matter in the least in any case.[3]

Ever yours,
[T.]

1–I. G. Bartholomew, *The Cause of Evil; Or, the Values of Nature and the Values of Religion* (1927). Bartholomew was Lady Rothermere's sister.

2–JMM responded (10 Oct.): 'I will get "The Cause of Evil" by Bartholomew.'

3–JMM was hospitable (10 Oct.): 'Of course, it goes without saying that The Adelphi would like to have what you will write on Babbitt's "Democracy & Leadership".'

## TO *Wyndham Lewis* TS Cornell

10 October 1927 Faber & Gwyer Ltd

My dear Wyndham,

I am glad if you are, in principle, satisfied with Thorpe. I myself was not particularly glad of either Thorpe or Birrell, but could not at the moment think of anyone better than either. I shall however try to see Thorpe in the meantime and find out what he is up to.

I am very sorry indeed to hear about your Eyes. I should much like to see you before you go away. Owing to previous circumstances, I have had rather to fill up this week, but could manage a Lunch this week or preferably a Dinner next week if possible. Ring me up at Museum 9543 in the afternoon or at Sloane 3184 before 12 a.m.

Yours etc.
T. S. E.

## *I. P. Fassett* TO *Harold Monro* CC

12 October 1927 [London]

Dear Mr Monro,

Mr Eliot has asked me to send you the enclosed. As he was talking to you today about Robert Graves and Laura Riding, he thought that you might be interested to see this typical specimen of her manner of correspondence.[1]

Yours faithfully,
[I. P. Fassett]
Secretary

1 – Laura Riding had sent to TSE on 12 Oct. this missive: 'Dear Mounseer / So sorry you couldn't publish my letter – I read with much interest Humbert Wolfe's review of Chesterton! / L. R.' Monro replied to TSE on 24 Oct., 'I return the enclosed vile and insolent document which Miss Fassett kindly sent me to see as you may want to place it among your archives. At a certain type of joke one finds oneself completely unable to laugh but I feel rather sorry for Robert Graves for he surely must have ruined himself.'

## TO *Osbert Sitwell*[1] CC

13 October 1927 [London]

Dear Osbert,

Thank you very much for sending me your Volume of Poems, which I shall read with interest.[2] It is thoughtful of you to remember me.

I might have communicated with you long since, but I seem to remember clearly that Vivien wrote to you – against my Counsel – over a year ago from Rome, and that you did not reply.[3]

Yours sincerely
[Tom]

1 – Osbert Sitwell (1892–1969), poet, novelist, man of letters: see Biographical Register.

2 – *England reclaimed*: a book of eclogues.

3 – OS replied ('Fri'): 'I am glad you mentioned that letter, for I never knew if you were aware of it as an incident.

'How could I answer it? In it V. stated that unless she heard from me within 3 days certain ~~incidents~~ things would follow. It reached me on the first day of the General Strike: for 10 days there were no letters or cable! Further I could not advise her with absolute disregard of what you might wish, and knew nothing of yr wishes. And I never heard, and have never since heard, of any scandal connected with either of you.'

Much later, in an unpublished memoir of TSE written on 19 Feb. 1950, OS recalled: 'The occasion I now set out to describe exhales its own flavour of comedy, albeit that it is rooted in the tragedy of the Eliot situation . . . In 1926, on the first or second day of the General Strike, my sister in her flat on Moscow Road, Bayswater and I in my small house in Chelsea, both of us received long and incoherent letters from Vivienne, couched in almost identical terms. She wrote from Rome, where she had gone to stay, and declared that we should have inevitably heard of the scandal to which she was referring, and in which she was involved. We should be aware, however, that if she returned to Tom, it would inevitably bring disgrace upon him, of which he would never be able to rid himself. She appealed to us, in consequence, as old friends of his, to tell her what to do. Unless, she proceeded, she heard from us by cable ot letter, advising her to go back to him, she would continue to remain abroad. We were on no account to let him find out that she had written to us.

'We were cognisant of no rumours – indeed there were none – but the letters were those of an unhappy, distracted, almost demented person, and we felt ourselves bound to give considerable attention to them. Indeed, they caused us much worry, as we did not know how to act. For one thing, here was Vivienne, demanding an immediate answer, yet we could not judge what would be Tom's feelings in the matter: he was the chief person to be considered, and yet we could not talk about it to him without admitting that his wife had written to us. Eventually, as it seemed to us that he very probably might not want her to go back to him, we decided not to answer her – in any case, from a practical point of view, owing to the General Strike, no letter or telegram from us could reach her . . . Vivienne, who, of course, returned on her own initiative as soon as it was possible to travel, subsequently, it transpired much later, told Tom that when, finding herself in an agonizing personal quandary she had appealed to us for counsel, neither of us had troubled to reply. As a result he was for some months angry with us, and the coolness made itself evident. I pressed him to say what had gone wrong, and when I heard, felt that I was at liberty to explain the circumstances I have just outlined . . . Soon afterwards, Tom, in token of reconciliation, invited me to a dinner party [Thurs., 25 Jun 1931] at Clarence Gate Gardens. Vivienne had just finished a course of treatment in a home, and we were to celebrate her recovery.

'This in itself imparted a certain awkwardness to the festive occasion that had been arranged . . . When I was shown into the drawing-room, I found that for once I was not the first arrival, and Mr Faber, James Joyce and Mrs Joyce, were already talking to our host. A few moments later, Vivienne entered in a flustered manner, on her lips her rather twisted smile, which was opposed by the consternation and suspicion in her greenish eyes . . . Not quite certain what tone was suitable to adopt, I opened, by remarking to her with heartiness, '"It *is* splendid to see you again, Vivienne."

Looking me straight in the eye, she replied slowly,

'"I don't know about *splendid*: but it is strange, *very* strange."

'Thereupon we went in to dinner. The table seemed set for a gala: for by each place was set a bouquet or a large buttonhole, of sweet-peas, struggling through a white misty rash of gypsophila. The food was good, and accompanied by an excellent hock – a wine that James Joyce liked. I sat on Vivienne's right. Faber, opposite to me, proved to be a typical publisher and university-man, a pillar of Church and State. All the views he held were rooted in strong moral principles. (He probably believed quite genuinely that, from an ethical point of view, authors *ought* to be paid as little as possible; that it would ruin both their work and their characters if they were to be given a fair price). When he talked, he hit the right nail on the head so often that it became like a man playing the xylophone. Mrs Faber, ostentatiously conventional, was dressed in black, but sported a row of pearls resembling the shark's teeth necklaces worn by Polynesian warriors. She spoke of domestic problems with knowledge and concentration: of the difficulty, for example, that she found in moving her servants from her castle (in Wales, I think), to London and back again: yet in such days, she added, it was impossible to find and maintain two separate staffs for each residence . . . Mrs James Joyce was a particularly charming woman, but both she and her husband were a little depressed that night; because, I found out later, they had recently recollected that they had forgotten to get married thirty years or so before, and were off to a registry-office the next morning to repair this omission. (So the marriage-register would date the dinner-party). As for our hostess, she was in high spirits, but not in a good mood. She showed an inclination to "pick on" Tom across the table, challenging his every statement, and at the same time insinuating that the argumentativeness was his; that he was trying to create a scene. All this he parried with his calm and caution, remaining patient and precise, with on his face an expression of wary good nature. Indeed, it was impossible, except for those who knew them both well, to tell when he was put out with her. Her name was usually pronounced *Vivien*: but if he were irritated by her, we would notice that he would call her Viv*ienne*. However, on this occasion he allowed no faintest sign of strain to escape him. And, as dinner went on, things became a little better, she began to leave him alone, and instead talk to me about him. He was being very difficult, she averred; only one human being [Janes] seemed now to interest him, an ex-policeman of about seventy years of age, who acted as odd man, and was an habitual drunkard.

'When after dinner the men came in from the dining-room, in an effort to win our sympathy, our hostess alleged that Tom would never give his guests enough to drink, and that she was always having to complain about it. Tom stayed on in the drawing-room, to talk to Mrs Joyce and Mrs Faber, but looked rather as if he were keeping an eye open for a squall, while Vivienne led us into the dining-room, found another bottle of hock for us, and left us at the table in order to join her other guests. The door was open on to the passage, and, while Joyce was talking to us of Italian Opera, which he so greatly loved, and was even singing passages to us from his favourite works, a door in the further wall of the passage suddenly swung back, and out stepped the figure of an elderly man [Janes] in a dark suit with white hair and moustache, blinking as if he had suddenly emerged from darkness into a strong light, and – rather singularly in a house – crowned with a bowler hat. My attention had been focussed on him from the moment he appeared, as it were out of his trap-door, since I had at once identified this rather tortoise-like individual as the ex-policeman of whom Vivienne had spoken. Silence now fell on the company. The newcomer stopped in the doorway opposite us for a moment, and made to each of the three of us – Joyce, Faber and me – a sweeping bow with his hat, saying as he did so "Goo' night, Mr Eliot!", "Goo' night, Mr Eliot", "Goo' night, Mr Eliot", and then, while the last syllable was still on his lips, and without giving himself time to discover the failure of his ingenious method of insurance by address in triplicate against the possible charge of inebriation, he turned and went on his way, humming loudly to himself.

'The incident possessed atmosphere, and I was delighted by it, as was Vivienne when we returned to the drawing-room and told her about it. For once Tom refused to see the joke, looking rather as I imagine Dante would have looked had someone ventured to make a stupid pun in his presence.

'Soon the moment came for the party to break up; Mrs Faber rose, rattled her sharks' teeth round her neck with one hand, and observed "It's been lovely, Vivienne."

'Vivienne looked at her mournfully, and replied, "Well, it may have been lovely for you, but it's been dreadful for me."

'Mrs Faber, rather at a loss, rapped out at her,

"Nonsense, Vivienne, you know it's been a triumph."

'Vivienne repeated in desolate tones "'A triumph'! . . . Look at Tom's face!"

'Tom saw us to the door, and his voice sounded into the darkness, with its firm and wary tones. Indeed his character was firm, mild for all its fire, subtle and cautious. Much had happened to make him cautious – not least, his swift marriage as a young man, and its aftermath and outcome.'

GCF was less possessed by Vivien's demeanour and antics than by James Joyce, as he recorded in his diary for 25 June 1931: 'Dined with the Eliots, & met James Joyce & Mrs. J. & Osbert Sitwell. An interesting party, & Mrs E amazingly much better. Osbert very much the adequate man of the world – likeable. Joyce, a little tired-looking man, wearing glasses, evidently physically under the weather, talking little & quietly, perfect manners. One couldn't but like him, & feel his quality. I asked him about his friend, Sullivan, the tenor, whom he has tried & failed to place on the map of Covent Garden. He was suspicious of my source of knowledge; but I steered him past that, & he talked on his favourite subject with passion. So much did he impress me, that I dreamed of him off & on all night!'

Two weeks earlier, on 10 June, at a dinner party celebrating the second anniversary of F&F, Faber noted: 'A full house, all the directors & their wives or sisters – incl. mirabile dictu Mrs Eliot, who arrived – hour late, & very nervous: but she apparently enjoyed herself. The rest of the party didn't break up till 1.30 a.m.!'

On 2 Feb. 1933 VHE sent a copy of *Marina* (1930) to Joyce, inscribing it: 'To James Joyce *from Vivienne Haigh Eliot*' (R. A. Gekoski catalogue, 2009).

## TO *Claude Collier Abbot*[1] TS Durham

13 October 1927 *The Monthly Criterion*

Dear Sir,

I am sorry that I was unable to answer immediately your letter of the 15th September, and perhaps I am now too late to be of any use for your purpose.[2] I am pleased that you like *The Waste Land* and wish that I could tell you more about it. It is not an evasion, but merely the truth, to say that I think in these cases that an explanation by the author is of no more value than one by anybody else. You see, the only legitimate meaning of a poem is the meaning which it has for any reader, not a meaning which it has primarily for the author. The author means all sorts of things which concern nobody else but himself, in that he may be making use of his private experiences. But these private experiences are merely crude material, and as such of no interest whatever to the public. About the best thing that has been written about this poem is an introductory essay by Professor E. R. Curtius in the *Neue Schweizer Rundschau*, but I do not know whether you know German.

Yours faithfully,
T. S. Eliot

## TO *Louise Alvar*[3] CC

13 October 1927 [London]

Dear Madame Alvar,

My only reason for venturing to hope that you have not completely forgotten me is that I received your kind invitation for Monday evening to meet Monsieur Valéry.[4] I am much looking forward to seeing you

1–Claude Collier Abbot (1889–1971), Lecturer in English, University of Aberdeen, 1921–32; Prof. of English, Univ. of Durham, 1932–54; editor of *Durham University Journal*, 1939–52. A collector of manuscripts, books and Pre-Raphaelite art, he was to edit *The Correspondence of Gerard Manley Hopkins and Richard Watson Dixon* (1935).

2–Abbot, who was about to give a talk to the literary society at Aberdeen University, asked TSE: 'If you can help my stupidity (it is not, believe me, laziness) & refer me to any interpretation [of *The Waste Land*] that has your approval, I shall be very grateful.'

3–Louise Alvar (1884?–1966), Swedish soprano renowned for her recitals of Ravel (who would often stay with Alvar and her English husband on his visits to London). A friend of Conrad, she lived at 14 Holland Park, London W11, and was hospitable too to other writers including von Hofmannsthal and Valéry.

4–Valéry was visiting England for a tightly scheduled programme of talks and social events, 12–18 Oct. On Mon., 17 Oct., he was due to attend a dinner at the French Institute, London: see Michel Jarrety, *Paul Valéry* (2008), 691–2.

again, and hope that you will not mind if I bring with me two friends and colleagues, Mr Herbert Read and Mr Frederic Manning, both of whom I hope you may care to meet.

Yours very sincerely,
[T. S. Eliot]

## TO *D. S. Mirsky* CC

14 October 1927 [*The Monthly Criterion*]

Dear Prince Mirsky

I am very sorry to hear that you are doing the 'Tolstoy' for the *Observer*, but I had feared that something of the sort would happen as you are so much in request.[1] I should not have minded myself, if you were interested to do it, but I have recently been lecturing one or two younger contributors for reviewing the same book elsewhere without letting me know, so I am afraid that I must reconsider. But is there, by the way, any other book of any kind on any subject that you would care to do fairly soon? I should so much like to have you contribute more or less regularly.

Sincerely yours,
[T. S. Eliot]

## TO *Arnold Bennett* TS Beinecke

14 October 1927 *The Monthly Criterion*

My dear Bennett,

This is to let you know that I have just heard from Pinker's that the *American Bookman* is publishing your *Florentine Diary* in November; Pinker's do not know whether all together or in how many instalments. So I shall begin with about a third of it in December and shall shortly be sending you proof.

Sincerely yours,
T. S. Eliot

1 – Mirsky volunteered (13 Oct.) to review Fausset's *Tolstoy* for *MC* but regretted that he was already reviewing it for the *Observer*.

## TO *Lord Halifax* CC

15 October 1927 [London]

Dear Lord Halifax,

At the risk of overwhelming you with printed matter, I am sending you another pamphlet, *Maurras et son temps*, by Gonzague Truc. It is the best non-partisan criticism of the man that I have seen. Truc is neither Royalist nor Catholic, though he is an enthusiast who has helped in the revival of Scholasticism.[1]

It is very difficult even for a person in my position, to make up one's mind about this affair. For the man Maurras himself – a much bigger figure than Daudet – I have great respect. Both Maurras and Daudet have suffered for their opinions. Maurras's life has been attacked by Communists more than once. But for his opinions, he should certainly have been in the Académie. And whatever the truth may be, I am sure that Daudet and his wife truly believe that their son Philippe was killed by Communists, who did everything possible afterwards to blacken his memory. It is incontested [uncontested] that Maurras is a great prose writer, or that he has, in forty years, done much and sacrificed much for the good of France. His case is therefore *sui generis*.

As for Maurras' private opinions, there is no doubt that they are such as should rightly, in part, be condemned.[2] Maurras is a genuine atheist, a real Pagan; not merely a Low Church fanatic like Bertie Russell. His view is that of a Greek, with all of the pre-Christian strength and weakness: to Christianity he is simply blind.

But from a condemnation of Maurras to a condemnation of the *Action Française* is a long step. The *Action Française* may be accused of excessive nationalism. I should say that that was true; though my opinion is modified by a suspicion that the paper's constant warnings against danger from Germany are partially justified. But I have been a reader of the paper for several years, and I have never found in it anything fundamentally prejudicial to either Faith or Morals. I should even say that Maurras had been scrupulous to reserve his private opinions to his own books, and to respect the convictions of the Catholic youth that supported the royalist movement. Many of the objections to the paper seem to me very petty. It is objected to Bainville (a man of about my own age who will probably

1–TSE made use of Gonzague Truc's edition of *Les Mystiques espagnols: Sainte Térèse–Saint Jean de la Croix* (1921), and other works, in the preparation of his Clark Lectures; he had written to HR on 11 Dec. 1925: 'I think rather well of him.'

2–Maurras's *Action Française* was condemned by Pope Pius XI in 1927.

succeed Maurras one day) that he has edited and praised the tales of Voltaire – as if every man of letters, of whatever beliefs, did not admire the writing of Voltaire.

Gordon George makes several remarks which I should question. He says that the *Action Française* was 'infuriated' by the Pope's efforts for peace in 1916. I was not at that time reading the paper regularly, but I should be very much surprised to find that it had openly opposed itself to the Pope. He says that the *Action Française* is 'nominally' monarchist. I should like to know why 'nominally'. It is true that the paper cannot be taken as representing the old type of royalists by heredity; in spite of Maurras's belief in the value of aristocracy, his movement is almost entirely a middle-class movement, and is in many ways radical rather than reactionary. But I do not believe for a moment that Maurras aims at a dictatorship for himself. But what is more extraordinary in Gordon George's summary is the suggestion that these troubles began only last Christmas, after the Pope had patiently endured the aggressions of the *A.F.* for a long time. As you will see from the documents, the trouble began with the wholly unexpected public letter of Cardinal-Bishop of Bordeaux Andrieu in October, a year ago.[1] Nothing of this sort could have been expected, for Maritain (who is a professor at the Institut Catholique) had only fairly recently before that, become very intimate with the *A.F.* He was present at a dinner which I attended, at which the other guests were only Maurras, Pujo,[2] Bainville, Daudet and Massis – the real leaders of the *A.F.* That was in July 1926. Not only Maritain, but many Roman priests and dignitaries were completely taken by surprise.

The reception of Mons. Maglione by Briand took place after the trouble had begun, and had therefore no causal relation to it.[3]

What is omitted, in the account of Gordon George and of Catholic opponents, is the statement that the *A. F.* offered submission and asked that the Vatican should appoint teachers of doctrine for its school of political science in Paris and for its groups. What also the opponents do not answer is the contrast between the attitude of the Vatican towards

1–Pierre-Paulin Andrieu (1849–1935), Cardinal and Bishop of Bordeaux, had issued in 1926 the first ecclesiastical-official condemnation of the *Action Française*.

2–Maurice Pujo (1872–1955), journalist and co-founder in 1898 of the *Comité d'Action Française*, forerunner of the nationalist and royalist *Action Française*.

3–Luigi Maglione (1877–1944) worked in the Vatican Secretariat of State before being appointed in 1920 Nuncio to Switzerland and Titular Archbishop of Cesarea di Palestrina. He was Apostolic Nuncio to France, 23 June 1926–22 July 1938. Back in Rome, he became Prefect of the Sacred Congregation of the Council, and from 1939 until his death he served as Vatican Secretary of State under Pius XII.

Maurras and towards the public statements of Governor Smith of New York, who is a candidate for the presidentship. Smith is a R.C. (the first who has ever been candidate for the Presidency in America), and in response to enquiries from anxious protestant supporters declared, in several headlines, his independence from the Vatican as a man of politics.[1]

I think that George's term 'dangerous' applied to the *A.F.* is permissible; but he has no justification for calling it an 'immoral party'.

What I cannot help asking is why the blow to the *A.F.* should have fallen at this moment? What has altered since 1916 or since 1914, when some of Maurras's works were condemned, but when the promulgation of the condemnation was withheld? I cannot help thinking (though with regret) that what has changed is the attitude of the Vatican towards the Republican government of France.

I think I told you that I had always expected eventual difficulty between the *A.F.* and the Holy See. I foresaw that the religious programme of a Nationalist party would require a kind of Gallican Establishment. The success of the *A.F.* would I think tend to make France more Christian and more Catholic, but certainly far less ultramontane. And the Congress in Chicago last year strengthened my fears. I suppose that there is no doubt that the two strongest countries, from the point of view of blind ultramontane devotion to the Papacy, are Poland and the United States: and we must add that South Germany and Austria are now Republican, even Socialist, and likely to remain so. (I do not believe that what has just happened to the *A.F.* would have happened if the Hapsburgs had still been on the Kaiserliche Königliche Throne).[2] It seems to me (who have no inner knowledge of the Vatican whatever, and am therefore perhaps presumptuous in putting these considerations to you who know it intimately) that the Vatican *must* hereafter be hostile to any country which has a Monarchy, or to any party in a republican country which advocates a Monarchy. I know that other people who have followed recent movements have come to the same conclusion. And I believe that the condemnation of the *A.F.* was merely part of a movement of conciliation between the Vatican and the Socialist-Republican régime in France.

Feeling as I do, you will see that I believe that the immediate difficulties in the way of Anglo-Roman reconciliation are great. I fear Rome at

1 – Alfred Smith, Jr. (1873–1944) – universally known as Al Smith – 42nd Governor of New York (1 Jan. 1923–31 Dec. 1928), was the first Roman Catholic to run for President as a major party (Democrat) nominee. He lost to Herbert Hoover in 1928.

2 – *Kaiserlich und königlich* ('Imperial and Royal'): the Dual Monarchy of 1867–1918, when the Hapsburg monarch was Emperor of Austria and King of Hungary.

present, because I fear that it would welcome any movement towards the abolition of the Kingship in Britain; and I think not only persons of my own complexion, but really the great majority of the population, has [have] a genuine attachment to the Crown.

Forgive me if I have exceeded the limits within which I ought to speak to you about such matters; and believe that I am actuated by great admiration for yourself, and a conviction that the work you have done is of great and permanent value and present benefit, whatever happens in the future.

I should like to send my copy of this letter to my friend Henri Massis, for his observations, but if you prefer me to keep it to myself, I will of course show it to no one.[1]

Yours very sincerely,
[T. S. Eliot]

1–TSE would later characterise Maurras, in *The Christian News-Letter* no. 44 (28 Aug. 1940), as 'a middle-class, meridional, free-thinking man of letters'. And he went on: 'Maurras – who now, I hear, supports the Pétain *régime* – is a man of powerful but narrow mind, who used to hate Germany, dislike (unless my suspicions were wrong) England; and who, because of his southern Provençal origins, was strongly pro-Italian in the dubious cause of "Latin Mediterranean culture". Like most of his group, he was ill-informed on foreign affairs; and he did not know enough of England to understand either the good or bad of British policy. The one man in his group with some understanding of foreign affairs was Jacques Bainville, a writer of brilliant and lucid mind, whose early death is much to be regretted, but who was, like Maurras, a free-thinker and a product of post-Revolution bourgeoisie.

'The attitude of Maurras towards the Church was simple: he made no pretence of Christian belief, but supported the Church as a social institution making for stability. How many of the hereditary Catholics, of the old families, he was able to attract I do not know. At the time when I was personally acquainted with him and with his entourage, I think that his following was more from the middle and lower middle classes. He waged, it is true, an incessant journalistic battle against political corruption – somewhat indiscriminately and with excessive violence. The more pious of the royalist aristocracy may have hesitated to associate themselves with this outspoken agnostic who made no bones about his lack of faith. He, on the other hand, with honest naivety, could see no reason why Catholics could not support him if he supported them; and when his movement was condemned, and his newspaper put on the Index, by Pius XI in 1927, I am sure that he was genuinely surprised. (The interdict has since been lifted, on the basis, I believe, of certain assurances given; but he has never attracted back to him such uncompromising Catholics as Jacques Maritain and Georges Bernanos.) In imposing his censure, the Pope was doing more than simply reaffirming the policy of reconciliation with the Republic entered upon by Leo XIII: he was condemning a heresy which asserted that only one form of government, the monarchical, was compatible with Catholicism. Perhaps also condemning a dangerous intolerance which classified Jews, Protestants and Freemasons in one comprehensive condemnation. I defended the *Action Française* when it was put upon the Index; my *particular* defence may or may not stand; but I believe now that the Pope understood its tendencies better.'

A few years later, TSE was to write of Maurras to Adrian Earle (30 June 1944): 'The weakness of that admirable writer was always that he was himself a product of the post-

Revolution mentality of France, with a background of Voltaire, Taine, Renan and Comte: so that his royalism was utilitarian and not traditional. And I do not think that any analogy of l'Action Française could provide a very helpful start. It would be desirable, certainly, that people of the right type of mind should study and expound the monarchical society, going back through Burke to the régime mixte commended by Aquinas. But such a movement could not be, at this time, directly political: it must be educative first, for the majority, at the present time, can only be directed from one kind of totalitarianism towards another, and they must be taught to think in different terms altogether. I do not think that the royalism of Maurras, any more than that of Bolingbroke, is what is wanted, but something more scholastic and Catholic.'

A few years later again, TSE was to write a brief essay on Maurras at the request of Henri Massis – 'I do not consider that it has any value except as the symbol of a kind of loyalty to a great writer,' TSE noted in his covering letter (1 Apr. 1948) – pointing out that the primary texts by Maurras that he had read were *L'Avenir de l'Intelligence*, *Anthinéa*, *Les Amants de Vénise* and *La Leçon de Dante*, and going on to compare Maurras with his teacher, Irving Babbitt: 'one thing that he had in common with Charles Maurras was an inability to accept Christianity. In Babbitt the alternative was a kind of Buddhism which I find romantic; in Maurras, a romantic neo-Hellenism, an idealization of the Mediterranean pre-Christian world. My view may be mistaken; but the reader will be better able to judge if he is put in possession of it; and this view is that the only "classicism" possible for modern man is one which embraces the Christian faith. I believe this in spite of the fact that there can be a romantic Catholicism, and that this is an aberration: for romantic Catholicism always involves being a Catholic partly for the wrong reason.

'And yet, for some of us, Maurras was a kind of Virgil conducting us almost to the doors of the temple. The forces which impel a man from agnosticism or denial, to the point at which he finds the last step inevitable, are numberless; a man finds himself at one moment directed by influences from without, at another moment led by an inner destiny; and this ends in the mystery of grace. To a large extent also a man may be moved by his reaction *against* outside forces and personalities, rather than by positive attraction. But as for the positive forces which *impel* some men towards the Christian Faith – in distinction from those which *draw* – may be reckoned the influence of certain other men who have not themselves escaped the bondage of disbelief; and surely, from a Christian point of view, this influence must be accounted to them for righteousness.

'I have been trying to suggest, by these remarks, what is for me the essential Maurras – the ideas which point in the direction of Christianity and Catholicism. Apart from that – which is implicit in his criticism of literature, and especially perhaps in *La Leçon de Dante* – I could do no more than enumerate ideas, and disengage what I accept from what I do not. The conception of the function of the monarchy, and of social rank, is naturally more congenial to a certain type of conservative of English opinion untouched by the doctrines of the modern world, than it can be to others; but on the other hand I can only note with regret the absence of sympathy, which Maurras has sometimes manifested towards my country.

'Finally, there is the style. A foreigner, and one who is by no means bi-lingual, cannot pretend to appreciate the precise and delicate choice of words, the fine construction of sentences, into which the excellence of a style can be analysed. Yet I think that he can, in a general way, recognize the style of a master . . . [F]or the delight of style I am likely to turn again, from time to time, at longer or shorter intervals, to one or another of these books of Maurras which I have cited.'

## TO *The Editor of* The New Statesman[1]

15 October 1927 24 Russell Square, W.C.1.

Sir,

I congratulate Mr Campbell upon his poem, 'Tristan da Cunha', in *The New Statesman* of today. His control of the metre is remarkable, and his language stronger and less flamboyant than in some of his earlier work. The poem has a curious resemblance – not in detail, but in rhythm and in general spirit – to a German poem which is almost unknown even in Germany, the *Tristan da Cunha* of Johannes Th. Kuhlemann (*Der Strom*, Cologne, 1919).[2] I once attempted to translate this poem, which is very fine, but abandoned the attempt. I do not know whether Mr Campbell knows German; but if he does, he might make a very brilliant translation.[3]

Yours, etc.,
T. S. Eliot

## TO *Horace M. Kallen*

TS American Jewish Archives

17 October 1927 *The Monthly Criterion*

Dear Horace,

I am afraid I have owed you a letter for nearly five months, and I am quite certain that I owe you profuse apologies not only on that account but

1–Published in the issue of 22 Oct. under the heading 'Tristan da Cunha'.

2–Johannes Theodor Kuhlemann (1891–1939) published 'Tristan da Cunha' in the first issue of *Der Strom* (1919), 23–6.

3–In an undated letter (?Oct. 1927), Roy Campbell was to tell TSE, 'I have just been shown your letter about my Tristan da Cunha in *The New Statesman*. I value your encouragement very highly and I am honoured by your letter.' In about Aug. 1928 he wrote to TSE: 'I was very unsure of myself when I returned from Africa, as I had been out of touch with decent criticism and intelligent company for so long . . . Your letter to the *Statesman* about *Tristan da Cunha* reassured me a good deal . . . I do not read German well enough to attempt a translation of Kuhlemann. I find I can read odd sentences in German through knowing Afrikaans. In any case I shall try to get Kuhlemann's *Tristan da Cunha* and get someone to give me a literal translation. I read in South Africa [in Aug. 1926] a letter to my friend William Plomer from a man named [J. R.] Gillie in Germany who said he was going to translate the poem. He gave one verse of his translation: I think it was this verse that set me off on my poem, though I don't think I actually imitated it. I had already done five verses of my poem in the same metre under the title of Kerguelen. But I doubt if I should have continued or altered them if Plomer had not produced this letter and suggested *Tristan* as being a better subject . . .' In his memoirs, *Broken Record* (1934), Campbell says that 'Beyond Kerguelen' by the Australian poet Henry Kendall (1839–82), 'is the father of my "Tristan da Cunha". He seized first of all in verse that mystery of the lonely island walking on the sea' (126). See further Peter Alexander, *Roy Campbell: A Critical Biography* (1982), 62–3.

for having unintentionally deceived you about the immediate prospects of a lecture tour in America. I have consequently given you and Alvin Johnson unnecessary trouble. I had a very pleasant letter from him, and I must apologise all round.[1]

I need not say that when I can be certain long enough in advance of getting to America I will notify the School for Social Research first. The terms are quite satisfactory, and I only hope that the School will not change its mind in the interval.

The reasons which make it impossible at present are two. One my wife is ill in France, and I should not like to pin myself down to such a long time in America definitely. Secondly my mother is ill in Boston, and I cannot make any engagements because I want to be able to run over to see her for a short time at any moment necessary.

I hope that by 1929 the situation will be simpler. In any case I have so much to do with *The Monthly Criterion* that it is difficult to neglect it; but I hope that I shall be able to get that machinery running more automatically in the next six months.

Ever yours cordially, & very grateful thanks

T. S. Eliot

## TO *George Williamson* — TS Williamson

17 October 1927 — *The Monthly Criterion*

Dear Mr Williamson,

Thank you for your letter of the 3rd September enclosing your very interesting essay comparing my verse with that of Donne.[2] I will certainly show it to Herbert Read, and thank you for it. There is nothing in it which I should regard as anything but complimentary to myself; beyond that point I find it almost impossible to think of anything intelligent to say in response to criticism of myself.

I should like very much to see some of your book on Donne before it appears.[3] It is difficult to think of any suggestions without knowing

1 – Alvin Johnson, Director of The New School for Social Research, New York, had urged TSE on 22 Sept. to come and lecture there for a 6–month period starting perhaps early in 1928: 'your coming will be an event of the greatest importance' to the students.

2 – 'The Talent of T. S. Eliot', *The Sewanee Review* 35 (July 1927), 284–95; rev. and repr. as *The Talent of T. S. Eliot* (Univ. of Washington Chapbook no. 32, 1929).

3 – *The Donne Tradition: A Study in English Poetry from Donne to the Death of Cowley* (1930).

exactly how you are tackling the subject. But be sure that I shall be most interested. I am writing, or ought to be writing, a book largely dealing with Donne and his contemporaries myself, but you need not fear any overlapping, as I am not concerned with the Donne tradition beyond the death of Cowley.

Sincerely yours,
T. S. Eliot

## TO *Richard Cobden-Sanderson* TS Texas

Wednesday, 19 Oct[ober 19]27 *The Monthly Criterion*

Dear CS:

Just to tell You we as ad a Fair Wind to Church St. Kens. where we Hove to and signalled a Pilot to take a passenger Ashore which done we laid a Course NE by E ¼ E & struck it not thick of Fog but kind of Smurry whch is natural this Time of year hit a bad Cross Rip in Kensington Gore whch was probly an unfavrable Tide coming out of Brompton Rd. short Squall off Sloane Street whch moderated so we ad to Claw Off Cadogan Gardens but was Glad to sight Holy Trinity ¼ off the Port Bow Hove to in Sloane Sq. abt. 4 Bells in a bit of a Breeze of Wind battnd down Hatches & went Blow for a cup of Coffee I tell you was glad to hitch up to the old Wharft and thankfull no Casualties though light cargo ave entred on Log 2nd Nov. 12th Nov. & 16 Dec.* being 3d in Advent 5 for 7:30 So will now close Hoping you are Well & yr Good Lady and Famly yrs, respecfly

T. S. Eliot

* This seems like abusing your hospitality. I was rather surprised to find my Diary so full. I hope I have not accepted one or two of your invitations which were meant for someone else.[1]

## TO *Osbert Sitwell* CC

20 October 1927 57 Chester Terrace, Eaton Square

Dear Osbert,

I am glad that you have cleared up this little matter.[2] I did not know exactly what Vivien had said in her letter; but I had seen a letter which

1 – The dates refer to social occasions organised by RC-S: the event on 12 Nov., for example, was a drinks party in celebration of RC-S's 43rd birthday.
2 – See TSE's letter to OS, 13 Oct.

she had written to Edith a few days before, and inferred that the letter to you was in the same strain. As Edith replied at once, and very charmingly and tactfully, I naturally could not understand why you could not do the same.

I have not the slightest idea what she could have meant in saying that anything was going to happen within three days. The notion of some scandal was of course entirely a creation of her own brain. I quite accept the attitude you adopted.

Vivien is at present in a sanatorium in France, by her own wish; I expect she will be back in London soon after Christmas, unless they advise her to go south until the spring.[1]

Yours ever,
[Tom]

## TO *Ellen Sollory* CC

21 October 1927 [London]

Dear Ellen,

I am very glad to hear from you but sorry that you cannot give me better news.[2] I wish I could be of some real use, but I doubt whether I know anybody in Mr Sollory's line of business. Perhaps, however, if I knew more exactly what his special line of work is, I might be able to get

1–A year later, on 19 Oct. 1928, VHE was to write to Sacheverell Sitwell's wife Georgia: 'I have been complaining for a very long time that I have not seen or heard anything about the Sitwell family . . . I shd like to know you very much indeed. Yrs sincerely, *Vivienne H. Eliot*' (Texas).

2–Ellen, the Eliots' former maid, had written from Bushy, Herts, on 20 Oct.: 'I was very pleased to get your Letter but very sorry indeed to hear that Mrs Eliot is away again did hope to get better news but your Letter is not so cheerfull as when at Eastbourne so it do not done much good. I did not write again to Mrs Eliot as I [did] not mean to worry her and was hoping to see her in town. You say that you are alone at Chester Terrace all I hope is that you have someone there to look after you and take care of yourself and eat well, I don't expect Mrs Eliot will stay away long from you but I do hope all is doing well. I have not written lately as I have no good news to send, for Mr Sollory as been out of work now 5 weeks and as no prospects of getting any at least not in his line so he is trying hard to get and the trade into something he has often spoke of you and wondered if you could help him but owing to Mrs Eliots Illness he did not like to worry you for we know quite well what a strain it is for you without us sending our troubles glad to say we are all keeping well, and I hope that you are keeping in good health. [Illegible word] all our Family ar home glad to hear that you have still got Peter and George I should love to see them. I pray to hear better news next time Will now close With kind Regards from Mr Sollory give my kind Love to Mrs Eliot when writing her.'

in touch with somebody who could help. If he cared to do so, I should be very glad if he would drop me a line and give me some idea of the kind of work he would be open to accept. I am sorry I have not very good news either.

My mother, Madam Eliot, who remembers you so well and often speaks of you, is very ill in America. So, as I may be going to France very soon to see Mrs Eliot, and then on to America for a short visit to my mother, I do not know where I shall be about Christmas time. I am therefore sending you my Christmas present now. Perhaps it will be more useful now than at Christmas.

Yours very truly,
[T. S. Eliot]

## TO *The Editor,* The Times Literary Supplement CC

21 October 1927 [London]

Dear Sir,

In returning to you my corrected proof of *Nine Essays*[1] I wish to say that I am taking the liberty of sending you back, under separate cover, the book *O Rare Ben Jonson*.[2] It seems to me utter trash.

Yours faithfully,
[T. S. Eliot]

## TO *Hugh Macdonald*[3] CC

21 October 1927 [*The Monthly Criterion*]

Dear Macdonald,

Thank you very much for lending me the W. P. Ker edition which will be very useful to me and which I will return to you as soon as I can. When

1–'A Scholar's Essays' – review of Arthur Plat's *Nine Essays*, with a preface by A. E. Housman – *TLS*, 27 Oct. 1927.

2–Byron Steele, *O Rare Ben Jonson* (1927).

3–Hugh Macdonald (1885–1958), who trained as a solicitor, went into partnership with Frederick Etchells to produce fine editions under the imprint of The Haslewood Books, 1924–31. His own works include *England's Helicon* (1925), *The Phoenix Nest* (1926), *John Dryden: A Bibliography of Early Editions and of Drydenianae* (1939), *On Foot: An Anthology* (1942), *Portraits in Prose* (1946), *Andrew Marvell's Poems* (1952) and *Bibliography of Thomas Hobbes* (1952).

you get Thorn-Drury's[1] opinion, perhaps you will let me know so that we can discuss the text. I quite agree that the text ought to be the best possible. If not, some reviewer is bound to devote about three lines to my essay and half a column to the textual errors. I accept your terms as laid down in your letter of the 19th instant. They are quite satisfactory.[2]

Yours sincerely,
[T. S. Eliot]

## TO *Rt. Hon. Viscount Halifax* CC

21 October 1927 [London]

My dear Lord Halifax,

Thank you very much for your kind letter of the 18th.[3] I should not have troubled you with all this reading matter and correspondence at a time when I realise how busy you must be. But of course I had not foreseen what was going to happen. I look forward eagerly to seeing your letter in *The Times*. I suppose a letter from the Archbishop will appear tomorrow.[4]

Thank you for your kind expressions about my letter. I did not mean you to return it as I have kept a carbon copy. I therefore send your letter back herewith. Remember that I do not want to impose on your time or good nature, but when this infernal business in England has settled down a bit I should be indeed grateful to have some comments from you.

Yours very sincerely,
[T. S. Eliot]

1–George Thorn Drury, editor, an authority on Caroline and Restoration literature.
2–Macdonald, who had lent to TSE Ker's edition of John Dryden's *Essays*, wrote on 19 Oct.: 'The question of the text to be used is rather more difficult than I had thought. I have talked to Thorn-Drury about it & I should like some time to speak to you on the subject. Of course our reason for reprinting the *Essay* [*on Dramatick Poesie*] is to secure a parallel essay from you, but we may as well make the book as satisfactory as possible from every point of view . . . We offer you £20 down on the delivery of the MS & some share in the profits to be agreed on later. It is difficult to make a definite proposition until we have an estimate & settle what paper is to be used etc. Under any circumstances the copyright is to be yours at the end of 3 years from the date of publication.'
3–Lord Halifax had thanked TSE on 18 Oct. for his 'most *interesting* letter . . . a letter I should like to keep & have by me'.
4–'I am engaged in a cryptic war with Cardinal Bourne which interests & amuses me very much. My letter . . . I hope will appear in The Times on the day after tomorrow . . .' Under the headline 'Malines Report: Publication Delayed', Halifax published in *The Times* (22 Oct. 1927, 14) this letter addressed to the Archbishop of Canterbury: 'My dear Lord, – I have been sent from Rome the copy of an Encyclical letter of Pius XI, and in the interests

## TO *The Accounting Office, The Accounts Branch, The Home Office*

CC

21 October 1927 [London]

Dear Sirs,

REFERENCE 412614/4

In connection with my application for naturalisation with reference number as above, I have today received a letter from the Under Secretary of State directing me to forward to you the fee of £9 (nine pounds). I enclose my cheque herewith and should be obliged for the favour of your acknowledgement and receipt.

I am,
Your obedient servant,
[T. S. Eliot]

---

of that peace and reconciliation which, in the words of that Encyclical, "the King of Peace came to bring on Earth," I would ask your Grace to acquiesce in the delay for a few weeks of the dispatch of the advanced copies now about to be sent out of the English and French Reports of the Conversations at Malines.

'In the meantime, I send your Grace an extract from the Encyclical in question, which, though it has been published some time, touches the most urgent need of the present time and is one which must appeal to all Christian hearts throughout the world as it quotes the words: "For unto us a child is born, unto us a Son is given: and the government shall be on his shoulder: and his name shall be called Wonderful, Counsellor, The mighty God, the Everlasting Father, The Prince of Peace."

'I am your Grace's most devoted Halifax."

'Quotations from Encyclical referred to from above. (1) The Empire of Our Redeemer embraces all men. His Empire includes not only Catholic nations, not only baptized persons who, belonging to the Church, have been led astray, but also all those who are outside the Christian faith . . . Nor is there any difference in this matter between the individual and the family or the State; for all men, whether collectively or individually, are under the dominion of Christ. In Him is the salvation of the individual, in Him is the salvation of society. He is the author of happiness and true prosperity for every man and for every nation.

'With God and Jesus Christ excluded from political life . . . the basic authority has been taken away, and human society is tottering to its fall . . . when men recognize both in private and in public life that Christ is King Society will receive the blessings of real liberty, well-ordered discipline, peace, and harmony . . . Then will the law regain its former authority . . . and peace, with all its blessings, be restored . . . What happiness would be ours if all men, individuals, families, and nations would let themselves be governed by Christ!'

## TO *The Under Secretary of State, The Home Office* CC

21 October 1927 [London]

Sir,

REFERENCE 412614/4

I have to thank you for your letter of the 20th instant and to inform you that I am accordingly forwarding a cheque for £9 (nine pounds) to the accounts branch of the Home Office.

I return herewith the Memorial and Statutory declaration which I have identified before the commissioner for oaths. I cannot quite understand why you believe that the correct spelling of my wife's second name is 'Haig'. I know that it has been spelt 'Haigh' for many generations; I would point out that it is not the Scottish family of 'Haig' but the Yorkshire family of 'Haigh'.

I have the honour to be, Sir,
Your obedient servant,
[T. S. Eliot]

## TO *Horace M. Kallen* TS The American Jewish Archives

22 October 1927 *The Monthly Criterion*

Dear Horace,

Your letter of the 12th October seems to have crossed my own. I am much interested to hear your criticism of my geographical ignorance.[1] Theoretically I believe one ought to make verse as watertight as prose on such points. On the other hand, if I had bothered about the topography and archaeology of Asia Minor, I should have had to omit a good deal of detail which really is meant to be symbolical.

You will by now have heard both from me direct and through Mr Johnson why I cannot make any definite plans at present for lecturing in America. I very much regret that I cannot. It is extremely generous of you to invite me to stay with you while in New York and nothing would please me more than to take advantage of your invitation. I therefore

1 – Of *Journey of the Magi* Kallen declared: 'It has a bitter beauty and is intended, I assume, to be like the landscape of Roland at the Dark Tower, all symbol. For there is no way that men travelling with horse and camel can pass from snowline to vegetation overnight and reach Bethlehem. That sink lies in the arid Judean hills, which stick up sharp and nude all around. They slope eastward to the waste lands of the Dead Sea, south to the Desert. There is no snow nearer than Hermon, to the north, several camel journeys away.'

accept in principle. Please by the way, give my kind regards to your sister whom I remember very well, though I do not suppose she will remember me. Your book has not yet turned up but I look forward to it eagerly.[1]

Yours ever,
T. S. Eliot

## TO *Montgomery Belgion* CC

22 October 1927 [*The Monthly Criterion*]

Dear Mr Belgion,

Thank you for your letter of October 11th and for your very interesting essay in *The Saturday Review of Literature*.[2] I think your essay is a valuable contribution to this subject and ought to do much good. I am sorry that you had to make the cuts.

I am not surprised that *Messages* has not succeeded in England; I am afraid there is only a very small public for this sort of thing.[3]

No, I don't suppose that Murry is even a good Bergsonian.[4] I did not happen to be criticising him from a Bergsonian point of view myself, and indeed was anxious to make my note as brief as possible, but of course the point was worth taking up.

Yours sincerely,
[T. S. Eliot]

## TO *Ray Strachey* CC

24 October 1927 [London]

Dear Mrs Strachey,

I am writing to you on behalf of the firm to ask whether you have ready, or in preparation, or in your mind, another novel. We should very much like to have the first sight of your next piece of work.

1–Kallen had sent TSE a copy of *Why Religion?* (1927).

2–'In Memory of T. E. Hulme', *Saturday Review of Literature* 4 (1 Oct. 1927), 154–5.

3–'In spite of the numerous reviews, *Messages* has been an utter failure in England.'

4–'I am rather surprised no one has pointed out, in passing, that Murry's proposed terminology, Reason for both Intelligence and Intuition, is not merely not Thomist; it is not even Bergsonian.'

I must add that everyone I know who has read *Shaken by the Wind* has been immensely interested in it.[1]

Yours sincerely
[T. S. Eliot]

## TO *John Gould Fletcher* CC

24 October 1927 [London]

Dear Fletcher,

I was delighted to have the two books and am very pleased to possess that copy of *Nerval* with your inscription in it.[2] I have had two copies of *Nerval* in my lifetime, both of which I gave away. But neither of them was nearly so nice or so complete as this little edition which I have never seen.

I will read the Henry Adams book and return it to you as soon as possible. Also I will try to ship you the Guénon books very soon.[3]

About the poems, I did not quite understand the message and was going to write to you. I did not remember that there had been a suggestion of cutting the book down. Certainly I will look over it and make suggestions, but you must consider my suggestions and use your own judgment afterwards.[4]

1 – Rachel (Ray) Strachey, *Shaken by the Wind: A Story of Fanaticism* (F&G, 1927).

2 – Gérard de Nerval, *Poésies* (Paris: Editions d'Art Edouard Pelletan, 1924).

3 – TSE ordered from Adrienne Monnier, on 8 Oct., two books by René Guénon: *Introduction générale à l'étude des doctrines Hindoues* (1921) and *La Théosophie*. Guénon (1886–1951) was a French author and intellectual who specialised in metaphysics and Eastern philosophies and esotericisms (including Hindu doctrines).

4 – 'As you know, a manuscript volume of poems by me is now in Faber & Gwyer's hands. De la Mare thinks that they will publish it, but it seems too long – it will run to 208 pages. Could you possible go over the whole thing, and cut it down to 175 pages?'

TSE wrote in his reader's report (6 Sept. 1927) on *Poems of John Gould Fletcher*: 'I think that Mr Fletcher is one of the best and one of the most reliable of living poets. My opinion of his work, which is a high opinion, is not reduced by this MS, but as I was one who recommended "Branches of Adam" which has failed so conspicuously, I hesitate to urge this by myself. On the other hand, I think that one of the reasons why "Branches of Adam" failed is that it is a long, continuous and difficult poem, whereas the present MS is rather Mr Fletcher's collected works of the last few years and can for the most part be read a few pages at a time. I do not think that the public will consider anything in the way of verse which requires continuous effort, but I do think that the present book might have many more readers than "Branches of Adam". As verse, I recommend it strongly; as saleable matter, I should like another opinion. It will in the long run do no harm and may do much good to the standing of the firm. But in considering publication, I should not expect anything but some immediate financial loss. Personally, I should be very glad if the firm would publish it; especially if there is no important verse for the season in view' (Faber Misc. 5/4).

Yours ever sincerely,
[T. S. Eliot]

P.S. I spent the weekend at Oxford and met A. L. Rowse who is very young, very earnest and very likeable. I believe his father is a clay miner in Cornwall. He was immensely flattered to hear that you were interested by his letter[1] and would very much like to meet you when he is next in town.

## TO *Lady Rothermere* CC

24 October 1927 [London]

Dear L. R.,

I was terribly sorry to hear of your illness.[2] I know, not from my own experience but from having seen my brother in crises of ear trouble, what frightful agony these things are. I hope your doctor is really good and understands it as well as anybody would. Such a prolonged attack of acute pain leaves one very weak, and the danger is of abusing your strength during the following few weeks. I hope that you were really comfortable and well looked after in spite of the state of your house. I was under the impression that this time you had bought a house instead of building one, but I dare say redecorating and altering is as much of a business as building.

I shall do *The Cause of Evil* myself for the *Criterion* and shall certainly observe your hint to speak of the author as 'he'.[3] I thought myself that I did know who it was. Middleton Murry has promised to try to get it for his quarterly *New Adelphi* and I have written to *The Times* about it. I will also write to *The Nation*. Of course I should not mention to anyone who the author was. I merely say that it is someone I know about whose book is likely to be interesting.

I am not likely to get over to Paris much before the middle of November. I shall probably go over for a few days about that time, but my movements are rather complicated. I may have to take a month and go to Boston to see my mother who is very old and very ill. But I should pay a brief visit

1 – ALR's letter of protest at Fletcher's review of Laski's book *Communism*, published in *MC* 6 (Dec. 1927), 542–5. Fletcher had written on 9 Oct., of Rowse: 'He puts his argument very clearly and I hope to be able to reply to him without intrusion of those disagreeable absurdities that have marked my brush with Graves.' Rowse, he went on, 'is perfectly fair and puts forward some real arguments'.

2 – Lady Rothermere, who had an ear abscess, was being treated in Switzerland.

3 – She had written on 16 Oct.: 'You have probably guessed that The Cause of Evil is written by my sister! *Please* speak in your criticism as if she were <u>*He*</u>.'

to Paris before then as my wife has wisely gone back to her sanatorium for a time and I should come to see her. I should have loved to come to Fribourg. Where will you be after that date? Is there any chance of your being in Paris at all before the end of the year?

I have not had the *Criterion* sent to you because your postcard which reached me several days before your letter seemed nevertheless to have been written afterward. I hope I was right; otherwise you must send me an imperative wire. Do tell me what you think of the *Criterion* when you have read it. There will be another number along in a few days and I shall have one copy sent to Fribourg and the rest to Miss Beach.

I do hope you will soon be as well as when I saw you last.

Ever yours sincerely,
[T. S. E.]

## TO *Bruce Richmond* CC

24 October 1927 [London]

Dear Richmond,

Many thanks for your letter. The printing supplement was very interesting notwithstanding the blunder which was perhaps a good thing if it gave you the impetus towards a week's holiday.[1] It didn't matter about cutting out the Dryden.[2] As a matter of fact, I wrote the review in what I intended to be a detachable form, and I think it was perhaps all the better for the detaching.

By the way, Heath Cranton have just published a book called *The Cause of Evil* by I. G. Bartholomew. I couldn't review it in any case, for you, as I know the author, but as it is a new name and not a very good publisher, I take the liberty of mentioning the book to you as it might be overlooked.

Yours ever,
[T. S. E.]

1–*Times Literary Supplement Printing Number*, 13 Oct. 1927 (a supplement). BLR had written on 23 Oct.: 'I have you on my conscience. I had to drop our city lunches because of sudden disasters and (at the same time) expansions to a special Supplement about Printing. This might have been (and, to some extent, was) a good thing. But at the last moment they printed it on blotting-paper . . . and three months' hard work was entirely wasted & made ridiculous. I turned my face to the wall – or, rather, the borders of Worcestershire & Shropshire – and hid myself for a week.'

2–'I'm sorry I cut out the Dryden – it was solely for fitting: & things *would* not shuffle properly.'

## TO *E. M. W. Tillyard*[1] TS King's

24 October 1927 Faber & Gwyer Ltd

Dear Tillyard,

Certainly, I should be delighted to give you my opinion for what it is worth on the thesis.[2] I hope, however, that the Board realises that I am not at all an authority on Roman Catholic dogma, or even on Emerson, so that my opinion would not in any case be a highly specialised one.

I should be glad if you would drop me a line immediately to say how soon you would be sending the dissertation because in a few weeks' time I may be out of London.

We are also very glad in London that Richards has returned, and I had an interesting evening with him last week.

Yours sincerely,
T. S. Eliot

## TO *Marguerite Caetani* TS Caetani

24 October 1927 *The Monthly Criterion*

Dear Marguerite,

I was very glad to get your letter. I can do nothing about the Colums[3] because they disappeared promising to send me an address from Paris and I have not heard from them. I am very much more sorry to find that I shall miss you in Paris. It is very sweet of you to suggest my coming down to Menton and I should like nothing better. I doubt if it is possible for the reason that at the first opportunity I shall have to go to Boston for a fortnight on account of my mother's being very ill, and that will take me

1–E. M. W. Tillyard (1889–1962): Fellow in English of Jesus College, Cambridge, 1926–59; Master, 1945–59. Publications included *The Personal Heresy: A Controversy* (with C. S. Lewis, 1939); *The Elizabethan World Picture: A Study of the Idea of Order in the Age of Shakespeare, Donne and Milton* (1942), *Shakespeare's History Plays* (1944), *Milton* (1946), *Shakespeare's Problem Plays* (1949) and *The Muse Unchained: An Intimate Account of the Revolution in English Studies at Cambridge* (1958).

2–Tillyard invited TSE (21 Oct.) to give his opinion on the PhD thesis of 'an American Jesuit [Father F. J. Yealy] entitled *Emerson and the Romantic Revival*'. He wrote again on 26 Oct.: 'The author is in America and as an oral examination is impossible he will have to undergo a written examination, should the reports of the two examiners be such as to justify the possibility of his being allowed the Ph.D. Degree. Perhaps, then, when you read the thesis you would consider any possible questions you would like to put in the written examination.'

3–Padraic Colum (1881–1972), Irish writer; Mary Colum (1884–1957), literary critic.

away from London for a month. I should certainly be coming to Paris for a few days before leaving for America, but the latter journey would of course put Menton out of the question. I am very sorry indeed.

Now about the cheque. You put me in rather a difficult position. You send back the cheque and at the same time give excellent reasons for not using the poem. If I had realised this at the beginning I should have asked you not to return the cheque at all. The only way out I can suggest is this: that you should have my next poem of about the same length exclusively, and that I should keep the cheque as payment in advance for a poem which is not yet written. I would only ask permission to arrange for publication in America within a month after *Commerce* was due to come out. This would be merely in order to protect my copyright as I have already had an unpleasant experience of New York Jewish piracy.

I trust that Léger's measles won't develop into something else and that he will be recovered by the time I get to Paris. I will certainly find my way into the Foreign Office as you suggest.

I have asked Faber & Gwyer to enter you for all the volumes of the new series. I believe it will be very beautifully printed but I have not yet seen sheets.

I saw Valéry just for a few moments at a reception. This sort of meeting is never very satisfactory and one only goes to please the people. He seemed to be in a great rush and was going off somewhere the next day, and I heard of him later in Oxford.[1]

Thank you *very much* for sending the flowers to Vivien. She was delighted to have them. I am posting you her letter from London as the sanatorium are sending her letters to me to look at first.

Yours ever affectionately,
~~T. S. Eliot~~ Tom

Sorry. I had just signed a dozen letters that way!

## TO *Richard Aldington* — TS Texas

24 October 1927 — Faber & Gwyer Ltd

My dear Richard,

This is just a line to say that Trend has written to ask me if I know of anybody who is capable of giving a course of twenty or thirty lectures

1 – On 18 Oct. Valéry talked to the French Society at Somerville College, Oxford: see Jarrety, *Paul Valéry*, 692.

on English literature at the University of Madrid. He says that it must be someone who can lecture competently either in French or Spanish <I mean, *either* would do>, and he had himself thought of you. He writes from Cambridge and gives no particulars about dates, or, what is the most important thing, the emolument, but if that is satisfactory, and it would have to be, is it a thing that you would consider?

I hope to see you on Thursday.

Ever yours,
Tom.

## TO *Richard Cobden-Sanderson* TS Texas

24 October 1927 *The Monthly Criterion*

Dear Cobden-Sanderson,

Thank you for your more or less reassuring letter. I was rather worried by the number of engagements, and suspected that some of them did not belong to me. I was sorry to hear from Tandy[1] that I had given my host and hostess some uneasiness by expressing some of my opinions in ignorance of the fact that I was sitting next to a Roman Catholic gentleman. For which many apologies all round.

Yours ever,
T. S. E.

I dare not come to your Rainbow Club tomorrow: I must see my mother in law directly after lunch. I'll come next week D.V.

## TO *Mario Praz* TS Galleria Nazionale d'Arte Moderna, Rome

24 October 1927 *The Monthly Criterion*

My dear Praz,

I cannot provide you with any evidence of Wyndham Lewis being either a Jew or not a Jew.[2] And as he would deny it violently, and as

1 – Geoffrey Tandy (1900–69), botanist, worked at the Natural History Museum, London.

2 – Praz asked on 23 Oct.: 'Could you let me know definitely whether Mr Wyndham Lewis is a Jew? – This question of mine might startle you, or simply amuse you: but I should like to be sure before writing for the *English Studies* my review of *The Lion & The Fox* & *Time & Western Man* . . . Of course, Lewis's *forma mentis* seems to me typically Jewish: I am not infrequently reminded of Weininger – of course, again, this fact can hardly distort my opinion of his work, which is rather a high one – : besides, were he not somehow only half-western, he would not insist with such relentless *gusto* in his defence of the white civilization

in any case you are not in a position to prove that he is a Jew, I should think it advisable for you not to touch upon that question at all. Several people have made the suggestion to me but it had never occurred to me independently.*

Your other questions I can't answer, I am sorry to say.[1] I shall write to you soon when I have had time to read Montale's poem.[2] I don't think I have any proof copy of my Preface, but if Constable's do not send it to *English Studies* I could lend you my copy.[3] I enjoyed very much seeing you the other evening.

Yours ever,
T. S. Eliot

* I mean, *I* have no reason to believe he has Jewish blood.

[P. S.] I have still to write in reply to your other letter, to thank you for yr offprint.

## TO *Bruce Richmond* CC

25 October 1927 [London]

Dear Richmond,

Thank you for your letter of the 24th. The choice is rather a difficult one, but I should say that of the two books the Beaumont and Fletcher book is the one which needs the more scholarly treatment, and therefore I should prefer to have Lucas's Webster. Unless I am mistaken, however, this is not merely a study but is a new critical edition published by Chatto and Windus.[4]

---

(*Paleface*): as you know, there is no worse antisemite than a converted Jew. His name and self-portrait would confirm my impression: but it may only be an impression, and I would feel very sorry if I called him a Jew – though with no other intention than a classificatory one – and he were not one. You needn't reply to this but with *Yes* or a *No*, or a *Non liquet* (at yr earliest convenience).'

1 –'[D]o you know what Lewis means by *altofronto*? This word puzzles me not a little (see for inst. *The Lion & the Fox* p. 248, 254). I suppose it is meant for Italian, perhaps in some hazy Ezra-Poundish way . . . Another funny word is *Atte* (*Lion & Fox* p. 256) i.e. obviously *Ate*, perhaps + *Attis*, the priest of Cybele (in other words, Ate *shamanized*!)'

2 –'Arsenio'.

3 –'The publisher of *Newton's Seneca* has not yet sent the book to *Engl. Studies*: I don't think he will send it: but if you by any chance have a typewritten copy of yr preface, I shd like to read it, & then I could return it to you.'

4 –'Lucas . . . has got a study of Webster, which is coming very soon. About the same time a book is coming from the Oxford Press which endeavours to establish the exact shares of Beaumont and Fletcher in their plays . . . Which of the two would you prefer?' See TSE, 'John Webster' – on *The Complete Works of John Webster*, ed. F. L. Lucas – *TLS*, 26 Jan. 1928, 59.

I have by no means forgotten that I have promised eventually to do a couple of columns on Jespersen for you.[1] But I am saving up my best energies for the Bradley.

Yours ever,
[T. S. Eliot]

## TO *His Mother*

TS Houghton

25 October 1927

*The Monthly Criterion*

My dearest Mother:

I have just got back from a weekend visit to All Souls College Oxford. My partner, or more correctly my Chairman, Geoffrey Faber, who has been a very good friend to me (did I tell you that I am God Father to his younger son Thomas?) is a Fellow of the college, and asked me for the weekend.[2] It is a peculiar college. There are no undergraduates at all, so it is more like a very small and rich and select club. There are some Fellows who are engaged in research work, and some Professors, and the rest are people who only go there for weekends. For instance, I met Sir John Simon, the Liberal Politician, there (he is not an interesting person) he is a Fellow,[3] and a lot of people of the same sort. But a few of the younger Fellows are very intelligent: I met one named Harris, with whom I had a long talk; found that he had been teaching at Princeton, knew and admired very much our old Paul Elmer More,[4] and also Irving

1–'The Problem of Grammar' – on *A Modern English Grammar on Historical Principles*, Part III, by Otto Jespersen; *The Soul of Grammar*, by E. A. Sonnenschein – *TLS*, 10 Nov. 1927. Not in Gallup.

2–GCF noted in his diary, Sat., 22 Oct.: 'met Eliot at Paddington, & we went down to All Souls together . . .' 23 Oct.: 'Ordinary sort of day. El. & I walked round by Iffley in afternoon.'

3–John Simon (1873–1954), lawyer and politician, was elected a Fellow of All Souls in 1897. Following a very successful period at the Bar (he was made KC in 1908), he was elected a Liberal Member of Parliament in 1910, serving in turn as Solicitor General (a post that brought with it a knighthood), Attorney General, and Home Secretary. After a period outside the House, he was returned as Member of Parliament for the Spen Valley at the General Election of 1922, and became Deputy Leader of the Liberal Party under Lloyd George. On 6 May 1926 he declared in the House of Commons that the General Strike was illegal. In later years he served as Ramsay MacDonald's Foreign Secretary in the National Government from 1931; at the Home Office, 1935–7; as Chancellor of the Exchequer, and ultimately as Lord Chancellor, 1940–5. Shy and coldly clever, he was not greatly liked. See D. Dutton, *Simon: A Political Biography of Sir John Simon* (1992).

4–Paul Elmer More (1864–1937), critic, scholar and prolific writer, had grown up in St Louis, Missouri, and attended Washington University before going on to Harvard; at one time he taught TSE's brother Henry: see Biographical Register.

Babbitt. It is a lovely place, and they keep up all the old ceremonies. After dinner, which is very formal, everyone goes into the Common Room, for the ceremony of drinking Port. You have to sit there, whether you want to drink Port or not, until the Warden of the College rises; then you may go to the Coffee Room to drink coffee; but it is only when you have left the Coffee Room and entered the Smoking Room that you may indulge in Tobacco, including the most ceremonious form of Tobacco – Snuff! I am more or less used to Snuff, as I had to partake of it at dinners at Trinity College Cambridge when I was lecturing there; but I don't like it!

I have been very busy this week clearing up arrears: wrote two reviews for *The Times* (which you will see) and two for *The Dial* (which you will see later on). Now I have three articles to write – one for *The Dial*, one for the *Neue Schweitzer Rundschau*, and the third an introduction to a new edition of some of Dryden's essays.[1] Thank goodness I have refused to give any speeches this year: not very important, but Undergraduate Societies at the universities keep applying.

I hope you have received safely my Seneca. Dear Charles Whibley, who is one of my greatest friends, and who gave me the job of doing that, has just got married. He is 67, and his Bride, I hear, is 24 – the daughter of the late Sir Walter Raleigh. But it may be a very good thing for both of them. I have not met her yet.[2]

Herewith the little book of Lancelot Andrewes's prayers. I thought it might interest you, because of my essay on him in *The Times* last year. Although translated from Latin and Greek, in which he composed them, I think they have a great deal of the distinction of his English prose, some of which is very lovely. The first 5 lines of my *Journey of the Magi* are quoted directly from one of his sermons. I had a very amusing letter from Horace Kallen, Sheff's[3] old friend, to whom I had sent a copy of *Journey*

1–John Dryden, *Of Dramatic Poesie an essay 1668 . . . Preceded by a Dialogue on Poetic Drama by T. S. Eliot* (Frederick Etchells and Hugh Macdonald, 1928). TSE's preface was reprinted as 'A Dialogue on Dramatic Poetry', *SE: 1917–1932* (1932).

2–CW married his goddaughter Philippa, daughter of the literary critic Sir Walter Raleigh. He confided to TSE (14 Oct.): 'I am going to be married on Wednesday next to Miss Philippa Raleigh, & I am full of foolish, necessary business. Don't say a word to anybody until the announcement is made in the *Times*.' On 25 Oct. he wrote, on honeymoon: 'Here we are, married & happy. It seems strange because we lost no time, & were formally engaged less than a fortnight . . . Never mind about a wedding present. I have your affection & sympathy, I know, & that is enough.'

3–Alfred Dwight ('Sheff') Sheffield (1871–1961), husband of TSE's eldest sister Ada (1869–1943), taught English at University School, Cleveland, Ohio, and was an English instructor, later Professor, of Group Work at Wellesley College. His publications include *Lectures on the Harvard Classics: Confucianism* (1909) and *Grammar and Thinking: a study of the working conceptions in syntax* (1912).

*of the Magi,* telling me that if I meant it to be accurate, my geography of the country about Bethlehem was completely wrong! There are no snow mountains anywhere about, it appears. The poem has sold very well.

I long for more news of you always, mother dear, and am looking forward eagerly to seeing you soon.

Devotedly your son
Tom.

## TO *R. Gordon George* CC

25 October 1927 [London]

My dear Gordon George,

Very many thanks for your letter and for letting me see the interesting and delightful letter from Halifax[1] which I return herewith. I hope that it is unnecessary to say that after my visit to Yorkshire I have had it in mind to write to you and thank you for an introduction of the greatest value. I have only been prevented by pressing work. I enjoyed the visit thoroughly and, as you say, his personality is a very great influence which I should have been sorry to miss in my life.[2]

I must tell you that Halifax showed me a copy of an interesting and valuable essay which you have written on the Vatican and Conciliation. With most of your essay I am in agreement, I think, though it deals with subjects with regard to which I am merely an ordinary member of the non-Roman public. But with some of your observations about the 'Action

1 – Not found.

2 – Robert Sencourt, in *T. S. Eliot: A Memoir*, wrote of Lord Halifax – 'the leading layman in the Church of England' – and of the impression Halifax had made on TSE: 'Although the old churchman was then on the verge of ninety, he was still a captivating and lively companion . . . He was a scholar who wrote delightful English. He carried on a continual correspondence with the Archbishops of Canterbury and York, impelling them towards Catholic unity. But above all, he was a master of the art of conversation, with a spirit of boyish fun and a taste for the jokes Tom loved.

'It was not long before Lord Halifax was writing to thank me for sending him someone so admirable and delightful in every way: one to whom he was immediately drawn, in reciprocity of friendship. Tom had hardly been a day at Hickleton before he came to a full identity of religious outlook with his host, who not only specialized on Catholic claims and developments within the Church of England but was actually head of its special organism, the Church Union . . .

'Tom . . . accompanied his host each day to Hickleton Church, the little church close by the Hall, where they worshipped in a form which only an expert could have detected was other than the Roman Catholic mass . . . Issuing from this worship, he bound himself to the causes of his host' (102–4).

Française' I found myself in disagreement, and took the liberty of giving Lord Halifax a brief memorandum of my objections. Of course I am quite aware that I approach the subject from an opposite point of view to your own. The 'Action Française' includes personal friends of mine, including Maurras himself, and I have known and admired and been influenced by his work for nearly twenty years. I have therefore personal feelings involved. And also I am aware that from your point of view I am distinctly Erastian, or from my point of view more interested in local politics than yourself.[1]

With these qualifications there are two or three questions I should like to ask. First, what is your evidence that the 'Action Française' was 'infuriated' by the Pope's efforts for peace in 1916? Second, why do you say that the 'Action Française' is 'nominally' monarchist, a statement which seems to imply that this monarchism cloaks merely the personal ambitions of its leaders; which I should deny. Third, why do you suggest that the 'Action Française' has been pursuing a policy of petty aggression and annoyance against the Vatican, and that it was this aggression which finally induced the Pope to make a statement? And you do not indicate that the beginning of the recent affair must be dated from the publication of the open letter from Cardinal Andrieu. I think that many people like myself are unable to see why this letter appeared when it did; and I believe that this condemnation took many supporters of the 'Action Française', even persons intimately associated with it, wholly by surprise. You omit also any mention of the efforts toward conciliation and submission made by the 'Action Française' itself. Finally, do you think you are justified in calling the 'Action Française' a 'dangerous and immoral party'? I think that you are justified from your point of view in calling it dangerous, though I do not think it dangerous myself, but I cannot see any justification for using such a word as 'immoral'. You might refer to some of the ideas of Maurras himself as 'immoral', but even this would be unfair unless you made very precise your use of the word 'immoral'. After all, you were presumably writing this essay for an ordinary English quarterly and not

1–Cf. TSE's statement, from 'The English Tradition' (1940): 'There was a good deal of what we should call Erastianism, certainly of nepotism, in the mediaeval Church. And for Erastianism itself there is something to be said . . . At least, we must recognize a wide difference, for good and for bad, between the situation of Church and State in the later eighteenth century and that of a Church in a modern state controlled by an openly, or almost openly, infidel government. There was a great deal of corruption in the Church, but a church can be corrupt without being Erastian . . . We must remember that the independence of the Church may be bought at too high a price too, if that independence relieves it of its contract with the mass of the nation' (*Christendom*, Dec. 1940, 229–30).

for a theological journal; and this use of the word 'immoral' seems to me to appeal to Protestant prejudice in favour of Catholic dogma.

I have further views about the whole matter but I do not think they would interest you as they are on those matters where my point of view would be most different from yours, and I am more interested in general to discuss with you those matters which we have in common.

It is extremely kind of you to suggest that I should visit you in the south and nothing could give me more pleasure or more profit. I have just had a similar invitation from some relatives in Menton, and if I could get away for a month it would be a great temptation to combine the two. But it is probable that I shall have to go to America for a few weeks to see my mother, and in that case I am afraid I cannot afford to take the time for a holiday in the south.

Do write to me as soon as you have time.

Yours ever,
[T. S. Eliot]

## TO *Henry Eliot* — TS Henry Eliot

25 October 1927 — *The Monthly Criterion*

My dear Brother:[1]

First about the Buchens. As they went to Paris first, they were only in London 3 days. Buchen rang me up and asked me to tea, and I went. I did my best to get them to come to lunch with me, but he was too busy. Had they been able to stay longer I should have wanted to take them about a bit, and perhaps arrange to have them meet some people. I congratulate you on your partner. I don't pretend to be a good judge of people at first sight, and I have never found anybody else who was, but I liked Buchen. He seemed to me intelligent, shrewd, kindly and humorous. She is very pretty, alert and pleasing. They are people who could mix with anybody, and I should [have] liked to have them meet a few of my friends. And he seems genuinely fond of you and appreciative of you.

I could not think of anything to do for them in the time. I sent them a couple of books to read on their journey to Amsterdam; I don't know whether they got them or not; would have sent flowers, but as they were leaving the next day I knew it would be only a nuisance.

1–Henry gave the original of this letter to his partner, Walter [Walther] Buchen, after making a copy from which this text is taken.

Especially in the circumstances, and in my case, I don't like you paying for my entertaining them, and I didn't entertain them. So, as you have also paid my insurance with Black, I shall be returning you a draft. I originally arranged that you should pay my insurance out of my bank balance; but you no longer have any bank balance with mine, so there is no point in it.

Please let me know where my Hydraulic share certificates are. I have but a few now, and am minded to keep these unless you see a chance of selling advantageously. But I should like to arrange to keep the certificates at the Old Colony, and have the Dividends paid in there for me, and have the Old Colony forward to me. At present Mother forwards the draft for the dividend, but I don't like that, and should like to put it on a business basis. Could you just see to this for me.

Vivien seems to have made some improvement. She writes to me, and I get reports from the sanatorium. But the condition is still bad. I shall try to arrange a visit of two weeks to mother before Christmas, and will *promise* her to come again in the spring. At the moment I am waiting (PRIVATE AND CONFIDENTIAL) for my British Passport, as I have applied for Naturalisation and been accepted, having pulled a few strings with the Home Secretary.[1] If this shocks you, I will present you my reasons; in any case, don't tell mother. So far as I know, I am not notorious enough to be bothered by Reporters etc. when I come, and should like to keep my visit as Quiet as possible; as I should just want to stay at home and not see people. I hope to hear again from the Home Office in about a week.

I have been in a rather tense state. As I could not go off for a rest cure, having too much to do in London, I have been seeing a good many people, and working hard. What I want to do is to go off to Dublin for a week's holiday, then go over to Paris for a few days to see about V., and then come on to Boston. I shd not have time to come to Chicago this time; of course IF you could run over to Boston for a few days during my stay I should be very happy.

I was happy to find that Buchen seemed to be so devoted to you.

Always your affectionate brother
Tom

1 – Valerie Eliot was to remark that for TSE 'becoming an English citizen and being received into the English Church' was a single step (Spender, *Eliot* [1975], 5). Later, TSE was reported as saying of his citizenship: 'In the end I thought: "Here I am, making a living, enjoying my friends here. I don't like being a squatter. I might as well take the full responsibility"' ('Reflections: Mr Eliot', *Time*, 6 Mar. 1950).

## TO *Rev. F. J. Powicke* CC

25 October 1927 [London]

Dear Sir,

I have read with much interest and pleasure your two books on the Cambridge Platonists and Richard Baxter. It would give me great pleasure if you had time and cared occasionally to review a book for *The Criterion*. I have at the moment a book which looks interesting and which I dare say you have seen – *William Law and Eighteenth Century Quakerism*.[1] I immediately thought of you.

If you do not know the *Criterion* I shall have pleasure in sending you a specimen copy. It is primarily a literary review but I aim to make its scope as wide as possible and to review a certain number of untechnical religious and theological works. Of course we do not, as a literary review, represent any religious sect or school: I do not expect or desire reviewers to conceal their individual points of view, but merely want to have reviews which would interest readers of any type of belief.

Yours very truly,
[T. S. Eliot]

## TO *Harry Crosby* TS Virginia

26 October 1927 *The Monthly Criterion*

Dear Mr Crosby,

Thank you very much for sending me the charming little book of Lautréamont which was entirely unknown to me.[2] I shall have much pleasure in examining it. I return your preface which I have read with much interest.[3] As I did not know the work of the man you are introducing there is very little that I can say about it. You ask about the quotations, I should say that if the book is intended for a small public, and I imagine that such a book could only have a small public, I should certainly advise leaving the quotations in French. They are a compliment to the literacy of the public which the public always enjoys. Also I think you should stick to the capital letters in question.

1–See F. J. Powicke's review of Stephen Hobhouse, *William Law and Eighteenth Century Quakerism*: *MC* 7 (Feb. 1928), 179–82.

2–Crosby sent (23 Oct.) 'the little Lautréamont *Préface à Un Livre Future*'. Comte de Lautréamont: pseudonym of Isidore Ducasse (1846–70).

3–Crosby, preface to his *Transit of Venus* (Black Sun Press, 1928).

I do not know whether R. N. D. Wilson has published any book.[1] If you are interested, why do you not write to him care of the *Criterion* and the letter will be forwarded. As for 'agon', you will find a full discussion of the word in Liddell and Scott's Greek-English lexicon.[2] I use the word in accordance with an analysis of F. M. Cornford in his very interesting book on the origins of Greek comedy.

Yours sincerely,
T. S. Eliot

## TO *Leonard Woolf*

TS Reading

26 October 1927

*The Monthly Criterion*

Dear Leonard,

In reply to yours of the 25th. Again I have no objection whatever.[3]

There is a suggestion of a book which I think is more in the way of the Hogarth Press than Faber and Gwyer's. William Stewart, who is a friend of Tom McGreevy but a very different sort of person being an Ulsterman, has translated one of Valéry's dialogues and written a long, and I think a good, introduction; and Madame Bussy has translated the other. Would the idea of uniting these two dialogues in one smallish volume and considering using the Introduction also in the same volume appeal to the Hogarth Press?[4] Stewart has left me a copy of his introduction which I could show you. He is a lecturer at the University of Sheffield, but was for three years lecturer at the École Normale, sent by Trinity College, Dublin. He seems to know French very well and also German. He is a friend of Curtius. If you ever wanted an extra man for German translations, I think he would be very glad of the work.

There is a book just come out called *The Cause of Evil* by I. G. Bartholomew, published by Heath Cranton. I venture to call it to your attention for *The Nation*, as coming from an unknown author and an inferior publisher it might get overlooked, and there may be something in it. I know something of the author, but my promise was merely to call

1–'Has R. N. D. Wilson published any of his poems in book-form?' Wilson, who was County Librarian of Sligo, Eire, published *The Holy Wells of Orris and Other Poems* in 1927.

2–'I can't find anywhere the meaning of Agon.'

3–LW thought (25 Oct.) to take sheets of the US edition of some of the Hogarth Essays and to bring out the volume in the UK also. 'Would you have any objection to this . . .?'

4–LW replied (27 Oct.) that he would be 'glad to consider the Valéry translation'. See *Eupalinos or The Architect*, trans. William McCausland Stewart (1932).

it to the attention of a few editors without soliciting any particular kind of notice.[1]

Yours ever,
T. S. Eliot

## TO *R. L. Mégroz* TS Reading

26 October 1927 Faber & Gwyer Ltd

Dear Mr Mégroz,

I have thought over your letter but I am afraid that I am a very poor dreamer and I can think of nothing that would be suitable or of any interest.[2] My dreams are very fragmentary and valueless. I hope, however, and believe that there are many people who dream much more profitably than I do.

With all best wishes,
Yours sincerely,
T. S. Eliot

P.S. In view of a recent book on the subject, which has aroused a good deal of interest, I suggest that if you could get together an anthology of anticipation dreams it would go particularly well.[3] I have never had any such myself, but I think that they are not uncommon.

## TO *Clive Bell* CC

26 October 1927 [London]

Dear Clive,

Herewith Miss Mayor's story returned.[4] Its length makes it absolutely impossible for the *Criterion*. You will say that I need not have kept the story for so long merely to discover that it was fifty-one typed pages, but I

1 – LW: 'I will have a look at The Cause of Evil, though I doubt whether Mr I. G. Bartholomew knows what it is.'

2 – R. L. Mégroz wrote (17 Oct.): 'I covet a dream of yours . . . I am trying to collect some interesting dreams (i.e. records from a number of well known people distinguished in different directions) for an anthology (critically arranged) of dreams & visions.'

3 – This refers to J. W. Dunne, *An Experiment with Time* (1927), which had been reviewed, under the headline 'Dreams of the Future', in *TLS*, 29 Sept. 1927, 659. (Mégroz published a letter on the subject of Dunne's book, *TLS*, 13 Oct. 1927, 715.)

4 – 'Virginia will print it I think,' said Bell in a card (21 Oct.). 'You will sympathise with the impatience of a half fledged authoress.'

wanted to read it with some care in order to see whether it could be cut or run in instalments. I do not believe that it could be cut and it is certainly not the type of story which could be run in instalments. It needs to be read at one sitting. I am doubtful if it would find a place in any periodical, and I do think the best way to publish it is to get the Hogarth Press to make a small book.

Thank you very much for letting me see it. It is extremely interesting and I intend no derogation to the story when I say that I wish you would scratch about and produce something for the *Criterion* yourself. I know that you are solicitous to preserve untarnished your high reputation for laziness, but as you have only given the *Criterion* one contribution in five years, I do not believe that your reputation would be damaged if you gave me something else. Believe me, I have no intention of converting you to industry, but you could, at a trifling expense of your valuable time, contribute to the success of a periodical which I believe to be deserving.

Ever yours,
[T. S. E.]

## TO *William Force Stead* CC

26 October 1927 [London]

Dear Stead,

Herewith your Ms returned. I would say definitely, include the poem about which you were doubtful.[1] I write in haste but I have read through the book at leisure, and with much enjoyment. As I am in rather a rush at the moment, I merely give you my opinion without going into the reasons. Primarily, I think this poem has its place in helping to make the book better balanced. If you are still doubtful, I will give you my reasons at greater length a little later. I do not *think* that the objections you suggest apply seriously. You might of course consider putting in a line at the beginning or at the end to say that this is a fragment of an unfinished and much longer poem. I think it sometimes helps one's own self-criticism to publish parts of unfinished work.

Ever yours,
[T. S. Eliot]

1 – WFS had sent the proof of his book on 19 Oct.: 'It seems to me that it needs the inclusion of the blank verse semi-philosophical poem at the end, "Uriel" – otherwise it is much too slight, & even of this more serious addition I am honestly disillusioned and wonder if it is worth printing.'

## TO *Ezra Pound* TS Beinecke

26 October 1927 Faber & Gwyer Ltd

Dear Ezra,

The point at which we have arrived is this: we quite definitely want to do the book providing that we can sell a sufficient number of sheets in America, and I think there is very little doubt that we can. The Bruce Rogers scheme is off for the reason that for very special editions they only want to have work never previously published in any form. There is, however, a suggestion that they would take sheets and we have actually taken the matter up with them. They seem to be pretty flourishing, and I believe they would be as good a firm as any to market a limited edition of poetry in America.

Our proposal is this: we can pay Dazzi ten guineas for his work and give you twenty five pounds advance on royalty. I believe the rate would be fifteen per cent on copies sold in Great Britain, but I cannot get hold of our manager at this moment and I must confirm this. We propose a limited edition of a thousand copies and would expect to dispose of two or three hundred copies at least in America. We should pay you royalty, I believe, at a slightly lower rate on copies sold in America, i.e., the whole business would be done through us. The only out about it is that they are very keen to have you sign the whole edition. For a book of this sort I hope you will; it would make a big difference to the sales.

If there is nothing doing in America with the people I mentioned, we will follow your wishes and try Covici[1] and then Liveright before tackling anyone else; and if you have any objection to any other particular publishers, let us know.

I understand that as most of the book was originally set up in America your copyright there will be adequately covered. You said you had written to the receivers of Small Maynard, and I should be very glad to know if you have had any reply.

Yours,
T.

P.S. When you have a new lot of cantos or any other unpublished stuff ready for publication, why don't you try these Bruce Rogers people?

1–Pascal ('Pat') Covici (1885–1964), Romanian-born US publisher; began publishing in Chicago in 1922, and set up Pascal Covici, Inc. in 1925. He later published many writers including John Steinbeck (with whom he forged a successful alliance). In 1938 Covici was to join Viking Press, where he published works by Lionel Trilling, Arthur Miller and Saul Bellow (who would dedicate *Herzog* to him). See *Pascal Covici 1888–1964* (1964).

They seem to pay higher prices than anybody and their books are in great demand. I believe they have an agent here whom I could tackle.

## TO *Mary Colum*[1] CC

27 October 1927 [London]

Dear Mrs Colum,

I am relieved to hear from you at last. After you disappeared leaving no address I began to feel as if the darkness had swallowed you up altogether. I am so very sorry to hear that you have had bronchitis; especially as I know that these small complaints are particularly tiresome and uncomfortable when one is ill in Paris.[2] I hope that you have been well looked after and are now taking care of yourself. I am only afraid that you will have missed Madame de Bassiano. I wrote to her about you and had a letter from her a few days ago saying that she was leaving for the south with her children tomorrow. So I am afraid you may miss her altogether.

I have read your review of Fernandez's book and think it is absurd of you to have any such scruples about meeting him.[3] It seems to me a very fair review and one that ought to please him rather than otherwise. At

1 – Mary Colum (1884–1957): Irish author and critic; married in 1914 to Padraic Colum (1881–1972), playwright, poet, and writer for children. She was co-founder of *The Irish Review*, 1911–14. In 1914 the couple emigrated to the USA (where she was to become Literary Editor of *Forum*, 1933–41, and to teach comparative literature at Columbia University). In the 1920s they made a number of return visits to Europe, where they became close to James Joyce: see their memoir *Our Friend James Joyce* (1958). Her other works include *From These Roots: The Ideas that have Made Modern Literature* (1937).

Colum wrote of TSE: 'He was not in the least like any Englishman I ever knew, yet that he was of clear English descent one could not but realize; one felt that England was his homeland; he needed it, not for his happiness, but to fulfill whatever dream of life he had . . . Nevertheless, Eliot looked a little alien in London; he was very carefully dressed, not in the *dégagé* British manner, but in the deliberate American way; his handsome face and figure had not at all the British look; he seemed to be aware of his own alienness, for he told us of the remark of a French writer of immediate American-Spanish ancestry, "All of us born in North or South America feel more at home with each other than we do with anybody in Europe." He seemed to quote this with approval and assent.

'We dined with him in a typical English restaurant, where in true British fashion we drank sherry before dinner and port after it – he loved the whole English civilization as did Elinor Wylie, and every custom belonging to it' (*Life and the Dream* [1947], 302).

2 – Mary Colum had written in an undated letter to say that she had had bronchitis and had not yet been able to make use of any of TSE's letters of introduction.

3 – 'Would you be so kind as to cast your eye on a few paragraphs of the enclosed review of Fernandez, and tell me if in the best of your belief, he might not like it, and if therefore I ought not to meet him.'

any rate, if he were annoyed by it he would be a much sillier fellow than I believe him to be. It would be a pity if you and your husband did not meet him as he is one of the people who talks English perfectly. Your mention of that point inspires me to send another note in case you care to use it to Charles Du Bos who also talks English extremely well – in fact his mother was English or Scotch. He is also a very good talker and I think at times an extremely good critic; he and his wife have a charming flat on the Ile Saint Louis and I am sure that they would like to meet you. As Maritain and Fernandez both live out of town you will of course have to write to them first and arrange meetings as best you can. But I hope that you will see all of these people.

Thank you very much indeed for your note of introduction to Dunsany.[1] I am not quite sure when I shall get over there, but I shall not fail to use it.[2] I should have written long before to thank your husband for his generous and numerous cards of introduction to very interesting people in Dublin but that I did not have his address. Please convey to him my cordial thanks.

But what is most pleasant is that you hold out some hope of my seeing you again in London.

Yours very sincerely,
[T. S. Eliot]

## TO *Mario Praz* CC

28 October 1927 [*The Monthly Criterion*]

My dear Praz,

I am glad that you have got the Seneca. I do indeed like Montale's poem very much.[3] I shall use it together with your translation early in the new year, you may tell him.

I am inclined to agree with you that your Preface should be in English rather than Italian, but of course I do not know what Partridge had in

1 – Edward Plunkett, 18th Baron Dunsany (1878–1957), soldier and writer, lived at Dunstall Priory, Kent, but also owned Irish estates including Dunsany Castle in County Meath.

2 – As an executor of his father-in-law, Charles Haigh-Wood, TSE anticipated that he would have to make a personal visit to the family properties in Dun Laoghaire.

3 – Praz had written on 25 Oct.: '*Engl. Studies* . . . have got the Seneca for me. I am very glad. I am looking forward to your opinion of Montale's *Arsenio*.'

mind and perhaps he has good reasons to offer.[1] The idea of such an anthology seems to me a good one.

Yours ever,
[T. S. Eliot]

## TO *René Julliard*[2] CC

Le 28 octobre 1927 [London]

Monsieur,

Je vous remercie de votre letter du 24 octobre. J'ai beaucoup réflechi et j'ai consulté mes collègues. J'espère que vous allez nous envoyer des propositions plus exactes, parce que vous envisagez une œuvre de grande envergure, et du point de vue d'une maison d'éditions anglaise je n'y vois pas encore très clair. Il me semble au premier abord que le public anglais qui appuierait un tel projet serait assez retreint. Mais je serai bientôt à Paris et je voudrais bien en causer avec Monsieur Massis et Monsieur Bainville.

Monsieur Richmond me dit que vous repasserez à Londres en peu de jours, et j'espère que vous pourrez faire un rendez-vous pour me voir.

Croyez, Monsieur, l'assurance de ma considération parfaite et de mes sentiments sympathiques.

[T. S. Eliot][3]

1–Eric Partridge had invited Praz to edit for his press an anthology of Italian sonnets; but Praz was unhappy about the suggestion that his preface should be published in Italian.

2–BLR told TSE on 25 Oct.: 'A very engaging young man . . . came to see me yesterday about the possibility of establishing a branch in London of a Society . . . for spreading the sale of the best French books in London. He wants, if possible, to link up with some publisher in London who might be interested in it. Whether Faber & Gwyer would or would not be interested in it I leave to you . . .' René Julliard (d. 1962) was to set up in 1942 the publishing house Éditions Julliard; his discoveries included Françoise Sagan.

3–*Translation*: Dear Sir, I wish to thank you for your letter dated October 24th. I have given it a lot of thought and consulted my colleagues. I hope you are going to send us more exact terms, as you envisage wide-ranging (ambitious) works and from the point of view of an English publishing house, I cannot see things clearly yet. It seems at first sight that the English public who would support such a project is rather restricted. But I will soon be in Paris and I would like to discuss it with Mr Massis and Mr Bainville.

Mr Richmond tells me that you will be back in London in a few days and I hope you will arrange an appointment to see me.

Be assured, Sir, of my perfect consideration and my friendly feelings, [T. S. Eliot]

## TO *Raymond Mortimer*[1] CC

28 October 1927 [London]

Dear Mortimer,

I am not quite sure from your letter whether your friend is a freshman or a Frenchman, or whether his name is Fry, or Fay, or Foy.[2] However, it would be very nice to come to tea with you on Tuesday.

Yours ever,
[T. S. E.]

## TO *Richard Aldington* CC

28 October 1927 [London]

My dear Richard,

Alas! I am afraid you have hit several nails on the head. I will digest and try to profit. I am afraid you are right about the translations; they are not very readable. But I got £50 for the essay, for which may I be duly thankful.[3]

1–Raymond Mortimer (1895–1980): literary and art critic; associate of the Bloomsbury group, being close friends with George Rylands, Duncan Grant and others (in 1924 he had begun an affair with Harold Nicolson); wrote for the *New Statesman* from 1927 (and for a while contributed the 'London Letter' to the *Dial*, in succession to TSE), becoming literary editor (in succession to Desmond MacCarthy), 1935–47; and later writing for the *Sunday Times*, 1948–80; author of two collections of essays, *Channel Packet* (1942) and *Try Anything Once* (1976). A lifelong Francophile, in 1955 he was appointed an officer of the Légion d'honneur; and in 1977 he received the prize of the Académie Française.

2–Mortimer wrote on 26 Oct.: 'There's a Frenchman called Bernard Fay, whom you probably know of, who is in London now & is very anxious to meet you. I doubt if you would get much pleasure or profit from his company, but if you would come to tea here next Tuesday or Friday to meet him, I should be honoured.' Bernard Fay (b. 1893) was author of *Panorama de la littérature contemporaine* (1925); *L'Esprit revolutionnaire en France et aux États-Unis à la fin du XVIIe Siècle* (1925; trans. by Ramon Guthrie as *The Revolutionary Spirit in France and America*, 1928); *Bibliographie critique des ouvrages français relatifs aux États-Unis, 1770–1800* (1925); *Notes on the American Press at the End of the Eighteenth Century* (1927); *Franklin, The Apostle of Modern Times* (1929); and *La Langue Française pour la Célébration du troisième Centenaire de Harvard* (1936). See also Antoine Compagnon, *Le Cas Bernard Faÿ: Du collège de France à l'indignité nationale* (Paris: Gallimard, 2010).

3–RA had complained, in a letter now lost, that TSE had wasted his talents in writing a poor introduction to a poor translation of Seneca in Whibley's 'tedious' series. See RA, 'Mr Eliot on Seneca', *N&A* 42 (29 Oct. 1927), 159. RA told HR it was a 'devilish job': 'I was set a nasty problem by the *Nation* – to review Tom's *Seneca*. I hope I have extricated myself honourably. The first difficulty was that I thought the *Tenne Tragedies* most appalling bilge, and I wonder why Whibley thought them worth printing at 42/-. The second difficulty

I wish they had sent you the enclosed paper to review at the same time. It is less formal than the Introduction.

Always yours,
[Tom]

## TO *William Stewart* CC

31 October 1927 [London]

Dear Stewart,

Please forgive my delay in replying to your letter.[1] I am very sorry to say that Valéry came and went without my having any opportunity to speak to him on these subjects. He was only in London a very few days. I was only able to see him at a reception on the Monday evening which was very crowded so that I could only speak a few rather formal phrases to him and he told me that he was leaving for Oxford the next day. So that it has all come to nothing. I am writing to McGreevy to explain.

I think your Introduction to the dialogues is very good and I think it ought to appear *as* an Introduction; it does not seem to me suitable for the *Criterion*. My suggestion would be that as Madame Bussy has already translated the other dialogue, the two ought to be published together, you and she of course dividing the royalties, if any, proportionately. If both dialogues were published together, it would balance the rather long Introduction much better. I think that the Hogarth Press would be the people for this, unless you cared to try Benn whom I do not know. I have spoken to Leonard Woolf about it and he is interested.

I should be delighted if you would let me see your translation when it is quite ready. Meanwhile I will send you back your Introduction which I like very much indeed.

Sincerely yours,
[T. S. Eliot]

---

was that I was greatly disappointed with Tom's Introduction, which read like an uneasily executed task. Altogether, the most difficult review I ever had to write' (*Richard Aldington: An Autobiography in Letters*, ed. Norman T. Gates [1992], 29).

1 – Stewart had asked (16 Oct.) about the fate of his translation of Valéry's *Eupalinos*.

## TO *A. L. Morton*[1] CC

31 October 1927 [London]

Dear Morton,

I am afraid that I cannot use any of these but I hope that you will send me some of your work from time to time. And will you suggest another book to review now and then?

Yours sincerely
[T. S. Eliot]

## TO *E. M. W. Tillyard* TS King's

31 October 1927 *The Monthly Criterion*

Dear Tillyard,

I have read your Jesuit's dissertation on Emerson and I think it ought to be accepted beyond doubt. But before I write my formal report on it I should be glad if you would enlighten me on one point. Is he to be examined solely on the direct subject matter of this thesis, or on some general field of study?[2] I should like to know, as you have asked me to give you any questions to be put to him which suggest themselves to me.

Yours sincerely,
T. S. Eliot

## TO *Rev. Geoffrey W. S. Curtis* CC

31 October 1927 [London]

Dear Mr Curtis,

I remember meeting you and should be glad to see you again if you ever come south. Many thanks for your kind expression about the *Criterion*.

1–A. L. Morton (1903–87) was to become a leading Marxist historian; educated at Cambridge, he worked in the 1930s for the *Daily Worker*. *A People's History of England* (1938) is a modern classic. His later works include *The English Utopia* (1952), *The Everlasting Gospel: A Study in the Sources of William Blake* (1958), *The World of the Ranters: Religious Radicalism in the English Revolution* (1970). See also *Rebels & Their Causes: Essays in Honour of A. L. Morton*, ed. Maurice Cornforth (1978), and *History and the Imagination: Selected Writings of A. L. Morton*, ed. Margot Heinemann (1990).
2–Tillyard (3 Nov.): 'The examination does not go beyond the direct subject matter of the thesis.'

Two of these poems are rather unsuitable for the *Criterion* by the nature of their subject matter. The third is interesting and I hope to see more of your work.[1]

Yours sincerely,
[T. S. Eliot]

## TO *Thomas McGreevy* TS TCD

31 October 1927 *The Monthly Criterion*

My dear McGreevy,

I was very glad to get the 'Gide' and have sent it to be set up for the January number. I like it very much indeed.[2]

My intentions of meddling in your business with Valéry came to nothing as I was only able to see him for a few moments at a reception and he was off to Oxford the next day. He seems to have filled up his time in England with official feasts and speeches. So I don't know what should be done next. Could you get in touch with Valéry's impresario, whose name, I believe is Monod?[3] I think Benn's would be all right if they cared to take it up. Otherwise, the Hogarth Press is certainly the most suitable place for it.[4]

Always yours sincerely,
T. S. Eliot

1–In a following letter (15 Nov.), Curtis – a 'de-intellectualised, clerical soul,' he called himself – acknowledged TSE's 'appreciative remark about my "Il Paradiso" doggerel'.
2–See McGreevy on Gide (inc. *Les Faux-Monnayeurs*), *MC* 7 (Jan. 1928), 65–9.
3–Julien-Pierre Monod.
4–McGreevy, who had translated Valéry's *Introduction à la Méthode de Léonard de Vinci*, said: 'before I went to Paris . . . a man at Benn's . . . gave me to understand that I had only to send the thing fairly adequately done and there would be no hitch. Leonard Woolf told me . . . that if I couldn't get a rich publisher . . . he'd be interested' (11 Oct.)

## TO *Olivia Shakespear*[1] CC

1 November 1927 [London]

Dear Mrs Shakespear,

It is very nice indeed to hear from you again.[2] I am very sorry indeed that I am engaged for Thursday evening, but I am more or less permanently in London and if you are in the same position I do not see any reason why we should not meet in a week or ten days, unless you change your mind about wanting to see me. I am so sorry that I cannot come this Thursday and see Miss Wood again. I did not know that Homer[3] was with you. When I do come to see you, I hope you will let me come at an early enough hour to inspect the son and grandson of genius before he retires for the night.[4]

With many thanks and all best wishes,

Yours sincerely,
[T. S. Eliot]

## TO *Richard Cobden-Sanderson* TS Texas

1 November 1927 Faber & Gwyer Ltd

Dear Cobden:

A Courteous letter requires a Reply. I could not have turned Up at the Rainbow today, for the reason that I did not know the Bearings of that Hostel. I am sorry about the Wednesday night, but I regard it as the Hand of God, and a Manifestation of Divine Will that I should do a little work and keep comparatively Sober. I was Signalled this afternoon (about 6 Bells) by a Vessell named the Tandy, master one Tandy A.B., and arranged to lay along side Chiswick Wharft one evening next week,

1–Olivia Shakespear (1864–1938), mother of Dorothy Pound and second daughter of Major General Henry Tod Tucker (1808–96), made an unhappy marriage in 1885 with Henry Hope Shakespear (1849–1923), a solicitor. She published several novels including *Love on a Mortal Lease* (1894) and *The Devotees* (1904). Through her cousin, the poet Lionel Johnson (1867–1902), she effected a meeting with W. B. Yeats, which resulted in a short love affair and a lifetime's friendship. WBY wrote at least two poems for her, and she was the 'Diana Vernon' of his *Memoirs* (ed. Denis Donoghue, 1972).

2–Shakespear invited TSE (31 Oct.) to dinner. 'The news from Buffalo is good – & "Omar" [son of EP] is doing well here, only teething at the moment. He is a lovely little thing.'

3–TSE meant to type 'Omar', EP's son. (Homer Pound was EP's father.)

4–Responding to this letter on 21 Nov., she commented: 'I am glad to see you still retain that mocking spirit, which teased me so in Paris.'

on the understanding that you and Mrs Cobden-Sanderson were likely to cross the bar Later in the Evening. I have arranged to arrive from the Continent in time for Supper or a shade sooner by Seaplane; so you may hear my engines.

Very many thanks for your kind despatches.

Yours ever etc.
T. S. E.

Re next week: If I get into foul water I may hail the Doves & pick up a Pilot.

## TO *His Mother* — TS Houghton

1 November 1927 — Faber & Gwyer Ltd

My dearest Mother:

I have just returned from a very pleasant weekend at Cambridge. I staid at Corpus Christi College, with a rather new friend of mine, one Kenneth Pickthorn (he has reviewed a little for *The Criterion*) who is a Fellow of the College and Tutor in History. It is a very small college, but a nice one. On Saturday night very few fellows were present: they had mostly gone up to Derby, where the President of the college was being instituted as Bishop of Derby. One man however was there whose accent puzzled me a little; a Law don; and he turned out to be a Yale man (and a Jew into the bargain). We spent the evening with another friend of mine whose name you may have seen: Ivor A. Richards a fellow of Magdalene College; I reviewed a book of his in *The Dial* for January, and he wrote an article in the September *Atlantic Monthly* which was partly about me. I shall be going down again to stay with Richards as soon as I can. Richards had just been in America: it is surprising how many people I meet who have been in America, and know somebody whom I know. (Today I met another person who had been to Harvard lately, and had met Irving Babbitt – a Frenchman named Bernard Fay, who has been lecturing at Columbia all the year). On Sunday we dined at Pickthorn's house with his wife; and on Sunday night we dined in hall, where there was a pretty full company. The President (now a Bishop) was back from his investiture; but as he was still to be President of the College until 3 p.m. on Monday, he was ceremoniously addressed by everyone as 'Mr President' and not as 'My Lord Bishop'. The titles of 'Heads of Houses' are rather confusing, both at Oxford and Cambridge: for at some colleges they are 'Warden', at some they are 'Master', at a few they are called 'Provost', and at a few they are called 'President'. I spent a long evening with the new President, the successor, a man named Spens[1] (Scotch); I only got to bed at 12; and up again at 7:30 to breakfast and catch my train.

I really find Cambridge more congenial than Oxford in these times. In Cambridge you find many more points of view, where in Oxford you only find a universal monotony; in Cambridge you find much more difference between colleges. There are more vigorous personalities in Cambridge. King's College, with Maynard Keynes and Lowes Dickinson[2] and such people, is distinct; Trinity is quite different; Jesus (Archbishop Stearnes' college[3]) is dominated by Charles Whibley; Magdalene is divided between two quite different but both positive personalities, Richards and Gaselee;[4] and Corpus is dominated by Spens and Hoskyns.[5] And each other college has its character. I had much rather get a job at Cambridge than at Oxford. The contrast was borne in upon me after passing one weekend at Oxford and the next at Cambridge; which I have never done before.

I long for more news of you. I may go to Paris for a few days to see Vivien. Otherwise I am very busy. I have to settle down to write a new introduction: this time to a new edition of Dryden's criticism. Unfortunately I promised to do it three years ago and must fulfil it; but it interferes with other things I want to do.

Your devoted son
Tom

1–Will Spens (1882–1962), Master of Corpus Christi College, Cambridge, 1927–52.
2–Goldsworthy Lowes Dickinson (1862–1932): Fellow of King's College, Cambridge; historian, pacifist, and promoter of the League of Nations; Apostle. OM thought him 'a rare and gentle Pagan Saint . . . by temperament religious and poetical' (*Ottoline at Garsington* [1974], 117–19).
3–Richard Sterne (1664–1683), Archbishop of York – great-grandfather of Laurence Sterne – was elected Master of Jesus College in 1634. TSE's spelling of the name seeks to flatter the claim of his mother, Charlotte C. Stearns, to be descended from Sterne.
4–Stephen Gaselee (1882–1943), librarian, bibliographer and classical scholar; Fellow of Magdalene College, Cambridge, from 1909; Pepys Librarian, 1909–19; Librarian and Keeper of the Foreign Office from 1920; later President of the Bibliographical Society, 1932; Honorary Librarian of the Athenaeum Club from 1928; President of the Classical Association, 1939; and Fellow of the British Academy, 1939. Publications include *The Oxford Book of Medieval Latin Verse* (1928). He was to be knighted in 1935.
5–Edwyn Hoskyns, 13th Baronet (1884–1937): theologian; Fellow of Corpus Christi College, Cambridge – which he served successively as Dean of Chapel, Librarian and President. His notable works in biblical theology, some of them published only after his death, include *The Fourth Gospel* (1940) and *Crucifixion–Resurrection* (1981). See G. S. Wakefield, 'Edwyn Clement Hoskyns', in E. C. Hoskyns and F. N. Davey, *Crucifixion–Resurrection* (1981); R. E. Parsons, *Sir Edwyn Hoskyns as Biblical Theologian* (1985).

## TO *James Smith* CC

1 November 1927 [London]

Dear Smith,

I am very glad indeed to hear from you. I did not know in the least what had happened and I am very sorry to hear of your lack of success. Of course, if the dissertation turned out to be entirely philosophical it would naturally not be sent to me.[1]

I will re-read your 'Pepys' as soon as I can and let you know about it. I can see, however, that in its present form it is much too long for the *Criterion* and would like to know whether you think it can be drastically cut. Either Beaumont and Fletcher or Wittgenstein would be very interesting. I hear that there is a new book on Beaumont and Fletcher coming out which will deal with the question of attributions. Perhaps you would like me to get it for you if I can. But I should particularly like you to do Russell's *Outline* when it appears.[2] I have had his *Analysis of Matter* reviewed by H. W. B. Joseph of Oxford. At any rate I shall always be glad to send anything I can in your direction.

I heard about Jack merely because I happened to see this summer the president of Michigan University who is an old friend of mine.[3] From Jack I have never heard a word. So I cannot give him any advice good or bad.[4]

What I particularly want to know is whether you would care to review a book called *Form In Gothic* by Professor Wilhelm Worringer. It has just been translated into English with an introduction by Herbert Read. You may have seen an essay by Worringer in the *Criterion* early this summer. He is a philosopher of art, and although his book does have a good deal to say about Gothic art, it is primarily a book for a philosopher rather than a mere art critic. Anyway I think Worringer is a good man and I doubt

1 – Smith had failed at his second attempt at a Fellowship. 'I must confess I completely neglected your advice: I allowed myself to become so interested in philosophical prolegomena that I had no time to rewrite the old thesis. The new one, "entirely philosophical" . . . was sent to new referees; and they were not very sympathetic.'

2 – Smith submitted a paper on Pepys that had formed part of the thesis seen by TSE; and he set out his plans: 'I project a paper on Beaumont and Fletcher . . . Many people have a gross respect for Wittgenstein: I think it can quite pleasantly be shown that he is neither new, trustworthy nor clear. Would this be too technical for you?' See Smith on Bertrand Russell, *An Outline of Philosophy*, *MC* 7 (June 1928), 419–21.

3 – Clarence C. Little.

4 – Peter Jack had 'been appointed Professor at Michigan': 'I am troubled about his thesis on Pater as I was never troubled before . . . You, I trust, will give him good advice.'

whether his book will be understood or properly noticed in this country and I should like to do our best about it. I should like you to look at it anyway, but I will not send it until I hear from you.[1]

Sincerely yours,
[T. S. Eliot]

## TO *Richard Aldington* TS Texas

1 November 1927 *The Monthly Criterion*

My dear Richard,

Thank you very much for your letter. I am delighted to find that you prefer my Shakespeare lecture to my Seneca introduction.[2] The latter, my small critical ability had already told me, is no great shakes. I think the idea of a cheap reprint of the old series is a good one, but I have not the slightest doubt that the publishers would lose any amount of money over it. You have no idea how few people care a damn about such things.

Certainly the party was a silly one, but I did not anticipate anything else.[3] Let us try to arrange a meeting alone, or of a maximum of four persons, the next time you come. Am I one of the irrepressible twins you mention, and if so who is the other? And do not father upon me any idea of the superiority of London *soirées*. I never said or intimated such a thing. I never go to a really social soirée myself and those I do attend, I attend primarily for the purpose of drinking beer in company. Doubtless I could do the same in a pub. in Aldermaston. The only point about London is that you can see the right people, one or two at a time, rather more often, and that you sometimes meet interesting people whom you would be willing to meet again alone.

Yours always affectionately,
Tom

1 – Worringer's book was not reviewed in *C.*

2 – RA wrote on 30 Oct., 'Your Shakespeare Society lecture is the true Thomas, and far superior to the Seneca Introduction.' See note on letter to RA 28 Oct.

3 – RA regretted that he and TSE had got separated at a 'rather . . . silly' party. 'I fancy those parties are too large and too disparate. At Harold's on Friday we had a much better one, for there were only about seven or eight people. It is true we lacked the irrepressible twins who make all coherent conversation possible. But, my dear Tom, this idea of the superiority of London Soirées is all nonsense.'

## TO *The Under Secretary of State, The Home Office* CC

3 November 1927 (of 57 Chester Terrace, Eaton Sq., S.W.1.)

Reference 412/614

Sir,

In accordance with your instructions of the 2nd instant I return herewith your Certificate No. 15337 with the oath of allegiance duly sworn before a Commissioner for Oaths. I am registering the letter but should be obliged by the favour of your acknowledgement of receipt.

I presume that it is my duty to notify the Aliens' Registration Office at Bow Street and that my next step should be to apply to the Passport Office for a British passport.

I have the honour to be, Sir,
Your obedient servant,
[T. S. Eliot]

## TO *Raymond Mortimer* CC

4 November 1927 [*The Monthly Criterion*]

Dear Mortimer,

I wonder if you would help me out with a few books unless you have already undertaken the same task for someone else. The books in question belong to this French translation series of Routledges, but the volumes I particularly must have dealt with are the two volumes of selections from Madame de Sevigne's letters edited with an introduction by Richard Aldington. It wouldn't matter whether your opinion was favourable or not, but I should like to get a notice of some sort on them. One could of course consider the whole question of whether such translations are useful or not, or on the other hand one could talk on Madame de Sevigne instead. I should be very glad indeed if you could do these books.[1]

I did not think that Fay was a bore at all; he seems to me quite as interesting as the majority of Frenchmen one meets.

Yours ever,
[T. S. Eliot]

1 – Mortimer replied on 6 Nov. that he could not 'very well deal with the Routledge translations. In the first place I have never read Madame de Sevigne right through . . . Secondly I am supposed to be translating Madame de Staal-Delaunay for that series, and I cannot very properly say how futile the production of such translations seems to me.' (The review of Madame de Sevigne was presently undertaken by Peter Quennell.)

## TO *John Hayward* TS King's

4 November 1927 Faber & Gwyer Ltd

Dear Hayward,

I am returning *Mont-Cinère*[1] under separate cover with many thanks. Our readers have found it interesting certainly, but we regard translations of French novels as a probable loss ninety nine times out of a hundred, and the approval was not strong enough to make us feel justified in launching this book. Many thanks for letting me see it.

When you are able to come to lunch or tea, do let me know.

Yours ever,
T. S. Eliot

## TO *John Gould Fletcher* CC

4 November 1927 [London]

Dear Fletcher,

Thank you for your reply to Rowse which I have sent to be set up for the January number.[2] The Guénon book which I sent you is not the one about which I spoke.[3] I have sent you the latter yesterday. I have not yet read it, but please keep it if you like until I ask for it; it will probably be a long time before I have time to read it. I am afraid it is in any case too late to suppress your reply to Graves as the December number is all in page.[4] I should have been very sorry to suppress it even if it had still been possible to do so. I don't think anything Graves could say would matter; he seems to have damaged his own case in the eyes of everybody. But unless he comes out with some very gross insult or other I hope we can avoid actually calling him a liar.

Yours ever,
[T. S. E.]

1 – Julian Green, *Mont-Cinère*, which JDH had lent to TSE in Oct. 1927.
2 – Fletcher, letter to the Editor, *MC* 7 (Jan. 1928), 62–4.
3 – Fletcher wrote on 30 Oct.: 'Thanks for forwarding me the Guénon book. I thought . . . that it was a sort of critical history of Indian philosophy – a subject in which I am interested, but on which I am very ignorant – but I discovered that it is a history of Theosophism [*La Théosophie*], which is a very different thing, and one in which I take little interest.'
4 – 'I think it would be perhaps better if you suppressed my reply to Graves. He might make some fantastic reply in the style of Murry's review of Santayana in your current issue – which is the sole blot on a very interesting number, in my opinion. Incidentally, I may remark to you that I have just heard from Allen Tate, to the effect that Graves' assertion that all the poems in the Close Chaplet were conceived and written by Miss Riding before she had ever met Mr Graves, is false.'

## TO *Marianne Moore* TS Rosenbach

Sunday, 6 November 1927 [London]

Dear Miss Moore,

I have several days ago your telegram reading MUCH DESIRE FROM YOU ARTICLE ON EZRA POUND TO ACCOMPANY AWARD PRESS CAN WAIT UNTIL NOVEMBER TWENTYTHIRD DIALPUBCO[1]

I have tonight replied

POSTING POUND NOTE TONIGHT ELIOT

I infer that Pound has received the (long overdue) *Dial* Award. If so, I am very glad. But I have sent herewith a note which I hope will do in any event. I have not given it a title, not knowing what precise use it was to serve. May I leave it to you to do so?[2]

I trust that you received my notes on Crashaw and v. Hügel, sent some weeks ago.[3]

Yours sincerely,
T. S. Eliot

## TO *His Mother* TS Houghton

6 November 1927 [London]

Dearest Mother:

I have passed a quiet Sunday this weekend at home. Next weekend I shall either go over to Paris to see Vivien, or if I cannot get to Paris for a few days after that, I shall go to Worcester College, Oxford, to stay with

1 – Telegram sent on 1 Nov.

2 – 'Isolated Superiority', *Dial* 84: 1 (Jan. 1928), 4–7. A paragraph from TSE's review, headed 'Ezra Pound and the Art of Verse', appeared in a broadside, *Clip-sheet from The Dial . . . December 27, 1927 . . .* (New York, 1927), by way of publicity for the Jan. issue.

3 – 'The Poems English Latin and Greek of Richard Crashaw', *Dial* 84: 3 (Mar. 1928), 246–50; reprinted as 'A Note on Richard Crashaw' in *FLA*. 'An Emotional Unity' – on *Selected Letters of Baron Friedrich von Hügel (1896–1924)* – *Dial* 84: 2 (Feb. 1928), 109–12. The two reviews were commissioned by Moore on 10 Aug. On receipt of the piece on von Hügel, Moore told IPF (28 Oct.): 'We feel memorably enriched by the sense he gives of emotional unity in Baron von Hügel and by the very thoughtful implication of the closing sentence. We should like to publish the article as an essay and wonder if Mr Eliot might think well of *An Emotional Unity* as a title?' (The closing sentence of TSE's review reads: 'We demand of religion some kind of intellectual satisfaction – both private and social – or we do not want it at all.') On 3 Nov. Moore wrote further: 'We are almost abashed to realize how much we have been asking, and how much more we have received even than we have asked – in Mr Eliot's article on Crashaw. The consideration of Dante in connexion with this poetry, we feel to be singularly appropriate.'

a friend there and talk to the undergraduates. I have spent part of this Sunday afternoon writing a short article on Ezra Pound: I had a cable from *The Dial* asking for it, from which I gather that he has been given their Prize. I hope so, he deserves it. I don't know whether he will like my article, if they publish it; for I have been frank and said what I think both for and against him. In any case I shall use the same note as a review in *The Criterion*, and will send you a proof copy: at the moment I have sent one copy to *The Dial* and must send the other to be set up for *The Criterion*.

I am always very busy. My next job is to write my introduction to Dryden, because I promised it two years ago; it is a nuisance, as I have other things I much more want to do. And I have to see a good many people: tomorrow I must lunch with the Master of Corpus Christi College (Cambridge) whom I met last week as I told you on my visit to Cambridge. By the way, I always impress Cambridge people very much by claiming descent from Archbishop Stearnes, whose portrait hangs in Jesus College, so I hope there is no doubt about it! I have never seen a complete family tree from him; is there one? I have another connexion with Cambridge in President Charles Chauncy, who was a fellow of Trinity College.[1] As I have said, I should like, and even hope, eventually to get a job or an honorary Fellowship in Cambridge; I like Cambridge much better than Oxford.

My memory is not what I imagine it was; but, as the old saying is, 'it never was'. I cannot remember whether I told you how much I liked Buchen (Henry's partner) and his wife: I liked them much better than Henry had led me to expect; and as I wrote to Henry, I am glad on his account that he now has such a partner (he is much more likeable than Joe Husband, who is not bad); and I was very sorry that they were not in London longer, so that I could have them meet a few of my friends. They both seemed very fond of Henry indeed, and even appreciative of him.

Dearest mother, I pray for you and thank God for you, every day.

Your devoted son,
Tom.

1–Charles Chauncy (1592–1672), nonconformist divine, was second President of Harvard University, in succession to Henry Dunster. TSE wrote to BD on 31 Dec. 1935: 'When you next visit me in my eyrie at Russell Sq. I shall be able to show you a photograph of the portrait [artist unknown] of the Revd Charles Chauncy D.D., Fellow of Trinity College and Tutor of Hebrew in the University of Cambridge, and second President of Harvard. A Schismatic. Original in the common Room of Dunster, Cambridge (Mass.).'

I was very sorry not to see Elizabeth Wentworth again before she left; I hope you or Marion will see her when she gets back. It was a great pleasure to see a little of her. I have lunched again with Mark (whom I like very much) and his wife (whom I had never met before) a few days ago.

Vivien is much better, and has asked me to send you her Love.

## TO *G. C. Robertson* CC

7 November 1927 [London]

Dear Mr Robertson,

Please excuse me for not having answered sooner your pleasant and welcome letter of the 25th October. I must say that I found my tenants at least as satisfactory as they could have found their landlord. I have not only visited the flat myself, but Mrs Haigh-Wood has been to see it (who is a much more severe critic than myself) and she was astonished to find that anyone could leave a flat in such a perfect condition of order and cleanliness. I suppose that there are inevitably a few breakages and so on which it is the business of Clymo's to deal with.

I am glad to have your address and I certainly hope that I may see you now and again. Very many thanks for your suggestion about electrical fittings. I shall remember it and take your advice when I need anything.

I hope your new flat is everything that you desire and also that you have found a quieter neighbourhood than Clarence Gate Gardens.

With all best wishes to Mrs Robertson and yourself,

Yours very sincerely,
[T. S. Eliot]

## TO *Alfred Zimmern*[1] CC

7 November 1927 [*The New Criterion*]

Dear Mr Zimmern,

I am very glad to hear from you and most grateful to you for your remarks and the pamphlet which I had not seen and will certainly read.[2] I shall be very glad to recur to the matter as soon as possible in my Commentary, and if you should care to frame any remarks in the form of a letter to the Editor I should be very glad of that too.

If you are more or less established in Paris, I hope I may have the pleasure of seeing you on one of my occasional visits. The last time I saw you, as a matter of fact, was an occasion on which Jean de Menasce was staying with you and Mrs Zimmern at Queen Anne's Gate and I called on you there.

Yours sincerely
[T. S. Eliot]

1–A. E. Zimmern (1879–1957) – Fellow and Tutor of New College, Oxford, 1904–9; enthusiast for working-class education (serving as an inspector of the Board of Education, 1912–15) – had written in a testimonial, 22 Aug. 1918: 'Mr T. S. Eliot is well-known to me. He has done successful work as a lecturer to working men under the auspices of London University. I have the highest opinion of his character and ability.' (See TSE's letter of thanks, 27 Oct. 1916: *L* I, 172.) In 1920 he was a founder of the Institute of International Affairs (Chatham House); and after teaching as Wilson Professor of International Relations at the University College of Wales, Aberystwyth, and at Cornell University, he became Deputy Director of the League of Nations' Institut International de Coopération Intellectuelle (forerunner of UNESCO). He was the first Montague Burton Professor of International Relations at Oxford, 1930–44; Deputy Director of Chatham House, 1943–45; and in 1945 he became Secretary-General of UNESCO. Publications include *The Greek Commonwealth* (1911), *Europe in Convalescence* (1922), and *The Third British Empire* (1926).

2–Zimmern thanked TSE (4 Nov.) for 'calling attention to [the Institute], even if with a shade of criticism'. He enclosed a document of his own which was 'unofficial (so far as the League is concerned)', and in which TSE would find (pp. 10–11) 'his views on the place of the teacher in connexion with efforts to inculcate ideas from outside.'

## TO *Edmund Wilson* CC

7 November 1927 [London]

Dear Mr Wilson,

Thank you for your cable about my note on Whitehead.[1] I have no idea when that is likely to appear as Wyndham Lewis's *Enemy* is not a very punctual publication, but I have thought over your suggestion. On the whole I think I should much prefer not to publish this note elsewhere. I am not satisfied with it and if I had had time I should already have revised it. I should much prefer to offer you something else. I am going to write a note on Irving Babbitt for publication in *The Adelphi* here and I think that I could easily arrange so that you could publish it at the same time. Would you care to have that?[2]

Yours sincerely,
[T. S. Eliot]

## TO *R. Gordon George* CC

7 November 1927 [London]

My dear Gordon George,

I have had these essays for some little time and still see no immediate prospect of using any of them. I think, therefore, that it is only fair to let

1–TSE's review of A. N. Whitehead's *Science and the Modern World* and *Religion in the Making* – 'The Return of Foxy Grandpa' – was never published. The galley proof is kept in the Wyndham Lewis Collection at Cornell University Library. WL had acknowledged the piece for *The Enemy*, in an undated letter: 'I like what you say about Whitehead very much. It is a very important contribution.' TSE argued in his review, apropos Whitehead's supposed 'rehabilitation of religion', that it seemed to him 'very doubtful' that 'there is such a thing as "religion" above the various particular religions'. Furthermore, he maintained, 'The conflict between religion and science is a conflict between two quite unreal phantoms . . . But Professor Whitehead is wholly occupied with phantom conflicts. He assumes that "science" (a fiction) is in conflict with God (another fiction), and he proceeds to show that science is far from being hostile to God, that on the contrary it requires Him, as the principle of Order . . . For Professor Whitehead seems to think that you can make a perfectly good substitute religion if only you provide a GOD of some kind. He is all in the tradition of the late William James, and of Professor Bergson, with the patronage of one who was, in his time, an admirable political philosopher, but a very feeble-minded theologian – the respected Matthew Arnold . . . But the most important things in any religion . . . are not derivative from the notion of God . . .' TSE argued in conclusion: '[F]or anyone who is seriously concerned, not with "religion", that gelded abstraction, but with Christianity, there is far more to be learned from Irving Babbitt's *Democracy and Leadership* than from Professor Whitehead's soporific elixirs.'

2–Wilson said (25 Nov.) they would be very glad to have the Babbitt article.

you have them back. As I explained to you verbally, my list had already been filled with essays of the general and rather philosophical type which it will take me some months still to work off, and the great problem of an editor is to distribute material so as not to give the readers too much of any one type of thing at a time. Besides, I shall want, and have room for, your *Maupassant* before I could use any of these. In spite of your assurances, I still feel that you are a very inaccessible person and have grave doubts always in writing to you whether my letters will be received, and if received, whether they will be answered. Do let me hear from you, even briefly, as soon as you get this note. Particularly because you are a person with whom I do not want to lose touch even though our meetings seem condemned to be few and hurried.

Yours ever sincerely,
[T. S. Eliot]

## TO *Charles Smyth*[1] CC

7 November 1927 [London]

Dear Mr Smyth,

I venture to suggest to you that I should be very much pleased if you cared occasionally to review historical books for the *Criterion*.

If you have never seen this review I shall be very glad to send you a copy; but you can probably find out most quickly and easily about it from Pickthorn who can also give you some idea of our tendencies and directions and who will also, I am sorry to say, be able to tell you that our emoluments are very small.

I do not know whether you have time to do anything of this sort. I have nothing very important on hand at the moment. If you are favourably

1 – Charles Smyth (1903–87) was an eminent ecclesiastical historian and a fine preacher in the Anglican communion. In 1925 he gained a double first in the History Tripos at Corpus Christi College, Cambridge, winnng the Thirlwell Medal and the Gladstone Prize, and was elected to a Fellowship of Corpus (R. A. Butler was elected a Fellow on the same day). He edited the *Cambridge Review* in 1925, and again in 1940–1. He was ordained deacon in 1929, priest in 1930; and in 1946 he was to be appointed rector of St Margaret's, Westminster, and canon of Westminster Abbey. (On 28 Apr. 1952 TSE expressed the view, in a letter to Janet Adam Smith, that Smyth should be 'moved up to where he so eminently belongs, an episcopal see'.) Smyth's publications include *Cranmer and the Revolution under Edward VI* (1926); *The Art of Preaching (1747–1939)* (1940); the Birkbeck Lectures, *Simeon and Church Order*, given at Trinity College, Cambridge, 1937–8; and a biography of Archbishop Cyril Garbett (1959).

disposed I have two books which I should like to send you to look at. One is the new *Letters of Warren Hastings* which is probably interesting but from our point of view is not of sufficient momentary interest to require anything but a very short notice; the other is a book about which I know nothing called *The American Heresy*, which is a more serious study of American history than the title would suggest. It deals with several prominent figures from Thomas Jefferson on, and appears to be quite a serious book. This, if it is really good, would merit a longish review which it very likely will not get anywhere else. I am always particularly anxious to review the occasional good books which are overlooked by everyone else.

Yours sincerely,
[T. S. Eliot]

## TO *James Smith* CC

7 November 1927 [London]

Dear Smith,

I hope you will not be too alarmed by the Worringer book or by my commendation of it.[1] As a matter of fact I have not read this book and have only glanced at it and was speaking from my general opinion of Worringer. And he is a man of whom the late T. E. Hulme had a high opinion. So please tackle the book if you possibly can.

I think that I might as well return the 'Pepys'. I don't know what ought to be done with this essay. I should like to see it published but it is not really quite the sort of thing for a review, except perhaps for such as the *Modern Language* review. It really ought to be published as a pamphlet by the Shakespeare Association but I am afraid it is rather too long for that.

Yours very sincerely,
[T. S. Eliot]

1–Smith had written on 6 Nov.: 'Worringer's article greatly interested me. Let me see his book, and I will tell you within a week whether I consider I should review it, or not. I feel a greater responsibility than usual towards a book you so highly recommend. I am much flattered that, having so recommended a book, you offer it to me.'

## TO *A. D. Peters*[1] TS Texas

7 November 1927 *The Monthly Criterion*

Dear Sir,

After having troubled you and Mr Coppard I am very sorry to have to return these two stories to you, but the fact is that neither of them is quite what the *Criterion* wants.[2] I based my request to Mr Coppard largely upon a previous story of his which we published entitled 'The Field of Mustard', which I still think is one of the finest stories in English which has appeared for many years. I should like very much to get something more of the same kind. 'The Ape and the Ass' is definitely too fantastic and allegorical, and 'That Fellow Tolstoi' is a story which I think would appeal primarily to a different and probably a larger audience than that of the *Criterion*. Especially as I think 'That Fellow Tolstoi' is probably a very saleable story to periodicals of wider circulation than ours, I have less regret in returning it, and I hope that if Mr Coppard produces something more of the type of 'The Field of Mustard' that I may have the first examination.

Yours very truly,
T. S. Eliot

## TO *Leonidas Warren Payne Jnr* TS Texas

7 November 1927 *The Monthly Criterion*

Dear Professor Payne,

Thank you for sending your book and for your letter of the 11th September.[3] In spite of your modesty, I should imagine that your book was

1–A. D. Peters (1892–1973), Prussian-born literary agent (formerly August Detlef). Educated at St John's College, Cambridge, he worked in early years as a literary editor and drama critic before founding in 1927 his literary agency which came to represent authors including Hilaire Belloc, Edmund Blunden, Alec Waugh, J. B. Priestley, Rebecca West, Terence Rattigan, A. E. Coppard, Evelyn Waugh, C. Day Lewis and Frank O'Connor. In the 1950s he worked with Norman Collins and Lew Grade in forming the Associated Television (ATV) company, which enjoyed considerable commercial success.

2–IPF had written to Peters on 12 Oct.: 'Mr Eliot would like to retain this script ['The Ape and the Ass'] for the moment, but he would be very glad if you could let him see the story called "That fellow Tolstoy!" which Mr Coppard mentioned to him. He thinks that it is likely to be more suitable for his programme than "The Ape and the Ass" which, by reason of its subject matter, is rather out of line with the *Criterion*.'

3–L. W. Payne (University of Texas at Austin) sent TSE a copy of his secondary school anthology, *Selections from Later American Writers* (Chicago), and asked of him: 'I confess

admirable for its purpose. Not having been for some time in touch with American education, I cannot of course be quite sure what the purpose is, and therefore of course cannot criticise your book like an expert. The method seems to me extremely ingenious. As for myself, I must express a slight regret that you have thought fit to select as representative of my work a rather insignificant poem like 'Cousin Nancy'. In this connection I can correct you on one point. The niece was not called 'Cousin Nancy' by her aunts; indeed in New England it is uncommon for an aunt to address a niece as 'Cousin'. My reference was to the extensive consanguinity in New England where everybody, if not nearly related, is at least a cousin of everybody else.

'Cousin Nancy' is therefore an imaginary cousin of the author of the lines; but I must add emphatically that you must understand that the lady in the verses is an entirely imaginary character and in no way a portrait of any of my female relations.

I am,
Yours very sincerely,
T. S. Eliot

## TO *E. M. W. Tillyard* CC

7 November 1927 [London]

Dear Tillyard,

I am returning to you today under separate cover Father Yealy's essay. As I said in my previous letter, there is not the slightest doubt in my mind that the essay is quite adequate for its purpose, and I recommend the author for his degree. I enclose herewith my report on it which seems to me rather inadequate, but you must remember that I am not a specialist on early American history or on Emerson. But even if none of the questions which I have suggested can be worked in to the examination paper, I think that I have indicated two possible lines along which to question the examinee. When I first wrote to you I had in mind that the questions might be so worded as to test Father Yealy's knowledge in a wider field: such as his general knowledge of Liberal German theology at the beginning of the 19th century. But I see that this is not what is wanted.

---

that I am never sure of myself in interpreting the highly condensed and ironic modern poetry, but I am eager to learn. If I have made any egregious errors in trying to elucidate your work for young readers, I shall be grateful if you would set me right.'

If my remarks are of no use to you I should like to be told so.

Yours sincerely,
[T. S. Eliot]

*Report on a Dissertation Entitled 'Emerson and the Romantic Revival'*

The author has done his work thoroughly, so thoroughly that the effect is that of bringing together a whole modern navy to sink a single Chinese junk.

His account of the origins of New England Unitarianism (an indigenous growth) is, so far as I can check it, accurate, well-informed, and fair. I think the author tends to overestimate the proportion of Calvinism among the New England colonists. After the first wave of immigration, the new colonists represented nearly every type of English Protestantism and Anglicanism, and the tendency towards democracy and individualism in Church government was largely due to the same geographical and economic causes which induced democracy in political government (see Gooch: *The Growth of English Democracy*, pp. 67 ff.). Otherwise, the author has given an excellent summary of events and persons.

I think that the author might be asked a few questions (1) concerning Emerson's study and reading and (2) concerning his influence. Emerson boasted that he never read anything in a foreign language that he could get in translation: but did he know any foreign language, and what did he get in translation, and did he in fact read anything at all? Father Yealy might, I think, fairly be asked to take any one or two of Emerson's 'Representative Men' and tell us from what sources Emerson informed himself. How did he acquaint himself with the text of Plato, and what commentaries, if any, had he read on that author? What were his sources of information about Napoleon? Such questions should bring to light the extreme poverty of Emerson's scholarship. Here is another point: how far are Emerson's real notions of 'scholarship' those of the America of his day – i.e. did not Emerson actually set up a new standard of Ignorance in America: and was not American scholarship before his time superior to American scholarship after his time? (My grandfather, a contemporary of Emerson and a Unitarian clergyman of no particular philosophic gifts, had I know read more or less of Kant, Hegel and Fichte in German before 1835). What had Emerson actually read of Berkeley, and to what extent did he understand him? What had he actually read among 'Sacred Books of the East', and in what form? To what extent did he misrepresent them? What had he read of Rousseau and of Schleiermacher, the two Romantic theologians with whom he seems to have most in common?

Another group of questions might concern his influence. Father Yealy seems to incline to the view that he had none to speak of, but I am not sure. Did he not have some influence on heretical cults and tendencies; if perhaps only in stimulating an interest, of a more or less undesirable kind, in Oriental religion and philosophy. He may have also inspired H. C. Warren, the pioneer of Pali scholarship. He at least has affinities with Walt Whitman, which Father Yealy has not brought out. In any case Emerson is himself a 'Representative Man', of a deplorable variety, representative of much modern American 'spirituality'. A more special influence would be that upon liberal theology, e.g. the Harvard Divinity School: certainly Unitarianism has been intellectually inferior since Emerson's time to what it was in the time of Channing.

An interesting, and I think a just essay on Emerson is that of J. M. Robertson in *Modern Humanists Reconsidered.*

A closer comparison with Carlyle would also be interesting.

## TO *Charles Whibley* CC

10 November 1927 [London]

My dear Whibley,

I was very glad indeed to get your letter but in spite of that temptation refrained from bothering you with a reply. I feel that I must now write you a short note, however, merely to say that my naturalisation is now completed and that I have even obtained a passport, so that I can visit my wife or my mother at any time. I am sure that it is only owing to your intervention, and at a time when you must have been extremely busy, that this has been accomplished so soon and I am very deeply grateful to you.[1]

I was only disappointed to find the oath of allegiance a very disappointing inferior ceremony. I expected to be summoned to the Home Office at least, if not before the Throne. Instead I merely had to swear an ordinary oath before an ordinary commissioner, just as one does in ordinary life.[2]

I have much to talk to you about but will wait until you are settled again at home.

Yours ever affectionately,
[T. S. Eliot]

1 – TSE became a British subject on 2 Nov.

2 – Whibley cheered TSE on 15 Nov.: 'I am delighted that you are an Englishman at last. I am proud & pleased to welcome you as a compatriot.'

## TO *Thomas Sturge Moore* TS Valerie Eliot

10 November 1927 Faber & Gwyer Ltd

Dear Mr Sturge Moore,

Although the matter has long since passed out of my hands, I am writing to express our regret at the delay in coming to a decision about your book.[1] We have now reached the point of deciding that we should very much like to publish it but are not sure that we could afford to do so without some support from America and are waiting to hear from America about the possibility of sale of sheets in that country.

Yours sincerely,
T. S. Eliot
Director.

## TO *Leonard Woolf* CC

10 November 1927 [London]

Dear Leonard,

I tried to get you on the telephone yesterday afternoon to mention this matter to you so that you might speak of it to Herbert Read; but you were out. Some time ago, Herbert Read gave me a manuscript of a translation of Machiavelli's only play, *Mandragora*, made by Eric Maclagan.[2] The original idea was that we might print the whole in the *Criterion*, but it is much too long for one number of the *Criterion* and would suffer very much by being serialized, so that I handed it over to the firm to consider making a small book. After long deliberation, the firm decided that it would be too small a book for us to do. I think that is a mistake, and in any case Maclagan, who is now at Harvard, might be induced to write a longer Introduction. I think the play very amusing. I believe this is the only translation. And it is a thing which few people can read in Italian (I cannot for one) because it is largely in dialect. If the idea interests you, I suggest that you might write to Read and ask him to instruct me to send it on to you.

Yours ever,
[T. S. Eliot]

1–*In Defence of Beauty*.

2–Eric Maclagan (1879–1951), an authority on Italian sculpture, was Director of the Victoria & Albert Museum, 1924–45. He made translations from the work of French poets including Rimbaud and Valéry, but his translation of *La Mandragola* (1518), by Niccolo Machiavelli (1469–1527) – not his only play – was not published.

## TO *Bruce Richmond* CC

10 November 1927 [London]

Dear Richmond,

I have just read the article in today's *Times* that you mention.[1] It will not conflict with my purposes in the least. And I do not think there will be any appearance of overlapping.

I think I know my Bradley pretty well and have a general idea of what I want to say, so it should not take me long to do the article.[2] Only it is just that particular book which is so inaccessible and which I have not read for a long time.

I could promise a review of the Lawrence book within ten days if you sent it to me.[3] I cannot promise it sooner because I am going to Paris on Sunday and may be there for perhaps a week. I am not sure, however, that I know a great deal about this particular topic of the playhouse, and Lawrence is rather a heavy weight; but if you want me to tackle it I will do my best.

Yours sincerely,
[T. S. E.]

P.S. I have no idea when The Moonstone is coming out. It ought to have been out long since but I am not sure if I have even had a complete set of proofs of the text.

1–BLR wrote on 9 Nov.: 'An article towards the end of tomorrow's Supplement will probably surprise you as much as it surprised me. But a man who, to my great relief, actually offered to review a book on Grammar by Sonnenschein (!) has taken French leave to drop in a volume of Jespersen. He only deals with this particular volume; so don't let it put you out of your stride for the more general article on him that you are meditating for us.' ('The Problem of Grammar' – on Otto Jespersen, *A Modern English Grammar on Historical Principles, Part III* [Heidelberg: C. Winters, 1927], and E. A. Sonnenschein, *The Soul of Grammar* [Cambridge University Press] – *TLS*, 10 Nov. 1927, 815.)

2–BLR asked TSE to review Bradley's new book soon after its appearance. See 'Bradley's "Ethical Studies"', *TLS*, 29 Dec. 1927, 981–2; repr. as 'Francis Herbert Bradley' (*FLA*).

3–'Stage Studies' – on *Pre-Restoration Stages Studies* and *The Physical Conditions of the Elzabethan Public Playhouse*, by W. J. Lawrence – *TLS*, 8 Dec. 1927, 927.

## TO *C. W. Stewart* TS Faber

11 November 1927 London

Dear Stewart,

In connection with the enclosed letter which you have seen, here are the advance proofs of the French text of Julien Benda's *Propertius* book.[1] I have read them through rather hastily. I think we ought to consider the book not merely on its own merits but in connection with the other two books by the same author, one of which I believe you have arranged for, and the other of which I am rather keen to get. It is also a question of our general business with Payson and Clark.

I enjoyed this book but am not quite certain whether it would appeal so much to a British public as the other two which are heavier in style. In any case, if Payson and Clark are going to do this, I should certainly *not* recommend going further than taking a few sheets from them. If this did not cost much it might be worth while. But we certainly could not afford to take sheets from Payson and Clark without having examined the translation itself. The book is easy reading but would not be easy translating.

If you have not time to read it yourself, perhaps you can think of someone to give it to before the next book committee.

Yours,
T. S. Eliot

## TO *Ezra Pound* TS Beinecke

[? November 1927] [London]

Cherr Ezra Episc.

I am glad to have one letter from you that I nedd not esquive but can answer directkly, glad yr last arrived in time as have been able to add new footnote to say that the Propertuis which I think impproper to British pubblic to see and which as I have observed is obbtainable from Faber & Gwyer in a vollume called *Quia Pauper Amavi* but of course we prefer you should not see this book but if you ask for it we cannot refuse it etc. Another Footnote says one Benda (anglice <Julius or Joe> Bender) has done a book on Proptertius which is less Sound, & that Mr Pound has the

1 – *Properce, ou, Les Amants de Tibur* (1928). Benda had first told TSE on 6 July 1927 that he had written on the Roman poet Propertius.

responsibility of having introjuced this jew politician to the anglosaxon pub lic.[1] I happened to read ProPerse which its publishers sent to us to consider Eng. translation: can testimony that it is usual french dung on clasical sibjects.

POS

HIS ——+—— MARK.

SUM

## TO *Allen Tate* CC

11 November 1927 [London]

Dear Mr Tate,

Yes, I have your essay on my mind and to some extent on my conscience, but as I am quite certain that I want to use it some time (as soon as I can) it is not so much on my conscience as a great many other contributions which lie before me.[2] I am afraid it will be impossible until the spring or early summer. If this seems to you outrageous, I shall have no grounds for complaint if you publish it somewhere else; only in that event I should depend upon your letting me know.

I have very little room for poetry at present and think it best to return you these with the hope that you will let me see something more in three or four months' time.

Yours sincerely,
[T. S. Eliot]

1–Benda, *Properce*. TSE, in a footnote to his edition of EP's *Selected Poems* (1928, 1964), remarked of *Homage to Sextus Propertius*: 'It is, in my opinion, a better criticism of Propertius than M. Benda's *Properce*. I observe in passing that it was Mr Pound who introduced Benda to England and America' (20). Of Propertius, TSE noted too, in *VMP*, 145: 'The young Propertius is far more mature, with a Latin maturity, far more experienced in disillusion and disgust, than the young Donne; he writes of experience that made and spoilt his life, Donne only, at most, of a passing adventure.'
2–Tate wrote (17 Oct.) to ask after the fate of his essay 'Poetry and the Absolute' that TSE had accepted in the spring of 1926. It was not published in *The Criterion*.

## TO *Mario Praz* cc

11 November 1927 [London]

My dear Praz,

Thank you very much for sending me your article on Wyndham Lewis which I have read with much interest and return herewith.[1] It is an extremely good article and there is much in it with which I am cordially in agreement; though at the same time I consider it rather unfair. I am aware that Lewis is a very difficult writer to consider quite judicially, if that is possible at all; the critic will be prejudiced either in his favour or against it. You are certainly right as against Humbert Wolfe's hurried opinions. The only thing that I really regret in your essay is that you have given so much space to *The Lion and the Fox* which, apart from many brilliant incidental observations is, I think, not only an inferior book but a by-product on which he ought not to have wasted so much time. All that you say of it would, I think, be quite fair had you reviewed this book by itself; but criticised in conjunction with his two other books, it casts a shadow on them which they do not deserve. I have felt myself that his knowledge was too rapidly assimilated and his reading excessive. But I think that it will be another five or ten years before we have enough data about him to criticise him properly. He needs a great deal of room to move about in, and he has at least this characteristic of the pamphleteer, that he has to do his thinking and preparatory work more or less in public. That is, in order to get to his conclusions he has to put many things into pen and ink and then into print which another type of person would reserve for his own conversations with himself. But if a man is like that, that is what he is: and I believe that Lewis may do something very remarkable which will justify all that he is doing now. I believe that a man who has anything to say either can say it in a hundred pages or else he needs perhaps a hundred volumes, and that the mediocrity writes always too much or too little.

I have not yet thanked you for your note on Schoell's book.[2] I am very gratified to find that you like this book as much as I do and I think we are substantially in agreement. I do *not* think, however, that Schoell's discoveries dispose of my comparison of Chapman with Dostoevski. They would only do that if they disposed of Chapman as merely a compiler, which he certainly is not; we have to remember that Chapman was

1 – Praz's article on WL was to be published in the Dutch *English Studies* in Feb. 1928.

2 – Praz had sent (14 Oct.) an offprint of his review of Schoell's book on Chapman. 'On p. 160 there is a passage which can be closely paralleled with a passage in yr lecture, p. 16. Of course when I wrote it I had not read yr lecture; otherwise I wld have quoted it.'

not merely a pirate but a great poet. I maintain that my comparison is unaffected by Schoell's discoveries.

I will keep your friend Hawley in mind for anything that may turn up which he could do.[1]

Yours ever,
[T. S. Eliot]

## TO *Orlo Williams* CC

11 November 1927 [*The Monthly Criterion*]

Dear Williams,

I see that this German Jew, Lion Feuchtwanger, is bringing out another book. Lady Rothermere has been pestering me because we never reviewed *Jew Süss*[2] about which she is very enthusiastic. I simply put it to you whether the appearance of a new book by the same person makes necessary a consideration of his work. I am always prejudiced against such people, but I have never read anything by this man.[3]

Yours in haste,
[T. S. Eliot]

1–Praz recommended an 'exceptionally promising student of mine, Frank Hawley (a Yorkshire man), who is studying Oriental languages in Paris, and now (with a scholarship) in Berlin, asks me whether I can get him some hackney work (mainly translating into English) . . . [H]e has really a genius for linguistics. He . . . could be relied upon entirely for French, German, Russian . . .'

2–*Jew Süss: A Historical Romance*, trans. Willa and Edwin Muir (London, 1926). Published in German in 1925, this historical novel by Lion Feuchtwanger (1884–1958) concerns the career of a seemingly unscrupulous Jewish businessman, Joseph Süss Oppenheimer, who secures the corrupt state of the Duke of Württemberg. Proud of his Jewishness, Oppenheimer keeps to himself the revelation that he is in fact the son of a nobleman. When the Duke betrays him by seeking to rape his daughter, whom he kills by accident, the Jew Süss successfully engineers his revenge and brings about the death of the Duke. Although he cannot be proven guilty of a crime, let alone murder, the pressure of popular anti-Semitic prejudice prevails and he is sentenced to death by hanging. Even then, however, he does not disclose his noble birthright nor renege on the Jewishness which is his secret pride. The novel went through twenty-seven printings by Apr. 1928.

3–Williams responded: 'Feuchtwanger's books don't happen to appeal to me, but they are having a great success, not only in England. To that extent I suppose his work deserves consideration. People say his reconstruction of a period with its mentality is very powerful. I hate reconstructions.

'Why not put Frederick Manning on to him? I think he might do Jew Suss, and the Ugly Duchess together rather well.' (12 Nov.)

## TO *His Mother* TS Houghton

12 November 1927 *The Monthly Criterion*

Dearest Mother:

I am so delighted to have your letter of the Friday (two weeks ago?) in your own handwriting. I am sure you must be much stronger. It is very silly of you to worry about my sending you my books etc., for if I did not have you to send them to, what should I do? That is one of the chief pleasures in doing them, that you will see them afterwards. I wish I could do more, but my life, although interesting, is full of interruptions. You do not say if you have had any letters from me, but I have written twice a week. I am going over to Paris for a few days tomorrow to see Vivien, and will write as soon as I return. It has been fearfully cold here, I hope not with you.

Your devoted son,
Tom

## TO *Olaf Stapledon*[1] CC

12 November 1927 [*The Monthly Criterion*]

Dear Mr Stapledon,

I am returning to you the 'Metaphysical Posters' after long consideration.[2] My general feeling is that you are still a little too metaphysical. I mean that if one is going to be metaphysical in poetry it seems to me that the abstractness must be compensated by a definite and even startling concreteness, which I think is what you will find in Donne; and also by a very definite and very interesting rhythm. That is the harm which so-called Imagist poetry has done. The right Imagist poetry is almost purely

1–Olaf Stapledon (1886–1950), science fiction writer and philosopher, took a degree in History at Balliol College, Oxford, and then worked for a while in his father's shipping company in Liverpool. But in 1913 he abandoned his father's business in favour of making his living by teaching for the Workers' Educational Association (WEA). After WW1 (he served as a conscientious objector in the Friends' Ambulance Unit), he earned his doctorate at Liverpool University and subsequently essayed poetry and philosophy: *A Modern Theory of Ethics* was to be published in 1929. However, fame and fortune came to him in 1931–44, when he produced a series of celebrated works of science fiction (including *Last Men in London*; *Last and First Men*; *Sirius*) and books of philosophy and cultural criticism.

2–Stapledon had submitted his essay on 28 Sept.: 'it is upon the border land between philosophy and literature that I work best.' Earlier he had posted (28 May) a 'sequence of poems in vers libre' which he called 'a unit, though its members also are units . . . All that I send herewith is the first movement of an extensive enterprise, not yet completed, in which I deal, in a medium of my own, with contemporary man's relation to his world.'

sensuous and therefore I think can dispense, as it has dispensed, with interesting rhythm; but the more abstract and thoughtful one makes one's verse, the more it stands in need of rhythm. I find your poem so interesting that I am compelled to make these comments which I hope you will not think impertinent. But I do feel that the content is valuable enough to make it worth a great deal more work.

I am retaining your essay on Europeanism and Modern Science which I find very interesting. I cannot quite make up my mind about it at the moment. I have had, as you will see, other essays covering similar ground. This is both an advantage and a disadvantage, but I think it very likely, if you will leave it in my hands, that I shall be able to use it in a few months; so I hope you will let me keep it.

Whenever you come to London I hope you will let me know.

Yours sincerely,
[T. S. Eliot]

## TO *F. S. Flint* CC

12 November 1927 [*The Monthly Criterion*]

Dear F. S.,

Would you be so kind, at your leisure, as to look over the two MSS enclosed? I have read them myself and think there is something in it; I have also shown them to Herbert who thinks there is something in it; but we cannot agree as to *what* there is in it or whether it is good enough to publish in its present form.[1] You will remember that there is so little stuff available that my standards for fiction or semi-fiction are probably lower than yours or Herbert's. Anyway, we agreed to leave the matter to you to arbitrate.

I am at present engaged on a poem about a Channel Swimmer which I will send when completed. It is called 'How we Brought the Good Sole from Dover to Calais'.

Yours in haste,
[T. S. E.]

1 – Precise details of these submissions are not known, but HR's letter (11 Nov.) reveals that one essay was by Charles Mauron, the other two by Laura Riding Gottschalk: 'Mauron, I think, is very good & I should publish it as soon as possible.

'The other things [by Riding] are surely just verbiage. In the first of them there is no real understanding of Hulme's point of view, & in any case it has nothing to do with the *Criterion*'s point of view. The article about anthologies is sound enough but too obvious. And both essays are much too long & I don't see why you or anyone else should be put to the trouble of reducing them to concision.'

## TO *Bonamy Dobrée* TS Brotherton

12 November 1927 *The Monthly Criterion*

Dear Buggamy:

I am relieved to hear from you at last, and to know that you have forgiven me my trespasses. It is also pleasing to hear that you have had nothing but Rain at Giza (by the way, is it pronounced Geezer or Gyser, and have you a nasty Cough as I have have, and are you eyeless in Giza, at the mill, with Slaves?) (and speaking of slaves, I think you are extreamly Lucky to have a Gander who can speak nothing but Arabic, it must make you feel at Home I suppose he eats slugs).

Yes Kipling[1] appears as a Christmas Gift to the Public. I was restored by your Wire; for to tell the truth I had after deep thought decided to cut out the Gloria at the end and tell you afterwards. I quite understood the sentiment myself but was not Sure that others would. Within about 3 months I want to print the Congreve,[2] which as you say is superior to the Converxation; and the latter can I presume wait.

The weather is extreamly Cold, but I am off to Paris which I dread for a few days in my heaviest Flannels with long sleaves.

You will be missed at the Xmas Frolix. The Bolovian Cult progresses, and threatens to Sweep England. There is no reason why you should Not lecture on the subject in Egypt, on the contrary. But you are Wrong about Bergsohn. I mean you have mistaken his meaning. It was what the French call a *jeu d'épices*. For Wux is essentially reversible. Did I tell you that the Male Bolovians were divided equally at Puberty into Modernists and Fundamentalists, but that the Females communicated in both Kinds? But even Ovid pointed out that the Female has the best of it. I am very busy writing a Poem about a Sole. That is, it is about a Channel Swimmer who has a Sole as a mascot; you see it is allegorical, and everything can be taken in an allegorical, analogical, anagogical, and a bolovian sense. So it is giving me much trouble. There is also a Dove that comes in, but I dont understand how

The Dove dove down an oyster Dive
As the Diver dove from Dover . . .

then the sole

1 – 'Rudyard Kipling', *MC* 6 (Dec. 1927), 499–515.
2 – 'William Congreve: A Conversation between Swift and Gay . . .', *MC* 7 (June 1928), 295–305.

was solely sole
Or solely sold as sole at Dover . . .

you get the drift of it, but it is Difficult. When he reaches the other side

'He's saved his sole whole!' Cry'd the Priest;
Whose Sole? OUR Sole! the folk replied . . .
His balls are Bald! the people Bawled . . .

This Sole, which had been Dover bred,
Was shortly cooked with chips In Greece . . .

It is very difficult to put all this together; it is called How we Brought the Dover Sole to Calais.

DONT try to pronounce Wux. I cautioned you. Else you will suffer the same fate as dear old Profer. Krapp of Koenigsberg, who died a Martyr to the cause of Bolovian Phonetics. He lived for 3 months on Beans, then on Asparagus, then on Chestnuts etc. trying to get the right accent. And then he got acute dyspepsia and colic, which spoilt his temper, so that he swallowed his front Teeth and so died in a Phrensy.

I think there is some misprision on your Part about my Truth. I would not wish to make truth a function of the will. On the contrary. I mean that if there is no fixed truth, there is no fixed object for the will to tend to. If truth is always changing, then there is nothin to do but sit down and watch the pictures. Any distinctions one makes are more or less arbitrary. I should say that it was at any rate essential for Religion that we should have the conception of an immutable object or Reality the knowledge of which shall be the final object of that will; and there can be no permanent reality if there is no permanent truth. I am of course quite ready to admit that human apprehension of truth varies changes and perhaps develops, but that is a property of human imperfection rather than of truth. You cannot conceive of truth at all, the word has no meaning, expect by conceiving of it as something permanent. And that is really assumed even by those who deny it. For you cannot even say it changes except in reference to something which does not change; the idea of change is impossible without the idea of permanence. E.& O.E., and without prejudice.

Oh I suppose the only thing to be done about W. Civilisation is to think as clearly as one can. The first thing is to understand the disease, if there is a disease. Benda is rather sound this way.

Must answer the theological and other parts of yr letter on return. I hope yr father in law is better?

Ever yrs.
T.S.

The Sole –

Although it hung about the Plaice
'Twas solely sold as Sole at Dover . . .

## TO *Richard Aldington* MS Texas

12 November 1927 *The Monthly Criterion*

My dear Richard,

Go ahead.[1] I'll swear to anything. *But* do his backers have to be U.S.A. Citizens? Because I'm a British subject. Oh – I see you are recommending too – so that's all right.

I see *Transition* but never open it.[2] I will look up Abe – it does sound like one of E.P.'s pseudonyms.[3]

I am off for 4 days, but after that will send testimony whenever you want it. Why not try Fletcher? Osbert?

Yours in haste, aff
Tom.

## TO *Lady Rothermere* CC

12 November 1927 [London]

Dear L. R.:

Now then. I am delighted to have so much correspondence from you, I should never have thought it possible. NO! there is nothing wrong with your brain – at any rate, your letters have given much pleasure!

1 – RA asked TSE on 11 Nov. if he would support Glenn Hughes, a professor of English at the University of Washington, in his quest for a Guggenheim Travelling Fellowship. Hughes was proposing to write a book on 'the Imagists and later Anglo-American poets'.

2 – *Transition*, edited in Paris from 1927 to 1938 by Eugene Jolas and Elliott Paul, carried contributions from writers including Gertrude Stein, William Carlos Williams, Rainer Maria Rilke, Max Ernst, Allen Tate, Giuseppe Ungaretti, Laura Riding and JJ ('Continuation of a Work in Progress', which was to form part of *Finnegans Wake*).

3 – 'Do you see an American periodical called "transition"? Have you observed the contribution of one Abraham Lincoln Gillespie, Jr.? Is not this our old friend E. P.?'

Let me run through your comments, taking the easiest first, before I start on my own.[1]

MURRY: I CAN'T agree with you at all! but [as] I don't know where to begin this must wait until I see you.

LEWIS: Very glad to agree. A long review of the book will appear in the Jan. number. If you find the review 'dry' don't blame me; I asked Lewis to choose his own reviewer, which he did (Thorpe). But I have not yet received the review. Lewis is now abroad somewhere, but I saw him just before he left, and we decided that we must make plans for some closer cooperation in a campaign of some kind.

GERTRUDE BELL: I gave this book to Bonamy Dobrée, who is now in Egypt, and who went through the Mesopotamian campaign. I have only just received his note, for January.

DAVID NEELS (?) I cannot trace such a book. When did it appear?

YOUR SISTER: I am finding difficult and not to be dealt with in a hurry. Incidentally, I wish she might know that I spell my name with one L, that my poem is *not Waste Lands*, and that Joyce's book is <u>Ulysses</u>, not *Odyssey*!

1–Lady Rothermere had written two letters, the first on 26 Oct.: 'Dear friend T. S. I think the Criterion is awfully "dry". That is my candid opinion & I understand it is shared by others! – (even Faber himself!! But don't say I said so! please).

'You know I still think *The Dial* is on the whole much more interesting & readable. The last number had a *most interesting* article by Bertrand Russell.

'I am much amused to hear that the *Adelphi* has been put on its legs again – *by whom?* You know I was much tempted to do that & asked you when I was last in London – if you remember – to find out what M[iddleton] M[urry] was going to do! *Yes* please send it to me also *The Enemy* – I have ordered W[yndham] L[ewis's] new book . . .

'You are a dear about my sister's book & she will be most grateful – although you may not agree with all she says!! I'm sure you will consider the book well worthwhile . . .

P.S. I told Faber I considered the printing matter badly placed on page. Not enough room between *title* and matter – .'

The second letter, dated 5 Nov. commented on the latest *Criterion*: 'I like the leading article! Don't think much of Arnold Bennett. Vulgar little man! Like *immensely* Murray's "Concerning Intelligence" & entirely agree with him . . . Lawrence is boring!

'The great thing I think is to have <u>short</u> articles. So far they have all been too long. The Rudyard K. is on the long side!

'Poor T. S.!! You *asked* for my views & here they are! I should really like to see our Criterion get a little less "grave" – serious it should be –

'I am so sorry you won't come & see me here [at Fribourg]. You would so enjoy it – (& you don't enjoy much in your life – it's rather like The Criterion – a bit dry! That's what's wrong with your work, lack of emotion in your life). Oh, dear what am I talking about – I think my illness must have upset my brain!! – Forgive me cher ami & believe me always to be your friend (& in spite of all!) admirer.'

She added on the back of her letter: 'You have had no notice of *David Neels* Travels to Mecca nor of *Gertrude Bell's Letters* (very interesting books) – .'

*NEW ADELPHI*: Don't know who has re-financed it. J.M.M. always very secretive. Most secretive person I know. Think it now emulates the *Criterion* in dryness, and not nearly so interesting as the monthly *Adel.*

*CRITERION*: Sub-heading Printing. Yes, I had already made the same observation about high spacing and am glad you mentioned it.

Sub-heading Dryness. Was much afflicted by this remark, more especially as I had worried about the fact already. Went out for a drink, came back and looked at the *Criterion*, came to no conclusion, went out again, after which it looked less dry; but it seemed dryer than ever in the morning. Candidly, I don't know quite what to do. It is damnably difficult to get short things. Many of those I have I have cut down considerably. I put Bennett in to see if he would send up the circulation. Of course the *Dial* and other American papers get the pick of things because they can pay high prices; it is awfully difficult fitting in people like Lawrence and Yeats, because the *Dial* gets everything of theirs first and I can only have them if I can fit in with the *Dial*. But frankly I don't find the *Dial* interesting except in fiction. The *Dial* never discovers anything, they merely play all the reputations which are played out in Europe. Another advantage the *Dial* has: their public is not very particular, being so far from Europe, and will take things out of books, whereas our public wants everything fresh and unpublished. For instance, we 'found' Fernandez and gave him what reputation he has in England and America, and I have never taken anything from him unless he wrote it specially for the *Criterion*; but the *Dial* was quite willing to publish as an article a section from his book which had already appeared. That is the advantage of an ignorant but eager public. I suppose the *Dial* will discover Curtius and Massis and Maritain and Scheler in time. They are only just celebrating Valéry now, and I should be a laughing stock if I did that at so late a date. I am just going to introduce Léger, whom they will say is a great poet, about a year hence.

I have another story by Liam O'Flaherty;[1] one by Carlo Linati;[2] and am looking for some good German fiction. Capek has become a bore; the last thing he sent was poor stuff.[3] Coppard is sometimes good; he just sent two stories he thinks are good, and they are rotten. There are two good men I have not got yet: Scott Fitzgerald and Hemingway.

1–O'Flaherty, 'The Letter', *MC* 7 (June 1928), 346–51. A. A. Kelly notes (*The Letters of Liam O'Flaherty* [1996], 217): '26 April . . . Eliot wrote to A. D. Peters returning "The Alien Skull", which he liked, in favour of "The Letter" which he liked even more . . .'

2–Linati, 'One of the Claque: An Improbable Story', trans. Orlo Williams, *MC* 7 (Mar. 1928), 232–46.

3–Karel Čapek, 'Helena', *MC* 5 (June 1927), 314–26.

NOW to another sort of Business. You SAID that you would be in Paris for a time from the 18th Nov. This [It] is important that I should see you. I am going there tomorrow, but must return for *Criterion* Meeting on Thursday, but must go back in any case the following week. I particularly must see you. COULD YOU send me a wire to 24 Russell Square as soon as you are sure of being in Paris on any given date? One problem is: Faber now wants to turn the *Criterion* back into a Quarterly, as he finds it very expensive to finance. Now so far as I am concerned personally, there are so many considerations both ways that they cancel out, so that it is really and truly a question to be decided entirely between you and Faber without worrying about me. On the one hand I hate to retreat from any position once taken up; and I think it would envelop the *Criterion* in an atmosphere of failure. I think that people like a monthly better; and a monthly can have a controversial tone which is impossible to a review appearing less frequently. On the other hand I could hardly continue with a monthly for more than another year without some kind of assistance or relief; it is alright most of the year, but under present conditions I can never take a real holiday, as I cannot be absent more than 3 or 4 days without arranging carefully beforehand and then having a parcel of stuff sent me daily; when I was in the country early this summer for three weeks I had about two hours work every morning. Also I want to go to Boston to see my mother etc. So I am divided, although as I say I should hate to give up the attempt so soon.

Hereunder the figures:

| | Trade Orders | Returns | Sold |
|---|---|---|---|
| May | 2553 | 1683 | 870 |
| June | 2441 | 1640 | 801 |
| July | 2274 | 1311 | 963 |
| August | 2036 | 1221 | 815 |
| September | 1332 | 254 | 1078 |
| October | 1267 | 56 | 1211 |
| November | 1204 | 6 | 1198 |

The November figures are not reliable, as they are not complete, either in sales or returns. The early orders were obviously excessive; it would appear that both orders and returns diminish; and that on the whole sales increase. These figures do not include subscriptions; they have remained fairly constant at about 200; but within the last few weeks have increased considerably, especially from America.

It is Faber's opinion that the sales have not increased, as a result of making it a monthly, in proportion to the increase of expense; he has to look at it primarily from the point of view of Faber & Gwyer, and finds that the firm under the present arrangement of half yearly settlement with The New Criterion Ltd. has to suffer by advancing the running expenses for half a year ahead, when the firm needs the cash for financing other things.

Now, if there is any hope of seeing you in Paris and talking the thing out, that would be much better than correspondence; so if I can see you in Paris, will you think this over and let us discuss it there. If you send me a wire to London, I can come over to Paris for several days (I shall come anyway) at a time to suit you, as soon as possible after the 18th.[1]

Always yours sincerely
[T. S. E.]

[*Extract*]

NEW CRITERION LIMITED

Memorandum of a Discussion at the Directors' Meeting held on Thursday, November 17th, 1927.

*Present*: Mr Faber, Mr Eliot and the Secretary. Mr Horne was prevented from attending at the last moment. Mr Stewart, a Managing Director of 'Faber & Gwyer Ltd', was also present at the discussion.

The questions under discussion were:

What further amount of capital should be called up; and

Whether *The Criterion* should be continued as a Monthly, or should revert to a Quarterly.

It was recognised that these questions could not be settled without the concurrence of Lady Rothermere and Mr Horne; and for that reason it was thought desirable to draw up the following statement for their benefit.

The change over to a Monthly took place in May 1927. The support of the newsagents for the new policy had been secured, and a very satisfactory show was made on the book-stalls. The distribution in this way of *The Monthly Criterion* for the months of May, June and July amounted to

1–Lady Rothermere responded ('Wednesday'): 'There is *only* one thing to do – you must come *here* [Domaine de Brunisberg, Fribourg en Suisse] to see me – I am probably staying until the end of the month . . . I think the *Criterion* could easily bear your expenses with me – tell Faber so – as *he* wants you to *persuade me to something* (which entre-nous I shall *never* consent to!) will probably agree! If not cher ami count on LR!

'Your position *is* difficult & we must talk it over immediately.'

some 2,500 copies an issue. The services of an expert sales canvasser were employed at the cost (after June) of Messrs Faber & Gwyer Ltd; and a considerable amount of press advertising and circularisation was undertaken. There can be no question that a very full chance was given to The Criterion to establish itself as a Monthly, provided that a sufficient public was in existence willing to buy and read the magazine if it was brought to their notice.

The results of the campaign have been extremely disappointing. In spite of the large distribution, the net sales of *The Monthly Criterion* have little exceeded those of the Quarterly *Criterion*. The net figures up-to-date are as follows:

May, 864; June, 769; July, 905; August, 766; September, 890; October, 1198; November, 1207.

A few returns of the May issue are still being sent in, and of course a large number of returns in respect of the following issues are to be expected. It may be taken that the net average sale of *The New Criterion*, including subscribers' copies, will be found to be between 700 and 800 copies a month.

The plain fact which emerges from this experiment is that *The Criterion* is a magazine for a very limited, highly educated public; and that there is no possibility whatever of its achieving a more popular success as a Monthly.

This fact has reacted strongly on the possibility of obtaining advertisements. It is impossible to secure advertisements without a more substantial circulation. The receipts for the May issue were nearly £40; for the June issue, £23; for July and August, £20; for September, £13; and for October, £9. An improvement on these later figures is expected for November and December; but the difficulty of obtaining enough advertisements to put *The Monthly Criterion* on a satisfactory financial basis is insuperable. It has been suggested that more advertisements might be secured if the canvassing was placed in the hands of an Advertisement Agency. But whereas the present canvassing commission is only 5%, no advertisement agency would take on the business at less than 25%; and it is more than doubtful if they would be able to effect any improvement.

The financial position of 'The New Criterion Ltd' may be briefly stated as follows: For the period from January 1926 to June 1927 the total net loss amounted to £2,315. 5. 7. For the period from June to December 1927 the estimated total net loss is £790. 4. 9. An accurate estimate for the latter period is difficult to make, in view of the impossibility of saying accurately what the sales are until all the returns have come in. Taking these two totals together, the total net loss up till the end of 1927 from the inception of the Company is £3,105. 10. 4.

To meet this loss the amount of capital called up when the Company was floated was £2,000. There will therefore be at the end of the year a deficiency of about £1,100. The uncalled capital amounts to £3000. There is, therefore, a balance of about £1900 to finance the magazine after 1927.

The first question to be discussed was therefore this: How long would this balance of £1,900 enable *The Criterion* to be continued after the end of the present year, first as a Monthly, and second as a Quarterly?

[The full ensuing discussion – omitted here – covered the relative financial merits of continuing the magazine as Monthly or as Quarterly. One of the factors to be borne in mind, Faber recorded, was that 'the editor's salary of £400 a year is guaranteed up to the end of 1931, by agreement between the Company and the present editor. Of this, Messrs Faber & Gwyer Ltd have made themselves responsible for £75, so that the actual amount of salary payable by the Company is £325 . . . Mr Eliot, however, said that if the magazine ceased to appear, and his work as editor therefore ceased, he would not press for the full amount due to him under the agreement, but would be content with £250 a year, which, together with his director's fees from Faber & Gwyer Ltd, would make up the guaranteed amount to £400.']

The discussion then followed the question – which of these courses was, in the opinion of those present, the most desirable; and it was realised that the final decision could not be come to without consultation with Lady Rothermere. But the alternative that seemed the most preferable was that of reverting to a Quarterly, making the December issue the last monthly issue, the next quarterly issue to be in March, and thereafter in June, September and December. This course would have the following advantages: In the first place it would definitely prolong the life of the magazine for a year; secondly it would be more convenient for the editor; thirdly it would leave open the possibility of continuing the magazine after 1929, if the present proprietors wished to do so.

It was therefore decided that the above Memorandum should be drawn up, and should be communicated by Mr Faber to Mr Horne, and that Mr Eliot should take the earliest possible opportunity of taking Lady Rothermere's views. It was also agreed that if the reversion to a Quarterly form were confirmed, a notice should be inserted in the next issue of *The Criterion*, notifying that the change would be made, and giving as the reason for doing so, the fact that many subscribers to *The Criterion* had expressed their preference for the quarterly form.

## TO *Alsina Gwyer* CC

17 November 1927 [London]

My dear Mrs Gwyer,

I have just got back this morning and find your kind letter.[1] It would have given me very great pleasure to dine with you on next Tuesday and it is most unfortunate that I have an engagement for that evening which was made three weeks ago so that I cannot very well break it. I should have been so happy to come.

I shall be in London until next Thursday when I must go away again; first for a flying business visit to Lady Rothermere in Switzerland, and then I shall naturally stop in Paris for a few days on the way home. But I do not expect that the whole journey will take me more than a week and I very much hope that I may see you on my return.

Yours very sincerely,
[T. S. Eliot]

P.S. I have been with my wife in Paris and am glad to say that she is very much better. And I do find these little voyages beneficial.

## TO *John Gould Fletcher* CC

18 November 1927 [London]

My dear Fletcher,

If you are in town I wonder if you could spare a moment to write me a line to say whether you know anything about an American poet named Robinson Jeffers and whether you like his work. We have the chance of publishing a book of his and I have not had the time to read it; apart from the fact that I am extremely diffident about my own opinions. But I know that I have heard his name favourably mentioned.[2]

At present I am rather unsettled. I have just got back from a short visit to Paris and have got to go away again in a few days for a rapid visit on business to Switzerland. I shall try to get hold of you about the end of the week after next.

Yours ever,
[T. S. Eliot]

1–Mrs Gwyer invited TSE (16 Nov.) to dinner on 22 Nov., in company with the Fabers and Dr & Mrs A. S. Hunt from Oxford.

2–Robinson Jeffers (1887–1962), American poet. Works include *The Women at Point Sur* (1927), *Cawdor and Other Poems* (1928) and *Dear Judas and Other Poems* (1929).

## TO *F. L. Lucas* CC

18 November 1927 [London]

Dear Lucas,

I am sorry to have troubled you with a rumour. I was dining with the Woolfs a few days ago,[1] before I left for Paris, and I understood from them, as I had already understood from Richmond, that your Webster had not yet appeared. Now it happened that I had that same day seen a catalogue of an Edinburgh bookseller named Thin in which your Webster was advertised; and as Richmond had promised it to me to review for the *Times* I expressed surprise at it being offered already for sale in a second hand bookseller's catalogue. I was in error, however, in supposing that it was offered at two guineas. I find that it was actually advertised at £3. 12. 0. which as you tell me is the published price. Therefore the only surprising thing is that a second hand bookseller should be able to offer it before it is published.

As Richmond has asked me to review it for the *Times*, I thought for the moment that he must have forgotten and sent it to someone else. I am relieved to find that it has not yet appeared. This leaves the question open why booksellers in Edinburgh should offer, apparently for immediate delivery, books that have not yet come out. If I do get the book for *The Times*, I shall not feel justified in reviewing it myself for the *Criterion*. Can you suggest a good reviewer? If you have anyone in mind I will take your advice; otherwise I think I will send the book for review in the *Criterion* to my friend Mario Praz in Liverpool.[2]

Yours very sincerely,
[T. S. Eliot]

1–TSE attended a party thrown by Clive Bell on 20 Oct.; the other guests were Harold Nicolson and LW and VW – who noted on 22 Oct.: 'Tom, of course, in white waistcoat, much the man of the world; which sets the key & off they go telling stories about "Jean" (Cocteau) about Ada Leverson, Gosse, Valéry, &c. & L. & I feel a little Bloomsburyish perhaps; no, I think this sort of talk is hardly up to the scratch' (*Diary* III, 163).

2–Lucas replied on 19 Nov. that he would look into 'the goings-on of Mr. Thin.' In the event, Chatto & Windus was obliged to TSE for bringing the matter to their attention. Praz, he reported, had undertaken to review *Webster* for the Dutch periodical *English Studies*; but he thought George Rylands might be a suitable reviewer of his edition for *MC*: 'a critic who knows enough of the period without being a pedant'. In a later, undated note, Lucas suggested 'Saintsbury; or Professor Gordon at Oxford'.

## TO *F. S. Flint* CC

18 November 1927 [London]

Dear Frank,

Herewith proof of a review which I have written of Ezra's latest collection. This is to appear both in the *Dial* and in the *Criterion* so I want to have it fairly right; and I am never very happy in anything that I say about Ezra. I should be very grateful if you would glance over it merely from the point of view of considering whether I have said anything better not said in Ezra's or the general interest.[1]

Yours ever,
[T. S. E.]

## TO *Alsina Gwyer* CC

18 November 1927 [London]

My dear Mrs Gwyer,

I am indeed very very sorry. The facts are as follows: next Thursday I must dash over to Switzerland on behalf of the *Criterion* to see Lady Rothermere, and I do not know just when I shall be back. Meanwhile I am not quite sure about next Wednesday. I have agreed to lunch with Charles Whibley but was not certain from his letter whether he meant Wednesday or Thursday. I think he meant Wednesday; if not, I should like very much to lunch with you. Perhaps you will allow me to ring you up as soon as I hear from him again. Owing to my recent absence and to my next departure, I have had to crowd things up. I have a lunch engagement for tomorrow and for Monday and Tuesday; a dinner engagement for

1–Flint (19 Nov.) considered TSE's essay on EP a poor effort. TSE claimed 'certain excellencies' for EP 'in much the same way as he does himself, and that, notoriously, is a bad way, and, in fact, with him, is a somewhat childish way'. Flint thought that 'no harm will be done by publication in the *Dial*. But, in the *Criterion*, the review, *even if every claim made in it were a true claim*, will be taken as evidence of crankiness . . . The finest ear for verse since Milton? There is only good verse and bad verse? . . . You have evaded . . . Ezra's real personality – in fact, just as you have, once more, set up the Ezra myth . . . Restless? Fidgety is truer. Ezra has the itch and the reddish nostrils of a pregnant woman. He is always big with other men's fecundations, and always crying for apricots. His influence is like his erudition – patchy. And he reconciles none of his interests: they ferment in him . . . I should define Ezra as a poet with a fine ear and eye and no brains. Hence his skimming of the cultures and the poetries, and his feverish acceptance of *any* new thing, however outrageous it may be. Fundamentally, he is uncritical; but he cannot always deceive that ear and eye. Hence the fine things he has done. Hence the rubbish.'

Tuesday and Wednesday. So if there isn't any time when we could meet between now and next Thursday I hope I may see you as soon as I return.

With many thanks,

Yours very sincerely,
[T. S. Eliot]

P.S. Please excuse my frequently typing my correspondence as I am somewhat bothered by a kind of writer's cramp.

## TO *R. Gordon George* cc

18 November 1927 [London]

Dear Gordon George,

I was very glad indeed to get your letter of the 11th November which gave me both pain and pleasure.[1] Pleasure indeed to hear from you and pain that I should not have made my editorial motives quite clear. I entirely agree with everything that you say about your essays and I value

1 – George (Sencourt) had replied to TSE's letter of 7 Nov.: 'It is a blow to get back at once three essays taken by you a year ago, and I cannot pretend to feel no chagrin at your giving me no opportunity to say a word about applying Thomistic standards to literary and artistic criticism. If I had not been so busy since I came back here [Hyères] . . . you would already have had my "Reason and the Arts" which is the first step in that direction in the *Supplement*. And I think I can say that no one now writing in England, even yourself, has given more attention than I to the idea of so founding criticism on firm intellectual ground, the firm ground of metaphysical truth, as opposed to leaving it in the air like the last generation of critics, and still more to this cheap nonsense, which is Middleton Murry's speciality, and which you have been devoting yourself to exposing.

'I have given all the weight I can to what you wrote about Maurras. It must have been a blow to you to read what I wrote, and any friend must have felt as you felt: only a friend, and one with your fine sincerity, would have taken the trouble to write to both Lord H. and me, and with the care you have done. I am always particularly grateful for anyone who writes to criticize an article of mine before it is published. But looking carefully into each point you mention, I feel convinced that the difference between my statements and your judgements is a difference of point of view. No immorality to my mind is so insidious as political immorality, and to write with great literary skill and attractiveness to urge that the supreme authorities of the Church are wrong in putting peace and forgiveness about militant patriotism is so dangerous as to be immoral. That article was written with more vigour than I realised at the time: on re-reading it, however, I feel that the force of my life is behind it. That within the Holy Roman Church there should be so many opposed to that universal unity by which the Church shows her Divine nature among peoples, nations, and languages demands surely from a Catholic the strongest possible assertion of her duty and prerogatives. My article is an attack upon the spirit of sectarianism and nationalism by which certain Catholics nullify the faith they profess. If later you would allow me to send you other things I have written in this sense, I think you would see just where it fits in. But do let me hear as soon as you can if there is to be any hope of seeing you. You can be quite sure of your letters reaching me, and surer still that they will be appreciated.'

them very highly. And if you do not publish them elsewhere, I hope that you will let me have one or all of them again in another six months. I thought, however, as I could not see my way to publishing any of them within that period that it was only fair to let you have them back so that they might appear elsewhere.

Of course, I have as an editor to consider not only what I want to impress upon the public but also the size of dose which the public can take. I have felt that I have already been a little imprudent; that is to say that the reviewers have already associated the *Criterion* so openly with Scholasticism that, at the moment, anything further in the same direction would only arouse that attitude of animosity among our readers which is known by the name of Protestantism and connected with the influence of the present Dean of St Pauls. And if a review like mine is to be of any use at all it must avoid being pigeon holed.

I appreciate very much your clemency and tolerance in the matter of the 'Action Française'. It is quite true that we approach the question from very different points of view, but that fact only makes, I think, our communications the more valuable and important. For after all, it is the same central problem that occupies both of us, and there are none too many intelligent people today who have grasped this problem. We must endeavour, I feel, to arrive at an understanding.

As I have already said, I am afraid that there is scant hope of my getting to the Riviera this winter. Next week I shall have to go to Switzerland for a few days, then to Paris, and on my return I shall have to pay a visit to Dublin. And later on I must go to Boston. But if we can keep in communication by letter, that is something, and I shall write to you again before long whether I hear from you or not.

Yours ever sincerely,
[T. S. Eliot]

## TO *Mario Praz* CC

18 November 1927 [London]

My dear Praz,

Thank you for your letter.[1] I would agree and would go even farther and say that you are more fair to Lewis than he is to the authors whom

1–Praz protested on 14 Nov., apropos TSE's comments (letter of 11 Nov.) on his essay on Wyndham Lewis: 'I have not certainly been more unfair to Lewis than he is to practically all the authors he is discussing. What I really wanted to expose was his method: his presumption

he discusses. I would only add that there is a very subtle difference, at any rate for the intelligent reader. One feels immediately that Lewis is not fair and one does not expect him to be fair, and indeed one would hardly wish him to be fair because if he were more fair he would be less Lewis. Therefore his unfairness does not seem to matter. But you, on the other hand, *are* fair and are unprejudiced and are obviously not airing any violent opinions of your own; therefore the effect, on myself at least, is rather more unfair to Lewis than the effect of Lewis is unfair to anyone else. Have I made myself clear? As for Humbert Wolfe, his opinions on such a matter are of course totally negligible.

As for Chapman, I only meant that what strikes me as puzzling in Bussey d'Ambois remains the same for me in spite of Schoell.[1]

Schoell explains for me a great many of the gnomic and sententious passages of Chapman in his plays as well as in his other verse; but he does not explain for me the plan of the Bussey d'Ambois plays with their surprising changes of attitude which I do not think can be explained by borrowings. After all, Chapman was a great poet as well as a great plagiarist.

Ever yours,
[T. S. E.]

P.S. At the moment I am not at all sure that I shall be able to use Montale before February or March. I hope that he will not mind. In any case I have noted that proofs are to be sent to you.

## TO *Rev. Geoffrey W. S. Curtis* CC

18 November 1927 [*The Monthly Criterion*]

Dear Mr Curtis,

I hope very much that you *will* let me know when you come to town so that we may meet; particularly as I do not in the least understand your letter. I am quite at a loss to understand why you should call me an Agnostic; as for the word 'uncreaturely', it seems to have a meaning to

---

in making cocksure judgements on everything. I think he ought to be warned against this, in his own interest, and certainly the best way to warn him is not the facile flattery of H. Wolfe . . . But Lewis is indiscriminate, like a cataclysm . . .'

1–Praz wrote: 'As for my remarks on Chapman and Dostoevski, I did not imply more than you do when on p. 16 of your lecture [you] say: ["]Schoell . . . suggests that the 'profundity' and 'obscurity' of Chapman's dark thinking are largely due to his lifting etc. and incorporating them in his poems largely out of their context."'

you which I cannot yet penetrate.[1] Anyway, I assure you that I am much more interested in Christianity than I am in Thomism and that I hope to see you in London.

Yours sincerely,
[T. S. Eliot]

## TO *I. A. Richards*

TS Magdalene

20 Nov[ember] 1927 *The Monthly Criterion*

Dear Richards,

I am sorry I did not get back till Thursday, and so could not answer your letter in time. (I must go away again on Thursday next, and so am rather rushed). But, if still of any use –

I am sorry that you gave me the advantage of identifying the quotations.[2] Still, I am surprised at the students' opinions. Of VI I should have said:

1 – Curtis noted (15 Nov.) that TSE's letter rejecting the verses he had submitted arrived on All Saints' Day. 'Your own agnostic, uncreaturely Catholicism has not yet won for you the childlike genius that would enable you to apprehend in such a coincidence the kindly play of the free, patterned, living harmony which pervades all our "multi-levelled" existence. (Sad that a catholic must be verbose! But the fourth dimension mocks at language!) . . . I am one who claims to have discovered or rather developed an orthodoxy that can be believed, and I am in its grip. But the gift comes only to the "creaturely".'

2 – IAR delivered his series of lectures on 'Practical Criticism' for the first time in the Michaelmas Term (Oct.–Nov.) of 1925, when the Examination Hall was packed with 120 students from English and other disciplines. Those in attendance included Mansfield Forbes, E. M. W. Tillyard, H. S. (Stanley) Bennett, Joan Bennett and F. R. Leavis. It is widely maintained that TSE came to at least one lecture, and handed in a 'protocol' (from the German *protokoll*: record, transcript of proceedings) on one or more of the unattributed poems that IAR handed out – the point of the exercise being to generate independent and discriminating readings. This letter by TSE may go to prove that TSE did not attend any of IAR's lectures, but it remains possible that he had gone to one or more of the lectures IAR had given in Mar. 1926 – when TSE himself was delivering his Clark Lectures. After taking an extended leave (Mar. 1926–Sept. 1927), Richards gave the course again in Oct.–Nov. 1927, when a remarkable generation of students – they included William Empson, Muriel Bradbrook, E. E. Phare, Jacob Bronowski, Humphrey Jennings, Hugh Sykes and Alistair Cooke – all flocked to have their efforts flayed by the Welsh prophet. John Constable reports that IAR recorded in 1971 that the contributors included writers and scholars from 'T. S. Eliot down' but added that 'no one will ever know who wrote which'. Constable notes too that Elsie Duncan-Jones in her annotated copy of *Practical Criticism* attributed protocol 13: 46 to TSE, and comments: 'The attribution of 13.46 to T. S. Eliot appears to me uncertain on the grounds of content, though as is evident from Eliot's letter . . . he did contribute comments. Joan Bennett . . . has reported that Eliot certainly sent a protocol, presumably the latter, and that "I. A. R. told some of us that he and Eliot differed in their evaluation", but whether the piece was used in Practical Criticism is not known' (*Practical Criticism*, ed. John Constable [2001], xxix–xxx).

'First rate 18th century work, solid, well-written'. Of VII: 'Rubbish. *Sweet communion* definitely bad, also *silver rain*. Late 19th century or more likely still worse 20th century piece'.[1] VIII is of course Whitman at his best.

I don't know the tomb he is talking about. Those that I remember in Cambridge Mass. are I am afraid only those in Mt. Auburn cemetary, which are as hideous as any in the world.[2]

I seem to have put this in a rather dogmatic way: let us add Without Prejudice or Responsibility and E. & O. E.[3]

Yours ever
T. S. E.

## TO *His Mother* — TS Houghton

21 November 1927 — *The Monthly Criterion*

My dearest mother:

I am delighted to have such good news of you, and I am looking forward eagerly to seeing you early in the new year. I am as always very busy. I went to Paris last week, as I told you, for a few days. I saw a few of my friends there, with whom I had some interesting talk about French

1–Two of the three poems mentioned by TSE did not make it into *Practical Criticism* (1929). In his second set of lectures, IAR made use of just eight poems, but only five of them are known: they were by Alfred Noyes, G. H. Luce, Thomas Hardy, Wilfred Rowland Childe and Henry Wadsworth Longfellow. 'Of the other three there is only very scant evidence in the surviving Richards papers,' says Constable – and most of what is known comes from this letter by TSE. 'Attempts to trace a work containing both "silver rain" and "sweet communion", both of which are common terms in isolation, have failed. Of the Whitman no trace survives beyond this remark, and a very brief annotation, almost certainly dating from 1927, mentioning Whitman in the "Practical Criticism" lecture notes.' Constable remarks further: 'Richards seems to have used this letter from Eliot in a lecture on the 1st of December', as Dorothy Richards noted down in her diary that same day: '[The students] seemed mystified by T. S. Eliot's support of the Longfellow.' (*Practical Criticism*, ed. Constable, xxii–xxiv.)

2–In fact, the poem was not by Whitman: it is Longfellow's 'In a Country Churchyard'. Elsie Duncan-Jones was to recall in a memoir, 'From Devon to Cambridge, 1926: or, Mentioned with Derision': 'I usually saw that the bad poems were bad, but not always that the good were good. Longfellow's "In a Village Churchyard", for instance – the best account of that poem, baffling if one didn't know that the churchyard was in America, since the lady in the poem was buried with her slaves, I think is from the pen of T. S. Eliot, but I don't know how I know' (*Cambridge Review*, 103: 2267 [26 Feb. 1982], 147).

3–TSE wrote about *Practical Critcism* in three places: (i) 'Poetry and Propaganda', *Bookman*, 70: 6 (Feb. 1930), 595–602; (ii) 'Note to Chapter II', *Dante* (1929), 57–60; repr. in *SE* (1932, 1934, 1951); (iii) 'The Modern Mind', *TUPUC* (1933), 121–42.

and international politics, and I saw Vivien of course each day. She is very much stronger, but I doubt whether they will think that she ought to come back to London before the spring. She sent her fond love, and asked me to explain that she is not yet supposed to write letters; she writes to me twice a week, and once a week to her mother, but it is very tiring for her to write, and they do not like her to write much.

Now I have been very rushed since my return, particularly as I have to rush off to Switzerland on Thursday for three days to see Lady Rothermere on business. She lives in Switzerland most of the time now, as she has a great deal of trouble with her ears, and she has found a doctor there whom she believes in. Of course I am going at her expense. I shall stop in Paris on my way home, and see Vivien again for a few days. I shall be away about a week.

It is difficult to avoid social engagements, and keep to work. I have written nothing for *The Times* lately, and I have about four books on hand from there to deal with; to say nothing of *The Nation*, and that essay I have promised to write about Dryden for a book. I have my own two or three books to get into order for publication, and something always interferes. I have not been dining out very much, but one cannot avoid it altogether. Yesterday I had to go to lunch with Mrs Gwyer (one of the proprietors of Faber and Gwyer); tomorrow with Faber; all this is part of my business; and I had to dine with someone named the Hon. Mrs Wentworth Chetwynde, who is really an American woman from Virginia whose name was Randolph.

Everything goes on at home, except that my poor old Janes has met with an accident. One evening when I was in Paris he came in the evening as usual, tripped over the cat on the stairs, and fell down the kitchen stairs and through the backyard door window. Apparently he lay there for about half an hour bleeding before he came to. So he had to have several stitches taken in his head and is in bed, and lost no end of blood. I go round to see him every night, and I have arranged to pay his doctor's bill; but it is very worrying to have an accident like that happen to a servant on one's own premises.

I will try to drop you a line before I leave, and will write again as soon as I get back. And I always long for more news, either from you or about you.

Your very devoted son,
Tom.

## TO *The Editor of* The Church Times CC

21 November 1927[1] [London]

Sir,

I was glad to see, in your issue of the 18th November, an editorial paragraph on the subject of the *Action Française*.[2] This affair, of the greatest moment to all French Catholics, has been ignored by English newspapers, and I am glad to see that you have not overlooked its importance.

I have followed the affairs of the *Action Française* for some years, and I hope that you will allow me to make a few comments on your excellent article. I should not venture to speak to English Romanists on this subject, as their point of view is already decided for them. But I have found, amongst Anglo-Catholics, a tendency to assume that this was a simple case, in which the Vatican was quite right in reproving an immoral doctrine. But it is by no means a simple case. I have, as recently as last week, discussed the affair with Romanist friends in Paris; and they admit that the affair is not only so complicated as to pass the comprehension of foreigners, but complicated enough to baffle the understanding of Frenchmen. It is, in short, a matter in which no foreigner can come to an opinion unless he has a considerable knowledge of the social, political and religious history of France since the French Revolution to the present day.

I do not wish, in this letter, to enter into these matters thoroughly; and it could not be done in the space of a letter. I wish only, first, to caution your readers against a hasty and summary conclusion; and second, to protest against your intimation that the doctrines of Daudet and Maurras have had a bad influence. I speak as one who cordially regrets the religious views of Charles Maurras, but who is at the same time proud of having his acquaintance and friendship. No one can understand Maurras who does

1–Published in the issue of 25 Nov.

2–*The Church Times* adjudged ('Summary', 18 Nov. 1927, 579): 'The intelligence that Rome, through the French hierarchy, proposes to inflict certain further penalties, extending even to excommunication, on the readers and supporters of the *Action Française* is of interest outside the Roman communion . . . We hold the Nationalist philosophy of M. Maurras to be uncatholic, and, in great measure, anti-Christian; and we consider that the Pope would have failed in his duty had he not warned the faithful against its teaching and tendencies. On the other hand, we confess that the attempt to inflict ecclesiastical penalties on the readers of a daily newspaper, perhaps no more anti-Christian than many other French newspapers, appears very unwise . . . The denunciation of the *Action Française* was right. We understand and sympathize with the proper fear of the influence of Mr. Maurras and M. Daudet on French Catholic youth, but we doubt whether the evil will be destroyed by the threatened excommunication.'

not understand the anti-clerical age, in France, in which he was educated. He belongs to what I should call a 'sacrificed generation': a generation brought up in the shadow of Renan. He belongs to a generation for which religious belief never came into consideration. Almost alone of that generation, Maurras perceived the defects of that mentality; and without religious belief himself, and without the support of any constituted authority, took upon himself to aim at the recovery of that social order without which the Catholic Church cannot flourish. It is owing to the fact that he came to the same conclusion by different processes, that he has attracted so many devout catholics to his cause.

Other men of the same intellectual generation – men, as I think, of partially pernicious influence, such as Anatole France[1] and Maurice Barrès[2] – have been accepted and (in the French political sense) canonised; Maurras, whose teaching is far more moral, more austere, than that of either of these – ~~less~~ not corrupt ~~than~~ like France, less nationalistic than Barrès – has been denied the Academy, and even any decoration.

I am moreover more than sceptical, when anyone suggests that Maurras has inclined a single young man to religious doubt. He has had, certainly, great influence on men in France, from men of my own age down to youths of eighteen or twenty at the present time. But my strong impression is, that the youth of the present day accepts the positive, rather than the negative side of his teaching; and that those young men who regard him as their master are fortified, rather than weakened in their religious faith, by what they take from him. A generation which, like the present generation, has utterly repudiated Anatole France, could hardly fail to be uncritical in its attitude towards Maurras.

I have, in this letter, deliberately omitted consideration of the Vatican policy, which is another, and a very complicated and obscure question. But many people must wonder why the condemnation occurred just at the moment when it did, and took just the form that it took.

I am, Sir,
Your obliged obedient servant,
[T. S. Eliot]

1–Anatole France (1844–1924), French novelist, journalist, poet; author of *Les Opinions de Jerôme Coignard* (1893) and *La Révolte des Anges* (1914). Nobel Laureate, 1921. In 1922 his corpus had been placed on the Roman Catholic *Index Librorum Prohibitorum*.
2–Maurice Barrès (1862–1923), novelist, journalist and politician, who declared for nationalism and anti-Semitism. In the 1890s he was a vocal Anti-Dreyfusard.

## *The Master, University College Oxford*[1] CC

22 November 1927 [London]

Dear Master,

I must apologise for not having answered your letter immediately.[2] I have been abroad.

I appreciate very highly the compliment which you pay me and it would give me great pleasure indeed to come and meet your Undergraduate Society. I should like very much to accept in principle, but I hesitate at present to accept as I cannot be quite sure of any fixed date. I have lately been obliged, and shall be obliged for some time to come, to go abroad now and then at short notice, and it is possible that I may have to pay a short visit to America during next Hilary term. In the circumstances, therefore, I am obliged with great regret to decline; but I shall probably be more certain of my movements and able to make definite engagements early in the new year.

With many thanks,

I am,
Yours very truly,
[T. S. Eliot]

## TO *F. S. Flint* CC

22 November 1927 [*The Monthly Criterion*]

Dear Frank,

I wrote to Benda as soon as I had read the first section of the *Trahison des Clercs* and secured an option from him as soon as the book was ready.[3] I am very keen about it. It is possible that we may be taking it in association with an American firm who are already doing *Belphégor*,[4] and I believe his *Propertius*; but if so, I shall do my best to see that the translation is made in this country and, if you will do it, by yourself.

Yours ever,
[T. S. E.]

1 – Sir Michael Sadler (1861–1943), Master of University College, Oxford, 1923–34.
2 – M. E. Sadler had written on 12 Nov. to invite TSE to dine with the 'Martlets', a long-established and active literary society in the college – 'the cleverest undergraduates of the time . . . and a few dons who are honorary members'. (He was to write again on 22 Nov.)
3 – Flint recommended F&G to publish Benda's *La Trahison des clercs*. 'It has a a clear central idea, clearly expounded and well illustrated . . .'
4 – *Belphégor: essai sur l'esthétique de la présente société française* (1918).

## TO *Herbert Read* CC

22 November 1927 [*The Monthly Criterion*]

Dear Herbert,

I shall be very grateful if you will read and perpend[1] the two enclosures and let me have your unvarnished opinion. Frank speaks with great conviction and I hesitate to ignore his opinion. Meanwhile, I have withdrawn this review from the January number, and it is not a vital matter to me that it should appear at all. The question is, is there anybody else who would and could review Ezra's book with less bias than myself?

Yours ever,
[T. S. E.]

## TO *James Smith* CC

22 November 1927 [London]

Dear Smith,

I am glad that you will do Worringer. As I believe I told you, I suspect that it is a book which will be overlooked or misunderstood by ordinary reviewers and I am all the more anxious to have it done.

The Pepys article is not dull but it suffers from the contagion of dullness which invariably affects every dissertation that I have ever seen which has been produced for such a purpose.[2] It need not cause you any anxiety about your own style because your Bosanquet review was anything but dull. All you need is practice in writing other things besides dissertations. They always have a temporary bad effect on one.

Yours ever,
[T. S. Eliot]

1–Assess or consider (archaic); from classical Latin *perpendere*: to weigh carefully. A favourite term with HR.

2–'I am afraid my Pepys article seemed to you deadly dull,' Smith ventured (25 Nov.). 'If the task is not too gross, will you tell me what I must henceforward avoid if I am to write magazine articles? I must write with greater ease, I suppose, and at greater length.'

## TO *Kenneth Pickthorn* CC

22 November 1927 [London]

Dear Pickthorn,

Very many thanks for your review.[1] I am afraid that you took more trouble over the book than it is worth. Anyway, I like the review and have sent it to the printers. Possibly you would not mind its being moderated slightly, merely by omitting one or two paragraphs at the end; but we will take that up later. I am afraid that the Guedalla book[2] is not worth your attention. But if you cared to dispose of it in one short and acid paragraph, I should be glad of that. Or you could turn it over to Smyth.

I hope the whiskey arrived eventually, as they assured me that it had been sent.

Yours ever,
[T. S. Eliot]

<Your note [on] the book since received.>

## TO *Sylvia Beach* TS Princeton

22 November 1927 *The Monthly Criterion*

Dear Miss Beach,

Thank you very much for your letter. I am very sorry indeed to hear of the death of your mother, and in the circumstances you need not have bothered to write to me at all.[3]

I shall be delighted if you and Mr Joyce can make any use of my Roth correspondence.[4] Have you seen an article of about two columns which appeared in the *New York Evening Post* at the time? I believe that I told you that I had returned Roth's cheque, or rather that I had sent it to the

1–Pickhorn wrote on 15 Nov.: 'I'm afraid this won't give very much pleasure to Burdett: suppress it if you like: I hate writing anything I'm not getting money for, but I could bear it once. As to Guedalla's latest performance, I gather that it's a collection of essays about his American experiences: I doubt my qualifications for dealing with such a work, but will try if you like!'

2–*Collected Essays* (1927), by the historian Philip Guedalla (1889–1944).

3–Eleanor Beach (1864–1927) had committed suicide.

4–Beach had written (19 Nov.): 'Samuel Roth's treatment of you was horrifying and Mr Joyce and I were very glad you took up the matter. As you gave me permission to use the letters in the campaign against Samuel Roth, they have been handed to Mr Joyce's lawyers to be used in the case which is to come up this winter in New York.'

*Evening Post* asking them to return it to him. Since then I have heard nothing more of the matter.

With many thanks,

Sincerely yours,
T. S. Eliot

## TO *Olivia Shakespear* CC

22 November 1927 [London]

Dear Mrs Shakespear,

Alas! I am sorrier than ever.[1] The fact is that I am leaving London again on Thursday afternoon, this time to see Lady Rothermere on business in Switzerland and for other business in Paris on my way back. I shall be away, I suppose, about a week, but I cannot tell to the day. May I be permitted to drop you a line as soon as I return, in the hope that you will open another date for me?

Yours sincerely
[T. S. Eliot]

P.S. Is the full name of the infant Omar K. Pound?[2]

## TO *Clive Bell* CC

22 November 1927 [London]

Dear Clive,

I am very much tempted to accept your invitation for dinner on Friday, December 2nd but having turned the matter over repeatedly in my mind I am bidden by my conscience to decline on the ground that I cannot be quite sure of arriving. I have got to go on Thursday next to Switzerland and then to Paris, on business, and although I expect to be back the following Thursday or Friday I cannot be quite certain. If I decline your invitation, therefore, you will understand that it is merely an attempt at scrupulous behaviour toward the most charming of hosts.

Yours sincerely
[T. S. E.]

1 – She had invited him (21 Nov.) to dinner on 29 or 30 Nov.

2 – In response to TSE's mistake in his previous letter to her, she explained: 'Ezra's father is Homer, & his son is Omar – it will cause a fine confusion when the two meet.'

## TO *Owen Barfield* TS Barfield

23 November 1927 *The Monthly Criterion*

Dear Mr Barfield,

I have been extremely busy for some time past and have been, and still am, obliged to be away from London a good deal. Hence my delay in acknowledging your Ms.[1] Even now I have not had the time to read it through carefully, but I think that I ought to return it to you as it is obviously an impossible length for the *Criterion* and poetry cannot be serialised. I wish that I had the time to criticise it in detail, although as a matter of fact you have not asked for criticism. I congratulate you on the poem, however, and would only make two suggestions. One, that I believe that the only way to publish it is to publish it by itself as a small book, and for this purpose I might recommend the Hogarth Press. Two, I think that you would be well advised to change the title. Unfortunately Mr Yeats has not only written a short poem of the same name which was published in the *Criterion*, but has called his latest book of poems by the same title. A change of title would be particularly urgent if you succeeded in publishing the poem as a small book by itself.

Sincerely yours,
T. S. Eliot

## TO *Orlo Williams* CC

23 November 1927 [*The New Criterion*]

Dear Williams,

Thank you for the proofs received. I am sorry to hear of the accident to your mother-in-law which must obviously have given great anxiety.[2] I hope that she will improve very rapidly.

Yes, I should very much like to have both the Italian Periodicals and the review of Forster by the 15th December. That is to say I should like to have the Italian Periodicals in any case; but if you are at all pressed for time, the review can easily wait several weeks longer as I shall have enough review material. I think that the review of Forster might be anything up to 1500 words according to your opinion of what the book deserves. As for the Foreign Periodicals, that depends so much on what the reviewer has

1 – A long poem (1,500 lines) in blank verse, entitled 'The Tower'.
2 – Williams's mother-in-law, who was over 80, had broken her hip in a fall.

in hand and what he finds interesting that I like to allow a good deal of latitude in space. On the other hand, that is a particular reason for having the Foreign Periodicals early; so that the rest of the paper can be fitted in. I should say roughly that three or four pages (i.e. the equivalent of three or four of our small-type pages) was about right. Read usually needs six pages for his American Periodicals because they are so numerous and so vast; Cournos is apt to take six pages because he is long-winded. But I should imagine that three or four pages would be all that you need.

I have to go abroad tomorrow on business for a week but I should like very much to see you early week after next if I can.

Yours ever,
[T. S. Eliot]

## FROM *Henry Eliot* TS Valerie Eliot

26 November 1927 2620 Lakeview Avenue, Chicago

Dear Tom,

I am afraid that the news is out.[1] I have revealed nothing, even to Theresa, and I will not send the news on to Cambridge. However, I do not anticipate any great shock to them.

They do not subscribe to 'Time'.[2] I subscribed to it for a year to help out a poor clergyman, but it irritated me by its style, its facetiousness and its triviality. It has a circulation of perhaps 200,000, and many people seem to like it immensely.

I should like you to have sent to me a copy of the September and of the October Criterion. In some way they got thrown out by the maid with other magazines. I had started some articles which I wanted to finish. I enclose $2.00, which I think the American Express (or any bank) will exchange for you.[3]

I am expecting to go on to Cambridge about December 16, and hope you are coming some time between then and the first of the year.

1 – TSE wrote on this letter: '(Re Nationality)'.

2 – *Time* magazine reported in its issue of 28 Nov.: 'Last week a sleek, brilliant citizen of the U.S. became a subject of His Britannic Majesty King George V. He is Thomas Stearns Eliot, relative of the late Charles William Eliot, President Emeritus of Harvard University . . . His many adverse critics, in no wise surprised by his change of nationality, hint that a certain superciliousness toward U.S. letters caused him to feel more at home in England, where neo-literary figures abound profuse as the autumnal leaves' (14).

3 – See TSE's letter to IPF of 20 Dec.

Mother apparently continues to improve greatly, gaining weight and energy, though her letters show that she misses her former activities.

Affectionately,
Henry

## TO *Mary Hutchinson* TS Texas

2 December 1927 *The Criterion*

Dear Mary,

You will let me know at what time to be at your house for high tea? <Thursday, the 9th.> I suppose I had better dress (it seems less unnatural at this time of year to dress in the middle of the afternoon) because we shall be famished with exhaustion I expect by the end of the performance, and will want supper. Unless you have more recent information, we will not attempt to find anything else but the Savoy.

Affectionately
Tom

The stalls are rather nearer the front than I really like.

## TO *Wyndham Lewis* TS Cornell

3 December 1927 *The Monthly Criterion*

Dear Wyndham,

I have returned on Friday from abroad. If you are in London, I should particularly like to see you. Dinner any evening next week, except Thursday.[1]

Yours ever
T. S. E.

1–WL told HR (16 Dec.) after dining with TSE and discussing the suspension of *The Criterion*: 'I suggested that he and a few of the more important of his staff of reviewers, should come over into The Enemy lock stock and barrel. I especially had you in mind and Thorpe, who I believe is a friend of yours' (*Letters of Wyndham Lewis*, 173).

## TO *The Editor of* The Church Times CC

3 December 1927[1] [London]

Sir,

*L'Action Française*

Having just returned from abroad, I saw only yesterday your issue of November 25, in which you kindly printed my letter. I should be greatly obliged if you would print a correction to one sentence which as it stands, says exactly the opposite of what I meant. I wrote: 'A generation which like the present has utterly repudiated Anatole France, could hardly fail to be uncritical in its attitude towards Maurras.' What I meant, of course is: 'could hardly fail to be critical' etc.

As for Mr Boulter's letter in your issue of December 2,[2] I must assume that Mr Boulter has read Maurras's pamphlet of 1903, *Le Dilemme de Marc Sangnier;* but I would ask whether the 'quixotic' attitude of Sangnier and his friends would in his opinion have been beneficial to France? And if Mr Boulter expects us to believe that *Le Sillon* was suppressed by the influence of the French *haute noblesse* at the Vatican, is he not inciting us to believe that the attack upon *L'Action Française* may spring from some other 'influence', no more noble? With Mr Ward's

1 – Unpublished.

2 – B. C. Boulter wrote: 'Like Mr Eliot, I have long been interested in the progress of French Catholicism and its reaction to differing social ideals. I remember the pain with which I heard of the suppression of that promising movement known as *Le Sillon* some quarter of a century ago. Marc Sangnier and his friends had attempted, somewhat quixotically at that time, to dissociate Catholicism from royalism, nationalism, and militarism, to which it was traditionally allied, and to give it an active social tendency. Unfortunately, the *haute noblesse* was strong enough at the Vatican to procure the suppression of the movement. A great opportunity was lost, and at a time when such action was urgently needed. Persuasive writers like Anatole France, eager for reform, openly derided the Church, and atheistic Communism began to spread.

'Today in France there are two movements at work, both full of interest. Marc Sangnier, now an older man but as vigorous as ever, has rallied together a growing number of Catholics who are devoutly orthodox in religion, who are Republican by conviction, and who are actively working for international amity, religious freedom, industrial justice, and social purity . . .

'There is also a movement, known as *l'Action Française*, which, in the face of post-war chaos, has, under the leadership of Daudet and Maurras, rallied together those Catholics to whom Catholicism still bears the old imprint. To them the Church is the obvious upholder of the traditional social order. It stands for nationalism, militarism, and royalism . . . In fact, the leaders of the movement, interesting personalities and writers of distinction, are carrying on that all too easy, but most sinister, task of establishing nationalism and reaction on a basis of orthodox religion.'

letter I have no fault to find, especially as I do not know how he arrives at his figures.[1]

As evidence of the complexity of which I spoke, I would point out that some of the most vociferous denouncers of *L'Action Française* issue their projectiles from the publishing house of Bloud & Gay, the firm which has always been associated with certain exponents of Modernism, including MM. Blondel and Le Roy.[2]

Two books giving interesting information are *Cinquante ans de politique*, by Tavernier, and *Le Ralliement et l'Action Française* by Merleix.[3]

I am, Sir,
Your obliged obedient servant,
[T. S. Eliot]

## TO *R. Ellsworth Larsson* CC

6 December 1927 [London]

My dear Larsson,

I am very sorry that I happened to be abroad when you wrote to me and so have only just seen your letter yesterday.[4] It is a very puzzling and perplexing case. I have been trying to think what can be done. Possibly there will have been developments in the meantime to alter the affair, but if so you will no doubt tell me of them. Personally I very much hesitate to encourage you to come to England at the present time. I dislike to

1 – Leo Ward wrote from London on 25 Nov. (above TSE's first letter): 'As in your Summary of last week you express sympathy with the Pope's desire to counteract the influence of a movement dominated by so anti-Christian a thinker as M. Charles Maurras, it may interest your readers to know that the policy you suggest – that of denunciation, without disciplinary sanctions – was that actually adopted by the Holy See until the open and organized rebellion of the *Action Française* made sterner measures necessary.

'The great majority of its Catholic supporters (about two-thirds it is estimated) have now abandoned the movement. But it required the fullest enforcement of ecclesiastical discipline to make the condemnation effective.'

2 – The French publishers Bloud et Gay, established in 1911 by the politicians Edmond Bloud (1876–1948) and Francisco Gay (1885–1963), specialised in works of Roman Catholic persuasion and were to become a centre for resistance to Nazism.

3 – Mermeix, *Le Ralliement et l'Action Française* (Paris, 1927).

4 – On 28 Nov. Larsson wrote from the Commissariat Special, Gare Principale, Dieppe, that he had been detained by the French authorities in Paris and taken to Dieppe because his English visa had expired and he had run out of money. He asked TSE to do him the favour of writing 'a letter . . . asking me to stop with you for some particular period, dating the letter some time in the past and addressing it to me in Paris . . . Once I am in England, I shall be all right, I am sure, for I think I can manage some sort of work there.'

throw cold water on an idea with which I am so much in sympathy in principle, but I am rather worried to think how you will possibly be able to make a living in this country unless you already have some pretty definite promise of work. I once tried to make a living by miscellaneous journalism myself, and although I had already published my first book of poems, I found the task quite impossible. I dare say that I could just get along by miscellaneous writing now; but even now I could only make a very small income in that way. So for two years I was a schoolmaster and for eight years I was a bank clerk. And it took me a good deal of time and no little luck even to get those jobs. And that was during the war when there were many more vacancies than there are now. Candidly, I do not want to invite you to England merely to see you starve here. But if you have any offers of work, I could probably make a rough guess at what income you could make.

This all seems very cold comfort. I should of course be glad to contribute anything within my means towards helping you to get back to New York, where it seems to me, not knowing anything of your personal affairs, you would probably be better off for the present. If you had even a very small private income, I should certainly encourage you to come here; knowing that in five or ten years you might be able to do very well. But what I advise is that you should try to establish your reputation in New York first; then when you return to England you will be able to keep up your New York literary connections which are very much more lucrative than those in this country where payment rates are low.

As your letter is now a week old, I should be very glad to hear from you again about your extremely trying situation.[1]

Sincerely yours,
[T. S. Eliot]

1–Larsson wrote on 8 Dec. 1927 that the American consul in Dieppe had told him to go back to Brussels; he would not be assisted to return to London or the USA. 'I am very grateful for your kindness. Your offer is extremely generous and gracious.' By 15 Dec. he was back in Belgium, where the consul was helping him to find a job.

## TO *I. A. Richards* CC

6 December 1927 [London]

Dear Sir,[1]

Mr Eliot has asked me to inform you that owing to differences of opinion between the Proprietors on matters of policy *The Criterion* will be suspended from the current issue.[2] Mr Eliot therefore regrets that he will be unable to make use of any more reviews. He asks me to say that contributors who have received review books should retain the books which have been sent to them.

Yours faithfully,
Irene Fassett
For and on behalf of
T. S. Eliot
Director of Faber & Gwyer Ltd.

## TO *Messrs Chatto & Windus* CC

6 December 1927 [*The Monthly Criterion*]

Dear Sirs,

Enclosed herewith you will find a circular letter which is being sent out by the *Criterion* to all publishers. I am writing to you personally as well inasmuch as we had only just received your valuable edition of the works of John Webster. In fairness to Mr Lucas and to yourselves I think that this copy of an expensive and important work ought to be returned. If you will let us know when you can send a messenger for the four volumes I shall be pleased to have them ready for you.

I will add my personal regrets at being unable to present a notice of this work in the *Criterion*.

Yours faithfully,
[T. S. Eliot]

1 – This letter was sent out to all the contributors to *MC*.

2 – Later, on 30 Apr. 1935 TSE was to write to Sydney Schiff, who had reported that Lady Rothermere was unwell, that he had not seen her 'for about eight years, and indeed we did not part on the best of terms, but I am extremely sorry to hear of her illness. It is all the sadder to think of it for a person who valued good health so highly and who had hitherto enjoyed so much vigour.'

## TO *G. B. Dangerfield* CC

7 December 1927 [*The Monthly Criterion*]

Dear Sir,

Thank you very much for your letter which arrived while I was abroad. I have heard also from Larsson and am very sorry indeed that he has got into such a trying predicament.[1] I agree with you that in the circumstances it is very much better for him to go back to America and wait until he has accumulated a little money before he returns, but I am extremely sorry for him indeed.

Yours very truly,
[T. S. Eliot]

## TO *John Gould Fletcher* CC

7 December 1927 [London]

My dear Fletcher,

I can fully assure you that the difficulties of the *Criterion* have nothing to do with your own activities. On the contrary, your letter in reply to Rowse[2] was actually the only contribution in the last number for which Lady Rothermere had a good word. May I say also that your cordial and unfailing support in the *Criterion* has been a very great help to me personally and that I hope our collaboration will continue in some way or another. Monday evening would suit me very well for dinner. If we dine in town, perhaps you will pick me up at my house; if you wish me to come to you, will you let me have directions for getting there? As I am near to Victoria station, I don't suppose that it would be difficult.

Yours ever,
[T. S. Eliot]

1–Larsson had returned to England, but since his visa had elapsed he was deported to France where he was momentarily detained by the French authorities: it was expected that he would be sent back to the USA.
2–Fletcher, letter to the Editor, *MC* 7 (Jan. 1928), 62–4.

## TO *William Aspenwall Bradley* CC

7 December 1927 [London]

Dear Mr Aspenwall,[1]

Thank you very much for your letter of the 4th instant. We are very much interested in *Le Trahison des Clercs*. As for *Properce*, we have come to the conclusion after much deliberation that this is a book for too small a public in English-speaking countries to justify our taking it on. We felt quite certain that the people who are interested in such a book of Propertius would certainly want to read M. Benda in French. *Le Trahison des Clercs,* however, like *Belphégor,* should have a very much wider appeal. As you know, I was so much interested in the first instalments in the *Nouvelle Revue Française* that I wrote to M. Benda and obtained an option on the translation rights. I have now read all of the three instalments in the *Nouvelle Revue Française*. Can you tell me if these three instalments make up the whole book or whether there is to be any more? That is to say, before closing with you I think that we ought to know just how large a book we should be taking on, and if possible we should of course like to see the other material if any is to be included. Our preference, of course, would be to have a rather bigger book than would be made by these three instalments alone.

Yours sincerely,
[T. S. Eliot]

P.S. I shall also be writing to M. Benda about this matter.

## TO *Virginia Woolf* CC

8 December 1927 [London]

My dear Virginia,

I should be very happy if you could come and have tea with me at Russell Square one day next week. Would Tuesday or Thursday be possible? I will buy a Cake.[2]

Yours ever,
[T.]

1–C. W. Stewart wrote at the head: 'Mr Eliot, I return Mr Bradley's letter & proof of Properce in case you wish to write. I have not written to Mr Bradley or to Payson & Clarke.'
2–VW replied (undated): 'I should like to come to tea on Tuesday very much. No cake needed. A penny bun is what I like most of anything in the world.'

## TO *Messrs James & James* CC

8 December 1927 [London]

Dear Sirs,

*Miss Emily Spencer Wood Deceased.*

I have this day returned to you the eight transfer forms signed by Mrs Vivienne Haigh Eliot and duly witnessed, together with the instructions to pay dividends to her bankers.

I observe that the majority of transfers, with the exception of the Manchester & County Bank and the District Bank Shares, have been executed. On behalf of my wife, I recognise the matter of the liability on these Country Bank and District Bank shares, amounting to some £300. I am presently taking the advice of Mrs Eliot's brokers on this matter; but if you do not hear from me in the course of two days, you may assume that Mrs Eliot assumes the liability on these uncalled shares. In any case I am ready to assume that liability myself, so that you may freely proceed with the transfers.

It seems, according to my records, that there are still four other securities (besides the two Banks mentioned) of which my wife has not had [typing runs off the foot of the carbon copy] myself, were to be sold, have been sold. And I assume that any dividends from other stocks have accumulated in the Trustees' Account. Presumably there will be a cash balance, in consequence, to be divided between Maurice and Vivien?

Yours faithfully,
[T. S. Eliot]

## TO *Messrs The New Criterion Limited* CC

8 December 1927 [London]

Dear Sirs,

I give herewith details of the expenses of my journey to Switzerland:

| | |
|---|---|
| Return fare London–Berne | £10. 2. 11. |
| Wagon-Lit Berne–Paris | £ 1. 8. 0. |
| Incidental expenses | £ 1. 12. 0. |
| Total: | £13. 2. 11. |

Less cost of ticket London–Paris which I should have taken in any case

£ 5. 5. 0.

Total: £ 7. 17. 11

I have kept this expenditure as low as possible and have included no expense which I should have made in any case by going to Paris that week. You will observe the share due by yourselves if £3. 19. 0. As in order to reclaim the rest I should be obliged to communicate with Lady Rothermere, I propose to let the matter drop.

Yours faithfully,
[T. S. Eliot]

## TO *Ezra Pound* — TS Beinecke

8 December 1927 — Faber & Gwyer Ltd

Dear Ezra,

Having been abroad on business I was delayed in answering your letter. I have put up the matter of the facsimile.[1] The present situation is this. We should hear in a day or two from the American people I spoke of and we have already communicated to Liveright that he shall have the next chance at it if the offer falls through. The great difficulty at present is merely one of time. We have unfortunately two sets of heavy and very expensive books to bring out in 1928 and the cost of the Guido, even with only one facsimile page of the Ms., is estimated at £400. They simply can't lock up so much money at once and they could not guarantee publication of the book until some time in 1929. Of course if the other books went very well we should certainly produce it sooner as it is to our interest to bring it out as quickly as possible. But there you are. So if you want to bring it out sooner and care to try somebody else with it immediately, you can of course go ahead; but I shall be very disappointed if we lose the book.

More information about other matters later. Delighted to hear of the *Dial* prize.

Yours ever,
T.

1–EP wrote on 26 Nov., apropos his projected edition of the poems of Cavalcanti, that sound commercial instinct made him believe 'that the reprods will more'n pay for themselves in surety of sale. To say nothing of the aera perennius side of the matter.'

## TO *Charles Whibley* CC

8 December 1927 [London]

My dear Whibley,

Thank you very much for your kind letter.[1] I should like very much to come down on the afternoon of Wednesday the 14th until the following morning. I have not yet looked up the trains but I seem to remember that there is one which does get in about tea time.

Yours ever affectionately,
[T. S. E.]

## TO *Frank Morley*[2] TS Berg

9 December 1927 57 Chester Terrace, Sloane Square

Dear Mr Morlaix:

One thing did not occur to me, that is that the Payt. for contributions for January properly belongs to the Old *Criterion,* i.e. Lady R. as that would in honour have had to be paid for in any case. If we can work that it would reduce the Jan. expences to £40. The only thing is that she may make a fuss being that kind of person who would willingly spend £10,000 in order to save 30 thirty [*sic*] cents in which case we should probably let her have the 30 cents thirty rather than litigation. But properly and Honourably honora bely we shd only be lible for £40, but I *cant* assure that.

The Manager and Assistants of the CAMBDEN HOTEL wish to notify Mr Morlaix that owing to the Man having forgot it Off his Van this morning the two pieces of Merchandise Invoised were not delivered, but the Manager Apologisung and having received from an unknown Source

1–Whibley had written from his home at Great Brickhill, Bletchley, in response to a (now lost) letter by TSE telling him of the Rothermere débâcle: 'I am much interested to hear about Lady R. & the *Criterion*. On the whole, I am pleased. It means more leisure & less anxiety for you. That is a good thing. Also it means that you will work for yourself & publish a book before long. I like in general the scheme of your book, but we will talk about that when we meet.

'To come back to the *Criterion* for a minute. I think you may take an honest pride in the retrospect. You have edited a magazine, wh. is distinctively your own, & which nobody else could have edited, & it is secure of memory. And to be rid of the Rothermere connection is a clear gain.'

2–Frank Morley (1899–1985), editor, publisher, author: see Biographical Register.

Mr Morlaix' address 10 Essex Street[1] will Bill the two pieces to that Adress tomorrow (Sat.) morning & hope he will accept Apologies for Delay.

I have told Erbert that Anonymous Friends wish to Present him with a Young Talking Parrot for Xmas. Please do not give me Away. I Guarantee the Parrot.

Yours etc.
T. S. E.

## TO *Richard Cobden-Sanderson* TS Texas

10 dec. this day of
St Melchisedech 1927 *The Monthly Criterion*

Dear Cobden:

I shd like to celebrate with you (apart from the Feast of S. Achilles 16 dec.) either (1) Demise of *Criterion* or (2) Resurrection of *The Criterion*. Not that it matters a Damn to me or to You except To Hell with the Harmsworths but will You Suggest Two Days Next Week upon Either of Which you could meet me at HENEKEYS at 12.30 p.m. that is Noon to Toast the King.

Yours etc.
T. S. E.

<P.S. My Respex to Mrs Cobden.
In Haste.>

## TO *James Smith* CC

12 December 1927 [London]

Dear Sir,[2]

Mr Eliot has asked me to inform you that owing to certain concurrences of opinion *The Criterion* is to be continued. The January number will appear and probably the February, and it is hoped with some confidence that the capital which has been withdrawn by one of the Proprietors will be replaced from other sources.

Yours faithfully,
[Irene P. Fassett]
Secretary.

1 – The address of The Century Company, of which FVM was London manager.
2 – This letter was sent out to all the contributors to *MC*.

## TO *R. Gordon George* CC

12 December 1927 [London]

My dear Gordon George,

Thank you very much for your kind letter.[1] I am sorry to know definitely that there is no chance of seeing you as unfortunately I shall not be able to get to Paris again for about ten days. You will have received another circular letter and will understand that this business of stoppage and reorganisation has taken the whole of my time. What is going to happen is that the *Criterion* will certainly continue for a month or two and we hope during that time to accumulate capital to replace that which was suddenly withdrawn by one of the Proprietors. So I cannot say definitely to you 'Go ahead with the Maupassant'; but I will leave that to you and will in any case notify you immediately the periodical is definitely on its feet. The rest of your letter gave me very much pleasure and I am anxious not to answer it until I can give more time to it.

Ever yours,
[T. S. Eliot]

P.S. This letter is not an answer to your last letter, but merely an acknowledgment of your letter of November 23rd, but I must thank you for the enclosures that you sent which I shall read with great interest, and I shall write to you later.

T. S. E.

1 – George had written on 23 Nov.: 'I am very glad to have your letter of the 18th. The earlier letter had given me the impression that you had tired of my essays, and only wanted to shelve them – and I could not help feeling that I had something of my own to say, and was in fact the first mover in this direction in England, though, in the *Criterion*, you have since become its leader . . . I am now sending you a recent essay of mine in *transition*, and my "Reason and the Arts" in the *Supplement* which dealt with so many of the points which have been since discussed in the *Criterion*.' He hoped to meet TSE in Paris, 5–12 Dec.: 'I love conversation with you . . . When you have read more of what I had been writing earlier, you would find no difficulty in seeing why I wrote with such vigour against Daudet and Maurras. We have come to a great turning point in the history of the Universal Church of Rome. Is the Latin tendency to be dominant, or is there to [be] freedom for the growth of national lives which are widely different? And with this rises the other side – are nationalisms to be absolute, or is there not one universal law for all men, divinely instituted and sacramentally uniting inward and outward forms? I look with hope for the gradual development of immense gifts of life in the present policy of the Papacy, and it is for these reasons that I am at once so interested in Church unity, in peace, and in the Orient.'

## TO *Richard Cobden-Sanderson* TS Texas

Monday, 12 December 1927 *The Monthly Criterion*

Dear Cobden,

Yes, do come to the GROVE on Thursday if you possibly can. Beauchamp Place is near Brompton Road station, and when you get to the GROVE you ask for the dugout. We much need the advantage of your sapient council. This is not a frivolous meeting, but a Tridentine conclave, re. *Criterion.*

It is just possible that occasion will be taken to present a small ichneumon[1] to Mr Read, but this is more likely to happen a fortnight later, as Selfridges have no ichneumons in stock at the moment.

Yours etc,
T. S. E.

My previous letter explaining this letter follows.

## TO *Richard Cobden-Sanderson* TS Texas

13 December 1927 *The Monthly Criterion*

Dear Cobden,

Being now at my office and perfectly sober, I find that I had already made a very boring engagement for Friday lunch. On Thursday, there is, as you say, the lunch at the Grove. I should very much appreciate it if you could find time to come all that distance to lunch with the party there. Your presence would be more than welcome any Thursday but would

1–'A small brownish-coloured slender-bodied carnivorous quadruped . . . closely allied to the mongoose and resembling the weasel tribe in form and habits. It is found in Egypt, and is noted for destroying the eggs of the crocodile, on which account it was venerated by the ancient Egyptians' (*OED*). See TSE's uncollected poem 'Montpellier Row' – on Walter de la Mare – including the lines 'Vista of Hanoverian trees / His right décor . . . which yet / The old enchanter, if he please / May change to haunt of marmoset, Amphisbaena, or ichneumon', plus this note: 'For the habits of the ichneumon, and its behaviour at windows, see *The Crooked Man* (in "The Memoirs of Sherlock Holmes").' The passage in question from Arthur Conan Doyle's story 'The Crooked Man' reads:

'The man leaned over and pulled up the front of a kind of hutch in the corner. In an instant out there slipped a beautiful reddish-brown creature, thin and lithe, with the legs of a stoat, a long, thin nose, and a pair of the finest red eyes that ever I saw in an animal's head.

'"It's a mongoose," I cried.

'"Well, some call them that, and some call them ichneumon," said the man. "Snake-catcher is what I call them, and Teddy is amazing quick on cobras. I have one here without the fangs, and Teddy catches it every night to please the folk in the canteen."'

be particularly useful on this Thursday as it will not be a frivolous party but a serious conclave to discuss ways and means, and your counsel and support would be very much respected by all present. So do come on Thursday to the Grove if you can any time between one and one-thirty.

Yours ever,
T. S. E.

P.S. When you speak of a morning session in the Doves, do you imply that the Doves is conducted with complete disregard to the licensed hours for the sale of liquor, or alternatively that in order to attend a morning session at the Doves you never go to Thavies Inn except between 3. pm. and the reopening of the Doves at 5.30? <This is the previous letter which I said would follow the preceding letter.>

## TO *Thomas McGreevy* TS TCD

13 December 1927 *The Monthly Criterion*

My dear McGreevy,

I should have answered your letter of the 28th November much sooner but that I have been exceedingly rushed and preoccupied with our recent crisis.

I have made a few enquiries about the firm in which you are interested and have heard nothing against them. They are said to be solvent and certainly of good intentions so far as the quality of their literature is concerned. I have a suspicion that there may be some Jewish interest, but I am not sure; anyway I am glad to hear that it is a little more promising.

There is certainly no objection to your reprinting any part of the note on Moore which you did for us.

I am sorry that the Valéry matter is still so mixed up. I cannot think of anything that we can do.

A fortnight ago the *Criterion* was about to close down altogether because Lady Rothermere wishes to withdraw her capital. However, a collection has been made for the purpose of bringing out one or two more numbers, during which time it is confidently hoped that other support will be forthcoming. I will let you know what happens, but meanwhile you can rely on your 'Gide' appearing in the January number, and on getting paid for it.

Yours sincerely,
T. S. Eliot

TO *Sally Cobden-Sanderson*[1] MS Beinecke

Tuesday [13 December 1927?] *The Monthly Criterion*

Dear Sally,

I hope Rchd has remembered the message, but I forgot to add that Mongeese (Ichneumons) are very *Usefull* (see Oxford Dictionary) for they eat Crocodiles' Eggs.

Yrs. etc.
T. S. E.

TO *Richard Aldington* TS Texas

13 December 1927 Faber & Gwyer Ltd

My dear Richard,

Thank you for your letter.[2] I will certainly see Miss Wilde when she turns up and see what can be done about this. Thank you very much for giving us the chance of the Gourmont books. I will let you know about this in a short time too. What gives me particular pleasure in your letter is to hear that you are going to be in London for a time.[3] That is delightful. I am leaving London on the 20th or 21st to spend Christmas in Paris but I shall be back again before the end of the month and hope to see a good deal of you while you are in London.

So much has happened lately, and so rapidly, that I have had no time to let you know about it. In brief, we have fallen out completely with Lady Rothermere, who, it appears, dislikes the *Criterion* intensely and who wishes to withdraw her capital from it immediately. We at first intended to shut up shop at once, but a number of people have objected and

1–TSE wrote to HWE on 1 Jan. 1936, of Richard and Sally Cobden-Sanderson: 'Richard has a certain convivial charm; Sally is a little too boisterous for my taste. They are very jovial company, but of course have little intellectual interest.'

2–RA wrote that Dorothy Wilde had brought to England the manuscript of 'a novel, by Natalie Barney, the Amazon of our cher maître, R. de. G [Rémy de Gourmont]. I have promised to assist in arranging the publication of this work in the U.S. and England . . . I forget if I told you, but I am issuing from U.S. a two volume anthology of Rémy, and, in separate volumes, translations of the Lettres à l'Amazon and Lettres Intimes à l'Amazon, for which Miss B. is writing prefaces . . . I have not yet arranged definitely with any English publisher about these Gourmont books, though I have practically promised Allen and Unwin first refusal. However, if Faber and Gwyer wanted them, and would promise to take 750 sheets of each of the three Gourmont books, I think I could arrange this . . .'

3–The Aldingtons were renting a flat at 3 Mecklenburgh Square, London, for a month from 22 Dec.

interposed so that a small collection has been made in order to run the January number at least, while a few people are scurrying about to see if the capital which has been withdrawn can be replaced from other sources. I am naturally pessimistic and therefore not as hopeful as the others. But I must say I am thankful to get rid of the Harmsworth connection, and if the *Criterion* is re-established, it will be in a much stronger position than before. All this has happened within the last two weeks and you will understand how very rushed I have been. Particularly as I have many other things to keep in my head which have no connection whatever with this matter.

Yours ever affectionately,
Tom

## TO *Alan Porter* CC

13 December 1927 [London]

Dear Porter,

I am sorry that I did not get your letter in time to accept your invitation, and since I have been back I have been too busy with the question of the reorganisation of the *Criterion* to write to you. I shall be very busy from now until just before Christmas when I must go abroad again. Perhaps you will ask me again next year.

Thank you for expressing yourself so fully about my Christmas poem.[1] I value all that you say in praise of it, but I must say quite ingenuously that your interpretation of it gave me rather a shock. No doubt that is partly

1 – Alan Porter's letter of 25 Nov. was largely devoted to his reading of TSE's poem *Journey of the Magi*; beginning from this second paragraph:

'I thought it was rather awkward and cowardly to leave you without saying how I *had* criticized "The Journey of the Magi". I took it as a very important poem, and tried to exhibit *why*, from the substance of what you wrote – not from technique or vividness or lyric quality at all. That is, as if you were *doing* something, as if the poem were an action.

'And I said, "Alas for this nostalgia", very much as Richards seems to have said, "Hurrah for this nostalgia". Here is a myth, and you are remaking it, just as a Greek poet remade the myths he told. And what falls out of the story, what is put into it, how is it changed?

'There is no star, there are no gifts, there is actually no birth and no worship (or perhaps there was a birth, yes, certainly there was one; but not an overwhelming and ever remarkable birth).

'How would I like to see the myth? Or rather, how do I see it? As in fact the Three Magi *were* Zoroaster and Pythagoras and Buddha. As if the mysteries of the ancient world *were* something of supreme dignity and truth. As if this were the order of Melchizedec; suffering the shock of becoming Christian and having its meaning fulfilled, and transcended in fulfillment.

because we start with quite different fantasies of what such an occurrence would have been like. But as the whole story of the Magi is not, I believe, an essential matter of Christian doctrine, I felt a certain liberty to treat it according to my own fantasy of realism. I did not intend to put forward, and still do not believe that I did put forward, any view which would either conflict with Christian doctrine or any imagination which would tend to weaken belief. The notion that the three Magi were the three religious leaders whom you mention does not appeal to me because what little I know of their religions makes me unable to accept the imaginative possibility of such a tribute. I certainly do not accept the interpretation, interesting as it is, which you put on my verses in the third paragraph of your letter. If I may say so, I think that this interpretation is due rather to a reading of my previous verses than to this. I meant that the Magi were drawn by a power which they did not understand, and I used them as types of a kind of person who may be found at almost any period of history. I meant them to be pathetic as Dante's Virgil is pathetic.

When you speak of the Cairnses, do you mean the Cairds? I know the Cairnses only as a breed of terriers.

I certainly acquit you of everything if you will acquit me; but if the poem continues to make the impression on you that it did – then there is no possibility of acquitting it.

Sincerely yours,
[T. S. Eliot]

---

'Into Christianity came Plato and Aristotle, Trismegistus, Eleusis, the Vedas . . . It was something to take the breath away, and make them humble; but are we to say they had nothing to bring, and they were left *rootless* after it had happened. I see it as if it were mankind at its firmest and greatest that was here confessing its insufficiency, and receiving its justification.

'I think you saw it as if the world were at a dead end; as if it were superseded rather than transcended; as if these were three more Jews, or rich young men.

'And if I am to take the poem as an attitude to life, I believe it would go like this – "The world certainly happens, and has to be accepted: but there is no certain perfection. It comes difficultly to us, and even trivially. I don't know whether there is an absolute meaning to it. I am forced to certain conclusions. Is there any guarantee that they are Right? And suppose they are right: are they very exhilarating?

'It was one of the Cairnses, I think, who used to get indignant at the phrase "too good to be true", holding that we should rather say "not good enough to be true". This looks to me like a good, buoyant, and creative feeling.

'Will you acquit me of impertinence in writing this? If I said "blasphemous", I must apologise; it was a swear word. Some-one asked me, "But do you think all that has anything to do with it as a *poem*?"; and that is a point of view which is beyond me to handle.'

TO *His Mother* TS Houghton

14 December 1927 *The Monthly Criterion*

My dearest mother,

I know I have not written to you for a long time now, not for about a fortnight I think, but I have never been more busy with more things than I have within that time. I was very happy to get your note, and delighted to hear from Mrs Haigh-Wood that she has had a long letter from you written in ink. I am happy that you are so well. I have been too busy to get any Christmas presents yet, so anything I send will be very late. I did send you one small genealogical book which may amuse you, unless you have a copy already.

The chief point is that the Rothermere interest is out of *The Criterion,* and we are looking for other capital to replace it. I am very thankful to get her out of it, and in any case I do not worry, as my salary is guaranteed for three years more. I found that she was very sick of *The Criterion*, and did not mind saying so, to such an extent that it would have been impossible to go on that way. In fact, I am sure that she lost all interest in it from the moment she had to share it with Faber & Gwyer. It never really interested her, and I wonder that she did not try to withdraw long ago. So long as she felt that she had a review and an editor all to herself, I think she took a certain pride of possession, but when that was gone there was nothing else left. I must say that the connection was always a great strain, as she is not only an eccentric person, but belongs to a world from which we should never choose our friends, a world of millionaires with no social background or traditions and no sense of public responsibility. One should make every allowance for a woman who had to live so long with Lord R. as she did, as my opinion of him could not be put on paper. Certainly, if *The Criterion* is put solidly on its feet again, it will be in a much more solid and respectable position than ever before, as the previous association was not one to impress the public favourably, and the brief rumour that it was going to stop has rallied opinion in its favour. I have had numerous letters and verbal expressions to protest strongly against stopping it, and saying that it would be an irreparable loss. Bruce Richmond is very anxious to help by interesting suitable capitalists in it, and a committee has been formed.

I have made it clear that I have not time to do anything but the minimum of work of this sort myself, and must leave it to others.

From my personal point of view, I should really have been rather glad to have it come to an end, so long as I was sure of drawing the salary. One gets very tired in time of doing a job in which oneself is so submerged; fighting other people's battles, and advertising other people's wares. Of course it is pleasant to do something that many people think useful, and to have people depend on you is perhaps the most substantial and solid human relationship, in general, that there is; for you can depend on people's dependence more than on their affection. And I suppose that if one gets these things it is because one wants them. I never thought I wanted to do anything but write poetry and some philosophic prose, and just do enough practical work to be free from financial worry; and never to meddle in affairs at all. Instead, I have had a pretty active life, at least. Perhaps it is just as well; I have had a much wider experience of men and things. I should once have protested if anyone had told me that I should be running a review, and having to advise young men and find work for them, and keep in touch with various foreign writers and see about the exploitation of their work in English, and help to direct a publishing company, and deal with its policy and advise Faber, and Gwyer, and Mrs Gwyer, and keep up with French politics in order to defend the policy of my French friends in this country in connection with their row with the Vatican, and correspond with damned English papists about it, and interest myself in the repair of a local church, and be trustee of an estate, and see that old Janes gets properly looked after, and write reviews and articles at the same time. But I suppose it is a family characteristic and can't be helped.

I have just written a long essay on F. H. Bradley's Ethics for *The Times*.[1] And I think there will be things of mine in the January and the February and possibly the March *Dial*, so look out for them, as you can get them in Cambridge much quicker than I can send them. And I have just done a note on Chesterton for *The Nation* which I will send you.[2]

I am going down tonight to stay with Charles Whibley and his new wife, but must be back by lunch time tomorrow. On Wednesday 21st I and Mrs Haigh-Wood are going to Paris for one week, as I must be in London again on the 29th for a board meeting. Maurice was to have come too, but we thought it might be too exciting and tiring for Vivien to see so many of us at once – Lucy Thayer is staying in Paris too – and as Maurice would have had to travel at night and would have had only two days there anyhow, it would have been very tiring for him as he is very

1 – 'Bradley's "Ethical Studies"', *TLS*, 29 Dec. 1927, 981–2; repr. in *SE* as 'Francis Herbert Bradley'.

2 – 'Mr Chesterton (and Stevenson)' – on G. K. Chesterton, *Robert Louis Stevenson* – *Nation & Athenaeum*, 42: 3 (31 Dec. 1927), 516.

busy in the British-Italian Bank in London. Vivien is very much better, and is trying to make and to buy a few small Christmas presents in the village, as it would be too tiring for her to shop in Paris. I have not told her anything about *The Criterion* crisis, because she has the *Criterion* so much at heart that it would have distressed her, and she is always terribly inclined to worry, and to convince herself that everything is her fault, and as *The Criterion* is going on for the present there is no need to tell her.

Well, I will write again either just before I leave or in Paris. I shall think of you all the time at Christmas and try to picture your Christmas gathering. With very much love to all

your devoted son,
Tom

## TO *Rev. M. C. D'Arcy* CC

15 December 1927 [London]

Dear Father D'Arcy,

First of all I wish to say that I hope you will be in London at least until the New Year. I must go to Paris on the 21st for about a week but on the other hand I must be in London again on the 29th. If you are to be in London for a week or two at the beginning of January I will hope to see you then and will write again to suggest your lunching with me. If, however, there is no chance of seeing you after the 29th of December, I hope you will let me know, and if possible I will write or wire you to suggest a meeting before I leave. But I should prefer to see you upon my return as I shall then have more leisure. I should be grateful if you would drop me a line in reply to this and let me know how long you are to be in London.[1]

As for the *Duns Scotus*: if the *Criterion* continues we shall certainly want it. But in the circumstances it will be too late for the January or February numbers and I am not quite in a position to ask for contributions for the March number as I am not yet sure whether the March number will appear. I can only say that I very much hope you will proceed with the review when you recover your papers.[2] If it were possible for you, and

1–D'Arcy went to lunch (Herbert Read was also a guest) at 57 Chester Terrace on Mon., 9 Jan. 1928. He also took tea at TSE's office in the first week of Jan.

2–D'Arcy posted his regrets (13 Dec.) from 114 Mount Street, Grosvenor Square, London (where he was staying for about six weeks)): 'I have left the two volumes at Oxford, & my notes are somewhere there or in a trunk which has not arrived here yet.'

if you were willing, to let me have something by the middle of January for the hypothetical March number, I should be very grateful. In any case, I am fairly confident that the *Criterion* will continue, and if it does not continue then I shall not blame myself for having charged you with this book as I shall hope you will publish something about it elsewhere. I will let you know as soon as anything is settled, but meanwhile I hope you are willing to take the risk of letting me have something by the middle of January.

Sincerely yours,
[T. S. Eliot]

P.S. I hear that Mr George Santayana says that you know nothing about St Thomas. I should also like to know whether he knows anything about St Thomas himself.[1]

1–D'Arcy replied on 16 Dec.: 'Santayana! I did not know he was an authority on St. Thomas. I have never found much of the wisdom of St. Thomas in his writings.'

Santayana (1863–1952), Spanish-born American philosopher, studied at Harvard under William James and Josiah Royce, and was the author of numerous philosophical, literary and autobiographical books, including *The Sense of Beauty* (1896), *The Life of Reason* (1905) and *Three Philosophical Poets: Lucretius, Dante, and Goethe* (1910). At Harvard, TSE took Santayana's courses in the History of Modern Philosophy, 1907–8, and the Philosophy of History ('Ideals of Society, Religion, Art, and Science, in their historical development'), 1909–10. Following his mother's death in 1912, Santayana moved to Europe and lived in Paris and Oxford before settling in Italy. Conrad Aiken called him 'that Merlin, that Prospero, with his wizard mantle from Spain'; and he was deeply influential in Harvard philosophy during TSE's time there. The *Harvard Monthly* declared in Mar. 1912 that Santayana had 'attained a following which in enthusiasm and intensity . . . is impossible to parallel'. In 1918 TSE remarked upon the 'imperial and slightly amused gaze of Mr Santayana', while in *The Varieties of Metaphysical Poetry* he said that, though *Three Philosophical Poets* was 'one of the most brilliant' of his books, he was 'more interested in poetical philosophy than philosophical poetry'. TSE never changed his poor opinion of Santayana. On 12 Oct. 1961 he disclosed to William B. Goodman (Harcourt, Brace & World, Inc.): 'While Santayana's *Three Philosophical Poets* did make a deep impression on me, I never regarded myself as to any degree a disciple of Santayana himself. As a matter of fact, I thought the man rather a poseur, who chose to look down upon New Englanders as provincial Protestants. <Unjust, no doubt: it is merely what I thought when I was an undergraduate!> Most of his early books, *The Life of Reason*, seem to me very dull, and he was certainly much at his best on the borderline between philosophy and literary criticism.' He told Robert Fitzgerald in 1962: 'As for Santayana, I always thought that he had a strong theatrical streak, that he liked to pose as the noble Spaniard to look down on us Puritan New Englanders from the point of view of a Catholic who had lost his faith, but retained his culture, and to dress like a man of mystery. Furthermore, I did not like his literary style at the time. His earlier works seem to me rather in the style of Emerson's, that is to say each sentence carefully chisled, but you had to leap from one sentence to another. Perhaps his later work has more charm. I liked some of his essays on the borderline of literary criticism. There was an amazing one called "The Genteel Tradition in American Philosophy". He was at his best I think when he was slightly mischievous, not to say malicious, as about Josiah and about Bertrand Russell.' On 15 Aug. 1963, he told Robert H. Wilbur: 'There were two lecturers . . . whom I disliked because they seemed to me to have a touch of charlatanism about them; one was C. T.

## TO *Montgomery Belgion* CC

16 December 1927 [*The Monthly Criterion*]

Dear Mr Belgion,

The essay by Rivière is called 'Sur la Crise du Concept de la Littérature' and it was published in the *Nouvelle Revue Française*, I think about a year before his death.[1] I cannot give you the exact date at the moment as I have lent my copy, but I will let you know as soon as I can get it back.

I am not quite sure what article I wrote about *Ulysses* in 1922.[2] I certainly have no copy of such an article. It may be something that I wrote for the *Nouvelle Revue Française* or it may be in the *Dial*; but I do not think I ever devoted a whole article to *Ulysses*. It may well have been mentioned in the course of some other article.

I am sorry not to be more helpful. If I have an inspiration I will write to you again.

Yours sincerely,
[T. S. Eliot]

## TO *Ottoline Morrell* CC

16 December 1927 [London]

My dear Ottoline,

It is very kind of you to ask me to Garsington for Christmas and I appreciate it very highly. Were I to be in England for Christmas I should certainly accept with great pleasure and a very quiet Christmas would have suited me better than an uproarious one; but I am going over to Paris on Tuesday or Wednesday next and expect to stay there for a week. I suppose you will be back in London by the end of December? I will ring you up as soon as I get back.

With very many thanks and best Christmas wishes,

Affectionately yours,
[T.]

---

Copeland and the other George Santayana . . . Santayana's earlier work, *The Life of Reason*, seemed to me very difficult reading because of a sort of Emersonian style.' On 3 Apr. 1964 TSE moved to alter the blurb that Harcourt Brace & World proposed to print on a Harvest edition of TSE's plays: 'At Harvard I did follow one or two courses given by Professor Santayana, but I did not like him or admire him and it is irrelevant to mention him. If any one teacher of mine at Harvard is to be mentioned it should be Irving Babbitt, the man who had the greatest influence on me.'

1–Jacques Rivière, 'La Crise du concept de littérature', *NRF* 125 (Feb. 1924), 159–70.

2–'Ulysses, Order, and Myth', *Dial* 75 (Nov. 1923), 480–3.

## TO *Alvin Johnson*[1] CC

18 December 1927 [London]

Dear Mr Johnson,

Your letter of the 18th ultimo – which pressure of circumstances has continually postponed answering – has caused me considerable distress of conscience, as I feel that you have had a great deal of probably fruitless trouble on my account.[2] I understand the situation. But it is simply impossible for me – for both public and private reasons at present – to make definite engagements so long ahead; I simply do not know whether I shall be in a position, at the beginning of 1929, to come for the necessary length of time to New York, or not. Rather than make an engagement which I might have to break to your greater discomfiture, I prefer to risk the probability of missing this opportunity altogether. I am very anxious to come, and should much prefer lecturing under the auspices of your school to those of any other; but whether I could be in New York for 8 or 10 weeks at that time, is entirely unknown. So all I can do is to thank you, and to say that if I can and do come to New York, I shall be very happy if I [runs off end of page] handsome that what you offered for 1928.

With very grateful thanks,
Yours sincerely,
[T. S. Eliot]

## TO *John Gould Fletcher* TS Arkansas

18 December 1927 *The Monthly Criterion*

Dear Fletcher,

I should have written to you before to express my appreciation of your great generosity. You ask me not to divulge it, but I have had to do so to Morley, as he is in charge of the fund. I hope too that it will help to release two or three of the most impecunious of our members. Personally I am delighted in such a sign of faith; anyway it is extremely generous.

1–Alvin Saunders Johnson (1874–1971), American economist; co-founder of the New School for Social Research, New York, of which he was director from 1922.

2–Johnson asked TSE to tell him 'as soon as possible when you will come and what the general content of your course will be'; he hoped TSE would teach in the fall of 1928. TSE had been prompted too by his brother-in-law 'Shef', on 1 Nov.: 'About ten days ago I saw Alvin Johnson at the New School of Social Research. He seemed in some anxiety as to the time when they could count on having your course of lectures here in New York.' Johnson said (28 Dec.) they could manage if TSE gave them one month's notice.

Certainly I will bring the Stained Glass[1] to the office; and I shall be very much interested to know what you think of it. As I have a few matters to clear up before I leave on Wednesday, I am not quite sure of my movements tomorrow. I am pretty sure to be in from 4.30; I have an appointment in the City for 3, but mean to come back to the office for tea.

Yours ever,
T. S. E.

## TO *Richard Aldington* CC

18 December 1927 [London]

My dear Richard,

Many thanks for your letter, which seems to have crossed one of mine (which should have reached you before you wrote) as you do not allude to one or two matters I mentioned.

I have not discussed this question with anyone in the firm yet, and shall not have time to do so till I get back. I leave on Wednesday morning, and return on the 28th to London.

My private opinion is that I should warmly recommend them to take your Gourmont Anthology, and possibly the *Lettres*, but of these I cannot judge with conviction not having read them. But if, as I understand, you are generously tying up your own translations with Miss Barney's works, then I am much more doubtful.[2] I don't think I can recommend 'em to take Miss B. on; I don't think there would be a penny of profit on Gourmont, only glory; and with Barney it would certainly be losing money. Even if there is a scabrous sale for the *Inteems*, we are the last people to swing it; F. & G. are too bloody respectable to sell anything except the Life of Joynson-Hicks[3] or something of that sort. I am trying to make them less respectable, but it would be unfair to the *Inteems* to start them off with such a blessing as ours.

1–*English Stained Glass*, by Herbert Read.

2–RA wrote on 11 Dec.: 'Of course, I don't mind a bit if you prefer not to touch the Gourmont books. I only suggest it, because I think it might be an inducement to your board to do the Barney novel, the publication of which in England would be a condition of the whole deal.'

3–William Joynson-Hicks (1865–1932), solicitor and Conservative politician. As Home Secretary, 1924–9, he earned a reputation as a reactionary on account of his personal commitment in the banning of Radclyffe Hall's *The Well of Loneliness*, though he would redeem himself in part with his strong support for the Equal Franchise Act (1928); he was also passionately in favour of penal reform. He was created Viscount Brentford in 1929.

So if the stuff goes severally, may we see the Anthology first [typing runs off the page]. In any case, they have rather choaked their 1928 list, and nothing but a Winner would persuade them to promise publication of anything before 1929.

Ever yours although in great haste and with Best Xmas wishes to Both,

[Tom]

## TO *I. P. Fassett*

TS Valerie Eliot

20 December 1927 *The Monthly Criterion*

Dear Miss Fa ssett:

(This typewriter has sta rted skipping, I dont know why). The enclosed letter, with two one dollar bills, both beautiful and new, explains itself. I should be very grateful if, at your leisure, you would transpose these two dollar bills into sterling and see that the two numbers of *The Criterion* are sent to my brother. I think that there should be a substantial balance, which can be added to my personal petty cash account.

Yours faithfully,
T. S. Eliot

## TO *Edwin Muir*

CC

20 December 1927 [*The Monthly Criterion*]

Dear Muir,

I should have replied to your letter very much sooner but for the fact that I did not know whether the *Criterion* was to continue or not.[1] You may or may not have heard that one of its supporters has suddenly withdrawn support which caused a crisis. Owing to the activities of a small number of generous friends, the January number is certain and the February number probable; and during that time it is hoped that more substantial support can be obtained.

If you would like to have Macleod's book on the understanding that your review may or may not be published and paid for, please drop a line to my secretary who will send it to you. I am just going abroad for a week

1–Muir had asked on 5 Dec. if he might review Joseph Gordon Macleod's *Beauty and the Beast: Essays on Literature* (1927). 'It is an essay on the aesthetics of the novel, and as I am at present writing a volume on much the same subject for the Hogarth Lectures, it would interest me greatly.'

and will write to you again on my return and suggest that you come to lunch or tea one day when you are in London.

Yours sincerely,
[T. S. Eliot]

P.S. I have glanced at the book and am not at all sure that it is a good book. In fact I think it is a very immature book. Perhaps something better will occur to you as well.

## TO *Rev. Arthur E. Massey* CC

20 December 1927 [London]

Dear Sir,

Thank you very much for your kind letter of the 15th instant.[1] I am of course pleased and flattered that you should care to take so much trouble to obtain my signature for my book of poems. It would also be a pleasure to me to comply with your request, but the situation with regard to my volume of poems is rather different from that with regard to my *The Journey of the Magi*. Of *The Journey of the Magi* there was, it is true, a limited edition, but this limited edition was not a signed edition. Of my collected poems there was a signed edition. I do not say that I approve of signed editions or of the public interest in them. But the fact that I have signed a certain number of copies which the publishers sell at a higher price for this reason obviously makes it impossible for me to sign other copies, except for presentation to personal friends. Otherwise purchasers of the signed copies would have a right to complain. I hope that you will understand my position and accept my thanks and apologies.

I am,
Yours very truly,
[T. S. Eliot]

1 – The Revd Arthur E. Massey, Hon. Sec. of the Peacehaven Literary, Scientific and Debating Society, said he had been so 'struck & charmed' by *Journey of the Magi* that he had resolved to give a copy of *Poems 1909–1925* to 'a dear friend who is a student and lover of poetry' as a New Year's present. Would TSE be so gracious as to 'add to it a favourite quotation with your autograph'? He would not send the book till TSE said so. In the event, TSE would despatch a signed copy to Massey. A few months later, when Massey asked TSE to sign his copy of *A Song for Simeon*, TSE was again obliging; and in Dec. 1928 Massey was gratified, yet again, to receive a signed copy of *For Lancelot Andrewes*.

## TO *Ezra Pound* CC

20 December 1927 [London]

Cher Ezra,

Your letter arrives just as I am on the point of leaving for Paris for a week, V being at present at Malmaison. I am very much relieved to hear that you do not object to the delay in publication.[1] As you have now made your journey to Florence, so that there seems to be no hurry, will you permit me to defer the matter until my return? I shall ask my people to make as near an estimate as possible of your suggestions, and upon my return shall have more leisure and energy for urging what you suggest. With best Wuxmas wishes to D. and yourself,

I am, Sir,
Yours etcetera,
[T.]

## TO *Wyndham Lewis* MS Cornell

29 December 1927 Faber & Gwyer Ltd

Dear Wyndham,

I have returned to London. If you are in town will you dine early next week or this week? <Or this week.> Shd like to see you. I am free at present any night exc. Tuesday.

Yours,
T. S. E.

Sloane 3184

1 – EP had written on 14 Dec.: 'Not so much question of time that worries me. In some ways spring of 1929 wd suit my schedule better, as I have the CANTOS 17–27 and Machine Art, and How To Read scheduled for 1928.

'What I do care about is doing the job right . . .

'Delay means I shall dodder over the damn book, and spend much more time on it than I intended, which is, after all, to F. and G.'s profit, and prob. to general quality of woik . . .'

## TO *William Force Stead* — TS Beinecke

29 December 1927 — Faber & Gwyer Ltd

My dear Stead:

Having been abroad for 8 days and just returned very seasick yesterday I have just received and answer your kind letter. I was sorry you could not lunch that day. I very much appreciate your hospitality. I could not come at once, but could probably come any later weekend in January, but then if you will might come to fulfil my engagement towards yr young friends at Worcester. Will you hint the most convenient date for you?

I am at the moment at a loss to think of a Christian anthropologist; the book has arrived, but, as you know, the crisis in the *Criterion* has made me hesitate for the moment to send out for review any books, when I am not sure that there will be any review to print 'em in. Your point about Polynesians and Christianity is a good one, and ought to have been made by someone before.

I had to leave for Paris a couple of days after I saw you, and did not make any Christmas communion. I went to St Sulpice on Saturday night and to the British Embassy Church on Sunday, but had breakfasted so did not communicate. But (strictly private) I communicate three times a week anyway, so I hope that does not matter.[1]

Congratulations on the *Times* review, which was at least as favourable as the *Times* ever is to any poetry. Yes, I do think it is a good book and deserves success.[2]

Ever yours most cordially
T. S. E.

1–WFS had written (undated): 'I am most interested to hear that you have made your communion and having tried it find it "indispensable". The great thing is to get outside of our own skins and there is something about the communion that draws us out toward the centre of things. Let the sceptics say what they like; there is something there to be discovered and the trouble with them is that they have not discovered it. As Rawlinson said, when we try to explain the metaphysics of it to the man in the street, he gets the impression that we have explained it away . . . But the simple Catholic who simply believes and *sees* that Christ is in the Sacrament, is as wise in his moments of communion as the Angelical Doctor, and far wiser than the ingenious sceptic who curls his lip and walks away . . .'

2–'Mr Stead's New Poems' – on *Festival in Tuscany*, by WFS – *TLS*, 29 Dec. 1927, 988. WFS had written on 22 Nov.: 'Alan Porter tells me he was talking with you the other day and that both of you agreed it is a fairly good book. And this, which might seem damning with faint praise if it came from others, seems almost reckless enthusiasm coming from such diabolically severe critics.'

TO *T. Sturge Moore* TS Texas

30 December 1927 Faber & Gwyer Ltd

Dear Mr Sturge Moore,

I am with great regret returning *In Defence of Beauty* to you on behalf of the firm. I may say that everyone who looked at the book was very much aware of its importance and also very sensible of the value to the firm of having your name on our list; but as they decided after several enquiries that the prospects of American support were inadequate, the majority agreed that it would be inadvisable for them to contemplate publication at the present time. I am personally extremely sorry, and I must also apologise to you for the firm on account of the delay in coming to a decision.

The January and I believe February number of the *Criterion* will appear, and we are hopeful of enlisting sufficient powerful support to enable the review to continue indefinitely. If, therefore, you have written the *Blake* review which you have in hand, and are willing to risk the possibility of no March number appearing, I should be very happy to have it for that number.[1]

With many thanks for the interest you have taken in the *Criterion*.

Yours sincerely,
T. S. Eliot

MS under separate cover

1–Moore's review of several books on Blake, *MC* 7 (Mar. 1928), 272–81.

# BIOGRAPHICAL REGISTER OF PRINCIPAL CORRESPONDENTS

**Conrad Aiken** (1889–1973), American poet and critic. Though he and Eliot were a year apart at Harvard, they became close friends, and fellow editors of *The Harvard Advocate*. Aiken wrote a witty memoir of their times together, 'King Bolo and Others', in *T. S. Eliot: A Symposium,* ed. Richard Marsh and Tambimuttu (1948), describing how they revelled in the comic strips of 'Krazy Kat, and Mutt and Jeff' and in 'American slang'. In the 1920s he settled for some years in Rye, Sussex. His writings include volumes of poetry including *Earth Triumphant* (1914); the Eliot-influenced *House of Dust* (1921); *Selected Poems* (1929), which won the Pulitzer Prize; editions of *Modern American Poets* (1922) and *Selected Poems of Emily Dickinson* (1924); and *Collected Criticism* (1968). His eccentric autobiographical novel *Ushant: An Essay* (1952) satirises TSE as 'Tsetse'. On 7 Nov. 1952 TSE thanked Aiken for sending him an inscribed copy: 'It is certainly a very remarkable book. After the first few pages, I said to myself, this is all very well for a short distance, but can he keep it up through 365 pages without the style becoming oppressive? Anyway, you have done it, and I have read the book through with unflagging interest and I hope that it will have a great success.' However, TSE was to write to Cyril Connolly on 17 Apr. 1963: 'Aiken is an old & loyal friend – I don't think he is a booby, though *Ushant* is a curiously callow work.' Stephen Spender noted in 1966 that Eliot 'once told me that he always felt disturbed and unhappy that . . . Aiken had had so little success as a poet. "I've always thought that he and I were equally gifted, but I've received a large amount of appreciation, and he has been rather neglected. I can't understand it. It seems unjust. It always worries me"' ('Remembering Eliot', *The Thirties and After* [1978], 251). See too *Selected Letters of Conrad Aiken*, ed. Joseph Killorin (1978); Edward Butscher, *Conrad Aiken: Poet of White Horse Vale* (1988).

**Richard Aldington** (1892–1962), poet, critic, translator, biographer, novelist. A friend of Ezra Pound, he was one of the founders of the Imagist movement; a contributor to *Des Imagistes* (1914); and assistant editor of *The Egoist*. In 1913 he married the American poet H.D., though they became estranged and were separated (albeit they did not divorce until 1938). In 1914 he volunteered for WW1, but his enlistment was deferred for medical reasons: he went on active service in June 1916 and was sent to France in December. (TSE replaced him as Literary Editor of *The Egoist*.) During the war, he rose from the ranks to be Acting Captain in the Royal Sussex Regiment. He drew on his experiences in the poems of *Images of War* (1919) and the novel *Death of a Hero* (1929). After WW1, he became friends with TSE, working as his assistant on the *Criterion* and introducing him to Bruce Richmond, editor of the *TLS* (for which TSE wrote some of his finest essays). From 1919 Aldington himself was a regular reviewer of French literature for the *TLS*. In 1928 he went to live in France, where, except for a period in the USA (1935–47), he spent the rest of his life. He is best known for his early Imagist poetry and translations (see for example his edition of *Selections from Rémy de Gourmont*, 1928), for his WW1 novel *Death of a Hero* (1929), and for the controversial *Lawrence of Arabia: A Biographical Inquiry* (1955), which is widely held to have damaged his own reputation. In 1931, he published *Stepping Heavenward*, a lampoon of TSE – who is portrayed as 'Blessed Jeremy Cibber': 'Father Cibber, O.S.B.' – and Vivien ('Adele Palaeologue'). This ended their friendship. His estrangement from Eliot was further publicized in an essay written in the 1930s but published only in 1954, *Ezra Pound and T. S Eliot: A Lecture*, which takes both poets to task for their putatively plagiaristic poetry. He published further biographies, including a controversial study of his friend D. H. Lawrence, *Portrait of a Genius, But . . .* (1950); *Complete Poems* (1948); and *Life for Life's Sake* (memoirs, 1941). See also *Richard Aldington: An Intimate Portrait*, ed. Alister Kershaw and Frédéric-Jacques Temple (1965), which includes a brief tribute by Eliot (with a comment on the 'cruel' *Stepping Heavenward*); 'Richard Aldington's Letters to Herbert Read', ed. David S. Thatcher, *The Malahat Review* 15 (July 1970), 5–44; Charles Doyle, *Richard Aldington: A Biography* (1989); *Richard Aldington: An Autobiography in Letters*, ed. Norman T. Gates (1992); and *Richard Aldington & H. D.: Their lives in letters 1918–61*, ed. Caroline Zilboorg (2003).

**W. H. Auden** (1907–73), prolific poet, playwright, librettist, translator, essayist and editor. He was educated at Gresham's School, Holt, Norfolk, and at Christ Church, Oxford, where he co-edited *Oxford Poetry* (1926, 1927), and where his friend Stephen Spender hand-set about thirty copies of his first book, a pamphlet entitled *Poems* (1928). After going down from Oxford with a third-class degree in English in 1928, he visited Belgium and then lived for a year in Berlin. He worked as a tutor in London, 1929–30; then as a schoolmaster at Larchfield Academy Helensburgh, Dunbartonshire, 1930–2; followed by the Downs School, Colwall, Herefordshire, 1932–5. Although Eliot turned down his initial submission of a book of poems in 1927, he would presently accept 'Paid on Both Sides: A Charade' for the *Criterion*; and Eliot went on for the rest of his life to publish all of Auden's books at Faber & Faber: *Poems* (featuring 'Paid on Both Sides' and thirty short poems, 1930); *The Orators* (1932); *Look, Stranger!* (1937); *Spain* (1936); *Another Time* (1940); *New Year Letter* (1941; published in the USA as *The Double Man*); *The Age of Anxiety* (1947); *For the Time Being* (1945); *The Age of Anxiety: A Baroque Eclogue* (1948); *Nones* (1952); *The Shield of Achilles* (1955); *Homage to Clio* (1960); and *About the House* (1966). Eliot was happy too to publish Auden's play *The Dance of Death* (1933), which was to be performed by the Group Theatre in London in 1934 and 1935; and three further plays written with Christopher Isherwood: *The Dog Beneath the Skin* (1935), which would be performed by The Group Theatre in 1936; *The Ascent of F6* (1936); and *On the Frontier* (1937). In 1935–6 Auden went to work for the General Post Office film unit, writing verse commentaries for two celebrated documentary films, *Coal Face* and *Night Mail*. He collaborated with Louis MacNeice on *Letters from Iceland* (1937); and with Isherwood again on *Journey to a War* (1939). His first libretto was *Paul Bunyan* (performed with music by Benjamin Britten, 1941); and in 1947 he began collaborating with Igor Stravinsky on *The Rake's Progress* (performed in Venice, 1951); and he later co-wrote two librettos for Hans Werner Henze. Other works include *The Oxford Book of Light Verse* (1938); *The Enchafèd Flood: The Romantic Iconography of the Sea* (1951); *The Dyer's Hand* (1963); and *Secondary Worlds* (1968). See further Humphrey Carpenter, *W. H. Auden: A Biography* (1981); Richard Davenport-Hines, *Auden* (1955); and Edward Mendelson, *Early Auden* (1981) and *Later Auden* (1999).

**Montgomery ('Monty') Belgion** (1892–1973), author, was born in Paris of British parents and grew up with a deep feeling for the language and culture of France. In 1915–16 he was editor-in-charge of the European edition of the *New York Herald*; and for the remainder of WW1 he served first as a private in the Honourable Artillery Company, and was later commissioned in the Dorsetshire Regiment. Between the wars he worked for the Paris review *This Quarter* and for newspapers including the *Daily Mail, Westminster Gazette* and the *Daily Mirror*, and for a while he was an editor for Harcourt, Brace & Co., New York. In WW2 he became a captain in the Royal Engineers, and he spent two years in prison camps in Germany. In 1929 Faber & Faber brought out (on TSE's recommendation) his first book, *Our Present Philosophy of Life*. Later writings include *Reading for Profit* (1945) and booklets on H. G. Wells and David Hume.

**Julian Benda** (1867–1956), journalist, political-social philosopher, and critic. Born into a Jewish family in Paris, he studied history at the Sorbonne, and was recognised as a noted essayist and '*intellectuel*', writing for a variety of periodicals including *Revue Blanche*, *Nouvelle Revue Française*, *Mercure de France*, *Divan* and *Le Figaro*. A passionate upholder of the Graeco-Roman ideal of rational order and disinterestedness – Eliot said Benda's 'brand of classicism is just as romantic as anyone else's' – his works include *Dialogues à Byzance* (1900), complete with pro-Dreyfus pieces; *Le Bergsonisme: ou, Une Philosophie de la mobilité* (1912); *Belphégor: Essai sur l'esthétique de la présente société française* (1918); and *Le Trahison des clercs* (*The Treason of the Intellectuals*, 1927) – trans. Richard Aldington in 1928. See further Ray Nichols, *Treason, Tradition, and the Intellectual: Julian Benda and Political Discourse* (1978).

**Arnold Bennett** (1867–1931), author and journalist (and son of a weaver and tailor who eventually qualified and practised as a solicitor), grew up among 'the five towns' of the Potteries and began work at the age of 16 in a solicitor's office; but he swiftly made a name for himself as journalist and prolific author. His best-selling novels include *A Man from the North* (1898), *Anna of the Five Towns* (1902), *Whom God hath Joined* (1906) and *The Old Wives' Tale* (1908) – the first book in the Clayhanger trilogy. His plays, including *The Great Adventure* (1913), were just as successful, with naturalistic and effective dialogue; and it was in his capacity as a capable dramatist that TSE consulted him in the early 1920s – ironically when Eliot was attempting to write a determinedly (and ultimately uncompleted) experimental play, *Sweeney Agonistes*. It says much for Bennett that he took TSE seriously and gave him advice that was valued – though Bennett was not keen on the *Criterion*. See *The Journals of Arnold Bennett*, ed. N. Flowers (3 vols, 1932–5); and Margaret Drabble, *Arnold Bennett: A Biography* (1974).

**Marguerite Caetani**, née Chapin (1880–1963) – born in New London, Connecticut, she was half-sister to Mrs Katherine Biddle, and a cousin of TSE – was married in 1911 to the composer Roffredo Caetani, 17th Duke of Sermoneta and Prince di Bassiano (a godson of Liszt), whose ancestors included two Popes (one of whom had the distinction of being put in Hell by Dante). A patron of the arts, she founded in Paris the review *Commerce* – the title being taken from a line in St-John Perse's *Anabase* ('*ce pur commerce de mon âme*') – which ran from 1924 to 1932; and then, in Rome, *Botteghe oscure*, 1949–60, a biannual review featuring poetry and fiction from many nations – England, Germany, Italy, France, Spain, USA – with contributions published in their original languages. Contributors included André Malraux, Albert Camus, Paul Valéry, Ignazio Silone, Robert Graves, Archibald MacLeish, E. E. Cummings, Marianne Moore.

**Richard Cobden-Sanderson** (1884–1964), printer and publisher, was the son of the bookbinder and printer, T. J. Cobden Sanderson (1840–1922), who was Bertrand Russell's godfather; grandson of the politician and economist Richard Cobden (1804–65). He launched his publishing business in 1919 and was publisher of the *Criterion* from its first number in Oct. 1922 until it was taken over by Faber & Gwyer in 1925. He also published three books with introductions by TSE: *Le Serpent* by Paul Valéry (1924), Charlotte Eliot's *Savanarola* (1926) and Harold Monro's *Collected Poems* (1933). In addition, his firm produced books by Edmund Blunden and David Gascoyne, editions of Shelley, and volumes illustrated by Rex Whistler. He became a dependable friend as well as a colleague of TSE's. His wife was Gwladys (Sally) Cobden-Sanderson.

**Jean Cocteau** (1889–1963), playwright, poet, librettist, novelist, film-maker, artist and designer, was born near Paris and attracted notice with two volumes of verse, *La Lampe d'Aladin* ('Aladdin's Lamp', 1909) and *Prince Frivole* ('The Frivolous Prince', 1910). Becoming associated with many of the foremost exponents of experimental modernism – Proust, Gide, Picasso, Stravinsky, Satie, Modigliani, Diaghilev – he turned his energies to multiple modes of artistic creativity ranging from ballet-scenarios to opera-scenarios, fiction and drama. 'Astonish me!' Diaghilev urged of him. A resourceful collaborator, his works embrace stage productions such as the ballet *Parade* (1917, produced by Diaghilev, with music by Satie and designs by Picasso); *Les Biches* (1924); *Oedipus Rex* (1927, music by Stravinsky); and *La Machine infernale* (produced at the Comédie des Champs-Elysées, 1934); novels including *Thomas l'imposteur* (1923) and *Les enfants terribles* (1929); and films including *Le Sang d'un poète* (1930; 'The Blood of a Poet', 1949).

**R. G. Collingwood** (1889–1943), philosopher and historian; Fellow of Pembroke College, Oxford; later Waynflete Professor of Metaphysical Philosophy, Magdalen College. On 8 Mar. 1938 Collingwood would send TSE a copy of *The Principles of Art* (1938) – which declared: 'In literature, those who chiefly matter have made the choice, and made it rightly. The credit for this belongs in the main to one great poet, who has set the example by taking as his theme in a long series of poems a subject that interests every one, the decay of our civilisation' – with the personal comment: 'in a sense the book is dedicated to you; the concluding pages are all about *The Waste Land*, regarded . . . as a demonstration of what poetry has got to be if my aesthetic theory is to be true! I hope you will be able to forgive me for treating you as a *corpus vile*, and will understand that it is the highest compliment a poor devil of a philosopher has it in his power to pay you.' (TSE wrote to Thomas Stauffer, 17 Aug. 1944: 'Aesthetics was never my strong suit. In fact, it is one department of philosophy which I always shied away from, even in the days when I thought I was going to be a philosopher, and that is a long time ago. I think that instinct told me that the less I thought about general aesthetic theory the better for me. (Incidentally, do you know Collingwood's book *In Praise of Art*? <*Principles of Art* – I am not sure of the title, but I have the book somewhere> To a plain literary practitioner like myself, who, as F. H. Bradley said of himself, has no capacity for the abstruse, Collingwood seems very good.') Collingwood's other works include *Speculum Mentis, or, The Map of Knowledge* (1924), *Outlines of a Philosophy of Art* (1925) and *The Idea of History* (1945). See Fred Inglis, *History Man: The Life of R. G. Collingwood* (2009).

**John Cournos** (1881–1966) – Johann Gregorievich Korshune – naturalised American writer of Russian birth (his Jewish parents fled Russia when he was 10), worked as a journalist on the *Philadelphia Record* and was first noted in England as an Imagist poet; he became better known as a novelist, essayist and translator. After living in England in the 1910s and 1920s, he emigrated to the USA. An unhappy love affair in 1922–3 with Dorothy L. Sayers was fictionalised by her in *Strong Poison* (1930), and by him in *The Devil is an English Gentleman* (1932). His other publications include *London Under the Bolsheviks* (1919), *In Exile* (1923), *Miranda Masters* (a *roman à clef* about the imbroglio between himself, the poet H.D. and Richard Aldington, 1926), and *Autobiography* (1935).

**Ernst Robert Curtius** (1886–1956), German scholar of philology and Romance literature. Scion of a family of scholars, he studied philology and philosophy at Strasbourg, Berlin and Heidelberg, and taught in turn at Marburg, Heidelberg and Bonn. Author of *Die Französische Kultur* (1931; *The Civilization of France*, trans. Olive Wyon, 1932); his most substantial work was *Europäische Literatur und Lateinisches Mittelalter* (1948; trans. Willard R. Trask as *European Literature and the Latin Middle Ages*, 1953), a study of medieval Latin literature and its fructifying influence upon the literatures of modern Europe. In a letter to Max Rychner (24 Oct. 1955) Eliot saluted Curtius on his seventieth birthday by saying that even though he had met him perhaps no more than twice in 35 years, he yet counted him 'among my old friends', and owed him 'a great debt': 'I have . . . my own personal debt of gratitude to acknowledge to Curtius, for translating, and introducing, *The Waste Land*. Curtius was also, I think, the first critic in Germany to recognise the importance of James Joyce. And when it is a question of other writers than myself, and especially when we consider his essays on French contemporaries, and his *Balzac*, and his *Proust*, I am at liberty to praise Curtius as a critic . . . [O]nly a critic of scholarship, discrimination and intellect could perform the services that Curtius has performed. For his critical studies are contributions to the study of the authors criticised, which must be reckoned with by those authors' compatriots. *We cannot determine the true status and significance of the significant writers in our own language, without the aid of foreign critics with a European point of view*. For it is only such critics who can tell us, whether an author is of European importance. And of such critics in our own time, Curtius is one of the most illustrious.' He praised too 'that masterly work, *Europaeische Litteratur und Lateinisches Mittelalter*, on which he had been at work during the years when freedom of speech and freedom of travel were suspended. It bears testimony to his integrity and indomitable spirit . . . Curtius deserves, in his life and in his work, the gratitude and admiration of his fellow writers of every European nation' (Eliot's letter is reproduced in full, in English, in 'Brief über Ernst Robert Curtius', in *Freundesgabe für Ernst Robert Curtis zum 14. April 1956* [Bern, 1956], 25–7.) See also J. H. Copley, '"The Politics of Friendship": T. S. Eliot in Germany Through E. R. Curtius's Looking Glass', in *The International Reception of T. S. Eliot*, ed. Elisabeth Däumer and Shyamal Bagchee (2007), 243–67.

**Martin D'Arcy** (1888–1976), Jesuit priest and theologian, entered the Novitiate in 1906, gained in 1916 a first-class degree in Literae Humaniores at Pope's Hall – the Jesuit private hall of Oxford University – and was ordained a Catholic priest in 1921. After teaching for a while at Stonyhurst College, in 1925 he undertook doctoral research, initially at the Gregorian University in Rome, then at the Jesuit House at Farm Street in London. In 1927 he returned to Campion Hall, Oxford (successor to Pope's Hall), where he lectured and tutored in philosophy at the university. He was Rector and Master of Campion Hall, 1933–45; and Provincial of the British Province of the Jesuits in London, 1945–50. Charismatic and immensely influential as a lecturer, and as an apologist for Roman Catholicism (his prominent converts included Evelyn Waugh), he also wrote studies including *The Nature of Belief* (1931) and *The Mind and Heart of Love* (1945). Lesley Higgins notes: 'Five of his books were reviewed in *The Criterion*, some by Eliot himself; his twenty-two reviews and articles in the latter certainly qualify him as part of what Eliot termed the journal's "definite . . . [and] comprehensive constellation of contributors".' See further H. J. A. Sire, *Father Martin D'Arcy: Philosopher of Christian Love* (1997); Richard Harp, 'A conjuror at the Xmas party', *TLS*, 11 Dec. 2009, 13–15.

**Bonamy Dobrée** (1891–1974), scholar, editor and critic, was to be Professor of English Literature at Leeds University, 1936–55. After service in the army during WW1 (he was twice mentioned in despatches and attained the rank of major), he read English at Christ's College, Cambridge, and taught in London and as a professor of English at the Egyptian University, Cairo, 1925–9. His works include *Restoration Comedy* (1924), *Essays in Biography* (1925), *Restoration Tragedy, 1660–1720* (1929), *Alexander Pope* (1951), and critical editions and anthologies. From 1921 to 1925 Dobrée and his wife Valentine resided at Larrau, a village in the Pyrenees, where he worked as an independent scholar. He was one of TSE's most constant correspondents. On 8 Sept. 1938, TSE would write to George Every SSM on the subject of the projected 'Moot': 'I think [Dobrée] would be worth having . . . He has his nose to the grindstone of the provincial university machine . . . but he is not without perception of the futilities of contemporary education. His mental formation is Liberal, but he has the rare advantage of being a man of breeding, so that his instincts with regard, for instance, to society, the community and the land, are likely to be right. He is also a person of strong, and I imagine hereditary, public spirit.' On 23 Feb. 1963, TSE urged his merits as future editor of Kipling's stories: 'He is far and away the best authority on Kipling . . . I have often discussed Kipling with him, and know that we see eye to eye about the stories. As for Dobrée's general literary achievements, they are very high indeed: his published work is not only very scholarly, but of the highest critical standing, and he writes well . . . If this job is ever done – and I should like to see it done during my lifetime – Dobrée is the man to do it.' See also Jason Harding, *The 'Criterion': Cultural Politics and Periodical Networks in Inter-War Britain* (2002).

**Charlotte Champe Stearns Eliot** (1843–1929), the poet's mother, was born on 22 October in Baltimore, Maryland, the second child and second daughter of Thomas Stearns (1811–96) and Charlotte Blood Stearns (1818–93). She went first to private schools in Boston and Sandwich, followed by three years at the State Normal School, Framlingham, Mass., from which she graduated in 1862. After teaching for a while at private schools in West Chester, Pennsylvania, and Milwaukee, Wisconsin, she spent two years with a Quaker family in Coatesville, Pa. She then taught at Antioch College, Ohio, 1865–7; at her Framingham School; and at St Louis Normal School. It was while she was at the last post that she met Henry Ware Eliot, entrepreneur, whom she married on 27 October 1868. She was Secretary of the Mission Free School of the Church of the Messiah for many years. As her youngest son was growing up, she became more thoroughly involved in social work through the Humanity Club of St Louis, whose members were disturbed by knowing that young offenders awaiting trial were being held for long periods with adults. In 1899, a committee of two was appointed, with Mrs Eliot as chairman, to bring about reform. It was in large part due to her campaigning and persistence over several years that the Probation Law 1901 was approved; and in 1903, by mandate of the Juvenile Court Law, a juvenile court was established with its own probation officer and a separate place of detention. As a girl, Charlotte had nursed literary ambitions, and throughout her life wrote poems, some of which (such as 'Easter Songs' and 'Poems on the Apostles') were printed in the *Christian Register*. In 1904 she published *William Greenleaf Eliot: Minister, Educator, Philanthropist*, a memoir of her beloved father-in-law (TSE's grandfather); and it came as a great joy to her when TSE arranged for the publication of her *Savanarola: A Dramatic Poem*, with an introduction by himself (London, 1926). When she was shown the issue of *Smith Academy Record* containing TSE's 'A Lyric' (1905), she said (as TSE would remember) 'that she thought it better than anything in verse she had ever written'. TSE reflected further on that fine declaration: 'I knew what her verse meant to her. We did not discuss the matter further.' Inspired by a keen ethic of public service, she was a member of both the Wednesday Club of St Louis and the Missouri Society of the Colonial Dames of America, serving successively as Secretary, Vice-President and President. She chaired a committee to award a Washington University scholarship that required the beneficiary to do a certain amount of patriotic work; and in 1917-18 she did further service as chair of the War Work committee of the Colonial Dames. After the death of her husband in January 1919, she moved home to Cambridge, Mass.

**Henry Ware Eliot, Jr** (1879–1947), TSE's elder brother, went to school at Smith Academy and passed two years at Washington University, St. Louis, before going on to Harvard. At Harvard, he displayed a gift for light verse in *Harvard Celebrities* (1901), illustrated with 'Caricatures and Decorative Drawings' by two fellow students. After graduating, he spent a year at Law School, but subsequently followed a career in printing, publishing and advertising. He attained a partnership in Husband & Thomas (later the Buchen Company), a Chicago advertising agency, 1917-29, during which time he gave much financial assistance to TSE and regularly advised him on investments. He accompanied their mother on her visit to London in the summer of 1921, his first trip away from the USA. In February 1926, he married Theresa Anne Garrett (1884–1981), and later the same year the couple went on holiday to Italy along with TSE and Vivien. In 1932 he displayed a different side to his talent when he brought out a detective novel, *The Rumble Murders* (Houghton Mifflin), under the nom de plume Mason Deal. But it was not until late in life that he found his true calling, as a Research Fellow in Anthropology at the Peabody Museum, Harvard: see his posthumous work *Excavations in Mesopotamia and Western Iran, Sites of 4000 to 500 B.C.* (Peabody Museum of American Archaeology and Ethnology, 1950). He was one of TSE's most regular and trusted correspondents; and he was instrumental in building up the T. S. Eliot collection at Eliot House (Houghton Library). Of slighter build than his brother – who remarked upon his 'Fred Astaire figure' – Henry suffered from deafness owing to scarlet fever as a child, and this may have contributed to his diffidence. Unselfishly devoted to TSE, whose growing up he movingly recorded with his camera, Henry took him to his first Broadway musical, *The Merry Widow* (which remained a favourite). It was with his brother in mind that TSE wrote: 'The notion of some infinitely gentle / Infinitely suffering thing' ('Preludes' IV).

**Charlotte Eliot** (1874–1926), third child in the Eliot family ('my favourite sister', said TSE), married George Lawrence Smith, an architect, on 5 September 1903. She studied art at college in St Louis and in Boston, with sculpture being her especial interest. She died of peritonitis.

**Margaret Dawes Eliot** (1871–1956), second child in the Eliot family: never married. In an undated letter (1952) to his Harvard classmate Leon M. Little, TSE wrote: 'Margaret is 83, deaf, eccentric, recluse (I don't think she had bought any new clothes since 1900).'

**Marion Cushing Eliot** (1877–1964), fourth child of Henry Ware and Charlotte Champe Eliot, studied at Miss Folsom's school for social service in Boston. She visited TSE in London with his mother in 1921.

**Vivien Eliot,** née Haigh-Wood (1888–1947). Born in Bury, Lancashire, on 28 May 1888, 'Vivy' was brought up in Hampstead from the age of 3. After meeting TSE in company with Scofield Thayer in Oxford early in 1915, she and TSE hastened to be married just a few weeks later, on 26 June 1915. (TSE, who was lodging at 35 Greek Street, Soho, London, was recorded in the marriage certificate as 'of no occupation'.) The marriage was not a happy one for either of them. She developed close friendships with Mary Hutchinson, Ottoline Morrell and others in TSE's circle. Despite chronic personal and medical difficulties, they remained together until 1933, when TSE resolved to separate from her during his visit to America. She was never to be reconciled to the separation, became increasingly ill, and in 1938 was confined to a psychiatric hospital, where she died (of 'syncope' and 'cardiovascular degeneration') on 22 January 1947. She is the dedicatee of *Ash-Wednesday* (1930). She published sketches in the *Criterion* (under various pseudonyms with the initials 'F.M.'), and collaborated on the *Criterion* and other works. See Carole Seymour-Jones, *Painted Shadow: The Life of Vivienne Eliot* (2001).

**Geoffrey Faber** (1889–1961), publisher and poet, was educated at Malvern College and Christ Church, Oxford, where he took a double first in Classical Moderations (1910) and Literae Humaniores (1912). He was called to the bar by the Inner Temple (1921), though he was never to practise law. In 1919 he was elected a prize fellow of All Souls College, Oxford, which he went on to serve in the capacity of Estates Bursar, 1923–51. Before WW1 – in which he served with the London Regiment (Post Office Rifles), seeing action in France and Belgium – he spent 18 months as assistant to Humphrey Milford, publisher of Oxford University Press. After the war he passed three years working for Strong & Co. Ltd., brewers (there was a family connection), before going in for publishing on a full-time basis by joining forces with his All Souls colleague Maurice Gwyer and his wife, Alsina Gwyer, who were trying to run a specialised imprint called the Scientific Press that Lady Gwyer had inherited from her father, Sir Henry Burdett: its weekly journal, the *Nursing Mirror*, was their most successful output. Following protractedly difficult negotiations, in 1925 Faber became chair of their restructured general publishing house which was provisionally styled Faber & Gwyer. After being introduced by Charles Whibley to T. S. Eliot, Faber was so impressed by the 37-year-old American that he chose both to take on the running of the *Criterion* and to appoint Eliot to the board of his firm (Eliot's *Poems 1909–1925* was one of the first books to be put out by the new imprint, and its first best-seller), which was relocated from Southampton Row to 24 Russell Square. By 1929 both the Gwyers and the *Nursing Mirror* were disposed of to advantage, and the firm took final shape as Faber & Faber, with Richard de la Mare and two additional Americans, Frank Morley and Morley Kennerley, joining the board. Faber chaired the Publishers' Association, 1939–41 – campaigning successfully for the repeal of a wartime tax on books – and helping to set up the National Book League. He was knighted in 1954, and gave up the chairmanship of Faber & Faber in 1960. His publications as poet included *The Buried Stream* (1941), and his works of non-fiction were *Oxford Apostles* (1933) and *Jowett* (1957), as well as an edition of the works of John Gay (1926). In 1920 he married Enid Richards, with whom he had two sons and a daughter. He died at his home in 1961.

**John Gould Fletcher** (1886–1950), American poet and critic, scion of a wealthy Southern family, dropped out of Harvard in 1907 (his father's death having secured him temporarily independent means) and lived for many years in Europe, principally in London; a friend of Ezra Pound, he became one of the mainstays of Imagism and published much original poetry. In later years he returned to his native Arkansas and espoused agrarian values. His *Selected Poems* won the Pulitzer Prize in 1939. Fletcher wrote of TSE in *Life Is My Song: The Autobiography of John Gould Fletcher* (1937): 'As an editor, I found him to be practically ideal, willing for opinions to be mooted that ran contrary to his own avowed toryism, so long as those opinions were not merely emotional prejudices, but were backed up by something resembling intellectual judgment'

(308). See also Fletcher, *Life for Life's Sake* (1941); *Selected Letters of John Gould Fletcher*, ed. Leighton Rudolph, Lucas Carpenter, Ethel C. Simpson (1996) – 'One of my difficulties with Eliot, whom I knew fairly well for nearly 15 years, was his intellectual snobbery'; Lucas Carpenter, *John Gould Fletcher and Southern Modernism* (1990); and Ben F. Johnson III, *Fierce Solitude: A Life of John Gould Fletcher* (1994).

**Frank Stuart ('F. S.') Flint** (1885–1960), English poet and translator, and civil servant, grew up in terrible poverty – 'gutter-born and gutter-bred', he would say – and left school at 13. But he set about to educate himself in European languages and literature, as well as in history and philosophy. In 1908 he started writing articles and reviews for the *New Age*, then for the *Egoist* and for *Poetry* (ed. Harriet Monroe). Quickly gaining in reputation and authority (especially on French literature – his influential piece on 'Contemporary French Poetry' appeared in Harold Monro's *Poetry Review* in 1912) – he soon became associated with T. E. Hulme, Ezra Pound, Richard Aldington and Hilda Doolittle; and he contributed poems to the *English Review* (ed. Ford Madox Hueffer) and to Pound's anthology *Des Imagistes* (1914). In 1920 he published *Otherworld Cadences* (The Poetry Bookshop); and with TSE and Aldous Huxley he was one of the contributors to *Three Critical Essays on Modern English Poetry*, in *Chapbook* II: 9 (March 1920). Between 1909 and 1920 he published three volumes of poetry, though his work as essayist, reviewer and translator was the more appreciated: he became a regular contributor to the *Criterion* from the 1920s – and a member of the inner circle gathered round TSE – even while continuing to work in the statistics division of the Ministry of Labour (where he was Chief of the Overseas Section) until retiring in 1951. See also *The Fourth Imagist: Selected Poems of F. S. Flint*, ed. Michael Copp (2007).

**E. M. Forster** (1879–1970), novelist and essayist, was educated at King's College, Cambridge, where he gained a second in the classics tripos (and where he was elected to the exclusive Conversazione Society, the inner circle of the Apostles). Though intimately associated with the Bloomsbury group in London, where his circle of friends and acquaintances came to include Edward Marsh, Edward Garnett, Duncan Grant, Roger Fry, Lytton Strachey and Leonard and Virginia Woolf, he derived much from visits to Italy, Greece, Egypt and India – where he worked for a while as private secretary to the Maharaja of Dewas: that experience brought about one of his most acclaimed novels, *A Passage to India* (1924), which sold around one million copies during his lifetime. His other novels include *Where Angels Fear to Tread* (1905), *A Room with a View* (1908), *Howards End* (1910) and the posthumous *Maurice* (1971, written 1910–13), a work that addressed his homosexuality. He gave the Clark Lectures at Cambridge in 1927 – in succession to TSE – which were published as *Aspects of the Novel* (1927). He turned down a knighthood, but in 1953 he was appointed a Companion of Honour; and he received the OM in 1969. See also Forster, 'Mr Eliot and His Difficulties', *Life and Letters*, 2: 13 (June 1929), 417–25; P. N. Furbank *E. M. Forster* (2 vols, 1977, 1978); *Selected Letters of E. M. Forster*, ed. Mary Lago and P. N. Furbank (2 vols, 1983–5); Nicola Beauman, *Morgan: A Biography of E. M. Forster* (1993).

**Robert Graves** (1895–1985), poet and novelist. Educated at Charterhouse and St John's College, Oxford, he served during WW1 with the Royal Welch Fusiliers (being wounded at the battle of the Somme in 1916, and hospitalised with shell-shock in 1917). In 1918 he married Nancy Nicholson (1899–1977), but he then lived for several stressful but collaboratively fertile years in a *ménage à trois* with the American poet and critic Laura Riding (1901-91). Graves lived with his wife and Riding during his time as a Professor of English literature at Cairo University from January 1926 till July 1926. Riding became Graves's mistress in 1926 and stayed with him until 1939: among other achievements, they co-authored *A Survey of Modernist Poetry* (1927). Other major writings include *Good-bye to All That* (memoir, 1929), *I, Claudius* (historical fiction, 1934), which won both the Hawthornden Prize and the James Tait Black Memorial Prize, and which was adapted as a television series starring Derek Jacobi in 1976; *Wife to Mr Milton* (novel, 1941); *The Long Weekend* (social history, written with Alan Hodge, 1941); *The White Goddess: A Historical Grammar of Poetic Myth* (1948); *The Nazarene Gospel Restored* (1953); *The Greek Myths* (1955); *Collected Poems* (1959); and *The Crowning Privilege* (1956). In 1961 he was awarded the Gold Medal of the National Poetry Society of America; and he held the Oxford Chair of Poetry, 1961–6. It was in 1966 too that he was honoured by the award of the Queen's Gold Medal for Poetry.

**H. J. C. Grierson** (1866–1960): Regius Professor of Rhetoric and English Literature, University of Edinburgh, 1915–35; knighted in 1936; celebrated for his edition of *The Poems of John Donne* (2 vols, 1912) and *Metaphysical Lyrics and Poems of the Seventeenth Century* (1921)

– which TSE reviewed in the *TLS*, 21 Oct. 1921. Cairns Craig, in 'The Last Romantics: How the Scholarship of Herbert Grierson influenced Modernist poetry' (*TLS*, 15 Jan. 2010, 14–15), argues that '*The Waste Land* is saturated with echoes of Grierson's *Metaphysical Lyrics and Poems*. When Eliot sent a copy of his *Collected Poems* to Grierson, it was inscribed "to whom all English men of letters are indebted".' (Letty Grierson remembers a slightly different wording, 'to whom all poets of today are indebted': noted in the Grierson catalogue issued by James Fergusson Books & Manuscripts, 2010.) TSE contributed to *Seventeenth Century Studies Presented to Sir Herbert Grierson* (1938).

**Maurice Haigh-Wood** (1896–1980), TSE's brother-in-law. He was six years younger than his sister Vivien, and after attending Ovingdean prep school and Malvern School, trained at Sandhurst Military Academy, before receiving his commission on 11 May 1915 as a Second Lieutenant in the 2nd Battalion, The Manchester Regiment. He served in the infantry for the war, and on regular visits home gave TSE his closest contact with the nightmare of life and death in the trenches. After the war, he found it difficult to get himself established, but became a stockbroker, and he remained friendly with, and respectful towards, TSE even after his separation from Vivien in 1933. In 1930 he married a 25-year-old American dancer, Ahmé Hoagland, and they had two children.

**John Hayward** (1905–65), editor, critic and anthologist, read modern languages at King's College, Cambridge. Despite the early onset of muscular dystrophy, he became a prolific and eminent critic and editor, bringing out in quick succession editions of the works of Rochester, Saint-Évremond, Jonathan Swift, Robert Herrick and Samuel Johnson. Other publications included *Complete Poems and Selected Prose of John Donne* (1929), *Donne* (1950), *T. S. Eliot: Selected Prose* (1953), *The Penguin Book of English Verse* (1958) and *The Oxford Book of Nineteenth Century English Verse* (1964). Celebrated as the learned and acerbic editor of *The Book Collector*, he was made a Chevalier of the Légion d'honneur in 1952, a CBE in 1953. Writers including Graham Greene and Stevie Smith valued his editorial counsel; and Paul Valéry invited him to translate his comedy *Mon Faust*. Hayward advised TSE on various essays, poems, and plays including *The Cocktail Party* and *The Confidential Clerk*, and most helpfully of all on *Four Quartets*. See also Helen Gardner, *The Composition of 'Four Quartets'* (1978).

**Mary Hutchinson**, née Barnes (1889–1977), a half-cousin of Lytton Strachey, married St John ('Jack') Hutchinson in 1910. A prominent Bloomsbury hostess, she was for several years the acknowledged mistress of the art critic, Clive Bell, and became a close, supportive friend of TSE and VHE. TSE published one of her stories ('War') in *The Egoist*, and she later brought out a book of sketches, *Fugitive Pieces* (1927), under the imprint of the Hogarth Press. She wrote a short unpublished memoir of TSE (Harry Ransom Humanities Research Center, Austin). See David Bradshaw, '"Those Extraordinary Parakeets": Clive Bell and Mary Hutchinson', *The Charleston Magazine*, in two parts: 16 (Autumn/Winter 1997), 5–12; 17 (Spring/Summer 1998), 5–11.

**Aldous Huxley** (1894–1963), novelist, poet and essayist, whose early novels *Crome Yellow* (1921) and *Antic Hay* (1923) were immensely successful satires of post-war English culture. While teaching at Eton, Aldous told his brother Julian in December 1916 that he 'ought to read' Eliot's 'things', which are 'all the more remarkable when one knows the man, ordinarily just an Europeanized American, overwhelmingly cultured, talking about French literature in the most uninspired fashion imaginable'. For his part, Eliot thought Huxley's early poems fell too much under the spell of Laforgue (and of his own poetry), but Huxley went on to become not only a popular comic novelist, but, as the author of *Brave New World* and *The Doors of Perception*, a highly influential intellectual figure. See Nicholas Murray, *Aldous Huxley: An English Intellectual* (2002); and Aldous Huxley, *Selected Letters*, ed. James Sexton (2007).

**Horace Meyer Kallen** (1882–1974), German-born philosopher, taught at Harvard, Princeton and Wisconsin before co-founding in 1918 the New School for Social Research, New York. Educated at Harvard (where William James was his mentor), he was an ardent cultural pluralist. His numerous works include *William James and Henri Bergson: A Study in Contrasting Theories of Life* (1914); *The Book of Job as a Greek Tragedy* (1918); *Judaism at Bay: Essays Toward the Adjustment of Judaism to Modernity* (1933); *Art and Freedom* (1942); *Modernity and Liberty* (1947); *Ideals and Experience* (1948); *The Liberal Spirit* (1948); *Patterns of Progress* (1950); *Secularism is the Will of God* (1954); *Cultural Pluralism and the American Idea* (1956). Fellow of the Jewish Academy of Arts and Sciences, and Fellow of the International Institute of Arts and Letters, he was a leader of the American Jewish Congress, a member of the executive board of the World Jewish Congress, Chair of the YIVO

Institute for Jewish Research. TSE wrote in his Faber & Faber reader's report (16 June 1929) on Kallen's book *Frontiers of Hope*: 'Kallen, whom I have known for many years, was a favourite disciple of William James, and a brilliant philosopher, until he abandoned metaphysics for Zionism and social reform. He is a Jew who has abandoned the faith but retained the race. I began the book with a prejudice against it, however; but found it extremely interesting. It is well written, and the personal sketches of travel blend in well with the social study. He visited Palestine as a Zionist, and Italy, Poland and Russia; and his observations and reflections on the present status of Jews in those countries are well worth reading. It is really an interesting document. Of course it must be remembered that Kallen is very well known in New York, the largest Jewish town in the world . . . If the book can be sold, I recommend it strongly. It should at least have another reading, unless it is decided a priori unmarketable.' (Faber Misc. 5/2). See also *The Legacy of Horace Kallen*, ed. Milton R. Konvitz (1987); Sarah L. Schmidt, *Horace M. Kallen: Prophet of American Zionism* (1995); and Ranen Omer, '"It Is I Who Have Been Defending a Religion Called Judaism": The T. S. Eliot and Horace M. Kallen Correspondence', *Texas Studies in Literature and Language* 39: 4 (Winter 1997), 321–56.

**Wyndham Lewis** (1882–1957), painter, novelist, philosopher, critic, was one of the major modernist writers. A friend of Ezra Pound, Lewis was the leading artist associated with Vorticism, and editor of *BLAST*, the movement's journal (1914–15), in which TSE's 'Preludes' and 'Rhapsody on a Windy night' appeared (July 1915). Lewis served as a bombardier and war-artist on the Western Front, 1916–18, and wrote memorable accounts of the period in his memoir *Blasting and Bombardiering* (1937), including brilliant portraits of TSE, Pound and Joyce, and wartime and modernist London. TSE reviewed Lewis's first novel *Tarr* (1918) in *The Egoist* 5: 8 (Sept. 1918), describing him as 'the most fascinating personality of our time', in whose work 'we recognize the thought of the modern and the energy of the cave-man' (106). In turn, Lewis considered Eliot 'the most interesting man in London society' (7 Nov. 1918). TSE, who thought Lewis's work 'so imaginative and visually concrete' (letter to Philip Lane, 4 Dec. 1934), published pieces by him in the *Criterion* and, even though Lewis was notoriously cantankerous, kept up a lifetime's friendship with him. Lewis did a number of drawings of TSE, one of which hung in his flat – reproduced in vol. 2 of *Letters* – and his best-known portrait of him (rejected by the Royal Academy) is now in Durban. On Lewis's death, TSE wrote 'The Importance of Wyndham Lewis' in *The Sunday Times*

(10 Mar. 1957), and a memoir in *Hudson Review* X: 2 (Summer 1957): 'He was . . . a highly strung, nervous man, who was conscious of his own abilities, and sensitive to slight or neglect . . . He was independent, outspoken, and difficult. Temperament and circumstances combined to make him a great satirist . . . I remember Lewis, at the time when I first knew him, and for some years thereafter, as incomparably witty and amusing in company . . . ' TSE wrote too, for *Spectrum*: 'Wyndham Lewis was in my opinion one of the few men of letters of my generation whom I should call, without qualification, men of genius. It is for other painters and draughtsmen to praise his genius as a painter and draughtsman. I would only like to repeat what I have said several times before, that Lewis was the most prominent and versatile prose-writer of my time. I would also like to pay a special tribute to the work he did after he became blind. In *Self-Condemned* he seems to have written a novel greater than *Tarr* or *The Revenge for Love*; in *Monstre Gai* a sequel to *The Childermass* more remarkable than *The Childermass* itself. It is a great artist and one of the most intelligent men of my age who is dead' (letter to Hugh Kenner, 27 Mar. 1957). See *The Letters of Wyndham Lewis*, ed. W. K. Rose (1963); Paul O'Keeffe, *Some Sort of Genius: A Life of Wyndham Lewis* (2000).

**Thomas McGreevy** (1893–1967) – the family name was 'McGreevy', but by the 1930s he would assume the more Irish spelling 'MacGreevy' – Kerry-born poet, literary and art critic, and arts administrator, worked for the Irish Land Commission before serving in WW1 as a Second Lieutenant in the British Royal Field Artillery: he fought at Ypres and the Somme, and was twice wounded. After reading History and Political Science at Trinity College, Dublin, he moved in 1925 to London, where he met TSE and started to write for the *Criterion*, the *TLS* (with an introduction from TSE) and *Nation & Athenaeum*. His poem 'Dysert' appeared in *NC* 4 (Jan. 1926) under the pseudonym 'L. St. Senan' (the title was later changed to 'Homage to Jack Yeats'). In 1927 he took up teaching English at the École Normale Supérieur in Paris, where he became friends with Beckett and Joyce (to whom he had been introduced in 1924) and with Richard Aldington. (His promotional essay on Joyce's incipient *Finnegans Wake* – 'The Catholic Element in Work in Progress' – appeared in *Our Exagmination round his Factification for Incamination of Work in Progress* in 1929.) In addition, he journeyed through Italy with W. B. Yeats. Back in London in 1933, he lectured at the National Gallery and wrote for *The Studio*. Ultimately he was appointed Director of the National Gallery of Ireland, 1950-63. He was made Chevalier de la Légion d'Honneur, 1948;

Cavaliere Ufficiale al merito della Repubblica Italiana, 1955; and Officier de la Légion d'Honneur, 1962. In 1929 he published a translation of Paul Valéry's *Introduction à la méthode de Léonard de Vinci* (*Introduction to the Method of Leonardo da Vinci*); and in 1931, two short monographs, *T. S. Eliot: A Study* and *Richard Aldington: An Englishman*; and his *Poems* would appear in 1934. His publications on art include *Jack B. Yeats: An Appreciation and an Interpretation* (1945) and *Nicolas Poussin* (1960). See also *The Collected Poems of Thomas MacGreevy: An Annotated Edition*, ed. Susan Schreibman (Dublin, 1991).

**Frederic Manning** (1882–1935), Australian writer who settled in 1903 in England, where he came to know artists and writers including Max Beerbohm, William Rothenstein, Richard Aldington and Ezra Pound (the latter would compliment him as 'the first licherary ComPanionship in Eng/ of Ez'); author of *Scenes and Portraits* (1909; 2nd edn, revised and enlarged, 1930). Despite being an asthmatic, he served in the ranks (Shropshire Light Infantry) in WW1, being involved for four months in heavy fighting on the Somme: this experience brought about his greatest achievement, a novel about the Western Front, *The Middle Parts of Fortune* (privately printed, 1929; standard text, 1977; expurgated as *Her Privates We*, credited pseudonymously to 'Private 19022', 1930; republished in full, with intro. by William Boyd, 1999) – 'the best book to come out of the First World War,' Eliot is said to have said of it. In a letter to Aldington (6 July 1921), Eliot described Manning as 'undoubtedly one of the very best prose writers we have'; and he wrote of him in a later year: 'I did not know him well myself, though I have met him – I think directly after the first World War – and I have a precious copy which he gave me of *Her Privates We* and later I went to his funeral in Kensal Green . . . I remember him as a very careful and meticulous letter writer – one of few people I knew who put the first word of the next page at the bottom of every page of their letter' (letter to L. T. Hergenhan, 26 Oct. 1962). See Verna Coleman, *The Last Exquisite: A Portrait of Frederic Manning* (1990).

**Henri Massis** (1886–1970), right-wing Roman Catholic critic: contributor to *L'Action Française*; co-founder and editor of *La Revue Universelle*. Closely associated with Charles Maurras, his writings include *Jugements* (2 vols., 1924), *Jacques Rivière* (1925), and *La Défense de l'Occident* (1928). A defender of Mussolini and Salazar, his later works include *Chefs: Les Dictateurs et nous* (1939) and *Maurras et notre temps* (2 vols, 1951). On 1 Nov. 1945 TSE wrote the following testimony: 'I, Thomas Stearns

Eliot, British subject, of 24 Russell Square, London, W.C.1., England, doctor honoris causa of the Universities of Cambridge, Edinburgh, Leeds, Bristol, Columbia, Honorary Fellow of Magdalene College, Cambridge, a member of the board of directors of the publishing house of Faber & Faber, Ltd., London, testify that I have known Monsieur Henri Massis for over twenty years. The firm of publishers of which I am a director published an English translation of his *Défense de l'Occident*; and M. Massis was a contributor to a quarterly review, *The Criterion* of which I was the editor. I saw M. Massis whenever I visited Paris, and when he visited London. I also received regularly *La Revue Universelle* of which on the death of Jacques Bainville he became the editor. The intellectual bond between myself and M. Massis was the common concern for the civilisation of Western Europe, the apprehension of the Germanic danger, and a similar diagnosis of its nature . . . We were also in accord in attaching great importance to the development of the closest possible relations in every way, between France and England. My conversations with M. Massis, as well as his writings, left me with the strongest impression that he was not only a man of clear vision in these matters, but also a patriot of integrity and probity, who would never hesitate to sacrifice his own interests to those of his country. I should always have said that the love of France was one of his most conspicuous characteristics. And I cannot believe that so passionate a nationalist can be suspected seriously of having used his editorship of *La Revue Universelle* in order to ensure anything but the consolidation of an intellectual resistance to the plans of Germany for the subordination of his country.'

**Charles Maurras** (1868–1952): French poet, critic, political philosopher and polemical journalist; founding editor and moving spirit of the monarchist paper, *L'Action Française* (1908–44) – which was ultimately to support Pétain and Vichy during WW2. TSE was to write of Maurras, in a letter to Vernon Watkins dated 10 Apr. 1946: 'He was condemned as a collaborator and is in prison for the rest of his life unless he is later released on compassionate grounds. Maurras was one of those whose collaboration, if it can be called that, was the result of mistaken judgement and certainly not unpatriotic or self-interested motives.' Building on 'three traditions' – classicism, Catholicism, monarchism – Maurras's ideology was to become increasingly right-wing, authoritarian and anti-democratic. In 1925 TSE planned to write a book about Maurras; and he later wrote 'The *Action Française*, M. Maurras and Mr. Ward', *MC* 7 (Mar. 1928). TSE said he had been 'a reader of the work of M. Maurras for eighteen years', and, far from 'drawing him away from' Christianity – during 1926 Maurras was even condemned by the Pope, with five of his books being placed on the Index – it had had the opposite effect. (Paul Elmer More wrote to Austin Warren on 11 Aug. 1929, of Eliot: 'some time between *The Waste Land* and *For Lancelot Andrewes* he underwent a kind of conversion, due largely I believe to the influence of Maurras and the Action Française' – quoted in Arthur Hazard Dakin, *Paul Elmer More* [Princeton, 1960], 269. However, Eliot would write this comment in the margin of his copy of Dakin's book on More: 'Hardly possible. But Maurras convinced me, as he convinced my friend Massis, of the social importance of the *Church*. But there is a gap here which Maurras could not bridge.') In a later essay, TSE cited Léon, Whibley, Daudet and Maurras as the 'three best writers of invective of their time' (*SE*, 499). Eliot would ultimately write of Maurras to William Force Stead, on 19 Mar. 1954: 'I am a disciple of Charles Maurras only in certain respects and with critical selection. I do owe Maurras a good deal, and retain my admiration for him, but I think he had serious errors of political judgment – in fact, he should have confined himself, I think, to the philosophy of politics, and never have engaged in political agitation at all. In that, however, I may be wrong – one never knows what things would have been like, had they been different.' See also James Torrens, SJ, 'Charles Maurras and Eliot's "New Life"', *PMLA* 89: 2 (Mar. 1974), 312–22.

**Jean de Menasce** (1902–73), theologian and orientalist (his writings include studies in Judaism, Zionism and Hasidism), was born in Alexandria into an aristocratic Jewish Egyptian family and educated in Alexandria, at Balliol College, Oxford (where he was contemporary with Graham Greene and took his BA in 1924), and at the Sorbonne (*Licence ès Lettres*). In Paris, he was associated with the magazines *Commerce* and *L'Esprit*, and he translated several of TSE's poems for French publication: his translation of *The Waste Land* was marked '*revué et approuvée par l'auteur*'. He became a Catholic convert in 1926, was ordained in 1935 a Dominican priest – Father Pierre de Menasce – and went on to be Professor of the History of Religion at the University of Fribourg, 1938–48; Professor and Director of Studies, specialising in Ancient Iranian Religions, at the École Pratique des Hautes Études, Paris. Eliot came to consider him 'the only really first-rate French translator I have ever had' (letter to Kathleen Raine, 17 May 1944).

**Harold Monro** (1879–1932), poet, editor, publisher, bookseller. In 1913 he founded the Poetry Bookshop at 35 Devonshire Street, London, where poets would give readings and lectures. In 1912 he briefly edited *The Poetry Review* for the Poetry Society; then his own periodicals, *Poetry and Drama*, 1913–15, and *The Chapbook* (originally *The Monthly Chapbook*), 1919–25. From the Poetry Bookshop, Monro would put out a remarkable mix of publications including the five volumes of *Georgian Poetry*, ed. Edward Marsh (1872–1953), between 1912 and 1922 (popular anthologies which sold in the region of 15,000 copies), the English edition of *Des Imagistes*, and the first volumes by writers including Richard Aldington, F. S. Flint and Robert Graves, along with some of his own collections including *Children of Love* (1915) and *Strange Meetings* (1917). TSE was to accept *The Winter Solstice* for publication by Faber & Gwyer as no. 13 of the Ariel Poems. Though a homosexual, Monro was to marry the sister of a friend, 1903–16; and in 1920 he wed Alida Klemantaski (daughter of a Polish-Jewish trader), with whom he never cohabited but who was ever loving and supportive to him: both of them endeared themselves to Eliot, who would occasionally use the premises of the Poetry Bookshop for meetings of contributors to the *Criterion*. After Monro's death, TSE wrote a 'Critical Note' for *The Collected Poems of Harold Monro*, ed. Alida Monro (1933). See Joy Grant, *Harold Monro and the Poetry Bookshop* (1967); and Dominic Hibberd, *Harold Monro: Poet of the New Age* (2001).

**Marianne Moore** (1887–1972), American poet and critic, contributed to *The Egoist* from 1915. Her first book, *Poems*, was published in London in 1921. She went on to become in 1925 acting editor of *The Dial*, editor, 1927–9, and an important and influential modern poet. Eliot found her 'an extremely intelligent person, very shy . . . One of the most observant people I have ever met'. Writing to her on 3 April 1921, he said her verse interested him 'more than that of anyone now writing in America'. And in Eliot's introduction to her *Selected Poems* (1935), which he brought out from Faber & Faber, he stated that her 'poems form part of the small body of durable poetry written in our time'.

**Thomas Sturge Moore** (1870–1944), English poet, playwright, critic and artist – and brother of the philosopher G. E. Moore – was christened Thomas but adopted his mother's maiden name 'Sturge' to avoid confusion with the Irish poet Thomas Moore. A prolific poet, author of 31 plays, and a loyal contributor to the *Criterion*, he was also a close friend of

W. B. Yeats, for whom he designed bookplates and bookbindings. He published his first collection of poems, *The Vinedresser and Other Poems*, in 1899. See also *W. B. Yeats and T. Sturge Moore: Their Correspondence, 1901–1937*, ed. Ursula Bridge (1953); Frederick L. Gwynn, *Sturge Moore and the Life of Art* (1951).

**Paul Elmer More** (1864–1937), critic, scholar and prolific writer, had grown up in St Louis, Missouri, and attended Washington University before going on to Harvard; at one time he had taught Greek to TSE's brother Henry. Initially a humanist, by the 1930s he assumed an Anglo-Catholic position not unlike that of TSE (who appreciated the parallels between their spiritual development). See also 'An Anglican Platonist: The Conversion of Paul Elmer More', *TLS*, 30 Oct. 1937, 792. At the outset of his career, More taught classics at Harvard and Bryn Mawr; thereafter he became a journalist, serving as literary editor of *The Independent* (1901–3) and the New York *Evening Post* (1903–9), and as editor of *The Nation* (1909-14), before finally turning to freelance writing and teaching. TSE keenly admired More's many works, in particular *Shelburne Essays* (11 vols, 1904–21), *The Greek Tradition* (5 vols, 1924–31) and *The Demon of the Absolute* (1928); and he went to great trouble in the 1930s in his efforts to secure a publisher for *Pages from an Oxford Diary* (1937), which More stipulated he would only ever publish in anonymity. In 1937, TSE wrote in tribute: 'The place of Paul More's writings in my own life has been of such a kind that I find [it] easiest, and perhaps most effective, to treat it in a kind of autobiographical way. What is significant to me . . . is not simply the conclusions at which he has arrived, but the fact that he *arrived* there from somewhere else; and not simply that he came from somewhere else, but that he took a particular route . . . If I find an analogy with my own journey, that is perhaps of interest to no one but myself, except in so far as it explains my retrospective appreciation of *The Shelburne Essays*; but my appreciation of the whole work cannot be disengaged from the way in which I arrived at it. . . . It was not until one or two of the volumes of *The Greek Tradition* had appeared, that More began to have any importance for me. It was possibly Irving Babbitt himself, in a conversation in London, in 1927 or '28, during which I had occasion to indicate the steps I had recently taken, who first made me clearly cognizant of the situation. In the later volumes of *The Greek Tradition*, and in the acquaintance and friendship subsequently formed, I came to find an auxiliary to my own progress of thought, which no English theologian could have given me. The English theologians, born and brought up in surroundings of private belief and public form, and often themselves descended from ecclesiastics, at any rate living mostly in an environment of religious practice, did not seem to me to know enough of the new world of barbarism and infidelity that was forming all about them. The English Church was familiar with the backslider, but it knew nothing of the convert – certainly not of the convert who came such a long journey. I might almost say that I never met any Christians until after I had made up my mind to become one. It was of the greatest importance, then, to meet the work of a man who had come by somewhat the same route, to the same conclusions, at almost the same time: with a maturity, a weight of scholarship, a discipline of thinking, which I did not, and never shall, possess. I had only met More once in earlier years . . . My first meeting with him in London, however, seemed more like the renewal of an old acquaintance than the formation of a new one: More was a St. Louisan, and had known my family; and if he had remained a few years longer, I also would have learned my Greek from him, as did my brother' (*Princeton Alumni Magazine* 37 [5 Feb. 1937], 373–4).

**Frank Vigor Morley** (1899–1980), son of a distinguished mathematician – his brothers were the writer Christopher, and Felix (who was to become editor of *The Washington Post*) – was brought up in the USA before travelling as a Rhodes Scholar to New College, Oxford, where he earned a doctorate in mathematics. After working for a while at the *Times Literary Supplement*, he became London Manager of The Century Company (Publishers) of New York. In 1929 he became a founding director of Faber & Faber, where he would be a close friend of TSE: for ten years they shared a top-floor office at Russell Square. In 1933, when TSE separated from Vivien, Morley arranged convivial temporary accommodation for him near his farmhouse in Surrey. In 1939 Morley moved to New York, where he became Vice-President of Harcourt Brace and Company (and during the war he served on the National War Labor Board in Washington, DC). In 1947 he returned with his family to England to take up the post of Director at Eyre & Spottiswoode. A large, learned, ebullient figure, he earned the sobriquet 'Whale' – though not merely on account of his manifest corpulence: in his youth he had spent time working aboard a whaling ship (being revolted by the killing of the whales), and wrote (with J. S. Hodgson) *Whaling North and South* (1927) – which was reviewed in the *Monthly Criterion* by his friend Herbert Read. Later publications include *The Great North Road*, *The Long Road West* and *Literary Britain*. Morley Kennerley told *The Times* (25 Oct.

1980) that 'one of his hobbies was to work out complicated problems for his friends, and for those baffled there were amazing practical jokes. Convivial lunches with interesting people were a joy to him . . . He found jobs for many and squeezed me into Fabers where he generously put up with my sharing a corner of his room for some years. I was present all day during his interviews, dictation, visitors and often lunch. How he put up with all this I do not know. His correspondence with Ezra Pound was quite something, and I think he out-Pounded Pound. As his family say, he was a compulsive letter writer and was rarely without a pencil in his hand or pocket.'

**Lady Ottoline Morrell** (1873–1938), daughter of Lieutenant-General Arthur Bentinck and half-sister to the Duke of Portland. In 1902 she married Philip Morrell (1870–1941), Liberal MP for South Oxfordshire, 1902–18. A patron of the arts, she entertained a notable literary and artistic circle, first at 44 Bedford Square, then at Garsington Manor, near Oxford, where she moved in 1915. She was a lover of Bertrand Russell, who introduced her to TSE, and her many friends included Lytton Strachey, D. H. Lawrence, Aldous Huxley, Siegfried Sassoon and the Woolfs. Her memoirs (ed. Robert Gathorne-Hardy) appeared as *Ottoline* (1963) and *Ottoline at Garsington* (1974). See Miranda Seymour, *Life on the Grand Scale: Lady Ottoline Morrell* (1992, 1998).

**Edwin Muir** (1887–1959), Scottish poet, novelist, critic; translator (with his wife Willa) of Franz Kafka. TSE was to write to LW on 22 Aug. 1946: 'I am anxious to do anything I can for Muir because I think highly of his best poetry and I think he has not had enough recognition.' To his cousin Eleanor Hinkley, 25 Dec. 1955: 'I have always found Willa rather oppressive. Edwin is a sweet creature, who never says anything when his wife is present, and only an occasional word when she isn't. An evening alone with him is very fatiguing. But he is a good poet, and I believe, what is even rarer, a literary man of complete integrity. He is not really Scottish, but Orcadian – in other words, pure Scandinavian.' And in an obituary tribute: 'Muir's literary criticism had always seemed to me of the best of our time: after I came to know him, I realised that it owed its excellence not only to his power of intellect and acuteness of sensibility, but to those moral qualities which make us remember him, as you say justly, as "in some ways almost a saintly man". It was more recently that I came to regard his poetry as ranking with the best poetry of our time. As a poet he began late; as a poet he was recognised late; but some of his finest work –

perhaps his very finest work – was written when he was already over sixty . . . For this late development we are reminded of the later poetry of Yeats; and Muir had to struggle with bad health also: but in the one case as in the other (and Muir is by no means unworthy to be mentioned together with Yeats) we recognise a triumph of the human spirit' (*The Times*, 7 Jan. 1959). Willa Muir privately commented on TSE's plaudits: 'Eliot, in his desire to present Edwin as an orthodox Christian, overdid, I think, the desolations and the saintliness. Edwin's wine could never be contained in any orthodox creed' (letter to Kathleen Raine, 7 Apr. 1960). TSE would later say of Muir: 'He was a reserved, reticent man . . . Yet his personality made a deep impression upon me, and especially the impression of one very rare and precious quality . . . unmistakable integrity'; and of his poems: 'under the pressure of emotional intensity, and possessed by his vision, he found almost unconsciously the right, the inevitable, way of saying what he wanted to say' ('Edwin Muir: 1887–1959: An Appreciation', *The Listener*, 28 May 1964, 872). Muir's publications include *First Poems* (Hogarth Press, 1925); *Transition: Essays on Contemporary Literature* (1926); *An Autobiography* (1954); *Selected Poems of Edwin Muir*, preface by TSE (1966); *Selected Letters of Edwin Muir*, ed. P. H. Butter (1974).

**John Middleton Murry** (1889–1957): English writer, critic and editor; founded the magazine *Rhythm*, 1911–13; worked as a reviewer for the *Westminster Gazette*, 1912–14, and the *Times Literary Supplement*, 1914–18, before becoming editor from 1919 to 1921 of the *Athenaeum*, which he turned into a lively cultural forum – in a letter of 2 July 1919, TSE called it 'the best literary weekly in the Anglo-Saxon world'. Richard Church thought him 'a dark, slippery character, who looked over my shoulder (probably into an invisible mirror) when talking to me, and referred to himself always in the third person . . . In spite of these characteristics . . . he was possessed by a strong literary sensibility.' In a 'London Letter' in *Dial* 72 (May 1921), Eliot considered Murry 'genuinely studious to maintain a serious criticism', but he disagreed with his 'particular tastes, as well as his general statements'. After the demise of the *Athenaeum*, Murry went on to edit *The Adelphi*, 1923–48. In 1918, he married Katherine Mansfield. He was friend and biographer of D. H. Lawrence; and as an editor he provided a platform for writers as various as George Santayana, Paul Valéry, D. H. Lawrence, Aldous Huxley, Virginia Woolf and Eliot. His first notable critical work was *Dostoevsky* (1916); his most influential study, *The Problem of Style* (1922). Though as a Romanticist he was an intellectual opponent of the avowedly 'Classicist' Eliot, Murry offered Eliot in 1919 the post of assistant editor on the *Athenaeum* (which Eliot had to decline); in addition, he recommended him to be Clark lecturer at Cambridge in 1926, and was a steadfast friend. Eliot wrote in a reference on 9 Sept. 1945 that Murry was 'one of the most distinguished men of letters of this time, and testimony from a contemporary seems superfluous. Several volumes of literary essays of the highest quality are evidence of his eminence as a critic; and even if one took no account of his original contribution, his conduct of *The Athenaeum*, which he edited from 1919 until its absorption into *The Nation*, should be enough to entitle him to the gratitude of his contemporaries and juniors. His direction of *The Adelphi* should also be recognised. Since he has devoted his attention chiefly to social and religious problems, he has written a number of books which no one who is concerned with the same problems, whether in agreement with him or not, can afford to neglect. I am quite sure that no future student of these matters who wishes to understand this age will be able to ignore them, and that no future student of the literary spirit of this age will be able to ignore Mr Murry's criticism.' He wrote to Murry's widow on 29 May 1957: 'The friendship between John and myself was of a singular quality, such that it was rather different from any other of my friendships. We did not often meet. We disagreed throughout many years on one point after another. But on the other hand, a very warm affection existed between us in spite of differences of view and infrequency of meetings. This affection was not merely, on my part, a feeling of gratitude for the opportunities he had given me early in my career during his editorship of *The Athenaeum*, but was something solid and permanent. He was one of the strangest and most remarkable men I have known, and no less strange and remarkable was the tie of affection between us.' See F. A. Lea, *The Life of John Middleton Murry* (1959); and David Goldie, *A Critical Difference: T. S. Eliot and John Middleton Murry in English Literary Criticism, 1919–1928* (1998).

**F. S. Oliver** (1864–1934), businessman and polemicist, was educated at Edinburgh and Trinity College, Cambridge, before joining forces in 1892 with Ernest Debenham in the firm of Debenham and Freebody (drapers, wholesalers, manufacturers), which they caused to flourish and expand (buying up Marshall and Snelgrove and Harvey Nichols); Oliver, who had become a wealthy man, retired as managing director in 1920. A radical Tory, he engaged himself in many public issues. His publications included *Alexander Hamilton* (1906), *Ordeal by Battle* (1915) and *The Endless Adventure* (3 vols, 1930–5).

**Kenneth Pickthorn** (1892–1975), historian and politician; Fellow of Corpus Christi College, Cambridge, from 1914; Dean, 1919–29; Tutor, 1927–35; President, 1937–44. From 1950 to 1966 he was to be the Conservative MP for a Midlands constituency; an independent-minded and outspoken parliamentarian, critical of cant, he was made a baronet in 1959, Privy Councillor in 1964. His publications included *Some Historical Principles of the Constitution* (1925) and *Early Tudor Government* (2 vols, 1934).

**Ezra Pound** (1885–1972), American poet and critic, was one of the prime impresarios of the modernist movement in London and Paris, and played a major part in launching Eliot as poet and critic – as well as Joyce, Lewis and many other modernists. Eliot called on him at 5 Holland Place Chambers, Kensington, on 22 Sept. 1914, with an introduction from Conrad Aiken. On 30 Sept. 1914, Pound hailed 'Prufrock' as 'the best poem I have yet had or seen from an American'; and on 3 October called Eliot 'the last intelligent man I've found – a young American T. S. Eliot . . . worth watching – mind "not primitive"' (*Selected Letters of Ezra Pound*, 40-1). Pound was instrumental in arranging for 'Prufrock' to be published in *Poetry* in 1915, and helped to shape *The Waste Land* (1922), which Eliot dedicated to him as 'il miglior fabbro'. After their first meeting, the poets became friends, and remained in loyal correspondence for the rest of their lives. Having initially dismissed Pound's poetry (to Conrad Aiken, 30 Sept. 1914) as 'well-meaning but touchingly incompetent', Eliot went on to champion his work, writing to Gilbert Seldes (27 Dec. 1922): 'I sincerely consider Ezra Pound the most important living poet in the English language.' He wrote an early critical study, *Ezra Pound: His Metric and Poetry* (1917), and went on, as editor of the *Criterion* and publisher at Faber & Faber, to publish most of Pound's work in the UK, including *Selected Shorter Poems*, *The Cantos* and *Selected Literary Essays*. After his move to Italy in the 1920s, Pound became increasingly sceptical about the direction of TSE's convictions and poetry, but they continued to correspond. TSE wrote to James Laughlin, on the occasion of Pound's seventieth birthday: 'I believe that I have in the past made clear enough my personal debt to Ezra Pound during the years 1915–22. I have also expressed in several ways my opinion of his rank as a poet, as a critic, as impresario of other writers, and as pioneer of metric and poetic language. His 70th birthday is not a moment for qualifying one's praise, but merely for recognition of those services to literature for which he will deserve the gratitude of posterity, and for appreciation of those achievements which even his severest critics must acknowledge' (3 Nov. 1955). After Eliot's death, Pound said of him: 'His was the true Dantescan voice – not honoured enough, and deserving more than I ever gave him.' See A. David Moody, *Ezra Pound: Poet: A Portrait of the Man and his Work*, I: *The Young Genius 1885–1920* (2007), Humphrey Carpenter, *A Serious Character* (1988), and *The Selected Letters of Ezra Pound 1907–1941*, ed. D. D. Paige (1950).

**Mario Praz** (1896–1982), scholar and critic of English life and literature; author of *La Carne, la Morte e Il Diavolo nella Letteratura Romantica* (1930), trans. as *The Romantic Agony* (1933). Educated in Bologna, Rome and Florence, he came to England in 1923 to study for the title of *libero docente*. He was Senior Lecturer in Italian, Liverpool University, 1924–32; Professor of Italian Studies, Victoria University of Manchester, 1932–4; and Professor of English Language and Literature at the University of Rome, 1934–66. His many other publications include *Il giardino dei sensi* (1975). In 1952 he was conferred by Queen Elizabeth II with the title of Knight Commander of the British Empire (KBE). In 'An Italian Critic on Donne and Crashaw' (*TLS*, 17 Dec. 1925, 878), TSE hailed Praz's study *Secentismo e Marinismo in Inghilterra: John Donne – Richard Crashaw* (1925) as 'indispensable for any student of this period and these authors'. Later, in 'A Tribute to Mario Praz', he noted: 'His knowledge of the poetry of that period in four languages – English, Italian, Spanish and Latin – was encyclopaedic, and, fortified by his own judgment and good taste, makes that book essential reading for any student of the English "metaphysical poets" ' (*Friendship's Garland: Essays presented to Mario Praz on His Seventieth Birthday*, ed. Vittorio Gabrieli [1966].)

**Alec (later Sir Alec) Randall** (1892–1977), diplomat and writer, entered the Foreign Office in 1920. In the early 1920s he was Second Secretary to the Holy See. He ended his career as Ambassador to Denmark (where he was awarded the Grand Cross, Order of Dannebrog), 1947–52. He wrote on German literature for the *Criterion* and *TLS*. Later works include *Vatican Assignment* (1956) and *The Pope, the Jews and the Nazis* (1963).

**Herbert Read** (1893–1968), English poet and literary critic, and one of the most influential art critics of the century. Son of a tenant farmer, Read spent his first years in rural Yorkshire; at sixteen, he went to work as a bank clerk, then studied law and economics at Leeds University; later still, he joined the Civil Service, working first in the Ministry of Labour and then at the Treasury. During his years of service in WW1, he rose to be a Captain in the Yorkshire regiment, the Green Howards (his war poems were published in *Naked Warriors*, 1919); and when on leave to receive the Military Cross in 1917, he arranged to dine with TSE at the Monico Restaurant in Piccadilly Circus. This launched a lifelong friendship which he was to recall in 'T.S.E. – A Memoir', in *T. S. Eliot: The Man and his Work*, ed. Allen Tate (1966). Within the year, he had also become acquainted with the Sitwells, Ezra Pound, Wyndham Lewis, Richard Aldington and Ford Madox Ford. He co-founded the journal *Art & Letters*, 1917–20, and wrote essays too for A. R. Orage, editor of the *New Age*. In 1922 he was appointed a curator in the department of ceramics and glass at the Victoria and Albert Museum; and in later years he was to work for the publishers Routledge & Kegan Paul, and as editor of the *Burlington Magazine*, 1933–9. By 1923 he was writing for the *Criterion*: he was to be one of Eliot's regular leading contributors and a reliable ally and adviser. In 1924 he edited T. E. Hulme's posthumous *Speculations*. His later works include *Art Now* (1933); the introduction to the catalogue of the International Surrealist Exhibition held at the New Burlington Galleries, London, 1936; *Art and Society* (1937); *Education through Art* (1943); and *A Concise History of Modern Painting* (1959). In 1947 he founded (with Roland Penrose) the Institute of Contemporary Arts; and in 1953 he was knighted for services to literature. Eliot, he was to recall (perhaps only half in jest), was 'rather like a gloomy priest presiding over my affections and spontaneity'. According to Stephen Spender in 1966, Eliot said 'of the anarchism of his friend Herbert Read, whom he loved and esteemed very highly: "Sometimes when I read Herbert's inflammatory pamphlets I have the impression that I am reading the pronouncements of an old-fashioned nineteenth-century liberal"' ('Remembering Eliot', *The Thirties and After* [1978], 251). Joseph Chiari recalled TSE saying of Read: 'Ah, there is old Herbie, again; he can't resist anything new!' See Herbert Read, *Annals of Innocence and Experience* (1940); James King, *The Last Modern: A Life of Herbert Read* (1990); and *Herbert Read reassessed*, ed. D. Goodway (1998). Jason Harding (*The 'Criterion'*: see citation under Dobrée) calculates that Read wrote 68 book reviews, 4 articles and 5 poems for the *Criterion*.

**I. A. Richards** (1893–1979), theorist of literature, education and communication studies. At Cambridge University he studied History but switched to moral sciences, graduating from Magdalene College, where in 1922 he was appointed College Lecturer in English and Moral Sciences.

A vigorous, spell-binding lecturer, he was to the fore in the advancement of the English Tripos. His early writings – *The Foundations of Aesthetics* (with C. K. Ogden and James Wood, 1922), *The Meaning of Meaning* (also with Ogden, 1923), *Principles of Literary Criticism* (1924), *Science and Poetry* (1926), *Practical Criticism: A Study of Literary Judgment* (1929) – are foundational texts in modern English literary studies. After teaching at National Tsing Hua University in Peking, 1929–30, he repaired for the remainder of his career to Harvard University, where he was made a university professor in 1944. His other works include *Basic Rules of Reason* (1933), *Basic in Teaching: East and West* (1935), *Mencius on the Mind* (1932), *Coleridge on Imagination* (1934), *The Philosophy of Rhetoric* (1936), *Interpretation in Teaching* (1938), *Speculative Instruments* (1955), and translations from Plato and Homer. He was appointed Companion of Honour in 1963, and awarded the Emerson-Thoreau medal of the American Academy of Arts and Sciences, 1970. Out of the teaching term, he enjoyed with his wife Dorothea (1894–1986) an adventurous life of travel and mountain-climbing. See *Selected Letters of I. A. Richards, CH*, ed. John Constable (1990); John Constable, 'I. A. Richards, T. S. Eliot, and the Poetry of Belief', *Essays in Criticism* (July 1990), 222–43; *I. A. Richards and his Critics*, ed. John Constable (vol. 10 of *I. A. Richards: Selected Works 1919–1938* (2001); John Paul Russo, *I. A. Richards: His Life and Work* (1989).

**Bruce Richmond** (1871–1964), literary editor, was educated at Winchester and New College, Oxford, and called to the Bar in 1897. However, he never practised as a barrister; instead, George Buckle, editor of *The Times*, appointed him an assistant editor in 1899, and in 1902 he assumed the editorship of the fledgling *Times Literary Supplement*, which he commanded for 35 years. During this period, the *Lit Sup.* established itself as the premier academic and critical periodical in Britain. He was knighted in 1935. TSE, who was introduced to Richmond by Richard Aldington in 1919, enthused to his mother that year that writing the leading article for the *TLS* was the highest honour 'in the critical world of literature'. In a tribute, he recalled Richmond as possessing 'a bird-like alertness of eye, body and mind . . . It was from Bruce Richmond that I learnt editorial standards . . . I learnt from him that it is the business of an editor to know his contributors personally, to keep in touch with them and to make suggestions to them. I tried [at the *Criterion*] to form a nucleus of writers (some of them, indeed, recruited from *The Times Literary Supplement*, and introduced to me by Richmond) on whom I could depend, differing from each other in many things, but not in love of literature and seriousness of purpose. And I learnt from Richmond that I must read every word of what was to appear in print . . . It is a final tribute to Richmond's genius as an editor that some of his troupe of regular contributors (I am thinking of myself as well as of others) produced some of their most distinguished critical essays as leaders for the *Literary Supplement* . . . Good literary criticism requires good editors as well as good critics. And Bruce Richmond was a great editor' ('Bruce Lyttelton Richmond', *TLS*, 13 Jan. 1961, 17).

**Laura Riding**, née Reichenthal (1901–91), a child of Austrian Jewish immigrants, was an American poet and essayist. Married to Louis Gottschalk but divorced in 1925, she published her first poems as Laura Riding Gottschalk. Educated at Cornell, she was associated with the *Fugitive* magazine, which published her early poetry. From 1929 to 1939 she lived and worked with Robert Graves (for a while, in a *ménage à trois* with Graves's wife Nancy). In collaboration with Graves she set up the Seizin Press and wrote *A Survey of Modernist Poetry* (1927) and *A Pamphlet Against Anthologies* (1928). In 1941 she marred Schuyler B. Jackson and would thereafter publish under the name Laura (Riding) Jackson. Works include *Anarchism is Not Enough* (1928); *The Poems of Laura Riding: A Newly Revised Edition of the 1938/1980 Collection* (ed. Mark Jacobs, 2001); and *The Word 'Woman' and Other related writings* (1993). See Richard Perceval Graves, *Robert Graves: 1926–1940, The Years with Laura Riding* (1990); and Elizabeth Friedmann, *A Mannered Grace: The Life of Laura Riding* (2005).

**J. M. Robertson** (1856–1933), author, journalist, politician, began his career as a clerk; then worked on newspapers including the *Edinburgh Evening News* and *National Reformer*. He was Liberal MP for Tyneside, 1908–18. Though self-taught, he was a prolific writer, publishing over 100 books and pamphlets including *The Problem of Hamlet* (1919), *Hamlet Once More* (1923), *Mr Shaw and the Maid* (1926) – a study of *St Joan* which TSE reviewed in the *Criterion* (Apr. 1926) – *and The Problems of Shakespeare's Sonnets* (1927), which TSE reviewed in *The Nation* (12 Feb. 1927). A fervent disintegrationist, Robertson sought to isolate the pure Shakespeare. TSE wrote to Duff Cooper on 30 Nov. 1949, in response to his book *Sergeant Shakespeare*: 'I must let you know that I am no longer under the influence of Robertson, and no longer quite agree with what I said about *Hamlet*.' See also Leo Storm, 'J. M.

Robertson and T. S. Eliot: A Note on the Genesis of Modern Critical Theory', *Journal of Modern Literature* 5: 2 (Apr. 1976), 315–21; Martin Page, *Britain's Unknown Genius: The Life-Work of J. M. Robertson* (1984); *J. M. Robertson, 1856–1933: Liberal, Rationalist and Scholar*, ed. G. A. Wells (1985); Odin Dekkers, *J. M. Robertson: Rationalist and Literary Critic* (1998).

**Mary Lilian Rothermere,** née Share (1874–1937), Viscountess Rothermere. The daughter of George Wade Share, she married in 1893 Harold Sydney Harmsworth, first Viscount Rothermere (1868–1940). It was owing to Scofield Thayer, whom she met in New York, that she became the patron of Eliot's quarterly review *The Criterion* 1922–5. Discussion of her support for the review, a successor to Schiff's *Art and Letters*, was first floated in July 1921, and it became a reality when the first issue of the *Criterion* appeared in October 1922, featuring the first UK publication of *The Waste Land*.

**A. L. Rowse** (1903–97), Cornish historian, was educated at Christ Church, Oxford, and elected a Prize Fellow of All Souls in 1925. He was a lecturer at Merton College, 1927–30, and taught also at the London School of Economics. His numerous books include *Sir Richard Grenville of the Revenge* (1937), *The England of Elizabeth* (1950), *William Shakespeare: A Biography* (1963), *Shakespeare the Man* (1973), *Simon Forman: Sex and Society in Shakespeare's Age* (1974), *All Souls in My Time* (1993) and volumes of poetry gathered up in *A Life* (1981). Though he failed in 1952 to be elected Warden of All Souls, he was elected a Fellow of the British Academy in 1958 and made a Companion of Honour in 1997. See Richard Ollard, *A Man of Contradictions: A Life of A. L. Rowse* (1999) and *The Diaries of A. L. Rowse* (ed. Ollard, 2003). TSE was to write to Geoffrey Curtis on 1 May 1944: 'Rowse is an old friend of mine, and a very touching person: the suppressed Catholic and the rather less suppressed Tory (with a real respect for Good Families), the miner's son and the All Souls Fellow, the minor poet and the would-be politician, the proletarian myth and the will-to-power, are always at odds in a scholarly retiring mind and a frail body. He is also very patronising, and one likes it.'

**Bertrand Russell** (1872–1970): one of the most influential twentieth-century British philosophers; co-author (with Alfred North Whitehead) of *Principia Mathematica* (1910–13), and author of innumerable other books including the popular *Problems of Philosophy* (1912), *Mysticism* *and Logic* (1918) – which was reviewed by TSE in 'Style and Thought' (*Nation* 22, 23 March 1918) – and *History of Western Philosophy* (1945). In 1914, Russell gave the Lowell lectures on 'Our Knowledge of the External World' at Harvard, where he encountered Eliot. On 27 March 1914, Russell described Eliot as 'very well dressed and polished, with manners of the finest Etonian type'. He later characterised him as 'proficient in Plato, intimate with French literature from Villon to Vildrach, and capable of exquisiteness of appreciation, but lacking in the crude insistent passion that one must have in order to achieve anything'. After their accidental meeting in 1914, Russell played an important role in introducing TSE to English intellectual life, as well as getting him launched as a reviewer for *International Journal of Ethics* and *The Monist*. However, it has been alleged that, not long after TSE's marriage, Russell may have had a brief affair with his wife Vivien – though in later years Russell would deny any such thing; on 28 May 1968 he wrote to Robert Sencourt: 'I never had any intimate sexual relations with Vivienne. The difficulty between Eliot and Vivienne sprang chiefly from her taking of drugs and the consequent hallucinations.' The three friends had shared lodgings for a period in 1916 at Russell's flat in London. Russell was a Conscientious Objector and vocal opponent of WW1, which led to a brief prison sentence in Wandsworth. In later years, TSE saw little of his one-time professor and friend, and he attacked Russell's philosophical and ethical views, in his 'Commentary' in the *Criterion* (April 1924), and elsewhere. Russell provides a partial account of his relationship with the Eliots in *The Autobiography of Bertrand Russell* II: *1914–1944* (1968). See also Ray Monk, *Bertrand Russell: The Spirit of Solitude* (1996).

**George 'Dadie' Rylands** (1902–99), Shakespearean scholar and theatre director, was educated at Eton and King's College, Cambridge: he gained a starred First in the English Tripos and was elected a Fellow of King's in 1927 on the strength of a dissertation that was published as *Words and Poetry* (1928). An associate of the Bloomsbury circle, he worked as assistant to LW and VW – 'a very charming spoilt boy . . . pink as a daisy and as proud as a wood-lion,' said VW of him – at the Hogarth Press, which published his early verse, *Russet and Taffeta* (1925) and *Poems* (1931). But he earned a major reputation through his passion for nurturing plays and speaking verse (he acted and produced at the Amateur Dramatic Club and Arts theatres, and succeeded John Maynard Keynes as chairman of the Arts). Actors and directors including Michael Redgrave, Peter Hall, John Barton and Ian McKellen learned their craft under his direction at Cambridge. In 1961 he was appointed CBE for his services to Shakespearian studies; and in 1987 he was made a Companion of Honour.

**Alexis St Léger Léger** (1887–1975) – pen name **St-John Perse** – poet and diplomat. Scion of a Bourgignon family, he passed his early years on an island near Guadeloupe in the West Indies, but the family returned to France in 1899. After studying law at the University of Bordeaux, he joined the Foreign Office as an attaché and worked for six years as Secretary at the French Legation in Peking: his poem *Anabase* is inspired by aspects of his life and observations in China, which included a journey to Outer Mongolia. In 1921, at a conference in Washington, DC, he was recruited by Aristide Briand, Prime Minister of France, as his *chef de cabinet*; and after Briand's death in 1932 he retained high office, serving as Secrétaire Générale of the Foreign Office, 1933–40. Dishonoured by the Vichy regime (he was a Grand Officier of the Légion d'honneur), he spent the years of WW2 in the USA (serving for a time as a 'consultant' to the Library of Congress); and he went back to France only in 1957 (he had formally closed his diplomatic career in 1950, with the title of Ambassadeur de France). His publications include *Éloges* (published with help from André Gide, 1911), *Anabase* (1924; trans. by TSE as *Anabasis*, 1930), *Exil* (1942), *Pluies* (1943), *Vents* (1946), *Amers* (1957) and *Oiseaux* (1962). In 1924 he published in *Commerce* a translation of the opening section of 'The Hollow Men'. He was made Nobel Laureate in Literature in 1960. In a copy of *Anabase* (Paris: Librairie Gallimard/ Éditions de La Nouvelle Revue Française, 1925: limited edition copy no. 160), St.-John Perse wrote: 'À T. S. Eliot / dont j'aime et j'admire l'oeuvre / fraternellement / St. J. Perse.' (TSE Library). In 1960 TSE was to recommend St-John Perse for the Nobel Prize. When requested on 10 Mar. 1960 by Uno Willers, secretary of the Svenska Akadamiens Nobelkommitté, to 'write down a more detailed motivation for your suggestion', TSE responded on 23 Mar. 1960: 'My interest in the work of St-John Perse began many years ago when I translated his *Anabase* into English. This task gave me an intimacy with his style and idiom which I could not have acquired in any other way. It seemed to me then, and it seems to me still, that he had done something highly original – and in a language, the French language, in which such originality is not easily attained. He had invented a form which was different from "free verse" as practiced in France today, and different from the "prose-poem" in which some French writers, anxious to escape the limitations of the conventional metrics of their language, take refuge. He is the only French poet among my contemporaries, with the solitary exception of Supervielle, whose work has continued to interest me. With some of my contemporaries writing in other languages I feel a certain affinity – with Montale, for example, and with Seferis so far as I can judge from translations – with Perse, I have felt rather an influence which is visible in some of my poems written after I had translated *Anabase*.' He added: 'My remarks are, of course, to be taken as confidential, as I am always careful never to express in public my opinions of the relative value of the works of poets who are contemporaries or my juniors.' See also Richard Abel, 'The Influence of St.-John Perse on T. S. Eliot', *Contemporary Literature*, 14: 2 (1973), 213–39.

**Gilbert Seldes** (1893–1970), journalist, critic and editor, was a war correspondent before becoming editor of *The Dial*, 1920–3. His works include *The Seven Lively Arts* (1924) – an influential study of popular arts embracing the comic strip and popular songs as well as cinema and vaudeville – and *The Stammering Century* (1928). He wrote a number of 'New York Chronicles' for the *Criterion*. In later years he was a prolific essayist; he also wrote for the Broadway theatre, and became the first director of TV programmes for CBS News, and founding Dean of the Annenburg School for Communication, University of Pennsylvania. See Michael Kammen, *The Lively Arts: Gilbert Seldes and the Transformation of Cultural Criticism in the United States* (1996).

**Robert Esmonde Gordon George – Robert Sencourt** (1890–1969), critic, historian and biographer. Born in New Zealand, he was educated in Tamaki and at St John's College, Oxford. By 1929 – perhaps to avoid confusion with Professor George Gordon (President of Magdalen College, Oxford) – he was to take the name of Robert Sencourt. He taught in India and Portugal before serving as Vice-Dean of the Faculty of Arts and Professor of English Literature, University of Egypt, 1933–6. *The Times* obituarist noted that he was 'born an Anglican [but] was converted to Roman Catholicism which alone could inspire him with the spiritual dimension of the life of grace . . . [He] was the most fervent and devout of religious men, with the same personal mysticism which makes his life of St John of the Cross a joy to read. Never fearing to speak his mind in religious matters, even when (as often) his view ran counter to the Church's, he was intolerant of any form of ecclestiastical cant or humbug.' His books include *The Genius of the Vatican* (1935), *Carmelite and Poet: St John of* *the Cross* (1943), *St Paul: Envoy of Grace* (1948), biographies of George Meredith, the Empress Eugénie, Napoleon III, King Alfonso and Edward VIII, and *T. S. Eliot: A Memoir*, ed. Donald Adamson (1971). On 17 July 1936 TSE was to write to the Master of Corpus Christi College, Cambridge, in support of Sencourt's application for the Chair of English at Bucharest: 'I don't know anything about the job in Bucharest, but I should think Sencourt would do admirably for it. He is a New Zealander, and has lived abroad a great deal, largely in Italy and France, and has what would be called a cosmopolitan mind. He gets on well with foreigners – he had three years as Professor of English in Cairo, and is very tolerant of inferior races, and gets on well with them. He is an R.C. convert. He knows everybody or nearly everybody. George Gordon will probably speak for his work as an undergraduate at Oxford (some years ago). He is very much more than competent in English literature (you will learn his official qualifications from other sources), is I believe a firstrate horseman, and of physical courage to the point of recklessness. He is regarded as an odd creature, and a snob: but I know that his kindness and generosity are boundless. I will also say what one could not very well say in a formal testimonial, that I think he is absolutely good enough, and *not too good*, for such a position. It wouldn't be a question of blocks being chopped (rather badly) with a razor; he is just the right sharpness and weight; he wouldn't despise the job and he would do it thoroughly; and he would do his best to like and to understand his pupils. I think the Roumanians would be lucky to get him.' Sencourt wrote to TSE in Oct. 1930, after staying for a few days with him and VHE: 'I could hardly imagine a spirit more congenial and refreshing than yours . . . I know I can count on you both to give me more of what means so much to me.'

**Edith Sitwell** (1887–1964): poet, biographer, anthologist and novelist; editor of *Wheels* 1916–21. Her collection, *The Mother and Other Poems* (1915), was followed by *Clown's Houses* (1918) and *The Wooden Pegasus* (1920). In 1923, her performance at the Aeolian Hall in London of her cycle of poems, *Façade* (1922), with music by William Walton, placed her briefly at the centre of modernistic experimentation. Other writings include *Gold Coast Customs* (1929), *Collected Poems* (1930), *Fanfare for Elizabeth* (1946), *The Queens and the Hive* (1962) and *Taken Care Of* (memoirs, 1965). She was appointed a DBE in 1954. See John Lehmann, *A Nest of Tigers: Edith, Osbert and Sacheverell Sitwell in their Times* (1968); and John Pearson, *Façades: Edith, Osbert and Sacheverell Sitwell* (1978). TSE published one of her poems in the *Criterion*.

**Osbert Sitwell** (1892–1969), poet, novelist and man of letters. Early in his career, he published collections of poems, including *Argonaut and Juggernaut* (1919), and a volume of stories *Triple Fugue* (1924), but he is now celebrated for his memoirs, *Left Hand, Right Hand* (5 vols, 1945–50), which includes a fine portrayal of TSE.

**James Smith** (1904–72): critic and educator; won a double first in English and Modern Languages (French and German) from Trinity College, Cambridge. According to a profile in *Granta* (which he edited, 1925–6), he revived the Cam Literary Club, 'and even presided over it for a year, in order to introduce Cambridge to T. S. Eliot' (cited in John Haffenden, *William Empson: Among the Mandarins* [2005], 603). He was Vice-President of the Club (the President being Professor Sir Arthur Quiller Couch). Empson was to recall having his weekly supervisions with I. A. Richards and then treacherously 'listening to the James Smith group, who favoured T. S. Eliot and Original Sin' (195). Smith was to become an occasional contributor to the *Criterion* and to *Scrutiny*: he wrote on Empson's *Seven Types of Ambiguity* and on metaphysical poetry; and his other essays included studies of Croce, Wordsworth, Marlowe, Chapman, Webster and Shakespeare (collected in the posthumous *Shakespearean and Other Essays*, 1974). In the 1930s he taught at King Edward VII School in Sheffield before becoming an HMI. During WW2 he was Director of the British Institute at Caracas; and after the war he became Professor of English at Fribourg. F. R. Leavis petitioned TSE on 19 Nov. 1946 to support Smith's application: 'He is, in my opinion, an incomparably well-equipped man, but, by a series of accidents, he didn't start a university career when he ought to have done, & so has never held a university post before . . . (He's a Catholic, so would fit in at Freiburg, which is Dominican, I'm told.)' TSE replied to Leavis on 21 Nov. 1946, 'I have hardly been in touch with [Smith] for a number of years but I have enough confidence in him from my knowledge in the past to be very glad to give him this support', and he enclosed a testimonial: 'I have known Mr. Smith ever since he was an undergraduate at Cambridge where I formed a high opinion of his abilities. A little later I was a referee in connection with a dissertation which he submitted and was to report very favourably thereon. I regard Mr. Smith as a man of quite first rate abilities, and of exceptionally wide knowledge and interests.'

**Willliam Force Stead** (1884–1967), poet, critic, diplomat, clergyman, was educated at the University of Virginia and served in WW1 as Vice Consul at the American Foreign Service in Liverpool. After working for a while in Florence, he was appointed in 1927 Chaplain of Worcester College, Oxford, where he became a Fellow. While in England, he befriended literary figures including W. B. Yeats, John Masefield and Robert Bridges, as well as TSE – whom he was to baptise into the Anglican Church in 1927. In later years, after living through WW2 in Baltimore, he taught at Trinity College, Washington, DC. His published poetry included *Moonflowers* (1909), *The Holy Innocents* (1917), *Uriel: A Hymn in Praise of Divine Immanence* (1933) and an edition of Christopher Smart's *Rejoice in the Lamb: A Song from Bedlam* (1939) – a work which he discovered. TSE was to write a testimonial for WFS on 9 Dec. 1938: 'I have known Mr. William Force Stead for over eleven years and count him as a valued friend. He is, first, a poet of established position and an individual inspiration. What is not so well known, except to a small number of the more fastidious readers, is that he is also a prose writer of great distinction: his book [*The Shadow of*] *Mt. Carmel* is recognised as a classic of prose style in its kind. And while the bulk of his published writing on English literature is small, those who know his conversation can testify that he is a man of wide reading and a fine critical sense. Mr. Stead is, moreover, a man of the world in the best sense, who has lived in several countries and is saturated in European culture. By both natural social gifts and cultivation, accordingly, he has a remarkable ability of sympathy with all sorts and conditions and races of men. I would say finally that I know from several sources, that Mr. Stead was most successful as a teacher of young men at Oxford; that he gained both the affection and the respect of his students; and that he exercised upon them a most beneficial influence. He has the scholarship necessary to teach English literature accurately, and the personal qualities necessary to make the subject interesting to his pupils; and I could not recommend anyone for the purpose with more confidence' (Beinecke). See 'Mr Stead Presents An Old Friend', *Trinity College Alumni Journal* 38: 2 (Winter 1965), 59–66; 'William Force Stead's Friendship with Yeats and Eliot', *The Massachusetts Review* 21: 1 (Spring 1980), 9–38.

**Allen Tate** (1899–1979), poet, critic and editor, grew up in Kentucky and attended Vanderbilt University (where he was taught by John Crowe Ransom and became associated with the group of writers known as the Fugitives). He taught at various universities before becoming Poet-in-Residence at Princeton, 1939–42; Poetry Consultant to the Library of Congress, 1944–5; and editor of *The Sewanee Review*, 1944–6; and he was Professor of Humanities at the University of Minnesota (where colleagues included Saul Bellow and John Berryman), 1951–68. Eliot wrote of him in 1959: 'Allen Tate is a good poet and a good literary critic who is distinguished for the sagacity of his social judgment and the consistency with which he has maintained the least popular of political attitudes – that of the sage. He believes in reason rather than enthusiasm, in wisdom rather than system; and he knows that many problems are insoluble and that in politics no solution is final. By avoiding the lethargy of the conservative, the flaccidity of the liberal, and the violence of the zealot, he succeeds in being a representative of the smallest of minorities, that of the intelligent who refuse to be described as "intellectuals". And what he has written, as a critic of society, is of much greater significance because of being said by a man who is also a good poet and a good critic of literature' (*The Sewanee Review*, 67: 4 [Oct.–Dec. 1959], 576). Tate's publications include *Ode to the Confederate Dead* (1930), *Poems: 1928–1931* (1932), *The Mediterranean and Other Poems* (1936), *Reactionary Essays on Poetry and Ideas* (1936), and *The Fathers* (novel, 1938).

**Harriet Shaw Weaver** (1876–1961), English editor and publisher, whom Virginia Woolf described as 'modest judicious & decorous' (*Diary*, 13 April 1918). In 1912, Weaver began by giving financial support to *The Freewoman*, a radical periodical founded and edited by Dora Marsden, which was renamed in 1913 (at the suggestion of Ezra Pound) *The Egoist*. Weaver became editor in 1914, turning it into a 'little magazine' with a big influence in the history of literary Modernism. TSE followed in the footsteps of Richard Aldington and H.D. to become assistant editor in 1917 (having been nominated by Pound), and remained so until it closed in 1919. When Joyce could not secure a publisher for *A Portrait of the Artist as a Young Man*, Weaver in 1917 converted *The Egoist* into a press in order to publish it. She went on to publish TSE's first book, *Prufrock and Other Observations* (1917), Pound's *Dialogues of Fontenelle* and *Quia Pauper Amavi*, Wyndham Lewis's novel *Tarr*, and Marianne Moore's *Poems*, and other notable books. (She played a major role as Joyce's patron and confidante, and went on to be his literary executor and to help to put together *The Letters of James Joyce*.) TSE wrote in tribute in 1962: 'Miss Harriet Shaw Weaver . . . was so modest and self-effacing a woman that her generous patronage of men of letters was hardly known beyond the circle of those who benefited by it . . . Miss Weaver's support, once given, remained steadfast. Her great disappointment was her failure to persuade any printer in this country to take the risk of printing *Ulysses*; her subsequent generosity to James Joyce, and her solicitude for his welfare and that of his family, knew no bounds . . . [Working for her at *The Egoist*] was all great fun, my first experience of editorship. In 1932 I dedicated my *Selected Essays* to this good, kind, unassuming, courageous and lovable woman, to whom I owe so much. What other publisher in 1917 (the Hogarth Press was not yet in existence) would, I wonder, have taken *Prufrock*?' See also Jane Lidderdale and Mary Nicholson, *Dear Miss Weaver: Harriet Shaw Weaver, 1876–1961* (1970).

**Charles Whibley** (1859–1930) took a first in Classics in 1883 from Jesus College, Cambridge, and embarked on a career as journalist, author and editor, and as a well-connected social figure (his intimates were to include Lord Northcliffe and Lady Cynthia Asquith). After working briefly for the publishers Cassell & Co., he wrote for the *Scots Observer* and the *Pall Mall Gazette* (for a while in the 1890s he was Paris correspondent, a posting which enabled him to become acquainted with Stéphane Mallarmé and Paul Valéry), for the *Daily Mail*, and above all for *Blackwood's Magazine* – where he produced for over 25 years a commentary, 'Musings without Method', comprised of sharp high-Tory substance and style. TSE hailed his column as 'the best sustained piece of literary journalism that I know of in recent times'. Richard Aldington thought Whibley 'a pernicious influence' on Eliot: 'Eliot was already too much influenced by Irving Babbitt's pedantic and carping analysis of Rousseau – indeed to some extent he founded his prose style on Babbitt – and in Whibley he found a British counterpart to his old Harvard professor. Whibley was . . . a good scholar, but a hopeless crank about politics. He was the very embodiment of the English Tory don, completely out of touch with the realities of his time. "Whig" and "Whiggism" were his terms of contempt and insult to everybody he disliked, and anybody can see how Eliot picked them up. But Whibley took Eliot to Cambridge, where his conversation enchanted the dons and procured him friends and allies, vastly more important and valuable than the Grub Street hacks who had rejected him.' His friend F. S. Oliver wrote (17 April 1930), in some personal reminiscences put down at TSE's request, of 'the apparently impulsive and prejudiced character of C. W. that when he came to deal with the craft of writing he had no favour, or fear, or anger for friends or enemies. I never knew him once to praise good-naturedly a book because it was written by a very close friend; nor have I ever known him to dispraise a book with real merits, but which happened to be written by someone whose character and opinions he held in detestation. Contrary to the general idea of him he was one of the most *tolerant* people (as regards literature) that I have ever known

. . . [I]t is this quality of truthful, courageous, penetrating, sympathetic literary criticism which I should put first among all his brilliant capacities . . . [H]e was I think the best critic who lived in my time.' Whibley's books included *William Pitt* (1906), *Political Portraits* (1917, 1923) and *Lord John Manners and his Friends* (1925). See TSE, *Charles Whibley: A Memoir* (English Association Pamphlet no. 80, Dec. 1931).

**Orlando (Orlo) Williams** (1883–1967): Clerk to the House of Commons, scholar and critic; contributor to *TLS*; Chevalier, Légion d'honneur. His publications include *The Clerical Organisation of the House of Commons 1661–1850* (1954); *Vie de Bohème: A Patch of Romantic Paris* (1913); *Some Great English Novels: The Art of Fiction* (1926).

**Edmund Wilson** (1895–1972): influential literary critic, social commentator and cultural historian; worked in the 1920s as managing editor of *Vanity Fair*; later as associate editor of *The New Republic* and as a prolific book reviewer. Major publications include *Axel's Castle: A Study in the Imaginative Literature of 1870–1930* (1931) – which includes a chapter on TSE's work, sources and influence – *The Triple Thinkers: Ten Essays on Literature* (1938) and *The Wound and the Bow: Seven Studies in Literature* (1941). TSE was to write to Geoffrey Curtis on 20 Oct. 1943: 'Edmund Wilson is a very good critic except that, like most of his generation in America, he has mixed his literary criticism with too much political ideology of a Trotskyite variety and perhaps he is also too psychological, but I have a great respect for him as a writer and like him as a man.'

**Humbert Wolfe** (1885–1940) – originally Umberto Wolff (the family became British citizens in 1891, and he changed his name in 1918) – poet, satirist, critic, civil servant. The son of Jewish parents (his father was German, his mother Italian), he was born in Bradford (where his father was a partner in a wool business), and went to the Grammar School there. After graduating from Wadham College, Oxford, he worked at the Board of Trade and the Ministry of Labour, and spent time as UK representative at the International Labour Organisation in Geneva. He found fame with *Requiem* (1927), and in 1930 was mooted as a successor to Robert Bridges as Poet Laureate. He edited over 40 books of verse and prose, and wrote many reviews. See Philip Bagguley, *Harlequin in Whitehall: A Life of Humbert Wolfe, Poet and Civil Servant, 1885–1940* (1997).

**Leonard Woolf** (1880–1969): writer and publisher; husband of Virginia Woolf, whom he married in 1912. A friend of Lytton Strachey and J. M. Keynes at Cambridge, he played a central part in the Bloomsbury Group. He wrote novels including *The Village and the Jungle* (1913), and political studies including *Socialism and Co-operation* (1919) and *Imperialism and Civilization* (1928). As founder-editor, with Virginia Woolf, of the Hogarth Press, he was responsible for publishing TSE's *Poems* (1919) and *The Waste Land* (1922). In 1923 he became literary editor of *The Nation & Athenaeum* (after TSE had turned it down), commissioning many reviews from him, and he remained a firm friend. See *An Autobiography* (2 vols, 1980); *Letters of Leonard Woolf*, ed. Frederic Spotts (1990); Victoria Glendinning, *Leonard Woolf: A Life* (2006).

**Virginia Woolf** (1882–1941), novelist, essayist and critic, was author of *Jacob's Room* (1922), *Mrs Dalloway* (1925) and *To the Lighthouse* (1927); *A Room of One's Own* (1928), a classic of modern feminist criticism; and *The Common Reader* (1925; 2nd series 1932 ). Daughter of the biographer and editor Leslie Stephen (1832–1904), she married Leonard Woolf in 1912, published her first novel *The Voyage Out* in 1915, and founded the Hogarth Press with her husband in 1917. The Hogarth Press published TSE's *Poems* (1919), *The Waste Land* (1922), and *Homage to John Dryden* (1923). TSE published in the *Criterion* Woolf's essays and talks including 'Kew Gardens', 'Character in Fiction' and 'On Being Ill'. Woolf became a friend and correspondent; her diaries and letters give first-hand accounts of him. Woolf wrote to her sister Vanessa Bell on 22 July 1936: 'I had a visit, long ago, from Tom Eliot, whom I love, or could have loved, had we both been in the prime and not in the sere; how necessary do you think copulation is to friendship? At what point does "love" become sexual?' (*Letters*, vol. 6). Eliot wrote in 1941 that Woolf 'was the centre, not merely of an esoteric group, but of the literary life of London. Her position was due to a concurrence of qualities and circumstances which never happened before, and which I do not think will ever happen again. It maintained the dignified and admirable tradition of Victorian upper middle-class culture – a situation in which the artist was neither the servant of the exalted patron, the parasite of the plutocrat, nor the entertainer of the mob – a situation in which the producer and the consumer of art were on an equal footing, and that neither the highest nor the lowest.' To Enid Faber on 27 Apr. 1941: 'she was a personal friend who seemed to me (mutatis considerably mutandis) like a member of my own family; and I miss her dreadfully, but

I don't see her exactly as her relatives see her, and my admiration for the ideas of her milieu – now rather old-fashioned – is decidedly qualified.' See also Hermione Lee, *Virginia Woolf* (1996).

# INDEX OF CORRESPONDENTS AND RECIPIENTS

CORRESPONDENTS



RECIPIENTS

# GENERAL INDEX

Page references in **bold** indicate a biographical note